Gender and sexuality give rise to passionate debates among contemporary Mormon studies scholars and the communities they study. This handbook serves as an indispensable orientation to these complex issues and as a springboard for future research. I highly recommend this volume for anyone interested in the history, culture, theology, and future prospects of the Latter-day Saints.

Patrick Q. Mason, Utah State University, USA

THE ROUTLEDGE HANDBOOK OF MORMONISM AND GENDER

The Routledge Handbook of Mormonism and Gender is an outstanding reference source to this controversial subject area. Since its founding in 1830, the Church of Jesus Christ of Latter-day Saints has engaged gender in surprising ways. LDS practice of polygamy in the nineteenth century both fueled rhetoric of patriarchal rule as well as gave polygamous wives greater autonomy than their monogamous peers. The tensions over women's autonomy continued after polygamy was abandoned and defined much of the twentieth century. In the 1970s, 1990s, and 2010s, Mormon feminists came into direct confrontation with the male Mormon hierarchy. These public clashes produced some reforms, but fell short of accomplishing full equality. LGBT Mormons have a similar history. These movements are part of the larger story of how Mormonism has managed changing gender norms in a global context. Comprising over forty chapters by a team of international contributors the Handbook is divided into four parts:

- Methodological issues
- Historical approaches
- Social scientific approaches
- Theological approaches.

These sections examine central issues, debates, and problems, including: agency, feminism, sexuality and sexual ethics, masculinity, queer studies, plural marriage, homosexuality, race, scripture, gender and the priesthood, the family, sexual violence, and identity.

The Routledge Handbook of Mormonism and Gender is essential reading for students and researchers in religious studies, gender studies, and women's studies. The Handbook will also be very useful for those in related fields, such as cultural studies, politics, anthropology, and sociology.

Amy Hoyt as Visiting Scholar of Religion at Claremont Graduate University, USA. Her work specifically focuses on issues of gender within Mormonism in North America and Africa. She has published in *Feminist Theology, Mormon Studies Review,* and *Gender & History.*

Taylor G. Petrey is Associate Professor of Religion at Kalamazoo College, USA and editor of *Dialogue: A Journal of Mormon Thought*. He is the author of *Tabernacles of Clay: Gender and Sexuality in Modern Mormonism* (2020).

Routledge Handbooks in Religion

The Routledge Handbook of Muslim–Jewish Relations
Edited by Josef Meri

The Routledge Handbook of Religious Naturalism
Edited by Donald A. Crosby and Jerome A. Stone

The Routledge Handbook of Death and the Afterlife
Edited by Candi K. Cann

The Routledge Handbook of Religion and Animal Ethics
Edited by Andrew Linzey and Clair Linzey

The Routledge Handbook of Mormonism and Gender
Edited by Amy Hoyt and Taylor G. Petry

For more information about this series, please visit:
www.routledge.com/Routledge-Handbooks-in-Religion/book-series/RHR

THE ROUTLEDGE HANDBOOK OF MORMONISM AND GENDER

Edited by Amy Hoyt and Taylor G. Petrey

LONDON AND NEW YORK

First published 2020 by Routledge

2 Park Square, Milton Park, Abingdon, Oxon OX14 4RN
605 Third Avenue, New York, NY 10017

Routledge is an imprint of the Taylor & Francis Group, an informa business

First issued in paperback 2022

Copyright © 2020 selection and editorial matter, Amy Hoyt and Taylor G. Petrey; individual chapters, the contributors

The right of Amy Hoyt and Taylor G. Petrey to be identified as the authors of the editorial matter, and of the authors for their individual chapters, has been asserted in accordance with sections 77 and 78 of the Copyright, Designs and Patents Act 1988.

All rights reserved. No part of this book may be reprinted or reproduced or utilised in any form or by any electronic, mechanical, or other means, now known or hereafter invented, including photocopying and recording, or in any information storage or retrieval system, without permission in writing from the publishers.

Notice:
Product or corporate names may be trademarks or registered trademarks, and are used only for identification and explanation without intent to infringe.

Publisher's Note

The publisher has gone to great lengths to ensure the quality of this reprint but points out that some imperfections in the original copies may be apparent.

British Library Cataloguing-in-Publication Data
A catalogue record for this book is available from the British Library

Library of Congress Cataloging-in-Publication Data
Names: Hoyt, Amy, editor. | Petrey, Taylor G., editor.
Title: The Routledge handbook of Mormonism and gender / edited by Amy Hoyt and Taylor G. Petrey.
Other titles: Routledge handbooks in religion.
Description: Milton Park, Abingdon, Oxon ; New York, NY : Routledge, 2020. | Series: Routledge handbooks in religion | Includes bibliographical references and index. |
Identifiers: LCCN 2019055856 | ISBN 9780815395218 (hardback) | ISBN 9781351181600 (ebook)
Subjects: LCSH: Church of Jesus Christ of Latter-day Saints–Doctrines. | Gender identity–Religious aspects–Church of Jesus Christ of Latter-day Saints. | Gender identity–Religious aspects–Mormon Church. | Women–Religious aspects–Church of Jesus Christ of Latter-day Saints. | Women–Religious aspects–Mormon Church. | Mormon Church–Doctrines.
Classification: LCC BX8643.S49 R68 2020 | DDC 289.3/32081–dc23
LC record available at https://lccn.loc.gov/2019055856

ISBN: 978-0-815-39521-8 (hbk)
ISBN: 978-1-03-233626-8 (pbk)
DOI: 10.4324/9781351181600

Typeset in Bembo
by Wearset Ltd, Boldon, Tyne and Wear

CONTENTS

List of illustrations   *xi*
Notes on contributors   *xiii*

   Introduction   1
   Amy Hoyt and Taylor G. Petrey

PART I
Methodological issues   9

1   Gender and culture in a global church   11
    Laurie F. Maffly-Kipp

2   Race and gender in Mormonism: 1830–1978   26
    Amanda Hendrix-Komoto and Joseph R. Stuart

3   Intersectionality   38
    Chiung Hwang Chen and Ethan Yorgason

4   Femininities   50
    Amy Hoyt

5   Masculinities   60
    Sara M. Patterson

PART II
Historical approaches   73

6   Joseph Smith, plural marriage, and kinship   75
     Benjamin E. Park

7   Mormon gender in the age of polygamy   86
     Laurel Thatcher Ulrich

8   Mormon women and scripture in the nineteenth century   100
     Amy Easton-Flake

9   Mormonism, gender, and art in nineteenth-century Scandinavia   114
     Julie K. Allen

10   Mormon gender in the progressive era   129
     Matthew Bowman

11   Mormon gender in the mid-twentieth century   143
     Colleen McDannell

12   Mormon feminism after 1970   157
     Claudia L. Bushman

13   Gender and missionary work   169
     David Golding

14   Homosexuality and therapeutic culture in Mormonism   187
     Eric G. Swedin

15   Homosexuality and politics in Mormonism   205
     Neil J. Young

16   Mormon LGBTQ organizing and organizations   221
     John Donald Gustav-Wrathall

17   Mormonism, gender, and art   239
     Mary Campbell

18   Mormon literature and gender   258
     Fara Anderson Sneddon

19   Sexual purity and its discontents in Mormonism   271
     Sara Moslener

20 Mormonism and sexual violence   284
    Andrea G. Radke-Moss

PART III
Social scientific approaches   303

21 Women and religious organization: a "microbiological" approach to
    influence   305
    Melissa Wei-Tsing Inouye

22 Global Mormon perspectives and experiences of familial structures   321
    Caroline Kline

23 Structures of home and family: North America   336
    Megan Stanton

24 Non-traditional families   350
    Ryan T. Cragun and Giuseppina Valle Holway

25 Social science perspectives on gender and Mormon orthodoxy   364
    Jana Riess and Benjamin Knoll

26 Gender and mental health in Mormon contexts   378
    Rebekah Perkins Crawford

27 Women's gender roles and Mormonism in England   392
    Alison Halford

28 Institutional gender negotiations within Irish Mormon congregations   405
    Hazel O'Brien

29 Peruvian Mormon matchmaking: the limits of Mormon endogamy at
    Zion's border   419
    Jason Palmer

30 Mormon women at work in Nicaragua   432
    Amanda Talbot Tew

31 Mormon masculinity, family, and kava in the Pacific   449
    Arcia Tecun and S. Ata Siu'ulua

32 Gendered dynamics and institutions within Nigerian Mormonism   464
    Russell W. Stevenson

PART IV
Theological approaches — 481

33 Scripture and gender — 483
    Joseph M. Spencer

34 Theology of the family — 495
    Rosalynde Welch

35 Theology of sexuality — 509
    Taylor G. Petrey

36 Queer Mormons — 525
    K. Mohrman

37 Trans and mutable bodies — 539
    Kelli D. Potter

38 Feminism and Heavenly Mother — 553
    Fiona Givens

39 Women and priesthood — 569
    Jonathan A. Stapley

40 Men and the priesthood — 580
    Margaret Toscano

41 *Mujerista* theology — 598
    Sujey Vega

Index — *608*

ILLUSTRATIONS

Figures

9.1	Christen Dalsgaard, *Two Mormons Have ... Entered the Home of a Country Carpenter ...*, 1856. Image courtesy of the Danish National Art Museum	117
9.2	C.C.A. Christensen, *Reunion of the Saints*, 1878. Image courtesy of the Daughters of the Utah Pioneers	120
17.1	Anonymous portrait of an LDS family, Busath Photography, Salt Lake City, Utah, ca. 1989	240
17.2	David W. Rogers (attributed), *Emma Smith*, ca. 1842. Courtesy, Community of Christ Library-Archives, Independence, Missouri	241
17.3	David W. Rogers (attributed), *Joseph Smith Jr.*, ca. 1842	242
17.4	Marsena Cannon, *Portrait of Wilford and Phebe Woodruff and family*, 1849. Courtesy, Ronald Fox Collection, Salt Lake City, Utah	244
17.5	Effie Huntington, *Untitled*, n.d. Courtesy, Tom Perry Special Collections, Harold B. Lee Library, Brigham Young University, Provo, Utah	246
17.6	Harriet Harwood, *The Pumpkin and the Cauliflower* (Still Life), 1892. Courtesy, University of Utah Collection	247
17.7	Mary Teasdel, *Mother and Child*, 1920. State of Utah Alice Merrill Horne Collection, Courtesy Utah Arts & Museums	248
17.8	Minerva Teichert (1888–1976), *Loading the Ship*, 1949–1951, oil on masonite, 36 × 48 inches. Brigham Young University Museum of Art, 1969	250
17.9	Trevor Southey, *Eden Farm*, 1971. Courtesy, Trevor Southey Estate	254

Tables

24.1	Current marital status of adults (18+) in the U.S., in Utah, and of Mormons and non-Mormons	351
24.2	Household types in Utah and the U.S., 2017 (ACS)	353
24.3	Cohabiting households in Utah and the U.S. and mean number of children, 2017 (ACS)	354
24.4	Percentage of GSS respondents with no children by religion and marital status	354

24.5	Percentage of GSS respondents who have divorced by year, religion, and marital status	355
24.6	Number of marriages in Utah and the U.S., 2017 (ACS)	356
24.7	Work status of participants and spouses, Mormons and non-Mormons in GSS and Utah and U.S. in ACS	358
25.1	Mormon testimony statements by gender	369
25.2	Mormon spirituality by gender	370
25.3	Troubling issues in the Church, by gender	371
25.4	Mormons and popular culture consumption in the last six months, by gender	372
25.5	Word of Wisdom adherence, by gender	373

CONTRIBUTORS

Julie K. Allen is the Don R. and Jean S. Marshall Professor of Comparative Literature and Scandinavian Studies at Brigham Young University. She is the author of *Danish but Not Lutheran: The Impact of Mormonism on Danish Cultural Identity, 1850–1920* (University of Utah Press, 2017) as well as many articles on Danish culture, literature, film, and migration.

Matthew Bowman holds the Howard W. Hunter Chair of Mormon Studies at Claremont Graduate University. He is the author of *The Mormon People: the Making of an American Faith* (Random House, 2012) and the co-editor of *Women and Mormonism in Historic and Contemporary Perspectives* (University of Utah Press, 2015).

Claudia L. Bushman, Wellesley College, BYU and Boston University, writes on Mormonism and nineteenth-century social history. A veteran Mormon feminist, she was the founding editor of *Exponent II*. Retired from teaching, most recently at Columbia University, she remains interested in women's stories. She is telling her own in her autobiographical, "I, Claudia."

Mary Campbell is an associate professor of American art history at the University of Tennessee, Knoxville. A lawyer as well as an art historian, she focuses on the intersections of American visual, legal, and religious culture.

Chiung Hwang Chen is a professor of communication, media, and culture at Brigham Young University–Hawai'i. Her research interests include media-related religion, gender, and race issues, as well as cultural studies in the Pacific and Chinese-speaking regions.

Ryan T. Cragun is a professor of sociology at the University of Tampa. His research focuses on Mormonism and the nonreligious.

Rebekah Perkins Crawford earned her Ph.D. in communication studies at Ohio University. She studies discourses about mental health within religious communities and focuses on how peoples' talk and interaction enable or constrain access to formal and informal mental healthcare resources. She is a visiting professor of community and public health in the College of Health Sciences and Professions at Ohio University in Athens, Ohio.

Contributors

Amy Easton-Flake is Associate Professor of Ancient Scripture at Brigham Young University. Her research focuses on nineteenth-century women's reform literature and biblical hermeneutics. Her work can be found in the *New England Quarterly, American Journalism, Women's History Review, Symbiosis, Journal of Book of Mormon Studies*, and multiple edited volumes.

Fiona Givens graduated with B.A. degrees in German and French from the University of Richmond, followed by an M.A. in European history. Her work has been published with Greg Kofford Books, *Exponent II, LDS Living, Journal of Mormon History*, and *Dialogue*. In addition to co-writing *The God Who Weeps* (Ensign Peak, 2012), she is the joint author of *The Crucible of Doubt: Reflections on the Quest for Faith* (Deseret Book, 2014), and *The Christ Who Heals: How God Restored the Truth that Saves Us* (Deseret Book, 2017).

David Golding is a historian in the Church History Department, Salt Lake City, Utah. He holds a Ph.D. from Claremont Graduate University and serves as a review editor for the *Journal of Mormon History*.

John Donald Gustav-Wrathall earned his doctorate in American social and religious history at the University of Minnesota and is author of *Take the Young Stranger by the Hand: Same-Sex Relations and the YMCA* (University of Chicago Press, 1998). He is a former president and served as the first full-time executive director of Affirmation, LGBTQ Mormons, Families & Friends.

Alison Halford is based at the Centre for Trust, Peace and Social Relations, Coventry University, U.K. Her research interests are gender, Mormonism, religion in public spaces, and interfaith initiatives.

Amanda Hendrix-Komoto is Assistant Professor at Montana State University, where she researches the racialized intersections of sexuality and religion in the American West. Her first book *Imperial Zions: Race, Religion, and Family in the American West and the Pacific* is forthcoming with the University of Nebraska.

Daniel Hernandez (Arcia Tecun) is Wīnak (Mayan) and uses the publishing name Arcia Tecun after his grandmothers. He was raised in Rose Park, Utah, and is married with four children, remains a Mormon, completed doctoral research on contemporary kava, and is currently lecturing at the University of Auckland.

Giuseppina Valle Holway is an assistant professor of sociology at the University of Tampa. Her research focuses on sexual and reproductive health, demography, and the family.

Amy Hoyt is as Visiting Scholar of Religion at Claremont Graduate University, USA. Her work specifically focuses on issues of gender within Mormonism in North America and Africa. She has published in *Feminist Theology, Mormon Studies Review*, and *Gender & History*.

Melissa Wei-Tsing Inouye is a senior lecturer in Asian studies at the University of Auckland. Her areas of research interest include religion in China, global charismatic religious movements, and global Mormon studies.

Caroline Kline is a research assistant professor in the Department of Religion at Claremont Graduate University (CGU). She earned her Ph.D. in religion with a focus on women's studies in religion at CGU. She co-edited with Claudia Bushman the book *Mormon Women Have Their Say: Essays from the Claremont Oral History Collection.*

Benjamin Knoll is the John Marshall Harlan Associate Professor of Politics at Centre College in Danville, Kentucky. He is the co-author, with Cammie Jo Bolin, of *She Preached the Word: Women's Ordination in Modern America* (Oxford University Press, 2018). He holds a Ph.D. in political science from the University of Iowa.

Laurie F. Maffly-Kipp is the Archer Alexander Distinguished Professor at the John C. Danforth Center on Religion and Politics. She also serves as the director of the Religious Studies program in Washington University in St. Louis Arts & Sciences.

Colleen McDannell is Professor of History and Sterling M. McMurrin Professor of Religious Studies at the University of Utah. Her book *Sister Saints: Mormon Women since the End of Polygamy* (Oxford University Press, 2018) won the Organization of American Historians best 2019 book award for U.S. Women's and/or Gender History.

K. Mohrman is a clinical teaching track assistant professor in the Ethnic Studies program at the University of Colorado Denver. Her manuscript *Exceptionally Queer: Mormon Peculiarity and US Exceptionalism* argues discourses about Mormonism have played a central role in shaping culture, nationalism, and imperial power in the U.S., specifically through the (re)production of sexual normativity and racial hierarchy.

Sara Moslener is a lecturer in the Department of Philosophy and Religion at Central Michigan University. She is the author of *Virgin Nation: Sexual Purity and American Adolescence* (Oxford University Press, 2015).

Hazel O'Brien is a lecturer in sociology at Waterford Institute of Technology, Ireland. She has a particular interest in minority religions, and the intersections of national, religious, and ethnic identities.

Jason Palmer is a Ph.D. candidate in anthropology at the University of California, Irvine. His dissertation project on Peruvian Mormon migration, kinship, and place-making was partially funded by a Global Mormon Studies Research Grant from Claremont Graduate University.

Benjamin E. Park is an assistant professor of history at Sam Houston State University. He is the author of *American Nationalisms: Imagining Union in the Age of Revolutions, 1783–1833* (Cambridge University Press, 2018) and *Kingdom of Nauvoo: The Rise and Fall of a Religious Empire on the American Frontier* (W.W. Norton/Liveright, 2020).

Sara M. Patterson is a professor of theological studies and gender studies at Hanover College in Indiana. She is the author of *Pioneers in the Attic: Place and Memory along the Mormon Trail* (Oxford University Press, 2020). She also continues to write about the intersections of religion and gender and sexuality.

Taylor G. Petrey is an associate professor of religion at Kalamazoo College and editor of *Dialogue: A Journal of Mormon Thought*. He is the author of *Tabernacles of Clay: Gender and Sexuality in Modern Mormonism* (University of North Carolina Press, 2020).

Contributors

Kelli Potter is Associate Professor of Philosophy and Associate Director of Religious Studies at Utah Valley University. Her research focuses on the philosophy of religion and Mormon theology.

Andrea G. Radke-Moss is a professor of history at Brigham Young University-Idaho. She has published widely on the history of women and higher education, Mormon women and sexual assault in war, and women's experiences at the 1893 World's Columbian Exposition.

Jana Riess is the author of *The Next Mormons: How Millennials Are Changing the LDS Church* (Oxford University Press, 2019). She holds a Ph.D. in American religious history from Columbia University and is a senior columnist at Religion News Service.

S. Ata Siuʻulua is Tongan and doing doctoral research on Tongan families and music at the University of Auckland. He was raised in South Jordan, Utah. He is no longer active in the church, but considers himself a cultural Mormon, and is reclaiming his ancestral spirituality.

Fara Anderson Sneddon is an independent scholar with a M.A. from BYU in American literature and completed Ph.D. coursework in multicultural American literature at the University of Georgia.

Joseph M. Spencer holds a Ph.D. in twentieth-century philosophy from the University of New Mexico and is Assistant Professor of Ancient Scripture at Brigham Young University. He is the author or editor of seven books and of many articles. Spencer serves as the editor of the *Journal of Book of Mormon Studies* and also edits, with Matthew Bowman, the book series *Introductions to Mormon Thought* for the University of Illinois Press.

Megan Stanton is a historian of American religion and kinship. She received her Ph.D. in history from the University of Wisconsin-Madison in 2018. Her research examines how nineteenth-century theologies of the family affected general authorities' church governance in both the Church of Jesus Christ of Latter-day Saints and the Reorganized Church of Jesus Christ of Latter Day Saints, now known as the Community of Christ. She received the Mormon History Association's Best Dissertation Award in 2019.

Jonathan A. Stapley is an award-winning scientist and historian. His most recent volume, *Power of Godliness*, was published by Oxford University Press in 2018.

Russell W. Stevenson is the author of *For the Cause of Righteousness: A Global History of Blacks and Mormonism,* 1830–2013 (Kofford Books, 2014), winner of the 2015 Mormon History Association Best Book Award. He has authored multiple articles on race, sexuality, Nigeria, and Latter-day Saint identity. A recipient of the Fulbright-DDRA fellowship, he is completing his Ph.D. in African History at Michigan State University.

Joseph R. Stuart is a Ph.D. candidate in history at the University of Utah. His research analyzes the construction of race and gender in twentieth-century African American history. His work has been published in the *Journal of Mormon History* and *Church History: Studies in Christianity and Culture.*

Eric G. Swedin is a professor of history at Weber State University. His doctorate is in the history of science and technology. His publications include numerous articles, six history books, four science fiction novels, and a historical mystery novel. His website is www.swedin.org.

Contributors

Amanda Talbot Tew is an independent scholar with interests in Mormon and gender studies in Latin America. She completed her Master of Arts in musicology and Bachelor of Arts in music at Brigham Young University.

Margaret Toscano is an associate professor of classics and comparative studies at the University of Utah. Her research centers on myth, religion, and gender in both ancient and modern contexts. She is the co-editor of the book *Hell and Its Afterlife: Historical and Contemporary Perspectives* (Ashgate, 2010) and has published extensively on Mormon feminism for over thirty years.

Laurel Thatcher Ulrich is 300th Anniversary University Professor, emerita, Harvard University. She is the author of numerous books and articles on early American history, women's history, and material history. Her latest book is *A House Full of Females: Plural Marriage and Women's Rights in Early Mormonism* (Knopf, 2017).

Sujey Vega is an associate professor of women and gender studies at Arizona State University. Using ethnography, oral history and archival analysis, Professor Vega's research includes Latina/o expressions of ethnic identity, immigration politics, ethno-religious practices, and intersectional theory.

Rosalynde Welch is an independent scholar of Latter-day Saint theology, holding a Ph.D. from the University of California at San Diego. She is the author of numerous articles on LDS topics, and is a co-director of the Theology Seminar in Latter-day Saint Scripture, a member of the advisory board of the Neal A. Maxwell Institute for Religious Scholarship, and an associate editor at the *Journal of Book of Mormon Studies*.

Ethan Yorgason is an assocaite professor of geography at Kyungpook National University in Daegu, South Korea. In addition to Mormon studies, he is particularly interested in eastern Asia's cultural and political geography.

Neil J. Young is an independent historian of twentieth-century US politics and religion and an affiliated research scholar with the Schar School of Policy & Government, George Mason University. He is the author of *We Gather Together: The Religious Right and the Problem of Interfaith Politics* (Oxford University Press, 2015).

INTRODUCTION

Amy Hoyt and Taylor G. Petrey

This volume offers specialists and general readers updated treatments of the most pressing issues in the scholarship on gender and Mormonism. It brings together the culmination of so much research over the past several decades, but also charts future directions. Building on the feminist foundations of scholarship on women, this volume also features a queer analytic and attention to men and masculinity. The designation "gender studies" refers to this expanded vision of a whole range of perspectives on sexual differences.

Feminist thought is deeply important for framing this collection of chapters. Since its founding in 1830, the Church of Jesus Christ of Latter-day Saints has engaged gender norms in surprising and sometimes controversial ways. The LDS practice of polygamy in the nineteenth century both fueled rhetoric of patriarchal domination as well as gave many polygamous wives greater autonomy than their monogamous peers. LDS women were present and active in suffrage, especially in the newspaper *The Woman's Exponent*, and even participated in the Seneca Falls convention with their contemporary thought leaders on women's rights. After polygamy was abandoned, the church's conflicts over women's autonomy continued and have become a central issue in recent decades. Feminist activists in the 1970s founded *Exponent II*, hearkening back to their feminist forebears, and began to publish edited books examining an array of institutional issues through a feminist lens. In the 1970s, 1990s, and 2010s, these tensions flared up when Mormon feminists came into direct confrontation with the male Mormon hierarchy. Such public clashes produced some reforms, but fell short of accomplishing equality. Gay, lesbian, and trans Mormons share a similar history of tensions with church leaders, clashes, and some modest reform. These confrontations are part of the larger story of how Mormonism has positioned itself in the context of changing gender norms in a global context.

While scholars of religion and of Mormonism have long seen the importance of gender as a lens on their traditions, it has not necessarily been a reciprocal relationship from women's and gender studies departments. Religious studies and women's studies both came about in the late 1960s and early 1970s on college campuses, but mostly evolved as separate disciplines. In fact, the two editors of this volume were trained in the only two schools that have a women's studies and religion program, at Claremont and Harvard respectively. Women's studies and gender studies still rarely include scholars of religion into their academic conversations. This volume is also an effort to contribute to these conversations as well.

Despite the dearth of formal academic venues, the feminist intellectual revolution made its mark in all sorts of fields. Women's studies in particular has had an important impact on Mormon studies and continues to wield influence. The second wave in the U.S. brought about revelatory and controversial books for LDS readers. These included various activist and scholarly texts, such as Sonia Johnson's fiery, *From Housewife to Heretic: One Woman's Struggle for Equal Rights and Her Excommunication from the Mormon Church*, Maureen Ursenbach Beecher and Lavina Fielding Anderson's scholarly edited volume *Sisters in Spirit: Mormon Women in Historical and Cultural Perspective* (1987), and Maxine Hanks' feminist anthology *Women and Authority: Re-emerging Mormon Feminism* (1992). In addition, Margaret and Paul Toscano's *Strangers in Paradox: Explorations in Mormon Theology* (1990) pushed on openings for women's theological expansion and D. Michael Quinn's *Same-Sex Dynamics among Nineteenth Century Americans: A Mormon Example* (1994) challenged the heterosexualist history that preceded it. These formative texts helped set the agenda for the study of gender and sexuality within Mormonism.

After several LDS scholars were excommunicated in the 1990s, presumably for their critical gaze at institutional gender norms, others working within gender studies fell fairly quiet. During this time the online community of Mormon feminists began to grow as the information age made connecting with other feminists accessible in a way that previously was not. However, most of these conversations were published in blogs, rather than within the academy. In recent years, however, gender studies approaches have become mainstream at academic conferences on Mormonism. In the past decade, even the Church History Department, the official historians of the Church of Jesus Christ of Latter-day Saints, have made women's history a priority in hiring, publishing, and research. There are also a handful of recent volumes on Latter-day Saint women and Mormon feminism that demonstrate a renewed commitment to these topics.

Ultimately, however, there has been a lag in publishing about issues of gender and sexuality within Mormon studies. The present volume seeks to accomplish two goals, (1) providing a useful overview of the study of gender in the LDS tradition and (2) charting a future for such a field of inquiry. This Handbook attempts to address the many gaps in literature that exist within Mormon studies and gender and also, when possible, help the reader understand what has already been done within the area. Some of the chapters cover well-worn topics. Others are not able to draw upon multiple published sources to talk in generalities about the trends in Mormonism and gender since the chapter may be the first of its kind within the academic sphere. By assembling many of the best scholars of gender and Mormonism, the editors provide a volume that brings the scholarship up to date, engages with broader questions, and demystifies the tradition to insiders and outsiders alike. From nineteenth-century Mormon feminism and suffrage movements to contemporary debates about trans identity, the contributions of this volume are timely, comprehensive, and cumulative of scholarship on these topics.

Scholarship on Mormonism and gender in the past five decades has centered primarily on history, theology, and sociological approaches. In addition to these areas, this multidisciplinary volume discusses some of the foundational issues and guiding questions that stretch across these methods. Our work builds on these studies and pushes scholars and readers to consider issues in a wider and more contemporary context, including how masculinity is shaped and perpetuated historically and contemporarily within Mormonism, how sexual orientation and identity, particularly LGBTQ issues, are grappled with theologically and through lived religion within the LDS Church, and how shifting the scholarly gaze away from presumed whiteness and outside of North America adds nuance to scholarship regarding gender and sexuality within the Mormon tradition. Intersectionality in all forms is optimal and we aim to bring layered and complicated insights into topics that have been debated within Mormonism for years.

Introduction

Methodological issues

As gender studies has developed and matured as a field of inquiry, the topics and questions have changed. This transition is reflected in the title of this volume focused on "gender," a catch-all term for the diverse subjects and approaches. "Women's studies" was inaugurated in response to the androcentric curriculum of history, literature, religious studies, psychology, and other fields. Pioneering scholars argued that the scholarship and courses most male faculty offered simply ignored the women who also contributed to these fields, giving students and readers a false understanding that only men were relevant agents of history and culture. In response to this pressure from (mostly) female faculty, colleges and universities around the United States and in the U.K. established women's studies courses and eventually departments with the objective to incorporate women into the curriculum.

However, the field itself has undergone radical reorganization, as the superficially simple objective became much more theoretically rich. As the field developed, it was shaped by several complexities that called into question some of the assumptions about women as a category of analysis. This challenge came from several different quarters, including non-heterosexual women, transwomen, scholars working on critiques of class, as well as non-white and global feminists who often had different priorities and perspectives than many of the white North American feminist activists. "Women" was not, it seemed, a singular category, but one that was embedded and layered with multiple other identities, and must be regionally, historically, socially, and racially located.

A further development in gender studies has been the inclusion of sexuality and the inclusion of men and masculinity. As scholars of sexuality noted that the heterosexual order was closely linked with the patriarchal order, the two fields of inquiry began to overlap. Additionally, scholars increasingly began to investigate the social construction of masculinity and maleness. Rather than replicating the older androcentric approaches prior to women's studies, masculinity studies offers a critical approach to maleness, emphasizing contested options, provisionality, and instability.

This change is also reflected in the approach that many scholars of Latter-day Saint history, thought, and culture have taken in their work. Today these scholars are trained and teach in a variety of academic programs that reflect the methodological and theoretical diversity of the topic itself. Women historians in the 1970s were part of the trends of the feminist critique of academic history. Feminist theologians also became active during this period, flourishing in the 1980s and early 1990s. Attention to the social categories of femininity and masculinity mark some evolution in the field. In the 1990s, studies of LDS sexuality and masculinity began to appear. The turn to masculinity in the scholarship has produced important insights, especially about the fractured and paradoxical masculinity of LDS men in the United States. As masculinity is increasingly pluriform, and as heterosexuality is decoupled from normative maleness, these tensions are increasingly acute.

Today, gender studies often takes an intersectional approach to gender, seeing it as situated within broader structures like race, nationality, class, and sexuality. This sort of meta-analysis is often baked into the scholarship, not content to simply reproduce past categories and assumptions. Sensitive to the multiple, overlapping ways that marginalization may occur, the concept of intersectionality accounts for a more dynamic theory of subjectivity. Such a view also holds that the voices of marginalized people offer important counternarratives and ethical insights into dominant discourses. New scholarship on Latter-day Saints is taking these perspectives as a starting point.

The essays in this volume reflect on some of the broader theoretical and topical shifts in gender studies, including sexual violence, theorizing and complicating the supposed binary of masculinity and femininity, global approaches, and intersectionality. As a global church, global perspectives are increasingly important in the study of the Latter-day Saint story. These global perspectives complicate the idea of a uniform Mormonism, as the cultural context greatly shapes how Latter-day Saints embrace and embody gender performances. Such perspectives resist essentializing cultures and recognize transnationality, migration, and postcolonialism.

The global focus arises in tandem with a methodological shift that would incorporate analysis of race alongside analysis of gender. Latter-day Saint teachings about gender have often implicitly and explicitly been racialized by either assuming certain kinship dynamics as normal and normative or by privileging whiteness over others in practice and policy. Such analysis not only responds to the global context, but might help retell the history of the Church of Jesus Christ of Latter-day Saints in the United States. The racialized teachings about those of African descent, Native Americans, and Pacific Islanders show how race and gender are necessarily intertwined.

Historical approaches

Historical approaches to gender have not only been an important methodology in Mormon history, but to the field of gender studies itself. Histories of gender are keen to focus on change, development, and sometimes radical reversals. Many contemporary LDS members believe that in general, Mormon religious ideas are somewhat stable and unchanging. This includes ideas about homosexuality, modesty, race, and kinship, all of which are carefully mapped out and examined within this volume, offering readers new insights into the fragility of religious ideas and norms. History often tells a different story.

The resources for doing Mormon history are incredibly rich. The Church of Jesus Christ of Latter-day Saints is notorious for keeping meticulous records. Scholars who study members of this tradition, the largest branch of Mormonism, are fortunate to have a plethora of documents to consult. However, those that are examining gender and sexuality within the LDS Church also have a challenging time gaining institutional permission to access the records, as the more sensitive the subject matter is, the tighter the institution seems to control the information. Gender and sexuality certainly fall into this category.

Scholars in the Handbook examine official church teachings as well as church leaders to grasp how the global church expanded and changed as it was steered by different men. Understanding how an institution came to be and the ideals that shaped its trajectory are important in complicating historical narratives. While the LDS Church is unapologetically patriarchal, scholars can look to the shadows to sketch women's complex lives and interactions with institutional authority.

The chapters in this section reflect contemporary historical conversations in religious studies such as intellectual history, institutional history, cultural studies, and activism. Postmodern theory is a powerful analytical tool to trace how an idea has developed, shifted, and even been reconceptualized within a faith tradition. Relatedly, the poststructuralist turn towards examining and deconstructing systems of power has deeply influenced the way in which scholars approach institutional history. Since institutional self-reflection is atypical, this work serves to deconstruct the dynamics of power that are inherent in institutional life, and point towards possibilities.

Within these historical approaches, many of the chapters focus on art and literature. Scholars of material and cultural studies have called attention to the salience of these objects for interpreting the past. Material culture scholars approach objects as part of meaning making and within religious studies this rings particularly true. Understanding how Mormon and anti-Mormon popular literature communicated ideas about Mormon sexuality historically is important for understanding how other Americans and Europeans interacted with early Saints and draws attention to the trope of women as sexual victims of the religious elite.

Social scientific approaches

The use of anthropological and sociological research is growing in Mormon studies. Social scientific methods work well for studying the intersection of religion and gender and can help scholars understand how theology is being actualized by believers. In this volume, there are three main sociological methods that have been used: ethnography, lived religion, and sociological surveys. While these methods have different disciplinary genealogies they share a common aim of attempting to understand both what individuals believe and how they practice their religious convictions. They differ from historical and theological methods in that they decenter the institutional narrative by looking to the people "on the ground" who are living the religion and examining what practices are being internalized, resisted, and upheld by the members.

Ethnography is a method that encourages living among the people and conducting in-depth field research, including interviews and participant observation. This method aims to help scholars capture the culture and worldview of those they study. Ethnography can be a method used to privilege people and groups that operate on the margins of a religious community. Within Mormonism, communities that live outside of North America fall into this category, and the further one travels from the Utah headquarters of the LDS Church the less likely one is to find communities and groups of LDS that have been studied. This volume addresses this challenge by presenting both new and expanded ethnographic research on communities in Peru, Nicaragua, Ireland, the U.K., South Africa, New Zealand, and more. Ethnography is also helpful when studying groups of people that are bound by identity and not necessarily living far from the geographical center of the church. In this way, non-traditional families and non-traditional expressions of gender and sexuality are captured through ethnographic methods.

Coming out of the field of history of religions, the newer methodology "lived religion" seeks to decenter the narratives of religious institutions. Lived religion challenges high theology and seeks to understand how religion is actually practiced by people, not simply how it is idealized by leaders. The newest of the sociological methods in the volume, lived religion has become popular with scholars, including those who examine Mormonism and gender. Lived religion also gives scholars of Mormonism insight into how rapidly changing policies about sex, gender, and sexuality are digested and actualized by followers of the tradition.

Survey research offers another approach to analyze trends and shifts among Latter-day Saints. Much of this research has been conducted through broad national surveys that sample a few Latter-day Saints. Authors in this volume also reflect new and innovative ways to fund and conduct sociological research. Crowdfunding in order to pay for professional data collection provides scholars important data that have been missing from the research. Similarly, sociological tools give us excellent data that have been gathered by other institutions but used for varying purposes. Synthesizing these different data sets and finding patterns within the LDS population helps move the field forward in helpful ways.

The important common denominator among these methods is that they aim at getting at the way in which sex and gender are shaped by institutional teachings, as understood by individuals and smaller groups within the Church of Jesus Christ of Latter-day Saints.

These methods prioritize the experiences of people, and secondarily examine official texts, declarations and policy. In this way, such methods contribute to a type of "ground up" theology where adherents implement adaptations and eventually some of these shifts work their way up to institutional leaders and become part of the official policy. Within the LDS Church, change is slow and there often exists a lag between the changes that members make in their lives and official acknowledgment of the social and cultural changes, let alone policy changes. Social scientific data round out scholarly sources to include "real" people and give a much more robust portrait of the religion.

Theological approaches

Theology is a mode of thinking that Latter-day Saints have used to explain, support, and resist the gender and sexual norms around them. At the same time, theology is often a marginal discourse in contemporary Mormonism. Latter-day Saints have not really engaged with broader theological movements except in niche academic venues. There are almost no trained theologians employed by the church's curricular and academic institutions, nor have any of the senior church leaders seriously engaged with contemporary academic or political theology in their writings or sermons. Some scholars have even claimed that Mormonism has no theology.

This lack of engagement with theology has happened primarily because Mormonism has populist roots that are suspicious of religious professionalism and the tradition of Christian thinking that tended to look down on Mormonism's heterodox teachings. This has not necessarily been cause for embarrassment, but rather a source of pride. Because Latter-day Saints think of themselves as distinctive religiously, they have often done theology differently as well. In this way, the study of LDS theology has to theorize up from the practices and teachings that are not expressed in these terms. A secondary, but important, reason for lack of theological engagement by feminist theorists has been the fear of suffering institutional consequences, as several academics in the 1990s experienced.

LDS beliefs about gender and sexuality also rest on a theological foundation that is quite distinct from other Christian faiths. For instance, LDS theology draws on an extensive reformulation of traditional doctrines of God, including the idea that God is a male-gendered person of material substance, that he is married to a female companion (at least one), that human souls have the potential to become like God, and that there was a pre-mortal drama for human souls and an extensive elaboration of what post-mortal heavenly existence may be like. There is also additional scripture to the Bible in the Book of Mormon, Doctrine and Covenants, and the Pearl of Great Price. On top of this, the teachings of past church leaders form a deuterocanonical tradition that shapes contemporary interpretations. These narratives, visions, revelations, texts, and interpretive traditions then must be reapplied to present concerns to give them meaning and relevance.

While these alternative sources for theological reasoning make Mormonism distinctive relative to other Christians, not everything in LDS theologies is entirely distinctive. Indeed, despite all of these unique sources, since the outset of the twentieth century when the faith abandoned the practice of plural marriage, Latter-day Saint teachings on gender and sexuality have mirrored other conservative religious groups on issues such as birth control, sex outside of marriage, same-sex relations, transgender identity, and gender roles. The distinctive elements of Mormonism's theological tradition are nearly always put to use to make Mormonism conform to traditionally conservative social norms. Official LDS theology then uses its theological distinctiveness to emphasize aspects of its social normality by adopting conservative gender norms.

The essays in this volume explore these themes, as well as more recent trends in LDS theology on gender and sexuality that have expanded beyond the interests of North American feminists. Queer, trans, transnational, racial, and class concerns have sparked new theological questions about reproduction, belonging, materiality, and essentialism. These approaches have troubled the essentialist ontology of what it means to be "male" and "female." Gender analysis in these approaches is more intersectional, less heteronormative, and less constrained by present problems. Theology in this case is then as constructive as it is critical, seeking resources within the tradition to make the case for a more inclusive Mormonism that expresses its greatest virtues.

Just as the conservative interpretations of Mormonism have mirrored broader social movements, so too have the critical engagements of these teachings been influenced by modernist and postmodernist reform movements in Christianity. Indeed, the overlap over concerns between LDS women and other Christian women in North America in the last two centuries has produced a confluence of agendas, vocabulary, and perspectives. North American Mormon feminists have focused much of their attention on egalitarian solutions to patriarchal Mormonism. They have focused on traditional theological resources like scripture to find alternative perspectives. Mormon feminists have also focused on other concerns of Christian feminists, like gender roles, a divine feminine, and women's ordination. These theological issues in particular have been central to Mormon feminist scholarly and activist concerns since the 1980s, but have their roots in nineteenth-century feminist agitation.

In modern contexts, Mormon feminists have used the church's distinctive teachings as a basis for rejecting conservative interpretations of gender and sexuality. For instance, the tradition of a Heavenly Mother in Latter-day Saint thought has rallied Mormon feminists to new theological possibilities for complementary egalitarianism. These feminists have also looked to early Mormonism and scripture as a precedent to break down the structural hierarchies that favor men in marriages and ecclesiastical settings. Thus, while challenging current practices, Mormon feminists often rely heavily on Mormon tradition and sources of authority to make their claim. But these efforts have also exposed new dangers as the church has set limits about such reinterpretations of the faith. Women's ordination has been a particular source of tension; LDS activists for women's ordination have faced discipline from church leaders.

Some church members have attempted to use these distinctive theological foundations to critique official LDS teachings on gender and sexuality. Scholarly approaches to LDS theology then seek both to elaborate how the intellectual tradition and theological framework have thought about gender and sexuality and to critically engage these teachings for alternative possibilities. This theological orientation is often critical of racialized patriarchy and/or heteronormativity with a view that such ideologies are inconsistent with a more fulsome understanding of justice. Thus, rather than a secular critique, theological readings offer constructive alternatives within the tradition as a framework for internal reform.

Conclusion

Scholarship and activism on gender have sometimes been in conflict, with the stakeholders prioritizing different goals. While activists are often seeking to make substantive changes to culture and institutions, many scholars are more content with accurate descriptions or theoretical musings. Within religious studies it is widely accepted that contemporary social movements in the U.S. relied upon religious actors for their success. Black churches were at the center of the Civil Rights movement and scholars have demonstrated that religious women were involved in the second wave of the American women's movement from the beginning. Examining activism and social movements within a faith tradition also reminds the reader of the necessity of activism to bring about institutional change. The scholars in this volume represent various positions on that continuum and often hold different goals.

Regardless of the competing interests, history has demonstrated that cultures and communities are reluctant to include people who seem different and activism has helped to pry open the gates of privilege, even if only incrementally. There is a price within the LDS tradition for public activism and that can come in the form of one's membership. Former LDS bishop Sam Young was excommunicated for his advocacy of curtailing the ability of bishops to interview children and teenagers about sexual matters. Similarly, Kate Kelly, who led the Ordain Women movement, was excommunicated after leading protests and inquiries requesting that the prophet and Quorum of the Twelve Apostles seek revelation sanctioning women's ordination.

Despite these excommunications, the church sometimes accommodates change. Recently the church changed the policy for one-on-one interviews by ecclesiastical leaders of young men and women, opening them up to include a third party if the parent or child request it. Similarly, women leaders in the church experienced an expanded public presence at senior and local levels. These small changes would not have occurred without activism, yet the LDS leadership discourages any type of campaigning for social change by excommunicating those at the head of the movements who are most vocal and visible and thus sending a message that if one values one's membership, they should not publically demand/ask/beg for it. These censures always have a temporary chilling effect within the activist community but eventually a new movement is formed or reinvigorated and micro changes within the institution are often evident.

What will happen as the Church of Jesus Christ of Latter-day Saints continues to adapt to changing social norms cannot be fully predicted, but the conflicts over gender and sexuality have become increasingly acute in recent years. This volume contributes to an understanding of the past and the present, and offers scholars and other readers new insights for making sense of the future.

PART I

Methodological issues

1
GENDER AND CULTURE IN A GLOBAL CHURCH

Laurie F. Maffly-Kipp

The teaching of leaders of the Church of Jesus Christ of Latter-day Saints on matters related to gender roles is fairly straightforward: men and women serve different ultimate purposes, both on this earth and in the life hereafter. Since 1995, as elaborated in "The Family: A Proclamation to the World," official LDS teaching has declared that gender roles are both essential and eternal characteristics of individuals, attributes that shape domestic, ecclesiastic, and sacramental obligations. In this formulation, a woman's highest calling is motherhood, and her duty if possible is to stay home and care for her children while her husband earns a living, supports the family, and serves as its spiritual head. Within the church, males alone (if deemed worthy) may serve in the priesthood, an office linked to specific ritual functions, and men comprise the organizational hierarchy. Women serve church offices as well through the female Relief Society and callings in localized settings. In its ideal form, this version of gender describes a religious community in which sex-specific roles are organized into parallel and complementary structures that determine the most basic of daily activities. Young boys and girls are educated and socialized into roles within the church and family that stress their differing religious and familial obligations.

Although its theological underpinnings are quite distinctive, Mormon understandings of male and female roles are not unlike those in many conservative Christian churches that celebrate the primacy of the nuclear family and the complementary roles of men and women (Griffith, 2017; McDannell, 2018). As in other American-based churches, moreover, the emphasis on adhering to those roles has increased dramatically within Mormon communities since the 1970s, as feminism, gay rights, and other related social issues have prompted clearer articulation of gendered boundaries by those dedicated to upholding distinctive roles for men and women.

These ideals, with a basis in divine mandate, are also presumed to be universally applicable. At the conclusion to the 1995 Proclamation, President Gordon B. Hinckley advised his worldwide followers to promote these values: "We call upon responsible citizens and officers of government everywhere to promote those measures designed to maintain and strengthen the family as the fundamental unit of society." In practice, however, applying these principles both within and outside of the U.S. has entailed considerable negotiation. Simply put, men and women in different parts of the world understand their social roles in distinct ways, and thus the notion of what is required of one's gender is not a settled matter. Of course, this is true even within the United States: as David Knowlton observes, divergent discourses of manhood and womanhood, promoted by institutions, the media, and various communities, also shape

American society (Knowlton, 1992, p. 22), and Mormons are not exempt from the din of that cacophony of expectations. He notes that U.S. church members learn to be Mormon and to be American simultaneously, but the gendered expectations of those identities are not indistinguishable (Knowlton, 1992; see also Grimshaw, 2015).

In important respects the Mormon tradition has always been global, and therefore to distinguish too clearly between gender roles within and outside the U.S. is somewhat artificial. Further, local expressions of gendered ideals are shaped not simply by religious mandate but by class, ethnicity/race, economics, and political processes that may have little relationship to American patterns. The number of examples of cultural difference in gender roles is endless, and rather than provide a laundry list survey of the ways that Mormon assumptions have confronted these myriad constructions, it is more illuminating to outline some of the dynamics that govern decisions made within local communities as they encounter LDS religious ideals about male and female roles. With the rapid growth in the numbers of Mormon communities outside the United States since 1960, the disconnect between religious ideals and social possibilities—as well as the "Americanness" of Mormon gender norms—has come into even sharper relief. That disjunction has elicited a variety of responses from non-U.S. Mormons, from quiet dismissal to defiance to creative adaptation. While it is impossible to fully capture the many ways that a focus on gender plays out in Mormon communities throughout the world, several key points illustrate the dynamics involved. In turn, those varying rejoinders are challenging and even reshaping the intricate negotiations between official teachings and localized practice.

The building up of Zion by the Latter-day Saints was a global religious project from the start. In September 1830, six months after the founding of the church, Joseph Smith, Sr. and Don Carlos Smith, the father and brother of the Prophet, embarked on a preaching journey north of the St. Lawrence River. By 1834, missionaries had established four branches in the eastern towns of Ontario, and Canadian believers had begun migrating to Kirtland, Ohio, to join the body of the Saints. In 1837 the mission spread to Britain, where Mormons achieved even greater success in attracting and baptizing new members. By the 1850s, over half the membership of the church lived in the British Isles, a population that fed the pool of European emigrants embarking for the United States. Throughout the nineteenth century, steady streams of baptized members from western Europe replenished the pews and brought to the growing community in Utah a culturally diverse mix of members, many with familial ties to other places.

Since 1960, international membership has increased markedly faster than domestic growth; by 1996, the number of baptized members outside the U.S. had surpassed the number within. The growth of Mormon communities in Latin America, West Africa, and Asia, as well as the growth of the church in transnational migrant communities, has raised even more pointedly questions of how to disseminate and promote standardized gender ideals. Yet despite these swiftly changing demographic realities, the vast majority of scholarship on gender and Mormonism focuses on the familial and ecclesiastical status of women in the Church of Jesus Christ of Latter-day Saints, and nearly all of those studies address the topic of Euro-American women. Until the past decade, discourses about gender roles in the church outside the U.S. have been virtually untouched as a subject of analysis (Haglund, 2012; Zeveloff, 2012). As a result, this essay focuses most extensively on women's roles within the faith, since this is where research is the most illuminating and tensions are most pronounced. This comes with the caveat that understandings of female gender roles bear directly on men's experiences, inasmuch as gendered identities are "co-constructed" and defined in relation to one another (Dawley and Thornton, 2018).

European progressivism and American mores

Although the vast majority of Mormons in the U.S. today are Euro-American, it is precisely in the Western European context that many aspects of the Mormon focus on complementary gender roles is most often seen as a U.S. imposition, if not a distillation of conservative American values. This impression likely reflects the ways that Mormonism in the U.S. has diverged from European social democratic patterns in the last half of the twentieth century. These patterns are also true of some of the wealthier former colonial possessions of European powers such as New Zealand, Australia, and South Africa. Carine Decoo-Vanwelkenhuysen, a Belgian transplanted to Utah, reflected on her move from Antwerp to the Mormon Corridor in the early 2000s: "I thought I had a Mormon identity until I moved to Utah," she wrote (2015, p. 135). It was only in that move that she realized that Mormon female identity was not universal. From her perspective, Utah Mormon identity was routinely conflated with right-wing conservatism and Republican party politics. Her own experiences in a local ward in Belgium had been much more politically diverse, and the corresponding understanding of women's roles in Utah seemed far too limiting.

In a survey of sixty women in seventeen European countries, Decoo-Vanwelkenhuysen mapped Mormon women's experiences and compared them to what she had encountered in the U.S. She noted striking differences in life choices, in which European Mormon women conform more closely to other European choices than to U.S. Mormon norms: European Saints tend to marry later and delay childbirth for a few years after marriage, focusing instead on acquiring formal education before motherhood. They also continue to work outside the home by choice—in fact, the employment rate of Mormon women in Europe was even higher than European averages. Decoo-Vanwelkenhuysen reasoned that European female Saints pursue work not just for economic reasons, but to feel involved socially in their communities. In Western Europe's social democracies, generous health care, parental leave policies, and child support make a balance of work and family life easier, and women liked this level of support. Some, she reported, are openly critical of what they perceive to be anti-family policies in the U.S. (2015, pp. 136–37).

The lessening of gender distinctions in work and family life also carries over into church responsibilities and theology. According to some European observers, many church members feel that gender equality is already a given in European countries, so there is no need to fight for it, and they report that women already enjoy healthy participation in decision-making in their local wards. Most don't want to hold the priesthood (and, as in the U.S., a number of them rationalize that men need it more than they do), but they tend to minimize the theological significance of gender difference. They are also critical of the "American" emphasis on modesty in dress, the "odd" dating and courtship patterns, and the lack of robust sex education for young people in the U.S., to which they attribute the higher rates of teen pregnancy, births, and abortions in the U.S. (Decoo-Vanwelkenhuysen, 2015, pp. 140, 142).

Other research on European Mormons reinforces this data. Wilfried Decoo estimates that perhaps only 10–15 per cent of European membership lives in traditional Mormon family arrangements. He attributes this in part to family disruptions caused by conversion, as well as the lack of a surrounding Mormon culture that makes it more difficult to keep children in the faith. The question, then, of what Mormon women's experience can and should look like in Europe is intriguing. The Correlation Movement beginning in the 1960s that was intended to make the church less "American" by paring down the gospel message to "essential elements" is still, to Decoo's way of thinking, filled with American ideals and behaviors that aren't recognized as such. In many parts of Europe, the initial organizers of branches and wards are white, middle-class Americans, and they bring with them "American" advice on dating, dress, and grooming

(Decoo, 2015, pp. 549, 551–52). For women these differences have particular salience, since their own sense of what it means to gain agency or self-reliance can be very much at odds with church teachings for women.

This is not to say that European Mormons downplay or ignore the teachings of church leadership regarding gender. There are plenty of stories of struggle, for example, with same-gender attraction among church members across the Atlantic (and the same advice is dispensed by local leaders there as it would be in the U.S., i.e., while the feelings *themselves* are not considered sinful, one is expected to resist acting upon those inclinations as one of the "challenges" that God gives us in this mortal life), and the church has posted numerous descriptions of believing Saints who seek to conform to heterosexual norms in its social media (Church of Jesus Christ of Latter-Day Saints, 2016; Hafen, 2009). But some observers have noted that in European countries that are openly accepting of homosexuality and same-sex partnerships, many church members themselves support the more fluid understandings of gender in the surrounding society—fearing, perhaps, the stigma of being labeled intolerant. Walter Van Beek asserts that in Holland, many LDS church members view homosexuality as an acceptable form of difference: "tales of American institutions … that tried to 'heal' this 'affliction' by deprogramming are whispered about with some horror by Dutch members." As a result, Dutch Saints tend to avoid discussion of such issues in church contexts. Even in the years prior to the campaign against same-sex marriage in California in 2008 (Proposition 8), a cause in which church members were actively mobilized, stake presidents in Europe "conveniently" ignored the call of Utah leadership to fight against such legislation in their own countries: "No LDS voice was heard when those laws were passed in Europe," and more important still, "the stake presidents felt no reason at all to be against those laws" since they represented what, from a Dutch standpoint, was a backward American ideology (Van Beek, 2005, p. 31).

Conservatism and abundant gifts in the Global South

The situation in the Global South[1] stands in stark contrast to the relatively flexible attitudes of European gender norms. For the most part, Global South regions exhibit much more conservative attitudes about sexuality and gender. Homosexuality is illegal in over seventy countries in Africa, the Middle East, and South and Southeast Asia, and in a handful of places is punishable by death (Avery, 2019). While women's economic roles are highly variable, the preponderance of childcare and domestic work is seen as falling within their domain. As such, attitudes in these areas are often more congruent with American Mormon values, and therefore traditional church teachings are welcomed as a means of supporting and stabilizing nuclear family structures. Rather than seeing women's proscribed roles as mother and domestic worker as an oppressive possibility, female members in the Global South are more likely to welcome the clarity and relative safety promised by Mormon gendered ideals. That difference is illustrated succinctly by a speech delivered in 2014 by Sharon Eubank, currently the first counselor in the Relief Society General Presidency of the Church of Jesus Christ of Latter-day Saints.

> I am going to tell you a story, and it actually happened to Lillian DeLong, a friend of mine. She served on a Relief Society board years ago. And she was assigned to go to Ghana. And she had her husband with her. And they were in a very rural part of Ghana. So, they did their training. She was there to do Relief Society Training. And it is a very simple structure and they were in different rooms, and her husband was in Priesthood and she was in Relief Society and they did their training. After it was over, a woman came up to her, in her beautiful Ghanaian church dress, and she shook her

hand and she kept saying "This is a woman's church." She's just crying and tears are just streaming down her face. She kept saying, "This is a woman's church." Lillian didn't really know what she was talking about. And she's smiling and saying, "Yeah." But the woman just kept pumping her hand and saying over and over again, "This is a woman's church." And finally Lillian said, "What do you mean, 'This is a woman's church?'" And she said, "We have just been in the marvelous Relief Society that teaches us not only spiritual things but temporal things about how to make our lives and our children and our families better. And at the same time your husband is in the Priesthood room and he is teaching our husbands that the culture of the church does not allow for them to beat their wives and their children."

(Eubank, 2014)

Eubank's story was celebrated with a standing ovation at the conference. It was later posted on the Mormon Newsroom's website, and reprinted in the *Ensign* magazine. The excitement with which this address was received, according to one observer, is unparalleled by that of any address given by any other speaker at a FairMormon conference (Densley, 2017). It served as a demonstration, in Eubank's estimation, of the universality of church teachings about the eternal significance of gender. The knowledge that church teachings had some effect on ameliorating deeply entrenched social problems—and to hear that stated in such a moving way from the Ghanaian woman—undoubtedly provided listeners with confirmation that the role of the church in other parts of the world, by teaching men and women appropriate ways of interacting in their families, can be salutary.

Mormon gender patterns in the Global South also track closely with those of other conservative Christian groups, especially the new charismatic (or 'Neo-Pentecostal') churches, which are currently among the fastest growing movements in these regions. Like the charismatic churches, Mormon teachings emphasize individual moral agency and complementary responsibilities of men and women within the household. They also shift spiritual priority toward the maintenance of nuclear family systems, while still acknowledging broader kinship ties as spiritually significant. This can be useful in many parts of the world, such as Latin America, in which conversion to Mormonism can precipitate profound disruption of kinship ties; sometimes the extended church family then fills in as kin in place of biological relations. However, in West Africa and Oceania, where religious affiliation tends to be quite fluid, it is more common for extended family members to attend different churches, or even multiple churches at the same time.[2] Still, the acute focus in Mormon life on nuclear family practice does at times rub up against localized kinship patterns of obligation and friendship (Thornton, 2016; Soothill, 2007, pp. 219–30).

Despite relatively conservative common teachings about gender roles and sexuality, one particular aspect in which Mormon ideals differ dramatically from charismatic patterns comes in the role of women's spiritual authority. Ghana provides a case in point. Many of the newer charismatic churches emerging there exhibit a highly decentralized ecclesiastical structure. Some, such as Ghana's Lighthouse International, promote loose ties to international organizations such as the Pentecostal World Fellowship, but many are single megachurches led by charismatic individuals that are not under the jurisdiction of larger governing bodies. It is in these localized congregations, some of which have thousands of members, that women's spiritual authority as leaders and even founders can be fully exercised (Soothill, 2007; Ampofo, 2017). The majority are male led, but a significant minority of newer organizations in Ghana have been founded by female leaders, whose spiritual authority is declared and widely recognized. A larger number of religious congregations with male pastors nonetheless treat with great deference the position of the "First Lady," the wife of the pastor, who exercises considerable independent command both within the church and beyond its walls (Soothill, 2007, p. 155; 2010, pp. 83–87). Whether one calls this female "empowerment" is a contested question, but women in these churches undoubtedly perform religious roles accompanied by considerable power and social standing, and are even represented in social media and on the ubiquitous billboards in cities like Accra as having co-equal standing with their husbands.

The Church of Jesus Christ of Latter-day Saints in Ghana has developed in a very different way. Although the Mormon tradition shares with charismatic Christian groups a longstanding emphasis on the power of individual spiritual revelation and gifts, it began to downplay the more enthusiastic potential of teachings in the early twentieth century. Those shifts in practice were never completely eradicated, but the rise of a centralized bureaucratic structure in Utah over the following century had the effect of curbing women's prophetic opportunities, in particular, within ritual and formal occasions (anointings, healings, and presiding over organized religious life). By the post-World War II era, increasing emphasis on the standardization and correlation of church practice has also made it easier to enforce gendered rules about participation. In contrast to independent charismatic female preachers, who are beholden to no one except their followers and to their God, women within the LDS Church, even if they desired to, have little room to push the bounds of conservative social and sacramental roles. Recall the woman quoted by Sharon Eubank, who expressed delight with the ways the church was helping her family to conform to fairly traditional patterns; her main concern was not to shift roles but to school her husband in how to be a better husband and father.

Global South Mormonism was not always born into these patterns, however. When the LDS Church first entered Ghana in the 1970s, it bumped up against a society in which women also engaged in other kinds of spiritual leadership alongside the role of wife and mother. Beginning in the early 1960s, some Ghanaians, armed with the Book of Mormon and a few instructional manuals, began to form religious communities and take the name of the LDS Church for their own. It was only after 1978 with the lifting of the ban on temple participation for peoples of African descent that the Utah church began to send missionaries to West Africa; before that time, in the absence of oversight, these small churches tried as they could to adapt Mormon practices to their own setting. This led to some distinctive hybrid church procedures. Members actively incorporated enthusiastic dancing, drumming, and women's participation into their Mormon practice. Perhaps the most unusual was a church organized and led by a woman named Rebecca Mould, who was known to her followers as "Prophetess Rebecca." Her leadership, in this regard, conformed to traditional patterns of women's authority in southern Ghanaian society. The first constitution of this new eclectic "Mormon" church in 1969 makes no mention of gender differences in terms of the priesthood, and women in this church and others like it led prayer groups and performed ritual cleansings and baptisms for both male and female congregants. At times female authority was questioned: in 1972, male leaders discussed a proposal to bar women from "giving revelations and prophecies" (Meeting Minutes, n.d. Dadzie papers, p. 240). They did not pursue this option, but instead instructed that dreams and revelations had to be reported to the pastor. Still, Prophetess Rebecca was elected to a national "high council" of twelve apostles in 1972 with no dissent.

When the LDS missionaries arrived and set about regulating church practices, they had to confront the "problem" of Prophetess Rebecca, who also happened to own the building in which the church met. Meeting minutes and journals reveal a delicate process of negotiation. Initially, Rebecca welcomed the LDS missionaries and was one of the first baptized into the young church. President Spencer W. Kimball sent along a special commendation to her, and she was set apart as Relief Society president. Her title was changed to "Mother Rebecca," although many followers continued to call her a prophetess and she continued to occupy a prime seat on the dais in the front of the meeting house. Still, efforts to nudge her out of a position of spiritual authority began to chafe, and her leadership became less visible. The missionaries explained to her that the baptisms she had performed were not valid because they had to be conducted by a member of the priesthood. When they departed in late 1979, arguments broke out in the church as several male members tried to convince her to donate her building to the church. When she refused, she was accused of "abusing" the Presidency, and soon thereafter she left the church to reclaim the title of independent church leader (Stevenson, 2015, pp. 254–55).

While her role as Prophetess Rebecca was relatively unusual, the circumstances surrounding her departure suggest that she was far from alone in wanting to retain women's ecclesiastical authority in the church. Her sister, Comfort Mould, had already split away and formed her own charismatic congregation. When Rebecca left the LDS Church, she took a substantial number of her followers with her and continued to use LDS church materials. She considers herself a Mormon. "The Lord knows that I'm a Mormon … In my heart, I'm a Mormon; I'm a Latter-day Saint" (Johnson, n.d., p. 37).

In many parts of the Global South, this culturally specific form of women's religious authority continues to exist alongside—and not necessarily in tension with—very traditional models of womanhood. In Ghanaian society, both seem to be acknowledged and respected. Even Prophetess Rebecca's former church members who stayed in the LDS fold still acknowledged her as a healer and prophetess, and continued to visit her every so often to pay their respects. But this example also suggests that some Mormon Ghanaians remained mindful of prior cultural practices with respect to gender that continued to influence their religious behavior—many of which were either purposely stifled by, or perhaps not even visible to, American missionaries, stake presidents, and others tasked with building up local branches of the church.

Those less visible patterns of behavior and belief that slip under the radar of many American Mormons have also shaped the development of the church among indigenous peoples in the Americas and in Oceania, in ways that scholars are only now beginning to trace. Mormons arrived in New Zealand in the 1880s, at a time of considerable conflict between British colonizers and those they were attempting to subjugate. There, they encountered receptive indigenous Maori who had grown dissatisfied with both British colonial overreach and Anglican worship. The Mormons presented a fresh alternative unencumbered by imperial politics, one that seemed to fit neatly with Maori prophetic traditions. What did not fit neatly was traditional Maori social organization. Scholarship on precolonial Maori society indicates that prior to Christian influence, women held many positions that were, at least in theory, hardly compatible with Mormon doctrines: they retained their names as well as their property upon marriage, wore similar clothing to men, and remained, for all intents and purposes, closely identified with their natal *whanau*, a term denoting "kinship group" that has no direct parallel in American usage (Walker, 2017), but that denotes both spiritual obligations and geographical responsibilities to sacred land as well as people. Because homes were kept and children were often raised by a network of relatives beyond the biological parents, women could fulfill many social roles in addition to childrearing and domestic tasks. Women and men thereby both exercised patterns of leadership, or *rangatira*, that were linked to their prophetic gifts, or *mana* (Lineham, 1991; Mikaere, 1994).

Unlike Anglican ministers, the first Mormon missionaries brought a message of prophecy and healing, one that proved compatible, for a sizeable number of Maori, with their older cosmology. Their distance from Utah also made it possible, up until World War II, to creatively combine Mormon and Maori teachings, allowing them to keep alive ritual aspects of language, music, and dance that Protestant missionaries had been intent on stamping out. Many members lived together in a settlement near their church and attended schools run by the LDS Church, cementing connections between the *whanau* and the sacred body of believers. Some Maori today, who were raised in this mid-century Mormon Maori communal environment, credit Mormon missionaries with keeping alive their traditional ways of life, including the importance of women to the social and spiritual life of the group. Rather than categorically stamping them out, American missionaries, as Ian Barber has written, demonstrated a "range of conflicting cultural behaviours" (Barber, 1995, p. 147) in response to Maori practices. He notes that perhaps the single greatest conflict in the early twentieth century arose over the role of the *tohunga-Maori*, or traditional religious practitioners, men and women who engaged in healing practices among their people. Both Mormon and non-Mormon Maori would visit them, and some *tohunga* themselves blended their rites with Christian teachings. Missionaries tried to insist that healing ordinances could only take place through the authority of the priesthood, a rule that would effectively have prevented women from serving as healers at all. By all reports these efforts were sporadic, and even countered by a redoubled commitment in the 1930s and 1940s to the use of Maori language, music, and cultural displays in church gatherings.

Data on the meaning of gender roles in this context, as is the case in other areas of the Global South, is suggestive and fragmentary. But it is certainly true that the arrival of Mormonism has had multiple and perhaps even contradictory effects within indigenous communities, leading to creative improvisation that can, at times, fall outside the bounds of official oversight.

Mobility, gender, and transnational religious community

Up to this point, we've been discussing elements of Mormonism and gender from a perspective of cultural stasis, i.e., we have assumed, for the purposes of generalization, that there are separable and discrete cultures located in different regions that reflect distinct social practices, beliefs, and values. And we have seen how the Mormon global project has promulgated a universalized "gospel culture" in congregations through the inculcation of shared teachings about male and female purposes and goals, one that cuts across cultural boundaries and acknowledges only limited forms of cultural distinctiveness. That process has been neither complete nor consistently applied, but it remains an important ideal within the LDS Church.

The world, however, is a much more mobile place than this model of cultural encounter can accommodate. Increasingly, people move around to metropolitan centers such as New York, London, Barcelona, Dubai, Hong Kong, Auckland, or Singapore. Some move with families for jobs in finance or banking and stay only a short amount of time. Others come without family as migrants, and send money home to support their kin, often returning for extended periods of time but living, in a sense, betwixt and between cultures. A growing number of urban centers are hardly monocultural. Somalis live in Minneapolis, Japanese live in Accra, and Filipinos live in Sydney. These transnational hubs present a different sort of challenge for any definition of "gospel culture," an increasingly common issue that relates directly to the social roles that people inhabit. Will the church have enough members of the priesthood to carry out the most basic functioning? Will the Relief Society be able to gather if women need to work on Sundays? What languages will be spoken at church, and who will be most affected by those choices? What does family even mean when people cannot be held together in this life?

All of these issues arise in a mobile world, and they take on added significance the further away from areas of Mormon demographic strength that one travels. Mormonism, as we have seen, is a tradition premised on the dissemination and fortification of heterosexual, monogamous family life, which in turn relies on a relatively balanced gender ratio for its endurance. This is especially true at early life stages, when balanced gender growth facilitates marriage and childbirth, the moments at which family religious involvement is at its most robust (Sloan,

Merrill, and Merrill, 2014, p. 141). The sacramental life of local congregations is also dependent on both leadership from male holders of the Melchizedek Priesthood and women's involvement in the Relief Society, the Young Women program, and Primary. A large imbalance within a Mormon population, then, can dramatically affect the ability for growth. At times, it even hinders congregations from carrying out the most basic daily and weekly practices. At the very least, severe gender imbalance can necessitate adaptation of Mormon norms and practices as they are promulgated by church leadership, causing a disconnect between proscribed religious ideals and local possibilities (Stark, 2002).

That situation already exists in peripatetic communities such as Hong Kong, an example that is perhaps predictive of future issues to come. As populations become more mobile, less fixed to national geographies or boundaries, it becomes challenging even to figure out what a normative expression of gender roles, that would be more discernible in stable populations, looks like. From her vantage point in Hong Kong, Staci Ford has begun to trace a community of "flexible citizens," groups of mobile inhabitants that give rise to entirely new cultures linked to transnational Asian capitalism. In these settings, economic necessities fundamentally reshape individual and family identities as transnational flows of people, goods, and capital create Mormon wards in China, Singapore, and Hong Kong (and many other metropolitan centers) made up of multiple worlds. Melissa Inouye has written poignantly about the challenges of flexible citizenship, a vantage that allows her to see into many cultural worlds simultaneously but also marginalizes and stereotypes people into a nebulous category of "Asianness."

In Hong Kong, Ford notes that flexible citizenship is not a one-size-fits-all designation. Inhabitants range from upwardly mobile and highly educated workers following jobs in finance or marketing to domestic workers living on very little means (who are technically not citizens at all). While wealthier workers can blend into the many ex-pat wards in these cities (wards that include many American workers living abroad, where services are generally conducted in English), people of lesser circumstances and education find themselves in settings where proscribed LDS practices are exceedingly difficult, if not impossible, to maintain. One district, the Hong Kong China District, will serve as an example. In this area, domestic workers comprise the majority of the church membership. They are migrant workers, with most coming from the Philippines but some others from Indonesia, Thailand, and Nepal. Ford notes that it is "arguably among the most gender-imbalanced entity of its type in the LDS Church anywhere in the world." Approximately 75 per cent of the 1,800 members are women, and roughly 1,000 make their living as domestic workers (Ford, 2018, p. 216).

It is hard to overstate the disparities between the life led by these women and those of other Asian ex-pats—not to mention North American Latter-day Saints. These workers present a particular challenge in a church committed to specific ideals of what constitutes "family." Their migration typically was compelled by high unemployment and social instability in their home countries. In Hong Kong, they live with their employers in variable conditions; quite often, they sleep on the floor, in closets, or in bathtubs, performing work for which they are paid less than the Hong Kong minimum wage. Much more could be said about their material circumstances and their distance from gendered norms of family life. But Ford's point is that at the local level, the church adapts to the gender disparities and working hours of these women. Women there occupy more decision-making roles than would be common among women in Utah, for example, and are set apart for roles that would otherwise be occupied by priesthood holders. The Hong Kong temple opens on Sundays once per quarter to accommodate different work schedules. In other words, local leaders improvise to meet the needs of a "Woman's Church" in this setting. But Ford also observes matters in which church leadership has been reluctant to "flex." She concludes by urging readers to "consider the ways in which culturally bound LDS ideals of motherhood and fatherhood, manhood and womanhood, family, and patriarchy may constrain rather than empower" (Ford, 2018, p. 224).

Transnational families are quickly becoming the norm in many parts of the world, a fact that will continue to reshape gendered experiences in the LDS Church. The faith has experienced tremendous growth over the last forty years in West Africa and in parts of Asia, and the little research that has been published on regional variability among LDS gender ratios demonstrates considerable diversity. Women outnumber men in membership in Christian organizations throughout the world, and the LDS Church generally is no exception. But in Africa, there are 118 males for every 100 female members, a figure that has considerable significance for the smooth operation of local congregations. In Asia, the disparity skews in exactly the opposite direction (Sloan, Merrill, and Merrill, 2014, p. 144).

U.S. responses and domestic divides

One could easily overstress both the ways in which Mormons outside the U.S. have reacted against aspects of the tradition that seem culturally retrograde or been attracted to the LDS Church because it provides a bulwark against change. The church has continued to grow, and in order to be a member in good standing and "temple worthy," one must conform to particular standards of behavior and dress. Nonetheless, as Melissa Inouye has commented, "Mormonism is administered centrally but experienced locally" (Inouye, 2018, p. 258), and that measure of decentralization leaves plenty of room for individual discernment and adaptation. The church hierarchy must decide, in multiple situations, how—or whether—to challenge variation in social and even sacramental roles; at times, this strategic flexibility results in "looking the other way," or simply quiet adaptation, and there will always be disagreements over how much improvisation is acceptable.

From a global perspective, there are only a few lines, mostly related to sexuality and ritual life, that have been consistently and universally inviolable. These moments of rupture are instructive in what they reveal about the relative flexibility of teachings on gender. Eternal gender identity is either male or female, with the concomitant biological imperatives to procreate and raise children if possible. Homosexual behavior is forbidden. Only worthy males may be ordained to the priesthood. Beyond these gender rules, much is advised but little is mandatory. In practice, enforcement of dress codes, dating, and even ward callings (as we have seen in Hong Kong) is left to the discretion of local bishops and social discouragement from one's friends (which can be more constraining at times than official dicta).[3]

In non-Mormon-dominant communities, such as Ghana or Maori New Zealand, those social pressures can run in the opposite direction, leading members to feel the pressure of local customs that run against typical (Euro-American) Mormon patterns. Clearly, the presence of female sacramental leadership in Ghana in the 1970s was seen as a bridge too far, and was therefore banned from the LDS Church. In like manner, the gendered roles of Maori Mormons shifted in the 1950s. After decades of actively encouraging Maori Mormons to retain many of their traditional ways of life, the newly appointed mission president Gordon C. Young, who had long expressed concern about the sad moral state of the Maori, changed tactical course and circumscribed the bounds of "gospel culture" in ways that delegitimized many Maori customs and eroded gendered authority. Elderly male *rangatira*, revered for their age and *mana* among their people, were replaced in church leadership by younger men of lesser status. Traditional funerary customs were phased out in favor of Mormon ritual patterns (especially after the opening of the New Zealand temple in 1958). Most significant for Maori women was the new enforcement of civil marriages, even among couples who, in keeping with Maori ways, had lived together for decades without legal proceedings. Since the 1890s Mormon missionaries had expressed contradictory but generally lax attitudes toward the marriage status of members, since Maori traditionally did not formalize marriage arrangements and had few concerns about pre-marital relations. Under British law the Maori had been exempted from the 1880 Marriage Act, which enforced coverture laws among white women; that exemption enabled Maori women to continue to conduct business and hold property outside the purview of their husbands, a right that Maori women valued greatly. Under Young's leadership, Mormon members, even those in longstanding relationships, were compelled to be legally married or face excommunication. Barber estimates that Young excommunicated between 100 and 200 members for "sexual immorality" between 1950 and 1952 (Barber, 1995, p. 164).

The rise of dissent about gender and sexuality back in the U.S., including confrontations over the ERA in the 1970s, homosexuality and same-sex marriage in the 1990s and 2000s, and women's ordination in the 2010s, have also redoubled efforts by Utah leadership to impose international standards of gender comportment. The introduction of the Proclamation on the Family in 1995 had at least some of its roots in the growth of the church outside the U.S., as male leadership faced challenges from multiple directions on its stances on women's roles. In the early 1990s, Relief Society President Elaine L. Jack and her two counselors, Chieko Okazaki and Aileen Clyde, conducted an international survey of the Relief Society—quite likely the only one of its kind. It was an ambitious and thorough undertaking: they directed stake Relief Society presidents to organize twelve-person focus groups to answer questions about their experiences in the organization. They also encouraged women to suggest changes and improvements. What they discovered, however, was that women didn't discuss the Relief Society; instead, they focused on women's myriad concerns and the gap that many of them felt between church ideals and the reality of women's lives. One woman apparently reported that she simply didn't go to church "because what they tell me about myself, it's just too painful."

To report back to the church, President Jack, Okazaki, and Clyde planned a General Relief Society Conference in the fall of 1995 that would celebrate the diversity of women's experiences and family structures that were anchored within the faith. Two weeks before the meeting, Gordon B. Hinckley called them into his office and advised them that they would need to change the theme. He instructed them that they should instead address the "traditional" family, and not demonstrate the many kinds of families within the church. One of his associates also intimated that the Brethren had discussed the matter amongst themselves and would have further instruction forthcoming soon. It was at the following General Conference that President Hinckley presented "The Family: A Proclamation to the World," a document that thereafter became the dominant statement of gender and family norms in Mormon discourse. None of the Relief Society leaders had been consulted ahead of time about the document—and indeed, in later years both Okazaki and Clyde expressed their frustrations in not being consulted during the process (McDannell, 2018, pp. 153–72).

Acknowledgment of diverse life experiences in the globalizing church were not entirely stifled, however. Jack, Okazaki, and Clyde all managed, in their own addresses to the General Relief Society that fall, to name some of the disjunctions between the reality of women's lives and church ideals that they had uncovered in their survey. In her characteristically cheerful way, Okazaki first thanked President Hinckley for his inspired words: "We all have a clear vision of the ideal, gospel-centered home; and the women in the Church work toward that ideal, yearn for it, pray for it, and rejoice in it." Yet she continued by noting that mortality brings with it experiences of both good and evil so that we may learn from our choices.

> And many of these experiences are painful. In most congregations of sisters, even in hearts and homes in apparently ideal circumstances, there are hidden heartaches and

taxing challenges. At least some among you are survivors of abuse and other crimes of personal violence. Death or divorce can visit any home … In your family, or in the family of someone close to you, is someone dealing with chronic mental, physical, or emotional illness; chemical dependency; financial insecurity; loneliness, sorrow, or discouragement? Many sisters are in second marriages, with the triple challenges of healing from the loss of a first marriage, working to build a strong second marriage, and compassionately providing part-time mothering to children of the husband's earlier marriage.

(Okazaki, 1995)

Okazaki thereby acknowledged the realities that she had charted in the survey while still honoring the value of the scripted ideal.

Since the 1990s, as women's work opportunities and social influence has expanded in American society more broadly, a significant number of U.S. Mormon women have continued to seek change in LDS definitions of appropriate gender roles. Recent studies indicate that there is a wide generation gap among U.S. Mormon women over their traditional roles in all aspects of church life, with younger women much more likely to be bothered by their inability to hold the priesthood and assume other responsibilities normally given to male members (Riess, 2018). Female agency has a very different meaning to the more progressive flanks of the U.S. church, many of whom request equality of social and ritual roles, not simply the freedom to fulfill maternal and domestic callings. These groups of critics do not speak with a single voice. Instead, we can see their concerns ranging from advocacy for women's ordination to the priesthood, to those gently seeking more gender equality and a greater sphere for women's input in institutional leadership.

The U.S. Mormon progressive perspective on gender is thus very different from the concerns of many Mormons in transnational and Global South settings. In responding to Sharon Eubank's story of the woman in Ghana, one American woman commented on a blog site that, while she was happy that this woman's life was improving because of the church, she felt that her experience was precisely the opposite:

Women in America go to church and experience a contrast—but in the opposite direction. I recognize many American female members are not pained by the male-oriented nature of the current church, but I for one walk in to church and feel nearly suffocated by culture shock—utter shock at how little women are utilized, recognized, conferred with, and so on. I don't want the church structure to feel like something a woman ultimately outgrows once she finally recognizes and honors her true worth. It's wonderful that the church is helping men in third-world countries learn it's not acceptable to beat women and children with their fists, but women still feel beat up by "patriarchy" in the capital state of our religion.

(Johnson, 2017)

In response, the LDS Church has supported and even sponsored discussion of women's issues, presenting, as did Eubank, the argument that complementary gender roles are the most liberating path for Mormon women. The Ghanaian example allowed her to emphasize the universal applicability of Mormon gender roles.

Because we are conservative morally, a lot of people thought that our doctrine about women and men was conservative. Far from being restrictive and conservative, and we sometimes get labeled that way, my contention is that the Church's doctrine about the roles of women in the family, and the church, and the community, and the nation, and the temple and how men and women relate to each other and interplay and support each other and work together is the most moderate, and powerful, and enlightening and energizing doctrines that I know about. And if people truly understood it, it would blow their mind.

(Eubank, 2014)

And it is true that many Mormon members outside the U.S., those in both the more traditionally inclined Global South and the progressive Western European settings, simply do not share American concerns over holding the priesthood or incorporating a Heavenly Mother into their worldview.

Ironically, however, the church-related "pro-family" organizations dealing most directly with the promotion of traditional gender roles are staffed almost exclusively by white North American (and mostly Utah-based) women. These include groups such as Latter-day Saint Women Stand and United Families International, both of which defend a traditionalist reading of the Proclamation on the Family, including women's roles. The website of United Families International (UFI) has a section devoted to "world family news," and the contributors, as indicated by their online representation, are all North American and white. UFI's informational online articles consist of studies on abortion, cohabitation (parts I and II), "Divorce 100 reasons not to," pornography, and "the Marriage Advantage." At FairMormon, where Sharon Eubank spoke, a panel discussion in 2013 on "Seeking Sisterhood among Different Perspectives on Mormon Feminism" included five prominent LDS women, all very accomplished, and all U.S. based. The ideals of appropriate Mormon female responsibility presented in these settings, in other words, is premised on a limited range of possibilities.

I do not mean to suggest that U.S.-based initiatives with respect to Mormon gender ideals—either those of the official church leadership and its proponents, or those of progressives seeking radical change—merely employ the needs and desires of men and women in the Global South to adjudicate their own internal disagreements. But at times the U.S.-based discussion of gender ideals can sound both needlessly narrow in scope, and not attuned to the many different sorts of cultural expectations, demographic realities, and economic pressures that shape human lives outside of the Mormon Corridor. The ideological thrust of the Mormon global project has been deeply molded by the metaphors of gathering, extending, and reaching out, bringing to others the truths of the gospel and principles of right living. It will take still larger structural transformations in church organization, if they are to occur, to change that pathway into a multi-directional thoroughfare.

Notes

1 I use the term "Global South" in a descriptive way to refer to industrializing or newly industrial countries in Asia, Latin America, Africa, and the Caribbean. A term intended originally to replace the more value-laden labels "underdeveloped" or "third world," Global South has also come under considerable critique as a way of distinguishing among nations (some of which are in the hemispheric north). Nonetheless, it suffices here as a way to denote countries that share certain common challenges.
2 This is not true, however, in the conversion of West Africans from Islam to Christianity, a less common transition that can lead to prolonged family stress.
3 This is not to discount the stresses of local pressure. Anecdotes abound of men not being called as bishops because they sport beards, or women being consigned to lesser callings because they insist on wearing pants to sacrament meeting.

References

Ampofo, A.A., 2017. Africa's Fast-growing Pentecostal Mega Churches Are Entrenching Old Injustices against Women. *Quartz Africa*. June 16. https://qz.com/africa/1007819/pentecostal-churches-in-ghana-and-nigeria-are-entrenching-sexist-gender-roles-for-women/.

Avery, D., 2019. 71 Countries Where Homosexuality Is Illegal. *Newsweek*. April 4. www.newsweek.com/73-countries-where-its-illegal-be-gay-1385974.

Barber, I., 1995. Between Biculturalism and Assimilation: The Changing Place of Maori Culture in the Twentieth-Century New Zealand Mormon Church. *New Zealand Journal of History* 29(2): 142–69.

Church of Jesus Christ of Latter-Day Saints, 2016. Mormon and Gay. https://mormonandgay.churchofjesuschrist.org/articles/church-teachings?lang=eng.

Dawley, W., and Thornton, B.J., 2018. New Directions in the Anthropology of Religion and Gender: Faith and Emergent Masculinities. *Anthropological Quarterly* 91(1): 5–23.

Decoo, W., 2015. Mormons in Europe. In T. Givens and P.L. Barlow, eds. *The Oxford Handbook of Mormonism*. New York: Oxford University Press, pp. 543–58.

Decoo-Vanwelkenhuysen, C., 2016. Mormon Women in Europe: A Look at Gender Norms. In M. Bowman and K. Holbrook, eds. *Women and Mormonism: Historical and Contemporary Perspectives*. Salt Lake City, UT: University of Utah Press, pp. 219–29.

Densley, Jr., S.T., 2017. Should We Apologize for Apologetics? *Interpreter: A Journal of Mormon Scripture* 27: 107–42.

Eubank, S., 2014. This Is a Woman's Church. 2014 FAIR Mormon Conference. August. www.fairmormon.org/conference/august-2014/womans-church.

Ford, S., 2018. Sister Acts: Relief Society and Flexible Citizenship in Hong Kong. In J. Brooks and G. Colvin, eds. *Decolonizing Mormonism: Approaching a Post-Colonial Zion*. Salt Lake City, UT: University of Utah Press, pp. 202–28.

Griffith, M., 2017. *Moral Combat: How Sex Divided American Christians and Fractured American Politics*. New York: Basic Books.

Grimshaw, J., 2015. The Lindsey Stirling Effect. *Dialogue: A Journal of Mormon Thought* 48(4): 69–88.

Hafen, B.C., 2009. Bruce C. Hafen Speaks on Same Sex Attraction. Evergreen International Annual Conference. September 19. https://newsroom.churchofjesuschrist.org/article/elder-bruce-c-hafen-speaks-on-same-sex-attraction.

Haglund, K., 2012. Why Mormon Men Love "Church Ball" and Are Scared of Homosexuality. *Religion and Politics*. September 10. https://religionandpolitics.org/2012/09/10/why-mormon-men-love-church-ball-and-are-scared-of-homosexuality/.

Inouye, M.W.-T., 2018. A Tale of Three Primaries: The Gravity of Mormonism's Informal Institutions. In G. Colvin and J. Brooks, eds. *Decolonizing Mormonism: Approaching a Postcolonial Zion*. Salt Lake City, UT: University of Utah Press, pp. 229–62.

Johnson, C., 2017. Comment series at By Common Consent. https://bycommonconsent.com/2017/12/17/wholl-be-a-witness-for-my-lord/#comment-395268.

Johnson, J.W.B., n.d. Interview transcript, Church History Library OH 4021.

Knowlton, D., 1992. On Mormon Masculinity. *Sunstone*. August, pp. 19–31.

Lineham, P., 1991. Tanner Lecture: The Mormon Message in the Context of Maori Culture. *Journal of Mormon History* 17: 62–93.

McDannell, C., 2018. *Sister Saints: Mormon Women since the End of Polygamy*. New York: Oxford University Press.

Meeting Minutes, n.d. Dadzie Papers. Black Cultural Archives.

Mikaere, A., 1994. Maori Women: Caught in the Contradictions of a Colonised Reality. *Waikato Law Review* 2. www.waikato.ac.nz/law/research/waikato_law_review/pubs/volume_2_1994/7.

Okazaki, C., 1995. A Living Network. General Conference. October. www.lds.org/general-conference/1995/10/a-living-network?lang=eng.

Riess, J., 2018. Younger Mormons Far More Likely to Be Troubled by Women's Roles in the LDS Church, Study Shows. *Religious Studies News*. November 26. https://religionnews.com/2018/11/26/younger-mormons-far-more-likely-to-be-troubled-by-womens-roles-in-the-lds-church-study-shows/.

Sloan, A.A., Merrill, R.M., and Merrill, J.G., 2014. Gender Distribution of the Church of Jesus Christ of Latter-day Saints Worldwide. *BYU Studies Quarterly* 53(1): 141–51.

Soothill, J.E., 2007. *Gender, Social Change and Spiritual Power: Charismatic Christianity in Ghana*. Boston, MA: Brill.

Soothill, J.E., 2010. The Problem with "Women's Empowerment": Female Religiosity in Ghana's Charismatic Churches. *Studies in World Christianity* 16(1): 82–99.

Stark, R., 2002. Physiology and Faith: Addressing the "Universal" Gender Difference in Religious Commitment. *Journal for the Scientific Study of Religion* 41(3): 495–507.

Stevenson, R., 2015. "We Have Prophetesses": Mormonism in Ghana, 1964–79. *Journal of Mormon History* 41(3): 221–57.

Thornton, B.J., 2016. *Negotiating Respect: Pentecostalism, Masculinity, and the Politics of Spiritual Authority in the Dominican Republic.* Gainesville, FL: University Press of Florida.

Van Beek, W.E.A., 2005. Mormon Europeans or European Mormons? An Afro-European View on Religious Colonization. *Dialogue: A Journal of Mormon Thought* 38(4): 3–36.

Walker, T., 2017. Whānau – Māori and Family: Contemporary Understandings of Whānau. *Te Ara: The Encyclopedia of New Zealand.* www.TeAra.govt.nz/en/whanau-maori-and-family/page-1 (accessed August 24, 2019).

Zeveloff, N., 2012. The Ultimate Mormon Male. *Salon.* February 6. www.salon.com/2012/02/05/the_ultimate_mormon_male/.

Further reading

Barber, I., 1995. Between Biculturalism and Assimilation: The Changing Place of Maori Culture in the Twentieth-Century New Zealand Mormon Church. *New Zealand Journal of History* 29(2): 142–69.

Ford, S., 2018. Sister Acts: Relief Society and Flexible Citizenship in Hong Kong. In J. Brooks and G. Colvin, eds. *Decolonizing Mormonism: Approaching a Post-Colonial Zion.* Salt Lake City, UT: University of Utah Press, pp. 202–28.

Lineham, P., 1991. Tanner Lecture: The Mormon Message in the Context of Maori Culture. *Journal of Mormon History* 17: 62–93.

Riess, J., 2018. Younger Mormons Far More Likely to Be Troubled by Women's Roles in the LDS Church, Study Shows. *Religious Studies News.* November 26. https://religionnews.com/2018/11/26/younger-mormons-far-more-likely-to-be-troubled-by-womens-roles-in-the-lds-church-study-shows/.

Sloan, A.A., Merrill, M.R., and Merrill, J.G., 2014. Gender Distribution of the Church of Jesus Christ of Latter-day Saints Worldwide. *BYU Studies Quarterly* 53(1): 141–51.

Soothill, J.E., 2010. The Problem with "Women's Empowerment": Female Religiosity in Ghana's Charismatic Churches. *Studies in World Christianity* 16(1): 82–99.

2

RACE AND GENDER IN MORMONISM

1830–1978

Amanda Hendrix-Komoto and Joseph R. Stuart

Latter-day Saints have defined racial and gender categories through interpretations of their sacred texts, particularly the Book of Mormon and the temple liturgy. Readings of these texts have explained differences in skin color by defining whiteness as evidence of personal righteousness and Blackness as evidence of individual sinfulness. For instance, the Book of Mormon repeatedly highlights how faith, practice, and obedience to God shape relationships within families. God marks the Lamanites with dark skin after they abandon their family members and their ancestors' religion. The Book of Mormon articulates a vision of the family that is consonant with white, middle-class understandings of the domesticity from the nineteenth century. To cite one example, the prophet Jacob castigates the Nephites for failing to uphold the same standards of familial love as the Lamanites. "Behold," he chastises them, "their husbands love their wives, and their wives love their husbands, and their husbands and their wives love their children." The Lamanites are further used to shame the Nephites shortly after the wicked Lamanites separate from the righteous Nephites, "O my brethren, I fear that unless ye shall repent of your sins that their skins will be whiter than yours" (Jacob 3:7–8). The Book of Mormon's narrator describes people by their relationship to the male head of household. Women and children become men's wives, daughters, and sons.

The patriarchal understanding of the family that Latter-day Saints derive from the Book of Mormon fails to account for the complexity of families within American history. People who aspired to genteel respectability often spurned extramarital sex and regulated interactions between men and women. Poverty often prevented working-class families from fulfilling these expectations. They did not have the money to fully separate the interactions between men and women and often embraced older understandings of sexuality, in which extramarital sex could be countenanced in certain situations. The Book of Mormon would have labeled many of their activities as licentious. The vision of the family within Mormonism's sacred text was also implicitly racialized. As several historians have argued, Native American families can rarely be reduced to the nuclear family and frequently include kinship obligations that extend to grandparents, cousins, and aunts and uncles. Some tribal nations define kinship through matriarchal lines. The Book of Mormon also fails to reflect the fragile nature of African American families under slavery. In the nineteenth century, white enslavers could break apart Black families for financial gain, which meant that few African Americans would have recognized their own families within the Book of Mormon. Even today, many members of the African Diaspora understand kinship as extending beyond the nuclear family to include "aunties" and "uncles" who may or may not be biologically related. By sacralizing the nuclear family, the Book of Mormon presents a vision of the family that fails to match the lives of many Mormons both in the past and in the present day.

In some ways, the LDS temple provides a universal vision of what constitutes a family. The uniformity of LDS temple clothing, for example, is meant to erase racial and class distinctions. Their sameness also reflects the Church's stance that "all are alike unto God" and that class, nationality, and ethnicity do not matter in God's eyes (2 Nephi 26:33). The temple, however, does not dissolve all differences. Before 2019, women made covenants to their husbands. Although they became "queens" and "priestesses" in the temple, they fulfilled these roles only in relationship to their husbands. This language reinforced hierarchies between men and women. Recent changes to the temple liturgy have tried to emphasize humanity's essential equality. Since 2019, women have made their covenants directly with God. These changes, however, are too recent to assess their long-term effects on LDS culture (Reiss, 2019).

The changes to the Church's temple liturgy highlight a tension within the Mormon tradition. Since its birth in the nineteenth century, Mormonism has struggled to reconcile the universal parts of its vision with those that support patriarchy and racism. For example, early Mormons endowed some Black men with priesthood authority while they applauded Andrew Jackson's Indian removal policies. In this chapter, we explore the tensions between Mormonism's universalism and its acceptance of racial and gendered hierarchies from 1830 to 1978. Most scholars who have examined the intersections of race and gender in Mormon history have focused on the policy excluding peoples of Black African descent from receiving priesthood ordination or full participation in the temple liturgy. In this essay, we argue that a variety of religious texts and practices shaped the LDS Church's interactions with people of color in the United States and throughout the world. We first examine how white Mormons considered the place of Native Americans and peoples of Black African descent before Joseph Smith's introduction of the endowment and sealing ordinances. Next, we investigate how the Mormon exodus from the Midwest to the Great Basin shaped Mormon interactions with Native peoples in the American West and Mexico. We then scrutinize the place of missionary work among peoples of Asian descent, giving special attention to the first decades of Mormon missionary work in Japan. Finally, we consider the role of the Indian Placement Program and Official Declaration 2 in the late twentieth century.

Introduction of the sealing ordinance and eternal gender roles

The temple has had wide-ranging effects on how Mormons understand race, family, and gender. Mormonism emerged in the industrial revolution of the nineteenth century, which transformed family life and gender definitions. The movement of adult children away from family farms to cities challenged traditional patriarchal authority. Children no longer relied on their fathers to provide them with enough land and capital to establish their livelihoods. Historians Samuel Brown and Richard Bushman have argued that many of Joseph Smith's religious innovations were therefore designed to ensure that family bonds would last into the eternities, cementing connections that Latter-day Saints had made during mortality (Bushman, 2005, pp. 422–23; Brown, 2012, pp. 232–47).

Smith's innovations depended upon male-administered liturgy and patriarchy. The most notable of these new practices was the sealing ritual, which he introduced in Nauvoo, IL, in 1841. Smith taught that the sealing ritual preserved the bonds between individuals and families before and after death and that it ensured humankind would live together in eternal kinship networks. These networks would expand as people sealed themselves to one another. In Joseph

Smith's expansive theology, this ritual would eventually bind humanity together and ensure that *all* people would be redeemed (Brown, 2012, pp. 203–47). Smith used these familial connections to create links between his closest friends and confidantes, with the belief that those relationships would continue in the eternities. Strategic sealings allowed him to be at the head of all of these kinship networks.

The sealing ritual is (and was) implicitly gendered. Individuals could only create eternal relationships by being incorporated into a heterosexual family. Beginning in 1846, Mormon couples could ritually adopt other adults as their children. The head couple received honor for their place within this network and became responsible for the salvation of their new kin. Smith did not organize sealings based on notions of romantic love; the liturgy functioned to organize the eternities under couples, operating under the authority of male-only priesthood authority. Accordingly, early Latter-day Saints understood the family as extending beyond biological ties to include the creation of kin through what Joseph Smith called the "welding links" of Mormon liturgy (Smith, 1841–1842, p. 199).

Nineteenth-century Mormon thought on indigenous peoples

Mormon ideas about Native Americans often aligned with their contemporaries. In the late eighteenth century, Thomas Jefferson laid out his vision for the emerging United States. He hoped that the former colonies would spurn industry and embrace small farmers. "Let our workshops remain in Europe," he wrote in his 1785 book *Notes on Virginia*. "The mobs of great cities" would eventually prove "a canker" on the American body politic and would "[eat] to the heart of its laws and constitution" (Jefferson, 1787, p. 275). In Jefferson's expansionist vision, Native Americans would become "civilized" farmers who adopted white cultural norms. Although Smith rejected Jefferson's rural ideal, he also followed other missionaries in evangelizing Native people, whom he called "Lamanites." Smith sent missionaries to various tribal nations with a message charging them to remember their lapsed relationship with God. Upon conversion, he promised, they would become "white and delightsome." Their white brethren would see them as models of racial uplift and godly piety who would seamlessly integrate into white American culture.

Scholars disagree over the complicity of white Mormons in the dispossession of American Indians and whether the Book of Mormon reflects an anti-Native bias. Jared Hickman (2014) has provocatively argued that the Book of Mormon functions as an anti-colonial text that upends assumptions about nineteenth-century American expansion. He points out that the book ends with an "Amerindian apocalypse" in which Native people take control of the continent. His reading, however, downplays the role that whiteness plays in the text. Although the Book of Mormon imagines a future in which God reclaims Native Americans as a "Chosen People," Hickman admits that nineteenth-century Mormons would have believed redemption could only come after Native people abandoned their culture and their skin became white. Ideas surrounding racial redemption resulted in a double bind for indigenous people. Although the Book of Mormon invested Native Americans with a sacred history, scholars like Elise Boxer (2009 and 2018) have highlighted the collusion of Mormonism with American settler colonialism, showing how white Latter-day Saints denigrated indigenous bodies and argued that Native people must abandon their culture

White Mormons found that their scripture could support both the veneration and eradication of indigenous people. In 1830, Mormon missionaries traveled to Ohio where they hoped to convert Native Americans the United States had expelled from their homelands. The mission failed to produce Native American converts, but nevertheless demonstrates early Mormonism's focus on American Indian communities. When the missionaries preached in Kirtland, Ohio, they managed to baptize local white people. Their ecstatic spiritual practices included moments when they assumed "Indian" identities. Local newspapers reported they preached in imagined Native languages and moved along the ground in an act they called "sailing in the boat to the Lamanites" (Givens and Grow, 2011, p. 51). Although the men and women who participated in these spiritual practices eventually repented or were reprimanded, their focus on Native Americans in their religious practices was only an extreme manifestation of what was a common belief in the early Church.

Before his death in 1844, Joseph Smith founded the Council of Fifty, an organization that was meant to be a political counterpart to the spiritual Kingdom of God, which would work in concert to usher in Jesus' Second Coming. Within that council, Smith argued that Mormons should supervise the evangelization of Native peoples and collaborate with them in matters of politics, whether they converted or not. Their centering on Native identity, however, did not mean that Mormons opposed U.S. Indian policy. Instead, they saw themselves working within it by awakening Native people to their supposed Book of Mormon past. Mormons interpreted the 1830 Indian Removal Act, which expelled tens of thousands of Native Americans from their homes and killed several thousand more, as an act of God. The LDS newspaper the *Millennial Star* assured Native peoples in 1832 that they would "soon be convinced that [removal was] the best thing that has come to pass among them for many generations" (quoted in Underwood, 1993, p. 82). Their willingness to see removal as an act of God dismissed Native suffering. White Mormons failed to recognize the profound effect that their settlement had on Native communities in the Great Basin.

After Joseph Smith's death in 1844, Mormons fled from Nauvoo, Illinois, which began an exodus that culminated in the creation of Mormonism's "Great Basin Kingdom." Mormon settlements displaced Native Americans, who found that European cattle and plants fundamentally altered the ecosystems that had sustained their communities for centuries. Historians Jared Farmer (2010), Ned Blackhawk (2008), and John Peterson (1999) have traced the rising violence that occurred after Mormon settlement. The Mormon eagerness to adopt Indian children heightened the existing slave trade, as the Ute and other mounted tribes raided neighboring communities for children to sell them to Mormon communities. In the mid-nineteenth century, intensifying conflicts between white Mormons and Native Americans caused the former to re-evaluate the role that indigenous peoples played in their theology. Confronted with flesh-and-blood Native Americans who refused to conform to Mormon redemption narratives, many white Mormons began to see Native Americans as less a "Chosen People" and more as a people marked for eradication (Reeve, 2015, pp. 75–105).

Even those white Mormons who continued to call Native Americans a "Chosen People" believed that their culture needed to be transformed before they could be integrated into the Church or American society. Beginning in the 1850s, Mormons worked with the federal government to create Indian Farms throughout the Utah Territory. They hoped that Utah's Native American communities would adopt settled agriculture. Moving between places, however, had long allowed the Shoshone, Ute, and Paiute to subsist in the Great Basin's arid climate without straining the area's resources. They were reluctant to transform their cultural practices to match those of Mormons and other white settlers. The gendered cultural transformations that Mormons sought asked Native men to abandon hunting, which would emasculate them within their tribes. Mormons also aimed to transform Indian marital practices. Utah newspapers described Native American marriages as abusive relationships and exoticized non-white polygamy. The fact that non-Mormon publications used similar language to deride Mormon polygamy did little to stop newspaper editors in Utah from publishing the stories.

White Mormons also believed that they could quicken the civilizing of Native Americans by absorbing Native women and children into their families. In the nineteenth century, Mormon leaders encouraged their followers to marry Indian women and adopt Indian children in hopes that these close, familial relationships would teach Native Americans the habits of civilization. Historian Dawn Peterson (2017) has shown that people as diverse as white missionaries and Southern plantation owners adopted Native children to instill them with white values and culture.

The willingness of Mormons and other Americans to absorb Native Americans into their families rested on patriarchal assumptions. White Mormons believed that authority lay in the figure of the father, who, invested with the power of God through the priesthood, would teach his children obedience and ensure that they became faithful members of the kingdom of God. Because of their God-given authority, white fathers could ensure that the children within their household would adopt white customs regardless of their actual skin color. For white women married to Indian men, the lack of a white father in the household meant there was no guarantee that their children would be considered white.

Native Mormonisms in nineteenth- and early twentieth-century Oceania and Mexico

Mormon attempts to "civilize" local Native American communities were ultimately no more successful than those of other white settlers. Hundreds of Native Americans accepted Mormon baptism in the nineteenth century, but most did not. Perhaps because of this failure, coupled with eschatological expectations for Native conversions, white Mormons celebrated the baptizing of people they considered to be descendants of the peoples of the Book of Mormon more than they did white baptisms. White Mormons traveled to the Pacific Islands, Latin America, and other places where they believed they could find the descendants of American Israelites. The conversion of these people allowed them to imagine Lamanite conversions that fulfilled the promises found in the Book of the Mormon. Mormonism, however, changed as it moved across imperial borders. Native people read the Book of Mormon through their own cultures and created indigenous Mormonisms that would have been unrecognizable to white Mormons living in the Great Basin.

In the 1840s, Addison Pratt served a mission in French Polynesia with a handful of other men. They eventually managed to convert large segments of the population on the Austral Islands and the Tuamotus. The Church's most long-lasting successes, however, occurred elsewhere in the Pacific. In 1850, a group of Latter-day Saint missionaries traveled to the Hawaiian Islands in hopes of converting the white men who worked there to Mormonism. Their message, however, was ill-received. After prayer, some of the men received a revelation that Polynesians were descendants of American Israelites. By the end of the nineteenth century, significant communities of Native Hawaiian Mormons lived throughout the Hawaiian Islands. They had similar success in New Zealand. In the 1880s, Mormon missionaries shifted their efforts from the area's white population to the Maori. Historians have argued that the faith's emphasis on spiritual gifts may have resonated with Maori culture, which accepted prophesying and faith healing as reality. Mormon missionaries also integrated themselves into local communities to the extent that they "began to think like Maori, to feel like Maori, and no doubt look like Maoris" (Morrison et al., 2012, p. 68). The result was a religious faith enmeshed in Maori identity and politics.

Mormons also evangelized indigenous people in Mexico. In 1875, Mormon missionaries traveled to Chihuahua to distribute selections from the Book of Mormon to government officials and other local elites. The retreat of white Mormons to Utah during the Mexican Revolution allowed a vibrant indigenous Mormonism to develop. Suspicious of foreign influence, the Mexican government expelled foreign missionaries from the country in 1926. Consequently, Anglo-American leadership only sporadically assumed control of the LDS Church in Mexico throughout the twentieth century (Flake, 1972). In their absence, Mexican members of the LDS Church adapted the faith to their own circumstances.

One local leader named Margarito Bautista argued in the 1930s that the focus of the Book of Mormon on the Lamanites revealed that God had focused his attention on indigenous people and saw them as the leaders of his church. The leadership of the LDS Church rejected his claims and those of Native Mormons who tried to foreground the experience of indigenous people. Although many Native members of the Third Convention eventually reintegrated into the LDS Church, an anthropologist located a Mexican community in 1996 that continued to follow Bautista called El Reino de Dios en su Plenitud (Murphy, 1998, pp. 1, 8–11). Their existence suggests the continued resonance of Mormonism's theological focus on indigeneity for Native Mormons.

In the early twentieth century, mainstream Mormonism sat uneasily with the experiences of Mormons of color in Mexico, Polynesia, and the small Native American communities who accepted the LDS faith. In Mexico, for example, white Mormons tended to see all Mexican Mormons as "Native" despite a local culture that recognized a diverse array of skin colors and racial gradations. Distance and the relatively small numbers of Mormons of color allowed white Mormon leaders to downplay these tensions. That would change in the mid-twentieth century with the rise of a self-conscious Civil Rights Movement and an explosion of Mormons of color abroad and at home. In the last decades of the twentieth century, the LDS Church saw dramatic growth in Latin America. In 1980, there were several hundred thousand Mormons in Latin America. By 2004, there were 4.5 million (Ayala, 2004). Latinx scholars like Ignacio Garcia have called for a renewed emphasis on people of color within the Church and have critiqued the Church's unthinking embrace of white American culture (Garcia, 2017).

Native American Mormons have lodged similar concerns with LDS Church leadership. In 1968, a group of Native activists, including Dennis Banks and Clyde and Vernon Bellecourt, founded the American Indian Movement. Their movement called on the U.S. federal government to honor the treaties that it had contracted with Indian nations and pushed for the decolonization of American society. They also criticized the LDS Church, and in the 1970s issued statements demanding Latter-day Saints repatriate Native remains from its museums and donate ten million dollars to Native-run social programs. Native activists also spoke out about the Indian Placement Program, which removed Native children from their homes and placed them with white Mormon families during the school year. Many white Mormons viewed the program as an act of altruism that provided Native children with opportunities they would otherwise never have, but Native activists saw it as an extension of the attempt of white settlers to destroy Native culture. The Navajo communities that provided the majority of the children to Mormon social services had mixed reactions to the program. While some saw it as a transformative experience that allowed their children to obtain excellent educations and build social capital, others were suspicious of the LDS Church.

Native Mormons have found solace in the LDS Church and often see their Mormonism and their identity as indigenous people as tightly intertwined. Still, Native activists have continued to criticize the LDS Church. In 1989, the LDS Church excommunicated a Native American General Authority George P. Lee who had vocally reminded members that Native people were at the heart of Mormonism's eschatology and thus should be better represented in local and global leadership. Although it is likely that charges that he molested a twelve-year-old girl played an important role in his excommunication, his downfall represented a real loss for Native Mormons who no longer had someone who represented their culture and perspective to Mormon leadership. In 2012, Larry Echo Hawk became a General Authority. He has been less vocal, however, about the place of Native Americans within the LDS faith than Lee was. Polynesian activists, including some within the LDS Church, have also criticized the church-owned Polynesian Cultural Center for displaying Polynesian bodies and promoting an exotic, sexualized vision of Oceania (Hendrix-Komoto, 2016). The Mormon emphasis on modesty has added an edge to these critiques. Ultimately, the LDS Church has found these criticisms challenging to answer. LDS theology foregrounds Native people, but the LDS Church's embrace of whiteness in the twentieth century has shifted their focus elsewhere.

The LDS Church's racial restriction and the temple liturgy, nineteenth and early twentieth centuries

The LDS Church's colonial practices have created levels of privilege within its membership. For instance, the Church barred Mormons of Black African descent from participating in its temple liturgy for more than 125 years. The ban began during Brigham Young's administration, though indigenous peoples could gain access to these rites. Interestingly, there is some evidence that Joseph Smith's wife, Emma Hale Smith, invited a woman of African descent named Jane Manning James to be sealed to the Smiths in their eternal kinship network. In her remembrance of the invitation, James recalled that Emma had asked her to be adopted as a "child" by the Smiths.

The details surrounding that invitation are unclear, but it is notable that Emma Smith invited a person of African descent during Joseph Smith's lifetime. This reflects the universalist strains in his theology, not only in matters of salvation but in terms of race. Smith's "white universalism" defined non-whites as degraded, but not beyond redemption (Mueller, 2017, p. 30). Eternal kinship networks, in theory, if not in practice, were available to all people during the lifetime of Joseph Smith. It is notable that Smith did not inform any of his fellow male Mormon leaders what his wife had done (if he knew). Smith's teachings on race throughout his prophetic career were inchoate and his successors had no concrete plan to follow upon his death in June 1844.

Smith's universalism began to fade soon after Brigham Young and the Quorum of the Twelve Apostles took the reins of leadership within the LDS Church. Several apostles formulated theories about the origin of black skin in premortal life or shared their belief in the Curses of Ham or Cain. Young did not withhold temple ordinances or priesthood ordination from Black Mormons until a meeting at the Utah legislature in February 1852. Speaking both as territorial governor and President of the LDS Church, Young justified the existence of slavery in Utah and articulated a rationale for restricting peoples of Black African descent from holding priesthood office or participating in temple liturgies. His arguments drew on a reading surrounding the biblical figure Cain and the Latter-day Saint belief, Law of Adoption. According to Young, Cain had not just committed murder; he had cut Abel off from the blessings of his posterity. "In the kingdom of God on earth," he said, "a man who has the African blood in him cannot hold one jot nor tittle of priesthood" (Young Speech, 1852). Because ordination to priesthood office was essential to receiving the temple ordinances of endowment and sealing, Young's pronouncement effectively barred Black Mormons from participating in LDS temple liturgy for more than a century. However, Young also stated that the opportunity would come for Black people to receive priesthood authority and temple rites but framed it as something that would happen far in the future, perhaps after the Second Coming of Christ.

This decision had far-reaching effects for Black Mormons, even though it did not affect other non-white Mormons. First, other than the few Black men ordained to the priesthood before 1852, they were not able to participate in the rituals of Mormon masculinity, including priesthood ordination and having his patriarchal authority solemnized through the sealing ordinance. He was also not permitted to serve in male-only callings in the Church, which limited their influence and social standing within Mormonism. Men and women of Black African descent could not meet the gender roles attainable to white Mormons, because they did not have access to the temple liturgy, which added a stamp of legitimacy to families. Although Black female converts participated in Relief Society meetings, they never occupied local leadership positions in mixed-gender or women-only meetings. Furthermore, as Quincy Newell has argued, Black women like Jane Manning James became known as "Aunts," which de-sexualized them and framed them as sexless adults rather than women possible of conceiving and rearing children like white women. This perception models how whites labeled Black women as "Mammies," able to perform the domestic tasks of womanhood while also presenting them as sexually unavailable (Newell, 2019, p. 129).

Jane Manning James recognized that black people were not permitted to participate in the temple liturgy, but it did not stop her from regularly petitioning LDS Church Presidents for the opportunity. She found a sympathetic ear in Wilford Woodruff, who was President from 1887–1898. Woodruff had considered and enacted two highly significant actions within Mormonism. First, he released a "Manifesto," promising that he would use his influence as the Mormon prophet to stop the public practice of plural marriage. Second, in 1894 he ended the hierarchical Law of Adoption, which placed church leaders as heads of eternal kinship networks. Beginning in April of that year, he stipulated that sealings would follow genealogy—children to parents back to Adam. This revolutionary change altered how Mormons conceived of gendered responsibilities. Though men and women were no longer the head of eternal kinship networks guaranteeing the salvation of those sealed to them, they were now responsible for seeking out their deceased ancestors and offering them the temple liturgy by proxy.

James petitioned Woodruff to receive her temple rites in 1895, the year after the Mormon prophet had ended the Law of Adoption. Woodruff worked with his apostles to find a way for her to receive temple ordinances and ultimately settled on a plan that allowed James to be sealed to Joseph and Emma Smith. In the end, James did not have to wait until she had died to enjoy these blessings, they would be performed for her by proxy by living Mormons. So, while James remained outside of the temple and could not participate in its ordinances, LDS leaders found a way for her to gain the blessings associated with Mormonism's crowning liturgy. However, they still found a way to mark her non-whiteness. In an unprecedented decision, Woodruff authorized James' sealing to the Smiths as a "servitor" rather than as a child, marking her forever as non-white. They also used the verb "attach" rather than "seal," verbiage that the written record does not show has been used after the proxy performance of James' rite. Ironically, had Woodruff considered the question before ending the Law of Adoption, it is possible that he would have suggested that James be sealed as a "child," as thousands of white Mormons had been ritually linked to other white Mormons.[1]

James lived long enough to see the crystallization of Mormonism's racial restriction by the LDS First Presidency in 1908 (it had been informal throughout the nineteenth century). As historian Paul Reeve (2015) has shown, Joseph F. Smith, nephew of Mormonism's founder, endorsed a "one drop" policy that mirrored American racial policies at the time. Under the "one drop" policy, possessing even one person of Black African ancestry in one's family lineage made one Black. One could not be white and have any sort of biological link to Blackness. Whiteness, or the expectation that one could attain righteousness through conversion to Mormonism, remained the determinant measure for one's potential for godliness.

The LDS Church's first years in Japan, 1901–1945

Following the Mormon persecution and prosecution for plural marriage in the late nineteenth century, the LDS Church's leadership took steps to define Mormons as the "right" (white) type of American citizen. As a part of these changes, the LDS Church began to participate in the United States' empire-building project. As a part of that project, the LDS Church sent out more missionaries, including to Japan. Led by Apostle Heber J. Grant in 1901, missionaries embarked across the Pacific Ocean, knowing that they would encounter people who did not look, talk, or worship as they did.

Several historians have defined the Japanese mission as Mormonism's first multi-year foray to a non-Christian country. As historian Reid Neilson has argued, "Latter-day Saints ... rendered non-Christians as capable of salvation and partakers of divine light," and thus worthy of the time and manpower it took to proselyte in Japan" (Neilson, 2010, pp. 14–15). They also believed that Asian people were, like Native Americans, descendants of Book of Mormon peoples. However, this does not tell the entire tale. White Mormon missionaries also went to a nation whose social and gendered order was quite different from the United States' gendered ideals, much less Mormonism's. At the end of the nineteenth century, the patriarchal order of Japan had begun to shift. Traditional patriarchal domestic arrangements gave way to shared responsibilities between men and women in the home. The Meiji, Taisho, and Showa governments (1868–1989) asked men to serve as soldiers and breadwinners, building the nation through the masculine duties of military service and economic productivity.

Mormons, were not as prepared as Protestant missionaries might have been to preach their gospel to the Japanese. They believed that they preached Christ and not culture, which led them to overlook the differences between the industrializing, modernizing Japanese people and their own frontier lives. Due in part to these differences, Mormon missionaries converted few Japanese to the LDS Church from 1901 to 1924 (even fewer baptisms took place from 1924 to 1945). Latter-day Saints had tried to "reformulate their evangelical outlook or practices for an Asian audience," but without understanding that Japanese gendered, familial, and religious cultures differed from the United States and Western Europe. Mormons viewed the Japanese as "morally decayed" and did not work to become familiar with Japanese politics, government, or economies, foregoing the opportunity to make appeals to Japanese men or women based upon their gendered roles (Neilson, 2010, p. 89).

The gendered road to Official Declaration 2, 1949–1978

The LDS Church's First Presidency did not publicly or officially sanction the Church's racial restriction until 1949. In that year, shortly after the United States Armed Forces moved to desegregate its ranks, they claimed that the Church's beliefs on "Negroes" had begun from the organization of the Church and that they were "not entitled to the Priesthood at the present time." They turned to Brigham Young for justification and to Wilford Woodruff to show that Church leaders had decreed that one day Black people would "be redeemed and possess all the blessings which [Mormons] now have" (Statement of the First Presidency, 1949).

The interpretation of the 1949 statement shortly after the *Brown v. Board of Education* (1954) decision reveals how central gender and sexuality were to the restriction. In 1954, Apostle Mark E. Peterson taught church instructors that the root of the civil rights struggles was not equality, but intermarriage. "The Negro seeks absorption with the white race. He will not be satisfied until he achieves it by intermarriage. That is his objective and we must face it" (Peterson, 1954).

This statement, along with further statements by other male church leaders in the 1950s and 1960s reveals the gendered panic beneath Mormon beliefs about people of Black African descent, as well as American conservative fears about civil rights. Mormons were not nearly as nervous about Black men holding ecclesiastical office as they were of interracial courtship, marriage, and dating. This matches other white attitudes at the time concerning interracial marriage between whites and Blacks. For instance, the Supreme Court did not declare prohibitions on interracial marriage unconstitutional until *Loving v. Virginia* (1967). As seen in statements like Peterson's, Mormons also rejected the legitimacy of interracial marriage. Mormons used the Bible to justify their aversion, but, importantly, also drew upon the liturgical rites of the temple. White relationships could hold up to the gendered ideal in Mormonism: powerful patriarchs leading their families and matriarchs as faithful wives and mothers, bound together in family relationships that would endure after death.

Amidst protests for a change to the LDS Church's policy on race from within and without the Church, Latter-day Saint scholars demonstrated popular resistance to the racial restriction. Perhaps most notably, a medical student at the University of Virginia named Lester Bush, Jr. wrote an extensive article showing that Mormonism's priesthood and temple restriction did not originate with Joseph Smith. Importantly, more than any other of the dozens of academic articles written on the restriction, Bush argued that Black Mormons viewed the temple restriction as "even more serious than the policy of priesthood denial, for in Mormon theology these ordinances were necessary for ultimate exaltation in the life hereafter" (Bush, 1973, p. 32). Bush's article, published in *Dialogue: A Journal of Mormon Thought*, made its way to the desk of LDS Church President Spencer W. Kimball. According to his son and biographer Edward Kimball, the Mormon prophet likely read the article as he decided whether worthy Black Mormons could participate in temple liturgy or whether Black men could hold the LDS Church's priesthood offices (Kimball, 2008, p. 54). Kimball and his counselors in the LDS First Presidency announced in June 1978 that all those declared worthy, regardless of race, nationality, or color, should have access to the temple rituals.

Black Mormons interviewed by student journalists at Brigham Young University bear witness to how the restriction had affected their gendered participation in Mormonism. Black women spoke to the ways their sons would be able to perform masculine roles in Mormonism. Said Marilyn Y. Smith, "When [my son] is twelve years old, he can hold the priesthood and be ordained a deacon. Now he won't have to live through the ridicule and downgrading that others of us have." One Black man, Robert Stevenson, anxiously awaited the opportunity to "do proxy endowment work in the temple." Mrs. Shirley Frazier, a Black woman in an interracial marriage, told reporters that she had long waited to be sealed to her husband and for the chance to see her male children pass the sacrament" (Extra!, 1978). Kimball's revelation, canonized as Official Declaration 2, made Black men and women eligible for the temple liturgy, but also made it possible for Black men and women to live up to Mormon ideals for masculinity and femininity through service and religious ritual.

Conclusion

In the past forty years, scholars have grappled with how to explain Mormonism's history of race both to Latter-day Saints and to the academy. Many of these studies have focused on the restriction on ordination for black men, rather than on black women and children, who were also barred from Mormon temple rituals. By rarely including women or children in histories of race, scholars of Mormonism have not fully explored the effects of past racism on people of color. This sort of gendered framing reveals the limits of previous scholarship: studies have been so narrow that there are many more avenues open for study. Fortunately, scholars have begun to examine the intersections of race and gender in Mormon history. Quincy Newell's (2019) work on Jane Manning James and the lived experiences of black Mormons promises to re-shape the ways that scholars of Mormonism and nineteenth-century religion understand the intersections of race, gender, and sexuality. Caroline Kline's (2018) dissertation on Mormon women and their religious lives across the globe also brings Mormon Studies outside of the United States without turning to missiology. Janan Graham-Russell's future work on Haitian women, colonialism, and the LDS experience also promises to open scholars' eyes to the intersection of race and gender in modern Mormonism. Even with these important projects, it is essential to remember that there are few studies of Mormon masculinities, race, and sexuality, particularly in areas where historical research has not received its due attention, such as Asian Mormonism.

We look forward to the development of future studies that bring together Mormonism, race, gender, and sexuality in ways that build upon existing scholarship and push the field forward.

Note

1 Adoption Record, Book A, 26, Church History Library, Salt Lake City, UT. Cited in Newell (2019, p. 115).

References

Ayala, L., 2004. Mormon Conversions Surge in Latin America. *NBC News*. July 13. www.nbcnews.com/id/5378318/ns/world_news/t/mormon-conversions-surge-latin-america/#.W4iutegzqUl (accessed June 14, 2019).

Blackhawk, N., 2008. *Violence over the Land: Indians and Empires in the Early American West*. Cambridge, MA: Harvard University Press.

Boxer, E., 2009. "To Become White and Delightsome": American Indians and Mormon Identity. Ph.D. dissertation. Arizona State University.

Boxer, E., 2018. "This Is the Place!" Disrupting Mormon Settler Colonialism. In G. Colvin and J. Brooks, eds. *Decolonizing Mormonism*. Salt Lake City, UT: University of Utah Press, pp. 77–99.

Brown, S., 2012. *In Heaven as It Is on Earth: Joseph Smith and the Early Mormon Conquest of Death*. New York: Oxford University Press.

Bush, L., 1973. Mormonism's Negro Doctrine: An Historical Overview. *Dialogue: A Journal of Mormon Thought* 8: 11–68.

Bushman, R., 2005. *Joseph Smith: Rough Stone Rolling*. New York: Alfred A. Knopf.

Extra!, 1978. *The Daily Universe* (Brigham Young University Student Newspaper). June 9.

Farmer, J., 2010. *On Zion's Mount: Mormons, Indians, and the American Landscape*. Cambridge, MA; Harvard University Press.

Flake, G., 1972. Mormons in Mexico: The First 96 years. *Ensign*. www.churchofjesuschrist.org/study/ensign/1972/09/mormons-in-mexico-the-first-96-years?lang=eng.

Garcia, I., 2017. Thoughts on Latino Mormons, Their Afterlife, and the Need for a New Historical Paradigm. *Dialogue: A Journal of Mormon Thought* 50(4): 1–30.

Givens, T., and Grow, M., 2011. *Parley P. Pratt: The Apostle Paul of Mormonism*. New York: Oxford University Press.

Hendrix-Komoto, A., 2016. "Mahana, You Naked!": Modesty, Sexuality, and Race in the Mormon Pacific. In P.Q. Mason and J.G. Turner, eds. *Out of Obscurity: Mormonism since 1945*. New York: Oxford University Press, pp. 173–97.

Hickman, J., 2014. The Book of Mormon as Amerindian Apocalypse. *American Literature* 86(3): 429–61.

Jefferson, T., 1787. *Notes on the State of Virginia*. London: John Stockdale.

Kimball, E., 2008. Spencer W. Kimball and the Revelation on Priesthood. *BYU Studies* 47(2): 4–78.

Kline, C., 2018. Navigating Mormonism's Gendered Theology and Practice: Mormon Women in a Global Context. Doctoral Dissertation, Claremont Graduate University.

Morrison, H., Paterson, L., Knowles, B., and Rae, M., 2012. *Mana Maori and Christianity*. Wellington, NZ: Huia Publishers.

Mueller, M., 2017. *Race and the Making of the Mormon People*. Chapel Hill, NC: University of North Carolina Press.

Murphy, T., 1998. "Stronger than Ever": Remnants of the Third Convention. *Journal of Latter-day Saint History* 10: 1, 8–11.

Newell, Q., 2019. *Your Sister in the Gospel: The Life of Jane Manning James, a Nineteenth-Century Black Mormon*. New York: Oxford University Press.

Nielson, R., 2010. *Early Mormon Missionary Activities in Japan, 1901–1924*. Salt Lake City, UT: University of Utah Press.

Peterson, D., 2017. *Indians in the Family: Adoption and the Politics of Antebellum Expansion*. Cambridge, MA: Harvard University Press.

Peterson, J., 1999. *Utah's Blackhawk War*. Salt Lake City, UT: University of Utah Press.

Peterson, M.E., 1954. Race Problems—as they Face the Church. Mark E. Peterson Papers, Box 1, Special Collections and Archives, University of Utah, J. Willard Marriott Library, Salt Lake City, UT.

Reeve, W., 2015. *Religion of a Different Color: Race and the Mormon Struggle for Whiteness*. New York: Oxford University Press.

Riess, J., 2019. Major Changes to Mormon Temple Ceremony, Especially for Women. *Religion News Service*. https://religionnews.com/2019/01/03/major-changes-to-mormon-temple-ceremony-especially-for-women/ (accessed June 14, 2019).

Smith, J., 1830. *The Book of Mormon*. Palmyra, NY: E.B. Grandin.

Smith, J., 1841–1842. *Journal, December 1841–December 1842*. The Joseph Smith Papers. www.josephsmithpapers.org/paper-summary/journal-december-1841-december-1842/76 (accessed January 21, 2020).

Statement of the First Presidency of The Church of Jesus Christ of Latter-day Saints, August 17, 1949. Church History Library, The Church of Jesus Christ of Latter-day Saints, Salt Lake City, UT.

Underwood, G., 1999. *The Millenarian World of Early Mormonism*. Urbana, IL: University of Illinois Press.

Young, B., 1852. Speech. February 5. Papers of George D. Watt, MS 4534 box 1 folder 3; transcribed by LaJean Purcell Carruth, corrected February 26, 2014. Church History Library, The Church of Jesus Christ of Latter-day Saints, Salt Lake City, UT.

Further reading

Aikau, H., 2012. *Chosen People, a Promised Land: Mormonism and Race in Hawai'i*. Minneapolis, MN: University of Minnesota Press.

This book examines the relationship of Native Hawaiian Latter-day Saints to the white-led Great Basin LDS Church of the nineteenth century.

Bowen, D., and Williams, C., 1992. Women in the Book of Mormon. In D. Ludlow, ed. *Encyclopedia of Mormonism*, vol. 1. New York: Macmillan, pp. 1577–80.

This short article provides an overview of the treatment of gender within the Book of Mormon.

Newell, Q., 2019. *Your Sister in the Gospel: The Life of Jane Manning James, a Nineteenth-Century Black Mormon*. New York: Oxford University Press, ch. 6.

This chapter explores how the Church of Jesus Christ of Latter-day Saints' racial restriction affected the ability of Latter-day Saints of Black African descent to perform gender roles related to church service and marriage. It uses the life of Jane Manning James and her husband, Isaac James, to examine how Black Latter-day Saints may have lived with such impediments to racial integration in Utah and within the LDS Church.

Reeve, W., 2015. *Religion of a Different Color: Race and the Mormon Struggle for Whiteness*. New York: Oxford University Press.

This book examines how Americans constructed Latter-day Saints as a racially corrosive religion that turned people considered "white" into racial inferiors. It has several chapters on how fears surrounding interracial marriage foregrounded many of the LDS Church's religious proclamations concerning race.

Weisenfeld, J., 2017. *New World-A-Comin': Black Religion and Racial Identity during the Great Migration*. New York: New York University Press.

This book examines the co-constructed relationship of religion and race through the case studies of New Religious Movements that arose in the Great Migration.

3
INTERSECTIONALITY

Chiung Hwang Chen and Ethan Yorgason

If "Mormon feminism" and "black Mormon" are rare enough formulations to be regarded by some as oxymorons, Mormon intersectionality must seem doubly strange. Mormonism seldom makes appearances in discussions of intersectionality. Studies of Mormonism likewise do not often incorporate the concept of intersectionality. Our premise is that the two should be brought into closer conversation. Intersectionality points to the compound effects of multiple identity positions as well as the impacts of conjoint axes of social-cultural marginalization. This chapter examines the application, or lack thereof, of intersectionality to Mormonism. It identifies work and activism—both potential and actual—that utilize intersectional approaches or perspectives. Its conclusions are more programmatic than substantive, in part because very little truly intersectional analysis has yet been undertaken on Mormonism, and in part due to the complexity of summarizing the variety of intersections that could and should be studied. Above all, it calls for greater attention to intersectional concerns among those who study Mormonism. We begin by defining and contextualizing the concept of intersectionality. We then suggest two ways in which Mormonism may be considered intersectionally: with Mormonism as one of many (often marginalized) identities and with Mormonism as its own socio-cultural system that produces its own (often intersectional) marginalizations. Within the latter approach to LDS intersectionality, we focus first on responses to Mormonism's marginalizations, and second on the role of intersectionality within Mormon Studies. Along the way, and especially in the conclusion, we propose directions for future research.

The concept

Intersectionality is a widely popular but somewhat misconstrued analytical framework. In a nutshell, it offers a way to examine interlocking systems of power and oppression. Rooted in black feminism, intersectionality argues that various forms of hierarchized social categories/identities, such as gender, race, class, sexual orientation, and so on, complexly intersect within social systems. These intersections affect how individuals are treated, are assigned social status, and create identity within the system. For those whose intersecting identities produce multiple instances of marginalization within the social hierarchies, the resultant interlocking oppression, according to intersectionality scholars, is significantly more damaging than that of so-called "single axis" oppression (e.g. gender- or race-based discrimination alone; see Crenshaw, 1989).

That is, the more types of marginalization an individual/group faces in society, the more severe the discrimination and disempowerment is likely to be. In other words, people who are marginalized in multiple ways (e.g. lower-class black women) often encounter the negative effects of "double jeopardy" or "multiple jeopardy" (Carastathis, 2014).

The concept of simultaneous interlocking systems of oppression developed in the 1970s through the early 1990s as black feminism took shape and challenged white feminists' assumption of a universal women's experience (Beale, 1970; Combahee River Collective, 1977; hooks, 1981; Lorde, 1984; King, 1988; Collins, 1990). The black feminist legal scholar Kimberlé Williams Crenshaw's notion of intersectionality (1989; 1991) caught on as the term for the collective thinking. In analyzing black women's difficulties in employment discrimination lawsuit cases, she noted that the American legal system sees gender and race as two totally separate categories. Black women's identity is often reduced to either one or the other of these classifications and associated with either white women's or black men's experiences. As a result, black women's uniquely disadvantaged position, being both black and female, is rendered invisible. She therefore called for an acknowledgment of "gendered racism" in which black women face an environment more hostile than does someone who is singularly exposed to gender- or race-based discrimination (Crenshaw, 1989; 1991).

The concept's scope has since expanded beyond the intersection of sexism and racism in understanding systems of discrimination and oppression to also include classism, heteronormativity, ableism, ageism, and the like. According to Leslie McCall, intersectionality emerged as "a major paradigm of research in women's studies and elsewhere" and is "the most important theoretical contribution that women's studies, in conjunction with related fields, has made so far" (2005, p. 1771). Valerie Smith sees intersectionality as a reading strategy to unpack ideologies "in which relations of domination and subordination are produced" (1998, p. xxiii; see also Cooper, 2016). Kathy Davis claims that intersectionality may have provided a solution to "the most pressing problem facing contemporary feminism—the long and painful legacy of its exclusions" (2008, p. 70). Intersectionality's popularity has grown such that it has become a "citational ubiquity" and as a concept has been applied by academics, activists, political theorists and many others (Wiegman, 2012, p. 240). Intersectionality has become a "buzzword" in and out of the academic realm (Davis, 2008); it provides a "handy catchall phrase" to make identity-based power relations visible and explainable (Phoenix, 2006, p. 187).

Despite its importance and popularity, intersectionality is not without critics, especially among feminists themselves. One key issue is that the concept is not well defined. The idea started from the intersection of gender and race. Other social categories and identities, such as class, age, sexuality, disability, religion, and colonialized status, have been added to the list. Some scholars worry that the proliferation and claiming of possibly endless new identities seem to have taken priority (Butler, 1990; Yuval-Davis, 2006). Others are less concerned; Kathy Davis argues that it is precisely the concept's perceived problematic characteristics—being ambiguous and open-ended—that make the theory a success (2008, p. 77).

Sumi Cho, Kimberlé Williams Crenshaw, and Leslie McCall (2013) prefer a tight definition. They insist that intersectionality's main concern is structures of inequality, not categories of identity. Those who claim that all identities are intersectional or ask "what about white men?" they argue, are fundamentally confused about the relationship between identity and power. In their minds, intersectionality is "an analytic sensibility," "a way of thinking," a "political intervention," and a type of social activism. Therefore, scholars should emphasize "what intersectionality does rather than what intersectionality is" in order to "illuminate how intersecting axes of power and inequality operate to our collective and individual disadvantage" (2013, p. 795).

Brittney Cooper (2016, p. 392) responds to the debate over intersectionality similarly, with only slightly more of a nod toward discussion of identity:

> Intersectionality's most powerful argument is not that the articulation of new identities in and of itself disrupts power arrangements. Rather, the argument is that institutional power arrangements, rooted as they are in relations of domination and subordination, confound and constrict the life possibilities of those who already live at the intersection of certain identity categories.

Diverging from those who focus on structural oppression are intersectionality scholars who prioritize personal identity. Utilizing standpoint theory, some feminists highlight the complexity of individuals' subject positions as they experience the world. Nash's goal, for example, is disrupting "race/gender binaries in the service of theorizing identity in a more complex fashion" (2008, p. 2). Jakeet Singh (2015) further suggests that identity-focused intersectionality allows us to see various types of personal agency, an important feminist objective in and of itself. However, Cooper calls this way of theorizing—applying intersectionality to situations in which no jeopardy or systematic oppression exists—"postintersectional" and "a mistake" (2016, pp. 400, 393; see also Carastathis, 2016; Tomlinson, 2013).

This chapter assesses intersectionality's application for Mormonism through reference to these two perspectives: personal identity and structural oppression. Although including both, we prioritize the structural-oppression approach. Thus we embrace a vision in which intersectionality is more than an apolitical concept, more than a recognition of finer categories of identity. Rather it is also a perspective on oppression and an analytical tool that illuminates how power operates through social hierarchy. Exploring various aspects of Mormonism, we argue that this vision of intersectionality has not been fully realized or utilized in either Mormon scholarship or activism.

Mormonism as a social category/identity

Religion is one of several lines of difference intersectionality may invoke. The anthropologist Saba Mahmood (2005) was a leading voice incorporating religion within feminist projects by analyzing Egyptian Muslim women's agency and authority in Cairo's piety movement. Her ethnography problematizes feminist theory specifically and secular liberal thought generally by showing how religious women advocate for ethical norms that are considered patriarchal or even oppressive to women. Salem (2013) further critiques Western feminists' lack of engagement with women of faith, reasoning that those feminists do not want to deal with the inherently patriarchal nature of many organized religions. Through the case of Islamic feminism, she suggests intersectionality may provide a solution to the exclusion. Weber (2015, p. 23) similarly calls for "intersectional frameworks that recognize the gendered racializations of Islam" in German feminisms. Analyzing hijab bans in Scandinavia and the Netherlands, Halrynjo and Jonker (2016) argue that awareness of the intersection between gender and religion is required to fully understand Western society's discrimination against Muslim women.

Intersectionality of identity

Mormon identity contributes to intersectional subjectivity within the societies in which it finds itself. If one regards intersectionality as primarily about personal identity rather than structural oppression, many examples of Mormonism's intersection with other identities can be identified or imagined. For example, any study of Mormon women's experiences in the larger society involves the intersection between religion and gender. Examination of women adjusting to new gender role expectations after converting to Mormonism fits this framework. Analysis of American/Utah Mormon gender norms, dating rules and rituals diffusing to other cultural settings can also provide intersectional insight. Another possibility includes profiles of famous Mormons. Stories on athletes (such as Jabari Parker) that emphasize the interaction between ethnic (in Parker's case, black/Tongan) and LDS religious affiliations as they navigate American society incorporate intersectionality (Thompson, 2014). Or similarly, discussions that emphasize how Tyler Glenn (the rock group Neon Trees' lead singer) brings his gay and LDS identities to bear not only on each other, but also on his life more generally, utilize intersectionality (Ganz, 2014). In addition, the "I'm a Mormon" campaign features scores of famous and non-famous Latter-day Saints who discuss how their Mormon faith combines with other identities within their societies.

Intersectionality of structural oppression

However, within intersectionality's structural oppression framework, Mormonism as a social category becomes trickier. Yuval-Davis (2006, p. 203) advises that social divisions should be examined critically because not all categories affect individuals equally. In addition, these categories often affect people differently in different (geographical, temporal, and social) locations. Gender, age, ethnicity, and class, she argues, "tend to shape most people's lives in most social locations, while other social divisions ... affect fewer people globally." A specifically Mormon religious identity might not participate as deeply in structural oppression in some places as other identities do. Yet Mormonism likely qualifies as a marginalized group in most places. Americans have viewed it as a cult since its origin. And according to a recent study, Mormons remain one of the least liked religious people in America, only slightly more favorable than Muslims and atheists (Pew Research Center, 2017). People in almost every other country similarly regard Mormons as a minor and/or distrusted minority. Even in the two nations where Mormons cannot be called a small minority (Samoa and Tonga), accusations of Mormonism's non-Christianity create Mormon "otherness." Thus, Mormons in most parts of the world likely have experience with at least occasional discrimination relating to their religion.

There is more to Yuval-Davis' point, however. She adds that "the ways different social divisions are constructed by, and intermeshed with, each other in specific historical conditions" also vary (2006, p. 202). In other words, Mormonism's role in this type of intersectionality must be demonstrated rather than assumed. In the USA, we would argue, being Mormon and female does not typically produce the same type of double jeopardy that being black (or Latina, etc.) and female have within legal and employment structures. The lack of physical markings associated with Mormon identity allows that identity to be irrelevant in many circumstances. A gay Mormon man may not face challenges that multiply together with each other in everyday American life any more than a non-religious or a mainstream Christian gay man does (though he may encounter more issues within Mormonism specifically). In other words, Mormon identity likely leads more often to additional, but separate oppressions than to simultaneous, conjoint, multiplicative oppressions. We are not sure, for example, that Latter-day Saint identity multiplied every burden that former Utah Congresswoman Mia Love faced because of her gender, national background, and race. (This was not always true. National controversy over polygamy during the late 1800s meant that gender and nationality intersected with religious oppression to place Mormon women and immigrants in multiplied structural jeopardy; Gordon, 2002). We suspect that this lack of strong intersectionality also largely holds in countries where

Mormons constitute smaller minorities. Mormon identity there may be neither visible nor stereotyped enough to produce intersectional consequences. However, there are places where Mormonism more likely participates in intersectionality effects, places where Mormonism's stereotypes or visibility are strong enough to combine with other lines of disadvantage and oppression. Among the most likely, we suspect, are countries where Mormons are a relatively larger percentage of the population than in most countries—Mexico, the Philippines, New Zealand, or Uruguay, for instance—or some European countries where the dominant cultures deeply frown upon non-traditional belief.

But these are empirical matters. Mormon identity in many countries produces strong connotations of white American culture. That association may or may not be a burden, depending on place and time (in some situations it can be a benefit). In any case, the role of Mormonism in intersectional oppression cannot simply be read off of its position as a single-axis minority category. Mormon identity does not always magnify the burden of those who are subject to other types of discrimination, even if it often adds separate oppressions. Consequently, the issue of Mormonism's role in structural-oppression intersectionality deserves further research. Scholars have seldom asked these questions.

Mormonism as a social system

Conceiving of Mormonism as a social system in and of itself gives a second perspective on Mormonism's role in intersectionality. Mormonism is not a complete social system; Mormons always operate within larger social contexts. But Latter-day Saints devote much physical, emotional, spiritual, social, cultural, psychological, and sometimes even economic and political energy toward Mormonism. Mormonism is complex and powerful enough to create its own hegemonic values, structures of power, and senses of centrality and marginality. Thus, in addition to Mormon identity's combining with other social identities, intersectionality exists within Mormonism itself. Social centrality and marginality within Mormonism share similarities with the American culture from which it stems. Whiteness, maleness, Americanness, and married heterosexuality hold particularly privileged positions within its structure of culture and authority. Middle-class values, political and social conservatism, able-bodiedness, and certain age characteristics at times also position individuals more toward the center of Mormon ideology and activity. Latter-day Saints who differ from these characteristics can still achieve great meaning, value, and social solidarity from their church experiences, but the deviations are typically obstacles that must be overcome or barriers preventing full participation within social-cultural and authority structures. Strength of belief itself—or "testimony" in LDS terminology—can also be regarded as an axis of hierarchical centrality, though we do not dwell on it in this chapter.

Intersectionality of identity

Compared to viewing Mormonism as one axis of identity within larger social systems, it is perhaps easier to see how intersectionality operates within Mormonism as a system. Much more scholarly attention has already been given to "intersectional" issues, even if not labeled as such. In relation to personal-identity intersectionality, many possible topics exist. Recent changes in missionary ages and Young Women's involvement in temple baptisms and "Ministering" programs, for example, highlight intersections between gender and age. Similarly, the April 2017 callings to the General Relief Society Presidency of a single woman and a Latina opened intersectional possibilities. Chieko Okazaki was, during the 1990s, the first non-Caucasian woman called to the church's general leadership. Her life and teachings embody intersectionality; they added space within Mormonism for greater prominence of non-hegemonic gender and national/ethnic identities. Jane Manning James, one of the most celebrated nineteenth-century black Mormons, provides another example. Many black women today regard her as a model who helps them valorize their LDS identity. And of course scholars could easily find intersectional stories in the lives of hundreds of thousands of less famous, ordinary Saints.

Studying this personal identity-based type of intersectionality can be quite illuminating, by offering a clearer vision of types of Mormon experiences that are not yet well known or understood. Nevertheless, we submit, it is the second type of intersectionality—the kind that focuses on structures of oppression—that may be even more important and more in line with the original aims of those advocating for the intersectionality concept. We explore this idea in two ways: first by focusing on intersectional responses to the marginalizations within LDS Church culture, and second by viewing Mormon Studies, as an academic field, through an intersectional lens.

Intersectionality of marginalization: responses to church culture

Individuals and groups attempting to counter aspects of LDS hegemonies have long existed. Their prominence has grown owing partly to the larger impact of identity politics in recent decades and partly to the church's increased stability over time, since relatively stable social systems/institutions are more likely to generate internal movements for reform and not just movements that oppose the whole system. For example, Mormon feminists used polygamy to argue for expanded gender roles during the 1870s and 1880s. Later, after the nominal end of polygamy, they advocated against many fellow church members in favor of continuing female suffrage as part of the Utah statehood convention. The so-called 1936 "Third Convention" of Mexican Mormons is another example. Drawing on racial/national identity, these Saints protested the relative paucity of local leaders in comparison to those sent from Utah (Tullis, 1997). Feminist activism and questioning of LDS structures of gender authority re-emerged especially strongly during the 1970s around the Equal Rights movement. More or less radical, more or less confrontational, and more or less visible movements have since continued to arise around issues of female roles, influence, and authority within Mormonism itself. Movements highlighting power and privilege relating to race emerged since the 1960s. Struggle preceded the 1978 overturning of the ban on temple access for blacks and priesthood authority for black men, in particular. More recently, oppressions within Mormonism toward sexual minorities have gained significant attention. The LGBT+ community along with its allies have made those oppressions visible.

Nevertheless, most of these and other LDS movements relating to centrality and marginalization—Mormonism's privileges and oppressions—focus on single-axis issues. They typically address race independent of gender, for example. They seldom connect sexuality to social class or nationality. In other words, movements addressing power within Mormonism are not often truly intersectional. We recognize that individual Mormons may think and sometimes act intersectionally, as is clear in the Latter-day Saints who have advocated for increased equality relating to gender, race, and sexual orientation. However, the movements themselves typically operate separately, although intersectional possibilities within Mormon movements are rising. We here highlight three groups that typify this not-yet-fully-realized potential: Sistas in Zion, Affirmation, and Mama Dragons.

Sistas in Zion may not be best labeled an activist group. The Sistas are just two people—Zandra Vranes and Tamu Smith. They do not strongly advocate institutional change. Their orientation is perhaps more "faithful" than many activist groups, strongly supporting basic Mormon narratives and truth claims. However, as two African American Mormon women, they make visible an identity/experiential perspective relatively unfamiliar to most Mormons. Their primary platform is Facebook, with a timeline full of thoughts and wisdom intended to help Mormons see things differently. Nevertheless, the Sistas' intersectionality is perhaps not equally balanced. That is, their focus is much more race than gender. Their commitment toward greater equality and stronger female voices within Mormonism occasionally becomes apparent. But many more of their posts (and most of the reaction from Facebook followers) highlights African American identity. They do not frequently emphasize the dual/simultaneous identity or marginalizations of black women within Mormonism.

Affirmation supports LGBT+ Latter-day Saints. Created in the late 1970s, the group established chapters in just a few American cities at first, but grew larger and more visible over time. It now even includes members from Latin America and Great Britain. These members embody identity intersections of many different kinds between LGBT+ sexuality and Mormonism, including strongly active, disaffected, and former Mormons. Not originally established around ideas of intersectionality (if Mormonism is conceived of as a system of power), it has developed more of an intersectional sensibility as it has grown. It works, for example, toward respect and empowerment based on differently abled status and differing nationalities (Noyce and Stack, 2018) in conjunction with its sexual-identity focus.

Mama Dragons, formed in 2014, also organizes around LGBT+ issues. But rather than mainly LGBT+ individuals themselves, Mama Dragons membership is primarily mothers of LGBT+ persons with some LDS association. It thus explicitly links a gendered identity with concern through direct family connection for people subject to Mormonism's sexual-orientation structural oppressions. Despite intersectionality in its identity, however, similar to both Sistas in Zion and Affirmation it advocates primarily around a single axis (sexuality). Thus like other possible examples within Mormonism, each of these groups have opportunities to operate intersectionally but they have not fully realized a sustained intersectional commitment.

Intersectionality of marginalization: Mormon Studies

Just as with Mormonism generally, we can regard Mormon Studies as a system possessing its own power dynamics, centralities, and marginalities. This system is not particularly independent; it derives especially from the ecosystems of Mormonism and American higher education. In Mormon Studies, certain topics, regions, and perspectives receive much more attention than others, creating a privileged center for the field. Origin stories, institutional church history, and (for post-exodus matters) a Utah/American West focus still soak up much of the attention. When scholars discuss Mormon women the experiences of white American women are typically used as an overall representation of Mormon women's experiences. When the focus turns to Mormonism outside the United States, analysis often utilizes a missiology framework, with its frequent bias toward experiences and viewpoints of people from the "center" of the church. The temple and priesthood ban against black men and women or the Old Testament/Book of Mormon-tinged notion of lineage is usually the backdrop for discussions of race. Additionally, certain types of people (especially white, American men) involve themselves more centrally in Mormon Studies' production and consumption while others are more marginal.

Mormon Studies has doubtless opened toward other issues and perspectives in recent decades. Almost all corners of the field accommodate discussions of discrimination, community, and identity organized along various axes of difference, such as race, gender, class, nationality, and sexuality. Even the *Journal of Mormon History*, a publication that may be expected to hold to the historically traditional center of Mormon Studies, has recently published several articles on various "non-traditionally" conceived topics. Nevertheless, the aggregate focus of Mormon

Studies still does not come close to mirroring the church membership's diversity; nominally about 60 percent reside outside the United States.

To take one example, the recently published *Oxford Handbook of Mormonism*, edited by two of Mormon Studies' pre-eminent scholars (Givens and Barlow, 2015), will likely be a leading introduction to and definition of the field over the next several years. Out of 41 chapters, just four focus primarily on the church outside the United States. A handful of other chapters' sections discuss the international church generally or some aspects of it, but broad generalities rather than specifics about Mormons' experiences there are the rule. Beyond the topics themselves, Mormons Studies in that *Handbook* appears to be the domain of primarily white Americans, overwhelmingly men. As best as we can figure, the forty-five contributors to the volume include one non-American and one non-white scholar. There are even more non-Mormon authors (seven, if our reckoning is correct). Our point is not to criticize the editors' author choices for individual chapters; all make good sense on their own. Rather it is to emphasize that for all the increased attention to diversity within Mormon Studies, clear patterns of centrality and marginality persist.

Thus we agree with Elise Boxer who stated at a recent roundtable on Mormon history: "Mormon studies need to include scholars, including scholars of color, whose perspectives are not only different, but which challenge widely accepted narratives … that do not fit neatly into a Mormon-American perspective or experience" (Colvin, 2015, pp. 259–60). Even though much of that roundtable's discussion focused on race/ethnicity/nationality, especially by critiquing white American centrality, participants made gestures toward fuller intersectionality. Gina Colvin (2015) did so most directly. She noted that historical research, with its priority on documentary evidence, generally makes black and brown women invisible. She thus argued that scholars should more carefully attend "to the multicultural, biracial, intersectional experience and the way in which these identities are understood in Mormon contexts" (p. 261). In fact, we argue, a true intersectional spirit that is attuned to multiple, simultaneous discriminations and oppressions is difficult to find within Mormon Studies. Where scholars move beyond dominant narratives and types of experiences, attention to single axes of diversity takes priority. Individual readers might bring intersectional insight to their own interpretation of Mormonism through this scholarship, yet the research itself rarely explicitly highlights the intersections.

Hopefully this is beginning to change since some Mormon Studies scholars increasingly articulate intersectional concerns, vocabulary, and perspectives. But producing true intersectional research remains difficult, including for the very mundane reason that norms of scholarship often lead researchers to "narrow their topic" in a way that precludes intersectionality. Nevertheless, we want to point to, among other candidates, three articles that bear an intersectional spirit effectively. Each emphasizes personal stories. Such a focus may especially usefully sustain discussions of LDS intersectionality. Perhaps unsurprisingly, two come from a book co-edited by Gina Colvin (a Maori woman who has long been interested in issues of social power within Mormonism), while a third comes from a *Journal of Mormon History* special issue she co-edited. That edited book, *Decolonizing Mormonism*, more generally lends itself well to discussions of intersectionality (Colvin and Brooks, 2018).

First, Ignacio Garcia (2018) recollects how, as a young bishop several decades ago, he sought to decolonize the minds of members within his largely lower-class, Latino ward in Tucson, Arizona. Many of them, along with some stake and area leaders, felt that due to race and class they were destined to simply follow instructions and models from those with higher status within Mormonism. Their race seemed to confine them to the continually deferred promise that the Lamanites would become more "white and delightsome," while their economic status made it hard for them to believe that they could truly lead within the church. Garcia recounts the slow process by which ward members began to understand that their own value within Mormonism need not be defined by white, middle-class cultural models.

Second, Stacilee Ford (2018) draws on years of participant observation in Hong Kong to analyze the varieties of LDS sisterhood within that very cosmopolitan city. National difference plays a major role; LDS women inhabit local (Cantonese), mainland Chinese, and white American identities and experiences, among others. The presence of some of those others in Hong Kong stems from disadvantaged positions within the global economy. This group, composed especially of Filipinas, is marginalized because of nationality, economic class, and gender. Their presence as transnational workers in Hong Kong complicates roles within a church that prioritizes mothers' duties in their own homes. Like Garcia, Ford attends to how marginalized Saints seek value and unique identity within their Mormonism. Both scholars celebrate the flourishing of LDS faith. However, they both also carefully describe and critique the structural oppression of intersectionally marginalized LDS groups. Even more than Garcia, Ford (2018, p. 223) situates her account through the concept of intersectionality.

> The intersectional analysis … is unfortunately something we do not implement as often as we might within Mormonism for a number of reasons, including that we are keen to celebrate a unified sisterhood and church membership. That is a noble ideal, but in so doing, we may be ignoring economic, historical, political and personal realities that shape us in profoundly different ways and that demand more thoughtful attention and action.

The third article does not prioritize faithfulness as much; the story it conveys might be less of a success story from the perspective of the institutional church. Russell Stevenson (2015) uses historical/archival methods to tell of the 1960s–1970s ascension and then marginalization of local forms of Mormonism in Ghana. Rebecca Mould was widely regarded as a prophetess in a local Mormon branch there. Stevenson highlights her role both before and after the church's introduction of missionaries and central institutional authority subsequent to the 1978 ending of the racial priesthood ban. In spite of the institutional church's hands-off attitude during the late 1960s and most of the 1970s, Mormonism flourished in Ghana. It was one of many indigenized Christian movements offering hope for personal and community success in the confusing socio-economic aftermath of political decolonization. Ghanaians attracted to Mormonism, including Mould, established structures of authority based on their own spiritual experiences. While seeking greater connection with Salt Lake City, they seemed to have little knowledge and/or concern about American Mormonism's racialized and gendered priesthood. Once the ban was removed, the church sent senior missionaries who strongly wished for greater black involvement in the LDS community. Yet those early missionaries quickly set about changing structures and practices in the Ghanaian branches they found foreign. The institutional church did not support Mould's authority over the branch she had led. While calling her as Relief Society president staved off dissention initially, eventually she and nearly 70 percent of the branch dissociated themselves from the institutional church.

Conclusion

Intersectionality concerns the mutual, simultaneous impact of multiple identities or structural axes of power within society. Emerging out of black feminist scholarship and activism, it now refers to many forms of combined minority status. We have argued that both the identity and the structural-oppression conceptions of intersectionality (and their combinations) illuminate

LDS experiences. Whether Mormonism is regarded as an identity within larger societies or a social system itself, it participates in the hierarchical prioritization and marginalization of social groups. Nevertheless, we believe intersectionality is not sufficiently utilized within either Mormon life generally or Mormon Studies particularly. Sistas in Zion, Affirmation, and Mama Dragons point to activism's intersectional potential while Colvin, Garcia, Ford, and Stevenson provide useful examples for scholarship. By helping us see how identities and oppressions are co-constituted (Cooper, 2016), intersectionality may help us begin the process of imagining more productive ways of relating to one another.

Intersectional exploration of Mormonism is still in its infancy. This is in part because proliferation of even single-axis identities within the LDS rubric is itself in its early stages. Mormonism generally prizes unity within its community. It finds both scriptural and cultural-political justifications to discourage identity positions that derive from outside its hierarchical organization. But discouragement of identity positions, many scholars argue, reinforces unacknowledged marginalizations. Garcia, for example, predicts that Latinos will not be de-marginalized within the church through stronger universalistic assertions of the insignificance of race and ethnicity to LDS identity (2018, p. 159). Instead, de-marginalization requires finding a voice to "push back against the racial assumptions that undergird much of Mormon historicity." This voice is lacking, in part because so few scholars of color (Latino or any sort) are currently being read or published. Interpretations by white Mormon scholars or Latino anti-Mormons, he argues, are insufficient to create a Latino Mormon voice. Thus, we submit, in an environment where single-axis identities are weak or discouraged, it is hard to see strong intersectional discourses developing within or about Mormonism.

Above all, we advocate intersectionality as a perspective/outlook/approach. Scholars of intersectionality provide useful advice for those who want to use this perspective to better understand and navigate Mormonism. One suggestion to move from single-category, to multiple-category, eventually to intersectional research (Hancock, 2007) is to ask an additional question. Matsuda relates, "When I see something that looks racist, I ask, 'Where is the patriarchy in this?' When I see something that looks sexist, I ask, 'Where is the heterosexism in this?' When I see something that looks homophobic, I ask, 'Where are the class interests in this?'" (1991, p. 1189). Intersectionality additionally involves, in bell hooks' memorable phrase (1984), a willingness to move "the margin to the center." Perspectives typically seen as marginal within LDS narratives assume new importance within this outlook. The transnational experiences of LDS Filipina domestic workers become central to the contemporary LDS story, not just an interesting side note. An intersectional approach, finally, also prioritizes building coalitions with other (often differently) marginalized groups (Carastathis, 2016; Cho, Crenshaw, and McCall, 2013; Chen and Yorgason, 1999). An intersectional Mormonism means not just pointing to discrimination toward Mormonism that formally resembles oppression of other minority groups, not just allying socially-politically with other religious groups who share similar beliefs, but also creating linkages that prioritize eradicating discrimination and marginalization of many (all?) sorts, both within and outside of LDS society. The LDS Church's recent agreement with the NAACP on anti-poverty initiatives in the USA draws on an intersectional impulse (Walch, 2018). But it will retain that attitude only to the extent that Mormons assume they have as much to learn as to teach within the partnership. We hope this chapter encourages readers to pursue this intersectional spirit.

References

Beale, F., 1970. Double Jeopardy: To Be Black and Female. In B. Guy-Sheftall, ed. *Words of Fire: An Anthology of African American Feminist Thought.* New York: New Press, pp. 146–55.
Butler, J., 1990. *Gender Trouble: Feminism and the Subversion of Identity.* New York: Routledge.
Carastathis, A., 2014. The Concept of Intersectionality in Feminist Theory. *Philosophy Compass* 9(5): 304–14.
Carastathis, A., 2016. *Intersectionality: Origins, Contestations, Horizons.* Lincoln, NE: University of Nebraska Press.
Chen, C.H., and Yorgason, E., 1999. "Those Amazing Mormons": The Media's Construction of Latter-day Saints as a Model Minority. *Dialogue: A Journal of Mormon Thought* 32(2): 107–28.
Cho, S., Crenshaw, K.W., and McCall, L., 2013. Toward a Field of Intersectionality Studies: Theory, Applications, and Praxis. *Signs: Journal of Women in Culture and Society* 38(4): 785–810.
Collins, P.H., 1990. *Black Feminist Thought: Knowledge, Consciousness and the Politics of Empowerment.* London: Unwin Hyman.
Colvin, G., 2015. Roundtable Discussion: Challenging Mormon Race Scholarship. *Journal of Mormon History* 41(3): 258–81.
Colvin, G., and Brooks, J. eds., 2018. *Decolonizing Mormonism: Approaching a Postcolonial Zion.* Salt Lake City, UT: University of Utah.
Combahee River Collective, 1977. *Combahee River Collective Statement.* Combahee River Collective. https://combaheerivercollective.weebly.com/the-combahee-river-collective-statement.html (accessed June 29, 2018).
Cooper, B., 2016. Intersectionality. In L. Disch and M. Hawkesworth, eds. *The Oxford Handbook of Feminist Theory.* Oxford: Oxford University Press, pp. 385–406.
Crenshaw, K.W., 1989. Demarginalizing the Intersection of Race and Sex: A Black Feminist Critique of Antidiscrimination Doctrine, Feminist Theory and Antiracist Politics. *University of Chicago Legal Forum*, pp. 139–67.
Crenshaw, K.W., 1991. Mapping the Margins: Intersectionality, Identity Politics, and Violence against Women of Color. *Stanford Law Review* 43(6): 1241–99.
Davis, K., 2008. Intersectionality as Buzzword: A Sociology of Science Perspective on What Makes a Feminist Theory Successful. *Feminist Theory* 9(1): 67–85.
Ford, S., 2018. Sister Acts: Relief Society and Flexible Citizenship in Hong Kong. In G. Colvin and J. Brooks, eds. 2018. *Decolonizing Mormonism: Approaching a Postcolonial Zion.* Salt Lake City, UT: University of Utah Press, pp. 202–28.
Ganz, C., 2014. Neon Trees' Tyler Glenn: Gay, Mormon and Finally Out. *Rolling Stone.* March 25. www.rollingstone.com/music/music-news/neon-trees-tyler-glenn-gay-mormon-and-finally-out-235705/ (accessed August 14, 2018).
Garcia, I., 2018. Empowering Latino Saints to Transcend Historical Racialism. In G. Colvin and J. Brooks, eds. 2018. *Decolonizing Mormonism: Approaching a Postcolonial Zion.* Salt Lake City, UT: University of Utah Press, pp. 139–59.
Givens, T.L., and Barlow, P.L. eds., 2015. *The Oxford Handbook of Mormonism.* Oxford: Oxford University Press.
Gordon, S.B., 2002. *The Mormon Question: Polygamy and Constitutional Conflict in Nineteenth-Century America.* Chapel Hill, NC: University of North Carolina Press.
Halrynjo, S., and Jonker, M., 2016. Naming and Framing of Intersectionality in Hijab Cases—Does It Matter? An Analysis of Discrimination Cases in Scandinavia and the Netherlands. *Gender, Work and Organization* 23(3): 278–95.
Hancock, A.M., 2007. When Multiplication Doesn't Equal Quick Addition: Examining Intersectionality as a Research Paradigm. *Perspectives on Politics* 5(1): 63–79.
hooks, b., 1981. *Ain't I a Woman: Black Women and Feminism.* New York: South End Press.
hooks, b., 1984. *Feminist Theory from Margin to Center.* New York: South End Press.
King, D., 1988. Multiple Jeopardy, Multiple Consciousness: The Context of Black Feminist Ideology. *Signs: Journal of Women in Culture and Society* 14(1): 42–72.
Lorde, A., 1984. *Sister Outsider.* Berkeley, CA: Crossing Press.
Mahmood, S., 2005. *Politics of Piety: The Islamic Revival and the Feminist Subject.* Princeton, NJ: Princeton University Press.
Matsuda, M.J., 1991. Beside My Sister, Facing the Enemy: Legal Theory out of Coalition. *Stanford Law Review* 43(6): 1183–92.

McCall, L., 2005. The Complexity of Intersectionality. *Signs: Journal of Women in Culture and Society* 30(3): 1771–800.

Nash, J.C., 2008. Re-thinking Intersectionality. *Feminist Review*, 89: 1–15.

Noyce, D., and Stack P.F. 2018. Is LGBTQ Support Group Affirmation Getting too Tight with the Mormon Church. *The Salt Lake Tribune Mormon Land*. July 18. www.sltrib.com/podcasts/mormon-land/ (accessed July 20, 2018).

Pew Research Center, 2017. Americans Express Increasing Warm Feelings toward Religious Groups Pew Research Center. www.pewforum.org/2017/02/15/Americans-express-increasingly-warm-feelings-toward-religious-groups/ (accessed July 16, 2018).

Phoenix, A., 2006. Editorial: Intersectionality. *European Journal of Women's Studies* 13(3): 187–92.

Salem, S., 2013. Feminist Critique and Islamic Feminism: The Question of Intersectionality. *The Postcolonialist* 1(1). http://postcolonialist.com/civil-discourse/feminist-critique-and-islamic-feminism-the-question-of-intersectionality/ (accessed July 10, 2018).

Singh, J., 2015. Religious Agency and the Limits of Intersectionality. *Hypatia* 30(4): 657–74.

Smith, V., 1998. *Not Just Race, Not Just Gender: Black Feminist Readings*. New York: Routledge.

Stevenson, R.W., 2015. "We Have Prophetesses": Mormonism in Ghana, 1964–79. *Journal of Mormon History* 41(3): 221–57.

Thompson, A., 2014. For Many Mormon Athletes, Mission Is to Play. *The New York Times*. June 25. www.nytimes.com/2014/06/26/sports/basketball/jabari-parker-heeds-nba-draft-call-bypassing-formal-mormon-mission.html (accessed August 14, 2018).

Tomlinson, B., 2013. To Tell the Truth and Not Get Trapped: Desire, Distance, and Intersectionality at the Scene of Argument. *Signs: Journal of Women in Culture and Society* 38(4): 993–1017.

Tullis, F.L., 1997. A Shepherd to Mexico's Saints: Arwell L. Pierce and the Third Convention. *BYU Studies* 37(1): 127–57.

Walch, T., 2018. Inside the Collaboration between the LDS Church and the NAACP. *Deseret News*. June 22. www.deseretnews.com/article/900025670/inside-the-collaboration-between-the-lds-church-and-naacp.html (accessed August 15, 2018).

Weber, B.M., 2015. Gender, Race, Religion, Faith? Rethinking Intersectionality in German Feminisms. *European Journal of Women's Studies* 22(1): 22–36.

Wiegman, R., 2012. *Object Lessons*. Durham, NC: Duke University Press.

Yuval-Davis, N., 2006. Intersectionality and Feminist Politics. *European Journal of Women's Studies* 13(3): 193–209.

Further reading

Colvin, G., and Brooks, J. eds., 2018. *Decolonizing Mormonism: Approaching a Postcolonial Zion*. Salt Lake City, UT: University of Utah.

Cooper, B., 2016. Intersectionality. In L. Disch and M. Hawkesworth, eds. *The Oxford Handbook of Feminist Theory*. Oxford: Oxford University Press, pp. 385–406.

Crenshaw, K.W., 1991. Mapping the Margins: Intersectionality, Identity Politics, and Violence against Women of Color. *Stanford Law Review* 43(6): 1241–99.

Mahmood, S., 2005. *Politics of Piety: The Islamic Revival and the Feminist Subject*. Princeton, NJ: Princeton University Press.

Stevenson, R.W., 2015. "We Have Prophetesses": Mormonism in Ghana, 1964–79. *Journal of Mormon History* 41(3): 221–57.

4
FEMININITIES

Amy Hoyt

Introduction

It is almost impossible to talk about women within the Church of Jesus Christ of Latter-day Saints as a monolith and futile to think it can be done without somehow eliding various subjectivities for the comfort of classification. A unified definition of any group is difficult, particularly when they span the globe and include multiple races, ethnicities, socioeconomic classes, and sexual orientations. An additional challenge in defining a group of women is that within the fields of women's and gender studies the term "femininities" is contested as it has not been as thoroughly interrogated and deconstructed as the binary term "masculinities" has been. Despite the limitations of the term, and the challenges inherent in describing LDS women as a stable, unified cohort, this essay tentatively employs the category of "femininities" in order to examine the institutional ideal of a feminine subject and the competing reality of various Latter-day Saint female subjectivities. Using an intersectional approach that attends to agentive adaptations within networks of power, this essay observes the disconnect between the ideal feminine subject developed within hegemonic American masculinity and the lived practices of Latter-day Saint female subjects that span the globe. Relying upon ethnographic research in multiple countries this essay offers an alternate notion of multiple LDS femininities with just two connected threads: a belief of being a daughter of God coupled with a deep commitment to family.

Theoretical framework

Several conversations within feminist theory are particularly generative for understanding the multiple challenges of defining a unified feminine subject, particularly from a male, American perspective. Gender studies has spent limited academic space theorizing the category of femininities, partially because some consider it a "site of struggle" as it can imply the white, heterosexual feminine identity that is hierarchically in relation to the Other. Femininities then remains largely uninterrogated, and by default often becomes defined as the lack of masculinity. It is the shadow side of maleness; the less desirable, less important aspects of humanity (Dahl, 2018). This is reflected within almost every society and community around the world, as patriarchy is the de facto organizational system used within government, business, religion, families, higher education, and endless subgroups and communities. The lack of focus on the category of femininities within the discipline of gender studies reveals the pervasive nature of patriarchy as a system of power that functions to legitimate the hierarchical norms of maleness, thus imitating the very structures it is attempting to destabilize (Paechter, 2018).

While femininities is underdeveloped in the field, the category of gender is not. The decoupling of gender from biological sex and the related idea that binary gender norms inevitably devalue the feminine began with the advent of women's studies courses in the late 1960s and early 1970s on college campuses in the Global North. Although scholars identified early on the difference between biological sex and socially constructed gender norms, most early feminist theorists presumed a white, female subject from the Global North. This theory considered all other women as merely slight deviations of the consummate woman. She, of course, was heteronormative, white, and privileged. Women who embodied different subjectivities, and multiple subjectivities, including women of color, working-class women, queer women, and women with differently abled bodies, began to call attention to this oversight and added nuanced theories to the larger body of literature.

Postcolonial feminist theory was born from the need of feminist scholars in the Global South to call attention to the false notion of sisterhood that European-American feminists espoused while they continued to devalue women outside of these locales. In this way, scholars pointed out that they were discursively colonizing women in the Global South and replicating colonial and patriarchal patterns (Mohanty, 1984). The theory points to the ways in which colonial legacies are replicated and sustained through liberative movements who imagine that they share unified experiences and desires for autonomy. The notion that patriarchy and empire are in a symbiotic relationship is particularly useful for studying women in a global religion.

Queer theory helped to further theorize sexuality and gender as a set of behaviors. Recognizing the social construction of gender led to the theoretical observation that gender is a performance that is steeped in heteronormative sexual desire. In other words, gender is constructed from social expectations that are locally specific and then actualized, or lived out, by most men and women in ways that are distinct so that they demonstrate their commitment to heterosexual romantic relationships (Butler, 1990). Binary gender norms are fragile and precarious and as such, they need to be repeated, propped up, and stabilized frequently. This happens in both conscious and subconscious ways wherein subjects perform gender in socially constructed behaviors that are transcribed onto a body in order to convey a particular gendered identity. In other words, gender performances are how "being a woman" or "being a man" are presented, displayed, and rehearsed moment to moment. Within this system, two distinct genders are defined and reified against one another as they are bound together in heteronormative culture. These performances, or behaviors, may shift depending upon time and place, but they are always defined in relation to one another. Locked in dualistic interplay, the binary gender system requires meticulously constructed actions, speech, and even sexual desire in order to elide the unstable nature of the system.

The performative nature of gender has been used by scholars to examine the religious practices that help form female subjectivity within various faith traditions. This has illuminated agentive female religious acts, but it runs the risk of eliding the power dynamics that operate within institutional religious settings. Recent research examining LDS women has called attention to the ways in which performativity theories gloss over systemic power relations and have advocated for pressing through the limits of simply reporting how women "do religion" in order to interrogate mechanisms of power that minimize the value of the female subject (Sumerau and Cragun, 2015; Kane, 2018).

Antonio Gramsci's concept of hegemony, originally developed as a critique of capitalism in the early twentieth century, is instructive for examining systemic relations of power. Gramsci identified hegemony as ideology created by the ruling class within a society that is then transmitted as truth to the collective so that it is naturalized and adopted by most of the community. Hegemony consists of a reciprocal relationship between consent and coercion so that the effect is to convince the subordinate group that it is in their best interest to be governed by the ruling group (Gramsci, 1971, p. 80). At the same time, coercion appears as if it is sanctioned by much of the group. Hegemonic ideals often include a deep investment in the normative ideologies by most members of the group because they are seen as the way things "ought to be."

Hegemonic masculinity, the collective agreement that the ascendancy of men is natural and in the best interest of society, supports the use of other hierarchies as normative. These can include hierarchies based upon race, ethnicity, geographical location, class, and sexual orientation. This does not mean that *all* males within the construct adhere to the socially expected masculine norms, but that they are measured against these ideals and potential power is implied to all within the dominant group, even if they are not recognized as wielding overt power. By virtue of performing and projecting the masculine values that are seen as normative, they benefit from the regimes of truth that claim the superiority of a particular type of subject.

It is important to be attentive to the shifting hegemony within local contexts as microcommunities are often formed within large organizations, particularly based on physical, economic, and geographical distinctions. It is also important to note that individual female subjects are capable within a hegemonic structure of wielding power. It would be theoretically incomplete to discount that women have participated in violence against others historically and the way in which individual female subjects access some authority. However, within hegemonic masculinity feminine subjects do not possess the characteristics needed to be given universal authority.

Within this structure, gendered subjects receive value, and thus access to potential authority, by virtue of their compliance with the ideological truth that it is in the best interest of society that males have universal authority. Within the Church of Jesus Christ of Latter-day Saints many members consider male authority to be the will of God.

LDS gender constructs

Leaders within the faith routinely use the terms "sex" and "gender" interchangeably and conflate biological sex with the heteronormative gendered behaviors. The idea that biological sex and gender are fused demonstrates a theological belief that in a pre-mortal drama, gendered spirits chose corporeality. In other words, the corporeality of gender is simply a manifestation of a spiritual nature. Binary gender constructs are sanctified by these teachings and males and females are considered to have opposite sacred duties that complement one another's divine purpose (Chen, 2014).

Somatic female subjects are tasked with bearing and rearing children. Motherhood is considered a sacred role due to the theological belief that spirits are "waiting" to obtain physical bodies and have a mortal experience (Hoyt, 2009). Bearing and raising children is the most sanctified duty within LDS femininities and is considered a divine calling (Chen, 2014). Male subjects are tasked as patriarchs within both the domestic and religious spheres. Thus, patriarchal leadership within the institution, congregation, and home are not only the way things "ought to be" but they are considered preordained, timeless patterns that God has sanctioned. It is important to understand that although not every white North American man has institutional authority within the faith community, every male over the age of eleven has the potential to be given the holy priesthood in order to officiate religious rituals. Male access to institutional authority is available should he claim it or be "called" to it by a higher ecclesiastical body. While the priesthood is only given to qualified males and is described in terms of authority, it acts to keep males in charge of all institutional decisions, policies, and ideologies, thus becoming a very powerful mechanism of masculine hegemony. There are masculine subjects who attempt to minimize their privilege in an effort of solidarity with LDS women, although they are in the minority. Despite these aberrations, institutional and ideological power resides exclusively with males and is transmitted to those with less power.

Ideological power translates into actualized power, especially within a religious setting where compliance with ideological and theological norms enhances one's value and dissent can decrease one's value, and potentially lead to expulsion. In LDS discourse priesthood power is presented as "authority" vis-à-vis the male priesthood. Relatedly, although the priesthood is considered a sacred duty as it is "the authority to act in the name of God," only those that possess the priesthood are able to lead in institutional settings. This acts to foreclose female participation in ecclesiastical leadership, thus foreclosing the possibility of the female perspective being represented in leadership forums where decisions are made for the body of the church, including what constitutes an ideal LDS female subject. Nevertheless, hegemonic power is derived from the consent of the majority of the group to allow the ruling group to use coercion in order to define and transmit truth.

Coercion can take the form of leaders censoring women's and allies' voices, both individually and collectively. Scholars and news outlets have documented multiple instances of contemporary LDS women and men being summoned to meet with their male ecclesiastical leaders because they had privately or publicly behaved in ways that seemed incongruent with LDS female ideals or outright questioned beliefs, rituals, and practices that erase or devalue women's contributions (Hoyt, 2007; Kane, 2018). Male leaders have restricted access to temple rituals, public prayers, and Sunday rituals, such as taking the Sacrament, when women or men have vocalized dissent over harmful patriarchal practices. Excommunication has also been utilized to censor feminist intellectuals and discredit members who question patriarchal norms.

The use of intimidation and coercion acts to silence those who disagree with the seemingly naturalized masculine hegemony. These practices maintain religious boundaries and ultimately the ascendancy of male authority. In instances of coercion and intimidation the consent of the majority is not obtained through a vote, but through the chilling effect these actions have on others. Private intimidation and censorship is not as noticeable and in these cases the private nature of the interaction works to maintain the status quo, unless the individual chooses to make it public since the LDS Church will not comment on disciplinary proceedings of members. This policy is important for the protection of the majority of those members who are not being coerced or intimidated for intellectual disagreements; nevertheless, the private nature of the proceedings also obscure the way in which feminist activists are censored. When the general membership is aware of formal sanctions being enacted on women, such as when Kate Kelly was excommunicated for leading a group that asked the highest ecclesiastical leaders to seek revelation from God about the ordination of women, the community often explicitly supports these sanctions as they support an all-male priesthood; they believe it is a sacred order of authority. Relatedly, when the general membership is not explicitly supportive, the lack of major blowback to the leadership implies agreement that the ecclesiastical sanctions were necessary in order to maintain the spiritual integrity of the group. Most members of the LDS community support the use of disciplinary councils and courts in order to ensure the naturalized, spiritual order of patriarchy is maintained (Kane, 2018).

White hegemony

Hegemonic masculinity is not the only regulating hierarchical structure that is used to construct LDS femininities. An intersectional approach attends to other hierarchies that are at play, including those based upon the categories of race and ethnicity, especially within a global religion. A white hegemony functions alongside hegemonic masculinity and influences the way in which ideal LDS femininities are constructed. The majority of the male leaders within the Quorum of the Twelve, the second highest governing ecclesiastical body of the Church of Jesus Christ of Latter-day Saints, are white and were raised in the U.S. Likewise, the majority of the other high ecclesiastical bodies are composed of white, American men. Recently leaders have been chosen who represent different locales, ethnicities, and races but the majority is still white, American, or European businessmen.

There are a few female leaders within the highest ranks of the LDS church. While they have the responsibility to manage the women's organization, the children's organization, and the young women's organization, these women do not have autonomous control over the curriculum, budgets, or programmatic specificities of their respective organizations. However, they are the public faces of these organizations, and stand as models of representative femininity for all LDS women. Almost every female leader in this elite group is North American and white.

The way in which this democratic, capitalist, racialized, heteronormative, patriarchal structure influences all Latter-day Saints cannot be underscored enough. Most high-ranking church leaders are forged within this environment and the leaders that were raised outside of the U.S. are often former business executives or were educated in the Global North. They are influenced by the culture of American capitalism that is reflected in the majority of the leadership corpus, and naturalized impulses of this economic system seep into the LDS religious culture (Brooks, 2018). These leaders create ideal femininity. In this way, Latter-day Saint ideal femininity is created at the center and measured by criteria that are explicitly and implicitly communicated from a predominantly North American, white, male, heterosexual, middle-class leadership.

Despite the fact that many iterations of devout femininities exist within the religious hierarchy, the ideal unified LDS feminine subject gets transmitted publicly, as an affluent, white, American who is a demure wife and devoted full-time mother. She is strong in her devotion to God and spiritually capable, but ultimately submissive to male authority. This ideal becomes reinforced by female leaders embodying the very characteristics, mannerisms, and appearance that are seen as part of a devout female subject. This collection of traits, formulated by male leaders and taught as spiritually sanctioned, becomes viewed as a cohesive, stable, ideal LDS female subjectivity and transmitted to a global audience. Due to the rapid transmission of information through multimedia channels this unidimensional LDS woman is broadcasted as the LDS female *par excellence*, as she represents the most valid LDS female performance.

For women who live outside of the U.S., which constitute the majority of female members in the church, this contributes to a type of intersectional oversight. As women, and as women living outside of the U.S., they are given an ideal to strive for that is based upon a femininity that is largely unattainable. This potentially keeps other ways of knowing and doing the feminine inaccessible, unofficial, and even unacceptable. In short, any femininity that isn't aligned with the dominant North American model of ideal LDS femininity is irregular, or other.

Lived LDS femininities

When the ideal LDS female subject is compared to the realities of embodied female subjects, fissures become apparent. The remainder of this essay draws upon the scholarly literature as well as the ethnographic work I completed in North America, Botswana, Rwanda and South Africa. Scholars have documented the disconnect between official rhetoric of LDS male leaders and the actual lives of LDS women by analyzing public talks given by male leaders, discourse within official church magazines, and church-sponsored media campaigns (Vance, 2002; Chen, 2014). These studies have shown that official teachings about what constitutes an ideal Latter-day Saint femininity have shifted over time. Like all new religions, early Mormonism was open and accepting of all types of converts in order to grow. The undervalued within a society typically find acceptance within new religious movements and Joseph Smith provided a refuge for those seeking a spiritual space regardless of race, ethnicity, gender, and socioeconomic status. Women in the early church had a wider range of acceptable duties, roles, and responsibilities that were not confined to nurturing children at home.

Rhetoric that narrowed women's roles to an almost exclusive focus on motherhood as an all-consuming duty did not start until the end of World War II (Vance, 2002). Prior to this period, women's roles were expansive within the LDS tradition, and included titles and roles of "priestess" and "prophetess." Women were given much more latitude in performing spiritual rituals up until the mid-twentieth century although it had always been a practice met with some controversy (McBaine, 2017).

The byproduct of priesthood correlation, undertaken in the 1960s and completed in the 1970s, by the LDS Church headquarters in an effort to streamline and duplicate itself easily in distant locales, brought a further narrowing of female roles. Women were instructed to have a male priesthood holder officiate all blessings and spiritual rituals, leave the paid labor force, and protect their families from the ills of society. These edicts were a reaction against the social movements sweeping the U.S. in the latter half of the twentieth century as people of color, women, and LGBTQ persons sought social access to the rights and status of heteronormative, white males. While the official narrowing of women's roles eased up somewhat in the 1990s and at the beginning of the twenty-first century, church-sponsored media campaigns pushed hegemonic motherhood as the ideal LDS femininity. While they depicted motherhood in different ways, ultimately the campaign reinforced a particular type of motherhood, that of the stay-at-home mother (Chen, 2014). Even though the campaign appeared to convey acceptable differences in the ways LDS women inhabited the female subject, a specific ideal was privileged, and it was not radically different than the male leadership had been espousing since the end of World War II. The reaction against these social movements by the LDS male leaders coupled with the solidification of "priesthood correlation" acted to contract the ideal feminine subject to a fraction of what she once was in the early years of Mormonism. Thus, as masculine hegemony became more concretized within the LDS Church, the plethora of ideal femininities became a unified ideal femininity. Despite the shifts in authorized femininity over the past seventy years, one thing has remained the same—the construction of what constitutes an ideal LDS femininity has always been managed ultimately by men.

It is well documented that official rhetoric and reality do not match when it comes to femininities in the Latter-day Saint faith. There are several main points of disconnect. First, the majority of LDS women are not married; over half of all women in the church are single due to never marrying, divorce, death of a spouse, or by choice.[1] Most of these women are still highly invested in heteronormative marriage as an ideal; however, the way they construct family is distinct based upon locale. In Botswana, for instance, child fostering is common so that mothers can work while relatives take care of their children (Kline, 2018). In another example, migrant labor patterns have separated Filipina LDS mothers from their children for months and years, as they work and send money home to their relatives who are raising them (Ford, 2018). Second, many LDS women are wage earners outside of the home, either by choice or necessity (Riess,

2019; Kline, 2018). Third, the LDS ideal of women as stay-at-home mothers is a luxury of the upper-middle class in almost all nations. Many families around the world rely on at least two wage earners in order to provide shelter, food, and the necessities for sustaining life. Even when women are able to afford to stay home full time with their children, some choose to enter the labor force as they find purpose in developing their careers. In Rwanda, the notion that women would not participate in public life is extremely out of place. In the post-genocide period Rwanda leads the world in women in parliamentary positions and women have been instrumental in rebuilding the government, economy, and infrastructure of the nation over the last twenty years (Hoyt, 2019). In South Africa, often multi-generational family members help take care of the children of the younger generation (Hoyt, 2019).

The women in Botswana, South Africa, and Rwanda I have worked with do not have overt criticism of the patriarchal system within Mormonism. In fact, many of these women report that while they may not have an ideal home relationship, they believe that the church provides males with a model for masculinity that values women and family. For these women, "benevolent patriarchy" is a vast improvement when compared to the models of masculinity that preceded conversion to the Latter-day Saint faith (Kline, 2018). When asked specifically about patriarchy, exclusive male leadership, and if they feel valued as women, the vast majority of women I worked with in these three nations reported that they were grateful for the "Family Proclamation" document (The Church of Jesus Christ of Latter-day Saints, 1995) which instructs men and women in their respective gendered roles within the heteronormative family. They also felt an affinity for the male leadership of the church and felt valued as women. This coincides with other research on women in the Global South, where benevolent patriarchy is seen as a blessing as it is a more palatable authoritative relationship between men and women. Regardless of the lack of obvious criticism by most of the women who do not embody the ideal LDS female subject, many of the women I spoke with outside of North America are aware that their circumstances are different from the model espoused by LDS leaders, making the ideal somewhat inaccessible.

These disconnects point to the need for constructs of LDS femininities to be attainable and achievable for the women who are part of the LDS tradition. Validating the pious choices that LDS female subjects make around the globe, even if they do not reflect white, American, capitalist ideals and hegemonic masculine norms is desperately needed so that women don't feel as if they can never measure up. It is perplexing in that while the official masculine hegemonic rhetoric centers on familial constructs that are heteronormative and North American in origin, the reality of most LDS women is that they do not have familial constructs that mirror the official rhetoric. This could be extremely damaging to some women who long for the ideal.

Given the limitations of the ideal construct developed within a hegemonic masculinity to portray LDS women in an authentic way that still attends to unifying features of a feminine subject, I propose that scholars report genuine reflections of the Latter-day Saint feminine subject that acknowledges the multiple inhabited realities of women around the globe.

Threads of unification

Throughout my fifteen years of conducting ethnographic research on Latter-day Saint women in North America and different African nations, there are only two themes that remained consistent throughout every community, regardless of race, ethnicity, economic background, education, marital status, sexual orientation, and nationality. These two themes seem to be the essence of a female subjectivity within the Church of Jesus Christ of Latter-day Saints. First, these women all express a conviction that they are daughters of God, typically expressed as a daughter of a "Heavenly Father." Not every woman spoke specifically about her identity as a "daughter of God" but all of the women I interviewed spoke of their "Heavenly Father," which in LDS discourse implies an accepted belief in the father/daughter relationship. Women utilize this familial construct with deity to seek comfort, ask for blessings, seek safety, and to ask for forgiveness in an effort at personal and spiritual improvement. Women in Rwanda and South Africa prayed to forgive others, women in Botswana prayed for protection of their children who were with relatives. Women in North America prayed to understand the direction they should go in their lives. This belief that unifies all Latter-day Saint women is not simply an idea. It is attached to practices such as prayer, reading scriptures, and performing volunteer religious jobs in their local congregation.

This first unifying theme of LDS femininities sets the foundation for the second unifying theme: the importance of family. Again, regardless of the vast differences among the hundreds of women I have worked with, the importance of family is a central part of their subjectivity. The women I worked with in North America between 2004 and 2006 and then re-interviewed in 2016 identified family as what was most important, valuable, and pressing for them. When I asked them to update me on what had changed in their lives over the past ten years, since our first interview, every single woman I interviewed structured her narrative around what had changed within her family. She did not discuss what changed in her career, job, or volunteer positions and she did not discuss what had changed in her community or congregation. She also did not discuss what had changed in her extra-curricular hobbies or interests. Tales of births, deaths, marriages, divorce peppered every interview. When pressed about changes that were not related to family, women discussed changes in their health and wellness. These women are all different ethnicities, ages, and range from career women to stay at home moms. Some are married, single, divorced and some are still active participants in the LDS faith while others consider themselves "Mormon" but don't attend church very much. Regardless of all of the differences between these women, family was the one commonality. Not simply that they had a family, but that family structured how they viewed their worlds and measured success.

The way in which female subjectivity is closely linked to commitment and connection to family is not unique to LDS women. Women I have interviewed in other faith traditions in similar locales also construct a large part of their personal narrative around themes related to family. While not unique to LDS women, it is a unifying feature of LDS women that I have worked with and as such, remains an important thread of femininity, one of only two constants that the research shows.

Most, but not all, of the women I worked with discussed motherhood. Some of the women were single, never married, or divorced without children. Women speak of mothering their own children and mothering other children. Women who do not have children or are not married typically speak of receiving the "blessings" of a spouse and offspring in the next life. However, while motherhood remains extremely important within the official LDS ideal of what constitutes a female subject, it is not a universal experience and thus I have not included it as such. It is a very common part of many LDS women's subjectivities, although the way in which they enact motherhood is very diverse, as other scholars have pointed out (Chen, 2014; Kline, 2018). The women who do not explicitly articulate a spiritual future that includes a husband and children often remain deeply connected to their family of origin—their siblings and parents. LDS femininities are constructed within a familial structure and live out their subjectivity in terms of connection to and commitment to their family, whether it is the family they were born into or the family they have created, or the generational family that they are deeply invested and entrenched in. Family looks different for almost every LDS woman that I have interviewed, but family is the most important construct in their subjectivity.

Conclusion

The official LDS feminine subject is decidedly North American. She is privileged enough to stay at home and raise children; she does not need to spend her day seeking water, shelter, or food. She is able to read and has a heteronormative marriage in which her partner provides substantially for her. She is a consummate nurturer to her children, she dresses modestly, she is soft spoken and obedient (Kline, 2014). She is deferential to her male authorities, who she believes are God's authorized spokespeople on the earth.

These institutional ideals reflect the reality of a minority of LDS women. Instead, the threads that connect all LDS female subjects, regardless of any distinguishing factors, are not about proper behavior, employment, or appearances. Femininities within the Church of Jesus Christ of Latter-day Saints are a true mosaic of female subjects, connected by two threads: the belief that she is a daughter of God and the resulting deep commitment to her family.

Systems of power and dominance are a primary concern within gender studies and call attention to the mystery of why LDS women accept secondary status in the church. I have argued that the Gramscian feminist concept of hegemonic masculinity can explain the disconnect between the secondary status of Latter-day Saint women and the majority of women abstaining from mobilizing to seek change. Scholars have noted that leaders within the church embed socially constructed binary, hierarchical gender ideals into theological norms which have "ultimately sanctified gender inequalities by granting God's blessing to women's subordination" (Sumerau and Cragun, 2015). It is critical to the health of a religious group that institutional hierarchies are carefully examined when a minority is appointed to disseminate ideological truth to the other members, despite members agreeing to their secondary role within the organization.

Note

1 Please see www.ldsliving.com/Sister-Stevens-Shares-51-Percent-of-the-Women-in-the-Church-Are-Single-How-This-Affects-the-Ideal-Family/s/84962 (accessed November 10, 2019).

References

Brooks, J., 2018. Mormonism as Colonialism, Mormonism as Anti-Colonialism, Mormonism as Minor Transnationalism: Historical and Contemporary Perspectives. In J. Brooks and G. Colvin, eds. *Decolonizing Mormonism: Approaching a Postcolonial Zion*. Salt Lake City, UT: University of Utah Press, pp. 163–85.
Butler, J., 1990. *Gender Trouble: Feminism and the Subversion of Identity*. London: Routledge.
Chen, C.H., 2014. Diverse Yet Hegemonic: Expressions of Motherhood in "I'm a Mormon" Ads. *Journal of Media and Religion* 13(1): 31–47.
The Church of Jesus Christ of Latter-day Saints, 1995. The Family: A Proclamation to the World. www.lds.org/topics/family-proclamation?lang=eng&old=true.
Dahl, U., Kennedy-Macfoy, M., Sundén, J., Gálvez-Muñoz, L., Martínez-Jiménez, L., Gopinath, G., Hemmings, C., and Tate, S.-A., 2018. Femininity Revisited: A Roundtable. *European Journal of Women's Studies* 25(3): 384–93.
Ford, S., 2018. Sister Acts: Relief Society and Flexible Citizenship in Hong Kong. In J. Brooks and G. Colvin, eds. *Decolonizing Mormonism: Approaching a Post-Colonial Zion*. Salt Lake City, UT: University of Utah Press, pp. 202–28.
Gramsci, A., 1971. *Selections from the Prison Notebooks of Antonio Gramsci*, ed. Q. Hoare and G. Nowell-Smith. London: Lawrence and Wishart.
Hoyt, A., 2007. Beyond the Victim/Empowerment Paradigm: The Gendered Cosmology of Mormon Women. *Feminist Theology* 16(1): 89–100.
Hoyt, A., 2009. Maternal Practices as Religious Piety: The Pedagogical Practices of American Latter-day Saint Women. In K.J. Torjesen and C.A. Kirk-Duggan, eds. *Women and Christianity*. Santa Barbara, CA: Praeger, pp. 305–27.

Hoyt, A., 2019. Epistemic Humility: LDS Notions of Family in Africa. Paper presented at *Mormonism in Africa: A New Religious Movement*, World Christianity Conference. Princeton Theological Seminary. Princeton, New Jersey. March 15–18.

Kane, 2018. "Priestesses unto the Most High God": Gender, Agency, and the Politics of LDS Women's Temple Rites. *Sociological Focus* 51(2): 97–110.

Kline C., 2014. The Mormon Conception of Women's Nature and Role: A Feminist Analysis. *Feminist Theology* 22(2): 186–202.

Kline, C., 2018. Navigating Mormonism's Gendered Practice and Theology: Mormon Women in a Global Context. PhD Dissertation, Claremont Graduate University. Copy given to me by author May 25, 2018.

McBaine, N., 2017. Mormon Women and the Anatomy of Belonging. *Dialogue: A Journal of Mormon Thought* 50(1): 193–202.

Mohanty, C.T., 1984. Under Western Eyes: Feminist Scholarship and Colonial Discourses. *boundary 2* 12(3)/13(1): 333–58.

Paechter, C. Rethinking the Possibilities for Hegemonic Femininity: Exploring a Gramscian Framework. *Women's Studies International Forum* 68: 121–28.

Riess, J., 2019. *The Next Mormons: How Millennials Are Changing the LDS Church*. New York: Oxford University Press.

Sumerau, J.E., and Cragun, R.T., 2015. The Hallmarks of Righteous Women: Gendered Background Expectations in the Church of Jesus Christ of Latter-Day Saints. *Sociology of Religion* 76(1): 49–71.

Vance, L., 2002. Evolution of Ideals for Women in Mormon Periodicals, 1897–1999. *Sociology of Religion* 6(1): 91–112.

Further reading

Brooks, J., Steenblik, R.H., and Wheelwright, H., eds. 2016. *Mormon Feminism: Essential Writings*. Oxford: Oxford University Press.

Hanks, M., ed. 1992. *Women and Authority: Re-emerging Mormon Feminism*. Salt Lake City, UT: Signature Books.

Holbrook, K., and Bowman, M., eds. 2016. *Women and Mormonism*. Salt Lake City, UT: University of Utah Press.

5
MASCULINITIES

Sara M. Patterson

When he converted from being a black Baptist missionary to a member of the Church of Jesus Christ of Latter-day Saints (LDS), Wain Myers did not realize that he was converting into a new understanding of masculinity. Instead, what brought him to the church were a new understanding of God as one who communicated directly with believers, a new vision of community, and a version of the priesthood that seemed to fit Myers' own vision. Myers didn't know that he was converting into a new understanding of masculinity; nonetheless, he found one. And it sounded pretty good. His wife Sebrina, who had been LDS much longer than he had, had already embraced the gender norms of the LDS Church. When the couple began to have their own children together, Myers had a different way of doing things: "I was used to changing diapers, cleaning, cooking, caring for the children, and having a full-time job," Myers wrote about his children from a previous relationship. Yet Sebrina "didn't appreciate my hands-on style: she had her own idea of what our roles should be. I was the man, and she was the woman. She took care of the babies, the cooking, the cleaning, and all the other domestic things that needed to be done. My role was to go to work and provide." After their different visions of gender roles collided over an incident in which Myers attempted to change their infant's diaper, Myers came to a new realization: "*Wait a minute!* I thought. *I don't have to get up in the middle of the night and fix bottles anymore. I don't have to change dirty diapers anymore! All I have to do is go to work, play with the kids, and teach them things from time to time. Sebrina will take care of the rest! Why am I fighting this?*" Myers finally understood that Sebrina's desire to be the nurturer for their children was her role and that "This was an amazing deal. As soon as I let these thoughts sink into my thick skull, I realized it was time for me to stand up and be the man, father, husband, and son God created me to be" (Myers, 2015, italics in original). For Myers, this model of gender complementarity, where women and men took up roles that complemented one another, seemed like a dream come true. The model gave him a sense of exactly who he was in the divine plan for humanity.

Myers' perspective echoed a number of theologies of gender offered by the LDS Church hierarchy in the past several decades. In official statements and General Conference talks, the church seemed to double down on the idea of gender complementarity to the extent that that model was seen as divinely ordained, essential to human nature, and a part of identity *before, during, and after* life in this world. In the 1995 "The Family: A Proclamation to the World," often referred to as "The Family Proclamation," then-prophet Gordon B. Hinckley declared that "gender is an essential characteristic of individual premortal, mortal, and eternal identity and purpose." In so doing, Hinckley held up gender as the most salient aspect of individual identity. Hinckley went on to claim that "marriage between a man and a woman is ordained of God and that the family is central to the Creator's plan for the eternal destiny of His children." In the Family Proclamation, the highest leaders of the church articulated that a monogamous, heterosexual marriage was the only form of family that was pleasing to God and that it was the type of family that could receive exaltation, or the highest level of reward in the next life. Further, they characterized each gender's role: "By divine design, fathers are to preside over their families in love and righteousness and are responsible to provide the necessities of life and protection for their families. Mothers are primarily responsible for the nurture of their children" (The Family Proclamation, 1995).

Myers' revelation about his own family structure and how it should work mirrored the understandings of gender and family set forth by the highest church officials. It is at this level that it is perhaps easiest to see the construction of a singular, fairly uniform notion of Mormon masculinity. Yet we must also take into account the way that that prescribed "official" masculinity—the "on paper" masculinity of the LDS Church—gets played out in the lives of individual Mormon men. For this reason, I have examined statements made by church officials, and I have turned to modern Mormon autobiographies and memoirs, primarily, but not exclusively to Mormon men's memoirs, to help understand how they experience Mormon masculinity on the individual level. In this essay, I will focus on two particularly descriptive memoirs about life as a Mormon man, Wain Myers' and William Shunn's, both of whom embraced certain aspects of Mormon masculinity and rejected others. It is at the individual level, where masculinity shifts from paper to practice, that more multiplicity is possible. In life, masculinity intersects with the lived realities of men who are not just religious beings but who also have cultural, regional, and socio-economic expectations woven into their notions of manhood. It is at these intersections and at the boundaries of the official Mormon manhood offered by the church hierarchy that the notions of masculinity may be fraying at the edges. In particular, it is at the level of practical, lived religion that the church's "official" masculinity is being challenged because of its assumed heteronormativity, the limitations and exclusions it places on women in their religious lives, and its markedly American characteristics.

In the beginning ...

When Joseph Smith founded the church in 1830, there was no doctrine about the meaning of what it meant to be a man or a woman in the church. Yet as Smith began to have continuing revelations about what the church would look like during the restoration, aspects of masculinity began to be defined. First and foremost, Smith had revelations about the role of the priesthood that was given to all worthy men. Smith instituted two forms: the Aaronic Priesthood, which allows holders to administer the sacraments and ordinances of the church, and the Melchizedek Priesthood, which allows holders to participate in church leadership and to teach and take the gospel to the world. These roles, referred to as the "keys and power of the priesthood," were placed in the realm of masculinity and have been there ever since. Within the Latter-day Saint tradition, the priesthood has stood at the center of constructions of masculinity from the very beginning.

Smith also taught about and had revelations that applied to understandings of the family. These, of course, also defined what masculinity should look like in the tradition. First only revealed to a small circle of trusted friends and family members, Smith proclaimed that in the restored church, plural marriage—the practice of polygamy—would be part of the family structure. And so, a believing and worthy man would participate in multiple marriages. It was not until after Smith's death, when many believers had followed Brigham Young to Utah, that Young made a public announcement of the practice in 1852. In 1876, it became an official part of the Doctrine and Covenants, a collection of canonized revelations for the restored church. Doctrine and Covenants 132, Smith's revelation on plural marriage, likened church members to the biblical Israelites and declared that they must marry just as God's chosen people Abraham, Isaac, Jacob, Moses, David, and Solomon, did. Participants in restoring the true church would embrace plural marriage as a religious duty. The revelation said of priesthood holders that

> if any man espouse a virgin, and desire to espouse another, and the first give her consent, and if he espouse the second, and they are virgins, and have vowed to no other man, then is he justified; he cannot commit adultery for they are given unto him; for he cannot commit adultery with that that belongeth unto him and to no one else.

Priesthood holders who abided by the rules laid out for them were promised that in the next life

> shall they be gods, because they have no end; therefore shall they be from everlasting to everlasting, because they continue; then shall they be above all, because all things are subject unto them. Then shall they be gods, because they have all power, and the angels are subject unto them.

Thus, priesthood holding and proper sexual practices were tied to an individual man's (and therefore his household's) ability to reach exaltation, or the highest level of heaven. While not everyone in the community practiced plural wifery, it came to define the community as a people set apart from the larger culture. It showed that as a collective, they were God's chosen people. For other Americans, polygamy made Mormons an intolerable peculiarity.

In 1890, when the American government put such pressure on the church for its practice of polygamy, threatening to seize its property and its finances and jail many of its members, church president Wilford Woodruff made a public announcement that the practice would be ended. Over the course of the next three decades, the church gave up the practice and a new masculinity was fashioned in the rubble. During this "era of transition," the role of the priesthood became the solid foundation on which Mormon masculinity continued to stand even as sexual practices changed. As Amy K. Hoyt and I have argued,

> The new Mormon masculinity that developed from 1890 to 1920 was also rooted in divine revelation, but consisted of four pillars: a changed notion of priesthood; adherence to the Word of Wisdom (a divinely revealed health code that prohibits alcohol and tobacco use); an increased expectation that young LDS men would go on missions (which was understood as the time a Mormon man would stand against the wider culture); and monogamous heterosexuality. On these four pillars, Mormons constructed a new man who, they asserted, was the ideal American citizen.
>
> *(Hoyt and Patterson, 2011)*

I will explore each of these pillars in the period from the early twentieth century through the early twenty-first.

Priesthood

As stated earlier, the priesthood was and has been the central pillar of Mormon masculinity. It was this pillar that provided stability as the church transitioned out of polygamy and to monogamous heterosexuality in the early twentieth century. Even so, that pillar saw some changes during the era of transition. Because of concern for "wayward boys" during that time, the church shifted the offices of the priesthood downward, ritually inducting boys into the adult practices of the priesthood at earlier ages. Even today, worthy male eleven-year-olds in the church can participate in the Aaronic Priesthood. The idea behind this shift was that it would give young boys a sense of responsibility and a role within the church, hoping to offer stability during a time when Mormon youth were asking questions and potentially being peer-pressured into activities that would make them "unworthy" of the priesthood office (Hoyt and Patterson, 2011). Usually, young men receive the Melchizedek Priesthood around the age of 18 or before they go on missions.

This age structure continues to this day. The priesthood—its structures and roles—was one of the things that appealed to Wain Myers when he was investigating the church. The democratic nature of the priesthood, in that all men could participate in the calling, and the fact that the priesthood holders were not paid, seemed to Myers to maintain the "purity" of the call. He appreciated that each calling was valued and seen as integral to the workings of the church. He liked the idea that each person contributed to the community's success without an expectation of praise or compensation, but rather out of a sense of responsibility and calling from God.

Even so, when Myers found out about the church's historical priesthood and temple ban—the ban that prohibited Africans and African Americans from the priesthood and temple blessings, based on an understanding of cursed biblical lineages, which had been in place from the mid-nineteenth century until 1978—Myers was stumped. He first blamed God: "I found it hurtful that my Father, the Omnipotent One, was at one point a racist and had only changed His way of thinking about people of color like me in the not-to-distant past." In a church based on continuing revelation, Myers first felt that the explanation for the ban had to reside in God's hands. Noting that the ban was not lifted until 1978, only then making it a truly democratic office *for men*, Myers finally came to a different understanding of how to explain the priesthood ban. He came to believe that it was tied to the human fallibility of church leaders. It was church leaders living in a racist society that maintained the ban for over a century—it was in 1978 that they finally heard God's protest that had been going on for so long.

> When people ask me how I got over the pain I felt about the priesthood ban, I tell them that I haven't yet—and hope I never will. This pain and confusion fuel my testimony and further solidify my knowledge that God is great and that His work will go forth no matter the weaknesses of mortal man.
>
> *(Myers, 2015)*

Myers' faith in God had been restored.

Even though the priesthood is democratic, at least for all worthy male church members, it is also hierarchically structured. In his memoir of his time as a Mormon missionary, William Shunn felt this structure profoundly and was overwhelmed by the expectations: "Christ in heaven was the living, breathing head of our church, however difficult I found that to imagine. A straight line ran from him to our new prophet … then down through the apostles and other General Authorities" and further down to Shunn (Shunn, 2015). This hierarchy not only structures the institution of the church, it also shapes and dictates how the religious experience of divine revelations works. That is, revelations can only apply to the people over whom the individual has priesthood authority. As Myers put it to someone inquiring about the structure:

> The formula is simple, beautiful, and leads down a straight and narrow path back to our Heavenly Father. Personal revelation should be in accordance with the family patriarch's. The patriarch's leadership should line up with the prophet's. The prophet's instructions and counsel will align with God's instructions. If followed by faith, the formula is perfect. It's man and his many faults that complicate the process.
>
> *(Myers, 2015)*

Thus, the offices are placed in relationship to one another and each male priesthood holder has a domain over which he can have revelations. In this instance, religious experience is gendered, structured, and limited in its power. This formula allows for the institution to maintain authority while also encouraging individuals to seek revelations about God's will in their own lives and the lives over which they hold priesthood authority.

When Sebrina, Myers' future wife, explained the priesthood to him, she described it as "the power and authority from God to act in His name." Before moving on to other aspects of masculinity, it is important to note the "His" in her statement, which is so often overlooked. The emphasis is on the maleness of Heavenly Father. As other essays in this handbook have noted, in LDS cosmology, Heavenly Father and Heavenly Mother are both divine figures. This theological structure emphasizes complementarity, but it is Heavenly Father to whom believers are supposed to direct their attention and their prayers. Because both beings are recognized, Heavenly Father's gendered identity is not metaphorical, as some Christians of other denominations have claimed about their traditions; rather Heavenly Father's gender is literal. He is male. And it is from this source that the power of the all-male priesthood is drawn. He is the ultimate model—as patriarch, authority, and protector—for Mormon masculinity. For Wain Myers, this was part of the appeal of the Mormon system. Myers hadn't had a stable male role model in his life as he grew up. Heavenly Father stepped in and provided this stability, offering him the roles of protector, provider, corrector, and guide, all of the traits that are used to describe masculinity in the Family Proclamation. For Myers the idea of a Heavenly Father who oversaw his life and provided him with guidance when he was lost was an appealing and important aspect of the LDS tradition (Myers, 2015).

Missions

Beginning in the twentieth century, missionary work became an expectation for most Mormon men. Church leaders declared that "it was on a mission that the Mormon boy truly became a man—a faithful man professing his faith *in the gentile* [non-Mormon] *world*." And so it was as the young man went out in the world as a representative of his faith that, at least according to the stories offered by the church, he became confident in his faith and began to stand up for what he believed. It was his testimony, his knowledge that the claims of the church were true, that allowed him to stand in the face of any opposition he might encounter.

Testimonies themselves are not the exclusive realm of men in the church; each mature member is supposed to have a testimony. Yet the idea that that testimony would be expressed to outsiders, that it would mark a man as a representative of the tradition, was primarily focused on the male experience of missionary work. "Testimonies should be tried and tested," wrote Wain Myers, "because that's how we grow them and increase our conviction that the gospel is true" (Myers, 2015). For Myers, at least, opposition and questioning allows an individual's testimony to be strengthened. Surety is the primary result. Shunn explained that

> Saying you *have* a testimony implies that diligent study and prayer have instilled in you an unshakeable assurance that the Book of Mormon and the gospel of Jesus Christ as restored by the prophet Joseph Smith are true, correct, and authored by God.
>
> *(Shunn, 2015)*

Shunn wanted that surety and hoped that his mission would help solidify his belief. It didn't end up that way for him, and his understanding of truth changed over time. Nevertheless, the testing of testimony and sacrificing time in his young adult life was seen as an important aspect of creating manhood.

On his mission, Shunn experienced these kinds of sacrifices. After spending three intensive weeks training at the "spiritual boot camp" of the Missionary Training Center in Provo, Utah, Shunn went to his mission field in Canada. He had been told that

> each of us would have 70 proselytizing hours a week to look forward to, at least eighteen of them knocking on doors. Ten solid Book of Mormon placements would be the minimum weekly goal, along with six first discussions. The monthly goal would be two convert baptisms.
>
> *(Shunn, 2015)*

Thus, the missionaries' lives are heavily scheduled with goals that are, for many, unrealistic. Yet the mission is not just about gaining converts; if it was, it would mean that many missionaries were and are unsuccessful, failures, in fact. Rather, the mission is as much, if not more, about identity formation *for the missionaries* as it is about achieving all the goals laid out before them. In this way, the church can understand all missions as successful because they are expected to take a young Mormon man and turn him into *a man*.

There is immense pressure within the LDS community for men to go on missions. Although women can be missionaries too, that pressure does not exist for them. In Shunn's case, the pressure came in many forms. First, it came in the pressure to go:

> I fantasized about skipping out on mission service, but I couldn't see a way to make that happen in real life. I was too afraid of my father's reaction, too reluctant to shame myself before my family, too unwilling to shame my family before the community.
>
> *(Shunn, 2015)*

In this instance, Shunn was reacting to a church hierarchy, in his case the prophet Spencer W. Kimball laying out the expectation. Kimball had declared "Every young man should serve a mission. It is not an option; it is your obligation" (Kimball, 1983). Later in his mission, when Shunn ponders and then attempts to leave early, he met with the mission president.

> He observed that any woman who would have me after I'd abandoned a mission was not the sort of woman who would inspire me to the great achievements of which I was capable. He predicted that my dereliction of duty would cast a shadow as long as my life, impairing my ability to finish what I started, crippling my sense of self-worth, setting a precedent for failure over which I would never triumph. No worldly success, he said, could ever compensate for this one preeminent defeat.
>
> *(Shunn, 2015)*

Although Shunn's experience may not be a common one—most missionaries do not try to leave their missions, and those who do consider leaving don't always receive the same reaction from their mission president—his comments point to the high stakes associated with the mission experience for males. It is there that Mormon boys become men—they demonstrate discipline, they set goals for themselves, they learn life experiences, they become sure of their testimonies, and they are taught they will become optimal marriage material.

This last idea, that men who have gone on missions are more attractive to faithful, Mormon women, is one that was promoted early in the twentieth century in church periodicals and continues to this day. In a 1900 article in the *Improvement Era*, a returned missionary was described: "His shoulders were straighter and broader ... His steps had lost their hesitancy and now he walked as though he was sure of the ground upon which he trod." For Shunn, the promise came from another missionary, who told him "Believe you me, Elder, you've never *seen* girls go crazy like they do for that black name tag ... you're prime husband material. You're what she's been taught all her life to set her sights on" (Shunn, 2015). The promise here is an intriguing one yet knowledge of the assumptions about what a mission will do for a young man helps explain it. If it is on a mission that he learns faith, responsibility, discipline, and fortitude, all traits that young Mormon women are taught to seek in a mate, then the assumptions make more sense. Young missionaries are even promised that their mothers will notice and respect them more (Hoyt and Patterson, 2011). For Shunn, this came through when he called his mother from his mission. "Hello, Bill," she said, "Or rather, I mean, Elder Shunn" (Shunn, 2015). Recognizing his role as a missionary as his defining characteristic, his mother changed her behavior toward him, offering a new level of respect and a recognition of his adulthood.

Even Shunn saw the changes that missionary work could have, and it made him long for the transformative effects. "The elders who most attracted my attention were the two-year vets checking in for their last night before shipping home." Shunn noted that they were different from the "greenies" like himself and his fellow missionaries who had just arrived.

> Beaming, confident men, looking hale and fit, *ages* more godly and mature than the greenies ... I couldn't imagine ever being one of them, with their easy, solemn camaraderie, couldn't imagine crossing the vast gulf of time that lapped at their backs, landing on that distant shore a new man.
>
> (Shunn, 2015)

Thus, in Shunn's case, the implicit and explicit promises made both by church authorities and the culture of missionary storytelling, seemed to be true. During his mission, a Mormon male *became a man* and he did that in response to the critiques of Gentiles, the strengthening of his testimony, and the promise of what was to come next in life.

Bodies

While the priesthood and missions offer young men *roles* that can shape their identities as men in the faith, those men still need to show that they are *worthy* of those roles. That worthiness is very much tied to their bodies. In the early twentieth century and in the church's efforts to fit in with the broader culture, church authorities began to focus on the Word of Wisdom as a key aspect of worthiness. An 1833 revelation given to the prophet Joseph Smith, the Word of Wisdom told believers that they should abstain from alcohol, tobacco, tea, and coffee. In the nineteenth century, that revelation was often viewed as a guide, but in the twentieth century it came to be read as a set of commandments. And the church focused much of its energies on policing the male body, assuming that females naturally avoided such substances. Instead, young women were counseled to help their male peers observe the standards in the revelation (Hoyt and Patterson, 2011).

The rhetoric surrounding church authorities' counsel focused on the importance of self-discipline for young men. And self-discipline has been an important topic in the description of masculinity by church leaders in the late twentieth and early twenty-first centuries (Sumerau et al., 2017). In a discussion with his fellow missionaries about drinking alcohol, Shunn recalled,

> A Mormon commandment called the Word of Wisdom strictly forbids the use of alcohol—no ifs, ands, or buts. Had I so much as looked sideways at a bottle of beer, my father would have knocked me into the next century.
> *(Shunn, 2015)*

In Shunn's case, the warnings worked; unlike his fellow missionaries, he had never even thought to have a drink. Being able to abstain from tobacco and alcohol is a marker that the church assumed and assumes will mark Mormon men as distinct from other men in their cultures and will develop the kinds of self discipline that they will find helpful in their lives as adults.

In the late twentieth century, another expectation for the male body appeared. Just as "The [early twentieth century] model of Mormon masculinity was critical to the maintenance of a distinct religious identity; Mormon men and their bodies bore the markers of this identity" (Hoyt and Patterson, 2011). In a large turn from its namesake's choices, Brigham Young University (BYU), the flagship university of the church, required that men shave their beards. This 1960s policy was put in place because it was believed that beards "were seen as a symbol of anti-authoritarian rebellion" or in the words of Apostle Dallin Oaks, then president of BYU, who gave a speech in 1971,

> the beard and long hair are associated with protest, revolution and rebellion against authority. They are also symbols of the hippie and drug culture. Persons who wear beards or long hair, whether they desire it or not, may identify themselves with or emulate and honor the drug culture or the extreme practices of those who have made slovenly appearance a badge of protest and dissent.
> *(Stack, 2017 and Oaks, 1971)*

Tellingly, the beard restrictions were part of BYU's Honor Code, suggesting that being beardless was an important sign of a man's morality, of his honor. In 2017, political science professor Kelly Patterson defended the beard code against rising critiques, for precisely these reasons. The code, Patterson wrote, entails "an idea of what students can and should become." She argued that being beardless is an "acceptance of responsibility and a bulwark against the strong predilection expressed in modern society that institutions no longer have any say in or responsibility for the development of individuals" (qtd in Stack, 2017). There are currently three exceptions to the beard code: theatrical, religious (non-LDS students who wear beards "as part of their faith ... [and] must secure the blessing of the university's chaplain"), and medical (which must be diagnosed by a university doctor). Thus, the university (and subsequently the church more broadly) attempts to mark Mormon masculinity in an era when beards are hip, a remarkable turn for a church whose past prophets and practitioners often sported beards and long hair that set them apart in their own historical contexts.

Sexuality and fatherhood

As the church shifted away from polygamy to monogamy, it faced a particular challenge. In the shift, the church was becoming more like its Protestant contemporaries, yet it was important to maintain a distinctiveness, even if that distinctiveness didn't play out in actual practices. For this reason, monogamy "had to be reconceived as a *Mormon* religious practice" (Hoyt and Patterson, 2011). In the pages of the *Improvement Era*, boys were taught that they would be held to high standards in terms of their sexual choices. They were to remain sexually chaste. When they entered into a courtship with a girl, they were to do so with the intention of getting married. Within the system of eternal progression, the Mormon cosmological vision, bachelorhood was perilous as it left men in a precarious spiritual state. Without a wife, they would not be able to progress to the highest level of heaven, achieving exaltation. And so, heterosexual monogamy became a religious imperative—chastity outside of marriage and then procreation within a temple marriage were the highest ideals for young men and for young women.

For William Shunn, these institutional dictates seemed quite serious and he understood his sexual choices to be choices about his spiritual well-being. "It may seem like a quaint belief to people who weren't raised with it," Shunn wrote,

> but I was taught from a young age that your virginity was the greatest gift you could bring your partner on your wedding day. Nobody wants to eat off a used plate, we were told. No one wants a wad of gum that's already been chewed. Boys were told to stay clean and avoid girls who were too aggressive or dressed immodestly or did not attend church. Girls were told to defend their precious virtue with their lives. Any deviation from the straight and narrow would destroy lives and reverberate through eternity.
>
> (Shunn, 2015)

The choices that Shunn made were heavily prescribed. Boys and girls were taught that potential mates had a particular set of traits and that their choices would "reverberate through eternity," a heavy burden to carry as he navigated his teenage years. In addition to this, he was told that he should not have too close a relationship with a young woman until after his mission. After their missions, young men were counseled to marry. In a devotional given by Elder Earl C. Tingey, emeritus member of the First Quorum of the Seventy,

> There may seem to be less encouragement for returned missionaries to get married. If that is your understanding, it is false. All returned missionaries should be encouraged when they return home to remain active in the Church, secure an education, acquire employment skills, and move in the direction of finding an eternal companion.

Tingey went on to write that marriage should not be placed on the back burner in terms of personal goals: "An emphasis on education or career may put marriage in a lesser role. Marriage, education, and career can go together. A career without family, where family is possible, is a tragedy" (Tingey, 2013).

In this imagined system, marriage inevitably leads to fatherhood, an important goal for men who wish to progress in their spiritual lives. In addition to the Family Proclamation's description of a father as one who provides for his family, it is important also to note that a man is described as one who *presides* over his family. This role can mean that he serves as the family's priesthood holder, having revelations for and making the ultimate decisions about the family's future. In addition to practicing authority over family and relationships, men are taught in official venues that they must exercise self-control, "control over sexual and emotional expression, and control of others" (Sumerau et al , 2017). They must avoid being controlled by the outside world. Thus, Mormon masculinity is defined as standing independently in a world and set of relationships that may try to control him. Making sure that he polices his own urges and behaviors is practice for being able to stand firm and maintain control in precisely those settings.

Training for citizenship and success

As the era of transition from polygamy to monogamy ended and the church sought to become more like its Protestant American peers, but with a distinct Mormon flavor, a partnership developed between the institution and the Boy Scouts of America (BSA) that was important to the training of young Mormon men. Blending LDS religious training of young men with the BSA curriculum allowed the church to blend "patriotism, religion and wholesome endeavours, all while contributing to the solution of young wayward Mormon boys through character-building experiences." Because the BSA promoted the idea that it was in the wilderness that American manhood was shaped through toil and hard work, the Latter-day Saints had a particularly strong connection. Heralding the pioneers who had traveled westward to Utah as trailblazers and models of thrift, sobriety, and hard work, the LDS community had at its disposal countless stories that lifted up Mormon pioneers as the epitome of American masculinity and citizenship (Hoyt and Patterson, 2011). Since the merger, the relationship has been a strong one, making LDS troops a substantial portion of the total number of troops in the United States. These programs were designed to teach young Mormon men moral expectations and shape them into tough, rugged future Americans.

During that same period, the church came to embrace the idea that it was through recreation activities that masculinity would be molded. Because of this idea, programs that focused on athletics, hiking, games, and social activities became important programs at local wards. Through athleticism, the church was able to promote the healthy bodies, minds, and spirits of Mormon boys (Kimball, 2003). Sports allowed Mormons to connect with the rest of "sports-mad American society" and, even to this day, athletics offers Mormonism "a mechanism to show real-world examples of Mormons succeeding in the wider society" (Kimball, 2003). Athletes such as Merlin Olsen and Steve Young end up standing as representatives of their faith and of their physical abilities.

The century-long, intimate relationship with scouting changed in 2019. The church transitioned out of its relationship with BSA. Some have suggested that current changes in the BSA have been the cause, notably its 2013 decision to allow members to be openly gay, its 2015 decision to allow openly gay troop leaders, and its 2017 decision to allow girls and transgender children to join, all decisions that directly challenge the theologies of gender and sexuality set forth in the Family Proclamation. The church maintains, though, that these aren't the reasons. Rather, it asserts that

> For years, Church leaders have been preparing a new initiative to teach and provide leadership and development opportunities to all children and youth, to support families, and to strengthen youth everywhere as they develop faith in our Lord and Savior Jesus Christ ... This new approach is intended to help all girls and boys, young women and young men discover their eternal identity, build character and resilience, develop life skills, and fulfill their divine roles as daughters and sons of God.
> *(Church Announces, 2018)*

Tellingly, the statement emphasizes the eternal identities of Mormons as divine daughters and sons as key to the lessons. A joint statement made by the LDS Church and the BSA about the break-up, says that the church "continues to support the goals and values reflected in the Scout Oath and Scout Law" (Joint Statement, 2018). According to the statement, the church upholds the core documents of the BSA while distancing itself from recent developments in its practices tied to gender and sexuality.

Conclusions

While the model of Mormon masculinity offered by church authorities has changed only in relatively small ways since the shift from polygamy to monogamy, there is evidence that that model may be fraying at the edges. First, the model is a decidedly American one. It was forged in a time when Latter-day Saints were trying to fit into the larger American culture, trying to create a tolerable difference. Since that time, the church has globalized in new ways, and over half of its membership resides outside of the United States. Local cultures will necessarily play a role in constructing masculinity even as the institutional church may offer up the same understanding of what a Mormon man should be. It is to these globalized and local masculinities that scholars must begin to turn their attention.

Second, the church's complementary gender model and its intersection with heteronormativity, both theologically dictated, is being challenged on a number of fronts. In a complementary gender system, where the two sides, male and female, are imagined as opposites—two halves of a pie, if you will—when one side expands, the other side necessarily contracts. It becomes a gender battlefield. In that situation, groups such as OrdainWomen.org—which at face value appear to be about women seeking the priesthood in a tradition that gives it to all worthy boys and men—come to be interpreted as aggressive organizations. Granting women the priesthood would necessarily appear to collapse the dualism; women's piece of the pie would expand and men's would contract. The priesthood would no longer be a defining trait of masculinity as it has been for so long. As long as the church imagines gender in this way, as two halves of one pie, any movement for expanding women's roles in the church beyond motherhood and nurturing, a movement that many modern Mormon women welcome, will necessarily appear to be an attack on masculinity.

In a somewhat similar fashion, groups like Affirmation: LGBTQ Mormons, Families, and Friends, a Mormon LGBTQ+ organization, challenges the church's entrenched theological stance that one's heavenly reward is tied to one's participation in the *right* form of sexuality. As more and more LGBTQ+ Mormons seek to reconcile their identities, to see the identities as both/and rather than either/or, the expectations about Mormon men's masculinity and sexuality, at least on the level of lived religion, if not institutional expectation, will be challenged as well. And so, the question is still very much open: who will the Mormon man be in the twenty-first century?

References

Church Announces Plan for Worldwide Initiative for Children and Youth, 2018. *Church News*. May 8. www.churchofjesuschrist.org/church/news/church-announces-plan-for-worldwide-initiative-for-children-and-youth (accessed June 9, 2019).

The Family Proclamation, 1995. www.lds.org/topics/family-proclamation (accessed August 1, 2018).

Hoyt, A., and Patterson, S.M., 2011. Mormon Masculinity: Changing Gender Expectations in the Era of Transition from Polygamy to Monogamy, 1890–1920. *Gender & History* 23(1): 72–91.

Joint Statement: Church and Boy Scouts of America, 2018. www.churchofjesuschrist.org/youth/childrenandyouth/joint-church-bsa-statement (accessed June 9, 2019).

Kimball, R.I., 2003. *Sports in Zion: Mormon Recreation, 1890–1940*. Urbana and Chicago, IL: University of Illinois Press.
Kimball, S., 1983. *Church News*. October 9.
Myers, W., with Martinez, K.L., 2015. *From Baptist Preacher to Mormon Teacher*. Springville, UT: CFI.
Oaks, D., 1971. Talk of the Month: Standards of Dress and Grooming. www.churchofjesuschrist.org/study/new-era/1971/12/standards-of-dress-and-grooming (accessed June 9, 2019).
Shunn, W., 2015. *The Accidental Terrorist: Confessions of a Reluctant Missionary*. New York: Sinister Regard.
Stack, P.F., 2017. Pressure Builds for BYU to Scrap Its Beard Ban—But if It Does, Don't Expect the Mormon School to Become a Haven for the Unshaven. *Salt Lake Tribune*. December 8.
Sumerau, J.E., Cragun, R.T., and Smith, T., 2017. "Men Never Cry": Teaching Mormon Manhood in the Church of Jesus Christ of Latter-day Saints. *Sociological Focus*. March.
Tingey, E., 2013. The Right Time to Marry. www.lds.org/ensign/2013/03/the-right-time-to-marry (accessed September 10, 2018).

Further reading

Brooks, E.M., 2018. *Disenchanted Lives: Apostasy and Ex-Mormonism among the Latter-day Saints*. New Brunswick, NJ: Rutgers University Press.
The Family Proclamation, 1995. www.lds.org/topics/family-proclamation.
Hoyt, A., and Patterson, S.M., 2011. Mormon Masculinity: Changing Gender Expectations in the Era of Transition from Polygamy to Monogamy, 1890–1920. *Gender & History* 23(1): 72–91.
Kimball, R.I., 2003. *Sports in Zion: Mormon Recreation, 1890–1940*. Urbana and Chicago, IL: University of Illinois Press.
Myers, W., with Martinez, K.L., 2015. *From Baptist Preacher to Mormon Teacher*. Springville, UT: CFI.
Shunn, W., 2015. *The Accidental Terrorist: Confessions of a Reluctant Missionary*. New York: Sinister Regard.
Sumerau, J.E., Cragun, R.T., and Smith, T., 2017. "Men Never Cry": Teaching Mormon Manhood in the Church of Jesus Christ of Latter-day Saints. *Sociological Focus*. March.

PART II

Historical approaches

6

JOSEPH SMITH, PLURAL MARRIAGE, AND KINSHIP

Benjamin E. Park

By the time of his death in June 1844, Joseph Smith, the founding prophet and president of the Church of Jesus Christ of Latter-day Saints, had been married to somewhere between thirty and forty women. Nearly all of these unions took place in the final three years of his life, and around half were in 1843 alone. Except for his first wife, Emma, all of these relationships were secret and only known to a couple-dozen people. However, despite these clandestine origins, Smith's actions and ideas laid the foundation for Mormonism's polygamous practice, which in turn set the boundaries for how believers understood gender, marriage, and the eternities ever since.

Historians have devoted extensive attention to all facets of Smith's polygamous experiment, often in contention with one another. Debates have centered, among other things, on when the practice began, the exact number of plural wives, whether Smith had intercourse with these women (and if so, which ones), as well as the entire theological foundation for the unions. Many of these studies can be classified as either apologetic or critical, with both academics and amateur researchers placing enormous significance on the answers (Compton, 1997; Smith, 2008; Hales, 2013). Indeed, much of the literature is reflective of the very same stakes originally introduced by Smith's first defenders and antagonists. The scandalous nature of polygamy has hardly subsided since the antebellum period.

A general consensus has developed concerning the cultural context for the practice, however, as well as its broad parameters. Similar to other sexual experiments that took place during the antebellum era—like the Shakers and the Oneida—Mormonism's earliest polygamous teachings were a reaction against a mainstream domestic culture that they found simultaneously too fragile as well as too narrow. It was also part of a broader patriarchal backlash against a democratic culture that had become feminized and egalitarian. Smith's unions, then, were understood as a way to create familial and kinship linkages that transcended death as well as reintroduce male-controlled order in an anarchic world. They also reflected a deep commitment to communal salvation, a belief that redemption could only be achieved through the connection to other faithful believers and their families. And finally, despite the parochial nature of the earliest plural sealings, the legacies of Smith's polygamous teachings have persisted to the present time.

Historical overview

Rumors concerning experimental sexual practices haunted the LDS faith since the first few years of its existence. Many new religious movements during the era were accused of transgressing social norms, particularly boundaries of gender, and Mormonism easily slid into that narrative, whether justified or not. Gossip became so pervasive that church leaders published an official statement in 1835 that proclaimed their belief in traditional monogamous unions between one man and one woman. Despite the accusations, Mormon marital rituals remained customary: even when Joseph Smith presided over a wedding ceremony, he merely performed the typical role of a preacher and left the actual rites to civic authorities. Mormon men and women fulfilled standard expectations for couples during the era, albeit with sometimes strained financial relations as the husbands were called on frequent missions.

It was around this time, however, that some historians locate Smith's first plural union. Fanny Alger, born in 1816, was a teenager when her family joined the Mormon faith and migrated to the church's then-headquarters in Kirtland, Ohio. She even lived in the Smith home and helped Joseph's wife, Emma, with domestic affairs. Though she did not remain a member and quickly left the city and church in 1836, later reminiscences from family and familial friends claimed she was married to Smith as a polygamous wife, and was then evicted by Emma as soon as she had discovered her husband's relationship. Contemporary documentation for this association being a form of marriage is exceptionally sparse. Oliver Cowdery, at one time Joseph Smith's close assistant, accused him of an "affair" in 1838—an accusation that, in part, led to Cowdery's excommunication. But the details concerning what Cowdery knew, and even what he was accusing Smith of, remain opaque. Scholars still debate whether this relationship between Smith and Alger was a formalized union, a fleeting affair, or even a later construction with little historical basis.

If there was some form of polygamous union between Smith and Alger during the 1830s, it was likely built on a primitivistic commitment to biblical mimesis—that is, a desire to replicate the actions of biblical patriarchs. Mormonism, in general, was a restorative tradition that believed in reconstituting God's true order that had been lost from the earth; just as Smith believed he was a prophet like the dominant figures in the Old Testament, it is possible he similarly believed in the right to accumulate multiple wives, and perhaps even concubines. Indeed, much later reminiscences from Smith's close associates claimed he received his first revelation concerning polygamy while working on his translation of the Bible, which took place between 1830 and 1833. The restoration of God's will, they believed, included living the marital structure of antiquity.

According to more reliable records, however, polygamy truly began in earnest in 1841, after Joseph Smith and his followers settled in Nauvoo, Illinois. On or around April 5 of that year, Smith met with Louisa Bemon and Joseph Noble in a clandestine rendezvous amidst the trees outside the city, where Noble married Bemon, his sister-in-law, to Smith as a plural wife. Smith was then married to at least two more women, Zina and Presendia Huntington, by the end of that year, as well as a handful more in the first few months of 1842. These were the first official polygamous unions in the church, yet they remained shrouded in secrecy and were rarely recorded in the moment. Most details come from later accounts and indirect sources, making it impossible to reconstruct an entire picture.

Some themes for these early marriages were consistent and clear, however. First, the unions were closely related to new temple rituals that were being introduced around the same time. Construction had begun on what was to be a magnificent temple structure in 1840, the same year that Smith announced new rituals that allowed members to be baptized for deceased relatives. Human society, these new teachings emphasized, transcended the grave and could link families together within the gospel for eternity. These plural marriages were similarly seen as "sealings," meaning that death could not dissolve their familial link. They were a way to ritualize and assure eternal stability within a society concerned with loss and disruption. Further, the women who were sealed to Smith were among the most spiritually active and zealous in the community, and likely saw an attachment to the prophet as a vindication of their devotion.

Most, though not all, of Smith's first plural wives were already married at the time of their sealing, several of whom denied any conjugal relations with the Mormon prophet. Their unions, then, seemed to be based more on sacred pairings than physical intimacy. To enact Smith's vision of united families gaining salvation through shared redemption, couples were united together by these welding links. Some of these women, like Sylvia Sessions Lyon, were married to men outside the faith, which Smith believed necessitated their attachment to him so as to grant them a binding covenant; others, like Mary Elizabeth Rollins and Marinda Nancy Johnson, were already married to active members of the church, which made their unions all the more complicated. Nearly all of them hailed from families that boasted deep ties and close relations to the prophet, which seemed to justify deeper familial connections. After the first year, however, Smith mostly ceased courting married women in 1842 and was instead sealed to an increasing number who were young and single.

As Joseph Smith's conception of priesthood governance, the authority that ruled the Mormon cosmos, evolved, so too did his polygamous practice. Smith formulated and implemented a series of theological ideas in 1842 that were designed to reform society and place it in providential order. Drawing from new scriptural texts that were published as the later chapters of a scriptural text known as the Book of Abraham, this new order included new fraternal rituals for men called the endowment, an energetic organization for women, and an expansion of participants within the polygamous circle. Besides Smith, a growing yet contained number of other Mormon leaders, including Brigham Young, took additional wives. One of the women sealed to Smith during this period was Eliza R. Snow, a famous poet and leader within the LDS community. Educated, talented, and respected, Snow's intense religiosity and commitment to the prophet made her willing to enter into what she knew to be a scandalous practice. She subtly mused on her clandestine sealing in her diary, where she compared the stability of God's kingdom and patriarchal order to the chaos and winds of the tumultuous world. Polygamy, for these participants, brought order to a disorderly society.

Not everyone was as amenable to Smith's proposals. Several women rejected both Smith and Young in early 1842 when they were approached as potential brides. Further trouble began when John C. Bennett, a recent convert who had quickly gained status in Nauvoo and became mayor within the civic sphere and assistant president in the religious, capitalized on the rumors concerning polygamy to commence his own sexual dalliances. When discovered and disciplined, he threatened to expose Smith's "spiritual wife" practice. The extent of his knowledge concerning Smith's sealings is debated, but his risk of damaging the prophet and the church through scandalous accusations was real. Coupled with the political and legal fallout from Bennett's exposés, Mormon leaders were put on the defensive for the second half of 1842, and Smith was forced to pause his polygamous activities.

That pause did not last for long. By January 1843, once he felt safe from Bennett's rumors, Joseph Smith continued the polygamy project in earnest. He was sealed to around twenty women that year, and the number of other men and women who entered the practice numbered nearly thirty. Several of these brides were teenage girls. One of these young women, Sarah Ann Whitney, was the daughter of Newell K. and Elizabeth Whitney. Though members of the faith for over a decade, and both Newell and Elizabeth had held significant positions within the community, Smith's proposal to be sealed to their daughter caused immense turmoil. In order to console their grief and appease their hesitancy, Smith dictated a revelation that contained the text for the ritual, a rare contemporary document detailing the theological foundations for polygamy that has survived until the present. The manuscript is both revealing and instructive.

> Verily thus saith the Lord unto my se[r]vant N. K. Whitney the thing that my se[r]vant Joseph Smith has made known unto you and your [Family] and which you have agreed upon is right in mine eyes and shall be crowned upon your heads with honor and immortality and eternal life to all your house both old & young because of the lineage of my Preast Hood saith the Lord it shall be upon you and upon your children after you from generation to generation By virtue of the Holy promise which I now make unto you saith the Lord.
>
> [T]hese are the words which you shall pronounce upon my se[r]vant Joseph and your Daughter [Sarah Ann] Whitney. They shall take each other by the hand and you shall say: you both mutu[al]ly agree calling them by name to be each others companion so long as you both shall live presser[v]ing yourselv[es] for each other and from all others and also through [o]ut all eternity reserving only those rights which have been given to my servant Joseph by revelation and commandment and by legal Authority in times passed. If you both agree to covenant and do this, then I give you [Sarah Ann] Whitney my Daughter to Joseph Smith to be his wife to observe all the rights betwe[e]n you both that belong to that condition. I do it in my own name and in the name of my wife your mother and in the name of my Holy Progenitors by the right of birth which is of Priest Hood vested in me by revelation and commandment and promise of the living God obtained by the Holy Melchizedek [Jethro] and other of the Holy Fathers commanding in the name of the Lord all those powers to concentrate in you and through to your po[s]terity for ever all these things I do in the name of the Lord Jesus Christ that through this order he may be [glorified] and through the power of anointing [David] may reign King over Iseral which shall hereafter be revealed let immortality and eternal life henc[e]forth be sealed upon your heads forever and ever.
> (Smith, 1842)

The entire Whitney family, as a result of this ritual, was assured salvation due to their connection to Smith's priesthood structure. The sealing served as a welding link that bound the families together for all eternity.

Even as Smith expanded his polygamous system, his first wife, Emma, remained largely ignorant of these activities. When she did learn some details, she was likely shielded from others, which led to a series of confrontations and reconciliations. At one point in May 1843, she acquiesced to Joseph being sealed to a set of sisters, Emily Dow and Eliza Maria Partridge, only to later find out he had already been sealed to them a few months previous. She was also deeply distraught to learn that some of her closest friends, including Eliza R. Snow, had been secretly sealed to Joseph without her knowledge. The frequently tense relationship between the Smiths remained rocky for several months, including a moment when Emma threatened divorce and Joseph was forced to sign over valuable property and land to acquiesce her demands. They finally settled later that year when Joseph promised not to take another plural wife.

In the midst of one of their confrontations, Hyrum Smith, Joseph's brother and himself a recent convert to the practice, urged the prophet to dictate a revelation that justified the practice. The result was an expansive, detailed, and circular text that exceeded 3,000 words and connected polygamy to the Old Testament, eternal marriage, and post-resurrection glory. The revelation opens with a direct appeal to ancient patriarchs, justifying biblical prophets like Abraham, Isaac, and Jacob taking plural wives because it was God's revealed command. Later believers and some contemporary scholars have claimed that this implies the revelation was first received during Smith's work with the Bible a decade earlier, yet it also fits with the patriarchal-centered focus Smith exhibited throughout Nauvoo, including the production of the latter chapters of the Book of Abraham in 1842. Regardless, the bulk of the revelation is best understood as intimately tethered to its Nauvoo-era climate (Bushman, 2005).

This revelatory text also emphasized the eternal nature of priesthood covenants. Any contract or oath between individuals not sealed by priestly authority was destined to perish at one of the party's death, yet those who entered the ordinance through Smith's ritual power were assured perpetual stability. Both men and women sealed under this covenant were promised to become "gods," which meant "inherit[ing] thrones, kingdoms, principalities, and powers, dominions, all heights and depths." Both men and women were included in a royal "they," though the role of husbands as sovereign was clear while that of women remained inchoate. While the promised blessings were immense, so were the required sacrifices. After detailing the eternal nature of marriage covenants, the revelation dictated its polygamous dimensions. Referred to as "the law of my Holy Priesthood" and "the works of Abraham," the divine voice approved of men taking a plurality of wives as part of God's heavenly order; conversely, if a woman were to take a second man, she "hath committed adultery and shall be destroyed" (Smith, 1843). While it supplied a provision for wives to approve of any addition to their family, it reaffirmed that they could not reject additional women that God had appointed. Reflecting the particular circumstances of the document's production, the revelation closed by explicitly vindicating Joseph Smith and chastising Emma for refusing to follow his counsel.

Emma Smith was not convinced. She sternly rebuked her brother-in-law Hyrum for even raising the issue, and the next day Joseph allowed her to destroy the revelation. (But only after they had made an additional copy.) News of the revelation slowly spread throughout Nauvoo, with some authorities accepting its ideas while others refused. A number of Nauvoo's ecclesiastical and civic leaders, when confronted with the text, determined Smith was a fallen prophet. As tensions mounted in the spring of 1844, dissenters threatened to reveal the teachings, and followed through by publishing the newspaper *Expositor* in June. Smith continued to publicly deny his involvement in the practice and, acting as city mayor, ordered the press's destruction. These actions played a significant role in his eventual arrest and death at the hands of a mob later that month.

Once Smith was deceased, Brigham Young and the Quorum of the Twelve Apostles moved swiftly to wrest control from any potential inheritors of church leadership. One of the ways they emphasized their authority was through the expansion of Smith's priestly rites, including polygamy. Publicly, they worked feverishly to finish the temple, where thousands of Saints eventually gained the opportunity to be sealed to their spouses; privately, they rapidly grew the number of polygamous unions. Young and Heber C. Kimball, another senior member in the quorum, also took the occasion to be married to the women who were already sealed to Smith. Even if the women would remain sealed to Smith in the eternities, Young and Kimball served as guardians until their death. It was a very literal way to carry on Smith's mantle.

Cultural context

The antebellum period featured a number of substantive challenges to traditional domestic order, both radical and conservative. The American Revolution and expansion of political rights raised significant questions concerning the role of women, the relationship between husband and wife, and the division between public and private, particularly within the domestic sphere. These developments took place simultaneously with a revival of religious fervor that swept the nation during the early republic and cultivated intense spiritual regeneration. Women played an important role in all these advances, and denominations were forced to react in ways that reflected the new cultural climate. This led to a number of controversial evolutions and experiments, of which Mormon polygamy was merely one example.

Among mainstream evangelical denominations that quickly came to shape mainstream culture, monogamous marriage remained crucial. However, single women and wives were provided new responsibilities to both shape congregational messages as well as reform surrounding society. Several denominations even featured women preachers, an activity that transgressed traditional boundaries. As part of the cultural compromise that attempted to keep women out of the public sphere and dedicated to domestic work, women were now seen as guardians of the home, which included obligations like policing and improving virtue. This responsibility empowered women to enter the public sphere and participate in societal discussions. Capitalizing on this responsibility, activists sought new avenues that expanded gendered expectations and duties. All religions attempted to respond to these developments in order to address their modern constituents. There was a spectrum for results, ranging from the feminine divinity of the Moravians to the entrenched female activism of the Methodists. Everywhere, it seemed women were achieving more rights within the religious sphere.

A number of groups were not satisfied with these more conventional approaches, however. The formality of the domestic home appeared to be too stifling and stagnant, and true liberation required a more radical dissolution of gender roles. Several of these reformers were, like the Mormons, communitarian in approach. By creating their own societies divorced from the wicked world, they felt free to implement revised gender norms better equipped to meet spiritual needs. Most notably, the Shakers rejected sexual intercourse altogether and instead instituted a regimented code of celibacy and a strict separation of the sexes. Sanctification, they believed, could only be achieved through segregated gendered experience. Conversely, John Humphrey Noyes founded what came to be known as the Oneida Community, a society that welcomed open marriage yet regimented male countenance. Procreation was to be controlled, but sexual activity was still diversified and expanded. Divinity, from the perspective of both movements, could not be contained within traditional, monogamous relationships.

Other contemporaries believed the mainstream changes were moving society too far along from traditional wisdom. In New York, a renegade prophet by the name of Matthias—born as Robert Matthews—organized a cult that featured, among other things, domineering patriarchal rule. In Matthias' eyes, America's modernization had only led to chaos. Closer to the Mormons in Nauvoo, an Illinois resident named Udney Hay Jacobs wrote an extensive manuscript about how America's democratized culture had provided women too much freedom, and the only solution was to return to biblical gender boundaries. Though both men had connections to Joseph Smith—Matthias met him in 1835, and excerpts from Jacobs' book first appeared in a Nauvoo newspaper—the Mormon prophet did not move as far in their direction. For example, he emphasized a woman's right to divorce, which granted them the opportunity to leave their husbands and choose their eternal mate. Unlike Matthias and Jacobs, Smith maintained a woman's choice and framed his marital structure as a system that could empower all those who entered.

Mormonism's polygamous project shared many elements with these contemporaneous movements. Like the Shakers, they were unwilling to give up traditional gender spheres and merge men and women into a homogeneous experience. Like the Oneida, they believed that the opportunity for chosen and elite men to sire children from different women took precedence over the basic confines of monogamous marriage. And like the Moravians, their conception of deity, while still gendered male or female, was closely connected to sexuality: a man and woman could only be sanctified as husband and wife, and their glory perpetuated through reproduction. Together, these groups signify that the antebellum period provoked a number of religious challenges to traditional domesticity, sexuality, and gendered norms. Joseph Smith's polygamous experiment can only be understood as one part of a broader chorus.

Yet Smith's beliefs still held unique elements. Unlike the radical reformers of his day, Smith used traditional means to address modernity's ills: a primitivist restoration of biblical traditions. And unlike the more conservative retrenchments, Smith maintained a commitment to choice and free will as a crucial element of the practice. Polygamy was a conservative means to promote radical ends. Notably, of all the sexual experiments promulgated by religious groups during the era, Mormonism's drew the most converts and sustained the longest success.

Polygamous kinship

The practice of polygamy in Mormon Nauvoo opened new possibilities, though rarely definitive answers, for how believers understood gender and kinship. While the husband was to be a patriarch akin to the biblical prophets of old, his relationship to wives and their families was more assumed than outlined. Given most of Smith's first plural wives were already married, there was some question as to how their two unions related to one another. Some believed their first husband would take precedence for time, and Smith for eternity, and they therefore lived with their original families without much change. Others, like Sylvia Session Lyon, witnessed their relationship with their civic husband evolve as a result of the sealing, and at one point she left her first husband and made Smith her primary relation. These were important decisions, as the lack of these sealings could prove deleterious—Smith, speaking of fellow apostle Parley Pratt, said that if one were not sealed to a woman for eternity their glory would be clipped.

The fathers of some of Smith's teenage brides viewed the unions more in terms of familial rather than marital terms, with children serving more as religious linkages within a family saga than actors within their own marital narrative. For example, the Apostle Heber C. Kimball was anxious for his fourteen-year-old daughter, Helen Mar Kimball, to be sealed to the prophet. Likely prompted by the sealing performed between Smith and Sarah Ann Whitney the previous summer, where the whole Whitney clan was assured salvation, Kimball believed that his entire family's eternal progression would be curtailed if not for the union. For Helen, then, she was expected to forgo the societal expectations of courtship, marriage, and a traditional domestic life in order for her extended family to gain eternal glory. It is possible she did not fully understand the implications at the time. She later wrote about the experience as akin to Abraham offering up his son, Isaac, to the Lord, only in this instance the sacrifice was the patriarch's daughter, and there was not a lamb provided in her stead. For many of the women who were sealed to Smith, the only justification came through prophetic obedience, spiritual renewal, and eternal assurance.

The men who desired these sealings, including husbands like Smith as well as fathers like Kimball and Newell Whitney, understood salvation as a communal experience. Exaltation, the highest reward for those most faithful, was reserved to those who were bound together through priesthood keys. Besides polygamy and vicarious baptisms, both rituals that emphasized the connectivity between families and generations, Mormons in Nauvoo also introduced a ritualized adoption that achieved these goals. The Law of Adoption, as it came to be known, implied the sealing together of couples to other priesthood leaders. But rather than a linear hierarchy, with children connected to their literal parents, adult men and women were instead sealed to contemporary men who then served as their spiritual patriarch within the grand Mormon chain of belonging. Saints could only be saved when welded into a consanguineous web of relations and devotion. As his biography once put it, Joseph Smith "yearned for familial plentitude. He did not lust for women so much as he lusted for kin" (Bushman, 2005, p. 440). Plural wives were one part of that equation, though certainly a crucial and most controversial one.

The principle of polygamy was still rooted in sexuality, however. Though there has not been any evidence to prove Joseph Smith sired any children from his polygamous unions, a number of his wives later admitted to conjugal relations with the prophet. Other men and women who entered the practice in Nauvoo under Smith's direction did reproduce, though the principle's secrecy limited the number until the church left Nauvoo for the West. When his secretary, William Clayton, told Smith that his plural wife was pregnant, the prophet promised private support even if he were forced to publicly discipline him due to political conditions. Some later recalled that there were physical spaces set aside from the public's eye in order to handle these controversial forms of pregnancy.

Though many of the men would later claim their disgust upon originally learning of polygamy, most jumped into the practice with enthusiasm. Sometimes it brought them trouble. Brigham Young's first attempt at courting a plural wife, a recent British immigrant named Martha Brotherton, ended in disaster when Brotherton rejected his proposal, left the faith, and allowed an anti-Mormon author to print her affidavit detailing the episode. At one point in the spring of 1842, as an influx of new immigrants, many young women, flooded Nauvoo, rumors concerning polygamy likely sparked an upswing in extramarital relations, and dozens were tried before the city's ecclesiastical court. Even some of Smith's closest advisors, like those in the Quorum of the Twelve Apostles, moved at such a speed that it caused concern. For the rest of his life, Smith attempted to simultaneously expand his polygamous project while also policing the morals and activities of those who were not yet authorized to participate. The desire for eternal kinship cannot explain all the zeal behind the practice.

For a number of women in Nauvoo, polygamy offered the paradoxical opportunity for spiritual fulfillment, external rewards, and even social advancement. It also provided an avenue to enter into new relationships when previous unions had failed. Augusta Cobb, a well-educated and established convert who left her husband when she joined the faith, believed polygamy to be the key to her religious and temporal salvation. Not only could she form a new relationship with someone who shared her faith, but she had the choice of several prominent apostles who were willing to make her a queen in their expanding kingdom. Though rebuffed by her friends in Boston when she tried to share the news and entice more women to join her in Nauvoo, Cobb was eventually sealed to Brigham Young.

The men and women who embraced polygamy as God's will defined it as the mechanism through which they could figuratively and literally conjoin a community together. While most antebellum Americans triumphed in their belief concerning individualism and self-reliance, the Mormon practice of plural marriage emphasized the need for communal stability and spiritual networks. Individuals, families, and generations could only be exalted through shared sanctification. Polygamy was not merely about sexual partners, but familial roots and branches. Once Mormonism gave up this communal perspective of salvation—including the adoption ordinance—and embraced the more traditional form of traditional and companionate unions, the mental world of early polygamy appeared even more foreign.

Theological legacy

Joseph Smith's teachings concerning polygamy were products of a particular time and context, yet they created a foundation for Mormon understandings of gender ever since. This is particularly true concerning the revelation he dictated in June 1843. The document remained a secret for the next few years, even as the number of polygamous participants quickly ballooned. However, in 1852, once the Saints were settled in Utah, Brigham Young announced the practice to the world and made the revelation public record. It was then used as a theological defense for the practice in both public and private discourse. Finally, in 1878, it was added to the church's scriptural book, the Doctrine and Covenants, along with most of Smith's other revelations. This meant it was now binding as part of the Mormon canon. Even after the church publicly denounced the practice of polygamy in 1890, the revelation still remained, though somewhat curtailed by the proclamation that supposedly ended the practice.

Besides the text itself, other aspects of polygamy's theological legacies persist. Though men are not allowed to be married to multiple women at the same time while they are still alive, they are able to be sealed to a new wife if their first wife is deceased or their first marriage ended in a divorce. It is understood that both unions are eternal in nature. For example, Russell M. Nelson, who became president of the church in 2018, is currently sealed to both Dantzel White, his first wife who passed away in 2005, as well as Wendy Watson, to whom he was sealed in 2006. Conversely, if a woman's husband were to die, she would not be allowed to be sealed to a second unless the first union is annulled. So while polygamy *during life* is still forbidden, a version of Smith's eternal polygamy remains fully in force. As long as the 1843 revelation remains in the LDS canon, elements of its teachings will continue to permeate Mormon thought.

Joseph Smith's polygamous theology also shapes how believers conceive of their roles in the afterlife. During the final months of his life, Smith taught that human beings were destined to become gods just like the divine being they currently worship. Indeed, he reasoned, the being that is currently known as "God" was once a man in a similar earthly experience, and it is humanity's job to mimic his progress and evolve into a similar type of deity. That implied not only receiving a body that could be resurrected and sanctified but also, according to his closest interpreters, uniting with plural wives who would reign over new worlds and populations. Fulfilling a literalistic reading of Abraham's promise, exalted Mormons had the destiny to become divine parents with posterity greater than the stars in the sky or sand on the seashore.

But what did it mean to produce other humans in one's new dominion? Smith's teaching was somewhat vague. At times he taught that all human spirits were, at their core, "intelligences" that were self-existent with God, and therefore cannot be created or destroyed. This would seem to imply that once an individual progressed to Godhood they would serve more as guardians than parents over intelligences that are ready to gain a mortal body and experience life on an earth. This theology seems to relate to the adoption-based rituals of Nauvoo, in which individuals and families are sealed within a web of kin underneath a presiding patriarch. Alternatively, Smith's polygamy revelation, as well as the interpretations of those who learned the doctrine first-hand from Mormonism's first prophet, seemed to imply that polygamous unions enabled patriarchs to produce literal children through their plural wives, even into the eternities. As an extension of earthly experience, this model included sealed parents creating spirit children who could inhabit new worlds.

These competing ideas, though abstract, have substantial implications for how Mormon women view their own activities in the afterlife. Will they be co-rulers with their husband over already-existent spirits? Or will they be expected to serve as mothers and birth billions of spirits, along with a myriad of other wives, to populate worlds over which their husband reigns? Beyond theological musing for the afterlife, these exegetical questions also either reaffirm or challenge domestic expectations during their earth existence. Given Mormons pattern their lives, obligations, and relationships off what they believe to be a heavenly model, determining what, exactly, Joseph Smith taught concerning plurality in the cosmos determines how they understand their position as women within the faith. The legacy of Smith's polygamous experiment in Nauvoo, which often developed within a particular context and in response to unique concerns, still shapes gender roles today. When Russell M. Nelson spoke at his first press conference after becoming the new LDS prophet, he drew on language from Smith's 1843 polygamy revelation to justify the traditional role of wives and mothers. The stakes remain high.

Outside the mainstream Church of Jesus Christ of Latter-day Saints, other Mormon groups have also wrestled with Smith's polygamous teachings. Though the Community of Christ, previously known as the Reorganized Church of Jesus Christ of Latter Day Saints, staked much of its early reputation on the argument that Smith never practiced plural marriage, other groups have tried to maintain the "principle" with earnest. Most famously, the Fundamentalist Church of Jesus Christ of Latter-Day Saints, until recently led by Warren Jeffs, has made news due to their commitment to "pioneer" clothing and lifestyles, including polygamy. Other, more mainstream fundamentalist groups, most of whom are located in the Utah region, also practice polygamy. Some of the individuals within these movements, like those who have been featured in American reality television shows, have tried to adapt to modern culture while also classifying any estrangement from Smith's polygamous system as heresy. Wives wear modern clothes, enter the modern workforce, and even make modern arguments concerning gender rights, but still share a husband. Even in twenty-first-century America, the marital experiment inaugurated in Nauvoo influences many lives.

Conclusion

As much as Smith's beliefs concerning gender, marriage, and kinship were rooted in antebellum America, their implications became much grander. Particular principles held relevance with contemporary movements, but also diverged in order to formulate Smith's unique answer to what he believed to be the nation's problem of domesticity. He argued the only solution to the world's chaos was the stability gained through eternal sealings authorized by priesthood power, and the primary form to save the most people was through a communal system of polygamous linkages. The practice simultaneously rooted women within a patriarchal network, while also promising an abstract form of empowerment, glory, and godhood. It was, paradoxically, both conservative in approach yet radical in implications. Though these ideas remained secret during his lifetime, and only a few dozen were initiated into the sacred circle, after Smith's death the practice became a primary element for tens of thousands of men and women ever since. Both scholars outside the faith and believers within are still debating its implications.

References

Bushman, R., 2005. *Joseph Smith: Rough Stone Rolling*. New York: Knopf.
Compton, T., 1997. *In Sacred Loneliness: The Plural Wives of Joseph Smith*. Salt Lake City, UT: Signature Books.
Hales, B., 2013. *Joseph Smith's Polygamy*, 3 vols. Sandy, UT: Kofford Books.
Smith, G., 2008. *Nauvoo Polygamy: "... But We Called It Celestial Marriage."* Salt Lake City, UT: Signature Books.
Smith, J., 1842. Revelation, July 28. LDS Church History Library. Salt Lake City, UT: CHL.

Smith, J., 1843. Revelation July 12. *Joseph Smith Papers Project.* www.josephsmithpapers.org/paper-summary/revelation-12-july-1843-dc-132/1.

Further reading

Bushman, R., 2005. *Joseph Smith: Rough Stone Rolling*. New York: Knopf.
   The definitive biography of Joseph Smith, this book is an introduction to both his life as well as his ideas, including polygamy. It pays particular attention to the cultural context in which Smith lived.
Compton, T., 1997. *In Sacred Loneliness: The Plural Wives of Joseph Smith*. Salt Lake City, UT: Signature Books.
   This is a group biography of the women who were sealed to Joseph Smith. It draws extensively from their later writing, as well as their experiences concerning how polygamy shaped their lives. Also includes an introduction that frames Smith's polygamist experiment as a dynastic project.
Flake, K., 2015. The Development of Early Latter-day Saint Marriage Rites, 1831–1853. *Journal of Mormon History* 41(1): 77–103.
   This article details the evolution of Mormon polygamy during its first decade, particularly during Joseph Smith's era. By focusing on marriage rites, Flake contextualizes Mormon marital practices within a Protestant tradition.
Smith, M., 2013. *Revelation, Resistance, and Mormon Polygamy: The Introduction and Implementation of the Principle, 1830–1853*. Logan, UT: Utah State University Press.
   This book focuses on the role that secrecy and fraternity played during polygamy's first years, especially in Nauvoo. It argues that the clandestine practice influenced how Mormons understood the world around them.
Ulrich, L., 2017. *A House Full of Females: Plural Marriage and Women's Rights in Early Mormonism, 1835–1870*. New York: Knopf.
   Though it deals with a chronological scope beyond just Joseph Smith, the early chapters are the best analysis of the lived reality of polygamy during the Nauvoo period. Particular attention is given to individual families, like those of Wilford Woodruff and William Clayton.

7

MORMON GENDER IN THE AGE OF POLYGAMY

Laurel Thatcher Ulrich

In *Public Vows*, historian Nancy Cott argued that in the United States monogamous Christian marriage structured the "system of attribution and meaning that we call *gender*." By turning men into husbands and women into wives, it shaped the way both sexes acted in the world, dispensing privileges and constraints, obligations and rewards. The unmarried as well as the married felt its "ideological, ethical, and practical impress." This does not mean that marriage has ever been a static institution. Debates over laws governing marriage have been a perpetual element the nation's history (Cott, 2000, p. 3).

In the nineteenth century, that was nowhere more evident than in the conflict between the United States government and the Church of Jesus Christ of Latter-day Saints over the practice of polygamy. That conflict played out in the courts, in the halls of Congress, and in the press. As Cott explains, Americans, like their European predecessors, assumed a "thematic equivalency between polygamy, despotism, and coercion on the one side and between monogamy, political liberty, and consent on the other." Thus the Latter-day Saints inhabitants of Utah acquired a place in public imagination once reserved for Turks and Asians (Cott, 2000, pp. 23, 105–31). They became the *other* against which to measure the nation's values. If true Americans were democratic, individualist, and monogamous, Latter-day Saints were collectivist, theocratic, and polygamist (Gordon, 1996; 2002; Fluhman, 2012; Talbot, 2013; Reeve, 2015).

But what if, at its root, the marital system in Utah was much the same as elsewhere. After visiting the territory in 1871, Elizabeth Cady Stanton surprised reporters by refusing to make a distinction between polygamy and monogamy. In her view, the condition of women had been the same "in all ages and latitudes, under all forms of government and religions, alike under heathenism, Catholicism, Protestantism, and Mormonism—the divinely ordained subjects of man." The problem was not polygamy, but patriarchy. Women everywhere were taught "to be subservient on earth in order to win a place in heaven." Even in the supposedly democratic United States, they were denied the right to vote and were "shut out of the world of work—helpless dependents on man for bread" (Ulrich, 2017a, p. xiii). Her traveling companion, Susan B. Anthony, made a similar argument. To become free, women "must be able to live honestly and honorably without the aid of men" (Talbot, 2013, p. 67).

Stanton and Anthony had come to Utah because its territorial legislature had in 1870 passed a law enfranchising women. They assumed that a nascent reform movement in the territory had initiated the change and that with the vote, women would rise up against polygamy. They soon discovered that the situation was more complicated. In Utah the most ardent advocates for woman suffrage also defended plural marriage, and in time some of them even became officers in the National Woman Suffrage Association led by Stanton and Anthony. Were women like Emmeline Wells, the articulate editor of the *Woman's Exponent* or Sarah Kimball, the impassioned president of the Utah Woman Suffrage Association, mere pawns of the patriarchy as their opponents imagined? Or was there something about their experience as Latter-day Saints that gave them the power to assert their equality as citizens?

Behind that question is a larger one. If the "system of attribution and meaning that we call *gender*" was sustained by marriage, did the form of marriage matter? In other words, did the practice of plural marriage change gender roles in any fundamental way?

That question is intriguing but difficult to answer with any certainty because the variables spin out in so many directions. This is not just because the earliest members of the Church of Jesus Christ were born and raised in monogamous societies and therefore shared many values with their opponents, but because polygamy as practiced in Utah territory was neither uniform nor universal. At its peak around 1860, almost half of the inhabitants (men, women, and children) lived in polygamous households. These were not, however, the expansive *harems* of popular imagination. Two-thirds of polygamous men had only two wives. Another 20 percent had three. Men who had more than four wives were a distinct minority (Bennion, 1984, p. 17; 2013, pp. 122–25; Bennion et al., 2005, p. 26; Cornwall et al., 1993, p. 149; Daynes, 2008, pp. 101, 123–33)

The big households nevertheless had an enormous impact on the church and on opposition to it, not only because they were led by powerful men but because they included powerful women. Outsiders could not understand how women could simultaneously embrace plural marriage and stand up for women's rights. At one level, the answer was obvious—their own community was threatened. Plural marriage had become one of the markers of their community and an assault on it became an assault on their identity and faith. The most visible female leaders in Utah in 1870 had long since demonstrated their ability to push against the grain. Some had fled abusive or alcoholic husbands. Others had defied parents and community norms by embracing Mormonism. All had faced scandal and mob violence. They had worked beside men and without them to build homes and communities in four states. By the time they arrived in Utah, many of them already knew how to circulate petitions, sign affidavits, lobby public officials, and employ the power of the press. More importantly, through their organizations they had learned to work together across household boundaries (Ulrich, 2017a, pp. xiii–xiv, 53–55, 73–83, 111–14; Derr et al., 2016, pp. 136, 142–44, 151–56, 168–72)

Given the complexity of early Mormon history, it is difficult to sort out the relative importance of religious commitment, frontier adversity, plural marriage, and outside opposition in shaping values and behavior in early Utah. Still, if Cott is right about the power of marriage to define the ways the sexes "act in the world," then a closer look at similarities and differences between Latter-day Saints and their neighbors might tell us something about the stability or the mutability of the construct we call *gender*. This essay will explore four arenas where Latter-day Saints appear to have deviated from broader ideas about gender: in their approach to divisions of labor and responsibility within households, in their understanding of sexuality, in their acceptance of divorce, and in their eventual embrace of woman suffrage.

Divisions of labor in the household

In the early United States, a new emphasis on representative government forced Americans to consider both the relationship between the household and the state and the division of authority within households. Did rules demanding consent of the governed apply within as well as beyond the family? If male heads of household had the right and responsibility to govern their children, servants, slaves, and other dependents, did they also have the right to govern their wives? If so, what was the line of demarcation between a wife and a servant or slave? These questions and others were raised in the immediate aftermath of the American Revolution.

By the 1820s, most opinion-makers had settled on a division of responsibility that reaffirmed the time-honored responsibility of men to govern households and represent them in the economy and state. At the same time they elevated the potential power of women by "ascribing world-historical importance to women's maternal role, and claiming for women a nature less sexual and more self-controlled than the nature of men." This social construct, often termed "Republican Womanhood" (or alternatively "Republican Motherhood"), valorized the *indirect* power of women to influence the nation by employing moral authority as Christians and mothers (Kerber, 1988, p. 20).

The contrasting spheres of males and females were honored in civic performances, such as the one held in the Salt Lake Valley on July 24, 1849 to celebrate the anniversary of the arrival of the first pioneer company two years before. In the formal program, a procession of young women in white dresses carried Bibles and Books of Mormon in chaste dignity while young men marched with swords and copies of the Constitution and the Declaration of Independence. The parade probably mimicked July 4 celebrations that at least some of the organizers had witnessed in the Midwest. Two easily overlooked details marked it as a specifically Mormon event. By holding their celebration on July 24 rather than July 4, the Saints distinguish their independence from a nation they believed had abandoned them, and the banners honoring Brigham Young acknowledged the union of civil and religious authority. The young men's banners designated Young as "The Lion of the Lord." The women's mimicked civic processions with "Hail to our Chief" (Ulrich, 2017a, pp. 204–8). To hostile observers, the new holiday exemplified a potentially dangerous "theocracy." But the symbols reified a conventional gender order. Males carried the nation's founding documents. Females symbolically assumed responsibility for morality and Christian nurture.

Nor, on the surface at least, was there anything unusual about the sermon Young preached in roughly the same spot two years later. "The man is the Head of the family and should Govern it," he began, as though anyone within the sound of his voice might doubt it. He continued with a typically rough-hewn image: "Let the wife rule the Husband & she will keep him tied to the dish cloth & kitchen all the days of his life." Then he turned to the women seated before him. "Do you know your calling as Mothers?" he asked. "It is your duty to Brace up your feelings as men have to do & Be Mystress of your House" (Ulrich, 2017a, p. 233). Like the parade, Young's sermon evoked time-honored notions about the appropriate division of authority within families, ideas embedded in Anglo-American law and in the lived experience of the mostly white, small-holding farmers and craftsmen who were part of the Latter-day Saints movement and who, though dependent on the labor of their wives and children, never questioned a husband's right to govern his household and a woman's right—and responsibility—to command her kitchen.

But there was more to Young's sermon than might appear. He was not just a pastor offering a homily. He was the President of the Church of Jesus Christ of Latter-day Saints, a prophet charged with building God's kingdom on earth. When he warned men about being "tied to the dish-cloth" or told mothers to brace-up their feelings and take control of their houses, he was less concerned about women usurping authority that belonged to men than about men refusing responsibilities he believed God had given them. The Church of Jesus Christ of Latter-day Saints did not have a professional clergy. From the foundation of the church in 1830, ordinary men—farmers, tradesmen, and common laborers—were ordained to a "priesthood" that allowed them to draw down the powers of heaven in the most ordinary acts of their lives and prepare themselves and their families for salvation. With power came responsibility.

To build God's kingdom, Young needed men willing to leave their own wives and children to serve proselyting missions, lead exploring expeditions, lay out new settlements, build roads and bridges, negotiate with neighboring Indians, and if necessary take up arms in defense of their people. When Young said he wanted women who could brace up their feelings "as men had to do," he imagined wives who were capable of supporting themselves and their children, who could function with or without a husband, who could teach school, take in sewing, plant a garden, milk a cow, press a cheese, drive an ox team, and weave a carpet out of old clothes, who could, in short, become the "Mystress" of a house (Ulrich, 2017a, pp. 30–56).

Both Brigham's sermon and the July 24 processions were in that sense misleading. As mothers, women were responsible for reading scriptures and passing on religious teachings to their children, but men, not women, carried the Bible and the Book of Mormon to the world. In a special conference held in the summer of 1852, church authorities called one hundred men, almost all of them husbands and fathers, to leave their unfinished farms and houses to preach Latter-day Saints doctrine, including plural marriage, to the world. Forty-one of these special missionaries went to the British Isles, still the most productive area for Mormon proselyting. The others were scattered from Continental Europe to Hawai'i and from Hong Kong and Calcutta to the Cape of Good Hope. In a send-off speech, Heber Kimball told them, "*go, if you never return*, and commit what you have into the hands of God—your wives, your children, your brethren." Before leaving, only a third of the men had embraced plurality. When they returned, almost all of them accepted "the principle" (Ulrich, 2017a, pp. 239–42).

The phenomenon of men leaving their families in the service of a higher cause is not in itself a violation of gender boundaries. In persuading men to respond to the church's call, leaders used an argument that has been employed in virtually every American war from the Revolution onward, that no women would want to marry a man who refused to serve his country. Nor was it unheard of for a wife to assume her husband's responsibilities if he went to war or to sea or died young. But Latter-day Saints enlarged the realm of public duty by taking men away from their day-to-day labors, leaving wives and other family members to assume the burdens they left behind. In essence, they made men more accountable religiously and women more responsible for the economic support of their families (Ulrich, 2017a, pp. 32, 46–56, 247–50, 259).

The higher up a man was in the church hierarchy the more likely he was to have responsibilities that took him away from home, if not for missionary service then for management of the secular or ecclesiastical work of the church. Since leaders at this level generally had multiple wives, this produced complex rearrangements of domestic affairs. Who was to be the mistress of the house? And how many houses should there be? Only a few men followed the example of Brigham Young who built a multi-gabled house near the site of the Temple in Salt Lake City where a dozen wives lived communally, dividing responsibility for teaching children, preparing meals, gardening, weaving cloth, and producing clothing on a newly acquired sewing machine. More commonly, men built separate dwellings for their wives, sometimes in different neighborhoods or towns. Even when wives cohabited, they had private spaces in the house and wherever possible separate fires or kitchens. Whatever the arrangement, husbands moved between houses or parts of houses in regular or random patterns (Carter, 2000; 2015, pp. 133–61; Embry, 1987, pp. 73–84).

Dispersal of wives accelerated as leading men opened enterprises in new parts of the territory. Having wives in different towns, gave them surrogates and a home in more than one place. Separate dwellings did not preclude economic cooperation among wives. The letters of George Albert Smith and his wives provide lively evidence of such a pattern. Bathsheba Smith, the first wife, had a home of her own near the temple in Salt Lake City, while Lucy, Hannah, Zilpha, and Sarah lived as pairs in different parts of the town and eventually in different towns. Although there are many examples of sister-wives forming strong bonds with each other, there is also plenty of evidence, even in the life histories of revered leaders, of conflict among wives, neglect by husbands, and unequal treatment of children. Perhaps the trend toward separate households was an attempt to lessen conflict (Ulrich, 2017a, pp. 233–36, 357–58, 366).

Plural marriage also reshaped relationships between husbands, wives, and household servants. In the United States in the nineteenth-century, even families of modest income often had some sort of household helper. In rural settings, these were often teen-age daughters of neighbors, although as education became more important for daughters of well-to-do families, servants or "helpers" typically came from disadvantaged or immigrant families, accentuating class differences between the mistresses of households and their workers. Nineteenth-century periodicals addressed to middle-class housewives were filled with anecdotes about the difficulty of finding good servants (Dudden, 1983).

Similar patterns emerged as single women embraced Mormonism in their native countries and immigrated to Utah. In Utah, however, these same women frequently moved upward, within the same household, from servant to wife. For some women that not only represented economic security but upward mobility, since men with the largest number of plural wives were often among the economic and religious elite. But to outsiders, nothing seemed more repellent. From early-modern ballads to sentimental novels, English literature is filled with stories about powerful men preying on innocent maidservants. Consciously or not, Latter-day Saints rearranged the old plot, by portraying a master's courtship of a household servant as a God-sanctioned way of ensuring that every woman, no matter how poor, might become a wife.

Demographic realities underlay this rearrangement of conventional household relations. By increasing the demand for wives, plural marriage radically reduced the number of single women in early Utah. For the system to work at all, older men almost always had to marry younger women. But the market operated in different ways depending on the social status and national origin of potential wives. A detailed study from Manti, Utah shows that girls from well-established families usually became wives. Although their husbands might later enter plurality, the initial marriage was monogamous. In contrast, women who immigrated without a father or who came from a poor family were far more likely to enter marriage as plural wives. As a consequence, there were not only age differences among wives but class or ethnic differences as well. Although religious women prided themselves on treating their husband's other wife or wives with kindness, it cannot have been easy for any of those involved, including the husband (Daynes, 2008, pp. 116–27; 2012, p. 72; Ulrich, 2017a, pp. 273–79).

Sexuality

Demographers have long puzzled over the nature of the "demographic transition" that began in the United States around 1800. In most societies a reduction in the number of children born in a society correlates with an increase in the number who survive infancy or early childhood. In the United States fertility decline actually *preceded* mortality decline. Whether the driving force was economic or cultural remains a matter of debate, but since effective contraception was largely unavailable, reduced fertility was likely achieved by some sort of reduction in sexual activity, not full-scale abstinence, as among the Shakers, but a perhaps barely noticed but no less significant accentuation of self-restraint within marriage (Haines, 2000, pp. 157–69; Klepp, 1998, pp. 910–45).

Historians have long-since abandoned the label "Victorian" to characterize attitudes toward sexuality in the early nineteenth century. There were by the 1840s a variety of "frameworks" for understanding the physiology and moral meaning of sex. These ranged from folk survivals of old ideas about different levels of "heat" in male and female bodies to self-consciously scientific descriptions of reproductive organs. As one scholar has put it, published works spanned the full spectrum "from sexual restriction to sexual enthusiasm." Although written sources on the topic are abundant, the challenge is determining the relationship between what people said and what they actually did (Horowitz, 2002, pp. 3–15).

Many experts believed that the sexual capacities and needs of males and females were different, that women's primary fulfillment came in motherhood, and that sexual arousal during pregnancy or lactation might damage a developing infant. Writers varied in their opinions about male sexual expression. Nearly everyone condemned masturbation. Some warned against too frequent seminal emission even in marriage, arguing that the paroxysms of sexual congress could lead to debility or early death. Among the most radical of the sex reformers was Sylvester Graham, whose famous diet of whole grains and cold water was designed to tamp down lust. William Alcott, a physician classed among the moderates, believed that a man might safely sleep with his wife once in a lunar month. Some educated Americans, including Thomas Kane, a Philadelphia reformer famous for his friendship with Brigham Young, embraced these ideas, not only for health, but to control the spacing and number of their children (Horowitz, 2002, pp. 92–100; Ulrich, 2017a, pp. 269–70; Grow, 2009, pp. 140–48).

In contrast Latter-day Saints were enthusiastic about reproduction which they imagined as continuing into the eternities for those who remained true to covenants made in a temple. Like Abraham, the righteous might see their progeny become as numerous as the grains of sand on the seashore or the stars in the heavens. Mormon patriarchs denied being driven by lust. They claimed that sexual intercourse had one purpose, to build God's kingdom by bringing pre-existent spirits to earth (Doctrine and Covenants 132, p. 19). When called upon to defend polygamy, they drew upon some of the same reform literature embraced by their opponents. Although they rejected extreme abstinence, they embraced the sanctity of motherhood and the importance of exercising restraint in the timing and frequency of intercourse. Some argued that because there were far more righteous women than men on the earth, plural marriage was an essential part of the work of salvation. It harmonized the physical differences between the sexes and allowed spiritual love to blossom. When blessed by the Holy Spirit, sexual expression produced loving connection (Hardy and Erickson, 2001, pp. 45–50).

Latter-day Saints added a layer of spiritual meaning to themes in contemporary advice literature that they found congenial. Like other nineteenth-century Americans they celebrated motherhood. But though they appeared to embrace some notions of restraint in marriage, they liberated and indeed sanctified the notion that men had greater sexual capacities than women. It is hardly surprising that critics accused them of lechery. Respectable Americans were quite aware of seemingly respectable men who kept mistresses or patronized houses of prostitution (and some of those men actually turned up in Utah as federal officials), but they preferred to look the other way. The idea that a Christian church would actually condone, even celebrate, such behavior by promoting polygamy seem outrageous.

Mormons responded with equal fervor. Plural marriage was not prostitution. In 1854, two years after the church officially announced its support for plural marriage, Belinda Marden Pratt published a little tract written in the form of a letter to her sister in New Hampshire. Called *A Defence of Polygamy*, it emphasized the different reproductive capacities of males and females. In the bloom of adulthood, she explained, the female body was "designed to flow in a stream of life … till mature age and approaching change of worlds … render[ed] it necessary for her to cease to be fruitful." In contrast, the male capacity for reproduction had no end. With multiple wives, a righteous man might become "the prince or head of a tribe, or tribes … like Abraham of old." He could protect each wife during the sacred periods of pregnancy and lactation and share with them joy in their collective posterity (Ulrich, 2017a, pp. 267–68, 270–72).

Belinda's treatise was among the most widely distributed of the pro-polygamy defenses that emerged after the public announcement of plural marriage in 1852. Her husband, Apostle Parley P. Pratt, pronounced it "one of the Little entering wedges of a worlds Revolution." She herself was a bit of a revolutionary. She had left a legal husband in Massachusetts in 1844 in order to join the saints in Nauvoo, and then married Parley in secret (Givens and Grow, 2011, pp. 327–31). Her celebration of her husband's Mormon kingdom must have horrified her sister. But for her it promised a glorious future.

In letters to their relatives, Latter-day Saints defended polygamy. In the privacy of their own diaries or in discussions with other women, they revealed the persistence of romantic fantasies, sexual jealousy, and status anxiety in a system ostensibly devoted to reproduction and service to God (Ulrich, 2017a, pp. 343–51; Harline, 2014, pp. 77–79). These themes were not unique to Latter-day Saints or to plural wives. They were part of a larger discourse on marriage that leaks through the idealizations in nineteenth-century sentimental literature. In an undated handwritten poem in the papers of Vilate Kimball a woman begs her husband not to succumb to the attractions of a younger woman, lest he "drive a faithful wife/Forever from your arms!" Vilate's descendants assumed she had written in anguish over plural marriage. It was actually composed by a now forgotten male poet from Ohio and published widely in eastern periodicals with the title "A Lady to Her Husband." Vilate may have copied it directly from one of these publications or from a handwritten copy passed on to her by someone else (Ulrich, 2017a, p. 230).

It nevertheless resonated with her own situation. Heber and Vilate Kimball were among the first to embrace Joseph Smith's teachings on plural marriage, but though Vilate embraced the principle she clearly struggled with her own feelings. In 1850, at the age of forty-four, she delivered her tenth and last child. But her husband's reproductive work continued. In 1850 and 1851, Heber Kimball fathered nine other children, including a pair of twins, by eight plural wives who were in their twenties and early thirties. In their monogamous years, Heber had been a devoted and sentimental lover. As they entered polygamy, he had struggled to maintain his once deep relationship with Vilate, refusing to blame her when she felt discouraged. But in a moment of frustration (and perhaps guilt over his seeming abandonment of the wife of his youth), he fell back on preaching. He assured his wife that

> every son and daughter that is brought forth by the wives that are given to me will add to your glory as much as it will to them. They are given to me for this purpus and for no other. I am a Father of lives to give lives to those that wish to receive. Woman is to receive from Man.

He signed himself "your true friend and husband in Christ" (Ulrich, 2017a, pp. 99–101, 172–74, 230–31).

Kimball's missive suggests that fatherhood rather than motherhood was the active principle in plural marriage. Vilate would do her part, but in the end it would be his progeny, not hers, that would fill the earth.

Divorce

In the years following the American Revolution, writers of both sexes drew upon the language of marriage and family to describe the nature of a democratic society. Just as a happy marriage depended on the consent of the parties involved, good government required the consent of the governed. Describing freely chosen government as essentially benign, moralists turned the analogy in both directions. In the shadow of the French and Haitian revolutions, moralists urged Americans to honor the governors they had freely chosen. In a similar manner, newspaper essays urged restive wives to submit cheerfully to their husbands, explaining that "women by entering upon the marriage state, renounce some of their natural rights (as men do, when they enter into civil society)" (Cott, 2000, p. 17). Writers in this period rested rather comfortably on the power of consent, barely noticing the revolutionary origins of their own governments nor acknowledging that the covenant of marriage did not allow for a regular election.

As Nancy Cott has written, a nascent women's rights movement in the 1830s "threw a wrench into the sentimental national conversation about marriage and the household" (Cott, 2000, p. 67). Close examination of state laws from the period that idealized visions of monogamous marriage found in poetry, popular songs, and engravings obscure the many ways in which old-fashioned patriarchy persisted in state laws in the nineteenth century. Except when challenged by married women's property laws, the common-law notion that a woman's legal existence was "suspended' in marriage prevailed. In most states a married woman could not sue or be sued in her own name nor vote or sit on juries. Although judges were uncomfortable with the notion that a husband might physically discipline or constrain a wife, they were loath to intervene in what they considered private matters. In cases of assault, courts still focused not so much on the violation of a woman as on the property right her husband held in her body. In custody disputes, judges assumed that fathers, not mothers, had first claim on children. Although most states legalized divorce at some point after the Revolution, the process was adversarial and the outcome never assured (Reilly, 2013, p. 69; Hartog, 2000, pp. 106–10, 122–31, 150–55; Cott, 2000, pp. 56–70).

That may be why well into the nineteenth century, desertion by one party or the other remained an oft-used solution to an unhappy marriage (Schwartzberg, 2004, pp. 573–600). Although it was easier for a husband than a wife to simply leave and take up a new identity elsewhere, some women did manage to escape abusive or alcoholic husbands. Some of them cast their lot with the Saints. In the first marriage Joseph Smith performed, the bride was still legally married to the husband she had left in another state. According to the common law, she was a bigamist. But in the eyes of the Mormon prophet, God's mercy overruled the laws of men. A worthy man wanted her for his wife. Her early marriage destroyed by alcohol and violence had effectively ended. The practice of overlooking previous marriages persisted, which is why Belinda Marden had been able to marry Parley Pratt even though she was still legally bound to a husband in New Hampshire (Ulrich, 2016).

In Utah, the territorial legislature systematized the ability to escape an unhappy marriage by creating one of the most liberal divorce laws in the nation. In addition to the usual grounds, "impotence, adultery, habitual drunkenness," it allowed full divorce "when it shall be made to appear to the satisfaction and conviction of the court that the parties cannot live in peace and union together, and that their welfare requires a separation." Brigham Young himself authorized more than 1,645 divorces by 1866. One of his clerks said, he never refused a request when a plural wife insisted upon it. In most cases, the couple simply parted by mutual consent. Wives did not receive alimony, but husbands were required to continue supporting minor children. Most divorced women appear to have remarried rather quickly, sometimes going from one plural marriage to another (Ulrich, 2017a, pp. 280–83; Pearson and Madsen, 2005; Embrey, 1987, p. 178).

To critics, easy access to divorce seemed every bit as reprehensible as polygamy. Both violated what many considered the fundamental premise of Christian marriage, a life-long commitment to having sexual congress with only one person. One clergyman asked rhetorically, "What made Mormon polygamy *possible* in this country?" His answer: the "*unchastity* that makes divorces easy and popular" (Gordon, 2002, p. 173). Although Mormons were in some respects in the vanguard in authorizing divorce, they were not alone. Divorce expanded much more rapidly in the United States than in Catholic countries or in Britain, much to the consternation of conservatives. In an influential book published in 1869, the president of Yale College argued that adultery was the only legitimate ground for divorce and even then only the innocent party should be allowed to remarry. Other writers concurred. That most petitioners for divorce were women reinforced their concern. Writers associated divorce with "free love, polygamy, or a world in which husbands no longer controlled their wives, household, dependents, and property" (Cott, 2000, pp. 106–7).

In this era, the label "free lover" was attached to anyone who argued for easier access to divorce. Superficially at least, Latter-day Saints fit into that category. In a sensational divorce case widely reported in the press, one writer claimed that a woman who had traveled without her husband had fallen into the company of "Fourierites, agrarians, Mormons, spiritualists, [and] free-lovers" (Fox, 1999, pp. 233–36; Basch, 1999, pp. 70–71; Hartog, 2000, p. 227). In arguing that it was a sin for a couple to continue living together when their affections were alienated, some Latter-day Saints came close to an argument made by health reformer Mary Gove and her second husband, Thomas Nichols. They argued that if marriage were defined as "the real union of two persons in mutual love" and adultery as "any gratification of mere lust" then "a true marriage may be what the laws call adultery, while the real adultery is an unloving marriage." Interestingly, Gove had once been a friend of Augusta Cobb, who in 1843 left her own husband to become a plural wife of Brigham Young (Ulrich, 2017a, p. 106). For them, marriage was both a means of salvation and the foundation of the new Zion they were attempting to create in their desert enclave.

Latter-day Saints believed that there was a kind of optimism among the Saints that allowed them to embrace second chances in many aspects of ordinary life and in faith. In practice, divorce seems to have been a safety valve that allowed plural marriage to endure. In Utah, pressure from church authorities sometimes pushed the boundaries of consent to a breaking point. This was especially so during the so-called "Mormon Reformation" of 1856–1857, when Brigham Young and others threatened damnation for those who resisted God's law. One result of bombastic preaching was a significant expansion in the number of plural marriages. Another was an equally dramatic increase in divorce two years later (Daynes, 2012, p. 70). In combination with plurality, divorce may or may not have made lives easier for women, but it did validate the broader concept of choice for those who might otherwise have remained single and it allowed women caught in a difficult marriage a way out.

Woman suffrage

Although women did not have the right to vote anywhere in the United States in the 1830s, female voluntary societies of various kinds were already having a profound impact. Women raised funds to support local clergy, sewed clothing for orphans, made flags for local militia companies, and promoted temperance, Sabbath observance, and other modes of social reform. But as the national conflict over the expansion of slavery heated up, voluntarism began to assume political significance. Women, including African-American women began to form their own antislavery societies, publishing their minutes in *The Liberator*. Angelina and Sarah Grimke, sisters who had grown up in a slave-owning family in South Carolina, began to speak about what they had seen. In February 1838, Angelina became the first woman to address the Massachusetts legislature. She carried with her antislavery petitions signed by 20,000 women. In the midst of the conflict, Catharine Beecher, the daughter of a prominent evangelical minister, engaged Angelina Grimke in a pamphlet debate. Beecher believed that Grimke was violating God-given boundaries by engaging in public agitation. "Woman is to win every thing by peace and love; by making herself so much respected, esteemed and loved, that to yield to her opinions and to gratify her wishes, will be the free-will offering of the heart." To which Grimke responded, "When I look at human beings as moral beings, all distinction in sex sinks to insignificance and nothingness; for I believe ... whatever it is morally right for man to do, it is morally right for woman to do." Their argument was not about slavery, but about gender, and it helped to stimulate the beginning of what came to be known, somewhat inaccurately, as "first wave feminism" (Ulrich, 2007, pp. 132–37).

In 1838, the year Angelina Grimke addressed the Massachusetts legislature, 10,000 Latter-day Saints were facing mob violence in Missouri. Driven across the river into Illinois, they gathered petitions for redress. Although most were signed by male heads of households, widows who submitted testimony also claimed to have lost "rights of citizenship." For Mormon women, political conscience grew out of their own life experience. In the next seven years, they helped build a new city, raise money for a massive temple, and with Joseph Smith's support organize themselves into a charitable organization they called the "Female Relief Society of Nauvoo." Joseph Smith's wife Emma became its president. Eliza Snow, a poet who had once acted as secretary to her father, who was a Justice of the Peace in Ohio, kept the minutes. The Nauvoo society was dedicated to the relief of the poor, but internal conflicts in the community over the secret practice of plural marriage as well as disagreement with outsiders over the growing power of Nauvoo in local politics, brought women into the heart of the battle. The Relief Society created and signed petitions defending Joseph Smith and their own reputations, and when their community seemed threatened, Emma and Eliza visited the governor of Illinois (Derr et al., 1992; Derr et al., 2016, pp. 3–17; Ulrich, 2017a, pp. 57–83, 108–34).

After Joseph Smith's death in 1844, a conflict between Emma Smith and Brigham Young ended meetings of the Relief Society. Emma remained in Nauvoo. Eliza was among the majority of women who followed Young to Utah. Although they made no effort to reconstitute the Relief Society, they did not give up religious practices they believed had been ratified by Smith and by God. Nor did they abandon volunteerism. In refugee camps on the Missouri River, along the overland trail in 1847, and in rude cabins and adobe houses in early Utah, they blessed one another, healed the sick, spoke in tongues, and in private meetings quietly read the promises Eliza had recorded in the minutes of the first Relief Society. Over the next few years, informal association flourished alongside organized voluntarism of various kinds, including relief for Paiute women and children. Female leadership flourished despite uneven support and occasional push back from male leaders (2017a, pp. 127–30, 175–82, 192–97, 305–11; Derr et al., 2016, pp. 177–234).

In 1867–1868, as the church faced new challenges from internal dissent over economic policy, the coming of the railroad, and growing national concern over polygamy, Brigham Young asked Eliza Snow to help reconstitute the Relief Society throughout the territory (Derr et al., 2016, pp. 235–55). She already had a network of like-minded supporters, including Sarah Kimball, who had been instrumental in organizing the society in Nauvoo. Less than eight months after assuming the presidency of the Fifteenth Ward Relief Society, Kimball laid the cornerstone for an "unpretending edifice" to be paid for and used by women. She told the assembled crowd that the rock on which she stood was a "consecrated rock" and a stepping stone to "a more extended field of useful labor for female minds and hands." Some of the speeches she gave at Relief Society meetings might have been published in women's rights newspapers (Butler-Palmer, 2013, pp. 72–78).

That Snow was herself interested in women's rights is clear from a poem she published in Utah in 1850 in response to news of the first national convention held in Worcester, Massachusetts in 1850. Given the negative view of female activists in this period, she was surprisingly gentle in her response. Utah women, she argued, had no need to become "conventionists" because they lived among superior men. Like Catharine Beecher, Snow believed in God-given differences between the sexes. She also knew how to win "by peace and love," if not open flattery (Ulrich, 2017a, pp. 210–11). Anti-Mormon writers parodied her old-maid demeanor and her "strong-mindedness." But to her fellow Saints, she was not only a *poetess*, but a *priestess* and *prophetess*. One of her more enthusiastic contemporaries described her as "the president of the female portion of the human race." Because of her resolute defense of the church from its earliest days, her eventual support for woman suffrage mattered (Beecher, 1991, p. 5).

When the U.S. House of Representatives in December of 1869 passed a draconian anti-polygamy bill Salt Lake City's female leaders met in the upper room of the new Relief Society Hall to plan a mass meeting to protest federal action and to ask the territorial legislature to give them the vote. Their meeting, which was followed by similar gatherings in fifty-eight Utah towns, attracted attention in the national press and apparently helped to prevent final passage of the anti-polygamy bill. Their plea to the legislature also worked. A few weeks later, they returned to the Relief Society Hall to celebrate their success. Kimball openly declared herself "a woman's rights woman." Others followed. Within a few weeks Bathsheba Smith was writing the editor of the Boston-based *Woman's Journal* to announce the creation of a new constitution for Utah, the "first constitution in the history of the world" that women had participated in creating. By then the passage of woman suffrage had attracted the attention of Elizabeth Cady Stanton and Susan B. Anthony, who visited Utah in the following summer. In 1872, *The Woman's Exponent*, the longest-lived woman's rights newspaper west of the Mississippi was launched (Ulrich, 2017a, pp. 376–83).

Their energetic defense of plural marriage was impressive, but ultimately in vain. In 1878, the Supreme Court validated Congress's intervention in Utah affairs beginning a long struggle between the government's effort to enforce anti-polygamy laws and Mormon resistance. Women paraded and protested while continuing to expand the charitable and cooperative manufacturing work of the Relief Society and other female-led organizations. In 1880, Eliza Snow set out to visit every Relief Society in the territory. By December 1881, she had covered the full distance from Malad City, Idaho in the north to Bunkerville, Nevada in the south, a span that via today's interstate highways encompassed 452.4 miles, but surely much longer along Utah's winding roads. A newly built railroad facilitated part of the journey, but most of it required tedious travel in a horse-drawn "spring wagon" (Derr, 2012, pp. 102–3).

In 1887, the Edmunds-Tucker Act disenfranchised Utah women. Despite protests from many national woman suffrage leaders, even some advocates for women's rights argued that ridding the nation of the scourge of polygamy was more important than the franchise. In 1890, Church President Wilford Woodruff, pushed to the brink by Federal confiscation of church property and a threat to take over the temple, decided that in order to save the church he had to give in on polygamy. He issued a Manifesto promising to obey the law.

It took another five years to convince Congress that Utah was worthy of statehood. As the time for submitting a new constitution approached, dissension broke out among territorial leaders over the wisdom of including woman suffrage in the proposed constitution. Some may have opposed it on principle. Others believed it might doom the bid for statehood. In response, Apostle Joseph F. Smith delivered a forceful speech that might have come from one of the pamphlets of the National American Woman Suffrage Association:

Woman may be found who see to glory in their enthralled condition, and who caress and fondle the very chains and manacles which fetter and enslave them! Let those who love this helpless dependent condition … enjoy it; but for conscience and for mercy's sake let them not stand in the way of those of their sisters who would be, and of right ought to be, *free!*"

Smith may have had a bit of help from his friend Emmeline Wells, the editor of the *Woman's Exponent* (Madsen, 2017, pp. 350–51).

In 1896, Utah entered the union as a woman suffrage state, only the third in the nation to do so. For anti-suffragists, the Mormon embrace of woman suffrage was a powerful reason to oppose it. To them, woman suffrage, like polygamy, was a radical attempt to destroy unity in marriage and order in the state. To many Americans, their arguments were persuasive. Voting was one of the last planks in the woman's rights platform to succeed. By the time the nation ratified the Nineteenth Amendment in 1920, scores of American women had graduated from college, become physicians, organized reform movements, established independent businesses, worked as journalists, funded museums and monuments, driven automobiles, married and divorced and married again. Yet to some of the wealthiest and best-connected Americans, female voting threatened social order.

Polygamy may or may not have reshaped gender in nineteenth-century Utah but it certainly pushed the weakest edges of the broader system (Ulrich, 2017b). The fight *against* polygamy provided the opportunity for Mormon women to rediscover and assert their political rights. It also gave male leaders an incentive to support them. That Latter-day Saints women seized the moment in 1869 can be seen as a logical extension of their well-documented resilience in the face of opposition. But when seen as part of the larger story, it provides evidence of the fungibility of gender roles when a community faces new challenges.

This brief survey has suggested some of the ways that the system of marriage in nineteenth-century Utah subtly challenged conventional notions of gender. Plural marriage elevated the status of leading men while flattening the distance between wives and servants. It loosened bonds between husbands and wives and created complicated new relationships among women. It liberated male sexuality by broadening the boundaries of marriage, a practice that also allowed women who might otherwise have remained single to become mothers. By sanctifying both marriage and reproduction, it encouraged population growth and accommodated geographic expansion. In combination with divorce it enlarged the principle of consent in marriage. Every one of these conclusions, however, needs to be qualified by time, place, and the particulars of individual families.

References

Basch, N., 1999. *Framing American Divorce: From the Revolutionary Generation to the Victorians*. Berkeley, CA: University of California Press.
Beecher, M.U., 1991. *Eliza and Her Sisters*. Salt Lake City, UT: Aspen Books.
Bennion, L.C., 1984. The Incidence of Mormon Polygamy in 1880: "Dixie" versus Davis Stakes. *Journal of Mormon History* 11: 27–42.
Bennion, L.C., 2013. Plural Marriage, 1841–1904. In B.S. Plewe, ed. *Mapping Mormonism: An Atlas of Latter-day Saint History*. Provo, UT: Brigham Young University Press, pp. 122–25.
Bennion, L.C., Morrell, A.T., and Carter, T., 2005. *Polygamy in Lorenzo Snow's Brigham City: An Architectural Tour*. Salt Lake City, UT: Western Regional Architecture Program, University of Utah.
Butler-Palmer, C., 2013. Building Autonomy: A History of the Fifteenth Ward Hall of the Mormon Women's Relief Society. *Buildings and Landscapes* 29: 69–94.
Carter, T., 2000. Living the Principle: Mormon Polygamous Housing in Nineteenth-Century Utah. *Winterthur Portfolio* 35: 223–51.

Carter, T., 2015. *Building Zion: The Material World of Mormon Settlement*. Minneapolis, MN and London: University of Minnesota Press.

Cornwall, M., Courtright, C., and Van Beek, L., 1993. How Common the Principle? Women as Plural Wives in 1860. *Dialogue* 26: 139–53.

Cott, N., 2000. *Public Vows: A History of Marriage and the Nation*. Cambridge, MA: Harvard University Press.

Daynes, K.M., 2008. *More Wives Than One: Transformation of the Mormon Marriage System, 1840–1910*. Urbana and Chicago, IL: University of Illinois Press.

Daynes, K.M., 2012. Striving to Live the Principle in Utah's First Temple City: A Snapshot of Polygamy in St. George, Utah, in 1880. *Brigham Young University Studies* 4: 69–95.

Derr, J.M., 2012. The Relief Society, 1854–1881. In B.S. Plewe, ed. *Mapping Mormonism: An Atlas of Latter-day Saint History*. Provo, UT: Brigham Young University, pp. 102–3.

Derr, J.M., Cannon, J.R., and Beecher, M.U., 1992. *Women of Covenant: The Story of Relief Society*. Salt Lake City, UT: Deseret Book.

Derr, J.M., Madsen, C.C., Holbroke, K., and Grow, M., 2016. *The First Fifty Years of Relief Society*. Salt Lake City, UT: Church Historian's Press.

Dudden, F.E., 1983. *Serving Women: Household Service in Nineteenth-Century America*. Middletown, CT: Wesleyan University Press.

Embry, J., 1987. *Mormon Polygamous Families: Life in the Principle*. Salt Lake City, UT: University of Utah Press.

Fluhman, S., 2012. *"A Peculiar People": Anti-Mormonism and the Making of Religion in Nineteenth-Century America*. Chapel Hill, NC: University of North Carolina Press.

Fox, R.W., 1999. *Trials of Intimacy: Love and Loss in the Beecher Tilton Scandal*. Chicago, IL and London: University of Chicago Press.

Givens, T., and Grow, M., 2011. *Parley P. Pratt: The Apostle Paul of Mormonism*. New York: Oxford University Press.

Gordon, S.B., 1996. "The Liberty of Self-Degradation": Polygamy, Woman Suffrage, and Consent in Nineteenth-Century America. *Journal of American History* 85: 815–47.

Gordon, S.B., 2002. *The Mormon Question: Polygamy and Constitutional Conflict in the Nineteenth Century America*. Chapel Hill, NC: University of North Carolina.

Grow, M., 2009. *"Liberty to the Downtrodden": Thomas L. Kane, Romantic Reformer*. New Haven, CT and London: Yale University Press.

Haines, M.R., 2000. The Population of the United States, 1790–1920. In S.L. Engerman, and R.E. Gallman, eds. *Cambridge Economic History of the United States*. New York: Cambridge University Press, vol. 2, pp. 157–69.

Hardy, B.C., and Erickson, D., 2001. "Regeneration; Now and Evermore!": Mormon Polygamy and the Physical Rehabilitation of Humankind. *Journal of the History of Sexuality* 10: 40–61.

Harline, P.K., 2014. *The Polygamous Wives Writing Club: From the Diaries of Mormon Pioneer Women*. New York: Oxford University Press.

Hartog, H., 2000. *Man and Wife in America: A History*. Cambridge, MA: Harvard University Press.

Horowitz, H.L., 2002. *Rereading Sex: Battles over Sexual Knowledge and Suppression in Nineteenth-Century America*. New York: Knopf.

Kerber, L.K., 1988. Separate Spheres, Female Worlds, Woman's Place: The Rhetoric of Women's History. *Journal of American History* 75: 9–39.

Klepp, S.E., 1998. Revolutionary Bodies: Women and the Fertility Transition in the Mid-Atlantic Region, 1760–1820. *Journal of American History* 85: 910–45.

Madsen, C.C., 2017. *Emmeline B. Wells: An Intimate History*. Salt Lake City, UT: University of Utah Press.

Pearson, L.M., and Madsen, C.C., 2005. Innovation and Accommodation: The Legal Status of Women in Territorial Utah, 1850–1896. In P.L. Scott and L. Thatcher, eds. *Women in Utah History: Paradigm or Paradox?* Logan, UT: Utah State University Press, pp. 36–81.

Reeve, W.P., 2015. *Religion of a Different Color: Race and the Mormon Struggle for Whiteness*. New York: Oxford University Press.

Reilly, K.A., 2013. Wronged in Her Dearest Rights: Plaintiff Wives and the Transformation of Marital Consortium, 1870–1920. *Law and History Review* 31(1): 61–99.

Schwartzberg, B., 2004. "Lots of Them Did That": Desertion, Bigamy, and Marital Fluidity in Late-Nineteenth-Century America. *Journal of Social History* 37(3): 573–600.

Talbot, C., 2013. *A Foreign Kingdom: Mormons and Polygamy in American Political Culture, 1852–1890*. Champaign, IL: University of Illinois Press.
Ulrich, L.T., 2007. *Well-behaved Women Seldom Make History*. New York: Knopf.
Ulrich, L.T., 2016. Runaway Wives, 1830–1860. *Journal of Mormon History* 42: 1–26.
Ulrich, L.T., 2017a. *A House Full of Females: Plural Marriage and Women's Rights in Early Mormonism, 1835–1870*. New York: Knopf.
Ulrich, L.T., 2017b. Afterword: Useful History. *Gender & History* 29(3): 732–41.

Further reading

The following works provide comparative frameworks for understanding the practice of plural marriage in nineteenth-century Utah.

Bennion, J., and Joffe, L.F. eds., 2015. *The Polygamy Question*. Boulder, CO: University of Colorado Press.
Carter, S., 2008. *The Importance of Being Monogamous: Marriage and Nation Building in Western Canada to 1915*. Edmonton: University of Alberta Press.
Hyde, A.F., 2011. *Empires, Nations, and Families: A History of the North American West, 1800–1860*. Lincoln, NE: University of Nebraska Press.
Pearsall, S.M.S., 2019. *Polygamy: An Early American History*. New Haven, CT: Yale University Press.
Witte, J., Jr., 2015. *The Western Case for Monogamy over Polygamy*. New York: Cambridge University Press.

8
MORMON WOMEN AND SCRIPTURE IN THE NINETEENTH CENTURY

Amy Easton-Flake

To inspire Mormon women to study the scriptures, Hannah Tapfield King penned the following lines for the *Woman's Exponent* in 1878:

> There is ever an inspiration in the Scriptures that I feel in no other book … These Scriptures have fed the world for generations with "food convenient to them," and many have been enlightened, strengthened and invigorated by them for the journey of life, and the trials that "flesh is heir to." There they have beheld themselves as in a mirror, their experience has been mapped out before them, and there they have also found the panacea for them.
>
> *(1878a, p. 11)*

King's assertion of the scriptures' divine authority and ability to enlighten, strengthen, console, and guide readers places her in the mainstream of nineteenth-century American religious thought. Despite the gradual erosion of the Bible's significance in American consciousness after the Civil War, the Bible remained "the most imported, most printed, most distributed, and most read written text in North America up through the nineteenth century" (Gutjahr, 1999, p. 1). Consequently, studies of how individuals used and interpreted the Bible may provide significant insights into how religious individuals understood and navigated their lives. This chapter examines nineteenth-century Mormon women's use of scriptures—the Bible as well as scriptures particular to The Church of Jesus Christ of Latter-day Saints—as recorded in journals, autobiographies, and the *Woman's Exponent*.[1]

The Bible in nineteenth-century America

Scholars have long recognized the broadly based and widely shared biblicism that superseded racial, gender, and class divisions in nineteenth-century America. The Bible's significance in American consciousness prior to the Civil War is difficult to overstate, as it served as the main source of learning in schools and homes, laid forth the terms by which one earned and accounted for authority, and taught a language of self-understanding. The Bible's authority was not static but was continuously established as individuals and the nation turned to it for direction on living a Christian life as well as for the answers to religious, social, and political issues (Noll, 2002, pp. 375–79; Perry, 2018, pp. 1–9, 76; Kaestle, 1983, pp. 45–51). Mormons shared the populist, literal hermeneutic that dominated nineteenth-century American understanding of the Bible (e.g., Eve was created from Adam's rib) (Barlow, 2013, p. 10). Informed by the most influential epistemologies in early nineteenth-century America—Scottish Common Sense Realism and Baconian Science, which emphasized that individuals' senses could provide direct and uncomplicated knowledge of the world that was available and comprehensible to all—Americans privileged common sense or "literal" readings of the Bible that were thought to be apparent to everyone. They believed that the Bible had direct application to modern times, the meaning of scripture was clear and unchanging, biblical narratives were real and accurate, religion and science were compatible, and prophetic statements were the word of God and were to be fulfilled exactly as written, often in nineteenth-century America (Marsden, 1982, pp. 80–84; Noll, 2002, pp. 376–85).

In the last third of the nineteenth century, Americans' understanding of the Bible underwent significant changes as new findings from historians, archaeologists, and world travelers provided access to the ancient world of the Bible and allowed it to be approached in scientific, historical, and new theological terms. The discovery of earlier New Testament manuscripts and the project of revising the King James Version of the Bible in light of new understanding of Hebrew and Greek eroded some people's belief in the Bible's infallibility as transmission and translation issues came to light. Greater acceptance of Darwin's theory of evolution and geological evidence that pointed to the earth being millions of years old also led some to question the veracity of the Bible (Taylor and Weir, 2006, pp. 11–12). Where the Bible and science had previously been seen as compatible, the two now seemed to some to be at odds. Scholars of the Bible now engaged in "so-called lower criticism—textual criticism that aimed at establishing the original text of scripture free from mistranslations—and higher criticism which sought to discover the historical background of the biblical texts, their authors, sources, and literary characteristics" (Gifford, 1985, p. 22).

However, the writings of laypeople—both men and women—found within the popular press reveal that, although individuals at times brought insights from science, history, and geography to inform their reading of the Bible, the focus remained on spiritual and theological understandings of the text (de Groot and Taylor, 2007, p. 9). Some of the most common features of this noncritical approach were searching for timeless and universal truths; emphasizing connections between biblical characters' lives and the lives of the readers; drawing moral inferences; using the New Testament as a lens to interpret the Old Testament; and employing various modes of interpretation including typology, association, and proof texting (Taylor and Weir, 2006, pp. 15–17). For most believers throughout the nineteenth century, the Bible remained the infallible word of God and practical uses of scripture dominated. Individuals appropriated the text to make sense of their own lives as they turned to it for guidance and comfort (Noll, 1986, pp. 11–12, 27–31). Though significant differences do exist in the biblical exegesis written at the beginning and the end of the nineteenth century, differences over time become much less significant when we focus on ordinary individuals' use and appropriation of the Bible in their daily writings and lives.

Nineteenth-century Mormons and scripture

By and large, members of the Church of Jesus Christ readily fit within this overview of Americans' use and interpretation of scripture in the nineteenth century. What most differentiates them from their Christian contemporaries was their acceptance of the Book of Mormon and Doctrine and Covenants as scripture. Throughout the 1830s and 1840s as Joseph Smith introduced new works of revelation and religious counsel; these works were regarded as scripture by adherents of the faith and incorporated into religious worship (Johnson, 2018). Nevertheless, the Bible, as judged by the frequency of its incorporation into religious sermons and writings intended for both public and private consumption, remained the primary religious text for members of the Church of Jesus Christ of Latter-day Saints throughout the nineteenth century (Underwood, 1984; Easton-Flake, forthcoming). When one considers both the Bible's preeminent status in nineteenth-century America and the vast number of Mormons at this time who were converts from Protestant faiths, this finding is unsurprising. What is perhaps surprising is that no definite distinction can be made between why and how Mormons used and incorporated these different works of scripture. Such a finding reinforces that all these texts were considered scripture and indicates that the decision of which scriptural text to incorporate was likely simply a matter of familiarity and expediency.

Similar to the laity's use of scripture in Protestant faiths, Mormons' use and interpretation of scripture remained relatively consistent throughout the nineteenth century. The one notable exception to this narrative of continuity was the gradual decline of what American religious historian David Hall calls "patchwork quoting"—the incorporation of language, phrases, and allusions from biblical texts into their own writings—over the course of the nineteenth century (1989, p. 28). Lucy Mack Smith's 1853 family memoir provides an excellent example of "patchwork quoting" as scriptural references are a defining characteristic of her writing—a single sentence frequently contains multiple scriptural allusions. For example,

> [Smith] reproaches the three men who have purchased their farm by fraudulent means of thrusting the family "straightway into the common air like the beasts of the field or the fowls of Heaven with naught but <the> earth for a resting place and the canopy of He the skies for a covering." Compare Daniel 2:38 ("the beasts of the field and the fowls of the heaven"), Numbers 10:33 ("a resting place"), Proverbs 20:14 ("it is naught ... but"), and Psalms 105:39 ("a cloud for a covering").
>
> *(Quoted in Anderson, 2001, p. 14)*

Smith's ability to effortlessly blend Bible references together to describe feelings and events reflects both the importance of the Bible to her personally and "the nearly ubiquitous bearing of the Bible on American consciousness" prior to the Civil War, as observed by Noll (2002, p. 371). That Smith's memoir and letters also abound in Book of Mormon phraseology illustrates that it too was accepted as scripture (Johnson, 2018, pp. 34–36). While some Mormon women born a generation after Smith (b. 1775), such as Eliza R. Snow (b. 1804) and Hannah Tapfield King (b. 1808), still displayed great knowledge and use of the Bible by frequently integrating scripture into their writings, a notable distinction in their use of scriptural references remains. While Snow and King most often attended to one scripture at a time and often placed quotation marks around a scripture to set it off from surrounding text, Smith effortlessly blended multiple scriptural passages and used almost no quotation marks. This difference exemplifies the decline in "patchwork quoting" noted by David Hall and other scholars of American religious history.

Yet notably while the frequency of scriptural usage subsided over the nineteenth century, the principal reasons why Mormon women referenced and used the scriptures remained constant. Similar to their Protestant contemporaries, Mormon women throughout the nineteenth century primarily used scriptures to praise God, provide comfort, encourage desired behaviors, fashion their lives, explain religious doctrine, and argue for the correctness of certain political or social views (Easton-Flake, 2017, p. 91). Likewise, the methods they employed to understand scripture remained fairly consistent throughout the century as they too shared the common nineteenth-century sensibility that scriptures may be interpreted without any mediating guide. Consequently, this analysis of nineteenth-century Mormon women's use of the scriptures does not track changes over the century but rather focuses on providing insights into why and how Mormon women incorporated scripture into their lives as preserved in their writings while noting significant points of connection and divergence between Mormon and Protestant women, Mormon women and men, and public and private writings.

Biblical usage within the mainstream

As evidenced in both their public and private writings, Mormon women frequently turned to scriptures to find comfort amidst difficulties. Most prevalent are scriptures asserting God's control and watchful care of his people. Whether it was the persecution in Nauvoo, the harsh conditions of Winter Quarters, or the struggles of daily life in territorial Utah, women found comfort in remembering that "not a hair of your head shall fall to the ground unnoticed" (Luke 21:18; Ruth, 1886, p. 51). By viewing their suffering as trials intended to purify and qualify them, women found purpose in their extremities: "It is through suffering that we are to be made perfect" (Hebrews 2:10; Tracy, 1816–1846, pp. 60–68). Similarly, they reminded themselves and one another that "God has promised that all things shall work together for the good of those who love Him and keep His commandments" (Romans 8:28; Tanner, 1980, p. 71; Beecher, 2000, p. 133; Cuyler, 1891, p. 130). Even in the face of death and immense suffering, they asserted, "He hath done all things well" (Mark 7:37; King, 1864–1872, pp. 82, 134; E.C.F, 1889, p. 32; Alder, 1893, p. 166).

In Mary Jane Tanner's letter to her aunt (August 6, 1879), we see how she combined counsel found in different scriptures to create the comfort she needed following the deaths of three of her eight children. "I would rather bear children to die than not bear them, for I am laying up treasure in heaven where wealth nor rust doth corrupt, and some day they will be stars in my crown of glory" (1980, p. 176; phrases found in Matthew 6:19–20, Revelation 12:1, Doctrine and Covenants 75:5, and 1 Corinthians 9:25). This merging of different phrases scattered throughout scriptures to create the rationale needed to face a current difficulty was a common practice among Mormon women, as was applying scriptures to circumstances not intended by the original writer. As Tanner wrote, "It is hard to lay our beautiful ones away, but they are in God's keeping. Christ said let little children come to me" (1980, p. 176). When Christ spoke these words to his disciples (see Luke 18:16), he spoke of children coming to him in life, not in death. But here Tanner extracted Christ's words from their original context to make them speak to her own contemporary need. In doing so, she exemplifies the fact that most laymen and laywomen, members of the Church of Jesus Christ and those of other faiths, were not primarily concerned with scriptures' original meanings but rather their practical uses.

One way in which this is displayed repeatedly in women's private writings, but also on occasion in their public writings, is in their use of scriptures to narrate their lives. For instance, Hannah Tapfield King used Proverbs 31:27 to describe her mother: she "looked well to the ways of her household and ate not the bread of idleness," and Matthew 18:4 to describe her father: he was "humble before his God as a little child!" (1864–1872, p. 2). When King chose whom to marry, she described herself as "halting between two opinions" from 1 Kings 18:21 (p. 6). And later in life when her only son left to serve a mission for the Church, she described herself as being like both "Hannah of old who gave her son to the Lord" and Abraham who was willing to sacrifice Isaac for the Lord (p. 131). These examples illustrate how women turned to the Bible not only for comfort and religious instruction but also for a language of self-understanding. Women sanctified their lives, finding greater purpose and connection to God as they saw themselves as offering their "widow's mite" or being like Abraham following the Lord "not knowing whither we go," but trusting that the "Lord will go before us, and be our frontward and rearward" (Jolley, 1880, p. 2; Randall, 1846, p. 144).

In writings intended for public consumption, the dominant practical use of scriptures shifted from describing life events to teaching what it meant to live a sanctified life and providing encouragement to do so. Christ's Sermon on the Mount as recorded in Matthew 5–7 was the most frequently cited scripture block (referenced at least 170 times) in the *Woman's Exponent*. Women turned to it to encourage readers to be meek, merciful, pure in heart; to be peacemakers, to love their enemies, to live the higher laws of the Gospel, to have correct motives, to be the salt of the earth and the beacon set upon a hill. Readers were reminded to "seek ye first the kingdom of God, and his righteousness, and all these things shall be added unto you" (Matthew 6:33). Scriptures throughout the New Testament were used to encourage faith, repentance, forgiveness, and gratitude; while scriptures in the Old Testament, Book of Mormon, and Doctrine and Covenants were more often used to warn of pride, vanity, and idleness (e.g., Proverbs 16:18, Doctrine and Covenants 90:17, 1 Nephi 12:18, Job 5:7, Proverbs 31:26–27, and Doctrine and Covenants 88:124). Women were regularly encouraged to devote their lives to performing good works and laboring in the Lord's vineyard—to be constantly vigilant and to "hold to the iron rod" (Anon, 1890a, p. 52). And above all other qualities, they were instructed to develop the Christ-like attribute of charity. Paul's hymn of charity recorded in 1 Corinthians 13 was frequently quoted, as were specific moments in Christ's life that displayed charity in action (Kimball, 1881, p. 187; Myers, 1887, p. 51). Charity was used both in the sense of physical charity (giving to the poor, comforting people) and also in the sense of the love Christ has for everyone (including enemies and persecutors) (Richards, 1899, p. 28; Kimball, 1882, p. 169).

Women encouraged others to develop charity and the other attributes of a saint by citing scriptures that spoke of the blessings that would come from following God's counsel and the punishments that would come if they did not. While occasionally scriptures would refer to blessings and punishment that could occur in this life (for example, the deserts of Utah now "blossom like the rose" [Isaiah 35:1]), most often scriptures referred to the next life (Anon, 1880, p. 20; Pulsipher, 1799–1886). Various scriptures from Christ's Olivet Discourse were frequently cited to incite readers to constant vigilance as "no man knoweth the hour of his coming" (Matthew 24:36; Wells, 1893, p. 115). The most oft cited scripture from Christ's Olivet Discourse, however, was one of hope. "Well done good and faithful servants: enter thou into the glory of thy Lord" (Matthew 25:21; B.M., 1881, p. 50). Focusing on promised rewards of "rest," "glory," and being "joint heirs with Christ," writers motivated their readers to live more consecrated lives and rely more fully on the Lord.

As discussed to this point, Mormon women's deployment of scriptures could effectively describe nineteenth-century Protestant women as well. The focus on finding comfort in scriptures by pointing to God's watchful care; the call to develop Christ-like attributes such as love, mercy, humility, and obedience; and the mention of rewards or punishments waiting in the next life are also found in the numerous Protestant journals published throughout the nineteenth century. Similar to the *Woman's Exponent*, Protestant journals ran and edited by women proliferated, at least in part, because of women's self-understanding that they were to teach and minister to the young, the poor, the sick, the uneducated, and the nonreligious. Having become the moral guardians of the home at the beginning of the nineteenth century, women soon extended this role outside the home to become the moral guardians of society, and in this position, they gained the authority to instruct and influence society (Frank, 1998, pp. 26–35; Ryan, 1981, pp. 75–98). That the bulk of women's scriptural usage, no matter the religious affiliation, was dedicated to teaching and promoting moral conduct underlines how this pervasive self-construct created points of connection among nineteenth-century women.

Distinguishing scriptural usage

The differences between nineteenth-century Mormons' and Protestants' use of scriptures surface when one looks at doctrines peculiar to the Church of Jesus Christ of Latter-day Saints, such as the practice of polygamy; their understanding of themselves as part of God's covenant relationship with Israel; their teachings on apostasy and restoration; and their emphasis on priesthood, proper authority, and continuing prophets, prophecies, and revelation. It is noteworthy that, with the one prominent exception of polygamy, articles and scriptures devoted to explaining these unique Church doctrines appear only sporadically in the writings of Mormon women but proliferate in the publications of Mormon men. To say that women did not write about the doctrines that distinguish Mormons would be inaccurate, as scriptures on baptism, apostasy, and restoration appear a handful of times in their writings, while scriptures on the need for priesthood, proper authority, prophets, and continual revelation make a more frequent appearance. However, the vast statistical discrepancy between occurrences in the *Millennial Star* and the *Woman's Exponent* indicates that this was not a central function of women's scriptural engagement (Easton-Flake, 2020). Given women's societal place and self-understanding at the time, Mormon women's decision to focus on scriptures that promoted the accepted and common morality of nineteenth-century America is fitting.

The one glaring exception to this rule was the abundance of scriptural exposition dedicated to supporting and explaining plural marriage. From 1880 to 1889 14 percent of all biblical passages cited in the *Woman's Exponent* dealt with polygamy (Easton-Flake, 2020). Though at first this may seem like an aberration from women chiefly using scriptures for practical uses, when one considers the intense persecution that Mormons faced for this practice in the 1880s and the effect of this persecution on the daily lives of the people as a whole, one realizes it is not. The Edmunds Act passed by Congress in 1882 made polygamy a felony. Many polygamists were imprisoned, went into hiding, or cut off relations with plural wives. Five years later, persecution intensified when the passing of the Edmunds-Tucker Act in 1887 stripped Utah women of their right to vote and dis-incorporated the Church of Jesus Christ of Latter-day Saints. Though historians estimate that in the late nineteenth century only 15–20 percent of Mormon women were plural wives, monogamous and polygamous women saw this as an attack on their community and freedom to worship (Embry and Kelley, 2005, pp. 11–12). Writers for the *Woman's Exponent* vigorously defended the practice in nearly 10 percent of the *Woman's Exponent* editorials from 1871 until 1890 (Madsen, 1992, p. 72). Strikingly, after the 1890 Manifesto, a declaration offered by Church President Wilford Woodruff that officially ended the practice within the faith, not a single scriptural reference to polygamy appeared in the *Woman's Exponent*.

The Mormons' choice of defense for plural marriage was the biblical precedent; consequently, the *Woman's Exponent* and other publications of the Church of Jesus Christ of Latter-day Saints contain numerous references to the plural marriages in the Bible as well as Christ's polygamous lineage (Smith, 2014, p. 112). Speaking directly to those who tried to stop polygamy, Mormon writers warned, "What God has joined together let no man put asunder" (Mark 10:9; Pratt, 1882, p. 91). Many Mormons regarded plural marriage as evidence that they were the inheritors of the Abrahamic covenant, and they frequently cited Peter's words from Acts that "all things [must] be restored again as they were in the beginning" (Acts 3:21) to explain why they believed God had commanded Joseph Smith to restore the ancient practice (Whitney, 1881, p. 66). Seeking other explanations from the Bible as to the purpose of plural marriage, writers repeatedly cited Isaiah's words of warning about the dearth of righteous men, "That seven women will take hold of one man, saying, we will eat our own bread and wear our own apparel, only let us be called by thy name, to take away our reproach" (Isaiah 4:1) as well as the words of Jacob from the Book of Mormon, "For if I will, saith the Lord of Hosts, raise up seed unto me, I will command my people [to practice plural marriage]; otherwise they shall hearken unto these things [the law of monogamy]" (Jacob 2:30; M.F., 1882, p. 135; Tanner, 1980, p. 188; Pratt, 1884, p. 99). Both of these scriptures point to a common perception among the Mormon people that the Lord needed them to practice plural marriage at this time in order to, as Susa Young Gates wrote, "raise a righteous and numerous seed for the fulfilling of his great latter-day purposes" (1882, p. 82). In defending polygamy, men and women used similar scriptures and rationales. The one noteworthy distinction along gender lines was the higher rate at which women mentioned specific women who practiced polygamy anciently. Women writers, for instance, were particularly fond of interpreting the Lord's answering of Hagar's, Sarah's, and Hannah's prayers as evidence of his divine approval of plural marriage and his watchful care over plural wives both in ancient times and in the nineteenth century (Easton-Flake, 2017, pp. 97–98). Given that the *Woman's Exponent* was regarded as a space where Mormon women could represent themselves and their religious beliefs to the world, it is not surprising that virtually every reference to polygamy is positive.

Women's private writings provide a more balanced view of women's attitude towards polygamy—here they record how they used scriptures to both sacralize this practice and to help them through their struggles with this practice. Sarah DeArmon Pea Rich, for instance, saw her actions as linking her to the ancient matriarchs: "Like Sarah of old, I had in that temple given to my husband four other wives" (1885). Phoebe W. Carter Woodruff described the "wrestle" she had with "Heavenly Father in fervent prayer" to gain her own spiritual witness that plural marriage was of God (quoted in Tullidge, 1877, p. 413). The decision for her was not an easy one. Mary Jane Mount Tanner expressed the challenges and sorrows that came for her when her husband married a second wife and explained how "we carry our burdens to Him. For He has said, 'Come unto me all ye who are weary and heavy laden. For my yoke is easy and my burden is light'" (Matthew 11:30; Tanner, 1980, p. 189). Being in a polygamous marriage was clearly difficult for Tanner, but she found comfort in the promises she read in the scriptures. Mary Lois Walker Morris' description of entering plural marriage as "drink[ing] this bitter cup" is particularly interesting because even as it sacralized the action by linking it with Christ's ultimate act of love and submission to God's will, it also emphasized Morris' abhorrence of plural marriage and her view of it as her ultimate act of submitting to God's will (quoted in Milewski, 2007, p. 123). Studying Mormon women's use of scripture in relation to plural marriage provides a microcosm of the ways women used scriptures to find comfort, explain religious doctrine, encourage desired behaviors, and—most significantly in this case—argue for the correctness of certain political and social views.

Scripture usage to aid women

What is perhaps most intriguing from a gender perspective is how some nineteenth-century Mormon women used scriptures to assert women's equality, gendered capabilities and worth, and increasing expansion into public realms. As the *Woman's Exponent*'s stated purpose was to build one another through the "diffusion of knowledge and information" and to correct the "gross misrepresent[ations]" of Mormon women found within the popular press (Greene, 1872, p. 8), it is fitting that over 10 percent of all scriptures referenced in the *Woman's Exponent* were employed to improve the status of women. In contrast, Mormon women rarely used scriptures for this purpose in their private writings. This marked variance not only underlines the different purposes that motivated women to write for public as opposed to private audiences but also demonstrates women's awareness of scripture as a powerful rhetorical tool. By and large, writers for the *Woman's Exponent* sought to portray Mormon women as capable, intelligent, independent agents with crucial roles to play in society and God's kingdom. They often sought to raise the status of motherhood and women's domestic labor even as they advocated expanding women's field of action. Likewise, they extolled women's unique virtues in relation to men's, even as they asserted her fundamental equality with men. As scriptures represented truth and the word of God for these believers, writers turned to them often for examples of the Lord's regard for woman, her contributions to building God's kingdom, and her equality with man (Easton-Flake, 2017, pp. 92–95; 2018, p. 1104). For instance, a number of writers recounted Paul's words, "Man is not without the woman, nor the woman without the man in the Lord" (1 Corinthians 11:11) to validate their argument that men and women are equal before God (L.E.H., 1882, pp. 17–18; Anon, 1887, p. 63).

The creation narrative in Genesis was the scripture block Mormon women most frequently enlisted in the service of women's advancement. This is to be expected as it was the foundational text used for debating and defining the status and role of women in nineteenth-century America. The discrepancies between the two creation stories in Genesis 1 and 2 as well as the significant ambiguities within them allowed all sides to use this section to promote their views on the question of women's position in the nineteenth century (Taylor and Weir, 2006, pp. 21–24). Mormon women, similar to other nineteenth-century women who used this narrative to advocate for women's increased status, focused on the creation account in Genesis 1 in which male and female are created together rather than Genesis 2 in which Eve is created only after all other creatures have been eliminated as adequate companions for Adam (Genesis 2:20; Horne, 1895, p. 77; Richards, 1890, p. 71; Kimball, 1892, p. 149). Writers used this initial creation passage to affirm the equality of the sexes—God established equality between man and woman at the beginning when he made them both simultaneously in his image and gave them both dominion over every living thing. As Mary Ann M. Pratt emphasized, "And God said I have given you (not him), speaking to the man and woman, all things bearing seed upon all the face of the earth." Pratt then used this as evidence that women should have the vote and an equal voice in politics and society (1891, p. 189).

Recognizing that other readings of the creation narrative were possible, some women refuted or revised these other interpretations in their writings and in the process, at times, emphasized doctrine particular to their faith. Ruby Lamont, for instance, reinterpreted what it meant for Eve to be made out of Adam's rib: "May we not read an *equality* in the glorious symbol, a side by side companionship, an 'I am king and thou my sister queen,' (for God bade *them* have dominion)," and in the process possibly alluded to Mormons' belief in being kings and queens, priests and priestesses in the next life (1895, p. 7). Mormons' view of the Fall as a planned and necessary part of God's plan—an understanding that stems from restoration scripture—provided Mormon women with a framework that enabled them to more easily dismiss the issue of Eve's culpability and to see her in a heroic light. The views of Eve, the Fall, and "the curse" preserved in the *Woman's Exponent* are fascinating and far from monolithic (Petersen, 2014, pp. 135–74). Collectively, they also offer a significant example of how Mormons' expanded canon and unique doctrines—such as their teachings on apostasy and restoration, their understanding of themselves as part of God's covenant relationship with Israel, and their beliefs in regard to premortal and postmortal life—often impacted their readings of the Bible and set them apart from their fellow Christians (Easton-Flake, 2018, pp. 1107–10).

Common ground among Mormon women and their fellow nineteenth-century Christians is again found, however, when one looks at how they used biblical women and Christ's interactions with women to bring increased recognition to women's gendered attributes and the crucial roles women play in family, public, and religious life. Irrespective of their religious tradition, women most often used their readings of biblical women, as Joy A. Schroeder found, "to elevate their audience's view of women, encourage female readers to appreciate their gifts and recognise that they had a worthy heritage," a view in full accordance with nineteenth-century women's understanding that their primary responsibilities lay within the family (2014, p. 161; cf. Rose, 1995; Newton, 1994, pp. 43–46).

Mormon women's exegesis of biblical women adds further evidence to Schroeder's finding, as they at times read against the grain or pointed out oft neglected aspects of the text to help their readers see and celebrate the influence and power women could wield within familial roles and relations. For instance, in relating the family dynamics of Rebekah and Isaac, Adelia B. Cox Sidwell explained how "God not only acknowledged, approved and honoured [Rebekah's] will, but relied upon her fine powers of discretion, and discernment of character" to ensure that Jacob, who was God's son of choice, received the birthright blessing (1890, p. 136). At another time, Sidwell reframed Peter's injunction, "Wives obey your husbands even as Sarah obeyed Abraham," by reminding her audience what Sarah's obedience looked like in the narrative: "We read that Sarah wanted Abraham to do something that was 'very grievous' to him, and that God said unto him, 'In all that Sarah hath said unto thee, hearken unto her voice,' and Abraham did accordingly; comment is unnecessary" (1889, p. 1). Mormon women also echoed the expressions of women's exalted piety and purity that were standard fare in nineteenth-century America and Great Britain and showed biblical women to be influential as they remained "pure, chaste, and good" (King, 1878b, p. 14; cf. Hogan and Bradstock, 1966, pp. 1–5; Welter, 1966). Thus, most Mormon writers fit nicely within the ranks of the nineteenth-century interpreters and female activists who used scripture to illustrate the power women wielded within traditional gender behaviors and relationships and to show that familial roles were not limiting or disempowering but expansive (Brekus, 1998, pp. 149–53; Taylor and Weir, 2006, pp. 84–90, 269–80, 377–82; Easton-Flake, 2018, pp. 1106–16).

Likewise, Mormon women echoed an oft used argument of female activists when they explained that their public activism was simply an extension of their familial roles and listed biblical women who had played prominent political and/or religious roles to justify their own seemingly unconventional public behavior (Easton-Flake, 2018, p. 96). Deborah, a judge in Israel for forty years, was the favorite proof text not only of God's approval of female political leadership but also of society's need for motherhood and feminine virtue in the political sphere (Schroeder, 2014, pp. 155, 161, 180–84; Anon, 1876, p. 84; Anon, 1890b, p. 149; Anon, 1879, p. 76). As one *Woman's Exponent* author wrote, "So beautiful in character, so noble in life, her genius was superior to any recorded in the history of the Hebrews, and she alone has escaped unreproved by prophets and historians" (Smith, 1890, p. 177). Similarly, the regard men displayed in the ancient world to the prophetesses Huldah and Miriam was used as rationale for men in the nineteenth century to give women the vote (Woodmansee, 1890, p. 29; Easton-Flake, 2017, p. 96).

Perhaps most persuasively, Mormon women joined women of other faiths in using Christ's interactions with women to argue for the Lord's great regard for women and their position as integral actors in helping God achieve his purposes in ancient and modern times (Hardesty, 1984, p. 63; Bidlack, 2010, p. 140). As one Mormon woman wrote, the Bible provides "abundant testimonies that God acknowledges woman as capable of thinking and acting for herself" and that he trusts them and uses them as significant actors in his work (Anon, 1879, p. 76). As multiple *Woman's Exponent* authors recounted, "It was a woman who oftenest ministered to the wants of the son of God, who believed in and followed him, but it was not a woman who betrayed him" (Young, 1889, p. 139).

> Woman alone pressed her way to the very foot of the cross ... Woman embalmed his precious body. Woman first greeted him when he burst the bonds of death and triumphed over the grave ... Twas woman who was first commissioned to go and proclaim the glad tidings of his resurrection, And woman today stands among the foremost in her Master's work.
>
> *(Smith, 1890, p. 177)*

As another *Woman's Exponent* writer elaborated,

> In fact one cannot help thinking the Savior himself set this glorious example of giving to woman a divine mission, when he said to Mary and other women who were with her, "Go tell my brethren &c." There have been times in the history of the world as recorded in the Scriptures when the most important questions have been settled by women.
>
> *(Anon, 1891, p. 164)*

Nineteenth-century Mormon women joined with women of other faiths in viewing themselves not as second-class citizens but as valued members of God's kingdom who could actively take part in Christian duties, family life, and civil affairs as did their foremothers in biblical times (Easton-Flake, 2017, pp. 92–97; 2018, p. 1116).

Conclusion

As Philip Barlow writes, "The Mormon identification with biblical peoples, events, and prophecies was experientially more all-encompassing than that of any other major group during the nineteenth century" (2013, p. 109). Unsurprisingly then, when nineteenth-century Mormon women sought to find models for themselves and create their own space within their community, they often turned to the same place where their male counterparts found a sense of identity: the scriptures. While members of the Church of Jesus Christ of Latter-day Saints throughout the nineteenth century continued to reference the Bible more frequently in their writings than they did restoration scripture, they clearly embraced their extra-biblical canon and read the different works in relation to the others. As Helen Mar Whitney wrote in 1884,

> Had we nothing more than the present translation of the Bible to depend upon we should be as much at sea concerning the Gospel and our future state as the rest of the world appear to be. But the revelations given to us through the Prophet Joseph Smith throw new light upon the Scriptures, and a great deal that was once a dead letter can now be interpreted; and we, therefore, take a more consistent and enlightened view of the Scriptures, which previous to this was as a sealed book.
>
> *(1884, p. 145)*

The Church's emphasis on an expanded canon and prophetic and personal revelation to facilitate the meaning of scripture had, at times, a significant impact on their reading of scripture. This may be seen whenever a doctrine particular to the faith tradition is discussed, but it is particularly noticeable in nineteenth-century Mormon women's discussions of polygamy and Eve.

More often than not, though, Mormon women's exposition of scripture remains undifferentiated from their Protestant contemporaries as they primarily used scriptures to praise God, provide comfort, encourage desired behaviors, fashion their lives, explain religious doctrine, and argue for the correctness of certain political and social views. They shared the populist, literal hermeneutic that dominated nineteenth-century Americans' understanding of the Bible, and they primarily took a noncritical approach to scriptures as they sought for timeless and universal truths, found connections between biblical characters' lives and their own, and drew moral inferences. Mormon women, similar to women of other faith traditions, appropriated scriptures to make sense of their own lives as they turned to them for guidance and comfort. As Hannah Tapfield King wrote to her readers at the end of *Women of the Scriptures*, "The models are fine and we should copy them" (1878b, p. 23).

Note

1 The *Woman's Exponent* was a bimonthly newspaper that played a significant role in Utah and in the Mormon Church from 1872 to 1914. Never owned or officially sponsored by the Mormon Church—although Church leadership did approve of it—the *Woman's Exponent* was run entirely by women and provided a space for them to freely express their viewpoints and interests.

References

Alder, L.D., 1893. To My Dear Friend, Camilla C. Cobb. *Woman's Exponent* 21(22): 166.
Anderson, L.F. ed., 2001. *A Critical Edition of Lucy Mack Smith's Family Memoir*. Salt Lake City, UT: Signature Books.
Anonymous, 1876. Be Wise and Hearken to Counsel. *Woman's Exponent* 5(11): 84.
Anonymous, 1879. Wise Women of Scripture. *Woman's Exponent* 8(10): 76.
Anonymous, 1880. Jubilee Celebration. *Woman's Exponent* 9(3): 20.
Anonymous, 1887. Woman's Voice. *Woman's Exponent* 16(8): 63.
Anonymous. 1890a. The Times in Which We Are Living. *Woman's Exponent* 19(7): 52.
Anonymous, 1890b. The Days of the Judges. *Woman's Exponent* 18(19): 149.
Anonymous, 1891, Woman's Special Mission. *Woman's Exponent* 19(21): 164.
B.M., 1881. Woman's Voice. *Woman's Exponent* 10(7): 50.
Barlow, P., 2013. *Mormons and the Bible: The Place of the Latter-day Saints in American Religion*. 2nd ed. New York: Oxford University Press.
Beecher, M. ed., 2000. *Personal Writings of Eliza Roxcy Snow*. Logan, UT: Utah State University Press.
Bidlack, B., 2010. Olympia Brown: Reading the Bible as a Universalist Minister and Pragmatic Suffragist. In N. Calvert-Koyzis and H. Weir, eds. *Breaking Boundaries: Female Biblical Interpreters Who Challenged the Status Quo*. New York: Bloomsbury, pp. 125–43.
Brekus, C.A., 1998. *Strangers and Pilgrims: Female Preaching in America 1740–1845*. Chapel Hill, NC: University of North Carolina Press.
Cuyler, 1891. Faces in the Clouds. *Woman's Exponent* 19(17): 130.
De Groot, C., and Taylor, M.A., 2007. *Recovering Nineteenth-Century Women Interpreters of the Bible*. Atlanta, GA: Society of Biblical Literature.
E.C.F., 1889. Our Baby Girl. *Woman's Exponent* 18(4): 32.
Easton-Flake, A., 2017. Biblical Women in the *Woman's Exponent*: Nineteenth-Century Mormon Women Interpret the Bible. In P. Goff, A.E. Farnsley II, and P.J. Thuesen, eds. *The Bible in American Life*. New York: Oxford University Press, pp. 89–100.
Easton-Flake, A., 2018. Merging Mormon Women and Women of Genesis: Hannah Tapfield King's "Women of the Scriptures." *Women History's Review* 27(7): 1103–22.
Easton-Flake, A., 2020. The Bible in the *Millennial Star* and *Woman's Exponent*: Biblical Use and Interpretation in the Church of Jesus Christ in the Late Nineteenth Century. *BYU Studies* 59(4).
Embry, J.L., and Kelley, L., 2005. Polygamous and Monogamous Mormon Women: A Comparison. In P.L. Scott and L. Thatcher, eds. *Women in Utah History: Paradigm or Paradox?* Logan, UT: Utah State University Press, pp. 1–30.
Frank, S.M., 1998. *Life with Father: Parenthood and Masculinity in the Nineteenth-Century American North*. Baltimore, MD: Johns Hopkins University Press.
Gates, S.Y., 1882. Homespun Talks to Mrs. Scott. *Woman's Exponent* 11(11): 82.

Gifford, C.S., 1985. American Women and the Bible: The Nature of Woman as a Hermeneutical Issue. In A.Y. Collins, ed. *Feminist Perspectives on Biblical Scholarship*. Chico, CA: Society of Biblical Literature, pp. 11–33.

Greene, L.L., 1872. A Utah Ladies' Journal. *Woman's Exponent* 1(1): 8.

Gutjahr, P.C., 1999. *An American Bible: A History of the Good Book in the United States, 1777–1880*. Stanford, CA: Stanford University Press.

Hall, D., 1989. *Worlds of Wonder, Days of Judgment: Popular Religious Belief in Early New England*. Cambridge, MA: Harvard University Press.

Hardesty, N., 1984. *Women Called to Witness: Evangelical Feminism in the Nineteenth Century*. Nashville, TN: Abingdon Press.

Hogan, A., and Bradstock, A., 1966. *Women of Faith in Victorian Culture: Reassessing the Angel in the House*. Charlottesville, VA: University of Virginia Press.

Horne, M.I., 1895. Remarks. *Woman's Exponent* 24(11–12): 77.

Johnson, J., 2018. Becoming a People of the Books: Toward an Understanding of Early Mormon Converts and the New Word of the Lord. *Journal of Book of Mormon Studies* 27: 1–43.

Jolley, C.A., 1880. A Mother's Reflection. *Woman's Exponent* 9(1): 2.

Kaestle, C.F., 1983. *Pillars of the Republic: Common Schools and American Society, 1780–1860*. New York: Hill and Wang.

Kimball, M.E., 1881. Charity—How Defined. *Women's Exponent* 9(24): 187.

Kimball, M.E., 1882. True Charity. *Woman's Exponent* 10(22): 169.

Kimball, S.M., 1892. Relief Society Notes. *Woman's Exponent* 20(19): 149.

King, H.T., ca. 1864–1872. *Hannah Tapfield King Autobiography*. [manuscript] Church Archives. 628. Salt Lake City, UT: Church History Library.

King, H.T., 1878a. The Holy Scriptures. *Woman's Exponent* 7(2): 11.

King, H.T., 1878b. *The Women of the Scriptures*. Salt Lake City, UT: privately published.

L.E.H., 1882. Woman in Politics. *Woman's Exponent* 11(3): 17–18.

Lamont, R., 1895. Women's Suffrage. *Woman's Exponent* 24(1): 7.

M.F., 1882. Celestial Marriage. *Woman's Exponent* 10(16): 135.

Madsen, C.C., 1992. Voices in Print: The *Woman's Exponent*, 1872–1914. In D.H. Anderson and M. Cornwall, eds. *Women Steadfast in Christ*. Salt Lake City, UT: Deseret Book, pp. 69–80.

Marsden, G.M., 1982. Everyone One's Own Interpreter?: The Bible, Science, and Authority in Mid-Nineteenth-Century America. In N.O. Hatch and M.A. Noll, eds. *The Bible in America: Essays in Cultural History*. New York: Oxford University Press, pp. 79–100.

Milewski, M.L. ed., 2007. *Before the Manifesto: The Life Writings of Mary Lois Walker Morris*. Logan, UT: Utah State University Press.

Myers, E.M., 1887. Charity. *Woman's Exponent* 16(7): 51.

Newton, S.E., 1994. *Learning to Behave: A Guide to American Conduct Books before 1900*. Westport, CT: Greenwood Press.

Noll, M., 1986. *Between Faith and Criticism: Evangelicals, Scholarship, and the Bible in America*. San Francisco, CA: Harper & Row.

Noll, M.A., 2002. *America's God: From Jonathan Edwards to Abraham Lincoln*. New York: Oxford University Press.

Perry, S., 2018. *Bible Culture and Authority in the Early United States*. Princeton, NJ: Princeton University Press.

Petersen, B.J., 2014. Redeemed from the Curse Placed upon Her: Dialogic Discourse on Eve in the "Woman's Exponent." *Journal of Mormon History* 40(1): 135–74.

Pratt, M.A.M., 1882. In Answer. *Woman's Exponent* 11(12): 91.

Pratt, M.A.M., 1884. Scripture Testimony for Plural Marriage. *Woman's Exponent* 13(13): 99.

Pratt, M.A.M., 1891. Woman's Vote. *Woman's Exponent* 19(24): 189.

Pulsipher, M.B., 1799–1886. *Pulisipher, Mary Brown, 1799–1886*. [typescript, autobiography] Writings of Early Latter-day Saints and Their Contemporaries, Special Collection. Provo, UT: Harold B Lee Library. Accessed boap.org.

Randall, S., 1846. [Letter.] June 1. Published in K.W. Godfrey, A.M. Godfrey, and J.M. Derr, 1982. *Women's Voices: An Untold History of the Latter-day Saints, 1830–1900*. Salt Lake City, UT: Deseret Book, p. 144.

Rich, S.D.P., 1885. *Sarah DeAnnon Pea Rich, 1814–1893 Autobiography*. [typescript] Writings of Early Latter-day Saints and Their Contemporaries, Special Collection. Provo, UT: Harold B. Lee Library. Accessed boap.org.

Richards, L.L.G., 1899. Charity and Labor. *Woman's Exponent* 28(4): 28.
Richards, S.W., 1890. Woman's Rights. *Woman's Exponent* 19(9): 71.
Rose, J.E., 1995. Conduct Books for Women, 1830–1860: A Rationale for Women's Conduct and Domestic Role in America. In C. Hobbs, ed. *Nineteenth-Century Women Learn to Write*. Charlottesville, VA: University Press of Virginia, pp. 37–58.
Ruth, 1886. An Emphatic Protest. *Woman's Exponent* 15(7): 51.
Ryan, M.P., 1981. *The Cradle of the Middle Class: The Family in Oneida County, New York, 1790–1865*. Cambridge: Cambridge University Press.
Schroeder, J.A., 2014. *Deborah's Daughters: Gender Politics and Biblical Interpretation*. Oxford: Oxford University Press.
Sidwell, A.B.C., 1889. Woman's Influence. *Woman's Exponent* 18(1): 1.
Sidwell, A.B.C., 1890. Women of the Bible. *Woman's Exponent* 18(17): 136–37.
Smith, A.C., 2014. Hagar in LDS Scripture and Thought. *Interpreter: A Journal of Mormon Scripture* 8: 87–137.
Smith, E.F., 1890. Woman's Mind Equal to Man's. *Woman's Exponent* 18(22): 177.
Tanner, M.J.M., 1980. *A Fragment: The Autobiography of Mary Jane Mount Tanner*, ed. M.W. Ward. Salt Lake City, UT: Tanner Trust Fund University of Utah Library.
Taylor, M.A., and Weir, H.E., 2006. *Let Her Speak for Herself: Nineteenth-Century Women Writing on the Women of Genesis*. Waco, TX: Baylor University Press.
Tracy, N.N.A., 1816–1846. *Nancy Naomi Alexander Tracy, 1816–1902*. [typescript, autobiography] Writings of Early Latter-day Saints and Their Contemporaries, Special Collection. Provo, UT: Harold B. Lee Library. Accessed boap.org.
Tullidge, E.W., 1877. *Women of Mormondom*. New York: Tullidge and Crandall.
Underwood, G., 1984. Book of Mormon Usage in Early LDS Thought. *Dialogue* 17(3): 35–74.
Wells, C.C.R., 1893. The Close of the Year 1892. *Woman's Exponent* 21(15): 115.
Welter, B., 1966. The Cult of True Womanhood: 1820–1860. *American Quarterly* 18(2): 151–74.
Whitney, H.M., 1881. Scenes in Nauvoo. *Woman's Exponent* 10(9): 66.
Whitney, H.M., 1884. Answers to Woman and Sin. *Woman's Exponent* 12(19): 145.
Woodmansee, E.H., 1890. Lawn Fete. *Woman's Exponent* 19(4): 29.
Young, P.C., 1889. Woman and Her Sphere. *Woman's Exponent* 17(18): 139.

Further reading

Barlow, P., 2013. *Mormons and the Bible: The Place of the Latter-day Saints in American Religion*. 2nd ed. New York: Oxford University Press.

This book, originally published in 1991, remains the seminal text on understanding how Mormons have used and interpreted the Bible from the religion's founding in the 1830s through the end of the twentieth century.

Easton-Flake, A., 2017. Biblical Women in the *Woman's Exponent*: Nineteenth-Century Mormon Women Interpret the Bible. In P. Goff, A.E. Farnsley II, and P.J. Thuesen, eds. *The Bible in American Life*. New York: Oxford University Press, pp. 89–100.

This article focuses on how Mormon women used and interpreted the Bible in the last quarter of the nineteenth century. More particularly, it focuses on Mormon women's use of biblical women to promote their ideals of Christian womanhood, their arguments for gender equality and expansion of women's sphere, and their defense of the Mormon practice of polygamy.

Easton-Flake, A., forthcoming. Nineteenth-Century Mormon Biblical Interpretation. In T. Petrey and C. Crawford, eds. *Bible in Mormonism*. Oxford: Oxford University Press.

This chapter examines Mormons' similarities to and differences from Protestants' use of the Bible and provides a highly contextualized look at how Mormons interpreted the Bible from the founding of the Church (1830) until the end of the nineteenth century when higher criticism had made significant inroads into how Americans interpreted the Bible. In contrast to this chapter, it emphasizes change over time: 1820s–1840s, 1840s–1870s, and 1870s–1900.

Johnson, J., 2018. Becoming a People of the Books: Toward an Understanding of Early Mormon Converts and the New Word of the Lord. *Journal of Book of Mormon Studies* 27: 1–43.

This article focuses on Book of Mormon reception history in mid-nineteenth-century America. It looks at how Mormons came to accept and use it as scripture. Similar to the Bible, Mormons used the Book of Mormon to order and understand their lives.

Taylor, M.A., and Weir, H.E., 2006. *Let Her Speak for Herself: Nineteenth-Century Women Writing on the Women of Genesis.* Waco, TX: Baylor University Press.

This book provides an invaluable collection of rare primary sources. There are fifty different nineteenth-century female interpreters, of various religious backgrounds, represented in this book, which is divided into sections based on stories or characters from Genesis. The introduction offers a succinct overview of biblical interpretation and women's approaches to interpretation in nineteenth-century America.

9

MORMONISM, GENDER, AND ART IN NINETEENTH-CENTURY SCANDINAVIA

Julie K. Allen

When the first representatives of the Church of Jesus Christ of Latter-day Saints arrived in Copenhagen, Denmark in June 1850, they encountered a society transitioning from absolute monarchy to constitutional democracy. The Danish Constitution adopted a year earlier, in June 1849, had created a parliament and extended the right to vote to male heads of household, as well as establishing religious freedom and other civil rights. As tens of thousands of Danes—and soon thereafter Icelanders, Norwegians, and Swedes as well—began to exercise their right to choose a religion radically different from the Evangelical Lutheranism sponsored by the state, they were forced to reevaluate not just their doctrinal beliefs, but also their cultural, national, gender, and social identities, many of which were shaped by their religious traditions and practices. The dramatic numbers of Scandinavian converts to Mormonism in the nineteenth century and their influence as the largest non-Anglo-American ethnic group in territorial Utah make the connections between Scandinavia and Mormonism highly relevant to discussions of gender politics in the LDS Church. However, with few first-hand accounts that reflect explicitly on such negotiations, the most productive source for exploring the wide-ranging ramifications of conversion for nineteenth-century Scandinavian converts is art, both visual and literary, which can capture and render visible contemporary ideas and concerns about gender and sexuality, particularly with regard to religion. Artistic texts about and by Mormons in late nineteenth- and early twentieth-century Scandinavia, primarily Denmark, provide critical insights into how cultural norms about gender intersected with LDS doctrine, policies, and culture. This chapter will begin by examining representative works by Scandinavian visual artists that engage affirmatively with Mormon theology, gender norms, and history before turning to lesser-known literary and cinematic texts that complicate those narratives.

Rendering Mormon theology and gender ideals visible

Although they belong to the twentieth century, the works of painter Arnold Friberg (1913–2010) offer a useful starting point for reflections about Mormonism, gender, and art in nineteenth-century Scandinavia. Born in the U.S. to a Swedish father and Norwegian mother who joined the LDS Church in Phoenix, Arizona in 1920, Friberg is one of the most influential and best-known shapers of gendered Mormon art in the twentieth century. His works, in particular the illustrations of the Book of Mormon he created on commission for Adele Cannon Howells in the 1950s and 1960s, are notable for the vivid physicality of their male figures, especially the muscular depictions of scriptural heroes like Nephi, Ammon, and Captain Moroni. In the artist's own view, the muscularity in his paintings was "intended to physically portray the inward greatness of the men he depicts" (Carmack, 2000, p. 40). Friberg explained, "When I paint Nephi, I'm painting the interior, the greatness, the largeness of spirit. Who knows what he looked like? I'm painting a man who looks like he could actually do what Nephi did" (Osborne, 1984, p. 51). Some of Friberg's paintings include female figures, such as his depiction of the prophet Lehi surrounded by his sons and daughters finding the Liahona, but these women are visually as blandly nondescript as their textual equivalents. It is the men, large of stature and taut with righteous purpose, who dominate both Friberg's canvases and the scriptural stories they bring to life.

Friberg's equation of masculinity, physical strength, and spiritual stature echoes the preoccupation with physical and spiritual well-being promoted by the turn-of-the-century American religious movement known as Muscular Christianity. Although the movement was primarily a Protestant phenomenon, the LDS Church enthusiastically affirmed similar ideals of robust manliness in connection with its own attempts to join the American religious mainstream. In a *Juvenile Instructor* article in 1904, for example, LDS leader George Reynolds declared that Jesus Christ "would have been a vigorous, deep chested, broad shouldered man, with well-cut features and above the medium height, with his bodily energies developed through a life of youthful labor in Joseph's carpenter shop at Nazareth" (Reynolds, 1904, pp. 498–99). The institutionalization of the Word of Wisdom as a non-negotiable facet of Mormon identity in this era likewise coincided with more widespread American fervor for healthy living, exemplified by vegetarianism and abstinence from alcohol. Yet although Friberg's images clearly reflect their American context, as fellow LDS artist Minerva Teichert observed with approval (Barrett and Black, 2005, p. 75), they are also, particularly in the aspirational perfection of their human forms, rooted in a nineteenth-century northern European tradition of portrayals of religious subjects in both the neoclassical and realist styles.

Tracing the Scandinavian antecedents of Friberg's art back to the early nineteenth century leads to one of the most significant objects for Mormon art in the European neoclassical tradition, namely the marble statue of the *Christus* created by the Danish sculptor Bertel Thorvaldsen (1770–1844) for Vor Frue Kirke (The Church of Our Lady) in Copenhagen. Although he received his earliest artistic training from his Icelandic woodcarver father, Thorvaldsen was able to transcend his family's poverty by studying art at the Royal Danish Academy of Art in the 1780s, with such Danish masters of neoclassical painting as Nicolai Abildgaard and Johannes Wiedewelt. He traveled to Rome on a royal stipend in 1797 and spent much of his working life there, developing a distinctive heroic neoclassical style. On a visit to Denmark in 1819, he received a commission to sculpt a series of statues of Jesus Christ and his twelve apostles for the rebuilt Church of Our Lady, which had been destroyed by the British bombardment of the city in 1807. He created the statues in Rome and returned with them to Copenhagen in 1838, where he was lauded as a national hero. In its original location, the *Christus* stands in a gilded niche adorned with the words, "Kom til mig" (Come unto me), stepping forward with hands outstretched, palms up, toward the viewer. This visual depiction of a physically imposing but emotionally gentle Christ has come to exemplify the Mormon conception of deity. A lone female angel bearing a shell-shaped basin kneels in front of the *Christus*, while the twelve apostles stand in two rows down the nave, mutely testifying to Christ's divinity and visually affirming the exclusively masculine character of Christian religious authority.

Thorvaldsen's statues of Christ and his apostles have long resonated—on both a visual and a theological plane—with Mormon theology and authority. A few weeks after his arrival in

Copenhagen in the summer of 1850, LDS apostle Erastus Snow wrote in his diary of visiting the cathedral, which struck him unfavorably with its elegance and pomp. He noted that, "At the head of the main Saloon before the Alter [sic] stands Jesus in Statuary in the act of preaching & on either side of the room are the full-size statues of the 12 Apostles which were carved in marble in Rome." Reflecting on the Lutheran church's divergence from the gospel as restored by LDS founder Joseph Smith, Snow concluded that "after the 'Mother of Harlots' had made war with the Saints & overcome them slain Jesus and his apostles ... she had placed their Statues in her Temples to 'Grace her Triumph'" (Snow, 1850). Snow seemed to regard the statues purely theologically, with little appreciation for their aesthetic merits, as trophy captives of a discredited faith tradition (which he describes as female). Similarly, when LDS Church President Spencer W. Kimball toured the cathedral in 1976, he was preoccupied with the doctrinal significance of the statues. According to LDS apostle Boyd K. Packer, Kimball pointed to the keys held by Thorvaldsen's Peter and announced, "I want you to tell every Lutheran in Denmark that they do not hold the keys! ... We hold the real keys and use them every day" (Tanner, 2001, p. 161). Yet alongside these theological concerns, LDS Church leaders have long prized Thorvaldsen's *Christus* for its balanced, symmetrical depiction of a serene, beatific Christ. They commissioned Aldo Rebechi to create a full-sized replica for use in the Mormon Pavilion at the New York World's Fair in 1964–65 (Carmack, 2000, p. 43) and have since placed additional replicas in LDS temple visitor centers around the globe, from Laie, Hawaii to Salt Lake City, Utah to Rome, Italy. In the latter, the *Christus* replica is surrounded once more by his apostles, but some of their identifying symbols, such as the winged cherub at Matthew's feet, have been modified to suit LDS theological parameters.

Produced a generation after Thorvaldsen's *Christus* in a more realist artistic tradition, the works of Danish painter Carl Heinrich Bloch (1834–1890) also occupy a central place in the Mormon art canon for their depictions not only of Christ, but also of the world of the New Testament. Born to a merchant family, Bloch studied at the Royal Danish Academy of Art in the 1850s, traveling to the Netherlands to learn from the works of Rembrandt and other Dutch realist painters. Aside from several popular genre paintings, Bloch dedicated most of his work to religious subjects. He frequently reproduced scriptural scenes, most impressively in the series of twenty-three paintings illustrating the ministry of Christ that hang in the royal chapel in Frederiksborg Palace north of Copenhagen, but also in several altarpieces and other devotional works. In these depictions, it is less the unmistakable physical dominance of the depictions of Christ that resonates with LDS teachings than the balanced composition, rich color palette, and harmonious but meticulous realism of each scene. Carmack attributes the popularity of Bloch's works in the LDS Church to their acute realism in depictions of biblical scenes. He cites Doyle L. Green, managing editor of the LDS magazine *Improvement Era* from 1950 to 1970, who praised Bloch's "fascination with detail, his powerful use of light and shadow, his dramatic animation and heroic vision, his accurate draftsmanship, and the all but perfect structural qualities of his figures, combined with the skillful use of vivid color" (Carmack, 2000, p. 22).

In contrast to Friberg and Thorvalden's male-focused works, Bloch's religious paintings feature several beautifully drawn and vividly-gowned women, including Mary and Elizabeth greeting each other joyfully, Mary listening gravely to the angel Gabriel, and the woman at the well listening intently to Christ preach of living water, in addition to several golden-haired angels of indeterminate gender. Although graceful and poised, many of these figures are shown in profile or have their faces turned away from the viewer and, as a result, lack the intimacy and personality of, for example, Bloch's popular 1866 genre painting of two women in a Roman osteria, who look directly and even a bit coquettishly at the viewer. One notable exception to this pattern is Bloch's depiction of the Nativity, in which a red-gowned Mary looks directly out of the canvas, her candle-illuminated face composed but unmistakably delighted. Bloch's images of biblical men and women are used widely in LDS contexts, from educational art kits to the cover of the *Ensign* magazine, although his angels' wings have sometimes been removed, in keeping with LDS doctrine of wingless angels, and their shoulders covered, in order to conform to prevailing notions of modesty.

Creating a visual record of Mormon history

Scandinavian visual arts have also played a significant role in creating a visual record of Mormon history. Bloch's contemporary, the Danish painter Christen Dalsgaard (1824–1907), shared the former's attention to realistic detail and interest in well-balanced compositions, but unlike his countryman, Dalsgaard took Mormonism itself as his subject, exploring its appeal to Danish men and women. The son of a landed family, Dalsgaard had trained at the Royal Danish Academy of Art in Copenhagen for six years with many of Denmark's leading painters, including private lessons with Martinus Rørbye. His breakthrough painting, first exhibited in 1856, is titled *Two Mormons Have, in the Course of Their Wanderings, Entered the Home of a Country Carpenter, Where They Seek to Win New Followers by Means of Preaching and Exhibiting Various of Their Sect's Scriptures* (Figure 9.1).[1] The eponymous Mormon missionaries are the focal point, surrounded by a group of listeners that includes an attentive blind girl, her skeptical father, the carpenter reading through a Mormon tract, a small girl hiding under the table, and three women along the periph-

Figure 9.1 Christen Dalsgaard, Two Mormons Have ... Entered the Home of a Country Carpenter ..., 1856

Image courtesy of the Danish National Art Museum.

ery of the scene—one leaning against a wall, another bending over a cradle in another room with her back turned, and the last peering through the window. Although a mundane subject, Dalsgaard's painting, like Bloch's devotional images, is highly detailed, with vivid colors, deft use of lighting, and the inclusion of many small details, such as wood shavings, everyday household implements, and folk costumes, that give the scene the stamp of authenticity and an air of immediacy.[2] In 1937, the Danish author and critic Johannes V. Jensen argued that the value of Dalsgaard's paintings lay precisely in their richness as culture-historical source material: "It is the clothing, the characters, the room, and the period-specific attitude toward life that modern viewers will pay attention to" (Bucka, 2001, p. 51). This assessment also applies to the painting's relevance to Mormonism and gender.

In a May 1856 letter to the picture's original purchaser, N.L. Høyen, Dalsgaard explains the thoughts and emotions that informed his depiction of each of the figures in the scene, which are reflected in their physical characteristics. He describes how Mormon missionaries always travel two by two, but distinguishes between the two Mormon missionaries depicted in the painting, describing one as "young, convinced of the truth of his teachings, and fanatically enthusiastic; the other old, hardened, sly, an altogether bad person" (Rostrup, 1942, p. 146). The younger missionary's ramrod posture, well-tailored coat, thick hair, rosy cheek, straight nose, and earnest expression convey his uprightness and sincerity, while the older missionary's body is obscured, leaving his rather hunched shoulders, thinning red hair, bulbous nose, double chin, and dour expression to convey his lack of character. The young missionary seems to be directing his words toward the young blind girl and her father; her expectant, upturned face, framed by an elaborately patterned scarf, conveys her hopeful interest, while the soaring white wings of her collar catch the viewer's eye. In his letter, Dalsgaard attributes the girl's interest in the Mormons to her blindness and physical weakness. The missionaries' promise of healing has captivated her completely, but her father, who is the central figure in the scene, with the light full on his keen eyes, bright hair, and wizened but firmly-set mouth, is more cautious, though the hope that his daughter could be healed does tempt him. He is impressed by the Mormons' energy, which contrasts favorably with "the lassitude of habitual Christianity," but, Dalsgaard assures Høyen, "like the five wise virgins, he has managed to preserve the true oil in his lamp" and resists being persuaded. Mormonism is thus shown to be of interest primarily to the weak or the sick, those for whom reality falls short, while those with strength of body and character are wary of such promises.

Dalsgaard's narrative is more concerned with the distinction between healthy and weak individuals than with gendered expectations about susceptibility to religious belief. According to Dalsgaard, the blind girl's scowling father finds the unfamiliar Mormon faith "unethical and worldly." Dalsgaard describes the robust carpenter, in whose home the Mormons are preaching, as "too healthy a nature to want anything to do with this sect, without even really knowing why." His wife has retreated to the bedside of her young child, "irritated over or indifferent to the preacher's speech." On the girl leaning against the wall, a sister of the carpenter's wife, the speech "makes no positive impression," for the "new doctrine has as little relevance [for her] as for the wife. She listens to the preacher with a mixture of curiosity and mockery, secure in the naïve strength of her childhood faith" (Rostrup, 1942, p. 147). Coming from a member of the increasingly areligious Danish elite, Dalsgaard's description of the girl's simplistic faith sounds rather condescending, but he invests her, as all of the characters in the room, with an active, curious mind, despite her plain clothing and non-descript features.

Mormon history received a more empathetic, comprehensive portrayal in Scandinavian art by a young Danish convert named Carl Christian Anton (C.C.A.) Christensen (1831–1912), who worked in the same period and style as Bloch and Dalsgaard. In contrast to Dalsgaard's patrician origins, Christensen came from an impoverished family in Copenhagen in 1831, the oldest of four sons. His mother supported the family, including Christensen's alcoholic father, by taking in laundry. Each of the boys was accepted into a boarding school for poor children, which C.C.A. attended from December 1842 to April 1846. He was to be apprenticed to a carpenter, but a chance encounter with the painter Eleanore Christine Harboe (1796–1860), who happened to see some of his sketches and silhouettes on a visit to the school, changed his course in life. Harboe's patronage gave Christensen the opportunity to study at the Royal Danish Academy of Art, where he, alongside Dalsgaard and Bloch, studied with some of Denmark's leading painters, including C.W. Eckersberg. Yet Christensen's rags-to-riches story was disrupted when his mother, who had joined the first Baptist congregation in Copenhagen in 1848, converted to Mormonism in late 1850, which C.C.A. and his brothers soon did as well.

Joining the LDS Church distracted Christensen from pursuing a career as a painter in Denmark, however, which distressed his mentor Harboe. Christensen left the art academy in June 1853 to serve as an unpaid missionary on the island of Zealand. In his memoirs, Christensen recalled Harboe's disappointment at his decision to abandon his artistic work in order to proselyte, noting, "It came like a clap of thunder for her and caused her great sorrow, because she regarded Mormonism as a deception, and because she did not understand my simple testimony because of her great worldly knowledge" (Schmidt, 1984, p. 7). In ways Harboe could not have foreseen, however, Christensen was able to develop his artistic skills through his church membership, including writing several hymns for the LDS hymnal, publishing numerous poems, and receiving additional artistic training while serving a mission in Norway between 1865 and 1867. In territorial Utah, where the harsh conditions of frontier life inhibited the kind of vibrant artistic life Christensen had been part of in Copenhagen, Christensen attempted to fill this void by becoming the first artist to paint the epic migration of the Mormons across the Great Plains to Utah, a journey Christensen himself undertook on foot with a handcart in 1857, just a year after Harboe herself moved to Rome, where she died of cancer in 1860.

In Utah, Christensen became well known for his historical paintings of the early history of the LDS Church, using the skills he had honed in Scandinavia. Unlike Dalsgaard and Friberg, Christensen generally painted group scenes in which individual figures receive little attention. In the early 1860s, Christensen painted murals in LDS temples around Utah and did decorative painting for the Salt Lake Theater, before turning, in the 1870s, to iconic images of pioneer life, as well as depictions of his own missionary work in Scandinavia. One of his most beloved paintings, from 1878 (Figure 9.2), depicts the warm welcome awaiting Scandinavian immigrants arriving in Utah, a reception he had experienced first-hand after his harrowing journey across the plains. In this image, Christensen uses warm brown tones to evoke the desert landscape in Utah that surrounds the bustling group of people in the lower half of the frame, focusing on a woman wearing traditional black Danish peasant clothing with a blue apron embracing her white-clad daughter. The three covered wagons in the background evoke the storied prairie crossings of the 1850s, though the woman's fashionable dress and the date of the painting could easily refer to a time after the arrival of the railroad made the journey to Utah much easier and faster. What is decisive for Christensen in this scene is the emotional accuracy of the reunion between aged parents and their children, as well as the sense of community provided by the townspeople, neatly dressed and busily engaged in their affairs, and the tidy houses that contain the scene.

Like Dalsgaard and Bloch, Christensen's style—albeit rather "homespun" (Jensen, 1983, p. 401)—reflects the preoccupations of Danish realist painting, with the difference in Christensen's case that his painterly gaze was "directed not toward Denmark but rather toward the Mormon experience" (Schmidt, 1984, p. 32). Christensen painted a few scenes of missionary

Figure 9.2 C.C.A. Christensen, *Reunion of the Saints*, 1878
Image courtesy of the Daughters of the Utah Pioneers.

labor in Denmark and Norway, but dedicated most of his efforts to documenting Mormon history and doctrine. In this way, Christensen was able to leave a much more significant artistic legacy than if he had stayed in Copenhagen. In 1878, he was commissioned by Dimick B. Huntington to make a series of eleven small canvases of scenes from the Bible and the Book of Mormon, which he then sewed together and rolled up like a scroll, with handles on either end, so that the images could be displayed one at a time. He completed a similar panorama, consisting of seven larger canvases depicting the early history of the church, in 1879. He gradually added more canvases to the roll until it contained 23 scenes in all. He then took the panoramic paintings on several exhibit circuits across the Utah territory with his brother Frederik, leaving his two Norwegian-born wives, Elise Sheel and Maren Pettersen, and their children to tend the farm. When these canvas scrolls, long forgotten, were rediscovered in Sanpete County in the mid-twentieth century, LDS apostle Boyd K. Packer stated, "Brother Christensen was not masterful in his painting, but our heritage was there. Some said it was not great art, but what it lacked in technique was more than compensated in feeling" (Packer, 1976).

Complicating the Mormon narrative

Without interpretative commentary like Packer's, the feelings conveyed through Christensen's Mormon history paintings depend on the viewer's own attitudes toward the subject matter, whereas literary texts tend to state their biases more explicitly. Although a great deal of anti-Mormon propaganda was published in Scandinavian newspapers, very few narrative treatments of Mormonism in nineteenth-century Scandinavia attempted to convey a more balanced perspective. One exception to this norm is an unpublished manuscript, titled simply "Mormonism," written by the Danish noblewoman Kirstine Marie Elisabeth Stampe (1824–1883) in about 1859, just a few years after Dalsgaard's painting of the Mormon missionaries and Christensen's emigration. Stampe's book illuminates the disdain which most elite Danes felt about this new, American religion, but it demonstrates remarkable sensitivity and empathy, unlike any of Stampe's male contemporaries. Her open-minded, thoughtful approach to this highly controversial topic was likely shaped in part by the artists and thinkers she encountered in the home of her parents, Baron Henrik Stampe and his wife Christine Dalgas, who were the patrons of Thorvaldsen, for whom they built an atelier at Nysø, where he lived from June 1839 until his death in 1844. Their home was a gathering place for artists and intellectuals in nineteenth-century Denmark, with not only Thorvaldsen but also the writers Hans Christian Andersen and Adam Oehlenschläger, and the poet and pastor N.F.S. Grundtvig, among many other notables and dignitaries, in frequent attendance. As a member of such a culturally sophisticated household, Stampe enjoyed opportunities for international travel, artistic education, and cultural exchange that were rare at the time, including a trip in 1842, at age eighteen, with her parents and Thorvaldsen to Rome, where she interacted with the artists working there.

Despite her class privilege, Stampe's positionality as a woman on the periphery of male society informed her intellectually generous approach to Mormonism. Her interest in Mormonism derived from her friendship with another woman, who had joined the LDS Church in the mid-1850s. By studying Mormonism, Stampe hoped to be able to persuade her friend of the error of her ways. In a 1857 letter to Pastor Grundtvig, by whom she had been confirmed in the Lutheran church in 1841, Stampe reports that her sister Jeanina had informed her "how much Pastor Grundtvig was opposed to my visiting the Mormon woman of whom I am so fond," but she goes on to explain her compassionate motivation for continuing the relationship: "I am so happy and peaceful about having had a good talk with her and I am certain that it will prove itself one day not to have been in vain, when the hour of the Lord arrives" (Stampe, 1857). In a letter dated October 11, 1858, Grundtvig validates the importance of such emotional connections, while expressing confidence that the friend's recent death was divinely decreed:

> I may have wondered a bit over your fascination with the Mormon woman, but I would hardly have let you see that, since matters of the heart are as necessary for us as our eyes. Based on your report, it seems reasonable to me that Our Lord, by cutting her earthly sojourn short so abruptly, has mercifully removed her as a piece of wood from the fire.
>
> (Grundtvig, 1858)

It may have been sorrow at the loss of her friend and perhaps also distress at the common misrepresentations of her friend's beliefs that prompted Stampe to write her book that fall, though she never published it, perhaps due to the disapproval of such high-profile figures in Danish society as Grundtvig and Pastor Peter Christian Kierkegaard, elder brother of the philosopher Søren Aabye Kierkegaard.

Although Stampe makes it clear that she does not endorse Mormon theology, she is explicit about her determination to approach the subject objectively. She prefaces the manuscript with a challenge to her readers to live up to their own intellectual standards of inquiry:

> It would be asking a great deal of the reader to digest an entire book about Mormonism. And what would he say to see Mormonism presented as a great spiritual curiosity,

even as something extraordinary!—Mormonism, which only attracts ignorant, uneducated wretches with no prospects, which is rarely even mentioned in the civilized world and even those who most fervently oppose false sects and doctrines cannot be bothered to waste more than at most a little, tossed-off pamphlet on! Mormonism! It is said of it that it defeats itself, but even this self-defeat is not worth attending to; Mormonism, which everyone has the right to laugh at and say "God save us!" about without knowing anything about it; Mormonism, which would make a despised social outcast of any person who dared to talk about it with the same interest that one talks of Platonism, Islam, or any religion that might be of interest to learn about. One will find this Mormonism presented here, not just as a highly interesting and enlightening phenomenon, but also as not exactly a theology but rather a combination of doctrines that poses quite serious questions, for which we need to find answers, whether it be in Mormonism itself or somewhere else.

(Stampe, [1859])

Rejecting the idea that Mormonism can simply be mocked and dismissed, Stampe acknowledges the validity and importance of the spiritual questions Mormonism poses and declares her intention of identifying "the strings of truth upon which Mormonism plays," that is to say, the elements of commonality between Mormonism and Danish Lutheranism, "that which blinds about Mormonism, which gives it the appearance of truth in the eyes of many seeking the truth."

More than any other nineteenth-century Danish commentator on Mormonism, Stampe does not dismiss Danish Mormons as deluded or ignorant fools, but attempts instead to account for Mormonism's appeal to respectable, intelligent people, like her friend. This is her audience, she explains, for it is "with regard to those souls both among the Mormons and the non-Mormons who have some truth in them that this entire book has been written." Stampe defends her decision to look for the truths contained in Mormonism with the explanation that "those things that are true in themselves can more easily attract a mind in which there is some truth than outright lies are able to." Her intention, as she states on several occasions, is to show how these leavening elements of truth are distorted or corrupted in Mormon doctrine, but her willingness to admit to their existence and their attractive power for truth-seekers is remarkable for her time and place.

With considerable philosophical finesse, Stampe distinguishes between not just truth and lies, but also between truths that can become untruths in particular circumstances. She explains,

> Although that which is true in and of itself can more easily appeal to what we people would call an honest mind than that which is entirely false, it does not necessarily follow that that which is true on its own merits is therefore always true.

As an example, she notes that even though it is true that the earth needs rain for grains to grow, too much rain at one time can cause seed corn to rot, making the statement "it is good that it is raining, for the earth needs rain to grow to enable the grain to grow" untrue in that context. By the same token, she notes, the fact that something is approved by the world does not make it true, nor does being persecuted by the world make something false. "Even though the world, civilization, and the bourgeoisie's common opinion brand something as despicable, it can still appeal to the truth in a mind that has the courage to defy the world, civilization, and the bourgeoisie."

Applying this principle to Mormonism, Stampe exhibits empathy, even admiration, for the courage it required for her countrymen to convert to a religion as unpopular as Mormonism, whatever its flaws might be. Such determination, she explains, requires "a conscience that dares to stand against the opinion of all the people in the whole wide world, resting in God." Stampe seems to suggest that the complete social isolation that results from embracing Mormonism gives the convert access to a powerful spiritual experience and undermines attempts to disprove Mormonism out of hand:

> Most people who condemn Mormonism with the most sincere conviction of their entire souls and have never felt a moment's pang of conscience in that regard do so, however, without the same kind of peace of conscience that … comes from having experienced what it is like to have no other witness on your side except God.

In Stampe's view, having "no other witness on your side except God" brings with it an inner peace that can serve to strengthen an individual's faith, even if the particular doctrines that a person believes are untrue. By contrast, Stampe deems reflexive, unconsidered rejections of Mormonism to be inconsistent with a Christian's responsibility to consult with God on matters of faith. Her goal is therefore to show the elements of "absolute truth" contained within Mormonism in order to demonstrate, with the peaceful consciousness of having God on her side, "that the [Mormon] doctrine has nonetheless been weighed and found wanting," with the goal of leading truth-seekers back into the fold of the Danish Lutheran church.

Stampe's approach is scholarly, rather than dogmatic, and she takes a particular interest in the elements of beauty that she finds within Mormonism. Although she acknowledges the centrality of the Book of Mormon, she focuses particularly on the book of Doctrine and Covenants, which she describes as "the Mormon Book of Revelation." Compiled of revelations received by LDS founding prophet Joseph Smith between approximately 1830 and 1844, it illustrates, in Stampe's view, how modern Mormon revelation "lives and works within living people." She finds the Doctrine and Covenants to be "a much more tasteful and spiritual application of Biblical style, tone, and character than anything I have found in The Book of Mormon." She cites several passages of Doctrine and Covenants that she describes as particularly beautiful and argues that such poetry ought to be acknowledged by Danish educated society, if only on aesthetic grounds:

> Even in the old pagan myths and heretic beliefs, the founders of which died many centuries ago, one can find beautiful elements and bring out something or other as a pleasant thought, such as, for example, Ingemann has done by bringing to our attention Mohammed's beautiful description of the two angels on his right and left shoulders. The fact that the thought occurred to Mohammed did not prevent any of us, although we regarded him as a false prophet, from giving widespread approval to the lovely idea, while now as soon as the conversation turns to the heretic religion that is widely despised by the educated, every thought that it contains is mocked as ridiculous, even as sheer nonsense, even when thoughts are found within it that would be praised to the skies if they had been uttered by one's own poets or in other places.

This line of argumentation recalls author Johannes V. Jensen's above-mentioned comments about the aesthetic merits of Dalsgaard's painting, which seemed to the critic to compensate for its somewhat bizarre subject matter. Both Stampe and Dalsgaard seem willing to suspend judgment on the theological validity of Mormon doctrine long enough to acknowledge the ways in which it can contribute to the beauty and complexity of Danish culture.

Mormon emigration and the white slave trade

In education, fortune, and social standing, Elise Stampe enjoyed a level of independence greater than most other Scandinavian women of her time, but as political and social reforms swept Scandinavia in the late nineteenth century, women of all social classes enjoyed increased freedom, particularly in terms of employment and mobility but also with regard to sexuality and marriage. These increased opportunities for women occasioned considerable public discussion in the arts about the changing roles of women, which the Danish literary critic Georg Brandes (1842–1927) kindled with his 1869 translation of John Stuart Mill's essay "The Subjection of Women," accompanied by a preface calling for women's emancipation and the legalization of both divorce and civil marriage. Norwegian playwright Henrik Ibsen (1828–1906) resoundingly endorsed women's empowerment with his provocative play *Et dukkehjem* (*A Doll's House*) in 1879, while his countryman Bjørnstjerne Bjørnson (1832–1910) used his 1883 play *En handske* (*A Gauntlet*) to argue, like the Danish feminist Elisabeth Grundtvig (1856–1945), for greater sexual accountability for men rather than greater sexual freedom for women. While Brandes and Bjørnson defended their respective positions in newspaper debates, the Swedish playwright and artist August Strindberg (1849–1912) entered the fray with his 1884 short story collection *Giftas* (*Getting Married*), in which he denounces Ibsen's story as hypocritical and lays out a series of blunt suggestions for ensuring actual equality between the sexes. Swedish feminists and moralists, represented by the Society for the Married Woman's Property Rights and the Federation, a society working for the abolition of prostitution, brought a blasphemy lawsuit against him, of which he was acquitted on November 17, 1884.

Suspicion of Mormonism, particularly due to the practice of polygamy, as exploitative of women raised concerns among many observers in northern Europe, from the popular Danish songwriter Julius Strandberg (1834–1903), whose penny street ballads were the era's equivalent of YouTube, to the German novelist Balduin Möllhausen (1825–1905), whose 1864 novel *Das Mormonenmädchen* (The Mormon Girl) chronicles the disillusionment of a young female Swedish convert to Mormonism who first learns about Mormon polygamy after making the arduous journey to Utah. Strandberg wrote several ballads mocking Mormon polygamy, such as "Jeg er Mormon, Som du Nok Ved" ("I Am a Mormon, You Surely Know") from 1871, which deals with "the Mormons' High Priest Brigham Young and his 16 wives" (Strandberg, 1871). In the first verse, the speaker explains, "I am a Mormon, you surely know, and therefore I have a lovely flock of wives—sixteen, I believe." He then acknowledges, with an implicit wink and nudge, "But one can't always stay at home, of course, and so I naturally have a little on the side; since a man ought to have two mistresses for each of his wives, I've got 32 mistresses, 64 girlfriends, and 96 acquaintances." The promiscuous Mormon polygamist is the villain of this piece, much like the immoral men Bjørnson castigated in his play. In another ballad, from 1884, Strandberg takes aim at immoral men who sacrifice women to the Mormons in order to indulge their own desires. This song carries the unwieldy title, "Den Sidste Nye Vise om de to Kjøbenhavnske Murersvende der Solgte Deres Koner" ("The Most Recent New Song about the Two Journeymen Masons from Copenhagen Who Sold Their Wives"), with the subtitle, "For 2,000 crowns to a Mormon priest, who journeyed to Utah with them" (Strandberg, 1884). Once their wives are gone, the Danish men get drunk on their profits.

Other ballads made a more explicit connection between Danish Mormon emigration, polygamy, and the endangerment of women. Given the relative frequency with which Mormon convert women emigrated without husbands or fathers, under the protection of LDS missionaries, accounts of exploitation and abuse seemed plausible. C.O. Jordan's popular, widely reprinted "Mormonpigens Klage" ("The Mormon Girl's Lament") from the early 1870s, is intended to warn virtuous Danish girls away from the Mormon missionaries' promises of paradise in America. The song is prefaced by the summary:

Including a detailed and truthful account of a rich farmer's daughter from Fyn, who a short time ago was lured by the Mormons, so that she journeyed with them to Utah, after having sacrificed great sums of money to the priests; and about how she was forced to marry a man who already had seven wives, and about how after innumerable trials she returned impoverished to her home.

(Wright, 1983, pp. 142–44)

It resembles an anonymously published song from 1865, "Lykke og Ulykke Eller: Saltsøens Mysterier. En smuk historie om en ung Pige, der blev forført af Mormonerne til at rejse til Saltsøen og hvad hun dér oplevede" ("Happiness and Unhappiness; or the Mysteries of the Salt Lake. A lovely story of a young girl who was persuaded by the Mormons to travel to the salt lake and what she experienced there"). In all of these accounts, vulnerable young women who take advantage of the increased speed and decreased cost of trans-Atlantic migration in the late nineteenth century come to regret their rashness and independence.

This fear of the negative consequences of women's emancipation not only persisted throughout the final decades of the nineteenth century, it intensified as more and more Scandinavian women pursued employment opportunities in large cities, from Stockholm to Chicago. Swedish maids were in such high demand in Chicago households at the turn of the century, for example, that specialized employment offices existed just to facilitate such contracts. Enough of these women had negative experiences, either with unsavory agents or exploitative employers, that all manner of rumors about kidnapping and human trafficking gained currency. By the early twentieth century, national and international organizations had been established across Europe, including the French Les Amies de la Jeune Fille (Friends of Young Women), the German Jungfrauenverband (Young Women's Association), and the Danish National Committee for Combating the White Slave Trade, to raise public awareness of the existence of the white slave trade, protect young women from falling victim to it, and bring its perpetrators to justice.

Danish committee chairman Axel Liljefalk described the committee's task as a crusade to help "the human race ... cleanse itself of the shame, infamy, and unhappiness that the white slave trade brings upon it" (Liljefalk, 1911, p. 7). In his 1911 report to the Danish parliament, Liljefalk, while admitting that sex trafficking has occurred since the beginning of human existence, argues that its particular incarnation in the early twentieth century is closely connected to the changing social conditions, global criminal networks, and increased physical mobility of the industrialized world. He enumerates the false promises made by agents of white slavery, who recruit women to work in restaurants, hotels, pubs, dance halls, music halls, and female orchestras, and warns against schemes by masseuses, midwives, impresarios, retail merchants, and emigration agents that force women into compromising situations and make them vulnerable to white slavery. Although his 1911 report does not mention Mormons, in his discussion of unreliable emigration agents Liljefalk warns that "an offer of marriage, made at the proper moment, rarely misses its mark" (Liljefalk, 1911, pp. 15–16). A few years later, however, he alleged that Mormon missionaries in Denmark were directly responsible for the disappearance of more than 10,000 Danish women per year. When an LDS member of the Danish Parliament, F.F. Samuelsen, challenged Liljefalk to prove his allegations, he was unable to do so. However, the association between Mormonism and the white slave trade was already well established in the public imagination, in part because of allegations made by former Mormon Hans P. Freece, who toured the Nordic region in 1910–1911 on behalf of the Danish Lutheran Utah Mission, that Mormons were still practicing polygamy, despite the 1890 manifesto from LDS Church president Wilford Woodruff abandoning the practice, and abducting young Danish women to do so.

This controversy, which involved a number of highly-publicized speeches by Freece and rebuttals by Andrew Jenson, president of the LDS Scandinavian Mission, attracted the attention of the Danish film industry, which had begun to make a global name for itself with erotic melodramas about the white slave trade. These films essentially picked up where the street ballads left off, depicting Mormonism as a dangerous foreign element that could ensnare unwary women into unwanted polygamous marriages. Building on the success of the film *Den hvide slavehandel* (*The White Slave Trade*), which was produced twice in the same year by two different film companies in Denmark—Aarhus-based Fotorama in April 1910 and Copenhagen-based Nordisk a few months later—and its sequel *Den hvide slavehandels sidste offer* (*In the Hands of Imposters*, 1911), Nordisk made the world's first anti-Mormon film, *Mormonens Offer* (*A Victim of the Mormons*, 1911), which became a blockbuster hit around the globe.[3] As Nordisk's marketing materials for *The White Slave Trade* explain, the phrase "the white slave trade" contains "three words full of unease and horror, which cause the fearful motherly heart to tremble and brings a flush of shame and indignation to a father's cheeks; three words that impertinently strip away all of the twentieth century's civilization and progress!" (Nordisk, 1910). The allegation that the trafficking of white women was particularly uncivilized evokes charges made against the LDS Church by its American critics in the previous century about polygamy being a relic of barbarism, just adapted for a different cultural context.

A Victim of the Mormons conforms to the parameters of the earlier white slave trade films in nearly all respects, replacing brothel owners with Mormons. Subtitled "A Drama of Love and Sectarian Fanaticism," it stars the popular Danish actors Valdemar Psilander and Clara Wieth. Psilander plays a Mormon priest named Andrew Larsson who persuades a young woman named Nina, played by Wieth, to run away with him to Utah. Larsson's behavior in the film follows the pattern laid out in Liljefalk's report, namely "seeking out the necessary prey, catching it in his net, developing a relationship that inspires trust, and then delivering the victim to the transportation agents" (Liljefalk, 1911, p. 16), except that Larsson accompanies Nina overseas. When Nina changes her mind about leaving shortly before boarding the ship, Larsson confines, drugs, and smuggles her on board. Once they get to Utah, he confines her in his house while he goes to the Salt Lake Temple to perform baptisms. Meanwhile, Nina's desperate brother Olaf and her fiancé Sven Berg pursue her all the way to Utah, where they succeed in rescuing her—after a harrowing car chase—with the assistance of the police and a compassionate housekeeper. In the scuffle, Nina opens a trapdoor in the living room and Larsson shoots himself as he falls through it. With its robust international distribution networks, Nordisk was able to sell this film to markets from Albany, NY to Australia, despite efforts by the LDS Church to have it banned in the U.S.

Fotorama produced its own anti-Mormon film in 1911, *Mormonbyens Blomst* (*The Flower of the Mormon City*), depicting the travails of a Danish Mormon girl in Utah who narrowly escapes a forced marriage with a Mormon polygamist. Unlike Nordisk's film, *The Flower of the Mormon City* does not conform to the conventions of the white slave trade, but, as the program notes confirm, it deliberately engages with contemporary concerns:

> The Mormon question has likely never been more current than at the moment. Time after time, Mormon propaganda has taken root here, as in other countries, and since people from Utah are energetic folks, it's hard to get rid of them. Thus they even force their way into idyllic domestic spaces, as we see here.
>
> (Fotorama, 1911)

The film opens with the visit of Mormon missionaries to Danish blacksmith Jens Olsen's home, where his ailing wife is receptive to their teachings. After her death, their young daughter Kristine Olsen accompanies her father to the Mormon settlement in Utah, to honor her mother's wishes. At first, Jens is content in his new home and Kristine, played by Jenny Roelsgaard, grows up to be the lovely "flower of the Mormon city." However, her father's antipathy to polygamy and refusal to be baptized eventually antagonizes the leaders of the isolated Mormon frontier community. When John, a local Mormon man with one wife already, decides to force Kristine to become his second wife, even though she loves the non-Mormon cowboy Tom Carter, played by Aage Schmidt, the town leaders threaten vigilante justice if Jens doesn't force his daughter to comply. With Tom's help, Kristine and Jens flee into the desert, where Jens dies and Kristine is abducted by the Mormons while Tom is out hunting. At the altar, Kristine faints before she can be forced into this unwanted marriage, giving Tom time to rescue her once more. They establish themselves as a family in New York, but Tom ultimately gives in to Kristine's desire to return to Denmark, where they purchase her father's abandoned smithy and integrate themselves into rural Danish society.

Both films' association of Mormonism with the white slave trade position the LDS Church in Scandinavia in the early twentieth century as a threat to women that must be defeated by the aggressive intervention of male protectors. This strategy reflects the broader cultural discourses about gender roles and modernity in early twentieth-century Scandinavia discussed above. At a time when women's suffrage movements were gaining momentum, these films reflect a lack of confidence in women's mental and physical abilities to make the best choices for either themselves as individuals or society as a whole. When Nina Gram chooses to run away with Andrew Larsson to Utah, her susceptibility to making such a choice is attributed to her irrational, emotional reactions to her fiancé's boorish behavior and her seducer's aura of mysticism. When she changes her mind, her physical weakness and timidity prevent her from being able to escape successfully, even when Andrew's housekeeper tries to help her flee through her open, unbarred window, until her brother and fiancé arrive. Similarly, Kristine Olsen is depicted as unable to resist either the lure of Mormonism or the coercion to marry against her will, until assisted by men and restored to her native cultural environment.

Conclusion

The introduction of Mormonism into Scandinavia in the second half of the nineteenth century bore unexpected fruit in the rich, varied artistic legacy described above, which reveals how notions of gender in Mormonism intersected with artistic practice, historical context, and social transformations in the region, as well as how the Scandinavian artistic tradition has shaped visual representations of Mormon theology and history. Some works created originally for a Lutheran Scandinavian context later came to occupy a prominent place within the Mormon artistic canon, reinforcing LDS doctrine and gender norms, while others were created with direct reference to Mormon culture, history, and practice. The questions of female agency, male physicality, and sexuality these works explore resonate with the concerns of the times and places in which they were created, but also with the challenges Mormon culture faces today.

Notes

1 The original title in Danish is *Tvende Mormoner ere paa deres Vandring komne ind i et Tømrehus paa Landet, hvor de ved Prædiken og ved Fremvisning af nogle af deres Sekts Skrifter søger at vinde nye Tilhængere*.
2 Friberg was, in fact, so taken with this painting that he copied it in 1964, but without noticeably altering the physiognomy of any of the figures.
3 These first Danish anti-Mormon films were quickly followed by a host of French and American productions, including *The Mountain Meadows Massacre* (1912, Pathé Frères, director unknown), *The Danites* (1912, directed by Francis Boggs), and *Riders of the Purple Sage* (1918, directed by Frank Lloyd), based on Zane Grey's 1912 novel of the same name.

References

Barrett, R.T., and Black, S.E., 2005. Setting a Standard in LDS Art: Four Illustrators of the Mid-Twentieth Century. *BYU Studies* 44(2): 24–80.

Bucka, I., 2001. Værk og Virkelighed—Realismen i Christen Dalsgaards Billeder. In C. Sabroe, C.B. Andersen, and I. Bucka, eds. *Christen Dalsgaard 1824–1907*. Vestsjællands Kunstmuseum.

Carmack, N.A., 2000. Images of Christ in Latter-day Saint Visual Culture, 1900–1999. *BYU Studies* 39(3): 18–76.

Fotorama, 1911. *Mormonbyens Blomst. En ung dansk Piges dramatiske Oplevelser i Mormonbyen Utah*. Aarhus, Denmark.

Grundtvig, N.F.S., 1858. Letter to Elise Stampe. October 11. Manuscript Department, Royal Danish Library, Copenhagen, NKS 3946 kvart.

Jensen, R., 1983. C.C.A. Christensen on Art: From the Salt Lake City *Bikuben*, February–March 1892. *BYU Studies* 23(4): 401–24.

Jordan, C.O., [1870s]. Mormonpigens Klage. *Dansk Folkemindesamling* Z 190/915.

Liljefalk, A., 1911. *Den Hvide Slavehandel*. Copenhagen: E. Jespersens Forlag.

Nordisk Films Compagni, 1910. Publicity materials for *Det hvide slavehandel*. Copenhagen.

Osborne, S., 1984. Arnold Friberg: The Master's Touch. *This People* 5: 44–51.

Packer, B., 1976. The Arts and the Spirit of the Lord. Speech given at Brigham Young University. February 1. https://speeches.byu.edu/talks/boyd-k-packer_arts-spirit-lord/.

Reynolds, G., 1904. The Personal Appearance of the Savior. *Juvenile Instructor* 39: 497–500.

Rostrup, H., 1942. Et Brev fra Christen Dalsgaard. In *Kunstmuseets Aarsskrift*. Copenhagen: Nordisk Forlag, pp. 145–47.

Schmidt, J., 1984. *C.C.A. Christensen. Dansk-amerikansk maler, digter, samfundsrevser og missionær*. Aalborg: Forlaget Moroni.

Snow, E., 1850. Papers: 1836–1888. L. Tom Perry Special Collections, Harold B. Lee Library, Brigham Young University, Provo, Utah.

Stampe, E., 1857. Letter to N.F.S. Grundtvig, September 14. Grundtvig Collection G 466.VI.d.6, Manuscript Department, Danish Royal Library, Copenhagen.

Stampe, E., [1859]. Mormonismen. Constantin Hansen Family Collection NKS 4987 4, Manuscript Department, Royal Danish Library, Copenhagen.

Strandberg, J., 1871. Jeg er Mormon, Som Du Nok Ved. *Dansk Folkemindesamling* 1970/16, XI: 80. Danish Royal Library, Copenhagen.

Strandberg, J., 1884. Den Sidste Nye Vise om de to Kjøbenhavnske Murersvende der Solgte Deres Koner. Danish National Library.

Tanner, J.S., 2001. Of Men and Mantles: Kierkegaard on the Difference between a Genius and an Apostle. *BYU Studies* 40(2): 149–64.

Wright, R., and R.L., 1983, *Danish Emigrant Ballads and Songs*. Carbondale, IL: Southern Illinois University Press.

Further reading

Allen, J., 2017. *Danish but Not Lutheran: The Impact of Mormonism on Danish Cultural Identity, 1850–1920*. Salt Lake City, UT: University of Utah Press.

This book situates the arrival of Mormonism in Denmark in its sociohistorical context, exploring the factors leading up to the establishment of religious freedom, the initial theological concerns of Danish Lutheran clergy, a more in-depth description of popular cultural responses to Mormonism, and the cultural negotiations required of Danish Mormon convert-emigrants.

Mulder, W., 1957. *Homeward to Zion: The Mormon Migration from Scandinavia*. Minneapolis, MN: University of Minnesota Press.

Mulder's meticulous historical account of the conversion and emigration of more than 17,000 Scandinavian converts is an invaluable source for the lived experience of Scandinavian Mormons in the nineteenth century and their contributions to building up both the Utah Territory and the LDS Church.

10
MORMON GENDER IN THE PROGRESSIVE ERA

Matthew Bowman

More than any other single factor, the slow abandonment of polygamy transformed the ways in which Mormons thought about gender in the late nineteenth and early twentieth centuries. Mormon men were accustomed to viewing themselves as figures akin to the patriarchs of scripture and thus had to reframe what it meant to be religious in an American society suspicious of Mormon patriarchy. Mormon women, who had imagined themselves as simultaneously participants in the patriarchal order of polygamous marriage but also members of an activist female community centered upon the church-sponsored Relief Society, similarly found themselves stripped of older institutions and norms. Mormon men and women, then, had to adapt to new gender norms as their church sought greater integration into American life, and Mormon leaders, male and female, sought to implement reforms in order to guide their flock as they worked out precisely what those might be. They drew both on ideas embedded within Mormonism itself and on the norms and mores of American culture, and worked out a new gendered cultural synthesis which incorporated elements of each.

The end of plural marriage

In 1890, Wilford Woodruff, the 83-year-old president of the church, issued what has come to be called the "Manifesto," canonized in Mormon scripture as "Official Declaration 1." Understood by members of the church as written in response to direction from God, and under intense legal pressure from the United States government, Woodruff stated that "my advice to the Latter-day Saints is to refrain from contracting any marriage forbidden by the law of the land." He later claimed he had received revelation indicating that should the church persist in practicing plural marriage, it would be destroyed by the federal government. Over the next fourteen years, the practice of polygamy slowly ground to a halt; plural marriage numbers declined sharply, and in 1904 then-president of the church Joseph F. Smith announced that any who performed or participated in a polygamous marriage henceforth would be excommunicated. In 1911, the first such disciplines were executed. Historians have long emphasized the ways in which polygamy shaped Mormon gender roles, helping to define what Latter-day Saints believed to be the proper roles of women and men. Thus, the end of polygamy also forced Mormons to reconceive what those roles meant.

Polygamy helped to define Mormon manhood because it linked men's roles as polygamous husbands and fathers both to their leadership in the church's priesthood and to their afterlives as deified patriarchs ruling over kingdoms in God's celestial realm. Thus, Mormon men reified their roles as patriarch to their families and understood that dominating their social and familial worlds was the natural unfolding of the cosmos. Brigham Young had taught that "the only men who become Gods, even the Sons of God, are those who enter into polygamy" (Daynes, 2001, p. 73). Young understood polygamy to be the ultimate expression of Mormon patriarchy, in which men on earth imitated the divine presidency of God himself. Such teachings also applied to one's daily life. John Taylor claimed that "Celestial Marriage ... was binding on all Latter-day Saints, [and] no man was entitled to the right of presiding without abiding this law" (Daynes, 2001, p. 72). Polygamy thus was linked to a man's prestige and authority in the church hierarchy in which all men held one role or another. Because polygamy emphasized men's roles as leaders and patriarchs, it was a site for the expression of other manly virtues: strength and vigor chief among them. For Taylor, defense of and participation in polygamy was a mark of vigor, assertiveness, and a laudable lack of shame; as he asked,

> Are we ashamed of anything we have done in marrying wives? No ... Would you have no fears? None. All the fears that I am troubled with is that this people will not do right—that they will not keep the commandments.
> *(Watt, 1854–1886, vol. 11, pp. 224–25)*

Similarly, Mormon women had been taught that participation in polygamy was a mark of faith and true femininity. While men celebrated masculine dominance and assertiveness, women were taught endurance and sacrifice, and their role as Mormon women was linked to their willingness to enter into a social structure many found emotionally painful. Helen Mar Kimball Whitney, a plural wife both to Joseph Smith and later to Horace Kimball, summarized the ways many Mormon women thought about polygamy in her 1884 memoir and justification *Why We Practice Plural Marriage*. Frequently Mormon women spoke of entering into polygamous marriages as a test of their faith. God would, Whitney said, "receive none but the willing and obedient. When Abraham had made his sacrifice, the Lord restored it, which ought to be lesson enough for the rest of us." To so willingly submit, she said, would gain Mormon women social acceptance and divine favor. Whitney claimed of husbands that "to see such a great sacrifice made by the wife ... has increased his love and exalted her" (pp. 9, 22).

At the same time Mormon women like Whitney spoke of polygamy as a test of faith which would humble them, Mormon women and men alike believed that polygamy would secure for women their traditional roles in the home and hence elevate the moral temper of society generally. As Whitney put it, "through the wicked and unnatural course," as she called monogamy, "thousands of women are denied their privileges and are forced to seek employment outside the home" (p. 7). Polygamy would provide for every woman the role of wife and mother—and indeed in at least one Mormon community marriage rates for women were astronomically high. In so promoting frequent marriage, Mormons believed polygamy would restrain the opportunities and desires that drove men to sin with both prostitutes and other unattached women (Nichols, 2002).

And yet, despite all such language of submission and sacrifice, many historians have observed the ways in which polygamy also empowered women, fostering a community of plural wives bound together by their shared experience of commitment to their faith and distant relationships with their husbands. Centered upon the Relief Society, an official church organization for women, these women pursued social activism, women's suffrage, and community reform. Through the vehicle of the Relief Society, Mormon women participated in broader national movements centered simultaneously on female political activism, community organization, and the promotion of public improvement and health. Mormon women then both lobbied for women's suffrage and cared for the poor, sponsored a hospital and joined national organizations dedicated to promoting international peace. They constructed and ran church organizations like a Primary association for children and youth programs for young women. Mormon femininity under polygamy, then, was marked by a pairing of independence and submissiveness, activity and stoicism.

For Mormon men, the seeming reluctance of Woodruff's concession, and his insistence that the abandonment of polygamy was coerced rather than sought out, left many who had been raised on declarations like Taylor's, that polygamy and Mormon masculinity were closely bound, feeling as though their identities were threatened. Brigham Henry Roberts, a member of the Presidency of the Seventy (the lowest tier of the General Authorities of the Church), wrote in his diary how aghast he was at Woodruff's announcement. "I was in quite an exasperated mood, and felt crushed and humiliated," he wrote.

> I thought of all the Saints had suffered to sustain that doctrine ... we had preached for it, sustained its divinity from the pulpit, in the press, from the lecture platform ... to lay it down like this was a kind of cowardly proceeding.
>
> *(Walker, 1982, p. 2)*

Roberts' language, contrasting humiliation and cowardice with the boldness with which Roberts himself (one of Mormonism's most prominent public apologists) had once defended the policy, indicates the strain the Manifesto placed upon his sense of his role as a man, which was closely bound to his identity as a Mormon.

Roberts' distress was not his alone. Many Mormon men felt ashamed, abandoned, and weakened; some, as did Roberts, believed Woodruff's decision was unmanly and craven. This was often because they associated polygamy with the fulfillment of their priesthood obligations. This number included several members of the Quorum of the Twelve Apostles. John W. Taylor, for instance, was dropped from the Quorum of the Twelve in 1905 for performing plural marriages after the Manifesto and was excommunicated in 1911. In a hearing before the Quorum of the Twelve, Taylor cited a revelation he believed his father, John Taylor, the second president of the church, had received concerning polygamy. In the revelation God declared "How can I revoke an everlasting covenant? For I, the Lord, am everlasting, and My everlasting covenant cannot be abrogated nor done away with." Taylor insisted that under the right circumstances it was possible for a man with priesthood office to "solemnize plural marriages with authority now." For Taylor, as for other Mormon men, polygamy was a manifestation of their priestly authority; Woodruff's abrogation, then, was a blow to what they believed that authority to be, and hence, what they understood their priestly duties as men to be (Collier, 1987, p. 7).

Mormon women also found Woodruff's Manifesto disruptive. Many were as stunned as was Roberts, and equally distressed in ways that signaled they perceived a threat to the particularly gendered virtues polygamy exalted. While Mormon men felt their vigor and assertiveness threatened, Mormon women worried that their sacrifices had been for naught. Lorena Washburn Larsen, the second wife of Bent Larsen, wrote that when her husband informed her of Woodruff's Manifesto, she felt a wave of bitterness. "It is easy for you, you can go home to your other family and be happy with her," she remembered thinking. "I fancied I would see myself and my children, and many other splendid women and their children turned adrift" (Larsen, 1962, p. 105). She ended up raising her children alone, with sporadic contact from her husband, who had decided the Manifesto required him to cease cohabitation with both his wives. Many other plural wives found themselves in similar situations; absent any specific direction from church leadership as to how plural wives were to be treated, some husbands abandoned them, while others simply took their relationships underground.

Mormon women also faced disruption in the particular domestic relationships which polygamy had created. As polygamy had been promoted in part to generate familial loyalty to the church and to provide opportunities for young Mormon women to live in faithful households, its termination, thus, seemed to some a threat to that domestic order. Susa Young Gates, daughter of Brigham Young and a prominent Mormon writer, also worried that the end of polygamy would disrupt women's opportunity to find an appropriate domestic life. "Just wait ten years," she warned a hypothetical young woman,

> and then see if this manifesto hasn't as much significance for you, sitting at home with your empty dreams, as it has for the young married man, who has had his choice from a surplus of girls as good and good-looking as you are.
>
> (Gates, 1891, pp. 283–85)

Gates worried that the number of righteous young men was limited, and thus faithful young women would find their opportunities to enact the gendered norms expected of them to be limited.

The gendered disruptions polygamy caused, then, left Mormons feeling disconnected from those gendered virtues and roles that lay closest to their notion of how someone was to be a Mormon man or a Mormon woman. This was not to say that Mormons were left entirely separated from gender proscriptions; there were many ways that Mormons understood gender that were similar to those Americans around them. But it did mean that the specific relationships between gender and Mormonism were left to be rebuilt.

The reconstruction of Mormon masculinity

In 1913 the church officially affiliated with the Boy Scouts of America and began encouraging young Mormon men to participate in the Scouting movement. Founded by a British soldier named Robert Baden-Powell, Scouting organized boys into military-like troops for outdoor activities, dressed them in uniforms, and set before them a series of tasks and skills to master, from knot tying to civic involvement. Mormon leaders like Roberts emphasized the virtues that Scouting would inculcate in young Mormons: in addition to the discipline, patriotism, and self-sufficiency that the leaders of Scouting extolled, Mormons in particular celebrated the movement because they found in it a usable Mormon past that offered a vision of Mormon manhood distinct from polygamy. Mormon boosters of Scouting like Brigham Henry Roberts praised it for offering to young Mormon men the refining experience of their ancestors' migration across the plains of the American West. They thus found in Scouting a renewed Mormon masculinity (Kimball, 2003).

While assumptions of male headship and patriarchy remained, the older language linking plural marriage to the divinization of Mormon patriarchs faded; replacing it emerged instead a language of personal ethics and self-discipline, a masculinity closer to that of American Protestants than that of the polygamous era had been. Mormon men began valuing social respectability and the virtues that went along with it, discarding the defiant separatism leaders like John Taylor had extolled. Instead they created a Mormonism consonant, as some historians have argued, with the progressive-era Muscular Christianity movement, which emphasized that Christianity was a faith of vigor and action, and that male Christians were to be strong leaders, capable fathers and husbands, and disciplined, successful citizens in a capitalist, democratic, American society. (Kimball, 2003; Alexander, 1985)

However, this growing consonance with the United States was not uncomplicated. At the same time Mormon leaders prized patriotism and American innovations like Muscular Christianity, they feared the encroachment of American commercialized culture. This fear became particularly pressing as the tension between the church and the American state diminished, and hence as American cultural institutions—businesses, entertainment, and media—pressed further and further into Mormon communities. As did many other American religious leaders, Mormon leaders worried that these institutions were promoting immorality. They worried about immodest clothing and improper depictions of courtship in movies and plays and art; they feared the sexual possibilities in dance houses and billiard halls, and they worried about the spread of prostitution, the sexual availability of women that they had believed polygamy eradicated. In part, church-sponsored institutions like Scouting were attempts to replace such forms of leisure, and indeed, they reflected Mormon concern for the morality of their young men.

Thus, the rise of a new Mormon masculinity targeted especially Mormon young men. In 1877, Brigham Young had directed that ordination to the Mormon priesthood be adapted in order to allow teenage boys to participate in its rituals; thirty years later, in 1908, Joseph F. Smith regularized ordination patterns so that beginning at age 12, Mormon men would progress through its offices as they aged. The reasoning Young, Smith, and other Mormon leaders gave was a need to socialize young Mormon men, inculcating them with Mormon norms and values at a youthful age. As one Mormon leader observed,

> it was just as necessary for the young men to be ordained Deacons, Teachers, and Priests, as it is for school children to study in the 1st, 2nd, and 3rd readers, for we must start at the lower round of the ladder and work up step by step.
>
> (Hartley, 1996, p. 109)

The language of progression through effort and education reflects a new masculinity of discipline and commitment and linked this scale of priesthood advancement to the work of Scouting, as young Mormon men were encouraged to enter the Scouting program at the same time as they entered priesthood quorums.

This reconfiguration of priesthood affected Mormon understandings of masculinity in a number of ways. While the induction of younger and younger men into the priesthood conceptualized it as a socializing and training institution for Mormon boys, other discussion around the priesthood increasingly emphasized its administrative and leadership function. Through the period, the leadership of various priesthood offices—seventy, priests, high priests, elders, and so on—sought to establish regularized meetings, curricula, and purpose. More, under the leadership of Joseph F. Smith, president of the church from 1901 to 1918, a Correlation-Social Advisory Committee began to assert greater priesthood authority over the various auxiliaries of the church: the Relief Society, the Sunday School, and youth programs. Combining two initial committees, one designed to coordinate the work of the church with civic and welfare agencies and the other designed to coordinate the curricula of the various auxiliaries to avoid overlap, the Correlation-Social Advisory Committee ended up making a series of recommendations which received in their specifics little support from the church's First Presidency. However, in general, the First Presidency used the committee to assert its authority over the various auxiliaries, and over the course of the 1920s laid down the lines of the parameters of what each auxiliary should concern itself with.

Just as young Mormon men were given new institutions to replace polygamous marriage in order to socialize them into the expectations accorded their gender, so were they also increasingly exhorted to embrace behavioral expectations that were marked as manly. In particular, after the end of polygamy, Mormon leaders accelerated emphasis on the Word of Wisdom, Joseph Smith's health code. Traditionally understood to proscribe alcohol, tobacco, coffee, and tea, Mormons in the nineteenth century understood the Word of Wisdom to be wise counsel, but not formally binding. In 1921, however, Heber J. Grant, president of the church, directed that adherence to the Word of Wisdom henceforth be required for temple worship, the highest and most important ordinances in the church, including marriage.

Though formalized in 1921, church leaders had already begun encouraging adherence to the Word of Wisdom with greater enthusiasm. Many American Christian churches had embraced the broader Prohibition movement seeking to ban the sale of alcohol in the United States, arguing that alcohol wrecked the formation of Christian character. Just so, beginning soon after the Manifesto, Mormon leaders did the same, emphasizing that it was the responsibility of men called to leadership in the church to respect the Word of Wisdom, because the moral self-discipline it demonstrated was associated with the character of Mormon leadership. "Men who have had experience in the Church should not be ordained to the Priesthood nor recommended to the privileges of the House of the Lord unless they will abstain from the use of tobacco and intoxicating drinks," said Joseph F. Smith in 1915 (Alexander, 1985, p. 264). Grant in particular linked adherence to the Word of Wisdom to the new masculine values of self-discipline, ethical behavior, and loyalty to the church that were becoming markers of Mormon manhood in the early twentieth century. In 1916, shortly before he became president of the church, Grant spoke to the youth of the church and endorsed the prohibition of alcohol, declaring that supporting a ban on alcohol was prerequisite for young men who wished to lead. "No man should ever represent Utah in any place or position of trust unless he has stood up and declared ... that he will stand for this thing," said Grant, who also blasted young men who believed they could drink and also take on the responsibilities of marriage. Scathingly sarcastic, Grant quoted a tale told by prohibitionist Frank Hanly, and took on the voice of such a young man addressing the father of his wife. "I have accepted her under the sanction the highest and holiest of covenants," Grant mimicked.

> But the next day I come back to you and say ... I have a right to drink a thing that will make it impossible for me to perform my part of the covenant—come to you and say I have a right to drink a thing that will send me home to her, your daughter, whom I have so taken, a frenzied fiend.

Grant exalted the self-discipline it took to fulfill the Mormon obligations of sacramental marriage and feared the lack of discipline that he believed drink both marked and facilitated. "That thing is not liberty! It's crime! Crime before God!" he quoted Hanly (1916, p. 403). In such a way did adherence to the Word of Wisdom become a marker for the new Mormon masculinity.

The revitalization of Mormon courtship

Grant's insistence that drink interfered with a Mormon man's obligation to treat with fidelity the marriage covenant reflected a reorientation in Mormon commitment to marriage. The abandonment of polygamy did not diminish Mormon commitment to marriage. Rather, Mormon leaders simply transferred their theological allegiances from polygamous to monogamous marriage, and the ways in which they defended it and exhorted their followers illustrate how Mormon leaders imagined what it meant to be a Mormon man or Mormon woman in the early twentieth century. Meanwhile, young Mormon men and women sought to balance the new demands their leaders were making of them with attraction to broader American ways of thinking about courtship and marriage, which included flirting, courtship, and romance, often in venues and styles their leaders found threatening (Inouye, 2004; de Schweinitz, 2011).

For both Mormon men and women, marriage was still taken to be an important sign of maturity and faithfulness to the church. The apostle James Talmage insisted even after the end of polygamy that "marriage is not, can never be, a civil compact alone; its significance reaches farther than the earth; its obligations are eternal; and the Latter-day Saints are notable for the sanctity with which they invest the marital state" (Talmage, 1907, p. 87). In order for a marriage to fulfill its true sacred potential, Mormons were taught that their choice of a marriage partner must exemplify gendered expectations; Mormon women were taught to marry only Mormon men who were faithful church members. Susa Young Gates, a leader in the church's programs for young women, wrote vividly that the question of whether to marry a non-Mormon or a Mormon who "smoke, drank and swore, and would not go to the Temple" was no different from the question of "which I would rather have, the small-pox or the diphtheria" (Tait, 2013, p. 116). Gates exhorted young women to give their favor only to Mormon men who met the expectations of the new Mormon masculinity.

Mormon men were also admonished that their opportunities to enter a sacred marriage were dependent upon their exercise of self-restraint and moral discipline. Joseph F. Smith declared "man is largely responsible for the sins against decency and virtue, the burden of which is too often fastened upon the weaker participant in the crime" (Hoyt and Patterson, 2011, p. 86). Smith, and other Mormon leaders, often blamed negative courtship patterns for male immorality, fearing that young people too often socialized in places that encouraged immorality, such as dance rooms and billiard halls. Mormon men were not to indulge their appetites in the ways that other young men did; rather, they were to court women in restraint and self-discipline. To counter these temptations, Mormon leaders sought instead to exalt the home as the locus of morality and the family, encouraging what one church periodical called "Home Nights," entertainment and parties hosted in private homes, which would, the magazine observed, "outdraw the public dance hall, the public resort and the moving picture show, and every other form of entertainment that takes our boys and girls away from the home" (Talbot, 2017, p. 316).

Mormon wariness of American cultural practices was also expressed in concern for proper dress. If Joseph F. Smith held men accountable for righteous courtship, other Mormon leaders believed that modest dress was primarily the responsibility of Mormon women. The dance hall and other public entertainments were suspect in part because they were associated with improper clothing, which in turn was linked to faithfulness to Mormonism. Mormon leaders thus linked clothing with spirituality for both men and women, arguing that not only would modest dress mark a faithful Latter-day Saint, but also would contribute to a spiritually healthy community and foster righteous marriages. Conversely, immodest clothing would draw Latter-day Saints away from righteous behavior and hence away from the church. In 1916, the apostle George Richards blasted the fashion industry for perverting the nation's morality. What "is or is not modest and proper?" he asked. "I would much rather leave the answer to that question to the conscience of our girls than to Dame Fashion." He went on to link the "immodest" clothing he saw popular in "our new dances" to the "demi-monde of Paris." For Richards, fashionable but immodest clothing was alien to the values of the Mormon community.

More, Richards argued that clothing was important because it would affect the spiritual vitality of men and women alike. "Fallen women wear such immodest dresses," he declared. "The lewd and immodest dress of the demimonde is to indicate a lewd person." He worried that wearing such clothing would degrade the faith of Mormon women—but he also held it accountable for the diminished spirituality of Mormon men. "The lustful eye caused by immodest dress," he indicated, "means a loss of spirituality and in some cases a loss of virtue." Finally,

Richards connected modest dress to, again, the success of proper Mormon courtship. "What would one of our girls think," he asked, "if after marriage she should learn from her husband that before marriage by reason of her immodest dress and exposed person he had been so overcome by lust as to resort to haunts of vice?" (1916, pp. 323–24). Unlike Smith, Richards placed responsibility for male chastity upon women, but asserted with Smith that a virtuous Mormon courtship would not be driven by sexual desire.

Home Nights served another function as well: in addition to encouraging Mormon youth to resist worldly trends, they would offer Mormon women a venue for demonstrating homemaking skills. Just as it did with Mormon men, marriage discourse offered women a set of prescribed gender roles, which emphasized that performance in a woman's role as wife and mother were linked to her faithfulness as a Latter-day Saint. "The perfect woman was not only righteous and talented but desirable," one Mormon periodical instructed (Hoyt and Patterson, 2011, p. 86). But what it meant to be "talented" and "righteous" was still, in the early twentieth century, in flux.

The transformation of Mormon femininity

The sentiments of these church leaders reflected what some historians have called the "cult of true womanhood," or the concept of "separate spheres" which moved to the fore of American culture in the late nineteenth century. These ideas, most prevalent among white middle- or upper-class Protestant Americans, maintained that men and women inhabited different and separate spheres; it fell to men to venture into the public realm to do battle in politics or business, to steer the nation and to earn the money that supported their families. Women, on the other hand, were not emotionally, mentally, or physically equipped for such fights; instead, their presumed gentle temperaments and strong moral compasses best equipped them for the private sphere of the home, where they would provide their families with a firm moral foundation and their children with a primary nurturer and parent (Edwards, 1997; Smith-Rosenberg, 1985).

After the end of plural marriage, as Mormons sought greater integration into American society, their expectations of women shifted accordingly, and they began to adopt the notion of separate spheres. This did not, though, mean that the activism of nineteenth century Mormon women was entirely forgotten. Indeed, a notable feature of much Mormon writing on womanhood in the years immediately following polygamy was the suggestion that Mormonism better empowered women than any other philosophy on earth, even as women were encouraged to take seriously their roles as mothers. As Susa Young Gates wrote in 1911,

> the sex lines can be drawn safely only when occupation, not natural dominance, draws them. It is right enough for men to classify themselves on sex lines, when war and protection from inimical force is the motive; and, too, it is proper enough for women to consider by themselves questions pertaining to the conduct of home labors and duties. But there are certain large questions which pertain to public as well as individual policy which can never be left safely to the consideration of either sex alone.

Given the "superior opportunities" Mormonism offered women, Mormon women sought both "social equality and a strong religious sense," and celebrated "reformatory work," "civic and labor leagues," and "social settlement work," the projects of Mormon women in the early twentieth century (1911, pp. 1, 189, 211). For Gates, also a defender of Mormon women's roles as wife and mother, the two could co-exist; this meant that men and women held complementary roles.

Consonant with such beliefs, sociologists have observed that the rhetoric of Mormon leaders after World War I increasingly emphasized women's roles in the home and family, rather than the public activism that characterized earlier periods, though the transition was gradual rather than sudden (Vance, 2002). The dominant figure in the early twentieth century Relief Society was Amy Brown Lyman, who served in various high leadership positions in the Relief Society until becoming its president in 1940. Lyman's career offers a useful illustration of the gradual shift in Mormon femininity away from its activist nineteenth-century past toward increasing emphasis on the cult of true womanhood by the mid-twentieth century (Hall, 2015; McDannell, 2018; Derr, Cannon, and Beecher, 1993).

During the 1910s and 1920s, Lyman sought out training in the burgeoning field of social work, and pushed successfully for the establishment of a Church Social Services department, which she directed. Using the principles of social work, this department sought to relieve economic suffering by building alliances with government agencies and other relief organizations. Lyman insisted upon training, sending a number of members of the Relief Society to Denver to attend classes and participate in fieldwork. Lyman argued, following the language of many activist women in the American progressive era, that such efforts derived from the notion of civic housekeeping, in which women took to the public square because they sought to defend the traditionally female sphere of motherhood (Skocpol, 2009).

In that spirit, under Lyman the Relief Society continued its activism, though its work increasingly focused on tasks that civic housekeeping could be invoked to justify. They erected milk stations throughout Salt Lake City, which provided both support for poor breastfeeding mothers and a food supply for the infants of impoverished families. They taught classes in mothering skills, they raised money and supplies for refugees in Europe during World War I, working closely with the federal government and the Red Cross. During the 1920s, the Social Services department would begin sponsoring, with a community organization, a Community Clinic that provided free healthcare in the city, and agreed to an arrangement to provide evaluations and monitoring of the families of juvenile delinquents. The same decade, Lyman instituted a Relief Society curriculum that recruited professionals to write lessons about social issues like malnutrition, poverty, and other social afflictions. Lyman also lobbied the state government for improved regulation and funding of social welfare programs. By 1921, with Lyman's support, the Relief Society endorsed and began implementing the Sheppard-Towner Act, a federal law which sought to organize alliances between the federal government, local governments, and community organizations to provide better neonatal and infant care throughout the United States. Through the 1920s, Lyman's life got busier and the Social Services department expanded.

In many ways, Lyman's activism reflected the tradition of public involvement among Mormon women; it also reflected the common American trend of civic housekeeping, which was drawing many American women into politics. And yet, from the beginning of her career in the 1910s, Lyman faced obstacles. One of her prime opponents was Susa Young Gates. Gates believed that Lyman's impulse toward professionalism and training hampered the spiritual justification behind the work of the Relief Society and would lead to a diminution of the familial responsibilities of Mormon women. Gates and Lyman each argued for their positions before Heber J. Grant, who became president of the church in 1919, and Gates ultimately resigned her position on the Relief Society Board, implying capitulation to Lyman's point of view. However, it is important to recognize the two were not so far apart as they might have seemed; Lyman's civic housekeeping rhetoric allowed her to speak the idiom of motherhood, while finding in it consonance with her activism. Indeed, much of the work the Relief Society did in the 1920s was centered upon care for children. Lyman's early career, then, reflected the ambiguity of shifting gender roles in early twentieth-century Mormonism.

The church welfare plan and the solidification of gendered spheres

Lyman soon discovered that other church leaders were growing suspicious of her activist conception of Mormon femininity, and began pressuring the Relief Society toward an increasingly privatized vision of a woman's proper role. When the Great Depression began in late 1929, Lyman continued to pursue the model of charity and social work she was accustomed to, seeking alliances with government agencies and organizing the Relief Society to canvass Mormon communities for need. She worked with the state of Utah to disperse federal aid and coordinated training efforts with the governments of Salt Lake City and local counties.

In 1936, however, spearheaded by First Counselor J. Reuben Clark, the First Presidency announced a new Church Security Program, which soon was renamed the Church Welfare Plan. The Plan sought to coordinate church-wide efforts to aid needy church members, but it was also shot through with assumptions about the proper role of men and women, and the Mormon priesthoods and Relief Society, that marginalized Lyman's vision of civic housekeeping in favor of domestic motherhood. Clark, who had spent most of his time outside Utah and had little experience with the vitality of the Relief Society there, was instead steeped in traditional American gender roles; he was a deep believer in the notion of separate spheres and had strong opinions about how Mormon men and women were to relate that fell closely in line with such traditional notions. As he told the Relief Society in 1940, "Do not try to be anything else but good mothers and good homemakers, for that will exhaust all the time, all the effort, and pay the greatest dividends of anything else you can do in the world" (Hall, 2015, p. 152).

When the Welfare Plan was announced, then, it was a surprise to Lyman that the Relief Society was almost entirely shut out of its administration. The Plan bypassed the Relief Society, ignoring the existence of the Social Services Department and instead erecting a new system for distributing church welfare that focused on the traditional responsibility of bishops, who each supervised a congregation, to distribute church offerings. The Plan directed bishops and stake presidents, who supervised several congregations that together made up a stake, to create welfare committees. These committees would finance farms or small manufactories where Mormon men who needed money because of unemployment could find work; in exchange, they would be given a portion of what the welfare farm or manufactory produced. This process would be supervised by bishops and stake presidents, who were priesthood officers and therefore male. The Relief Society was an afterthought and was asked to fulfill its traditional position of canvassing congregations for families or individuals in need, and to aid Mormon women receiving welfare assistance in formulating family budgets (Mangum and Blumell, 1993, pp. 142–44).

In part, the Welfare Plan focused on male leadership in church and family because the priesthood leadership of the church saw the Plan as a vehicle to promote an image of the Mormon man as a father and provider. "Only in extreme cases should women with young children be provided with work outside the home," stated one early Welfare Plan handbook (First Presidency, 1952, p. 2). Instead, the Plan was structured, and its administrators directed, to provide work for fathers first, in order to strengthen not only the financial health of the Mormon community but also to bolster the strength of the monogamous family, which was enjoying the sort of theological and cultural celebration that polygamous marriages had enjoyed fifty years prior. J. Reuben Clark observed in 1944 that the Welfare Plan was designed so that Mormons would "quit drawing on the national stock pile" of government resources and build up the "family stock pile" instead. Reliance on Mormon masculinity, then, was linked to independence from the state and reliance instead on the male-led Mormon community. Mormons, he said, should look to their fathers, both familial and ecclesiastical, for help when they needed it. "The bishop is the father of his ward," Clark explained, drawing on a familiar metaphor, "and as any good father would do if part of his family is not very prosperous and another part is, he would try to see that the part that is prosperous helps the part that is not" (Clark, 1944, pp. 3–4).

The gendered transformation of Mormon priesthood

Clark's emphasis on the authority of the priesthood drew institutional authority away from the Relief Society, a process that continued into the middle of the twentieth century. This process increasingly equated Mormon manhood with priesthood and administrative authority, and Mormon womanhood with the home. These changes happened along at least two lines: the formal delineation of what the "priesthood" was and the rhetoric of Mormon publications and leadership.

Sociologists have observed that, beginning around the time of World War I, Mormon periodicals increasingly emphasized the domestic responsibilities of Mormon women, and earlier language, like that of Gates which found that role compatible with public activism began to fade (Vance, 2002). Instead, by the middle third of the century, Mormon periodicals were emphasizing that a woman's primary duties were those of wife and mother, and that other pursuits should be subordinated in service to those callings. Mormons came to affirm the distinction between the private and public spheres that characterized much of American culture more broadly. Indeed, the distinction came to be drawn within Mormonism itself, as administration and leadership in the church came to be associated with manhood. In 1926 Gates and the Mormon writer Leah Widtsoe drew the parallel.

> No woman could safely carry the triple burden of wifehood, motherhood and at the same time function in priestly orders. Yet her creative home labor ranks side by side, in earthly and heavenly importance, with her husband's priestly responsibilities. His in the market place—hers at the hearthstone ... That he would bungle and spoil home life if he sought to enter woman's sphere is as sure as it is that she would emasculate his affairs if, or when, she attempts to prove her equality by crowding man out of his place.
>
> *(1926, p. 5)*

Increasingly as the twentieth century went on, Mormon leaders began to emphasize this complementarianism, arguing that Mormon women were as uniquely suited to the tasks of the home as Mormon men were for the tasks of leadership in the church. In 1940, John A. Widtsoe, an apostle and husband to Leah Widtsoe, echoed his wife's earlier claims: "In the divine economy, specific duties are assigned to the different members of the family," Widtsoe wrote. "In the case of women, the natural and most satisfying career is the home" (1940, p. 587). The language here, that women possessed special inherent gifts which uniquely suited them for motherhood, grew increasingly common by the 1930s and 1940s, and affirmed anew Susa Young Gates' earlier suspicions of professionals usurping womanly responsibilities. By the 1940s, the First Presidency of the church insisted that the

> divine service of motherhood can be rendered only by mothers. It may not be passed to others. Nurses cannot do it; public nurseries cannot do it; hired help cannot do it ... the mother who entrusts her child to the care of others, that she may do non-motherly work, whether for gold, for fame, or for civic service, should remember that "a child left to himself bringeth her mother to shame."
>
> *(First Presidency, 1942, p. 12)*

The narrowing of acceptable roles for Mormon women reflected the growing institutionalization and delineation of Mormon priesthood. The standardization of priesthood organization and leadership that characterized the early years of the twentieth century (the progression of young men through priesthood offices as they grew; the assertion of priestly authority over the auxiliaries of the church), was likewise accompanied by language that asserted that priesthood was uniquely suited for male nature. "All men who have experience hold or should hold the Priesthood," wrote Widtsoe. "In the family the man is the spokesman and primary authority, and therefore the Priesthood is bestowed upon him." For Widtsoe, priesthood work "intensifies family loyalty and devotion, from which virtues proceed" (1915, pp. 97, 144). Thus, priesthood and male authority in both the private and public spheres were drawn in parallel to each other. More, he believed priesthood authority was a way for Mormon men to develop character and virtue, which in turn would intensify their devotion to their families. Priesthood and family were connected together, and male authority was the link.

This process of delineating priesthood between public and private spheres was most obvious in the regularization of Mormon practices of blessing the sick or infirm. For many years both men and women had performed such blessings of healing by laying on of hands. Men had traditionally done so according to the authority of their priesthood office. Female authority for such blessings was more ambiguous. Many women were blessed by authority of their faith in Jesus, but some women, like the prominent nineteenth-century leader Eliza R. Snow, had associated such blessings with the authority women received in the rites of Mormon temple worship, which included washing and anointing, rituals that accompanied many blessings of the sick. Men and women also gave somewhat different blessings: women in particular blessed other women in the Relief Society, particularly in the confinement ritual, given to pregnant women about to give birth (Stapley and Wright, 2011; Newell, 1981).

During his presidency (1901–1918) Joseph F. Smith was a staunch supporter of these practices, though he also offered clarification and regulation, reserving the right to "seal" blessings to priesthood holders. But after his death the priestly leadership of the church began to grow uncomfortable with them. During his presidency, Heber J. Grant (1919–1945) standardized many liturgical practices, eliminating redundancies and issuing standard directives on how to perform many rites. This standardization accompanied the clarification of priesthood authority over the various auxiliaries of the church that also marked Grant's presidency, and perhaps unsurprisingly, increasingly leading members of the Mormon hierarchy began to insist that blessings of healing were best administered by male priesthood holders who had formal ordination. By the 1930s, local priesthood leaders, like bishops and stake presidents, had begun to regulate Relief Society blessing practices, and soon, John Widtsoe wrote in his manual *Priesthood and Church Government* that the gifts of the spirit—like speaking in tongues, prophecy and blessings—were "properly exercised under the power of the Priesthood" (1939, p. 246). In 1946, the apostle Joseph Fielding Smith wrote to the Relief Society General Board that women should offer blessings and anointings only under the direction of priesthood leaders, but also discouraged them from the practice. By the middle of the century, the practice had lost official sanction altogether (Stapley and Wright, 2011; Stapley, 2018).

Conclusion

The era between the end of polygamy and World War II was marked by transition between two periods of relative stability: the age of plural marriage and the conservative postwar Mormon culture the correlation movement created in the 1960s. As such, Mormon gender norms in the period reflected a certain ambiguity, as Mormon men and women wondered how to balance the changing demands of their faith with the pressures of American culture writ large.

References

Alexander, T.G., 1985. *Mormonism in Transition: A History of the Latter-day Saints, 1890–1930.* Urbana, IL: University of Illinois Press.
Clark, J.R., 1944. Address Given by President J. Reuben Clark at the Salt Lake Regional Welfare Meeting, Monday, February 7. Church History Library and Archives, pp. 3–4.
Collier, F., 1987. *The Trials of Apostles John W. Taylor and Matthias F. Cowley.* Salt Lake City, UT: Collier's Publishing Company.
Daynes, K.M., 2001. *More Wives Than One: The Transformation of the Mormon Marriage System, 1840–1910.* Urbana, IL: University of Illinois Press.
de Schweinitz, R., 2011. Preaching the Gospel of Church and Sex: Mormon Women's Fiction in *The Young Woman's Journal*, 1889–1910. *Dialogue: A Journal of Mormon Thought* 33: 27–54.
Derr, J.M, Cannon, J.R., and Beecher, M.U., 1993. *Women of Covenant: The Story of Relief Society.* Salt Lake City, UT: Deseret Book.
Edwards, R., 1997. *Angels in the Machinery: Gender in American Party Politics from the Civil War to the Progressive Era.* New York: Oxford University Press.
First Presidency of the Church of Jesus Christ of Latter-day Saints, 1942. Parenthood. *Conference Report* 47: 12–13.
First Presidency of the Church of Jesus Christ of Latter-day Saints, 1952. *Welfare Plan of the Church of Jesus Christ of Latter-day Saints.* Salt Lake City, UT: Church of Jesus Christ of Latter-day Saints.
Gates, S.Y., 1891. Editor's Department. *Young Women's Journal* 2: 283–85.
Gates, S.Y., 1911. *History of the Young Ladies' Mutual Improvement Association.* Salt Lake City, UT: Deseret News Press.
Gates, S.Y., and Widtsoe, L., 1926. *Women of the Mormon Church.* Salt Lake City, UT: Deseret News Press.
Grant, H.J., 1916. Prohibition. *Young Women's Journal* 17: 402–6.
Hall, D., 2015. *A Faded Legacy: Amy Brown Lyman and Mormon Women's Activism, 1872–1959.* Salt Lake City, UT: University of Utah Press.
Hartley, W.G., 1996. From Men to Boys: LDS Aaronic Priesthood Offices, 1829–1996. *Journal of Mormon History* 22: 80–137.
Hoyt, A., and Patterson, S.M., 2011. Mormon Masculinity: Changing Gender Expectations in the Era of Transition from Polygamy to Monogamy, 1890–1920. *Gender and History* 23(1): 72–91.
Inouye, M., 2004. What a Girl Wants: LDS Women's Courtship and Marriage, 1890–1930. In C. Bushman, ed. *Latter-day Saint Women in the Twentieth Century.* Provo, UT: Joseph Smith Institute for Latter-day Saint History at Brigham Young University, pp. 75–92.
Kimball, R.I., 2003. *Sports in Zion: Mormon Recreation, 1890–1940.* Urbana, IL: University of Illinois Press.
Larsen, L., 1962. *Autobiography of Lorena Eugenia Washburn Larsen.* Provo, UT: Brigham Young University Press.
Mangum, G., and Blumell, B., 1993. *The Mormons' War on Poverty: A History of LDS Welfare, 1830–1990.* Salt Lake City, UT: University of Utah Press.
McDannell, C., 2018. *Sister Saints: Mormon Women since the End of Polygamy.* New York: Oxford University Press.
Newell, L.K., 1981. A Gift Given, a Gift Taken: Washing, Anointing and Blessing the Sick among Mormon Women. *Sunstone* 29: 16–25.
Nichols, J., 2002. *Polygamy, Prostitution and Power: Salt Lake City, 1847–1918.* Salt Lake City, UT: University of Utah Press.
Richards, G.F., 1916. Modesty. *Young Women's Journal* 17: 323–24.
Skocpol, T., 2009. *Protecting Soldiers and Mothers: The Political Origins of Social Policy in the United States.* Cambridge, MA: Harvard University Press.
Smith-Rosenberg, C., 1985. *Disorderly Conduct: Visions of Gender in Victorian America.* New York: Oxford University Press.
Stapley, J.A., 2018. *The Power of Godliness: Mormon Ritual and Cosmology.* New York: Oxford University Press.

Stapley, J.A., and Wright, K., 2011. Female Ritual Healing in Mormonism. *Journal of Mormon History* 37: 1–85.
Tait, L.O., 2013. The 1890s Mormon Culture of Letters and the Post-Manifesto Marriage Crisis: A New Approach to Home Literature. *BYU Studies Quarterly* 52: 1–27.
Talbot, C., 2017. Mormons, Gender, and the New Commercial Entertainments, 1890–1920. *Journal of the Gilded Age and Progressive Era* 16(3): 302–24.
Talmage, J.A., 1907. *The Story of Mormonism*. Salt Lake City, UT: Deseret News Press.
Vance, L., 2002. Evolution of Ideals for Women in Mormon Periodicals, 1897–1999. *Sociology of Religion* 63(1): 91–112.
Walker, R.W., 1982. B.H. Roberts and the Woodruff Manifesto. *BYU Studies Quarterly* 22: 363–66.
Watt, G.A., 1854–1886. *Journal of Discourses*, 26 vols. Liverpool: A. Calkin.
Whitney, H.M.K., 1884. *Why We Practice Plural Marriage*. Salt Lake City, UT: Deseret News Press.
Widtsoe, J.A., 1915. *A Rational Theology as Taught by the Church of Jesus Christ of Latter-day Saints*. Salt Lake City, UT: Deseret News Press.
Widtsoe, J.A., 1939. *Priesthood and Church Government*. Salt Lake City, UT: Deseret News Press.
Widtsoe, J.A., 1940. Women's Greatest Career. *Improvement Era* 43(10): 587.

Further references

Holbrook, K., and Bowman, M. eds., 2015. *Women and Mormonism in Historic and Contemporary Perspectives*. Salt Lake City, UT: University of Utah Press.

A collection of essays, many of which deal with the transformation of Mormon femininity between the end of plural marriage and the mid-twentieth century and which emphasize the tensions Mormon women have felt between American culture and their faith.

Shipps, J., 1984. *Mormonism: The Story of a New Religious Tradition*. Urbana, IL: University of Illinois Press.

Shipps discusses in broader strokes a transition in Mormon society, culture and doctrine similar to the one outlined here: from a intensely communal religion centered upon polygamy to an emphasis upon moral behavior and individual rectitude.

11
MORMON GENDER IN THE MID-TWENTIETH CENTURY

Colleen McDannell

The postwar Mormon culture constructed between 1945 and 1970 was so secure and vibrant that it flourished throughout the tumultuous years of the 1960s and provided a workable ideal until the end of the century. In conference addresses, *Relief Society Magazine* fiction, advice columns, hymns, personal diaries, and dramatic performances, Latter-day Saints delivered a consistent message of who women and men were and what they should be doing. Caring for large families and participating in ward activities became so all-encompassing that most Latter-day Saint women had little time or energy for anything else. Mormon men were to be the sole financial providers for their families, but they also were expected to be fully involved in the church and active in the home. Sexual discipline was required of both genders and an elaborate language of purity was developed to instill appropriate heterosexual behavior.

Even when women and men detailed their struggles to uphold gender standards in their private letters and diaries, they made no request to fundamentally change Mormon culture. Obviously, high standards were hard to meet and many Saints, in spite of their best intentions, could not practice their ideals. Mothers could be severely tested by their home lives, but they sought strategies for domestic improvement not for radical restructuring. Most Latter-day Saint women ignored the structural changes promoted by the burgeoning feminist movement. Men may have sought callings with fewer responsibilities, but they acknowledged that the "priesthood" was the foundation of the church. Some Mormons might leave the church altogether, or, like the historian Fawn Brodie in 1946, be excommunicated, but most accepted Latter-day Saint gender roles as difficult but virtuous.

Tumultuous mid-century

Latter-day Saints constructed this formidable culture during two decades of profound national unrest. Historians have overturned the notion that the 1950s were a halcyon era, instead arguing that the postwar years profoundly transformed how many Americans understood their place in society and culture. Women in particular were experiencing worlds markedly different than their mothers did. Even though the white, middle-class home was idealized, married women increasingly worked outside of the home and expected their husbands to help—at the very least—with child rearing. In 1963 Betty Friedan's *Feminine Mystique* helped catalyze a renewed feminist movement—which would call for a realignment of both female and male behavior. By

1970 some women embraced the sexual liberation of a "counterculture" while other more conservative women had long since mobilized to fight communism, abortion, and sexual liberation. Some men had rejected their father's commitment to marital fidelity, self-denial, and corporate loyalty choosing instead to experiment with self-expressive lifestyles. As women increasingly moved into the workforce, as well as into politics and education, defining appropriate gender roles became more complex.

During the postwar decades, many American women and men asked the "who am I" question. For many, there was no clear answer. For Mormon women and men of this era, there was. At the beginning of the 1950s, Latter-day Saints shared notions about gender roles with middle-class Americans. Two decades later, many Americans had adopted more fluid notions of gender and sexual expressions—comportment that would be unacceptable in orthodox Mormon households.

Domesticity after World War II

In August 1945, Japan surrendered to the Allied forces, and American soldiers slowly came home. The war industry converted to peacetime production and families longed to get back to normal. However, exactly what was "normal" was not clear. Two powerful and overlapping desires dogged America's families. Political discourse, the media, pop psychology, and religious rhetoric presented a familiar and comforting image of a father earning a living for his family, nurtured by a loving mother. Insecurity, felt by individual traumatized soldiers or by Cold War fears, would be relieved through family stability, womanly graces, Godly piety, and capitalist consumption. Almost every aspect of American culture taught that when women crossed into the male sphere—and certainly vice versa—disaster ensued. Mental breakdowns, children transformed into juvenile delinquents, and political disorder inevitably would ruin the nation if "natural" gender roles were not upheld.

At the same time that popular culture extolled mothers for their domestic abilities, married women were increasingly entering the marketplace as workers. During World War II, millions of women had answered the call to join the labor force (often doing traditionally male jobs) in spite of the pressures it placed on home life. At the war's end, female workers quit (or were fired) to make room for returning soldiers. The growing economy, however, needed more workers. Since the G.I. Bill had made homeownership a reachable dream for more families, advertisers targeted female consumers, hoping to convince them to buy their products and thus make their homes modern, efficient, and beautiful. To afford postwar products, women joined their husbands in the labor force but understood their outside employment to be simply "a job," while their career was being a mother. Pink-collar work was not perceived as a revolt against domesticity but rather as a means to augment home life. Consequently, during the 1950s the employment of married women grew by 42 percent. Companies abandoned their rules against hiring wives. Thirty percent of married women were employed by 1960, and 39 percent of all mothers with school-age children were in the labor force (Hartmann, 1994, p. 86).

To secure this consumer-oriented home life, breadwinner masculinity flourished. At least it was presented as a desirable goal in popular culture. For many African-American families, however, racism kept them from achieving such ideals. Men were expected to submit their personal desires for the collective good of their family. If need be, a second job could be taken on or a tedious one endured. For white men, hard work often helped them take advantage of a growing American economy. For black men, they continued to labor in a segregated, unjust, workplace. As white men moved into the middle class, men discovered that the camaraderie that they shared with their working-class male friends could not be easily duplicated in the suburbs. The sex segregation of ethnic neighborhoods, where men socialized in taverns, unions, and clubs was replaced by couple-based activities focused on church, school, and sports. In this "Father Knows Best" world, men were to be fully engaged with their families, if not with housework.

Changes in the Intermountain West

Latter-day Saints also benefited from the expanding postwar economy. Utah's population grew by 25 percent during World War II as people migrated to the state to work in war industries (Christensen, 1978, p. 510). Rural Utahans also moved to the cities for work. Before the war, the state's per capita income was 20 percent less than the national average. By 1943 it was almost 3 percent greater (Christensen, 1978, p. 505). Like much of the American West, Utah benefited from the growth of the federal government. Cold War fears brought contracts for missile systems, facilities for chemical weapons storage, and the expansion of military bases.

Utah women participated in this bourgeoning economy. During the war, women's employment had peaked in 1943 at 64,510 workers but it declined to nearly 46,000 by the spring of 1946 (Murphy, 2005, p. 210). However, as in the rest of the country, Utah women were going back to work. In 1950 the state had a female workforce of 57,294, and half of those were married and living with their husbands. That number was an 87 percent increase over the 1940 figure (Murphy, 2005, pp. 211–12). The next decade brought even steeper increases, and by 1970 half of Utah's women over 16 were employed (Beecher and MacKay, 1978, p. 577). Some Latter-day Saint women married educated men and moved out of state with their husbands when opportunities arose. Moving up the social scale or away from the community of the Saints was both exciting and terrifying.

Utah men who took advantage of the G.I. Bill by attending college developed wider skills and credentials than their fathers possessed. Mormonism's stress on knowledge, thrift, and hard work also facilitated their ability to take advantage of postwar affluence and move into the middle class. A common pattern of male leaders and members was a boyhood spent on the family's farm, youth studying at college, and adulthood working in an office. The sons of hard-working farmers joined corporations and government agencies. As the church expanded its missionary activities and experienced member growth, it not only required a more sophisticated bureaucracy but also individuals to staff church-owned, for-profit, businesses. Latter-day Saint men managed church real estate, media, insurance, and retail organizations. Men oversaw the church's thirty-two food canneries, clothing and furniture factories in California, and even a sugar plantation in Hawaii. Self-sufficiency was still promoted, but mid-century Mormon men were increasingly enmeshed in organizational networks that valued teamwork and monetary success. The Progressive Era values of efficiency, centralization, and rational religion became even closer aligned with masculinity.

In 1951, Relief Society President Belle S. Spafford accurately recognized the reconfiguration of postwar America. Women were being lured into the workforce by "vocational opportunities ... increased living standards and high living costs, requiring greater income than one member of a family can provide." At the same time, women saw "increased opportunities to transfer child-care functions to child-care centers" and "strong community appeals [for work]." More perceptively, Spafford recognized that Latter-day Saint women like other women had "desires for independence, yes, and in some instances a sense of discontent and fear of missing something in the seclusion and the unrecognized activities of household routine." Still, Spafford concluded, women should resist such enticements because employment came "at too great a cost to their children, at the too costly sacrifice of a full realization of the joys and blessed privileges of motherhood" (Spafford, 1951, p. 725). Barely into the 1950s, Spafford was well aware of the challenges that a changing American society posed to Latter-day Saint women.

Anxieties over consumer culture

Changes in the texture of Mormon culture and of American society raised anxiety among church leaders and members. Consequently, delineating the duties and capabilities of faithful Mormon women and men became a preoccupation of the postwar Latter-day Saints Church. Teaching appropriate gender roles became ubiquitous. Commemorative biography, semi-annual conference talks, and popular fiction all articulated what might be thought of as a theology of gender for a growing Latter-day Saints community. It made no difference if a Saint lived in Salt Lake, Boston, or Mexico City, the message was the same.

For instance, in 1950 Vesta Crawford, an associate editor of the *Relief Society Magazine*, wrote an essay about her friend Virginia Clark. In it Crawford presented Clark as the ideal Latter-day Saint mother, an image frequently duplicated in Mormon literature throughout mid-century. Clark was the mother of six and had experienced the death of one son. She had been a missionary and then married a righteous Mormon man. He, too, had given two years of his life to the church and eventually became a ward bishop. No farmer, Clark's husband would wear the academic robes that she faultlessly sewed for him. Virginia Clark confided to her friend that her life "had been satisfying and complete, full of joy and fulfillment." The same certainly would have been said by her husband (Crawford, 1950, p. 296).

Virginia Clark stood in sharp contrast with another woman described that same year by David O. McKay, soon to become church president. McKay told the story of a woman who had been married five years, worked, went skiing and skating, and enjoyed dinner out followed by a movie. She and her husband were "crazy about each other," but they did not want a family. Children would be "a foreign element in this little world that is so perfect and so all our own." McKay notes that the man had a job but nothing is said of his commitment to religion. The couple's modern, carefree life could not produce happiness, however. Soon the man was looking at other women because, he has "unconsciously grown to miss the things that Nature knows a woman should be giving to her husband." Childless women, the president believed, will "lose their beauty, their alertness, their interest in life. Their faces are so often empty and vacuous, even if pretty." These women were not a credit to their sex. "Wifehood is glorious," McKay concluded, "but motherhood is sublime" (McKay, 1950, p. 800).

In the case of Virginia Clark, her life circled around the traditional triad of home, children, and church. The childless woman, in contrast, focused exclusively on herself and excluded all that did not give her pleasure. In neither caricature, do we see a glimpse of the Progressive Era Mormon woman who sought to improve the community, promote cultural refinement, or broaden the intellect. Nor do we see the productive pioneer male who can make, as well as organize. Both Mormon and national cultures valorized the home, but Latter-day Saints were especially suspicious of modern forms of leisure or consumption that detracted from the home's centrality and seriousness. Stories in church literature warned against the mother who went to work to pay for a new washing machine or a father who spent too many hours at work. "Homemaking is a joint enterprise," Relief Society President Spafford would explain, "with divinely ordained division of labor for forming, maintaining, and projecting the family unit" (Spafford, 1958, p. 354).

Postwar babies

In 1950, McKay's worries about childless women seemed blind to the postwar baby boom. However, a decade later birth rates were cooling and more Americans worried about global overpopulation. By 1965 one out every four married women under 45 years of age had used the newly approved Birth Control Pill (Watkins, 1988, p. 34). Mormon teaching, however, tightly connected male and female gender roles to motherhood and fatherhood. Raising large families were visible signs of men and women fulfilling their spiritual roles. Apostle Ezra Taft Benson pithily observed in 1969 that, "The Lord did not say to multiply and replenish the earth if it is convenient, or if you are wealthy, or after you have gotten your schooling, or when there is peace on earth, or until you have four children" (Benson, 1969, p. 44). Benson continued the belief cultivated during the polygamous nineteenth century that having numerous children enabled spirits to come to earth, increased the community of the Saints, and was essentially an act of worship. Latter-day Saints believed that blessings would come to those who had a large posterity and who raised them up in righteousness.

Church leaders thus worked against the popular understanding that parents could more effectively address their children's material, educational, and emotional needs through maintaining a small family size. Likewise, Latter-day Saints rejected the postwar goal of a labor-free home. Since Mormons have always linked religion and work, for the home to have a spiritual focus it must also be the center of meaningful labor. Rather than mutely stand by and let the mass media erase household industry, Latter-day Saint women wrote themselves into a productive, pious, and praiseworthy domestic world. Women penned lyrical evocations of neatly folded bed linens, enticing rows of canned peaches, and aromatic, brown-crusted bread, hot from the oven. As late as 1965, *The Improvement Era* claimed that no French perfume could "possibly compete with the captivating power held by the aroma of bread baking in the oven when a hungry man enters the door of a home" (Anon, 1965, p. 78). Canning, bread baking, quilting—these activities held symbolic value that connected modern Latter-day Saint women to the foundational era of their religion and the efforts of their pioneer foremothers. Virtuous men appreciated the care their wives took in domestic production but consuming tasty pies and bread, not their production, underscored their masculinity.

Domesticity's dark side

Although domesticity was a Mormon idea, not all women found the role meaningful and natural. Some mid-century women wrote to "Mary Marker," the advice columnist for the church-owned *Deseret News* about the stresses they experienced at home. "I hate everything about baking bread," observed a letter writer from the late 1940s, "but I was so sold on the idea that any good wife and mother baked bread for her family that I forced myself to do it." It was only after electric shock treatments, six months in a psychiatric hospital, and "an awful lot of therapy" that this woman began to "not feel guilty about not liking housework" (Anon, ca. 1948–49). In 1951, Madelene Scott found an apt image of her life with three young children: a "mechanical rabbit being chased around and around by the greyhounds" (Scott, 1951). A mother from Ely, Nevada, wrote about spending a tedious evening with other young mothers. She marveled at the change in her life: a few years earlier she and the same friends were at college reading Proust in the original French but now after a day of caring for babies, "we're almost dead at night." "We're losing interest in ourselves," she observed, "and we're becoming real bores. What can we do?" (Ely, ca. 1948–49). A writer from Hurricane, Utah, signed a 1955 letter "Lazy Susan." "I have stomach ulcers and other nervous disorders," she confessed, "which

I feel like I can never overcome until I learn to either become more efficient or not to let my undone work bother me." She ended her letter by revealing that "I pray about this all the time, but I guess I lack faith. Can you help me?" ("Lazy Susan," 1955).

Both Mary Marker and the other Mormon women who wrote in with their suggestions reflected decades of practical advice on housekeeping contained in the pages of the *Relief Society Magazine*. The home should be a productive unit not a perfect system, so it did not pay mothers to become overly concerned with achieving perfection. It was much better for women to have a specialized understanding of domesticity and then to acknowledge their own limits as individuals. The struggles of motherhood and housekeeping could be kept under control if women cultivated a spiritual orientation, organized themselves, and balanced the various demands of home life. Domesticity and motherhood were a part of woman's natural make-up; they could be improved upon but not eliminated.

Improved systems of housekeeping, appropriate mindsets about home, and a realistic perspective on family life would enable the joy of motherhood to materialize. Mrs. O.H. Lamoreaux responded to "Lazy Susan" by expounding on her system for conquering domestic woes: "I scrub and wax [the floor] once a week and wash and iron weekly and have stopped worrying about whether the house is neat or not. If not every pillowcase was ironed or every toy picked up, so be it" (Lamoreaux, 1955). In 1955, Elise E. Hart suggested ripping up the carpet and putting in linoleum (Hart, 1955). Mrs. E.F. Kehl told another mother that she woke an hour before her babies in order to iron, sew, and mend. "Have a *system*" she stressed, "Made to your order but have *one*" (Kehl, n.d.). In 1963, Deseret Book published Daryl Hoole's *The Art of Homemaking* and it became an instant bestseller. Hoole insisted that women find a system for household management and give up the search for perfection. From her perspective as a mother of eight, she knew that organization was the key to making happy families.

Other women believed that positive attitudes made for strong families. In 1958, "A Happy Wife" wrote in to the *Deseret News* to respond to a letter sent in by "Bitter." "Happy Wife" asked mothers to "try to see the beauty in a sunny day, your flowers, the clouds, sunset or just a clothesline of pretty white clothes, or a door of freshly ironed clothes, or a story your child has to tell." If "Bitter" would greet her husband looking cheerful and happy, make him a surprise meal, and stop looking for his faults, "most husbands would come to their senses" ("A Happy Wife," 1953). Women needed to cultivate patience and understanding. Leola Curtis wrote in to agree: "What you haven't learned is how to handle a man. It's the oldest, and hardest to learn, art." Women needed to be sweet, but sincerely sweet (Curtis, 1958).

Commodifying womanhood

While many Mormon women assumed that it was *their* responsibility to improve their attitudes, it would be one particular Mormon woman who would commodify those sentiments into a commercial business. At the same time that Daryl Hoole was promoting household organization as the key for happy homes, another Latter-day Saint, Helen Andelin, took a different approach. In 1962, Andelin first met with a small group of women from her ward, and, not unlike a Relief Society class, she taught lessons in what she called "Fascinating Womanhood." Andelin had based her ideas on a set of booklets printed in the 1920s that stressed the distinctive roles of men and women. The response of her neighbors was exceedingly positive. Soon Andelin needed to rent space at a local YMCA to accommodate all of the women who wanted to attend her workshops. In 1965, Andelin and her husband self-published *Fascinating Womanhood*, a book to accompany the workshops. Within a year, the couple had sold over 40,000 copies and 900 women per week were taking their classes (Neuffer, 2007, pp. 102–4). Andelin's perspectives on gender roles struck a chord with Mormons and non-Mormons alike.

Helen Andelin drew from Latter-day Saint understanding of male and female characteristics but significantly reworked them. She downplayed women's roles as an efficient and productive homemaker and instead stressed her role as a romantic partner to her husband. Women did not need to learn how to be better housewives, they needed to learn how to be better wives. To be a good wife, women should cultivate their adorable, childlike natures and present themselves as charming, helpless, and dependent. Wives ought to smile and be ever beautiful. Andelin provided a well-defined picture of what this beauty entailed: women must only wear light or bright colors and patterns. They should avoid masculine attire like trousers and choose instead delicate and silky fabrics that enabled them to walk, gesture, and sit in a feminine way. Expressing strong opinions or displaying flashes of intelligence were unbecoming of a lady. Men were drawn to women who looked feminine, and femininity meant the opposite of whatever men thought was manly. The wife needed to be happy with anything her husband did: adjusting her likes to his, her hobbies to his, her pleasures to his. Women must praise their husbands and admire them as providers, even if they were not.

From Andelin's perspective, men were naturally insecure and tended to be lazy. Yes, men were to be domestic and religious leaders but not all men were eager to take up their authoritative positions. Women needed to take control—gently—and encourage men to express their God-given capabilities. If men shirked their leadership roles, women must not compensate and take on male responsibilities. "When you work," Andelin wrote, "you rob your husband of his right to meet ordinary challenges, and to grow by these challenges. And, as you become capable, efficient, and independent, he feels less needed, and therefore less masculine. This weakens him. As you lift, he sets the bucket down" (Andelin, 1965, p. 317). From the perspective of Fascinating Womanhood, church literature that rendered women as competent achievers missed the key point: men chaffed at knowing their efficient and useful wives could survive without them. Helen Andelin—perhaps the most famous Mormon woman that no one knew was Mormon—not only rebuked feminist notions of fluid gender roles but traditional Mormon ones as well.

Masculine Mormons

Helen Andelin and Daryl Hoole both believed that women shaped the spiritual realm of the home. Men, in turn, were expected to bring their faith to the world. After World War II, the church revitalized its domestic and foreign missionary activities. David O. McKay, who had been in the First Presidency since 1937 and served as president from 1951 to 1970, was a firm believer in the global expansion of Mormonism. McKay understood missionary work as specifically a male priesthood activity and having such experience increasingly became a critical part of being a faithful Mormon man (Evans, 1985, p. 153). During the two decades of McKay's leadership, the church would put almost 90,000 missionaries in the field (*Annual Report*, 1972). In spite of the high birth rate of Latter-day Saints, during this time church membership increased more by adult converts than by children being baptized (Shepherd and Shepherd, 1998, p. 4).

Church leader Henry D. Moyle fueled member expansion, and his efforts reflected his own understanding of mid-century Mormon manhood. In 1959, Moyle headed the Missionary Department committee and served as both First and Second Counselor to President McKay until Moyle's death in 1963. As with other Latter-day Saint men, Moyle came from a farming family but studied engineering in college and attended law school. After serving in World War I, he became a successful businessman, working in oil, banking, ranching, and insurance. Scorning the frugality and austerity of his father, Moyle argued that Mormons needed to make an impression in the world. He encouraged the rebuilding of crumbling mission homes into impressive and somewhat extravagant edifices. Believing that mission presidents should reflect the active virility of their religion, Moyle sought out younger men for the position who could demonstrate male religious conviction and authority. Even the age of male missionary service was lowered from 21 to 19. A sports fan, Moyle encouraged his missionaries to use baseball to lure potential youthful converts into church. Sport became a missionary tool and intrinsic to Mormon notions of manliness.

As proselytizing gained more prominence in Mormon life, male missionaries became the heroic exemplars of the righteous Saint. Men sacrificed their personal comfort and independence (as they had fighting two world wars) in order to march with the Army of the Lord and conquer the world for Christ. In addition to the military, church leaders also took inspiration from American capitalism to facilitate member growth. Standardized manuals and unified approaches were promoted. Like efficient salesmen, missionaries memorized dialogues, collected statistics, utilized flannel boards and flip-charts for illustrations, and dressed in business attire. Rather than spontaneously preaching in the streets, as they had done previously, they systematically knocked on doors and hoped to deliver standardized lessons. Accruing a growing number of baptisms, rather than the quality or duration of the conversion, became the goal. Men who met their quotas as missionaries were celebrated, those who did not, ignored. As in the secular world, achievement made the man.

The unified model of missionary work played to the linguistic strengths of men. Clear-cut, memorized dialogues gave the impression of certainty. Missionaries addressed vague or uncomfortable questions with prescribed responses or ignored the queries as irrelevant. The missionary knew the truth by heart, and he worked diligently to convince those who did not have the truth that he was right. With the non-Mormon in the subordinate position, the missionary was center stage. Teaching aids and statistics gave the aura of a science, and missionaries could compete with one another by tallying baptisms.

Women assumed an awkward place in this male world of religious soldiers and salesmen. Since women could not baptize converts (because only men had the power of the priesthood) and accumulating baptisms was the goal, female missionaries actually were a liability. As we have seen, the church presented the family—not preaching—as women's highest calling. In 1951 the official age for a woman missionary was set at 23, to encourage women to concentrate on marriage not mission. Women were to raise mission-bound sons and wait for mission-bound boyfriends, not dream of mission service for themselves. Although in 1964 the church lowered the age limit for women to 21, most members still assumed that sister missionaries were women with spotty marriage prospects. Missionary work was a masculine activity and women were indulged but not encouraged.

Ward culture climax

Although Henry Moyle's "baseball baptisms" were less than successful, mid-century Mormonism was marked by serious growth. In 1940, there were 862,600 Saints living mostly in the Intermountain West (Reeve and Parshall, 2010, p. 57), but by 1970 church membership tripled to a global 3 million (Givens, 2007, p. 231). To encourage converts to remain in place, church leaders ratcheted up its building program. By 1964, more than 60 percent of all church buildings had been constructed within the previous ten years (Givens, 2007, p. 245). A growing church sought to secure the commitments of new converts through a myriad of ward activities. While "correlation" (an organizational movement devised by leaders in Salt Lake City) sought to consolidate and simplify, on the local level ward life was a dizzying array of social events that engaged every age group.

From Salt Lake City to Boston to Cape Town, Mormons organized dances, dinners, holiday parties, road shows, pageants, musicals, speech contests, rummage sales, and summer camps. Young ladies wearing formals were presented to Mormon society in Gold and Green balls where they danced with their fathers to orchestral music. Women provided food for funerals and arranged music to be presented by the ward's "Singing Mothers." In places without Latter-day Saint mortuaries, Relief Society women prepared bodies for burial. While men may have initiated and overseen such events, women provided most of the labor. Social events certainly functioned to reinforce feminine values such as beauty and domesticity, but they also illustrated to women that they could be efficient, creative, and productive organizers. Ward life kept women constantly busy.

In addition to social activities, fundraising was also the job of women. Before 1970, the women's Relief Society raised money for its own projects as well as the ward's. Goods sold at bazaars were often made during Tuesday afternoon Relief Society "work meetings." They raised money by selling crafts, foods, and services to other members of their ward or stake. Women's efforts were creative and relentless. Zina Burr from Alberta, Canada, described in her diary how for one Relief Society bazaar she made more than fifteen pounds of chocolates, a doll cradle out of a grape basket, two nylon dress slips, and two aprons. Other women in her ward made lampshades and ice cream. Burr was proud of her accomplishments but she admitted, "My eyes are suffering from so much strain. Lot of fine hand work to [sew] those doll dresses" (Burr, 1953). Bazaars encouraged women to be imaginative. A woman from Cape Town, South Africa, remembered having an "ankle beauty contest" where, dressed in their favorite shoes, women stood behind a curtain and modeled their feet. Relief Society sisters sold tickets to vote for the shapeliest ankle (Dalhender, 2015).

For women immersed in family life, ward activities broke the isolation of the home and encouraged them to make friends with their Latter-day Saint sisters. Women learned homemaking skills but also money management. Although family and home were valorized, mid-century Mormonism was a ward-centric culture. For both men and women, activities kept people together and solidified their identity as Mormons. Especially in an era of rapid convert growth, creating a discernible culture of "sisterhood" and "priesthood" was critical to keep people connected to their new religion. Ward culture served as an instant community for Latter-day Saints who had either recently converted or moved out of the Intermountain West. Directed from Salt Lake City, church materials carried American postwar domestic culture to the far reaches of the globe.

Craft making and party activities duplicated what middle-class women did in the home, but Relief Society meetings also introduced women to more intellectual undertakings. In 1963, for instance, Relief Society women read lessons about *Moby-Dick* (*Relief Society Magazine*, January 1963, p. 66), Walt Whitman (*Relief Society Magazine*, January 1963, p. 66; February 1963, p. 147), and Willa Cather (*Relief Society Magazine*, June 1963, p. 475). Women who taught theology, literature, or social science lessons were expected to be confident and knowledgeable. Preparing lessons, clarifying concepts, and generating cogent discussions engaged women's minds and helped them see themselves as thinkers in addition to doers. For women who had never been to college, or who had gone and then turned to full-time motherhood or pink collar jobs, Relief Society meetings provided the rare opportunity to explore thoughts and ideas.

In 1966, the Relief Society general board modified the heavy emphasis on American history, literature, and culture in its materials. Church leaders hoped to make the Relief Society lessons less specifically American so as to better engage a global membership. The academic nature of Relief Society meetings, which harken back to an earlier age of "cultural uplift," was perceived to estrange members. In addition, correlation sought to present basic and accessible messages to all Latter-day Saints. Then, in 1970, male church leaders decided that the women of the Relief

Society would no longer produce the curriculum for its meetings. The *Relief Society Magazine* was ended. Until that point, however, Latter-day Saint women remember their wards as being places for the mind, as well as the spirit.

Mid-century modesty

The ward was also a place for defining the body. Mormon women and men learned in the ward (with reinforcement in the family) that the Saints needed to create pure bodies as well as pure homes. Mid-century Mormonism, far more than at any other point in Latter-day Saint history, circled around the spiritual importance of cleanliness. Modesty, chastity, and following of the dietary rules of the Word of Wisdom became conflated with the benefits of personal and domestic order. In 1955, Ruth Chapman wrote that she lived as if Christ was in her home at all times. "It helped me keep my house cleaner," she explained, "and say only the things that he would be able to hear" (Chapman, 1955). That same year, "Fed Up With Smoking" also conflated physical cleanliness, moral cleanliness, and the presence of Christ. "We are taught to keep our homes clean so that the spirit of the Lord will be our constant companion," she advised. "We are also taught that He will not dwell in unclean places. I can't for the life of me, imagine the Savior's presence in a lot of filthy cigarette smoke or a place where alcoholic fumes are" ("Fed Up With Smoking," 1955). Cleanliness meant proper living, sexual purity, and verbal restraint. Latter-day Saint women of the Progressive Era had extended housekeeping outward to include clean streets and water, and mid-century women moved "being clean" inward into the body.

In a 1951 devotional address to Brigham Young University (BYU) students, church apostle Spencer W. Kimball warned that "unchastity is the great demon of the 1950s." As with the case of Pompeii, Sodom, and Babylon, rejecting purity would lead to societal destruction. By wearing too-short dresses, too-tight sweaters, or too-revealing evening gowns, women risked their chastity by tempting men. Without mincing words, Kimball told college women that if they wanted to be respected not to let their boyfriends "fondle you, don't let them touch you." Boys were tempted to break the law of chastity because girls flaunted their bodies. "Evening gowns can be the most beautiful thing in the world," but "the Lord never did intend that they should be backless or topless. I want to tell you it's a sin." Kimball appealed for a "style of our own" (Kimball, 1951).

Some BYU women remember rushing out and buying matching sweaters for their fancy dresses, but Kimball was not satisfied (Blakesley, 2009, p. 22). He continued to decry the state of cleanliness, modesty, and chastity. Three years later, he gave another address to the BYU student body called "Be Ye Clean." The address was eventually published and distributed to young male missionaries. Kimball told the story of a couple who had come to him for counseling and for forgiveness of a terrible act. The boy explained that they engaged in "necking" and "petting" following a school dance. Eventually, the couple "continued on and on and the terrible thing happened." They had come to Kimball to seek forgiveness because the girl in particular was tormented by sleepless nights and horrible dreams. After listing the sexual sins cited in the New Testament (Colossians 3:5) Kimball explained, "Today we call these same sins: necking, petting, fornication, sex perversion, masturbation, included are every hidden and secret sin and all unholy and impure thoughts and practices." Forgiveness certainly was possible, but it was equally important for Latter-day Saints to control their instincts, strive to become perfect, and "control and master the self" (Kimball, 1954). Kimball, who would become church president in 1973, spoke relentlessly about the impure tendencies of youth and inspired other leaders to do the same.

During the 1950s, Latter-day Saints developed a rich set of metaphors for cleanliness and freshness, enabling them to talk quite imaginatively about inappropriate sexual behavior. Adults presented to young Saints physical examples of goods that could be crushed, sullied, or tainted (like illicit sex). The inventory of ruined articles if dirtied was evocative: a piece of gum chewed and then passed around, a licked cupcake to be shared. Purity metaphors were woven into stories and creatively expanded. "If you had an exquisite rose and you pulled off a few of the fragrant petals," observed the advice columnist for the *Deseret News* in 1952, and you passed them around to friends, 'you could never restore that rose or have a complete and beautiful flower again." Her message was clear: "Keep it intact for marriage" (Mary Marker, 1952). Since everyone supposedly knew what "it" was, the object lesson was clear. Sexual behavior was so powerful and intimate it was best to use euphemisms.

Mormons were hardly unique in assuming that girls were responsible for unruly male desire or that women should be virgins before they married. Female sexual purity has been a long-standing value of many cultures. However, after each world war, chastity rhetoric became more intense in the United States. After World War II, America again became preoccupied with all types of non-marital sexual activity. Cold War anxieties manifested in fears of sexually charged, dangerous, and destructive women and communist-inspired homosexuals. Sexual containment, not unlike communist containment, required female bodies to be bound by girdles and padded brassieres. Rhetoric about "good girls" and "bad girls"—from women's magazines to high literature—was as flamboyant as Mormon metaphors of dirty party dresses and plucked roses.

Where Latter-day Saint attitudes differed from most Americans was their insistence that purity was a requirement for women *and* men. Mormon men were not given the benefit of the "double standard" whereby their sexual activity was dismissed with a casual "boys will be boys." In addition, after the war middle-class men increasingly engaged in behaviors once believed to be beneath them. Hugh Hefner's magazine *Playboy* (1953) flaunted the female body, embraced cosmopolitan hedonism, and decried Victorian prudery. The Playboy lifestyle became semi-legitimate for the middle-class male and linked to upward mobility. Smoking also became popular and the rugged Marlboro Man helped push Philip Morris tobacco sales from $5 billion in 1955 to $20 billion in 1957 (Roman, 2009, p. 120). Swearing, which previously was a sign of a man who was not raised as a "gentleman," became commonplace among all classes. The middle-class rejection of the courtly ways of their fathers continued into the 1960s, when the men of the counterculture moved on to illegal drugs and casual sex.

Such conduct, however, was not appropriate for Mormon men. Mormon ethics held purity as a masculine as well as a feminine virtue. Mormon men were expected to uphold standards typically associated with "lady-like" women and "good girls." Not only were men to be chaste, they were not to smoke, drink, swear, lose their tempers, or be disinterested in home life. They were to be fully involved with their ward callings and with family prayer and instruction. Gender differences did not include different levels of purity or piety. "There is but one standard for men and for women," Joseph L. Wirthlin told Relief Society women in 1950, "and rather than lose one's virtue, better one lose his life, for at least he will die clean in the sight of God" (Wirthlin, 1950, p. 294). Domesticity, purity, piety, and even obedience—female virtues from a past era—were admired because Latter-day Saint *men* were also expected to uphold these values. Female purity was thus given additional relevance because it was associated not simply with women but also with men.

A key figure in this universalizing of purity codes was Church President David O. McKay. Born in 1873, McKay brought to mid-century Mormonism the chivalrous values of an earlier America. McKay was a young man when fraternal societies, "muscular" Christianity, and proponents of Theodore Roosevelt's strenuous life were at their peak. In these years, gentlemen were to exercise their manliness by controlling their emotions and guiding the development of the weak (women, children, the "dark" races). True men of the turn of the century—the white men of the middle class—had a measured and appropriate sexuality.

McKay never moved away from such virtues. In a 1963 conference address given when he was 90 (seven years before his death), McKay urged men to guard their behavior. He reminded the Saints, "No member of this church—husband, father—has the right to utter an oath [to swear] or ever to express a cross word to his wife or to his children." Men were told to contribute to the ideal home via their character and by "controlling your passion, your temper, guarding your speech." Mothers and fathers were never to express "a condemnatory term, an expression of anger or jealousy or hatred" in their homes. "Control it!" McKay demanded, "Do not express it!" McKay specifically told fathers to do whatever they could "to produce peace and harmony, no matter what you may suffer" (McKay, 1963, p. 130). Shortly after the address, Wander Lifferth wrote to the *Deseret News* that her home life changed because of President McKay. She was grateful to the prophet because "almost instantly, my husband ceased to find fault with my housekeeping" (Lifferth, 1963). The Mormon masculinity of mid-century, in contrast to evolving American norms of male behavior, required men to be chaste and self-controlled. Men were to discipline what the church defined as the detrimental and base elements of the male disposition.

Obedience, also a value traditionally associated with women, had its place in Mormon masculinity. Within a hierarchically organized church structure, men needed to be obedient to those above them in callings. "The priesthood" was bound together through layers of authority, and a righteous man assented to the directions given by other men over him. Communal harmony could only be achieved if both women and men tempered their lust for individual acclaim and disruptive pride.

Volunteerism, an aspect of both of mid-century American society and of pioneer Mormonism, was reinforced after the war. Bishops and stake presidents took on nurturing roles as they distributed food, cared for the old and infirm, and guided the young. In other Christian denominations, clergy were salaried professionals—not unlike doctors or lawyers—but in Mormonism the day-to-day church was run by volunteers. Like mothers, men were not paid for accomplishing these duties. Sacrifices of time and assertion of self-discipline was Christ-like behavior required of men and of women. Under the impact of correlation, church leaders asked Latter-day Saint men to take on more and wider responsibilities. This trend would culminate in 1970 when some Relief Society activities were folded into general church duties overseen by men.

While nineteenth-century polygamy continues to be associated with the Latter-day Saints, that social arrangement did not last long enough or was widespread enough to mold Latter-day Saint culture. Even the patriarchal pioneer is more a figment of the imagination than of historical reality. Contemporary gender roles in Mormonism are much more indebted to the 1950s when aging church leaders reached back into their own childhoods to forcefully articulate appropriate behavioral patterns at the precise time when American society was undergoing sweeping change. It is the tenacious quality of mid-century Mormonism, especially regarding sexuality and motherhood, which endures.

References

"A Happy Wife" to Mary Marker, December 27, 1953. ACCN 1862 Box 34 Folder 6, Ramona W. Cannon Letters, Special Collections, Marriott Library University of Utah [hereafter abbreviated as UU].

Andelin, H., 1965. *Fascinating Womanhood*. 1990 ed. New York: Bantam Books.

Annual Report of the Church. July 1972. www.lds.org/ensign/1972/07/the-annual-report-of-the-church?lang=eng.

Anon to Mary Marker, [circa 1948–49]. ACCN 1862 Box 36 Folder 2, UU.

Anon, 1963. *Relief Society Magazine*. January, p. 66.

Anon, 1963. *Relief Society Magazine*. February, p. 147.
Anon. 1963. *Relief Society Magazine*. June, p. 475.
Anon, 1965. Did You Know That ... *The Improvement Era*. January, p. 78.
Beecher, M.U., and MacKay, K.L., 1978. Women in Twentieth-Century Utah. In R. Poll, T. Alexander, E. England, and D. Miller, eds. *Utah's History*. Provo, UT: Brigham Young University Press, pp. 563–86.
Benson, E.T. 1969. *One Hundred Thirty Ninth Annual Conference*. April, p. 12.
Blakesley, K.C., 2009. "A Style of Our Own": Modesty and Mormon Women, 1951–2008. *Dialogue: A Journal of Mormon Thought* 42(Summer): 20–53.
Burr, Z.P.H., 1953. Diary, November 15. [Church of Jesus Christ of Latter-day Saints] Church History Library [CHL].
Chapman, R. to Mary Marker, 1955. ACCN 1862 Box 35 Folder 4, UU.
Christensen, J., 1978. The Impact of World War II. In R. Poll, T. Alexander, E. England, and D. Miller, eds. *Utah's History*. Provo, UT: Brigham Young University Press, pp. 497–514.
Crawford, V., 1950. Household of Faith. *Relief Society Magazine*. May, pp. 295–98.
Curtis L. to Mary Marker, July 17, 1958. ACCN 1862 Box 35 Folder 5, UU.
Dalhender, V., February 11, 2015. Interview by Colleen McDannell.
Ely, Nevada to Mary Marker, [circa 1948–49]. ACCN 1862 Box 36 Folder 2, UU.
Evans, V., 1985. Women's Image in Authoritative Mormon Discourse: A Rhetorical Analysis. Ph.D. dissertation.
"Fed Up With Smoking" to Mary Marker, October 5, 1955. ACCN 1862 Box 35 Folder 4, UU.
Givens, T., 2007. *People of Paradox: A History of Mormon Culture*. New York: Oxford University Press.
Hart, E. to Mary Marker, March 18, 1955. ACCN 1862 Box 35 Folder 6, UU.
Hartmann, S., 1994. Women's Employment and the Domestic Ideal in the Early Cold War Years. In J. Meyerowitz, ed., *Not June Cleaver: Women and Gender in Postwar America, 1945–1960*. Philadelphia, PA: Temple University Press, pp. 84–100.
Kehl, E. to Mary Marker, [no date]. ACCN 1862 Box 36 Folder 3, UU.
Kimball, S.A., 1951. Style of Our Own. BYU Devotional. Available only in audio https://speeches.byu.edu/talks/spencer-w-kimball_style/.
Kimball, S., 1954. Be Ye Clean. Addresses to student body, May 4. Brigham Young University, American Collection.
Lamoreaux, O. to Mary Marker, March 16, 1955. ACCN 1862 Box 35 Folder 6, UU.
"Lazy Susan" to Mary Marker, March 9, 1955. ACCN 1862 Box 35 Folder 4, UU.
Lifferth, W. to Mary Marker, June 26, 1963. ACCN 1862 Box 38 Folder 1, UU.
Mary Marker column, September 8, 1952. ACCN 1862 Box 33a Folder 4, UU.
McKay, D., 1950. A Woman's Influence. *Relief Society Magazine*. December, p. 800.
McKay, D., 1963. *One Hundred Thirty-Third Annual Conference*. April, p. 130.
Murphy, M., 2005. Gainfully Employed Women, 1896–1950. In P. Scott and L. Thatcher, eds. *Women in Utah History: Paradigm or Paradox?* Logan, UT: Utah State University Press, pp. 183–222.
Neuffer, J., 2007. Fascinating Womanhood: Helen Andelin and the Politics of Religion in the "Other" Women's Movement, 1963–2006. Ph.D. dissertation.
Reeve, P., and Parshall, A., 2010. *Mormonism: A Historical Encyclopedia*. Santa Barbara, CA: ABC-Clic.
Roman, K., 2009. *The Kings of Madison Avenue: David Ogilvy and the Making of Modern Advertising*. New York: Palgrave Macmillan.
Scott, M to Mary Marker, November 2, 1951. ACCN 1862 Box 34 Folder 7, UU.
Shepherd, G., and Shepherd, G., 1998. *Mormon Passage: A Missionary Chronicle*. Carbondale, IL: University of Illinois Press.
Spafford, B., 1951. If You Live Up to Your Privileges. *Relief Society Magazine*. November.
Spafford, B., 1958. The Place of Latter-day Saint Woman [sic], *The Improvement Era*. May.
Watkins, E., 1998. *On the Pill: A Social History of Oral Contraceptives, 1950–1970*. Baltimore, MD: Johns Hopkins University Press.
Wirthlin, J., 1950. A Mother's Influence, *Relief Society Magazine*. May. Wirthlin continued a thought developed by J. Reuben Clark and published in *One Hundred Ninth Semi-Annual Conference*. October 1938.

Further reading

Derr, J., Cannon, J.R., and Beecher, M.U., 1992. *Woman of Covenant: The Story of Relief Society*. Salt Lake City, UT: Deseret Book, pp. 304–39.
Surveys the major accomplishments of the Latter-day Saint women's organization. Strong description of women's ward culture before correlation.

Holbrook, K., 2016. Mormons and Housework during Second Wave Feminism. In P. Mason and J.G. Turner, eds. *Out of Obscurity: Mormonism since 1945*. New York: Oxford University Press, pp. 198–213.
Discusses LDS attitudes towards housework. Particularly important in connecting the architecture of the Relief Society building with the middle-class home.

May, E.T., 1988. *Homeward Bound: American Families in the Cold War Era*. New York: Basic Books.
This book makes the important connection between the private world of the home and the public world of American politics. It is especially strong on illustrating how notions of domesticity promoted anti-communism.

McDannell, C., 2011. *The Spirit of Vatican II: A History of Catholic Reform in America*. New York: Basic Books.
Catholic lay women at mid-century shared many similarities with Mormons. However, the changes that occurred for Catholic women in the early 1960s enabled them to better adapt to feminism, unlike Latter-day Saint women.

McDannell, C., 2019. *Sister Saints: Mormon Women since the End of Polygamy*. New York: Oxford University Press.
This books surveys the main currents of Mormon women's history from the late nineteenth to the early twenty-first century. This essay is based on Chapter 5: "A Style of Our Own."

12
MORMON FEMINISM AFTER 1970

Claudia L. Bushman

Although Joseph Smith set out an expansive feminist model in his June 1830 revelation to his wife Emma, that she should be "ordained … to Expound scriptures, and to exhort the church" and that her time should be given "to writing, and to learning much," and that this was the "Lord's voice unto all" (Doctrine and Covenants, 1981, 25:7–8), the plan was never fully realized. Women's spiritual meetings have been gradually discouraged. Women's domestic labors were valued and encouraged, but their ecclesiastical responsibilities have been steadily downgraded and phased out.

Brigham Young gave women faint praise, allowing them useful involvement in the home and in the public sphere, but no space in the church leadership.

> We believe that women are useful, not only to sweep houses, wash dishes, make beds, & raise babies, but they should stand behind the counter, study law or physic [medicine], or become good bookkeepers & be able to do the business in any counting house, and all this to enlarge their sphere of usefulness for the benefit of society at large. In following these things, they but answer the design of their creation.
> *(Young, 1951, pp. 216–17)*

Nevertheless, Latter-day Saint women were active in many religious realms, teaching and preaching and had extensive involvement in public affairs through the Relief Society. In the early twentieth century, male leaders moved toward limiting women's activities, taking over some autonomous women's church work. Relief Society women were edged out of the administration of the Utah social welfare they had engaged in. Their duties in 1940, according to J. Reuben Clark of the First Presidency, were to serve as a "handmaiden to the priesthood." They could be "aids and helps," but the priesthood was responsible for the instruction and salvation of church members. Women should maintain the modesty and chastity of youth, create a righteous home, and keep the world from sinking into a "welter of sin and corruption" (Clark, 1940, p. 802). In public life, they could serve as workers and volunteers, not as officials.

There was a respite during World War II as women moved into the public work arena. The war required their work, as men were in short supply. But the end of World War II and the return of weary veterans from the front brought the glorification of domesticity in the nation as a whole. For the first time in their century plus of existence, Mormons, who were experienced in homemaking and family rearing, marrying young and with large families, were seen as role models, supporting traditional domestic tasks and church activity. Mormons exemplified the ideal family for twenty years before awakenings of feminism sowed discontent in the minds and hearts of some housewives.

For most LDS women, family life was the ideal. But in the 1960s, they were affected by the reaction to post-war domesticity in the nation as a whole, as married women began to return to the workforce, some for freedom, others for income. *The Feminine Mystique*, published in 1963, suggested to many mysteriously dissatisfied women that they might have satisfying careers outside the home. In 1950 Utah had a female workforce of 57,294, and half of those were married and living with husbands. That was an 87 percent increase over the 1940 figure (Murphy, 2005, p. 210). By 1970, half of Utah's women over 16 were employed. The Mormon population of the state would have been between 60 and 70 percent (Beecher and MacKay, 1978, p. 577).

During these years, the church, governed by a male priesthood hierarchy, introduced "correlation," a program that standardized church practices, further limiting female activity. Priesthood leaders sometimes feared that women were taking over congregational life and moved to rein them in. In 1967, a church directive announced that the opening and closing prayers of the church's sacrament meeting were to be pronounced only by priesthood holders—boys and men. In 1969, the Relief Society social service programs for unwed mothers, young people, and Native Americans were shifted away from women to male priesthood leaders. In 1970, the church determined that LDS women married to inactive or non-members were not to participate in the temple rituals known as the endowment. Church leaders began to criticize the radical ideas of women's liberation. In 1970, in an effort to restructure church leadership in the name of efficiency and coordination, priesthood leaders took over the leadership of the Relief Society which had been independent since its inception, financing and spending its resources as members saw fit. The Relief Society was "correlated" into the greater church organization, surrendering its assets and agency. In the future, priesthood leaders would organize and supervise the group and put the women on an allowance. The *Relief Society Magazine* was discontinued. The church firmly established the male priesthood as the center of authority with existing organizations as auxiliaries (McDannell, 2019, pp. 85–94).

It is ironic that the church hierarchy should take over the Relief Society, its leadership, its funds, and its activities when women were finding in their church work a Mormon answer to "The Feminine Mystique." LDS women were making valued and valuable careers out of their church work and doing much good. They were certainly capable of carrying out such responsibilities, though it is also true that many women, setting high standards for themselves, felt overworked and leaders feared that they were slighting their home responsibilities.

In 1971, Apostle Thomas S. Monson spoke about "The Women's Movement: Liberation or Deception?" He foresaw a society with women who refused motherhood, where pornography, crime, delinquency, and materialism flourished. Monson declared that women, casting off their true identities, had not been liberated but deceived (Monson, 1971). It was difficult for senior church leaders to see that women had anything good to gain from the life envisioned by feminism. Such women, in questioning the traditional gender roles enshrined in LDS song and story, had lost not only their good sense but their identity as true women.

Notwithstanding the warnings, women began reaching out for something else. In Boston in 1970, Relief Society sisters published a critically acclaimed and financially successful guidebook, *A Beginner's Boston*, which they also wrote, illustrated, and distributed, after their priesthood brothers had dismissed the idea as too risky and too much work. In Salt Lake City, Leonard Arrington, the church historian, who served from 1972 to 1982, had publicized the little-known economic contribution of LDS pioneer women. He gave new identity to their female descendants, hiring some women to work in his historical shop. Spots of organized female activity encouraged LDS women to reach beyond the hearth and the cradle.

Rebirth of Mormon feminism

The year 1970 was a moment of change. The nature of the change can be glimpsed in one microcosmic group in Boston. The group began to meet in June of 1970 to discuss their lives as Mormons. They sought discussion, enlightenment, and mutual support. They began with tears and headaches, hopes and fears. They wondered what they should do with their lives. They knew about the LDS pioneer women's publication, *The Woman's Exponent* (1872–1914), and after discovering bound volumes available for loan from Harvard's library, they were set on fire by the early feminist rhetoric. *The Exponent* had represented and reported on all Latter-day Saint female organizations, although it was never an "official" publication. *The Exponent* was a feminist publication by definition, encouraging women to speak for and to women, speaking up against injustice and inequality of opportunity, and about the equality of the genders (Bushman, 1974, p. 181). The Boston women's view was notably expanded. They found that in working together, they could manage events and projects that they could not have done individually. They produced an annual Exponent Day dinner and lecture with a female speaker. Important LDS women achievers traveled east to address appreciative audiences.

Independent LDS publishing had by then provided a voice for Mormons exploring new ideas. *Dialogue: A Journal of Mormon Thought* began publication in California in 1966. The Boston women's group offered to edit a women's issue of *Dialogue*. Editor Eugene England immediately agreed. Working on the issue kept the women busy examining the lives of others. The explorations of this group, of which I was a part, led us to feature diversity rather than homogeneity. The message is one that Mormon feminists continue to stress: let us broaden the definition. The introduction of the "pink" issue stated, "We argue then for acceptance of the diversity that already exists in the life styles of Mormon women." My favorite sentence in the introduction to that issue is this modest musing: "Does it undercut the celestial dream to admit that there are occasional Japanese beetles in the roses covering our cottages?" (Bushman, 1971, pp. 5–8).

When the manuscript was finally submitted, the newly appointed *Dialogue* editor was not enthusiastic. He said that the group had not dealt with the real issues of Mormon women which were patriarchy and polygamy. His comment came as a surprise. Those were not our issues. Here we were, a group of real Mormon women trying to understand the lives of Mormon women, who were told by one of the church's male liberals that we did not know what our issues were. Nor did he think it presumptuous to spell them out for us. Poor LDS women, infantilized from all sides. But he published the issue, dated Summer 1971, and it was very popular.

The Boston women's group continued to meet, persuaded by their success that they could do more. They explored the past, looking at polygamy and patriarchy which had been suggested for their attention. They chose topics, researched them, taught a class for the LDS Institute students, wrote up papers and self-published a book of their essays as *Mormon Sisters, Women in Early Utah*, in 1976. This, they thought, and still think, was big-time feminism.

The group began publication of the newspaper *Exponent II* in 1974, in tribute to the pioneer publication, the *Woman's Exponent*. We used the Mormon past to illustrate and encourage contemporary female strengths, which, the editors felt, were not being sufficiently publicized. The opening editorial stated that *Exponent II* was "a modest but sincere newspaper ... faithful but frank ... poised on the dual platforms of Mormonism and Feminism" aimed "to strengthen the Church of Jesus Christ of Latter-day Saints, and to encourage and develop the talents of Mormon women. That these aims are consistent we intend to show by our pages and our lives" (Bushman, 1974, p. 2). I admit here that these phrases were my own. The group did not debate or vote on them, but we did believe that Mormonism and feminism were compatible. *Exponent II* has been in steady publication for more than forty years.

Equal rights amendment

The women's issue that attracted the most attention, publicity, and contention at that time was the proposed Equal Rights Amendment (ERA) to the United States Constitution. The amendment, proposed by Alice Paul in 1921, approved by both houses of the United States Congress in 1972 and sent to the states for individual ratification reads "Equality of rights under the law shall not be denied or abridged by the United States or by any State on account of sex."

Women familiar with the active and productive lives of LDS women of previous generations assumed that the amendment would sail through the ratification process; a majority of Utah Mormons polled favored it (Bradley, 1995, p. 94). The first issue of *Exponent II* had an article on "What the ERA Will Mean to You." But to some, the amendment threatened LDS and American life. Some quiet opposition began to be heard. General Relief Society President Barbara Smith, influenced by a meeting with senior male church leaders and her own research, came to believe that the ERA would be destructive to families and women (Bradley, 2005, pp. 105–67).

Not all agreed. In 1975 Elouise Bell, an English professor at Brigham Young University (BYU) who believed in the "righteous goals of feminism," addressed the BYU community in a Forum address, the first female faculty member to do so. She urged the audience to "examine the issues" and memorably proclaimed, "Let it not be said that BYU or the Latter-day Saint people stood on the sidelines while great and needed social reforms were taking place" (Bell, 1976, pp. 527–40).

In 1975, a *Church News* editorial by the First Presidency stated their opposition to the ERA, citing the differing divine roles for men and women. "We recognize men and women as equally important before the Lord, but with differences biologically, emotionally, and in other ways ... The ERA, we believe, does not recognize these differences." Church opposition to the ERA built steadily. In October 1976, the First Presidency issued an official statement predicting that the ERA would "strike at the family, humankind's basic institution," and "stifle many God-given feminine instincts." Church anti-ERA activity gathered steam in 1977 when active campaigning by Elder Boyd K. Packer and Barbara Smith persuaded the Idaho state legislature, heavily LDS, to rescind their pro-ERA vote (Huefner, 1978, pp. 58–76).

Meanwhile, the United Nations proclaimed the International Woman's Year (IWY) and invited the states to organize committees to discuss national and international women's rights. Ambitious suggestions for improving the lives of women world-wide were proposed for discussion.

At the Utah meeting, the debate became a battle as Relief Society women, ten quietly recruited from each congregation, attended with orders to vote down all proposals. The organizers, who had expected about 2,000 women to gather for a reasoned discussion of important issues, were overwhelmed by 14,000. The chaotic and disruptive sessions shocked and dismayed the organizers and many others.

Ratification of the ERA stalled. The deadline for ratification was 1979. In 1978, Mormons for the Equal Rights Amendment was organized in Washington, D.C. The group accused the church of unsuitable involvement in politics. Mormons for the ERA was provocative and outspoken, chartering airplanes to tow banner statements like "Mother in Heaven Loves the ERA," over the LDS Church's General Conference. Although they may have wished to do so, in an age of wide public communication, the church could not silence the words and actions they labeled as heresy and apostasy. The leader of the organization, Sonia Johnson, previously the pianist in the primary organization for LDS children in her congregation, spoke out and would not back down. Fast on her feet and with a good ear for quotable language, Johnson used the words of the leaders against them. When Church President Heber C. Kimball warned supporters of the ERA that they should be "very, very careful" because "the Church is led by strong men and able men [who feel they are] in a position to lead properly," she responded. "The threat here is open and clear. We had better be very, very careful because the men at the head of the Church are strong and the patriarchs have for millennia crushed those women who escaped from their mind-bindings." Unable to convince or silence her, the church excommunicated her in 1979. She had "spoken evil of the Lord's anointed" (Brooks, Steenblik, and Wheelwright, 2016, pp. 63–73). The Equal Rights Amendment was not added to the U.S. Constitution.

Official opposition occurred at a moment when in other spheres, the church was liberalizing its policies. Even as leaders attempted to stamp out feminist reforms, a major liberal realignment welcomed Black men and women to full fellowship in the church. Although Black members had been involved from the earliest days of the church, Brigham Young had limited their participation. Black men were not ordained to the priesthood. Black couples could not participate in temple rituals. In 1978, President Spencer W. Kimball announced a new revelation securing access for Black members. Church members, many of whom had justified their racist inclinations and behavior by church teachings, quickly accepted the new doctrine. The church was liberalized in one realm while it remained conservative in another.

Opposition to the ERA heralded two decades of struggles centered on individuality, obedience, and religious power. The secure faith of many LDS women was shaken and crystalized by Sonia Johnson's excommunication. Faithful members believed that the president of the church, inspired by deity, could not err or go astray. And as the church opposed the ERA, it must be evil. Yet they believed that the legitimate rights of women should not be "denied or abridged." Some began to favor their own revelation and exercise their own agency over the direction of church authority. Apostle Ezra Taft Benson gave church members a stark warning about the "living prophet and the First Presidency—follow them and be blessed—reject them and suffer" (Benson, 1981).

The scars caused by political intervention in the ERA debate remained years later. Church members have since been enlisted and encouraged to take sides on other contentious issues, notably the efforts to defeat bills in Hawaii and California that would legalize same-sex marriage. While Mormon women are and have been generally faithful and obedient, some felt that this behavior countered their understanding of their identity as followers of Jesus Christ and his teachings. Some began to question what they were told, resulting in their being sidelined and shunned.

One result of the friction between women's groups in the church was an additional set of unofficial women's meetings where women formed independent cells that were sometimes critical of church action. Feminist women have organized unofficial groups, partially or completely distancing themselves from obedience to church leaders. Although some of these women have left the church, they maintain their relationships to old friends. For many years now, these feminist groups have gathered informally in forums, or symposia, as "Pilgrims," or for "retreats." They spend a weekend each year camping out at a rustic location, singing songs, listening to talks, getting to know others who share their opinions. These are times of good cheer and companionship, nevertheless, they are underground events, unofficial and somewhat suspect.

Alternative voices

In 1980 various LDS church meetings held throughout the week were consolidated into one, three-hour-long Sunday block. Weekly religious meetings were systematized for efficiency and standardization. This move further reduced church activities where women had been leaders and teachers; Relief Society meetings became more like Sunday School classes. The new scheme acknowledged the demands made on church members in an increasingly global church and also implicitly recognized that many women who had been available for heavy church responsibilities were now working. The previous emphasis on domesticity was reduced. The Relief Society and the priesthood were taught the same lessons.

Ezra Taft Benson, aged 86, named president of the church in 1985, preached a reactionary message: "Contrary to conventional wisdom, a mother's calling is in the home, not in the marketplace, the counsel of the Church has always been for mothers to spend their full time in the home in rearing and caring for their children." Women should only work outside the home if the situation demanded it. "Have your children and have them early" (Benson, 1987).

These trends occurred against a background of increasing openness in the examination of the church's past. A simplified, positive, and standardized view of Mormon history had been taught for many years, a view that ignored awkward and difficult episodes or considered them the creations of enemies. In the last quarter of the twentieth century, church historians explored what came to be called the "new Mormon history" where the good and the bad were brought into the open.

In 1980, conservative leaders, disapproving of this new and revealing Mormon history, moved to relocate the church's historical division to Brigham Young University and to reduce its size. Two years later, Leonard Arrington, who had ushered the new history into the church, was removed as head of the division. In 1981, Apostle Boyd K. Packer addressed educators of the church's young. In his talk, "The Mantle is Far, Far Greater," he regretted that writers told so much about church history, "whether it is worthy or faith promoting or not." He said that "some things that are true are not very useful," and he wanted those left out (Packer, 1981, pp. 259–71).

The study of women's roles in the church participated in the new openness and the negative reaction it initially evoked. At first women's scholarship met resistance. As female scholars engaged in serious research and publication, conservative church leaders moved to control the flow of information. In 1985, when Linda King Newell and Valeen Tippetts Avery wrote a sympathetic book about Joseph Smith's wife Emma, a woman long castigated for failing to move west with the Mormons after the murder of her husband, the authors were banned from speaking in official church meetings.

In 1989, Apostle Dallin H. Oaks warned church members against listening to alternate voices that promote such selfish personal interests as "property, pride, prominence, or power" or the voices of "lost souls" or "false prophets," deceivers all (Oaks, 1989). In 1993, Apostle Boyd K. Packer defined the dangerous "alternate voices" that were upsetting church members and leading them astray. Those voices were emanating from three sources: the gay and lesbian rights movement, the feminist movement, and the "so-called scholars or intellectuals." He saw these messages as invasions of the church's values and standards (Packer, 1993).

In 1993, six church members, now known as the September Six, were excommunicated from the church for heresy, apostasy, and speaking out. They were told that they were free to hold views differing from church positions, but not free to speak out and publicize them. Several notable and productive feminist authors who had been writing about women's issues were among those singled out for excommunication during that period, including Lavina Fielding Anderson, Maxine Hanks, Janice Allred, and Margaret Toscano. The church acted to stamp out heresy and independent thinking about questionable topics like praying to a Heavenly Mother, and the possible ordination of women. There were objections to, and sorrow for, the excommunication of these members. Several feminist professors left BYU, by their own choice or at the request of the university. Women became more cautious.

But this opposition was not to last as the church gradually moved toward historical transparency. When Gordon B. Hinckley ascended to the church presidency in 1995, he began a new era, more open, less tense, somewhat diminishing previous controversy. More new scholarship was accepted on the less attractive aspects of the past, which had previously been denied and minimized. Some international leaders were called into higher office in the church, recognizing its global nature. The attacks of the church on the liberal community ceased. The church began to publish all the papers relating to Joseph Smith in an extensive and highly professional multi-volume series. More recently, the church has also published the Gospel Topics essays, a series of position papers dealing with the best, most complete, most honest, and most authoritative answers to some of Mormonism's thorniest problems, such as Joseph Smith's polygamy, and the restriction of priesthood ordinances to Black members before 1978. The alternate voices now speak officially. Emma Smith has been repatriated into the church story.

Though encouraging to those who wish to speak out about women's rights, transparency has not necessarily guaranteed women a larger voice in church policies. A notable confrontation took place in October 1995, as the General Presidency of the Relief Society planned a women's conference. They researched the lives of international LDS women, and realizing the variety in female life styles, chose to speak on the diversity they had found. Two weeks before the meeting, President Hinckley met with the women and told them to focus on the traditional family. The Relief Society leaders were not to deliver the addresses they had planned on the problems they saw. He would introduce an official new document, "The Family: A Proclamation to the World," which references many past church teachings. Since then, this document has achieved almost canonical standing, although its origin has not been revealed. LDS scripture is generally identified by author, date, and circumstance. Questions about the Proclamation's origin have remained unanswered. And neither has it been called or considered revelation. Male leaders introduced a document that would govern women's behavior in the future without consulting them about it. The women did not see the Proclamation until the evening before the General Relief Society Meeting where it was introduced (Okazaki and Prince, 2012).

The Proclamation refers to heavenly parents and declares that heterosexual marriage and gender are eternal and ordained of God. Men and women, united in marriage, are to reproduce. The family, rather than the individual, is the basic unit. A somewhat contradictory assertion is that fathers preside over their families even as men and women are obligated to help one another as equal partners (Kline, 2016). The proclamation is not specific, however, about how a mother is primarily responsible for the nurture of the children, leaving open many possibilities specifically denied in previous teachings. Married pairs are not told how many children to have or counseled on birth control, and they are not to judge others on family size. The document recognizes that circumstances require individual adaptation. Women are allowed some freedom of choice, but the presiding/equality tension at the center of the male–female relationship remains. And no freedom is allowed to gays or others outside of strict gender constructions.

Recent changes

In 2012, the church announced a welcome change in the eligibility ages for missionaries. The beginning age for men went down from 19 to 18. For women the more dramatic age-change was from 21 to 19, allowing girls to be missionaries before marriage, before graduation from college, and to be closer in age to male missionaries. The women still serve for only eighteen months compared to twenty-four for male missionaries, and they still cannot exercise the priesthood functions of baptizing the people they teach, but this plan allows many more girls to serve missions with their challenges and broadening experiences. The girls learn mission discipline and scriptural knowledge, making them more mature partners in marriage and stronger workers in Mormon wards as well as expanding their worldviews.

Activity on the internet, making possible the wide distribution of unofficial ideas and discussions, has led to new openness in the church. The internet has required the church to abandon its efforts to suppress potentially damaging information. The church now develops programs to use the internet for its own missionary purposes. The ease of reading freely transmitted material online and the proliferating groups that meet together there as well as physically in many locations such as the women's retreats, have made available much more information of a wider scope than the scriptures, conference talks, and approved sources. The alternate voices are widely available, and they are listened to.

In this era of increasing openness, some members have left the church. Others have determined that they can live with painful disclosures. Many believe that they can be feminists and faithful Mormons. This is more possible as they exercise their own agency, choosing which paths and leaders to follow. Women recreate their Mother in Heaven as they wish her to be. Others have maintained their Mormon identity with more of an opportunity to think twice before accepting what they are told. Others, in a more pragmatic mode, knowing now just where various teachings have come from, see new possibilities for individual action. They see that women's powers and participation in the church could easily be increased without resorting to new revelation or public demonstrations. Church leadership has made some changes. There has been some rewriting of the temple ceremony text elevating Eve and softening gender differences. On a congregational level, the governing committee of the congregation, the Priesthood Executive Committee, has been superseded by the more inclusive Ward Council consisting of female ward leaders as well as priesthood leaders. After open deliberation, the Ward Council speaks with one voice, the priesthood. But women are more involved at various levels.

The fast and cheap internet has given articulate women a platform of their own. The Bloggernacle is a friendly place for women to speak and be heard outside of the long arm of the priesthood. Blogging has turned into a lucrative job for stay-at-home moms, some rediscovering new aspects of creative domesticity. The web disseminates multiple voices, allowing a wider feminine presence in the greater church culture. The blogs have brought comfort and company to like-minded women (Haglund, 2016).

In addition to expressing themselves, Mormon women have also taken to the internet to organize for change. One group organized online and called All Enlisted invited LDS women to wear pants to church on a particular Sunday. Mormon women traditionally dress up for Sunday services, which generally means wearing skirts. The internet-driven movement garnered national press attention. Not every woman wore pants to church on that December day in 2012, but most everyone was aware that doing so would be noted.

Ordain Women, another well-publicized effort, used the internet to broadcast women's stories and impressed upon church leaders the importance of the skill and power of the female half of the congregation in leadership. They asked for inclusion in the church's male priesthood, striking directly at women's subordinate position in the church and seeking realization of the promise made to Emma Smith. The group requested tickets to attend the priesthood session of the General Conference in October 2013. This male-only gathering, a free-but-ticketed event, was one of the traditional five meetings of the twice-annual General Conference of the church. The request was denied. The women then stood in the standby ticket line. Wearing Sunday clothes, they politely requested admittance; it too was denied. They said that they were not demanding admittance but were pleading for the priesthood. Again, they were not admitted. Nor were they at the next conference. A female spokesperson for the church asked that they desist in this request.

Church leaders considered that the women were not behaving suitably for Latter-day Saint women. One of the organizers, Kate Kelly, was told that she was free to have such views but not to urge them on others. She was excommunicated, as others had been. Church leaders do not like to be confronted. Having oppositional ideas is acceptable, but urging them on others, and particularly carrying out actions in the eyes of the world, is considered apostasy or heresy. Priesthood leaders expect church members to listen and obey.

The church later moved toward equality by upgrading an existing woman's general meeting to be the sixth regular meeting of the General Conference. The leaders had earlier decided to broadcast the priesthood meeting on television and over the internet. All women are now free to tune into this once all-male meeting though they still lack the credentials to attend. Going forward, the church will alternate the gender-based meetings, holding one or the other at each General Conference, suggesting their equal importance.

Contemporary Mormon women

Mormon women have always been feminists in the sense of managing homes and families alone or equally yoked with husbands. Many are independent with advanced degrees and demanding work. They carry heavy administrative and teaching roles in the church and are essential temple workers. They serve missions and hold responsible roles in schools and the community. There have always been LDS spinsters, widows, maiden aunts, college professors, successful business women, and other variants, but the standard model that generations of young women have been taught to aspire to has been the married mother of many, excellent neighbor, church worker, and loving wife in a temple-married happy eternal family. Church leaders, fearing potential harm to children, have discouraged mothers from working outside their homes, considering the home and family as of first importance. A woman could be a successful executive in church organizations—and there have been many effective leaders—but the home and family and the husband's work have come first. Church rhetoric has valorized women's domestic role. Women have been expected to be mothers and home builders.

Today, the acceptable model for female behavior has been broadened. Economic, educational, and global realities have extended the possibilities, even as it is now clear that there are not enough noble, handsome, devoted male church members for the attractive, well-educated, single women in the church. An adequate number of qualified men simply does not exist, seriously undercutting the chances for women to realize the ideal. In addition, there are lots of widows and divorcees, not to mention people who have changed or announced their alternate genders. The church quietly acknowledges the diversity of conditions. The celestial dream of temple marriage to a strong priesthood holder followed by motherhood is not available to everyone. Church leaders now frequently stress that marriage may only be realized in the hereafter.

The church began, then, with partially realized feminist ideals which over a century and a half gradually wore away. In the years after World War II, the church opposed the stirrings of feminism, hoping to correct and quash them. Since then, there has been a gradual growth of acceptance, and an extension of feminism, even as traditionalists consider it negatively and as feminists find their church possibilities inadequate.

Where are LDS women today? Many are attempting to answer that question. Many LDS women find their roles within the church and Mormon culture to be rewarding. Lay participation allows them wide opportunities to carry out responsibilities in ways that reward their ingenuity, imagination, and responsibility. David Campbell, in summarizing female attitudes after a broad survey, notes that Mormon women see their faith grounded in personal revelation, rather than adhering to hierarchy. Women tend to see Mormonism as a community, their religion in terms of service to others. He finds about four out of five Mormon women as untroubled by the role of women in the church and not searching for change. Their reliance on personal revelation eases the discomfort they may feel with male authority (Campbell, 2016, pp. 199–212).

The posts on LDS blogs, however, indicate a "strain of discontent," a desire for a "greater voice." Some women feel that the church could easily grant them more equality and opportunities. Their voices are instructive. One life-long, faithful church member thinks that all LDS women should consider themselves feminists. Her words reflect the disgruntlement that many women feel.

> It seems like the brethren keep taking things away from women of the church. Women used to be encouraged to give blessings to other women. We used to have a Relief Society Magazine written by women. We used to have Relief Society lessons of interest to women about women. We used to have funds. There are so many things. Have they given us anything back? … What are they afraid of? Why do they need so much control?

She sees many easy and possible improvements.

> I think women and girls need visible role models. There are not a lot of stories of women in the scriptures, but every one that there is ought to be in every lesson manual. I am in Primary nowadays, and I shudder every time the Presidency goes on and on about the boys having the Aaronic Priesthood and mentions nothing about the girls … I wish the Young Women's theme would be changed to "We are daughters of Heavenly Parents" instead of just Heavenly Father. How easy is that! I wish we studied the lives of the Relief Society Presidents and the wives of the Prophets … I just don't see how women can continue to be limited going forward.
>
> *(Lauper, 2018)*

The church offers many potential blessings: something to believe in, a guide and purpose for living a good life, a pattern that avoids some of society's most debilitating ills. The church provides an opportunity for organized do-gooding, a community wherever a lonely and isolated Mormon may go. A large percentage of church members cling to their strong testimonies of the church's scriptures and leaders. But along with this preponderance of satisfied women, there are others who feel marginalized or unhappy about the church and wish to create an alternative LDS experience, a sisterhood and sometimes a brotherhood of their own. They form internet communities, retreats, and feminist groups with an LDS flavor.

A considerable number of others live with ambiguity, questioning some of the procedures, but too deeply involved by tradition and affection for Mormonism to give it up. One such sister gives a useful and memorable description of that state.

I often don't know which side of the [gay marriage] debate I am on. [On the one hand], I believe that our son's [gay] marriage will be good for him and good for society. His marriage will in no way undermine my marriage ... or male–female marriage in general. On the other hand, I believe that a prophet stands at the head of our church that has spoken out against same-sex marriage. It's a good thing I have two hands!

(Claremont Mormon Women's Oral History Collection, 2010, #71, pp. 23–24)

Many women, thinking of their own places in the church, are similarly grateful for two hands.

References

Beecher, M., and MacKay, K., 1978. Women in Twentieth Century Utah. In R. Poll, T.G. Alexander, E.E. Campbell, and D.E. Miller, eds. *Utah's History*. Provo, UT: Brigham Young University Press, pp. 563–86.
Bell, E., 1976. The Implications of Feminism for BYU. *BYU Studies* 16(4): Article 9.
Benson, E., 1981. Fourteen Fundamentals in Following the Prophet. Address given February 26 at Brigham Young University. *Liahona Magazine*. June.
Benson, E., 1987. To the Mothers in Zion. Fireside for Parents. February 22. www.lds.org/ensign/1987/05/news-of-the-church/president-benson-lauds-blessings-of-motherhood?lang=eng&_r=1.
Bradley, M., 1995. The Mormon Relief Society and the International Women's Year. *The Journal of Mormon History* 21(1): 105–67.
Bradley, M., 2005. *Pedestals and Podiums: Utah Women, Religious Authority, and Equal Rights*. Salt Lake City, UT: Signature Books.
Brooks, J., Steenblik, R., and Wheelwright, H. eds., 2016. *Mormon Feminism: Essential Writings*. New York: Oxford University Press.
Bushman, C., 1971. Women in *Dialogue*: An Introduction. *Dialogue: A Journal of Mormon Thought* 6(2): 5–8.
Bushman, C., 1974. Exponent II is Born. *Exponent II*. July, p. 2.
Campbell, D., 2016. LDS Women's Attitudes toward the Church: Satisfied with the Status Quo or Restless for Reform? In K. Holbrook and M. Bowman, eds. *Women and Mormonism: Historical and Contemporary Perspectives*. Salt Lake City, UT: University of Utah Press, pp. 199–212.
Claremont Mormon Women's Oral History Collection, #071, 2010. Library of the Claremont Colleges, Claremont, CA.
Clark, Jr., J.R. 1940. Our Homes. *Relief Society Magazine*. December.
Doctrine and Covenants of The Church of Jesus Christ of Latter-day Saints, 1981. Salt Lake City, UT: The Church of Jesus Christ of Latter-day Saints.
The Family: A Proclamation to the World, 1995. www.lds.org/topics/family-proclamation?lang=eng&old=true.
Haglund, K., 2016. Blogging the Boundaries: Mormon Mommy Blogs and the Construction of Mormon Identity. In P.Q. Mason and J.G. Turner, eds. *Out of Obscurity: Mormonism since 1945*. New York: Oxford University Press, pp. 234–56.
Huefner, D., 1978. Church and Politics at the Utah IWY Conference. *Dialogue: A Journal of Mormon Thought* 11(1): 58–75.
Kline, C., 2016. Saying Goodbye to the Final Say: The Softening and Reimagining of Mormon Male Headship Ideologies. In P.Q. Mason and J.G. Turner, eds. *Out of Obscurity: Mormonism since 1945*. New York: Oxford University Press, pp. 214–33.
Lauper, J., 2018. Personal Communication to C. Bushman. July.
McDannell, C., 2019. *Sister Saints: Modern Mormon Women from Polygamy to the Present*. New York: Oxford University Press.
Monson, T., 1971. The Women's Movement: Liberation or Deception? *Ensign*. January.
Murphy, M., 2005. Gainfully Employed Women, 1896–1950. In P.L. Scott and L. Thatcher, eds. *Women in Utah History: Paradigm or Paradox?* Logan, UT: Utah State University Press, pp. 183–222.
Oaks, D., 1989. Alternate Voices. General Conference. April. www.lds.org/general-conference/1989/04/alternate-voices?lang=eng.

Okazaki, C., and Prince, G., 2012. "There Is Always a Struggle": An Interview with Chieko Okazaki. *Dialogue: A Journal of Mormon Thought* 45(1): 112–40.
Packer, B., 1981. The Mantle Is Far, Far Greater than the Intellect. *BYU Studies* 21(3): Article 2.
Packer, B., 1993. Talk to the All-Church Coordinating Council. May 18. www.zionsbest.com/face.html.
Young, B., 1951. *Discourses of Brigham Young*. Salt Lake City, UT: Deseret Book.

Further reading

Bushman, C. ed., 1976. *Mormon Sisters: Women in Early Utah*. Cambridge, MA: Emmeline Press.
  Essays about nineteenth-century Mormon women.
Bushman, C., and Kline, C. eds., 2013. *Mormon Women Have Their Say: Essays from the Claremont Oral History Collection*. Draper UT: Greg Kofford Books.
  Topical essays using oral history materials.
Dew, S., 2013. *Women and the Priesthood: What One Mormon Woman Believes*. Salt Lake City, UT: Deseret Book.
  The positive case for women's rights in the church.
Hanks, M. ed., 1992. *Women and Authority: Re-emerging Mormon Feminism*. Salt Lake City, UT: Signature Books.
  Sources and essays.
Jergensen, S.C., and Miner, S.M. eds., n.d. c. 2018. *Seasons of Change: Stories of Transition from the Writers of Segullah*. El Cerrito, CA: Peculiar Pages.
  Personal stories of crisis and change by Mormon women.
McDannell, C., 2019. *Sister Saints: Mormon Women since the End of Polygamy*. New York City: Oxford University Press.
  An excellent new survey.
Shepherd, G., Anderson, L.F., and Shepherd, G., 2015. *Voices for Equality: Ordain Women and Resurgent Mormon Feminism*. Salt Lake City, UT: Greg Kofford Books.
  A collection of essays.
Ulrich, L.T., 2010. Mormon Women in the History of Second Wave Feminism. *Dialogue* 43(2): 45–63.
  From one present at the event.

13
GENDER AND MISSIONARY WORK

David Golding

Missionary work remains an enduring and dynamic feature of the Latter-day Saint experience. Joseph Smith's first followers preached with the Book of Mormon by canvassing the countryside of the 1830s United States. Within the decade, an institutional system around preaching developed: the Church of Jesus Christ of Latter-day Saints issued mission calls to volunteers who carried out proselytism as a temporary occupation, leaving their homeland and families for months or years to evangelize in pairs (Harper, 1998). By the 1970s, tens of thousands of young adults embarked on mission tours annually, fostering a subculture that treated men's two-year assignment as a rite of passage (Hoyt and Patterson, 2011; Shepherd and Shepherd, 1998). Latter-day Saints at large yet embraced the New Testament mandate to proclaim the Christian gospel. Regardless of formal ordination, lay missionaries participated in their local congregations by visiting proselytes and lapsed church members and delivering home lessons (Humpherys, 1977). The church continues this intricate program of assigning, training, dispatching, and supporting missionaries, who by 2018, numbered more than 67,000—around 15 percent of the worldwide Christian missionary force (*Church News*, 2018; Johnson et al., 2016).

Unlike the majority of highly active missionary organizations, Latter-day Saints launched into proselytizing without first considering the theological or theoretical implications. Joseph Smith's revelations urged the laity to "embark" as soon as they felt the desire to preach, and this practical approach precluded any effort to articulate a missiology or check missionary work against theology. The missionaries intrepidly went and preached, following the whims and circumstances that confronted them. Today's missionaries participate in a system that has evolved on perceptions of prior effectiveness. History, therefore, not only explains changes in the missionary program but also informs the mentality of Latter-day Saint missionaries—their activities derive from what earlier missionaries have done, almost never from an agenda set by theory or missiology. Whatever has appeared to garner more baptized church members has informed the proselytizing activities administrators and missionaries have employed.

The calculus of proselytizing effectiveness included changing conventions of behavior for women and men. Between 1830 and 1898, women participated as lay missionaries or in support of missionary husbands, but public reactions toward Latter-day Saint polygamy practices during the late nineteenth century prompted church officials to call single women as certified missionaries (McBride, 2018). Later systematic reforms struggled against female participation—in many settings, male missionaries doubled as local ecclesiastical leaders, roles reserved for the male priesthood. Yet the demands of evangelism and the perceived advantages of feminine preaching kept women at the front lines of the global mission effort. The settings in which the missionaries understood their commission to preach frequently nurtured the roles and agency of women and men during periods of adolescent development and young adulthood, ensuring that missionary patterns of devotion could endure in the culture of regular congregations (Riess, 2019, pp. 33–48).

Similar to the broader field of Mormon history, scholarship on missions has favored the nineteenth century. Works treating women's experiences in the missions lean toward the twentieth century, due to women's later participation. The general context for twentieth-century missions, however, has received little synthesis and almost no institutional development has been traced. This chapter proffers five periods for Mormon missions, each characterized by a main proselytizing strategy with ramifications on gendered discourse and effects in the broader church. The following sections examine the processes of masculinization and feminization that mission has inculcated by plotting Latter-day Saint mission history in the context of gender, reviewing the scholarly literature on gender and missionary work, and entertaining the frontiers of current studies.

Freelance prelude (1829–1832)

Immediately after Joseph Smith finished the manuscript of the Book of Mormon in 1829, his relatives and associates spread the word. Smith's mother shared news of the book with her siblings, but nearly all other documented evangelizers were men who visited churches, taverns, and cottages intending to preach. A revelation in 1830 called on four men to take the book to "the Lamanites," a Book of Mormon designation Smith and his followers ascribed to Native Americans. This "mission to the Lamanites" excited the new congregation, and women led by Smith's wife Emma sewed new clothes for the missionaries (Smith, 1845, p. 189). This mission ended abruptly due to a legal technicality with the United States government. But the missionaries had reason to celebrate the endeavor: a congregation of Reform Baptists in Ohio accepted the Book of Mormon and dozens joined Smith's young church (Underwood, 2005; Anderson, 1971).

Future missions followed this initial strategy of seeking out churched Christians and holding meetings to promote how the Book of Mormon had fulfilled biblical prophecy (Porter, 1988; Williams, 1969). The method of preaching reinforced roles of women participating as spiritually active recipients of the gospel message and men engaging as scriptural interlocutors. Prominent elders like Parley P. Pratt and William E. McLellin prepared sermons and arguments anticipating intense debates among clergymen and community leaders (Givens and Grow, 2011, p. 7; Baer, 1994); prominent women like Emma Smith and Eliza R. Snow exhorted fellow congregants in church gatherings and with poetry (Derr et al., 2016, p. 5; Waspe, 1942).

During this period, the term "priesthood" gained permanent traction within the nascent movement. For the Latter-day Saints, "priesthood" held together the wide concept of ecclesiology (i.e., the theological foundations for what constituted the church, body of Christ, or kingdom of God) and its application in missions. On a structural level, priesthood officers sustained the administration of church congregations and mediated disputes. The names and duties of these offices held theological significance for missionaries contending against critics: the *organization* of the church validated the truth claims of that church. They reasoned that the proper scheme of deacons, teachers, priests, elders, apostles, bishops, high priests (and later seventies and patriarchs) should correlate with scriptural definitions of Jesus' original church. While later scholars recognized various associations of New Testament terms (like deacon and priest) with women of late antiquity, Protestant North Americans of the early 1800s routinely ascribed such roles to men (Torjesen, 1993).

The Latter-day Saint priesthood order emerged in tandem with the first commissions to preach, inflecting mission with clerical expectations. Notwithstanding the neutral language in an early revelation about the missionary call—"O ye that embark in the service of God" (Doctrine and Covenants 4:2)—the attitude of framing official church procedures as priesthood functions precluded women from assuming the call. Not only did priesthood imbue missions with a masculine character on account of male access to priesthood office, but priesthood also cast missionary work in a biblical idiom already saturated in ancient patriarchal vocabularies. In a general sense, a Latter-day Saint man with any position in the church lived a priestly life traceable to the age of the patriarchs. Mission as an extension of priesthood order introduced men to a fraternity of sacrifice and discipleship.

Emigration era (1832–1898)

Joseph Smith dictated dozens of revelations within a couple of years, all rendered in the first-person voice of Jesus Christ and addressed variously to individuals, church leaders, and the church membership. The missionaries adhered to the revelations as both a scriptural mandate and a field manual (Ellsworth, 1951, pp. 41–42, 179–80). On several occasions, revelations directed the church to "gather" the covenant people out from "among the congregations of the wicked" and from the far reaches of the earth. The gathering would culminate in the Saints erecting a holy city called Zion, living in unity, and preparing for the imminent Second Coming of Christ. The missionaries sounded "the warning voice" by calling on their proselytes to leave home for Zion (Harper, 1998).

As the mandate to gather intensified in the mid-1830s, missionary work became highly transient, splitting the world into the domains of the gathered and the ungathered, the "stakes of Zion" and the "conferences" of the mission field. Under this scheme, missionaries were those identified with venturing outward from Zion, and the covenant faithful, those flowing inward to Zion. A group of twelve apostles served as the senior directors of the effort and the presiding officials over the church in the field (Whittaker, 2012a; 2012b; Ellsworth, 1951).

An early revelation promised an "endowment of power" that should precede "going forth among all Nations," what Smith and his associates interpreted to mean a Pentecost-like outpouring of the Holy Spirit that should empower missionaries ahead of departing on foreign missions. The Quorum of the Twelve Apostles particularly needed such "gifts of the Spirit" to fulfill its mandate to bear "special witness" of the resurrected Jesus Christ (Minutes and Blessings, 1835). In this season of fervent anticipation, church leaders sometimes took displays of ecstatic religious observances, like speaking in tongues or prophesying of the latter-day glory, as instances of an endowment of power. And the direct allusions the revelations made to Luke 24 (in which Jesus tells his disciples to wait in Jerusalem before taking the gospel to all nations until they should be "endued with power from on high") cast the present teaching model as something preliminary. The endowment of power, however it should manifest itself, would inaugurate the *global* mission effort (Smith, 1831).

This theological prerequisite for foreign missions rather exclusively involved men. Only in meetings of elders and high priests did church leaders watch for signs of the endowment of power (Staker, 2009, pp. 147–62). But with the construction and dedication of the church's first temple, the "House of the Lord" in Kirtland, Ohio, in 1836, both clergy and laity recognized several meetings of heightened spirituality as fulfilling the revelations' promise of the endowment of power. Many women participated in a series of Pentecostal phenomena, and reports told of an overall sense of God manifesting his presence to the general congregation (Harper, 2005; Stapley and Wright, 2009, pp. 63–66). While some Latter-day Saints spoke of their "solemn assembly" as an endowment for all the faithful, the effects on missionary work again enlisted men. Smith consequently dispatched an apostle to head the first foreign mission to Great Britain, a commission the whole group of Twelve Apostles viewed as a gateway to a truly global expansion of the church (Allen, Esplin, and Whittaker, 1992).

In the mission context, "priesthood," "endowment of power," and the foreign world all served a powerful millenarian concern for the end times, the latter days. The gathering held urgent significance: prophecies of worldwide tribulation portended terrible, even fatal, events that could befall any nation at any time, which obligated the elders to sound the warning to everyone. Should the elder neglect this mandate or somehow lapse in performing his duties, it stood to reason that the people he might have reached could blame their suffering or death on his inaction (Golding, 2015, pp. 215–18). Dark forces like the "man of sin" described in 2 Thessalonians drove the weak toward destruction and fought against the true church of Christ. The elders needed the endowment of power and priesthood authority to win in the battle for souls.

One revelation instructed the elders to establish a school for preparing each other for church leadership and mission service and made cleansing one another from "the blood of this generation" a centerpiece in the devotions of the group (Smith, 1833 [D&C 88]). Another ritual performed specifically by the missionaries responded to rejection by having the elder privately cast the dust off his feet as a testimony against the rejectors, thus absolving the missionary of any guilt at the judgment bar of God (Weber, 2013). In this priesthood capacity, the elder exercised a prerogative to "seal up" the righteous to salvation or the wicked to the day of God's wrath (Doctrine and Covenants 1:8–10). The gravity of such actions fit within codes of masculine honor of the 1800s—where death was on the line, men possessed both the burden and the authority to confront the situation. The priesthood concept suffused with apocalypticism premised the earliest missions on an exclusively masculine liability. On record, women as missionary wives or later as "sister missionaries" did not perform feet-dusting rituals.

Between the 1830s and the 1890s, three major efforts sustained missionary work abroad, all headed by the Twelve Apostles: the British mission; the European mission, which sprouted smaller missions in Scandinavia, Italy, and Turkey; and the Hawaiian mission, with its beginnings in Tahiti and other Pacific islands (Whittaker, 2012a; 2012b). Joseph Smith had dispatched elders to "Germany, Palestine, New Holland, the East Indies, and other places" by 1842, but these smaller circuits quickly fell defunct (Smith, 1842). Latter-day Saint resettlement in the North American West in the 1840s and 1850s shifted the base of missionary operations to Utah Territory, and though missionaries still worked in Britain and Western Europe, expansion stalled during and after the Utah War of 1857 and 1858 (a short confrontation between the United States Army and militias commanded by church president Brigham Young). Not until the 1870s did work outside Europe resume, but by then, the Latter-day Saint practice of polygamy had received international attention, and missionaries faced increasing resistance, even open hostility and mob attacks in the southern United States (Mason, 2011).

A tangled series of antipolygamy legislation and Latter-day Saint resistance to federal enforcement culminated in a powerful law and Supreme Court decision threatening to disenfranchise the church, and Church President Wilford Woodruff issued a manifesto leading to the end of Latter-day Saint plural marriages (Gordon, 2002). The siege lifted, and Latter-day Saints confronted the daunting prospect of assimilating into the broader society. Missions presented a key province for improving relations with neighbors and enhancing the reputation of the church (Embry, 1997, p. 107). Under Woodruff, administrators established permanent mission offices, further routinized proselytizing assignments and tours, and bureaucratized overall mission organization. The Quorum of the Twelve Apostles called mission presidents to supervise the increasingly systematic effort to proclaim the Book of Mormon and gather the faithful to Zion (Allen and Leonard, 1976, pp. 425–28).

All this while immigrant converts took the mandate to gather literally and personally, funding their own travel with whatever means they possessed. A significant number of converts struggled to afford or get outfitted for the migration, and the church eventually chartered the Perpetual Emigrating Fund that provided loans travelers could repay after integrating into Latter-day Saint communities. Emigration agents stationed at mission offices helped with purchasing supplies, booking passage on ships, and advising immigrants on their travel. Just as the church disavowed polygamy, its leaders began discouraging new members from relocating to Zion. Mission offices thereafter scaled down their emigration processing and instructed missionaries in building permanent congregations (Woods, 2011).

The shift from a localized to a universalized Zion—from a central and literal gathering place to a network of stakes all representing a global Zion community—was monumental. Nothing short of the social, economic, and theological dimensions of Mormon life experienced the effect, and the religious identity transitioned toward a more assimilated relationship with the outside world. For missions, the apocalyptic character of front-line proselytism suffered a conceptual blow, now that personal salvation replaced evading last-day calamities as the central objective. While stark militaristic rhetoric continued to ornament missionary discourse, the literal posture gave way to figurative tones: the battleground for souls resided primarily in the spiritual domain (Stimmler, 2003). Women could enter this contest where persuasive preaching dwelled more on accepting new doctrine than rejecting a wicked world.

System era (1898–1951)

In the aftermath of ending church-sanctioned plural marriages, reports persuaded most mission presidents that critics forced the issue of polygamy almost constantly. In determining a response, they began to consider women as not only missionary candidates, but church representatives ideally suited for an oppositional environment. After all, critics had commonly presumed that Mormon women lived in bondage to their husbands and secretly desired deliverance. Women missionaries, leaders believed, could counter these presuppositions in person by testifying of their pleasant homes and endorsing their family arrangements. Some mission presidents considered women's decorum and poise a potent challenge to prevailing stereotypes. Wilford Woodruff agreed, and in 1898, he enacted a new policy allowing leaders to set apart women as certified missionaries and mission presidents to employ "lady missionaries" abroad (McBride, 2018).

The new policy had a measurable impact on female enrollment as local church leaders who recommended women for missionary service processed more applications. In five years, married women made up over 60 percent of the female missionary force; but within another four years, this proportion flipped, with single women making up around 60 percent of women missionaries by 1908. Nearly 40 percent of all certified missionaries were women by 1918 (Sons of Utah Pioneers, 2016, pp. 28–29). With the greater proportion of single women in the field, this first generation witnessed a discursive shift—the common title "sister missionary" replaced "lady missionary" in parlance and curriculum. The change coincided as well with a cultural turn toward women entering the workplace in greater numbers. When the larger European and American societies called on women to assist in the war effort, the church closed sister missionary calls during World War II with the exception of women skilled in secretarial work, certified school teachers, or wives of men older than draft ages. The postwar environment noticed a retrenchment in tying women to motherhood and domestic work (Radke and Cropper-Rampton, 2005).

As women further proselytized, men tended to ask whether their "sisters" should engage in the same assignments and routines as the elders. Mission presidents offered a hesitant "yes and no": elders should "visit every reputable house" without "purse or scrip" (a practice dating to the early period of freelance missions in which elders relied on their proselytes for lodging and food); lady missionaries should do largely the same work as the elders, but limit their work to cities and "not travel without 'purse or scrip'" (McMurrin, 1904, p. 540).

These adjustments to eligibility allowances coincided with structural changes to the larger mission effort. Apostles at the turn of the twentieth century recognized irregularities across the missions and proposed forming a missionary committee to systematize and coordinate the missions (Alexander, 2012, p. 229). For some administrators, a slow-going bureaucratization ensued, the first indication of a reorienting of the mission scheme around developing rather than planting churches. In Protestant parlance, "church planting" described the strategy of orienting proselytism around galvanizing new congregations in areas without a parish or church presence. Through the Emigration Era, Latter-day Saint missionaries adhered to this strategy by taking as their principal objective reaching potential converts where no Latter-day Saint church or congregation existed and developing a congregation ready to support its members in emigrating to Zion. As missions further systematized around a scheme of perpetual (as opposed to transient) congregations, the missionaries and their administrators remained with converts and cycled personnel through defined zones. In this new self-sustaining environment, missions pivoted away from carrying out an urgent mandate of warning the nations of imminent calamity toward realizing a program of finding and baptizing converts (Golding, 2015, p. 217).

As women worked alongside men in expanding existing congregations, their presence entailed adapting the organization to missionaries not ordained to priesthood office. Aside from feet dusting, which by the 1890s had declined in practice enough for the First Presidency to discourage its frequent performance, not much else about proselytizing amounted to priestly rites or functions, especially with the dramatic pivot away from apocalyptic preaching (Weber, 2013, pp. 125–26). Like the elders, the first sister missionaries received setting-apart blessings and temple endowments prior to departure, and in the field, applied the elders' usual preaching methods (McBride, 2018, pp. 54–56). As preaching circuits aligned more directly with perpetual congregations, groupings of elders and sisters resembled the layout and geographic boundaries of wards and stakes. Missionary "districts" (separate from congregational districts formerly called "conferences") and parent "zones" brought elders and sisters in neighboring areas together, though under the leadership of an elder or pair of elders designated by the mission president the district leader or zone leader.

Though the proselytizing functions between elders and sisters differed very little, the chain of decision-making held women accountable to men and men accountable to rotating leadership. At least one mission president experimented with a sister missionary leader: in 1928, Marian Gardner was set apart as a "supervisory lady missionary" tasked with the same responsibilities as "supervisory elders," but only over women throughout the mission. When elders voiced confusion over Gardner's authority, the mission president conducted training meetings reiterating her role as an assistant to the president (Watt and Watt, 2017, pp. 140–41). Gardner's service proved the exception throughout the System Era as church leaders maintained the mission hierarchy as a training ground for young adult men to learn the order of the priesthood and receive preparation for future church leadership (Murdock, 1973, pp. 71–72).

Stake presidents in Utah—where greater than 92 percent of the total church membership resided in 1912—saw missionary possibilities in the heartland. They secured permission from the First Presidency to set apart local elders to proselytize within a stake (Keeler, Knight, and Merrill, 1912). Though the "stake missionaries" worked part-time, their deployment within congregations already deemed "gathered" and permanent shifted the scope of prior evangelism. Existing stakes seemed to require preaching regardless of the level of religious saturation in the locale. Such a model invited an assessment of how the ecclesiastical order should integrate with missionary organization patterns. The First Presidency, Quorum of the Twelve, and Missionary Committee revisited the scheme repeatedly, aiming to reduce the complexity of the missionary environment from a variable operation to a stable and replicable system. The trade-off meant an elaborate and highly defined matrix of church and mission units, church and mission leadership, and church and missionary activity.[1]

Apostle and member of the Missionary Committee, David O. McKay, commenced a worldwide tour of the missions in 1921 to survey the overall effort for systematic improvements. Sixty-one thousand miles and 366 days later, McKay returned to Utah reporting a somewhat dismal situation: local leadership struggled, infighting abounded, and congregations lacked adequate facilities (Cannon, 2011). Previously an accomplished businessman, Church President Heber J. Grant enacted corporate measures to streamline the missions. He maintained previous conventions, particularly categories of priesthood officers, while reconfiguring mission procedures around administrative efficiency.

Between 1925 and the late 1930s, broader Progressive Era influences had translated into a new mission system supervised more than ever before from Salt Lake City offices and subject to regular administrative calibrating. In 1925, the Missionary Home (a renovated house on the church headquarters campus in Salt Lake City) opened as a training center for outgoing missionaries. Each new class entered the Home for five to seven days of instruction by senior church leaders in policy, preaching methods, and general advice. Mission presidents praised the concentrated orientation newcomers received and suggested curriculum enhancements that led to standardized manuals and training reports (Snow, 1928; Cowan, 1984). That same year, Apostle Melvin J. Ballard traveled to Buenos Aires to dedicate South America for missionary work—the most conspicuous expansion of a new mission field since the ambitious opening of Asia in 1901. (Ballard's mission had followed Grant closing the Japan Mission due to political tensions, language difficulty, and purported minor church growth [Neilson, 2010].) Two years later, the church retired "conferences" and reformatted the hierarchy of units to proceed from mission to "district" to branch, with elders sometimes serving as district and branch presidents (Talmage, 1927). Elders noticed a fastening of leadership patterns to their status as missionaries. Sister missionaries heard more encouragement to lead women's Relief Society gatherings than to organize branch meetings; their numbers declined as mission calls overall dropped slightly throughout the 1920s (Embry, 1997, p. 110).

The updates overall adhered to a central and bureaucratic paradigm. The First Presidency increasingly sought for a reproducible scheme of personnel and activities, and a fundamental unit dating to Joseph Smith's grand Zion vision—the stake—emerged as the ideal cohort for consolidating such features. In 1930, stakes outside of Utah numbered only sixteen and had been organized only in Canada, Mexico, California, Colorado, Arizona, and Idaho. With sights on the Pacific and Latin American fields, Heber J. Grant anticipated stake growth emerging from within the missions and a proceeding from a model of expanding-then-dividing stake boundaries. The stakes should resemble each other in size, staff, activity, and devotion. No longer fully blended as in Brigham Young's pioneer "Deseret," church operations and the civic community separated, sometimes through active measures by Grant, the Twelve Apostles, and the Presiding Bishopric. Grant orchestrated the founding of the Corporation of the President of the Church of Jesus Christ of Latter-day Saints and through it started consolidating business components left over from the earlier Mormon enterprises. He oversaw the separation of administrative concerns into church departments and committees (Alexander, 2011, pp. 308–14).

Regular Latter-day Saints could recognize a new layering of occupations and programs, some centralized in a headquartered administration and others given to the purview of the stake to which they belonged. Missions overlapped with districts and stakes—the stake presidency and other stake officers served independently of the mission president and missionaries, but sisters and elders were dispatched to stakes in addition to unproselytized areas, increasingly assisting lay missionaries in ministering to proselytes, new converts, and lapsed church members. The Missionary Department, nothing more than a secretary and a couple of office assistants in Salt Lake City, suddenly noticed greater demands on processing mission calls, securing travel visas, planning itineraries, interfacing with mission presidents, and tracking statistics (Murdock, 1973, pp. 17–25, 61–68).

One elder in the largest and most active mission of the time, the British Mission, and future church president, Gordon B. Hinckley, caught attention for building rapport with local newspapers and successfully staging preaching and open house events. Apostles interviewed the missionary after his return to Utah, and decided to launch a new public relations committee with Hinckley as its executive secretary. The Radio, Publicity, and Mission Literature Committee began in 1935 developing broadcasts, public information campaigns, and new missionary curricula. By 1937, the committee had reviewed several plans circulating in the missions and published a standard manual, the *Missionary's Hand Book*, that set church-wide mission policies in writing for the first time. The handbook instructed mission presidents and elders to direct special attention to several routines in the districts, including a leadership pattern assigning sister missionaries to lead Relief Society groups and elders assuming ecclesiastical responsibilities under the mission president's direction. The pattern solidified the districts as proto-stakes headed by men and shepherded toward permanence and incorporating church programs (*The Missionary's Hand Book*, 1937; Dew, 1996, pp. 84–85).

The pace of mission work experienced a dramatic pause with World War II, particularly with the closure of the European field, male missionary candidates serving in war, and administrators passing on recruiting more women. When David O. McKay became church president in 1951, over 90 percent of total church members resided in the United States; over the next forty years, that percentage dropped by an average of about 1 percent per year. Targeted adjustments in the church and its missions inaugurated an era of coordinated and correlated programs created with a strong interest in expanding the church internationally (Boone, 2012).

Program era (1951–2012)

David O. McKay adopted a thoroughly bureaucratic structure and programmed routine into the missions. He sought to accelerate convert baptisms by coordinating closely with mission presidents to find the models that achieved higher growth church-wide. Reports persuaded McKay that missionary uniformity enhanced their presentation and curbed attrition. He advanced policies requiring uniform attire, curriculum, training centers, length of tours, application procedures, certification process, and field manuals (LoRusso, 2016; Prince and Wright, 2005, pp. 232–36). Whether in a mission, stake, district, or branch, each participant joined in a worldwide program, a unified effort to expand the church membership through proselytism. The features of that program came under scrutiny by an expanding Missionary Department managed by Gordon B. Hinckley who reported to the First Presidency (Dew, 1996, pp. 84–85, 143–58).

McKay marshaled the full membership into the program, declaring a motto that resonated for decades: "Every member a missionary." The structure for participating in mission had turned so routine, McKay could frame mission as a "responsibility" resting on all church members, a universal mandate touching all corners of the Latter-day Saint community (Prince and Wright, 2005, p. 230). Referring potential proselytes—what missionaries and laypersons increasingly called "investigators" for their having "investigated" whether to join the church—for in-home lessons emerged as a sign of discipleship and for some ardent "member-missionaries," a sacred duty. The distinction between full-time service and local or part-time volunteer work divided along gendered expectations: men of the priesthood possessed a duty to enter the mission field by virtue of their covenant of ordination; women's duty went only so far as that expected of all disciples and could be fulfilled by impromptu or local outreach.

Marriageability soon preoccupied senior church leaders deciding on destinations for missionary candidates, who noticed a wave of single women applying for missionary service. In 1951, McKay adjusted women's age of missionary candidacy from 21 to 23. "It is surprising how eagerly the young women and some married women seek calls to go on missions," he said of the new policy.

> We commend them for it, but the responsibility of proclaiming the gospel of Jesus Christ rests upon the priesthood of the Church. It is quite possible now, in view of the present emergency [i.e., influx of sister missionaries], that we shall have to return to the standard age for young women, which is twenty-three.
> *(Radke-Moss, 2016; Embry, 1997, p. 112).*

Another surge of female missionary participation did not occur again until 2012 and another change to the minimum age of service.

The steady growth of church congregations corresponded with predictable growth in missionary candidates, but a sharp increase in convert baptisms and missionary participation began to intensify in 1960. Stakes abroad started to multiply—in eleven years, a stake was organized on each continent. McKay and Hinckley encouraged a new paradigm in administration: instead of sending missionaries to canvass vast stretches, mission presidents should assign them to existing congregations and subdivide mission zones as growth happened. Even when opening a town or city to proselytism, the presidents should branch out from centers of planted groups. The days of a missionary pair wandering into distant, unevangelized areas diminished; adhering to more familiar extensions of staffed mission fields allowed sister missionaries into the intrepid work of opening a new area for the first time (Prince and Wright, 2005, pp. 227–55).

By the 1960s, a philosophical shift in how Latter-day Saints understood church programs gained momentum. This "Priesthood Correlation" effort sought to subsume all programs under a hierarchy of priesthood direction. The whole institution underwent a series of theological audits: how could this auxiliary or that procedure be integrated within a priesthood line of oversight? The centralized bureaucracy assembled several standing councils to set objectives and agendas for church departments. In 1971, a report solicited from third-party consultants recommended that the church staff its departments with professional employees (Prince, 2016, pp. 86–88, 193–94, 294). Socioeconomic norms of the time already favored men for executive and professional candidacy; women initially worked in the Missionary Department as secretaries, stenographers, and office assistants. The executive councils dispatching women and men on missions comprised men bearing elite ecclesiastical credentials. The missionary program reverted to a male-dominated scheme with women as auxiliary counterparts just as signs of growing missionary interest among young women had begun to surface (Lyon and McFarland, 2003; Payne, 2005, p. 128).

Professionalization encouraged an institutional separation of business concerns. Executives created new divisions within the Missionary Department based on strategic assessments of church-wide proselytization and program logistics. As the divisions within the department expanded, the number of infield experiments increased. Mission presidents attempted new door-to-door techniques, lesson scripts, teaching props, and public information campaigns, relaying a regular stream of reports to the Missionary Department. The variables of success revolved around missionary safety and rates of baptism. An ambivalent culture of creative experimentation on the one hand and strict adherence to battle-tested standards on the other modulated the mission experience through the 1970s and 1980s. Reports of fresh preaching methods placed rhetorical emphasis on personal obedience to mission rules (Shepherd and Shepherd, 1998; Adams and Clopton, 1990; Jensen, 1974).

The divide-and-conquer formula persisted, and the rate of splitting off new stakes and missions climbed. Latin America and the Philippines experienced unprecedented growth, and sensing the momentum, Church President Spencer W. Kimball demanded all hands on deck. He gave an impassioned plea to "lengthen our stride" and raise up powerful missionaries, calling on all young men to live a higher code of conduct and apply to serve a mission. The ratio of certified missionaries to total church members peaked in the late 1970s (Kimball, 2005, pp. 113–15; Boone, 2012). The strong 1970s rhetoric of all young men serving missions occasioned a rise in negative sister stereotypes like the "unmarried Old Maid," and cultural elements like the popular musical *Saturday's Warrior* reinforced women's role in supporting missionary boyfriends rather than applying for missions themselves. The effects more often delimited sister missionary agency along supporting men through marriage, home and family life, and menial office work. Winning over male counterparts in the mission field added stresses to sisters' routines between the 1970s and 1990s. The proportion of sisters to elders dropped below 20 percent, encouraging more young women to assent to a contingency plan mentality: a significant number of sisters opted for a mission after perceiving their window for courtship had closed. The (often militaristic) rhetoric that motivated elders to brave long hours of rejection cast sisters as delicate, thus circumscribing women's service around safe and controlled activities (Radke and Cropper-Rampton, 2005).

Kimball's greatest legacy came with a prophetic revelation he announced in 1978—a restriction against men of black African descent being ordained to the priesthood and against women and men of black African descent participating in temple rituals was lifted (Kimball, 2008). Missionaries who had labored over the policy's red tape—filing black proselytes' pedigrees to determine ancestry before baptism—could preach baptism, priesthood, and temple without regard to race. Baptism rates through the 1980s in Central and South America soared. By 1979, Latter-day Saints in Chile numbered more than half a million and represented more than 3 percent of the country's population, more per capita than in the United States (Cannon and Cowan, 2002, p. 286). More missionary candidates applied from outside North America, creating demand for additional training centers. The missiological phenomenon of "reverse missions" touched Latter-day Saints for the first time as sisters and elders from outside the Anglophone subculture received mission calls to the church's heartlands in Utah and the rest of the western United States. Language-specific branches, especially Spanish, proliferated across North American stakes and were regularly supported by certified missionaries (Embry and Richards, 2012).

By the 1980s, the church presented missionaries as official representatives bearing not only ministerial certificates but also name badges and a uniform appearance so recognizable, the male Mormon missionary sporting a white shirt, necktie, and black tag became the poster child of Mormon culture.[2] Sister missionaries weathered several iterations of dress and grooming standards, receiving at one point an experimental course in business fashion from modeling consultants, but settling on a conservative wardrobe of typical North American office wear (Blakesley, 2009, pp. 33–35; Buehner, 1982). Since 1901, the extent of proselytizing tourists at the most-visited site of the church, Temple Square in Salt Lake City, had involved a Bureau of Information distributing pamphlets, presenting short tours, and offering on-hand guides (Hafen, 1997, p. 362; Richardson, 2003, pp. 79–80). In 1989, around seventy sister missionaries replaced over 900 part-time volunteers in delivering all tours and presentations. Field evaluations had persuaded Temple Square administrators that visitors were "more quickly comfortable with a young lady" than with elders and senior couples. The church trusted its busiest interface with the public to young sister missionaries and their friendly demeanor, a plan still in effect (*Church News*, 1989; Bremer, 2000, p. 430).

Both sisters and elders beyond Temple Square negotiated standards of appearance and conduct, but codes differed depending on gender. Women not only coordinated their attire to match an acceptable fashion but also received instruction on their appearance that administrators linked with personal development. The initiative to improve feminine presentation of sister missionaries was titled the "Personal Development Program" and associated wardrobe decisions of color and dress ensembles with inner esteem and confidence. To dress mindfully was to display one's serious intention to live righteously. The "motley assortment of house dresses, jumpers, and little girl type clothes" evident in typical sister missionary dress reflected poorly on the gospel message, program developer Alice Buehner reported in 1982. A greater burden of nonverbal communication rested on women for how they could more effectively attract proselytes than men (Buehner, 1982, pp. 6–13). Standards evolved almost negligibly for elders.

When Gordon B. Hinckley became church president in 1995, the missionary force had never been larger, and convert baptisms exceeded 300,000 per year (Boone, 2012). Hinckley noticed in the upswell of converts a related rise in lapsed church members. Whereas a generation of missionaries had looked to expand wards and stakes, the latest corps received directives to locate and "reactivate" the "less-active." Several measures aimed at improving quality over quantity of conversions: more thorough proselyte instruction and interviews before baptism; shifting primary oversight of missionary work to ward bishops and local leaders; coordinating better with lay and certified missionaries; and revising curriculum to steer missionaries away from rote presentations toward adapted lessons and spiritual inspiration (Hinckley, 1999; Smith, 2015). Candidates for full-time service heard Hinckley announce greater insistence on missionary qualifications—"raising the bar"—to seek out "missionaries to match the message of salvation." Within three years, the number of certified missionaries dropped by 20 percent (Boone, 2012). The release of *Preach My Gospel*—a revised curriculum of missionary preparation, proselyte lessons, and field training—further emphasized a culture of skilled preaching and personal righteousness. Rhetoric of a "greatest generation of missionaries" supplanted the duty-speak of the 1970s and 1980s as young people spoke of valued experience over sacrifice (Riess, 2019).

Multifaceted era (2012–present)

In the Program Era, minor adjustments to minimum age requirements and length of service stabilized around 19 years old and twenty-four-month tours for men and 21 years old and eighteen-month tours for women. In 2012, Church President Thomas S. Monson inaugurated a shift in age standards, lowering the age of eligibility to 18 and 19 for men and women respectively. The change elicited a surge in sister missionary participation: in a year, fifty-eight new missions were created, bringing the total to 405, and total certified missionaries rose from 58,000 to over 80,000, the majority of the increase owed to a significant number of female applicants (Rabada, 2014, pp. 20–21; Toone, 2018).

Monson and other leaders followed the policy change with an initiative branded "Hastening the Work of Salvation." This multifaceted effort discouraged door-to-door proselytizing and called on church members and missionaries to combine their interactions with potential proselytes. Social media campaigns placed certified missionaries in contact with online inquirers and advertised the neighborly posture of regular Latter-day Saints with slogans "I'm a Mormon" and "Meet the Mormons." Other media initiatives orchestrated by the Missionary and Public Affairs departments followed, bringing highly coordinated and strategized public messaging into the mainstream of missionary proselytism (Hastening the Work of Salvation, 2013).

Though "the surge" reverted to an earlier mean average of personnel, sister missionaries maintained a greater proportion than previously, leading to adjustments in mission hierarchies. The position of "sister training leader" emerged, but not in precise parity with elders' leadership. While a sister training leader supervised sisters, she still answered to male district leaders, zone leaders, and assistants to the mission president (Rabada, 2014, pp. 21–25). Competitive rhetoric had appeared throughout history—among the first mission presidents to employ sister missionaries, some compared levels of usefulness between sisters and elders (McMurrin, 1904, pp. 540–41). "I used to like to challenge [the sisters] to beat the elders," one mission president reported in 1974, "because I think historically lady missionaries are kind of second-class citizens" (Winder, 1974, p. 89). Sisters before and after the surge often posted similar statistics as the elders but could sense jealousy from elders who remarked about perceived advantages (such as car privileges and more populated assigned areas) owed to common regulations designed to protect sisters from harassment or assault (Radke and Cropper-Rampton, 2005). Sister missionaries by 2013 reported a commensurate degree of spiritual intensity and proselytizing work ethic and exceeded elders in personal religiosity, yet combated both the regular rejection on the street and negative projections from the elders (Chou, 2013, pp. 215–16).

Though the stresses of missionary life did not appear to subside for sisters after the surge, the environment fostered greater collaboration between women in official council groups in the mission and unofficial support networks outside the mission. Personal blogs grew into a popular medium for missionaries to narrate their experiences and include their families and friends in their service. Sisters especially utilized blogs to connect with other women and claim an authoritative voice in reporting on local conditions and proselytizing effectiveness (Mormon Missionary Collection, 2013–2019). Advice books previously centered on elders' challenges were written by returned sister missionaries for young women, drastically altering the categories by which missionary preparation had been typically articulated. Women embraced the language of adventurous, physical, and combative settings, assuring potential missionaries they could conquer any insecurity and endure hardships for Christ. Sisters could claim virtually every blessing promised to men of the priesthood on account of their calling as certified missionaries, but they offered something unique: their own personality, all her traits and character in delivering ministerial service to people in need of connecting with the Holy Spirit (Hahl and Knight, 2014; Young, 2014). Sister missionaries by 2019 displayed a willingness to experiment in less formal proselytism and more humanitarianism, a mission approach resonating with Latter-day Saint Millennials more broadly (Riess, 2019).

Male returned missionaries occupied a class of pre-leaders groomed through the mission experience for callings and assignments reserved for members of the priesthood. They often enjoyed a privileged status during courtship, as many women ranked the qualities of honoring the priesthood and completing a mission at the top of their mate selection criteria (Stacy, 2004). A sample of returned elders attending Brigham Young University in 2007 did not appear to reciprocate, instead placing a priority on dating partners being accepting and friendly (McLaughlin, 2007). After the surge in 2012 and 2013, female returned missionaries, especially in the United States, appeared more normalized and brought a more even appraisal of sister contributions (Chou, 2013). Campus folklore indicated the cachet previously held by recently returned elders receded with the rise of returned sisters; stories of awkward dates arising from men betraying missionary quirks spread among female students, rendering the male returned missionary more of a klutz than a catch (Green, 2016). The surge has appeared to have altered the mission appeal in dating contexts and purchased for women greater influence in resetting values (Riess, 2019, pp. 40–44; Bordelon, 2013).

Studies and frontiers

Most studies that concentrate on gender in the Latter-day Saint mission experience focus on women and sister missionaries. Feminist theory has informed various works, but masculinities studies have remained largely absent. Without established fields of Latter-day Saint mission studies or missiology, the topic of gender in missionary work has been eclectic in the scholarly literature and predominantly studied by historians (see Whittaker, 2000). Several histories of female missionaries narrate the emergence of certified sister missionaries and the effects of their proselytism. Matthew S. McBride (2018) collects the correspondence between mission presidents and Church President Wilford Woodruff to document the development of the policy permitting certified sister missionaries. The article notes several episodes of gendered discourse that fashioned an ambiguous missionary identity for women, encapsulated in the phrase "female brethren" written by one sister to chide elders who had addressed assemblies of missionaries as "brethren" out of habit. Andrea G. Radke and Rebecca Cropper-Rampton (2005) notice the ongoing ambiguities and binds imposed on sisters throughout the Program Era, especially in the category of courtship—women could not completely escape assumptions that they had failed to attract a spouse in deciding to serve a mission, yet they also could not satisfy demands of piety when treated as a potential temptation for the elders. The bind of being projected as simultaneously unattractive and too attractive induced unique stressors not broadly reported by male missionaries. Tania Rands Lyon and MaryAnn Shumway McFarland (2003) analyze the tensions apparent in age policies and priesthood discourse: women received accommodation but not the invitation to represent the church to the world, particularly in the changing age standards that counteracted higher female participation.

Surveys of sister missionary history include Calvin S. Kunz (1976), Jessie L. Embry (1997), Tally S. Payne (2005), and a special issue of *Pioneer* (Sons of Utah Pioneers, 2016). Reid L. Neilson and Fred E. Woods (2012) offer an anthology of studies on latest topics of interest, particularly drawing more global and regional awareness of missions. Jana Riess (2019) presents data and recent historical context for changing attitudes toward missions and sister missionary participation in the Multifaceted Era among the rising generation of missionaries.

Sociological studies tend to examine gender dynamics within the broader concern for courtship and marriage cultures.[3] Hui-Tzu Grace Chou (2013) conducted a survey of returned missionaries and compares elder and sister responses to determine statistically significant differences. Religiosity before and after the mission factored prominently in the class of female missionaries, whereas pressure ranked higher for male missionaries. Nancy C. McLaughlin (2000 and 2007) tracks dating behaviors of male returned missionaries but researches the class of young adults rather than active missionaries.

The array of multilingual and multivocal sources typical of missionary encounters challenges scholars and promises fresh perspectives for gender studies. Globalization as a setting and process has gained considerable traction in mission studies and historiography, though reception history and processes of conversion and disaffiliation within mission fields, among proselytes, and about non-white missionaries have received minor attention. Some scholars have argued the state of the scholarship necessitates decolonization; bringing gender studies and missiology together could displace the dominant narratives favoring missionary administrators and elders (Colvin and Brooks, 2018). Postcolonialism, a theory and critique missiologists more broadly have deliberated since the 1990s (Grimshaw and May, 2010), has yet to inform studies of Latter-day Saint missions. As gender amounts to a core concern of postcolonial interventions (Mohanty, 1984; Donaldson and Kwok, 2002), questions of indigeneity, agency, and sovereign subjectivities in the missionary encounter invite considerations of gendering discourse and effects. A conspicuous omission in mission historiography remains integrating indigenous voices—especially indigenous women's voices—into analyses of change over time and space. Future studies should leverage the growing network of globalization specialists and diverse scholars listed on the Global Mormon Studies directory (globalmormonstudies.org) and build a source base from the already rich archive of digitized missionary blogs curated by the L. Tom Perry Special Collections at Brigham Young University (Mormon Missionary Collection, 2013–2019).

Due to a lack of formal missiology within the Latter-day Saint religious community and Mormon studies scholarship, the chance to build missiology with a sound postcolonial and feminist perspective awaits. Especially as parity between sisters and elders appears to increase with the "Hastening the Work of Salvation" initiative, women's agency in fashioning a missiology—in conceptualizing and executing a religious commission—invites exploration. The ways mission has capitalized on male labor and mission theology has articulated masculine identity deserve attention, especially if a systematic missiology is to parse patriarchal and sovereign discourses in the service of a transnational or global framework.

Notes

1 No study has yet tracked the development of the office of mission president or the bureaucracy of the Missionary Department (Whittaker, 2011, pp. 672–73).
2 The Provo Utah Missionary Training Center reported to librarians at the Church History Library in Salt Lake City that the Brigham Young University Bookstore began supplying standard-issue name tags to missionaries at the Center and throughout the world in August 1980; Jim Kimball, qtd. in Ryan Combs, email to author, May 15, 2019.
3 See Whittaker (2000) for an overview of sociological studies of Latter-day Saint missions.

References

Adams, W.A., and Clopton, J.R., 1990. Personality and Dissonance among Mormon Missionaries. *Journal of Personality Assessment* 54(3–4): 684–93.
Alexander, T.G., 2011. Church Administrative Change in the Progressive Period, 1898–1930. In D.J. Whittaker and A.K. Garr, eds. *A Firm Foundation: Church Organization and Administration*. Provo, UT: Religious Studies Center, pp. 295–317.
Alexander, T.G., 2012. *Mormonism in Transition: A History of the Latter-day Saints, 1890–1930*. 3rd ed. Salt Lake City, UT: Greg Kofford Books.
Allen, J.B., Esplin, R.K., and Whittaker, D.J., 1992. *Men with a Mission: The Quorum of the Twelve Apostles in the British Isles, 1837–1841*. Salt Lake City, UT: Deseret Book.
Allen, J.B., and Leonard, G.M., 1976. *The Story of the Latter-day Saints*. Salt Lake City, UT: Deseret Book.
Anderson, R.L., 1971. The Impact of the First Preaching in Ohio. *BYU Studies* 11(4): 474–96.
Baer, M.T., 1994. Charting the Missionary Work of William E. McLellin: A Content Analysis. In J. Shipps and J.W. Welch, eds. *The Journals of William E. McLellin, 1831–1836*. Urbana, IL: University of Illinois Press, pp. 379–405.
Blakesley, K.C., 2009. "A Style of Our Own": Modesty and Mormon Women, 1951–2008. *Dialogue: A Journal of Mormon Thought* 42(2): 20–53.
Boone, D.F., 2012. Missionary Work, 1900–Present. In B. Plewe, ed. *Mapping Mormonism: An Atlas of Latter-day Saint History*. Provo, UT: Brigham Young University Press, pp. 178–81.

Bordelon, E.D., 2013. An Exploration of the Lived Experiences of Returned Mormon Missionaries. Ph.D. Dissertation, Louisiana State University.

Bremer, T.S., 2000. Tourists and Religion at Temple Square and Mission San Juan Capistrano. *Journal of American Folklore* 133(450): 422–35.

Buehner, A.W., 1982. The Communicational Function of Wearing Apparel for Lady Missionaries of the Church of Jesus Christ of Latter-day Saints. Master's thesis, Brigham Young University.

Cannon, D.Q., and Cowan, R.O. eds., 2002. *Unto Every Nation: Gospel Light Reaches Every Land*. Salt Lake City, UT: Deseret Book.

Cannon, H.J., 2011. *To the Peripheries of Mormondom: The Apostolic Around-the-World Journey of David O. McKay, 1920–1921*, ed. R.L. Neilson. Salt Lake City, UT: University of Utah Press.

Chou, H.-T.G., 2013. Mormon Missionary Experiences and Subsequent Religiosity among Returned Missionaries in Utah. *Social Sciences and Missions* 26(2–3): 199–225.

Church News, 1989. Sister Missionaries to Be Only Guides on Temple Square. October 21, p. 4.

Church News, 2018. 2017 Statistical Report for 2018 April General Conference. https://perma.cc/S7BX-V6Q5.

Colvin, G., and Brooks, J. eds. 2018. *Decolonizing Mormonism: Approaching a Postcolonial Zion*. Salt Lake City, UT: University of Utah Press.

Cowan, R.O., 1984. *Every Man Shall Hear the Gospel in His Own Language: A History of the Missionary Training Center and Its Predecessors*. Provo, UT: Missionary Training Center.

Derr, J.M., Madsen, C.C., Holbrook, K., and Grow, M.J. eds., 2016. *The First Fifty Years of Relief Society: Key Documents in Latter-day Saint Women's History*. Salt Lake City, UT: Church Historian's Press.

Dew, S.L., 1996. *Go Forward with Faith: The Biography of Gordon B. Hinckley*. Salt Lake City, UT: Deseret Book.

Donaldson, L.E., and Kwok, P. eds., 2002. *Postcolonialism, Feminism and Religious Discourse*. New York: Routledge.

Ellsworth, S.G., 1951. A History of Mormon Missions in the United States and Canada, 1830–1860. Ph.D. Dissertation, University of California–Berkeley.

Embry, J., 1997. LDS Sister Missionaries: An Oral History Response, 1910–70. *Journal of Mormon History* 23(1): 100–139.

Embry, J.L., and Richards, A.L., 2012. Specialized Congregations, 1947–Present. In B. Plewe, ed. *Mapping Mormonism: An Atlas of Latter-day Saint History*. Provo, UT: Brigham Young University Press, pp. 154–55.

Givens, T.L., and Grow, M.J., 2011. *Parley P. Pratt: The Apostle Paul of Mormonism*. New York: Oxford University Press.

Golding, D., 2015. Mormonism. In A.J. Ghiloni, ed. *World Religions and Their Missions*. New York: Peter Lang, pp. 215–62.

Gordon, S.B., 2002. *The Mormon Question: Polygamy and Constitutional Conflict in Nineteenth-Century America*. Chapel Hill, NC: University of North Carolina Press.

Green, S.L., 2016. *Return with Bother: Awkward Dating Stories with Recently Returned Missionaries*. Snowbird, UY: Mormon History Association Annual Meeting.

Grimshaw, P., and May, A., eds. 2010. *Missionaries, Indigenous Peoples and Cultural Exchange*. Portland, OR: Sussex Academic Press.

Hafen, T.K., 1997. City of Saints, City of Sinners: The Development of Salt Lake City as a Tourist Attraction, 1869–1900. *Western Historical Quarterly* 28(3): 342–77.

Hahl, E.B., and Knight, J.R., 2014. *Do Not Attempt in Heels: Mission Stories and Advice from Sisters Who've Been There*. Springville, UT: Cedar Fort.

Harper, S.C., 1998. Missionaries in the American Religious Marketplace: Mormon Proselyting in the 1830s. *Journal of Mormon History* 24(2): 1–29.

Harper, S.C., 2005. "A Pentecost and Endowment Indeed": Six Eyewitness Accounts of the Kirtland Temple Experience. In J. Welch, ed. *Opening the Heavens: Accounts of Divine Manifestations, 1820–1844*. Provo, UT: Brigham Young University Press, pp. 327–71.

Hastening the Work of Salvation, 2013. www.churchofjesuschrist.org/training/wwlt/2013/hastening/members-and-missionaries.

Hinckley, G.B., 1999. Find the Lambs, Feed the Sheep. February 21. www.lds.org/study/general-conference/1999/04/find-the-lambs-feed-the-sheep.

Hoyt, A., and Patterson, S.M., 2011. Mormon Masculinity: Changing Gender Expectations in the Era of Transition from Polygamy to Monogamy, 1890–1920. *Gender & History* 23(1): 72–91.

Humpherys, A.G., 1977. Missionaries to the Saints. *Brigham Young University Studies* 17(1): 74–100.
Jensen, J.E., 1974. Proselyting Techniques of Mormon Missionaries. Master's thesis, Brigham Young University.
Johnson, T.M., Zurlo, G.A., Hickman, A.W., and Crossing, P.F., 2016. Christianity 2016: Latin America and Projecting Religions to 2050. *International Bulletin of Mission Research* 40(1): 22–29.
Keeler, J.B., Knight, J.W., and Merrill, A.N., 1912. Local Missionary Work. *Improvement Era* 15(4): 377–78.
Kimball, E.L., 2005. *Lengthen Your Stride: The Presidency of Spencer W. Kimball.* Salt Lake City, UT: Deseret Book.
Kimball, E.L., 2008. Spencer W. Kimball and the Revelation on Priesthood. *BYU Studies* 47(2): 4–78.
Kunz, C.S., 1976. A History of Female Missionary Activity in the Church of Jesus Christ of Latter-day Saints, 1830–1898. Master's thesis, Brigham Young University.
LoRusso, J.D., 2016. "The Puritan Ethic on High": LDS Media and the Mormon Embrace of Free Enterprise in the Twentieth Century. In P.Q. Mason and J.G. Turner, eds. *Out of Obscurity: Mormonism since 1945.* New York: Oxford University Press, pp. 104–22.
Lyon, T., and McFarland, M.S., 2003. "Not Invited, but Welcome": The History and Impact of Church Policy on Sister Missionaries. *Dialogue: A Journal of Mormon Thought* 36(3): 71–102.
Mason, P.Q., 2011. *The Mormon Menace: Violence and Anti-Mormonism in the Postbellum South.* New York: Oxford University Press.
McBride, M., 2018. "Female Brethren": Gender Dynamics in a Newly Integrated Missionary Force, 1898–1915. *Journal of Mormon History* 44(4): 40–67.
McLaughlin, N.C., 2000. Dating Behavior of Latter-day Saint Male Returned Missionaries: A Process of Managing Desires. Ph.D. Dissertation, Brigham Young University.
McLaughlin, N.C., 2007. Managing Desires: Dating Styles of Latter-day Saint Male Returned Missionaries. In M.J. Woodger, T.B. Holman, and K.A. Young, eds. *Latter-day Saint Courtship Patterns: Studies in Religion and the Social Order.* Lanham, MD: University Press of America, pp. 71–87.
McMurrin, J.W., 1904. Lady Missionaries. *The Young Woman's Journal* 15(12): 539–41.
Minutes and Blessings, February 21, 1835. *The Joseph Smith Papers.* www.josephsmithpapers.org/transcript/minutes-and-blessings-21-february-1835.
The Missionary's Hand Book, 1937. Missouri: Zion's Printing and Publishing Company.
Mohanty, C.T., 1984. Under Western Eyes: Feminist Scholarship and Colonial Discourses. *Boundary 2* 12(3): 333–58.
Mormon Missionary Collection, 2013–2019. L. Tom Perry Special Collections, Harold B. Lee Library, Brigham Young University. https://archive-it.org/collections/3609.
Murdock, F.J., 1973. Interview by Gordon Irving, Salt Lake City, Utah. OH 89. Church History Library, Salt Lake City, UT.
Neilson, R.L., 2010. *Early Mormon Missionary Activities in Japan, 1901–1924.* Salt Lake City, UT: University of Utah Press.
Neilson, R.L., and Woods, F.E., 2012. *Go Ye into All the World: The Growth and Development of Mormon Missionary Work.* Provo, UT: Religious Studies Center.
Payne, T.S., 2005. "Our Wise and Prudent Women": Twentieth-Century Trends in Female Missionary Service. In C. Cornwall Madsen and C.B. Silver, eds. *New Scholarship on Latter-day Saint Women in the Twentieth Century: Selections from the Women's History Initiative Seminars, 2003–2004.* Provo, UT: Joseph Fielding Smith Institute for Latter-day Saint History, pp. 125–40.
Porter, L.C., 1988. "The Field Is White Already to Harvest": Earliest Missionary Labors and the Book of Mormon. In L.C. Porter and S.E. Black, eds. *The Prophet Joseph: Essays on the Life and Mission of Joseph Smith.* Salt Lake City, UT: Deseret Book, pp. 73–89.
Prince, G.A., 2016. *Leonard Arrington and the Writing of Mormon History.* Salt Lake City, UT: University of Utah Press.
Prince, G.A., and Wright, W.R., 2005. *David O. McKay and the Rise of Modern Mormonism.* Salt Lake City, UT: University of Utah Press.
Rabada, C.L., 2014. A Swelling Tide: Nineteen-Year-Old Sister Missionaries in the Twenty-First Century. *Dialogue: A Journal of Mormon Thought* 47(4): 19–45.
Radke, A., and Cropper-Rampton, R., 2005. "On the Outside Looking In": A Gendered Look at Sister Missionary Experiences. In C. Cornwall Madsen and C.B. Silver, eds. *New Scholarship on Latter-day Saint Women in the Twentieth Century: Selections from the Women's History Initiative Seminars, 2003–2004.* Provo, UT: Joseph Fielding Smith Institute for Latter-day Saint History, pp. 141–51.

Radke-Moss, A., 2016. Pragmatism and Progress: Sister Missionary Service in the Twentieth Century. *Pioneer* 63(1): 40–43.

Richardson, M.O., 2003. Bertel Thorvaldsen's "Christus": A Mormon Icon. *Journal of Mormon History* 29(1): 66–100.

Riess, J., 2019. *The Next Mormons: How Millennials Are Changing the LDS Church*. New York: Oxford University Press.

Shepherd, G., and Shepherd, G., 1998. *Mormon Passage: A Missionary Chronicle*. Urbana, IL: University of Illinois Press.

Smith, A.N., 2015. Teaching for Conversion: Recent Refinements in Teaching and Learning. *Religious Educator* 16(3): 102–29.

Smith, Jr., J., 1831. Revelation, January 2, 1831 [D&C 38]. *The Joseph Smith Papers*. www.josephsmithpapers.org/paper-summary/revelation-2-january-1831-dc-38/1.

Smith, Jr., J., 1833. Revelation, January 3, 1833 [D&C 88:127–37]. *The Joseph Smith Papers*. www.josephsmithpapers.org/paper-summary/revelation-3-january-1833-dc-88127-137/1.

Smith, Jr., J., 1842. Church History. *Times and Seasons* 3(9): 709.

Smith, L.M., 1845. Lucy Mack Smith, History, 1845. *The Joseph Smith Papers*. www.josephsmithpapers.org/paper-summary/lucy-mack-smith-history-1845/197.

Snow, L.C., 1928. The Missionary Home. *Improvement Era* 31(7): 552–54.

Sons of Utah Pioneers, 2016. The History of Sister Missionaries [Special Issue]. *Pioneer* 63(1).

Stacy, M.J., 2004. Altar Bound: A Qualitative Study of the Unique Mate-Selection Criteria Used by Young Women in the Church of Jesus Christ of Latter-day Saints (Mormon). Ph.D. Dissertation, Capella University.

Staker, M.L., 2009. *Hearken, O Ye People: The Historical Setting of Joseph Smith's Ohio Revelations*. Salt Lake City, UT: Greg Kofford Books.

Stapley, J.A., and Wright, K., 2011. Female Ritual Healing in Mormonism. *Journal of Mormon History* 37(1): 1–85.

Stimmler, A.G., 2003. Missions and the Rhetoric of Male Motivation. *Dialogue: A Journal of Mormon Thought* 36(3): 103–11.

Talmage, J.E., 1927. Districts and Conferences. *The Latter-day Saints' Millennial Star*. 89(14): 216.

Toone, T., 2018. A "Spectacular Success": How Sister Missionaries Have Dispelled Myths for 120 Years. *Deseret News*. June 8.

Torjesen, K.J., 1993. *When Women Were Priests: Women's Leadership in the Early Church and the Scandal of Their Subordination in the Rise of Christianity*. New York: HarperCollins.

Underwood, G., 2005. The Mission to the Lamanites. In A.C. Skinner and S. Easton Black, eds. *Joseph: Exploring the Life and Ministry of the Prophet*. Salt Lake City, UT: Deseret Book, pp. 144–55.

Waspe, I.A., 1942. The Status of Woman in the Philosophy of Mormonism from 1830 to 1845. Master's thesis, Brigham Young University.

Watt, R.G., and Watt, B.F., 2017. "I Have Volunteered for a Mission": The Experiences of Marian Gardner, a Sister Missionary. *Journal of Mormon History* 43(4): 124–54.

Weber, S.R., 2013. "Shake Off the Dust of Thy Feet": The Rise and Fall of Mormon Ritual Cursing. *Dialogue: A Journal of Mormon Thought* 46(1): 108–39.

Whittaker, D.J., 2000. Mormon Missiology: An Introduction and Guide to the Sources. In S.D. Ricks, D.W. Parry, and A.H. Hedges, eds. *The Disciple as Witness: Essays on Latter-day Saint History and Doctrine in Honor of Richard Lloyd Anderson*. Provo, UT: Foundation for Ancient Research and Mormon Studies; Brigham Young University Press, pp. 459–538.

Whittaker, D.J., 2011. Mormon Administrative and Organizational History: A Source Essay. In D.J. Whittaker and A.K. Garr, eds. *A Firm Foundation: Church Organization and Administration*. Provo, UT: Religious Studies Center, pp. 611–95.

Whittaker, D.J., 2012a. Early Missions, 1831–1844. In B. Plewe, ed. *Mapping Mormonism: An Atlas of Latter-day Saint History*. Provo, UT: Brigham Young University Press, pp. 40–43.

Whittaker, D.J., 2012b. Missions of the 19th Century, 1849–1890. In B. Plewe, ed. *Mapping Mormonism: An Atlas of Latter-day Saint History*. Provo, UT: Brigham Young University Press, pp. 94–95.

Williams, R.S., 1969. The Missionary Movements of the LDS Church in New England, 1830–1860. Master's thesis, Brigham Young University.

Winder, E.C., 1974. Interview by Gordon Irving, Salt Lake City, Utah. OH 68. Church History Library, Salt Lake City, UT.

Woods, F.E., 2011. Men in Motion: Administering and Organizing the Gathering. In D.J. Whittaker and A.K. Garr, eds. *A Firm Foundation: Church Organization and Administration*. Provo, UT: Religious Studies Center, pp. 197–222.

Young, D.P., 2014. *How to Ride a Bike in a Dress: Lifelong Reflections of a Sister Missionary*. n.p.: Idea Creations Press.

Further reading

Golding, D., 2015. Mormonism. In A. Ghiloni, ed. *World Religions and Their Missions*. Oxford, Peter Lang, pp. 215–62.

Reviews and charts Mormon mission theology in the context of comparative missiology.

Kunz, C., 1976. A History of Female Missionary Activity in the Church of Jesus Christ of Latter-day Saints, 1830–1898. Master's thesis. Brigham Young University.

Provides the broadest survey and analysis of sister missionaries in the nineteenth century and addresses the gendered differences between earliest Latter-day Saint missionaries.

Lyon, T., and Shumway McFarland, M., 2003. "Not Invited, but Welcome": The History and Impact of Church Policy on Sister Missionaries. *Dialogue: A Journal of Mormon Thought* 36(3): 71–102.

Interrogates the ambivalent posture and sometimes in-field resentment toward sister missionary service in the years before the 2012 age policy change.

McBride, M., 2018. "Female Brethren": Gender Dynamics in a Newly Integrated Missionary Force, 1898–1915. *Journal of Mormon History* 44(4): 40–67.

Examines the origins of sister missionary work in the church and the implications of gender on early policy changes in the missionary program.

Radke, A., and Cropper-Rampton, R., 2005. "On the Outside Looking In": A Gendered Look at Sister Missionary Experiences. In C. Cornwall Madsen and C. Silver, eds. *New Scholarship on Latter-day Saint Women in the Twentieth Century: Selections from the Women's History Initiative Seminars, 2003–2004*. Provo, UT: Joseph Fielding Smith Institute for Latter-day Saint History, pp. 141–51.

Investigates the changing attitudes toward and among women in the mission field. Offers a historical overview of how gendered identities have been projected onto sister missionaries and consults oral history interviews from the 1990s for sister and elder perspectives.

14
HOMOSEXUALITY AND THERAPEUTIC CULTURE IN MORMONISM

Eric G. Swedin

AMCAP

The Association of Mormon Counselors and Psychotherapists (AMCAP) held its first conference in 1975. The new organization, which grew out of earlier efforts by Latter-day Saints in the helping professions to organize themselves, sought to apply LDS values and theology to psychotherapy and to build the confidence of church authorities in the helping professions. AMCAP published an academic journal and newsletters, sponsored local discussion groups, and held semi-annual conferences in Salt Lake City in conjunction with the semi-annual church conference. The editorial policy for the *AMCAP Journal* prohibited articles that questioned or contradicted the established doctrine of the Church of Jesus Christ of Latter-day Saints (Swedin, 2003, pp. 56–62).

The theme of AMCAP's inaugural conference was "Current Issues Facing Mormon Counselors and Psychotherapists." Two of these issues—homosexuality and feminism—were to persistently return and continue to vex the Latter-day Saint community. The keynote speaker, Carlfred Broderick (1975, pp. 31, 32), a nationally prominent family relations therapist at the University of Southern California, spoke introspectively about his profession and his religion: "I have a lively awareness that counseling can be lifesaving, soulsaving, or life destructive and soul destructive ... So I think, in the Church, the long-standing hostility between the ecclesiastical authorities and the counseling profession is not without cause." Yet AMCAP could change this, because as professional counselors, "become more trustworthy, I think we'll be more trusted."

The willingness of a church general authority to speak at every AMCAP convention became a good indication that the church hierarchy had become more receptive to the usefulness of professional psychotherapy. Vaughn Featherstone (1975), the general authority who addressed the first convention, encouraged the members of AMCAP and reminded them that they were "doing probably what the Savior spent his whole life doing, in just a little different way. You are healing souls." This definition fit the image which many counselors and therapists had of themselves.

The therapists of AMCAP drew emotional strength and professional courage from each other. Most had been trained in graduate programs where religion was rarely mentioned as a positive component in human relations. Many wanted to be more assertive about their Latter-day

Saint faith, yet to break so significantly with their professional training usually required encouragement from others. Two Latter-day Saint therapists, Genevieve De Hoyos and Arturo De Hoyos (1983), declared that

> teaching higher principles needs no apology. At any rate, whenever a therapist follows a persuasion he believes to be true (be it Behaviorism, Gestalt, T.A., or the Gospel) he naturally starts teaching that persuasion. Thus, choosing to teach the Gospel is no different in procedure from choosing to teach any other ideology.
>
> *(p. 22)*

Efforts at BYU

Beginning in the mid-1970s, various Latter-day Saint psychologists investigated the possibility of creating a unique gospel-oriented theory of human behavior. The creation at Brigham Young University (BYU) in 1976 of the Institute for Studies in Values and Human Behavior played a part of this effort. An eminent psychologist, Allen E. Bergin, served as the first director of the Institute. The institute's mission proved too ambitious, and after five years, the institute closed, though efforts at integration continued. One of the more significant outcomes of this effort was a push to encourage secular therapists to consider religious belief as an important element of a multicultural approach.

The broad conversation over how to reconcile LDS beliefs with the modern psychologies has continued, often in therapeutic settings or everyday life, but also among scholars. Much of this scholarly work happens within the context of BYU and its strong psychotherapy programs, which turn out numerous professionals that serve their clients, both LDS and non-LDS. The *AMCAP Journal* has continued as *Issues in Religion and Psychology*. Some of the more interesting work occurs when LDS therapists critique the secular ideas of psychology, such as in the edited volume, *Turning Freud Upside Down: Gospel Perspectives on Psychotherapy's Fundamental Problems* (Jackson, Fischer, and Dant, 2005). A recent survey that examined the relationships between priesthood leaders and psychotherapists found that the suspicions of the past have mostly abated, though bishops and stake presidents are often poorly informed as to how therapy works. The religious leaders also tended to refer members to LDS Family Services because of a fear that a therapist in another setting might be biased towards religious individuals (Allen and Hill, 2014).

Sexuality and Mormonism

As with the rest of American society in the past half-century, the conversations between LDS religious traditions and the modern psychologies have often been about the sexuality and gender roles. Within the Latter-day Saint community, procreation and chastity are the primary values which have defined the boundaries of sexuality. In 1975, Spencer W. Kimball, the president and prophet of the church, reaffirmed these values:

> The union of the sexes, husband and wife (and only husband and wife), was for the principal purpose of bringing children into the world. Sexual experiences were never intended by the Lord to be a mere plaything or merely to satisfy passions and lusts. We know of no directive from the Lord that proper sexual experience between husbands and wives need be limited totally to the procreation of children, but we find much evidence from Adam until now that no provision was ever made by the Lord for indiscriminate sex.
>
> *(Kimball, 1975)*

Of all the values which members of the Latter-day Saint community try to live, the value of chastity remained probably one of the most difficult. In the early 1970s, a member of the First Presidency estimated that "75 percent of the problems crossing his desk each day were sex-related" (Cannon, 1976, p. 58). The prevalence of sexual issues is certainly not unique to the Latter-day Saint community, but rather a reflection of the obsessions of mainstream America. As sexual mores changed in America, different Christian denominations struggled with how to change their own traditions and how to accommodate these new attitudes. R.M. Griffith (2017) argued this change is the basis of the current fractures in American culture and politics. The most contentious conversations came in dealing with LGBTQ+ issues.

Homosexuality

Latter-day Saint attitudes toward homosexuality within their own community have gone through four phases. The first, lasting until after World War II, was characterized by indifference. Same-sex sexual relations were considered a sin but not a serious concern compared to many other temptations that the Saints faced. Homosexuals who showed no remorse were excommunicated and rhetoric from the pulpit portrayed sexual orientation as a voluntary decision to follow a road of sin (Quinn, 1996). The second phase began in the 1960s as homosexuality gained greater prominence in both mainstream American culture and in the attentions of the church hierarchy. Homosexual behavior remained a sin and feelings of same-sex attraction were often considered sinful. Efforts to seek a cure occurred at BYU and in private practices, playing out against a background of LDS psychotherapists seeking to reconcile their community with the modern psychologies. Homosexuals were often encouraged to find their own cure through heterosexual marriage (O'Donovan, 1994). A third phase began in the 1980s as the influence of LDS therapists softened the harsh view towards same-sex attraction. A greater appreciation of the limitations of moral agency (called free agency within the Latter-day Saint community) developed by the 1990s. Homosexuals were now excommunicated for being unrepentant and acting on their impulses, not for merely feeling homosexual urges (Phillips, 2004, pp. 37–35). A fourth phase began in the 2000s as a faction of Saints sought a further step—accepting LGBTQ+ into the LDS community as full members—though a more numerous faction resisted this.

Though Latter-day Saint theology has always condemned same-sex sexual acts as a sin, based on biblical injunction, this was an issue which attracted little attention for the first century of the Latter-day Saint community's existence. In 1947, a new member of the Quorum of the Twelve, Spencer W. Kimball, was assigned to handle interviews with members involved in sexual transgressions, including homosexuality. These experiences prompted him to make admonishments on chastity a frequent theme of his sermons.

> Despite the frequent claim by homosexuals that they had no control over their sexual orientation, Spencer [Kimball] believed that this problem, like all others, would yield to the consistent prayerful exercise of self-restraint. He pointed out that homosexuals rarely were excommunicated for their past acts but usually only for their unwillingness to make the effort to change.
>
> *(Kimball and Kimball, 1977, p. 381)*

While many church authorities compared homosexuality to the other sexual sins of fornication and adultery, they usually went further and referred to homosexuality as a "perversion" or a "crime against nature" (Church, 1970, p. 15) in addition to being "an ugly sin" (Kimball, 1969, p. 78). Fornication and adultery, as heterosexual sins, were thought to be more understandable.

Most of the men making these pronouncements only had personal experience with heterosexual attraction and struggled to empathize with same-sex attraction.

In 1959, Kimball and another apostle, Mark E. Peterson, received a special assignment to counsel homosexuals. The church hierarchy noticed that this problem was appearing more and more frequently, and by 1968 the number of cases was considered so large that more general authorities were assigned to help with the responsibility. A pamphlet, *Hope for Transgressors*, published in 1970, encouraged homosexuals to repent by seeking the help of "a kindly Church official who understands," so that a "total cure" could be effected (Church, 1970, p. 1). While the pamphlet did not refer to gender, the cover is of a man with bowed head resting on one hand. The rhetoric coming from the pulpit also continued to focus exclusively on males. Lesbians were occasionally referred to in passing and never focused on as a problem in their own right, perhaps because of the lesser numbers of women who experienced same-sex attraction and because the church hierarchy was male and thus more focused on priesthood holders.

In 1972 responsibility for counseling homosexuals was turned over to what was later named LDS Social Services, a branch of the church bureaucracy staffed with social workers and other helping professionals. Two approaches were adopted: the development of literature and assistance for local priesthood leaders as they dealt with the problem on a ward or stake level, and the development of a "professional" therapy model to be used by therapists on the staff of Social Services. This approach assumed that homosexuals were in the grip of a mental pathology, usually came from a "disturbed family background," had a "lack of relationship with peers," and manifested "unhealthy sexual attitudes." Homosexuality was "a symptom of a more basic difficulty within the individual that he has grown up with." Clients were encouraged to gain control over masturbation and their sexual fantasies. These church-employed therapists believed that "homosexuals can be counseled with success if he so desires to accomplish this" (Blattner, 1975).

Aversion therapy at BYU

In seeking to find a cure for homosexuality, researchers at BYU turned to aversion therapy. This form of therapy was based on learning theory from behavioral psychology, which saw an unwanted behavior as a learned response to a stimulus. By conditioning a negative outcome—such as pain, not pleasure—with the stimulus, individuals would stop the behavior. As with much of behavioralism, all that mattered was behavior, not the internal mechanisms within the psyche that led to that behavior. Researchers had reported success using this therapy to treat negative habits, compulsive gambling, smoking, and alcoholism. Researchers had also turned this therapy on sexual behaviors, such as exhibitionism, pedophilia, and homosexuality (Feldman, 1966; Fischer and Gochros, 1977).

Experiments using this technique were conducted at BYU during the 1970s, where male homosexual subjects were shown homosexual pornography and given a variable electrical shock in association with the pictures (Prince, 2019, pp. 89–98). The erotic pictures became associated with anxiety in the subject as he anticipated the shock. After six sessions, the procedure was changed so that the subject could avoid the shock by pressing a button. This button instantly replaced the homosexual pornography with a picture of a nude female. A few studies concluded that this form of electric aversion treatment or aversion using induced vomiting effectively treated male homosexuality (James, 1978). Certainly this was not true from an early written account of a person who experienced electric aversion therapy at BYU. Though he had only experienced homosexual feelings and had not acted on them at the time of the therapy, he later embraced his gay identity and joined Affirmation, a gay rights group formed by excommunicated Latter-day Saints (Harryman, 1991). At least one therapist in private practice also used aversion therapy with gay men, reporting success (Card, 1975). Other stories about aversion therapy at BYU have emerged over the years, including a short documentary (Weakland, 1996).

A student in a BYU psychology class in 1977 found himself outraged by the insinuations of the instructor that homosexuality was chosen as a sexual orientation. He wrote in response an anonymous fifty-seven-page pamphlet, *Prologue: An Examination of the Mormon Attitude Towards Homosexuality*, and took the Latter-day Saint community to task, detail by detail, for its stance against homosexuality. He argued that homosexuality was not a matter of free choice, but had a biological basis; furthermore, not only were there many gay Latter-day Saints hiding in fear, but "very few psychiatrists claim any more that they can cure the homosexual" (Anonymous, 1978, p. 23).

The publication of *Prologue* was part of a growing national gay rights movement, which promoted an acceptance for gay identity and legal rights for gay citizens. Having successfully campaigned for the 1973 American Psychiatric Association decision that removed homosexuality as a psychiatric disorder listed in the official *Diagnostic and Statistical Manual of Psychiatric Disorder* (DSM), the gay rights movement continued to press its case with psychotherapists. The modern gay rights movement traces its origins to the Stonewall Riots in 1969 in response to a raid by New York City police on a gay bar. Building on the momentum and experiences of the civil rights, women's rights, and anti-war movements, the gay rights movement gradually obtained local and state laws to protect gay people from discrimination. The horror of the AIDS epidemic in the 1980s pushed the issue of gay rights to the forefront and sparked further organization and successes. In the 1990s, gay celebrities came out and broke new ground, with business leaders following in the next decade. A sea change had happened in attitudes towards LGBT people and efforts to create marriage equality also succeeded.

Latter-day Saint gay activism paralleled the rise of mainstream gay activism and assertions of gay pride. A group of gay men and women in Los Angeles in 1977 founded Affirmation, a support group for excommunicated Latter-day Saints. Satellite groups were formed in other locations, including Salt Lake City. A year later they began publishing a regular newsletter called *Affinity*. Many members of Affirmation hoped that by educating the church leadership about the true nature of homosexuality, the prophet would then seek a revelation from God to sanction homosexuality (Feliz, 1988).

New professional directions

Despite the efforts of the national gay rights movement to promote a view of homosexual orientation as innate and unchangeable, LDS Social Services continued to treat homosexuals who expressed a desire to change. A professional development booklet, *Understanding and Changing Homosexual Orientation Problems*, published in 1981 for use by Social Services personnel in counseling homosexuals, described homosexuality as resulting from a four-stage process: "confusion, filling the void, sexual identity crisis, and resolution" (pp. 6, 11). A variety of motivational and spiritual therapy approaches were suggested as cures. Therapists were warned that "teaching a homosexually oriented man to lust after women instead of men is inappropriate," an important change from the BYU aversion therapy approach.

The 1987 fall AMCAP Conference focused on homosexuality. The AMCAP president, Clyde A. Parker, did not want the conference to be confrontational:

> It is not intended to 'take a stand,' to challenge, contradict or to oppose. The difficulty, it seems to me, is finding some reconciliation of individual needs and gospel principles

> ... acceptance of others, pursuit of truth, obedience to principle, compassion rather than judgment.
>
> *(Parker, 1987)*

For the first time, a general authority was not asked to give the keynote address. Instead, AMCAP invited Carol Lynn Pearson, a noted LDS feminist and writer. Pearson had written a best-selling book, *Goodbye, I Love You* (1986), about her experiences with the death of her ex-husband to AIDS. She asked for people to understand and sympathize with the emotional toll that homosexuality took on homosexuals and the people around them as they struggled with their sexual identity. Pearson had married when the church still encouraged gay men to marry women as a cure. The act of marriage was seen as proof of a cure. Carol Lynn Pearson's life demonstrated that this approach did not work well and in a 1987 General Conference talk, the apostle Gordon B. Hinckley warned that "marriage should not be viewed as a therapeutic step to solve problems such as homosexual inclinations or practices" (p. 47).

Therapists in LDS Social Services and LDS therapists in other settings engaged in reparative therapy for homosexuals who did not want to accept a "same-sex orientation" (Pritt and Pritt, 1987, p. 37). Thomas Pritt and Ann Pritt were two Latter-day Saint therapists who specialized in "compulsive sexual disorders, particularly homosexuality" for much of their careers. Drawing on the work of the English psychoanalyst Elizabeth R. Moberly, the Pritts promoted a theoretical model to explain and treat homosexuality. They believed that "social learning etiological factors" are more important than "biological" factors in the origin of homosexuality, and that "homosexuality involves social role and identity issues more than problems of sexuality per se" (pp. 38, 39). To believe in purely biological causation would seriously call into question LDS assumptions about sexuality.

A common assumption about homosexuals at the time was that they have difficulty relating with the opposite sex. Moberly and the Pritts reverse this assumption, arguing that an inability to relate with members of their own sex in a non-erotized manner is what defines the homosexual. Homosexuals who "are encouraged to get aroused by women and marry to become straight" are likely to be miserable because *the primary and most critical problem facing homosexuals is not how to be sexually attracted to members of the opposite sex, but how to satisfy unmet, legitimate affectional needs with those of their own sex*" (p. 48).

Moberly and the Pritts argue that the roots of homosexuality are laid in childhood emotional trauma when the child is emotionally separated from his or her same-sex parent. This separation led to the "parent–child affectional bond" being "damaged or disrupted." When that bond cannot be reestablished, the child protects themselves from further trauma and "unwittingly insures that his attachment needs will not be met" (p. 49). This inability to form attachments to the same sex leads to difficulty in "sex-role identification." Men who later become homosexual "generally report that during their childhood they had not felt competent or happy and successful in many of those sports and rough-and-tumble bonding activities that preadolescent boys commonly enjoy together." Later, with adolescence, these boys experiment with masturbation and sexual fantasies: "their unresolved needs, when paired with self-gratification, can facilitate entrance into the addictive world of sexual deviation. Although these behaviors do nothing to improve self-esteem or counter relational deficits, they do easily become habitual and lead to compulsive, ritualized interactions" (p. 50).

Experiencing an "impoverished identity" and "role dysphoria," they compensate though "sexual interest" in same-sex interactions (p. 50). These are not conscious choices. Rather, the inability to find a masculine "identity and relational deficits and needs are developed long before these children reach eight years of age." Within Latter-day Saint theology, children are not capable of sin before the age of eight, the age of accountability. These children go on to "gradually discover their orientation rather than consciously choose it" (p. 45–46).

As part of therapy, homosexuals are taught that their "needs are legitimate" and that they are really misdirected heterosexuals, so homosexuals need to learn to satisfy their needs for same-sex relationships through non-sexual interaction. Hard work is combined with a belief that the "Savior's divinely decreed order for sexual relationships" is the correct path (p. 58). Because of the prevalence of homophobia, the Pritts discourage their clients from "coming out of the closet" (p. 59). If a person self-identifies as a homosexual their opportunities for same-sex non-sexualized relationships are diminished. The Pritts hoped that one of the results of their work would be a reduction in homophobia. This "would encourage heterosexuals to more comfortably establish healing relationships with identity-impaired individuals." Homosexuals and heterosexuals must "share" in efforts at reparation (p. 39).

Alternative modes of behavior must also be taught. When tempted by "an overwhelming compulsion" to engage in homosexual relations, the client is taught to resort to "a series of alternatives," such as "visiting a heterosexual friend or family member or engaging in sports or some other distracting activity." These alternatives are facilitated by "mainstreaming themselves as exclusively as possible with heterosexuals" (p. 61). A "healthy self-esteem" will develop when the client begins to value the masculine attributes within themselves instead of seeking out those attributes in fragmented sexual relationships. They learn that heterosexual friends can "satisfy emotional needs and that the comfort of these relationships can replace the pull toward debilitating sexual intimacies" (p. 60).

In keeping with their LDS focus, the Pritts argue that in order to become whole, homosexuals need the friendship of heterosexuals and the healing power of repentance and redemption. The homosexual must "become convinced in their hearts" of the truthfulness of the scripture, "the Lord giveth no commandments unto the children of men, save he shall prepare a way for them that they may accomplish the thing which he commandeth them" (p. 61; 1 Nephi 3:7). It is through such faith, based on an "application of gospel truths" that "a healthy sex-role identification will indeed occur" (p. 64). If one accepts the Pritts' explanation of not only the origin of individual homosexual behavior, but also the desired form of therapy, then previous approaches within the Latter-day Saint community were sorely misguided, and even harmful. Concentrating on heterosexual marriage and heterosexual arousal as a solution would only lead to widespread misery.

The explanations put forward by Moberly and the Pritts, as well as others, were used to explain homosexuality as a deviation from normal heterosexual feelings and behavior. In the 1960s and 1970s, the power of dogmatic theories of human behavior, like Sigmund Freud's psychoanalysis or B.F. Skinner's behavioralism, lost much of their influence. Psychotherapists tended to become eclectics, where they picked and chose from a variety of different theories and techniques based on the needs of the individual client. They often adhered to the ethos of person-centered therapy as taught by Carl Rogers, where the client defined what they wanted out of therapy and could choose how to define their own mental health. Many people with same-sex feelings wanted to avoid those feelings and theories advanced by theorists like the Pritts led to the rise of an approach called reparative therapy.

Reparative therapy

The entire 1993 issue of the *AMCAP Journal* was dedicated to the treatment of homosexuality, as Latter-day Saint psychotherapists wrote extensively on homosexuality. Twice as many copies were printed than usual and the journal was completely sold out within a year. By this time,

Latter-day Saint advocates of reparative therapy felt increasingly under siege. Not only had mainstream psychotherapy adopted a position of viewing homosexual behavior as normal, but some professional groups had been moving to declare reparative therapy unethical. One Latter-day Saint psychotherapist, P. Scott Richards, responded to this movement by declaring:

> I now find myself unwilling to accept the notion that gay affirmative therapy is the only treatment option we should offer clients, just because this is currently the "politically correct" thing to do. I believe that Latter-day Saint (and other) therapists have a right to offer reparative therapy as a treatment option to those who request help in understanding, controlling, and/or overcoming their homosexual tendencies. In fact, if we do not inform such clients of this option, I believe we are letting them down.

Richards also believed that "homosexual people have a right to live their lives free from discrimination and violence," and should not have reparative therapy forced upon them (Richards, 1993, p. 40).

Therapists attempting to help clients change their sexual orientation called the effort reparative therapy, using the sense of the word to mean to make a repair. They believed that sexual orientation was a matter of nurture, not nature, and that LGBT individuals were broken. Ecumenical-minded Christians founded Exodus International in 1976 (dissolved in 2013), to promote reparative therapy. The LDS community also founded a similar organization, Evergreen International, in 1989, which sponsored local group meetings to offer mutual support for homosexuals trying to change. Support group meetings for family members and friends were also provided and annual conferences brought many like-minded people together. The goal was to help men and women overcome their feelings of same-sex attraction. The group claimed to have success. A testimonial from a member of Evergreen expressed his gratitude:

> In early 1989, I was in serious trouble. I was married with children, active in church, and yet very involved in homosexual activity. I was literally in the depths of hell trying to deal with the issue by myself. I couldn't deal with the tremendous conflict going on inside me. I had decided to either take my life or leave my family. Although I was not close to the Lord, and avoided prayer, He heard the cries of my heart, and literally lifted me out of the mire. I knew I could not succeed without some kind of support system. In addition to some good therapy, Evergreen came into my life. I was then able to experience the beautiful principle of repentance, and develop a personal relationship with my Savior. I now have a peace of mind that I have never had before; plus a good relationship with my family, church, and the Lord. I could not have done it without the love and support of my wife, the Lord and His church, and Evergreen.
>
> *(Matheson, 1993, p. 108)*

Throughout the 1990s, the efforts of some Latter-day Saint psychotherapists to advocate reparative therapy expanded.

The reparative therapy movement changed their preferred term to "sexual orientation change efforts (SOCE)" to emphasize that individuals should have the right to change their sexual orientation if they wanted to. It was a matter of believing that humans had moral agency. Critics saw the SOCE movement as just reinforcing self-loathing that many LGBTQ+ people already felt because of the social discrimination they experienced (Human Rights Campaign, 2019). Both sides claimed the prestigious mantle of science in arguing for their point of view. Studies of therapeutic outcomes were conducted and published, but this clash of different cultures just proved that cultural biases are the bane of psychological studies. Many seek to find the answer in the psychological sciences, but the modern psychologies have not yet produced a coherent theory of sexuality that meets the ability to predict that the physical sciences have taught us to expect of science.

The rhetorical strategy of the gay rights movement was based on the argument that sexual orientation was innate and biological, nicely encapsulated into the defiant slogan, "Born this way." That meant that therapeutic efforts to change an individual's sexual orientation were not possible, were personally humiliating, and led to only more self-hate. When SOCE failed to change a client, suicide was an all too common outcome. The gay rights movement condemned reparative therapy as "gay conversion therapy" and campaigned effectively to end such forms of therapy. One of the chief complaints was that parents were taking their minor children to therapists for conversion therapy and this constituted child abuse (Young, 2006).

As the movement for reparative therapy grew in strength in the 1980s and 1990s, A. Dean Byrd became perhaps the most outspoken LDS psychologist advocating for reparative therapy if the client wanted such a change. An LDS convert, Byrd was a psychologist on the faculty of the University of Utah Medical School, and served on the board of trustees for Evergreen International. He also became active as a leader in NARTH (National Association for Research and Therapy of Homosexuality), a national conservative activist organization founded in 1992. Byrd was a prolific writer, publishing his views both academically and for an LDS audience, before his death from leukemia in 2012 at the age of 63. A posthumous article, "Moving Back to Science and Self-Reflection in the Debate over Sexual Orientation Change Efforts," reflected his belief that science was on his side and that the argument by SOCE opponents that people were born that way had not been proven (Rosik and Byrd, 2013). His *Mormons and Homosexuality: Setting the Record Straight* was a popular book promoting similar sentiments (Byrd, 2008). Byrd found support for his arguments in official statements from church leaders.

In a 1995 *Ensign* article on "Same-Gender Attraction," the apostle Dallin H. Oaks acknowledged that "perhaps" some people may be born "unusually susceptible to particular actions, reactions, or addictions" (p. 9). This was no fault of their own, just a different personal challenge to be overcome during the journey of mortal life. Oaks applied this idea to not just same-gender attraction, but also gambling, tobacco use, alcoholism, a hot temper, covetousness, and other flaws that a person may struggle with while others feel no temptation. Oaks did not care for the words "homosexual" or "lesbian" as nouns. He preferred to use the words as adjectives, since using them as nouns imply something permanent from birth instead of feelings that are acquired through the "complex interaction of 'nature and nurture'" (p. 9). Because science had not reached any answers about the origins of homosexuality, the only accurate information was to be found in the revelations of the Lord to the church. He condemned gay-bashing as contrary to the Lord's commandments and called on church members to understand that "those who are struggling to resist inappropriate feelings are not people to be cast out but people to be loved and helped" out of their sins (p. 13).

In conjunction with the article by Oaks, the church released "The Family: A Proclamation to the World." Such a proclamation was an unusual step for the church and though the document has not been added to official church scriptures, it has been treated as such by the general authorities in subsequent years. Besides defending the family unit, headed by a "marriage between a man and a woman," the First Presidency and Council of Twelve Apostles declared that "gender is an essential characteristic of individual premortal, mortal, and eternal identity and purpose." While this declaration of gender immutability was consistent with LDS doctrine, it was the first time that such a declaration had been included in a quasi-scriptural form (Church, 1995).

Rhetoric teaches us that words are weapons. The term "same-sex attraction" was preferred for some time by Latter-day Saints, before being replaced by "same-gender attraction," which was more accurate as the difference between sex and gender was developed by feminists and gender studies scholars. The institutional church preferred to use "same-gender attraction" over the more commonly used terms of gay or lesbian because the church wanted to emphasize the difference that they saw between feelings of same-gender attraction and personal identity. For example, a male may be attracted to other males, but declaring himself to be gay is viewed a step away from the Gospel. An official church website later explained the preference for the term "same-gender attraction" as "a technical term describing the experience without imposing a label." The term was used "to be inclusive of people who are not comfortable using a label, not to deny the existence of a gay, lesbian, or bisexual identity" (Church, 2019a). Perhaps a different term, sexual minorities, would be even more useful.

The prominent LDS psychologist, Allen R. Bergin, wrote a book in 2002 that provided a nice window onto the LDS therapeutic culture that he had helped create. He thought that psychology had helped teach Latter-day Saints that for "some people, pathological circumstances, evil environments, or biological defects can cause severe problems to become deeply embedded at an early age—before there is any chance for the developing child to alter them by exercising agency." While Latter-day Saints strongly believe in free agency, psychology has shown that there are limits, so some Saints might find it "difficult to reconcile clinical evidence that unconscious processes are real with gospel concepts that we can choose our thoughts and behavior." With regard to homosexuality, "most Latter-day Saint experts in human behavior agree that a strong preference for the same sex is not chosen but develops early in life and becomes prominent in adolescence." Unfortunately, Bergin had found that "many priesthood leaders are not informed about same-sex attraction and may counsel members awkwardly or insensitively." With regard to reparative efforts, Bergin thought that rates of homosexual reparation were good for individuals with bisexual tendencies, though "our knowledge remains limited" and "those with exclusive homosexual arousal and no heterosexual arousal have low rates of success" (Bergin, 2002, pp. 34, 44, 68, 69, 208).

Reaching out

In the first two decades of the twenty-first century, the church continued further efforts in reaching out towards gay church members and the gay rights movement. Doctrine had not changed, but sympathy had grown, as well as advice that effectively meant that members who felt same-sex attraction should remain true to the law of chastity and practice celibacy. The 2007 church pamphlet, *God Loveth His Children*, was directed at members who felt same-gender attraction. The pamphlet recognized the "deep emotional, social, and physical feelings" that came with same-gender attractions. All people

> desire to love and be loved, including many adults who, for a variety of reasons, remain single. God assures His children, including those currently attracted to persons of the same gender, that their righteous desires will eventually be fully satisfied in God's own way and according to His timing.
>
> *(Church, 2007, p. 4)*

The pamphlet encouraged members to remember their eternal identity as sons and daughters of God, to obey the commandments, and to develop "self-mastery" (p. 5). Chastity was emphasized in that "all sexual relations outside of marriage are unacceptable" (p. 6). Repentance was available through Christ's Atonement and members should strive to fill their lives with positive influences, avoiding "obsession with or concentration on same-gender thoughts and feelings." Furthermore, it was

> not helpful to flaunt homosexual tendencies or make them the subject of unnecessary observation or discussion. It is better to choose as friends those who do not publicly display their homosexual feelings. The careful selection of friends and mentors who lead constructive, righteous lives is one of the most important steps to being productive and virtuous.
>
> (p. 9)

One must avoid "despair" or succumb to discouragement as "The Spirit of God brings good cheer and happiness. Trust the Lord. Do not blame anyone—not yourself, not your parents, not God—for problems not fully understood in this life" (p. 10).

This pamphlet is exactly what LGBTQ+ activists rejected. The words of the pamphlet implicitly and explicitly rejected an LGBTQ-based personal identity. The dream of some gay Mormons that the church would find new revelation that created a comfortable home for LGBTQ+ relationships was not being realized. This happened at a time when the national gay rights movement in the twenty-first century had started to achieve many of its goals.

Much as feminists in the nineteenth century had concluded that their quest for equal rights with men could most effectively be won by gaining the right to vote, leading to the women's suffrage movement, the gay rights movement had concluded that gaining the right for same-sex marriages would be the most effective way to achieve equal rights for LGBTQ+ people. Though this also played out in an international arena, various states in the United States began to pass laws in the 1990s that moved towards marriage equality. At first, such efforts were confined to defining domestic partnerships or civil unions, but the continued push for full equality surged in the 2000s. Various groups fought such efforts by passing propositions or laws on both the federal and state levels. The 1996 Defense of Marriage Act created a federal law defining marriage, which had mostly been a state-level issue before that. This was fought in the courts, legislatures, and through propositions put on electoral ballots through signature campaigns.

Gay marriage (marriage equality)

In 2008, the LDS Church formally joined the Proposition 8 effort in California to push back against what at the time was called "gay marriage." The church recruited campaign volunteers and helped raise funding for the effort. Though Proposition 8 passed, it was later overturned in federal court and the Supreme Court. Gay marriage had passed, now called "marriage equality," and quite quickly became a federal civil right as various federal courts declared contrary local state laws unconstitutional. In 2014, marriage equality came to Utah.

The LDS Church had previous experience with alternate forms of marriage in that the church used to practice polygamy in the form of men having more than one wife. This practice was formally ended with the 1890 Manifesto, though members continued to take more wives outside of the United States, and that practice finally ended with the Second Manifesto in 1904. Some members of the church refused to believe that God would have withdrawn such a fundamental principle and concluded that the church had fallen into error. They founded separate polygamous communities or continued to secretly practice polygamy in their own families. The church moved vigorously to suppress any polygamy within the ranks of church members, excommunicating any man or woman who participated in polygamy. Children of polygamous marriages were required to disavow their parents' theological beliefs and marriage practices in order to be baptized into the LDS Church.

The church leadership chose to handle the new form of marriage in the same way that polygamist marriages and the children of those unions had been handled. The new policy was placed in *Handbook 1: Stake Presidents and Bishops*, colloquially known as the "bishop's handbook," because it was only made available to members of the lay leadership in bishoprics or stake presidencies. The purpose of the handbook was to provide consistency in how policies are implemented in the church regardless of where a ward or stake was located. The handbook also provided a strong level of discretion on the part of the lay leader, which was one of the reasons that it had remained a confidential source. Of course, in the modern world of a free press and the Internet, secrets rarely remain secrets, and within days of the change on November 5, 2015, church officials were forced to publicly defend what was normally only an internal matter (First Presidency, 2015).

The new change in the handbook specified how members who entered a same-sex marriage were to be handled. The act of such a marriage is apostasy, just as entering polygamy also remained apostasy, and "warrants a Church disciplinary council." Children whose "primary residence is with a couple living in a same-gender marriage or similar relationship," are restricted from priesthood ordinances. If they are already baptized, that status is not altered, but if not already baptized, they are not allowed to be baptized until they are adults. As adults they must reject their parent's form of marriage in order to be eligible for baptism. Children are allowed to attend church and participate in every way, receiving "priesthood blessings of healing and spiritual guidance," but not advancing further in the church until they are adults and can freely make such choices (First Presidency, 2015).

News of this change provoked outrage because it sounded like children of same-sex couples were being rejected. That perception was understandable. The church leaders strove to explain that the policies were motivated by concern for the children. For instance, "Church leaders want to avoid putting little children in a potential tug-of-war between same-sex couples at home and teachings and activities at church." The desire to not provoke disharmony in the home is also found in church policies that children may not be baptized "without parental consent, even if the children want to be associated with their LDS friends." An adult who wants to be baptized will not be "baptized if the spouse objects." By defining same-sex marriage as an act of apostasy, many people assumed that this was a new stance by the church. The leaders maintained that this was not new doctrine, but merely a clarification now that same-sex marriage had become a reality in the United States (Otterson, 2015).

Elder D. Todd Christofferson was featured in a video explaining the changes. He emphasized that adult children of same-sex couples were not required to disavow "their parents," but to disavow the "practice" of same-sex marriage (Christofferson, 2015). The apostle had personal experience with homosexuality in his family in that his brother, Tom Christofferson, was gay and in a committed relationship before he decided to return to the faith of his youth. The brother later wrote a book published by Deseret Book, *That We May Be One: A Gay Mormon's Perspective on Faith and Family* (2017).

In August 2018, Dallin H. Oaks defended the policy change of four years earlier: "We were sorry to see how many critics of that policy failed to consider its positive purpose, which was to follow the Church's long-standing effort to avoid creating conflicts between children and those who are raising them," he said. "Where children are being raised by custodians who do not have such a fundamental conflict with Church doctrine, there are ways to obtain approval for children to be baptized." Oaks also noted that there was a lot of pressure on the church to change their beliefs and policies on the issues of gender and sexual minorities (Weaver and Zullo, 2018). In a conference talk a year earlier, Oaks lamented that the church "must live with the marriage laws and other traditions of a declining world," but "personal choices in family life" must follow the "Lord's way whenever that differs from the world's way" (Oaks, 2017, p. 29). In April 2019, the First Presidency (2019) announced that they had changed this policy. Children of LGBT parents could now be baptized if the custodial parents gave permission. Same-gender marriage was not to be considered apostasy, but "a serious transgression." Actually participating in same-gender sex was still considered sinful, with "immoral conduct in heterosexual and homosexual relationships" to be "treated in the same way." Even with these latest changes, Latter-day Saint beliefs and practices remained out of step with larger national changes.

Ferment

In addition to the success that came with marriage equality, the gay rights movement found success elsewhere. In 2009, the American Psychological Association passed a resolution arguing against SOCE because

> same-sex sexual and romantic attractions, feelings, and behaviors are normal and positive variations of human sexuality regardless of sexual orientation identity … homosexuality per se is not a mental disorder … [and] there is insufficient evidence to support the use of psychological interventions to change sexual orientation.
> *(American Psychological Association, 2009, p. 121)*

The NARTH Institute, which later changed its name to Alliance for Therapeutic Choice and Scientific Integrity, was labeled a hate group by the Southern Poverty Law Center. In 2013, the governor of California signed into law a bill that outlawed the use of SOCE therapy on minors. Other states prepared to follow suit.

In the LDS community, Evergreen International merged with North Star in 2014, and moved away from advocating reparative therapy. Part of the reason for this change was that SOCE had not lived up to its promise. Ty Mansfield, a marriage and family therapist, who was gay and chose to marry a woman, was one of the founders of North Star. This was a grassroots organization that was not focused on pushing a particular flavor of therapy, but to increase understanding between the LDS community and the LGBTQ+ community. In his quest to increase understanding, Mansfield had published two books with the church-owned Deseret Book. The first included his own story, as well as the story of a couple whose gay son had committed suicide. The second was an anthology of essays on how Latter-day Saints could handle same-gender attraction within the context of remaining true to gospel doctrine (Matis, Matis, and Mansfield, 2004; Mansfield, 2011).

The MormonsandGays.org website was launched in December 2012 by the church, and was renamed MormonandGay.lds.org four years later. The site was provided to help members with same-sex attraction and emphasized the love the church has for gay people, emphasizing that same-sex attraction was not a sin, but behavior could be a sin. The website also encouraged members to seek professional help if they desired it, because "seeking insight from a professional counselor is a sign of strength and humility." A paraphrased insight from Elder Jeffrey Holland noted that "professional help can sometimes be just as important as spiritual help." The final paragraph subtly referred to reparative therapy:

> While shifts in sexuality can and do occur for some people, it is unethical to focus professional treatment on an assumption that a change in sexual orientation will or must occur. Again, the individual has the right to define the desired outcome.
> *(Church, 2019b)*

The struggle to implement church advice played out in the lives of individuals. Josh Weed was a young faithful Latter-day Saint who realized that he was gay after puberty when the expected interest in girls did not appear. He told his parents and they were loving and supportive of his efforts to cope with his feelings of same-sex attraction and remain committed to his faith. A neighborhood girl named Lolly Shea became his best friend and he told her that he was gay. They later married, fully knowing that his orientation would be a challenge, had four daughters, and both became marriage and family therapists. On their tenth anniversary, they decided to come out about their relationship and wrote about it in a blog, which attracted enough attention to lead to other publicity opportunities. They saw themselves as helping others in similar circumstances, though they did not advocate that gay men normally marry women (Weed, 2012).

Five years later, Josh and Lolly announced via a blog that they were divorcing. They had become prominent examples of how one couple had personally handled the issues of a faithful LDS marriage when one of the partners was gay. Major changes had happened in his life and he felt the need to be more authentic to himself and for his clients. He quoted a phrase that he had once heard: "single Mormons go to bed every night pleading with the Lord that they will fall in love with someone tomorrow; gay Mormons go to bed every night pleading with the Lord that they will never fall in love with someone" (Weed and Weed, 2018; Stack, 2018).

Conclusions

The American Psychological Association used the term "sexual minorities" in its study of SOCE issues. This term has been around for some time, since the 1960s, but is useful in that it is not a term loaded with all the rhetorical strategies that come from different factions pushing their activist agendas, such as all the variations of LGBTQ+, same-sex, same-gender, reparative therapy, gay conversion therapy, and the like. By lumping all forms of non-heterosexual identities or behaviors and orientations into the single term of "sexual minorities," the phrase emphasizes the common interests and common issues, as well as tying the gay rights movement to the more broadly conceived civil rights movement that began with race, moved to include women's issues, and then expanded into ethnic minorities and sexual minorities.

Reparative therapy is now neither sanctioned, nor regularly practiced, by either LDS Family Services or private therapists. Latter-day Saints who are a member of a sexual minority and desire to retain their faith seek therapists who will try to help them adapt to their emotions of same-sex attraction. The goal is coping skills, not a cure. While people have reported cures, where they no longer experience same-sex attraction, those reports are treated with skepticism and often ignored. Only the most irresponsible therapist would attempt a cure nowadays.

Most therapists today are eclectics and the ethos of person-centered therapy taught by Carl Rogers remains strong. If a client wants to remain a faithful Latter-day Saint and learn to cope with their feelings of same-sex attraction, then the therapist will attempt to respect those wishes in a non-judgmental manner. If a client wants help to accept their feelings and navigate the waters of disengaging themselves from the LDS community, and embracing their sexual orientation, the therapist will help them do that. From an ethical perspective, a therapist who cannot meet these standards should suggest that the client seek another therapist. There are still therapists who are so committed to their own point of view on sexual minority issues that they cannot approach their clients in a non-judgmental manner.

Church doctrine and practices, after the changes of the 1980s and 1990s to recognize that same-sex attraction was a difficult problem, and turning away from encouraging heterosexual marriage as a cure, have remained consistent. Soon after becoming president of the church, Russell M. Nelson, told a group of youth in Las Vegas in February 2018 that the Adversary

(Satan) "attacks us through our appetites. He tempts us to eat things we should not eat, to drink things we should not drink, and to love as we should not love" (Mims, 2018).

One of the more fascinating developments of recent years is the increasing numbers of people who self-identify as sexual minorities. From a historical perspective, does this mean that many people have always internally identified as one of these variations and are now coming out? That is certainly part of the reason, and perhaps even the whole reason. Such people may now feel it's safer to step out of the closet because the social cost of coming out has been reduced. My presumption, absent science being able to give us more information, is that human sexuality is very malleable, a mix of innate inclinations, biology, opportunities, obsessions, fantasies, cultural attitudes, and lived experiences.

I am going to do what no historian should ever do. I am going to predict that this development will continue and will grow as more people self-identify as a sexual minority. In the past, a primary drive for human beings was to reproduce and pass on their family connections and their culture. As over-population becomes an ever greater problem, many people choose not to reproduce and that will become even more common. In the past, the need to reproduce as heterosexual-based families often encouraged individuals to suppress their inclinations toward same-gender attraction or alternative sexualities. Rarely was there a place for someone who felt gender dysphoria and wanted to resolve it through being transgender, especially in Western culture. Some cultures in India and some Native American cultures had a culturally defined third sex that provided a refuge in those cultures. Now that we no longer have the need to increase our population, where a smaller subset of the population will reproduce, people no longer have to suppress their LGBTQ+ orientations. Sexual minorities will flourish as we move ever further away from the need to use sex for expanding the population. This will continue only if the larger culture respects the rights of individuals to walk their own unique paths. This argument does not mean to imply that sexual minorities cannot have children or raise families, only that in the past such options were usually only found in heterosexual-based families.

I will make one last prediction. The rhetoric of "born this way" has proven very successful for the gay rights movement, but it holds hidden dangers. Just because a trait is biological does not mean that everyone will accept that trait as useful or desirable. As medical science advances, "born this way" explanations could encourage anti-gay activists to turn to genetic engineering solutions. The argument would be that biological problems require biological solutions (Barasch, 2018). I predict that the gay rights movement, especially as the issues around transgendered individuals continue to be controversial, will increasingly move away from "born this way" rhetorical explanations to argue that sexual orientation and identity are choices. As with the previous strategy of "born this way," arguing for choice reduces a very complex process in which genetics, biological effects, psychology, culture, and personal experience all combine to make each individual's gender journey different and unique.

In sum, the modern psychologies have significantly changed the LDS community, helping Latter-day Saints to realize that people have inborn instincts that are not readily overcome and that mental illness is a serious problem. With regards to sexual minority issues, both the institutional church and the community of Latter-day Saints have evolved new positions. LDS Social Services became LDS Family Services in 1996 and remains active in the area of psychotherapy, as do numerous therapists in other settings, seeking to apply therapy within the context of LDS values and the law of chastity. Feelings of same-sex attraction are no longer considered a sin, though acting on those feelings is considered a sin. The law of chastity remains the bedrock of the LDS view of both gender and sex, a stance that will make Latter-day Saints ever more a "peculiar people" (1 Peter 2:9). For LGBTQ+ church members, the social costs of being openly part of a sexual minority remain significant.

References

Allen, G., and Hill, C., 2014. Exploring Perceived Attitudes of Counseling between LDS Religious Leaders and Mental Health Therapists. *Issues in Religion and Psychotherapy* 36(1): 71–82.

American Psychological Association, 2009. *Report of the APA Task Force on Appropriate Therapeutic Responses to Sexual Orientation*. www.apa.org/pi/lgbt/resources/therapeutic-response.pdf (accessed June 17, 2019).

Anonymous, 1978. *Prologue: An Examination of the Mormon Attitude towards Homosexuality*. Provo, UT: Prometheus Enterprises.

Barasch, A., 2018. Biology Is Not Destiny. *Washington Post*. June 27. www.washingtonpost.com/news/posteverything/wp/2018/06/27/feature/seeking-a-scientific-explanation-for-trans-identity-could-do-more-harm-than-good/ (accessed September 23, 2018).

Bergin, A.E., 2002. *Eternal Values and Personal Growth: A Guide on Your Journey to Spiritual, Emotional, and Social Wellness*. Provo, UT: BYU Studies.

Blattner, R.L., 1975. Counseling the Homosexual in a Church Setting. *AMCAP Journal* 1: 6–9.

Broderick, C., 1975. New Wine In New Bottles. *AMCAP Journal* 1 (October): 30–35.

Byrd, A.D., 2008. *Mormons and Homosexuality: Setting the Record Straight*. Orem, UT: Millennial Press.

Cannon, K.L., 1976. Needed: An LDS Philosophy of Sex. *Dialogue: A Journal of Mormon Thought* 10(2): 57–61.

Card, R.D., 1975. Counseling the Homosexual in a Private Practice Setting. *AMCAP Journal* 1 (October): 10–13.

Christofferson, D.T. 2015. *Church Provides Context on Handbook Changes Affecting Same-Sex Marriages*. November 6. https://newsroom.churchofjesuschrist.org/article/handbook-changes-same-sex-marriages-elder-christofferson (accessed June 17, 2019).

Church of Jesus Christ of Latter-day Saints, 1970. *Hope for Transgressors*. Salt Lake City, UT: Church of Jesus Christ of Latter-day Saints.

Church of Jesus Christ of Latter-day Saints, 1995. The Family: A Proclamation to the World. www.churchofjesuschrist.org/study/manual/the-family-a-proclamation-to-the-world/ (accessed June 17, 2019).

Church of Jesus Christ of Latter-day Saints, 2007. *God Loveth His Children*. www.churchofjesuschrist.org/bc/content/shared/content/english/pdf/language-materials/04824_eng.pdf (accessed June 17, 2019).

Church of Jesus Christ of Latter-day Saints, 2019a. *Mormon and Gay: Frequently Asked Questions*. https://mormonandgay.churchofjesuschrist.org/articles/frequently-asked-questions (accessed June 17, 2019).

Church of Jesus Christ of Latter-day Saints, 2019b. *Mormon and Gay: Seeking Professional Help*. https://mormonandgay.lds.org/articles/seeking-professional-help (accessed June 17, 2019).

De Hoyos, G., and De Hoyos, A., 1984. The Mormon Psychotherapists: An Addendum. *AMCAP Journal* 9(1): 21–22.

Featherstone, V., 1975. Transgression. *AMCAP Journal* 1 (October): 36–41.

Feldman, M.P., 1966. Aversion Therapy for Sexual Deviations: A Critical Review. *Psychological Bulletin* 65(2): 65–79.

Feliz, A.A., 1988. *Out of the Bishop's Closet: A Call to Heal Ourselves, Each Other, and Our World: A True Story*. San Francisco, CA: Aurora Press.

First Presidency of the Church of Jesus Christ of Latter-day Saints, 2015. First Presidency Clarifies Church Handbook. [press release] November 13, 2015. www.churchofjesuschrist.org/pages/church-handbook-changes (accessed June 17, 2019).

First Presidency of the Church of Jesus Christ of Latter-day Saints, 2019. First Presidency Shares Messages from General Conference Leadership Session. [press release] April 4, 2019. https://newsroom.churchofjesuschrist.org/article/first-presidency-messages-general-conference-leadership-session-april-2019 (accessed June 5, 2019).

Fischer, J., and Gochros, H.L., 1977. *Handbook of Behavior Therapy with Sexual Problems*, vol. 1: *General Procedures*. New York: Pergamon Press.

Griffith, R.M., 2017. *Moral Combat: How Sex Divided American Christians and Fractured American Politics*. New York: Basic Books.

Harryman, D.D., 1991. With All Thy Getting, Get Understanding. In R. Schow, W. Schow, and M. Raynes, eds. *Peculiar People: Mormons and Same-Sex Orientation*. Salt Lake City, UT: Signature Books, pp. 23–35.

Hinckley, G.B., 1987. Reverence and Morality. *Ensign* 17(5): 45–47.

Human Rights Campaign, 2019. *The Lies and Dangers of Efforts to Change Sexual Orientation or Gender Identity*. www.hrc.org/resources/the-lies-and-dangers-of-reparative-therapy (accessed June 17, 2019).
Jackson, A., and Fischer, L., with Dant, D. eds., 2005. *Turning Freud Upside Down: Gospel Perspectives on Psychotherapy's Fundamental Problems*. Provo, UT: Brigham Young University Press.
James, E.C., 1978. Treatment of Homosexuality: A Reanalysis and Synthesis of Outcome Studies. Ph.D. Dissertation, Brigham Young University.
Kimball, E.L., and Kimball, A.E., 1977. *Spencer W. Kimball: Twelfth President of The Church of Jesus Christ of Latter-day Saints*. Salt Lake City, UT: Bookcraft.
Kimball, S., 1969. *The Miracle of Forgiveness*. Salt Lake City, UT: Bookcraft.
Kimball, S., 1975. The Lord's Plan for Men and Women. *Ensign* 5(10): 2–5.
Latter-day Saint Social Services, 1981. *Understanding and Changing Homosexual Orientation Problems*. Salt Lake City, UT: Church of Jesus Christ of Latter-day Saints.
Mansfield, T. ed., 2011. *Voices of Hope: Latter-day Saint Perspectives on Same-Gender Attraction: An Anthology of Gospel Teachings and Personal Essays*. Salt Lake City, UT: Deseret Book.
Matheson, D., 1993. The Transition from Homosexuality: The Role of Evergreen International. *AMCAP Journal* 19(1): 105–12.
Matis, F., Matis, M., and Mansfield, T., 2004. *In Quiet Desperation: Understanding the Challenge of Same-Gender Attraction*. Salt Lake City, UT: Deseret Book.
Mims, B., 2018. Satan Tempts Us to "Love as We Should Not Love," LDS Prophet Russell M. Nelson Warns Mormon Millennials. *Salt Lake Tribune*. February 19. www.sltrib.com/religion/2018/02/19/satan-temps-us-to-love-as-we-should-not-love-lds-prophet-russell-m-nelson-warns-mormon-millennials/ (accessed September 21, 2018).
Oaks, D.H., 1995. Same-Gender Attraction. *Ensign* 25(10): 6–14.
Oaks, D.H., 2017. The Plan and the Proclamation. *Ensign* 47(11): 28–31.
O'Donovan, R., 1994. "The Abominable and Detestable Crime Against Nature": A Brief History of Homosexuality and Mormonism, 1840–1980. In B. Corcoran, ed. *Multiply and Replenish: Mormon Essays on Sex and Family*. Salt Lake City, UT: Signature Books, pp. 123–70.
Otterson, M., 2015. *Understanding the Handbook*. November 13. https://newsroom.churchofjesuschrist.org/article/commentary-understanding-the-handbook (accessed June 17, 2019).
Parker, C.A., 1987. President's Message. *AMCAP News*. August, p. 1.
Pearson, C.L., 1986. *Goodbye, I Love You*. New York: Random House.
Phillips, R., 2004. *Conservative Christian Identity and Same-Sex Orientation: The Case of Gay Mormons*. New York: Peter Lang.
Prince, G.A., 2019. *Gay Rights and the Mormon Church: Intended Actions, Unintended Consequences*. Salt Lake City, UT: University of Utah Press.
Pritt, T.E., and Pritt, A.F., 1987. Homosexuality: Getting Beyond the Therapeutic Impasse. *AMCAP Journal* 13(1): 37–66.
Quinn, D.M., 1996. *Same-sex Dynamics among Nineteenth-Century Americans: A Mormon Example*. Urbana, IL: University of Illinois Press.
Richards, P.S., 1993. The Treatment of Homosexuality: Some Historical, Contemporary, and Personal Perspectives. *AMCAP Journal* 19(1): 29–45.
Rosik, C.H., and Byrd, A.D., 2013. Moving Back to Science and Self-Reflection in the Debate over Sexual Orientation Change Efforts. *Social Work* 58(1): 83–85.
Stack, P.F., 2018. Yearning for a "Romantic Attachment" They Never Had: Gay Mormon Josh Weed and His Wife of 15 Years Are Divorcing. *Salt Lake Tribune*. January 30. www.sltrib.com/religion/local/2018/01/30/yearning-for-a-romantic-attachment-they-never-had-gay-mormon-josh-weed-and-his-straight-wife-are-divorcing-after-15-years/ (accessed September 30, 2018).
Swedin, E., 2003. *Healing Souls: Psychotherapy in the Latter-day Saint Community*. Champaign, IL: University of Illinois Press,
Weakland, S., 1996. *Legacies*. [video online] www.youtube.com/watch?v=F8Ihx2tBris (accessed June 15, 2019).
Weaver, S.J., and Zullo, M., 2018. President Oaks Talks Church History, LGBT Issues, Mental Illness. *Church News*. August 28. www.thechurchnews.com/leaders-and-ministry/2018-08-28/president-oaks-talks-church-history-lgbt-issues-mental-illness-at-los-angeles-devotional-47877 (accessed June 17, 2019).
Weed, J., 2012. Club Unicorn: In Which I Come out of the Closet on Our Ten Year Anniversary. *The Weed: All Kinds of Real*. June 8. http://joshweed.com/2012/06/club-unicorn-come-closet-ten-year-anniversary/ (accessed September 29, 2018).

Weed, J., and Weed, L., 2018. Turning a Unicorn into a Bat: The Post in Which We Announce the End of Our Marriage. *The Weed: All Kinds of Real*. January 25. http://joshweed.com/2018/01/turning-unicorn-bat-post-announce-end-marriage/ (accessed September 29, 2018).

Young, S., 2006. Does "Reparative" Therapy Really Constitute Child Abuse?: A Closer Look. *Yale Journal of Health Policy, Law, and Ethics* 6(1): 163–219.

Further reading

Christofferson, T., 2017. *That We May Be One: A Gay Mormon's Perspective on Faith and Family*. Salt Lake City, UT: Deseret Book.

The author is the gay brother of a church apostle and the book was published by the church-owned publishing company. The author left his gay partnership to return to the faith of his childhood, but still considers himself happy to be gay.

Cook, B., 2017. What Do We Know of God's Will for His LGBT Children?: An Examination of the LDS Church's Position on Homosexuality. *Dialogue: A Journal of Mormon Thought* 50(2): 1–54.

An excellent recent summary of the changing attitudes in the LDS community and institutional church on LGBT issues.

Pearson, C.L., 2007. *No More Goodbyes: Circling the Wagons around Our Gay Loved Ones*. Salt Lake City, UT: Pivot Point Books.

An extensive collection of personal stories that encourage church members to support their gay family members and gay friends.

Schow, R., Schow, W., and Raynes, M. eds., 1991. *Peculiar People: Mormons and Same-Sex Orientation*. Salt Lake City, UT: Signature Books.

An older collection of essays that covers many topics and argues for sympathy for sexual minorities.

Wikipedia, n.d. Homosexuality and The Church of Jesus Christ of Latter-day Saints. https://en.wikipedia.org/wiki/Homosexuality_and_The_Church_of_Jesus_Christ_of_Latter-day_Saints (accessed September 30, 2018).

This wikipedia entry is remarkably comprehensive and well-documented.

15
HOMOSEXUALITY AND POLITICS IN MORMONISM

Neil J. Young

Given the general belief among conservative religious churches, including the Church of Jesus Christ of Latter-day Saints, that homosexuality constitutes a sin, many assume that this moral objection has translated into an across-the-board political opposition to the question of LGBTQ political rights. Indeed the rise of the Religious Right, a core base of the Republican Party and one of the most powerful political movements of the last fifty years, has depended in part on mobilizing conservative Christians against changing political and cultural ideas regarding gender and sexuality, especially gay rights. Both the LDS Church and Mormon laypersons have been fundamental constituents of the Religious Right since the 1970s. More generally, LDS Americans often rank as the nation's most conservative demographic, and states with Mormon-heavy populations, including Utah, Idaho, and Wyoming, regularly provide the Republican Party with its most lopsided wins.

Conservatism, in both its political and theological forms, often insists on its own unchanging nature—that it is the preserver and defender of timeless truth. This is particularly so regarding ideas of the family and the related matters of gender and sexuality. For religious conservatives, including Mormons, the theological belief that God created and ordained the familial institution to carry out essential functions, especially procreation and childrearing, has often occasioned vibrant political activism against changing legal and social norms, including loosening divorce regulations, changing sexual standards, the legalization of abortion, and the increasing acceptance of homosexuality. All of these historical developments have posed challenges to Mormonism's highly gendered theology of the family and its culture of sexual conservatism. Yet the issue of homosexuality and the politics of gay rights may have prompted the LDS Church's most sustained and engaged political efforts. For nearly a half century, the LDS Church has been a leader in the fight against the legalization of gay marriage, anticipating its possibility and organizing against it before many of the church's conservative allies joined the efforts. Yet in that same period, the LDS Church showed important changes in its beliefs about homosexuality and became an advocate for a wide range of civil rights protections for LGBT Americans that it had once opposed, distinguishing the church from its political allies, like conservative evangelicals, who generally have not altered their theological or political stances on homosexuality. In this way, the LDS Church's politics of homosexuality demonstrate not a fixed position but rather an ongoing historical process, one shaped as much by secular trends and cultural changes as it has resisted those same developments.

Mormon beliefs on homosexuality

To examine the LDS Church's political activism around the issue of gay rights, it's important first to understand the church's beliefs about homosexuality. Perhaps surprisingly given Mormonism's general conservatism, LDS theology and practices regarding homosexuality have shown remarkable variations over time. Among nineteenth- and early twentieth-century Mormons, the historian D. Michael Quinn found a "range of same-sex dynamics" lived out by many Saints in "relative tolerance" (1996, p. 2). The LDS Church's decision to largely overlook (or ignore) homosexual behaviors among some members in this period may have owed in part to the silence of Mormon scriptures, including the Book of Mormon, on the matter. Joseph Smith also appears to have never addressed homosexuality.

Instead, Mormon authorities and church teachings focused on other sexual sins through the early twentieth century, particularly fornication, adultery, and masturbation. But starting in the 1950s, the LDS Church began emphasizing the sin of homosexuality, a shift brought about largely by the era's "Lavender Scare," the widespread paranoia during the Cold War that homosexual men and women needed to be rooted out of their positions in the federal government for fear that they were communist sympathizers. Similar efforts took place in the LDS Church, including the excommunication of gay and lesbian Mormons, the ban of homosexual students from the church's Brigham Young University, and the establishment of an "aversion therapy" program at BYU to change homosexuals into heterosexuals, often through electroconvulsive shock and other treatments that amounted to physical torture (Quinn, 1996, pp. 375–79).

All of this was accomplished alongside the development of a robust anti-homosexual theology. The church's first public pronouncement on homosexuality deemed it an "abomination" in 1952. Six years later, *Mormon Doctrine*, an unofficial but highly-regarded encyclopedia of Mormon theology, listed homosexuality as a sin. Church teachings against homosexual activity proliferated in the 1960s, led by Spencer W. Kimball, a high-ranking LDS apostle who had been tasked with overseeing the church's efforts against the scourge of homosexuality. In his 1969 book, *The Miracle of Forgiveness*, Kimball provided a blueprint for future LDS teachings regarding homosexuality. Kimball argued that masturbation could cause homosexuality and sometimes homosexuality could lead to bestiality. Homosexuality, however, could be cured through repentance, and homosexual Mormons were encouraged to force themselves into heterosexual relationships, including marriage (1969). Mormons were not alone in these beliefs; Protestant churches at the time, both conservative and liberal, regarded homosexuality as a psychological disorder that could be overcome (White, 2015). But Kimball's recommendation that homosexual Mormons make themselves enter into heterosexual marriage reflected Mormonism's unique theology of marriage-based salvation. Since Mormons believe that a heterosexual marriage performed in an LDS temple is required to reach the highest realm of the afterlife, church teachings about the sin of homosexuality also emphasized its profound eternal consequences as a barrier to exaltation to the Celestial Kingdom.

Those teachings accelerated through the 1970s largely in response to the decade's changing cultural ideas about gender and sexuality. The LDS Church's political activism at the time against the Equal Rights Amendment (ERA), a proposed constitutional amendment that would have guaranteed sex equality under the law, both revealed and reinforced its beliefs about the danger homosexuality posed to traditional gender roles and the monogamous heterosexual family unit. Church officials warned that should the ERA be ratified, sex differences between men and women would disappear, thus paving the way for rampant homosexuality, an argument that Spencer Kimball had advanced in his 1971 booklet *New Horizons for Homosexuals* where he contended that unchecked homosexuality would result in the earth's ultimate depopulation (1971).

Kimball's ascension to the LDS Church presidency in 1973 only enhanced the visibility and prominence of his anti-gay efforts. That same year, the First Presidency released a "Statement on Homosexuality" in its *Priesthood Bulletin*, instructing that homosexuality ran "counter to ... divine objectives." As LDS president, Kimball spoke out against homosexuality so frequently that it attracted national attention in outlets like the *New York Times*, and other church officials mirrored Kimball's focus on homosexuality in their own writings, General Conference talks, and in church publications. These teachings showed the influence of Kimball's ideas, particularly that homosexuality was a personal choice that could be changed rather than an inborn trait. This meant, according to Mormon thought, that homosexuality could be avoided by men and women who cultivated their masculine and feminine traits, respectively, and prevented in children by parents who modeled proper gender roles, including male patriarchal authority and female wifely submission. For those who had succumbed to the temptation of homosexuality, LDS officials stressed they could return to heterosexuality through repentance and moral fortitude (Young, 2016, pp. 150–51).

Developed in the 1970s, these LDS teachings remained relatively unchanged through the twentieth century, even as the nation's attitudes showed increasing acceptance of homosexuality through the same decades. Yet the early twenty-first century revealed an important shift in Mormon conceptions of homosexuality, a change that shaped the church's political actions. The church's 1998 *Handbook of Instructions* removed excommunication as the punishment for Mormons for what it described as "Homosexual Behavior." Twelve years later, the updated 2010 *Handbook* distinguished those who engaged in homosexual activity from those who experienced "same-gender attraction." Mormons engaging in homosexual behavior were subject to church discipline, although no longer excommunication, but the church's guidelines emphasized Mormon leaders should encourage sexually active gay Mormons towards repentance rather than punishing them (Young, 2016, p. 166).

The LDS Church's differentiation between homosexual behavior and sexual orientation had consequences for its institutional practices and its religious teachings. BYU's revised honor code made clear that celibate gay students were not in violation of the university's rules; only same-sex physical activity could qualify one for expulsion (Lyon, 2007). Similarly, chaste gay Mormons could hold temple recommends and serve in leadership positions throughout the church. Numerous church talks and publications now taught that homosexuality was neither a sin nor a choice; only the decision to engage in homosexual physical activity was sinful. Reinforcing the distinction between behavior and orientation, LDS publications and sermons in the 2000s advocated a compassionate tone and replaced earlier warnings about God's judgment on homosexuals with lessons that depicted God's love towards those afflicted by same-sex desires. Importantly, the LDS Church indicated most gay Mormons should not enter into heterosexual marriage, as Kimball had once advised, suggesting LDS leaders' new understanding of homosexuality as a "real" condition that should be resisted but was unlikely to be changed (Holland, 2007). Rather than presenting homosexuals as deviants or diseased, Mormon publications now held up gay Mormons who did not give in to sexual temptation as righteous examples that all Saints might emulate.

In 2013, the church released a new website, mormonsandgays.org, which compiled the church's updated teachings on homosexuality and offered support for gay Mormons. The use of "gay" in the website's name and throughout its contents represented a significant development in itself, as the church had generally avoided that term in the past. In 2016, the church decided to rename the website to mormonandgay.lds.org. In dropping the "S" from both "Mormons" and "gays" in the previous title, the church meant to clarify that it didn't see these two groups in opposition or that homosexuals were outsiders to Mormonism. Instead, the renamed website acknowledged and affirmed that gay and lesbian Mormons existed throughout the LDS Church. Since then, the website has been renamed once more as mormonandgay.churchofjesuschrist.org to reflect the new emphasis on the full name of the LDS Church.

The changes in Mormon theology regarding homosexuality and LDS Church practices concerning gay Mormons in the early twenty-first century owed in large part, perhaps paradoxically, to the church's political work against the legalization of same-sex marriage. Facing strong public condemnation for those efforts, especially the church's part in supporting California's 2008 ballot initiative Prop 8, explored later in this chapter, the LDS Church worked to demonstrate that, in the words of one Prop 8 training document for Mormon volunteers, it was "pro-marriage, not anti-gay" (McKinley and Johnson, 2008). While critics may not have appreciated the LDS Church's parsing of its position, Mormon leaders believed the church could defend traditional heterosexual marriage without demonizing gay and lesbian Americans, hoping this softer stance on homosexuality would also lessen public outcry against the church. In this way, the church's new teachings on homosexuality, apart from the question of same-sex marriage, tracked with the larger culture's changing attitudes, just as in an earlier era, the church's development of a virulent anti-gay theology ran alongside the nation's sentiments against homosexuality at midcentury.

The politics of homosexuality

While the LDS Church largely abstained from national politics until the late twentieth century, the church has exerted a powerful political influence in Utah and other states of the Intermountain West since the nineteenth century. In Utah, the LDS Church shaped the state's legal regime, especially around matters regarded as vice. Although LDS officials tended to tolerate evidence of homosexual activity, the church supported the enactment of the state's anti-sodomy laws. Yet the state's lenient enforcement of those laws through the early twentieth century also reflected the church's general laissez-faire approach to homosexuality until midcentury (Winkler, 2008, pp. 55–60).

Along with the turn to a more vigilant anti-gay outlook and theology in the 1950s and 1960s, the LDS Church coordinated with Utah law enforcement to crackdown on homosexuals and stem what it saw as an upturn in homosexual activity at the time. Salt Lake City police regularly turned over men arrested on vice charges to LDS bishops for counseling. At the same time, the church borrowed techniques from law enforcement and the U.S. military to root out homosexuals in its midst, including the use of surveillance, anonymous informants, and forced confessions (Winkler, 2008, p. 108). While these activities took place largely outside the realm of public life, they drew upon the state's political and legal networks to curtail the lives of gay men and women.

On the national stage, the church's first involvement in federal politics through its work against the Equal Rights Amendment in the 1970s also represented its initial foray into anti-gay efforts beyond its Utah base. While the ERA's supporters generally saw the amendment as concerned with women's equality, the LDS Church connected the amendment to homosexuality and the threat of gay marriage. Mormon officials argued that the ERA's eradication of sex difference under the law would create a unisex society where homosexuality would flourish in the absence of meaningful gender distinctions between the two sexes. A twenty-three-page anti-ERA booklet, *The Church and the Proposed Equal Rights Amendment*, sent to every Mormon family mentioned homosexuality almost a dozen times and predicted its passage "could extend legal protection to same-sex lesbian and homosexual marriages, giving legal sanction to the rearing of children in such homes" (First Presidency, 1980). In its pamphlets, publications, and public statements, and internal documents, the LDS Church showed it understood the defeat of the ERA as an essential setback for the ascendant gay rights movement (Young, 2016, pp. 149–53).

These anti-ERA efforts demonstrated how the LDS Church could position a seemingly unrelated constitutional amendment as a gay rights measure to incredible effect among its members. The church's message to LDS laypersons stressed that their involvement was on behalf of a moral cause not a political matter. In enlisting Mormon men and especially women into its anti-ERA efforts, the church declared that the "ERA is a moral issue with many disturbing ramifications … for the family," imbuing their political activism with religious meaning (First Presidency, 1978). In this way, LDS authorities presented the work as part of Mormons' service to their church rather than a secular political activity.

That work also established the church's operational strategy for political activism in the future. Across the nation, the LDS Church established grassroots anti-ERA organizations in battleground states with names that concealed their Mormon identity, such as the Illinois Citizens for Family Life and the Virginia Citizens Council. LDS authorities instructed individual Mormons to join these groups and lead the anti-ERA efforts, including holding public rallies, writing state legislators, and canvassing voters. Mormons also were encouraged to donate money to the political cause in offerings taken up during church services. The church then directed those dollars through its network, passing money from Mormon-heavy states like Utah and California to ERA battleground states like Florida and Virginia that had smaller Mormon populations (Young, 2007). This strategy proved effective in helping defeat the ERA. It also created the church's procedures for carrying out political work at the state and local level, a system the church would use in its work against gay rights. When local and state jurisdictions began considering extending civil rights to homosexuals in the 1970s, the LDS Church relied on this same grassroots network to push back through supporting anti-gay ballot initiatives, propositions, and referenda.

Those opportunities proliferated through the 1970s as almost thirty cities, like Austin and Minneapolis, passed gay rights ordinances between 1972 and 1977 (Chauncey, 2004, p. 38). Conservatives were largely caught unaware by this wave of civil rights extensions for gay men and women, but they quickly rallied a countermovement. In Dade County, Anita Bryant organized the "Save Our Children" campaign that overturned a gay rights ordinance there in 1977. Encouraged by this unlikely victory, conservatives defeated or rescinded similar ordinances in over a half-dozen other cities in the next three years (Fejes, 2008, pp. 153–212).

Conservative Catholics and evangelicals spearheaded these efforts while Mormons remained largely absent—a surprising fact considering the LDS Church's concerns about the burgeoning gay rights movement. For the time being, Mormon leaders preferred to keep church members focused on stopping the ERA's ratification, believing it represented the bigger threat to its ideas about the traditional family. But behind the scenes, LDS officials kept close watch over the political fights over gay rights ordinances around the country. In Hawaii, for example, the church used its anti-ERA organization there, the Hana Pono Political Action Caucus, to also closely monitor any push for gay rights measures in the state legislature. Church leaders also briefly debated working against California's 1975 Consenting Adult Sex Bill which struck down the state's sodomy law and decriminalized gay sex. The church's estimate that it would need to invest half a million dollars to defeat the bill may have influenced its decision to remain largely on the sidelines. However, Mormon officials in Salt Lake City did instruct their church leaders in California to give all their support to stopping the bill's passage (Young, 2016, pp. 152–53).

Publicly, though, the church offered its encouragements to anti-gay efforts across the nation, believing its authority as a major religious institution could benefit the cause while also intending its public pronouncements to reinforce the church's teachings about homosexuality among its members. A 1979 editorial in the church's *Deseret News* maintained that "the persistent drive to make homosexuality an 'accepted' and legal way of life should disgust every thinking person." "In self-defense," the editorial contended, "America must launch a major offensive for virtue" (*Church News*, 1979). Mark Petersen, the church apostle who had been appointed along with Spencer Kimball to oversee its work against homosexuality in the 1950s, authored this editorial and five others against the gay rights movement from 1977 to 1979 as a handful of cities defeated gay rights ordinances. In one, Petersen praised Anita Bryant for "waging a determined fight to keep this evil from spreading, by legal acceptance, through our society." "Every right thinking person," Petersen inveighed, "will sustain Miss Bryant, a prayerful, upright citizen, for her stand. Righteous people everywhere also should look to their own neighborhoods to determine to what extent the 'gay' people have infiltrated their areas" (*Church News*, 1977). Kimball also praised Bryant for "doing a great service." Privately, Barbara B. Smith, president of the church's Relief Society for women, telegrammed Bryant a note of support, commending her "for your courageous and effective efforts in combatting homosexuality and laws which would legitimize this insidious lifestyle" (O'Donovan, 1994, p. 150).

Developing an anti-gay political strategy

Although the LDS Church had been on the winning side of the fight over the ERA, the church suffered strong condemnation for its political efforts against the amendment. Bruised by this response, LDS leaders directed the church away from political involvement in the 1980s, a decade that saw the continuation of efforts by gay rights activists to repeal sodomy laws, pass anti-discrimination protections, and, in some cases, legalize same-sex marriage. Privately, LDS authorities continued to keep close watch over these efforts and to develop its positions on each question. Dallin H. Oaks, a member of the church's Quorum of the Twelve Apostles at the time, drew up a document in the summer of 1984 to suggest how the church might take a stand on such matters.

The document, titled *Principles to Govern Possible Public Statement on Legislation Affecting Rights of Homosexuals*, revealed an important evolution in LDS authorities' thinking on gay rights and demonstrated the development of a shrewd political strategy for opposing those rights should the church decide to enter the political fray. While Oaks pointed to biblical and LDS scriptural condemnations of homosexuality, he reasoned that any public position the church took on possible legislation should be "tied to the relationship of the homosexual behavior to the demonstrable public interests of our secular society, rather than to the seriousness of homosexual behavior as a sin under religious law." That approach likely influenced Oaks' proposal that the church stay out of public debates over the repeal or extension of sodomy laws, arguing that weighing in on this issue would make it look like the church cared more about homosexual rather than heterosexual sin. Oaks also rationalized that since sodomy laws were nearly impossible to enforce without some violation of a constitutional right to privacy, the church should instead reserve "its influence for more important matters." Lastly, Oaks believed the prosecution of sodomy laws would actually backfire in terms of pursuing those more important matters because, he maintained, "the enforcement of special criminal penalties against homosexuals makes them martyrs and wins them public sympathy and some powerful liberal support they can use to their advantage" for exactly advancing those bigger political objectives (1984).

In that vein, Oaks counseled the LDS Church to adopt a tactical approach against non-discrimination laws, making "well-reasoned exceptions rather than to oppose such legislation across the board." Given that the gay rights movement presented itself as a continuation of the civil rights movement, Oaks cautioned the church to not respond in a way that would validate such claims. By targeting specific scenarios, like arguing homosexuals should be excluded from any jobs that involved minors like teaching or counseling youth, the LDS Church could appear to be putting forward rational exceptions supported by most Americans at the time while avoiding being seen as supporting overall employment discrimination against all gay men and women. Doing so would ensure the church's involvement with only the legislation most likely to pass, always an important consideration for the politically cautious organization. It also undermined, in Oaks' estimation, the gay rights movement's attempt to use the fight for non-discrimination protections as a proxy battle for wider cultural acceptance. If the public debate became about whether homosexuals had the right to a job, Oaks contended, Americans will "see the debate as a question of tolerance of persons who are different, like other minorities. Perceiving the issue in those terms, the public will vote for tolerance, and those who oppose may well be seen as unmerciful persecutors of the unfortunate" (1984). On the other hand, by defeating seemingly small measures like permitting homosexuals to take jobs in education, they could thereby win the larger war over public approval of homosexuality. This framing of non-discrimination laws around the issue of protecting minors depended on the erroneous but persistent beliefs that linked homosexuality to pedophilia, but it also was an attempt to keep the debate away from the legal question of the basic civil rights of gay and lesbian Americans.

Lastly, Oaks' memo addressed the matter of what it called "homosexual marriages." Oaks reminded his readers that although most political observers viewed legalization as unlikely, passage of the ERA would very likely have made it possible, an accepted view within the LDS Church even if most legal scholars had argued otherwise during the amendment's ratification period. While courts had refused to consider legal challenges to same-sex marriage bans, Oaks pointed out that the Universalist Unitarian Association had recently become the first major Protestant denomination to allow gay nuptials, paving the way for its increasing practice. Drawing a distinction from the other political issues under consideration in his memo, Oaks argued that "the interests at stake in the proposed legalization of so-called homosexual marriages are sufficient to justify a formal Church position and significant efforts in opposition." Again, Oaks counseled the church to present its opposition in secular terms. "We therefore do not mention that, in religious terms," Oaks clarified, "homosexual 'marriages' would be a devilish perversion of the procreative purposes of God." Instead, the church ought to position its objections as concern over its costs to society rather than a debate about civil rights. Following this strategy, the church should "speak in defense of the family," argue publicly that all legal rights of marriage have been granted for the sole consideration of its procreative purpose, and warn about the risk that same-sex marriages would depopulate the nation and ultimately "extinguish its people." "Our marriage laws," Oaks concluded, "should not abet national suicide" (1984).

The Family: A Proclamation to the World

While the LDS Church remained politically inactive through the 1980s, the Oaks document provided the template for its political strategy as it moved into the 1990s, particularly its recommendation that the church "vigorously oppose the legalization of homosexual marriages" (1984). The decade provided plenty of opportunities for that opposition as various states considered bans on same-sex marriage. In preparation for the church's political involvement, the First Presidency released a statement in 1994 opposing same-sex marriage and reminding Mormons that marriage "between a man and woman is ordained of God to fulfill the eternal destiny of His children" (First Presidency, 1994). The statement also called on Mormons to engage in the political fight against same-sex marriage by imploring elected officials to defend traditional marriage and working against any efforts to legalize same-sex unions.

The following year, the First Presidency released another document, "The Family: A Proclamation to the World." Directly connected to the church's increasing political involvement against same-sex marriage, the proclamation quickly became one of the LDS Church's most important documents with many Mormon families displaying copies of it prominently in their homes. It is cited often in church manuals and publications, and quoted from frequently by leading LDS officials at General Conference meetings. While a short statement of only about 600 words, "The Family" nevertheless summarized Mormon beliefs on gender, sexuality, family, and marriage, and how each related to Mormonism's theology of salvation. In the proclamation's opening line, the church asserted that "marriage between a man and a woman is ordained of God and that the family is central to the Creator's plan for the eternal destiny of His children." The "divine design" of gender roles received attention throughout the document. Women's role concerned the care of children while men had been ordained to "preside over their families" (First Presidency and Council of the Twelve Apostles, 1995).

Declaring gender an "essential characteristic" of Mormon men and women's "eternal identity and purpose," the statement described marriage as fitting together two distinct partners into one whole unit. By implication, same-sex marriage was unnatural, and thus should not be made legal, because it could never take two same parts and unite them as an integrated whole, a rejoinder to pro-gay marriage arguments premised on notions of equality, fairness, and justice. While "The Family" reaffirmed long-standing Mormon ideas about the divine nature of heterosexual marriage, the statement's depiction of marriage during a time when many states were adopting Defense of Marriage Act (DOMA) bans against same-sex marriage heightened the political meaning of this religious teaching. It was also intentional, coming on the heels of the church's 1994 statement opposing same-sex marriage and calling on Mormons to work politically to defend traditional marriage. "The Family" closed with a similar appeal, though one addressed "to responsible citizens and officers of government everywhere to promote those measures designed to maintain and strengthen the family as the fundamental unit of society" (First Presidency and Council of the Twelve Apostles, 1995). If those words seemed to obliquely concern the politics of same-sex marriage, the LDS Church's direct involvement in state same-sex marriage battles in the 1990s and early 2000s left little to question.

State battles over the Defense of Marriage Act

The first testing ground for that activism came in Hawaii where the state Supreme Court cited Hawaii's Equal Rights Amendment protection against sex discrimination in its 1993 decision *Baehr v. Lewin* that ruled the state's denial of civil marriage to same-sex couples required justification under strict scrutiny. Since Mormon leaders had argued that a federal ERA would lead to the legalization of gay marriage, they were unsurprised to see that political logic play out in Hawaii. They were also ready. As the case was remanded to trial court and the state legislature considered a group of competing bills to create a constitutional amendment banning same-sex marriage, the LDS Church stepped up its involvement in Hawaii, relying on its strong presence and extensive political network in the state (Morris, 1997, pp. 138–40). Fifty thousand Mormons made up approximately 5 percent of Hawaii's population at the time, and the church had established a successful grassroots political organization, Hana Pono, during the ERA years. The organization, whose name meant "Do What Is Right," had remained active on behalf of conservative causes in the state since then, including closely monitoring gay rights legislation (Quinn, 1994, p. 127).

From its headquarters in Salt Lake City, the LDS Church ran a secret political operation in the Aloha State, hiding its involvement just as the church had done during the ERA battle. Key to this was the creation of Hawaii's Future Today (HFT), a seemingly grassroots organization that the LDS Church directed at every turn. In creating the new group, the church may have abandoned its established organization in the state, Hana Pono, because its connection to the church was public knowledge by the 1990s. Hana Pono was, however, the largest financial backer of HFT (Gordon and Gillespie, 2012, p. 355). Hawaii's Future Today described itself as "a coalition of Hawaii citizens" dedicated to opposing prostitution, casino gambling, and same-sex marriage.[1] To further obscure the church's involvement, LDS officials tapped a local Catholic priest to serve as the group's co-chairman. For the position of chair, the church wanted "an articulate middle-age mother who is neither Catholic nor L.D.S.," but when no such person could be found, Debi Hartmann, an LDS woman who had served on the state's Board of Education, filled the spot (Dunn, 1995a). Still, church leaders were pleased with the operation they'd established in Hawaii. "We have distanced the Church from the coalition itself but still have input where necessary," one internal letter noted (Dunn, 1995b).

That input remained extensive, including LDS President Gordon B. Hinckley's trip to Honolulu to meet with those leading the efforts there. Church officials also called Mormons from both Hawaii and elsewhere to serve short missions with Hawaii's Future Today, repeating the church's practice of extending callings to LDS women for work against the ERA (Semerad, 1996). In church meetings throughout Hawaii, Mormons listened to a letter from the First Presidency encouraging their involvement. Thousands of Saints attended public rallies and wrote letters to their legislators asking them to vote for the amendment. After the amendment's passage by the Hawaii legislature in 1996, the LDS Church donated more than half a million dollars to support a media campaign and voter turnout efforts in anticipation of the 1998 election where Hawaiians voted on whether to add the amendment prohibiting same-sex marriage to the state constitution. Seventy percent voted yes (Young, 2016, p. 156).

After its success in Hawaii, the LDS Church worked to support the passage of Defense of Marriage Acts in other states. Utah, the first state to pass DOMA in 1995, provided an easy early victory for the church. By 2003, thirty-seven states had enacted bans against same-sex marriage with the LDS Church providing critical support in many of those places, including Alaska, California, Nebraska, Nevada, New Mexico, Texas, and Washington (Quinn, 2000). In Alaska, the church donated $500,000 to back that state's successful voter ban on same-sex marriage in 1998 (Ruskin, 1998). In Texas, LDS leaders provided the Saints there with letter templates to send to newspapers and state legislators voicing their support for traditional marriage. As in Hawaii, the church established a grassroots organization, Coalition for Traditional Marriage, and urged all Texas Mormons to join the group. Training documents instructed church members to never reveal their LDS connections, but to instead present themselves as concerned citizens. Similar efforts were made in Washington, New Mexico, and Nebraska (Quinn, 2000, p. 10). In Nevada, the church established the Coalition for the Protection of Marriage as its organization there to back Question 2, the proposed amendment to the state's constitution defining marriage as between a man and a woman. Nevada law requires that ballot initiatives for constitutional amendments must be passed by a majority of voters in two successive elections, so the LDS Church focused on ensuring Question 2's success in 2000 and 2002 through its organization. Led by Richard Ziser, an evangelical businessman in Las Vegas, and joined by the Catholic Church, the Coalition for the Protection of Marriage touted itself as an ecumenical group, but the LDS Church remained in charge. Mormon volunteers ensured the initiative qualified for the ballot in 2000 by collecting two and a half times the requisite signatures, and their vigilant politicking helped the initiative pass with 70 and 67 percent support in the 2000 and 2002 elections, respectively (Damore, Jelen, and Bowers, 2007).

Internal documents reveal that in nearly twenty other states, like Alabama, Kentucky, New Hampshire, and Wisconsin, the church kept close watch and some involvement with same-sex marriage legislation, including calling church members to lobby for the legislation in their states. In several of these, Mormons worked with other conservative Christians who were leading the anti-gay marriage efforts in their particular states. These ecumenical outreaches met varying responses. The church's contact in West Virginia reported he had "formed a loose coalition with the Catholics and the So. Baptists," and the Alabama leaders responded that they had met with an influential "Baptist lobbyist/minister." In New Hampshire, the church was happy that their leader there could "successfully support the Catholics and other religious leaders in this effort without taking strong leadership." But in Kentucky, "the Catholics" wouldn't return calls to the church's representative there, and in New Jersey the church's contact blamed the Catholic Church for a "lack of urgency" on the issue.[2]

Proposition 8

As it directed political efforts on behalf of DOMA in states across the nation, the LDS Church closely monitored same-sex marriage developments in California. As the largest state, California was often believed to be the trendsetter for the nation politically and culturally. Because of this, anti-marriage equality activists, including the LDS Church, ranked California as the most important state for passing a Defense of Marriage Act. If California voters enacted DOMA, they reasoned, it would be a crushing loss for the gay rights movement and a significant setback for efforts to legalize same-sex marriage in any state. With nearly 750,000 Mormons in California, the LDS Church had a sizeable resource to carry out its mission.

That work began in preparation of the 2000 election where Californians would vote on DOMA that year. Two years earlier, California's DOMA sponsor, State Senator Pete Knight, had privately called LDS officials in Utah to let them know his plans to get the act, called Proposition 22, on the 2000 ballot. By the late 1990s, the LDS Church's involvement in passing Defense of Marriage Acts around the country was well known enough that, despite the church's efforts to conceal its work, a call from Sen. Knight to coordinate efforts made perfect sense. Up until Election Day, Knight's office and LDS leaders remained in close contact, updating each other on efforts to ensure Prop 22's passage.

For over a year, the LDS Church oversaw extensive work on behalf of the ballot measure. At the church's October 1999 General Conference, President Hinckley encouraged all Mormons to support Prop 22. "This is not a matter of civil rights," Hinckley argued, "it is a matter of morality" (Hinckley, 1999). In California, the church again attempted to camouflage much of its activities through the creation of the grassroots organization Defense of Marriage Committee. Mormons were instructed to donate directly to the committee via a letter from LDS officials read aloud in church meetings throughout the state. The letter reminded Mormons that marriage between a man and a woman had been designed by God for the purpose of procreation and that Mormons had a religious obligation to protect God's institution for the family. LDS leaders indicated they expected California's Mormons to contribute 4 million dollars to the Defense of Marriage Committee, and the church tasked individual Mormon stakes and wards throughout the state with raising targeted amounts. California's Saints were also pressured to generously donate their time to ensuring Prop 22's passage, including distributing materials supporting the proposition and leading "get out the vote" efforts in communities across California. On Election Day, Prop 22 passed with 61 percent support (Young, 2016, pp. 157–59).

Although a major victory for the anti-gay agenda, Prop 22's days were numbered. In May 2008, the state's Supreme Court struck down Prop 22 as unconstitutional, thereby legalizing gay marriage in the state. Thousands of same-sex couples rushed to get married, but conservative activists also were busy organizing support for the California Marriage Protection Act, otherwise known as Prop 8, slated for the election ballot in November. Prop 8, which would define marriage in California's constitution as only between a man and a woman, found a broad range of support from religious conservatives throughout the state, but the LDS Church was widely acknowledged as the leading organizer, and Mormons by far provided the bulk of work on behalf of Prop 8, running telephone banks, holding rallies, and writing legislators. The *New York Times* reported that Mormons had constituted between 80 to 90 percent of the volunteers in door-to-door canvassing efforts throughout the state (McKinley and Johnson, 2008). Mormons also dominated the fundraising for Prop 8. One study found that Mormons contributed $30 million of the $42 million collected for the initiative, with much of that money sent from LDS members living outside of California (Mencimer, 2010).

To augment its political work, the LDS Church developed resources to remind church members about the sacred nature of marriage and the church's position on Prop 8. (Voters in Arizona and Florida were also considering similar constitutional amendments which received the church's support, but national attention—and LDS primary efforts—focused on California.) The church directed members to consult its newly-created website, PreservingMarriage.org, to strengthen their knowledge of the church's teachings on homosexuality and marriage. A new church statement, "The Divine Institution of Marriage," reaffirmed "the Church's declaration that marriage is the lawful union of a man and a woman" and warned about "the harmful consequences" the legalization of gay marriage would bring about, including forcing public schools to teach about same-sex marriage and suggesting churches with religious objections to gay marriage could lose their tax exempt status. Such claims repeated the church's previous strategy of framing the debate over same-sex marriage in terms of its societal impact rather than moral opposition. Rather than a denial of gay men and women's civil rights, the church presented its work as merely an affirmation of traditional heterosexual marriage that "neither constitutes nor condones any kind of hostility toward gays and lesbians" (Mormon Newsroom, 2008).

But hostility towards gay and lesbian Americans is exactly how many interpreted the LDS Church's activities in California after Prop 8 won a surprising victory with 52 percent of the vote. The outrage towards the LDS Church prompted protest rallies outside LDS temples in cities around the country, including some 10,000 demonstrators in front of the church's temple in New York City. Evangelical leaders and Catholic bishops extended their support to the LDS Church, and the National Organization for Marriage (NOM) launched a website abovethehate.com where people could sign a letter thanking the LDS Church for its help in passing Prop 8 and decrying "attacks" against the church and its members for the "courage in standing up for marriage" (Mantyla, 2008).

In naming the website "Above the Hate," Prop 8's supporters sought to reset the conversation on marriage equality. Opponents of Prop 8 in California had branded the measure as an act of odious vengeance against gays and lesbians—supporting Prop 8 equated to hating one's gay friends, family, and fellow citizens. Prop 8's backers hoped instead that somehow voters would not see gays as the amendment's target. "It is not our goal in this campaign to attack the homosexual lifestyle … the less we refer to homosexuality, the better," a training document circulated among Mormon volunteers had explained (McKinley and Johnson, 2008). That distinction had seemed to work for the LDS Church during its involvement in the state DOMA fights of the 1990s when public opinion on gay marriage largely matched the church's position. But by 2008, many Americans had difficulty separating Prop 8's defense of traditional marriage from their conviction that gays had been unfairly persecuted, a perception shaped no doubt by the dramatic cultural shift toward acceptance of homosexuality the nation had undergone in the intervening years. A wildly successful media campaign launched by a group called the NoH8 Campaign in the days following Prop 8's passage capitalized on those sentiments as it formed a photographic record of protest. Thousands of Americans, including dozens of celebrities, posed for NoH8's signature photograph with silver duct tape covering their mouth and "NoH8" emblazoned in black and red makeup across their cheeks.[3]

Yet the protests outside LDS temples, some of which turned violent and destructive, and boycotts against businesses owned by people who had donated money for Prop 8 allowed the amendment's supporters to claim their status as the real victims. Branded as hateful and intolerant, Prop 8's supporters turned the script. Religious conservatives argued that they, not gays and lesbians, suffered the true persecution and vilification; that they were not the bigots in this battle, but that their foes who sought to silence religious voices were. In supporting Prop 8, they claimed, they had not sought to deny anyone their rights but instead simply defended a traditional foundation of society in heterosexual marriage. Now they were being attacked, threatened, and intimidated by the forces who claimed their own campaign was one of love and acceptance. Though typically critical of minority claims of victimization, Prop 8's supporters relished adopting the identity for themselves and delighted in pointing out what they saw as the hypocrisy of their foes. The attacks on the LDS Church were also useful in recasting the conversation about the minority class under attack by Prop 8. While the amendment's passage seemed to its opponents a clear affront to the civil rights of the minority group of gay and lesbian Californians, Prop 8's supporters highlighted Mormons' status as a "minority religion" to heighten sympathy in the weeks following the election. Depicted as a small, earnest group of devout Americans, Mormons' defenders hardly saw the LDS Church as the powerful political force gay marriage advocates accused it of being.[4]

The "Utah compromise"

The strong public reaction against the church's role in Prop 8 surprised LDS officials. "What exactly are they protesting," the LDS spokesperson Michael Otterson asked (Young, 2016, p. 162). For many Mormon leaders, the amendment's victory suggested to them that their church was on the right side of public opinion, but they began to recognize that non-Mormons might not appreciate the church's belief that it could both defend traditional marriage while also supporting the civil rights of gays and lesbians. As earlier documented, in the years prior to Prop 8 the LDS Church had made significant adjustments in its theology and practices that showed a less harsh stance than in previous decades. Following Prop 8, the LDS Church said it supported certain protections for gays and lesbians around employment, housing, and hospitalization. In 2009, LDS officials were able to demonstrate that support when the church backed two Salt Lake City non-discrimination ordinances for gays and lesbians regarding employment and housing. Perhaps reflecting the church's new position, five out of seven Mormon senators voted for the Employment Non-Discrimination Act (ENDA) that passed the U.S. Senate in 2013. The bill outlawed employment discrimination based on sexual orientation or gender identity.

Yet more than this support for extending civil rights protections to gay Americans, the LDS Church's decision to not involve itself in four states that were considering same-sex marriage bans in the 2012 election may have been the most surprising. Many pointed to the church's absence as the reason all four states defeated the bans. Yet the LDS Church had not abandoned the issue of gay marriage altogether. When Hawaii once again considered same-sex marriage in 2013, the church renewed its operations in the state, but this time Mormons could not stop Hawaii from legalizing gay marriage. In Utah that same year, the church mounted a defense after a federal district court struck down the state's constitutional amendment defining marriage as between a man and a woman, lending support to the state's appeal of the ruling and reminding Mormons to study church teachings on marriage.

As the 2015 legislative session opened in Utah, the LDS Church announced its support for proposed legislation that would extend protections in housing and employment to LGBT people while also providing protections for religious expression and exemptions to religious institutions. State Bill 296, known as the "Anti-Discrimination and Religious Freedom Amendments," was the result of negotiations between the state's gay rights organizations, including Equality Utah, and the LDS Church, a somewhat unlikely event given the recent animosity that had arisen between those parties over the events of 2013 in the state. In a press conference before the vote on Salt Lake City's Capitol Hill, LDS officials appeared with a group of Republican and Democratic lawmakers to offer their backing. That appearance and the church's endorsement of the legislation proved critical in pushing the Republican-majority legislature, most of whom were Mormons, to pass the bill overwhelmingly. An accompanying piece of legislation, SB 297, also passed with a large margin. That bill allowed county clerks who hold religious objections to not have to perform same-sex nuptials while also requiring counties have substitute officiants on hand to solemnize marriages in such circumstances.

Dubbed the "Utah Compromise" for the way the legislation brokered agreement between the state's gay rights advocates and Mormon authorities, the two bills also represented the LDS Church's own compromise with the issue of LGBT political rights developed over the past two decades. Merrill Nelson, a Utah state representative and Mormon, explained his support for the bills by arguing that while homosexuality was not a civil right, housing and employment were. His vote for the bills, Nelson explained, hadn't also meant the condoning of a particular sexual orientation, a comment that reflected both the LDS Church's political strategy regarding gay rights and its religious distinction between homosexual activity and those with same-sex attraction (Romboy, 2015).

Equality Utah and the Human Rights Campaign, the LDS Church, and many national political commentators hailed the bills as a good legislative compromise that could provide an example to other states about how to reconcile competing political objectives. But some progressive groups also took exception with the legislation, viewing it, as one liberal outlet put it, as enabling "the various forms of discrimination they're supposed to prevent," because of the bills' religious liberty carve-outs and failure to address the issue of public accommodations (Ford, 2016). The bills also found criticism from several conservative religious groups who were more used to finding themselves in alignment with the LDS Church politically. A political director of the Southern Baptist Convention told LDS leaders that the Utah legislation was "not the right strategy" because it did not sufficiently protect freedom of conscience for religious objectors. "I don't think this will be a model," the SBC's Russell Moore spoke of the bills. Catholic bishops also indicated their displeasure (Goodstein, 2015a).

Conclusion

While the LDS Church's somewhat progressive stance on non-discrimination protections for gay and lesbian Americans puts it in conflict with its strongest allies, conservative evangelicals and Catholics, the church's steadfast opposition to same-sex marriage has helped maintain that alliance while also putting it out of step with the majority of Americans. Even as the church has softened its general positions on homosexuality and its treatment of gay and lesbian Mormons, that trend has occurred alongside the development of other church policies that many view as particularly punitive. The church's 2015 *Handbook* said Mormons in a "same-gender marriage" were subject to excommunication and banned children living in same-sex households from church baptisms (Goodstein, 2015b). Critics both inside and out of the LDS Church pointed out that the latter policy seemed to contradict the church's emphasis on supporting its members who identified as gay, particularly underage minors. But others maintained the new rules simply revealed Mormonism's true anti-homosexuality. In an important development and perhaps under pressure, the church under the new direction of President Russell M. Nelson announced in 2019 it was reversing the 2015 policy, now allowing children of same-sex couples to be baptized and removing the threat of excommunication for church members in same-sex relationships (Dias, 2019).

Even with those changes, the reality indicates a church that is struggling to stake out its positions, both theological and political, regarding homosexuality. Yet the history of the LDS Church shows its approach to the religious and political consequences of homosexuality has required an ongoing reevaluation of its position. Although the church is unlikely to change its stance on same-sex marriage, it will likely continue to back civil rights extensions for LGBT Americans. In a different political context, one could imagine the LDS Church making peace with same-sex marriage's legalization even as it maintained its religious teachings against it and prohibited it within the church. But if conservatives gain ascendancy again and overturn the right of gay marriage, the LDS Church may once again find itself on the frontlines.

Notes

1 Hawaii's Future Today, "Mission Statement," at www.rightsequalrights.com/mormongate/church-documents.
2 See, "LDS Church Gay Marriage Lobbying Reports," www.documentcloud.org/documents/811352-lds-church-gay-marriage-lobbying-reports.html.
3 For examples, see the NoH8 Campaign website, www.noh8campaign.com.
4 See, for example, Maggie Gallagher, "Above the Hate," *Real Clear Politics*, November 26, 2008, www.realclearpolitics.com/articles/2008/11/above_the_hate.html; and Jonah Goldberg, "An Ugly Attack on Mormons," *Los Angeles Times*, December 2, 2008, www.latimes.com/news/opinion/commentary/la-oe-goldberg2-2008dec02,0,6411205.column?track=rss.

References

Chauncey, G., 2004. *Why Marriage? The History Shaping Today's Debate*. New York: Basic Books.
Church News, 1977. Unnatural, Without Excuse. *Deseret News*, p. 16.
Church News, 1979. Is It a Menace? *Deseret News*, p. 16.
Damore, D., Jelen, T., and Bowers, M., 2007. Sweet Land of Liberty: The Gay Marriage Amendment in Nevada. In P. Djupe, and L. Olson, eds. *Religious Interests in Community Conflict: Beyond the Culture Wars*. Waco, TX: Baylor University Press, pp. 51–71.
Dias, E., 2019. Mormon Church to Allow Children of L.G.B.T. Parents to Be Baptized. *New York Times*. www.nytimes.com/2019/04/04/us/lds-church-lgbt.html.
Dunn, L., 1995a. Report to the Public Affairs Committee on Same-Gender Marriage Issue in Hawaii. Rights Equal Rights. www.rightsequalrights.com/mormongate/church-documents.
Dunn, L., 1995b. Letter to Elder Neal A. Maxwell. Rights Equal Rights. www.rightsequalrights.com/mormongate/church-documents.
Fejes, F., 2008. *Gay Rights and Moral Panic: The Origins of America's Debate on Homosexuality*. New York: Palgrave Macmillan.
First Presidency, 1978. First Presidency Reaffirms Opposition to ERA. *Ensign*. October, pp. 63–4.
First Presidency, 1980. The Church and the Proposed Equal Rights Amendment: A Moral Issue. LDS.org. www.lds.org/study/ensign/1980/03/the-church-and-the-proposed-equal-rights-amendment-a-moral-issue?lang=eng.
First Presidency, 1994. First Presidency Statement Opposing Same Gender Marriages. LDS.org. www.lds.org/ensign/1994/04/news-of-the-church/first-presidency-statement-opposing-same-gender-marriages?lang=eng.
First Presidency and Council of the Twelve Apostles, 1995. LDS.org. www.lds.org/topics/family-proclamation.

Ford, Z., 2016. The "Utah Compromise" Is a Dangerous LGBT Trojan Horse. Think Progress. https://thinkprogress.org/the-utah-compromise-is-a-dangerous-lgbt-trojan-horse-db790ad3b69e.

Goodstein, L., 2015a. Utah Passes Antidiscrimination Bill Backed by Mormon Leaders. *New York Times*. www.nytimes.com/2015/03/12/us/politics/utah-passes-antidiscrimination-bill-backed-by-mormon-leaders.html.

Goodstein, L., 2015b. New Policy on Gay Couples and Their Children Roils Mormon Church. *New York Times*. www.nytimes.com/2015/11/14/us/mormons-set-to-quit-church-over-policy-on-gay-couples-and-their-children.html.

Gordon, E., and Gillespie, W., 2012. The Culture of Obedience and the Politics of Stealth: Mormon Mobilization against ERA and Same-Sex Marriage. *Politics and Religion* 5(2): 343–66.

Hinckley, G., 1999. Why We Do Some of the Things We Do. LDS.org. www.lds.org/ensign/1999/11/why-we-do-some-of-the-things-we-do.?lang=eng&_r=1.

Holland, J., 2007. Helping Those Who Struggle with Same-Gender Attraction. *Ensign*. October, pp. 42–45.

Kimball, S., 1969. *The Miracle of Forgiveness*. Salt Lake City, UT: Bookcraft.

Kimball, S., 1971. *New Horizons for Homosexuals*. Salt Lake City, UT: Deseret News Press.

Lyon, J., 2007. BYU Changes Honor Code Text about Gay Students. *Salt Lake Tribune*. http://archive.sltrib.com/story.php?ref=/news/ci_5684555.

Mantyla, K., 2008. Anti-Gay Forces Pretend to Rise "Above the Hate." Right Wing Watch. www.rightwingwatch.org/post/anti-gay-forces-pretend-to-rise-above-the-hate/.

McKinley, J., and Johnson, K., 2008. Mormons Tipped Scale in Ban on Gay Marriage. *New York Times*. www.nytimes.com/2008/11/15/us/politics/15marriage.html.

Mencimer, S., 2010. Of Mormons and (Gay) Marriage. *Mother Jones*. www.motherjones.com/politics/2010/02/fred-karger-save-gay-marriage.

Mormon Newsroom, 2008. The Divine Institution of Marriage. Mormon Newsroom. www.mormonnewsroom.org/article/the-divine-institution-of-marriage.

Morris, R., 1997. "What Though Our Rights Have Been Assailed?" Mormons, Politics, Same-Sex Marriage, and Cultural Abuse in the Sandwich Islands (Hawai'i). *Women's Rights Law Reporter* 18(2) 129–204.

Oaks, D., 1984. *Principles to Govern Possible Public Statement on Legislation Affecting Rights of Homosexuals*. www.ldspapers.faithweb.com.

O'Donovan, R., 1994. "The Abominable and Detestable Crime against Nature": A Brief History of Homosexuality and Mormonism, 1840–1980. In B. Corcoran, ed. *Multiply and Replenish: Mormon Essays on Sex and Family*. Salt Lake City, UT: Signature Books, pp. 123–70.

Quinn, D., 1994. The LDS Church's Campaign against the Equal Rights Amendment. *Journal of Mormon History* 20(2): 85–155.

Quinn, D., 1996. *Same-Sex Dynamics among Nineteenth-Century Americans: A Mormon Example*. Urbana, IL: University of Illinois Press.

Quinn, D., 2000. Prelude to the National "Defense of Marriage" Campaign: Civil Discrimination against Feared or Despised Minorities. *Dialogue: A Journal of Mormon Thought* 33(3): 1–52.

Romboy, D., 2015. Utah Legislature Passes Two "Historic" Anti-Bias, Religious Rights Bills. *Deseret News*. www.deseretnews.com/article/865623954/Utah-House-panel-to-hold-hearing-today-on-religious-rights-bill.html.

Ruskin, L., 1998. Same-Sex Marriage Foes Given $500,000. *Anchorage Daily News*, p. F2.

Semerad, T., 1996. A Mormon Crusade in Hawaii: Church Aims to End Gay Union. *Salt Lake Tribune*, p. B1.

White, H., 2015. *Reforming Sodom: Protestants and the Rise of Gay Rights*. Chapel Hill, NC: University of North Carolina Press.

Winkler, A., 2008. Lavender Sons of Zion: A History of Gay Men in Salt Lake City, 1950–79. Ph.D. Dissertation, University of Utah.

Young, N., 2007. "The ERA Is a Moral Issue": The Mormon Church, LDS Women, and the Defeat of the Equal Rights Amendment. *American Quarterly* 59(3): 623–44.

Young, N., 2016. Mormons and Same-Sex Marriage: From ERA to Prop 8. In P. Mason, and J. Turner, eds. *Out of Obscurity: Mormonism since 1945*. New York: Oxford University Press, pp. 144–69.

Further reading

Fejes, F., 2008. *Gay Rights and Moral Panic: The Origins of America's Debate on Homosexuality*. New York: Palgrave Macmillan.

A history of the debates in the 1970s and 1980s about the civil rights of LGBT Americans, although one that gives little attention to the involvement of the LDS Church in these political contests.

Gordon, E., and Gillespie, W., 2012. The Culture of Obedience and the Politics of Stealth: Mormon Mobilization against ERA and Same-Sex Marriage. *Politics and Religion* 5(2): 343–66.

This article finds connections between the LDS Church's political efforts against the equal rights amendment and same-sex marriage, especially the church's habit of disguising its political activities through grassroots organizations.

Morris, R., 1997. "What Though Our Rights Have Been Assailed?" Mormons, Politics, Same-Sex Marriage, and Cultural Abuse in the Sandwich Islands (Hawai'i). *Women's Rights Law Reporter* 18(2): 129–204.

An exhaustive examination of the LDS Church's sustained involvement in opposing same-sex marriage in Hawaii. This article shows how Hawaii served as a critical testing ground for the church's political activism against gay marriage that it then exported to other states.

Quinn, D., 2016. *Same-Sex Dynamics among Nineteenth-Century Americans: A Mormon Example*. Urbana, IL: University of Illinois Press.

This chapter examines the history of early Mormonism's surprising tolerance of homosexual activity among its members, a striking contrast from the LDS Church's stance in the twentieth century.

16
MORMON LGBTQ ORGANIZING AND ORGANIZATIONS

John Donald Gustav-Wrathall

Mormon LGBTQ organizing and organizations

The existence of individuals sexually oriented toward members of the same sex as well as individuals expressing gender identities other than that assigned at birth have been documented to be a part of the Church of Jesus Christ of Latter-day Saints since its early history in the nineteenth century. But LGBTQ Mormons did not begin to organize until the 1960s. LGBTQ Mormon organizing is undeniably the result of intensifying social concern about homosexuality in the United States that came to a boil after World War II. The reaction of Latter-day Saint leaders and members to the increasing visibility of LGBTQ people was consistent with the historical response of Western Christianity, which associated homosexual and transgender phenomena with sin, heresy, and diabolical influences. LGBTQ Mormons, on the other hand, were motivated by a yearning to understand themselves, and by their faith and by a love for their church.

A trend has played out in the histories of almost every LGBTQ Mormon organization. These organizations began with an initial quest for integration of one's sexual or gender identity with one's faith, followed by disillusionment in the face of rejection and entrenchment on the part of the Church's hierarchy, followed by bifurcation into LDS-rejecting and LGBTQ-rejecting responses. Some prioritized the quest for holiness and sought conformity to LDS community norms. Some prioritized the quest for happiness and pursued authentic existence as a lesbian, gay, bi, trans, or queer person, however self-defined. Organizations would often start out faith-friendly and faith-affirming, optimistic about finding an authentic spiritual path rooted in LDS doctrine and within the ecclesiastical structure of the Church. This would be very congenial to faithful members of the Church. As time went on and hopes for integration and acceptance by the Church diminished, the organization would become more pessimistic and angrier at the Church, and would be increasingly less congenial for faithful members of the Church, and more congenial for disaffected former members. However, over time, LGBTQ organizations have mostly thrived as they have held the tension of being both LGBTQ-affirming and LDS-affirming.

Contrary to popular stereotype, Latter-day Saint rejection of homosexuality and transgender is as much a product of the twentieth century as was the mass movement for LGBTQ rights. D. Michael Quinn, in *Same-Sex Dynamics among Nineteenth-Century Americans: A Mormon Example*

(1996), documented the leniency with which same-sex sexual activity was treated throughout the nineteenth century among Mormons. As Latter-day Saints established settlements throughout the Intermountain West under the leadership of Brigham Young, "sodomy" was not proscribed in the territorial legal code. It was not until after the Utah War and the imposition of a non-Mormon territorial government that same-sex sexual behavior was proscribed by statute in Utah. Quinn found that to the extent the statute was enforced, it was used to punish religious outsiders—Mormons enforcing it against non-Mormons and vice versa. Quinn found that Mormons tended to view homosexual behavior as "youthful indiscretion" rather than as "grievous sin" during this era (Quinn, 1996, pp. 265–89).

A groundbreaking study by Mildred Berryman in 1929 in Salt Lake City established the existence in early twentieth-century Utah of a community of gay men and lesbians (including individuals of Mormon background) whose testimony was that they had been aware of their same-sex attraction since early childhood, who saw themselves as sexual minorities, and who connected with others like themselves through clubs such as "The Bohemian Club" in Salt Lake City. Berryman and other gay and lesbian Utahans saw their homosexuality in non-stigmatic terms, as something that was found naturally occurring in creation (Bullough and Bullough, 1977). Quinn has argued that same-sex oriented individuals were active in the Church, probably forming same-sex relationships, and saw themselves in non-stigmatic terms and may even have been, in their own way, trying to promote understanding of same-sex love. These individuals for the most part stayed off the radar of Church leadership (Quinn, 1996, pp. 231–47).

The Church of Jesus Christ of Latter-day Saints didn't really begin to deal with homosexuality in any concerted way until the 1950s. In 1959, Elders Spencer W. Kimball and Mark E. Petersen were assigned specifically to counsel individuals with homosexual inclinations. The Church Handbook of Instructions—a manual for Church leaders on how to administer the Church according to governing principles established in scripture—was revised in 1968 to include, for the very first time ever, "homosexuality" as one among a list of offenses that could lead to excommunication. Handbook treatment of homosexuality and eventually of transgender has become increasingly more elaborate in the years since then (O'Donovan, 2004; Prince, 2019, pp. 15–18). In late 1969, Spencer W. Kimball published *The Miracle of Forgiveness*, which helped, in the words of Mormon historian Gregory A. Prince, bring "homosexuality" into "the Mormon lexicon." He did so in terms that described it as an "ugly sin," "unnatural," an "abomination," and "second only to murder" in its gravity (Prince, 2019, pp. 31–37).

Growing ecclesiastical efforts to deal with homosexuality coincided with a growing concern about homosexuality in the broader American society, and the emergence, for the first time ever in the United States, of a visible, vocal, and broadly based movement for homosexual emancipation. U.S. military screening for "latent homosexuality" during World War II exposed millions of American service men and women to the concept of homosexuality for the first time, and spurred a growing self-awareness of gay and lesbian Americans that laid the groundwork for a gay and lesbian civil rights movement (Bérubé, 1990). The McCarthy-era "lavender scare" in the 1950s had a similarly galvanizing effect (Johnson, 2006). When a riot broke out in June 1969 at the Stonewall Inn in Greenwich Village in New York City, as drag queens and homosexual patrons of the bar fought back against a routine police raid of the establishment, LGBT people across the country were ready to begin organizing to fight for their rights. LGBT community and political advocacy groups began springing up all over the U.S., and the modern "gay liberation" movement was born (Adam, 1987; Duberman, 1993; Carter, 2004).

LGBT organizing shortly before and in the wake of Stonewall included religious organizing. Metropolitan Community Church, a Protestant denomination ministering to lesbian, gay, bisexual, and transgender people, was founded in 1968 in Huntington Park, California by former Pentecostal minister Troy Perry (Wilcox, 2001; Kohl, 2019). Dignity, an organization for gay and lesbian Catholics, was founded in Los Angeles in 1969 (Dignity USA, 2007). American Baptists Concerned was founded in 1972 (Rainbow Baptists, 2015), Lutherans Concerned in Minneapolis in 1974 (Janson, 2008, pp. 4–5). The following year, in 1975, similar ministries were organized for Evangelicals (Blair, 2013) and United Methodists (Affirmation: United Methodists for Lesbian, Gay, Bisexual, Transgender and Queer Concerns, 2011). All of these and other similar groups were organized because of the misunderstanding and intense hostility openly gay, lesbian, bisexual, or transgender people faced within their respective religious communities. They sought to promote greater understanding that could lead to full and equal participation of LGBTQ people within their respective faiths.

During the 1960s and 1970s, both before and after Stonewall, small, informal groups of LGBT Mormons were confidentially gathering for the purposes of conversation and social support. One such group was formed by a group of Brigham Young University (BYU) students in 1977. Matt Price (Steve Zakharias)[1] who was instrumental in organizing that group helped to organize other similar groups in Salt Lake City, Denver, and Dallas. An organizational charter was written, and these early groups called themselves "Affirmation—Gay Mormons United." After Affirmation garnered some national media attention in the gay press, Paul Mortensen of southern California contacted Price and organized in Los Angeles what was for a time to become the leading chapter of Affirmation. The L.A. chapter organized the first presence of Affirmation in a Gay Pride parade in 1979, and gave impetus to the organization of other chapters in San Francisco and Washington, D.C. In December 1979, representatives of the D.C., San Francisco, and L.A. chapters gathered in Los Angeles to organize a national structure and write a constitution. An early history of this meeting recounted: "Those in attendance started the two day meeting by kneeling in prayer and asking the Lord for guidance. The Lord responded in abundance; there is no question that the Spirit of revelation directed the proceedings." The organization was renamed "Affirmation: Gay & Lesbian Mormons" and a national newsletter, "Affinity," was launched (Affirmation: LGBTQ Mormons, Families & Friends, 2017).

Affirmation was founded with the premise that gayness was inherent. This premise followed from the experience of gay and lesbian individuals themselves that their sexuality was not something they chose, but rather something they discovered that was not amenable to change. If sexual orientation was rooted in one's being, that pointed to creation, to God as the source of human beings' sexual natures, and implied that God had a purpose for his LGBTQ children and a place for them in his kingdom, despite the fact that LGBTQ experience didn't seem to fit within current theological understandings. The original Affirmation charter included a "position statement" that "homosexuality and homosexual relationships can be consistent with and supported by the Gospel of Jesus Christ." If LGBTQ people existed, God had to have a place for them within his plan. The charter committed Affirmation "to work for the understanding and acceptance of gays and lesbians as full, equal and worthy persons within the Church of Jesus Christ of Latter-day Saints" (*Affirmation Gay and Lesbian Mormons General Charter*, 1979). The founders of Affirmation were not seeking a way out of the Church, but seeking full participation within it, in a way that was authentic for them as LGBTQ sons and daughters of God. Cloy Jenkins and Lee Williams, two of the founders of Affirmation at BYU, had drafted a kind of manifesto entitled "Prologue: An Examination of the Mormon Attitude towards Homosexuality" that made the case for a reevaluation of the assumptions made by Church leaders about homosexuality (Jenkins et al., 1978). Early Affirmation leaders requested direct, face-to-face meetings with Church leaders to make their case, but were harshly rebuffed (Thomas, 2013; Anzjøn, 2019).

Increasing numbers of LGBT Mormons felt impelled into one of two paths. One path was exile from the Church. Though the organization was founded for the purpose of creating a space within Mormonism for LGBTQ people, increasingly members of the organization saw themselves as "post-Mormon." A constant over the years has been tension within Affirmation between those who sought to stay creatively and constructively engaged with the Church and those who saw Affirmation as a support group for ex- or "recovering" Mormons. Church leaders and members, as well as a sizeable portion of the membership of Affirmation saw the organization as marginal with relation to the Church at best but more likely as "apostate" or in an oppositional or adversarial relationship with the Church.

LGBTQ Mormons found support among communities of Mormons that organized independently from the Church in the 1960s and 1970s for scholarly, intellectual and cultural exchange. *Dialogue: A Journal of Mormon Thought* was the first independent scholarly journal in Mormon studies, launched in 1966, and had a reputation for being willing to take on "difficult" topics (Anderson, 1999). In 1974, with the encouragement of Bob Rees, then editor of *Dialogue*, independent Mormon scholars launched *Sunstone* magazine, which also became a forum for discussion of controversial issues in Mormonism, including homosexuality. Bob Rees became one of the major contributors encouraging reevaluation of Mormon attitudes toward homosexuality. In 1979, the Sunstone Foundation began sponsoring annual symposia where scholars and community activists could engage in intellectual exchange. *Sunstone* and *Dialogue* began publishing a number of groundbreaking articles on homosexuality, the first ever to address the issue in a non-stigmatizing way in a Mormon context (MacMurray, 1977; Stout, 1987; Schow, 1990; O'Brian, 1993). LGBT scholars and writers were welcome and found heterosexual allies in these forums. Unfortunately, in the 1980s and 1990s, growing intolerance on the part of Church leaders for independent voices, or growing stridency of criticism from the intellectual community, or both, was contributing to tension between the leadership of the Church of Jesus Christ of Latter-day Saints and the *Dialogue* and *Sunstone* communities. In 1991, Church leaders advised Church members, particularly Church employees, not to participate in the *Sunstone* symposia (Stack, 2001), and in 1993 several prominent *Sunstone* contributors were excommunicated for apostasy (Stack, 2014b). This marginalized a significant LGBTQ supportive community from mainstream Mormonism.

In 1993 Gary and Millie Watts founded LDS Family Fellowship, an organization that provided support for Latter-day Saint families with LGBTQ members. Modeled somewhat after PFLAG (Parents and Friends of Lesbians and Gays) the organization sought to foster family support and acceptance of LGBTQ family members among Latter-day Saints (Wright, 2003). Initially strongly motivated to do outreach and education within the Church, many members of LDS Family Fellowship became discouraged with what they perceived as a lack of progress in the Church on LGBTQ issues, and members of the group became increasingly critical of and increasingly distant from the Church. Thus, by the early 2000s LDS Family Fellowship, like the *Sunstone* and *Dialogue* communities remained relatively marginal with respect to the mainstream LDS community. As the hopes of LGBT Mormon activists for dialogue with the Church were dashed, leaders and members of LGBTQ-affirming organizations like Affirmation and LDS Family Fellowship increasingly despaired of engaging in a productive dialogue with Church leaders.

The other possible path was denial of homosexual orientation or transgender identities as valid concepts and redoubled efforts to overcome "homosexual tendencies" or "gender dysphoria." Church leaders' response to the experience of LGBT Mormons who found their sexual orientation inherent and unchangeable was denial. Church leaders insisted that homosexuality was either the product of sinful choices that could be undone, or it was a form of mental illness that could be cured (Prince, 2019, pp. 25–30). Spencer W. Kimball, both in his work counseling individual "homosexuals" and in his book *The Miracle of Forgiveness*, counseled gay individuals to just get married, reassuring them that with faith they would be able to overcome their homosexuality and lead happy heterosexual lives both in time and for eternity (1969, pp. 77–90). Mormon bishops throughout the Church followed Kimball's lead on this. Struggling individuals were referred to therapeutic services (either under the aegis of LDS Social Services, later LDS Family Services, or to other agencies not affiliated with the Church) designed to help individuals attenuate or overcome their "same-sex attraction" or their "gender confusion." In the mid- to late 1970s, electroshock aversion therapy was practiced on gay students at the Provo campus of Brigham Young University (McBride, 1976; O'Donovan, 2004; James, 2011). In March 1978, Boyd K. Packer was assigned to address the issue, which he did in a talk given at a twelve-stake fireside at Brigham Young University entitled "To the One." The talk was eventually published as a pamphlet. In the talk, Packer condemned homosexuality as the product of "selfishness" (Packer, 1978). Later, Church leaders suggested that individuals were not "gay" or "lesbian." They were children of God struggling with the "affliction" of "same-sex attraction" (Lefevor et al., 2019). Church leaders rarely used the terms "gay" or "lesbian," and then only with the qualifier "so-called" (Larry King Live, 2004). Church leaders used the term "gender confusion" as a blanket term for any expression of sexuality or gender identity that didn't conform to heterosexual norms (Ballard, 2006).

In 1989, a dozen years after gay students at BYU organized Affirmation, Evergreen International, Inc. was founded in Salt Lake City with a mission of helping individuals "who want to diminish same-sex attractions and overcome homosexual behavior." Although not an official outreach of the LDS Church, and although not formally affiliated with the LDS or any church, Evergreen's board of trustees included general authorities of the LDS Church. LDS general authorities spoke at every Evergreen conference, and Evergreen adopted a formal position of upholding all doctrines of the Church. Evergreen's position as an organization was that homosexual attraction could be overcome through faith and through the Atonement. Individuals who questioned or rejected Church positions on the malleability or inherency of sexual orientation, or who insisted on an identity not sanctioned by Church leaders were not welcomed. Official terminology (such as "same-sex attraction" versus "gay" or "lesbian") was insisted upon. Both local church leaders and general authorities frequently encouraged individual gay men and lesbians they counseled to use Evergreen as a resource (Evergreen International, 2004).

Through the 1990s and early 2000s large numbers of LGBTQ Mormons started their journey of coming out and coming to terms with their sexual orientation or gender identity with Evergreen International, Inc. Evergreen was a safe place for individuals to acknowledge their feelings to others and to begin to compare notes. Many gay men and lesbians who eventually ultimately gave up hope of "attenuating" or "overcoming" their "same-sex attractions" and who left Evergreen in favor of coming out as gay or lesbian and seeking same-sex relationships described their time with Evergreen in positive terms as a time that enabled them to do due diligence with the Church and satisfy themselves that they had done everything possible to follow a Church-sanctioned path (Schow, 2005). Many reported extreme negative outcomes from their time with Evergreen: guilt and shame over one's inability to "overcome" their sexual orientation; failed marriages that were entered into under false premises; emotional damage from "conversion therapy" that didn't work. A handful claimed that Evergreen "worked" for them and helped them accomplish its stated goals (Wilcox, 2011–2015).

Just as Affirmation was one organization among many that drew inspiration from post-Stonewall gay rights activism, Evergreen International was one of a plethora of organizations that formed as a religious backlash against the LGBTQ rights movement. Its central claim was that homosexual orientation was not inherent and could be changed. Despite the American Psychiatric Association's removal of homosexuality from its list of disorders in 1973, conservatives continued to insist that it was a disorder and it could be cured. Evergreen International, in its approach to homosexuality, was closely aligned with and took its lead from Exodus International, founded in 1976 as an umbrella organization for hundreds of groups and ministries having a goal of helping individuals overcome their homosexuality. Evergreen was also closely aligned with the National Association for Research and Therapy of Homosexuality (NARTH), founded in 1992 by Joseph Nicolosi (Haldeman, 1999).

When Evergreen was founded, conversion therapy was already controversial and rejected by the mainstream of the American medical and psychiatric establishments. By the end of the 1990s LDS leaders were reluctantly beginning to accept that homosexuality might not be amenable to change. Much of the demonizing rhetoric of the Kimball era of the 1970s and 1980s about homosexuality characterizing it as "abomination" or "perversion" was dropped or deemphasized. Instead, leaders like President Gordon B. Hinckley stressed compassion and acceptance so long as individuals lived the law of chastity (Larry King Live, 2004). In 2006 LDS apostle Dallin Oaks and Quorum of the Seventy member Lance Wickman gave a public interview in which they distanced the LDS Church from conversion therapy, acknowledging that some forms of it (such as aversion therapy) were "abusive" and saying they could not "endorse" them. They also counseled against marriage as a "therapeutic step" and stated that an individual should not marry a member of the opposite sex unless they felt a "great attraction" to that individual. Celibacy was advised for those who could not heterosexually marry (Church of Jesus Christ of Latter-day Saints Newsroom, 2006).

The shift in LDS rhetoric away from conversion therapy as an acceptable way of dealing with homosexuality or transgender laid the foundation for a new organization aligned with the Church, but distancing itself from conversion therapy. In 2006, the same year as the Oaks and Wickman interview, Ty Mansfield and other gay Latter-day Saints who had a desire to stay active in the Church and "keep sacred covenants," sought to change the way LGBTQ Mormon ministry was conceptualized. Evergreen's focus on changing sexual orientation was abandoned; acceptance of LGBTQ identities, something the LDS Church had historically resisted, was given a nod. Though North Star provided forums for advocates of conversion therapy, the organization claimed agnosticism on the question of whether sexual orientation could or ought to be changed, preferring instead to focus solely on behavior that would enable individuals to remain in good standing in the Church. This was consistent with a growing emphasis by Church leaders on celibacy as the appropriate path for gay or lesbian individuals (North Star International, 2007).

By the 2010s, the concept of "conversion therapy" was under siege. Accumulating scientific evidence that it was damaging, and inability of conversion therapy practitioners to provide evidence of change, was leading to a discrediting of organizations focused on conversion therapy, and was encouraging a growing number of states and municipalities in the U.S. to pass laws banning, limiting. or heavily regulating the practice (Fadel, 2019). A landmark court case involving Mormon plaintiff Michael Ferguson found a major provider of "conversion therapy" guilty of fraud, striking a major blow to conversion therapy nationwide (Dubrowski, 2015). In 2013, the world's largest "ex-gay" organization, Exodus International, closed its doors as its president, Alan Chambers, formally apologized to the LGBTQ community for the harm they had done (Chambers, 2018). Evergreen, once enjoying the full and unqualified support of Church leaders, had been losing funding and Church leader support, and saw declining attendance at conferences. After Exodus International closed its doors, the handwriting was on the wall. In January 2014 Evergreen International followed suit and disbanded. Most former members of Evergreen joined North Star (Stack, 2014a). As the Church distanced itself from conversion therapy and from marriage "as a therapeutic step," the Church had shifted on LGBTQ issues, redefining the "orthodox" position to one better represented by the greater flexibility and openness of North Star.

The softening in LDS rhetoric about homosexuality was accompanied by a hardening of doctrinal and political positions. In 1995, partly in response to momentum in Hawaii behind legalization of same-sex marriage, the Church published its "Proclamation on the Family," which reinforced "traditional" heterosexual families, emphasizing men's roles as fathers and providers and women's as mothers and nurturers (First Presidency of the Church of Jesus Christ of Latter-day Saints, 1995), a document which has since been consistently used to reinforce the Church's political positions on same-sex relationships or transgender identities (Prince, 2019, pp. 44–66). In 2008, after the California Supreme Court overturned the state's legal ban on same-sex marriages, the LDS Church lent its full backing to the Proposition 8 campaign to amend the state's constitution to ban same-sex marriage. Californian Mormons were strongly encouraged by Church leaders, frequently over the pulpit, to donate money to the "Yes on 8" campaign and to participate in "get out the vote" efforts on its behalf that were coordinated by Church members and leaders. Mormons provided a disproportionate amount of the funding that backed the Prop 8 campaign (Prince, 2019, pp. 126–60).

Church support for Prop 8 sparked LGBTQ protests in Utah and California in the aftermath of Prop 8's victory in the polls. During the campaign, Church leaders had stressed that Church support for Prop 8 was a reflection of core beliefs and values related to marriage, and not a reflection of animus toward the LGBTQ community. They even expressed support for anti-discrimination and anti-violence legislation. In 2009, the Church of Jesus Christ of Latter-day Saints publicly backed an anti-discrimination ordinance in Salt Lake City that protected LGBTQ individuals from discrimination in employment and housing (GLAAD, 2009) and six years later backed a statewide anti-discrimination ordinance in Utah (Romboy, 2015). Significantly for LGBTQ Mormons, the Church also launched a new website in 2012 (NPR, 2012) that was significantly expanded and upgraded in 2016 (Zauzmer, 2016) emphasizing that while the Church still opposed same-sex relationships, Church members needed to accept and include LGBTQ individuals. Of particular significance was the fact that Church leaders emphasized the importance of listening and empathy toward sexual and gender minorities. This opened an unprecedented space for dialogue and understanding within the Church in place of decades of taboo and silence related to these issues. If the Church was ever to reconsider its stance, this was the necessary prerequisite.

In 2011, the Open Stories Foundation (formerly Mormon Stories) began sponsoring conferences where Latter-day Saints could hear the stories of LGBT Mormons. From this spun off a series of conferences (from 2011 to 2016) called the Circling the Wagons (CTW) conferences (Circling the Wagons, 2016). Circling the Wagons intentionally sought to build a bridge between liberals and conservatives, inviting voices from Evergreen, North Star, and Affirmation to the same rostrum. The organization was plagued by controversy from the beginning, accused by both conservatives and liberals of promoting a liberal or conservative agenda under pretext of neutrality. Even though the organization is now defunct, they did play an important role in promoting the value of open dialogue and mutual acceptance across even the most intense differences of opinion. Their role in fostering relationship and dialogue across difference had an impact on how other organizations like North Star and Affirmation thought about themselves and their constituencies and how they related to one another. One fruit of the CTW conferences was a growing dialogue between Affirmation, North Star, and former Evergreen leaders that has continued to the present both formally and informally.

CTW also played a role in fostering and providing a forum for the work of the Reconciliation and Growth Project, a group started in 2013 that included LGBTQ-affirming therapists and therapists who counsel individuals in "mixed orientation marriages" or who are "struggling with unwanted same-sex attraction" (Reconciliation and Growth Project, 2017). One of

Reconciliation and Growth's most important achievements was to develop a set of commonly agreed-upon ethical guidelines for therapists working with LGBTQ or same-sex-attracted clients. One important goal (in common with Circling the Wagons) was to decrease trauma caused by extreme rhetoric or divisiveness.

In the summer of 2012, a group of devout Mormons managed to grab national headlines when they organized a contingent of 350 or so to march in the Salt Lake City Pride parade under the banner "Mormons Building Bridges." Their goal was to communicate a message of love, support, and acceptance to the LGBTQ community, not in spite of their belief, but "because we believe" (Lyon, 2012; Mormons Building Bridges, 2019). Every year since then, Mormons Building Bridges (or "MBB") has organized a contingent of LGBTQ-affirming Mormons at Pride parades in Salt Lake and in other cities. It also sponsors annual retreats and an online social media presence where people can learn about LGBTQ experience and provides social support to LGBTQ Mormons and their families.

MBB was firm in excluding messaging from its Pride events that were critical of Church policies or teachings about sexual or gender identity, preferring instead quotations from scripture, General Authority quotes, or verses from hymns about love and inclusion. Individuals or groups wanting to organize MBB contingents at other Pride parades needed to satisfy the steering committee that they would enforce rules about messaging. However, MBB included all LGBTQ people, and encouraged them to share their stories, regardless of their church membership or relationship status. Thus, MBB became a forum for fully inclusive sharing of stories, even those that didn't fit nicely into orthodox paradigms.

Other local groups organized for the purpose of LGBTQ education, understanding, and support that were more closely aligned with the Church included ALL Arizona (organized in the Mesa area in the spring of 2012, around the same time Mormons Building Bridges was organizing) (Arizona ALL, 2018) and the Hearth (organized in the San Francisco Bay area in the spring of 2015) (Hearth, 2019). These organizations in their public messaging intentionally avoided statements critical of the Church or questioning of Church doctrine, emphasizing well established teachings and messages of General Authorities that were potentially welcoming or affirming of LGBTQ people. The goal of these groups was to enable as many mainstream Mormons as possible to receive and hear about the stories and experience of LGBTQ people, without judgment.

For example, "The Hearth" came into being when Jeff and Katherine Wise, devout LDS parents of a gay son, organized a "fireside" (the LDS term for informal educational or devotional gatherings organized by members) on LGBTQ issues. Jeff was serving as a bishop and felt obligated to clear the topic and speakers in advance with his stake president. With the stake president's approval, the speakers were Jeff himself, a counselor in the Stake Presidency, and an openly gay man who was active in the Church and had recently served as a ward executive secretary in a Bay Area ward. Over a hundred individuals attended the event, and there was strong interest expressed in doing it again. A steering committee was organized, and they began to hold monthly gatherings. There was communication and collaboration with local stakes to ensure that speakers and topics were acceptable. The Hearth organizers felt it important to maintain their independence from organizations such as Affirmation or Mormons Building Bridges so as to have more control over their messaging and their program, and to be able to maintain a positive relationship with the Church that was safe for active members of the Church.

Mormons Building Bridges had been preceded, in 2008, by a group calling themselves Mormons for Marriage. The group later changed its name to Mormons for Marriage Equality (M4ME) to avoid potential confusion about whether they were for or against same-sex marriage. M4ME began as a protest movement of Mormons who disagreed with the LDS Church's decision to back California's Proposition 8. Some Mormons who supported marriage rights for same-sex couples felt the need to speak out. Mormons for Marriage Equality ran a website and sought visibility by organizing contingents to march in Pride parades across the country. In the aftermath of the 2012 Salt Lake City Pride event and thereafter, leaders of Mormons for Marriage Equality harshly criticized Mormons Building Bridges, claiming that they had preempted more hard-hitting messages, critical of the Church's political opposition to same-sex marriage.

M4ME made no bones about criticizing the Church's political position on same-sex marriage. Their scuffles with MBB were emblematic of a feistier ethos among their members. One of the founders of the group, John Dehlin, was also the founder of the "Mormon Stories" community and had become openly critical of the LDS Church's policies and doctrinal positions. His open criticism of Church policies and doctrines led to his excommunication in the spring of 2015. M4ME had trouble keeping believing Mormons. Language on their website reflected a more "post-Mormon" ethos, describing themselves as "individuals associated with the Mormon faith and tradition" (Mormons for Equality, 2014). Former Church members in the organization didn't hesitate to engage in broadside attacks on the Church, its doctrines, policies, and leaders.

In 2012, as the marriage equality movement began to see some of its first victories in the courts, Mormons for Marriage Equality rebranded as Mormons for Equality, stating that they wanted to develop a permanent, politically progressive, LGBTQ-affirming Mormon presence. But after the Obergefell ruling in 2015 the group faded into inactivity. There are still Mormons who march under the Mormons for Equality banner at San Francisco Pride, but that is the extent of their activities (Harrison, 2017). In a recent interview with Spencer Clark, the last president of Mormons for Equality, he admitted that the organization was effectively defunct, though he felt that there was still much advocacy work that Mormons believing in LGBTQ equality needed to be involved in. For ex-Mormons who saw the organization as a vehicle to criticize the Church, it lost its appeal once M4ME was no longer in the spotlight after the effective resolution of the marriage equality issue in the Supreme Court.

Although LDS Family Fellowship had been in existence since the early 1990s, their marginalization from the mainstream LDS community made them unattractive as a resource for active or believing Mormons. In the late 2010s, three new groups for parents of LGBTQ Mormons were started, "Mama Dragons" (Mama Dragons, 2016), "Dragon Dads" (Kacala, 2019), and "I'll Walk With You" (I'll Walk With You, 2019). Mama Dragons came first on the scene, and provided the inspiration for Dragon Dads. Like LDS Family Fellowship before them, Mama Dragons and Dragon Dads quickly became forums for expressions of frustration and discontent with the Church's official policies and positions related to LGBTQ issues. It was a continuing struggle to find balance between uncompromising, "fierce" advocacy for their LGBTQ family members, and creating space for nonjudgmental dialogue with believing Mormons. In 2014, "I'll Walk With You—LDS Parents of LGBT" began with the promulgation of a series of videos on-line of parents sharing their stories of acceptance of their LGBTQ children, and a Facebook support group. "I'll Walk With You" made a more concerted effort to keep a space explicitly welcoming of parents who remain active in the Church, and "church-bashing" or criticism was labeled off bounds in their forums and heavily moderated.

By the early 2000s, Affirmation's membership consisted mostly of ex-Mormons. While there were members of Affirmation at the time who were believing Mormons and/or active in the Church, and while they periodically attempted to steer the organization back into a more LDS-Church-engaged course, Affirmation wasn't generally congenial for them. The prevailing assumption was that you couldn't be gay and Mormon. With the founding of Evergreen in

1989, the only two organizations positioned to serve LGBTQ Mormons were either for "ex-gay Mormons" (Evergreen) or "ex-Mormon gays" (Affirmation). However, the softening of LDS approaches to homosexuality and the emergence of new organizations (North Star, CTW, and Mormons Building Bridges) that allowed individuals to simultaneously claim a gay identity and affirm their faith as Latter-day Saints began to create openings for the kind of dialogical approach that had inspired the early founders of Affirmation.

A key moment was created when Affirmation leaders decided to hold their 2011 annual conference in Kirtland, Ohio, a key historic site for the Church and the location of the first temple built by the Church of Jesus Christ of Latter-day Saints. As part of the conference, Affirmation held a "testimony meeting" and devotional in the historic Kirtland Temple. I was invited to speak there on the theme of "Keeping the Spirit" (Gustav-Wrathall, 2011b). The conference drew significant numbers of LGBTQ Mormons who desired a renewed connection with their faith, and many experienced a spiritual outpouring at the conference (Gustav-Wrathall, 2011a).

Affirmation might have gone defunct around the same time that Evergreen closed its doors in 2014. At a meeting of the Affirmation board prior to the 2012 Affirmation conference in Seattle, Washington, the organization's treasurer reported that based on current trends in membership and financial giving, Affirmation would no longer be financially viable within three years. Randall Thacker and I were present at that meeting, and we shared our perception that Affirmation was viewed as an organization of "angry ex-Mormons," and that it would be difficult to reverse the current trends without a dramatic re-envisioning and rebranding.

Randall Thacker was a gay man who had been a key organizer of the Kirtland conference, and who had recently become active in his Washington, DC LDS congregation. He ran for president of Affirmation in 2012, and the centerpiece of his campaign was a vision of an organization that could celebrate being "LGBT *and* Mormon," an organization that had as a basic principle "following the Spirit." Randall invited me to serve as his senior vice president, and I campaigned vigorously on his behalf, believing in the urgency of having an organization that was both LGBTQ *and* Mormon. Part of the campaign involved me reaching out to LGBTQ Mormons across the country I had come to know through an LGBTQ Mormon blogging community who were similarly motivated to have an organization that was LDS-faith-positive and constructively engaged with the Church. The word was out that if you were LGBTQ and Mormon and you desired an organization with that kind of engagement, now was the time to join Affirmation!

Thacker won the election by a landslide. After a new leadership team, including a new board, was formed, a strategic planning gathering was held at the home of Greg Prince in Potomac, Maryland. A plan was created to more vigorously recruit new members and create on-line support, reach out to allies, and foster an earnest, non-confrontational dialogue with LDS leaders, with new messaging that emphasized full engagement with our faith as Mormons. Affirmation, among other things, organized a support group (dubbed "Prepare") for church-active and believing LGBTQ Mormons. It welcomed (and began to create resources for) individuals in "mixed-orientation marriages." It encouraged an ethic of "self-defining" and welcomed individuals who didn't identify with LGBTQ identities (such as individuals identifying as "same-sex attracted") and invited them to participate. Finally, it adopted a new name for the organization that emphasized recognition of bi and trans participation and emphasized the growing role of family and allies: "Affirmation: LGBT Mormons, Families & Friends."

The result of the rebranding and the new focus on constructive engagement with the Church was dramatic. A dynamic new leadership team came to the fore, willing to make incredible sacrifices to build the organization in new ways. Between 2012 and 2015, attendance at the

Affirmation Annual International Conference increased from around 100 to over 600. Conferences began to be attended by hundreds of heterosexual allies and – more significantly – growing numbers of youth. A small but significant number of LGBTQ Mormons turning to Affirmation were LGBTQ converts to Mormonism, individuals drawn to its teachings and ideals in spite of the challenges related to Church policy regarding LGBTQ people. Affirmation saw unprecedented growth internationally, with the revival of defunct organizations in Mexico and Chile, and the creation of new organizations in Argentina, Peru, Brazil, Colombia, Dominican Republic, and Ecuador. Within half a decade, two dozen Latin American chapters had come into being. A defunct UK organization was revived, with outreach happening in Spain, Germany, and Scandinavia. Social media connected thousands of new LGBTQ Mormons to the organization. Worldwide, Affirmation saw a twenty-fold growth in participation in conferences, retreats, and local gatherings. Affirmation began more earnest fundraising efforts, and saw its budget increase from less than $50,000 per year in 2012 to over $300,000 in 2018. "Big tent" LGBTQ Mormon organizing, in creating a space where LDS faith and LGBTQ identity could coexist, was resulting in a complete transformation of Affirmation's work and community.

Just as MBB and its leadership were criticized for being too lenient with the Church, and were accused of playing into the Church's hands or even of being operatives of the Church, Affirmation's new leadership was accused of betraying LGBTQ Mormons. The bitterness among some former leaders of Affirmation was intense. Baseless accusations were made that Affirmation leaders were on the payroll of the Church or that they were puppets of the Church. Ex-Mormons derisively referred to it as "Affirmation 2.0." However, unlike Evergreen, Affirmation did not need to abandon its premises in order to renew itself—it only needed to return to its original premises, premises it had (understandably) abandoned in the 1980s when the organization faced intense isolation from mainstream Mormonism and members of the LGBTQ Mormon community were dealing with intense, traumatic rejection by congregations and families.

It wasn't that Mormons didn't still hold homo- and trans-phobic attitudes in the 2010s. But shifts in attitude were observable among rank and file Mormons. LGBTQ Mormons in the 2010s were less likely to be excommunicated just for coming out, were more likely to encounter empathetic responses from Church members and leaders. Some stakes (such as San Francisco and Oakland) were implementing "no excommunication" policies, and were inviting their LGBTQ members to come back to church (Mosman, 2012). Increasing numbers of wards and stakes throughout the Church were sponsoring educational forums where LGBTQ members were invited to come and share their stories. These kinds of changes, accompanied by the kinder, gentler rhetoric of general authorities over the previous decade made Affirmation's more hopeful, optimistic approach appealing to a growing number of LGBTQ Mormons and their families.

While this was happening, an intensifying public political debate over same-sex marriage and transgender rights was creating rising tensions within the Church and rifts between liberal and conservative Mormons both in the Church as well as in independent Mormon intellectual, social, and service communities. After Prop 8, Church leaders continued making statements condemning same-sex marriage (Stack, 2010; Reeser, 2018). As cases involving freedom to marry in the U.S., including cases in Utah, made their way through the appellate court system on their way to the Supreme Court, the LDS Church filed *amicus* briefs in support of their position opposing same-sex marriage (*Church News*, 2015). After the *Obergefell v. Hodges* ruling in 2015, in which the U.S. Supreme Court declared same-sex marriage bans unconstitutional, the Church initially responded by sending out a letter to LDS congregations reaffirming the Church's position against same-sex marriage, and clarifying that LDS leaders were not to perform same-sex weddings, and chapels could not to be used as a venue for them (Woodruff, 2015).

Then, on November 5, 2015, a change in the LDS Handbook of Instructions was leaked on social media. The change named same-sex marriage a form of "apostasy," and denied rites of blessing and baptism to children of same-sex couples (Shill, 2015; Walch, 2015). This revelation (and subsequent public statements affirming the new policy) sent shock waves throughout LGBTQ Mormon communities everywhere, both liberal and conservative (Gustav-Wrathall, 2016).

MBB experienced mass resignations of members of their steering committee. About half of Affirmation's membership on the eve of the November 2015 policy were actively attending the LDS Church; and within one year of the policy change, half or more of those had dropped out, leaving only 20–25 percent of Affirmation's membership still active in the Church (Gustav-Wrathall, 2016). A rising tide of anger at and criticism of the Church among members and leaders of Affirmation caused some of the remaining Church-active members and leaders to withdraw from the organization. LGBTQ Mormons in every organization, from the most conservative to the most liberal were expressing hurt, anger, and despair. North Star leaders were reporting as much emotional turmoil in their organization as Affirmation leaders.

The two ally organizations most closely aligned with the Church, ALL Arizona and The Hearth actually experienced an influx of membership. Large numbers of mainstream Latter-day Saints were reporting feelings of hurt and confusion over the policy and were eager to learn more and to process difficult emotions. Jeff Wise, founder of The Hearth, reported that initially when he had approached his stake president about organizing monthly events so frequently, his stake president had resisted, but then changed his mind after the November 2015 Handbook policy change. Affirmation also, in the first year after the policy, experienced an increase in attendance at its conferences and an increase in donations from heterosexual Mormons who wanted to do something to support LGBTQ Mormons.

"The Policy" had created a paradoxical situation. On the one hand, it seemed to intensify the stigma attached to homosexuality in the Church by associating it with the worse sin of "apostasy," and by excluding from membership children raised by homosexuals. It was driving LGBTQ members away from the Church. On the other hand, it heightened the disconnect between the institutional LDS Church and the broader culture, intensifying a hunger on the part of mainstream Mormons to "build bridges" and understand. More mainstream Mormons than ever before in the history of the Church were ready for and wanting dialogue. The question was: Would there be any LGBTQ people left in the Church to engage in one with them?

The sense of urgency about organizing support for LGBTQ Mormons was heightened with the growing awareness of a dramatic increase in suicide among LGBTQ Mormon youth (Walch and Collins, 2016). Suicide had long been recognized as a problem among LGBTQ Mormons (Hilton, Fellingham, and Lyon, 2002). But anecdotal reports of dozens of youth suicides in late 2015 and early 2016 were confirmed by subsequent data to be part of a dramatic trend of a tripling in LGBTQ teen suicides between 2012 and 2016. Though there was a nationwide increase in suicide, nowhere was it as dramatic as in the Intermountain West, particularly in Utah (Parkinson, 2018). As many as 70 percent of LGBTQ Mormons were experiencing symptoms of post-traumatic stress disorder (PTSD) (Simmons, 2017). In response to the sense of crisis emerging from the awareness of this problem, in 2016 Stephenie Larsen opened the Encircle House in Provo, Utah, as an LGBTQ youth drop-in center. Their slogan was "No Sides, Only Love." In addition to providing a safe community space for LGBTQ youth, with a variety of social activities and an "Elevate" speaking series featuring "successful, thriving, inspirational LGBTQ+ individuals with diverse backgrounds and life journeys," they also provided free counseling services (Williams, 2017). In 2018, Encircle opened up a second community center in Salt Lake (Smart, 2018).

I became president of Affirmation in January 2016, a few months after the Affirmation community had been shaken by the November 2015 LDS Handbook policy change. I had run for president on a platform of engaging with Mormonism and with the LDS Church, making space for faith, and continuing dialogue. I was, and remain, active in my LDS ward and a "practicing" Mormon, to the extent possible for one who is also in a legal same-sex marriage and excommunicated. I was opposed by two candidates who had left the Church and were eager to increase the distance between Affirmation and the Church, particularly in the devastating wake of the 2015 policy. Though I won the election by a wide margin, the following years were characterized by increased tension over the "middle path" of Affirmation, with increasing numbers of members and leaders calling for a public divorce between Affirmation and the Church. Nevertheless, the organization thrived both financially and in terms of participation as we maintained the tension of that "middle" space.

Former Mormons who were the most alienated from the LDS Church felt abandoned by Affirmation, and no longer saw it as an organization that could serve their needs. Some of these gravitated to on-line groups like "Q-Saints," which have been harshly critical of Affirmation and the LDS Church. Still, Affirmation was serving growing numbers of former Mormons as well as active, believing Mormons, and "in-between." A major rhetorical shift in Affirmation in response to the November 2015 policy was to focus on healing trauma and preventing suicide. Between 2017 and the present, that emphasis came to replace the earlier emphasis on celebrating the possibility of being "LGBT *and* Mormon" and "following the Spirit."

In April 2019, the Church of Jesus Christ of Latter-day Saints announced that the November 2015 policy on gay families was being "updated." Both of the features of that policy—labeling legally married same-sex couples as "apostates" and denying membership to children of same-sex couples—were officially retracted. Despite this news, stories shared on the Affirmation website in response to the retraction of the 2015 policy overwhelmingly rehearsed stories of pain and trauma caused by the policy. Nathan R. Kitchen, who became president of Affirmation in January of 2019, has been harshly critical of the Church's treatment of its LGBTQ members. He published an Op Ed in the *Salt Lake Tribune* describing a "rainbow stained-glass ceiling" in the Church (Kitchen, 2019). It remains to be seen whether Affirmation will be able to maintain a dynamic tension between LDS faith and LGBTQ identity, or whether the scales will start to tip in a more post-Mormon direction again, and if so, what the impact will be for the organization.

After Evergreen closed its doors in 2014, there was an influx of former Evergreen International members and leaders into North Star. Some observed a conservative swing within North Star, and a growing focus on conversion therapy paradigms and approaches. In 2017, the North Star Board appointed Bennett Borden as president, and Bennett's wife Becky to the board of North Star. Bennett was a former HRC (Human Rights Campaign) attorney and a former member and activist within Affirmation. At first this looked like a conservative shift in the direction of conversion therapy. Both Bennett and Becky had been in previous same-sex marriages that they ultimately dissolved in order to marry. However, in his keynote address at the 2018 North Star conference, Bennett spoke about the special identities and the special callings of "gay and lesbian" sons and daughters of God. At a key moment in his address, he spoke of being "gay and Mormon and proud" to enthusiastic applause from conference attendees (Borden, 2018). This type of "gay pride" rhetoric would have been unthinkable in North Star only a few short years earlier. It was a sign that categories were shifting, and that the old days of complete rejection of LGBTQ identities were definitively gone.

As of the writing of this article, rapid and unpredictable change is the rule in relation to LGBTQ issues in the Church of Jesus Christ of Latter-day Saints. It is likely that the most interesting aspects of the story are still ahead of us.

The past, present, and future of Mormon LGBTQ organizing

Starting in the middle of the twentieth century, homosexuality came onto the radar of American society. It went from being virtually ignored to becoming an arena of intense struggle, both in the larger society and more intensely within religious communities. At stake in this struggle over the definition of homosexuality was the question of whether the lived experience of LGBTQ people could be factored into a collective understanding of the nature of sexuality and family broadly defined, and if so, how. The LGBTQ movement, which was already under way in the 1950s, gained urgency after the Stonewall event of 1969 and through the AIDS crisis of the 1980s. The legalization of same-sex marriage in the United States caused a hardening of lines within Mormonism, and high-profile LDS Church support of Prop 8 in California followed by the promulgation of the November 2015 Handbook changes was accompanied by a new suicide crisis among LGBTQ Mormons. Though in some ways these latest crises provoked an intensified willingness to engage in dialogue at all levels of the LDS Church and community, LGBTQ Mormon community organizing has continued to be plagued by bifurcation, by the belief on the part of both conservative Mormons and secular LGBTQ rights activists, that being Mormon is somehow inherently at odds with being LGBTQ, that you cannot be both. Yet, what has driven LGBTQ Mormon community organizing has ultimately been a deep yearning for integration of Mormon faith and spirituality with LGBTQ identities and relationships.

Organizations have waxed and waned, come and gone, either as institutional shifts in focus made their philosophy and approaches to the issue obsolete (such as Evergreen), or as frustration led activists to abandon an intersectional space in favor of an anti-Mormon space (such as Mormons for Equality). LGBTQ Mormon organizations tended to thrive when they focused on integration and dialog. They were attractive to believing members, and thus attracted more heterosexual allies. They were "safer" for LGBTQ Mormons who were still early in the process of coming out. And they responded to fundamental yearnings of LGBTQ Mormons for meaning and a sense of belonging within the community. For many LGBTQ individuals "Mormonism" provided answers to fundamental questions about life and about human nature and destiny (that we are children of God, acquiring a physical body and moral attributes so that we can be more like God) and a methodology for finding answers to difficult questions or facing life's existential dilemmas (through belief in "personal revelation"). As organizations abandoned the quest for integration and dialog, the "faithful" stopped seeing them as a resource. The disaffected, on the other hand, sometimes stuck around for the community, and appreciated being able to affiliate with and empathize with other "ex-Mormons." But many of these would drop out as well, not feeling inclined to affiliate with an organization that had any Mormon connection at all, and turning instead for support to resources within the secular LGBTQ community.

Nearly seven decades of LGBTQ activism—mostly LGBTQ individuals telling their stories and demonstrating the inadequacy of medieval theology or Freudian psychology to explain sexual or gender difference—has led to an erosion of the prevailing religious consensus. Growing numbers of churches and religious people are coming to the conclusion that they got homosexuality and transgender wrong, and are revising their views. A growing number of Protestant denominations, for example, are ordaining openly LGBT ministers and giving their blessing to same-sex marriage. Within the Church of Jesus Christ of Latter-day Saints, the subject remains emotionally charged, with endemic conflict resulting from the rise and success of the marriage equality movement in the United States. Until same-sex marriage became a viable political issue in the 1990s, there were two LGBTQ Mormon organizations: one conservative, denying LGBTQ identity and promoting conversion therapy, and one progressive, affirming the validity of LGBTQ Mormon identity and experience. As growing numbers of Mormons have come to support same-sex marriage, we've seen a multiplication of organizations seeking to address these issues, with dramatically increased numbers of heterosexual Mormons getting involved in organizations focused on understanding and listening to their LGBTQ brothers and sisters, sons and daughters. In a way, a growing disconnect between official policy and the views in the pews have been driving a new activism among Mormons to bridge the heartbreaking seeming chasm between LDS faith and human experience around this issue.

The "Mormon way" on this, as on any, issue would be grounded in a search for new revelation. Surveys of LGBTQ Mormons have documented hundreds seeking and finding the answers to their personal dilemmas through prayer and "personal revelation" (Dehlin et al., 2015). When I met with LDS apostle D. Todd Christofferson in 2013, I discussed the possibility of doctrinal change through new revelation. In his answer to my question, he paraphrased Jacob 4:10, from the Book of Mormon: "Seek not to counsel the Lord, but to take counsel from his hand." I responded, referencing 1 Nephi 15:8, "Yes, but we're allowed to ask the Lord questions, right?" He smiled, and replied, "Yes."

Note

1 At the time, it was common for LGBT Mormon activists and community organizers to use pseudonyms.

References

Adam, B., 1987. *The Rise of a Gay and Lesbian Movement*. Boston, MA: G.K. Hall & Co.
Affirmation Gay and Lesbian Mormons General Charter, 1979. Affirmation Gay and Lesbian Mormons. https://web.archive.org/web/20000301144936/www.affirmation.org/ (accessed July 21, 2019).
Affirmation: LGBTQ Mormons, Families & Friends, 2017. Our History. Affirmation: LGBTQ Mormon, Families & Friends. https://affirmation.org/who-we-are/our-history/ (accessed September 30, 2018).
Affirmation: United Methodists for Lesbian, Gay, Bisexual, Transgender and Queer Concerns, 2011. About Us. Affirmation: United Methodists for Lesbian, Gay, Bisexual, Transgender and Queer Concerns. www.umaffirm.org/site/about-us/1-about-us. (accessed September 30, 2018).
Anderson, D., 1999. A History of Dialogue, Part One: The Early Years, 1965–1971. *Dialogue: A Journal of Mormon Thought* 32(2): 15–66.
Anzjøn, M., 2019. Interview with John Gustav-Wrathall. February 26.
Arizona ALL, 2018. Home page. www.allarizona.org/.(accessed July 21, 2019).
Ballard, M.R., 2006. The Sacred Responsibilities of Parenthood. *Ensign*. March.
Bérubé, A., 1990. *Coming Out Under Fire: The History of Gay Men and Women in World War II*. New York: The Free Press.
Blair, R., 2013. *Gay and Christian?—You Are Not Alone*. Evangelicals Concerned Inc. http://ecinc.org/. (accessed September 30, 2018).
Borden, B., 2018. Awake and Arise: A Call to Action. Keynote Address. 2018 North Star Conference, Provo, Utah, March 16. https://youtu.be/_dUpvdXNLiE. (accessed August 27, 2018).
Bullough, B., and Bullough, V., 1977. Lesbianism in the 1920s and 1930s: A Newfound Study. *Signs: Journal of Women in Culture and Society* 2(4): 895–904.
Carter, D., 2004. *Stonewall: The Riots that Sparked the Gay Revolution*. New York: St. Martin's Press.
Chambers, A.M., 2018. Exodus Int'l President to the Gay Community: "We're Sorry." The Chambers Foundation. http://alanchambers.org/exodus-intl-president-to-the-gay-community-were-sorry/. (accessed October 1, 2018).
Church of Jesus Christ of Latter-day Saints Newsroom, 2006. Interview with Elder Dallin H. Oaks and Elder Lance B. Wickman: Same-Gender Attraction. Church of Jesus Christ of Latter-day Saints Newsroom. https://newsroom.churchofjesuschrist.org/article/interview-oaks-wickman-same-gender-attraction (accessed July 21, 2019).
Church News, 2015. Church Signs Amicus Brief Filed on Marriage. April 21. www.churchofjesuschrist.org/church/news/church-signs-amicus-brief-filed-on-marriage?lang=eng. (accessed July 21, 2019).

Circling the Wagons, 2016. Home page. http://circlingthewagons.org/.(accessed July 21, 2019).
Dehlin, J.P., Galliher, R.V., Bradshaw, W.S., and Crowell, K.A., 2015. Navigating Sexual and Religious Identity Conflict: A Mormon Perspective. *Identity: An International Journal of Theory and Research* 15(1): 1–22.
Dignity USA, 2007. Highlights of Dignity USA's History. Dignity USA. www.dignityusa.org/history (accessed September 30, 2018).
Duberman, M., 1993. *Stonewall*. New York: Penguin Books.
Dubrowski, P.R., 2015. The Ferguson v. JONAH Verdict and a Path Towards a National Cessation of Gay-to-Straight Conversion Therapy. *Northwestern University Law Review* 110(77): 77–117.
Evergreen International, 2004. About Us. Archived from the original on December 9. https://web.archive.org/web/20041209130109/www.evergreeninternational.org/about_us.htm (accessed August 26, 2019).
Fadel, L., 2019. Activists and Suicide Prevention Groups Seek Bans on Conversion Therapy for Minors. NPR. www.npr.org/2019/04/26/716416764/activists-and-suicide-prevention-groups-seek-bans-on-conversion-therapy-for-mino (accessed July 21, 2019).
First Presidency of the Church of Jesus Christ of Latter-day Saints, 1995. The Family: A Proclamation to the World. Church of Jesus Christ of Latter-day Saints. www.churchofjesuschrist.org/study/manual/the-family-a-proclamation-to-the-world/the-family-a-proclamation-to-the-world?lang=eng (accessed July 21, 2019).
GLAAD, 2009. Mormons Voice Support for Salt Lake City Anti-discrimination Law. GLAAD. November 13. www.glaad.org/2009/11/13/mormons-voice-support-for-salt-lake-city-anti-discrimination-law. (accessed July 22, 2019).
Gustav-Wrathall, J.D., 2011a. Kirtland. Young Stranger Blog. September 19. http://youngstranger.blogspot.com/2011/09/kirtland.html (accessed July 22, 2019).
Gustav-Wrathall, J.D., 2011b. On Keeping the Spirit. Young Stranger Blog. September 21. http://youngstranger.blogspot.com/2011/09/on-keeping-spirit.html (accessed July 22, 2019).
Gustav-Wrathall, J.D., 2016. Results of the Affirmation Survey on the Impact of the LDS Policy on Gay Families. Affirmation. https://affirmation.org/results-of-the-affirmation-survey-on-the-impact-of-the-lds-policy-on-gay-families/ (accessed July 21, 2019).
Haldeman, D.C., 1999. The Pseudo-science of Sexual Orientation Conversion Therapy. *Angles: The Policy Journal of the Institute for Gay and Lesbian Strategic Studies* 4(1): 1–4.
Harrison, P., 2017. Marching with Mormons for Equality. *HuffPost*. December 6. www.huffpost.com/entry/marching-with-mormons-for_b_10693284 (accessed July 21, 2019).
Hearth, 2019. About. The Hearth. www.ldshearth.org/new-page-1 (accessed July 21, 2019).
Hilton, S.C., Fellingham, G.W., and Lyon, J.L., 2002. Suicide Rates and Religious Commitment in Young Adult Males in Utah. *American Journal of Epidemiology* 155(5): 413–19.
I'll Walk With You, 2019. Home page. http://ldswalkwithyou.org/ (accessed July 21, 2019).
James, S.D., 2011. Mormon "Gay Cure" Study Used Electric Shocks against Homosexual Feelings. *ABC News*. https://abcnews.go.com/Health/mormon-gay-cures-reparative-therapies-shock-today/story?id=13240700 (accessed July 21, 2019).
Janson, J., 2008. *Lutherans Concerned for Gay People: The Beginning*. San Francisco, CA: Lutherans Concerned/North America.
Jenkins, C. et al., 1978. Prologue: An Examination of the Mormon Attitude towards Homosexuality. http://prologuegaymormons.com/the-book/ (accessed July 21, 2019).
Johnson, D.K., 2006. *The Lavender Scare: The Cold War Persecution of Gays and Lesbians in the Federal Government*. Chicago, IL: University of Chicago Press.
Kacala, A., 2019. The Dragon Dads Are an Online Community Offering Support to Fathers of LGBTQ Kids. *Hornet*. July 3. https://hornet.com/stories/dragon-dads-lgbtq-kids (accessed July 21, 2019).
Kimball, S.W., 1969. *The Miracle of Forgiveness*. Salt Lake City, UT: Bookcraft.
Kitchen, N., 2019. Nathan Kitchen: The Rainbow Stained-Glass Ceiling in the LDS Church. *Salt Lake Tribune*. August 23. www.sltrib.com/opinion/commentary/2019/08/25/nathan-kitchen-rainbow/ (accessed on August 23, 2019).
Kohl, D., 2019. *A Curious and Peculiar People: A History of the GLBTQ Community and the Metropolitan Community Church*. One Spirit Press.
Larry King Live, 2004. A Conversation with Gordon B. Hinckley, President of the Church of Jesus Christ of Latter Day Saints. *CNN*. http://transcripts.cnn.com/TRANSCRIPTS/0412/26/lkl.01.html (accessed October 1, 2018).

Lefevor G.T., Sorrell, S.A., Kappers, G., Plunk, A., Schow, R.L., Rosik, C.H., and Beckstead, A.L., 2019. Same-Sex Attracted, Not LGBQ: The Associations of Sexual Identity Labeling on Religiousness, Sexuality, and Health Among Mormons. *Journal of Homosexuality* Mar 8: 1–25.

Lyon, J., 2012. Mormons March in Gay Pride Parade to Build Bridges. *Salt Lake Tribune*. June 8. https://archive.sltrib.com/article.php?id=54225023&itype=CMSID (accessed July 21, 2019).

MacMurray, V.D., 1977. Warning: Labels Can Be Hazardous to Your Health. *Dialogue* 10(4): 130–32.

Mama Dragons, 2016. The Beginnings. Mama Dragons. https://mamadragons.org/our-origins/our-origins-our-origins-2/ (accessed July 21, 2019).

McBride, M.F., 1976. Effect of Visual Stimuli in Electric Aversion Therapy. Dissertation, Brigham Young University.

Mormons Building Bridges, 2019. Home page. http://mormonsbuildingbridges.org/ (accessed July 21, 2019).

Mormons for Equality, 2014. About us. https://web.archive.org/web/20141120215150/www.mormonsformarriageequality.org/about (accessed July 22, 2019).

Mosman, M., 2012. Learn to Labor and to Wait. Talk delivered at the Circling the Wagons Conference in San Francisco. August 12. http://mitchmayne.blogspot.com/2012/08/circling-wagons-mormon-lgbt-conference_14.html (accessed August 28, 2019).

North Star International, 2007. Who We Are. northstarlds.org. Archived from the original on October 6. https://web.archive.org/web/20071006161857/http://northstarlds.org/whoweare.php (accessed August 26, 2019).

NPR, 2012. Mormon Church Launches Website on "Same-Sex Attraction." *NPR*. December 6. www.npr.org/sections/thetwo-way/2012/12/06/166687164/mormon-church-launches-website-on-same-sex-attraction (accessed July 22, 2019).

O'Brian, T.J., 1993. You Are Not Alone: A Plea for Understanding the Homosexual Condition. *Dialogue* 26(3): 119–40.

O'Donovan, C., 2004. "The Abominable and Detestable Crime Against Nature": A Revised History of Homosexuality and Mormonism, 1840–1980. www.connellodonovan.com/lgbtmormons.html (accessed September 30, 2018).

Packer, B.K., 1978. "To the One": Address Given to the Twelve Stake Fireside, Brigham Young University. The Church of Jesus Christ of Latter-day Saints.

Parkinson, D., 2018. Utah's Escalating Suicide Crisis and LDS LGBTQ Despair. Rational Faiths Mormon Blog. https://rationalfaiths.com/utahs-escalating-suicide-crisis-lds-lgbtq-despair/ (accessed October 1, 2018).

Prince, G.A., 2019. *Gay Rights and the Mormon Church: Intended Actions, Unintended Consequences*. Salt Lake City, UT: The University of Utah Press.

Quinn, D.M., 1996. *Same-Sex Dynamics among Nineteenth-Century Americans: A Mormon Example*. Urbana and Chicago, IL: University of Illinois Press.

Rainbow Baptists, 2015. Who We Are. Rainbow Baptists. www.rainbowbaptists.org/ambaptists.htm (accessed September 30, 2018).

Reconciliation and Growth Project, 2017. Home page. https://reconciliationandgrowth.org/ (accessed July 21, 2019).

Reeser, A., 2018. Oaks Doubles Down on LDS Church Position on Gay Marriage, Gender Identity. *ABC 4 Utah*. October 6. www.abc4.com/news/local-news/oaks-doubles-down-on-lds-church-position-on-gay-marriage-gender-identity/ (accessed July 21, 2019).

Romboy, D., 2015. LDS Church, LGBT Advocates Back Anti-discrimination, Religious Rights Bill. *Deseret News*. March 5. www.deseretnews.com/article/865623399/Utah-lawmakers-unveil-anti-discrimination-religious-rights-legislation.html (accessed July 22, 2019).

Schow, R., 2005. *Go Forward*. LDS Resources video. www.youtube.com/watch?v=54QR_5k6qA8 (accessed on August 26, 2019).

Schow, W., 1990. Homosexuality, Mormon Doctrine, and Christianity: A Father's Perspective. *Sunstone* 75 (February): 9–12.

Shill, A., 2015. LDS Church Reaffirms Doctrine of Marriage, Updates Policies on Families in Same-Sex Marriages. *Deseret News*. November 5. www.deseretnews.com/article/865640835/Church-updates-policies-on-families-in-same-sex-marriages.html

Simmons, B.W., 2017. Coming Out Mormon: An Examination of Religious Orientation, Spiritual Trauma, and PTSD among Mormon and Ex-Mormon LGBTQQA Adults. Dissertation, University of Georgia.

Smart, C., 2018. Encircle, Where Families and Their LGBT Children Can Find Therapy and a Sense of Community, Is Coming to Salt Lake City. *Salt Lake Tribune*. February 5. www.sltrib.com/

news/2018/02/03/encircle-where-families-and-their-lgbt-children-can-find-therapy-and-a-sense-of-community-is-coming-to-salt-lake-city/ (accessed July 21, 2019).

Stack, P.F., 2001. *Sunstone*: Paying the Price of Intellectualism. Beliefnet. www.beliefnet.com/faiths/christianity/latter-day-saints/2001/08/sunstone-paying-the-price-of-intellectualism.aspx (accessed October 1, 2018).

Stack, P.F., 2010. Packer Talk Jibes with LDS Stance after Tweak. *Salt Lake Tribune*. October 25, 2010. https://archive.sltrib.com/article.php?id=50440474&itype=cmsid (accessed July 21, 2019).

Stack, P.F., 2014a. Longtime Support Group for Gay Mormons Shuts Down. *Salt Lake Tribune*. January 14. https://archive.sltrib.com/article.php?id=57344806&itype=cmsid (accessed July 21, 2019).

Stack, P.F., 2014b. Where Mormonism's "September Six" Are Now. *Salt Lake Tribune*. June 16. https://archive.sltrib.com/article.php?id=58060420&itype=CMSID (accessed July 21, 2019).

Stout, R.J., 1987. Sin and Sexuality: Psychobiology and the Development of Homosexuality. *Dialogue* 20(2): 31–43.

Thomas, O., 2013. Interview with John Gustav-Wrathall. January 2013.

Walch, T., 2015. Elder Christofferson Explains Updated LDS Church Policies on Same-Sex Marriage and Children. *Deseret News*. November 6. www.deseretnews.com/article/865640934/Elder-Christofferson-explains-updated-LDS-Church-policies-on-same-sex-marriage-and-children.html.

Walch, T., and Collins, L., 2016. LDS Church Leaders Mourn Reported Deaths in Mormon LGBT Community. *Deseret News*. www.deseretnews.com/article/865646414/LDS-Church-leaders-mourn-reported-deaths-in-Mormon-LGBT-community.html (accessed October 1, 2018).

Wilcox, K., 2011–2015. Far Between Movie Project. http://farbetweenmovie.com/ (accessed July 21, 2019).

Wilcox, M., 2001. Of Markets and Missions: The Early History of the Universal Fellowship of Metropolitan Community Churches. *Religion and American Culture: A Journal of Interpretation* 11(1), 83–108.

Williams, L., 2017. All for Love and Love for All: Provo's Stephenie Larsen Encircles LGBTQ Youth. *Utah Valley 360*. July 8. https://utahvalley360.com/2017/07/08/all-for-love-and-love-for-all-provos-stephenie-larsen-encircles-lgbtq-youth/ (accessed July 22, 2019).

Woodruff, D., 2015. LDS Church Issues Letter to Members in Response to Same-Sex Marriage Ruling. *KUTV*. June 30. https://kutv.com/news/local/lds-church-issues-letter-to-members-in-response-to-same-sex-marriage-ruling (accessed July 21, 2019).

Wright, J., 2003. Gay Mormons. *The Herald Journal*. July 27. www.hjnews.com/archives-2/article_7c8941a8-7250-5034-a959-d4fdb267badf.html (accessed August 26, 2019).

Zauzmer, J., 2016. "Mormon and Gay"? The Church's New Message Is That You Can Be Both. *The Washington Post*. October 25. www.washingtonpost.com/news/acts-of-faith/wp/2016/10/25/mormon-and-gay-the-mormon-churchs-new-message-is-that-you-can-be-both (accessed July 22, 2019).

Further reading

Dehlin, J.P., Galliher, R.V., Bradshaw, W.S., and Crowell, K.A., 2015. Navigating Sexual and Religious Identity Conflict: A Mormon Perspective. *Identity: An International Journal of Theory and Research* 15(1): 1–22.
This study of religious conflict among LGBT Mormons used a large sample (about 1,600). Though it has been criticized for its sampling methods, it was one of the first really in-depth, scholarly examinations of the challenges faced by LGBTQ Mormons.

Prince, G.A., 2019. *Gay Rights and the Mormon Church: Intended Actions, Unintended Consequences*. Salt Lake City, UT: The University of Utah Press.
Examines the history from the 1950s to the present of attitudes toward gender and sexual minorities in the Church of Jesus Christ of Latter-day Saints, including the Church's political involvement with gay and transgender rights.

Quinn, D.M., 1996. *Same-Sex Dynamics among Nineteenth-Century Americans: A Mormon Example*. Urbana and Chicago, IL: University of Illinois Press.
Examines the history of LGBTQ people's involvement in the Church of Jesus Christ of Latter-day Saints from the Church's foundation in the 1830s until the dawning of LGBTQ rights movement in the 1940s.

Schow, R., Schow, W., and Raynes, M., 1991. *Peculiar People: Mormons and Same-Sex Orientation*. Salt Lake City, UT: Signature Books.
In its day a groundbreaking anthology that began to address the theological, social, and cultural challenges faced by gay and lesbian members of the Church of Jesus Christ of Latter-day Saints.

17
MORMONISM, GENDER, AND ART

Mary Campbell

For $39.50 plus tax and shipping, the Church of Jesus Christ of Latter-day Saints' official bookstore, Deseret Book, will send you a decorative copy of the church's statement "The Family: A Proclamation to the World." "Family Proclamation (14×17 Framed Art) by the Cambridge Collection," Deseret Book's website announces, "Only ten left in stock—order now." The site doesn't provide much additional information about the Proclamation ("Production Description: This product has no description," the website flatly states) (Deseret Book, 2016). That said, most Latter-day Saints wouldn't need any. First delivered as an address by church prophet and president Gordon B. Hinckley at the 1995 General Meeting of the Mormon women's Relief Society organization, the Proclamation has since become a touchstone among Latter-day Saints. In my experience, it's the rare church member who isn't familiar with the text's declaration that "gender is an essential characteristic of individual premortal, mortal, and eternal identity and purpose," its insistence that "[b]y divine design, fathers are to preside over their families in love and righteousness and are responsible to provide the necessities of life," while "[m]others are primarily responsible for the nurture of their children" (First Presidency, 1995).

As Deseret Book's mention of its dwindling stock suggests, ornamental copies of the Proclamation have even become a standard part of Mormon visual culture. Stepping into an LDS family's living room, it's common to find a "Framed Art" version of the document hanging on the wall next to a large family portrait. When I was growing up in Salt Lake City, Utah, almost all of my friends—most of whom were Mormon—had pictures like these hanging in their houses (Figure 17.1). To my non-LDS ("Gentile") eyes, they seemed largely the same: studio photographs of a smiling husband and wife surrounded by five or six children, everyone looking happy and glossy and well groomed. Sometimes the photographs were printed on canvas, and sometimes they were displayed on formal easels, but they were always elaborately framed. Because my friends were relatively well-off, their parents commissioned these portraits from Busath Photography—as LDS families of a certain class still do. "You can't live [in Salt Lake's] East Bench [neighborhood] as a successful Mormon without having one of those Busath family portraits," the Utah painter and filmmaker Nathan Florence recently observed. "It's your family brand" (pers. comm. October 16, 2018).

As this chapter discusses, pictures like these also form a key part of a larger LDS brand. For the better part of two centuries, the institutional church and individual Latter-day Saints alike have turned to images and objects to promote the decidedly separate-spheres conception of

Figure 17.1 Anonymous portrait of an LDS family, Busath Photography, Salt Lake City, Utah, ca. 1989

gender that animates not simply the Proclamation, but the Mormon faith in general. Whether high art or pop cultural, such photographs, paintings, and sculptures have repeatedly enshrined the church's teachings that human beings are incapable of escaping their identity as male or female but must instead adhere to a conservative set of heterosexual (if not necessarily monogamous) gender roles in the afterlife (if not always in the here and now). In the process, the Saints have repeatedly marked themselves as the deeply photogenic standard-bearers of traditional family values.

At the same time, the visual has historically provided a particularly fertile site of what one might call LDS gender dissent—a place where certain Saints have struggled, whether intentionally or not, to exceed their church's vision of what a man or woman can be and should do. "There's something terribly tragic that not only Mormonism but most religions have such a hard time with the odd ducks," the LDS artist Trevor Southey remarked before his death in 2015 (*The Mormons*, 2007). Although the history of Mormonism, gender, and art comprises much more than a line-up of such peculiar people, they have certainly added to the richness of the field. They figure prominently here.

This is probably a good moment for a few clarifications, if only to avoid a flurry of emails updating me on Southey's standing within the church. I am fully aware that the LDS leadership excommunicated Southey in the early 1980s, after he abandoned its urgings to "become that wonder of wonders, a real man" (Southey, 2001) and instead accepted himself as a gay man. I also know that Southey later rejected Mormon officials' offer to rebaptize him, on the ground that for him to rejoin the faith would to be betray those who looked up to him as a gay role model. As he later explained, "through my work bearing testimony to all these younger people ... I [had become] a leader without intending to be so, and I had a responsibility to them" (*Art & Belief*, 2018).

It's a decidedly Mormon phrase, "bearing testimony," one you regularly hear Latter-day Saints use to describe the act of publicly sharing their conviction that their religion is true. The fact that Southey reached for this language in the context of such a different truth is one of the reasons I characterize him as an LDS artist. Regardless of his formal standing within the church, or even his religious beliefs, Southey was culturally Mormon; like so many people who have spent meaningful time in, or maybe even around, the Church of Jesus Christ of Latter-day Saints, he was fundamentally shaped by its ideas and modes of expression, verbal and otherwise. Just as my definition of "Mormon art" is expansive enough to include Busath portraits and $39.50 Proclamations, it makes room for images and objects created by such people. In this context, my argument depends less on whether a particular work qualifies as high art or was produced by someone who would have qualified for a temple recommend than on whether it deepens our understanding of LDS culture and theology.

The LDS family brand

According to *The Oxford Handbook of Mormonism*, "a pair of portraits of Joseph and his wife Emma may be regarded as the first masterpieces of Mormon art" (Anderson, 2015, p. 478). Generally attributed to the Gentile artist David W. Rogers (1807–1884), these paintings date to roughly 1842 and provide "handsome frontal views of the formally dressed couple" (Anderson, 2015, p. 478). The first LDS prophet and his wife appear as a matched marital set in these pictures, each dressed entirely in black and white, each seated in front of a slice of blank wall and a clouded landscape, each lifting a single hand as if to call attention to the marriage band encircling their respective fingers (Figures 17.2 and 17.3).[1] We know the pictures were intended to hang as a pair, most likely on the third floor of the LDS temple in Nauvoo, Illinois. We also know they never made it to this destination. Rocked by the crises that Joseph's 1844 murder unleashed within the church, Emma kept the two canvases with her at the Smith family home.

Figure 17.2 David W. Rogers (attributed), *Emma Smith*, ca. 1842
Courtesy, Community of Christ Library-Archives, Independence, Missouri.

Figure 17.3 David W. Rogers (attributed), *Joseph Smith Jr.*, ca. 1842

At some point she moved them from the family parlor to her bedroom, where they hung until shortly before her death (L. McKay, pers. comm. November 14, 2018).

Companion portraits like these were common in America during the early 1840s, as they had been since the colonial period. What weren't so ubiquitous were the actual facts of the Smiths' domestic situation. By early 1842, Joseph had married eight women: Emma plus seven sister wives. By the end of the year, he would add another nine women to his marital roster, and by the time of his assassination in the spring of 1844, he would count himself husband to thirty-eight (Smith, 2011, p. 622). It was not an arrangement that sat well with Emma. Far from it, she vehemently rejected the idea of polygamy, refusing to be soothed by her husband's protestations that it was God's will. Indeed, it appears that Joseph originally recorded his revelation on plural marriage in order to appease his first wife—or at least scare her into submission. "And let mine handmaid, Emma Smith, receive all those [wives] that have been given unto my servant Joseph," this revelation proclaims (D&C 132:52). "But if she will not abide this commandment she shall be destroyed ... for I am the Lord thy God, and will destroy her if she abide not in my law" (D&C 132:54). Threats of destruction notwithstanding, Emma remained unmoved. When Joseph sent his brother Hyrum to read the revelation to her for the first time, she chastised him so roundly that he ran back to Joseph complaining that "he had never received a more severe talking to in his life" (Hardy, 2007, p. 59).

Returning to the paintings of Joseph and Emma, we see little indication of such domestic strife. Although the dark clouds that gather in the distance behind each figure might be read to hint at the deep tension and sorrow that polygamy inflicted on the Smiths' relationship, they also invoke the works of the Hudson River School painter Thomas Cole and, in the case of Joseph's portrait, the landscapes of the celebrated Romantic artist William Turner. At the same time, we detect no traces of Joseph's multiple marriages in these images, no indication that a fuller accounting of his marital world would necessarily include many more portraits, many more painted female fingers to reach for his own raised hand. Despite the absolutely central role that plural marriage was coming to play in Joseph's theology during the period when he and Emma sat for their portraits—despite the fact that he was beginning to conceive of polygamy as the means by which a man could achieve deification, the practice through which righteous LDS men "shall be gods," blessed with "all power, and the angels ... subject unto them" (D&C 132:20)—the first prophet chose (or at least consented) to be memorialized as an ideal Victorian husband, one half of a harmonious monogamous duo.

Just as important, he and other prominent Mormons actively publicized this Victorian image of the Saints during the faith's Nauvoo years (1839–1846). Walking across the third floor of the Nauvoo temple as Joseph initially envisioned it, one would have found not only the twin pictures of him and Emma but multiple other companion portraits of various church leaders and their (first) wives hanging on the east and north walls. Although faithful church members went through their endowment ceremonies in this part of the temple, the building was not closed to the public, as large portions of LDS temples are today. Instead, it was relatively open, accessible to Mormons and non-Mormons alike (L. McKay, pers. comm. November 14, 2018). As a result, it's likely that Saints and Gentiles both found their way up to the third floor to gaze at the matching oil paintings of apostle John Taylor and his wife Leonora (the first of six women he'd married by the end of 1844) or Patriarch John Smith and his wife Clarissa (number one of three in 1843) (Major, 2002, p. 50; Smith, 2011, pp. 621, 627–28). It's likely that Saints and Gentiles both absorbed the vision of monogamous LDS domesticity that these images broadcast, regardless of the polygamous marriages that were taking place behind closed doors.

To be fair, most Latter-day Saints were monogamous at this point, as they would remain throughout the religion's polygamous period. Moreover, plural marriage was highly secretive in Nauvoo, and Joseph himself always publicly insisted that Emma was his only wife. Between her outrage at the practice and the fact that mere rumors of his sexual transgressions had previously gotten the prophet "tarred, feathered, and nearly castrated" (Campbell, 2016, p. 121) it's not surprising that he chose not to bring another dozen or so women with him to the painter's studio.

Nor is it surprising that the vast majority of plural families followed this example, even after the first Saints established themselves in the West (1847) and Brigham Young announced polygamy as an official church practice (1852). With Congress passing an increasingly brutal series of anti-polygamy statutes between 1862 and 1887, and federal courts beginning to accept photographs as admissible evidence during the late 1850s, posing for plural family portraits would have been a tremendous risk for the Saints—a risk they appear to have collectively declined. Rather than memorializing their religious dedication to the Principle in pictures, Mormon polygamists instead did what Joseph had back in Nauvoo, suiting up in their Sunday best and posing with one wife at a time or, alternately, sending a single wife to the photographer's studio with her children (Figure 17.4). In addition to acting as beloved mementos and reinforcing certain individuals' sense of their place in the social hierarchy, such proto-Busath images limited the Saints' legal exposure. For nineteenth-century Mormons, supposedly private pictures could carry enormous public consequences.

Figure 17.4 Marsena Cannon, *Portrait of Wilford and Phebe Woodruff and family*, 1849
Courtesy, Ronald Fox Collection, Salt Lake City, Utah.

Radiating saints

Even as such family portraits protected various LDS communities, however, they tore holes in the historical record. Just as Joseph and Emma's companion portraits effectively deny the existence of thirty-seven other Mrs. Smiths, the numerous photographs one finds of seemingly monogamous Mormon families banish countless plural wives to the unseen edges of the faith's history—much as the church itself exiles the prospect of its exalted goddesses in heaven to the undeveloped margins of its doctrine. Moreover, by repeatedly presenting LDS women solely as wives and mothers, these pictures give very little sense of the sort of female agency and autonomy that was developing throughout the Mormon West during the later decades of the nineteenth century. Like so many American women, female Saints actively sought to expand their sphere of influence during these years, pursuing careers outside the home, campaigning fiercely for female suffrage, and, in the case of Dr. Martha Hughes Cannon (1857–1932), becoming the country's first female senator in 1896. Despite the fact that their religion assigned them to a position of theological inferiority, in other words, "the so-called degraded ladies of Mormondom [proved themselves] quite equal to the Women's Rights women of the East" (*New York Herald*, 1870). As the LDS *Woman's Exponent* newspaper declared in 1875, "if woman cannot radiate beyond the domestic circle, then thousands are created for no purpose whatsoever" ("Woman's Work," 1875, p. 94).

The visual arts turned out to be a rich arena for such radiating female Saints during the Gilded Age and Progressive Era. In 1903, for example, the LDS artist Elfie Huntington (1868–1949) effectively heeded the *Woman's Exponent*'s insistence that a Mormon woman should "not bury [her] talent in a napkin, but improve upon it" ("Idleness and Unrest," 1875) by opening a professional photography studio with Joseph Bagley in the small town of Springville, Utah. Born in Springville in 1868, Huntington had lost her hearing to scarlet fever at the age of four and her mother to childbirth at age six. Living first with her grandmother and then with an uncle and aunt, she began working for a local photographer named George Edward Anderson when she was in her early twenties. In addition to managing numerous aspects of Anderson's studio, she bought a small view camera that she used to keep a visual diary of "the intimate lives of her friends and family and also the common street life of Springville" (Wadsworth, 1992, p. 200).

Examining these images, one encounters the sort of pictorial candor that nineteenth-century studio photographs tend to suppress, if not outright kill. A trio of young women in long skirts and elaborate hats struggle to pose on a boulder in one picture. A man lies passed out drunk in front of a tree in another. In yet a third image, a woman sits rather formally with a cat in her lap as her male companion turns away from the camera to lure one dog into a photo-worthy position while a second dog seems to contemplate running out of the frame. Peering closely at this photograph, one finds a third figure—or at least a disembodied arm and tiny triangle of skirt— hovering off to the far right. Such visual intrusions are common in Huntington's work. Repeatedly, small children and even adults edge their faces, bodies, and errant sleeves into her images as her official subjects fall out of photogenic arrangement. Like an early twentieth-century version of Lisette Model (1901–1983) or Robert Frank (b. 1924), Huntington seems to have been attracted to such in-between moments—to the broad swaths of awkwardness, strangeness, and sheer vulnerability that so often encase the perfectly composed moments we choose to memorialize.[2] Shooting a studio portrait of a man without legs, for example, she waited—or perhaps even asked—for him to remove his prostheses before exposing the plate (Figure 17.5).

Certain scholars have argued that Huntington was able to develop such an easy rapport with her subjects because she was so different from most of Springville's residents. Although she was a Latter-day Saint, she was also a single working woman with a physical disability and no children in a faith that makes very little theological room for those without spouses or offspring.[3] More than that, she appears not to have suppressed her deeply competent, adventurous nature. According to advertisements for the Huntington and Bagley studio, the duo was willing to "go anywhere, anytime, to photograph anything" in Utah County—usually on a motorcycle with Huntington driving and Bagley holding on as best he could in back. (Springville legend has it that Elfie once lost Joe going over a bump [Wadsworth, 1992, pp. 203–4].) Rather than alienating her neighbors, however, Huntington's version of independent New Womanhood seems to have drawn them closer to her. "Perhaps because she was deaf, perhaps because she was an anomaly in her town and in her time ... she was allowed into many lives" (Stevens Jones, 1988). Born only a year after the LDS leader George Q. Cannon announced "a great glory is bestowed on woman, for she is permitted to bring forth the souls of men" (Cannon, 1867, p. 338), Huntington seems to have received the support of the Mormon community as she used her camera to bring forth so many of its members, herself included.

Huntington was not the only LDS woman to pursue the arts this way. Nor did all such artists confine their focus to the towns where they were born. To the contrary, "between 1890 and 1920, at least a dozen Mormon women went to Paris to study the visual arts" (Jensen, 2017, p. 144). Seeking the sort of education, professional contacts, and institutional recognition the French system offered, these lady Saints joined an expanding community of female painters and

Figure 17.5 Effie Huntington, *Untitled*, n.d.
Courtesy, Tom Perry Special Collections, Harold B. Lee Library, Brigham Young University, Provo, Utah

sculptors who flocked to Paris from all parts of Europe and America during the decades surrounding the turn to the twentieth century. One of the first Utah artists to establish this pattern was Harriet Richards Harwood (1870–1922). Although Harwood was not a member of the church, she came from an LDS family. Moreover, she "was good friends with many ... Mormon women artists, and her journey was inspirational to them" (Jensen, 2017, p. 144, n. 21). Settling in France during the early 1890s, Harwood took classes at the Académie Julian, made weekly pilgrimages to the city's art galleries, and enjoyed at least one picnic lunch with the celebrated African-American artist Henry Ossawa Tanner (Gibbs, 1987, p. 29). Marrying fellow Utah painter J.T. Harwood in Paris in 1891, she spent the next four months honeymooning in "the quiet artists' haven of Pont-Aven," where she and J.T. painted every day (Gibbs, 1987, p. 28). The following year, she completed an exquisite still life of a pumpkin, cauliflower, and potatoes (Figure 17.6) that would become the only oil painting by a woman to be exhibited at the 1893 World's Columbian Exposition in Chicago. Unfortunately, Harwood's dedication to the arts did not last. "Despite her talents and critical success, [she] basically abandoned painting by the late 1890s, her energies spent on furthering her husband's artistic career and raising a family in the Mormon West" (Doss, 1994, p. 216). As J.T. asserted, "the duties of housewife took up so much of her time that art had to be a side issue" (quoted in Knecth, 1989). Unlike Elfie

Figure 17.6 Harriet Harwood, *The Pumpkin and the Cauliflower* (Still Life), 1892
Courtesy, University of Utah Collection.

Huntington, Harwood ultimately ceded her artistic aspirations to the demands of bourgeois womanhood.

This was not the case for every LDS painter who followed in her footsteps. As the art historian Erika Doss writes, "other Utah artists, such as Mary Teasdel (1863–1937) and Rose Hartwell (1861–1917)" were able to "resis[t] the power of Mormon theology" and its investment in the Cult of True Womanhood "by leaving the country and either remaining single or marrying late in life" (Doss, 1994, p. 218). Teasdel went first, moving to Paris in 1899 and studying with James Abbott McNeill Whistler, Benjamin Constable, and Jules Simon. Highly skilled in oils, watercolors, and pastels, she created land- and seascapes that evoke those of the French Impressionists Claude Monet and Alfred Sisley as well as the later work of Winslow Homer. In 1902, she became the first Utah woman (and second Utah artist) to exhibit at the prestigious Paris Salon. Moving in similar circles, Rose Hartwell took classes at the Académie Julian, showed at the 1903 Salon, and befriended the famed expatriate Impressionist Mary Cassatt. Like Cassatt, Hartwell and Teasdel are largely remembered for their scenes of mothers and children despite never having had children of their own. Teasdel's *Mother and Child* (ca. 1920) (Figure 17.7), in particular, shares something of the complicated view of maternity one finds in Cassatt's images. Sequestering the mother's body in shadow and the child itself in sleep, this painting focuses less on any sort of maternal connection than it does on the woman's face as she gazes out her small slice of window to the bright world that hovers just beyond.

Crucially, Teasdel, Hartwell, and their "sisters of the brush" (Jensen, 2017, p. 154) were not the only Mormon artists in France at this time. Having formally renounced polygamy in 1890, the turn-of-the-century church sought to repair the damage the practice had done to its reputation by self-consciously styling the Saints as a refined and artful people. As a part of this effort,

Figure 17.7 Mary Teasdel, *Mother and Child*, 1920
State of Utah Alice Merrill Horne Collection. Courtesy Utah Arts & Museums.

the LDS leadership sent four Mormon men on an official "art mission" to Paris between 1890 and 1893. Like so many of their female counterparts, these painters enrolled at the Académie Julian, absorbed the lessons of French modernism in the galleries, and painted the sort of *plein air* scenes that Monet had popularized. Unlike the LDS women, however, the art missionaries were funded by the church and received commissions to paint murals in the Salt Lake Temple upon their return. Although female artists like Teasdel also went home to Utah "to foster the arts among their people" (Jensen, 2017, p. 142), they never received the sort of institutional support the church bestowed upon its men.

Undeterred, these lady Saints set to work creating their own art infrastructure. Relying on the friendships they had formed during their time abroad as well as on longstanding LDS organizations like the female Relief Society, the church's Paris-trained women made substantial contributions to Utah's developing art scene (Jensen, 2017, pp. 470–84). Within a decade of her 1903 return from Europe, for example, Teasdel had become one of the ten founding members of the Association of Salt Lake Artists, as well as the director of the Utah Arts Institute. The Institute itself had been created by one of Teasdel's own students, Alice Merrill Horne (1868–1948). Born in a log cabin in Fillmore, Utah, Horne studied at the Art Institute of Chicago before "devoting her life to ennobling art in everyday Utah" (Black and Woodger,

2015, p. 135). This vocation took numerous forms, including running her own art galleries, creating a new art curriculum for the Relief Society, publishing articles about the arts, and attending "the International Congress of Women in Berlin, Germany, where she spoke on the progress of art in Utah and on women in politics" (Black and Woodger, 2015, p. 137). Elected to Utah's House of Representatives in 1898, Horne also "instigated the Utah Art Bill, establishing the nation's first state-sponsored art collection" (Doss, 1994, p. 216). (The fact that Horne managed all of this while raising six children makes it difficult to find a description of her that doesn't include the word "indefatigable.") As the LDS artist Minerva Teichert (1888–1976) declared at Horne's funeral in 1948, "Always was this great woman looking after the welfare of the artists, hoping they would be able to 'make a go of it' financially and still grow in spirit. Few people are so forgetful of self" (Black and Woodger, 2015, p. 138).

Miss Idaho

Teichert herself provides another example of the institutional church's failure to support even its best female artists. Growing up poor on a farm in southern Idaho, Teichert (née Kohlhepp) didn't go to an art museum until she was 14 years old. That said, she'd thought of herself as an artist since the age of 4, when her mother first gave her a set of watercolors. Determined to get a proper art education, Teichert saved enough money to enroll at the Chicago Art Institute after graduating from high school. There she became one of the last students of Georgia O'Keeffe's former teacher John Vanderpoel. By all accounts, Vanderpoel held Teichert to a higher standard than many of his other students, critiquing her work stringently even as he let weaker paintings slide. When Teichert demanded an explanation for the unequal treatment, he responded, "Miss Idaho, can it be possible you do not understand; they're not worth it, they will drop out, but you—ah, there is no end" (Teichert, 1917). Moving to Manhattan in 1915 to study at the Art Students League of New York, Teichert found another champion in the Ashcan School artist Robert Henri. According to Henri, Teichert was one of his three most promising students. "George Bellows, John Sloan, and Minerva Kohlhepp—those are my bets," he predicted. "This girl from Utah you're bound to hear from" (Doss, 1994, p. 209).

Unfortunately, Henri's forecast has yet to fully materialize. Although art historians are finally beginning to write about Teichert, she doesn't sit next to Bellows and Sloan in the art historical canon, nor does her work command nearly the same level of museum-and-market interest. Part of this is due to the fact that she left New York in 1916 to marry her "cowboy sweetheart," Herman Adolph Teichert. Trading her identity as "Miss Idaho" for life as "Mrs. Teichert," she returned to the family ranch outside of Pocatello and later moved to Cokeville, Wyoming. At this point, accounts of her life start to read like a rural version of Alice Merrill Horne's extreme working-mother vitae, with one scholar noting that by the early 1900s, Teichert "had reared five children, pitched hay, broken horses, raised chickens, homesteaded by herself, and all the while … painted in her living room and recited Book of Mormon scripture on almost any given occasion" (Johnson, 1990, p. 66).

Despite the intense demands on her time, Teichert managed to complete more than 500 works before her death in 1976. As Doss writes, these pictures tend to "focu[s] on Western women, showing them tall, strong, capable, and in control" in a way that disrupts both the Saints' "resoundingly patriarchal religion" and the nation's enduring fantasy of the West as a place inhabited solely by stereotypically masculine cowboys and savage Native Americans (Doss, 1994, p. 240). One finds a clear example of this attention to female worth in the series of paintings Teichert made of the Book of Mormon during the late 1940s and early 1950s. It was Robert Henri who first counseled her to turn to the Latter-day Saints' founding text for inspiration. "Has anyone ever told your great Mormon story?" he asked her during a painting critique. "Not to suit me," Teichert replied. "Good Heavens, girl, what a chance. You do it. You're the one," he exclaimed (Doss, 1994, p. 209). Three decades later, she fulfilled her mentor's vision with a series of forty-three murals. Not only do these images "portra[y] most of the instances where the Book of Mormon, however briefly, mentions women" (Wardle, 1997, p. 40), they include female figures in scenes where they do not explicitly appear in the text (Figure 17.8). With their luminous views of women caring for children, transporting water, and preparing for family journeys, Teichert's murals valorize the sort of quotidian domestic work that, despite its importance, so often goes unnoticed.

Importantly, the paintings themselves were designed to work. From the beginning, Teichert conceived of the images "as a missionary tool" and "dreamed of a temple of art in Salt Lake City where her Book of Mormon murals would … tell the scriptural story quickly and clearly to the visiting public" (Wardle, 1997, p. 41). Such dreams were not to be. Although church authorities commissioned a series of temple murals from her in 1947, they chose not to support her Book of Mormon project when she showed them her preparatory sketches in 1950. Rather than funding Henri's prodigy as she translated their "great Mormon story" into pictures, the LDS leadership left her to work in her living room, painting on cheap Masonite boards to cut costs and inspecting the murals through the wrong end of a set of binoculars to get a sense of how

Figure 17.8 Minerva Teichert (1888–1976), *Loading the Ship*, 1949–1951, oil on masonite, 36 × 48 inches Brigham Young University Museum of Art, 1969.

they would look from an appropriate distance (Wardle, 1997, pp. 30–31). Finishing all but one of the murals within a year, Teichert set out to find a home for them within the church's network of buildings and institutions, only to be met with more disinterest. After two decades of struggling to place her *chef d'oeuvre* in a site where it would be able to preach to her people, she simply "donated them to Brigham Young University" (Anderson, 2015, p. 480), noting in a letter to her family that she "was glad to be free from it" (Welch and Dant, 1997, p. 26). Although Teichert now stands with the LDS artist Arnold Friberg (1913–2010) as one of the two great illustrators of the Book of Mormon, the church continues to overlook her work when it comes to official publications and other educational materials. Of the forty Book of Mormon paintings included in the latest edition of the Gospel Art Book, for example, twenty are by Friberg while none are by Teichert.

Captain Moroni

Admittedly, Friberg's work delivers a very different image of Mormonism's New World Israelites than one finds in Teichert's lush arrangements of shape and color. Commissioned in 1950 to run in an LDS children's magazine, Friberg's suite of twelve Book of Mormon paintings "presented the book as a series of exciting adventure stories populated with muscular superheroes" (Anderson, 2015, p. 481). A brawny Nephi dominates his faithless brothers with a single outstretched arm in one canvas. A strappingly shirtless Ammon stands ready to protect a flock of sheep from invading Lamanites in another. In what is likely the most iconic image from the series, *Captain Moroni and the Title of Liberty*, the powerful Nephite commander towers above a phalanx of unsheathed swords, his own weapon hanging rather provocatively between his legs. Impressed by such arresting images of robust masculinity, the legendary filmmaker Cecil B. DeMille would eventually hire Friberg to design the costumes and general look of his 1956 religious epic, *The Ten Commandments*. "The God of the Bible is not a wishy-washy God," DeMille proclaimed in the souvenir handbook that accompanied the film (Friberg, 1956, unpaginated). As Charlton Heston's memorable turn as Moses reveals, the LDS artist didn't go in for the "wishy-washy" either—at least not when it came to his men.

According to Friberg, his figures' chiseled bodies spoke to their moral rectitude as much as their physical might. "The muscularity in my paintings is only an expression of the spirituality within. When I paint Nephi, I'm painting the interior, the greatness, the largeness of spirit," he insisted (Barrett and Black, 2005, p. 33). Viewed this way, Friberg's work channels the potent amalgam of male spirituality and (hetero)sexuality that necessarily runs through a religion that promises an eternity of polygynous godhood to men who live by its standards in the here and now. That said, Friberg's spiritual supermen also look like they stepped out of one of the mid-century physical culture magazines that "employed the alibis of art, health, and classicism to picture erotically exposed male bodies" for a largely gay audience (Meyer, 2002, p. 170).[4] Friberg might have been correct when he insisted, "I'm the only guy that can do a particular type of picture" (Barrett and Black, 2005, p. 33). As the plethora of Captain Moronis currently waving rainbow flags on the Internet reveals, however, even the most particular picture can satisfy a wide variety of needs.

Sturdy patriarchs

By the 1960s, Friberg's impulse to "portray the Nephites as an odd mixture of Vikings and Roman Centurions" (Goble, 2017) had fallen out of favor with the LDS leadership as a new ideal of Mormon manhood came to the fore. "The Mormon male, though he was to be a sturdy patriarch," was now to cultivate qualities like virtue and sensitivity rather than focusing exclusively on "athleticism and perfect health" (Carmack, 2000, p. 41). In keeping with this shift, the church increasingly turned to artists like the Seventh-day Adventist illustrator Harry Anderson (1906–1996) and, later, the LDS painter Del Parson (b. 1948) to translate its conception of warm-hearted manliness into images, and specifically images of "Christ as a compassionate ministering servant" (Carmack, 2000, p. 44). Even as Friberg's work continued to teach the Saints that boys were meant "to grow up and look like Nephi, this super buff righteous prophet who looks like He-Man" (Florence, pers. comm. October 16, 2018), Anderson's *Christ with the Children* depicted Jesus as an empathetic teacher while Parson's *The Lost Lamb* featured the savior cradling a baby sheep. Perhaps unsurprisingly, "the most reproduced Latter-day Saint picture of Christ" (Carmack, 2000, p. 59), Parson's *The Lord Jesus Christ* (1983), features a handsome man with gray eyes and a reddish beard who seems to smile slightly as he gazes into the distance. Appealing, approachable, and strikingly white, Parson's Jesus urges male Mormons to get in touch with their softer side.

It was this image of well-behaved LDS masculinity that the church publicized at the New York World's Fair. Held in Flushing Meadows, Queens between 1964 and 1965, the Fair gave the Latter-day Saints an unprecedented opportunity to present both their beliefs and themselves to the larger nation. Erecting an elaborate "Mormon Pavilion" on Robert Moses' fairgrounds, church authorities enlisted a fleet of young missionaries to guide the nearly six million visitors they received through an impressive arrangement of LDS-themed paintings, sculptures, and other exhibits. Although Mormon women participated in this effort, the World's Fair missionaries were overwhelmingly male and exclusively white (Eastern States Mission New York World's Fair Files, 1964–65). More than that, they turned out to be the Pavilion's most effective display. "The Elders [male missionaries] were the greatest asset we had at the Pavilion. If visitors were not particularly moved with the dioramas and the murals or the movie, they were always impressed with 'the wonderful clean-cut young men,'" a member of the church's full-time fair staff later remembered (Eastern States Mission New York World's Fair Files, 1964–65). The remarks left in the Pavilion's comment book support this observation. "Where in the world did you find all the presentable, personable clean-cut young men? I hope this work can expand to more greatness," one visitor enthused (Eastern States Mission New York World's Fair Files, 1964–65). "You certainly have inspired and dedicated men—there is hope for our country with people like that," another declared (Eastern States Mission New York World's Fair Files, 1964–65). Roughly a year after Betty Friedan published *The Feminine Mystique* and Martin Luther King Jr. marched on Washington, the church sold itself to countless Americans with its missionaries' demonstrations of wholesome white masculinity.[5] Cementing this performance of traditional gender roles, Mormon leaders arranged for several hundred LDS women to give a "Singing Mothers" concert in front of the Pavilion before the fair closed (Eastern States Mission New York World's Fair Files, 1964–65).

Eden Farm

Despite its success at the World's Fair, the church couldn't stave off the forces of historical change. As the developments of the 1960s and 1970s increasingly challenged Mormonism's white, patriarchal power structures, LDS authorities had two choices: accommodate or fight. They ultimately did both, admitting black men to the priesthood in 1978 but doubling down on their position that women were divinely designed to stay at home. Not only did "the church increas[e] its emphasis on motherly obligation and female subordination" (Young, 2007, p. 630) during these years, it eventually played a dispositive role in killing the Equal Rights Amendment, which would have added a prohibition against denying or abridging "equality of rights under the law ... on account of sex" to the Constitution (H.R.J. Res. 208 ..., 1971). Keenly aware that "a bid for constitutionally protected equality of the sexes struck at the very core of Mormonism's deepest beliefs about the gender-specific roles in life" (Young, 2007, p. 629), LDS leaders excommunicated a Saint named Sonia Johnson for publicly declaring that God supported the ERA and withheld temple recommends from other Mormon women who didn't fall into line (Young, 2007, pp. 637–38).

At the same time, the church erected a "Monument to Women" in Nauvoo, Illinois. Dedicated in 1978, this statuary plaza sits in a two-acre garden and includes eleven life-sized bronze castings of modestly dressed women engaged in activities like praying, quilting, and playing with children. Created by the LDS artist Dennis Smith (b. 1942), these sculptures effectively visualize then-prophet Spencer W. Kimball's pronouncement that "[by] staying home to care for her family, a woman will find greater satisfaction and joy and peace and make greater contributions to mankind" (Brigman, 1978).[6] Interestingly, the "Monument to Women" includes one statue that doesn't quite fit with Kimball's vision of woman's sacred domesticity. Of the eleven works Dennis Smith created for the garden, one depicts a female artist. As her fellow bronzes carry babies and sit shyly with boys, this figure appears to sculpt a woman's head. It's an oddly autobiographical piece for Smith to have included in the church's pantheon of acceptable female pursuits, even if it does comport with the centuries-long tradition of well-bred ladies who dabble in the arts.

Smith himself struggled with the "Monument to Women." Whereas the church originally "want[ed] one single monument of woman, a monumental woman" (*Art & Belief*, 2018), he "wanted to portray many different aspects of a woman's nature in her multifaceted experience" (Brigman, 1978). It was he who finally convinced the General Authorities it would take more than one sculpture to represent the gender as a whole. Moreover, Smith genuinely hoped the finished plaza would reflect "his own expanded view of the roles of women" (*Art & Belief*, 2018), as limited as those roles might seem today. Such religio-aesthetic tension is to be expected from a member of the Art and Belief Movement. Composed of artists like Smith, Trevor Southey, Neil Hadlock (b. 1944), and Gary Ernest Smith (b. 1942), the Art and Belief Movement coalesced at BYU during the mid-1960s. "We all did different things, but we just couldn't stay away from each other," Hadlock remembers (*Art & Belief*, 2018). At base, the Art and Belief artists wanted to contribute to the Mormon Kingdom of God by creating images and objects that would turn Zion into an art mecca on par with Vatican City. "They envisioned having an art center and seminars and making an influence on the church, influencing the way the church uses art in teaching the gospel," Southey's wife, Elaine, recalls (*Art & Belief*, 2018). At the time, however, "the General Authorities were thinking about how to communicate the [LDS] message" across both the nation and the larger world. In Florence's words, "they were interested not in high art but in PR and message control" (*Art & Belief*, 2018). Although Latter-day Saint leaders commissioned work from artists like Southey and Smith, the Art and Belief Movement made them slightly nervous.

In certain respects, the Movement's artists were fundamentally conservative. Male, Mormon, BYU-educated, and linked by their shared interest in figuration rather than abstraction, these painters, sculptors, and printmakers discussed aesthetics and theology late into the night while their wives congregated in the kitchen.[7] They were markedly free-thinking when it came to certain issues, however, including Southey's sexuality. A Rhodesian (now Zimbabwean) convert of European descent, Southey loved the sense of community and belonging the faith offered. "As strange as it seems today, I was comfortable [in the church]. Here I could be a gentle man and not feel that I was effeminate," he remembered toward the end of his life (Southey and Snow, 1998, p. 13). "I quickly learned that I could hide almost happily here" (Southey and

Snow, p. 33). As a gay man in a religion that would later declare homosexuality a sin second only to "murder and denying the Holy Ghost" (Church of Jesus Christ of Latter-day Saints, 2004, pp. 29–33), Southey had to hide. That said, he didn't conceal his sexuality from those closest to him, including his fellow Art and Belief artists and Elaine. "Everyone knew what the situation was," Dennis Smith recalled (*Art & Belief*, 2018).

Before they married, Southey and Elaine had spoken to Spencer Kimball, then an apostle, about the artist's attraction to men. Like the other Mormon counselors Southey consulted, Kimball maintained that marriage would solve his problems. "If I were simply to act the role, marry and settle down, it would all be fine. Practice would make me 'perfect,'" Southey later recalled (*The Mormons*, 2007). As it turned out, practice wasn't up to the task. Although Southey loved Elaine deeply, his feelings for her were purely platonic, and fifteen years of suppressing a fundamental part of himself eventually left him waking up every morning with the same phrase echoing in his mind: "and shot himself through the head" (*The Mormons*, 2007). Divorcing Elaine in 1982, he was excommunicated shortly thereafter.

Southey's work bears clear traces of his Mormon identity. Repeatedly, male and female figures float and sometimes fly across his pictorial surfaces as titles like *Into Mortality* (1968), *Embryo* (1977), and *Fatherhood* (1970) invoke the Saints' theological investment in the family as the basis of human exaltation. There is anguish in the work, too. Not just the overt emotional apocalypse of a painting like *Intercession at Gethsemane* (1981), but the quieter suffering one senses in *Union* (1972) and *Comfort Waiting* (1986) and even *Pieta* (1982), these depictions of men and women so brutally bare in their failure to fully connect. Finally, there is Southey's commitment to the human body—to the gorgeously delineated nudes that populated his work even during

Figure 17.9 Trevor Southey, *Eden Farm*, 1971.
Courtesy, Trevor Southey Estate.

his days at BYU, to the figures that, like Michelangelo's, always look a bit male even when they're not. One doesn't have to push hard at this work to find traces of the conflict and pain Southey experienced as a gay member of a homotoxic religion, the crippling internal collisions he endured as a result of his desire to live as both a family man and a queer man in a church that vehemently denies the two can ever be one and the same. "This is my ideal of a family," he once said of his 1971 work *Eden Farm* (Figure 17.9), pointing at the painting's two men, one woman, and small child standing naked in front of a cow. "It's only in the last little while I've had the courage to admit that I think what I was doing was saying, 'This is my family'" (*Art & Belief*, 2018).

It's an unorthodox family portrait, to be sure. But then, Joseph Smith's would have been, too, if he hadn't hidden the fullness of his family—and with it, the fullness of his theological desires for the sexualized male body—behind the polite façade of his companion portrait with Emma. Looking at *Eden Farm*, I think of Emma. I imagine her standing in her bedroom later in life, trying to decide where those portraits should go, trying to decide if the painting of her should hang on the left, so her picture would seem to face that of her dead husband, or whether it would be better to put herself on the right, so her painted hand would reach for his in a not-quite-yet-closed circuit of love. "This is my ideal of a family." Looking at *Eden Farm*, I think of Emma and Southey and all the other odd ducks like them, all of these imperfect Saints trying to make their families out of the remains their prophets left behind.

Notes

1 Joseph Smith's ring actually poses a thorny archival problem. Certain LDS scholars argue that it *isn't*, in fact, a wedding ring, while others maintain that it is. L McKay, pers. comm. November 14, 2018 (not a wedding ring); R Fox, pers. comm. 2018 (wedding ring). Because the portrait foregrounds this ring and, just as importantly, visually mates it to the ring Emma wears on her left ring finger, I've chosen to treat it as a wedding band.
2 I'm not the first to notice the parallels between Huntington's work and certain New York School photographers. In the catalog that accompanied her 1988 exhibition of Huntington's work, Cary Stevens Jones draws explicit comparisons between the two (see Stevens Jones, 1988).
3 Huntington did eventually marry Joe Bagley at the age of 68. He died six weeks later, however, and she declined to take care of his children after his death. She never had any children of her own (see Stevens Jones, 1988; Wadsworth, 1992, pp. 204–5).
4 Sixty years later, a Latter-day Saint named Chad Hardy would tap into this audience with a series of beefcake calendars of returned LDS missionaries (Friess, 2008). Tellingly, the 2010 calendar featured a photographic send-up of Captain Moroni on its cover.
5 In keeping with this attention to white manhood, the church also installed a replica of Bertel Thorvaldsen's nineteenth-century neoclassical sculpture of Christ, the *Christus*, near the Pavilion's entrance. Identical to the copy of the *Christus* that welcomes visitors to the LDS North Visitors' Center in Salt Lake City, Utah, this 11-foot marble statue presents Jesus as a towering white presence. As I've written elsewhere, it simultaneously casts male Mormons as the Mercury 7 of American religion—a set of traditional "men's men" up to the task of "protecting the country from Soviet attack and, beneath that, colonization by upstart women and minorities" (Campbell, 2017a; 2017b).
6 See also, Terry, Slaght-Griffin, and Terry (1980, p. 5): "Finite words cannot describe the soaring emotions felt by a woman who is completely caught up in fulfilling her eternal role. She is sweetheart, confidante, partner, friend to her husband, all the while molding, teaching, guiding her children." One wonders what the LDS artist Mabel Pearl Frazer (1888–1981), who created phenomenal modernist canvases and deserves much more than a footnote here, would have said. Despite her devotion to the church, Frazer never married and deemed housekeeping "an utter waste of intelligence." (She spent at least one period "living most on Cocoa-Cola [sic] and chocolate bars, with an occasional banana thrown in.") As her sister remembered, "statement [Mabel] made to a nurse in the hospital the day before she died pretty well sums up her character. She had been giving the nurse a bad time, and feeling a little remorseful for not having been more cooperative she suddenly grasped the nurse's hand

and said, 'I really have a lot of love in my heart, but I also have a lot of damn-it-to-hell'" (Waldis, n.d., pp. 25, 1).

7 Although Southey's wife, Elaine, wasn't an artist, she tended to join in the men's conversations. Florence, pers. comm. October 16, 2018.

References

Anderson, P.L., 2015. Mormon Architecture and Visual Arts. In T.L. Givens and P.L. Barlow, eds. *Oxford Handbook of Mormonism*. New York: Oxford University Press, pp. 470–84.

Art & Belief, 2018. Motion picture, rough cut. December 8. Directed by Nathan Florence and Matt Black.

Barrett, R.T., and Black, S.E., 2005. Setting a Standard in LDS Art: Four Illustrators of the Mid-Twentieth Century. *BYU Studies* 44(2): 24–95.

Black, S.E., and Woodger, M.J., 2015. *Women of Character: Profiles of 100 Prominent LDS Women*. American Fork, UT: Covenant Communications.

Brigman, J., 1978. Nauvoo Monument to Women. Internal quotation marks omitted. www.lds.org/ensign/1978/09/news-of-the-church/nauvoo-monument-to-women?lang=eng (accessed December 14, 2018).

Campbell, M., 2016. *Charles Ellis Johnson and the Erotic Mormon Image*. Chicago, IL: University of Chicago Press.

Campbell, M., 2017a. Saints in Space. *Cosmologics Magazine* (Harvard Divinity School). Fall. https://cosmologicsmagazine.com/mary-campbell-saints-in-space/.

Campbell, M., 2017b. Salt Lake City Spaceman. *Cosmologics Magazine* (Harvard Divinity School). Fall. cosmologicsmagazine.com/mary-campbell-salt-lake-city-spaceman/ (accessed May 27, 2017).

Cannon, G.Q., 1867. Discourse delivered on March 3. Reprinted in B. Young, G.D. Smith, and J.V. Long, eds. *Journal of Discourses*, vol. 11. Liverpool: F.D. Richards.

Carmack, N., 2000. Images of Christ in Latter-day Saint Visual Culture, 1900–1999. *BYU Studies* 39(3): 18–76.

Church of Jesus Christ of Latter-day Saints, 2004. *True to the Faith*. Salt Lake City, UT: Church of Jesus Christ of Latter-day Saints.

Deseret Book, 2016. Website. https://deseretbook.com/p/family-proclamation-14x17-framed-art-cambridge-collection-82130?variant_id=15034-framed (accessed December 14, 2018).

Doss, E., 1994. I Must Paint: Women Artists of the Rocky Mountain Region. In P. Trenton, ed., *Independent Spirits: Women Painters of the American West, 1890–1945*. Berkeley, CA: Autry Museum of Western Heritage in association with University of California Press, pp. 209–42.

Eastern States Mission New York World's Fair Files, 1964–65. Church History Library, Church of Jesus Christ of Latter-day Saints, Salt Lake City, Utah.

The First Presidency and Council of the Twelve Apostles of The Church of Jesus Christ of Latter-day Saints, 1995. The Family: A Proclamation to the World. www.lds.org/topics/family-proclamation?lang=eng&old=true (accessed December 14, 2018).

Friberg, A., 1956. *The Ten Commandments*. New York: The Greenstone Company.

Friess, S., 2008. Controversy over a Calendar of Mormon Men. *Newsweek*. July 17. www.newsweek.com/controversy-over-calendar-mormon-men-93027 (accessed December 14, 2018).

Gibbs, L.J., 1987. *Harvesting the Light: The Paris Art Mission and the Beginning of Utah Impressionism*. Salt Lake City, UT: Church of Jesus Christ of Latter-day Saints.

Goble, C., 2017. The Problem of Mormon Art. *Times and Seasons*. blog post, June 1. www.timesandseasons.org/harchive/2017/06/the-problem-of-mormon-art/index.html (accessed December 14, 2018).

Hardy, B.C. ed., 2007. *Doing the Works of Abraham: Mormon Polygamy; Its Origin, Practice, and Demise*. Norman, OK: Arthur H. Clark.

H.R.J. Res. 208, 92d Cong., 1st Sess. (1971); S.J. Res. 8.

Idleness and Unrest, 1875. *Woman's Exponent*. November 9, p. 110.

Jensen, H.B., 2017. Aesthetic Evangelism, Artistic Sisterhood, and the Gospel of Beauty: Mormon Women Artists at Home and Abroad, circa 1890–1920. In R. Cope, ed. *Mormon Women's History: Beyond Biography*. New York: Oxford University Press, pp. 470–84.

Johnson, M.A., 1990. Minerva Teichert: Scriptorian and Artist. *Brigham Young University Studies* 30(3): 66–70.

Knecth, P.L., 1989. Utah Impressionism, LDS Church History Library, M281 K68u 1989.

Major, J.C., 2002. Artworks in the Celestial Room of the First Nauvoo Temple. *BYU Studies* 41(2): 47–68.
Meyer, R., 2002. *Outlaw Representation: Censorship and Homosexuality in Twentieth-Century American Art.* New York: Oxford University Press.
The Mormons, 2007. Television program. PBS Television. New York. April.
New York Herald, 1870. Quoted in the Mormon Women in Council, Fairfield Herald Winnsboro, SC. February 2.
Smith, G.D., 2011. *Nauvoo Polygamy: … But We Called It Celestial Marriage.* Salt Lake City, UT: Signature Books.
Southey, T., 2001. The Choice. In A.L. Ellis, ed. *Gay Men at Midlife: Age before Beauty.* New York: Harrington Park Press, pp. 87–94.
Southey, T., and Snow, K.M., 1998. *Reconciliation.* Salt Lake City, UT: Signature Books.
Stevens Jones, C., 1988. *A Woman's View: The Photography of Elfie Huntington (1868–1949).* Springville, UT: The Springville Museum of Art.
Teichert, M., 1917. *Miss Kohlhepp's Own Story.* Pocatello, Idaho.
Terry, A., Slaght-Griffin, M., and Terry, E., 1980. *Mormons and Women.* Santa Barbara, CA: Butterfly Publishing.
Wadsworth, N.B., 1992. *Set in Stone, Fixed in Glass: The Mormons, the West, and Their Photographers.* Salt Lake City, UT: Signature Books.
Waldis, M.F., n.d. A Biographical Sketch of Professor Mabel Pearl Frazer, LDS Church History Library, M270.1 F847w 1984.
Wardle, M.E., 1997. That He Who Runs May Read. In J.W. Welch and D.R. Dant, eds. *The Book of Mormon Paintings of Minerva Teichert.* Salt Lake City, UT: BYU Studies and Bookcraft, pp. 28–45.
Welch, J.W., and Dant, D.R., 1997. *The Book of Mormon Paintings of Minerva Teichert*, Salt Lake City, UT: BYU Studies and Bookcraft.
Woman's Work, 1875. *Woman's Exponent.* November 9, p. 94.
Young, N.J., 2007. The ERA Is a Moral Issue: The Mormon Church, LDS Women, and the Defeat of the Equal Rights Amendment. *American Quarterly* 50(3): 623–44.

Further reading

Campbell, M., 2016. *Charles Ellis Johnson and the Erotic Mormon Image.* Chicago, IL: University of Chicago Press.
This book examines the work of a little-known Mormon photographer whose images of prophets, temples, half-dressed vaudeville actresses, and polygamous suffragettes worked in concert to mainstream the Latter-day Saints into the nation after the scandal of plural marriage.
Carmack, N., 2000. Images of Christ in Latter-day Saint Visual Culture, 1900–1999. *BYU Studies* 39(3): 18–76.
This article provides an overview of the evolution of both the twentieth-century church's preferred images of Christ and its ideals of masculinity.
Doss, E., 1994. I Must Paint: Women Artists of the Rocky Mountain Region. In P. Trenton, ed. *Independent Spirits: Women Painters of the American West, 1890–1945.* Berkeley, CA: Autry Museum of Western Heritage in association with University of California Press, pp. 209–42.
This chapter gives an excellent overview of the work of numerous female artists, many of them LDS, who worked in the Rocky Mountain era during the late nineteenth and early twentieth centuries.
Jensen, H.B., 2017. Aesthetic Evangelism, Artistic Sisterhood, and the Gospel of Beauty: Mormon Women Artists at Home and Abroad, circa 1890–1920. In R. Cope, ed. *Mormon Women's History: Beyond Biography.* New York: Oxford University Press, pp. 470–84.
This article provides an analysis of the friendships, networks, and organizations various Gilded-Age and Progressive-Era LDS women used to bring the art lessons they learned in Paris home to the Mormon West.
Southey, T., and Snow, K.M., 1998. *Reconciliation.* Salt Lake City, UT: Signature Books.
This catalogue accompanied Southey's 1998 retrospective and provides a solid introduction to both his work and his writing.

18
MORMON LITERATURE AND GENDER

Fara Anderson Sneddon

In an essay on women's autobiography, feminist theorist and scholar Susan Stanford Friedman posits that a woman writes the self as a communal act,

> [the female] autobiographical self often does not oppose herself to all others, does not feel herself to exist outside of others, and still less against others, but very much with others in an interdependent existence that asserts its rhythms everywhere in the community.
>
> *(Friedman, 1998, p. 79)*

In composing herself and her world into language, the author, then, acts as a gatherer, bundling her self together with the lives of the women surrounding her, creating community and collective identity, creating meaning. She writes "into history an identity that is not purely individualistic. Nor is it purely collective. Instead, this new identity merges the shared and the unique" (Friedman, 1998, p. 40).

The experiences of nineteenth-century Mormon women were certainly unique, and they were likewise highly communal. Having removed themselves from the world, these early women worked to create a utopian Zion founded upon the revolutionary theology of a new and charismatic religion. Relatively few of these women wrote autobiographies—for every ten early male Saints who kept a journal, only one sister did the same (Anderson, 2001, p. 67). Yet while their written texts hid in the shadows of words by their brethren, the Mormon female identity of today continues to be informed by the revolutionary literature that nineteenth-century Mormon women produced. They created a theology that elevated women, that connected them to a female deity, that reclaimed the female body from the male gaze, that won the vote and worked for suffrage throughout the world, and taught bravery in the face of fear. In writing for themselves, they were writing a new community into existence, and it would exert its rhythm for a century more.

There are four generally accepted periods of Mormon literature, first identified by Eugene England in his essay "Mormon Literature: Progress and Prospects" (1995) These periods are Foundations (1830 to 1880), Home Literature (1880 to 1930), the Lost Generation (1930 to 1970), and Faithful Realism (1960 to present). While the styles, themes, and rhetorical aims differ between periods, the writers all grapple with their place in both their Mormon communities and in larger Western culture. Each of these periods has its own specific genres and rhetorical purposes; likewise, each includes texts that grapple with the intersections of culture and values, identity, gender, and religiosity.

The last forty years of Mormon Studies have introduced the imperative of considering gender as essential to understanding Mormonism (Morrill, 2014). Scholars have brought to light more texts by LDS women, valuing their journals, diaries, and biographical sketches of daily life as well as finding value in the texts these women submitted to their own female-published periodicals. Subsequently, a far more nuanced and complicated Mormon identity has come to light. For the purposes of this chapter, our attention will be on the work of Mormon women of the Foundational and Home Literature periods, generally between 1830 and 1915. In considering their individual letters, meeting minutes, poetry, essays, ritual language, and short stories, an understanding of the voices of their wider female community arises.

While the Church of Jesus Christ of Latter-day Saints was (and continues to be) a top-down patriarchal organization, while the culture and theology were disseminated through the universalist male lens, and while those things most valued were male-centric history, experience, and voice, the real work of creation—of enlarging one's sphere, expanding identity, and elevating the human condition—was the work of early Mormon women.

The women who took up a pencil to write during the Foundational and Home Literature periods created themselves inside of Mormonism, inside a theology and culture that also maintained the separate spheres of Victorian gender construction. These female writers, deeply committed to their church and its patriarchal scaffolding and deeply committed to practices such as polygamy that appeared to the world to restrict and confine them, wrote for themselves identity, space, and opportunity that not only undergirded the entire Mormon experiment but also allowed them to construct their own reality of what it was to be a Mormon woman.

The Foundational Period of Mormon literature, 1830–1880

The first period of Mormon literature produced texts that were didactic and aimed at increasing testimony, righteousness, and conversion. Foundational period literature, comprising primarily scripture, sermons, poetry, letters, journals, and autobiography, found homes in Mormon publications. These newspapers and periodicals not only provided content for the converted but also served as a tool for missionaries who wanted to leave faith-building stories and theological lessons with those investigating the new religion. At this early moment in the church, members believed the literal gathering of Israel for the second coming of Christ was at hand. There was no time for leisure literature; instead, the Saints felt called upon to convert the world in preparation for a new dispensation. Their writings reflected such passion and faith, and they employed all the rhetoric at hand to convince others to follow.

The content of the *Millennial Star*, a periodical established in Britain in 1840, is representative of the early literature of the Foundational Period: there was no place for fiction or poetry that did not further the cause of Christ. The closest the *Star* came to creative or imaginative text were its sections of short first-hand accounts of miraculous happenings. These utilized dialogue, description, and even basic plot devices to capture readers' attention and create spiritual pathos (Clark, 1935, p. 3). While primarily written by men, such accounts told the stories of men, women, and children in common circumstances of hardship that were relieved by the miracles of God.

While not common, women's writing did appear in such periodicals, as did accounts—by writers of both genders—of women in the role of agents in God's work on earth. Eliza Jane Merrick was an English convert living in Windsor with her family. When her daughter, who had long suffered from lung congestion, became worryingly ill, Eliza remembered what Brother Booth had taught her about healing by faith and ritual. She wrote him a letter relating her experience with the miraculous, and he published it in the *Star*:

> Dear Brother Booth, I feel it to be my duty to inform you of the power of healing which has been manifested unto us during the past week. A youthful member of our family ... was obliged to be put in bed, and I anointed her chest with the oil you consecrated, and also gave her some inwardly. That was about four o'clock in the afternoon. She continued very ill all the evening: her breath was very short, and the fever very high. I again anointed her chest in the name of the Lord, and asked his blessing; he was graciously pleased to hear me, and in the course of twenty-four hours she was as well as if nothing had been the matter ... Though I have been but a short time in the church, I have received many blessings, and I hope soon to be able to stand up and testify of the same in Windsor.
>
> *(Merrick, 1849, p. 205)*

Merrick, a new convert who had been taught by missionaries that she had the authority to bless the sick, shared her story with the missionary who taught her. He went on to share it with a larger readership of women. This kind of dissemination germinated seeds that produced a culture of Mormon women engaging as agents in their new religion.

Such first-person stories, particularly those relating the stories of women, reveal an interesting intersect between the gendered separate spheres of Western culture and the surprising egalitarian gifts of the spirit of the early Mormon church. Women could actively participate in and create a lived religion in Mormonism; they were as free and empowered to lay hands to heal, expound scripture, and preach as Mormon men were. This differentiated Mormonism from other religious groups of the 1840s and 1850s that generally still saw suffering as sacred, miracles as ceased, and women as the audience rather than the agents of religious instruction.

Early Mormon literature was influenced foremost by the creativity of Joseph Smith's new theology, and this creative energy was infectious—both men and women felt empowered to speak and imagine with unfettered vision. Joseph Smith's mother Lucy Mack and his wife Emma both wielded considerable social power and force in the growing church—and rather than passive, idealized figureheads, they were publicly engaged in Joseph's work and in their running of the religious community. Lucy and Emma both claimed their voices, and both used them to construct greater space for women within Mormonism. Most influential to Joseph himself, however, was his mother Lucy Mack Smith. She was a storyteller, visionary, and healer.

Liberally educated, Lucy, far more than her husband Joseph Sr., ran the household finances and oversaw the religious upbringing of her family. She educated her children not just to read and write but also to interpret and draw conclusions from texts. She raised her family on stories of God's willingness to intervene in the lives of women: her aunt had been healed by faith—the dramatic story involved the woman rising from her bed for the first time in three years, running through town in her nightdress, opening the door to the church, and preaching the miracles of God. Lucy herself had two similar experiences, one when she had been dying and was lifted out of her body and healed after promising to raise her family to Christ, and another when she held her dying daughter in her arms and prayed to God to heal the child. She also told of having visions of a beautiful tree that connected her and her family to God—all experiences she told as stories to her children and, later, to the members of her son's church.

Lucy was also a regular speaker in church communities, often called upon to tell stories and to preach. On multiple occasions she recounted testifying to the people of Buffalo, New York, as she and a large group of Saints waited for river ice to break so they could board a boat and travel to Kirtland, Ohio. "Brethren and sisters," she called out,

> we call ourselves Latter-day Saints and profess to have come out from among the world for the purpose of serving God with a determination to serve him with our whole might, mind, and strength ... and will you suffer yourselves to begin at the very first sacrifice of comfort to complain ...? And ever worse, for here are my sisters fretting for the want of their rocking chairs! And brethren ... you are complaining that you have left a good house and now you have no home to go to ... How easy it would be for God to cause the ice to break away, and in a moment's time we could be off on our journey; but how can you expect the Lord to prosper you when you are continually murmuring against him?
>
> *(Smith, 1831, pp. 5–6)*

Lucy had stepped forward to head this group of converts when the presiding male church leader refused to do so. She chided the men and women equally and stood as an example of the authority and potential of Mormon women.

In Ohio, Missouri, and Illinois, Lucy bestowed blessings on both male and female church members. While her husband's blessings, being patriarch, were recorded, Lucy's appear only as mentions in journals and meeting minutes. These blessings were creative acts of skill and inspiration, crafted for an audience with rhetorical purpose, pathos, imagery and metaphor, and specific literary form.

As an orator and leader, Lucy's sermons and blessings helped develop a powerful female Mormon identity. Her dictated autobiography composed the narrative content of what would become the mythology of the church. *The History of Lucy Smith, Mother of the Prophet* stands parallel to the male-authored church history now canonized as scripture, providing a female framework that positioned the prophet Joseph first and foremost as her son and, secondly, positioned Joseph as beneficiary of the faith, wisdom, and status of her male and female Mack family progenitors. Her text, completed just over a year after Joseph's June 1845 martyrdom, immediately begins with a statement of her authority as a woman, a historian, and a writer:

> Having attained my 69 year, and being afflicted with a complication of diseases and infirmities many of which have been brought upon me by the cruelty of an ungodly and hard hearted world ... I feel it <a privilege as well as> my duty to ... trace carefully up, even from the cradle to the grave The footsteps of some whose life and death has been such as <are calculated> to excited an intense curiosity in the minds of all who ever knew them personally or shall hear of them hereafter. And ... no one on earth <is so thoroughly acquainted> as myself <with> the entire history.
>
> *(Smith, 1845, p. 220)*

Lucy immediately wrote herself as the only reliable narrator of the history of the prophet and the church. She underscored the careful crafting of her text and positioned the readers—even those who believed they knew and understood Joseph better—as curious outsiders. In her very first line, Lucy threatened any who might question or argue with her authority and her book: doing so would reveal themselves as belonging to the cruel, ungodly, and hard-hearted world. The true Saints, as she expressed in her sermon on the icy shores of Buffalo, were above the world.

Within a decade after its completion, Lucy's autobiography and family memoir was complicated by "layers of words" placed upon it by church leaders seeking a history that placed them and their leadership in better light; Lucy's voice was "obscured in the skirmishing of the men who took over the project" (Anderson, 2001, pp. 66–67). Lucy's original book is not extant; instead, there are competing versions produced between 1853 and 1945. Brigham Young, after the 1853 version published in the *Millennial Star*, demanded Lucy's book be kept from church members and destroyed, and he had George A. Smith make the revisions to the *Star*'s version; the LDS church leadership wanted control over the telling of its history. Leonard Arrington, church historian from 1972 to 1982, explained that Brigham suppressed Lucy's book "primarily because of the favorable references and space devoted to William Smith" (Lucy's son who she believed should lead the church instead of Brigham), and explained that Lucy's text "perhaps tells more about Mormon origins than any other single source" (Shipps, 1987, p. 91).

The church leadership has always had a vested interest in controlling its history, particularly as essential interpretations of central ideas such as priesthood and authority change over time—sometimes as quickly as over one or two decades. Considering that the mid-nineteenth century was pivotal in the cultural transformation of women's spheres, roles, education, and citizenship, it is not surprising that the revolutionary voice of Mormon women such as Lucy Mack and Emma Smith were of concern to later church leadership, specifically as church presidents sought to centralize and regulate power and authority.

Perhaps the clearest instance of women's voices being later over-written by male leadership during the Foundational Period is the revision of the minutes from the Female Relief Society of Nauvoo. As president of the Society, Emma oversaw a quorum of women, and her secretary, Eliza Snow, recorded all the sermons, prophecies, instructions, and conversation. "We expect extraordinary occasions and pressing calls," Emma told the women at their first meeting in 1842 (Derr et al., 2016, p. 35).

Eliza's Society minutes included almost every word the prophet Joseph told the sisters, including the things he told them regarding their new and empowered place in the restored church of Christ:

> This Society is to get instruction thro' the order which God has established—thro' the medium of those appointed to lead—and I now turn the key to you in the name of God ... This is the beginning of better days, to this Society.
>
> *(Derr et al., 2016, p. 59)*

The women of the Relief Society were now authorized to expound the scriptures, exhort the Saints, administer in the church—all responsibilities that had been structural male privileges in centuries of religious power that relied upon King James' New Testament.

Twelve years after Joseph's instructions to the Society, Church President Brigham Young called George A. Smith to compile a history of the church—the same man Brigham called to revise Lucy Mack's book. George A. made edits and changes to the Relief Society minutes that would stand for over 150 years. With Eliza's minutes in hand, he revised Joseph's instructions:

> [Emma Smith and her presidency] will receive instruction through the order of the Priesthood which God has established, through the medium of those appointed to lead guide and direct the affairs of the church in this last Dispensation and I now turn the key in your behalf in the name of the Lord ... this is the beginning of better days to the poor and needy.
>
> *(Derr et al., 2016, p. 207)*

George A. Smith had taken Emma and Eliza's texts of female empowerment and enfranchisement and rewritten them as a male-centric condescension to give the females something to do. No longer agents of their own, no longer the promise of better days for all women everywhere, George A. Smith's revised text re-circumscribed Mormon women into a separate sphere of caring for the poor and needy.

The nineteenth century saw unprecedented growth and changes in the culture and empowerment of women throughout Europe and North America, and Mormon women, though self-removed to the margins of American society, positioned themselves at the forefront of that promise. Emma Smith and the women of the Relief Society saw themselves as empowered by the prophet to open the door for the uplift of women throughout the world. For them, all the gains of the nineteenth and early twentieth centuries, from suffrage to increased educational opportunities, would come from the key Emma and her sisters turned for women (Madsen, 1982, pp. 173–74).

Despite repeated diminution, as the LDS Church moved west from Nauvoo, many of the Relief Society sisters grew into visionaries, perhaps even more so than their male counterparts. While the revolutionary promise of Mormonism was a direct humankind connection with a benevolent active deity, Mormon women were not just rewriting Christianity; they were revisioning the lived state of womankind. They were creating a Mother God. They had a vision of women with spiritual, ecclesiastical, secular, and political authority. They had accessed authority in Nauvoo, and they remembered the promises the prophet Joseph had made to them about better days.

The Relief Society sisters, regardless of how forward thinking many of them may have been about the place of women in society, were not so revolutionary when it came to racial and cultural diversity. Though early converts joined the church from Australia and the Pacific Islands, various European countries, and every region of the United States, members were almost entirely white. While arguably surprisingly egalitarian in their first decades, after the death of Joseph Smith they easily returned to the racial sentiments of the larger American society.

Eliza Snow, both as a poet and as the church's de facto female leader, constructed a lived religion that was privileged by its exclusion of color. In her 1864 poem, "The Lamanite" (an LDS term for an indigenous American), Eliza spoke of the whitening of a "red man" when he would choose to embrace the gospel:

> The night of ignorance, which deep shades distil'd/On the poor red man, nearly is fulfill'd:/Another key, the Priesthood turns, and lo!/The glimm'ring rays of light begin to flow/From the broad fountain of eternal day,/And hope is hov'ring o'er his darksome way./ ... ./The scales will fall, which now becloud their eyes,/And they, in truthful purity, arise;/And the now loathsome, savage Lamanite,/Will, when the Lord removes the curse, be white:/He'll learn our ways and feel as saints should do,/And will assist in building Zion too./He'll yet go forth and from his thicket den,/As a young lion, prowl on guilty men—/The scourge of justice—vengeance' rod, he'll be,/And smite with fearful, savage cruelty.
>
> (Snow, 1864)

Even in his purification, the indigenous man is helpful to white Zion not for his mimicry of the civilized or allegiance to his colonizer but for his innate, essentialized violence. He will take up his rod for an avenging God. What is most interesting, however, are not the tropes and stereotypes of red men and savagery but the specific language she employs to usher in a better day:

The time of ignorance for the indigenous people is almost gone, she explains, and it will end with "Another key, the Priesthood turns." This turning key evokes the very words of Joseph Smith that Eliza herself recorded in the minute book for the Relief Society of Nauvoo. Joseph turned the key to the women, giving them the agency and authority to act in God's kingdom for themselves. This is the same passage that George A. Smith altered and that Eliza certainly would have seen when the revised minutes were reprinted in the *Deseret News* in 1855. Having been officially erased from the authority to use the key Joseph turned to women, Eliza nonetheless wrote the Native American into a similar confinement—just one beneath her own.

Home Literature, 1880–1930

While the priesthood key to act without male intermediaries had been rewritten, Mormon women, particularly those who had received ritual endowments in the Nauvoo temple or Salt Lake endowment house, continued to claim empowerment and act with ritual authority in what they considered a sacred ordinance. While women such as Lucy Mack gave blessings, their words were very rarely recorded and certainly not published. However, since their time in Nauvoo, Relief Society sisters had begun composing an important and powerful oral text, passed from mother to daughter, matriarch to young woman. The confinement rituals were sacred administrations in preparation for childbirth, and by the end of the Foundational Period of Mormon literature, specific prescribed language had been attached. It wouldn't be until the second decade of the twentieth century that a few individual Relief Societies would record the words in their minute books. The language of the confinement rituals is, without question, high sacred literature. Filled with metaphor and imagery, the ritual language is a female writing of the body.

The ritual began as Mormon women gathered together to wash and anoint a pregnant woman's body as they, individually and in unison, recited ritual blessings over her and her unborn child:

> Sister Mary we wash you commencing at the crown of your head preparatory for your Annointing [sic] for your safe delivery speedy recovery life and salvation of your Offspring and we ask the Lord that all the faculities [sic] of your head that you may retain them through life your reverence for God and sacred things may increase with your days we wash your ears that you may retain your natural hearing your forehead that your intellect powers may never be impaired by accident or disease your eyes that you may retain your natural sight your nose the sense of smell your lips that you may praise God for his goodness.
>
> (*Tropic Ward, undated, pp. 248–49*)

The language is filled with repeated imagery of the body—blessings on the individual parts and their functions, blessings on the whole. The spoken physical inventory connected the recipient's womanly body directly to her spiritual self, creating a divine wholeness that worked to bless and heal the compartmentalization and divided attentions of female life.

The attention to physicality in LDS women's blessing and administration texts also speaks to the disconnect between a female body created in the image of a male God and calls forth the theology Mormonism offers of a divine Mother God. In blessing a woman's body, part by part, it was made sacred and pure. It was lifted out of the fallen world and redeemed, no longer a liability or commodity, no longer valuable only when deemed so by the male gaze. Instead, the female body became a reflection of the female God in whose image it was created.

In writing a space for themselves inside Mormon culture and theology, nineteenth-century Mormon women invoked the presence of the female divine by the act of gathering as women, making sacred the female body and touch, and creating a reality of authority that existed independent of a male filter. Their blessing and anointing literature spoke to their need to construct identity outside of the patriarchal order, to their need to claim their bodies as their own, and to their centrality in Mormon theology.

While sacred, unpublished Mormon texts in the nineteenth century may have been extraordinarily inventive and introspective—much like its creative and boundary-breaking theology, public literature valued scripture and personal experiences, rejecting fiction for truth and resplendence for the didactic. Primarily composed of theology, essays and articles, short fiction, and stories of real life, early Mormon literature was primarily utilitarian, aimed at providing instruction, converting the youth; averting obsolescence in leaders, parents, and lifestyle guidelines; and developing personal knowledge and skills. These texts were disseminated almost entirely through the explosion of LDS publications.

For adult Mormon women, the *Woman's Exponent* was essential in sharing instruction for Relief Society work from church leadership, organizing women and educating them regarding suffrage, and mobilizing them to get the vote. Established in 1872, it ran through the first three decades of the Home Literature period. The *Exponent* included some of the very best Mormon autobiography and history, publishing women's memoirs of their experiences in Nauvoo and Winter Quarters, printing their poetry, and providing them with access to high quality literature and biography from outside Mormonism. Although ostensibly for all Mormon women—on numerous occasions it published the comments of Jane Manning James, an African American member who regularly participated in its semi-monthly meetings—the *Exponent* assumed only a privileged white audience.

In an 1884 essay that included her instructions to Relief Society members, President Eliza Snow wrote regarding the confinement rituals:

> Any and all sisters who honor their holy endowments, not only have the right, but should feel it a duty, whenever called upon to administer to our sisters in these ordinances, which God has graciously committed to His daughters ... to apply them for the relief of human suffering.
>
> (Snow, 1884, p. 61)

The assumption—and the assertion—is that women who participate in the ritual must be endowed. Such instruction was news to many, going against the previous decades' practice. In one sentence, Eliza cut most Mormon women off from their ritual participation. Women who were not white could not attend the temple, so they could not be endowed. Women who were too poor to travel distances could not attend the temple, so they could not be endowed. For all intents and purposes, Eliza Snow relocated Mormon women's ritual access—its literature and its performance—to the space of white enfranchised privilege.

For Mormon writers after 1890 through most of the twentieth century, the deeply powerful foundational texts of Mormon women—Lucy Mack's autobiography, the Female Relief Society of Nauvoo minutes, and the confinement ritual texts—simply did not exist. Such literature had been co-opted, rewritten, or locked away "by church leaders to emphasize priesthood authority and order" (Derr et al., 2016). This authority, this order, was patriarchal. Early Mormon women, however forward thinking they may have been, were still products of their time and, committed to their faith and deeply respectful of their leaders, were complicit in their own circumscription. The pioneering Saints had purposefully constructed themselves as noble and sacred outsiders—

choosing to step out of a fallen world. But even in the process of locating themselves into the margins, they held tight to their privilege.

The *Woman's Exponent* was instrumental in white Utah women's suffrage and their growing political power. Emmeline B. Wells was an early contributor to the *Exponent*, writing essays, poems, and opinion pieces and, after taking the helm, editorials. She signed her work in three different ways, however. Her strong feminist pieces were ascribed to Blanche Beechwood, she used her given name to sign her first editorials, and later she published also as Aunt Em—a character whose strains hit the more sentimental and romantic notes of Home Literature (Madsen, 1982, pp. 166–67). The brilliance was that Emmeline was all these persons simultaneously, and her ability to speak in different voices to different audiences was essential in both the success of the *Exponent* and to the success of Mormon women's suffrage.

While much of the history of American women's rights has relegated the work of Mormon women to footnotes, the literature of suffrage was influenced in important ways by the words and work of LDS feminists. In 1902, Emmeline was an invited speaker at the National Council of Women; the *Exponent* published her address in its April issue:

> One of the tremendous forces more recently brought into active exercise, which had heretofore lain partially dormant, is this *awakening* of woman … She comes upon the stage of the great drama of the world's history at the most opportune time … and she has come to stay until all is accomplished that now lies hidden from view in the womb of the unborn years.
>
> *(Wells, 1902)*

Emmeline went on to explain that in the Garden of Eden, women and men were equal partners, created equally by God and honored equally in the creation of the world. She was using King James' Bible to fight for women's elevation, turning a tool of patriarchy upside down.

Emmeline then moved to the nineteenth century, explaining that women had been "instrumental in bringing about the restoration of that equality which existed when the world was created." Her use of the term restoration spoke to her LDS audience, calling forth the centrality of Mormon women in the prophet Joseph's promise that the Relief Society's turned key would open the door for all women throughout the world.

Emmeline closed her address with a scriptural reading that reflected a new feminist theology in Mormonism that had been percolating for over three decades. The promise of the restoration was that all people, male and female, could receive revelation, spiritual gifts, and empowerment from God; this promise elevated the potential and influence of LDS women, and it created an entirely new reading of the creation. She told her audience that women participated in the creation. Woman was made, by God, equal to man and was honored, as equal, by God. She asserted that Eve was a righteous ideal, and the glory of Eve's choice had been realized in the current day:

> It is this spirit stirring within women that is to bring her back again to that primeval state that existed in the Garden of Eden. It is the song of the poets ringing down the ages, and, as it were, the echoes of the divine music of a far-off region of sublime hopes and aspirations that had lingered in the soul without power of expression, a dim memory of something far distant, call it by what name you will, it is an incentive to higher thought—an idea, a superb height of excellence towards which we are climbing, slowly, may be, but surely.
>
> *(Wells, 1902)*

Eve was redeemed and, in doing so, Mormon women recreated themselves over again.

LDS publications were widely available to a growing Mormon audience, and they exerted significant influence on its culture and values. The development of literary standards and an excellence in craft began to accelerate—in thanks primarily to the growth of periodicals for Mormon adolescents. In 1890, the *Young Woman's Journal* and the *Contributor* (a magazine for young men) began publication. Both had a mission of developing young writers and providing quality literature—as well as building conversion, faith, and church participation in youth—and they mark the beginning of the Mormon short story (Gardner, 1979; De Schweinitz, 2000). They capitalized, of course, on the fact that young adults in Utah were reading fiction.

The California gold rush and the completion of the transcontinental railroad brought fiction to Utah. In addition to low-quality dime novels, Mormons were reading Dickens, the Brontes, George Eliot, and Stowe, and they were finding not only high-quality literature but also a vision of expanding the soul and becoming better as a people. By the 1890s, Mormons were writing and reading far beyond the scope and content of their first decades, and LDS leaders were encouraging them—especially those leaving for missions on the east coast and in Europe—to read history, science, and literature in order to make themselves more conversant and intelligent teachers of the gospel and to write literature in order not only to keep artistic pace with the larger culture but also to radiate the gospel truths through their texts (Clark, 1935, pp. 4–5).

The editors of the *Young Woman's Journal* and the *Contributor* capitalized on the shift in tone from church leaders. They did not warn the youth of the dangers of novels; in fact, they provided instruction and enccuragement to budding authors, poets, and dramatists. They solicited original texts from readers, and often editors would privately correspond with contributors, guiding the novice with lessons about writing styles, how to practice, and early semictics (Gardner, 1979, p. 4). Subsequently, their publications were filled with the efforts of Mormon youth, quite a few of whom had work that became quite skilled, even appearing in LDS periodicals for over five decades.

One of the strongest writers of this time was Josephine Spencer. Her poems and short stories were both a mainstay in Utah publishing and published in national reviews, and she herself was a celebrated editor with the *Deseret Evening News*. While her literature grew from her life within Mormonism and its culture, often utilizing LDS symbols and allusions, she did not shy away from themes and subject matter that pushed the conventional boundaries of Mormon literary and cultural norms.

Much like Emmeline and her multiple pseudonyms, Josephine played with genre conventions and expectations, often using a comfortable narrative voice that led readers to unexpected conclusions. When paired together, Josephine's short story "By Unmapped Paths" (1911) and her poem "A Knight of the Way" (1905) illuminate the kind of work she was doing to empower young women and move the Mormon female identity beyond sentiment and romanticism. Both pieces appeared in the *Young Woman's Journal*.

Loraine, the protagonist of "By Unmapped Paths," had grown up wealthy and privileged but finds herself destitute after her father's death, with no marketable skills. She lucks into a job as a house maid to the Cathcart family. When the son returns from college, however, he "commits siege to Loraine":

> He grasped her hand and Loraine tried to push past him in the hall … Cathcart caught her waist … Loraine tried to force herself free—but her efforts only serve to strengthen his persistence. Before she could move away, he had clasped her with both arms and kissed her.
>
> (Spencer, 1911, p. 7)

The assault is interrupted by his mother, who turns Loraine out. A time later, Cathcart finds her and attempts to sway her. "I don't want to boast," he says, "but you are not the first girl I have kissed—and, well, the 'highest society girl' is not above an innocent flirtation. You took it too seriously" (Spencer, 1911, p. 8).

Cathcart begs friendship and promises to marry her once he is no longer dependent on his father. He convinces her to move to his college town to be near him by promising her work and a loan for the trip. Despite letters with promises, the money and work never come. Loraine, in desperation takes her meager savings and instead travels to Colorado. Her train crashes, and the doctor who is tending to the victims happens to be a childhood friend from home. He instructs her how to nurse the patients, a skill which she develops quickly into a vocation. They marry, they have children. Happy ending.

At first glance, "By Unmapped Paths" is a standard sentimental piece of Home Literature. Yet Josephine depicts Cathcart with such realism and the assault with strong and powerful language, and in doing so underscores the violence of what in similar stories is merely an unsolicited embrace. Instead of being rescued into security by the son of her wealthy employer who promises her the world, Loraine chooses to move on into the unknown, and there she finds a vocation and a partner who supports her. Instead of giving young Mormon girls a story of sentiment and rescue, Josephine teaches them how to identify false love, how to be brave, and how to find value in their own work.

The same themes play out in her poem "A Knight of the Way," in which there are two characters, Hope and Fear:

> Hope came tripping down the road,/There upon the stile sat Fear;/Balefully his glances showed/At her tread of careless cheer./"Halt!" he shouted, as she came;/But Hope's footsteps never stayed—/Well she knew his evil fame/And the spell his sorceries laid./"One pace neared to the stile/And your life is in my hand!"/Loud Fear threatened. With a smile/Hope the little distance spanned/ ... /"Bog and Maze beyond thee wait."/Fear with fainter accent plead:/"Beckons there an evil fate/Where your careless steps are led."/But Hope passed with steady pace/To the turning in the lane/Where the sunrise kissed her face,/And there spread the blossoming plain.
>
> (Spencer, 1905)

The knight is, of course, the young woman Hope. Assaulted by the man Fear, she is confronted with the evils of the world that play upon her own self-doubt in an attempt to snare her and drag her low. Hope, however, even when presented with a turn in the road that she cannot see past, braves the unknown and is, in return, blessed with light.

There are, perhaps, few other Home Literature poems that better encapsulate the best of literature of Mormon women in the first eighty years of the LDS Church. They were creating their own world inside a growing patriarchal church. They were determining their own place in the theology, and building a female Mormon identity that could not be cowered and instead would reach beyond the blind turns and false promise of fear.

Conclusion

The study of Mormon literature going forward must grapple with its past. It must consider and value the Foundational and Home Literature periods and deal with the quality, content, and genres of Mormonism in the nineteenth century. These texts are essential to understanding the values and culture of their moments, and they have the potential to inform twenty-first-century

Mormonism in powerful ways that upset prevailing official historical narratives and assumptions that diminish the lives of early Saints. Scholars have been slow to approach Foundational and Home Literature with lenses of feminism, gender theory, post-colonialism, whiteness studies, etc.—all of which have the potential of illuminating meaning and Mormon identity in significant and important ways.

With no primary publisher, no uniquely Mormon literary criticism, and no way to ensure the physical longevity of a text outside of an archive, the first eighty years of Mormon literature, for all intents and purposes, disappeared from public memory. Unlike other subgroups of American literature such as Jewish and African American literature, there was no long tradition of Mormon storytelling. As a nascent religion without a single people, members were busy constructing a church that set them apart from the larger American community. Perhaps it was the women who understood that, before they could create a literature that was uniquely Mormon, they had to create a uniquely Mormon identity. While their texts may have been lost for a time, their influence on today's Mormon women has not.

The Mormon female identity of today is informed by the revolutionary work that nineteenth-century Mormon women undertook. They created a theology that elevated women, that connected them to a female deity, that reclaimed the female body from the male gaze, that won the vote and worked for suffrage throughout the world, and taught bravery in the face of fear. As Emmeline promised, as she stood overlooking the women gathered at the National Convention, "History may not have preserved it all, there may be no tangible record of what has been gained, but sometime we shall know that nothing has been irretrievably lost" (Wells, 1902).

References

Anderson, L.F., 2001. *Lucy's Book: A Critical Edition of Lucy Mack Smith's Family Memoir*. Salt Lake City, UT: Signature Books.
Clark, G., 1935. *A Survey of Early Mormon Fiction*. Provo, UT: BYU Thesis.
De Schweinitz, R., 2000. Preaching the Gospel of Church and Sex: Mormon Women's Fiction in the LDS *Young Woman's Journal*, 1889–1910. *Dialogue: A Journal of Mormon Thought* 33(4): 27–54.
Derr, J., Madsen, C.C., Holbrook, K., and Grow, M.J., 2016. *The First Fifty Years of Relief Society: Key Documents in Latter-day Saint Women's History*. Salt Lake City, UT: Church Historian's Press.
England, E., 1995. Mormon Literature: Progress and Prospects. In D.J. Whittaker. *Mormon Americana: A Guide to Sources and Collections in the United States*. Provo, UT: BYU Studies, pp. 455–505.
Friedman, S., 1998. Women's Autobiographical Selves: Theory and Practice. In S. Friedman. *Mappings: Feminism and the Cultural Geographies of Encounter*. Princeton, NJ: Princeton University Press, p. 79.
Gardner, A., 1979. *Representative Mormon Short Stories 1890 to 1940: Evolution of Sentimentalism Towards Realism*. Provo, UT: BYU Thesis.
Madsen, C.C., 1982. Emmeline B. Wells: "Am I Not a Woman and a Sister." *BYU Studies Quarterly* 22(2): 161–78.
Merrick, E.J., 1849. Several cases of Miraculous Healing by the Power of God. *Millennial Star* 2, p. 205.
Morrill, S., 2014. Gender in Mormon Studies: Obstacles and Opportunities. *Mormon Studies Review* 1: 63–69.
Shipps, J., 1987. *Mormonism: The Story of a New Religion*. Urbana, IL: University of Illinois Press.
Smith, L.M., 1831. Where Is Your Confidence in God. In J. Reeder and K. Holbrook. *At the Pulpit: 185 Years of Discourses by Latter-day Saint Women*. Salt Lake City, UT: The Church Historians Press, pp. 4–5.
Smith, L.M., 1845. Prologue. In L.F. Anderson. *Lucy's Book*. Salt Lake City, UT: Signature Books, p. 220.
Snow, E., 1864. The Lamanite. In J. Derr and K.L. Davidson. *Eliza R. Snow: The Complete Poetry*. Provo, UT: Brigham Young University Press, pp. 691–95.
Snow, E., 1884. To the Branches of the Relief Society. *Woman's Exponent* 13: 61.

Spencer, J., 1905. A Knight of the Way. *Young Woman's Journal* 16: 292.
Spencer, J., 1911. By Unmapped Paths. *Young Woman's Journal* 22(1): 3–14.
Tropic Ward Relief Society Minutes and Records, n.d. Salt Lake City, UT: Church History Library, Reel #5 1896 LR 9290 14, pp. 248–49.
Wells, E.B., 1902. The Age We Live In. *Woman's Exponent* 30(12): 89–90.

Further reading

Cracroft, R.H., and Lambert, N.E., 1979. *A Believing People: Literature of the Latter-day Saints*. Salt Lake City, UT: Desert Book.

This is the first anthology of Mormon literature, as such it has not yet ascribed developmental periods to the literature but instead approaches it by genre.

De Schweinitz, R., 2000. Preaching the Gospel of Church and Sex: Mormon Women's Fiction in the LDS *Young Woman's Journal*, 1889–1910. *Dialogue: A Journal of Mormon Thought* 33(4): 27–54.

This is one of the better treatments of women's fiction in early LDS periodicals. It considers specific pieces of short fiction and longer serialized pieces.

England, E., 1995. Mormon Literature: Prospects and Progress. In D.J. Whittaker. *Mormon Americana: A Guide to Sources and Collections in the United States*. Provo, UT: BYU Studies, pp. 455–505.

By far the most comprehensive treatment of Mormon literature, it establishes—for the first time—developmental periods, and it provides an overview of the problems in the field.

England, E., and Anderson, L.F., 1996. *Tending the Garden: Essays on Mormon Literature*. Salt Lake City, UT: Signature Books.

Authoritative collection of critical readings and scholarship on Mormon literature.

Peterson, B., 2014. Redeemed from the Curse Placed upon Her: Dialogic Discourse on Eve in the *Woman's Exponent*. *The Journal of Mormon History* 40(1): 135–74.

In depth discussion of Mormon women's construction of a theology of a redeemed Eve utilizing literary texts published before and in the *Woman's Exponent*.

19
SEXUAL PURITY AND ITS DISCONTENTS IN MORMONISM

Sara Moslener

Surveying the scholarship on sexual purity that has emerged in the last few years leads one to believe that evangelical Christians hold a monopoly on an industry that imbues adolescent sexuality with the gravity of eternal things. Though the influence of evangelical purity culture in the United States cannot be understated, it does conceal the efforts of other Christian churches with similar initiatives. For numerous historical reasons, the Church of Jesus Christ of Latter-day Saints has not had the degree of cultural and political power as evangelical Christians. However, within Mormon institutions and communities, sexual purity is a deeply embedded and theologized principle, not merely borrowed from evangelicals, but grown out of long-standing church teachings on the family and eternal salvation.

The purpose of this chapter is to examine how the LDS Church promotes sexual purity as a foundational theological principle. As a formalized church teaching, there is no effort to update the language to make it appeal to a young, contemporary audience. As this rhetoric intersects with the lived experiences of Mormons, it is left to believers, themselves, to articulate this principle in the contemporary world. Therefore, a second purpose of this chapter is to understand how church members negotiate these teachings alongside the questions posed by the world they live in. The most useful primary sources toward this two-fold end include church doctrine, youth magazines, blogs, and religious education curricula and resources. Careful analysis of these sources reveals a sustained commitment to sexual purity that is situated within a sophisticated theological understanding of family and eternal salvation. Far more than evangelical Christians who prioritize its temporal benefits, Mormons who embrace sexual purity articulate a relationship between earthly life and heavenly expectations. This is pointedly not a concession to the modern world, but an effort to maintain a strong institutional presence in the lives of Mormon believers.

A video created for LDS educational programs for young women nicely illustrates how Mormon advocates of sexual purity must negotiate the formality of church teachings while crafting a message that successfully communicates purity teachings to young people. In this video, young children are asked to participate in the variation of the social psychological experiment that requires them to make a choice between a small treat (such as a marshmallow or chocolate chip) or waiting for a more substantial treat (two marshmallows or a box with an unknown item inside.) The camera rolls for several minutes chronicling how the children endure their curiosity and impatience with some sniffing the box, others expressing boredom, or egging one another on with whispers.

Eventually, the video reveals that thirty-two out of the thirty-sex children did not opt for the chocolate chip. The virtuous thirty-two un-box their treat to discover a cupcake abundantly loaded with icing. Following this big reveal the video narrates the following:

> Why? They knew there was a much greater reward if they waited. Your Heavenly Father wants you to wait until marriage ... To use your procreative powers so He can bless you with something so much greater than a cupcake: Peace, Eternal Marriage, Power, Purity, Love, Sealed to Children Forever, Love, Joy, Eternal Life. It's worth waiting for.
>
> *(Phillips, 2011)*

At this point, the visual and audio motif shifts away from the happy children and their cupcakes, to a more somber image of the temple in Salt Lake City accompanied by seminary music, a genre of classical, religious music especially composed for the church. A list of blessings is superimposed as the camera pans upward toward the trumpeting Angel Moroni. Though the transition is somewhat jarring for the viewer, the effect demonstrates the challenges the church faces when attempting to maintain the gravitas and tradition of stated teachings, while also seeking to connect with its younger members. Unlike evangelical Christians who are not a singular church organization and have propelled their influence by crafting "culturally relevant" teachings for young people, the LDS Church situates its institutional power in the historicized rhetoric of doctrinal orthodoxies.

However, no religious institution, regardless of structure, is fully defined by formalized teachings articulated by its leadership. The institutional expectations are navigated by church members whose lived experiences shape how they articulate their own understandings of purity. In some cases, this means understanding young people who strive to live out stated principles in hopes of securing a happy married life and weathering the storms of adolescent life. For others, it means articulating critiques of church authority and resisting the patriarchal assumptions that accompany purity teachings. Though the LDS Church is an organization that requires a high level of institutional investment and, with that, daily practices of conformity and restraint, dissident voices are more than evident.

Celestial Marriage

The Law of Chastity is an official church teaching that supports one of the most fundamental ideals of Mormon theology, the concept of Celestial Marriage. Family life for LDS believers is not only an earthly arrangement, as it plays a significant role in the church's teachings about eternal life or the Celestial Kingdom. For Mormons, salvation and the rewards of Heaven are achieved through two institutions—the church and the family. "Only through celestial marriage can one find the straight way, the narrow path. Eternal life cannot be had in any other way. The Lord was very specific and very definite in the matter of marriage" (Kimball, 1976, n.p.). Couples who are married in the temple enter into an eternal relationship, bonding themselves to one another and to God. That is, they will remain married beyond their earthly existence. The two people are married according to temporal law, but also sealed together for the next life through the marriage ritual within the temple. Marriage, then, is a foundational component of LDS understanding of salvation, as marriage and child-bearing grant one access to greater levels of exaltation in the heavenly realm (Hoyt, 2007, p. 97).

A couple who seeks a Celestial Marriage must first demonstrate they are worthy of being married in the temple, much of their worth gained through obedience to the Law of Chastity.

As a teaching that requires abstinence from sexual activity before marriage, the Law of Chastity is not unique to the LDS Church. Like numerous other purity teachings, it names the benefits and detriments associated with sexual purity and sexual immorality. Those who are faithful to its teaching will enjoy a marriage of love, trust, commitment, happiness, and unity. For those who falter, relationships will be fraught with fear, guilt, and shame. To support this end, the Law of Chastity provides numerous guidelines for personal conduct to keep one away from situations that might tempt one to disobedience. These include a high level of self-monitoring including controlling one's thoughts, avoiding pornography and any activities that can stimulate sexual feelings including "passionate kissing, lying with or on top of another person, or touching the private, sacred parts of another person's body" (*For the Strength*, 2011, p. 36). Again, these requirements are not uniquely Mormon as they appear often in evangelical purity teachings. However, in the LDS Church these remain orthodox teachings, whereas for evangelicals they are cultural prescriptions that cannot be as easily monitored by institutional practices.

These earliest teachings on Celestial Marriage recorded in the church's Doctrine and Covenants assert that a man can only achieve the status of priesthood through Celestial Marriage. Without a family he cannot participate in the plan of procreation and thus his route to the eternal kingdom is limited, if not entirely stunted. The Celestial Kingdom comprises three heavens or levels of glory, the highest of which is attainable only through the covenant of marriage (The Church of Jesus Christ of Latter-day Saints, 2013). Thus, the primary purpose of Celestial Marriage is not to join two people, but for those two people to create a family through child-bearing. The importance of procreation to Mormon theology cannot be overstated, as it also plays a significant role in how believers enter eternal life. The church teaches that children who are born have pre-existed as souls in the pre-mortal realm. These children are sealed to their parents, the parents to one-another, and together they are blessed with joy and happiness, as promised by God. The entire family unit, when sealed, remains intact as its members pass from this world to the next.

The concept of "sealing" is unique to Mormon teachings. According to church teachings, the physical body is not a covering or just a component of the soul—it is an essential part of the soul. When couples are sealed, their physical selves become one, as described in Genesis when Adam and Eve become "one flesh." The use of the word "seal" is intentional as it communicates a spiritual and physical connection that is eternal. Sexual intercourse between husband and wife is a symbol of the physical unity of their sealing (Holland, 1999).

The institutional rhetoric of sexual purity, then, always refers back to the concept of Celestial or temple marriage and the procreative mandate. Physical immorality threatens more than the imminent health and happiness of individual believers, it threatens the spiritual status of the entire family, present and future. Sexual desire, also understood as the impulse to procreate, was created by God to be an overpowering force in order to demonstrate the divine mandate of child-bearing (Packer, 1972). Any interference with the procreative process, either through infidelity in marriage, extra-marital sex, and homosexuality is an "abuse of power he has given us to create life" (The Church of Jesus Christ of Latter-day Saints, 2016).

In the 1970s, the church introduced a magazine dedicated to young readers called *New Era*. As a church publication, its messaging reflects the institutional tone of church teachings. However, it is also a publication attempting to make church teaching more accessible to an adolescent audience and often creates space for younger members to voice their own views. Most importantly, *New Era*, from its inception has been dedicated to helping young people prepare to enter into a Celestial Marriage.

In one of the earliest issues of *New Era*, the publication ran the text of a sermon by Elder Boyd K. Packer entitled "Why Stay Morally Clean?" In his lesson, Packer explains why sexual morality is so essential to the care of Mormon bodies, physical and spiritual. A mortal body granted to those previously existing as souls was a gift from God, one that was stamped with God's own impression. Packer goes on to discuss how physical bodies were imbued with the power of procreation, "a light that has the power to kindle other lights" (1972). Thus, treating one's body, protecting it from contamination was necessary for achieving both physical and spiritual blessings. It is through the coupling of pure bodies that other spirits becomes embodied via procreation and enter into the world.

The February 1976 issue includes a sermon by President Spencer Kimball who was even more direct in his message to youth about the importance of preparing to enter into a Celestial Marriage. He narrates the story of a young man who did not prioritize marriage and is called to account for his decisions when facing his final judgment. Through this story, Kimball refers to marriage and procreation as a commandment, a responsibility, and a duty, not simply one life choice among many: "Your Heavenly Father expects you to marry and to rear a good, strong family. The Lord planned that men and women should find each other and have a happy family relationship and remain clean and worthy" (1976).

Celestial Marriage is "God's greatest blessing" and the only context in which the "sacred power of procreation" can be used (*For the Strength*, 2011). Therefore, the care of adolescent believers is the concern of both church and family. For this reason, the church articulates an understanding of adolescent spirituality focused on preparing one for an adulthood in which marriage and parenthood feature prominently. One such resource, *For the Strength of Youth*, demonstrates how church teachings assert a seamless understanding of adolescence, purity, and marriage.

Young people are taught that the Law of Chastity provides them with the necessary guidelines for earning the right to be married in the temple. Both formal and informal teachings offer rules and regulations on teenage behavior including clothing choice, dating, pornography, dancing, and much more explicit sexual behaviors. Adolescents learn that their bodies are temples, sacred sites where the holy is cultivated. Sexual purity protects one from disease as well as spiritual and emotional harm. But more importantly, purity assists adolescents in making choices that will make them worthy of a temple marriage.

In the life of the church, chastity prepares one for deeper institutional investment, namely temple recommendations and rituals. As part of this process, LDS members are expected to confess their sins to their bishop. By demonstrating their ability to live a life that reflects church teachings, Mormons gain greater spiritual status in the church. According to the Law of Chastity,

> Our Heavenly Father has given us the law of chastity for our protection. Obedience to this law is essential to personal peace and strength of character and to happiness in the home. Those who keep themselves sexually pure will avoid the spiritual and emotional damage that always comes from sharing physical intimacies with someone outside of marriage. Those who keep themselves sexually pure will be sensitive to the Holy Ghost's guidance, strength, comfort, and protection and will fulfill an important requirement for receiving a temple recommend and participating in temple ordinances.
>
> *(The Church of Jesus Christ of Latter-day Saints, 2016)*

Temple work is salvation work for Mormons and proving oneself worthy to participate is elemental to Mormon spirituality. The Law of Chastity provides a clear set of guidelines to help believers become "temple ready." This refers to a temple marriage, but also the numerous rituals and ordinances that occur within the grounds of the temple building, a site that is held as sacred by limiting those who may enter its premises. Though the Law of Chastity offers the gift of forgiveness for those who repent of sexual immorality, the process is presented as difficult, far more so than making an initial commitment to chastity.

The June 1980 issue of *New Era* articulated this for its readers in response to a question posed in their Q&A section: "What difference does a temple marriage make in this life?" Part of the answer included guidance on "Preparing for Marriage" which outlines the expectations of those seeking to be married in the temple and thus sealed for eternity. The answer assumes that young people desire a deeper relationship with the ministry of the institutional church through a temple marriage and understand that this choice has implications for both this life and the next. First and foremost, as young people enter into relationships they might consider worthy of marriage, they are required to "protect virtue and to avoid any improper use of the sacred power of creation" (Preparation for Marriage, 1980). At the time of this issue, young men and women focused their worldly ambitions on different tasks—young men on mission work and young women on motherhood—though in 2018 young women were equally encouraged to take a mission prior to marriage. These responsibilities prepare young people for their respective responsibilities within marriage. Men as holders of the priesthood retain the right and responsibility of leadership in both home and church with mission work giving them opportunity to practice the necessary leadership skills. Though these days it is just as common for men and women to do missionary work prior to marriage, the expectation of marriage remains a primary goal. When two young people decide to marry in the temple, family and church support networks offer "direction as to worthiness, but they also receive counsel on the importance of commencing a family, of raising a righteous posterity, and of establishing a priesthood-directed home" (Preparation for Marriage, 1980). Finally, the article reminds its readers that preparation for marriage is not a worldly activity, but one that fosters the spiritual growth and development necessary for entering the heavenly realm.

The next section will address the specific teachings that comprise these guidelines, however, at this point it is important to understand how sexual immorality poses a significant threat to the Mormon theological paradigm. *For the Strength of Youth* is just one of many sources that refer to Alma, a prophet whose teachings are recorded in the Book of Mormon. The story of Alma scolding his son, Corianton for "chasing after a harlot" has been interpreted by numerous LDS teachers to refer to an individual who has been overcome by lust (*For the Strength*, 2011, p. 39).

The text goes onto to say that such a sin is a grave one, second only to that of murder. Traditionally this text from Alma has been used to articulate the depth of sin one is cast into as a result of sexual immorality. Though forgiveness is available through repentance, other teachings warn believers that the process of being restored to holiness is a difficult path. Maintaining the Law of Chastity is more rewarding and requires less effort than seeking to repent from sexual sin.

The institutional rhetoric of sexual purity in the LDS Church is laden with formality and responsibility. The challenge of making these expectations appear accessible and attainable to young people is one that often falls to church members. The transmission of these ideas from institutional creed to adolescent lived experience is often bridged with an object lesson, a teaching that applies the theological principle to an everyday scenario. The next section will demonstrate how religious educators in the LDS Church attempt these translations, for better or worse, and offer a glimpse into the negotiations that everyday Mormons make as they practice their faith.

Object lessons

Chewed gum, used toothbrushes, crushed cookies, split wood, frozen lamp posts, used tape, squeezed toothpaste, a dirty dress, trampled flowers, licked cupcakes, run-away sleds, a camel and a tent: for better or worse, Mormon youth have endured having their bodies and sexual desires compared to all manner of food, hygiene, and lumber-based metaphors by well-meaning adults hoping to impart the urgency of sexual purity. The object lesson is a common pedagogical tool among purity advocates. Its purpose is to transmit a religious teaching as a form of common sense. Object lessons are an effort to make religious teachings or beliefs matter, by using material objects to demonstrate a far more valuable immaterial virtue. In the context of purity teachings they are especially interesting because they animate the essential tension at work in purity teachings—between flesh and spirit, heaven and earth. The quotidian objects of the lesson are put in relationship to one another, each item representing some aspect of experience of the individual believer. Sometimes the object lesson is accompanied by a narrative, but it is always presented as a representation of a particular moral value or theological teaching.

This chapter opened with a highly sophisticated object lesson presented as a video for use in LDS religious education. The scenario of small children sitting with hope and varying levels of patience was a depiction of adolescent sexual desire. They are presented with a chocolate chip and told they can enjoy the small treat now or wait for something even better—the contents of an unopened, white box. Giving into their desire means exchanging mystery and hope for immediate gratification. In this particular lesson, there is no punishment for choosing to have an early sexual experience, but there is the eventual disappointment of realizing what was unknowingly relinquished. Purity teachings hold human sexuality and intimacy at a premium. There is only so much to go around, so the maintenance of physical boundaries is a preservative measure. In LDS teaching where body and soul are intricately connected, preservation of the body is preservation of the soul. Waiting for the cupcake is rewarded with physical satisfaction and eternal happiness.

Adapting purity teachings into teen-friendly lessons is not unique to LDS religious educators. Evangelical organizations like Silver Ring Thing re-frame their pedagogical strategies regularly in order to maintain the attention of their adolescent audiences. A non-denominational organization, Silver Ring Thing (SRT) has traveled the nation since the early 2000s with an eighteen-wheeler packed with lights, lasers, and pyrotechnics. The goal of their national road-show has been to make their message culturally relevant while also encouraging their adolescent audiences to defy what they perceive to be a norm of sexual promiscuity. By utilizing popular cultural tropes, images, and narratives (in this case a horror-film mash-up) purity advocates connect with the world their young audiences inhabit. Yet they've also adapted the rhetoric of the counterculture and promote sexual purity as an act of resistance and individuality.

Their chosen object lesson involves a piece of wood, four unwitting audience members, pyrotechnics, and a chainsaw. Early in the live event, an SRT evangelist retrieves four volunteers from the audience: three young women and one young man. With humor, sincerity, and enthusiasm, he offers the young man a board on which was painted a half of a heart. He explains that this board represents the young man's emotional life. He then motions to each young woman and explains that throughout the course of his life the young man had engaged in premarital sexual activity with each of them. The evangelist then places the young man's heart-board into a vise, asks the volunteers to step aside, and retreats backstage. Seconds later pyrotechnics explode, lights flash, music thunders, and the evangelist reemerges, sporting a hockey mask and wielding a live chainsaw. As the audience screams and the volunteers fall to the floor, Matt hacks the heart-board into pieces.

As the noise subsides and the volunteers catch their breath, the evangelist explains once again that due to the young man's intimate relationships with each of these young women they will now each carry a piece of him for the rest of their lives. After he gives the pieces of the young man's heart-board to the other three, he holds up the piece of heart that remains. "This is what you will take with you when you get married," he says as he displays the remaining heart-board, reduced to a jagged-edged splinter of wood (Moslener, 2015, p. 122).

Because evangelicalism is a sub-culture of Christianity and not a single church organization, students who attend an SRT event come from a variety of religious backgrounds, including none at all. Thus, the organization incorporates evangelization of non-believers into their purity messaging. Though this is a very different approach than that taken by the LDS Church, the challenge is the same: how do you make church teaching accessible and attainable to young people weathering the storms of adolescence? In some ways the task for Mormons is simplified. First, evangelism work is fully integrated into the trajectory of adolescent spirituality via the church's well-established missionary program. While mission work and purity teachings are not wholly distinct in the larger project of Celestial Marriage, church doctrines and Sunday youth education programs provide the primary infrastructure whereby purity teachings are disseminated. Still, the work of making these standards relevant and intriguing to young people is a necessary task. Though Mormons are known for their large-scale productions of church history, when it comes to teaching the Law of Chastity, the more common approach is to make use of object lessons. The previous section on Celestial Marriage includes some mention of the specific stipulations of the Law of Chastity, but a deeper look into the practice of dating and the principle of modesty are necessary in order to begin analyzing how the teachings are translated into the more accessible object lesson.

Within evangelicalism, Christian courtship discourages young people from dating until they are prepared to consider a marriage partner. For many evangelical adolescents courtship has become the gold standard of the purity movement, some even choosing to reserve their first kiss for their wedding day. The LDS Church takes a very different approach, one that encourages dating for older teenagers, while being very clear to define the attitudes and behaviors appropriate for dating. Recommendations for dating are fully articulated in *For the Strength of Youth*, a text Mormon youth are encouraged to turn to with a variety of questions. Other publications point to this resource when addressing this topic, an indication that it holds a great deal of authority as a source of official church doctrine. In it, the church asserts that at the age of 16 young people are permitted to date. Though discouraged from dating one-on-one and dating the same person numerous times, Mormon youth are expected to spend the latter part of their teenage years beginning to think about the kind of person they would seek out as a partner. There is no expectation that adolescents find these partners, as serious relationships during the high school years are greatly discouraged. For those who do date, *For the Strength of Youth* admonishes its readers to protect the honor and virtue of those they date by maintaining careful physical boundaries and planning activities that encourage self-control (2011, p. 36).

Instructions for dating are extensive and clearly delineated, however, formal church teachings often miss the most pressing issues for young people by focusing on ultimate goals and behavioral ideals. This is where a magazine like *New Era* becomes a useful translator of church teaching—adapting the formalized rhetoric into more accessible language and addressing the realistic anxieties of adolescent dating culture. Nonetheless, the magazine maintains its strong connection to church teaching by always referring back to the *For the Strength of Youth* pamphlet. In the February 2018 issue, *New Era* raised a variety of questions young people have about dating including: Is it okay to date someone who is not LDS? How do you keep dating from being awkward? How do I avoid a steady relationship? It is okay to not want to date? Why is no one asking me out on a date? I don't want to ask girls on dates, is that ok? What if I really like someone—is it okay to steady date them? Is it okay to kiss someone as long as you aren't dating? In each case, the author guides readers back to *For the Strength of Youth*, encouraging young people to be familiar enough with the text so they can answer these questions as they are raised. However, the pamphlet also recognizes that official church teachings don't address each and every circumstance faced by young people navigating dating culture. Rather than supplementing the dating rules with more detailed regulations, the pamphlet provides broad principles and a blank space where adolescent readers can insert their own answers. The four principles are brief but all-encompassing: Have an attitude of faith; Try to see the issue from an eternal perspective; Seek advice from church teachings, church leaders, parents, and from God; and Be kind. This is one act of translation that makes church teaching accessible, but also empowers young people to investigate their own questions and take responsibility for the choices they make (Questions and Answers, 2018, n.p.).

A review of blogs dedicated to Mormon adolescent life reveals the only other topic given the same amount of attention as dating: modesty. The Mormon blogosphere is well-populated with a host of fashion sites accompanied by advice on the value of personal modesty. It's in these conversations that one particular element of the Law of Chastity becomes evident: the onus of maintaining purity is placed squarely on the shoulders of young women. *For the Strength of Youth* articulates different standards of modesty, understood as an essential part of purity, for young men and women. Women are given detailed instructions to "avoid short shorts and short skirts, shirts that do not cover the stomach, and clothing that does not cover the shoulders or is low-cut in the front or back." Immediately following are instructions for young men: "Young men should also maintain modesty in their appearance." This harsh discrepancy reveals an underlying gender inequality in church teaching. Young women are expected to monitor their bodies and behaviors as doing so contributes to the maintenance of purity and repression of desire in young men. This explains why both sexes are required to "be neat, clean, and avoid being inappropriately casual," but only the instructions for women indicate a connection between personal modesty and sexual purity (*For the Strength*, 2011, p. 7).

A young Mormon blogger named Whitney wrote extensively about her own commitment to modesty and the benefits she enjoys by obeying this church teaching. Her modesty decalogue includes comfort issues, body acceptance, resisting sexual objectification, personal and spiritual righteousness, ability to make good choices, and garnering the respect of others. She rounds out her list with a desire to please her Heavenly Father, "to show others that you are a princess ... born to be a queen" and to be found worthy to participate in temple rituals, though she does not particularly name marriage (Whitney, 2012).

In recent years, numerous women within the church have expressed substantial dis-ease about the ways that purity teachings have been transmitted. In the spring of 2013 Elizabeth Smart, speaking as a survivor of and advocate for victims of sex trafficking, relayed her own memories of an object lesson, one that informed how she made sense of the experience of being kidnapped, raped, and held captive for nine months. As a devout Mormon youth she has learned that sex outside of marriage is incompatible with her physical, emotional, and spiritual integrity. Like a lot of young religious people, she internalized this teaching as a spiritual axiom, one that when transgressed resulted in estrangement from God. In her LDS context, Smart learned that maintaining sexual purity was key to her ability to achieve Celestial Marriage and eternal happiness. However, purity teachings on the whole do not include lessons on consent or sexual violence. Often, any form of sex outside of marriage is seen as destructive, thus drawing no distinction between consensual pre-marital sex and sexual violence. As a 14-year-old making sense of her captivity, Smart was unable to articulate this distinction. However, she did remember a very effective object lesson. She remembered learning that having sex outside of marriage was like being chewed up like a piece of gum, leaving her dirty and unwanted and best suited for the garbage. She explained to her audience how this teaching informed her thoughts while she endured sexual violence as a young teenager:

> I thought, "Oh my gosh, I'm that chewed up piece of gum, nobody re-chews a piece of gum, you throw it away." And that's how easy it is to feel like you no longer have worth, you no longer have value. Why would it even be worth screaming out? Why would it even make a difference if you are rescued? Your life still has no value.
> (Dominguez, 2013)

Smart's critique echoes that of numerous others who recognize that purity teachings over-value female purity, often to the detriment of young women whose spiritual formation is closely tied to their sexual experience and sense of self. An institution like the Church of Jesus Christ of Latter-day Saints is highly invested in purity, as a form of patriarchal theology that serves to control women's behavior while simultaneously reinforcing the authority of the church. Though Smart, herself, has never challenged church teachings on chastity or purity, her critique of how those teachings are disseminated echoes a broader conversation among Mormons who are doing just that.

Chastity and its discontents

Within the LDS Church is a faithful opposition to its purity teachings. Comprising women and men who identify as hetero- and homosexual, trans- and cis-gendered, these Mormons press the institution to live according to a vision of gender and sexual justice they believe is consistent with an authentic Mormon faith. At the forefront of these initiatives are women and men who identify as both Mormon and feminist. Comprising academics, activists, bloggers, and housewives, their critiques of church purity teachings reject the patriarchal assumptions of LDS theology.

Mormon, feminist, scholar, Amy Hoyt describes this contingent as "authentically Mormon and authentically feminist." She explains that church doctrine supports feminist claims to gender parity, meaning that critiques of the institution's reliance on a patriarchal structure, of which purity teachings are considered an outgrowth, are an effort to encourage the church to live with greater authenticity. She asserts three foundational church teachings which challenge the portrayal of Mormon women as victims seeking empowerment through defying church laws. Rather, she asserts church teachings as the source of women's empowerment. Marriage and motherhood provide women equal spiritual status as men, one that reflects the divine marriage between Heavenly Father and Heavenly Mother. Celestial Marriage and the promises of entering the heavenly realm are achieved through the shared commitment of husband and wife. The highest levels of the heavenly realm, she argues, can only be obtained through Celestial Marriage, an arrangement that men and women must participate in equally. In Hoyt's estimation, church teachings present no barrier to gender parity. However, she also notes that these church teachings have been traditionally suppressed in favor of a patriarchal institutional structure. As a result, the liberatory aspects of Mormon faith practices emerge as challenges to the institution (Hoyt, 2007).

Other popular critiques take aim at the object lessons utilized to promote church teachings. Feminist scholar and author Jana Reiss and the online collective Mormon Feminist Housewives provide readers with tools to un-learn what they believe to be harmful church teachings about sex and sexuality and provide alternative models for framing the Law of Purity. Reiss, for her part, has developed alternative object lessons for Mormon girls. At a Mormon youth camp, Reiss prepared her activity by defiling five 20 dollar bills. She spit on them, stomped on them, smeared them with marshmallow, and then rolled them in the dirt. During the talk she selected five girls to receive these 20 dollar bills, but explained what she had done to them, how badly she had treated them. She then told each girl she could return her 20 dollar bill if she wanted. And, of course, no one did. Why? Because, the girls knew, regardless of how they've been treated, what had happened to them, those bills had not lost their value.

Reiss' object lesson turned numerous other lessons about purity on their heads. Without dismissing the purpose of the object lesson, Reiss utilized it to bring to the surface a lesson that often remains hidden under the dominant purity ideology.

> Some people may tell you that if your body has been sexually active, whether through your own choices or because you were violated by someone else against your will, that you are somehow deficient: you are the plucked rose, the chewed-up piece of gum.
>
> I want you to remember, though, why it was that none of you chose to return your twenty-dollar bill. It was because you know it has inherent value, that its worth had been guaranteed by something bigger. Your worth has also already been 100% guaranteed. You are created by Heavenly Parents and are backed by their full faith and credit. Nobody and nothing can take that away from you.
>
> (Reiss, 2018)[1]

Consistent among Mormon Feminist dissent is a desire to adhere to church teachings about the Law of Chastity. The purpose of their critique is not to upend the virtue of sexual purity, but situate it within a broader constellation of LDS theological claims. To take Reiss' example above, she employs this particular object lesson to discuss sex, but also to connect human sexuality with being a beloved and valued creation of the Heavenly Parents. In doing so, she affirms the most foundational teachings of the church, while resisting an ideological focus on young women's sexuality.

The online collective, Feminist Mormon Housewives (FMH), offers Mormon women a place to share similar critiques and strategies for advancing the church's theological foundations without sacrificing the bodily and sexual integrity of young women. A common feature of the redressing that occurs is re-hashing the object lessons used to promote ideals about sex as dirty and dangerous. One participant recounted a lesson in which the teacher hammered a nail into a block of wood, alluding uncomfortably to the phallic imagery and the notion that a hole once created can never be completely filled. Another reader discussed a story from the *Young Woman's Manual*, the resources used for religious education for girls/women aged 11–18. This story told of a camel and his owner caught in a sandstorm. The owner built a tent to protect himself from the wind and sand. The camel, left outside, begged to allow his nose inside the tent. The owner grants the animal's request, but then the camel slowly moves his entire body into the tent pushing the man outside and to his death. The next story in the *Young Woman's Manual* tells of Alice who attends a party, accepts an alcoholic drink, is date raped, and must therefore endure the loss of her purity (fmhLisa, 2012).

Another contributor remembers her Young Women's leader using a head of cabbage, the vegetable representing a teenage boy's brain. The leader removes a leaf and declares that the leaf represents the part of the boy's brain that thinks about school. Another leaf represents how much the boy thinks about sports. Then the leader holds up the remaining head of cabbage and declares that this is the amount of brain space teenage boys use to think about sex. The commenter goes on to challenge the myth of male sexual weakness that is used to burden young women with protecting themselves, and young men, from acting on their sexual desires (fmhLisa, 2012).

By re-telling their experiences through the memories of object lessons, Feminist Mormon Housewives and their readers participate in an act of faithful resistance. Their goal is not to dismiss church teachings, but to distinguish sound theology from fear-based misogyny. Sara Katherine Staheli Hanks speaks even more directly to the failure of these object lessons to articulate the deeper truths of Mormon theology and the spiritual lives of Mormon women. She, too, relates numerous object lessons using cupcakes, pies, flowers, bananas, handguns, pretzels, and chewed-up gum. Her article "There's Got to Be a Better Way to Teach This: Object Lesson and Chastity" was posted to Feminist Mormon Housewives shortly after Elizabeth Smart's public denouncement of feeling like that "chewed-up piece of gum" (Staheli Hanks, 2013).

Staheli Hanks recognizes the importance of visual lessons and their ability to remain embedded in one's memory. However, she also urged teachers to recognize that object lessons are not "a perfect comparison, because we are unique children of God with agency, not passive objects." She also notes that object lessons about chastity rarely include a discussion of repentance and atonement, church teachings that promise redemption for those who make bad decisions or are lost in confusion and self-doubt. Though situating her comments among other stalwart critiques of church teachings on purity, Staheli Hanks is not rejecting the Law of Chastity and its importance for youth, but raising questions about the impact of these teachings on marital sex, experiences of sexual assault, and sexual shame (Staheli Hanks, 2013).

FMH author, Lisa Butterworth crafted an alternative list of "Thirteen Articles of Healthy Chastity" which was later published in Joanna Brooks, Hannah Wheelwright, and Rachel Hunt Steenblik's, *Mormon Feminism: Essential Writings* (2015). Butterworth's suggestions address the deep flaws in how the church teaches chastity and provides a more nuanced understanding of sexual purity while pressing the church to institute practices that value women's bodily autonomy. Her third recommendation discusses the use and misuse of object lessons. She urges teachers to avoid object lessons that "demean our divine nature by comparing young women to objects." Moreover, she urges the use of lessons that are not rooted in fear of sex, but that offer the hope of redemption. Gender-based stereotypes (the myth of insatiable male sexuality), emphasis on outward appearance, neglect of experiences of sexual abuse and assault, and the requirement of women to confess to male church leaders fill out Butterworth's list of church practices that need to be changed in order to offer young people a theologically astute perspective on the Law of Chastity (Butterworth, 2015, pp. 243–45).

Conclusion

Sexual purity in the Church of Jesus Christ of Latter-day Saints is a highly formalized church teaching that represents a foundational theological principle. The Law of Chastity is preparatory work for young people seeking eternal salvation, a spiritual status in which marriage, childbearing, and family play a substantial role. It is no surprise that purity teachings strictly adhere to the formal rhetoric of the church. And yet, these teachings are not fully realized until they are lived out in the lives of the church body. Church leaders employ object lessons in an effort to materialize deeper theological truths in hopes they will embed themselves as memories preserved for later recall.

Recalling the numerous object lessons of their youth, many Mormon women have sorted through the underlying assumptions of these memories in order to distinguish between authentic theological claims and harmful, shame-based rhetoric that devalues women's bodies. Though most of these women self-identify as feminist, the most well-known critic, Elizabeth Smart, does not. Regardless, Mormon women's critiques and alternative pedagogical strategies do not reject the Law of Chastity. Rather they seek to re-frame this important teaching as part of the broader spiritual mandate of the LDS Church, one that requires and encourages the physical integrity of both men and women.

Note

1 The object lesson Reiss describes is used in other teaching contexts including sex education. Like many object lessons, its origin is unknown.

References

Butterworth, L., 2015. Thirteen Articles of Healthy Chastity. In J. Brooks, R. Hunt Steenblik, and H. Wheelwright, eds. *Mormon Feminism: Essential Writings*. New York: Oxford University Press, pp. 243–45.
The Church of Jesus Christ of Latter-day Saints, 2013. The Doctrines and Covenants of the Church of Jesus Christ of Latter-day Saints. www.lds.org/scriptures/dc-testament/dc/131?lang=eng.
The Church of Jesus Christ of Latter-day Saints, 2016. Chastity. LDS.org. September 1. www.lds.org/topics/chastity?lang=eng.
Dominguez, A., 2013 Elizabeth Smart Speaks on Human Trafficking. www.csmonitor.com/USA/Latest-News-Wires/2013/0504/Elizabeth-Smart-speaks-on-human-trafficking.
fmhLisa, 2012. 13 Articles of Healthy Chastity. www.feministmormonhousewives.org/2012/11/13-articles-of-healthy-chastity-2/ (accessed October 28, 2018).
For the Strength of Youth, 2011. Salt Lake City, Utah: The Church of Jesus Christ of Latter-day Saints.
Holland, J.R., 1999. Personal Purity. *Liohona*. January.
Hoyt, A., 2007. Beyond the Victim/Empowerment Paradigm: The Gendered Cosmology of Mormon Women. *Feminist Theology* 16(1): 87–98.
Kimball, S., 1976. Marriage the Proper Way. *New Era*. February.
Moslener, S., 2015. *Virgin Nation: Sexual Purity and American Adolescence*. New York: Oxford University Press.
Packer, B.K., 1972. Why Stay Morally Clean? *New Era*. July.
Phillips, J., 2011. Worth Waiting For. October 7. www.youtube.com/watch?time_continue=1&v=BR9UWj1q304.
Preparation for Marriage. 1980. *New Era*. June.
Questions and Answers. 2018. *New Era*. February.
Reiss, J., 2018. Dismantling Mormon Purity Culture. *Religion News Service*. October 28.
Staheli Hanks, S.K., 2013. There's Got to Be a Better Way to Teach This: Object Lessons and Chastity. www.feministmormonhousewives.org/2013/05/theres-gotta-be-a-better-way-to-teach-this-object-lessons-and-chastity/ (accessed October 28, 2018).
Whitney. 2012. Strength in Standards. Ask a Mormon Teen (blog). March 3. http://mormon-teen.blogspot.com/p/strength-in-standards.html.

Further reading

Brooks, J., Steenblik, R.H., and Wheelwright, H., 2015. *Mormon Feminism: Essential Writings*. New York: Oxford University Press.
   A collection of essays that chronicles the Mormon feminist movement from the 1970s to the present.
Klein, L.K., 2018. *Pure: Inside the Evangelical Movement that Shamed a Generation of Young Women and How I Broke Free*. New York: Atria Books.
   A memoir that includes a decade's worth of interviews and research on the evangelical purity movement with a special emphasis on how women have negotiated the negative messaging around sexuality, embodiment, and womanhood.

Moslener, S., 2015. *Virgin Nation: Sexual Purity and American Adolescence*. New York: Oxford University Press.
   A historical monograph of the evangelical purity movement from the nineteenth century to the early 2000s.

Staheli Hanks, S.K., 2018. *Where We Must Stand: Ten Years of Feminist Mormon Housewives*. CreateSpace.
   A collection of blog posts from Feminist Mormon Housewives organized to reflect the challenges of feminist activism in the LDS Church.

20
MORMONISM AND SEXUAL VIOLENCE

Andrea G. Radke-Moss

On March 12, 2003, police officers in Sandy, Utah discovered alive a 15-year-old kidnapping victim, Elizabeth Ann Smart, who had been missing since her June 5, 2002 abduction at knifepoint from her parents' Salt Lake City home. For nine months, Elizabeth suffered daily, repeated rapes, as well as other physical, emotional, and psychological torture by her kidnapper, Brian David Mitchell. Because Mitchell was a former, but now excommunicated, member and priesthood elder in the Church of Jesus Christ of Latter-day Saints, and because he had taken Elizabeth as a "second wife" to help secure his self-appointed messiah status, the specter of the Latter-day Saint theology of celestial marriage and polygamous practice hovered around this dramatic kidnapping and Elizabeth's eventual rescue.[1] Ultimately, Mitchell was found guilty and sentenced to life in prison, while Elizabeth went on to become known for her resilience and survival, using her experience as a wellspring for advocacy on behalf of other victims of sexual assault, childhood abduction, and sex trafficking. In 2011, she founded the Elizabeth Smart Foundation, which continues that work today.

Throughout the ordeal, the Church distanced itself from Mitchell, characterizing his actions as those of a deviant outsider (LDS Newsroom, 2003). Still the media tried to link Mitchell's actions to his religious background and identity, implying sinister undercurrents of sexual violence that drove him to Smart's eventual kidnapping and rape. One writer summarized that "there was the suggestion—at times the outright assertion—that this horrible incident was a product of Mormonism" (Duffy, 2003, p. 34). One editorialist called Smart's kidnapping a "Mormon's Mormon ordeal," suggesting that Mitchell was influenced by a religious context that had historically subjugated young women through coercion into polygamous marriages (Welker, 2010). The question arose of whether it was fair to see Mitchell as a product of a culture for which polygamy was a historical and doctrinal reality. While plural marriage was a well-known and important practice in the historical Church, the direct connection to Mitchell's crime was much less concrete, and most observers understood that he would have preyed upon Elizabeth no matter the religious association.

Some harsher critics took the censure even further, and sought to place responsibility on the religion's founder, Joseph Smith, who had among his plural wives two 14-year-old girls. One editorialist declared: "Smith established a script by which men exert sexual and physical control over women, and Mitchell followed it." However, when pressed on whether she was blaming the Church for Smart's abduction, she clarified, "I am not arguing that the mainstream church is responsible for his actions. I am arguing that his belief that he has a right to marry several 14-year-old girls is based at least in part in the doctrine of eternal or plural marriage" (Welker, 2010). Others suggested that Mormonism's emphasis on obedience to male authority also explained why Smart had been vulnerable to nine months of Mitchell's control. But Smart saw it very differently. In her own testimony, she insisted that his selfishness, domination, and violence were completely foreign to her in a Mormon context. Smart recalled Mitchell praying only for himself, while selfishly praying for others to "[fulfill] something for him." And when asked about the contrast between Mitchell's "spiritual blessings" and the blessings that Elizabeth had received from her father and other trusted church leaders, she remembered that her father's blessings were ones of "comfort and reassurance that I have my choices and I can make the right choice." In stark contrast, Smart described how Mitchell "told me what to do. He told me what was expected of me. He never said I had my agency to choose. It was all very dictated" (Smart, 2010).

Regarding suggestions that she had somehow accepted her abductor's authority over her, Elizabeth insisted that she never internalized Mitchell's control, and that her inability to leave or escape—even when she had the opportunity—was mainly due to raw fear and her survival instinct. In her mind, she never emotionally or intellectually succumbed, declaring, "I did not suffer from Stockholm Syndrome ... I despised them" (Smart, 2017). And when repeatedly asked why she didn't try to run away, she has insisted:

> It's not because any one of us enjoys being hurt. It's not because any one of us enjoys being raped or kidnapped. It's because we can. We do everything we can to survive, and there's reasons why we make those decisions.
>
> (Stump, 2017)

Ultimately, Smart attributed her faith in her religion and the love of her family for the spiritual power to endure months of sexual violence and terror, and to defy it. Her faith was what sustained her against violence, not what made her succumb to it.

Considering these different responses to Elizabeth Smart's captivity, it is important to note how this tension corresponds to or conflicts with reactions to sexual assault in a larger Mormon context, and particularly church leaders' responses to incidents of sexual violence today and in the past. Indeed, some have wondered how the Church of Jesus Christ of Latter-day Saints continues to grapple with its response to sexual assault, especially when it has historically been in the position of both victim and perpetrator.

Sexual violence typically enters the Mormon historical narrative in reference to the persecutions that early Latter-day Saints experienced during the Missouri War of 1838, in which some women were purportedly raped by members of the Missouri militias, as a violent tool of military aggression and religious persecution against the Church. Most members fled their homes around Far West, Missouri, and evacuated to the state of Illinois, eventually establishing a new community at Nauvoo, Illinois. The violence of the Mormons' famous expulsion from Missouri is "well documented," including "arson, destruction of property, the killing of livestock, confiscation of weapons, physical assaults, imprisonment, and murder" (Radke-Moss, 2017, p. 51). This violence also included the alleged rapes of Mormon women.

Although rape accounts were contested by observers and participants in the Missouri conflict, numerous witnesses attested to either observing the sexual assault of Mormon women or of receiving second-hand reports of the crimes. In a letter of December 1838, Parley P. Pratt wrote of the Saints' struggles in Missouri: "Much property has been plundered, provision destroyed Chastity of women violated houses burned, woman & Children fired <up>on &

some slain" (Pratt, 1838). These accounts made it into the Church's legal actions to gain redress for the crimes committed against its members in Missouri. Over the next few years, church leaders like Pratt, Sidney Rigdon, and Hyrum Smith continued to relate accounts of rapes against Mormon women as part of their testimony about the Missouri violence. On July 1, 1843, numerous leaders presented testimony before the Nauvoo Municipal Court, wherein Hyrum Smith described how "soldiers were permitted to patrol the streets of Far West to abuse and insult the people at their leisure, and enter into houses and pillage them, and ravish the women" (Smith, 1843).

These testimonies demonstrate how responses to sexual violence were very consistent with how other Americans treated rape in the nineteenth century. As a crime that was very difficult to prove and prosecute through formal legal channels, perpetrators were often acquitted, or not charged at all. Further, a culture of shame surrounded rape victims, which resulted in many remaining silent about their sexual assault or remaining anonymous even during the legal process. Rape accusations were often filed by men, for they held legal responsibility for their wives, daughters, and sisters. These factors resulted in no victims being identified by name, and most rape accounts coming from male witnesses' testimonies, based primarily upon hearsay. And because rape was not unheard of as a tool of war in group conflict, the Latter-day Saint Church leaders who sought redress for the Missouri violence typically conveyed rape accounts, not to gain justice for individual, unnamed female victims, but as part of a list of all crimes and persecutions committed against them, and as a symbolic attack against the whole community.

The sexual assault against women in Missouri became part of the Church's larger historical narrative, a collective memory that was told and retold over generations, which allowed Latter-day Saints to "build a community … around that shared suffering" (Radke-Moss, 2017, pp. 52–53). One event that cemented this construction of group identity is well-known to most members. Following their arrest and imprisonment after the siege of Far West in November 1838, Joseph Smith and other leaders had heard many rumors of sexual violence, accounts which threatened their confidence in their ability to keep their people safe. While in the Richmond Jail, Joseph Smith endured the first boastings about rape. Parley P. Pratt later immortalized the moment of Joseph's reaction in an 1853 *Deseret News* letter, fifteen years after the event. While lying on the floor in the jail, Pratt recounted, the men had to listen to the guards' "dreadful blasphemies, and filthy language," especially as they "recounted to each other their deeds of rapine, murder, robbery, etc., which they had committed among the 'Mormons,' while at Far West and vicinity. They even boasted of defiling by force, wives, daughters, and virgins." As the men lay in silence listening to these verbal persecutions, Joseph suddenly

> arose to his feet, and spoke in a voice of thunder, or as the roaring lion, uttering, as near as I can recollect, the following words: "SILENCE—Ye fiends of the infernal pit. In the name of Jesus Christ I rebuke you, and command you to be still; I will not live another minute, and hear such language. Cease such talk, or you or I die THIS MINUTE."
>
> (Radke-Moss, 2017, pp. 58–59)

The Majesty in Chains speech, as it has come to be known, has been told and retold in numerous media forms, persisting as one of the most defining experiences in the evolution of Joseph's prophetic role. As Terryl Givens and Matt Grow have argued, this Richmond Jail incident has become "the prime ingredient in the hagiographic tradition surrounding Joseph Smith" (2011, p. 144; cf. Baugh, 2012). The event has been reproduced in numerous dramatized and documentary films, curriculum materials, and literary works, including a famous multi-volume fictionalized account of early church history, called *The Work and the Glory*. The portrayal is always very similar: the guards boast about general atrocities committed against the Saints, and when the talk turns to Missourians raping unidentified Mormon women, Joseph Smith rises to his feet, incensed enough to stand up to his imprisoners. Feeling ashamed, the guards then cease their boasting, and even apologize. Smith's noble reputation is permanently affixed as an honorable, knightly defender of women's virtue; the memory of the Missouri rapes has helped to cement a group identity based upon a shared narrative of persecution, further drawing attention away from unnamed female victims.

As the Mormons moved to Utah in the nineteenth century, they carried with them not only the trauma of their sexual assault and other persecutions, but also the prevailing attitudes and legal approaches to rape common in America. When rape was a crime committed by outsiders against the group, church leaders responded with fierce indignation; but when sexual assault, statutory rape, and marital rape were committed within the Church's own ranks, and leaders responded with less outrage. The Church formally announced the practice of celestial, or plural marriage in 1852, which created possibilities for abusive situations, especially because marriage to underage wives was accepted and even encouraged. Like other nineteenth-century Americans, Mormons did not consider underage marriage a statutory sexual crime, or even marital rape, if the union was consensual or at least sanctioned by the bride's parents. In the cases of stranger rapes and other cases of sexual violence, Utah law treated rape as a crime, but in cases of underage marriage and nonconsensual sex in polygamous unions, Utah law allowed for a very liberal interpretation of the age of consent (Hendrix-Komoto, 2016).

Mormon response to sexual violence was even further complicated by race, as their experience with the indigenous tribes of the Great Basin often led to periods of violent conflict. Interactions between whites and natives already carried a highly sexualized and often imbalanced power dynamic in the West, considering church leaders' encouragement for Mormon men to marry Indian women as part of their missionary work among native tribes, whom they believed to be descendants of the "Lamanites" of the Book of Mormon. In intermarrying with native women, Mormons hoped to redeem the Indians by removing the curse of dark skin and whitening the race, even while white Mormon women lived in fear of being raped by Indian men, in ways that followed some of the stereotypical American perceptions about white–native encounters on the frontier. However, native women were more likely to be vulnerable to sexual violence, as in the case of the Bear River Massacre of January 29, 1863, in which Colonel Patrick Conner's volunteer force of 200 militiamen attacked a village of Northwestern Shoshones, killing an estimated 400 people. Locals in the Preston, Idaho area learned of female rape victims of the Massacre: Samuel Roskelley wrote that one Shoshone witness claimed that "the way the soldiers used the squaws after the battle was shameful … Says that there were from 20 to 30 squaws killed and many children" (Roskelley, 1863). In spite of leaders' apparent notice of the rapes of Indian women, no justice was sought for individual victims. Rather than issue significant protest against the rape of Shoshone women, instead Cache Valley settlers celebrated that Conner's actions had helped rid them of a troublesome problem.

The Mormon menace

Then, in one seemingly cool and smooth transformation, Latter-day Saints went from being the victims of sexual assault in the national imagination to the perpetrators of sexual assault, a public relations shift that continued to pivot around the Church's doctrine and practice of plural marriage. Negative attention swirled around Mormon polygamists for decades, culminating in the federal anti-polygamy Edmunds Act in 1882 and the Edmunds-Tucker Act in 1887. In the mid-nineteenth century, literally hundreds of examples of novels, editorials, cartoons, and public images reinforced the portrayals of Mormons as sinister kidnappers and traffickers of young women (Austin and Parshall, 2017). For example, one 1883 cartoon showed an uncivilized Mormon dragging his victims by their hair in defiance of civilized America as "lady liberty" (Reeve, 2015, p. 232).

And dime novels of the time also portrayed individuals or gangs of Mormon elders seeking to capture and enslave their future plural wives from among new white settlers to the West. These types of representations "served as a universally understood cultural discourse that equated Mormons with domineering male power, the subjugation of women, secret acts behind closed doors, and murderous defiance of federal authority" (Reeve, 2015, p. 232).

The threat of sexual violence as an implied or direct association with Mormon power in the West shifted the message: Mormons were not victims of murder and rape, but instead murderers and rapists themselves. This became even more pronounced when rumors circulated not long after the Mountain Meadows Massacre of September 1857 that perpetrators had raped some of the female victims, more specifically that John D. Lee himself was accused of raping one or two young women in the Fancher party. Historians have read these accounts with caution, and Lee himself defied the accusations against him: "It is published for a sworn fact that I violated two girls as [they] were kneeling and begging to me for life, and so help me God, it is an infernal lie!" (Walker, Turley, and Leonard, 2011, pp. 206–7).

It was difficult for members of the Church to avoid these associations with sexual assault in the nineteenth century. Because of the absolute centrality of polygamy to LDS religious practice, the religion's public image was already highly sexualized. Add to that the reality of murder committed by southern Utah leaders in 1857 and anti-polygamy sentiment that suggested the religion's danger to women as potential victims of rape and sexual slavery. Anti-Mormon attitudes even corresponded with anti-Chinese sentiment, wherein the Mormon Menace and the Yellow Peril grew almost side-by-side, connected mainly by a fear of the subjugation of women through both groups' polygamous practice. Politicians considered Chinese immigrants "lewd polygamists with low morals, proponents of a new form of slavery and adherents to despotic systems of government" (Reeve, 2015, p. 237). Even while Congress passed anti-polygamy legislation in the 1880s, it also passed the 1882 Chinese Exclusion Act which cut immigration down to a trickle, and enabled anti-Chinese violence in communities throughout the western United States.

Stereotypes about Mormon men kidnapping and enslaving women were further reinforced as the silent film era portrayed the sexual menace of Latter-day Saints. Anti-Mormon films gained popularity especially after the 1904–1906 Reed Smoot hearings which had redirected public attention to the rumors of continued polygamous practice among the Latter-day Saints. "Like many novels and magazine articles, films drew upon accounts of plural marriage, the Mountain Meadows massacre, and the highly secretive Danite activity as fodder for their sensational stories" (Olmstead, 2004, p. 203). In particular, Danish filmmaker Ole Olsen's film, *A Victim of the Mormons* was released in 1911, as "the first to cash in on the European concern over the 'Mormon problem' and the prevailing stories of missionaries absconding with young women to Utah" (Olmstead, 2004, pp. 205–6). Between 1911 and 1912, other silent films released in Europe and the United States further reinforced an image of Mormon sexual predation.

With the official end of polygamy at the turn of the twentieth century, the Church began its transition toward assimilation into mainstream American culture, and the stereotypes of "kidnappers of young women" lost some of the emphasis of previous years. The tensions of the post-World War II era turned church leadership's attention more to policing the sexual morality within its community, particularly because of the pressures of modernism, the rising youth culture, and increasing moral decay in American society. Spencer W. Kimball's *The Miracle of*

Forgiveness (1969) stood out as a major prophetic guidebook that addressed a litany of possible moral infractions and sexual behaviors, especially from a proscriptive point of view. Latter-day Saint understanding of sexual violence became even more muddied with the publication of Kimball's book, since he offered controversial counsel to rape victims. Kimball famously quoted Church President David O. McKay, who had declared that "Your virtue is worth more than your life ... preserve your virtue even if you lose your lives" (p. 63). Even more troublesome was Kimball's elaborative statement on a rape victim's suggested culpability, unless she resisted:

> Also far-reaching is the effect of the loss of chastity. Once given or taken or stolen it can never be regained. Even in a forced contact such as rape or incest, the injured one is greatly outraged. If she has not cooperated and contributed to the foul deed, she is of course in a more favorable position. There is no condemnation where there is not voluntary participation. It is better to die in defending one's virtue than to live having lost it without a struggle.
>
> (p. 196)

These statements have since been evaluated for the suggestion that the victim becomes responsible for her own rape if she does not physically resist, even to the point of death. This expectation of "better dead clean than alive unclean" was first introduced in a 1942 First Presidency statement, and repeated in some form by many general authorities over time, including McKay and Kimball (Harrison, 2016). Both seemed to follow common, but erroneous usage of "virtue" to mean "virginity," or something that can be "lost"—a definition which perpetuated a problematic, but enduring response to sexual violence. After years of church leaders suggesting that victims might be better off dead than to have been raped at all, the First Presidency again asserted in 1974 that "only if a woman resisted an attacker 'with all her strength and energy' would she not be 'guilty of unchastity'" (Stack and Alberty, 2016).

While Kimball may have intended a more sympathetic response to sexual assault, it is likely that he was informed by common early legal standards for rape, in which victims had to prove that they had resisted as hard as they could, even demonstrating signs of physical struggle, like bruises, cuts, finger marks, scratches, and ripped or torn clothing: all such markers were used as evidence in rape prosecutions. Because rape claims were difficult to prove, courts employed "specific criteria to evaluate the credibility of a woman's rape claim" (Block, 2006, p. 130). These included actions like screaming for help, making a complaint immediately after the assault, and showing "signs of the injury," all of which implied non-consent, and were used to "give greater probability to her testimony" (Block, 2006, p. 130). Thus the law required strong physical evidence, or eyewitness report of the rape to consider it a prosecutable offense.

Kimball's book left an impact during its years of high circulation, but a more charitable approach to sexual violence was already being formalized in official church policy. While the Church largely resisted feminist activism of the 1970s, still legislation like Title IX of the Education Amendments Act of 1972 and the proposed Equal Rights Amendment brought increased national criticism to problems of discrimination against women, along with attention to sexual crimes against women and children. But for the LDS Church, any concerns about ecclesiastical abuse or neglect of rape victims flew under the radar, with focus instead directed toward childhood sexual abuse. In 1978, Gordon B. Hinckley gave a stern public warning against the "ugly picture" of child sexual abuse, specifically calling out

> those vicious men and women who exploit children for pornographic purposes ... I wish to say that no man who is a professed follower of Christ and no man who is a

professed member of this church can engage in such practices without offending God and repudiating the teachings of his Son.

(1978)

He later repeated similar counsel in a 1985 General Conference talk, even adding potential consequences like excommunication and loss of priesthood ordination. Still, even as church leaders' awareness of child sexual assault was improving, they were less attentive about responding to adult victims. But new voices were offering important course corrections.

One clinical psychology faculty member at Brigham Young University, Maxine Murdock, had written a guide to helping sexual assault victims, published in the *Ensign* in 1981, with the support of the Relief Society General Board. In it, she attempted to counter some of the common myths surrounding sexual assault, such as the notion that a rape victim might be complicit in her own assault if she can't prove that she fought back. Murdock also gently chided male church leaders on whom victims hope to "count on for support" who are "either bewildered by the circumstances, or, through lack of understanding are only able to respond in an unsympathetic way," as well as others who "haven't had the experience to give the right kind of support" (Murdock, 2013).

In some cases, Murdock knew of victims who were told "No righteous Latter-day Saint man will ever want to marry you now"—an interesting and disappointing foreshadowing of the same self-doubting thoughts that would plague Elizabeth Smart over twenty years later. Murdock counseled,

> The truth is that no child of God, old or young, deserves this experience, no matter what the circumstances ... the idea that a woman actually "asks for" or invites and enjoys the kind of humiliating treatment that I deal with ... is simply not true.
> *(Murdock, 2013)*

Murdock's corrections were slow to catch on. For instance, the same year of Elder Hinckley's warning, he also signed a First Presidency letter to general authorities and stake and ward leaders which continued the notion that "persons threatened with rape or forcible sexual abuse should resist to the maximum extent possible or necessary," especially to show that they had "not willingly consented" (Kimball, Romney, and Hinckley, 2017). This counsel further confused many bishops, including Kent Harrison, who noted the "lack of availability of helps for Church leaders in handling cases of race, incest, or spouse abuse." He wrote to General Young Women President Ardeth G. Kapp that "There was a recent pamphlet ... on child abuse, but it said little or nothing about these other matters" (Harrison, 1986). Even as misconceptions about victim complicity persisted in many LDS circles, leaders eventually responded to requests for increased guidance on how to help victims with treatment, counseling, and legal action. In 1989, for the first time ever, the Church included adjustments to its Handbook, under the subheading "Victims of Rape or Sexual Abuse," which reminded leaders that rape victims were "not guilty of sin." Bishops and stake presidents were counseled to "treat such victims with sensitivity," but the Handbook stated little else (Harrison, 1990).

Some member-activists felt that the Church's actual response to child sexual abuse continued to be slow to meet leaders' counsel. In 1992, the Mormon Alliance began to publish accounts of what they considered both ecclesiastical and spiritual abuse by church leaders, including over thirty cases of child sexual abuse that were either committed or covered up by church leaders. The goals of the Alliance in releasing these accounts was to urge leaders to acknowledge that "spiritual abuse is systemic in the church," an admission that would require an institution-wide solution and not just case-by-case reprimands (Anderson, 1995). Members of the Mormon Alliance were excommunicated, in part for the publication of materials relating to institutional abuses. The drum beating continued, and 1992 proved a significant year for LDS response to sexual assault. Elder Richard G. Scott's April 1992 General Conference address offered a much-needed initiation toward greater understanding of a long-taboo subject; he also gave hope to victims of sexual abuse, with his assurance that "when another's acts of violence, perversion, or incest hurt you terribly, against your will, you are not responsible and you must not feel guilty." As groundbreaking as it was, Scott's counsel included an unfortunate and troubling hangover from past LDS teachings about victim responsibility:

> The victim must do all in his or her power to stop the abuse. Most often the victim is innocent because of being disabled by fear or the power or authority of the offender. At some point in time, however, the Lord may prompt a victim to recognize a degree of responsibility for abuse. Your priesthood leader will help assess your responsibility so that, if needed, it can be addressed.
>
> (Scott, 1992)

Scott's address is often cited as an important step toward better institutional ministering for victims of sexual abuse, but also as an example of how these early changes also came with setbacks.

Also in 1992, Brigham Young University held a workshop on the topic of sexual abuse, in conjunction with its annual Women's Conference, and later that year, Sister Chieko Okazaki, first counselor in the General Relief Society presidency, presented "Healing from Sexual Abuse" at a women's conference in Portland, Oregon. Because sexual abuse had only been discussed as "something that happened mainly to young children," Okazaki's talk was noteworthy since it "acknowledged the realities of sexual assault and rape in ways that no general authority of the Church had previously done." In fact, some observers have credited Okazaki for loosening the stigma surrounding sexual assault, so that "Church leaders began to respond to survivors of rape and sexual abuse with greater intensity and frequency" (Okazaki, 1992). The attention resulted in the 1993 publication of a guide for church leaders called *Confronting Abuse*, which was a "vast improvement" over anything previously released by the Church (Horton, Harrison, and Johnson, 1993). It contained thirty-one articles about "counseling and treating survivors of abuse." Other church leaders spoke more openly about the sin of sexual abuse: Howard W. Hunter articulated excommunication for perpetrators; Vaughn J. Featherstone first used the word "rape" to label any sexual abuse of a victim "against his or her will." President Gordon B. Hinckley continued to offer general warnings against spouse and child abuse.

In practice, church culture still struggled with appropriate responses to rape and other forms of sexual violence, much of which depended upon cultural assumptions, traditions, and teachings about female "virtue." Elizabeth Smart's 2002–2003 captivity and rescue shifted the ground considerably, by reigniting questions about institutional response to sexual abuse in both historical and contemporary contexts. Regarding the emotional aftermath of her sexual assault, Smart herself went on record critical of the unfortunate teaching she heard growing up, that in "losing her virginity"—even against her will, she would be undesirable as a future marriage partner. In a 2013 speech at Johns Hopkins University, Smart famously called out the troubling aspects of "abstinence-only education."

> I had a teacher who was talking about abstinence, and she said, "Imagine you're a stick of gum. When you engage in sex, that's like getting chewed. And if you do that lots

of times, you're going to become an old piece of gum, and who is going to want you after that?" Well, that's terrible No one should ever say that. But for me, I thought, "I'm that chewed up piece of gum." Nobody re-chews a piece of gum. You throw it away. And that's how easy it is to feel you no longer have worth. Your life no longer has value.

(Dominguez, 2013)

Smart's message drew particular attention to the negative effects of chastity rhetoric on victims of sexual assault. Even though she had been raped, the internalization of messages on virtue left her questioning her worth. Experts have questioned the effects of rigid abstinence education because "administering broad sexual shaming to children can have disastrous effects for victims of assault (Hess, 2013). Thus, while Elizabeth's faith in LDS theology sustained her during her ordeal, the unfortunate cultural teachings of the same belief system simultaneously retraumatized her.

The connection between rape and lost virtue was also informed by a well-known but problematic scripture in the Mormon canon. The prophet Mormon in the Book of Mormon tells of a final battle between Nephites and Lamanites, in which "many of the daughters of the Lamanites have they [the Nephites] taken prisoners ... depriving them of that which was most dear and precious above all things, which is chastity and virtue," suggesting that the physical rape of Lamanite women meant the loss of their actual purity (Moroni 9:9). When "Virtue" was added to the Young Women theme and values in 2009, this scripture was included as its reference in the Personal Progress Manual. Following Smart's 2013 public critique of victim-shaming culture, the discussion about Moroni 9:9 shifted, especially with some thoughtful critics questioning the scripture's use as another unfortunate case of "virginity" being used interchangeably for "virtue." Many offered needed clarification, that "[t]he chastity in which the Lord delights (Jacob 2) is not merely virginity, and cannot be taken away by another person, especially not by violence or abuse" (Haglund, 2013). After years of pushback, the scripture was removed from the Personal Progress curriculum in September 2016 (Stack, 2016).

The Smart case opened a floodgate of questioning about how Mormons individually and collectively respond to sexual assault. Over the years, attention to rampant clerical and sexual abuse in the Catholic Church had kept the drums beating on the dangers of male religious authorities having unchaperoned access to potential child victims. For the LDS Church, a smattering of sexual abuse scandals by church and Boy Scout leaders has gained some national attention, leading to either out-of-court settlements with victims, or ongoing legal defense efforts where the Church has fought the accusations. For example, a 1998 case of a Portland, Oregon victim showed how local leaders knew the perpetrator was a danger, but failed to inform other church members. The Church and victim settled for $3 million (Niebuhr, 2001). Around the same time, one teenage Idaho Boy Scout stood up against his abuser at Camp Little Lemhi in the late 1990s, which led to minor jail time for the abuser, but turned many in southeastern Idaho against the victim for being "disloyal" to the institutions, even as the Boy Scouts and the Church were forced to admit their failure to act on reports (Ames, 2013). Even now, two longstanding lawsuits by twenty-nine victims allege that the Boy Scouts and the LDS Church covered up sexual misconduct by BSA leaders in Idaho over three decades. Some of the victims have settled, while other cases have been dismissed or are pending (Sewall, 2019; cf. Dumas, 2014).

Few cases have had enduring impact on church policy, except that leaders and teachers of minor children are required to be "two-deep" in lessons and activities, and the Church maintains its hotline for ecclesiastical leaders, although some question the hotline's efficacy and intent, asking whether it is meant more to help victims or to warn church leaders and protect institutional reputation. In fact, a leaked 2018 document showed how the Church has sometimes gone out of its way to shield abusers from legal, criminal, or ecclesiastical responsibility, in actions that Jana Riess has described as choosing "the comfort of empire over the cause of justice" (Riess, 2018). But in the last few years, the actions of leaders have come under greater scrutiny, especially with the impact of social media exposure to the most problematic elements of church practices. To start, the absolute authority of male leadership at all levels of church hierarchy creates the backdrop for sexual abuse cases, because priesthood authorities hold the positions of questioner, prosecutor, advocate, judge, jury, and pardoner, with no formal oversight for abuse victims. A significant problem has been leaders not believing victims, or not taking a threat seriously, especially when the abuser is a known and respected husband, father, friend, priesthood leader, or prospective missionary (Meier, 2019; Park et al., 2019). Elder Richard G. Scott spoke to this problem in a 2008 follow-up address to his 1992 talk, even acknowledging the challenges of ecclesiastical leaders' mixed responses to sexual abuse. To victims, he counseled:

> Do not be discouraged if initially a bishop hesitates when you identify an abuser. Remember that predators are skillful at cultivating a public appearance of piety to mask their despicable acts. Pray to be guided in your efforts to receive help.

He then turned his instruction to the "judges in Israel," pleading for them to "painstakingly assure that every individual that is suffering from abuse receives appropriate help." He added a firm reminder to bishops about believing victims: "Recognize that it is very unlikely that a perpetrator will confess his depraved acts. Seek the guidance of the spirit when you feel that something may be amiss" (2008).

Resistance to believing victims has been one of the most impenetrable barriers to break down across the spectrum of sexual abuse cases in the Church. Some leaders have notoriously resisted proper intervention, even blaming or shaming victims, and ignoring criminal acts that have led to cover-ups and further enabling of abusers. In 2018, Kristy Johnson claimed that the Church had been told repeatedly of her father, Melvin Johnson's sexual abuse of herself and her sisters, but had refused to report him to the police. More troubling was that her father was a Church Education System employee who was moved around with each new accusation. Although he was finally excommunicated and divorced by his wife, he got rebaptized only one year later, and never faced criminal charges for the sexual abuse of his children (Kuruvilla, 2018; Tanner, 2018). However, other leaders have been sincerely motivated by a necessary attention to justice for victims, as in the 2010 case of Lone Peak High School Seminary teacher and principal Michael Pratt's statutory rape of a 16-year-old student. The Church immediately fired him and gave full support to the prosecution's efforts to convict Pratt (Israelsen-Hartley, 2010). Unfortunately, others have been driven by the desire to protect fellow leaders, or to defend the Church's institutional image over the interests of victims. Most egregious is when ecclesiastical leaders have committed their own acts of sexual violation against members, without an external process for investigation, reporting, or independent court of appeal.

A major catalyst for examining the Church's sexual assault policies came in the spring of 2016, when Brigham Young University came under fire for its botched responses to sexual assault cases. Students had reported their rapes to law enforcement, only to discover that their files had been referred to the Honor Code office, resulting in investigation, discipline, and even suspension for circumstances surrounding their assault, such as drug and alcohol abuse or curfew violations. Student Madi Barney became the public face of BYU's scandal, when the story of her rape and Honor Code investigation was first published by *Salt Lake Tribune* reporter Erin

Alberty on April 12, 2016.[2] Alberty's ongoing investigation led to many other rape victims coming forward with their stories, while the *New York Times*, the *Guardian*, *Washington Post*, *Time*, CNN, National Public Radio, and other news agencies added public exposure to the BYU cases. Critics protested that victims' fear of possible Honor Code punishment was a significant deterrent to sexual assault reporting and that by punishing victims, BYU was in violation of Title IX compliance. The university formed an advisory council to review sexual assault policies. In October 2016, the council published its report, with recommended changes such as amnesty for victims against possible discipline, and the separation of the university's Title IX office from the Honor Code office (Report of the Advisory Council, 2016). In May 2018, the Church released a formal announcement of policy changes at all three church universities which incorporated most of the advisory council's suggestions (Jenkins, 2018). However, the case of one BYU-Idaho rape victim exposed a troubling loophole for the Church's Title IX compliance, in which a victim might receive university immunity, but not a bishop's ecclesiastical endorsement, if he considered the sexual encounter consensual and not as an assault. "Bishops can revoke students' endorsement at any time, effectively kicking them out of school—a power that critics say pokes holes in amnesty and can be easily exploited by abusers who have compromising information about their victims" (Alberty, 2018).

As the Church has struggled to respond to public exposure around sexual assault, the 2014 #YesAllWomen social media campaign and the 2017 #MeToo movement both provided a new backdrop to further public awareness about violence toward women.[3] These campaigns have helped to destigmatize sexual assault, by encouraging public conversations about women's experiences; they have created an important context for LDS women to share their own stories of sexual abuse, while simultaneously exposing problems with church policy and action. The #MeToo movement unleashed a flood of Mormon women's and child survivors' testimonies, blogs, and stories about their experiences with ecclesiastical abuse. These range from bishops' inappropriate questioning about modesty and sexual practices, to victim shaming for reported sexual assaults, to sexual abuse reports being dismissed by ecclesiastical authorities, and even to a few leaders grooming and committing crimes themselves (Deitz, 2017; "Read the Stories," 2018).

The most shocking #MeToo moment came in March of 2018 when the Mormon Wikileaks site released a recording and transcript of former Missionary Training Center President Joseph Bishop admitting to sexual abuse of a former sister missionary back in 1984. The victim McKenna Dennison had reported the assault to Bishop's leaders in 2010, and then secretly recorded his confession to her in December 2017. The case produced a wave of shock at his admission, but also at the fact that LDS leaders had seemingly known about Bishop's abusive behavior and had not taken action against him (Stack, 2018a). The Church released a formal statement claiming its knowledge of the case and reaffirming a general commitment that "Sexual abuse cannot be tolerated in the Church … We continue to urge our leaders to take reports of abuse very seriously" (Newsroom, 2018a). Even as another victim came forward, records showed that complaints had been directed to law enforcement and high church leadership, but Bishop had avoided any disciplinary action or legal prosecution (Scoville, 2018). The press coverage produced conflicting reports, including some that questioned the victim's reliability, with others still suspecting some kind of institutional protection for Bishop. In the worst case scenarios like these, church leaders have again appeared to participate in active cover-ups of known sex abuse crimes.

The Joseph Bishop case contrasted to the Church's response to another mission president, just one month after the Bishop case broke. The *Salt Lake Tribune* reported on the recent release and excommunication of another mission president, Philander Smartt of the Puerto Rico San

Juan Mission, due to his inappropriate favors and overtures to female missionaries (Stack, 2018b). Thus, while President Smartt was summarily released and excommunicated, the Bishop case received the highest extent of LDS legal defense and even accusations that the Church had used nefarious methods to discredit the victim. The differing responses to the Bishop and Smartt cases showed how there might be conflicting facts in the different reports, but also that the Church seems more prepared to respond to current and future victims of sexual assault, but much less willing to look back and apologize for past failings.

Following months of public attention to these #MeToo moments, church leadership answered. In the April 2018 General Conference, Elder Quentin L. Cook of the Quorum of the Twelve Apostles gave a pointed, but somewhat awkward response. "It is commendable that nonconsensual immorality has been exposed and denounced [as] … against the laws of God and of society. Those who understand God's plan should also oppose consensual immorality, which is also a sin." Social media lit up with bewilderment, wondering whether Cook's use of "nonconsensual immorality" instead of just plain "rape" or "sexual assault," showed a continued problem of assigning responsibility to victims, and adding to an interpretation that "nonconsensual immorality" (i.e., rape) was "about the sex, and not about the assault" (Jensen, 2018). Others praised Elder Cook for responding at all, even if he used ambiguous wording, or was merely uncomfortable using the word "rape" in a conference setting.

Unfortunately, high-profile cases—if representative of a larger pattern—might portray an institutional church that has struggled to handle its sexual abuse cases, in part because of male authority structures, but also because of the difficulties in giving widespread institutional authority to unpaid and untrained lay leaders. In fact, the Church's common defense in sexual assault lawsuits is that it cannot possibly police the actions of all its members, even if they act in positions of volunteer service or local authority. In one Massachusetts case, church lawyers argued that the perpetrator "was a member like anybody else and … volunteered to do various things within the Church." Thus, while "'every church hopes that all of their members are wonderful, law-abiding citizens,' any church 'has members who sadly you find out later were not'" (Paige, 2008). Further, the Church's expanding presence as a global religion presents new challenges, including how to teach sexual and marital agency in systems based upon bride price, arranged marriages, child marriages, and patriarchal legal systems that marginalize victims of rape and domestic violence. Whatever the cultural framework, an institution that polices itself internally possesses little to no possible oversight for women and children, except to depend upon the expected moral integrity and sympathy of individual male leaders. And this continues to be the Church's greatest challenge in responding to victims of sexual violence—how much are lay leaders responsible for the institutional Church's response or non-response to members' stories of sexual violence?

The Church continues to insist upon its intolerance of abuse in any form, especially to avoid ecclesiastical exploitation, the potential for grooming children, and the appearance of sexual predation. Many caring leaders and professionals have responded with sympathy, awareness, and advocacy. In January 2018, BYU faculty member, Dr. Benjamin M. Ogles gave the most forceful and honest response for the Church's university-age students:

> Let me be very clear about the responsibility for sexual assault. The perpetrator is responsible for their actions. A victim was deprived of their agency, and they are not accountable for what happened to them without their consent—no matter what they were wearing, where they were, or what happened beforehand. They did not invite, allow, sanction, or encourage the assault.
>
> (Ogles, 2018,

The last two years have demonstrated a generally positive, but bumpy direction for the Church's approaches to sexual assault, with more public direction and awareness from leadership, LDS Newsroom statements, *Ensign* articles that address abuse, and improved Title IX training and response at church universities (Widdison, 2019). Officially, the Church encourages victims to report crimes through proper law enforcement channels; it maintains a hotline for leaders to seek help for sexual assault victims; and it refers victims to trained professional counselors at LDS Family Services and other counseling services. Most dramatic is the release of a church website dedicated entirely to information, training, resources, and services for victims of sexual abuse or assault, and their leaders (Church of Jesus Christ of Latter-day Saints, n.d.).

Even as the Church improves its sexual assault response, each new publicized case is a reminder of how much work still needs to be done. One gnawing problem remains, namely, the unaccompanied worthiness interviews with adult male leaders of minor children and youth. One former bishop Sam Young has protested to end bishops' interviews of male and female youth, first by circulating a petition through his website, "Protect the Children," and then leading a hunger strike and a march on Temple Square (Protect the Children, n.d.). The Church responded by revising its policies for youth interviews to permit that "another adult may be invited to be present during the interview (Newsroom, 2018b). But Young's local stake leadership excommunicated him, sending the message that the Church will revise its own practices, but punish those who demand change through external pressure or public embarrassment (Palmer, 2018; Walch, 2018). The recent announcement of a church survey regarding the feasibility of worthiness interviews for as young as 8- to 11-year old children has resulted in surprise that the Church would take even greater liberties with the perceived grooming of minors (Forgie, 2019b). It almost seems like each week brings a new case of sexual misconduct and even predation involving church leaders or high-profile Latter-day Saints. Recently, a bishop in Lehi, Utah, was arrested for leading a sex trafficking operation. That he was immediately released from his position shows the Church's increasingly swift response to abusive leaders; that he had even been a bishop to begin with shows the ongoing problem of potential sexual abuse by unvetted lay leadership (Curtis, 2019). Utah filmmaker and church temple filmmaker Sterling Van Wagenen's April 2019 arrest for sexually molesting a young girl between 2013 and 2015 brought another leaked revelation that he had also molested a teen boy in the early 1990s, but had never faced charges (Forgie, 2019a). And finally, BYU's problem with treating sexual assault cases is not completely resolved, as the state of Utah revoked the BYU Police Department's license for illegally and secretly reporting crimes to the university's Honor Code office, where the trouble had originally started. The accused officer and the department are currently appealing the license revocation (Harris and Rascon, 2019).

The Church of Jesus Christ of Latter-day Saints is an institution seemingly poised and willing to prevent and punish future problems of sexual abuse, even as it struggles with its past responses. Considering the Church's use of an untrained lay ministry, and a lack of oversight for ecclesiastical abuse, the challenges of responding to sexual abuse with the proper legal and spiritual advocacy is still mostly subject to local and high-level leadership lottery. The ongoing problem continues, that "men are put into positions of unaccountable authority over the vulnerable, and the faithful expect these men to police themselves and each other" (Sister's Quorum, 2019). Many fear that the Church will never be able to reform its larger culture of male leadership that defends men, which will continue to be an obstruction to progress on sexual assault response. In 2018, as Judge Brett Kavanaugh faced the Senate confirmation hearings for the United States Supreme Court, a former acquaintance testified that he had sexually assaulted her in high school. The timing of the accusation held up Kavanaugh's nomination, as the Senate debated whether to investigate the charges further. Notably, of the twenty-one members of the Senate Judiciary

Committee at the time, four of them—Orrin Hatch (R-Utah), Mike Lee (R-Utah), Mike Crapo (R-Idaho), and Jeff Flake (R-Arizona) were members of the Church of Jesus Christ of Latter-day Saints, meaning that "Mormons constitute almost a fifth of that body, and more than a third of the [eleven] Republicans." Indeed, some viewed the hearing as a "commentary on Mormonism," and the senators quickly gained the spotlight for how they might vote (Welker, 2018). In the meantime, a political action group called Mormon Women for Ethical Government (MWEG) wrote a letter appealing to the shared principles of the four senators, declaring that "[o]ur mutual faith teaches that any sexual abuse or assault in any context is contemptible and worthy of the most severe condemnation" (Mormon Women for Ethical Government, 2018a).[4] The fact that Mormon women were petitioning male political leaders of their own faith was groundbreaking, landing it on the pages of the *Washington Post*, *New York Times*, and other news outlets. The fact that only Flake appeared to have read the MWEG document, but that the other three senators ignored the women's petition completely was also telling, especially when they all voted to confirm Kavanaugh without additional investigation. For many LDS women, the MWEG petition represented a crushing and demoralizing moment, as high-powered Latter-day Saint men voted to uphold male privilege against a reasonable request by women of their own faith. It was a reminder to some that Mormon men are not really conditioned to listen seriously to women, even (or especially?) fellow Latter-day Saint women (Welker, 2018).

The Kavanaugh confirmation hearing also represented a hopeful moment, one to which many LDS women could look for the future of female voices in their church, as these women declared their own survival from sexual assault and demanded a change to the pervasive culture that silences and diminishes women both inside and outside of their faith. "This is not just about Judge Kavanaugh. This is about how men treat women in our society, particularly men who hold positions of power" (Mormon Women for Ethical Government, 2018b). An important model of communication and influence was laid down in that moment: with the help of social media and the online Mormon community seeking greater public awareness, Latter-day Saint victims' and advocates' voices are coming to the forefront of church discussions about sexual abuse. Survivor Elizabeth Smart has played a major role in this rising consciousness, with all of these conversations leading to demands for greater transparency in institutional sexual assault policies, changes in rhetoric about virtue and victimhood, more thorough and careful leadership accountability, and deeper access to education about sexual assault reporting, counseling, and intervention. In that hopeful direction, the Church issued an announcement in August 2019 that all leaders and teachers of children and adolescents would be required to complete a thirty-minute online training about preventing and responding to abuse (Walch, 2019). This policy has been heralded by many as a strong step toward proper sexual assault awareness and response, but criticized by others as a move that is too little too late. Still, a global and systematized approach for mitigating ecclesiastical abuse has some potential for institutional change. Like other patriarchal religions that have struggled with how to respond to sexual abuse of women and children, only when the Church of Jesus Christ of Latter-day Saints allows and even mandates greater inclusion of women's voices at all levels of ecclesiastical leadership will long-lasting solutions to sexual assault and sexual abuse be realized.

Notes

1 Polygamy is defined as a person having more than one spouse, whereas polygyny is the specific relationship of one man to more than one wife. Polyandry is when one woman has more than one husband. In the Mormon historical record, polygamy is often used interchangeably with polygyny.

2 Alberty and the *Tribune* won a Pulitzer for their investigation of BYU's sexual assault policies; see David Noyce, "*Salt Lake Tribune* Wins Pulitzer …," *Salt Lake Tribune*, April 26, 2017; found at https://archive.sltrib.com/article.php?id=5161643&itype=CMSID.

3 Since 2016, a flood of revelations about high-profile sexual offenders in the media and politics, especially presidential candidate Donald Trump's secretly taped admissions of forcibly grabbing and kissing women, drew particular attention to the pervasiveness of sexual assault in the workplace, education, politics, entertainment, and sports.

4 Mormon Women for Ethical Government, "Official Statement from Mormon Women for Ethical Government with Regard to the Brett Kavanaugh Confirmation Proceedings," September 24, 2018; found at www.mormonwomenforethicalgovernment.org/official-statement-from-mormon-women-for-ethical-government-with-regard-to-the-brett-kavanaugh-confirmation-proceedings/.

References

Alberty, E., 2018. Her Mormon College Upheld Her Sex Assault Complaint. *Salt Lake Tribune*. August 5. www.sltrib.com/news/2018/08/05/her-mormon-college-upheld/.

Alberty, E., 2016. BYU Students Say Victims of Sexual Assault Are Targeted by Honor Code. *Salt Lake Tribune*. April 12. www.sltrib.com/news/2017/07/27/byu-students-say-victims-of-sexual-assault-are-targeted-by-honor-code/.

Ames, M., 2013. Child Molestation at Idaho Scout Camp in the 90s Has Lasting Impact. *Daily Beat*. August 24. www.thedailybeast.com/child-molestation-at-idaho-scout-camp-in-the-90s-has-lasting-impact.

Anderson, L.F., 1995. *Case Reports of the Mormon Alliance*, vol. 1. https://web.archive.org/web/20080724171318/www.mormonalliance.org/casereports/volume1/part1/v1prolog.htm.

Austin, M., and Parshall, A.E. eds., 2017. *Dime Novel Mormons: The Mormon Image in Literature*. Salt Lake City, UT: Greg Kofford Books.

Baugh, A.L., 2012. "Silence, Ye Fiends of the Infernal Pit!" Joseph Smith's Incarceration in Richmond, Missouri, November 1838. *Mormon Historical Studies* (Spring/Fall): 134–59.

Block, S., 2006. *Rape and Sexual Power in Early America*. Chapel Hill, NC: University of North Carolina Press.

Brimhall, J.H., 2017. Historical and Contemporary Responses to Sexual Assault by the Church of Jesus Christ of Latter-day Saints. *Square Two* 10(3). http://squaretwo.org/Sq2ArticleBrimhallHistoricalOverview.html#backfrom19.

Church of Jesus Christ of Latter-day Saints, n.d. Abuse: Help, Healing, and Protection. www.lds.org/get-help/abuse?cid=rdb_v_abuse.

Curtis, L.D., 2019. Man Arrested in Undercover Human Trafficking Investigation Is an LDS Bishop in Lehi. *KUTV2*. February 20. https://kutv.com/news/local/man-arrested-in-utah-undercover-human-trafficking-investigation-is-an-lds-bishop.

Dietz, C.P., 2017. Not Better Off Dead: My BYU Rape Story. *Wheat and Tares* February 6. https://wheatandtares.org/2017/02/06/not-better-off-dead-my-byu-rape-story.

Dominguez, A., 2013. Elizabeth Smart Speaks on Human Trafficking. *Christian Science Monitor*. May 4. www.csmonitor.com/USA/Latest-News-Wires/2013/0504/Elizabeth-Smart-speaks-on-human-trafficking.

Duffy, J.-C., 2003. The Making of Immanuel: Brian David Mitchell and the Mormon Fringe. *Sunstone*. October, p. 34.

Dumas, G., 2014. Franklin Mathias—Boy Scouts Perversion Files. June 6. https://dumaslawgroup.com/boy-scouts-perversion-files-franklin-mathias.

Forgie, A., 2019a. Full Interview: Man Says He Was Molested by LDS Temple Video Director, Sundance Co-founder. *KUTV2*. May 1. https://kutv.com/news/local/full-interview-man-says-he-was-molested-by-lds-temple-video-director-sundance-co-founder.

Forgie, A., 2019b. Church Considering Lowering Age for Youth Interviews with Clergy to 8, Survey Says. *2KUTV*. July 9. https://kutv.com/news/local/lds-church-considering-lowering-age-for-youth-interviews-with-clergy-from-12-to-8.

Givens, T.L., and Grow, M.J., 2011. *Parley P. Pratt: The Apostle Paul of Mormonism*. New York: Oxford University Press.

Haglund, K., 2013. Dear Church Leaders, Fix This, Now. *By Common Consent*. May 6. https://bycommonconsent.com/2013/05/06/dear-church-leaders-fix-this-now/.

Harris, J., and Rascon, D., 2019. State Moves to Revoke BYU's Certification to Operate Its Own Police Department. *KUTV2*. February 26. https://kutv.com/news/local/state-moves-to-revoke-byu-certification-to-operate-its-own-police-department.

Harrison, B.K., 1986. Provo, Utah, to Ardeth G. Kapp ("Dear Ardie"), Salt Lake City. Letter. Quoted in J.H. Brimhall, 2017. Historical and Contemporary Responses to Sexual Assault by the Church of Jesus Christ of Latter-day Saints. *Square Two* 10(3). http://squaretwo.org/Sq2ArticleBrimhallHistorical Overview.html#backfrom19.

Harrison, B.K., 1990. Notes on Rape in an LDS Context. Personal notes, Provo, UT. Quoted in J.H. Brimhall, 2017. Historical and Contemporary Responses to Sexual Assault by the Church of Jesus Christ of Latter-day Saints. *Square Two* 10(3). http://squaretwo.org/Sq2ArticleBrimhallHistorical Overview.html#backfrom19.

Harrison, B.K., 2016. Rape and LDS Teachings. *Square Two* 9(2). http://squaretwo.org/Sq2Article HarrisonRape.html#backfrom5.

Hendrix-Komoto, A., 2016. 'The Sounds of Blasphemy Are Not Heard in Our Streets': Polygamy and the Response to Sexual Violence in Utah. Paper presented at the Church History Symposium, Brigham Young University, March 3–4.

Hess, A., 2013. Elizabeth Smart Says Pro-Abstinence Sex Ed Harms Victims of Rape. XXfactor on *Slate*. May 6. www.slate.com/blogs/xx_factor/2013/05/06/elizabeth_smart_abstinence_only_sex_education_ hurts_victims_of_rape_and.html.

Hinckley, G.B., 1978. Behold Your Little Ones. General Conference. October. www.lds.org/general-conference/1978/10/behold-your-little-ones?lang=eng.

Horton, A., Harrison, K., and Johnson, B. eds., 1993. *Confronting Abuse: An LDS Perspective on Understanding and Healing Emotional, Physical, Sexual, Psychological, and Spiritual Abuse*. Salt Lake City, UT: Deseret Book.

Israelsen-Hartley, S., 2010. Ex-Seminary Principal Michael Pratt Pleads Guilty in Sex Case. *Deseret News*. June 2. www.deseretnews.com/article/700036659/Ex-seminary-principal-Michael-Pratt-pleads-guilty-in-sex-case.html.

Jenkins, C., 2018. BYU Approves Updated Sexual Misconduct Policy. *Brigham Young University News*. May 24. https://news.byu.edu/news/byu-approves-updated-sexual-misconduct-policy.

Jensen, E., 2018. Mormon Leader's Comments about "Nonconsensual Immorality" Draw Fire. *Religion News Service*. April 3. https://religionnews.com/2018/04/03/mormon-leaders-comments-about-nonconsensual-immorality-draw-fire-and-new-questions-about-language/.

Kimball, S.W., 1969. *The Miracle of Forgiveness*. Salt Lake City, UT: Bookcraft.

Kimball, S.W., Romney, M.G., and Hinckley, G.B., 2017. Statement on Rape. Letter, Salt Lake City, Utah. Quoted in J.H. Brimhall, 2017. Historical and Contemporary Responses to Sexual Assault by the Church of Jesus Christ of Latter-day Saints. *Square Two* 10(3). http://squaretwo.org/Sq2Article BrimhallHistoricalOverview.html#backfrom19.

Kuruvilla, C., 2018. Woman Claims Mormon Church's Cover-Up Culture Protected Her Sexual Predator Dad. *Huffington Post*. June 29. www.huffpost.com/entry/mormon-church-cover-up-culture-sexual-predator_n_5b363f35e4b08c3a8f69aff1.

LDS Newsroom, 2003. Official Statement about Brian and Wanda Mitchell. March 3.

Meier, B., 2019. The Mormon Church Has Been Accused of Using a Victims' Hotline to Hide Claims of Sexual Abuse. *Vice*. May 3. https://news.vice.com/en_us/article/d3n73w/duty-to-report-the-mormon-church-has-been-accused-of-using-a-victims-hotline-to-hide-sexual-abuse-claims.

Mormon Women for Ethical Government, 2018a. Official Statement from Mormon Women for Ethical Government with Regard to the Brett Kavanaugh Confirmation Proceedings. September 24. www.mormonwomenforethicalgovernment.org/official-statement-from-mormon-women-for-ethical-government-with-regard-to-the-brett-kavanaugh-confirmation-proceedings/.

Mormon Women for Ethical Government, 2018b. Mormon Women Speak Out about the Brett Kavanaugh Proceedings. *Medium*. September 25. https://medium.com/on-common-ground/mormon-women-speak-out-about-the-brett-kavanaugh-case-bc078c3e9f70.

Murdock, M., 2013. When It Happens to One among Us … A Discussion of the Most Common Misunderstandings about Personal Assault. Republished in *Square Two* 6(1). http://squaretwo.org/Sq2 ArticleMurdockSexualAssault.html.

Newsroom, 2018a. Church Statement about Alleged Sexual Assault by Former Mission President. March 20 and 23. www.mormonnewsroom.org/article/statement-former-mission-president-alleged-abuse-joseph-l-bishop-march-2018.

Newsroom, 2018b. First Presidency Releases New Guidelines for Interviewing Youth. June 20. www.mormonnewsroom.org/article/new-guidelines-for-interviewing-youth#guidelines.

Niebuhr, G., 2001. Mormons Paying $3 Million to Settle Sex Abuse Case. *New York Times*. September 5. www.nytimes.com/2001/09/05/us/mormons-paying-3-million-to-settle-sex-abuse-case.html.

Ogles, B.M., 2018. Agency, Accountability and the Atonement of Jesus Christ: Application to Sexual Assault. Brigham Young University Devotional. January 30. https://speeches.byu.edu/talks/benjamin-m-ogles_agency-accountability-atonement-jesus-christ/.

Okazaki, C., 1992. Healing from Sexual Abuse. Presentation, Regional Women's Conference, Hillsboro, OR. Quoted in J.H. Brimhall, 2017. Historical and Contemporary Responses to Sexual Assault by the Church of Jesus Christ of Latter-day Saints. *Square Two* 10(3). http://squaretwo.org/Sq2Article BrimhallHistoricalOverview.html#backfrom19.

Olmstead, J.W., 2004. A Victim of the Mormons and the Danites: Images and Relics from Early Twentieth-Century Anti-Mormon Silent Films. *Mormon Historical Studies*. Spring, pp. 203–21.

Paige, C., 2008. Mother Sues Mormon Church in Abuse Case. *Boston News*. July 10. http://archive.boston.com/news/local/articles/2008/07/10/mother_sues_mormon_church_in_abuse_case/?page=full&fbclid=IwAR3s9cqhNN1nPe7PcxEzS11zwmvlqJXahMX1FNqdbElU4eAKVm3EfGzq0hQ.

Palmer, E., 2018. Mormon Bishop Facing Excommunication. *Newsweek*. August 30. www.newsweek.com/mormon-bishop-sam-young-excommunication-sexually-explicit-children-interviews-1096856.

Park, C., Brady, E., Chang, J., and McNiff, E., 2019. Families Speak Out against the Church of Jesus Christ of Latter-day Saints over Sex Abuse Allegations. *ABC News*. June 29. https://abcnews.go.com/US/families-speak-church-jesus-christ-day-saints-sex/story?id=63690802&cid=share_facebook_widget&fbclid=IwAR1J9tnI_zVtBB4DrP_GFwd61Z-x8BNp3LlagKlzjGYC2TNvbV-Lfkoe7Ao.

Pratt, P.P., 1838. Letter, Richmond, Ray County, to "Sister" [Manuscript 2], Dec 9, 1838. In D. Jessee and D. Whittaker. The Last Months of Mormonism in Missouri: The Albert Perry Rockwood Journal. *BYU Studies Quarterly* 28(1): 5–41.

Protect the Children, n.d. https://protectldschildren.org/.

Radke-Moss, A.G., 2017. Silent Memories of Missouri: Mormon Women and Men and Sexual Assault in Group Memory and Religious Identity. In R. Cope, A. Easton-Flake, K.A. Erekson, and L.O. Tait, eds. *Mormon Women's History: Beyond Biography*. Madison, NJ: Farleigh Dickinson University Press, pp. 49–82.

Read the Stories, 2018. https://protectldschildren.org/ (accessed January 20, 2020).

Roskelley, S., 1863. Smithfield, Cache County, Utah Territory, to Presidents E.T. Benson and Peter Maughan, February 8, 1863. Reprinted in N. Hart, 1982. *The Bear River Massacre*. Logan: Cache Valley Newsletter, p. 135.

Reeve, W.P., 2015. *Religion of a Different Color: Race and the Mormon Struggle for Whiteness*. New York: Oxford University Press.

Report of the Advisory Council on Campus Response to Sexual Assault, 2016. *Brigham Young University News*. October 7. https://news.byu.edu/sites/default/files/AdvisoryCouncilReport.pdf.

Riess, J., 2018. Mormonism and the Dangers of Empire. *Flunking Sainthood, Religion News Service*. September 12. https://religionnews.com/2018/09/12/mormonism-and-the-dangers-of-empire/.

Scott, R.G., 1992. Healing the Tragic Scars of Abuse. General Conference. April. www.churchofjesuschrist.org/study/general-conference/1992/04/healing-the-tragic-scars-of-abuse?lang=eng.

Scott, R.G., 2008. To Heal the Shattering Consequences of Abuse. General Conference. April. www.churchofjesuschrist.org/study/liahona/2008/05/to-heal-the-shattering-consequences-of-abuse?lang=eng.

Scoville, D., 2018. Timeline of the Joseph Bishop Sexual Abuse Scandal. *Medium*. March 24. https://medium.com/@davidscoville/timeline-of-the-joseph-bishop-sexual-abuse-scandal-77f39be1ef3a.

Sewall, C., 2019. Judge: Boy Scout Files Used to Track Sexual Misconduct Accusations Can Be Used at Trial. *Idaho Statesman*. April 22. www.idahostatesman.com/news/local/crime/article229436309.html?fbclid=IwAR0ewGZApc0UdPmVZt_-T8NSbOj7uBiRbWzxOVsWmELxwG-ioInndicLykw.

Sisters' Quorum, 2019. Sex Offenders in Church Leadership Is Not New. *Sisters Quorum*. February 28. https://sistersquorum.com/2019/02/28/this-is-not-news/.

Smart, E., 2010. Testimony, Day 3, November 10, 2010. Transcript reprinted in S. McFarland and A. Falk, 2010. *The Salt Lake Tribune*. November 12. http://archive.sltrib.com/article.php?id=50647494&itype=cmsid.

Smart, E., 2017. I Am Elizabeth Smart. Documentary. *Today Show*. Meghan Kelly. www.today.com/video/elizabeth-smart-i-couldn-t-go-back-to-who-i-was-before-i-was-kidnapped-1095584323741.

Smith, H., 1843. Testimony of Hyrum Smith. July 1. Nauvoo Municipal Court. Reprinted in C.V. Johnson, ed., 1992. *Mormon Redress Petitions: Documents of the 1833–1838 Missouri Conflict*. Provo, UT: Religious Studies Center, p. 639.

Stack, P.F., 2016. LDS Feminists Applaud. *Salt Lake Tribune*. September 29. www.sltrib.com/religion/2016/09/29/lds-feminists-applaud-as-church-removes-troublesome-book-of-mormon-verse-on-rape-from-youth-book/.

Stack, P.F., 2018a. Some Mormons Say Their Church Needs a Culture Change. *Salt Lake Tribune*. March 25. www.sltrib.com/religion/local/2018/03/24/after-watching-missionary-training-center-sex-abuse-scandal-unfold-some-mormons-say-their-church-needs-a-culture-change/.

Stack, P.F., 2018b. The Case of a Fallen Mission President. *Salt Lake Tribune*. April 26. www.sltrib.com/news/2018/04/26/the-case-of-puerto-rico-when-the-mormon-church-promptly-removed-a-mission-president-who-deceived-and-victimized-young-female-missionaries/.

Stack, P.F., and Alberty, E., 2016. How Outdated Mormon Teachings May Be Aiding and Abetting "Rape Culture." *Salt Lake Tribune*. May 6. Updated September 19, 2017. www.sltrib.com/religion/local/2017/07/27/how-outdated-mormon-teachings-may-be-aiding-and-abetting-rape-culture/.

Stump, S., 2017. Elizabeth Smart on the One Question That Won't Go Away: "Why Didn't You Run?" *Today Show*. November 14. www.today.com/news/elizabeth-smart-one-question-won-t-go-away-why-didn-t118795.

Tanner, C., 2018. Father Molested His Children for Years and Mormon Bishops Did Not Report It to Police, Lawsuit Says. *Salt Lake Tribune*. June 28. www.sltrib.com/religion/local/2018/06/28/father-molested-his/.

Walch, T., 2018. Sam Young Announces He Was Excommunicated. *Deseret News*. September 16. www.deseretnews.com/article/900032216/sam-young-announces-he-was-excommunicated-by-local-church-leaders.html.

Walch, T., 2019. Church Unveils Abuse Prevention Training for All Latter-day Saint Leaders of Children and Youth. *Deseret News*. August 16. www.deseret.com/2019/8/16/20808362/abuse-training-mormon-latter-day-saints-lds-church.

Walker, R.W., Turley, R.E., and Leonard, G.M., 2011. *Massacre at Mountain Meadows*. New York: Oxford University Press.

Welker, H., 2010. Elizabeth Smart: A Mormon's Mormon Ordeal. *The Guardian*. November 16. www.theguardian.com/commentisfree/cifamerica/2010/nov/16/elizabeth-smart-brian-mitchell-utah.

Welker, H., 2018. Kavanaugh Hearings Are a Commentary on Mormonism. *Religion Dispatches*. September 28. https://rewire.news/religion-dispatches/2018/09/28/kavanaugh-hearings-are-a-commentary-on-mormonism/.

Widdison, M., 2019. Protecting Children. *Ensign*. April. www.lds.org/study/ensign/2019/04/protecting-children?lang=eng.

Further reading

Block, S., 2006. *Rape and Sexual Power in Early America*. Chapel Hill, NC: University of North Carolina Press.

Brownmiller, S., 1975. *Against Our Will: Men, Women, and Rape*. New York: Simon & Schuster.

Henry, N., 2012. *War and Rape: Law, Memory, and Justice*. New York: Routledge.

Radke-Moss, A.G., 2017. Silent Memories of Missouri: Mormon Women and Men and Sexual Assault in Group Memory and Religious Identity. In R. Cope, A. Easton-Flake, K.A. Erekson, and L.O. Tait, eds. *Mormon Women's History: Beyond Biography*. Madison, NJ: Farleigh Dickinson University Press, pp. 49–82.

Smart, E., 2013. *My Story*. New York: Macmillan.

PART III

Social scientific approaches

21
WOMEN AND RELIGIOUS ORGANIZATION
A "microbiological" approach to influence

Melissa Wei-Tsing Inouye

> In the Church of Jesus Christ of Latter-day Saints, men have the priesthood, but women, who are naturally spiritual, have even greater influence: through service in church callings, sermons from the pulpit, and nurturing children.

All scholars who have spent time investigating the topic of women and authority within the Church of Jesus Christ of Latter-day Saints have heard this statement, or some variation of it, many times.[1] From a Western feminist point of view, this statement is a rather feeble argument of compensation. The church's formal structures for declaring doctrine, setting policy, and adjudicating individuals' membership status are restricted to men. Therefore, many conclude, Latter-day Saint women's charismatic activities and social influence at the grassroots do not measure up to a standard of gender equality or meaningful parity between men's and women's influence. From a position that values formal, hierarchical authority as the only meaningful indicator of power within a religious organization, statements like the one above deserve an exasperated roll of the eyes.

In this essay I would like to challenge—or at least moderate—this eye-roll (automatic dismissal of Latter-day Saint women's power), using the case study of the global Church of Jesus Christ of Latter-day Saints and drawing on a range of perspectives from existing scholarship in Mormon studies, the study of lived religion and culture, the study of organizations, and sociology and anthropology. A narrow focus on the visible, vertical structures of religious organizations and participation ignores the complexity of intraorganizational dynamics (Chaves, 1993a; 1993b). *Vertical structural power* is not the only *systematic power* at work within a religious community.

For me, the difficulty of arguing for the significance of women's informal or less-visible power within a patriarchal religion is that this tack is annoyingly similar to that taken by people who have not thought critically about women and internal religious dynamics, but simply want to defend the status quo of women's exclusion from administrative authority. To them, there is an essential distinction between men's and women's potential: by divine design, they argue, male authority is vertical, high-rise like the Church Office Building in Salt Lake City, and women's authority is horizontal, low-rise like the blocks of children's classrooms along the side of a typical Latter-day Saint chapel. This view, too, is flawed. Structures of vertical (highly visible, official) and horizontal (less visible, informal) authority within human organizations are not inherently gendered, and the gender essentialism found within Mormon discourse is problematic (Kline, 2014). Yet it would be a mistake to assume that, because women often act within horizontal or less visible systems of power, these hidden systems are insignificant.

In this paper, I use a loose analogy of microbiological systems in the human body to argue for the significance of the horizontal or less visible systems of power within religious organizations, and by extension the significance of women's influence within formally patriarchal religions. The particular case study of Mormon women, both historically and in the present, in diverse global contexts, powerfully demonstrates how even the most hierarchically oriented collective religious projects depend on other powerful systems to survive and thrive.

By challenging this eye-roll (a reaction that has often characterized my own response, as a feminist and practicing Latter-day Saint), I seek to broaden the ways in which scholars conceptualize the participation of actors with little formal power in highly centralized, hierarchical religious organizations (Giorgi, Guider, and Bartunek, 2014). My insistence on the gravity of women's influence even within a patriarchal religious organization like the global Church of Jesus Christ of Latter-day Saints is in the same vein as Saba Mahmood's goal, in her study of Egyptian Muslim women, to "redress the profound inability within current feminist political thought to envision valuable forms of human flourishing outside the bounds of a liberal progressive imaginary" (Mahmood, 2005, p. 155). The work of Mahmood and other scholars convincingly demonstrates that within patriarchal contexts such as Islam and Mormonism, women exercise agency and develop capacity as they cultivate moral discipline and maintain social structures and norms (Mahmood, 2005; Karim, 2009; Brekus, 2011). In this essay, my focus is not agency, but influence—the power not only to make choices for oneself, but to make choices that shape the lives, experiences, and expectations of *others*. Just as we would be simpletons to insist that the only thing that mattered about human life was having a skeleton clothed with muscles and sinew, we must not narrow our understanding of religion to formal administrative structures alone.

As the science of the human body has shown, what determines human survival and vitality is much more than a person's upright posture and muscle mass. Many of the body's internal systems, invisible to the eye, play a major role in physical survival, well-being, and identity, although these essential processes are incredibly complex. Immune and autoimmune responses can be a source of healing, illness, chronic pain, and dramatic survival. Mouth bacteria have recently been linked to Alzheimer's disease, and the balance of gut flora may be related to colon cancer occurrence. Memories of diving into cold water on summer days are not "stored" like a book on a shelf, but are actively reconstructed between various groups of neurons in different regions of the brain. These systems are much more difficult to understand than a stack of vertebrae in the spinal column, but they are just as important. Because of the complexity of the human body, the microbiological analogy that I will use throughout this essay depends less on detailed correlation and more on three images of complex systems within the body that, though not immediately apparent, are tremendously consequential.

There are three "microbiological" systems within a religious organization that I would like to discuss. This line of theorization is new and my own expertise limited, so I will not go so far as to assert that my categorizations are universal to all human religious experience. However, I believe that these three systems are present within the organized forms of the world religions that I have encountered in the course of my research career, including Christianity, Islam, and Buddhism. First, there is the *cultural* environment of images, music, rituals, practices, tastes, dispositions, and discourses. I link it to the immune system, which maintains the integrity of the body by making distinctions between native and foreign elements, creating bodies that directly engage with the external environment. Second, there are localized *relational* networks of interpersonal influence. I liken these shifting, spontaneous relational connections between individual believers to the colonies of bacteria in the gut. Third, there is the *ontological* reality that is the work of the shared religious endeavor, whereby that which cannot be seen or touched (the divine) is made real, almost tangible, and loyally taken for granted through constant acts of collective affirmation. I compare these to the neural networks of cells and synapses in the brain that store individuals' life experiences and hence their very sense of self and existence. Within the Church of Jesus Christ of Latter-day Saints all around the world, these microbiological systems facilitate women's pursuit of and influence over their collective religious existence.

While none of these three "microbiological" systems are inherently "male" or "female," the example of Latter-day Saint women demonstrates how these cultural, relational, and ontological systems can significantly influence the entire body of the church. While the structure of formal hierarchical authority is indisputably influential within the Church of Jesus Christ of Latter-day Saints—without it, the church would resemble the iconic bowl of Utah green Jell-O on a hot day—it would be a serious mistake to name it as the only influential system within Mormonism, and by extension to declare that Latter-day Saint women did not have access to systems of influence, or that a woman's participation in Latter-day Saint institutional and community life is only constraining, and not enabling. Just as Saba Mahmood in her study of Egyptian women asked what resources and capacities a pious lifestyle makes available, we might ask what resources and capacities the microbiological systems of complex religious organization make available to Latter-day Saint women, in their diverse situations around the world (Mahmood, 2005 p. 168).

At the outset I will state two things that seem obvious about organized religious movements, but which are quite important to keep in mind. In the first place, religious organizations are organized. Notwithstanding religious claims to divine genesis and direction, they behave like other kinds of large organizations, subject to the same pressures and constraints that come with scale, geographic distribution, bureaucracy, and so on. No matter how many multi-million-megawatts are available to leap down as divine power from on high, power must still be conducted through a manmade network of people held together by deadlines, meetings, schedules, telecommunications, flow charts, and the like.

In the second place, religious organizations are religious. They differ from political, civic, corporate, environmental, and other kinds of organizations in the particular orientation of their formation and ongoing life. For instance, while Latter-day Saint doctrines contain strong theological and cultural strains emphasizing the equality of all before God, or reverence for the natural world, the church is not primarily oriented toward achieving equality for all humankind or saving the planet. Although many jockey for power and status within the church's internal political and cultural hierarchies (despite scriptural injunctions to humility and modesty), people who convert usually do not do so because they aspire to local leadership positions, insisting on a guarantee of free and fair bishopric elections before accepting baptism. Religious projects depend on religious logics to solve religious problems. These logics can be multiplex and contradictory, but they are ultimately rooted in a particular religion's distinctive claims and concerns.

The Church of Jesus Christ of Latter-day Saints exemplifies both organizational and religious realities. Some observers have compared its highly centralized, bureaucratic, patriarchal structure to a multinational corporation or even a Stalinist regime. Its exclusivist religious claims assert the charismatic content of this bureaucracy. A separate structure exists for its volunteer-led local congregations that are generally more egalitarian, culturally adaptive, and erratic in personnel. Latter-day Saint women also present seeming contradictions, historically defending polygamy while fighting for women's rights, engaging in charismatic home practices while also asserting their desire for social influence on the national and world stage. Mormon practice ticks the boxes on both sides of the usual binaries: rationalized yet charismatic, hierarchical yet grassroots, global yet American, cosmopolitan but provincial, heavily mediatized yet also strikingly dependent on face-to-face interactions.

Yet I do not think that the existence of microbiological organizational systems is unique to the Latter-day Saint tradition. The example of Mormon women is simply useful because it tends to evoke a knee-jerk reaction that highlights some common assumptions about the structures and exercise of power. Research and analytical models in the study of organizations and anthropology, in particular, illuminate aspects of power relations (including relations with divine power) we might also consider.

Cultural

In the microbiological analogy, culture is like a religion's immune system: the system of the body whose "tasks are to determine friend from foe, innocuous from dangerous, inert from toxic," and which exhibits adaptive responses to changing environments (MacGillivray and Kollmann, 2014). Similarly, a religion's cultural systems engage with the external environment, curating and regulating an internal environment of circulating ideas, images, objects, ritual practices, dress, dietary practices, dispositions, and other symbols in a given place and time. For example, research on Christian movements within the Yoruba populations in West Africa highlights a "deep affinity" between the transplanted Christian message and local cultural resources. African Christian prophet movements made use of the "indigenous categories of religious life" (Sanneh, 1998, p. 221). Thomas Murphy's research on the overlap between Guatemalan Mormons' cultural understandings of "hot" and "cold" in medicine with the Word of Wisdom is another example of this negotiation between specialized religious cultures and the broader local culture (Murphy, 1997). Through their assignments to work with children and youth, women are primary models of Mormonism's ethos of organization. Their high level of social embeddedness within community networks adds to their influence in defining and regulating the boundaries of their religion (Stroope, 2012).

Mormons' emphasis on themselves as a "peculiar people" depends on a culture marked by difference from surrounding society. Charles L. Cohen has argued that, despite processes of assimilation, "Mormons ... retain their distinctive sense of peoplehood," a strong and unyielding "sense of who they know themselves to be" that leads them to "patrol their sociological boundaries" (Cohen, 2006, p. 63). Within the church, canonized scripture and central policy set out formal prescriptions and proscriptions regarding church members' beliefs, actions, and organizational participation. Even more extensive is the tangle of grassroots religious culture, which both marks the distinctiveness ("peculiarity") of the Latter-day Saints and exhibits affinities with host cultures around the world.

Historical scholarship on Mormon culture and lived religion has shown how early Mormonism developed a distinctive culture, intimately related to strong strains in the antebellum American religious culture in which it arose, including enthusiastic and emotional religiosity, Christian humanism, corporate organization, and a desire to unite material and spiritual life (Porterfield, 2018, pp. 103–5; Bushman, 2005; Ulrich, 2017). Scholars of Mormon material history have examined everyday objects such as quilts, brick molds, and butter churns, architecture, and ornamental art as evidence of "the day-to-day experience of Mormonism," with great relevance for ordinary women's lives (Probert, 2016; Carter, 2015). Ritual activity in temples in Kirtland, Nauvoo, St. George, Salt Lake City, Cardston, and other nineteenth-century edifices depended not only on stone and wood cut, hauled, and framed by men, but also on curtains, carpets, lace, veils, ceremonial clothing, and food for male laborers—all the work of women's hands.

Historically, organizations run by Mormon women, such as the Primary and the Young Women's Mutual Improvement Association (the historical predecessor to the modern Young Women program) had much more autonomy and official vertical authority than in the present. In their study of modes of power within Mormonism, Jill Derr and Brooklyn Derr pointed out that around the turn of the century, the female-led Relief Society and the Young Ladies' Mutual Improvement Association were calling their own missionaries, holding their own annual conferences, creating centrally prepared handbooks and lessons, and initiating their own programs across an increasingly international membership (Derr and Derr, 1982, pp. 23–25). Beginning in the early decades of the twentieth century, and accelerating during the Correlation movement of the 1960s, church growth prompted central streamlining efforts whereby these organizations, including those run by women, were gradually brought under the control of the centralized male priesthood hierarchy (Hatch, 2004; Bowman, 2012, pp. 184–215).

Contemporary Mormonism is also fertile ground for studying lived religion. Tona Hangen describes a vibrant culture always thrumming below the surface of official structures, "where improvisation, resistance, blending, and creativity are found in abundance" (Hangen, 2015, pp. 209–24). Provocatively, she observes, "If 'the laity' comprises nearly everyone in Mormonism, and leaders learn mainly by doing rather than through formal professional training, then lived Mormonism is, in that sense, the only kind there is" (Hangen, 2015, p. 210). In other words, grassroots cultural practices within Mormonism "involve processes of selection, repurposing, collage, and embellishment" that may stand in tension with existing official materials and messages (Hangen, 2015, p. 218).

While grassroots culture is not inherently or exclusively a feminine realm, it is clear that Latter-day Saint women play an outsize role in shaping their religious culture. In the first place, there are simply more female than male Latter-day Saints (Riess, 2019). In the second place, Latter-day Saint women are generally well-represented in positions managing the congregation's daily or weekly activities and interactions. As Tona Hangen notes, "uncorrelated" materials and autonomous approaches are especially prevalent in church lessons at the lowest levels of local organization, where women participate: children's and youth organizations, and private homes (Hangen, 2015, p. 218).

Of particular significance is women's participation in Primary, the Church's organization for children (girls and boys). While there are many worldwide variations, official guides on the church website state that ideally, Primary is to be led by an all-female presidency consisting of the Primary president, two counsellors, and a secretary. The music leader and pianist are usually, though not always, female. The majority of teachers tend to be female, though it is common to have some male teachers, especially for older classes. In large congregations it is often—though not always—the case that, as in the Elkton Ward documented by Susan Taber, "of all the organizations in the ward, the Primary has the largest staff" (Taber, 1993, p. 51). There are notable exceptions to this gendered arrangement. For example, in some church units in the Democratic Republic of the Congo, in which there is a chronic understaffing of women, Primary and Young Women are often taught by men. This is likely the case in areas of the world where women are systematically undereducated and where church units are small.

Beyond numerical mass, women are influential not so much for the doctrinal content of the lessons (which are standardized in lesson manuals and repeated year after year throughout a young person's childhood and adolescence), but for the strong, distinctive habitus that they create (Bourdieu, 1979, pp. 101–14, 466). Numerous studies have noted Mormonism's communitarian, collective, corporate character (Cannell, 2017; Fluhman, 2015; McDannell, 2018). For instance, in her study of American Latter-day Saints, anthropologist Fenella Cannell has described how "individual agency and responsibility are held in perpetual tension with a strongly desired and articulated collective salvational imperative" (Cannell, 2017, p. 154). This collective theology is articulated explicitly, to some extent, in some passages of scripture prescribing group unity and some aspects of the temple liturgy emphasizing family ties. However, the collective ethos is also expressed implicitly in the organizational form of Latter-day Saint worship and spirituality, which emphasizes deliberate gathering and organizing into cohorts and quorums. Laurel Thatcher Ulrich has pointed out that for Latter-day Saint women, "the concept of gathering that was at the heart of Mormon theology" was so important that "retreating into a private heaven was neither possible nor righteous" (Ulrich, 2017, p. xxiv).

The collective habits that shape Latter-day Saint realities both earthly and divine do not arise spontaneously but are the result of weekly training from a very young age, beginning in the local Primary organization (each of which has its own distinctive culture that varies not only from country to country but congregation to congregation) (Inouye, 2018). Within Primary, the female president models leadership and delegation, and her female counselors model leadership and deference to higher authority. Children learn to sit in chairs, to set up chairs in rows, put chairs away in stacks (i.e., to transform their space for shared reception of an authoritative lesson). They learn to speak in public, to play a part in a group performance, to fulfill rotating assignments. They learn to sing in a group, obeying the cues of the music leader and altering the pitch of their individual voices to match the voices of the leader and their peers. As Kristine Haglund has noted, mostly women have selected and composed Primary songs, through which children absorb core theological ideas, doctrinal precepts, positive associations, and understanding about how to live their religion in everyday life (Haglund, 2004).

While an adult Sunday School teacher can probably get away with droning directly from the official church-printed manual before an audience of listless but quietly seated adult Mormons, the interactive task of teaching children involves the teacher's personality and responds dynamically to that particular group of children's learning habits. For example, in a Primary meeting I attended in Likasi, the Democratic Republic of Congo, Primary was held in a stone garage, and there were no visual aids. Instead, the children were prompted to respond to questions in chorus, to chant in unison, and to occasionally clap and dance. It is in Primary where local leaders, usually women, most frequently do the work of translating centrally correlated directives into local idioms. As I have argued elsewhere with reference to Primary cultures in Hong Kong and New Zealand, it is often the case that instead of creating homogeneity, centralized, Utah-oriented authoritative structures provide justification or impetus for the creation of highly particularistic, localized, informal institutions within Latter-day Saint practice (Inouye, 2018).

In the informality of the home, such as "Family Home Evenings" and other devotionally oriented family settings, Latter-day Saint women teach their own children their values and beliefs, including not only religious doctrines but a broad range of ethical and social topics. Traditional Latter-day Saint attitudes about "homemaking" and gendered divisions of labor have also generally left women with the prerogative of shaping their home environments. In her recent book, *Sister Saints*, Colleen McDannell argues, "In a world in which images and objects are central to religion—as in every aspect of life—Mormon women have tremendous influence over how their religious life is lived." Women also shape Latter-day Saint culture through activities such as consumption, social and political activism, and participation in online forums. McDannell further argues,

> Mormon women are masters of the internet. Through social media, women decide which elements in a religion to "pin" or "post," and which to ignore. They decide which church leader's comments should be made into decorative plaques and which should be forgotten.
>
> *(McDannell, 2018, p. 199)*

Mormon women's initiative in framing the culture of the home to reference the larger religious community may yield both practical and strategic benefits in places or cultures characterized by relatively strong female subordination to men. As Elizabeth Brusco has shown in her studies of evangelical women in Colombia, women experienced a fairly socially conservative, patriarchal form of Christianity as empowering because church culture reined in husbands' drinking, gambling, and womanizing and created a new shared moral worldview in which the interests of husbands and wives became aligned (Brusco, 1995). Although a document such as "The Family: A Proclamation to the World," with its prescribed gender roles, appears deeply conservative within a Western liberal democratic context, its language of husband and wife as equal partners is radical in many other parts of the world where the church is growing rapidly.

Mormon women also have tremendous influence creating and policing internal cultural norms within the community. Recent research by Jana Riess shows that this culture of surveillance can be experienced negatively by millennial Latter-day Saints in the United States, and is a particularly widespread experience for women. "Feeling judged," was the number one reason cited by former millennial Latter-day Saint women in the United States for leaving their faith (Riess, 2019; McDannell, 2018). Assuming that this culture of judgment was indeed excessive, in the "immune system" analogy to Mormon culture, this would be a case of the immune system going haywire and attacking native bodies as if they were foreign (an autoimmune reaction).

In sum, Latter-day Saint women play an active role in shaping the internal cultural composition of their religious communities. Women with strong opinions and executive personalities may be as much a durable, persistent influence within local Mormon life as a provision in the official handbook.

Relational

A second powerful system within a religious organization is the network of personal relationships within the local community of believers. In our analogy of the body, this invisible but populous system is like the diverse, competing communities of microbes that occupy habitats such as the gut. Research shows the activities of fluctuating populations of individual strains of microbes, on and within the body, are surprisingly consequential in human health (Human Microbiome Project Consortium, 2012).

The usefulness of the microbiome model for our understanding of women's influence on religious systems is a model for how uncoordinated, somewhat unpredictable, fluid interactions of groups of individual believers can significantly affect a religious movement as a whole. In this section's emphasis on the messy, shifting state of affairs evoked by lowly colonies of microbes exuberantly competing and reproducing as they digest insoluble fiber in the colon, I draw on work from the field of organization studies (Derr and Derr, 1982; Johnson, 1979).

Studies of organizations provide numerous helpful analytical lenses for identifying power structures and relations within religious movements. One of the earliest theorists of organization was Max Weber, who identified three major sources of authority: rationalistic (official or bureaucratic), traditional (rooted in longstanding accepted practice), and charismatic (relating to a person's extraordinary personal character or ability). Charismatic authority in particular has long been claimed by Mormon women, and by women in religious movements more generally. Charismatic leadership of woman healers, spirit mediums, and prophetesses is well documented in religious studies literature (Wessinger, 2012; Cline, 2010; Porterfield, 2005).

Jill Derr and Brooklyn Derr's investigation into Mormon women's access to power concluded that opportunities for informal personal influence did exist for women, though these opportunities were not stable over time. Eliza R. Snow, for instance, by virtue of her marriage connections to Joseph Smith and Brigham Young (traditional authority) and her reputation for poetry, prophecy, healing, and blessing (charismatic authority), presided over the women's organizations of the church for years (1982, p. 31). Other Latter-day Saint women's leaders with official positions as "auxiliary" leaders, who had strong personal connections to prominent line-authority male leaders, such as Adele Howells, LaVern Parmley, and Belle Spafford, were able to win support for ambitious projects such as the founding of the Primary Children's Hospital in 1952, or the completion of the Relief Society Building in the same year (1982, pp. 32–34). In the late twentieth century, Sheri L. Dew and Chieko Okazaki were general officers within the Relief Society organization whose strong personal charisma and distinctive perspective amplified their influence beyond the official scope of their terms of organizational service. Personal relationships are especially influential within Mormonism's congregational structures, which juxtapose hierarchy and grassroots control. In this vein, Claudia L. Bushman in her study of contemporary Mormonism has noted, "Administration of the congregation is in the hands of the members. They are like shareholders in a large corporation with a stake in the company. They own it" (Bushman, 2006, p. 34).

Numerous studies of organizations demonstrate that instead of being directed by a rational, straightforward process of informed decision-making, organizations can often be described as "organized anarchies" in which many competing priorities, technologies, problems, solutions, and participants vie for institutional attention and support under changing, fluid conditions. An influential theoretical model, the "garbage can" model, posits that the rational-choice model of organizational leadership (a class of managers identifying a problem, researching solutions, and selecting the best outcome) does not always apply and may in fact be mythical. Instead,

> [t]o understand processes within organizations, one can view a choice opportunity as a garbage can into which various kinds of problems and solutions are dumped by participants as they are generated. The mix of garbage in a single can depends on the number of cans available, on the labels attached to the alternative cans, on what garbage is currently being produced, and on the speed with which garbage is collected and removed from the scene.
>
> *(Cohen and March, 1972, p. 2)*

This insight that organizations do not always function according to the ideals suggested by formal structures of decision-making has been corroborated by many studies highlighting the significance of participants' competing priorities, informal agendas, personal networks, and happenstance in shaping organizations.

The organized anarchy model emphasizes the significance of fluctuating time and energy constraints in shaping the quality of actors' participation in planning and implementation. Differences in time available to representatives of different interests or sub-organizations shape the dynamics of collaboration (DiMaggio, 1998). Because of Mormonism's lay priesthood and emphasis on traditional male breadwinner roles, at the local level the top decision makers are often ironically those with the least flexible schedules and hence the least time in which to participate in decision-making processes. Within the same traditional gender framework, women's more flexible schedules give them relatively more opportunities to participate in community life, through formal roles and informal social networks. Because of the time-intensive, highly differentiated nature of work with children and youth, women's activities may comprise the bulk of the total hours invested in congregational participation. Indeed, Colleen McDannell's 2018 study of modern Mormon women shows how the labor of Mormon community life, though directed by men, has been largely performed by women (pp. 73–76).

The garbage can model of organization emphasizes "inconsistent and chancy patterns of participation in choice situations, such that how a problem is resolved may hinge on whether one or another participant happens to come to the meeting at which it is discussed" (DiMaggio, 1998, p. 10). Some studies note that many people carry bundles of vexing problems and appealing solutions around with them from choice situation to choice situation and use every decision forum as an opportunity to bring them up. This inconsistency applies to Latter-day Saint women at the local level not only in terms of how powerful women influence their local congregational institutions, but also in a phenomenon that some online Mormon groups call "leadership roulette." Some leaders permit and even encourage women's active participation in collective decision making and cultural innovation. Others discourage it. From one point of view, this demonstrates women's marginal and tenuous situation, always dependent on getting a man in power to take them seriously, with their bundles of problems and solutions. From another perspective, it demonstrates a structural loophole in which official line-authority is not the only conduit to meaningful change.

Research on organizations has identified the significance of personal networks in facilitating the success of an organization or its initiatives. This research argues that a key factor in an actor's power, prestige, and effectiveness is centrality within his or her networks (DiMaggio, 1998, p. 18). The overlapping formal and informal networks within a Latter-day Saint congregation create multiple opportunities for women to occupy a central network position and influence the larger Latter-day Saint community. Research shows that "social embeddedness" (the strength of social networks within a religious congregation) affects both the religious activity and religious beliefs of congregational members (Stroope, 2012). Latter-day Saint women, by virtue of their formal roles organizing congregational activities and their informal roles coordinating the social and cultural lives of their families, are central to a congregation's collective life and shared assumptions.

The structural possibilities for local initiative within a Latter-day Saint congregation, accessible to women as well as men, suggest women's potential to exert influence within complex organizations. Studies emphasize the ways in which innovations diffuse gradually at sites where they solve concrete problems, at which point they become "institutionalized" and integrated more widely into the corporate culture. Gregory Prince notes in his article on Mormon authority and organizational structures that "trickle-up revelation" is as prevalent as prophetic directives. All church auxiliaries, from the Relief Society to the Sunday School to the Primary and Young Men and Young Women's organizations, began as local initiatives (Prince, 2015, p. 178). This sort of local improvisation is even more pronounced in church units that are recently developed, geographically remote, or sparsely populated (the reality for church units in most of the countries in which the church operates around the world).

Organization theory also reveals the significance of sometimes hidden and often contradictory "institutional logics," patterns of cultural symbols and material practices that provide meaning and order within an organization. Large, complex organizations are characterized by a "multiplexity of logics," meaning that logics can contradict each other, "sending conflicting or confusing signals about meaning or values to institutional inhabitants" (DeJordy et al., 2014, p. 304). At the same time, however, this multiplex and contradictory situation also enables agency. The presence of multiple logics "provide[s] actors embedded in these complex social structures with a choice of which logic or logics to focus on when taking action" (p. 304). Multiple logics within Mormonism help explain how, though excluded from administrative power, Mormon women frequently successfully leverage their moral and spiritual capital in order to exert influence. Since its founding in 2017 the activist group Mormon Women for Ethical Government (MWEG) has often advocated stances that put them at odds with the Republican–Mormon establishment in the state of Utah. However, their collective claim to the authentically

"Mormon" values of integrity, honesty, and charity cannot be automatically dismissed by conservative Mormon politicians who claim these same values (McDannell, 2018, p. 194). This moral solidarity has helped facilitate MWEG's success in gaining a national platform in the United States (for example, MWEG statements were entered into the official record during the Brett Kavanaugh Supreme Court confirmation hearings in 2018).

In sum, organization theories demonstrate ways in which the actions and interactions of individuals or groups within an organization can exercise enormous influence that is often overlooked with a focus only on the most obvious structures of power. Like the colonies of microbes that can determine robust health or life-threatening illness, these less-visible networks of relationships shape a religion's very life.

Ontological

The final "invisible system" in our microbiological analogy is the system comprising networks of neurons and synapses in various regions of the brain that store an individual's memories, and thus a sense of self and of existing as a unique personality (LeDoux, 2003). In our analogy, they represent religious believers' ontological project. Within Mormonism, women typically are those called to disseminate knowledge to the youngest of believers, and thus shape children's concepts of religious ideas or events. Above all else, religious organizations arise out of believers' collective desire to claim and perpetuate an extraordinary event or idea. As Ann Taves has put it in her study of religious experience, no experience is inherently religious, but must be deemed religious by one or more people. One person's special experience, such as a divine vision, or a heavenly voice, comes to be known and valued by others, who organize a religious community to protect and reproduce this special experience (Taves, 2009).

Without a chorus of supporting voices, the Jewish girl named Mary most likely was simply making excuses for her unwed pregnancy, a treasure-digging American boy named Joseph most likely invented a tale about an angel with golden plates, and the image of the Bodhisattva Guanyin most likely has no power or value beyond its thin veneer of gold leaf. The flame of charismatic power must be sheltered and sustained by organizational structures and processes, or else flicker out (Inouye, 2019, pp. 11–14). A religious believer, of course, would say that Christ's divinity does not depend on whether a large number of people believe in him or not, or that Joseph Smith's restoration project would have progressed even without the support of the friends and family members who formed the nucleus of his early church, or that the Bodhisattva Guanyin is a powerful being who, indeed, is overlooked by nearly all human beings caught in the cycle of delusion and suffering. However, the point is that different religious movements imagine the cosmos, the significant actors within it, and the purpose of an individual human life in distinctive ways that are not self-evident, but must be taught and reinforced through human work. Maintaining these diverse but interrelated understandings of the nature of reality, and the reality of the divine, is the most fundamental work of a religious community.

Talal Asad has observed how structures of power such as laws, schools, families, and so on create the conditions for experiencing particular religious truths. He used this argument to show how the category of "religion" as an object of scholarly inquiry was shaped by Western assumptions stemming from the Christian tradition. What is particularly interesting about this idea for the purposes of Mormon women's influence is the notion that everyday social structures are part of a powerful project that, indeed, allow certain kinds of truths to be experienced and therefore to exist in the world of believers (Asad, 1993, pp. 31–33).

Work in the anthropology of religion substantiates the real ability of religious communities to create reality, to train themselves to see God's face and hear God's voice. In her 2012 book on American evangelicals, *When God Talks Back*, Tanya Luhrmann argues that the process by which people come to experience divine power involves acquiring a skill. This skill of the intimate encounter with God is learned in the body and in the mind through repeated training and effort. Luhrmann writes, "the mental muscles developed in prayer work on the boundary between thought and perception, between what is attributed to the mind—internal, self-generated, private, and hidden from view—and what exists in the world" (p. 184). In Luhrmann's study, subjects who engaged in kataphatic discipline (guided imagination on the life of Christ as described in the Gospels) improved in tests of mental imagery vividness, became significantly more likely to say that they had had a near-tangible experience of God's presence, and that God had spoken to them at last. Even subjects who scored low on a standard psychological test measuring "absorption" (a person's ability to become intensely focused on the mind's object, closely correlated with the ability to be hypnotized, and the tendency to report having had an intimate experience of God's presence), after a month of exposure to the kataphatic discipline's imaginative, sensorily rich presentation of the Gospels' narratives, were more likely to say that "God had become more of a person to them" and that "they had felt God's presence" (p. 215). These practices of imagination, visualization, listening, and other forms of intense engagement with the Bible led to unusual and unintentional sensory experiences such as hearing an external voice say, "Excuse me," or opened their eyes to find that an angel had woken them from sleep (p. 216). They developed a capacity to experience God not only as internal to the mind, but as external in the world.

Overall, Luhrmann argues, certain practices of imagination, visualization, and auditory concentration increased subjects' intense spiritual experiences, showing

> how proclivity and practice shape the most basic ways we encounter our world: the way we perceive and judge what is real ... Each faith—to some extent, each church—forms its own culture, its own way of seeing the world, and as people acquire the knowledge and the practices through which they come to know that God, the most intimate aspects of the way they experience their everyday world change ... In some deep and fundamental way, as a result of their practices, they live in different worlds.
>
> (p. 226)

This research highlights the significance of repetitive, immersive religious practice in facilitating a person's experience of a particular religiously influenced reality. Within our case study of Mormonism, all over the world women play a key role in developing Mormonism's habitus—the acquired disposition to differentiate and appreciate, to establish and mark differences by a process of distinction—with regard not only to musical preferences or patterns of public address, but also the ways in which revelation through the Holy Spirit is experienced, and how the hand of God can be recognized in everyday life. Ontology, as Luhrmann's research shows, is not simply a matter of whether one believes sermons about how God created the world, but the fruits of hard training in a distinctive kind of reality. Within religious communities, this learning is mutually reinforcing.

In the earliest days of the church founded by Joseph Smith, women played a major role in validating Smith's claims and divine calling. They provided evidence for God's power within the church in their hearts, their tongues, and in their bodies as they prayed, blessed, and were healed (McDannell, 2018; Stapley, 2018; Derr et al., 2016). This same collective work of validation continues in the contemporary era, as Latter-day Saint women in New Zealand and Australia scrambled to follow the prophet by engaging in a ten-day social media fast, then testifying of its efficacy.

Luhrmann's finding about the power of sensory engagement and imagination to facilitate people's experience of religion as reality is significant because in their work in Primary and in their homes, Latter-day Saint women control the realm of Mormon spiritual training that is most dominated by images, imagination, movement, sensory stimulation, and bodily discipline. Because their students are young children, teachers may utilize a range of ingenious methods and props to keep and hold the children's attention. In "gospel lessons," they tell stories with the help of images and objects, encourage kinetic participation in learning activities, and train children to adopt certain bodily postures and even emotional modes in order to maintain "reverence." During "Singing Time," they train children to join their breath and energy in shaped musical melodies, and to commit to memory the lyrics of songs containing theological messages. It is significant that when church worship services transitioned from three hours to two hours, the only Sunday block of time that was not truncated or reduced was Primary Singing Time. This attests to leaders' understanding of the value of Singing Time in the formation of Latter-day Saints. It is the most sensorily and kinetically engaging of all modes of Sunday theological instruction, with tremendous power to permanently shape values, identity, and spiritual dispositions. In their homes, Latter-day Saint women display images, quotations, and other visual reminders of God's presence and involvement in the family's life. As they pray with their children, they are teaching not only a set of common phrases and patterns, but also certain expectations of God's availability, personhood, and power.

Religious neural networks (communities of believers that collaboratively store and recreate distinctive religiously inspired realities) are not directed solely at an external deity but also at their own internal authority structures. This work of making things real extends beyond divine power, but also the power of human leaders. Max Weber, in his study of different types of authority, put it this way: "the basis of every system of authority, and correspondingly of every kind of willingness to obey, is a belief, a belief by virtue of which persons exercising authority are lent prestige" (1947, p. 382). Claudia L. Bushman observed of Mormonism, "as in a democracy, the power of the leaders is derived from the consent of the governed who are free to follow their leaders or not" (Bushman, 2006, p. 34).

Mormon leaders may declare "thus saith the Lord," but it is up to the members of the rank-and-file to interpret these declarations as God's will for them. One example of divergence between members' actions and leaders' prescriptions is the practice of contraception. Leaders repeatedly condemned birth control in the strongest terms throughout most of the twentieth century, while the use of birth control steadily gained popularity within the Latter-day Saint population. Eventually, toward the end of the twentieth century, leaders reversed course and adjusted the official handbook to state that family planning was a matter between a couple and God. This change suggests that in some cases, leadership's failure to readjust authoritative pronouncements to adapt to seismic cultural shifts damages leaders' spiritual authority.

In addition to the positive work of making God's power real in individual and collective life, another form of ontological work that occurs within religious networks is rejecting and reframing rival sources of power (such as other deities, local religious rites, material resources, and so on). For example, in Taiwanese society, Latter-day Saints wrestle with the proper way to respond to the Chinese tradition of ancestor worship. Chiung Hwang Chen's 2008 discussion of Taiwanese Mormonism and indigenization suggests that Taiwanese members largely follow the Protestant hard line (originally introduced by European missionaries) of rejecting all forms of Chinese traditional ancestor worship, though the Latter-day Saint emphasis on genealogical research and family history softens this somewhat. Along the entire spectrum of Latter-day Saint responses to ancestor worship, from outright rejection to cultural accommodation, however, the character of the cultural and ontological work is the same: Latter-day Saints define through their discourse and actions which realities are valid, which are illusory, and which acts are efficacious or meaningless. Negotiating the double patriarchies of Euro-American Mormonism and Chinese Confucianism as they fulfill family roles may provide an opportunity for Taiwanese Latter-day Saint women to create an in-between space in which they assign their own values to competing ontological claims. Mormon women whose extended families still engage in traditional ancestor worship rites must draw these boundaries for themselves, sometimes going through the motions but denying the rites "in their hearts," or sometimes refusing to participate at all though this will incur the wrath of their extended non-Mormon families.

Other ways in which Mormon women, who have relatively little formal power, exercise informal power, and shape the scale of the believing Latter-day Saint reality, is by voting with their feet and disaffiliating from the church. Statistically speaking, the majority of people who were ever baptized as Latter-day Saints have done this (Charles et al., 2016). Disaffiliation is a common occurrence and has reached such a scale in the age of the internet that ex-Mormon communities now have their own distinctive culture.

Conclusion

In sum, the "microbiological mass" produced by individuals within religious organizations is tremendous. This has significant ramifications for our understanding of women's influence within religious organizations with vertical (formal) *and* horizontal (informal) dimensions, particularly within the case study of the Church of Jesus Christ of Latter-day Saints. In the first section of the paper we saw how in lived religious culture was largely modeled and curated by women; in the second, we saw how church life was shaped (and sometimes made more complicated) by networks of individuals and groups with diverse priorities and logics; in the third section, we saw the cosmic extent of the religious project's transformative aims. The religious project is not simply the maintenance of a religious community, but of an entire worldview and indeed an entire world or set of worlds, and this is reinforced daily and to the youngest believers by Mormon women.

Mormon women's exclusion from formal line-authority management does not prevent them from powerfully shaping the world in which all Latter-day Saints live: its cultural symbols, modes, and markers of belonging, its networks of relational influence, and its distinctive ontological possibilities. Religious organizations, by virtue of their organizational and religious character, open up fields of actions that go beyond advancement in formal administrative hierarchy. Since our subject is the participation of living beings in a collective religious project, we must explore not only narratives of constraint and control that are heavily influenced by our ideals for political governance, but also narratives of possibility and enterprise that are clearly a reality for the women who participate in Mormonism and other patriarchal religious systems. While structural inequality within religious organizations is indeed extremely significant, and something that I personally believe limits the flourishing of both women and religious organizations, it is short-sighted to view only "structural" (vertical, easily visible) power as power. We must begin to appreciate the power of horizontal, less-visible systems that define and animate the religious project, and within which women shape the worlds in which they live.

Note

1 Out of deference to the change in style preferences expressed late in 2018, I have used the full, official name of the church at this first mention. In this article, because of limitations in my expertise, I focus on women's access to power within the Church of Jesus Christ of Latter-day Saints and not other

traditions that originated with Joseph Smith. Throughout the rest of the article I will variously use terms such as "Latter-day Saints" (to refer to church members), "Mormon" (when an adjective instead of a long prepositional phrase is preferable for clarity and ease of reading, and when "Mormon" is part of an existing term, like "Mormon studies"), "the Latter-day Saint tradition" or "Latter-day Saint culture" (when referring to communities of practicing church members), "Mormon culture," and "Mormonism" (when referring very broadly to fields of culture, knowledge, lifeways, identity, and heritage that surround the religious movements established by Joseph Smith, especially the Church of Jesus Christ of Latter-day Saints).

References

Asad, T., 1993. *Genealogies of Religion: Discipline and Reasons of Power in Christianity and Islam*. Baltimore, MD and London: Johns Hopkins University Press.
Bourdieu, P., 1979. *Distinction: A Social Critique of the Judgement of Taste*, trans. R. Nice, R. London: Routledge.
Bowman, M., 2012. *The Mormon People*. New York: Random House.
Brekus, C., 2011. Mormon Women and the Problem of Historical Agency. *Journal of Mormon History* 37(2): 59–87.
Brusco, E., 1995. *The Reformation of Machismo: Evangelical Conversion and Gender in Colombia*. Austin, TX: University of Texas Press.
Bushman, C., 2006. *Contemporary Mormonism: Latter-day Saints in Modern America*. Westport, CT: Praeger.
Bushman, R., 2005. *Joseph Smith: Rough Stone Rolling, a Cultural Biography of Mormonism's Founder*. New York: Alfred A. Knopf.
Cannell, F., 2017. "Forever Families": Christian Individualism, Mormonism and Collective Salvation. In T. Thomas, A. Malik, and R. Wellman, eds. *New Directions in Spiritual Kinship: Sacred Ties across the Abrahamic Religions*. Cham, Switzerland: Springer International, pp. 151–69.
Carter, T., 2015. *Building Zion: The Material World of Mormon Settlement*. Minneapolis, MN: University of Minnesota Press.
Charles, C., Colvin, G., Decoo, W., Heiss, M., Ilunga, E., Inouye, M., Morris, D., Jun de Oliveira, M., Rutherford, T., Sono-Koree, C., and van Beek, W. (2016). Review of *Reaching the Nations: International LDS Church Growth Almanac*, by David Stewart and Matthew Martinich. *Mormon Studies Review* 3: 147–62.
Chaves, M., 1993a. Intraorganizational Power and Internal Secularization in Protestant Denominations. *American Journal of Sociology* 99(1): 1–48.
Chaves, M., 1993b. Denominations as Dual Structures: An Organizational Analysis. *Sociology of Religion* 54(2): 147–69.
Chen, C.H., 2008. In Taiwan but Not of Taiwan: Challenges of the LDS Church in the Wake of the Indigenous Movement. *Dialogue: A Journal of Mormon Thought* 41(2): 3–31.
Cline, E., 2010. Female Spirit Mediums and Religious Authority in Contemporary Southeastern China. *Modern China* 36(5): 520–55.
Cohen, C., 2006. Construction of the Mormon People. *Journal of Mormon History* 32(1): 25–64.
Cohen, M., and March, J., 1972. A Garbage Can Model of Organizational Choice. *Administrative Science Quarterly* 17(1): 1–25.
DeJordy, R., Almond, B., Nielson, R., and Creed, W.E.D., 2014. Serving Two Masters: Transformative Resolution to Institutional Contradictions. In P. Tracey, N. Phillips, and M. Lounsbury, eds. *Religion and Organization Theory*. Bingley, UK: Emerald, pp. 301–37.
Derr, J., and Derr, C.B., 1982. Outside the Mormon Hierarchy: Alternative Aspects of Institutional Power. *Dialogue: A Journal of Mormon Thought* 15: 21–43.
Derr, J., Madsen, C., Holbrook, K., and Grow, M. eds., 2016. *The First Fifty Years of Relief Society: Key Documents in Latter-day Saint Women's History*. Salt Lake City, UT: Church Historian's Press.
DiMaggio, P., 1998. The Relevance of Organization Theory to the Study of Religion. In N.J. Demerath III, P. Hall, T. Schmitt, and R. Williams, eds. *Sacred Companies: Organizational Aspects of Religion and Religious Aspects of Organizations*. New York: Oxford University Press, pp. 7–23.
Fluhman, J.S., 2015. Communitarianism and Consecration in Mormonism. In T. Givens and P. Barlow, eds. *The Oxford Handbook of Mormonism*. New York: Oxford University Press, 2015, pp. 577–90.
Giorgi, S., Guider, M., and Bartunek, J., 2014. Productive Resistance: A Study of Change, Emotions, and Identity in the Context of the Apostolic Visitation of U.S. Women Religious, 2008–2012. In P. Tracey,

N. Phillips, and M. Lounsbury, eds. *Religion and Organization Theory*. Bingley, UK: Emerald, pp. 259–300.

Haglund, K., 2004. "Who Shall Sing If Not the Children?": Primary Songbooks, 1880–1989. *Dialogue: A Journal of Mormon Thought* 37(4): 90–127.

Hangen, T., 2015. Lived Religion among Mormons. In T. Givens and P. Barlow, eds. *The Oxford Handbook of Mormonism*. New York: Oxford University Press, pp. 209–24.

Hatch, T., 2004. "Changing Times Bring Changing Conditions": Relief Society, 1960 to the Present. *Dialogue: A Journal of Mormon Thought* 37(3): 65–98.

Human Microbiome Project Consortium, 2012. Structure, Function and Diversity of the Healthy Human Microbiome. *Nature* 486: 207–14.

Inouye, M., 2018. A Tale of Three Primaries: The Gravity of Mormonism's Informal Institutions. In J. Brooks and G. Colvin, eds. *Decolonizing Mormonism: Approaching a Postcolonial Zion*. Salt Lake City, UT: University of Utah Press, pp. 229–62.

Inouye, M., 2019. *China and the True Jesus: Charisma and Organization in a Chinese Christian Church*. New York: Oxford University Press.

Johnson, F.R., 1979. The Mormon Church as a Central Command System. *Review of Social Economics* 37(1): 79–94.

Karim, J., 2009. *American Muslim Women: Negotiating Race, Class, and Gender within the Ummah*. New York: NYU Press.

Kline, C., 2014. The Mormon Conception of Women's Nature and Role: An Analysis. *Feminist Theology* 22(2): 186–202.

LeDoux, J., 2003. The Self: Clues from the Brain. *Annals of the New York Academy of Sciences*, 1001(1): 295–304. doi: 10.1196/annals.1279.017.

Luhrmann, T., 2012. *When God Talks Back: Understanding the American Evangelical Relationship with God*. New York: Alfred Knopf.

MacGillivray, D., and Kollmann, T., 2014. The Role of Environmental Factors in Modulating Immune Responses in Early Life. *Frontiers in Immunology*. September 12. https://doi.org/10.3389/fimmu.2014.00434.

Mahmood, S., 2005. *The Politics of Piety*. Princeton, NJ: Princeton University Press.

McDannell, C., 2018. *Sister Saints: Mormon Women since the End of Polygamy*. New York: Oxford University Press.

Murphy, T., 1997. Guatemalan Hot/Cold Medicine and Mormon Words of Wisdom: Intercultural Negotiation of Meaning. *Journal for the Scientific Study of Religion* 36(2): 297–308.

Porterfield, A., 2005. *Healing in the History of Christianity*. New York: Oxford University Press.

Porterfield, A., 2018. *Corporate Spirit: Religion and the Rise of the Modern Corporation*. New York: Oxford University Press.

Prince, G., 2015. Mormon Priesthood and Organization. In T. Givens and P. Barlow, eds. *The Oxford Handbook of Mormonism*. New York: Oxford University Press, pp. 167–81.

Probert, J., 2016. The Materiality of Lived Mormonism. *Mormon Studies Review* 3: 19–29.

Riess, J., 2019. *The Next Mormons: How Millennials Are Changing the LDS Church*. New York: Oxford University Press.

Sanneh, L., 1998. *Translating the Message: The Missionary Impact on Culture*. Maryknoll, NY: Orbis Books.

Stapley, J., 2018. *The Power of Godliness: Mormon Liturgy and Cosmology*. New York: Oxford University Press.

Stroope, S., 2012. Social Networks and Religion: The Role of Congregational Social Embeddedness in Religious Belief and Practice. *Sociology of Religion* 73(3): 273–98.

Taber, S., 1993. *Mormon Lives: A Year in the Elkton Ward*. Urbana, IL: University of Illinois Press.

Taves, A., 2009. *Religious Experience Reconsidered: A Building-Block Approach to Religion and Other Special Things*. Princeton, NJ: Princeton University Press.

Ulrich, L., 2017. *A House Full of Females: Plural Marriage and Women's Rights in Early Mormonism, 1835–1870*. New York: Alfred A. Knopf.

Weber, M., 1947. *Max Weber: The Theory of Social and Economic Organization*, trans. A.M. Henderson and T. Parsons. New York: Oxford University Press.

Wessinger, C., 2012. Charismatic Leaders in New Religions. In O. Hammer and M. Rothstein, eds. *The Cambridge Companion to New Religious Movements*. New York: Cambridge University Press, pp. 80–96.

Further reading

Bushman, C., and Kline, C. eds., 2013. *Mormon Women Have Their Say: Essays from the Claremont Oral History Collection*. Salt Lake City, UT: Greg Kofford Books.

Interpretive essays highlighting major themes and recurring narratives in hundreds of oral history interviews with Mormon women. These interviews are stored in a collection at Claremont Graduate University.

Haglund, K., 2004. "Who Shall Sing If Not the Children?": Primary Songbooks, 1880–1989. *Dialogue: A Journal of Mormon Thought* 37(4): 90–127.

A rare discussion of evolving Mormon children's culture and institutions. Haglund traces changes in the themes and pedagogical approaches appearing in songs in Primary children's songbooks over the years (for instance, a shift away from millenarianism, the influence of Progressive Era pedagogies, and an emphasis on sitting quietly to show reverence).

Hatch, T., 2004. "Changing Times Bring Changing Conditions": Relief Society, 1960 to the Present. *Dialogue: A Journal of Mormon Thought* 37(3): 65–98.

Weaves together two unfolding historical processes: the Priesthood Correlation movement that diminished the scope of Mormon women's formal autonomy and influence, and Mormonism's global spread and subsequent institutional accommodations to a more diverse membership.

Inouye, M., 2018. A Tale of Three Primaries: The Gravity of Mormonism's Informal Institutions. In J. Brooks and G. Colvin, eds. *Decolonizing Mormonism: Approaching a Postcolonial Zion*. Salt Lake City, UT: University of Utah Press, pp. 229–62.

Compares the annual "Primary Presentation" in three different congregations to demonstrate high levels of variability within local congregational cultures, even under highly centralized, correlated, programmed circumstances. This article discusses the gravity of local practices and personalities that exist alongside formal institutions.

Mahmood, S., 2005. *The Politics of Piety*. Princeton, NJ: Princeton University Press.

A seminal work problematizing Western liberal progressive assumptions about agency, power, and meaning for women in patriarchal religious traditions. Mahmood studies the piety and practices of Egyptian Muslim women.

22

GLOBAL MORMON PERSPECTIVES AND EXPERIENCES OF FAMILIAL STRUCTURES

Caroline Kline

In 1995, leaders of the Church of Jesus Christ of Latter-day Saints issued a statement entitled "The Family: A Proclamation to the World," which officially defined the church's stances on the primacy of family relationships, heterosexual marriage, gender roles, and proper sexuality. This nine-paragraph statement has since become a commonly cited document in Latter-day Saint church talks, conferences, and Sunday School lessons. So popular and so emphasized is "The Proclamation on the Family," as it is commonly known, that church members in the U.S. often display it on the walls of their homes. However, the Proclamation's injunctions for optimal married family living—including instructions for fathers to preside over, provide for, and protect their families while mothers are primarily responsible for nurturing children—have generated some controversy in intellectual and feminist Mormon circles uncomfortable with gender roles and exclusive allegiance to heterosexual marriage.

For Latter-Day Saints outside English-speaking North America, the nuclear two-parent, male-breadwinning, lovingly united vision of marriage and family stands as a (sometimes) alluring but often unattainable vision, given the particular and differing contexts in which these Saints navigate their lives. In this chapter, I examine the ways Latter-Day Saints outside the United States understand, navigate, experience, and create various structures of home and family, structures which at times resonate with the traditional LDS North American nuclear family model highlighted in the Proclamation and at other times, given diverse local contexts, diverge from it. In particular I examine three themes which characterize LDS family structures and experiences in various parts of the world: working mothers, the non-nuclear family, and patriarchal versus egalitarian marital power structures.

This chapter is qualitative in its methodology, drawing primarily from small samples of oral histories and interviews of Latter-day Saint women from Botswana, South Africa, Mexico, and Finland.[1] Secondary sources which discuss LDS family structures in Flanders, Hong Kong, the Philippines, Central America, and India shed additional light on LDS family structures throughout the world. I find that church members outside of the United States variously adopt and adapt North American LDS structures on home and family, depending on location and context. Economic realities, and at times personal preference, in Mexico, Finland, and Southern Africa lead many Latter-day Saint mothers to engage in breadwinning. Political unrest, globalizing forces, and/or strong cultural traditions in the Philippines, Botswana, South Africa, and India have led to the formation of non-nuclear LDS family structures. And in cultures that tend to support violent or domineering forms of familial patriarchy, Mormonism often encourages men to assume a more benevolent patriarchal style and family structure, though interviews attest that authoritarian male behavior and notions of female submission sometimes still remain in LDS families. In these various locations around the globe, many Latter-day Saints embrace the ideas in the Proclamation, even as they at times construct alternate structures and family practices that reflect their diverse contexts and realities.

Working mothers

Decades of rhetoric from LDS church leaders promoting full-time motherhood have produced among the U.S. Latter-day Saint faithful an idealized notion of the stay-at-home mother. A 2003 *Eternal Marriage Student Manual*, available currently at churchofjesuschrist.org, features the famous 1977 quote from President Spencer W. Kimball saying, "Wives, come home from the typewriter, the laundry, the nursing, come home from the factory, the café. No career approaches in importance that of wife, homemaker, mother—cooking meals, washing dishes, making beds for one's precious husband and children" (p. 237). Since the 1970s and 1980s, when church leaders doubled down on discourse promoting non-employed motherhood in the face of the surging Women's Rights movement, rhetoric from leaders on working mothers has become more conciliatory, opening up space for mothers who work out of necessity or who work part-time (Iannaccone and Miles, 1990).[2] In the United States the rates of LDS women who work full-time lag behind the national average—not surprising given the emphasis on the importance of in-home motherhood. Interestingly, Mormon women in the U.S. do work part-time at a higher rate than the national average—a compromise which enables women to still concentrate on home tasks and parenting while also earning some money and keeping a foot in professional doors (Riess, 2013). However, as Carrie Miles (2008) points out, the idealization of stay-at-home motherhood remains alive and well in contemporary Mormonism, even as people's individual circumstances may or may not allow for it. Wives of the highest-ranking church leaders in the U.S. seldom have professions, thus modeling idealized gendered family patterns for the tradition's adherents.

In various locales outside of the United States, the family model in which a male is the sole breadwinner is often viewed as less common, less possible, or less ideal. In her discussion on the church in Flanders, Ingrid Sherlock (2018, p. 194) notes that in the 1980s, some members in Flanders viewed the counsel for mothers to stay at home with children as American and somewhat alien. She writes,

> Flanders did not, and still does not, have a stay-at-home mom culture, not the least because people have to work to build up a pension. A lot of sisters, therefore, continued to work outside the home, which at times led to lively Relief Society lessons, but unfortunately also to recriminations and hurt feelings.

This reality of the importance of women working in various European contexts is echoed by Aada (Anonymous #2B, 2018), a Finnish woman I interviewed. She stated that in Finland,

> Most of the time you need to have both parents work, if you want to live comfortably and not rely on government welfare. Within the Mormon world, there's the idea of

being self-sustaining. So for many families, it's like either we're on government welfare or we both work. And they prefer both working.

Aada explained that government-subsidized high-quality childcare and generous parental leave policies also lead many women to choose to stay in the workforce. Among her Finnish LDS friends, Aada stated, it is common for women to take off between one and three years after having a child (the time which your job is guaranteed upon your return and in which you receive a percentage of your salary). The fact that government-subsidized day care is such high quality—all day-care workers have Master's degrees in elementary education—means that

> it's easier for Mormon moms to work because they know that they have this good day care ... They do naps there, they potty train, they cook food. It's perfect. You can drop off your child there before breakfast and they feed them warm breakfast and then you pick them up after work ... So it's a real help to families, and it makes it so that the moms when they do have to go to work don't feel so bad.

When asked about how Finnish Latter-day Saints feel about stay-at-home mother rhetoric from church leaders, Aada explained that such rhetoric tends to be downplayed:

> I don't think people emphasize that as much. Society [in Finland] is way more equal [in terms of gender than in the U.S.] and they view it as there should be good care for your children. When I was growing up my mom felt guilty that she had to work, but I think my generation doesn't so much feel guilty if they have to work. A lot of the women have goals and aspirations outside of home, but they still value and believe that raising kids is noble, staying at home is noble ... But it's not the only alternative.

In Finland, as in other European countries with strong social programs, LDS members embrace the principle that family is highly important, but they often understand that there is a variety of ways to uphold that principle, including both mothers and fathers engaging in careers. Also, they recognize that economic circumstances unique to Finland often make working motherhood preferable.

Oral histories I conducted in Mexico with LDS women likewise reinforce the point that context and circumstances unique to their countries make the American sole male breadwinning model less attainable. Latter-day Saint mothers in Mexico often feel that they must work due to generally low wages in the country (Kline, 2018, pp. 75–76). Eva (Anonymous #158, 2015, pp. 9–10) reported that in her suburb outside Mexico City, most mothers need to work:

> Even if church leaders tell us to stay at home, our reality is another. When the leaders speak to us, they speak from the U.S. reality. We live with poverty, unemployment, or really low wages—it's another reality. We try to adapt that to the direction from the leaders. Some women feel bad they have to work. Most of them see the reality, though. It's not optional—they need to work ... Eighty percent of the women worked outside the home in my old ward. It's a luxury to stay at home.

Other women in Veracruz mentioned institutional stay-at-home mother rhetoric, which prompted some women to give up careers. Others, however, felt that the best choice for their family was to continue to work, at least on a part-time basis.

One important finding in my work on Mormon women in Veracruz, Mexico is that the church in the 1980s and 1990s was often instrumental in helping women find ways to earn money for their families. Through Relief Society classes which taught them skills like baking pies, making soy milk, etc. many women began small businesses to supplement their family income. These classes were often life-changing for Mormon women as they led to improved financial situations, and none of the women manifested tension between this informal vending and LDS notions of stay-at home motherhood. I surmise this is because first, real necessity trumps notions of ideal family structure; and second, because much of this kind of production and vending takes place in or near the home on a part-time basis where women can simultaneously look after children if they need to. The church's helpfulness in assisting women to gain skills and improve their material circumstances was highly praised by some of the women I interviewed (Kline, 2018, pp. 71–79).

In Botswana, working mothers are the norm. Motherhood is a primary identity marker for Batswana women, but there is little sense in Botswana that motherhood should preclude paid labor. Women in Botswana associate motherhood not only with nurturing but also with production and provisioning of children (Suggs, 2002, p. 49). Such productive paid labor is often a necessity given the high rates of single mothers, and it is not unusual for mothers to work in cities while their own mothers care for grandchildren in the villages, supported by working daughters. Several LDS women I spoke with participated in this "child fosterage" practice. Even for LDS women who are married, working is often seen as the most viable option. For instance, Pearl, a married return missionary, told me that she would prefer to be at home with her young son, but at this point finances simply don't allow that (Kline, 2018, p. 142). In addition to providing necessary funds for the raising of children, working can also lend some women a sense of safety and self-sufficiency. Charity (Anonymous #22, 2015, p. 2), a single mom who converted to the church as a teenager, explained why stay-at-home motherhood is not always ideal in her context:

> There is this fear. As African[s] we have an issue of women being abused and needing to be on their own and needing to work so they are seen as independent. That comes through working so we don't have to depend on [a man]. It seems if you talk to most women being a housewife is least desirable because of her circumstances. Work makes us independent, out of oppression and self-reliant.

While Botswana has escaped much of the war and unrest that has characterized other African countries, its shift from a subsistence economy to a cash economy has disrupted traditional family units, leaving women to often shoulder the burdens of child provisioning. Even Latter-day Saint women with husbands often see working as the best option, given generally low wages and desire for security.

Black South African LDS mothers likewise tend to work due to the necessity of earning income. Interestingly, some of these women enthusiastically embrace the ideas of the Proclamation, finding the injunctions for parents to be loving and men to be involved, kind, and providing very positive. However, few of them live in situations in which a husband's salary could adequately support a family, and they feel little to no dissonance in their own choices or hopes to work. Amogelang (Anonymous #222, 2016, p. 7) responded this way when asked what she thought about mothers working outside the home:

> I think it's okay. If they're able and they're capable of doing it, why not? But if they choose to be stay home mothers, it's still okay. I would love to be a working mother. Of course, I would love to have time with my children and with my family as well.

Amogelang, like many other women around the world, hopes for a balanced life that includes time for both work and family. Minenhle (Anonymous #217, 2016, p. 9), who converted to the church at sixteen, responded this way when asked to envision her ideal future: "I would like to see myself working. I would be married, of course, with probably four kids. And in the church serving, of course." Minenhle expressed real surprise when her interviewer told her that in the U.S. there is some disagreement among Mormons about whether or not mothers should work, saying, "Really? ... Women here all work." As teenage converts, these women and many others in South Africa have been less exposed to emphases on stay-at-home motherhood, and notably, they find space within church teachings to envision ideal lives that include motherhood and career. The Proclamation's statement that women are primarily responsible for nurturing children is something these women embrace, but that statement does not necessarily imply to them non-working motherhood, a situation which is nigh but impossible for the majority of black women in the country. For these women, as for women in Botswana, an important way in which mothers fulfill their duty to nurture children is by providing for their physical needs.

Non-nuclear family structures

Related to the topic of working mothers is the topic of non-nuclear family structures, which defy the North American LDS emphasis on the male/female couple and their dependent children.[3] In various parts of the world, a nuclear family setup is compromised by poverty, war, violence, and other cultural factors which at times necessitate mothers and fathers leaving their children in order to either ensure survival or earn money that can be sent back to provide for children left behind. Changing societal factors which have likewise led to the weakening of bonds between mothers and fathers have led to many single-parent homes, and additionally, some cultures place greater value on extended family and multi-generational family structures. Some LDS families around the world are impacted by these factors or cultural considerations which lead them to live out their lives in non-nuclear families.

Particularly moving are Stacilee Ford's accounts of primarily Filipina domestic workers in Hong Kong, who often leave their own children behind with family members in order to find employment caring for others' children. These women therefore are, out of necessity, creating alternative family structures (transnational families, extended families caring for children) in order to ensure the survival of their families. As Ford (2018 p. 202) writes,

> High unemployment, corruption, poverty, and familial stress in their home countries fuel the continued migration of generally highly educated and multilingual women to Hong Kong and other global cities ... It is fair to say that by any standard, as a cohort, they are an exploited population who work long hours for less than the Hong Kong minimum wage.

Female domestic workers are a majority of LDS members in Hong Kong, comprising about 1,000 of the 1,850 Mormons in the area (Ford, 2018, p. 216). Church leaders in the area attempt to support and aid these domestic workers who live difficult lives separated from their own families and children, making several accommodations to building schedules and various LDS programs and practices to help these women participate in the life of the church in Hong Kong. Ford (2018, p. 226) comments on the discrepancy between LDS church rhetoric on families and the situations of these women:

> There is a real dilemma for a church that has become so closely associated with the post-World War II male-breadwinner/female-caretaker family model in North America. The individual and intersecting challenges of transnational families in globalization are often met, in part, by governments or institutions calling for a return to patriarchal traditions and conventional family structures as a way to soften the rough edges of globalization. But what if that strategy actually places families in more peril?

Ford is concerned that emphases on women's nurturing roles leave women unprepared for most employment in their own countries, thus forcing them to leave their families behind to engage in care work for other families. She understands that these women make such choices to leave children and family under strain so great that it threatens these families' survival. Ford (2018, p. 228) suggests the need for Mormons to do more to honor familial bonds (and alternative familial structures) "as they—like family members themselves—migrate and adapt in order to survive."

Many black South African Mormons also live in non-nuclear family contexts for a variety of reasons which range from Apartheid violence to societal factors. The oral histories of women who lived through the horrors of Apartheid highlight the ways violence and corrupt governments can disrupt nuclear family systems. Beatrice (Anonymous #212, 2016, p. 2) spoke of her mathematician husband getting involved in politics in the 1970s and having to flee for his life. She said, "The government wanted to get rid of him so he skipped the country in 1975." Her husband fled to Switzerland, leaving Dorothy with three children to raise and support alone. Her husband returned to South Africa in about 2005, but by that time, after thirty years of separation, there was no marriage to speak of, so they remain separated. Lesedi (Anonymous #218, 2016) also spoke of the toll on families under oppressive violent governments. Her father, also a political activist, "was a political elimination." After his murder, Lesedi's mother raised her young children alone. As an adult, Lesedi herself engaged in activist work against the regime, work which placed her in danger and threatened to lead to her own imprisonment and arrest. Fortunately, that did not happen despite some violent encounters with Boers, but the threat of that kind of separation hung over her head and the heads of her young children. These two South African oral histories show how oppressive governments and societal violence take significant tolls on nuclear families.

Cycles of poverty and lack of opportunity also lead to many single parent (usually mother-headed) households in South Africa. Samantha (Anonymous #155, 2016, p. 8) a Cape Coloured woman in her thirties, described this phenomenon in South Africa:[4]

> Growing up I've seen many single-parent families. Within my own extended family, I've seen people having babies when they are teenagers, not getting married, not staying married. I've just seen so many discarded children. I've seen so many children without a place. I've seen so many women so overwhelmed by their responsibilities of having to do family life all by themselves. So many. Especially in my extended family. These children often they get raised by granny, and mom drops out of school more times than not.

Samantha sees the church's focus on nuclear families as a liberating teaching in her context, because two parents living with and devoted to children lessens the burdens of childcare and ultimately opens up more possibilities for women to pursue their hopes and dreams. Single moms, in her experience, are often "stuck," as she says, living with or close to their own mothers and unable to pursue their own paths. For many women in South Africa, and in its neighbor to the north, Botswana, the church's emphasis on two-parent families with involved, present, breadwinning, and benevolent fathers is a very attractive family structure, though sometimes difficult to achieve.

Single parent families are also a common phenomenon in Botswana. Botswana did not experience the same kind of violence and oppression that was rampant in South Africa, but a changing economic system, as the country shifted to a cash economy in the latter half of the twentieth century, led to a breakdown of marital bonds. In the latter half of the twentieth century, many men began leaving their villages for cities looking for work, resulting in many single-parent households (Suggs, 2002, pp. 46–47). Out of the forty-eight oral histories my colleagues and I conducted with LDS women in Botswana, a third were single mothers who had never married.[5] Women in Botswana are expected to have children with or without a spouse in order to provide their own parents with grandchildren, to be fully considered adult, and to fulfill their culture's understanding of womanhood (Suggs, 2002, p. 30; Kline, 2018, pp. 100–101). The church's injunction to not have babies out of wedlock thus places some single women in difficult positions, as marriage is not easily achieved due to lower numbers of LDS men, to cultural expectations of sexual premarital relationships, and to expectations of bridewealth transfers, which could take years to amass. A few single Mormon women therefore have babies out of wedlock, while others navigate the difficult possibility of living out their lives without children or partners.

One facet of society in Botswana that makes single parenthood easier is the strong extended family network that still exists. The extended family is so important that single mothers can often count on very significant help from siblings and parents when they have children. Musa (Anonymous #1B, 2015), a single woman in Botswana, described how single mothers, even unemployed single mothers, manage to raise their children with the help of extended family: "Because in Botswana, you fall pregnant, you might not be working, and relatives and siblings will pitch in and help here and there, and life goes on! That's how we're raised." As Musa describes, tight bonds of obligation exist between extended family members in Botswana. These strong familial bonds are in some sense a product of the different notion of self that exists in Southern Africa. As John Mbiti (1969, p. 108) explained, community and group/familial/tribal identities and needs are often privileged over the individualized notions of the self, which are seen to be more Western. The importance of extended families is related to this more communal notion of self, and these extended families importantly provide funds for single mothers as well as childcare, sometimes for years at a time.

Several LDS women participated in child fosterage, which involves a parent or parents sending a child to be raised by a member of the extended family, often a grandmother living in a village. Such a system is often beneficial for both the mother and the grandmother, as the children provide the grandmother help with chores, and the mother is able to make and send money to the grandmother for child provisioning, though of course, it is not without its emotional difficulties and stresses. The importance of extended family is also reflected in norms which encourage adult children to financially provide for their parents. In their oral histories, some Batswana women spoke of wanting to work to accumulate enough money to someday provide a house for their mothers.[6]

The importance of the extended family structure in Botswana also emerges in the common practice of giving *lobola* or bridewealth, upon a woman's marriage. *Lobola* discussions traditionally take place between the uncles of the bride and groom, and when a settlement is agreed upon—often a lengthy matter—the marriage can move forward. *Lobola* is seen as a way to tie two extended families together. The practice is discouraged by church leaders because it tends to delay marriage, as grooms and their families work for years to earn enough money for it

(Oaks, 2012). However, to some Latter-day Saints in Botswana, it is a beloved tradition which unites extended families. As one woman (Anonymous #30, 2015, p. 17) told me,

> For me, [*lobola* is] a connection of families ... What makes my marriage significant is that on that day, we saw that token of appreciation go from his family to my family. The relations we make, the sounds we make of joy, of appreciation, of gladness, makes my [wedding day] unique.[7]

While Westerners tend to be uncomfortable with bridewealth traditions because they seem to commodify women, van Beek (2016, p. 83) explains that amongst Africans, "this marriage exchange is not a purchase but a relationship." As van Beek (2016, p. 89) and other scholars have noted, Africans often subscribe to a far broader notion of family, a notion that extends even to second cousins, unlike in the Western world where attention is primarily given to the nuclear family first and secondarily to aunts, uncles, and cousins. To Batswana, the practice of *lobola* demonstrates that fundamental importance of the extended family and its creation of bonds with other families.

Extended family relationships, particularly the relationship between adult children and their parents, are also very important in Indian Latter-day Saints' lives. In her dissertation on the LDS church in Hyderabad, India, Taunalyn Rutherford (2017, p. 272) discusses the way different conceptions of family structure might sometimes cause tension for LDS members, as young married couples have to decide whether to establish a nuclear family or a "joint family" (multi-generational family where the couple lives in the home of the husband's parents and often with other family members). Joint family structures are common in India. She explains:

> One of the mission presidents I interviewed expressed his frustration with the concept of joint families. He would often counsel young married couples to move out of the husband's family's home because he felt this improved marriages. I saw several variations in family structures in the church, however. Again, in the family sphere, members in Hyderabad seem to do what works for them. This may include a rejection of the "American" preference for nuclear families or a pushback against Indian traditions in order to prioritize the husband–wife relationship.

The bonds of obligation between adult children and their parents are also reflected in Indian marriage customs which emphasize marriages arranged by parents. Sometimes LDS young adults fall in love and then work to convince parents to come to an arrangement. But as Rutherford (2016, p. 87) explains, "There is still a strong submission to the will of parents and extended family in these cases." In India, the importance of parental authority is reflected in the various family structures and customs young adult LDS members adopt, adapt, or, with sometimes great familial tension, reject.

Patriarchal vs. egalitarian structures

The 1995 Proclamation states that "fathers are to preside over their families in love and righteousness." This language of benevolent male headship is reminiscent of language in conservative Protestant Christianity, which similarly describes male familial authority as "servant-leadership" (Wilcox, 2004, p. 172). However benevolent the description of male behavior, language which places men as presiders over their wives reflects a patriarchal view of familial structure.[8] Interestingly, however, within the next two sentences the Proclamation states: "In these sacred responsibilities, fathers and mothers are obligated to help one another as equal partners." This statement indicates an egalitarian marital structure, and equal partnership between husbands and wives has been emphasized for decades by the most powerful LDS church leaders. Contemporary Mormonism, therefore, occupies a discursive space that simultaneously and paradoxically embraces both the patriarchal narrative of male presiding and the egalitarian narrative of equal partnership in marriage (Kline, 2016).

Marital power dynamics play out differently in LDS communities around the world, affected greatly by individual personalities and the wider cultural context. One dominant theme I have found, however, is that in cultures that tend to display a more overt, rigid, or violent patriarchy, Mormonism often helps guide men to a more benevolent patriarchal style and family structure. In these contexts, husbands still often hold the majority of marital power, but they tend to wield it more benignly.

Oral histories I conducted in Mexico attest to LDS teachings pushing back on machismo behavior which includes alcohol abuse, familial abnegation, womanizing, and violence. Converting to the Church of Jesus Christ of Latter-day Saints was, for one woman I interviewed, a rejection of the damaging and neglectful male behavior and familial dynamics which had characterized both her childhood and her marriage (Kline, 2018, pp. 50–52). For women who endured these kinds of familial dynamics, LDS family structures were highly attractive as they encouraged male asceticism and devotion to their families, even if such devotion was sometimes couched in non-egalitarian terms.[9] While many of the older convert women I interviewed were not able to convince their husbands to embrace the church and its behavioral teachings, they did describe their LDS sons embracing more benevolent male behaviors, as they eschewed alcohol, remained committed to their marriages, and served in the church. However much the church helped in mediating the most severe and violent forms of patriarchal or machismo behavior, Ana's oral history did reveal that domestic violence and male authoritarianism remain a problem in some Mexican Latter-day Saint homes (Kline, 2018, pp. 60–67). The pervasiveness of domestic violence, even in LDS homes, became clear to Ana when she went to a workshop on domestic violence with other Mexican LDS women and realized almost every woman there had experienced violence in the home (Anonymous #173, 2015, p. 10).[10]

Latter-day Saint families in Central America often have a similar dynamic, according to Henri Gooren (2008), who studied Latter-day Saints in Costa Rica and Guatemala. He finds that LDS teachings tend to discourage machismo behaviors like alcohol consumption, womanizing, and familial abnegation, but that "the hierarchical, top-down organization of the LDS Church would seem to strengthen some elements of machismo (like the authoritarianism)." However, he goes on to say that that authoritarianism is somewhat mediated: "The LDS Church manuals and magazines stress family harmony and counseled couples to talk openly, respect each other's opinions, and share responsibilities. In Central America, this strengthens women's capability for empowerment" (2008, p. 376). Thus, while some elements of female subordination/male domination were present in Central American LDS marriages, the church's pragmatic emphasis on familial devotion and treating spouses respectfully often produced healthier and more functional marriages.

Taunalyn Rutherford (2017, p. 278) describes church teachings mediating the more violent forms of patriarchy which were common in segments of Indian culture. One interviewed woman describes the starkness of male dominance and violence in the home: "The men decide what has to be done for the family. I've seen my cousins and all they have been dominated and beaten. One of my uncles used to smoke and put his cigarette butt on my aunt." This kind of behavior, Rutherford explains, was described pejoratively by her Indian LDS interviewees as patriarchal and something that they were overcoming. She states, "They would contrast patriarchy with priesthood and the teachings of the church" which were considered to be enlightened and the opposite of patriarchy (2017, pp. 277–78). One Indian man Rutherford interviewed drew out the contrast between the wider culture of Hyderabad and church culture in terms of male dominance:

> Outside they don't give any respect to girls, and they abuse them ... But in church, every brother calls sister as sister, and we give them respect. We don't consider them as less than us; we consider them as equal to us because we have learned the gospel.
>
> *(2017, pp. 283–84)*

One male church leader in India also emphasized the ways church teachings encourage men to treat their wives benignly:

> The church standards teach us that we need to respect each other. There is no male domination. The scriptures teach us that we are equal and we need to respect each other. If I see my wife crying, I will be responsible for every teardrop that she sheds, so I don't want her to cry.
>
> *(2017, p. 284)*

For members in India, church emphases on marital cooperation and kindness could often significantly change oppressive patriarchal patterns.

In Botswana, LDS marriage norms were also generally considered to be liberatory when contrasted with wider patriarchal family structures. As one woman (Anonymous #23, 2015, p. 4) stated,

> Traditionally [in Botswana] you accept everything he [your husband] says with no questions. Gospel-wise that is not the case ... I am not commanded to obey. Sometimes people use scripture to justify this behavior but that's not the way. Love is the way to lead your home ... I started to realize that we are true partners.

Pearl (Anonymous #32, 2015, p. 10), a Batswana woman in her thirties, experienced a true partnership in her LDS marriage, much to the envy of other women who have less helpful and benign husbands. She explained,

> My friends will come to me and ask, "How do you get him to do this?" I don't get him to do anything. He just does things for me. Because when I do laundry ... before the mission, he wouldn't do it, now he will just put it in the machine and we come and fold it together. We'll clean together, we'll bathe the baby. We do everything together.

Pearl embraces the notion of him presiding, but it's clear that this presiding is limited in scope and highly benevolent.

While LDS marriage injunctions ideally cut back on patriarchal dominance in the family, one Batswana woman describes working with a difficult LDS husband whose inclination was to control his wife and act out angrily. She connects his eventual improved behavior to a *Strengthening Marriage* LDS pamphlet he was given one day, and while the marriage is not perfect and she still has to manage his controlling ways, she senses an improvement due to church teachings which emphasize kindness and give her leverage to press for an affectionate and united marriage (Kline, 2018, pp. 138–42).

In South Africa, church teachings are often considered helpful in encouraging more affectionate and less violent marriages, but black South African women report that there are still problems with patriarchal expectations and behavior, given an overall culture that places burdens of domestic work and expectations for deferential behavior on women. Mary (Anonymous #213, 2016, p. 7) described the submissive behavior she was brought up to embrace, and the way Latter-day Saint women contend with these messages that teach them to defer:

> Women face the challenge of not speaking out … In our culture, how we are brought up, women cannot say as much, especially when you are married … That's how we were brought up. So, that's still a challenge. It is still there and we can be abused physically or emotionally and we just keep quiet, saying, "Oh, this is life." Like in my ward we have had lots of programs of counseling. We would have those problems and we would go and have counseling, and that's when you understand. Mostly it's women who have been abused either physically or emotionally. And emotionally is a dangerous one because most of the time we don't realize that it's there. But it is. So that is a challenge even in the church—speaking out. We don't.

While there are powerful cultural forces that pressure women to act submissively and accept abuse, this woman's ward notably has counseling sessions that teach women what abuse is and presumably, that it is unacceptable. However, despite efforts made in church settings to teach about abuse, women still find it hard to speak freely, even in church settings.

While Mary still feels the weight of expectations for women to be submissive and quiet, Mpho (Anonymous #225, 2016, p. 5), another woman in South Africa, reported that church teachings have helped her to adopt a healthier self-image and attitude about her worth and potential. She states:

> I think that, for me, the church has helped me … to realize that, as a woman, I'm a daughter of God. I have the potential to reach where other people can reach, color or whatever, and where men can reach … [Also] we're here to help our husbands. Not to be a subject to your husband, but to be a companion, and that helps you realize that you can't keep on putting yourself down. If there's something that you feel you're capable of doing, you do it, you excel at it, and nobody will say anything about that.

In Mpho's experience, church teachings on women's divine worth and companionate marriage increase women's confidence and sense of possibility. Amelia (Anonymous #224, 2016, pp. 5–6), however, gives us a glimpse of what might happen at times when patriarchal church teachings that emphasize harmony in the home are layered onto cultural patriarchal notions:

> The church has taught me to be humble … I'm a very stubborn person, very stubborn. It has taught me to shut up, in some of the things, just shush. And listen to the counsels of the Lord. If my husband says [something] and I do not agree fully, I just keep quiet. To have peace. I have to say I have learned a lot, especially in Relief Society and Young Women, as to being a woman and embracing it and supporting it and being humble and being, you know, all of what the Lord wants me to be. I am not a master, but it has really humbled me. I'm very stubborn to a point that my husband will smack me, and I understand why, because I was very stubborn. I would say things that … But now I just zip it.

While Mary's ward has worked to end abuse and while church teachings have increased Mpho's sense of self-worth, Amelia's ward has taught her to adopt a submissive, quiet role for the sake of harmony in her marriage. Rather than speaking up as an equal in her marriage to her LDS husband, Amelia has embraced teachings of female humility and now often stifles her feelings and thoughts, believing that her husband was justified in striking her in the past when she stood firm on an issue. As R. Marie Griffith's study of evangelical women who embraced submission explains, attitudes of female submission can serve as a "strategy of containment" in contexts of male domination, as they ensure women's safety and preserve family harmony (1997, p. 181).[11] Nevertheless, that Amelia learned such a strategy from women in her ward is notable, and it indicates that within her ward, patriarchal messages of female submission were particularly potent, as they overwhelmed whatever messages there might have been about equal partnership and the atrocity of domestic violence. Thus, the dual discourse of LDS teachings on male/female marital roles (simultaneously patriarchal and egalitarian) play out in different ways for different women in South Africa, and no doubt the world at large, depending on women's circumstances, personalities, and the unique characteristics of their wards.

Conclusion

While the institutional LDS church promotes a North American model of the nuclear family with breadwinning father-leader and caretaker mother, LDS families around the world assume a variety of forms and structures, highly dependent on their particular cultural contexts. Working mothers, for instance, are the norm in many parts of the world, and many LDS mothers choose to be employed, given the economic realities of their countries. Some make this choice reluctantly, but others do so more enthusiastically, sometimes finding space within church teachings to assume breadwinning roles. Likewise, non-nuclear family structures are realities for many Latter-day Saints across the world. Many of these Saints are drawn to teachings about the importance of nuclear families, but contexts such as globalization, poverty, violence, and cultural considerations lead to reformations of family structures and care networks.

Finally, interviews, oral histories, and other scholarly works highlight that authoritarian and/or violent patriarchal family structures tend to be mediated by church teachings on family cooperation and affection. However, given the church's dual discourse on familial patriarchy and equal partnership, outcomes differ among individual families. Many LDS families around the world move away from abusive and controlling male behavior, but sometimes such behavior persists, justified by notions of female submission. Nonetheless, despite the male authoritarianism that still remains in some families, Mormonism does, by many accounts, provide a new mode of more benevolent masculinity. Thus, particularly in societies where colonialism has ravaged masculinity and destroyed traditional systems, LDS teachings about involved, kind, and benevolent husbands and fathers can transform family structures and offer men new and more benign ways to inhabit their masculine familial roles.

Notes

1 While my sample size is generally small—I draw from twenty-nine oral histories from Mexican women, forty-eight from Batswana women, twenty-one from South African women, as well as one interview with a Finnish woman—these interviews reveal patterns which reflect real differences across countries. We need a larger study to statistically analyze these patterns, but these interviews indicate important ways LDS members navigate their lives within particular and unique contexts of constraint. I assign pseudonyms to the women I and my colleagues interviewed.

2 For example, see the address by G. Hinckley (2001). Hinckley states, "The whole gamut of human endeavor is now open to women. There is not anything that you cannot do if you will set your mind to it." He goes on to discuss a nurse he met who had a wonderful life, working as much or as little as

she wanted. For a more systematic treatment of the change in institutional discourse on the subject of women working in the latter half of the twentieth century, see Iannaccone and Miles (1990).
3 Most scholars understand a nuclear family to consist of a mother, father, and children living at home. It stands in contrast to extended family. See Sarkisian and Gerstel (2012, p. 1).
4 Cape Coloured is a term used in South Africa to describe people of mixed African, European, and Asian descent.
5 Most of these single mothers were women who converted to the church after they had children with boyfriends.
6 See Allen (2016, pp. 9–10). Allen speaks of a Batswana Latter-day Saint woman in Denmark who feels a deep responsibility to provide for her mother and wants to build a house for her someday. She therefore struggles with stay-at-home mother church rhetoric.
7 For a more extended discussion of lobola and Latter-day Saints, see Kline (2018, p. 129).
8 I use the term "patriarchal" as sociologists do, to describe a "system in which power is secured in the hands of adult men" (Meagher, 2011, p. 441). Ideals of patriarchal family structure, until January 2019, were apparent in Latter-day Saint temple covenants, which subordinated wives to husbands (Buerger, 1994, p. 178).
9 This finding resonates with the work of Elizabeth Brusco (1995), who found that conversion to Evangelicalism among Colombians resulted in men becoming far more invested and helpful in the home. She argues that conversion "reconciles women's and men's divergent value systems by domesticating men" (p. 5).
10 Ana describes her own and other participants' reactions when the program leader discussed her experience with domestic violence:

> Everyone [in the audience] was like, 'Ah! [Gasp] I'm not the only one!' And we all started to write, and I turned around to look and saw everyone was writing it [their experience with abuse] down. And we were just fifteen women from the ward, so what about the rest? That's when I realized it's not just here or there, it's everywhere.
>
> [Cuando ella habla y cuenta su historia que fue de demasiada violencia, todas como que 'Ahh! No soy la única!' Y cuando todas empiezan a escribir y empiezo a voltear a ver y vi que todos están escribiendo. Y nada más fuéramos quince de barrio, ¿y las demás? Es cuando me di cuenta de que no es aquí, no es allá, es en todos lados.]

For a fuller discussion of Ana's experience with domestic violence, see Kline (2018, pp. 59–71).
11 Griffith studied evangelical women who often embraced postures of female submission.

References

Allen, J., 2016. Negotiating Belief and Belonging: Life Narratives of African LDS Women in Botswana and Denmark. Paper delivered at the American Academy of Religion conference 2016, San Antonio.
Anonymous, 2015. Unarchived interview #1B. Interview by Caroline Kline. June 2015, Botswana.
Anonymous, 2015. Oral History #22 (transcript). Interviewed by Jennifer Platt. June 7, 2015, Botswana. Gender, Narrative, and Religious Practice in Southern Africa Oral History Collection, Special Collections, The Claremont Colleges Library, Claremont, California.
Anonymous, 2015. Oral History #23 (transcript). Interviewed by Jennifer Platt. June 2, 2015, Botswana. Gender, Narrative, and Religious Practice in Southern Africa Oral History Collection, Special Collections, The Claremont Colleges Library, Claremont, California.
Anonymous, 2015. Oral History #30 (transcript). Interviewed by Caroline Kline. June 2015, Botswana. Gender, Narrative, and Religious Practice in Southern Africa Oral History Collection, Special Collections, The Claremont Colleges Library, Claremont, California.
Anonymous, 2015. Oral History #32 (transcript). Interviewed by Caroline Kline. June 14, 2015, Botswana. Gender, Narrative, and Religious Practice in Southern Africa Oral History Collection, Special Collections, The Claremont Colleges Library, Claremont, California.
Anonymous, 2015. Oral History #158 (transcript). Interviewed by Caroline Kline via Skype. February 9, 2015. Claremont Mormon Women Oral History Collection, Special Collections, The Claremont Colleges Library, Claremont, California.
Anonymous, 2015. Oral History #173 (transcript). Interviewed by April Carlson. March 2015, Veracruz, Mexico. Claremont Mormon Women Oral History Collection, Special Collections, The Claremont Colleges Library, Claremont, California.

Anonymous, 2016. Oral History #155 (transcript). Interviewed by Caroline Kline. December 2016, Connecticut. Claremont Mormon Women Oral History Collection, Special Collections, The Claremont Colleges Library, Claremont, California.

Anonymous, 2016. Oral History #212 (transcript). Interviewed by Elizabeth Johnson. May 30, 2016, South Africa. Transcript forthcoming in the Claremont Mormon Women Oral History Collection, Special Collections, The Claremont Colleges Library, Claremont, California.

Anonymous, 2016. Oral History #213 (transcript). Interviewed by Elizabeth Johnson. June 1, 2016, South Africa. Transcript forthcoming in the Claremont Mormon Women Oral History Collection, Special Collections, The Claremont Colleges Library, Claremont, California.

Anonymous, 2016. Oral History #217 (transcript). Interviewed by Elizabeth Johnson. June 5, 2016, South Africa. Transcript forthcoming in the Claremont Mormon Women Oral History Collection, Special Collections, The Claremont Colleges Library, Claremont, California.

Anonymous, 2016. Oral History #218 (transcript). Interviewed by Elizabeth Johnson. June 1, 2016, South Africa. Transcript forthcoming in the Claremont Mormon Women Oral History Collection, Special Collections, The Claremont Colleges Library, Claremont, California

Anonymous, 2016. Oral History #222 (transcript). Interviewed by Heather Sundahl. June 1, 2016, South Africa. Transcript forthcoming in the Claremont Mormon Women Oral History Collection, Special Collections, The Claremont Colleges Library, Claremont, California.

Anonymous, 2016. Oral History #224 (transcript). Interviewed by Heather Sundahl. June 5, 2016, South Africa. Transcript forthcoming in the Claremont Mormon Women Oral History Collection, Special Collections, The Claremont Colleges Library, Claremont, California.

Anonymous, 2016. Oral History #225 (transcript). Interviewed by Elizabeth Johnson. June 1, 2016, South Africa. Transcript forthcoming in the Claremont Mormon Women Oral History Collection, Special Collections, The Claremont Colleges Library, Claremont, California.

Anonymous, 2018. Unarchived interview #2B. Interviewed by Caroline Kline. August 13, 2018, Costa Mesa, CA.

Brusco, E., 1995. *The Reformation of Machismo: Evangelical Conversion and Gender in Colombia*. Austin, TX: University of Texas Press.

Buerger, D., 1994. *The Mysteries of Godliness: A History of Mormon Temple Worship*. San Francisco, CA: Smith Research Associates.

Eternal Marriage Student Manual, 2003. Salt Lake City: The Church of Jesus Christ of Latter-day Saints. www.churchofjesuschrist.org/bc/content/shared/content/english/pdf/language-materials/35311_eng.pdf (accessed June 14, 2019).

Ford, S., 2018. Sister Acts: Relief Society and Flexible Citizenship in Hong Kong. In G. Colvin and J. Brooks, eds. *Decolonizing Mormonism: Approaching a Postcolonial Zion*. Salt Lake City, UT: University of Utah Press, pp. 202–28.

Gooren, H., 2008. The Mormons of the World: The Meaning of LDS Membership in Central America. In C. Jacobson, J. Hoffman, and T. Heaton, eds. *Revisiting Thomas O'Dea's The Mormons: Contemporary Perspectives*. Salt Lake City, UT: University of Utah Press, pp. 362–88.

Griffith, R., 1997. *God's Daughters: Evangelical Women and the Power of Submission*. Berkeley, CA: University of California Press.

Hinckley, G., 2001. How Can I Become the Woman of Whom I Dream? *Ensign*. May, pp. 93–96.

Iannaccone, L., and Miles, C., 1990. Dealing with Social Change: The Mormon Church's Response to Change in Women's Roles. *Social Forces* 68(4): 1231–50.

Kline, C., 2016. Saying Goodbye to the Final Say: The Softening and Reimagining of Mormon Male Headship Ideologies. In P. Mason and J. Turner, eds. *Out of Obscurity: Mormonism since 1945*. Oxford: Oxford University Press, pp. 214–33.

Kline, C., 2018. Navigating Mormonism's Gendered Theology and Practice: Mormon Women in a Global Context. Ph.D. Dissertation, Claremont Graduate University.

Mbiti, J., 1969. *African Religions and Philosophies*. Oxford: Heinemann.

Meagher, M., 2011. Patriarchy. In G. Ritzer and J. Ryan, eds. *The Concise Encyclopedia of Sociology*. Oxford: Wiley-Blackwell, pp. 441–42.

Miles, C., 2008. LDS Family Ideals Versus the Equality of Women: Navigating the Changes since 1957. In C. Jacobson, J. Hoffman, and T. Heaton, eds. *Revisiting Thomas F. O'Dea's The Mormons: Contemporary Perspectives*. Salt Lake City, UT: University of Utah Press, pp. 101–34.

Oaks, D., 2012. The Gospel Culture. *Ensign*. March. www.lds.org/ensign/2012/03/the-gospelculture?lang=eng.

Riess, J., 2013. How Many Mormon Women Work Outside the Home? *Religion News Service*. July 19. https://religionnews.com/2013/07/19/how-many-mormon-women-work-outside-the-home/.

Rutherford, T., 2016. Shifting Focus to Global Mormonism: The LDS Church in India. In M. Goodman and M. Properzi, eds. *The Worldwide Church: Mormonism as a Global Religion*. Provo, UT: Religious Studies Center, Brigham Young University, pp. 71–94.

Rutherford, T., 2017. Conceptualizing Global Religions: An Investigation of Mormonism in India. Ph.D. Dissertation, Claremont Graduate University.

Sarkisian, N., and Gerstel, N., 2012. *Nuclear Family Values, Extended Family Lives: The Power of Race, Class, and Gender*. New York: Routledge.

Sherlock, I., 2018. The LDS Church in Flanders: Their Way, Our Way, or Their Way in Our Own Way. In G. Colvin and J. Brooks, eds. *Decolonizing Mormonism: Approaching a Postcolonial Zion*. Salt Lake City, UT: University of Utah Press, pp. 186–201.

Suggs, D., 2002. *A Bagful of Locusts and the Baboon Woman: Constructions of Gender, Change, and Continuity in Botswana*. Fort Worth, TX: Harcourt.

Van Beek, W., 2016. Church Unity and the Challenge of Cultural Diversity: A View from across the Sahara. In P. Mason, ed. *Directions for Mormon Studies in the Twenty-First Century*. Salt Lake City, UT: University of Utah Press, pp. 72–98.

Wilcox, W., 2004. *Soft Patriarchs, New Men: How Christianity Shapes Fathers and Husbands*. Chicago, IL: University of Chicago Press.

Further reading

Brusco, E., 1995. *The Reformation of Machismo: Evangelical Conversion and Gender in Colombia*. Austin, TX: University of Texas Press.

Brusco examines evangelicals in Colombia, finding that evangelical teachings often lead men to become more satisfactory husbands, as they eschew drinking, womanizing, and violence. She argues against notions that organized religion disadvantages women and that in fact, through its presentation of an alternate and more family-oriented form of masculinity, evangelicalism raises the standard of living for women and children.

Colvin, G., and Brooks, J. eds., 2018. *Decolonizing Mormonism: Approaching a Postcolonial Zion*. Salt Lake City, UT: University of Utah.

This edited volume addresses questions of Mormonism's American cultural imperialism, missiology, organizational structure, and theology through the perspective of members and scholars from around the globe.

Griffith, R., 1997. *God's Daughters: Evangelical Women and the Power of Submission*. Berkeley, CA: University of California Press.

Using participant observation, interviews, and textual analysis, Griffith explores the evangelical world of Women's Aglow, the largest women's evangelical organization. She finds that Aglow teachings do reinforce notions of women's dependence and submissiveness, but she also finds that women's submission to husbands often engenders better treatment and more satisfactory marriages. Thus, submission can lead to transformation and even power in their lives.

Kline, C., 2016. Saying Goodbye to the Final Say: The Softening and Reimagining of Mormon Male Headship Ideologies. In P. Mason and J. Turner, eds. *Out of Obscurity: Mormonism since 1945*. Oxford: Oxford University Press, pp. 214–33.

This paper traces the evolution of male headship ideologies in the LDS Church, as institutional church rhetoric shifted from overt male decision-making power to notions of equal partnership in marital decision making in the latter half of the twentieth century.

Miles, C., 2008. LDS Family Ideals Versus the Equality of Women: Navigating the Changes since 1957. In C. Jacobson, J. Hoffman, and T. Heaton, eds. *Revisiting Thomas F. O'Dea's The Mormons: Contemporary Perspectives*. Salt Lake City, UT: University of Utah Press, pp. 101–34.

This paper examines shifts in institutional LDS rhetoric on women working outside the home. Miles explains that church leaders have maintained the viability of their traditional claims about women's place in the home, even as their rhetoric has shifted to become more inclusive and understanding of working mothers, by emphasizing that mothers in the home are an ideal to strive for, but that different circumstances do not always allow for it.

23
STRUCTURES OF HOME AND FAMILY
North America

Megan Stanton

The home and family are integral to the religious practice of members of the Church of Jesus Christ of Latter-day Saints. Buildings such as temples and meetinghouses provide opportunities to enact sacred rituals and join together as a community of believers. Yet much of North American Latter-day Saints' religion is practiced not within these buildings, but instead with fellow family members and within the physical and cultural space of the home. Saints regularly express their daily worship and religious commitments in their living quarters. Given the prominence of the family in LDS theology, Saints' kin groups and domestic spaces are fundamental to their religious practice. In order to understand how Saints enact their religion, we must consider structures of home and family.

"Home" has a variety of meanings. It is not only a physical space, but also a cultural construct. Past generations of English speakers in North America often used the words home, household, and family interchangeably, imagining that these terms referred to all individuals living on a particular property. The meaning of these terms changed over time. After the mid-nineteenth century, the word "home" connoted a private domestic setting for many Americans. It was a protected space into which the public—representatives of the government, strangers, and even neighbors—should not intrude (Coontz, 1988; Shammas, 2002). Yet the home has not always been a private space. For a variety of reasons, it has also served public functions, into which any number of individuals might enter. The U.S. federal government's anti-polygamy legislation, for example, illustrates one historical intrusion into the privacy of LDS homes.

For scholars of American religion, "lived religion" is an interdisciplinary effort to understand people's daily experiences. As historians David Hall and Robert Orsi argued in the 1990s, lived religion emphasizes the actions and beliefs of the laity, including their performance of religion, their religious beliefs, and their relationships with leaders or institutions (Hall, 1997, pp. vii–xii; Orsi, 1997, pp. 6–9). Ethnographies and oral histories are particularly fruitful methods for understanding how people experience religion. Scholars also can uncover the daily practices of actual people through careful readings of sources such as institutional records, journals, and correspondence. Similarly, scholars find evidence of lived religion in material artifacts ranging from buildings to food to family scrapbooks.

This essay examines Saints' experiences in North America. It explores four major themes that have emerged in scholarly work: how the doctrine of gathering affected settlements throughout

North America; men's and women's gendered experiences of the home, family, and agency; the kinds of daily worship practiced in the home; and the home's function as a site of publicized cultural work.

North American settlements

Much of Latter-day Saint history revolves around the United States and especially the Great Basin region. This Utah-centrism is in part a legacy of the doctrine of gathering. Although LDS missionaries traveled the world in search of converts beginning in the 1830s, they directed new Church members to gather with the rest of the Saints in Utah during the nineteenth century (Arrington and Bitton, 1979, pp. 127–29). As a result, much of nineteenth-century LDS history unfolds through this process of migrating to and residing in the Great Basin region.

Upon arrival in the Great Basin region, these migrant Saints participated in settler colonialism. As Elise Boxer observes, Saints brought their cultural and religious practices into an already-inhabited environment by creating permanent settlements for themselves. American Indian groups such as the Ute people resided in the Great Basin region when the Saints arrived. Some Native people converted to the LDS Church, but many others did not. Regardless, Saints' settlements created a forced proximity among disparate peoples and cultural groups. The Saints' arrival altered the political, ecological, and economic trajectories of the region (Boxer, 2018, pp. 77–79).

The Saints' practice of polygamy resulted in settlements of Saints in Canada and Mexico by the late nineteenth century. These settlements provided shelter to people seeking to evade U.S. federal anti-polygamy prosecution. By living outside the political boundaries of the U.S., LDS settlers in Canada and Mexico escaped the reach of U.S. law. In these settlements, they continued practicing plural marriage for several more years. By the early twentieth century, however, leaders of the LDS Church came to forbid polygamous practice.

The LDS presence in areas outside the Great Basin region grew due to continued missionary work and the end of instruction about gathering. By the early twentieth century, the Church stopped encouraging converts to gather to Utah (Arrington and Bitton, 1979, p. 140). Instead, twentieth-century Saints remained in their places of origin in order to strengthen the Church's presence throughout North America and the world. In so doing, they created a North American diaspora of Saints spread across the continent. Native Hawaiians offer one extreme example of the end of gathering practices. Several hundred people had gathered from Hawaii to the Great Basin region in the late nineteenth century, settling in Salt Lake City and Iosepa, Utah. Yet in 1915, they followed President Joseph F. Smith's instruction to abandon their Utahan homes and return to Hawaii, where a new temple was under construction (Kester, 2013, pp. 5, 132–33). The end of gathering practices transformed the North American LDS experience from one organized almost entirely around a few specific regions into a transcontinental span of permanent settlements.

In the twentieth-century, Saints' experiences with family and home played out differently throughout North America. In the U.S., the LDS Church "Americanized." By the middle of the twentieth century, U.S. Saints conformed to normative American culture in their embrace of monogamous heterosexual marriage, adherence to complementary gender roles, and collective attainment of educational degrees and financial success (Hoyt and Patterson, 2011; Alexander, 1986; Mauss, 1989, pp. 41–42; Mauss, 1994). Although Saints in Canada prioritized values that mirrored those of U.S. Saints, they did not enjoy a parallel "Canadianization." Instead, their family practices kept them distinct from other Canadians without harming their cordial international relationships (Brassard, 2018). The Church in Mexico survived early twentieth-century political instability, but some Anglo settlers in the north returned to the U.S. during the Mexican

Revolution. Factors including the patronizing behavior of some Anglo LDS leaders who remained in the country, a national expulsion of foreign missionaries in the late 1920s, and a general lack of Church financial support contributed to a temporary rupture between central Mexican Saints and the LDS Church. About one-third of the Saints in central Mexico advocated in 1936 for a Mexican leadership and created their own movement, known as the Third Convention. In this conflict, Mexican Saints conveyed their frustration with an Anglo leadership that did not always acknowledge their needs. Some of these needs had to do with language and access to temple rituals. The introduction of the first Spanish-language temple services in the Mesa Temple in 1945 enabled Spanish-speaking Saints to take part in accessible temple ordinances and solemnize their family relationships in the eternities. The following year, most members of the Third Convention reconciled with the LDS Church (Tamez, 2015, pp. 78–80; Dormady, 2015, pp. 9–12; Pulido, 2015, pp. 96–97).

Compared to studies of the Great Basin region, relatively fewer scholarly works examine Saints' settlements in Mexico and Canada. Aside from polygamous practice, however, only a small number of these excellent scholarly works focus on structures of home and family. Sarah Carter's analysis of marriage offers a rare incorporation of LDS history into a broader Canadian national narrative (2008). Brooke Brassard's examination of Canadian Mormonism provides insight into how family practices affected Saints' interactions with other Canadians (2018). In an ethnographic study of global women of color, Caroline Kline found that women she interviewed in Mexico identified the Church as a liberating force in their lives. For example, support from paternal Church leaders aided them in challenging employment discrimination against their family members and in escaping domestic violence (Kline, 2018, pp. 48, 54–62). (In contrast, Jared M. Tamez determined that Mexican women historically have accommodated sexist, racist, and nationalist attitudes from some Anglo LDS leaders [2015, pp. 78–80].) Some studies of the LDS family and home likewise consider the experiences of Saints outside the Great Basin region. For example, Kristeen Black's ethnographic analysis examines kinship networks in both Utah and New Jersey (2016). Nevertheless, scholars might learn much more through further research on LDS homes or families outside the Great Basin region.

Family design and agency

Family design and the agency available to kin are integral to Saints' lived experience of religion. Family members' responsibilities within and without the home contributed to their religious practice, particularly during the nineteenth century when Saints in the Great Basin region infused tasks with religious meaning as they constructed their settlements.

The Saints treated even mundane tasks as religiously valuable for their contributions to building up Zion. Virtually all of the work that the Saints performed in creating and maintaining these early settlements was tinged with religious meaning. Men's and women's labor to sustain their bodies, for example, encompassed agriculture, food processing and storage, and cooking. These tasks were common among frontier societies, but the Saints saw this work as a means to sustain their fellow Church members. The sharing of food, including what men might catch while hunting, was a practical way to distribute food in an era lacking in refrigeration. However, it was also an expression of interdependence (Walker, 1999, p. 50). Similarly, the Saints saw women's work to prolong food supplies, either by canning produce or adding additional food items to flour in order to make the product last longer, as labor that contributed to the building up of Zion (Derr, 1999, pp. 237, 233).

Saints' homes reveal how they organized their daily life and conceptualized their family organization. In the Lion House, Brigham Young's wives pooled their resources and labor together. Meals were prepared for all residents of the house, with wives sharing meals together and splitting these housekeeping responsibilities among themselves and domestic servants (Carter, 2000, pp. 238–39; Hamilton, 1995, pp. 113–14).

The majority of families made other arrangements for their homes, however. The differences between homes for monogamous and polygamous families were often slight. Many polygamous families' homes were externally quite similar to monogamous families' homes (Carter, 2015, p. 136). At times, families added extensions to their homes as husbands married additional wives (Hamilton, 1995, p. 109). Buildings that housed monogamous families thus had the potential to accommodate plural families, provided the addition of more space. Other homes were designed for plural families, but nonetheless appeared similar to homes for monogamous families. Such similarity suggests that the Saints saw commonalities among their family experiences, even if households supported varied numbers of wives. Polygamous families nonetheless tended to provide wives with separate rooms and entryways into the home. Some homes even had separate living rooms and kitchens. These divisions enabled wives to maintain independence from one another even while sharing the same physical building (Carter, 2015, pp. 136, 138–39). Other wives possessed even more independence, for some polygamous families divided wives among different houses (Carter, 2015, pp. 148–49). These variations in polygamous housing demonstrate Saints' adaptations to individual circumstances.

Despite the patriarchal nature of nineteenth-century Mormonism and polygamous marriage, women's responsibilities were expansive. In addition to performing their own reproductive and productive labor, wives at times also took over their husbands' responsibilities. Women who did so worked as "deputy husbands," meaning that they acted on behalf of absent husbands (Ulrich, 1982, pp. 38–39). Wives of male missionaries often fulfilled their own and their husbands' responsibilities, in some cases without much ecclesiastical support (Ulrich, 2017, pp. 36–38, 46–47). Similarly, some polygamous wives residing in separate households cohabited with their husbands only some weeks out of the year. Such wives often assumed a variety of responsibilities on behalf of their households. And, in the last two decades of the nineteenth century, federal anti-polygamy prosecution resulted in men's absences from their homes, due to imprisonment or life underground. Wives functioned as heads of household in these cases too.

Nevertheless, polygamous family design raises an important question concerning agency. Women's accommodation of nineteenth-century polygamous patriarchal norms presents a puzzle for those who consider such norms to be oppressive. For example, women's expressions of support for plural marriage in public meetings beginning in 1870 were a surprise for nineteenth-century observers and later for academics. (Some non-Mormon Americans had assumed that the LDS women of Utah were in need of rescue from plural marriage. They thus interpreted the women's nineteenth-century activism as collaboration in their own oppression.) However, as Laurel Thatcher Ulrich notes, the women's activist support of polygamy was an outgrowth of the social radicalism of early Mormonism. Early LDS women in the U.S. had long expressed their support of a social system that differed from contemporary American models, even if their turn toward political organizing was new (Ulrich, 2017, pp. xiii–xvii). Women's support of plural marriage during the 1870s and 1880s, in other words, was an expression of their agency rather than evidence of their victimization.

Latter-day Saint women's agency remains a significant question for scholars of lived religion. As Catherine Brekus explains, academic depictions have represented "Mormon women as either deluded, downtrodden slaves or fiercely independent matriarchs" (2011, p. 61). Amy Hoyt traces the politicization of agency to liberal feminist theory, which has tended to restrict agency to acts of resistance of oppressive systems. Liberal feminist theoretical approaches are valuable, but they overlook the full, flexible spectrum of choice (Hoyt, 2007, pp. 2–4, 16–18, 28–30,

131; Hoyt, 2013, pp. 193–98). In other words, scholars cannot fully understand the choices that LDS men and women made until they recognize that agency includes not only resistance to but also cooperation with social structures (Hoyt, 2007, pp. 131–33; Brekus, 2011, pp. 74, 78–79; Haglund, 2016, pp. 234–35). Further, as Hoyt demonstrates in her ethnography of predominantly white Saints in the U.S., agency is fluid, "including resistance *and* maintenance of norms, which fall between the poles of autonomy and limited freedom" (2013, p. 198). Caroline Kline's ethnography of Mormon women of color offers a similar finding. She argues that women desired "non-oppressive connectedness," which blended interdependence with a rejection of injustice or violence (Kline, 2018, pp. 4–5, 41). Studies that treat agency broadly uncover the fluidity and messiness of lived experience. Evidence indicates that members of the LDS Church find meaning in their religious practice through a variety of points of connection.

Family design and roles evolved by the twentieth century after members of the LDS Church came to discontinue plural marriage. The work that people performed on behalf of their families likewise changed as fewer Saints established new settlements in the Great Basin region. Nevertheless, family roles remained important in Mormonism, particularly as the Saints came to embody a seemingly quintessentially American family structure by midcentury. Many LDS families adopted complementary gender roles. They asserted divisions between men's productive labor outside the home and women's reproductive labor, known by the Saints as homemaking, within it. By the mid-twentieth century, many Saints and other Americans argued that women belonged in the home, laboring on behalf of their husbands and children as homemakers. Such attention to women's place in the home grew increasingly defensive as feminists and gay and lesbian people—including Mormons and others—advocated for women's equality.

Popular books about homemaking illustrate a range of responses to the broader concerns that led to the women's liberation movement. In *The Art of Homemaking* (1962), Daryl V. Hoole recommended that her fellow LDS readers make homemaking more efficient so that they could dedicate time to other tasks that aided their communities (Holbrook, 2016, pp. 202–4). Helen B. Andelin, in contrast, valorized women's work in the home as she sold her *Fascinating Womanhood* (1965) marriage manual. According to Andelin, wives' disinterest in homemaking was damaging to their marriages and could be undone only when women created pleasant home atmospheres and offered admiration to their husbands. The Church supported the ideas of these LDS authors for some years. By 1970, however, the Relief Society underwent a curriculum shift that transformed official instruction (Neuffer, 2014, pp. 69–71, 97–99; Holbrook, 2016, pp. 205, 207–9). For example, the Relief Society's curriculum shifted from offering instruction about "Work" to "Homemaking." The forms of work that this curriculum sanctioned became narrow and gendered (Holbrook, 2016, pp. 210–11).

The LDS Church continued to promote complementary gender roles for men and women. President David O. McKay observed that men should prioritize their families over their wage work and socialization, explaining, "No other success can compensate for failure in the home" (McKay, 1964, p. 5). In February 1987, President Ezra Taft Benson instructed Saints to prioritize childbearing over financial and material goals. In addition, he told women to discontinue paid work and focus on rearing their children. Men, he argued, were the breadwinners of families, and women's participation in the workforce was a primary cause of divorce. This talk reiterated ideas he had shared earlier in the 1980s, and quoted liberally from instructions Spencer W. Kimball delivered as apostle and president in 1949 and 1977 (Benson, 1987b; McDannell, 2018, p. 165).

Benson also delivered a companion message to fathers in October 1987 that reiterated his instruction. He described fathers' role as breadwinners of the family, reminded them that their wives should not participate in the workforce, encouraged them to provide spiritual leadership within the home, and suggested that they participate in family activities. Fathers might also show their wives love with flowers and a "willingness to help with the dishes, change diapers, get up with a crying child in the night, and leave the television or the newspaper to help with the dinner" (Benson, 1987a). With these companion talks, Benson asserted his expectation that families would stay true to the structures that other LDS leaders had encouraged throughout much of the twentieth century.

Yet Benson's 1987 talks caused significant frustration among Saints, especially as women reacted to his discussion of motherhood. Lavina Fielding Anderson acknowledges that some women welcomed this instruction, in part because it affirmed their choices. Yet most of the women with whom she spoke responded to Benson's talk on mothers with a "reaction ... of pain and of anger" (Anderson, 1988, p. 105). They worried that Benson had overlooked the significant labor involved in creating and rearing children and failed to provide women with a standard by which to evaluate their mothering work. Instead, listeners feared that Benson set such high expectations that mothers' work was truly endless and never enough (Anderson, 1988, pp. 106, 110).

LDS women's work continues both outside the home and in homemaking, despite general authorities' instructions. Compared to other Americans, LDS women in the U.S. are more likely to be homemakers. One study found in 2008 that over one quarter of LDS women were homemakers, which was double the rate of other American women. This survey, in other words, determined that the majority of American women, LDS and not, were *not* homemakers (Phillips and Cragun, 2011, pp. 2, 6). A 2016 online public opinion survey determined that 75 percent of Millennial Mormons' mothers have worked outside the home since Millennials' births in the 1980s and 1990s, compared to just 57 percent of the mothers of Boomer/Silent Generation Mormons born prior to 1964 (Riess, 2019, pp. 237, 106–7, 6). LDS leaders' twentieth-century focus on women's work has pitted women against one another. Yet women's experiences are not as simple as a division between those who work outside the home and those who do not might suggest. Scholarship that reframes Mormon women's productive and reproductive labor could offer insightful new ways to recognize the value of LDS women's work.

Fewer studies have examined men's spiritual responsibilities within the LDS home. For much of the history of the LDS Church, leaders called for men to maintain clear leadership over their family members. Since the 1980s, the LDS Church has softened these instructions. Men began receiving recommendations not only to preside over their families, but also to invite their wives' input and participation. They remained the heads of their families, but they should not use their leadership to control their family members. As Caroline Kline notes, these changes in the LDS Church parallel conservative Protestants' use of the language of male headship (2016, pp. 214–21).

LDS leaders affirmed but also altered instruction concerning gender roles through "The Family: A Proclamation to the World." Announced in 1995 by President Gordon B. Hinckley, this statement was authored exclusively by men: namely the First Presidency and Council of Twelve Apostles (Prince, 2012, p. 136; McDannell, 2018, pp. 153–54). It reaffirmed complementary gender roles, inviting fathers to "preside over their families" and identifying mothers as "primarily responsible for the nurture of their children." Nonetheless, Colleen McDannell finds that the statement deescalated the gendered rhetoric of the 1980s. "The Family" fosters interdependence between husbands and wives, rather than the hierarchical headship that conservative Protestants such as the Southern Baptist convention have recently preached. Further, "The Family" is silent on whether women should work outside the home, thereby omitting instructions provided by Benson just one decade earlier (First Presidency, 1995; McDannell, 2018, pp. 159–60, 165–66). Instructions about gender-specific family roles, in other words, had shifted with this statement's publication.

The announcement of "The Family" was a flashpoint for the Saints. Although LDS leaders had condemned GLBTQ marriage previously, including in short texts produced in 1991 and 1994, "The Family" offered clear instructions about precisely why Saints should oppose any marriages that were not monogamous and heterosexual. As Colleen McDannell observes, the statement justified the LDS Church's opposition to GLBTQ marriage for Mormon as well as non-Mormon audiences (McDannell, 2018, pp. 156–57). It also bound the worldwide LDS Church to U.S. political developments. Soon after Hinckley read the statement to the Saints, Representative James V. Hansen (R-UT) submitted it into U.S. Congressional record. In 1997, the LDS Church submitted "The Family" in an amicus brief, designed to help convince the justices of Hawaii's supreme court to oppose gay marriage (Compton, 2015). In other words, "The Family" functioned in part to provide justification for American LDS leaders' opposition to the growth of gay marriage in the U.S.

Many members of the LDS Church endorse the claims made in "The Family." One study found that Mormon women mentioned Hinckley's statement more often than scripture in their blog posts. The statement was typically used to justify "non- or anti-feminist sentiments" (Haglund, 2016, p. 247). Another study explored Saints' views of the document through interviews with several heterosexual, married couples living in Utah Valley. These individuals differed in their valuation of the document and the extent to which they agreed with its message. Several agreed with "The Family" and considered it to be comparable to scriptural canon in importance. Others disagreed with the document, particularly in its rejection of gay marriage. One couple in fact observed regional differences in Saints' reactions. They explained that members of their former ward in Washington, DC regularly questioned "The Family," but that members of their new ward in Utah Valley seemed to accept the document wholesale (Scott and Petersen, 2018, pp. 177, 185, 188). Similarly, analysis of the Claremont Women's Oral History Project, which seeks understanding of contemporary LDS women's experiences, determined that women's views on the LDS Church's involvement with Proposition 8 varied widely (Rolapp, 2013). Support for "The Family" also contributed to Saints' support for California's Proposition 8 in 2008, which was written to repeal gay marriage in that state.

Nevertheless, the LDS Church's anti-gay marriage position has political ramifications. It has caused pain for GLBTQ Saints as well as for some of their heterosexual peers. Further, Hinckley's "The Family" and the LDS Church's encouragement of Saints' political work to support California's Proposition 8 reinforced the institutional rejection of non-heteronormative family models. In November 2015, months after the U.S. Supreme Court legalized gay marriage in *Obergefell v. Hodges* (2015), a handbook from the LDS Church revealed a new policy concerning gay marriage. The handbook instructed priesthood leaders to view gay marriage as equivalent to apostasy. The "November Policy" made adult Saints in gay marriages subject to disciplinary councils, and barred their children from full Church participation (Barrus, 2017). The provisions of the policy were defanged in 2019, but scholarship continues to develop on the ramifications of the policy and the LDS Church's continued restrictions on its GBLTQ members (Moore, 2019).

Research on family design and roles remains relevant as LDS people continue to negotiate general authorities' instructions about their family obligations. However, additional scholarship on men's roles in the home and on the variety of Saints' family patterns would provide important contributions to the study of LDS families and homes.

Domestic religious practice

Many acts of religious worship occur in the home or with family. North American Saints construct their religious worlds within their living spaces and in daily activities. They live their religion through their regular habits and actions. Saints' experiences of religion can be understood through attention to phenomena such as a home's religious iconography, families' food preparation and consumption, and how family members allot their shared time. Although ephemeral, these artifacts are far from trivial. They are key elements in how Saints practice their religion.

Physical decorations within homes convey the character of its residents and support religious worship. Religious wall hangings in LDS homes of the late twentieth and twenty-first centuries can include a variety of images and documents, including temple imagery, artwork of religious figures ranging from Jesus Christ to LDS prophets, crafts made by adult women in Relief Society meetings, and copies of "The Family: A Proclamation to the World." This variety of images serves several functions, both intended and not. The images foster remembrance of sacred buildings and the ordinances that family members have received within them. Similarly, the placement of LDS iconography allows guests to draw conclusions about a family's religious character or orthodoxy, as Colleen McDannell found in her examination of nineteenth-century Victorian domestic architecture (1986, pp. 25–28, 39–49).

These images also have unintended effects, particularly in their prescription of gender roles and sexuality. Photographs and artwork of predominantly male religious leaders can function to influence Saints' conflation of leadership with the male gender. Likewise, "The Family," when placed on the walls of LDS homes, supports leaders' instructions concerning gender and sexuality (First Presidency, 1995). Families tacitly endorse these claims by displaying "The Family" in their home or gifting copies of it to newlywed couples (Kline, 2016, p. 214).

Saints' experiences of religion in the home likewise include rituals such as food preparation and consumption. LDS meal preparation blends religiosity with sustenance. The consumption of food functions as a marker of religious identity and obedience through accordance with the Word of Wisdom, for example. Cookbooks published by LDS presses reveal that even Church-sanctioned authors struggle to resolve the tensions inherent in some of the instructions of the Word of Wisdom; eating meat sparingly or consuming produce only in seasons of harvest do not always sit easily with Americans' consumption habits and Saints' interest in canning (Holbrook, 2012, p. 140).

Families' daily religious experiences also include home worship. Worship within the home is a common experience shared by people of many religious faiths (McDannell, 1986, p. 77). LDS families arrange for a daily ritual, such as gathering for family prayer, scripture study, or a shared meal. Since 1915, the LDS Church has encouraged "home evening" gatherings in order to strengthen family unity and increase religious instruction (Goodman, 2011). These meetings were correlated in 1965, with published Family Home Evening manuals providing a recommended curriculum (Goodman, 2011). Some Saints coordinated their own lessons or events as well. These regular practices unite family members together in a shared activity.

Recently, even Saints not living with other kin can benefit from such group activities. As Kristeen Black observed in her ethnography of wards in Utah and New Jersey, single adults took part in Family Home Evening meetings together. In addition to providing some of the benefits that family units gained from these meetings, single adults gained opportunity to socialize with one another (Black, 2016, pp. 230–31). Nevertheless, oral histories collected and reviewed by Elizabeth J. Mott point to the ways that single women—including those widowed, divorced, and never-married—find themselves marginalized within their wards (2013, p. 48). Study of daily behavior reveals the variety of ways in which Saints conceptualize the family. Those not living with kin nonetheless find adaptations that provide them with the benefits of domestic worship.

The study of lived religion enables scholars of Mormonism to consider Saints' daily experiences. In so doing, scholars move beyond attention to statements made by LDS leaders and consider how Saints practiced and thought about their spirituality. Within the home, Saints' religious activities offer them opportunities to draw closer to God, to make connections with friends and family, and to communicate their religious identity to others. These activities can be understood through ethnographic studies, through analysis of material and cultural artifacts, and through examinations of liturgy. What people do when they practice religion offers insight into how Saints imagine their membership in their families as well as in their Church and cosmos.

The cultural meaning of domestic space

The home and family fulfill particular cultural roles in North America. Since the mid-nineteenth century, residents of the U.S. have divided political culture into two parts, known as the private and public spheres. Ideas about private and public spheres have divided individual citizens from their public government. They also have divided the home from the rest of the world. In short, the Americans who subscribe to the ideology of separate spheres have imagined that private domestic settings should be kept separate from the prying eyes of government officials, strangers, and even neighbors. The physical boundaries of the home—such as its exterior walls or its fencing—thus functioned also as social boundaries. These spheres also influenced American expectations of gender: although all people interacted with their worlds, sphere ideology associated men with the public sphere, and women with the private sphere. Americans believed that both spheres were necessary for a well-functioning society. Any loss of functionality in the private sphere, for example, damaged the public sphere as well. Nevertheless, these spheres were cultural constructs. In other words, they were not literal but instead were ideas that many Americans held in common.

However, these assumptions of privacy did not apply universally to all homes at all times. Some families, including LDS polygamous households, were stripped of opportunities for privacy. Scholars have also observed that these shared assumptions of privacy obscure our knowledge of the public and national projects that occur within homes. Scholarship on the North American LDS family and home provides opportunity to question our assumptions regarding the nature of cultural spaces.

In nineteenth-century Utah, the practice of plural marriage altered the application of private and public spheres within LDS political culture. Christine Talbot argues that the Saints broadened their shared understanding of the private sphere to encompass not only the home and family but also the LDS Church itself. This enlargement of the private sphere, Talbot asserts, was an effort to protect the LDS Church by marking it as a private space into which non-Mormons should not intrude. In short, the Saints argued that the private sphere applied to Saints' lives and their Church, and the public sphere encompassed all non-LDS peoples and institutions. In Talbot's analysis, the Saints' conflation of LDS families with the Mormon community resulted in the publicization of the family and privatized their territorial government (Talbot, 2013, pp. 1–2, 8–10, 34–35, 58). Critics of the LDS Church, in turn, drew from the ideology of spheres in their complaints about Mormonism. They characterized polygamy as harmful to social order through its violations of the private sphere: it eradicated domestic intimacy and disrupted the proper division between the private and public spheres. In this debate, the Saints and other Americans made competing claims about citizenship and political culture (Talbot, 2013, pp. 83, 95–104).

Many LDS families lost the benefits of privacy due to anti-polygamy legislation passed by the U.S. federal government in the late nineteenth century. Federal legislation criminalized polygamy beginning in 1862, but resulted in few prosecutions. Additional legislation, including the Edmunds Act of 1882, enabled federal officials to prosecute polygamy by focusing on the actions of cohabitation rather than on marital status. The Edmunds Act made plural cohabitation illegal: men could not live with more than one wife. The private decisions made by members of a plural household became, through this anti-polygamy legislation, a matter of federal attention. This legislation invited quite literal intrusions into families' homes. For example, some Saints complained that male federal officials searched women's bedrooms for evidence of unlawful cohabitation. This legislation illustrates the extent to which the federal government disrupted the privacy of Mormon families and homes. When a national American audience decried polygamy and determined that they should aid in its eradication, they made the activities taking place within Mormon domestic settings a matter of national interest. The Edmunds Act and other anti-polygamy legislation made issues that other Americans would consider private—namely, their marital choices and living arrangements—into potentially criminal actions.

The LDS home has also functioned as a site for racial assimilation, particularly through the incorporation of American Indian children into white families in the U.S. and Canada. Soon after arriving in the Great Basin region in the late 1840s, predominantly white Saints discovered that Indian traders in the region sold children taken captive from other tribes. The Saints began purchasing these children, believing that the captives otherwise would be tortured and killed. They thus became complicit in a complicated network of human trafficking already underway in the American West (Blackhawk, 2006, pp. 143–44, 230). They also received some children through other means, including as bounty from raids and battles with neighboring Indians. Over 400 children of Paiute, Goshute, Shoshone, Navajo, or Ute descent were incorporated into LDS homes as indentured servants in the nineteenth century. Within LDS homes, Indian servants entered formal agreements as wards who provided labor to their guardians in exchange for vocational training. They received religious instruction and were expected to assimilate to Anglo Mormon culture. Studies indicate that assimilation succeeded, as only about one-tenth of the captives chose to return to Indian communities upon reaching adulthood. Many of those who remained with white settlements never married, possibly due to a lack of potential mates in settlements opposed to interracial unions (Cannon, 2018, pp. 1–17, 20–21). Under these circumstances, predominantly white Saints encouraged American Indian children's assimilation within their homes and through household relationships.

The Indian Student Placement Program likewise illustrates the public function of domestic spaces. The program began informally in 1947 and held institutional support from 1954 to 2000. It transformed LDS, primarily white, homes in the U.S. and Canada into key sites of cultural assimilation. The placement program offered better educational opportunities to American Indian adolescents, and particularly residents of the Navajo reservation, who at midcentury had limited educational opportunities. Parents sent their children to live full-time with off-reservation LDS families during the school year. One requirement of the program was that American Indian participants and their parents be members of the LDS Church. Student participants included those who belonged already to the Church and those who converted in order to satisfy the program's requirement. The program reached its height in the early 1970s, placing nearly 5,000 students annually. It was phased out beginning in the 1980s, partially because on-reservation educational opportunities had improved (Boxer, 2015, pp. 132–33; Stanton, 2019, pp. 213–15, 222).

Although proponents of the program claimed that it enabled students to function successfully in both Indigenous and Anglo cultures, critics suggested that the program was instead an organized project in assimilation. George P. Lee, a Navajo participant who later served a mission, married in a temple, earned a Ph.D., and became a member of the Quorum of the Seventy, credited his success to the program. He argued that he gained a set of shared experiences with white people through his placement years that enabled him to succeed in predominantly white cultural spaces. In Matthew Garrett's analysis, some participants adopted a "Lamanite identity" and thus demonstrated agency in choosing to cooperate with the program's goals. Garrett's discussion mirrors recent scholarship on the reconceptualization of LDS women's agency. Other former placement participants have identified elements of the program as harmful, however. Many have claimed that they lost fluency in Native languages or felt distance from their communities of origin after spending so much of their childhoods living with other families (Stanton, 2019, pp. 216–17; Garrett, 2016, pp. 8, 10, 241–43; Boxer, 2015, pp. 163–65).

The placement program relied on the physical and cultural space of homes. The homes of the predominantly white "foster families" who sponsored Indian students functioned as sites of cultural assimilation. Students who enrolled in the program lived with families who expected adaptation to their way of life: mid- and late twentieth-century normative American middle-class culture. (Similar processes of Americanization occurred among non-Mormons. Indeed, many white families adopted Indian children at midcentury [Stanton, 2019, pp. 218–19].) Within placement homes, students learned to speak, dress, eat, and behave in the same manner as their placement families. Foster families and homes thus hosted much of the work inherent in students' cultural educations. It was within LDS homes that Native LDS children made individual cultural adaptations that collectively constitute one part of a larger national story of assimilation (Boxer, 2015, pp. 163–67). By bringing the assimilation of American Indian children into private LDS homes, the Church insinuated a larger public practice into the private sphere. The placement program disrupted the privacy of LDS domestic settings.

The publicization of LDS homes likewise occurs through objects as seemingly ephemeral as album collections. Historically, albums have contained autographs, newspaper clippings, and photographs that document family events. Since the 1990s, many LDS women have taken part in scrapbooking and, later, blogging. These documentary practices, Danille Elise Christensen observes, allow women to "claim value for *carework* and *kinwork*." They publicize the domestic relationships and experiences that, in the late twentieth and twenty-first centuries, are usually invisible outside of individual families. Scrapbooks and mothers' blogs are typically known for their focus on mundane aspects of life: on the everyday and unremarkable events that take place in domestic settings through routine childcare and home maintenance. Yet the seeming trivial nature of these albums performs cultural work: within them, authors document the work they perform for their families, articulate the value of caring for others, and seek out networks of like-minded caregivers. By sharing stories about their partners and children in scrapbooks and blogs, women affirm the value of the physical and emotional work conducted within families (Christensen, 2016, p. 45). The publicization of Mormon family life likewise enables bloggers to perform their LDS orthodoxy in others' eyes by emphasizing the ways in which their lives conformed to religious instruction (Haglund, 2016, pp. 239–40).

In North America, the home has acted as a site of significant cultural power. For many, it is a marker of boundary maintenance. It divides kin from non-kin. It creates a space for domestic intimacy that seems separate from the relationships and work of the broader world. And yet the home is not simply a private space. Studies examining the cultural space of domestic settings challenge us to question our assumptions about the home and the private sphere.

Conclusion

Within North America, LDS homes have accommodated the lived religious experiences of family members. They provided space for families to share rituals with one another and to take part in both private and public cultural projects. Nonetheless, scholars and students of the LDS home and family will find that much more research remains to be done. Ethnographies, oral history interviews such as those collected by the Claremont Women's Oral History Project, and written sources all have the potential to uncover LDS people's lived religion. The religious practices of families, particularly outside the Great Basin region and the U.S., especially warrant further examination. Similarly, scholars would benefit from paying closer attention to the domestic and spiritual responsibilities of LDS men in the home. The extent to which LDS families and homes have exceeded the boundaries of the private sphere deserve further consideration, for it is within these spaces that homes' broad impacts have been overlooked.

References

Alexander, T.G., 1986. *Mormonism in Transition: A History of the Latter-day Saints, 1890–1930*. Urbana, IL: University of Illinois Press.
Andelin, H.B., 1965. *Fascinating Womanhood*. Santa Barbara, CA: Pacific Press.
Anderson, L.F., 1988. A Voice from the Past: The Benson Instructions for Parents. *Dialogue: A Journal of Mormon Thought* 21(4): 103–13.
Arrington, L.J., and Bitton, D., 1979. *The Mormon Experience: A History of the Latter-day Saints*. New York: Vintage Books.
Barrus, C., 2017. Reactions to "The Policy": November 2015. *Worlds without End: A Mormon Studies Roundtable*. www.withoutend.org/reactions-the-policy-november-2015/.
Benson, E.T., 1987a. To the Fathers in Israel. www.lds.org/general-conference/1987/10/to-the-fathers-in-israel?lang=eng.
Benson, E.T., 1987b. To the Mothers in Zion. *Education for Eternity: Discipline-Specific Resources*. Brigham Young University. https://educationforeternity.byu.edu/w_etb87.html.
Black, K.L., 2016. *A Sociology of Mormon Kinship: The Place of Family within the Church of Jesus Christ of Latter-day Saints*. Lewiston, NY: Edwin Mellen Press.
Blackhawk, N., 2006. *Violence over the Land: Indians and Empires in the Early American West*. Cambridge, MA: Harvard University Press.
Boxer, E., 2015. "The Lamanites Shall Blossom as the Rose": The Indian Student Placement Program, Mormon Whiteness, and Indigenous Identity. *Journal of Mormon History* 41(4): 132–76.
Boxer, E., 2018. "This Is the Place!": Disrupting Mormon Settler Colonialism. In G. Colvin and J. Brooks, eds. *Decolonizing Mormonism: Approaching a Postcolonial Zion*. Salt Lake City, UT: University of Utah Press, pp. 77–99.
Brassard, B.K., 2018. Thirst Land into Springs of Water: Negotiating a Place in Canada as Latter-day Saints, 1887–1947. Abstract. Ph.D. Dissertation, University of Waterloo. www.researchgate.net/publication/325575963_Thirsty_Land_into_Springs_of_Water_Negotiating_a_Place_in_Canada_as_Latter-day_Saints_1887-1947.
Brekus, C.A., 2011. Mormon Women and the Problem of Historical Agency. *Journal of Mormon History* 37(2): 58–87.
Cannon, B.Q., 2018. "To Buy Up the Lamanite Children as Fast as They Could": Indentured Servitude and Its Legacy in Mormon Society. *Journal of Mormon History* 44(2): 1–35.
Carter, S., 2008. *The Importance of Being Monogamous: Marriage and Nation Building in Western Canada to 1915*. Edmonton: University of Alberta Press.
Carter, T., 2000. Living the Principle: Mormon Polygamous Housing in Nineteenth-Century Utah. *Winterthur Portfolio* 35(4): 223–51.
Carter, T., 2015. *Building Zion: The Material World of Mormon Settlement*. Minneapolis, MN: University of Minnesota Press.
Christensen, D.E., 2016. (Not) Going Public: Mediating Reception and Managing Visibility in Contemporary Scrapbook Performance. In J.B. Jackson, ed. *Material Vernaculars: Objects, Images, and Their Social Worlds*. Bloomington, IN: Indiana University Press, pp. 40–104.
Compton, L., 2015. From Amici to 'Ohana: The Hawaiian Roots of the Family Proclamation. *Rational Faiths: Keeping Mormonism Weird*. https://rationalfaiths.com/from-amici-to-ohana/.
Coontz, S., 1988. *The Social Origins of Private Life: A History of American Families, 1600–1900*. New York: Verso.
Derr, J.M., 1999. "I Have Eaten Nearly Everything Imaginable": Pioneer Diet. In R.W. Walker and D.R. Dant, eds. *Nearly Everything Imaginable: The Everyday Life of Utah's Mormon Pioneers*. Provo, UT: Brigham Young University Press, pp. 223–48.

Dormady, J.H., 2015. Introduction: The Mormons in Mexico. In J.H. Dormady and J.M. Tamez, eds. *Just South of Zion: The Mormons in Mexico and Its Borderlands*. Albuquerque, NM: University of New Mexico Press, pp. 1–22.

The First Presidency and Council of the Twelve Apostles of the Church of Jesus Christ of Latter-day Saints, 1995. The Family: A Proclamation to the World. www.lds.org/topics/family-proclamation?lang=eng.

Garrett, M., 2016. *Making Lamanites: Mormons, Native Americans, and the Indian Student Placement Program, 1947–2000*. Salt Lake City, UT: University of Utah Press.

Goodman, M.A., 2011. Correlation: The Turning Point (1960s). In S.C. Esplin and K.L. Alford, eds. *Salt Lake City: The Place which God Prepared*. Provo, UT: Religious Studies Center and Deseret Book, pp. 259–84. https://rsc.byu.edu/archived/salt-lake-city/13-correlation-turning-point-1960s.

Haglund, K., 2016. Blogging the Boundaries: Mormon Mommy Blogs and the Construction of Mormon Identity. In P.Q. Mason and J.G. Turner, eds. *Out of Obscurity: Mormonism since 1945*. New York: Oxford University Press, pp. 234–56.

Hall, D.D., 1997. Introduction. In D.D. Hall, ed. *Lived Religion in America: Toward a History of Practice*. Princeton, NJ: Princeton University Press, pp. vii–xiii.

Hamilton, C.M., 1995. *Nineteenth-Century Mormon Architecture and City Planning*. New York: Oxford University Press.

Holbrook, K., 2012. Religion in a Recipe. *Journal of Mormon History* 38(2): 139–43.

Holbrook, K., 2016. Housework: The Problem That Does Have a Name. In P.Q. Mason and J.G. Turner, eds. *Out of Obscurity: Mormonism since 1945*. New York: Oxford University Press, pp. 198–213.

Hoole, D.V., 1962. *The Art of Homemaking*. Salt Lake City, UT: Deseret Book.

Hoyt, A., 2007. Agency, Subjectivity and Essentialism within Traditional Religious Cultures: An Ethnographic Study of an American Latter-day Saint Community. Ph.D. Dissertation, Claremont Graduate University.

Hoyt, A., 2013. Agency. In C.L. Bushman and C. Kline, eds. *Mormon Women Have Their Say: Essays from the Claremont Oral History Collection*. Salt Lake City, UT: Greg Kofford Books, pp. 193–214.

Hoyt, A., and Patterson, S.M., 2011. Mormon Masculinity: Changing Gender Expectations in the Era of Transition from Polygamy to Monogamy, 1890–1920. *Gender & History* 23(1): 72–91.

Kester, M., 2013. *Remembering Iosepa: History, Place, and Religion in the American West*. New York: Oxford University Press.

Kline, C., 2016. Saying Goodbye to the Final Say: The Softening and Reimagining of Mormon Male Headship Ideologies. In P.Q. Mason and J.G. Turner, eds. *Out of Obscurity: Mormonism since 1945*. New York: Oxford University Press, pp. 214–33.

Kline, C., 2018. Navigating Mormonism's Gendered Theology and Practice: Mormon Women in a Global Context. Ph.D. Dissertation, Claremont Graduate University.

Mauss, A.L., 1989. Assimilation and Ambivalence: The Mormon Reaction to Americanization. *Dialogue: A Journal of Mormon Thought* 22: 30–67.

Mauss, A.L., 1994. *The Angel and the Beehive: The Mormon Struggle with Assimilation*. Urbana, IL: University of Illinois Press.

McDannell, C., 1986. *The Christian Home in Victorian America, 1840–1900*. Bloomington, IN: Indiana University Press.

McDannell, C., 2018. *Sister Saints: Mormon Women since the End of Polygamy*. New York: Oxford University Press.

McKay, D.O., 1964. Untitled talk. In *Conference Report, April 1964*. Salt Lake City, UT: The Church of Jesus Christ of Latter-day Saints, pp. 4–7.

Moore, L., 2019. Mormon Church Changes L.G.B.T. Policy, but Those Who Left Say This Isn't Enough. *New York Times*. www.nytimes.com/2019/04/06/reader-center/mormon-church-lgbt.html.

Mott, E.J., 2013. Singlehood. In C.L. Bushman and C. Kline, eds. *Mormon Women Have Their Say: Essays from the Claremont Oral History Collection*. Salt Lake City, UT: Greg Kofford Books, pp. 45–71.

Neuffer, J.D., 2014. *Helen Andelin and the Fascinating Womanhood Movement*. Salt Lake City, UT: University of Utah Press.

Orsi, R., 1997. Everyday Miracles: The Study of Lived Religion. In D.D. Hall, ed. *Lived Religion in America: Toward a History of Practice*. Princeton, NJ: Princeton University Press, pp. 3–21.

Phillips, R., and Cragun, R.T., 2011. Mormons in the United States 1990–2008: Socio-demographic Trends and Regional Differences. Trinity College. http://commons.trincoll.edu/aris/files/2011/12/Mormons2008.pdf.

Prince, G.A., 2012. "There Is Always a Struggle": An Interview with Chieko N. Okazaki. *Dialogue: A Journal of Mormon Thought* 45(1): 112–40.

Pulido, E., 2015. Solving Schism in *Neplanta*: The Third Convention Returns to the LDS Fold. In J.H. Dormady and J.M. Tamez, eds. *Just South of Zion: The Mormons in Mexico and Its Borderlands*. Albuquerque, NM: University of New Mexico Press, pp. 89–109.

Riess, J., 2019. *The Next Mormons: How Millennials Are Changing the LDS Church*. New York: Oxford University Press.

Rolapp, A.T., 2013. California's Proposition 8. In C.L. Bushman and C. Kline, eds. *Mormon Women Have Their Say: Essays from the Claremont Oral History Collection*. Salt Lake City, UT: Greg Kofford Books, pp. 285–301.

Scott, D.W., and Petersen, B.J., 2018. Defending the Family, Defending the Faith: An Analysis of "The Family: A Proclamation to the World," Religious Identity, and the Politics of Same-Sex Marriage in a Mormon Community. *Journal of GLBT Family Studies* 14(3): 175–95.

Shammas, C., 2002. *A History of Household Government in America*. Charlottesville, VA: University of Virginia Press.

Stanton, M.A., 2019. The Indian Student Placement Program and Native Direction. In J.P. Hafen and B. Rensink, eds. *Essays on American Indian and Mormon History*. Salt Lake City, UT: University of Utah Press, pp. 211–24.

Talbot, C., 2013. *A Foreign Kingdom: Mormons and Polygamy in American Political Culture, 1852–1890*. Urbana, IL: University of Illinois Press.

Tamez, J.M., 2015. "Our Faithful Sisters": Mormon Worship and the Establishment of the Relief Society in the Mexican Mission, 1901–1903. In J.H. Dormady and J.M. Tamez, eds. *Just South of Zion: The Mormons in Mexico and Its Borderlands*. Albuquerque, NM: University of New Mexico Press, pp. 73–88.

Ulrich, L.T., 1982. *Good Wives: Image and Reality in the Lives of Women in Northern New England, 1650–1750*. New York: Oxford University Press.

Ulrich, L.T., 2017. *A House Full of Females: Plural Marriage and Women's Rights in Early Mormonism, 1835–1870*. New York: Alfred A. Knopf.

Walker, R.W., 1999. Golden Memories: Remembering Life in a Mormon Village. In R.W. Walker and D.R. Dant, eds. *Nearly Everything Imaginable: The Everyday Life of Utah's Mormon Pioneers*. Provo, UT: Brigham Young University Press, pp. 47–74.

Further reading

Anderson, L.F., 1988. A Voice from the Past: The Benson Instructions for Parents. *Dialogue: A Journal of Mormon Thought* 21(4): 103–13.

This article describes men's and women's reactions to President Ezra Taft Benson's instructions on family roles within the LDS Church.

Boxer, E., 2015. "The Lamanites Shall Blossom as the Rose": The Indian Student Placement Program, Mormon Whiteness, and Indigenous Identity. *Journal of Mormon History* 41(4): 132–76.

This article analyzes the Indian Student Placement Program as a colonizing project. The author explores how the program used LDS foster families' homes as sites of colonization.

Christensen, D.E., 2016. (Not) Going Public: Mediating Reception and Managing Visibility in Contemporary Scrapbook Performance. In J.B. Jackson, ed. *Material Vernaculars: Objects, Images, and Their Social Worlds*. Bloomington, IN: Indiana University Press, pp. 40–104.

This article uncovers the purposes of scrapbooking through ethnographic interviews with members of the scrapbooking community, many of whom are women and some of whom are LDS.

Hoyt, A., 2013. Agency. In C.L. Bushman and C. Kline, eds. *Mormon Women Have Their Say: Essays from the Claremont Oral History Collection*. Salt Lake City, UT: Greg Kofford Books, pp. 193–214.

This chapter, which provides a published overview of Hoyt's 2007 dissertation, offers a new academic definition of agency that supports the study of women belonging to a traditional religion.

Talbot, C., 2013. *A Foreign Kingdom: Mormons and Polygamy in American Political Culture, 1852–1890*. Urbana, IL: University of Illinois Press.

This book examines how LDS and American notions of private spheres influenced nineteenth-century debates over American citizenship and Mormon family structure.

24
NON-TRADITIONAL FAMILIES

Ryan T. Cragun and Giuseppina Valle Holway

Introduction

Families in the United States have undergone significant transformations in the last several decades, leading to a growing array of living arrangements for children. For example, in 1960, approximately 88 percent of children under the age of 18 lived with two parents (biological, step, adoptive, or cohabiting parents); in 2018, this percentage had declined to 69 percent (U.S. Census Bureau, 2018a), representing a 22 percent decrease over the last half century. Although the two-parent family remains the most common living arrangement among children today, children are increasingly likely to spend some portion of their childhood in what have been historically considered "non-traditional" family forms.

The label "non-traditional" is somewhat of a misnomer as families have always been complex social structures with substantial variation. Since the mid to late 1800s, the nuclear family—heterosexual husband and wife with children where the husband works and the wife stays home to take care of the children—came to be seen as the ideal. The nuclear family model was never universal due to factors like maternal mortality and higher death rates for all individuals. Even so, by the middle of the twentieth century, the nuclear family had taken hold and came to be considered as the cultural standard against which all other families were then compared (Coontz, 1992). As a result, a heterosexual, two-parent household is considered "traditional" while any other family structure is now considered non-traditional. In this chapter, we focus on non-traditional Mormon families with the recognition that most if not all of these family structures have long existed; likewise, we are not making a normative evaluation about whether traditional families are preferred over non-traditional families.

To explore family structure among Mormons, we draw upon two data sources: the General Social Survey (GSS) and the American Community Survey (ACS). The GSS is a nationally representative survey of non-institutionalized Americans that is conducted every other year by the National Opinion Research Center. Each wave of the GSS contains between 2,000 and 5,000 participants from across the United States. There are several advantages to using the GSS, including its very high response rates (over 70 percent) and the detailed questions that are included. Of relevance to this chapter, the GSS includes questions about: religious affiliation, marital status, number of people in a household, total number of children, gender, and sexual identity, all of which are required to explore non-traditional families among Mormons. The primary limitation is that the number of Mormons in any given wave of the GSS is relatively small, which necessitates aggregating Mormons across waves of the GSS in order to have sufficiently large numbers to analyze them.

The GSS has been fielded consistently since 1972, with data gathered roughly every other year. During that time (1972–2018), a total of 764 Mormons have participated in the survey. Recognizing that Mormons in the 1970s are unlikely to look exactly like Mormons in the early twenty-first century, for most of our analyses we have separated the Mormon respondents into those who participated in the GSS prior to 2000 (n = 464) and those who have participated from 2000 on (n = 300). These are not extremely large samples, which means it can be challenging to get at fine-grained details as there are often just too few cases to make meaningful generalizations. Even so, the data are sufficient to present a general understanding of non-traditional families among Mormons in the U.S.

The ACS is a continuous survey project by the U.S. Census Bureau. Each year, data from over 3 million people (roughly 1 percent of the U.S. population) and 1.5 million households is gathered. The samples are very large but do not include substantial depth. The ACS includes key questions related to families, like household size, number of children in the household, household type (cohabiting, same-sex, married, single-parent, etc.), and work status. However, the ACS does not include questions about religiosity. As a result, the ACS cannot speak specifically to the characteristics of Mormon families. While not perfect, ACS data for the state of Utah can be used as a proxy for Mormons since members of the LDS Church make up more than 60 percent of the state's population (Phillips, 2018). In the most recently available ACS data for the state of Utah (2017), 56,380 households were surveyed, which included 147,655 Utahans (roughly 4.7 percent of the population).

Combined, the GSS and ACS can provide insights into the structure of Mormon families. As we have noted, the ACS is a very large sample, but lacks important details. The GSS, on the other hand, is a relatively small sample of Mormons, but includes far more questions, allowing for greater depth of analysis. The two data sets complement each other, compensating for the other's weaknesses. For this reason, we use both throughout this chapter to explore non-traditional Mormon families.

We begin by simply noting the breakdown of marital statuses of Mormons and non-Mormons and of the U.S. and Utah in the two surveys, as shown in Table 24.1. In 2017, 53.8 percent of Americans 18 and older were married; 26.5 percent had never married. In Utah,

Table 24.1 Current marital status of adults (18+) in the U.S., in Utah, and of Mormons and non-Mormons

Dataset	Year		Married	Widowed	Divorced	Separated	Never Married
ACS							
	2017	Utah	63.7%	4.3%	8.8%	1.3%	21.9%
	2017	U.S.	53.8%	6.7%	11.3%	1.8%	26.5%
GSS							
	1972–1999	Mormon	71.3%	6.8%	7.5%	0.8%	13.4%
	1972–1999	Non-Mormon	57.0%	10.4%	10.8%	3.5%	18.3%
	2000–2018	Mormon	61.3%	8.0%	13.3%	2.0%	15.3%
	2000–2018	Non-Mormon	46.0%	8.5%	16.1%	3.5%	26.0%

almost 10 percent more adults (63.7 percent) were married and fewer (21.9 percent) had never married. A similar pattern is found using the GSS. From 2000–2018, 61.3 percent of Mormons were married; 15.3 percent had never married. For non-Mormons in the same time period, 46.0 percent were married and 26.0 percent had never married.

Background section on Mormon families

The idea of family has been an important part of Mormon thought and doctrine since the very beginnings of the religion (Buerger, 1994; Bushman, 2007; Bowman, 2012). Unlike many other Protestant denominations, the LDS Church teaches that families are eternal, surviving into the afterlife (Howard, 2003). This doctrine was introduced by the founder of the religion, Joseph Smith, Jr., and played an important role in the early religion by helping to create a strong sense of community among the leaders of the religion and their family (Smith, 2011). The LDS Church is also known for its experiment with polygamous family structures in the nineteenth century (Van Wagoner, 1989), a practice the religion officially ended in 1890 (Quinn, 1998).

With the end of polygamy, the Mormon emphasis on family and marriage was clearly manifest in the higher rates of marriage among Mormons and their higher fertility rates (Heaton, 1986; Castleton and Goldscheider, 1989; Raynes, 1992; Heaton, Goodman, and Holman, 2001). Leaders of the LDS Church have taught and continue to teach that every member of the religion—with the exception of gay and lesbian individuals—has the obligation to marry and, if possible, have children (Shumway, 2004; Eyring, 2014; Sumerau and Cragun, 2015). While members of the LDS Church do not have the highest fertility rates of all religions in the U.S., they continue to have more children than the national average (Heaton, 1986; Heaton, Bahr, and Jacobson, 2005; Hostetler, 1997). As a reflection of this, Utah has a young population and has consistently had the youngest median age of any state in the U.S. (Castleton and Goldscheider, 1989; Heaton, Hirschl, and Chadwick, 1996; U.S. Census Bureau, 2019a) and, until recently, had the highest fertility rate of any state (as of 2017, it ranked second behind South Dakota, but first if Hispanic fertility is excluded; Phillips, 2018).

Given the heavy emphasis on marriage in the LDS Church, it is not surprising that members of the religion are more likely than the U.S. population, generally, to be married (Pew Research Center, 2015). The differences notwithstanding, Mormons are fairly similar to non-Mormons in the percentages who are widowed, divorced, and separated, suggesting general trends in marital formation and dissolution are also influencing Mormons.

Single-parent families and cohabitation

One of the most significant changes in family structure the U.S. has experienced in recent decades is the rise in single-parent families. Single-parent families make up the second most common living arrangement among children today, with more than one-quarter (27 percent) of children residing in this type of family structure (up from 9 percent in 1960). Although the percentage of children living in single father families increased from less than 1 percent to roughly 4 percent between 1960 and today, most single-parent families have been, and continue to be, headed by mothers (U.S. Census Bureau, 2018a).

Much of the increase in single-parent families can be attributed to two factors: nonmarital childbearing and divorce. Rates of nonmarital childbearing have increased over the past several decades. In 2017, nearly 40 percent of births occurred to unmarried women, compared to 5 percent in 1960 (Child Trends, 2018). More than half of these births, however, occurred in the context of cohabiting unions (Manning, Brown, and Stykes, 2015). Indeed, cohabitation, or "living together in an intimate sexual relationship outside of marriage" (Kroeger and Smock, 2014), has also increased rapidly in the United States and thus has become a common context in which adults and children reside (Bumpass and Lu, 2000; Bumpass and Sweet, 1989). In 1977, fewer than 1 million opposite-sex couples were cohabiting; today, more than 8 million opposite-sex couples are. During this same period, the percent of opposite-sex cohabiting unions with children increased, from 21 percent to 36 percent, respectively (U.S. Census Bureau, 2018b).

Data from the ACS illustrate that, in the state of Utah, the number of single-parent homes is similar to the percentage in the U.S. more broadly. Table 24.2 shows the different types of households in the U.S. and Utah. As noted above, just over 4 percent of U.S. households with children are headed by single fathers with no spouse or partner present and 11 percent are headed by single mothers. In Utah, 3.6 percent of households with children are headed by single fathers and 8.2 percent are headed by single mothers. More households in Utah are made up of married couples, 64.8 percent, compared to 51.0 percent in the U.S. generally. Fewer women are living alone in Utah (10.3 percent of households) than is the case nationally (15.7 percent of households). Likewise, fewer men are living alone in Utah (8.2 percent) compared to the U.S. generally (11.9 percent).

Not reflected in the previous table are rates of cohabitation. As noted, experience with cohabitation is widespread, with three-quarters of women aged 30 to 34 reporting having ever cohabited (Manning and Stykes, 2015). Although many single young women today express stronger expectations to marry than cohabit, most expect to cohabit with their future spouse (Manning, Smock, and Fettro, 2019). Indeed, cohabitation as a precursor to marriage has increased, with the share of women who cohabited with their spouse prior to marriage growing from 40 percent in the early 1980s to 70 percent in 2010–2014 (Hemez and Manning, 2017). Table 24.3 shows that about 6 percent of households in the U.S. are made up of cohabiting couples. The corresponding percentage in Utah is about 4 percent of households. Although the number of adults in cohabiting relationships is on the rise, particularly among adults aged 50 and older (Pew Research Center, 2017), and young adults aged 18 to 24, who are more likely to be living with a cohabiting partner than a spouse (Gurrentz, 2018; Nugent and Daugherty, 2018), cohabiting couples remain a minority of households in the U.S. and in Utah.

Also shown in Table 24.3 is the mean number of children in cohabiting households. Cohabiting heterosexual couples in Utah are more likely to have children than are cohabiting heterosexual couples in the U.S. generally. The average male-headed heterosexual cohabiting household in Utah has 0.69 children while the average for the U.S. generally is 0.52. Likewise,

Table 24.2 Household types in Utah and the U.S., 2017 (ACS)

	Utah	U.S.
	(*n* = 47,592)	(*n* = 1,243,840)
Married couple	64.81%	50.97%
Single father	3.60%	4.29%
Single mother	8.22%	11.09%
Male householder living alone	8.22%	11.88%
Male householder not living alone	2.61%	3.29%
Female householder living alone	10.31%	15.66%
Female householder not living alone	2.22%	2.83%

Table 24.3 Cohabiting households in Utah and the U.S. and mean number of children, 2017 (ACS)

	Utah (n = 47,592)		U.S. (n = 1,243,840)	
	%	mean # of children	%	mean # of children
Married and single households	96.34%	0.84	94.31%	0.45
Male householder, male partner	0.11%	0.02	0.17%	0.06
Male householder, female partner	1.74%	0.69	2.65%	0.52
Female householder, female partner	0.16%	0.32	0.17%	0.24
Female householder, male partner	1.66%	0.72	2.71%	0.65

female-headed cohabiting heterosexual households in Utah have a slightly higher number of children, 0.72, than do female-headed cohabiting heterosexual households in the U.S. generally, 0.65.

Another type of family structure that some might consider to be non-traditional is couples without children. Although the share of women in the U.S. without children has declined over the last few decades, in 2016, roughly 14 percent of women aged 40 to 44 had not given birth to any children (down from 20 percent in 2006, and up from 10 percent in 1976; Pew Research Center, 2018). Table 24.4, using data from the GSS, shows the percentages of each marital status category who do not have children by time period and whether or not they are Mormon. Married Mormons are slightly less likely than married non-Mormons to have no children, as are widowed Mormons (compared to widowed non-Mormons) in both time periods. However, in 2000–2018, never married Mormons are more likely than never married non-Mormons to have no children (80.4 percent versus 68.1 percent, respectively), suggesting that the rates of having children without being married or while cohabiting are lower among Mormons than they are among non-Mormons. Even so, close to 20 percent of never married Mormons report having a child.

Divorce

Also contributing to the increase in single-parent families is divorce. Rising divorce rates in the 1970s and 1980s meant that by 2010, nearly half of marriages ended in divorce or separation (Kennedy and Ruggles, 2014). Moreover, as divorce rates climbed during the second half of the

Table 24.4 Percentage of GSS respondents with no children by religion and marital status

		Married	Widowed	Divorced	Separated	Never Married
1972–1999						
	Mormon	11.2%	3.1%	17.1%	0.0%	91.9%
	Non-Mormon	14.0%	15.1%	17.9%	10.8%	83.6%
2000–2018						
	Mormon	11.4%	0.0%	17.5%	16.7%	80.4%
	Non-Mormon	13.8%	9.3%	16.1%	10.7%	68.1%

twentieth century, so did the share of children who resided in stepfamilies (Cherlin, 2010; Stewart, 2007). Determining the exact number of children living in stepfamilies is difficult to estimate, however, due to variations in definitions. Although stepfamilies have traditionally been defined as consisting of two married adults with stepchildren living in the household, many researchers have broadened this definition to incorporate stepfamilies that are formed through a variety of pathways, such as two-parent families formed via cohabitation (Brown, Manning, and Stykes, 2015; Stewart, 2007; Sweeney, 2010). Recent research indicates that an estimated 9 percent of children resided in a stepfamily in 2016, with 55 percent of those children (or 4.9 percent of all children) living in a married stepparent family (i.e., with a biological parent and their spouse), and 45 percent of those children (or 4 percent of all children) living in a cohabiting stepparent family (i.e., with a biological parent and their cohabiting partner; see Eickmeyer, 2017).

As noted in Table 24.1 above, Mormons are slightly less likely to be divorced than are non-Mormons. However, Table 24.1 is somewhat deceptive as it shows only an individual's current marital status. In effect, it hides whether individuals have ever divorced as someone could marry, divorce, and then remarry and, when asked their marital status, they could simply report that they are married without having to indicate that they have divorced in the past. Both the GSS and the ACS have attempted to address this issue. The GSS asked individuals who are currently married or widowed if they had ever divorced. Table 24.5 shows that Mormons are slightly less likely to have ever divorced than are non-Mormons in the U.S. In the 2000–2018 waves of the GSS, 20.2 percent of currently married Mormons had divorced, compared to 24.5 percent of currently married non-Mormons.

The ACS takes a different approach to capturing whether individuals have been divorced or married before with two questions. The ACS asked participants who reported their marital status as married, widowed, divorced, or separated, if they had divorced in the last 12 months. In both Utah and the U.S. in 2017, roughly 1 percent of individuals said that they had. The ACS also included a question asking how many times those who reported their marital status as married, widowed, divorced, or separated had been married. The results are shown in Table 24.6. Utahans are slightly less likely to have married more than once than is the case in the U.S. generally; 16.66 percent have married twice and 5.60 percent have married three times, compared to 19.70 percent and 5.74 percent in the U.S., respectively.

What Tables 24.5 and 24.6 suggest is that Mormons may be slightly less likely to divorce than are non-Mormons, but they are more likely to remarry (probably instead of cohabiting; Brown et al., 2019). As a result, looking just at the marital status of Mormons is somewhat deceptive as it hides the percentage of individuals who have ever divorced and the number of times such individuals have married, showing only their current marital status.

Table 24.5 Percentage of GSS respondents who have divorced by year, religion, and marital status

		Married	*Widowed*
1972–1999			
	Mormon	17.1%	40.6%
	Non-Mormon	18.2%	18.9%
2000–2018			
	Mormon	20.2%	25.0%
	Non-Mormon	24.5%	26.8%

Table 24.6 Number of marriages in Utah and the U.S., 2017 (ACS)

	Utah	U.S.
	(n = 80,942)	(n = 1,860,810)
One time	77.70%	74.50%
Two times	16.66%	19.70%
Three or more times	5.60%	5.74%

Same-sex couples

The number of same-sex couple households has grown over the past two decades. The U.S. Census Bureau estimates that in 2017, there were over 935,000 same-sex couple households, compared to just over 581,000 in 2009. Furthermore, 59 percent of these same-sex couple households today consist of married partners, compared to 26 percent of same-sex couple households in 2009 (U.S. Census Bureau, 2017a), thanks to the change in U.S. law in 2015 legalizing same-sex marriage nationwide. Many of these same-sex couple households include children: about 16 percent of same-sex cohabiting or married couples in the U.S. have biological, adoptive, or stepchildren under age 18 living with them (9 percent of male couples and 24 percent of female couples; U.S. Census Bureau, 2017b).

Given the LDS Church's fraught relationship with non-heterosexual individuals (Phillips, 2004; Sumerau and Cragun, 2014; Dehlin et al, 2015a; Dehlin, et al., 2015b), it's not surprising that very few individuals report that they are gay, lesbian, or bisexual (LGB) and also Mormon (Riess, 2019). The GSS began asking participants their sexual identity in 2008. Since then, just two individuals have reported being gay or lesbian and Mormon. Two other questions in the GSS asked since 1989 make it possible to determine whether a participant is sexually active with individuals of the same-sex by asking the number of male and female sexual partners they have had since age 18. Of the 230 Mormon women who have participated in the GSS since then, just eight (3 percent) reported same-sex sexual activity. Of the 153 Mormon men who have participated in the GSS since 1989, just seven (4.5 percent) reported same-sex sexual activity. These numbers are so small that it's impossible to conduct any meaningful analysis of them.

The ACS does include an estimate of the number of same-sex households. Cohabiting same-sex couples are shown in Table 24.3 above. In Utah, 0.11 percent of households were male same-sex cohabiting households, compared to 0.17 percent in the U.S. generally. The corresponding numbers for female same-sex cohabiting households were 0.16 percent in Utah and 0.17 percent in the U.S. generally. Per the ACS (and not shown in one of our tables), married same-sex households in Utah make up 0.37 percent of all households, which is slightly lower than in the U.S. generally, where same-sex households make up 0.49 percent of households. Collectively, then, same-sex households, both married and cohabiting, make up less than 1 percent of households in both Utah and the U.S.

Non-traditional work arrangements

One additional component to the make up of traditional families is labor force participation. In the nuclear family, only the husband works outside the home while the wife tends the home and takes care of the children. This ideal is what is taught by leaders of the LDS Church, though they recognize that there may be exceptions (The Church of Jesus Christ of Latter-day Saints,

1995). Yet, according to the latest data, the ideal is more of an exception as only about one-third of Mormon households in the U.S. have men working while women are out of the labor force (i.e., either going to school, retired, or taking care of the home), as shown in Table 24.7. Among non-Mormons, this is closer to 26 percent or 27 percent in the GSS, but across the entire U.S. in 2017 it was just 20.8 percent.

Unlike the other tables included in this chapter, in Table 24.7, all Mormons in the GSS (1972–2018) are included because of the numerous categories and small numbers. As a result, the GSS data underestimate current women's labor force participation, which has increased substantially since the 1970s (U.S. Department of Labor, n.d.). Table 24.7 illustrates that Mormons are not dramatically different from non-Mormons in their labor force participation. Close to one-third of Mormon households have both the husband and wife working whereas this percentage is closer to 44 percent among non-Mormons and close to 47 percent in ACS data (in both Utah and the U.S.).

Also of note in Table 24.7 is the inverse of the nuclear family work arrangement—households in which women are working while men are not in the labor force (i.e., either retired, going to school, or tending the home). In the GSS, between 5 percent and 6 percent of Mormon households had women working while men were out of the labor force, a number that was slightly higher than among non-Mormons in the GSS. According to 2017 ACS data, 5.86 percent of households in Utah had such an arrangement, while 8.26 percent of households nationally had the wife working while the husband was not in the workforce.

Discussion

While leaders of the LDS Church continue to urge members of the religion to marry, have children, and have women stay home to take care of the house and children (Eyring, 2014; The Church of Jesus Christ of Latter-day Saints, 1995), the data included in this chapter illustrate that a minority of Mormons are able to manage such an arrangement. In fact, of the 300 Mormons who participated in the GSS since 2000, 19.7 percent (59) are heterosexual, married individuals with children where the woman tends home and the man is either working full-time, part-time, retired, or temporarily unemployed. Given the relatively small number of Mormons in the GSS, this estimate is problematic. However, it does align with data from the U.S. as a whole that shows that only 23 percent of American households are now made up of heterosexual couples with children where the husband works outside the home and the wife takes care of the home (U.S. Census Bureau, 2018c). Assuming these estimates are accurate, somewhere between 20 and 25 percent of Mormon households align with the ideal family arrangement encouraged by LDS Church leaders, the nuclear family.

A number of forces have combined to force Mormons away from the breadwinner-homemaker model. Women's labor force participation increased during World War II, fell for a while after the war when they were forced out of the workforce, but began to increase starting in the 1950s with rapid growth thereafter. Today, a majority of women in the U.S., including women with children, work outside the home (U.S. Bureau of Labor Statistics, 2019). Women's mass entry into paid employment at the turn of the twentieth century occurred in response to broader economic and demographic trends (Coontz, 1992; Oppenheimer, 1973). With relatively stagnant male wages when adjusted for inflation since the 1970s (Moseley, 2013), women have entered the workforce in very large numbers in order to increase household incomes. Moreover, the shift from manufacturing to service occupations created a greater demand for female labor (Oppenheimer, 1973).

Women's labor force participation led to a greater degree of autonomy and less reliance on men. Coupled with less punitive divorce laws, women's greater autonomy contributed to higher

Table 24.7 Work status of participants and spouses, Mormons and non-Mormons in GSS and Utah and U.S. in ACS

	GSS (1972–2018)				ACS	
	Mormon		Non-Mormon			
	Females	Males	Females	Males	Utah	U.S.
Husband and wife in labor force, both employed	35.00%	32.90%	44.30%	44.20%	47.25%	46.68%
Husband and wife in labor force, wife unemployed	2.80%	1.70%	2.30%	2.60%	1.04%	1.28%
Husband in labor force, wife not, husband employed	33.20%	35.50%	27.50%	26.60%	28.77%	20.82%
Husband and wife in labor force, husband unemployed, wife employed	2.10%	1.70%	2.50%	2.60%	0.91%	1.04%
Husband and wife in labor force, both unemployed	0.00%	0.40%	0.60%	0.60%	0.09%	0.10%
Husband in labor force, wife not, husband unemployed	2.50%	3.10%	2.00%	2.10%	0.40%	0.42%
Husband not in labor force, wife in labor force and employed	6.40%	4.80%	4.20%	4.60%	5.86%	8.26%
Husband not in labor force, wife in labor force and unemployed	0.40%	0.80%	0.30%	0.10%	0.13%	0.21%
Neither in labor force	11.00%	16.40%	13.10%	14.80%	15.54%	21.19%
Total	93.40%	97.30%	96.80%	98.20%	100.00%	100.00%

Note: GSS numbers do not total 100% as there are additional possible job combinations not shown.

rates of divorce as they were able to leave abusive and domineering men (Schoen et al., 2002). Economic shifts, including an increased reliance on technological and skilled labor, have also spurred an increase in college enrollment. Currently, over one-third (37 percent) of 25-to-29-year-olds have completed four or more years of college, up from 8 percent in 1950 (U.S. Census Bureau, 2019b). This increase in college enrollment has lengthened the amount of time it takes to achieve financial independence (Tillman, Brewster, and Holway, 2019), which many Americans consider to be a prerequisite for marriage (Cherlin, 2010). Thus, it is not surprising that median age at first marriage has increased since the 1950s (U.S. Census Bureau, 2018d). The share of never married Americans has also increased during this time as well as the proportion of individuals who are living alone (U.S. Census Bureau, 2018e).

While Mormons have resisted these forces more than many other groups in the U.S., these forces have also influenced Mormons. The majority of Mormon women work (Phillips et al., 2011). Divorce rates among Mormons are close to the same as those for non-Mormons (see above). The average age at first marriage has increased among Mormons just as it has across the U.S. and more Mormons are living alone (Heaton, Bahr, and Jacobson, 2005; Phillips, 2018). Fertility rates have declined among Mormons as well (Phillips et al., 2011; Phillips, 2018). While Mormon families are still somewhat different from non-Mormons in the U.S., they are growing increasingly similar and a smaller and smaller percentage fits the ideal advocated by leaders of the LDS Church.

In two ways, Mormon families are not following broader social trends in the U.S. Because of the continued antipathy against lesbian, gay, and bisexual individuals by the leaders of the LDS Church, very few such individuals remain Mormon (Dehlin et al, 2015a; Dehlin et al., 2015b; Riess, 2019). The growth in the number of same-sex households that has occurred in the U.S. has not followed suit among members of the LDS Church. Likewise, while there has been some increase in cohabitation among members of the LDS Church, pressure to not engage in pre-marital sex has led to lower rates of cohabitation among Mormons compared to the U.S. population generally.

Some might hope that Mormon resistance on same-sex marriage and cohabitation means that there is hope for the traditional family yet. We are more skeptical because of the forces that are driving changes to the traditional family. As noted, the increase in women's labor force participation was largely driven by economic forces, as are lower fertility rates and delaying marriage. Without a dramatic shift in the economy that once again pays men a salary that allows families to live comfortably on a single income, it is highly unlikely that women will leave the labor force. While there is recent evidence that gender equality may lead to different aspirations for men and women (Falk and Hermle, 2018), without radical reforms, lower levels of economic inequality do not appear to be on the horizon and neither does an increase in traditional and nuclear family arrangements.

Ironically, LDS Church leaders are working against themselves on this front. The LDS Church's advocacy for conservative social and political ideas and the alignment of most Mormons with the Republican Party in the U.S. (Campbell, Green, and Monson, 2014) have resulted in Mormons and the LDS Church leadership supporting conservative economic policies that contribute to economic inequality. For instance, the leadership of the LDS Church has formally stated that it prefers private healthcare options, supports minimal government responsibility for healthcare (only for the poor), and encourages individual responsibility in health insurance (The Church of Jesus Christ of Latter-day Saints, 2014). Mormons are also substantially more likely to prefer smaller government with fewer services (75 percent) than are Americans in general (48 percent; see Pew Forum on Religion, 2012). Both universal healthcare and more government services are associated with lower economic inequality (Moseley, 2013). Whether intentional or not, LDS Church leadership and members of the religion support policies that increase economic inequality. Given that economic inequality is the primary factor leading to non-traditional family structures among heterosexuals in the U.S., LDS Church leaders are actually contributing to the claimed "breakdown" of the family that they so strongly oppose (Eyring, 2014). If leaders of the LDS Church want more individuals to be able to live comfortably in a two-parent household with children where the wife stays home, it would make more sense for them to advocate for political policies that reduce economic inequality rather than increase it (Falk and Hermle, 2018).

It may also make sense for leaders of the LDS Church to think about their messaging concerning families. Given the growth of non-traditional families in the U.S. generally and among Mormons specifically, it may make the religion more welcoming to non-traditional families if leaders of the religion began to recognize that the nuclear family is uncommon and need not be held up as the ideal. Divorce and remarriage are now pervasive and, at times, warranted (Schoen et al., 2002; Nason-Clark and Kroeger, 2004). Some women want to work outside the home (though, as noted, most work due to economic pressure; Coontz, 1992; Moseley, 2013). Young people are delaying marriage and childbirth while they get established in their careers (Muraco and Curran, 2012). None of these factors run counter to the values taught by the leaders of the religion. While changing Mormon policies concerning pre-marital sex and sexual identity would be more challenging, changing the conversation regarding divorce, smaller family sizes or having no children at all, women working outside the home, and young people delaying marriage are well within current policies, practices, and values. All that would really be needed is a shift in framing by leaders of the religion.

Conclusion

Broader social forces, particularly economic forces, have led to substantial shifts in family structures in the U.S. These forces have also led to changes in Mormon families. Mormons are about as likely to divorce as are non-Mormons but more likely to remarry. Mormon women are slightly less likely to work outside of the home than are non-Mormon women, but the majority of Mormon women now work outside the home. Fertility rates have declined among Mormons and an increasing percentage of Mormon young people are living alone and delaying the age at which they marry. Mormons are still less likely to cohabit than are Americans in general and very few lesbian, gay, or bisexual individuals remain in the LDS Church. All of this has resulted in the traditional, nuclear family now being a minority family arrangement among Mormons.

References

Bowman, M.B., 2012. *The Mormon People: The Making of an American Faith*. New York: Random House.
Brown, S.L., Manning, W.D., and Stykes, J.B., 2015. Family Structure and Child Well-Bring: Integrating Family Complexity. *Journal of Marriage and Family* 77(1): 177–90. doi: 10.1111/jomf.12145.
Brown, S.L., Lin, I.F., Hammersmith, A.M., and Wright, M.R., 2019. Repartnering Following Gray Divorce: The Roles of Resources and Constraints for Women and Men. *Demography* 56(2): 503–23. doi: 10.1007/s13524-018-0752-x.
Buerger, D.J., 1994. *The Mysteries of Godliness: A History of Mormon Temple Worship*. Salt Lake City, UT: Signature Books.
Bumpass, L., and Lu, H.-H., 2000. Trends in Cohabitation and Implications for Children's Family Contexts in the United States. *Population Studies* 54(1): 29–41.
Bumpass, L., and Sweet, J., 1989. National Estimates of Cohabitation. *Demography* 26(4): 615–25. doi: 10.2307/2061261.
Bushman, R.L., 2007. *Joseph Smith: Rough Stone Rolling*. New York: Vintage.

Campbell, D.E., Green, J.C., and Monson, J.Q., 2014. *Seeking the Promised Land: Mormons and American Politics*. New York: Cambridge University Press.

Castleton, A., and Goldscheider, F.K., 1989. Are Mormon Families Different? Household Structure and Family Patterns. In F.K. Goldscheider and C. Goldscheider, eds. *Ethnicity and the New Family Economy*. Boulder, CA, San Francisco, CA, and London: Westview Press, pp. 93–107.

Cherlin, A.J., 2010. *The Marriage-Go-Round: The State of Marriage and the Family in America Today*. New York: Vintage Books.

Child Trends, 2018. Births to Unmarried Women. www.childtrends.org/indicators/births-to-unmarried-women (accessed May 28, 2019).

The Church of Jesus Christ of Latter-day Saints, 1995. The Family: A Proclamation to the World. www.lds.org/topics/family-proclamation?lang=eng&old=true.

The Church of Jesus Christ of Latter-day Saints, 2014. Church Encourages Principled Approach to Health Care Coverage for Needy Utahns. https://newsroom.churchofjesuschrist.org/article/church-encour-ages-principled-approach-health-care-coverage-needy-utahns.

Coontz, S., 1992. *The Way We Never Were: American Families and the Nostalgia Trap*. New York: Basic Books.

Dehlin, J.P., Galliher, R.V., Bradshaw, W.S., and Crowell, K.A., 2015a. Navigating Sexual and Religious Identity Conflict: A Mormon Perspective. *Identity* 15(1): 1–22. doi: 10.1080/15283488.2014.989440.

Dehlin, J.P., Galliher, R.V., Bradshaw, W.S., Hyde, D.C., et al., 2015b. Sexual Orientation Change Efforts among Current or Former LDS Church Members. *Journal of Counseling Psychology* 62(2): 95–105. doi: http://dx.doi.org.esearch.ut.edu/10.1037/cou0000011.

Eickmeyer, K.J., 2017. American Children's Family Structure: Stepfamilies. www.bgsu.edu/ncfmr/resources/data/family-profiles/eickmeyer-stepparent-families-fp-17-16.html (accessed May 29, 2019).

Eyring, H.B., 2014. To Become as One. The Complementarity of Man and Woman: An International Interreligious Colloquium. Vatican City, Rome, November 18. www.lds.org/prophets-and-apostles/unto-all-the-world/renaissance-of-marriage?lang=eng (accessed May 24, 2019).

Falk, A., and Hermle, J., 2018. Relationship of gender differences in preferences to economic development and gender equality. *Science* 362(6412), p. eaas9899. doi: 10.1126/science.aas9899.

Gurrentz, B., 2018. Living with an Unmarried Partner Now Common for Young Adults. www.census.gov/library/stories/2018/11/cohabitaiton-is-up-marriage-is-down-for-young-adults.html (accessed May 29, 2019).

Heaton, T.B., 1986. How Does Religion Influence Fertility, the Case of Mormons. *Journal for the Scientific Study of Religion* 25(2): 243–58.

Heaton, T.B., Bahr, S.J., and Jacobson, C.K., 2005. *A Statistical Profile of Mormons: Health, Wealth, and Social Life*. Lewiston, NY: Edwin Mellen Press.

Heaton, T.B., Goodman, K.L., and Holman, T.B., 2001. In Search of a Peculiar People: Are Mormon Families Really Different? In M. Cornwall, T.B. Heaton, and L.A. Young, eds. *Contemporary Mormonism: Social Science Perspectives*. Urbana, IL: University of Illinois Press, pp. 87–117.

Heaton, T.B., Hirschl, T.A., and Chadwick, B.A., 1996. *Utah in the 1990s: A Demographic Perspective*. Salt Lake City, UT: Signature Books.

Hemez, P., and Manning, W.D., 2017. Thirty Years of Change in Women's Premarital Cohabitation Experience. https://scholarworks.bgsu.edu/cgi/viewcontent.cgi?article=1033&context=ncfmr_family_profiles (accessed May 29, 2019).

Hostetler, J.A., 1997. *Hutterite Society*. Baltimore, MD: Johns Hopkins University Press.

Howard, F.B., 2003. Eternal Marriage. *Ensign*. www.lds.org/study/ensign/2003/05/eternal-marriage?lang=eng (accessed May 24, 2019).

Kennedy, S., and Ruggles, S., 2014. Breaking Up Is Hard to Count: The Rise of Divorce in the United States, 1980–2010. *Demography* 51(2): 587–98.

Kroeger, R.A., and Smock, P.J., 2014. Cohabitation: Recent Research and Implications. In J.K. Treas, J. Scott, and M. Richards, eds. *The Wiley-Blackwell Companion to the Sociology of Families*. New York: Wiley-Blackwell, pp. 217–35.

Manning, W.D., Brown, S.L., and Stykes, B., 2015. Trends in Births to Single and Cohabiting Mothers, 1980–2013 (FP-15-03). www.bgsu.edu/content/dam/BGSU/college-of-arts-and-sciences/NCFMR/documents/FP/FP-15-03-birth-trends-single-cohabiting-moms.pdf (accessed May 29, 2019).

Manning, W.D., Smock, P.J., and Fettro, M.N., 2019. Cohabitation and Marital Expectations among Single Millennials in the U.S. *Population Research and Policy Review* 38(3): 327–46. doi: https://doi.org/10.1007/s11113-018-09509-8.

Manning, W.D., and Stykes, B., 2015. Twenty-five Years of Change in Cohabitation in the U.S., 1987–2013 (FP-15–01). www.bgsu.edu/content/dam/BGSU/college-of-arts-and-sciences/NCFMR/documents/FP/FP-15-01-twenty-five-yrs-cohab-us.pdf (accessed May 29, 2019).

Moseley, F., 2013. The U.S. Economic Crisis: From a Profitability Crisis to an Overindebtedness Crisis. *Review of Radical Political Economics* 45(4): 472–77. doi: 10.1177/0486613412475187.

Muraco, J.A., and Curran, M.A., 2012. Associations between Marital Meaning and Reasons to Delay Marriage for Young Adults in Romantic Relationships. *Marriage & Family Review* 48(3): 227–47. doi: 10.1080/01494929.2012.665013.

Nason-Clark, N., and Kroeger, C.C., 2004. *Refuge from Abuse: Healing and Hope for Abused Christian Women.* Downers Grove, IL: InterVarsity Press.

Nugent, C.N., and Daugherty, J., 2018. A Demographic, Attitudinal, and Behavioral Profile of Cohabiting Adults in the United States, 2011–2015. National Health Statistics Reports, no. 11, National Center for Health Statistics, Hyattsville, MD.

Oppenheimer, V.K., 1973. Demographic Influence on Female Employment and the Status of Women. *American Journal of Sociology* 78(4): 946–61.

Pew Forum on Religion and Public Life, 2012. *Mormons in America: Certain in Their Beliefs, Uncertain of Their Place in Society.* Washington, DC: The Pew Forum on Religion & Public Life, p. 125.

Pew Research Center, 2015. Mormons More Likely to Marry, Have More Children Than Other U.S. Religious Groups. www.pewresearch.org/fact-tank/2015/05/22/mormons-more-likely-to-marry-have-more-children-than-other-u-s-religious-groups/ (accessed May 29, 2019).

Pew Research Center, 2017. Number of U.S. Adults Cohabiting with a Partner Continues to Rise, Especially among Those 50 and Older. www.pewresearch.org/fact-tank/2017/04/06/number-of-u-s-adults-cohabiting-with-a-partner-continues-to-rise-especially-among-those-50-and-older/ (accessed May 29, 2019).

Pew Research Center, 2018. They're Waiting Longer, but U.S. Women Today More Likely to Have Children Than a Decade Ago. www.pewsocialtrends.org/2018/01/18/theyre-waiting-longer-but-u-s-women-today-more-likely-to-have-children-than-a-decade-ago/ (accessed May 29, 2019).

Phillips, R., 2004. *Conservative Christian Identity and Same-Sex Orientation: The Case of Gay Mormons.* New York: Peter Lang.

Phillips, R., 2018. Demography and Information Technology Affect Religious Commitment among Latter-day Saints in Utah and the Intermountain West. *The Journal of the Utah Academy of Sciences, Arts, & Letters* 95: 317–32.

Phillips, R. et al., 2011. *Mormons in the United States 1990–2008: Socio-demographic Trends and Regional Differences.* Hartford, CT: Institute for the Study of Secularism in Society and Culture.

Quinn, D.M., 1998. Plural Marriage and Mormon Fundamentalism. *Dialogue: A Journal of Mormon Thought* 31(2): 1–68.

Raynes, M., 1992. Mormon Marriages in an American Context. In M.U. Beecher and L.F. Anderson, eds. *Sisters in Spirit: Mormon Women in Historical and Cultural Perspective.* Urbana, IL: University of Illinois Press, pp. 227–48.

Riess, J., 2019. *The Next Mormons: How Millennials Are Changing the LDS Church.* New York: Oxford University Press.

Schoen, R., Astone, N.M., Rothert, K., Standish, N.K., and Kim, Y.J., 2002. Women's Employment, Marital Happiness, and Divorce. *Social Forces* 81(2): 643–62. doi: 10.1353/sof.2003.0019.

Shumway, W.D., 2004. Marriage and Family: Our Sacred Responsibility. *Ensign.* www.lds.org/study/ensign/2004/05/marriage-and-family-our-sacred-responsibility?lang=eng (accessed May 24, 2019).

Smith, G.D., 2011. *Nauvoo Polygamy: "... But We Called It Celestial Marriage."* 2nd updated ed. Salt Lake City, UT: Signature Books.

Stewart, S.D., 2007. *Brave New Stepfamilies: Diverse Paths Toward Stepfamily Living.* Thousand Oaks, CA: Sage.

Sumerau, J.E., and Cragun, R.T., 2014. "Why Would Our Heavenly Father Do that to Anyone": Oppressive Othering through Sexual Classification Schemes in the Church of Jesus Christ of Latter-Day Saints. *Symbolic Interaction* 37(3): 331–52. doi: 10.1002/SYMB.105.

Sumerau, J.E., and Cragun, R.T., 2015. The Hallmarks of Righteous Women: Gendered Background Expectations in the Church of Jesus Christ of Latter-Day Saints. *Sociology of Religion* 76(1): 49–71. doi: 10.1093/socrel/sru040.

Sweeney, M.M., 2010. Remarriage and Stepfamilies: Strategic Sites for Family Scholarship in the 21st Century. *Journal of Marriage and Family* 72(3): 667–84. doi: 10.1111/j.1741-3737.2010.00724.x.

Tillman, K.H., Brewster, K.L., and Holway, G.V., 2019. Sexual and Romantic Relationships in Young Adulthood. *Annual Review of Sociology*. doi: https://doi.org/10.1146/annurev-soc-073018-022625.

U.S. Bureau of Labor Statistics, 2019. Labor Force Statistics from the Current Population Survey. www.bls.gov/web/empsit/cpseea03.htm (accessed May 29, 2019).

U.S. Census Bureau, 2017a. Characteristics of Same-Sex Couple Households: 2005 to Present. Table 1. Estimates of Same-Sex Couple Households in the American Community Survey, by Marital Status: 2005 to 2017. Source: www2.census.gov/programs-surveys/demo/tables/same-sex/time-series/ssc-house-characteristics/ssex-hist-tables.xlsx.

U.S. Census Bureau, 2017b. Characteristics of Same-Sex Couple Households: 2005 to Present. Table 1. Household Characteristics of Opposite-Sex and Same-Sex Couple Households: 2017 American Community Survey. Source: www2.census.gov/programs-surveys/demo/tables/same-sex/time-series/ssc-house-characteristics/ssex-tables-2017.xlsx.

U.S. Census Bureau, 2018a. Historical Living Arrangements of Children. Table CH-1. Living Arrangements of Children under 18 Years Old: 1960 to Present. Source: www2.census.gov/programs-surveys/demo/tables/families/time-series/children/ch1.xls.

U.S. Census Bureau, 2018b. Historical Living Arrangements of Adults. Table UC-1. Unmarried Couples of the Opposite Sex: 1960 to Present. Source: www2.census.gov/programs-surveys/demo/tables/families/time-series/adults/uc1.xls.

U.S. Census Bureau, 2018c. Historical Families Tables. Table SHP-1. Parents and Children in Stay-at-Home Parent Family Groups: 1994 to Present. Source: www2.census.gov/programs-surveys/demo/tables/families/time-series/families/shp1.xls.

U.S. Census Bureau, 2018d. Historical Marital Status Tables. Table MS-2. Estimated Median Age at First Marriage, by Sex: 1890 to the Present. Source: www2.census.gov/programs-surveys/demo/tables/families/time-series/marital/ms2.xls.

U.S. Census Bureau, 2018e. Historical Households Tables. Table HH-4. Households by Size: 1960 to Present. Source: www2.census.gov/programs-surveys/demo/tables/families/time-series/households/hh4.xls.

U.S. Census Bureau, 2019a. American Fact Finder. https://factfinder.census.gov/faces/nav/jsf/pages/community_facts.xhtml?src=bkmk (accessed May 30, 2019).

U.S. Census Bureau, 2019b. CPS Historical Time Series Tables. Table A-2. Percent of People 25 Years and Over Who Have Completed High School or College, by Race, Hispanic Origin and Sex: Selected Years 1940 to 2018. Source: www2.census.gov/programs-surveys/demo/tables/educational-attainment/time-series/cps-historical-time-series/taba-2.xlsx.

U.S. Department of Labor, n.d. Civilian Labor Force by Sex. www.dol.gov/wb/stats/NEWSTATS/facts/women_lf.htm#CivilianLFSex (accessed May 29, 2019).

Van Wagoner, R.S., 1989. *Mormon Polygamy: A History*. Salt Lake City, UT: Signature Books.

Further reading

Heaton, T.B., 1986. How Does Religion Influence Fertility? The Case of Mormons. *Journal for the Scientific Study of Religion* 25(2): 248–58.

Heaton, T.B., Bahr, S.J., and Jacobson, C.K., 2005. *A Statistical Profile of Mormons: Health, Wealth, and Social Life*. Lewiston, NY: Edwin Mellen Press.

Heaton, T.B., Goodman, K.L., and Holman, T.B., 2001. In Search of a Peculiar People: Are Mormon Families Really Different? In M. Cornwall, T.B. Heaton, and L.A. Young, eds. *Contemporary Mormonism: Social Science Perspectives*. Urbana, IL: University of Illinois Press, pp. 87–117.

25
SOCIAL SCIENCE PERSPECTIVES ON GENDER AND MORMON ORTHODOXY

Jana Riess and Benjamin Knoll

Published in 1957, Thomas O'Dea's landmark book *The Mormons* set the standard for social science treatments of Mormonism in the second half of the twentieth century. Here for the first time was a mostly positive account of Mormon life written by an outsider and published by a respected academic press, the University of Chicago. O'Dea's treatment was a well-reasoned explanation of Mormons' history; unlike other accounts that focused on the faith's nineteenth-century origins, this book also took pains to explain the postwar growth and bureaucratic organization of the Church of Jesus Christ of Latter-day Saints. In fact, an entire chapter was devoted to "authority and government," and it is in this context that the book's sole paragraph devoted to women's experience can be found: a brief explanation of the function of the Relief Society. Beyond that, as anthropologist of gender Janet Bennion has observed, O'Dea's book had almost nothing to say about women (Bennion, 2008). It is therefore a live question to what extent this book titled *The Mormons* could indeed claim to address the slightly more than half of the Mormon people who happened to be female. (In various surveys through the years, women have been between 52 and 57 percent of the self-identified Mormon population, and men between 43 and 48 percent.)

What's more, O'Dea's interview pool failed to include a single female informant. In the 191 single-spaced pages of field notes that he and his wife Georgia compiled when conducting research in Utah in the summer of 1950, every scheduled interview was with a man, though women were sometimes present in the room (Bahr, 2008). This was a common procedure at the time; many midcentury sociologists and anthropologists based their research on male interviewees and respondents, and drew conclusions for entire societies based on what they learned from those men. Yet with the hindsight that we now have more than six decades after O'Dea's book, we can see that some of his most significant conclusions might have been very different if he had taken the time to consider gender as a fruitful category of research. He asserted, for example, that Mormons' increasing exposure to higher education could prove a source of significant tension for the religion in the future; education, he believed, would lead inevitably to liberalization (Jacobson, Hoffmann, and Heaton, 2008). This has not generally proven to be the case, as subsequent studies have demonstrated a persistent correlation between higher education and greater religious activity among Americans (Mayrl and Uecker, 2011; White, 2008). In fact, in the years following O'Dea's prophecy of potential decline, Mormonism actually enjoyed a remarkable resurgence, growing nearly 6 percent a year, on average, throughout the 1960s. We have to wonder how O'Dea's prognostication might have changed if he had consulted women, who are—as we will see in this chapter—typically more orthodox and active in the Church than men.

Gender, it turns out, is a vital factor in understanding a religious movement and its adherents, joining race, education, and other categories as something that must be discussed before we are qualified to proffer generalizations about an entire group. Just as historians of religion have challenged the absence of consideration of gender in their field—a turn made famous when Harvard historian Ann Braude demonstrated that "women's history *is* American religious history"—so too must social scientists add to their analysis of religion by exploring ways that women and men might express their faith differently (Braude, 1997). Unfortunately, social science has sometimes lagged behind other academic disciplines in paying adequate attention to gender as a category for understanding religious world views and behaviors. As sociologist Linda Woodhead has pointed out, "dominant theoretical frameworks within the Sociology of Religion often remain gender-blind"—and "gender-blind," in her analysis, is not a compliment.

> Although there has been some debate about why women, in the West at least, are more religious than men, this has largely taken place in isolation from what are still considered to be the "big" issues in the sociological analysis of religion, most notably issues concerning the growth and decline of religion in modern societies.

Writing in 2007, Woodhead noted that even at that late date we were likely to see only

> one member of a faculty working on gender, one paper in an edited collection dedicated to the topic, one stream on gender at a conference on the Sociology of Religion, and so on. The belief that attention to gender can and should inform and enrich all study of religion is not yet firmly established.
>
> *(Woodhead, 2007)*

While progress has been made since 2007, more attention needs to be paid to gender as a variable that affects religious behavior, attitudes, and outcomes.

It is our belief that gender is a fundamental category for understanding the Church of Jesus Christ of Latter-day Saints, and that both quantitative and qualitative analysis can contribute not only to our knowledge of the differences between Mormon women and men, but how Mormonism as a whole interacts with a changing culture. This chapter will therefore highlight several major sociological findings about American Mormonism and gender from recent years, organized into two common categories for discussing religion: believing and behaving. Special emphasis will be given to our own national study, the 2016 Next Mormons Survey (NMS), which included a nationally representative sample with 1,156 U.S. respondents who identified as Mormons and 540 who identified as former Mormons (total N = 1696).[1] The data of current and former Mormons is treated separately in the analyses that follow.

The demographics of Mormon women and men in the United States

Who are Mormon women in terms of race, sexual orientation, marital status, education, and employment? If we were to use the Next Mormons Survey to paint a portrait of a "typical" Mormon in terms of majority tendencies—keeping in mind the tremendous variation that exists even within those majority margins—he or she would be white, heterosexual, and married.

These tendencies hold true for both genders of Mormons. In terms of race, nearly nine in ten U.S. Mormons are white (87 percent), which is similar to findings from earlier studies, which have ranged from 85 percent white (Pew Forum, Mormons, 2014) to 91 percent white (Phillips and Cragun, 2008). Younger Mormons are a little more likely to identify as racially diverse than older ones, which reflects a national demographic shift and is true for both women and men. However, while Mormonism appears to be slowly diversifying, it is not doing so as quickly as the nation as a whole. For example, among the Millennial generation in the United States, nearly half (44 percent) are nonwhite, but this was true of only one in six (16 percent) Millennial Mormons in Pew's 2014 Religious Landscape Study, and only one in five (19 percent) of Millennial Mormons in the 2016 NMS.

Mormons' reported sexual orientation in the NMS is more in line with the nation's than its racial makeup is. About 5 percent of current Mormons say they are lesbian, gay, or bisexual, and this is the same for both women and men. Among younger Mormons, nonheterosexual orientation is slightly more common—8 percent for men and 11 percent for women, with the greatest gains coming in the category of bisexuality. This tendency for younger people to be more sexually diverse (or at least more open about it in an anonymous survey) is exactly typical of the nation of a whole, even down to the particular fact that bisexuality is the largest growth category (Gallup, 2017).

Where Mormons differ more markedly from national trends is in the percentage of adults who are married. In the NMS, two-thirds of currently-identified Mormons were married, either to their first spouse or to someone they remarried after a divorce or bereavement. While this represents a slight decline from the percentage of Mormons who were married in the early 2000s, it is still remarkably high. According to the Public Religion Research Institute, the only religious group to surpass Mormonism in its rate of married adults is Orthodox Judaism (Jones and Cox, 2016). In the NMS, roughly two of every three Mormons (whether male or female) reported being married endogamously—meaning, to someone of the same faith. Within those endogamous Mormon marriages, however, 16 percent of women say their spouse is either "not too active" or "not at all active" in the LDS Church, compared to just 9 percent of men who report this about their wives.

One interesting marital trend for both women and men is the rise of singleness, which was 12 percent in the 2007 Pew Religious Landscape Study but had grown to 19 percent when Pew repeated the RLS in 2014. The 2016 NMS similarly showed the "never-married" category to be 18 percent, or nearly one in five. So although Mormons are still outliers in the high percentage who are currently married, they also resemble national trends in the rise of single members. This has important implications for religious behavior, as the NMS shows that Mormons who are married (or remarried) are 10 points more likely to report attending church weekly than Mormons who have never been married (78 percent versus 68 percent), a pattern that holds true for both men and women.

Educationally, Mormons are largely on par with or even slightly above the achievement of other Americans, though there are gender differences. In the NMS, 38 percent of Mormon men had completed a college degree, compared to 32 percent of Mormon women. Men also were more likely to have obtained an advanced or professional postcollegiate degree. On the other hand, two-thirds of Mormon women had done at least some college (either an associate's degree or classes toward a bachelor's degree), compared to just over half of Mormon men. In general, then, Mormon women appear a bit more likely to start college than men, but less likely to complete a degree, particularly if they live in Utah, perhaps reflecting their culture's emphasis on women's role as primary caretakers of children (see also Heaton and Jacobson, 2015).

That role points to another salient demographic fact about Mormons compared to the national population: they are more likely to be parents. More than two out of every three

Mormon women in the NMS under the age of 45 have had at least one child, substantially higher than the national average, where roughly half of American women under 45 have had at least one child (Luckerson. 2015). There are indications, though, that Mormon family size is contracting. For example, in the 2007 Pew RLS, 49 percent of current Mormon respondents reported having children under the age of 18; when the survey was repeated in 2014, this had dropped to 41 percent. This is likely due to multiple factors: the slight aging of the Mormon population in the U.S. between surveys, the growing number of never-married Mormons, and a decline in the number of children Mormons are having.

In the NMS, we asked respondents to describe family size in three different ways: the number of siblings they had in their families growing up, the number of children they believe constitute the "ideal" family, and the number of children they have actually had themselves. Overall, the picture that emerges from these three data points supports the information from the RLS above. Mormon families in America, once known for being substantially larger than average, are getting smaller. While 35 percent of Mormons report having grown up in families of five or more children, just 12 percent have created such large families themselves. A growing number of Latter-day Saints now point to an "ideal" family size of two or three children, with younger adults more likely to say that zero, one, or two children is ideal (46 percent) than older Mormons are (32 percent). There are gender differences as well in that women appear to be more pronatalist than men: whereas nearly half of Mormon men say their ideal family has zero, one, or two children (48 percent), barely a third of Mormon women agree (34 percent). For women, the mean ideal family size is 3.4 children, while for men it is 2.8.

A key difference regarding children is that Mormon women are far less likely to have had their first child outside of marriage than American women as a whole; in 2017, four in ten live births in the United States were to unmarried women (CDC, 2017). Mormons typically wait until marriage to have children, but not long beyond the wedding: 2.3 years, on average, between the wedding and the birth of the first child for those whose first child was born in wedlock. In the NMS, just 11 percent of Mormon women report that their first child was born before they were married.

Finally, the demographic picture of Mormons in America includes information about employment and socioeconomic status. Mormon women are not as likely to work full-time (36 percent) as other women in America (61 percent), or when compared to Mormon men (70 percent) (BLS, 2017). But the percentage of Mormon women in the workforce has grown over time, as witnessed by the generational differences among Mormons when they reflect on their own mothers' employment status when they were growing up. Only 33 percent of Boomer/Silent Mormons say their mothers worked full-time outside the home when they were children, compared to 54 percent of Millennials. Overall, just a quarter of Millennial Mormons had mothers who did not work at all, either full- or part-time, compared to 44 percent of Mormons in the older generations. This reflects the large-scale increase in American women working outside the home in the 1980s and 1990s, when Millennials were children. It also points to an internal change in the Church itself. Historian Colleen McDannell has observed a reduction in anti-working-mother rhetoric from the General Conference pulpit when Mormonism began to succeed in winning converts in developing nations in which women working outside the home was a financial necessity, not a lifestyle choice (McDannell, 2018). In general, LDS leaders have in recent years ceased decrying the phenomenon of working mothers in their sermons and speeches, though they continue to emphasize the vital importance of women's primary role as mothers.

Believing: Mormon women as paragons of orthodoxy

"While I do not know all the Lord's reasons for giving primary responsibility for nurturing in the family to faithful sisters, I believe it has to do with your capacity to love," Henry B. Eyring of the LDS First Presidency told Mormon women and girls in the Church's October 2018 General Conference (Eyring, 2018). "As daughters of God, you have an innate and great capacity to sense the needs of others and to love. That, in turn, makes you more susceptible to the whisperings of the Spirit." Eyring stood in a long line of Mormon leaders who have used terms such as "innate" and "natural" to describe women's spirituality. "You sisters have divine attributes of sensitivity and love for things beautiful and inspiring," said Quorum member James Faust in 2005. "These are gifts you use to make our lives more pleasant" (Faust, 2005). He then complimented the sisters for dressing up their church lessons with a tablecloth and a vase of flowers, "which is a wonderful expression of your caring and conscientious nature. In contrast, when the brethren give a lesson they don't even decorate the table with so much as a shriveled dandelion!"

In Mormon sermons, it is common to hear men praise women for being closer to God, more open to the promptings of the Spirit, and more innately religious than men. Social science cannot investigate the "innate" aspect of such claims. (Are women more spiritual because they were born that way, or because a patriarchal religion has told them all their lives that they are *supposed* to be that way and applauded them when they complied?) But social science can attempt to quantify whether women do, in fact, report higher levels of religiosity and spirituality than men. In the Mormon case, it does seem to be statistically true: women are more religiously orthodox than men on many different measures of belief.

Let us consider basic testimony questions. In the NMS, these can be grouped roughly into two categories: general Christian beliefs (e.g., Jesus Christ was literally resurrected, there is life after death, God is real) and specifically Mormon ones (e.g., Joseph Smith was a prophet, the Book of Mormon is historically factual). Respondents were given a five-point scale of possibilities ranging from certain knowledge that the statement in question was true to certain knowledge that it was not. As evident in Table 25.1, women were noticeably more likely than men to choose the first option of "I am confident and know this is true." This does not mean that Mormon men are not believers; they just do not profess the same degree of theological certainty as Mormon women, particularly if they are younger.

Mormon women, then, express a greater degree of doctrinal certainty than men do, particularly on questions related to general Christian beliefs. Theological assurance is just one aspect of religious devotion, however. How do Mormon women compare in their sense of spiritual closeness to God? Once again, we see that women surpass men in their personal spirituality, though the differences are usually smaller than we saw for doctrinal certainty (Table 25.2).

These differences are not large, or at least in our view not quite enough to qualify as pedestal-worthy; Mormon women are not so spiritually elevated over Mormon men that they merit male leaders' exalted rhetoric about how women are far more naturally sensitive to the Holy Spirit than men are. It is true, though, that women are several points more likely to say they feel God's presence and love on a daily basis, are guided by God in their daily lives, and feel a deep sense of spiritual peace.

The NMS also showed that Mormon women are, in general, less troubled by controversial issues in Church history and theology than men. The NMS posed a series of fourteen such issues and asked whether respondents found them "very troubling," "a little troubling," or "not at all troubling." For example, 48 percent of Mormon men said they found it either "very troubling" or "a little troubling" that DNA evidence had not supported the Church's traditional claim that

Table 25.1 Mormon testimony statements by gender

	Men who are "confident and know this is true"	Women who are "confident and know this is true"	Delta (ordered from greatest to least difference)
Jesus Christ was literally resurrected and rose from the dead	61	76	+15
God is real	69	83	+14
There is life after death	63	76	+13
God has a plan for my life and I will be happier if I follow that plan	60	73	+13
God created Adam and Eve sometime in the last 10,000 years and humans did not evolve from other life forms	47	59	+12
Jesus Christ is the Savior of the world and died to reconcile humanity to God	68	79	+11
The LDS First Presidency members and apostles are God's prophets on the earth today	53	62	+9
The Book of Mormon is a literal, historical account	50	59	+9
Joseph Smith was a prophet of God	52	61	+9
God is an exalted person of flesh and bone	55	62	+7
God's priesthood authority is reserved only for men, not women	44	51	+7
The LDS Church is the only true faith leading to exaltation	48	53	+5
LDS temple sealings are ultimately the only way for families to be eternal	50	53	+3
The priesthood and temple ban on members of African descent was inspired of God and was God's will for the Church until 1978	37	36	–1
Average	54	63	+9

Note: This table has been reproduced from Riess (2019, p. 93). In this article, unlike in the book, half-point percentages have been rounded up to the nearest whole number.

Table 25.2 Mormon spirituality by gender

	Women	Men	Delta (ordered from greatest to least difference)
Feel God's presence and love daily	67%	57%	+10
Feel guided by God in the midst of activities or in answer to prayer daily	56%	51%	+5
Feel a deep sense of wonder and connection with the universe daily	45%	41%	+4
Feel a deep sense of spiritual peace and well-being daily	53%	50%	+3

modern-day Native Americans were the descendants of the Lamanites from the Book of Mormon; only 38 percent of women were bothered by that. Men were also more troubled by every other item in the series, as shown in Table 25.3, but to varying degrees.

Looking for patterns here, it seems that overall, a majority of Mormon men were at least a bit troubled by most of the items in the series. (Note that an admission of being troubled does not necessarily equate with agitation for change; the questions were simply about feelings and impressions, not about a desire to implement a different trajectory in the Church. Sometimes people's views are complex, even on the same issue.) Men achieved majority status for all but two of the items in the series, and in comparison to women were noticeably more troubled by historical issues like seer stones, conflicting accounts of the First Vision, and the DNA question referenced above, as well as by the Church's lack of financial transparency in how it spends tithing and donations. (The Church has not released an accounting statement to the public since 1959.)

Women, by contrast, achieved majority status on only a few items, all of which had to do with either modern-day exclusions in the Church (the priesthood/temple ban, excommunications, and LGBT rights) or polygamy/polyandry as practiced by Joseph Smith. Women were not as concerned as men about the ways the Church's teachings and practices have changed over time, or about the Mormon belief that human beings can become gods in the afterlife. Notably, they were also not as troubled as men about women not holding the priesthood, especially if they were of the Boomer and Silent generations; while a majority of younger women *were* troubled by women's lack of priesthood, older Mormon women were not.

What we can take from this is that most Mormon women appear to be strong believers in the Church's teachings and positions, as well as relatively tranquil about the messier details of its history, with the exception of polygamy and polyandry. And while we are not able to empirically assess the oft-repeated assertion by LDS Church leaders that women are more innately spiritual than men, we have seen that Mormon women are slightly more likely than Mormon men to report a daily feeling of personal closeness to God.

Behaving: gender differences in key areas of Mormons' religious practice

In addition to belief, behavior is a key area in which to understand the depth of individual religiosity. In general, Mormon women shine in several aspects of religious behavior. They pray daily at a slightly higher rate than men (70 percent vs. 66 percent). They are also more likely than men to say that they read the scriptures daily (40 percent vs. 36 percent) and study scriptures

Table 25.3 Troubling issues in the Church, by gender

	Men who found this "very" or "a little" troubling	Women who found this "very" or "a little" troubling	Delta (ordered from greatest to least difference)
Church teachings and practices changing over time away from how they were originally organized under Joseph Smith	55%	41%	+14
The use of seer stones in translating the Book of Mormon	51%	39%	+12
Lack of financial transparency with tithing, donations, and spending	58%	46%	+12
DNA evidence that Native Americans do not have Middle Eastern ancestry	48%	38%	+10
The Church's emphasis on conformity and obedience	52%	43%	+9
Multiple and somewhat conflicting accounts of the First Vision	57%	48%	+9
The Church's teachings about deification (becoming like God)	54%	37%	+7
The priesthood being reserved only for men in the Church	50%	43%	+7
Denial of priesthood and temple access to members of African descent before 1978	68%	63%	+5
Excommunications of feminists, intellectuals, and activists	60%	55%	+5
The Church's positions on LGBT issues	55%	50%	+5
The Church's strong culture of political conservatism	47%	43%	+4
Joseph Smith's polygamy (sealing himself to more than one woman)	60%	57%	+3
Joseph Smith's polyandry (sealing himself to women who were already married to other men)	66%	66%	+0

and General Conference talks on Sundays (42 percent vs. 32 percent). They are particularly pious in their entertainment and dietary choices, though in church attendance we see an unexpected twist.

Mormon leaders have consistently emphasized the need for Latter-day Saints to remain "unspotted from the world" in their choices of media and entertainment: sexually graphic or violent movies, pornography, and music with explicit content are to be avoided, while "wholesome" and family-friendly media choices are encouraged (Lds.org, 2011). As Table 25.4 shows, Mormon women appear to be more scrupulous in adhering to the Church's teachings on this matter.

In the first section of Table 25.4, we see that with only one exception (live sporting events), Mormon women consumed approved media at higher rates than men, including religious

Table 25.4 Mormons and popular culture consumption in the last six months, by gender

	Women	Men	Difference
Popular culture deemed acceptable by LDS leaders			
Animated movies	65%	54%	+11
PG-13 movies	67%	58%	+9
LDS Church videos	54%	45%	+9
LDS General Conference	57%	49%	+8
Live sporting event on television or online	49%	56%	−7
Popular culture deemed unacceptable by LDS leaders			
Video games with graphic or violent content	15%	31%	−16
"Soft" pornography	8%	21%	−13
Explicit pornography	8%	16%	−8
R-rated movies	34%	40%	−6
An HBO or Showtime series	23%	31%	−8
Music with sexually explicit or profane song lyrics	22%	25%	−3
Television with a mature rating	39%	41%	−2

content. Women were eight points more likely to watch the Church's semiannual General Conference and nine points more likely to have viewed LDS videos on the Church's website or on social media. By the same token, men were more likely to have consumed non-approved media such as pornography, R-rated movies, HBO, or graphic video games, though it should be noted that a majority of Mormon men appear to avoid these things. Women, overall, appear to be doing a slightly better job of keeping the Church's standards for appropriate viewing materials.

Another area where women excel is in upholding the Church's dietary code, also known as the Word of Wisdom. Modern leaders' interpretations of the Word of Wisdom forbid consumption of alcohol, tobacco, illegal drugs, caffeinated coffee, and caffeinated tea. Just as men in the general population are slightly more likely to consume some of these substances than women in the general population, so too are Mormon men when compared to Mormon women, though of course the overall Mormon rates of consumption are generally far lower than national averages. As seen in Table 25.5, the gendered pattern in which men are more likely offenders holds true with the notable (and entertaining) exception of caffeinated soda, which the Church clarified in 2012 was *not* contrary to the Word of Wisdom (Associated Press, 2012). Nearly two-thirds of Mormon women say they have consumed caffeinated soda in the last six months (64 percent), which is a bit higher than the rate among Mormon men (60 percent).

Pop culture consumption and Word of Wisdom adherence, then, are two areas of Mormon life in which women appear to surpass men in their religious obedience. One surprise in the data was that women do *not* outshine men in their self-reported church attendance. About 71 percent of Mormon women say they attend church weekly or more, compared to 77 percent of Mormon men. Moreover, sociological research out of Brigham Young University on LDS youth in six different areas (Mexico, Great Britain, the U.S. East Coast, the U.S. Pacific Northwest, and two Utah communities) found that boys were a bit more likely than girls to attend church meetings. The researchers acknowledged that this was a surprising finding given that girls scored higher on other indices of religious behavior and personal spirituality, and proffered the explanation that boys were perhaps more heavily supervised and "aggressively corralled by teachers" to get them

Table 25.5 Word of Wisdom adherence, by gender

Percent who had consumed the substance within the last six months	Men	Women
Substances explicitly forbidden by the Church's current interpretation of the Word of Wisdom		
Alcohol	29%	21%
Caffeinated coffee	39%	32%
Marijuana	14%	6%
Tobacco	22%	12%
Non-herbal tea	26%	24%
Psychedelic drugs	5%	1%
Heroin and other illegal drugs	7%	3%
Substances not explicitly forbidden by the Church's current interpretation of the Word of Wisdom		
Caffeinated soda	60%	64%
Decaffeinated coffee	18%	10%

from sacrament meeting to Sunday School class. "Girls, on the other hand, tend to gather in pairs and may more often leave to change their clothes or adjust their makeup," the researchers hypothesized (Chadwick, Top, and McClendon, 2010). This seems a strange and inadequate explanation, particularly given the fact that in four of the six geographical areas in which the research was conducted, ward boundaries would presumably have been too expansive to permit girls to leave church simply to stop at home to don a new outfit.

What, then, is the actual reason that Mormon men seem to attend church at slightly higher rates than Mormon women in these research studies, especially given that they also tend to show that women are slightly more religiously devout and spiritual than men? One explanation might be that men are more likely to "over-report" their levels of church attendance in the abstract, with more of them claiming to be weekly churchgoers than is actually the case. We see some evidence for this in an NMS follow-up question that asked respondents what Sabbath day activities they had engaged in over the last thirty days. Here, 61 percent of women said that they had "attended church meetings" compared to 52 percent of men. While this is suggestive of a higher likelihood to over-report church attendance among Mormon men, more research would be needed to confirm this.

Another explanation may relate to differences in religious activity related to leadership callings in the LDS Church, where only men are eligible to serve in the majority of time-intensive congregational leadership positions. Upon closer inspection of reported attendance rates in the NMS, about 52 percent of both men and women say that they attend church "once a week," but men are about 5 points more likely to say that they attend "*more* than once a week" (emphasis added) compared to women: 24 percent to 19 percent. Thus, the NMS shows that Mormon men are attending church more regularly simply because they are attending more than once per week, which is very likely due to their being more likely to be serving in a time-intensive leadership calling than women.

Gender as a factor in believing and behaving

Mormonism is not alone in having higher degrees of religiosity among women than among men; other religious groups, particularly other Christian ones, report the same phenomenon (Pew Research Center, 2018). Researchers have attempted various explanations as to why

(Trzebiatowska and Bruce, 2012). Of these, some of the more promising investigate the "gender order" of the religions in question, acknowledging that gender is one of many factors that people have to negotiate in the complex power structures that characterize functioning religions.

At base, we must ask: what do men and women *get* when they choose to inhabit different religious systems? In Mormonism, the benefits for men might appear to be obvious, since men have access to nearly every position of formal decision-making power in the Church of Jesus Christ of Latter-day Saints. Only men can be bishops, stake presidents, mission presidents, apostles, and even ward clerks. The roster of "callings" available to women is considerably more limited and local, with women placed (by men) in positions of authority over children, youth, and other women, but almost never over men. Even the handful of women who serve as "general officers" of the Church's auxiliary organizations do so at the pleasure of the all-male First Presidency: which women will serve, how long they will serve, and what programs they will pursue are determined by the male leaders who outrank them.

What is less clear is why women willingly assent to such a system. If women are stronger believers and behavers than men, why do they consent to having less of a voice in the Church? From the perspective of the faithful, one obvious answer might be that it is precisely the fact that women are more devout believers that results in their willingness to participate in a system in which they are excluded from many of the important and influential leadership positions and the decision-making process. Mormons are taught that God's plan for his children involves regular participation in religious worship activities and institutional service opportunities that are determined to a moderate extent by their gender, age, and marital status. From this perspective, Mormon women may be just as devout (if not more so) than men because they sincerely believe that their more limited opportunities for leadership, influence, and service have divine provenance and approval.

Interestingly, there is some research to bear this out: Mormon women, who are taught by the Church that their holiest and most noble calling is to be mothers, report their highest levels of religiosity when they are directly involved in raising their children. In a study of the religiosity of Mormon women and men through various stages of the life cycle, researchers discovered that women's "public devotion" (church activity rates, attendance, and callings) was more variable than men's, experiencing a rise during the childrearing years and a temporary decline in the early "empty nest" period. According to researchers James T. Duke and Barry L. Johnson, the decline in Mormon women's devotion was not due to aging, cohort, or period effects, but

> occurred specifically at the time that the Mormon mother lost her most consuming and responsible role, one she had played for twenty to thirty years and which had been a chief means by which status had been achieved within the Mormon community.
> *(Duke and Johnson, 1998)*

What this suggests is that Mormon women have tied their religious behavior to motherhood in a way that is inherently orthodox, since they have been taught that raising children is a divinely appointed task that is complementary to men's more public leadership roles in the Church.

As we consider the question of why women readily assent to a religious system that restricts their primary field of influence to the domestic sphere, it is worth keeping three things in mind. First, it seems that perhaps we are asking the wrong question—or asking the right question in the wrong order. Research by John Bartkowski and John Hoffmann has explored a dynamic among conservative Protestant American women, who evince greater religiosity and biblical literalism than their male counterparts despite being denied access to leadership positions. Bartkowski and Hoffmann say this is not a coincidence; rather, "conservative religious women's greater tendency to embrace literalist schemas is a compensatory mechanism that aims to offset their exclusion from positions of authority in patriarchal religious organizations" (Hoffmann and Bartkowski, 2008). In other words, it is *because* conservative religions deny women access to visible leadership and authority that women are more religiously orthodox than men; this is where women can distinguish themselves. If this "compensatory mechanism" theory is true of Mormonism as well, we begin to see that women's heightened religiosity can actually be read as a subversive expression of their desire for authority; those who choose to remain in the religion can exercise soft power by being more devout than men (Griffith, 1997). So rather than asking why women consent to a restricted role in the Church when they are stronger Mormons in terms of belief and behavior, we would turn the equation around, seeing their amplified devotion as a response to being barred from holding ecclesiastical authority. Women succeed by beating men at their own game.

Second, Mormon women may not be seeking the same things from religion as Mormon men, and in this they are not alone among religious women. In a small-scale ethnographic study conducted in the 1990s, psychologist Elizabeth Weiss Ozorak interviewed sixty-one women to understand what attracted them to different religious groups. Overall, she discovered that whereas men prioritized their own advancement as individuals in their chosen religions, women privileged relationships and the family. "Themes of relationship were far more prevalent than themes of individuation," the study found, emphasizing that while the interviewees were aware of patterns of gender discrimination, the women chose to employ coping strategies to reframe that discrimination (Ozorak, 1996). In the NMS, there is evidence that such a dynamic may be at work in the Mormon community. For example, while 51 percent of Mormon women named "the knowledge that families can be together forever" as one of their favorite aspects of being LDS, only 42 percent of men did. Women also scored higher on theological tenets such as "emphasis on the Savior" and "the comfort of having a prophet on the earth today." Men, by contrast, gravitated toward this-worldly choices, with 36 percent naming "the strong community I enjoy at church" (compared to 27 percent of women) and "the good health and freedom that comes with keeping the Word of Wisdom" (22 percent, versus 13 percent of women). Although these differences are modest, they are consistent: men seemed less interested than women in the familial and eternal components of the faith, and instead keener on the ways their membership might provide them with community support, health benefits, and opportunities to serve people outside the nuclear family.

Third, personality differences between men and women may play a role, specifically when it comes to their level of tolerance for risk. Examining survey data from over 20,000 American adolescents, sociologist John Hoffmann has found that at least part of the gender gap in levels of American religiosity is explainable by differences in risk tolerance (Hoffmann, 2018; Regnerus, 2007). In general, men are more likely than women to engage in risky behaviors and have higher levels of tolerance for risk and uncertainty. As Hoffman writes: "the philosopher and mathematician Blaise Pascal ... proposed that believing in God was a risk-avoidant strategy and not believing was risky" because if God exists and you choose not to believe, the eternal punishment could potentially be catastrophic (Dolan, 2019). In the case of Mormon doctrine, the potential risk of inactivity or nonbelief is high: one's exaltation in the Celestial Kingdom and ability to be with one's loved ones for all eternity is literally on the line (Nelson, 2019). Perhaps it is the case that Mormon women tend to be more devout than Mormon men because they are less willing to risk the possibility that they will be eternally cut off from their families or loved ones in the next life if they achieve anything less than faithful belief and activity in the LDS Church in this life.

In conclusion, Mormons as a rule are noticeably more religious than the general population in America, but women lead the way. This is particularly true in areas of doctrinal certainty, personal closeness to God, and some (though not all) aspects of religious behavior. Scholars who seek to understand Mormonism cannot, as Thomas O'Dea did, accurately base their conclusions about the Mormon people without a full accounting of the role and significance of Mormon women. What has passed for "gender-blindness" in social science about religion in general, and Mormonism in particular, has actually been another kind of blindness entirely: a refusal to recognize that an exclusively male perspective is not sufficient to capture the totality of religious experience.

Note

1 The 2016 Next Mormons Survey (NMS) is a nationally representative online public opinion survey designed and fielded by Jana Riess and Benjamin Knoll in 2016. Responses were gathered by the survey firm Qualtrics that uses a "panel matching" technique to obtain response samples. To ensure representativeness on key demographic and religious variables, a post-stratification sample weighting was applied to correct for over- or under-sampling on categories of age, gender, and education levels in the sample of current Mormons. It thus has a survey margin of error of ± 3 percent for current Mormons based on the sample sizes and the estimated size of those populations in the United States. For more information on methodology, see www.thenextmormons.org.

References

Associated Press, 2012. *LDS Church Clarifies Stance on Caffeine.* www.heraldextra.com/news/state-and-regional/lds-church-clarifies-stance-on-caffeine/article_e4e357d0-ba5d-5a6c-8e78-dd1e791a34b2.html (accessed September 1, 2019).

Bahr, H., 2008. Finding Oneself among the Saints: Thomas F. O'Dea, Mormon Intellectuals, and the Future of Mormon Orthodoxy. *Journal for the Scientific Study of Religion* 47(3): 463–84.

Bennion, J., 2008. Mormon Women's Issues in the Twenty-first Century. In C. Jacobson, J. Hoffmann, and T. Heaton, eds. *Revisiting Thomas F. O'Dea's The Mormons: Contemporary Perspectives.* Salt Lake City, UT: University of Utah, pp. 135–59.

BLS, 2017. Percentage of Employed Women Working Full Time Little Changed over Past 5 Decades. The Economics Daily: U.S. Bureau of Labor Statistics. Bls.gov. www.bls.gov/opub/ted/2017/mobile/percentage-of-employed-women-working-full-time-little-changed-over-past-5-decades.htm (accessed April 1, 2019).

Braude, A., 1997. Women's History Is American Religious History. In T. Tweed, ed. *Retelling U.S. Religious History.* Berkeley, CA: University of California Press, pp. 87–107.

CDC, 2017. FastStats. Cdc.gov. www.cdc.gov/nchs/fastats/unmarried-childbearing.htm (accessed April 1, 2019).

Chadwick, B., Top, B., and McClendon, R., 2010. *Shield of Faith: The Power of Religion in the Lives of LDS Youth and Young Adults.* Provo, UT: Religious Studies Center, Brigham Young University, in cooperation with Deseret Book.

Cox, D., and Jones, R., 2017. *America's Changing Religious Identity.* PRRI. www.prri.org/research/American-religious-landscape-christian-religiously-unaffiliated/ (accessed April 1, 2019).

Dolan, E., 2019. Willingness to Take Risks Could Explain a Small Part of the Gender Gap in Religiousness. PsyPost. www.psypost.org/2019/01/willingness-to-take-risks-could-explain-a-small-part-of-the-gender-gap-in-religiousness-52971 (accessed April 9, 2019).

Duke, J., and Johnson, B., 1998. The Religiosity of Mormon Men and Women through the Life Cycle. In J. Duke, ed. *Latter-day Saint Social Life: Social Research on the LDS Church and Its Members.* Provo, UT: Religious Studies Center, Brigham Young University, pp. 315–44.

Eyring, H., 2018. Women and Gospel Learning in the Home. General Conference. www.churchofjesuschrist.org/study/ensign/2018/11/general-womens-session/women-and-gospel-learning-in-the-home?lang=eng (accessed July 17, 2019).

Faust, J., 2005. Instruments in the Hands of God. General Conference. www.lds.org/general-conference/2005/10/instruments-in-the-hands-of-god?lang=eng (accessed April 1, 2019).

Gallup, 2017. In U.S., More Adults Identifying as LGBT. Gallup.com. www.gallup.com/poll/201731/LGBT-identification-rises.aspx (accessed April 1, 2019).

Griffith, R., 1997. *God's Daughters: Evangelical Women and the Power of Submission*. Berkeley, CA: University of California Press.

Heaton, T., and Jacobson, C., 2015. The Social Composition of Mormonism. In T. Givens and P. Barlow, eds. *The Oxford Handbook of Mormonism*. New York: Oxford University Press, pp. 309–33.

Hoffmann, J., 2018. Risk Preference Theory and Gender Differences in Religiousness: A Replication and Extension. *Journal for the Scientific Study of Religion* 58(1): 210–30.

Hoffmann, J., and Bartkowski, J., 2008. Gender, Religious Tradition, and Biblical Literalism. *Social Forces* 86(3): 1245–72.

Jacobson, C.K., Hoffmann, J.P., and Heaton, T.B., 2008. *Revisiting Thomas F. O'Dea's The Mormons: Contemporary Perspectives*. Salt Lake City, UT: University of Utah Press.

Jones, R.P., and Cox, D., 2016. *America's Changing Religious Identity: Findings from the 2016 American Values Atlas*. PRRI, 33.

Lds.org, 2011. *For the Strength of Youth*. www.lds.org/youth/for-the-strength-of-youth/entertainment-and-media?lang=eng (accessed July 18, 2019).

Luckerson, V., 2015. More Women Aren't Having Children, Survey Finds. *Time*. http://time.com/3774620/more-women-not-having-kids/ (accessed April 1, 2019).

Mayrl, D., and Uecker, J., 2011. Higher Education and Religious Liberalization among Young Adults. *Social Forces* 90(1): 181–208.

McDannell, C., 2018. *Sister Saints: Mormon Women since the End of Polygamy*. New York: Oxford University Press.

Nelson, R., 2019. Come, Follow Me. General Conference. www.lds.org/general-conference/2019/04/46nelson?lang=eng (accessed August 1, 2019).

Ozorak, E., 1996. The Power, but Not the Glory: How Women Empower Themselves Through Religion. *Journal for the Scientific Study of Religion* 35(1): 17–29.

Pew Forum, Mormons, 2014. Religious Landscape Study. www.pewforum.org/religious-landscape-study/religious-tradition/mormon/.

Pew Research Center, 2018. Christian Women in the U.S. Are More Religious Than Their Male Counterparts. www.pewresearch.org/fact-tank/2018/04/06/christian-women-in-the-u-s-are-more-religious-than-their-male-counterparts/ (accessed August 1, 2019).

Phillips, R., and Cragun, R.T., 2008. Mormons in the United States, 1990–2008: Socio-demographic Trends and Regional Differences. American Religious Identification Survey. http://commons.trincoll.edu/aris/files/2011/12/Mormons2008.pdf.

Regnerus, M., 2007. *Forbidden Fruit: Sex and Religion in the Lives of American Teenagers*. Oxford: Oxford University Press.

Riess, J., 2019. *The Next Mormons: How Millennials Are Changing the LDS Church*. New York: Oxford University Press.

Trzebiatowska, M., and Bruce, S., 2014. *Why Are Women More Religious Than Men?* New York: Oxford University Press.

White Jr., O.K., 2008. Thomas F. O'Dea and Mormon Intellectual Life. In C. Jacobson, J. Hoffmann, and T. Heaton, eds. *Revisiting Thomas F. O'Dea's The Mormons: Contemporary Perspectives*. Salt Lake City, UT: University of Utah, pp. 21–55.

Woodhead, L., 2007. Gender Differences in Religious Practice and Significance. In J. Beckford and N. Demerath, eds. *The Sage Handbook of the Sociology of Religion*. Los Angeles, CA: Sage, pp. 566–86.

Further reading

Bennion, J., 2008. Mormon Women's Issues in the Twenty-first Century. In C. Jacobson, J. Hoffmann, and T. Heaton, eds. *Revisiting Thomas F. O'Dea's The Mormons: Contemporary Perspectives*. Salt Lake City, UT: University of Utah, pp. 135–39.

Heaton, T., and Jacobson, C., 2015. The Social Composition of Mormonism. In T. Givens and P. Barlow, eds. *The Oxford Handbook of Mormonism*. New York: Oxford University Press, pp. 309–33.

Hoffmann, J., and Bartkowski, J., 2008. Gender, Religious Tradition, and Biblical Literalism. *Social Forces* 86(3): 1245–72.

Trzebiatowska, M., and Bruce, S., 2014. *Why Are Women More Religious Than Men?* New York: Oxford University Press.

Woodhead, L., 2007. Gender Differences in Religious Practice and Significance. In J. Beckford and N. Demerath, eds. *The Sage Handbook of the Sociology of Religion*. Los Angeles, CA: Sage, pp. 566–86.

26
GENDER AND MENTAL HEALTH IN MORMON CONTEXTS

Rebekah Perkins Crawford

Introduction: religion and mental health

Religious culture influences our physical health (Williams, 2013), and is especially significant when it comes to our mental health (Krok, 2014; Chen and VanderWeele, 2018). Because of this, psychologists have long studied religious communities for their roles in aiding recovery (Yangarber-Hicks, 2004), defining sexuality (Haque, 2013), and interpreting mental illness' stigma (Rogers, Stanford, and Garland, 2012). Religious leaders have been of particular interest because of the significant counseling role they play in some faith traditions. In the United States, for example, religious leaders remain the most frequently sought source of help for psychological distress (Stanford, 2007) with more people seeking mental health support from their spiritual advisors than from psychiatrists or primary care physicians (Wang, Berglund, and Kessler, 2003).

When studying the influence religion has on mental health it is important to differentiate not only between religious traditions but also between individual experiences within the same tradition (Dein, Cook, and Koenig, 2012). Indeed, it is essential to understand if minority subgroup status enables or constrains access to a religious community's assistance. Women, for example, must often navigate patriarchal and hierarchical religious organizational structures in order to find formal and informal support for their mental health needs. Thus, when gender blocks access to a religious group's support resources it is implicated not only as an ideological or philosophical barrier that women in religious communities must overcome, but also as an instrumental or social barrier that constrains women's holistic health and wellbeing.

Gender is a crucial factor to take into account when interrogating how religiosity affects mental and emotional wellbeing because both mental health indicators and experiences of religious group membership vary widely based on an individual's gender identity. For example, female members of religious organizations are more likely to report experiences of emotional or psychological distress then their male counterparts. Additionally, women who report that religious beliefs have a greater influence on their everyday lives are also more likely to report experiencing depressive symptoms (Lace, Haeberlein, and Handal, 2018). A strong sense of having meaning in life (which is a key component of religiosity) has been linked to greater depressive symptoms in women than in men (Yu et al., 2017). Women are not only more likely to experience mental health concerns, they are also significantly more likely to have those concerns dismissed by their religious leaders and to be advised not to take their medications (Stanford, 2007). Thus, female members of religious organizations consistently report greater experiences of mental illness then their male counterparts while simultaneously encountering decreased access to a religious organizations' support.

To acquire mental healthcare resources available in ecclesiastical contexts women must often communicate across a gender divide, surmounting cultural stigma to convince their (predominantly male) religious leaders that their needs are legitimate. The urgency to craft a persuasive appeal increases in situations where women's physical safety is also being threatened by gendered or sexual violence. Because women are most likely to report cases of domestic abuse or sexual violence to their religious leaders (Vaaler, 2008) those leaders' abilities to understand and appropriately respond to these reports becomes highly consequential not only to women's quality of life but also in some cases to their survival. Thus, understanding support-seeking communication patterns within religious institutions and acknowledging how these patterns are affected by gender illuminates different experiences within religious communities and highlights how gender enables or constrains members' ability to access support in a highly consequential non-clinical context of care.

The Church of Jesus Christ of Latter-day Saints is a religious community that illustrates how gender can play a complicating role in accessing mental health support resources. The LDS Church essentializes gender roles, teaching that gender is an eternal and unchangeable aspect of individual identity and that men and women[1] should play separate but equal roles in public and family life respectively (First Presidency of the Church of Jesus Christ of Latter-day Saints, 1995). Because of these gender roles, all church leaders who preside over LDS congregations, who have the authority to hear and absolve sin, and who have the power to grant access to church support resources, are male. The problems implicit in such limited representation in leadership are denied by a doctrinal ideology which claims that male leaders' authorization to receive revelation for all congregants will ensure that the inspiration of the Holy Ghost will overcome any lack of experience or perspective embodied in individual male leaders. Additionally, the rhetoric of radical spiritual equality, in which church members are constructed as "brothers and sisters" in Christ, all "children of God" and inheritors of an equal celestial legacy often normalizes the strict male hierarchical power structure and erases the unique vulnerabilities LDS women experience. This stark division of power coupled with the prominent role the LDS Church plays in defining health behaviors and providing health resources make it an important context in which to explore the way gender influences access to mental health support resources within religious organizations. Indeed, this context shows how essentialized gender norms coupled with a patriarchal, hierarchical organizational structure can create institutional barriers that can have profound implications for mental wellness.

Gendered access to mental health resources in Mormon communities

The Church of Jesus Christ of Latter-day Saints is an organization whose ideologies, structure, and resources have a dramatic influence on every aspect of members' lives. Indeed, some scholars have characterized the LDS Church as a totalizing institution (Goffman, 1990), or an organization whose "values, practices, rituals, and relationships ... not only extend to the member's everyday life but play a primary role" (Hinderaker, 2015, p. 93). The LDS Church, which has a history of founding pioneer settlements that relied on religious social services in the place of civic ones, still runs schools, hospitals, and social service agencies in parallel to government services. This prominent organizational influence means that Latter-day Saint leaders not only have the power to interpret what mental health means for specific individuals but also to decide who gets access to institutional resources which support mental wellness. In this way, the all-male LDS religious leadership acts as the exclusive gatekeeper to the vast array of member support resources available in Mormon contexts.

Latter-day Saint religious leaders have access to local networks and institutional assets that they can use to provide social and instrumental support to enable congregants' mental health. Leaders of local congregations, called bishops or branch presidents, are the main points of interaction between the church as an institution and the individual members. Bishops, who are untrained lay leaders that serve for roughly five years, have a variety of resources at their disposal to care for the holistic needs of their congregants. Bishops also have access to consecrated funds that they may use at their discretion to help members pay for short-term temporal needs such as rent, medical bills, medication, or therapy visits. Bishops themselves also act as a direct therapy resource, designating time for one-on-one counseling sessions with local members who are in distress, who are seeking pastoral counseling, or who feel the need to confess and repent of their sins. In addition, LDS bishops actively cultivate relationships with trusted professional mental healthcare providers who understand the culture and respect the lifeworld of Latter-day Saints. With the permission of their congregants bishops often refer members in need to these professional mental healthcare providers, help defray some of the costs, and sometimes even directly collaborate with professional caregivers to support recovery in the client's home community. Bishops in LDS-dominant communities also can refer members to short-term mental healthcare provided by LDS Family Services, can refer members to counseling clinics associated with church-owned universities, and can utilize a volunteer-led twelve-step recovery program administered by the church.

With so many therapeutic resources being activated only at the discretion of local religious leaders, communicative encounters in which members attempt to convince their bishop that they have credible needs and are making legitimate requests are highly consequential to mental wellness. Indeed, access to social and instrumental support in Mormon contexts rests on a relatively high-stakes interpersonal encounter in which the member in need must rely on their relationship with the leader, their personal credibility and their communicative resources to persuade the bishop to activate support. Once activated, the bishop plays the key role in coordinating the efforts of a variety of overlapping groups and institutions on the member's behalf. Unfortunately, gender often presents a poignant barrier that blocks female members' ability to utilize institutional resources that support mental health. For example, it is harder for women to get the bishop's time and attention, women who do achieve an appointment often have a harder time persuading bishops to accept their description of their needs, and bishops have a harder time understanding women's perspectives and experiences in general. Because of this, women can be less likely to get an appropriate response to their situation.

Interviews with bishops and professional mental healthcare providers who work with predominantly LDS clientele illuminated two main themes and two subthemes that specified how gender poses institutional barriers that block LDS women from full access to mental health support resources. The first main theme involved bishops' understanding of gender's influence on the interpersonal ecclesiastical interactions they have with women. The second main theme described how female leaders within the Church of Jesus Christ of Latter-day Saints are separate from, subordinate to, and dependent on the male leaders' authority, blocking them from acting as commensurate alternative sources of support. This second main theme can be divided into two subthemes that describe limitations LDS female religious leaders such as the Relief Society president face in their caregiving efforts. The first subtheme describes disclosure rules that limit Relief Society presidents' ability to keep women's information confidential from the male leaders. The second involves limitations to Relief Society presidents' authority which restrict their ability to hear women's confessions, provide female-specific pastoral counseling, and directly dispense money and other tangible resources without the permission of the bishop. These limitations to female leadership coupled with the complications women experience in their interactions with male leaders effectively narrows the gate through which Latter-day Saint women must pass to obtain help, and places it under constant male surveillance. In the following sections, I outline the discourses that illuminated these themes and provide examples from participants' voices which illustrate them.

Methodology

The themes listed above arose inductively out of twenty-three semi-structured open-ended interviews that I conducted with LDS bishops and professional mental healthcare providers (Crawford, 2018). These interviews resulted in twenty-seven hours of recorded conversation and 597 pages of double-spaced transcripts. I added to these transcripts ethnographic field notes, participant observation, autoethnographic reflection, and the analysis of pertinent cultural documents. Using NVivo coding software I engaged in five rounds of thematic coding, attending to patterns as they arose from the discourse. Consistent with Charmaz' (2006) Grounded Theory I used inductive responsiveness when necessary to change my inquiry practice to pursue new questions as they emerged.

My analysis used rhetorical and narrative sensibilities to interpret and share the themes, patterns, and meanings I gained from my research. I maintained the stringent standards of academic rigor for qualitative studies (Tracy, 2010) including using writing as a method of inquiry (Richardson, 2003), discovering as I progressed, and weaving the discourse and theory together until I was better able to see how the theory arose out of and was defined by the words and lived experiences of my participants. In the sections that follow, I describe and provide examples of each of the two main and subthemes that illuminate how gender enables barriers to accessing institutional mental health resources in local Latter-day Saint communities. I will use participants' own words to articulate the specifics of organizational structure, institutional behavior, and cultural expectations that implicate gendered power in communicative help-seeking encounters between male leaders and female church members, as well as between female and male church leaders. I will conclude by summarizing key points of interaction that are especially problematic for women trying to access mental health support resources and by suggesting cultural and institutional changes that might mitigate these barriers.

Gender in interpersonal ecclesiastical interactions

Because of their centrality in the LDS system of care and their role as financial gatekeepers, LDS bishops' awareness of gender's influence on interpersonal interactions in the ecclesiastical setting is key to enabling or constraining Latter-day Saint women's requests for support. Though a minority of white American bishops comes into their role doubting the legitimacy of mental health claims, overwhelmingly both LDS leaders and professional mental healthcare providers report that by the beginning of their second year, bishops are usually convinced about the reality of mental illness. Indeed, though white U.S. bishops consistently reported viewing general mental health claims as legitimate, their attitudes about the effects gender had on the interpersonal interactions necessary to access care varied more widely.

In their talk about the role gender plays in one-on-one care-seeking ecclesiastical interactions, LDS bishops enacted differing levels of awareness about the disempowered position female members inhabited when asking a male leader for support. Some LDS bishops, for example, continued to uneasily describe gender as non-influential in the interaction. Others expressed awareness and concern for the vulnerabilities women in need experienced but felt bound by organizational structures that made them unable to mitigate power imbalances. A very small minority of bishops reported purposefully circumnavigating institutional barriers or directly breaking organizational policies in order to better meet the needs of the women in their congregations. Below, I share examples and analysis of each of these attitudes about the role gender plays in interpersonal ecclesiastical contexts of care.

When I asked, for example, if gender was a problem or barrier women experienced in interpersonal ecclesiastical care situations most bishops I interviewed responded quickly with the answer that gender was not a problem. Usually, they immediately clarified their answer by stating that gender was not a problem *for them* as the bishop. Then they often followed this clarification with an open admission that gender could be a problem for the woman who was seeking help.

For example, one bishop said,

> For me, [communicating with women is] not an issue really. I get along well and they seem comfortable. And there are occasions where, maybe they've had a bad experience with a male figure ... and it takes a little while to build a relationship with trust. But I don't really notice a difference. Maybe there is but ...

This bishop's words take us along with him as he considers gender's role in his interpersonal ecclesiastical interactions, vacillating over its influence. First, he confidently states his perspective that gender is not powerful, before immediately qualifying it with an exception. Then, he reiterates his original view before undercutting his statement a final time with an expression of doubt. In his talk we can see this bishop representing the institutional stance—that requiring women to interact with an all-male leadership does not pose any barriers—before necessarily subverting it with expressions of doubt and articulations of contradictory examples from his own experience. In his verbal contradictions this bishop enacts the tension inherent to espousing an ideology that claims gender is inconsequential in ecclesiastical care-seeking contexts while simultaneously acknowledging individual examples that disprove this claim.

Other bishops acknowledged the barrier gendered power differentials posed in an ecclesiastical mental health interaction but expressed an inability to mitigate these problems because of the limitations placed on them by organizational policies and structure. For instance, one bishop said,

> Sometimes [women] have a problem talking to me because of my gender. For example, I think the abuse cases are the most obvious ones. When I've had a woman that was abused by a man, coming to talk to me is the last thing that they wanna do.

Though this bishop acknowledged gender as a barrier for women in the ecclesiastical interpersonal interaction, he stopped short of describing how to mitigate the context in order to accommodate individual needs. Another bishop concurred, admitting,

> An example of someone that had a really hard time with a priesthood holder and when she had to come in and work through things with me, it was a huge challenge and I think she would have done it sooner if I hadn't been a man.

In both these examples, though these leaders acknowledged the extra challenges women faced in this context, their talk stopped short of offering any solutions. Instead, they presented gendered challenges as inescapable and outside their power to mitigate.

Finally, a third category of LDS bishops, a very small minority, understood the gendered barriers women seeking help for emotional distress in the ecclesiastical setting experienced, and described using their authority to actively subvert institutional policies or cultural expectations in order to decrease the vulnerability of women in these interactions. For instance, one bishop described inviting the leader of the female auxiliary group, the Relief Society president into one-on-one interviews despite a current church policy prohibiting such actions. He said,

> I think, very understandably, many and maybe even most women would probably feel more comfortable talking to another woman about deeply personal matters of any stripe. And I am painfully aware of that because I feel so inadequate ... I acknowledge and understand the power imbalance, the gender difference, just everything that's all wrapped up into that. [And so] I try to use specifically my Relief Society president.

This bishop described understanding how the Relief Society president could be seen by female members as being compromised after working closely with him as a man, especially in situations where they were responding to domestic violence or a divorce. In these situations he assumed the "wife is gonna feel like I'm taking his side," adding, "and that's totally understandable." He then described his solution, one which expressly counter-demands church policy: "In that situation I've had the Relief Society president take a much stronger role in personally counseling and helping this [woman]," adding that the Relief Society president "doesn't need to talk to me about the person she is counseling." This interview is notable because of the bishop's awareness and openness about the way gender inhibits a woman's ability to access help in her local congregation. It is also remarkable because of the bishop's creative response to those barriers women experienced which included a willingness to subvert his own position as the sole authoritative spiritual counselor, to break norms about information disclosure between male and female religious leaders, and to directly counter demand church policy and official procedure.

Thus, even though LDS bishops' responses countenanced a spectrum of ideas about gender in the interpersonal ecclesiastical context, all the bishops' answers reflected some tension, complexity, or contradiction between the official ideologies and the lived realities of trying to negotiate a care context with a pronounced gendered power difference. Though bishops' talk evidenced differing levels of frankness about gendered barriers and different levels of willingness to subvert rules and policies to address those barriers, their descriptions of lived interactions implicitly acknowledged that an all-male religious hierarchy made interpersonal interactions between male leaders and female members more fraught and thus limited women's access to male-controlled organizational resources.

Mental healthcare provided by Relief Society presidents

Bishops described the involvement of the most prominent and powerful female leader of a local congregation, the Relief Society president, as helping to mitigate the gendered barriers women experience when seeking help in local Latter-day Saint congregations. Though few bishops utilized the Relief Society president as a full female counterpart, almost every bishop I interviewed mentioned the Relief Society president as a valuable asset that he employed in congregational care, especially on behalf of female members. As the bishops described Relief Society presidents' roles, contributions, and characteristics they also outlined ways the local female leadership were limited from directly and independently serving the needs of female members. Professional mental healthcare providers who also spoke about their experiences serving as Relief Society presidents corroborated the bishops' descriptions. Specifically, both bishops and

Relief Society presidents described a shared understanding that Relief Society presidents could not manage disclosure boundaries and experienced limits to their authority which prevented them from directly serving the complete needs of Mormon women. Indeed, though Relief Society presidents were praised almost unanimously for their resourcefulness and effectiveness, both male and female leaders described the Relief Society president as subject to the insights, agenda, and opinions of the bishop.

In general, male and female LDS leaders characterized the Relief Society president as fundamentally different from and beholden to the authority of the bishop. Most of these characterizations of the Relief Society president's role used taken-for-granted gendered assumptions about the differences between men and women to describe and justify the lower status, lack of authority, more "hands-on" duties, and greater amount of emotional labor that both male and female LDS leaders expected from Relief Society presidents. LDS religious leaders understood these gendered differences as a way to diversify both the types of care and the methods of delivery that they could offer within the local congregation.

Almost every bishop I interviewed mentioned his Relief Society president as a hands-on, "boots-on-the-ground" asset who was more integrated into the local congregation, less encumbered by the need to dispense institutional discipline, and more likely to be in touch with the everyday needs of women. Bishops described Relief Society presidents most commonly as the ones to go into a home to catalog physical and emotional needs, the ones most likely to fill out forms ordering food from church welfare resources, and the ones most likely to know when a woman and her family were navigating a major life event. Relief Society presidents were described by some bishops as a "third counselor" who acted as a sounding board beyond the bishop's two male assistants for how a bishop's ideas and policies would affect female members. Bishops described Relief Society presidents as acting in a more informal or "less official" church capacity. They described these female leaders as "implementer[s] of strong social networks," and as being on the "frontline of defense." One bishop praised the service orientation of his Relief Society president, describing how her instinct was to "take a step forward" towards women and families in need when others recoiled. This praise precludes claims that bishops might have doubts about a Relief Society president's ability to effectively provide direct, independent emotional and institutional emotional support for LDS women. Rather, descriptions of the different leadership roles women enact in LDS contexts points to gender as the main influence that limits the services female leaders can provide directly to Latter-day Saint women.

Relief Society presidents' descriptions of their own roles also reflected how gender constructed their church leadership role as more informal, integrated into the community, and focused on compassion over discipline. One Relief Society president represented her role as being "in the trenches dealing with individual people and cases." Though she strongly argued for the right of the Relief Society president to get revelation on behalf of Latter-day Saints despite her lack of priesthood ordination, she only expected that authority to extend to female members. Rather than an authoritative figure like the bishop, a Relief Society president, in her words, "can be a listening ear, a shoulder to cry on, a sounding board."

Even claims that the Relief Society president was a role endowed with respect and the right to inspiration were tempered by language that demarcated the female leader's position as deferential to and reliant on the bishop's authority. One female leader said being the Relief Society president is a position "not necessarily of power but of high visibility" and went on to list the limitations to her institutional power. She said, "I don't have any power in terms of church discipline" and described how she cannot help people financially because "that is the bishop's stewardship ... he has to know what's happening and he has to approve that." Thus, though they made claims about effectiveness and authority as female leaders, Relief Society presidents themselves qualified these claims by describing limitations to their power and expressing deference to male leaders.

Bishops' talk concurred with the Relief Society presidents' in expressing a limitation to Relief Society presidents' authority and an expectation that they will defer to bishops. One bishop described how he summarily dismissed a Relief Society president because he "completely disagreed with her philosophy in life." When he found out she had been counseling a female member to save her money in preparation for a possible divorce he said, "I didn't want her counseling the sisters if that was her perspective." Another bishop described how a Relief Society president's lower status in the religious hierarchy decreased her access to inspiration. He said, "It's true that a bishop gets more rights theologically toward inspiration for a person, but I think [Relief Society presidents] are entitled to divine assistance based on the position they've been placed in."

Thus, bishops and Relief Society presidents alike described the roles female leaders played in LDS congregations as fundamentally different from and subordinate to male leaders. Though interview participants consistently described Relief Society presidents as aware, responsive, and committed to service, their talk simultaneously limited the contributions LDS female leaders could make by defining their roles as lacking in authority and limited in scope. In some cases the decreased official capacity of LDS female leaders allowed Relief Society presidents to take a less threatening stance that increased their access to information about individuals' distress. However, the gendered limits placed on the female leaders' capacity also constrained their ability to directly support female members' mental health needs.

Two limitations emerged as especially consequential for Mormon women's mental wellbeing. First, disclosure rules which mandate that Relief Society presidents must reveal women's confidential information to bishops, and limits to Relief Society presidents' spiritual authority which make the bishop the sole person in the local congregations who can hear confessions, make disciplinary decisions about sin, and provide pastoral counseling and access to monetary support. These two limitations to female leadership roles maintain the bishop as the lynchpin to mental health resources by giving him access to all confidential information about relationship struggles, addiction, substance abuse, life crises, and psychological pain. In addition, the bishop's authority to literally pass judgment on the meanings of and appropriate responses to individuals' emotional distress situate him as the sole gatekeeper to social and functional support resources. While centering all local mental health support decision-making and dispensing power in the bishop is organizationally efficient, it can create barriers for women trying to access help. First, it forces women to access all resources through a male leader. Second, it discourages women who are trying to manage their privacy from asking for support from the Relief Society president. Finally, it can also enable misunderstandings when women try to communicate to their bishops about experiences of intimate partner violence. We will turn next to the discourses that elaborate on these specific subthemes and then conclude with some general recommendations.

Disclosure rules: Relief Society presidents must report to bishops

One key limitation that constrains a Relief Society president's ability to offer direct support for women's mental health concerns is her constant negotiation with people's confidentiality. Both bishops and Relief Society presidents expressed a belief that a Relief Society president must share everything she knows about members of the congregation with the bishop, even if the information was originally shared with her in confidence. One Relief Society president described feeling required to offer a disclaimer to female members in distress, saying, "I'm your Relief Society president and there might be some things that we need to be telling other people, either the police or the bishop, or whoever." Another example illustrates how a bishop instructed his Relief Society president in these disclosure expectations. He told how his Relief Society president was "suffering" because she was holding people's problems in confidence. She eventually confided in the bishop that the sisters "were telling [her] things like their immorality issues and their mental health issues," and the bishop chided her for keeping them confidential. He told her, "Why are you bearing this burden? It's not yours to bear, that's mine." She replied, "Really? I feel like I'm breaching confidentiality," and he responded, "That's not even your story to hear. If you feel someone is being bothered you need to come to me and I'll call that person in and then we'll let the Spirit do the rest." This bishop told his Relief Society president that she could listen "as a friend" but that she must tell women in distress, "It's important that you go see the bishop, 'cause if you don't see the bishop then I'm gonna go see the Bishop." Thus, both bishops and Relief Society presidents expressed a belief that the bishop's solitary spiritual role necessitated his access to congregation members' private information even if his access violated individuals' wishes. These examples also illustrate how Relief Society presidents are instructed in these disclosure patterns and how they communicate their information-sharing practices to the women they serve.

These unequal disclosure patterns between male and female LDS leaders were justified by both bishops and Relief Society presidents as existing to best serve the interests of people in need of help. Under this rationale, the bishop was the only person who could perform the services needed for spiritual healing and so sharing people's information with him could be the only way to help them. One Relief Society president described the way she made sense of the unequal disclosure rules in these words:

> In order to help this person I have to share [their information] with the bishop ... I am required to share with the bishop more than the bishop can often share with me ... Recognizing it's a one-way street and not being offended by that is a huge part of the job.

This Relief Society president understood the unbalanced disclosure boundaries as ultimately beneficial to the woman she was serving. However, later she also acknowledged that such disclosure patterns could compromise her ability to act as a confidant for women, admitting that disclosure expectation reduced the things women would tell her. She described how even informal friendships were affected by her role as the Relief Society president and her bishop's disclosure expectations, saying that "friends that I would talk to about my problems or their problems didn't want to talk to me anymore because I was the Relief Society president and [they thought that] maybe I was gonna tell the bishop." Thus, these Relief Society presidents expressed an awareness of how their close collaboration with the bishop and its associated disclosure expectations limited their own access to information about women's distress.

Having women feel hesitant to report their problems even to the Relief Society president because of confidentiality issues could pose an especially critical problem for women living with mental illness, substance use disorders, or relationship violence. For instance, one Relief Society president described how, "I had one sister come and say, 'Last night my husband threatened me with a gun and I don't know what to do.'" In contexts concerning women's safety, such as sexual assault, rape, domestic violence, and suicide the gendered organizational disclosure expectations make women effectively meeting the needs of other women organizationally unrealistic. Male leaders are the only ones with the authority to dispense church funds or provide other functional support that could promote women's safety. This makes it necessary for female leaders to report critically sensitive information to them if they are to have access to support resources.

Knowing that female leaders are bound to report information to male leaders could prevent women in distress who do not trust men from disclosing their needs or asking for help even from their female leaders. Allowing Relief Society presidents more autonomy in deciding what information to share with male leaders and allowing them access to support resources without having to gain the permission of male leaders could increase their ability to both hear about and meet the critical needs of the women in their congregations.

Gender, spiritual authority, and confession

Since confession is a main vehicle by which male leaders encounter (and sometimes discipline) emotional distress, the fact that Latter-day Saint women cannot hear confession is another limitation that blocks Relief Society presidents' ability to offer direct emotional support to Latter-day Saint women. Latter-day Saints believe that all spiritual authority in the local context centers in the bishop and that Relief Society presidents can only act with any power that he chooses to delegate to her. One bishop described it by saying, "I have the keys and through priesthood ordinance and through just simply delegation I set apart a Relief Society president ... and endow her with spiritual tools and authority." Thus, even when a Relief Society president serves the needs of LDS women, she does not draw on her own spiritual authority to do so but acts explicitly as a delegate who extends the bishop's power into the women's auxiliary. In this way Relief Society presidents only have spiritual authority insofar as they serve at the behest and pleasure of the bishop who acts as the ultimate religious authority in the local community.

This lack of explicit and independent spiritual authority blocks Relief Society presidents from hearing confessions of sin. As interpersonal situations that allow people in distress to communicate about mistakes, regrets, loss of meaning, and finding resolutions, confessionals are key contexts in religious communities that can address distress and provide emotional support. Relief Society presidents described how their lack of priesthood authority prevented them from interacting with women in distress and offering them comfort because they could not access God's power to officially absolve them after confession. In this way, the bishop's monopoly on spiritual authority situated him as the only avenue to resolve concerns about sins or mistakes.

Confessional communication can provide direct therapeutic relief that supports mental wellness (Pennebaker, 1995). Preventing women from hearing confession as religious leaders has ramifications for the mental wellness of female members. The problems associated with requesting support across the gender divide become pronounced especially in cases where women must "confess" experiences of sexual violence to their male leaders. Sometimes when male LDS leaders ask female members worthiness questions in connection to their sexual practices, the women will reveal guilty feelings about times when they were sexually assaulted, molested, abused, or raped. However, because many parts of LDS culture and doctrine emphasize female purity and denounce any sexual experience outside of marriage, cultural discourses about consent are often silenced or overlooked. Without consent as a diagnostic benchmark women's "confessions" of gendered violence can pass undiagnosed as such by male religious leaders. Unfortunately, in these cases of extreme trauma and vulnerability, male leaders often invoke institutional discipline where support, healing, and justice are required (Crawford, 2018).

For religious leaders to appropriately make sense out of women's physical and sexual vulnerability they must be able to adequately take the perspective of a survivor of gendered violence (Dougherty, 2001). Reports of sexual, domestic, or intimate partner violence are not only harder for female members to communicate across the gender divide, they are also harder for male spiritual leaders to hear and appropriately comprehend. Requiring survivors to report to male leaders because they are the only ones with the adequate spiritual authority to engage in confessional interactions multiplies the threats to LDS women's mental health. In the first place, it is much harder for survivors to disclose their sexual trauma to men. In the second, male leaders' perspectives are often limited by their gender, which makes them more likely to respond to reports of sexual violence inappropriately. Inappropriate response to disclosures that are already traumatizing to recount increases the likelihood that the hearer will perpetuate secondary trauma on survivors (Ullman, 2010).

If the leader listening to a report of sexual violence has institutional and spiritual power to fuel and validate his misinformed reactions to female members' reports of sexual violence, the extent of the secondary trauma inflicted on those members could be exponential. Secondary trauma compounds systemic weaknesses that already exist within the patriarchal hierarchy which increase survivors' vulnerabilities. For example, to access LDS organizational support and healing resources, survivors of gendered or sexual violence are ironically forced to navigate an all-male ecclesiastical power structure, which can be re-traumatizing just to interact with. One professional mental healthcare provider talked about how "church can be the worst place to be" for rape survivors, because they are "scared to death of men" and must meet alone with them behind closed doors in order to maintain access to their schooling and support resources. In this participant's words, LDS survivors experience "spiritual trauma" by belonging to a religious organization where the only leaders with enough authority to address their needs are men.

In cases where women report sexual violence to male leaders, Relief Society presidents are seldom described as being involved even peripherally since they do not have the authority to hear confessions nor vote in church disciplinary councils. Thus, denying female leaders' spiritual and institutional authority bars them from religious communication contexts where their perspective and advocacy are most acutely needed. Institutional rationalities that promote male spiritual leaders' misdiagnoses of gendered and sexual violence are among the most tragic examples of how essentialized gender roles and institutionalized gendered power imbalances interfere with mental health in Mormon contexts.

Conclusion

Religious organizations' rich holistic ideologies about health coupled with tight knit communities make them potential sites for the flexible, responsive, community-based mental healthcare that the World Health Organization (2001) described as the gold standard of care. The Church of Jesus Christ of Latter-day Saints encompasses a wide array of overlapping groups, resources, and services that can combine to effectively support the psychological wellness of individual members. Indeed, Mormonism is a faith tradition with rich cultural and institutional resources that its male religious leaders can dispense to provide social, emotional, and functional support for members living with mental illness or experiencing psychological distress. Because of ideologies about essential gender differences which starkly divide men's and women's roles in the religious organization, LDS conceptions about gender become highly influential to the lived experiences of those seeking mental health support in this ecclesiastical context. Gendered power imbalances often interfere when Latter-day Saint women seek direct pastoral care from male ecclesiastical leaders. Limits to the fiscal and spiritual power of female ecclesiastical leaders prevent Relief Society presidents from adequately compensating for the resources and support women may not be able to access through interacting with their bishop.

To fundamentally address the systemic mental health inequalities experienced by female members of the Church of Jesus Christ of Latter-day Saints, women in this organization would need to be given equal institutional power and voice. Female leaders would need to be included in every level of the ecclesiastical hierarchy and be able to lay claim to equal cultural and spiritual authority as they discharged their leadership roles. To mitigate some of the mental health inequalities perpetuated by the gendered ecclesiastical hierarchy as it now stands, Relief Society presidents should be encouraged to dictate their own disclosure rules rather than accepting a default expectation that bishops should have access to all female members' private information. This would not only shelter Latter-day Saint women against male leaders' oversight and potential discipline, it would also increase the likelihood that women would share their needs with their Relief Society president in the first place. Re-negotiating disclosure boundaries would only be effective, however, if Relief Society presidents had enough fiscal and cultural resources of their own to dispense financial and social support to female members in need without having to ask the bishop's permission. Finally, the organizational change with the largest potential to expand LDS women's access to ecclesiastical mental health support resources would be to invite female leaders to hear confession and grant absolution. Not only would this grant members greater access to confession as a potential therapeutic communication setting despite their gender identity, it would also decrease the likelihood that female survivors of sexual violence (and other forms of male aggression) would experience secondary traumatization in an ecclesiastical setting that is designed to promote recovery, healing, and community.

Barring widespread institutional reform, individual local leaders have enough autonomy and power to increase equity in access to ecclesiastical support resources by making themselves more approachable to women and by empowering their female counterparts with greater autonomy and resources to directly meet female members' needs. Male leaders can start conversations about how gender affects LDS membership experiences and opportunities and listen with the intent to improve their ability to take perspective. Bishops can also publicly communicate a "need to know only" disclosure expectation with the Relief Society president. They can designate funds in the ward budget for a Relief Society president to utilize with no questions asked. They can invite the Relief Society president into sensitive one-on-one conversations with the opposite gender or even just ask the Relief Society president to conduct them on her own. These small alterations would vastly increase the chances that the members who need the most mental health support are the ones getting access to the rich resources available in the LDS Church and culture, regardless of their gender.

In the current organizational structure, gender often constrains female members of the Church of Jesus Christ of Latter-day Saints from fully accessing mental health support resources in their local congregations. This is because the only leaders with the authority to hear confession and dispense functional support are men. In their discourse, LDS bishops expressed varying awareness of the communication barriers gender and power present to women who must ask a bishop for help with their mental or emotional distress. Bishops also described institutional policies as preventing them from mitigating power differentials and improving women's experience in the interpersonal ecclesiastical interaction. Thus, in their talk, LDS bishops described gendered barriers that female members experience when trying to access mental health support resources through their male leaders.

Limits to female leaders' spiritual and institutional power prevent Relief Society presidents from providing direct independent care to the LDS women that is commensurate with services the bishop could offer. Though participants described female spiritual leaders as passionate, aware, and reliable in the service of the mental and emotional needs of LDS women, they also described critical limitations that prevented LDS female leaders from adequately meeting all the emotional and mental health needs of LDS women. Specifically, the fact that Relief Society presidents were required to disclose all personal information to bishops compromised their ability to act as a confidant to women. Additionally, a lack of spiritual authority, which blocked Relief Society presidents from confessional contexts, prevented female Latter-day Saints in distress from having access to pastoral counseling that was adequately responsive to their experiences as women. Reports of gendered or sexual violence emphasize fundamental weaknesses inherent in a system dominated by a gendered power hierarchy, which ideologically masks male leaders' inability to fully understand women's experiences and perspectives. In these specific ways discourse from LDS bishops, Relief Society presidents, and professional mental healthcare providers reveal how gender enables barriers that make accessing LDS mental health support resources harder for women.

In this context we see a prime example of how religious organizations that are characterized by consistent gendered imbalances of power, a lack of institutional voice for women, and a culture which relegates women primarily to the private sphere, enable symptoms of mental illness in women while simultaneously constraining their access to institutional support. Indeed, the specifics about how gender influences mental health in Mormon contexts illustrate how ideological inequalities can be translated into institutional structures, which in turn have a tangible effect on the holistic wellness of human bodies. Latter-day Saint women's struggles to equally access mental healthcare resources in their religious communities points to the importance of understanding the integral relationships between symbolic worlds and physical realities.

Note

1 I acknowledge that gender is fluid and non-binary. However, the LDS community largely understands gender as existing in a male/female dichotomy that is inextricable from sex assigned at birth. For the purposes of this chapter, then, my discussion about gender will be limited to exploring women's experiences within the LDS lifeworld. This is because females constitute the only gender minority that is currently acknowledged by the dominant religious culture.

References

Charmaz, K., 2006. *Constructing Grounded Theory: A Practical Guide through Qualitative Analysis*. London and Thousand Oaks, CA: Sage.
Chen, Y., and VanderWeele, T.J., 2018. Associations of Religious Upbringing with Subsequent Health and Well-being from Adolescence to Young Adulthood: An Outcome-Wide Analysis. *American Journal of Epidemiology* 187: 2355–64. https://doi.org/10.1093/aje/kwy142.
Crawford, R.P., 2018. A Spectrum of Silence and the Single Storyteller: Stigma, Sex, and Mental Illness among the Latter-day Saints. Ohio University/OhioLINK. http://orcid.org/0000-0002-5508-0293.
Dein, S., Cook, C., and Koenig, H., 2012. Religion, Spirituality, and Mental Health: Current Controversies and Future Directions. *Journal of Nervous and Mental Disease* 200: 852–55.
Dougherty, D.S., 2001. Sexual Harassment as [Dys]Functional Process: A Feminist Standpoint Analysis. *Journal of Applied Communication Research* 29(4): 372–402. https://doi.org/10.1080/00909880128116.
The First Presidency of the Church of Jesus Christ of Latter-day Saints, 1995. The Family: A Proclamation to the World. www.lds.org/topics/family-proclamation?lang=eng.
Goffman, E., 1990. The Medical Model and Mental Institutions. In *Asylums: Essays on the Social Situation of Mental Patients and Other Inmates*. New York: Doubleday, pp. 321–86.
Haque, A., 2013. Psychology and Religion: Two Approaches to Positive Mental Health. *Intellectual Discourse* 8(1): 81–94. http://journals.iium.edu.my/intdiscourse/index.php/islam/article/view/483.
Hinderaker, A., 2015. Severing Primary Ties: Exit from Totalistic Organizations. *Western Journal of Communication* 79(1): 92–115. https://doi.org/10.1080/10570314.2014.943422.
Krok, D., 2014. Religiousness and Social Support as Predictive Factors for Mental Health Outcomes. *Archives of Psychiatry & Psychotherapy* 16(4): 65–76. https://doi.org/10.12740/APP/31319.
Lace, J.W., Haeberlein, K.A., and Handal, P.J., 2018. Religious Integration and Psychological Distress: Different Patterns in Emerging Adult Males and Females. *Journal of Religion & Health* 57(6): 2378–88. https://doi.org/10.1007/s10943-018-0608-0.
Pennebaker, J.W., 1995. *Emotion, Disclosure, and Health*. Washington, DC: American Psychological Association.

Richardson, L., 2003. Writing: A Method of Inquiry. In N.K. Denzin and Y.S. Lincoln, eds. *Collecting and Interpreting Qualitative Materials*. Thousand Oaks, CA: Sage, pp. 499–541.

Rogers, E.B., Stanford, M., and Garland, D.R., 2012. The Effects of Mental Illness on Families within Faith Communities. *Mental Health, Religion & Culture* 15(3): 301–13. https://doi.org/10.1080/13674676.2011.573474.

Stanford, M.S., 2007. Demon or Disorder: A Survey of Attitudes toward Mental Illness in the Christian Church. *Mental Health, Religion & Culture* 10(5): 445–49.

Tracy, S., 2010. Qualitative Quality: Eight "Big-Tent" Criteria for Excellent Qualitative Research. *Qualitative Inquiry* 16: 837–51.

Ullman, S.E., 2010. *Talking about Sexual Assault: Society's Response to Survivors*. Washington, DC: American Psychological Association.

Vaaler, M.L., 2008. Seeking Help from the Clergy for Relationship Violence. *Journal of Spirituality in Mental Health* 10(2): 79–100. https://doi.org/10.1080/19349630802074371.

Williams, J., 2013. Regional Cultures and Health Outcomes: Implications for Performance Measurement, Public Health and Policy. *The Social Science Journal* 50(4): 461–70. https://doi.org/10.1016/j.soscij.2013.09.007.

World Health Organization, 2001. *The World Health Report 2001—Mental Health: New Understanding, New Hope*. www.who.int/whr/2001/en/.

Yangarber-Hicks, N., 2004. Religious Coping Styles and Recovery from Serious Mental Illnesses. *Journal of Psychology and Theology* 32(4): 305–17.

Yu, E., Chang, E., Yu, T., Bennett, S., and Fowler, E., 2017. Examining Gender Differences in the Roles of Meaning in Life and Interpersonal Expectancies in Depressive Symptoms. *Gender Issues* 34(3): 203–22. https://doi.org/10.1007/s12147-016-9174-5.

Further reading

Compton, M.T., and Shim, M.P.H., 2015. *The Social Determinants of Mental Health*. Washington, DC: American Psychiatric Publishing.

Dougherty, D.S., 2001. Sexual Harassment as [Dys]Functional Process: A Feminist Standpoint Analysis. *Journal of Applied Communication Research* 29(4): 372–402. https://doi.org/10.1080/00909880128116.

Hattery, A.J., and Smith, E., 2019. The Catholic Church. In *Gender, Power, and Violence: Responding to Sexual and Intimate Partner Violence in Society Today*. Lanham, MD: Rowman & Littlefield, pp. 151–82.

Hinderaker, A., 2015. Severing Primary Ties: Exit from Totalistic Organizations. *Western Journal of Communication* 79: 92–115. https://doi.org/10.1080/10570314.2014.943422.

Rogers, E.B., Stanford, M., and Garland, D.R., 2012. The Effects of Mental Illness on Families within Faith Communities. *Mental Health, Religion & Culture* 15(3): 301–13. https://doi.org/10.1080/13674676.2011.573474.

Stanford, M.S., 2007. Demon or Disorder: A Survey of Attitudes toward Mental Illness in the Christian Church. *Mental Health, Religion & Culture* 10(5): 445–49.

Ullman, S.E., 2010. *Talking about Sexual Assault: Society's Response to Survivors*. Washington, DC: American Psychological Association.

Wang, P., Berglund, P., and Kessler, R., 2003. Patterns and Correlates of Contacting Clergy for Mental Disorders in the United States. *Health Services Research* 38: 647–73.

27
WOMEN'S GENDER ROLES AND MORMONISM IN ENGLAND

Alison Halford

Researching English Mormon women as a distinct group from North American Mormon women means identifying both the similarities and the points of departure in existing constructs of Mormon gender. For some English Latter-day Saint women constructing gender finds them confronting structures, lived practices and experiences in what can appear as "an American church with global outreach" rather than an international religion (Rutherford, 2016, p. 39). The close coupling of the Church of Jesus Christ of Latter-day Saints[1] (Mormons) and the United States is partly due to the origins of the Church emerging from a series of spiritual encounters received by a North American farm boy, Joseph Smith, in 1820, founding a discrete North American religion (Vance, 2015; Yeates, 1939). There is also the theological importance of one of the most sacred Church texts, the Book of Mormon, a scriptural account that claims Jesus Christ visited the Americas after his resurrection, positioning the United States of America as "Zion," as a Utopian concept and a physical location in Mormon discourse (Hartley, 1975; Jensen, 1987; Whittaker, 1987).

Mormonism may claim to be a global religion but it seems congregations outside of North America are often collapsed into a singular international narrative, with inevitably the United States being excluded from that definition. However, conceptualizing global Mormonism as discrete spaces serves the same purpose as "separate but equal" gender roles, that is to uphold primary authority and power within one group by claiming difference. Moreover, whilst there is a body of literature critiquing Church structures, polices, and leadership that reinforce cultural relativism (Decoo, 2013; Hawkins, 1988; Phillips, 2006; Van Beek, 2005), there is less written on the way that Mormon women outside of North America are having to navigate gender roles that are informed by North American exceptionalism.

This chapter is an attempt to address the gap in literature by discussing to what extent English Latter-day Saint women are negotiating gender roles that resist, comply, or embrace North American Mormonism. It means moving away from historic studies, that can be argued are a self-interested chasm, as English Latter-day Saint women only seem to feature when they cross the Atlantic (Arrington, 1987; Bartholomew, 1995). Instead, I will focus on the disconnections and connections between English and Utah Latter-day Saint women that link issues of identity, equality, and gender with Mormonism and North American cultural practices.

First, I will start the discussion at a point of interconnect for English and Utah Latter-day Saint women—the nineteenth-century Mormon practice of polygamy—but suggest the resultant tension from polygamy in the British context has facilitated contemporary English Mormon women reimaging Mormon gender norms to combat North American exceptionalism. Then, drawing upon thirty semi-structured interviews with Mormon women based in the Midlands region of England,[2] I will explore strategies of resistance that the women are utilizing to construct a regional gender role: the rejection of the Mormon gender model "Molly Mormon" and "It's a Utah thing," which positions Utah Mormon women as the object and the subject of Mormon female embodiment.

Finally, I will show how some English Latter-day Saint women are negotiating gender by creating a discrete third space between Church doctrine and policies and English secular societal values. In doing so, they are constructing gender roles that are informed by "pragmatic egalitarianism," whilst still claiming orthopraxis (Gallagher and Smith, 1999). In return, by departing from prescriptive gender roles, found in both Mormon and secular spaces, this allows English Mormon women to envisage a more nuanced, inclusive gender construction. Moreover, English Mormon women in resisting North American Mormon exceptionalism, rather than destabilizing Church narratives of a global cohesive sorority, are accommodating gender roles that acknowledge diverse, complex, contradictions that build spiritual resilience.

Pioneers, polygamy, and persecution: depictions of Mormon women in the English landscape

In England Mormonism is not taught within religious studies but is part of the history curriculum with a syllabus that covers Mormon theological discourse of Zionist gathering, along with the polygamy and the economic and social benefits of migration, which resulted in early Church colonization of mid-west North America (Head, 2009). Therefore, the Church of Jesus Christ of Latter-day Saints in England is not only inherently associated with quintessentially North American narratives of Mormon pioneers but it also reinforces continuing association between Mormonism and polygamy (Perkins, 2007). However, early English women converts differed from their North American counterparts, as they were "less submissive," more likely to be "politically active," and more "articulate" (Arrington, 1987, p. 73). This means rather than depicting early English Latter-day Saint woman, as Leonard Arrington (1987) suggests, as independent-thinking, politically engaged social actors, there is continuing institutional reproduction of English Mormon women as either economic migrants, sexualized polygamists' wives, or victims of religious persecution.

In the same way contemporary Islam, especially Muslim women, are seen by certain aspects of British media as destabilizing British collective identity (Crawley, McMahon, and Jones, 2016), women joining the Church in the nineteenth century were seen as rejecting English religious tradition, mainstream values, and culture (Perkins, 2007). The Victorian popular press held a deep suspicion of the American origins of the Latter-day Saint Church, which was further exacerbated when in 1852 news broke that the Church was practicing polygamy in North America (Grant, 1992; Parshall, 2009). The resultant enmity between mainstream English society and Mormonism escalated to such an extent that by 1910–1911 questions were asked in the Houses of Parliament on whether to expel all Latter-day Saints from Britain (Parshall, 2009).

During this time Mormon women were being singled out for the most critical media depictions, founded on anti-Mormon depictions of Mormon missionaries as predatory males, which positioned women as passive victims forced into polygamous unions (Lecourt, 2013). The continuing legacy of anti-Mormon propaganda was a "moral panic" (Cohen, 2002) that maintained the Mormon agenda in England was to sex-traffic young women to Utah (Perkins, 2007). This can be shown in the case of Gillian,[3] who was baptized in 1979. Gillian found parental resistance to her decision to join the Church was not only based on her father's fear that she was at a risk of being kidnapped and sent to Utah but he believed in a century-old myth that the Church had built a tunnel from the United Kingdom to the United States for that purpose.

> My father was quite a bit older than my mum and he had instructions from his parents not to talk to those Mormons. But back in the day, obviously, they didn't think much of Mormons in those days and I think it built up this idea that they should be avoided, plus he thought that I would up sticks and go to America. I mean he was around the days when they [Mormons] have this tunnel to whisk girls away, so he was frightened, he was in fear that I would leave.

Societal framing of Mormonism has shifted in England, as political institutions are increasingly legitimatizing diverse religious movements. Yet, demands for religious women's bodies to be policed and protected from what is seen as religious exploitation is still prevalent in post-millennial England. Thus, whilst the importance of faith beliefs for women may be recognized in British legislation, British societal structures reflect secular belief that religion is "seldom benign" as it continues to structurally reinforce gender inequality (Council of the European Union, 2005). This means English Latter-day Saint women constantly have to simultaneously resist and comply with gender roles in both secular and Mormon spaces, placing them at times in tension with both factions.

The early Church practice of polygamy continues to shape English societal attitudes to Mormon women, with several women I interviewed commenting they are still confronting religious illiteracy on Mormon family structures: "If only I had a pound for every time I am asked how many wives does your husband have, I would be a very wealthy woman" (Debbie, 42 years old, second generation). In addition, the consequences of early nineteenth-century emphasis on English converts relocating to North America, which saw the systematic dismantling of English Mormon congregations (Jensen, 1987), has shaped how English Latter-day Saint women view their spiritual authority in congregational spaces. In conditioning early converts to Mormonism that emigrating to Utah was evidence of the extent of their piousness, women who remained in England were seen as less faithful by members of the Church (Stenhouse (1889 [2008]). This is shown in the comments of one woman I interviewed, Bryony, when talking about the experiences of her husband's grandmother, who had joined the Church in 1915:

> It just seems in Utah they are interested only in their world, I mean look at Church history accounts, all about the pioneers who went to Utah, but my husband was baptised when he was 11 and his grandmother joined the church in 1915 and very little is written about the members that remained [in England]. She was stoned in the streets in Bradford in the 1920s as she did stay behind [not emigrate to Utah]; her best friend married an American and went to the States and most of the girls did marry missionaries who served here. But she stayed and despite what others thought she was still very faithful.
>
> *(Bryony, 68 years old, convert)*

For Bryony, not only is there a sense of betrayal that the institutional Church failed female converts that remained in England, subjecting them to persecution and alienation from English communities, she also feels she must defend her grandmother-in-law's piety. In conjoining English Mormon women with the history of early Mormon settlement in Utah, along with doctrinal concepts of a North America Zion and a lack of alternative narratives, the implication persists that faithful English Latter-day Saint women are those who relocate to Utah or desire to be like the women in Utah. This suggests to prove that in their religious credentials English Latter-day Saints may be more willing and anxious to comply and submit to Mormon gender roles.

Instead, as the following section shows, like early English Mormon women converts who were prepared to engage in political activism, English Latter-day Saint women are mobilizing resistance to certain Mormon gender roles and refusing to venerate Utah as a spiritual paradigm. By rejecting the Mormon gender role, "Molly Mormon," as an acceptable model, some English Mormon women are creating a counter-narrative, which is reimaging Utah as a contested Mormon identity that sees strategic collective resistance to North American exceptionalism. Moreover, having been subject to the consequences of early Church-sanctioned congregational asset stripping that rendered them vulnerable, implicit in these gender negotiations is a desire among English Mormon women to re-assert themselves as a legitimate religious authority in both public and Mormon spaces.

Molly Mormon: "it's a Utah thing"

Carine Decoo-Vanwelkenhuysen (2016), in her study of attitudes of European Mormon women, found it was the women's own mainstream culture rather than North American Church traditions that influenced how they constructed gender. Similarly, when asking about differences between Mormon women, several women I interviewed emphasized how Utah's concept of gender is counter-intuitive to English values and norms and not transferable outside of the Intermountain range, suggesting Utah is best understood as a "Mormon culture region" (Yorgason, 2003, p. 18). This means some English women conceptualize Utah women as symbolic of a privileged Mormonism that informs practice and policies with North American notions of gender.

The institutional Church claims Mormon ideals of gender are based on Mormon doctrine, with rhetoric that advocates that Mormon women will find the greatest fulfillment through marriage, domesticity, and motherhood and that conforming to these roles is a measure of their righteousness (Welker, 2016), a gender role, according to Sonia Johnson (1979, p. 75), which is designed to "reinforce the stereotype of the 'good' Mormon woman, acceptable to the brethren and therefore to God." But for some feminist scholars Mormon gender constructs are at times more reflective of a post-World War II North American idealized conceptualization of womanhood than divinely inspired (Brooks, 2016; Farnsworth, 1991).

The Mormon ideal of female embodiment, where a woman's primary function is reproduction, making them the gatekeeper for the families temporal and spiritual well-being, became known within North American and European Mormon communities as a "Molly Mormon." Gaining considerable traction in the Latter-day Saint congregations during the 1970s, it became a caricature of an orthopraxis Mormon woman (Farnsworth, 1991). Thus, when English Latter-day Saint women were asked to describe Molly Mormon, they described this gender role as embodying three characteristics: a woman's fertility, striving for perfection in the domestic space, and a representative of the archetypal Utah-based Latter-day Saint woman. Therefore for one interviewer, Emily, a 57-year-old divorced convert and mother of four, Molly Mormon is synonymous with a gender role that appears to be more reflective of nineteenth-century pioneer women: "I don't really know what it is like for those in other countries, but I get this impression of a Utah-Idaho Mormon woman. She must be absolutely perfect at baking bread, making all their children's clothes, having numerous children."

The work of Lori Beaman (2001) on Canadian Mormon women is instrumental for gaining a sociological definition of Molly Mormon. Beaman (p. 67) devised a typology of Mormon gender performance based on three broad categories: "Molly Mormon," "Mormon feminist," and "Moderate," which relate to the degree of willingness to accept and observe Mormon doctrine and practices in relationship to the broader societal expectations of gender. Beaman contends a Mormon feminist will exhibit secular views that may conflict with Mormon gender norms, an example of this is Mormon women who openly challenge the exclusion of women for positions of priesthood authority, putting them in direct opposition with the Church. By comparison, Moderate Mormon women negotiate gender enough to remain within mainstream and Mormon notions of gender. They may, for instance, be more likely to accept that women could be more visible in Church structures but are unlikely to agitate for change. In contrast, Molly Mormon is prepared, whether it is beneficial to her or not, to "obediently follow church leaders and teachings" (Beaman, 2001, p. 69).

The English Latter-day Saint women I interviewed, whether converts or generational members, did disassociate themselves from the ideals of Mormon feminists. For instance, there was little support for the extension of the priesthood to all, with the most common response being that even if women were given the priesthood it would not automatically equate to greater equality in institutional structures. As Evie, a 32-year-old mother of three, whose parents joined the Church before she was born, states: "Mormon feminism always stresses that because women don't hold the priesthood we are seen as less but they don't seem to realise that even if we hold the priesthood it doesn't mean that we will be seen as equal."

For a small but significant number of those I interviewed issues of gender inequality went beyond Mormon structures as they saw patriarchal exploitation manifest in domestic and public spaces, and within all religious and secular structures.

> Mormonism is male dominated, it means inequality and male dominated practices, so it automatically makes the assumption that the model is patriarchal. Yes, I do think there is a lot of disproportionate power to the men in the church and in the Mormon community, Mormon men do have access to power. But, I mean in my job where I have a lot of responsibility, I have a huge team, I have a huge budget, but it is still a male dominated arena. It's about recognising a male dominant culture but it's everywhere.
>
> *(Ellen, 56 years old, second generation)*

The heightened awareness among some English Mormon women of the extent to which gender inequality is omnipresent in all societal interactions but their reluctance to identify with feminism (secular or otherwise) correlates with European Latter-day Saint women's attitudes towards gender equality (Decoo-Vanwelkenhuysen, 2016). Furthermore, Decco-Vanwelkenhuysen contends that as Mormon women in Europe reside in countries where pay, health, education, and political engagement is moving towards greater gender equality than North America (World Economic Forum, 2018), gender roles such as either the Molly Mormon model or feminists are more pronounced in the United States.

It seems English Latter-day Saint women, like their European counterparts, are compliant to religious institutional constructs of gender whilst drawing upon secular notions of gender roles to further develop a less rigid gender construct. This allows them to remain within acceptable boundaries of both structures and according to Beaman's typology would frame English Mormon women as moderates. Forming gender roles through a moderate Mormon framework could result in English Mormon women reducing tension between the Church and mainstream cultural practices, but it fails to capture the extent to which English Latter-day Saint women not only advocate but are impassioned about the role of women inherently associated with being a wife and mother.

The women I interviewed, irrespective of their martial status or fertility, see the female body as an embryonic deity. Female embodiment is seen as a conduit for divine expression and experience through a woman's function to reproduce, then serve and nurture her family, which is far more suggestive of the ideals of the Molly Mormon model. Molly Mormon is not only a representation of a pious, hyper-feminine Mormon orthopraxis, who internalizes and reproduces uncritical Church practices, policies, and doctrine, but also positions women as "mothers primarily responsible for the nurture of their children" (First Presidency and the Council of the Twelve, 1995). This is because Molly Mormon as a gender construct maintains theological emphasis on biological essentialism and a separate but different narrative that co-conspires to uphold patriarchal hierarchy (Allred, 2015; Dworkin, 1983; Farnsworth, 1991; Johnson, 1979).

Molly Mormon becomes influential in boundary maintenance as the model is evoked to remind Mormon women that their key gender role is protecting and stabilizing the idealized family structure (Beck, 2007; Kimball, 1979; Packer, 1989). However, despite English Mormon women reproducing and replicating gender constructs based on the cruciality of women as wives and mothers, they view Molly Mormons with disdain as the model represents an unhealthy portrayal of womanhood. Bryony captures that when talking about her experiences of visiting her daughter's ward in Utah, where she sees women striving to be a Molly Mormon but instead cultivating exaggerated gender orthodoxies, which seldom bring happiness or increased piety:

> It's interesting because I was in my daughter's ward in Provo (an area of Utah) [and] everything they do every day is seen, they have to claim to have these perfect lives and feel that they have go to every [church] meeting, they must be seen going to the temple all the time. They are so Molly Mormon, but still they feel that they failed.
> *(Bryony, 68 years old, convert)*

Likewise, Lois feels that her siblings who migrated to Utah during the 1980s are centering their service on overt actions that improve their social standing rather than engage in meaningful charitable acts:

> I remember going to visit them [Lois' sisters] in Utah at Christmas time and they felt they had to give a gift to everybody, to every neighbour in the street, so stressed as they were baking mounds of cookies. I remember thinking that there is no need for that and that they were so busy doing that rather than feeding the homeless. But they're keeping up an appearance of what families do to serve others.

However, whilst Bryony and Lois critique Utah women as a visible promotion of a hyper-feminine, outwardly rigid performance of Mormonism, neither question what structural constructs are in place to cause Mormon women in Utah to act this way.

Brenda Brasher (1998) contends it is not unusual to see a lack of consciousness in religious women regarding the control a church institution has in prescribing and enforcing a singular narrative of women. She maintains that conservative religious women will reinvent perceptions of circumstances to position themselves as social agents, whilst avoiding conflict by failing to address embedded inequality and oppressive practices of institutional structures. Therefore, it seems that some English Mormon women are prepared to frame Molly Mormon as a product of Utah exceptionalism rather than accept that it reflects a patriarchal institutional strategy to introduce competition between women to isolate them from alternative models.

Moreover, a considerable number of interviewees associate the Latter-day Saint General Women's Leadership with a typical representation of Molly Mormon. For Mormon women the institutional reinforcement of Mormon female homogeneity comes through the worldwide women's General Female Latter-day Saint Presidencies, who represent Relief Society (women over the age of 18), Young Women (young women, 12–18 years old), and Primary (young children, 18 months to 12 years) at the highest level, overseen by the First Presidency, located in Salt Lake City, Utah. The role of the General Relief Society Presidency is to connect and inspire the global women-only church program Relief Society, which allows the institutional Church to claim a religious "imagined community" between women. Benedict Anderson (2006) defines an imagined community as the ability for individuals to feel an affinity for other individuals through creating group collective expression, such as anthems, national holidays, and generational connections without physically interacting with them in an intimate way. For the General Relief Society Presidency, becoming an imagined community means they establish practices, ideologies, and norms to cultivate meaningful connections between Mormon women (Burton, 2015).

However, for many women I interviewed the women's General Presidencies represent Molly Mormon to such a degree they expressed apathy rather than saw connections with their female spiritual leaders' leadership. This distancing between themselves and what they see as the antithesis of English Mormon women even extends to a critique of the leaders' clothing as it appears to exaggerate their Molly Mormon particularity:

> I don't know, this is difficult, and now I am being really honest, whilst I am all for women having a greater profile and everything, I really struggle to identify with the likes of general women's presidencies within the church. When we have the general women's meetings, I just can't get past the sickly sweetness, I mean, when they called the new primary presidency in those coloured jackets, it was just too much to bear.
> *(Tilly, 36 years old, second generation)*

Tilly's response to female Church leaders is reflective of many of the women I interviewed when discussing models of gender, yet there is little collective consciousness in the relationship between the highest female ecclesiastical leadership as an idealized form of Mormon womanhood and the maintaining of an all-male priesthood leadership. Instead, interviewees like Tilly and Mary, who held female leadership responsibilities in their local churches, will avoid listening to women leaders at conferences rather than question what causes these female leaders to become a material representation of Molly Mormon:

> I mean, sometimes the talk from the pulpit, like Julie Beck's talk on mothers staying at home with their children, we were away when she gave the talk, but when I looked it up on-line I was [rolls her eyes and sighs loudly]. When choosing the ones I am going to read I tend to go for the apostles rather than the general Relief Society presidency ... I am all for women talking more but those talks don't appeal to me.
> *(Mary, 71 years old, convert)*

However, as Lois' comments below suggest, the diminishing of the General Women's Presidency could also be symptomatic of discomfort at what they see as the homogeneity of female Church leaders that reinforce privileges of class, economic status, and race with positions of leadership:

It was a Sister's conference, when they first allowed 8-year-old girls to go to it and it was lovely because there was my daughter, with her daughter and me and also her mother-in-law, we were able to sit together, it was such a lovely feeling ... it was wonderful. But the conference, it did feel rather sugary whether it is because they are American, the American side of it or the Utah side of it, we didn't know ... it just felt a little bit earnest, you are not sure if they're in the real world. One of the Young Women presidents talked about a run she made up a mountain, that sort of thing but you get the impression it would be in her expensive new trainers and joggers.

(Lois, 62 years old, second generation)

By rejecting these female leaders as a distorted Utah Mormon gender performance, for some English women, this also means mobilizing opposition towards American exceptionalism in the Church, which is a political act. In order to reclaim power from a dominant narrative those outside of a main body can embrace the designated role of a "spoiled identity" and re-frame themselves as the norm and the main body as the deviant (Goffman, 1990, p. 17). Utah Mormons do have greater access to Mormon leadership, Mormon cultural capital, and institutional power (Quinn, 2001). Therefore, re-imagining Utah Mormon women as a stigmatized identity allows English Later-day Saint women, as a Mormon minority excluded from visible power, to propose that Utah hegemony is an issue when constructing Mormon gender roles.

The third space: pragmatic egalitarianism, the home, and shifting gender roles

Studies on Islamic women and Orthodox Jewish women have shown how religious piety in the domestic sphere can be a platform for empowerment when negotiating gender (Avishai, 2008; Mahmood, 2005). Similarly, English Later-day Saint women see the domestic sphere, in the mundane acts within homes, or in the communal connections that arise from that space, as a place where the intersection between gender and religion is more fully formed. In this regard, the home is becoming, for the women I interviewed, a "third space" (Bhabha, 2006, p. 155).

The concept of a third space is drawn from postcolonial studies on how displaced people navigate the new identities of the host country and their own previous national identity, "hence they create spaces that may be called 'third space'" (Aune, Sharma, and Vincett, 2008, p. 9). The use of the domestic sphere as a third space to re-configure Mormon practices and secularized gender discourses to create broader gender practices in the home sees some English Mormon women claim authority, rather than the structural Church, to dictate gender roles. This allows them to decide how their faith beliefs are translated in lived practices and shape gender constructs that benefit all members of the family.

Cultivating the home as a third space means English Mormon women are shifting away from patterns of Utah Mormon gender constructs to engage in a broader negotiated framework, which encourages diverse forms of identity and aims to navigate the tension between religious beliefs and societal changes. For instance, Evie feels residing in England, a partially secularized state, is not a barrier but an opportunity to access a more expansive gender construct as she is less constrained than Utah Mormon women:

I think there is a difference, especially between us and Utah, it is a culture that is completely Mormon, you know, like the perfect "Molly Mormon" woman. But it must be like living in a goldfish bowl, everybody watching you, whilst here we can be different, everybody can be accepted, it is easier to be a sinner.

(Evie, 32 years old, second generation)

The ability of English Mormon women to construct gender that traverses secular and sacred boundaries but which also appears as faithful adherence reflects what Sally Gallagher and Christian Smith (1999) term "pragmatic egalitarianism." This is where religious teachings, for example those that advocate male and female gender roles such as the male head of the household and the stay-at-home mother, are agreed in principle while lived practices are indistinguishable from secular norms. For example, Jill, a married mother of two children and a teacher, is acutely aware of the societal shifts in women's roles but still sees that her primary function is as a wife and mother. However, she believes that her role is not restricted to remaining in the domestic sphere and that working outside of the home does not undermine her commitment to her faith or family, it merely alters how it is manifested:

> I think, having talked to my sister in Utah, it's still very traditional rules over there, there is an expectation that the family is falling apart if the wife goes out to work, whereas I think the norm here is that women can go and do go out to work. And we have had a period where we have those [traditional] roles here, but things are changing. So, I don't feel so much that I'm not being faithful but I am acting out what is expected of me [by looking after my family].

Pragmatic egalitarianism operates in the domestic space as an ability among Mormon women to move beyond Church ideals or prescribed behavior to exercise agency that makes family structures robust when encountering secular and religious arenas. This can be seen in the negotiations undertaken by Debbie, a second-generation member and mother of five children who interprets responsibility for her children's spiritual well-being, alongside their temporal needs, to mean focusing on them becoming "good" people rather than restricting their growth to being good members:

> I've been given this chance to have all these children, who are just loaned to me on earth and it's up to me to bring them up to be good people, to be their own person but a good person as well.
>
> *(Debbie, 42 years old, second generation)*

For Debbie, and other women I interviewed, pragmatic egalitarianism formed in the domestic space is constructing gender roles into lived practices that allow Mormon women in England to function with less tension in the wider community as it serves to mediate between conflicting secular/sacred ideals of gender. Moreover, like the early English Mormon converts, they contradict depictions of religious women being submissive and forced to remain in the domestic sphere by owning the home as a site of transition and transformation when constructing gender practices and expressions. This indicates that as Britain becomes increasingly "religious indifferent" (Bruce, 2018, n.p.), English Latter-day Saints will increasingly "pick and choose" secular norms and faith ideals that can accommodate and validate expansive family structures that do not reflect Church ideals (Bushman, 2016, p. 265). Furthermore, as the institutional Church structure is promoting family-centered gospel learning, it may also see homes be used by Mormon women as politicalized spaces as they select and develop spiritual resources that address gender inequality and challenge Mormon gender roles.

Conclusion

Mormon women in England are constantly navigating increasingly secularized civic society, institutionalized state-approved religious orthopraxis, and North Americanized Mormon doctrine and practices. To understand English Mormon women, their lived practices, experiences and expressions of gender, means to see them as "subjects who are actually engaged in intricate, highly gendered theological world views" (Hoyt, 2007, p. 90). Moreover, to see how English Mormon women construct gender can be instrumental, in not only exploring the relationship between North American ideals and Mormonism, but in understanding how religious women monitor and enforce gender roles as acts of resistance and signs of emancipation.

By challenging some aspects of the Molly Mormon model, English Mormon women are "less submissive" than their North American counterparts in relation to traditional expectations of gender (Arrington, 1987). Yet, English Mormon women still ascribe to some key ideals, as being a wife and mother is a core aspiration and there is still inherent in that construction of gender a female dependence on being an object of affection and sexual desire for men. This means that whilst English Later-day Saint women develop strategies that make them appear more emancipated than Utah Latter-day Saint women, they still support the continuation of an all-male Church leadership. For some English Latter-day Saint women, the justification for complying with Church structures that are fundamentally unequal is gender inequality is found in all societal structures. In addition, English Latter-day Saint women appear to be disinclined to acknowledge the extent to which existing models of gender could be the result of a systemic patriarchal ideology that produces gender roles that maintain competition between women to isolate them from collective action.

For some English Mormon women, the highest level of Mormon female leadership is a material representation of a hyper-feminine caricature of Mormon female embodiment, and many are reluctant to engage with such models of American female authority as they perceive them as symbolic of and inherent to Utah Mormon culture. However, in challenging rigid, imposed American-centric concepts of gender as counter cultural to gospel principles, English Latter-day Saint women are generating their own hierarchy of what are acceptable representations of Mormon women, which raises questions regarding issues of power in relationship to Euro-American privilege.

Creating a third space means the domestic sphere becomes for English Mormon women a place where religious and societal gender norms collide to provide practices, and ways of thinking, that inform their gender performances in public and private arenas. This allows some English women to reconfigure their own positionality regarding valid Mormonism, which sees them reclaim and dismantle institutional structures of power by diminishing the authority of North America Mormonism to dictate gender roles. It also sees Mormon women in Britain engaging in acts of pragmatic egalitarianism, which in some respects, such as mothers working outside the home, are indistinguishable from secular norms of gender. As a result, English Latter-day Saint women, by incorporating regional practices, are developing a distinctive gender construct that has more porous boundaries but still connects with their faith beliefs and Mormon practices. Notwithstanding, for most English Latter-day Saint women I interviewed, gender roles are a series of complex constructs navigating multiply demands to reflect the diversity of Mormon women's lived experiences and practices in a global religion.

Notes

1 In this chapter I will alternate between Mormon and Latter-day Saint when talking about members of the Church of Jesus Christ of Latter-day Saints. This is to recognize that my field research pre-dates the Church's announcement that Latter-day Saints is the preferred shortened name for members. In using both terms, I am aiming to acknowledge current demands by the organizational Church for members to no longer be called Mormons but show respect for the women who I interviewed during 2016–2017, who self-identified as Mormons.

2 The Midlands area (West and East) of England comprises Derbyshire, Leicestershire, Nottinghamshire, and Warwickshire. This area has historic association with early missionary efforts of the Church, with some of the longest established units found within the area. The oldest continuous Mormon congregations in England include Preston, near Manchester, that dates back to 1837, followed by Eastwood and Derby (1841 and 1842 respectively) (Cuthbert, 1987).
3 Pseudonyms have been given to protect the identity of the women interviewed.

References

Allred, J., 2015. LDS Gender Theology: A Feminist Perspective. In G. Shepherd, L. Anderson, and G. Shepherd, eds. *Voices for Equality: Ordain Women and Resurgent Mormon Feminism*. Salt Lake City, UT: Greg Kofford Press. (E-Book).
Anderson, B., 2006. *Imagined Communities*. Revised ed. London: Verso.
Arrington, L., 1987. Mormon Women in Nineteenth-Century Britain. *BYU Studies Quarterly* 27(1): 67–83.
Aune, K., Sharma, S., and Vincett, G., 2008. Introduction: Women, Secularization: "One Size fits All." In K. Aune, S. Sharma, and G. Vincett, eds. *Women and Religion in the West: Challenging Secularization*. Aldershot: Ashgate, pp. 1–23.
Avishai, O., 2008. "Doing Religion" in a Secular World: Women in Conservative Religions and the Question of Agency. *Gender & Society* 22(4): 409–21.
Bartholomew, R., 1995. *Audacious Women: Early British Mormon Immigrants*. Salt Lake City, UT: Signature Books.
Beaman, L., 2001. Molly Mormons, Mormon Feminists and Moderates: Religious Diversity and the Latter-day Saints Church. *Sociology of Religion* 62: 65–86.
Beck, J., 2007. *Mothers that Know*. LDS General Conference. October 4. Salt lake City, Utah. www.lds.org/general-conference/2007/10/mothers-who-know?lang=eng (accessed May 12, 2016).
Bhabha, H., 2006. Cultural Diversity and Cultural Differences. In B. Ashcroft, A. Griffiths, and H. Tiffin, eds. *The Post-Colonial Studies Reader*. New York: Routledge, pp. 155–57.
Brasher, B., 1998. *Godly Women: Fundamentalism and Female Power*. London: Rutgers University Press.
Brooks, J., 2016. Mormon Feminism: An Introduction. In J. Brooks, R. Steenblik, and H. Wheelwright, eds. *Mormon Feminism: Essential Writings*. Oxford: Oxford University Press, pp. 1–24.
Bruce, S., 2018. *Professor Steve Bruce*. www.chester.ac.uk/cfpp/research/staff/prof-s-bruce.
Burton, L., 2015. I Was a Stranger. LDS Conference. October 2. www.lds.org/general-conference/2016/04/i-was-a-stranger?lang=eng (accessed May 20, 2017).
Bushman, C., 2016. Agency in the Lives of Contemporary Women. In J. Holbrook and M. Bowman, eds. *Women and Mormonism: Historical and Contemporary Perspectives*. Salt Lake City, UT: University of Utah Press, pp. 263–273.
Cohen, S., 2002. *Folk Devils and Moral Panics*. Oxon: Routledge.
Council of the European Union, 2005. *Council of the European Union Resolution*, 1464. http://assembly.coe.int/nw/xml/XRef/Xref-XML2HTML-en.asp?fileid=17372&lang=en (accessed May 9, 2019).
Crawley, H., McMahon, D., and Jones, K., 2016. *Victims and Villains: Migrant Voices in the British Media*. Coventry: Coventry University.
Cuthbert, D., 1987. *The Second Century: Latter-day Saints in Great Britain 1937–1987*. Cambridge: Cambridge University Press.
Decoo, W., 2013. In Search of Mormon Identity: Mormon Culture, Gospel Culture, and an American Worldwide Church. *International Journal of Mormon Studies* 6: 1–53.
Decoo-Vanwelkenhuysen, C., 2016. Mormon Women in Europe: A Look at Gender Norms. In K. Holbrook and M. Bowman, eds. *Women and the LDS Church: Historical and Contemporary Perspectives*. Salt Lake City, UT: University of Utah Press, pp. 213–30.
Dworkin, A., 1983. *Right-wing Women: The Politics of Domesticated Females*. London: The Women's Press.
Farnsworth, S., 1991. Mormonism's Odd Couple: The Priesthood–Motherhood Connection. In J. Brooks, R. Steenblik, and H. Wheelwright, eds. *Mormon Feminism: Essential Writings*. Oxford: Oxford University Press, pp. 165–69.
First Presidency and the Council of the Twelve, 1995. The Family: A Proclamation to the World. Salt Lake City, UT: The Church of Jesus Christ of Latter-day Saints.
Gallagher, S., and Smith, C., 1999. Symbolic Traditionalism and Pragmatic Egalitarianism: Contemporary Evangelicals, Families and Gender. *Gender and Society* 13(2): 211–33.

Goffman, E., 1990 [1968]. *Stigma: Notes on a Management of Spoiled Identity*. London: Penguin.
Grant, B., 1992. The Church in the British Isles. In *The Encyclopaedia of Mormonism*. https://eom.byu.edu/index.php/British_Isles,_the_Church_in (accessed May 10, 2019).
Hartley, W., 1975. Coming to Zion. *Ensign*. www.lds.org/ensign/1975/07/coming-to-zion-saga-of-the-gathering?lang=eng (accessed July 23, 2016).
Hawkins, J., 1988. Behavioral Differences Are Like Language Differences; or, "Oh, Say, What Is Truth?" vs. "Do as I'm Doing." In M. Stovall, and C. Madsen, eds. *A Heritage of Faith*. Salt Lake City, Utah: Deseret Book, pp. 157–72.
Head, R., 2009. The Experience of Mormon Children in English School-Based Religious Education and Collective Worship. *International Journal of Mormon Studies* 2: 196–205.
Hoyt, A., 2007. Beyond the Victim/Empowerment Paradigm: The Gendered Cosmology of Mormon Women. *Feminist Theology* 16(1): 89–100.
Jensen, R., 1987. Truth Will Prevail: The Rise of the Church of Jesus Christ of Latter-Day Saints in the British Isles 1837–1987. In B. Bloxham, J. Moss, and L. Porter, eds. *Truth Will Prevail: The Rise of the Church of Jesus Christ of Latter-Day Saints in the British Isles 1837–1987*. Salt Lake City, UT: The Church of Jesus Christ of Latter-day Saints, pp. 165–98.
Johnson, S., 1979. *From Housewife to Heretic*. New York: Anchor Press/Doubleday.
Kimball, S., 1979. The Role of Righteous Women. *Ensign*. November, pp. 100–107.
Lecourt, S., 2013. The Mormons, the Victorians, and the Idea of Greater Britain. *Victorian Studies* 56(1): 85–112.
Mahmood, S., 2005. *Politics of Piety: The Islamic Revival and the Feminist Subject*. Princeton, NJ: Princeton University Press.
Packer, B., 1989. Tribute to Women. *Ensign*. May. www.churchofjesuschrist.org/study/ensign/1989/07/a-tribute-to-women?lang=eng (accessed June 1, 2019).
Parshall, A., 2009. *Winston Churchill Investigates the Mormon Question, 1910–1911*. June 12. www.keepapitchinin.org/2009/06/12/winston-churchill-investigates-the-mormon-question-1910-1911/#more-2164 (accessed May 14, 2019).
Perkins, J., 2007. The Story of the British Saints in Their Own Words: 1900–1950. In C. Doxey, R. Freeman, R. Holzapfel, and D. Wright, eds. *Regional Studies in Latter-Day Saint Church History: The British Isles*, Salt Lake City, UT: Brigham Young University, pp. 149–71.
Phillips, R., 2006. Rethinking the International Expansion of Mormonism. *Nova Religio: The Journal of Alternative and Emergent Religions* 10(1): 52–68.
Quinn, M., 2001. LDS "Headquarters Culture" and the Rest of Mormonism. *Dialogue: The Journal of Mormon Thought* 34(4): 137–52.
Rutherford, T., 2016. The Internationalization of Mormonism: Indications from India. In P. Mason and J. Turner, eds. *Out of Obscurity: Mormonism since 1945*. Oxford: Oxford University Press, pp. 37–63.
Stenhouse, F., 1889 [2008]. *Expose of Polygamy: A Lady's Life among the Mormons*. https://digitalcommons.usu.edu/cgi/viewcontent.cgi?article=1038&context=usupress_pubs.
Van Beek, W., 2005. "Mormon Europeans or European Mormons?" An "Afro-European" View on Religious Colonization. *Dialogue: A Journal of Mormon Thought* 38(4): 3–36.
Vance, L., 2015. *Women in New Religions*. New York: New York University Press.
Welker, H., 2016. *Baring Witness: 36 Mormon Women Talk Candidly about Love, Sex and Marriage*. Chicago, IL: University of Illinois Press.
Whittaker, D., 1987. The "Articles of Faith" in Early Mormon Literature and Thought. In D. Bitton and E. Beecher, eds. *New Views of Mormon History: A Collection of Essays in Honour of Leonard J. Arrington*. Salt Lake City, UT: University of Utah Press, pp. 63–92.
World Economic Forum, 2018. *The Global Gender Gap Report*. www3.weforum.org/docs/WEF_GGGR_2018.pdf (accessed May 10, 2019).
Yeates, T., 1939. Count Tolstoy and the American Religion. *The Improvement Era*. 1(1). February. https://archive.org/stream/improvementera4202unse#page/n31/mode/2up (accessed May 12, 2019).
Yorgason, E., 2003. *Transformation of the Mormon Culture Region*. Chicago, IL: University of Illinois Press.

Further reading

Bartholomew, R., 1995. *Audacious Women: Early British Mormon Immigrants*. Salt Lake City, UT: Signature Books.

Drawing on over a hundred journals and accounts, this book is one of the most comprehensive and commanding overviews of early British Latter-day Saint women's lived experiences.

Beaman, L., 2001. Molly Mormons, Mormon Feminists and Moderates: Religious Diversity and the Latter-day Saints Church. *Sociology of Religion* 62: 65–86.

Eighteen years on, Lois Beaman's definitive study of Canadian Latter-day Saint women that conceptualizes a typology of Mormon women gender roles continues to resonate.

Decoo, W., 2013. In Search of Mormon Identity: Mormon Culture, Gospel Culture, and an American Worldwide Church. *International Journal of Mormon Studies* 6: 1–53.

A European perspective on the power dynamics in developing a gospel culture in a global religion, which is shaped by North American exceptionalism.

Farnsworth, S., 1991. Mormonism's Odd Couple: The Priesthood–Motherhood Connection. In J. Brooks, R. Steenblik, and H. Wheelwright, eds. *Mormon Feminism: Essential Writings*. Oxford: Oxford University Press, pp. 165–69.

This small but perfectly formed article uses the Mormon couplet; "men have Priesthood; women have motherhood" to show how Mormon gender roles are shaped by North American conservatism.

28
INSTITUTIONAL GENDER NEGOTIATIONS WITHIN IRISH MORMON CONGREGATIONS

Hazel O'Brien

HAZEL: Would you consider yourself a feminist? Can you be a feminist and be in the Church?
MARY: I think you can be a feminist anywhere. I think you are what you are. Do I see myself as a feminist? No. I see myself much more as a person who is into social justice. I think I have a sense of fairness across the board, be it in church, be it in government, be it in work, be it in any situation.

The above quote from Mary, an Irish Mormon convert in her fifties, illustrates the complexity and contradiction inherent in Irish Mormonism's understandings and practices of gender. Whilst Mary maintains that one can be feminist anywhere, including within Mormonism, and is passionate about social justice and fairness for all, she rejects such self-identification. A year of ethnographic fieldwork within Irish Mormonism demonstrated to me that complexity in the articulation and management of individuals' Mormon identities was the norm, not the exception. Thus, Mary's nuanced feelings about feminism and Mormonism is not unusual.

This chapter identifies that gendered Mormonism is locally negotiated and contested in Ireland within *both* a traditional Mormon doctrinal framework, and a rapidly liberalizing and progressive Irish society. By analyzing how gender is experienced within Irish Mormonism's local congregations, we can observe the negotiation of this particular juxtaposition. Irish Mormon congregations become sites where the commonalities and differences between these two gender frames collide. Members bring the progressive perspectives of the majority society which they are a part of and live within, into a space in which traditionally gendered understandings of power are sustained. Local Mormon congregations are spaces in which religious actors create and sustain meaning, develop and build community, and enact, adapt, or confront the doctrine of their church (Black, 2016). They are prime locations in which modern Irish Mormons' understandings and enactment of their gendered identities can be observed and understood.

Mormonism has undergone significant change in recent decades. Most significantly, Mormonism has become a global church, and must now reconcile a diversity of cultures and perspectives within a common faith. This chapter will firstly consider how these challenges are experienced by Mormon adherents who negotiate gender between "church culture" and their own cultures. Following this, a broad overview of gendered Mormonism in an Irish context is provided which emphasizes the transformation of Ireland from Catholic-controlled state to liberal nation, and the place of Mormonism within this shift. I then explore how Irish Mormons experience their gendered identities within their congregations.

Within scholarly literature the debate regarding the feminist credentials of Mormon theology is complex. In recent times, Hudson (2015) has argued that Mormon doctrine on gender is conservative but also radically feminist, citing Mormon reverence of Heavenly Mother and the role of Eve as evidence of the strong position of women within Mormon theology. However, Hoyt (2007) argues that Heavenly Mother's treatment in Mormon theology is less a symbol of female power and autonomy in the Church, as it is a symbol of the Mormon belief system pertaining to immortal kinship and Mormon beliefs regarding complementary gender roles. Brooks, Hunt Steenblik, and Wheelwright (2016) have observed that the key principles of the Mormon faith; love for all humankind, personal agency, and Heavenly Mother as Creator, are inherently compatible with the principles of feminism. Yet they observe that in spite of this, Mormon feminists have been marginalized by the Church for many decades. Perhaps this may explain Mary's and many other Mormon women's reticence with identifying as feminist, whilst still espousing feminist principles.

With regard to the experience of gender within Mormon *culture* rather than Mormon *theology*, we can see that gender is used as a tool by the Church to shape and control Mormon identity more broadly. To understand this, we must look to Heaton, Goodman, and Holman (1994) who demonstrated in the 1990s that Mormon families do maintain traditional beliefs and behaviors with regard to appropriate gender roles, and that they do so in distinctive ways. Mormon gender roles have helped to make Mormon culture distinct. More recently, Chen (2014) finds that the Church's recent "I'm a Mormon" campaign—designed to present a modern, diverse, and non-traditional representation of contemporary Mormonism—nonetheless still reinforces traditional understandings of gender, motherhood, and family.

An explanation for this continuing focus on traditional understandings of gender can be found within Bengtson, Putney, and Harris' (2013, p. 168) comprehensive survey of religious transmission within families in the United States. They find that Mormon families have some of the highest rates of intergenerational religious transmission, arguing that the Church and Mormon families work together to deliver this religious "continuity." Through this lens, we can understand the Church's continuing suspicion of Mormon feminism and its celebration of traditional roles for men and women as part of the Church's efforts to maintain strong common understandings of a Mormon identity, and thus to ensure the transmission of this identity through the generations.

The maintenance of traditional gender roles forms part of Church efforts to control the expression of Mormon identities in an era of unprecedented challenges as Mormonism continues to grow globally. The rise of global Mormonism directly challenges such identity management on the part of the Church. The growing field of Global Mormon Studies, and other studies, identifies that the lived experience of Mormonism in a variety of cultural settings is diverse and capable of wonderful adaptation (Wei-tsing Inouye, 2014; Rutherford, 2016; Benally, 2017; Uluave-Hafoka, 2017; Rutter Strickling, 2018). Such adaptation may be perceived by the Church as a threat to its continuity, but it is also clear that these ongoing changes reflect the future of the Church. Thus, this chapter seeks to examine how gender within Irish Mormonism is experienced at a congregational level in order to understand how contemporary Mormons outside of the U.S. interpret and experience Mormonism's traditional teachings on gender in their everyday lives.

A correlated Church in a global era?

Introduced in the 1960s, the Church policy of Correlation supported a standardization of the Mormon experience and facilitated a common understanding of Mormonism amongst its members (Allen, 1992; Phillips, 2008). Certainly, it is evident that Mormonism has within it a core "church culture" (Davies, 2003; Givens, 2007; Mason, 2016). However, the shift within Mormonism from small sect to global diverse church has caused scholars of Mormonism to reflect on the future of the Church as it now navigates multiple and conflicting cultural expectations across the globe. Davies (2000; 2003) has reflected upon the potential for the Church in the future and proposes that the Church "will appeal to and attract people in need of a distinctive identity and who are prepared to be different from their neighbours" (Davies, 2003, p. 248). Indeed, the stigma of being part of a small yet distinct religious minority has been identified as a key explanation for the Church's struggle to retain members in Europe (Decoo, 2013).

Yet, Rutherford (2016) suggests that scholars of Mormonism have hitherto underestimated the capacity of local members to adapt their faith to the environment which surrounds them in ways which may ultimately influence the "center" of the faith itself. She argues that "Mormonism is lived at the local, not general, level … policies are interpreted and applied by local leaders who are products of their own culture … The outcomes of this dynamic translation of the general to the local often surprise everyone" (Rutherford, 2016, pp. 57–58). From this perspective, Mormon faith and culture is not experienced as a simple one-way system from center to peripheral regions. Rather, it is a dialectic system of interactions, where each is shaped by the other. There is no reason to believe that the same cannot be true of the Church's experience of gender within diverse cultures.

Rutherford's argument that a hybridity of Mormonism with local culture creates an adaptation of Mormon tradition may seem as though its sits in contrast to the comments of Davies (2003) who argues that Mormonism is likely to develop in the future by keeping a identity distinct from the majority society wherever it grows. Yet I demonstrate in this chapter that both Davies (2003) and Rutherford (2016) are correct, and that the two positions can be reconciled in the everyday experiences of Mormons in "peripheral" regions such as Ireland.

Whilst experiences of stereotyping and stigmatization leave no doubt as to the Mormon position as Other in Ireland (Cosgrove, 2013), members are also re-creating Mormonism for an Irish milieu, reshaping it in ways which assist in a reconciliation of Irish and Mormon identities (O'Brien, 2018). Davies (2007) acknowledges this re-making of tradition which occurs within Mormonism. He notes that a re-invention of tradition often occurs within religions, including Mormonism, and that "just how that renegotiation takes place is, itself, of prime importance" (Davies, 2007, p. 59). Below, I provide an overview of Ireland's rapid shift from a state controlled by the Catholic Church with restrictive and punitive female gender roles (Inglis, 1998), to an increasingly progressive nation which has begun to reject religious influence on state affairs (Anderson, 2012).

The Irish context: a society transformed

Since the 1990s, Ireland has undergone rapid and significant economic modernization which has reshaped the cultural landscape of the country. The "Celtic Tiger" period from the mid-1990s to 2008 saw unemployment and poverty levels plummet (Kuhling and Keohane, 2007, p. 1), and Ireland become a globalized economy (Riain, 2014). This caused the reversal of generations of emigration, and mass immigration to Ireland for the first time from both inside and outside of the EU (Ruhs, 2005; Quinn and Ruhs, 2009). Though Ireland underwent a significant economic recession from 2008 to 2012, the economy has largely recovered, and Ireland remains a wealthy globalized economy.

Keohane and Kuhling (2004; Kuhling and Keohane, 2007) discuss the changing cultural environment in Ireland as a result of this economic shift. They observe that "the 'Celtic Tiger' is a striking example of an image in which are condensed elements of tradition and modernity, the global and the local, community and society, as they are in flux in the liminal contexts of collision culture" (2004, pp. 141, 142). Ireland's "collision culture" is evidenced through rapid social change as whilst these economic changes were underway, Ireland was also undergoing a considerable liberalization of its social attitudes and behaviors.

During the "Celtic Tiger" era, as the influence of the Catholic Church declined, Irish family life transformed as Catholic teaching regarding family and sexuality became less influential in people's decisions. People began to marry later or to abstain from marriage altogether. The average age at which women marry has increased from 24 years in 1980 (Central Statistics Office, 2000), to 33.2 years in 2015 (Central Statistics Office, 2016a). Births outside of marriage increased from just 5 percent of all births in 1980, to 28 percent of all births in 1998 (Central Statistics Office, 2000, p. 30). By 2016, 36 percent of all births in the state were outside of marriage (Central Statistics Office, 2016c). The introduction of divorce was seen to be a symbolic statement of Ireland's increasing liberalization. Divorce was legalized in Ireland in 1996, passed by a margin of just 1 percent of the electorate by referendum (James, 1997). However, Ireland maintains the lowest divorce rate in Europe at 0.6 percent per 100,000 people, significantly lower than the EU average of 2.0 percent (Central Statistics Office, 2016b).

Other key developments which reflect Ireland's increasingly liberal attitudes towards social and family life include fast-changing attitudes and polices towards homosexuality. Until 1993, homosexual acts were criminalized in Ireland. By 2011, Ireland had introduced Civil Partnership for gay men and women and in a high-profile referendum in 2015, Ireland became the first country in the world to legalize same-sex civil marriage by popular vote. Ireland's most recent significant change in social attitudes has been that of attitudes towards abortion, which was previously banned in almost all circumstances and which had been a key point of activism of Irish feminist groups for many years. A 2018 referendum resulted in agreement to legalize abortion up to twelve weeks, and in exceptional cases thereafter. This change was broadly interpreted as a significant symbol of Ireland's changing attitudes towards women.

Ireland's changes have resulted in a society which has been economically and socially transformed since the 1980s. However, although liberalizing policies have rapidly occurred, Ireland is still more conservative than its European neighbors on many issues. This can be seen in the very narrow passing of the divorce referendum, the low divorce rate, higher fertility rates, and broad restrictions on abortion until recently. Additionally, Ireland continues to have one of the highest rates of belief in God in Europe (O'Mahony, 2010) whilst recent census figures indicate that although adherence to Catholicism is decreasing, 74 percent still identify as Catholic (Central Statistics Office, 2017). Thus, Ireland remains a spiritual and religiously homogenous country in spite of rapid change. From this perspective we can see that Ireland's move towards wealth and liberalization has led to the emergence of both traditional and modern, conservative and liberal, socio-cultural perspectives which now exist alongside one another, occasionally in confrontation.

It is important to note that it is within this broad context of rapid change—including simultaneous liberalization and continued conservatism—that Mormonism in Ireland is experienced. In the following sections, I demonstrate the ways in which Mormon understandings of gender are re-shaped and even challenged within a wider context of rapidly liberalizing Ireland.

Development of Irish Mormonism: conforming and subverting gendered expectations

The first official missionaries to the island of Ireland arrived in County Down, Northern Ireland in 1840 (Barlow, 1968; Card, 1978). The first missionaries did not arrive in Dublin in the south until 1850 and set about conducting their work of informing and converting the mainly Catholic population. They received much opposition to their work, with organized anti-Mormon campaigns attempting to subvert their attempts to inform the population about Mormonism. Barlow (1968) recounts from original sources several testimonies of abuse, threats, and violent mobs that made the missionaries in Dublin fear for their lives. It was not until the 1960s that we see renewed interest from the Church in further developing missionary efforts in what was now the Republic of Ireland. In 1963, six missionaries were sent to the Republic of Ireland as part of a renewed focus on Ireland on behalf of the Church. In Cork and Limerick small congregations were established, the first outside of Dublin. By the end of 1967 there were 107 members within the Republic of Ireland, half of them based outside of Dublin (Barlow, 1968).

According to the 2016 census, there are now 1,332 Mormons in Ireland, an increase of 3.7 percent on 2011. This is three times less than the figure reported by the Church (Stewart and Martinich, n.d.b) but is a more reliable indicator of active membership as it relies on self-identification. There has been growth in Irish membership since the mid-twentieth century, however, the population of the Republic of Ireland has also grown substantially over the same time period. Thus, recent census figures estimate the Mormon population to be just 0.03 percent of the general population (Central Statistics Office, 2017).

Mormons in Ireland are significantly more diverse than the general population of Ireland, where in 2016, 92.2 percent of the population identified as white, and 82 percent identified with the census category of "white Irish." In contrast, 72 percent of Mormons in Ireland identified as white, and 57 percent as "white Irish." Eight percent of Mormons in Ireland identified as black in comparison to just 1.3 percent of the general population. Similarly, 7 percent of Mormons in Ireland identified as Asian in comparison to 2 percent of the general population (Central Statistics Office, 2017). The higher levels of ethnic diversity within Irish Mormonism are largely explained through conversions achieved from recent migrants to Ireland, and in Mormon missionary efforts being mainly concentrated in cities and large towns where ethnic diversity is greater (Stewart and Martinich, n.d.a). An analysis of Mormon membership in Ireland by social class shows that roughly one-third of members are concentrated in the three highest socio-economic groups (Central Statistics Office, 2017).

There is a fairly even gender breakdown amongst church members in Ireland. The Irish census indicates slightly more female than male members in 2016 (Central Statistics Office, 2017). The numbers of men and women stating that they were studying, unemployed, and retired, were broadly similar between the genders. It is the category of "looking after home or family" which reveals significant gender differences. Of all Mormon women over the age of 15 included in the 2016 census 15.5 percent reported themselves to be looking after home or family in comparison to just 0.9 percent of Mormon men. Just six Mormon men reported their status in this way in the latest census. Mormon men were also far more likely to be in some form of employment than women, with 55.5 percent of Mormon men over 15 being in the labor force in comparison to 40.8 percent of women (Central Statistics Office, 2017).

This difference between men and women is reflective of key values within the Church, where traditional family and gender roles are celebrated. "By divine design, fathers are to preside over their families in love and righteousness and are responsible to provide the necessities of life and protection for their families. Mothers are primarily responsible for the nurture of their children" (The Church of Jesus Christ of Latter Day Saints, 1995). Mothers are not prevented from working outside the home, but are encouraged by Church leaders to do so only if it is necessary for financial reasons (Ballard, 2006). On the basis of the figures above, we could infer that in this respect, Mormon men and women in Ireland are often adhering to Church guidance on this issue.

However, a wider analysis indicates that across the general population of Ireland, 14.8 percent of women over 15 stated that they were looking after home or family compared with 1.1 percent of men (Central Statistics Office, 2017). Thus, although there is a clear gender difference in work and family roles within Irish Mormonism, it is reflective of the wider gender norms within Irish society, where figures indicate that the gender divide with regard to these tasks is not dissimilar. These figures also illustrate significant negotiation on the part of Irish Mormon women regarding the Church's entreaties of women to avoid work outside the home, as the census indicates that 40.8 percent of Mormon women are working and another 8.7 percent are retired (Central Statistics Office, 2017). We can conclude that roughly half of Mormon women in Ireland do work outside the home either through choice or necessity. In cross-national comparison, these figures are actually lower than the rates of formal employment among U.S. Mormon women. Recent data indicates that an average of 68 percent of current Mormons report that their mother worked outside the home on either a full- or part-time basis (Riess, 2019, p. 107). Thus, on the issue of gendered roles for family and work, Irish Mormons are broadly keeping with the norms of wider Irish society, and are also aligned with U.S. Mormon women on this issue.

Contested understandings of female leadership in Church

The men are the priests, the women have the children.

(James, thirties, convert)

All worthy boys and men in the Church are allowed to hold the priesthood. This sacred power known as "priesthood authority" or "priesthood power" allows men who hold the priesthood to conduct blessings for new babies, baptisms for young children, and allows them to offer a blessing for any member who might request one. They can conduct Sacrament ceremony, which takes place each Sunday, and hold most of the key positions of responsibility within the local congregation. The concept of "priesthood authority" or "priesthood power" goes to the heart of Mormon doctrine.

The Church's position on the relationship between priesthood power and gender has been articulated by Dallin H. Oaks, a member of the Quorum of the Twelve, a group of the most senior leaders in the Church:

> Priesthood authority functions in both the family and the Church. The priesthood is the power of God used to bless all of His children, male and female. Some of our abbreviated expressions, like "the women and the priesthood," convey an erroneous idea. Men are not "the priesthood." Priesthood meeting is a meeting of those who hold and exercise the priesthood.
>
> *(Oaks, 2005)*

The Church argues therefore, that it is not men who are powerful, but the priesthood, which works through male members. Whilst these distinctions might be made, the reality is that it is only men who can hold this special power, and so there is a significant symbolic difference between the genders on the basis of the ability to hold priesthood power.

Additionally, there are practical ramifications leading out of this distinction which affect how men and women experience leadership at a local level. The Church's hierarchical system is designed so that top leadership positions are priesthood positions. Therefore, key roles are out of bounds for women, even at branch and ward levels. Female members are acutely aware that leadership in the Church is skewed towards the men. Not long after I arrived in her congregation Maureen, an Irish convert in her sixties, told me that I should try to observe the priesthood meeting despite it being male-only because "the men run the Church you know." When I told her that the Branch President had already approved my access to this meeting she was pleased, telling me "that's good."

However, when I have discussed gender and leadership with female members, many like to point out that women do hold leadership positions both at local and higher levels. Women such as Stephanie reminded me that women hold auxiliary organization positions such as Relief Society President. However, they are leadership roles looking after groups of other women and children. Women never hold leadership positions overseeing men, yet men hold leadership positions over women. This is problematic for some women I spoke with, such as Mandy, an American convert in her forties who was living in Ireland for a year at the time of our conversation. She says "I think that definitely women should have a bigger say in the Church. Like, I see no reason why a Sunday School President can't be a woman. Like, there is no rhyme or reason for stuff like that." In explaining her opinion she tells me that her concerns with the place of women within the Church go beyond just accessing positions of power. She tells me:

> I just feel like that sometimes in the Church they tend to put these women on a pedestal, as wives and mothers. They say, "you're so great, we're just so not worthy of you" but I just feel like that is patting them on the head, patting *us* on the head saying "you stay there" you know? ... I would appreciate more visibility of women leaders in the Church ... and having more influence in the way wards and branches and stakes are run.

Yet, many women I spoke with do not personally feel a need to hold the priesthood. In trying to understand why this might be, I found that women often cite their feeling of equality within their local congregations as justification for their opinions. Stephanie, a young second-generation Mormon in her twenties and a Relief Society President, told me how she feels about women and priesthood power. She tells me about a discussion with the Branch President, whom I've named Jason, after she had been called to the role of Relief Society President:

> Personally I don't mind. I know one or two Sisters that do mind and that's fine. This is the way Jason said it to me, he said "there is a Branch President and his counsellors and then there is the Relief Society President and hers." He said, "I would never do anything to your organisation without your say-so, that is totally yours. He said "we will decide together" that's the way the he put it, "together." He said "this is Heavenly Father's church, but together we will put it in the order that it supposed to be." So I don't feel that I am excluded or anything like that ... I feel okay about it. I can get up and talk on the Sunday if I want to, I can have input into lessons, I can ask questions, I feel like I have a calling, and I'm totally part of this Church, I am a president! Maybe you might disagree with that or whatever but that's how I feel.

Stephanie's anecdote shows that the attitude of the Branch President regarding gender influences how the women of the branch feel about their place in the congregation, and by extension, in the Church. In Stephanie's case, she feels equal to the men in the congregation because of the example Jason provides to all members. Mary, whose quote about feminism opened this chapter, is a convert in her fifties in the same branch as Stephanie. She holds similar opinions about women and the priesthood:

> It's never actually bothered me. It bothered Peter [her husband] when he joined church … because he was taught by Sister Missionaries. And then he thought well why can't they baptise me and stuff? I feel no matter what you do in the world men are men, and women are women … Women are nurturers, not every woman can give birth or have a child, but it is a role that no man can have … For me, the priesthood never, it was never something … Because I have always felt that women are equal in church and that we are able to have an opinion, we are able to say what we feel in meetings and in everything else … I don't think the priesthood would bring anything to my life.

Stephanie and Mary have clearly had a positive experience of gender at a local level in their congregations which, for them, alleviates their obvious exclusion from the hierarchical structures of power in the institutional Church. This confirms previous scholarship which has noted that "Mormonism feels to insiders more egalitarian in practice than it appears to outsiders in theory" (Riess, 2019, p. 97). The divergence of opinion between Stephanie and Mary, and Mandy on this topic is not unusual. I encountered a variety of perspectives on this issue, showing that despite clear doctrine and church guidance on the role of women, this is regularly negotiated and even disputed at a local level thereby confirming the presence of "local creativity" within a heavily standardized Church (Ammerman, 1998, p. 79). Thus, we can see that local congregations become key sites of gender negotiation which have the opportunity to heavily influence how men and women consider the issue of gender within the Church more broadly.

These diverse experiences and opinions on gender also illustrate that maintaining a common understanding and practice of differing roles for men and women may be more difficult in the modern global Church. Despite clear hierarchical structures built upon gender and which inform the structures of the branch, local experiences can both disrupt or maintain this, sometimes simultaneously. In Stephanie's particular case, her role as Relief Society President is still below the Branch President in the hierarchy of the Church, thus maintaining a Mormon tradition of female subservience. Yet, her lived experiences contradict this, as she told me she feels "equal" in church. Perhaps Stephanie and Mary were simply presenting me with an ideal of gender equality for the purposes of the research, or perhaps they wanted to present the Church and their local branch in a positive light. Yet, during my fieldwork I often saw male leaders challenged by female members. These instances occurred frequently during discussions on doctrine in Sunday School, and during discussions about decisions to be taken for the future of the branch, to be discussed further below.

It seems then, that Stephanie and Mary's protestations of equality could not simply have been for my benefit as a researcher of their faith and culture. I suggest that this grassroots renegotiation of gender and power at a congregational level may be as a result of the inter-relationships between "Church culture" and the culture of wider Irish society. Ireland's rapid modernization and liberalization has led to dramatic changes in the position of women in Irish society. It is likely that local congregations, who do not exist in isolation from the wider society of which they are also a part, are consciously or not, recreating this shift in gender relations within church.

Indeed, Mary mentioned to me that discussion of gender and religion within the wider society does cause her to reflect upon her own position within Mormonism; "at times there is a big flare up in the media, you have women priests and stuff like that, and you know then, it would make you reflect on your own religion."

Certainly, Church members in Ireland often recognize that the official position of the institutional Church on the issue of female leadership is out of step with many of the societies which the Church now exists within worldwide, including Ireland. James is a convert in his thirties and when speaking about the prohibition on a female priesthood told me "I know it seems very old fashioned" whilst astutely observing the phenomenon of assimilation versus distinction that has been a key analytical point amongst scholars of Mormon Studies (Mauss, 1994; 1996; 2011). He observed "there is definitely a feeling that the Church and society are splitting apart more and more, which is interesting because it's going to lead to certain issues in the future."

James understands the growing distance between the Church and Irish society, predominantly on issues of gender and sexuality, and the effects that may have on people's experiences both inside the Church and outside of it. James tells me "when I joined the Church, the society was much more traditional and the Church was quite close in that sense ... but now the opposite has happened, it's moved further away." James is adamant in his discussions with me that the Church's position on female leadership will not change in the future. He tells me that although he thinks the Church is progressive on some issues, it is "very firm" on this:

> There is a group of members in America who are women who want the priesthood and they campaign for it; I never understood that, because it will never change. It's not something that say "ok we'll just let them off to priesthood," that's not the way it's viewed, it's viewed coming from God.

James is clear that the institutional Church has differentiated itself from the values and norms of wider Irish society and he is appreciative of this distinction, as Davies (2003) predicted. Yet, as Mandy's opinion and Stephanie's experience of leadership show, at a local level adaptation is still possible, as Rutherford (2016) maintains. James believes that the institutional Church will not sway from its position on the place of women in the Church, but on this point too there is localized disagreement. Others told me that they see the Church as being in an era of transition, and that as the current leadership of the Church passes away, so too will the Church's traditional stance on gender and sexuality. Mandy tells me:

> I feel like the men that run the Church right now, the apostles and prophets, they are all men in their eighties, a few in their sixties. But for the most part, they are of that generation where no one is gay, no one is different, women stay at home, so I feel like as they start to pass away, and then the younger generations who were raised with strong females in the home, and who were raised in a world where homosexuality is okay, where their best friends could have two dads, as the leaders become younger and more exposed to the world, I feel that ... the Church will slowly started to progress a little bit.

Here we see that both Davies (2003) and Rutherford (2016) are correct; the Church is indeed attractive to those who seek a place in which traditionally conservative gender roles are praised and the Church's distinction from the values of wider society are a point of celebration for some. Yet, within local congregations members and their leaders bring with them the values they have absorbed elsewhere, and interpret for themselves the meaning of Church guidance on gender. The experiences of the Murphy family outlined below, demonstrate this point.

Who has the power to speak truth to power?

I would like to apologise for that man.

(Sue, thirties, second generation)

During this research, I spent time with one Mormon family who encapsulate much of the complexity inherent in how Mormon women in Ireland experience their church. John and Maureen Murphy are a well-known couple in Irish Mormonism and are well respected in their local branch. They have been fundamental in sustaining the small branch of about seventy regularly attending members. When their children were young, those attending in their congregation would often consist of just themselves and their children and one or two others. During this era, church was held in a small home in a suburban housing development. The church building for the congregation is now in an industrial estate in a modern but clinical building, and the lack of suitable premises for the branch in spite of its long history is a key point of concern for the Murphy family.

I came to understand through the Murphys just how women's status within the Church may be connected to aspects of their identity which are entirely unconnected to their gender, and which may be directly informed by their status "outside" of church. Maureen and John's two adult daughters, Diane and Sue, are active in the Church and well regarded. They have held all the key callings available to women, and benefit from the status that comes with being such longstanding members of the Church in a congregation that is majority first-generation converts. All three Murphy women are also white Irish, educated, and middle class and so able to benefit from the privilege that being part of the majority in terms of class and race brings. Both within and outside of church, the Murphy women are empowered to be confident in their voice in ways that other more vulnerable men and women in church may not be.

During the time I spent attending church in this congregation I saw that all three Murphy women were vocal in their criticisms of the Church as an institution and of key leaders in the Church. This is not to imply the women were generally unhappy *in* church or *with* the Church, they all were clearly very committed members and firm in their faith. However it was precisely this commitment that led the women to feel that they were justified in making their views known, and in challenging those men in positions of power with whom they happened to disagree. Three instances exemplified this.

Firstly, all three Murphy women were present during a Branch Council meeting in which the Mission President and District President were attending to inform the group about new plans being implemented to encourage more people to join the Church. The Mission President laid out the new plans, discussing specific numerical targets that the branch and its various organizations should aim to achieve. He emphasized that the priority for the Church under the new system was to get new members "through" the temple; in other words to complete their temple endowment. Diane Murphy spoke up immediately; "if I was inactive I would see it that I am a business plan, and I am just needed to get to the chapel and to the temple. I wouldn't see any love. Where is the love?" Her sister Sue agreed:

SUE: We need to be careful about how we do it because someone could join because they are lonely and they want friends, or because they fancy [are attracted to] the missionaries or whatever. If they get pushed through to the temple then they are accountable now, and that is not fair on them.

DIANE: Yes and that has happened here to two people. They were pushed through to temple, and we all said that was what was happening and sure enough, two weeks later they were gone and are now very inactive and back to a sinning life. We need to be concerned about keeping people *after* they join, and not just getting more to join.

The Mission President responded by encouraging the Branch Council not to be overly concerned with new members becoming inactive; "Let's not beat ourselves up about the fact that some people will go through temple and then be inactive." Overall, I felt that it was a fraught meeting filled with tension. The Mission and District Presidents spoke to defend the Church's new strategy, but many of the other men present did not speak or spoke more rarely. The Murphy women in contrast were active in the discussion and clearly deeply unhappy with the way in which the strategy was being presented.

The following week, I was scheduled to conduct an in-depth interview for my research with Sue. During this interview she brought up the previous week's meeting and told me how unhappy she was with the Mission President:

SUE: I would like to apologise for that man.
HAZEL: Don't apologise! Why would you have to apologise for him?
SUE: It's the first time in my life I felt I was part of a cult ... He came across so badly and I just wanted to stop him and say "I know you were a very successful businessman at home and this is how you talk to your people on your team at home, but we are not them!" That's all I wanted to say and I sat there going "shut up, shut up!" I could see Mam's blood pressure boiling, and I could see Diane the way she was moving in her seat, she was so uncomfortable.

A similar incident occurred around this same time period during a joint Priesthood and Relief Society meeting in which the Mission President was present. During a discussion about how to encourage more people to church, the Murphy women once more directly challenged the Mission President. This time, they pointed out that they were being encouraged by the Church to increase membership whilst simultaneously being refused ward status and a purpose-built church building (which the members often described as a "chapel"). Diane said "in [another congregation], the group was half the size, and they have a chapel. People in the community see it, they see a chapel." In biting tones she proffered "maybe we need to know someone somewhere to get the chapel." The Mission President suggested that if the branch were to get more members it could be eligible for a chapel. Maureen Murphy quickly interrupted him; "but it used to be 40, 60, then 80, to have a chapel. The goal posts are moving all the time."

Another example of the Murphy women's lack of fear in challenging men in power occurred during a joint Priesthood and Relief Society meeting for a lesson from Elder Herbertson, a member of the Quorum of the Seventy who was visiting Ireland. Although all present seemed to be honored to be in the presence of Elder Herbertson, Diane Murphy still interrupted his lesson on what the congregation should be doing to ensure they reached the Celestial Kingdom. She said "I think one thing that would help with the branch here would be a chapel." She received applause and laughter from the congregation for her interjection, the only time in one year of attending church that I ever witnessed applause in church. A few weeks later Elder Ballard, a member of the Quorum of the Twelve, visited Ireland and many of the congregation made the journey to attend the very special evening of prayer and celebration. Diane Murphy managed to briefly meet Elder Ballard in the corridor after the event and quickly told him that Ireland needed a temple. I was fascinated that of all the things that Diane could have chosen to say to such a high-ranking leader during what might be a once in a lifetime encounter, she chose to make her opportunity a moment of Irish-focused activism.

Conclusion

In evaluating the position and influence of the Murphy women's gender in these examples, we must consider not simply that they are women in a hierarchal institutional church that does not allow for these women to hold key leadership roles. We must also consider that they are women working in professional occupations in modern Ireland—they are used to speaking and to being listened to. We must consider that they are white Irish, within both a congregation and a society which are both becoming increasingly diverse yet remain white-centered. We must consider that they are educated, middle class, able to articulate themselves, and not intimidated by wealth or success. We must ask ourselves if one of the black migrant women in their congregation happened to share the Murphy women's opinions would she feel able to challenge her leaders as they do? This point of course also holds true for marginalized men. These men may be eligible for more "prestigious" callings and can hold the priesthood, but are they more powerful than the Murphy women? How can power be defined within the modern global Church, when such terms are operationalized in different ways by different groups, often within the one congregation?

To truly evaluate the place of gender in Irish Mormonism, we must not consider it in isolation. To do so would be to tell too simplistic a story about women and men in the Irish Church, too simple a story about the Murphys. The Murphy women are simultaneously privileged *and* marginalized within their Church. They have the ability to speak truth to power and show little fear in doing so. Yet despite their clear status within the congregation, and in spite of their committed efforts to improve the Church in Ireland for all its members, they can never lead a congregation themselves. To understand the experience of modern Mormon women in liberal societies we should be mindful to avoid "a dichotomous paradigm of victim/empowerment" which "hides their complexity" (Hoyt, 2007, p. 92). Such is the intricacy of being a woman within Irish Mormonism, both powerful and powerless, striving for "fairness" but accepting of inequalities in Church structures and doctrine. Such complexity should be celebrated as evidence of modern Mormon women developing their identities in ways which are authentic for them, within an increasingly diverse Church.

References

Allen, J.B., 1992. On Becoming a Universal Church: Some Historical Perspectives. *Dialogue: A Journal of Mormon Thought* 25(June): 13–36. www.dialoguejournal.com/wp-content/uploads/sbi/articles/Dialogue_V25N01_15.pdf.

Ammerman, N.T., 1998. Culture and Identity in the Congregation. In N.T. Ammerman, J.W. Carroll, C.S. Dudley, and W. McKinney, eds. *Studying Congregations: A New Handbook*. Nashville, TN: Abingdon Press, pp. 78–104.

Anderson, K., 2012. Ireland in the Twenty First Century: Secularization or Religious Vitality? In D. Pollack, O. Muller, and G. Pickel, eds. *Social Significance of Religion in the Enlarged Europe: Secularization, Individualization and Pluralization*. Farnham: Ashgate, pp. 66–109.

Ballard, M.R., 2006. The Sacred Responsibilities of Parenthood. *Liahona*. March. www.lds.org/liahona/2006/03/the-sacred-responsibilities-of-parenthood?lang=eng&query=gender+roles.

Barlow, B.A., 1968. History of the Church of Jesus Christ of Latter-day Saints in Ireland since 1840. M.A. Thesis, Brigham Young University. http://contentdm.lib.byu.edu/cdm/ref/collection/MTAF/id/15538.

Benally, M., 2017. Decolonizing the Blossoming: Indigenous People's Faith in a Colonizing Church. *Dialogue: A Journal of Mormon Thought* 50(4): 71–78. www.dialoguejournal.com/archive/dialogue-premium-content/winter-2017/.

Bengtson, V.L., Putney, N.M., and Harris, S., 2013. *Families and Faith: How Religion Is Passed Down across Generations*. Oxford and New York: Oxford University Press.

Black, K.L., 2016. *A Sociology of Mormon Kinship: The Place of Family within the Church of Jesus Christ of Latter-day Saints*. Lewiston, NY: Edwin Mellen Press.

Brooks, J., Hunt Steenblik, R., and Wheelwright, H. eds., 2016. *Mormon Feminism: Essential Writings*. Oxford and New York: Oxford University Press.

Card, O.S., 1978. The Saints in Ireland. *Ensign*. www.lds.org/ensign/1978/02/the-saints-in-ireland?lang=eng.

Central Statistics Office, 2000. *That Was Then, This Is Now: Change in Ireland, 1949–1999*. Cork: Government of Ireland. www.cso.ie/en/media/csoie/releasespublications/documents/otherreleases/thatwasthenthisisnow.pdf.

Central Statistics Office, 2016a. *Marriages and Civil Partnerships 2015*. Dublin. www.cso.ie/en/releasesand publications/er/mcp/marriagesandcivilpartnerships2015/.

Central Statistics Office, 2016b. *Measuring Ireland's Progress 2014*. Cork. www.cso.ie/en/releasesand publications/ep/p-mip/mip2014/.

Central Statistics Office, 2016c. *Vital Statistics Q3 2016*. Cork. www.cso.ie/en/releasesandpublications/ ep/p-vs/vitalstatisticsthirdquarter2016/.

Central Statistics Office, 2017. Details of Census. Cork: Government of Ireland. www.cso.ie/px/ pxeirestat/Database/eirestat/Profile 8 – Irish Travellers, Ethnicity and Religion/Profile 8 – Irish Travellers, Ethnicity and Religion_statbank.asp?SP=Profile 8 – Irish Travellers, Ethnicity and Religion=0.

Chen, C.H., 2014. Diverse yet Hegemonic: Expressions of Motherhood in "I'm a Mormon" Ads. *Journal of Media and Religion* 13(May): 31–47. doi: 10.1080/15348423.2014.871973.

The Church of Jesus Christ of Latter-day Saints, 1995. The Family: A Proclamation to the World. Salt Lake City, UT: The Church of Jesus Christ of Latter-day Saints. www.lds.org/bc/content/shared/ content/english/pdf/36035_000_24_family.pdf.

Cosgrove, O., 2013. The Experience of Religious Stigma and Discrimination among Religious Minorities in Ireland: A Multi-Faith Approach. Ph.D. Dissertation. University of Limerick. http://rian.ie/en/ item/view/73067.html.

Davies, D., 2007. *The Invention of Sacred Tradition*. Cambridge and New York: Cambridge University Press.

Davies, D.J., 2000. *The Mormon Culture of Salvation*. Aldershot and Burlington, VT: Ashgate.

Davies, D.J., 2003. *An Introduction to Mormonism*. Cambridge: Cambridge University Press. doi: https:// doi.org/10.1017/CBO9780511610028.

Decoo, W., 2013. In Search of Mormon Identity: Mormon Culture, Gospel Culture, and an American Worldwide Church. *International Journal of Mormon Studies* 6. www.ijmsonline.org/archives/3276.

Givens, T.L., 2007. *People of Paradox: A History of Mormon Culture*. Oxford and Cambridge, MA: Oxford University Press.

Heaton, T.B., Goodman, K.L., and Holman, T.B., 1994. Are Mormon Families Really Different? In M. Cornwall, T.B. Heaton, and L.A. Young, eds. *Contemporary Mormonism: Social Science Perspectives*. Urbana and Chicago, IL: University of Illinois Press, pp. 87–117.

Hoyt, A., 2007. Beyond the Victim/Empowerment Paradigm: The Gendered Cosmology of Mormon Women. *Feminist Theology* 16(1): 89–100. doi: 10.1177/0966735007082519.

Hudson, V.M., 2015. Mormon Doctrine on Gender. In T.L. Givens and P.L. Barlow, eds. *The Oxford Handbook of Mormonism*. Oxford and New York: Oxford University Press, 349–62.

Inglis, T., 1998. *Moral Monopoly: The Rise and Fall of the Catholic Church in Modern Ireland*. Dublin: UCD Press.

James, C.P., 1997. Cead mile failte? Ireland Welcomes Divorce: The 1995 Divorce Referendum and the Family (Divorce) Act of 1996. *Duke Journal of Comparative and International Law* 8: 175–228. http:// scholarship.law.duke.edu/cgi/viewcontent.cgi?article=1277&context=djcil.

Keohane, K., and Kuhling, C., 2004. *Collison Culture: Transformations in Everyday Life in Ireland*. Dublin: Liffey Press.

Kuhling, C., and Keohane, K., 2007. *Cosmopolitan Ireland: Globalisation and Quality of Life*. London: Pluto Press.

Mason, P.Q., 2016. Introduction. In P.Q. Mason and J.G. Turner, eds. *Out of Obscurity: Mormonism since 1945*. New York: Oxford University Press, 3–14.

Mauss, A.L., 1994. *The Angel and the Beehive: The Mormon Struggle with Assimilation*. Urbana and Chicago, IL: University of Illinois Press.

Mauss, A.L., 1996. Identity and Boundary Maintenance: International Prospects for Mormonism at the Dawn of the Twenty-first Century. In D.J. Davies, ed. *Mormon Identities in Transition*. London and New York: Cassell, pp. 9–20.

Mauss, A.L., 2011. Rethinking Retrenchment: Course Corrections in the Ongoing Campaign for Respectability. *Dialogue: A Journal of Mormon Thought* 44(4): 1–42. www.dialoguejournal.com/store/premium-digital-articles-2/premium-digital-articles-vol-44-num-4-winter-2011/#_am.

O'Brien, H., 2018. Being Mormon in Ireland: An Exploration of Religion in Modernity Through a Lens of Tradition and Change. Ph.D. Dissertation, University of Exeter.

O'Mahony, E., 2010. *Religious Practice and Values in Ireland: A Summary of European Values Study 4th Wave Data*. Irish Catholic Bishops' Conference. www.catholicbishops.ie/wp-content/uploads/images/stories/cco_publications/researchanddevelopment/evs_4th_wave_report.pdf.

Oaks, D.H., 2005. Priesthood Authority in the Family and the Church. LDS General Conference. Salt Lake City, Utah. www.lds.org/general-conference/2005/10/priesthood-authority-in-the-family-and-the-church?lang=eng.

Phillips, R., 2008. "De facto Congregationalism" and Mormon Missionary Outreach: An Ethnographic Case Study. *Journal for the Scientific Study of Religion* 47(4): 628–43. doi: 10.1111/j.1468-5906.2008.00431.x.

Quinn, E., and Ruhs, M., 2009. *Ireland: From Rapid Immigration to Recession*. Dublin. www.migrationpolicy.org/article/ireland-rapid-immigration-recession.

Riain, O., 2014. Where Is Ireland in the Worlds of Capitalism? In T. Inglis, ed. *Are the Irish Different?* Manchester: Manchester University Press, pp. 22–33.

Riess, J., 2019. *The Next Mormons: How Millennials Are Changing the LDS Church*. Oxford: Oxford University Press.

Ruhs, M., 2005. Managing the Immigration and Employment of Non-EU Nationals in Ireland. *Studies in Social Policy*. Dublin. http://edepositireland.ie/handle/2262/60230.

Rutherford, T.F., 2016. The Internationalisation of Mormonism. In P.Q. Mason and J.G. Turner, eds. *Out of Obscurity: Mormonism since 1945*. Oxford and New York: Oxford University Press, pp. 37–60. doi: 10.1093/acprof:oso/9780199358212.003.0003.

Rutter Strickling, L., 2018. *On Fire in Baltimore*. Draper, UT: Greg Kofford Books.

Stewart, D., and Martinich, M., n.d.a. *Reaching the Nations: Ireland, Cumorah*. http://cumorah.com/index.php?target=countries&cnt_res=1&wid=105&cmdfind=Search (accessed March 16, 2015).

Stewart, D., and Martinich, M., n.d.b. *Statistical Profile: Ireland, Cumorah*. www.cumorah.com/index.php?target=countries&cnt_res=2&wid=105&cmdfind=Search (accessed January 12, 2014).

Uluave-Hafoka, M., 2017. To Be Young, Mormon, and Tongan. *Dialogue: A Journal of Mormon Thought* 50(4): 99–104. www.dialoguejournal.com/archive/dialogue-premium-content/winter-2017/.

Wei-tsing Inouye, M., 2014. The Oak and the Banyan: The "Glocalization" of Mormon Studies. *Mormon Studies Review* 1: pp. 70–79. https://publications.mi.byu.edu/fullscreen/?pub=2402&index=7.

Further reading

Allen, J.K., 2019. Neither Fairyland nor Dystopia : Taking Western Europe Seriously in Mormon Studies. *Mormon Studies Review* 6: 34–45. www.jstor.org/stable/10.18809/mormstudrevi.6.2019.0034#metadata_info_tab_contents.

Barlow, B.A., 1968. History of the Church of Jesus Christ of Latter-day Saints in Ireland since 1840. M.A. Thesis, Brigham Young University. http://contentdm.lib.byu.edu/cdm/ref/collection/MTAF/id/15538.

Card, O.S., 1978. The Saints in Ireland. *Ensign*. www.lds.org/ensign/1978/02/the-saints-in-ireland?lang=eng.

Decoo, W., 2015. Mormons in Europe. In T.L. Givens and P.L. Barlow, eds. *The Oxford Handbook of Mormonism*. Oxford and New York: Oxford University Press, pp. 543–59.

Harris, C.W., 1990. Mormons on the Warfront: The Protestant Mormons and Catholic Mormons of Northern Ireland. *BYU Studies Quarterly* 30(4): 7–19. http://scholarsarchive.byu.edu/byusq/vol.30/iss4/2.

29
PERUVIAN MORMON MATCHMAKING
The limits of Mormon endogamy at Zion's border

Jason Palmer

Introduction

Ofelia Dominguez, a 40-year-old single mother, told me the following story in Arequipa, Peru in February 2018.

> One day the bishop calls me in for an interview and tells me, "Ofelia, look, the bishopric and I are worried that you are still not married. What is wrong? ... We have a brother [fellow church member] lined up for you ... He is the ideal person for you." ... I saw who this brother was and there wasn't any affinity on my part [laughs] so I kept rejecting his invitations ... He complained to the bishop, and the bishop called me back in for an interview. "Look, Ofelia, you are being too harsh, the Lord is giving you the last chance you are going to have." And I was like [sarcastically], "Oh really, the last chance of the Lord, you say? How interesting, continue." He says, "this brother has asked you out three or four times and you are rejecting him, and he is sad." "Alright. Bishop, do you love me?" "What? Why that question?" "Again, do you love me?" "Of course. I love all of my, my– little sheep and I have to guide them." "I don't think you love me, Bishop, because you are setting me up with a man who is not faithful to the church. Why do you draw distinctions between people?" "I don't draw distinctions." "Yes you do, because when the youth are courting someone you see if that person is worthy, if they go to the temple, if they are full tithe-payers or if they are constant in their church obligations. Nevertheless, you are directing me towards a brother who is not going to support me spiritually ... Is that the type of man you want for me, Bishop?"

Ofelia's resistance to the matchmaking efforts of a Mormon bishop in Peru is symptomatic of the kinship tensions created when Peruvians become Mormons. Arranged marriage is as uncommon in most Andean Catholic communities as it is in most U.S. Mormon communities. Why then does matchmaking emerge in this particular convergence of the two? A partial answer stems from Peruvian coresident siblingship and how it complicates the probability involved in finding an eligible Mormon to marry. However, this answer unearths a deeper question: what defines Mormon eligibility? In exploring the unanswerability of this question through the contradictory love lives of Peruvian Mormons in the Periféricos Ward of Arequipa, I uncover an underlying paradox at the core of Mormon kinship, one generated by the dynamic tension among lineage and love and among conversion and covenant birth. I argue that channeling this tension into the exclusion of unworthy marriage partners creates a sieve that determines who gets to be "Mormon" enough to enter Zion.

The Mormon concept of Zion encapsulates this tension and the paradox at its source. Administratively, Zion is the name Mormons give to any polis with enough "active" Mormons to form a confederation of cartographically bounded *wards* (congregations) called a "Stake of Zion." Metaphysically, Mormon Zion is paradoxical because it aims to achieve universal inclusivity by creating a tribalism that accentuates difference. Zion, like Audre Lorde's (1984) concept of radical love, is supposed "to recognize the notion of difference as a dynamic human force, one which is enriching rather than threatening to the defined self" (p. 45). Yet, at the same time, Zion appears to be equally founded upon "the belief in the inherent superiority of one pattern of loving and thereby its right to dominance" (p. 45). In Mormonism, nuclear marriage is the only correct pattern that can lead to full Zion citizenship in this life and godhood in the next. Even though this form of marriage is not universally present throughout the Andes (Canessa, 2012) or the U.S. (Sarkisian and Gerstel, 2012), much less the rest of the world, Zion claims that it is precisely through nuclear marriage "sealings" that universal kinship will be achieved. "We don't just seal nuclear families together in our temples. The utterly breathtaking goal of our faith is to seal the family of humanity together" (McKay-Lamb and Jensen, 2015, p. 191).

One paradox of Mormon Zion is that the only place on earth where this inclusive sealing of all humanity can happen is inside one of the most exclusive places on the planet. The Mormon temple—the architectural manifestation of Zion's culmination within a city—only validates two types of relationships in its sealing ritual: husband–wife and couple–child. All other relationships, including sibling–sibling, mother–child, and grandmother–grandchild are excluded unless they can be linked to the nuclear couple. This means that the vast majority of the families I interviewed in 2018 during my six months of ethnographic and ecclesiastical membership in Periféricos Ward do not have "sealed" relationships to the ones they love the most.

Wrong kind of love

As a Mormon Zion, Arequipa is Peru's second largest city and contains Peru's third Mormon temple. It has a population of over 800,000, is home to approximately 20,000 Mormons, and sits at the 7,400-foot mark on a volcano rising 19,000 feet above sea level in Peru's southern Andes. It is not uncommon in Arequipa to find conglomerated dwellings where Peruvian Mormons reside with married and unmarried siblings, nieces, parents, and cousins for the rest of their lives. They hope to continue this togetherness into eternity.

Ofelia is one such Mormon. Her 21-year-old daughter, Shannon, lives with her, her mother, and a constantly variable assortment of her nine siblings and their spouses and children. Ofelia also provides three square meals a day to four constantly transferring missionaries, any two of whom are usually from Utah. Since kinship in much of the Andes is constructed through the sharing of food and drink rather than essentialized in the sharing of DNA and the kinship idiom of "blood" (Weismantel, 1995), all who have eaten together often enough in Ofelia's home are kin to both her and the earth surrounding her home in a concept contemporary Andean philosophers call *Pacha* (Marin Benitez, 2015). "Pacha should be understood as home, in which everything and everyone belongs to one family under one roof" (p. 81). Ofelia seeks a Mormon temple marriage if only so that she can seal that marriage to her relationship with Shannon, so that mother and daughter can continue *Pacha* in the afterlife. Such a marriage is difficult to achieve because she must marry a Mormon to fulfill the demands of religious endogamy, yet if she meets one at a ward dance, she will be faced with the even stricter demands of familial exogamy: many otherwise eligible partners will be her cousins, siblings, or uncles. This happens because the Utah-centric model of ward districting catered to nuclear family units was transplanted onto the Peruvian reality of "extended family" coresidence. Mormons do not simply attend whatever church services they happen upon each Sunday. They belong—everyday—to the ward assigned to the boundaries within which their residence falls. In Peru, this model often translates to "ward boundaries" drawn around three or four large familial complexes that end up constituting over half a ward's membership.

The Abedul family alone provides Periféricos Ward with 15 percent of its active membership and a significant portion of its top leadership positions. The widowed matriarch of this family, living in the original home at the heart of a complex that is now growing up because it can no longer grow out, is not a Mormon, but most of her coresident six children and multitudes of grandchildren are. The Abedul complex is more centrally located within the ward boundaries than the chapel to which the ward is assigned and so has become the de facto recreation center for ward activities. In fact, one of the matriarch's sons-in-law, a successful civil engineer and former bishop of the ward, constructed a spacious party room—complete with bathroom, kitchenette, and entertainment center—on the fourth floor of one of the structures. Satirically christened *El Bunker*, it is the venue of near daily use for fundraiser cook-offs, youth slumber parties, ward council meetings, and church Self-Reliance courses. If the civil engineer's son, Marco, wanted to find an eligible Mormon mate, he would not have to look further than his own fourth floor on a "single young adults" activity night. However, of the ten or so young ladies he might find there, chances are that five would be his cousins and one would be his sister.

What about the other four? Therein lies a familial exogamy expectation that is more individually felt than socially defined. Through all the shared activities, lifestyle changes, and rites of passage that create the Mormon solidarity necessary to replace the loss of connection with surrounding Andean Catholic society, sometimes Peruvian Mormons do too good a job at forming what they call "ward families." When Zion is united, marrying outside the religion feels sinful, but marrying within the ward can feel downright incestuous. Like Romeo and Juliet, but in reverse, stories like the following abound.

OFELIA: Well, since Shannon was a very little girl, about 3 years old, she grew up with the Abedul kids in The Primary, so when they started getting older their parents told me, "hey, Ofelia, we want Shannon to be the wife of our son Marco," so I was like, "but she has to be the one to decide." "Yes, but we have to help her out." And so when she entered Young Women's they started to invite us to all their family parties … So the friendship grew and they would play and joke all up until that little young man went on his mission. His parents were so excited that their oldest was going on his mission and that Shannon was going to wait for him that they started to talk weddings, and his little brothers actually started calling her "*cuñis*" [sis'-in-law]. Just before Marco came back, his parents said, "Shannon, look, you know that Marco is about to come home and that you are going to have to get close to him, right?" … "But, it's that I don't know, and what if he doesn't like me? Plus, I see him as a brother." "No, but, it will be different now because he has to return and he has to have a fiancé." And I would ask her, "*Hijita* [little daughter of mine], do you feel any affinity for him?" "But, it's just that, *Mamá*, you know that we've grown up together. I love him as a brother but nothing more." And when he came back they said, "Shannon, you have to go to the airport to welcome him back," and she didn't go, she was embarrassed. Marco got back. His parents said, "hey, Marco, take a look at Shannon." "*Mamá, Papá*, she is like my sister. I would never fix my eyes on her like that, so please stop, just stop incentivizing this. No."

JASON: So they had done their job too well?

OFELIA: Yes, and in fact the same thing happened with Flavio [Marco's little brother] because he went on his mission six months before she went on hers, so they went at the same time and were writing through the internet ... So when she commented off hand to me one day in one of her emails, "*Mamá*, I am writing Flavio," I immediately thought, "oh, this could be Plan B." Right? And his parents were the same way, they got all excited and said, "yes, Plan B, Plan B! Yes, there is still hope!" And when we found out they were going to return from their missions on the exact same day we were like, "coincidences don't exist, there is a reason for this." And this time we were really sure that, "yep, this is it, you really are going to be an Abedul now, it's unavoidable." But, the same thing happened. I mean, they [Shannon and Flavio] are siblings after all. So the parents say, "*ay*, it would have been great." "Yeah, it's too bad," I tell them. But that's what happens when there is too much friendship.

As this story of backfired matchmaking exemplifies, Mormonism can be a flashpoint of endogamous paradox that further accentuates the counterintuitive way in which tribalism is supposed to bring about unity. Mormons can only marry within their own global "tribe" of coreligionists, which is why Marco's parents had to act early to reserve one of the few eligible mates for their son. Yet, Mormons also claim to be utterly inclusive about who can be worthy of their love. From the Abedul perspective, Shannon was a Mormon, therefore she was an eligible daughter-in-law. It turns out, however, that many Periféricos Ward members draw the borderline of endogamy's precise threshold much more closely around themselves than the relatively inclusive maxim "thou shalt marry a Mormon" would imply.

Covenant boundaries

Mormons want someone who is not only a Mormon, but a "full" Mormon, especially when finding a mate for someone they care about such as their own daughter or parishioner. In the eyes of many, Ofelia herself does not meet this ambiguous criterion. By virtue of being baptized at age 24, already a single mother, she was late for many important Mormon rites of passage including being "born in the covenant," a rite that points directly to the paradox at Zion's heart.

Not being "born in the covenant" refers to the fact that Ofelia's parents had not been sealed in the temple before she was born. Mormons born to temple-sealed parents come into the world already sealed to those parents. No future sealing rite is necessary for them to live together in the eternities. Ofelia missed out on this because she is a first-generation Mormon, or a *conversa* (convert). In much the same way that Indians under British colonialism were seen as "the effect of a flawed colonial mimesis, in which to be Anglicized, is *emphatically* not to be English" (Bhabha, 1984, p. 128) *conversos* are sometimes seen as more Mormonized than Mormon. Ofelia rejects this view.

OFELIA: A lot of times, before I understood such things, members of the church would always ask us that question, "hey, um, are you of the covenant?" And I would say, "what do you mean 'of the covenant?'" "I'm just asking if your parents were sealed in the temple and then you were born from them." "Oh, no then. No, I'm not of the covenant." "Oh, so you are of the baptized." And they would always ask me that question and I'd say, "ah, yes, I guess you're right because I just got baptized." And so time went on and during a lot of years they'd always ask that question, "are you of the covenant?" or, "is your daughter of the covenant, was she born in the covenant?" And with sadness or sometimes even shame I would say, "no, my daughter is not of the covenant." But then I started wondering, "why do they ask that?" And when I studied about it, I said, "what!?" I mean, how dare they make me think that I'm not of the covenant when I'm just as much of the covenant as they are. Those who have been chosen as people of the covenant who have been born in the covenant, and those who accept the gospel after repenting and entering into the baptismal waters, are all equal. Don't give me any talk about difference and, "we are the real people of the covenant, but since you were baptized it means you were only adopted by us," it's not like that. We are all part of the covenant, right? So I don't see why they have to make differences like that. It's a stupid question that they start asking.

JASON: And, do you know what that implies? What is going on in their heads when they ask that question?

OFELIA: Yes. That they feel superior for having been born in the covenant of marriage and temple sealing ... sometimes the parents of my seminary students tell me, "my kids were born in the covenant so they already know everything." Mistake. Right? Gargantuan mistake! Why? Because there are many brothers and sisters, Shannon's contemporaries, who, while it is true that their parents were sealed in the temple, born in the covenant themselves even, and I guess from inside the womb they were grasping gospel concepts [laughs], BUT, their kids have come home early from missions, sometimes not even gone on missions, been dishonorably discharged from missions, and their daughters have gone astray and all of that, right? So that is why I say emphatically, "no." I mean, it is not an indispensable requirement that one be of the covenant people, right? What matters is how one goes about guiding one's kids, whether they were born in the covenant or not.

JASON: Is it possible that they think they were born in the covenant because their spirits were more valiant in the preexistence?

OFELIA: Of course. It's not just possible, that is precisely what they think. They think they are more choice spirits, "the elect," right? They think they've been chosen, but—MISTAKE!

Ofelia makes a joke about the womb as part of her strong statement against those who look down on her *conversa* status. She makes fun of the idea that one could exercise agency before birth because she knows that this notion is partially from whence the Mormon doctrine of "the elect" emerges. Ironically, however, stories of humanity's pre-birth existence also provide her with pride in being a *conversa*—using her agency to choose Mormonism. After all, Mormonism's original sibling rivalry, Lucifer versus Jesus, was about agency. As my Mormon friends recount, Heavenly Father and Heavenly Mother's second-born spirit son, Lucifer, planned to force human beings to be good inhabitants of the new planet Earth. The first born, Jesus, wanted goodness to be a choice. The two brothers could not find a compromise and fought a primordial war over this question of agency. Those on Earth today with physical bodies fought on the winning side. The losers never got bodies; they are Satan's demons.

There is a divide in the Periféricos Ward between those who think that the more valiant soldiers in the war were rewarded with birth into a Mormon home and those who think that choosing Mormonism during Earth-life represents true valiance. In this debate, generational Mormonism becomes a contested requirement for "full" Mormonism. The implications of this requirement deepen as the divide between generational Mormons and *conversos* subdivides further into tribes. Tribes relate covenant birth to evangelization economics. More Mormon births means more Zion citizens, so it is vitally important for Mormons that they count themselves among biological lineages that are divinely designated to multiply. The lineage most anciently linked with such a promise is that of the Jewish patriarch Abraham: "I will multiply thy seed ... as the sand which is upon the sea shore ... and in thy seed shall all the nations of the earth be blessed" (Genesis 22:17–18). For this reason, Mormons receive a "patriarchal blessing" in which the knowledge of their tribe of Israel is revealed to them and in which they are proclaimed heirs to the Abrahamic blessings. In this way, as Ofelia advocates, all Mormons become a covenant people, not just those of "covenant birth." However, the ambiguity between biological descent and spiritual adoption in Israelite tribe ascription, as further refracted through The Book of Mormon's creation of Lamanite identity, causes even Ofelia to stop short of claiming that everyone is born with an equal potential to become full gospel keepers.

OFELIA: Like it says, "the Lamanites will blossom as the rose in the desert," right? And it says the gospel will be preached to the Lamanites in the last days. I mean, I am a *conversa*, so this gospel has only recently come to me. In the scriptures it says that the Lamanites will not just listen to the gospel, but that they will be the strongest ones in keeping it. The ones to take charge. And I stop and think about that. Sometimes I have even made some comparisons because there are people who are born in the covenant here in Arequipa, they have grown in it, but they are not strong in some things. My daughter has grown up with a lot of them, and as time goes on many of these youth go inactive. Like she says, "they are lost in the world." And she always asked me, "how did they end up like that if they are the ones who were born in the covenant? If their father was a stake president or their parents were returned missionaries, how could this happen?" And sometimes I didn't know what to tell her, right?

For Ofelia, birth or pre-birth circumstances should not influence destiny, and yet she finds it more inexplicable for a covenant-born Mormon to leave the church than for a *conversa* to do the same. Furthermore, she believes a tribe called Lamanite was destined to receive the gospel. This contradiction between what is innate and what is chosen stems from the way Israelite covenant lineages are simultaneously pathologizing and vitalizing in The Book of Mormon. The book tells the story of Lehi and his family escaping Jerusalem and coming to America in 600 B.C.E. Lehi is of the Israelite tribe of Manasseh. Once in America, Lehi's son Laman is cursed, his skin is darkened, and according to many Peruvians, he becomes the principal ancestor to all Amerindians, including Ofelia. The reason for Laman's curse was that he tried to kill his brother Nephi. In other words Laman, and his descendants the Lamanites, did not know the proper way to be kin. However, Nephi foretold that a future group—often interpreted as European carriers of a "believing-blood" (Mauss, 2003) bio-spiritually descending from Ephraim, Manasseh's brother—would come and cure Amerindian kinship with a better way. Ofelia believes herself to also carry the believing-blood of this Israelite lineage, meaning she was predisposed to accept this better way and become a *conversa*.

Per anthropologist Fenella Cannell (2013), Mormonism's "lineage thinking reinforces the experience of kinship as sacred, which is also pursued through genealogical work and many other aspects of LDS practice ... [holding open] kinship as an arena of mystery, in which agency, relatedness, creation, and destiny endlessly collide" (p. 90). This mystery is "the mystery of transmission" (p. 91), which is neither genetic nor spiritual making it the key to why there are so many conflicting unities and divisions in Zion regarding lineage.

> I have sometimes asked Latter-day Saints whether it is possible to transmit goodness in a family line; people usually pause, then answer that it is not ... The Mormon emphasis on the centrality of individual agency ... makes ideas of pure ancestral determination impossible. At the same time, the pause before the answer acknowledges the idea of elite lines, of chosen lineages, and of noble intelligences whose destiny was fixed before the mortal world began.
>
> (p. 90)

The space between believing and blood and between conversion and covenant birth in lineage discourse entails what Ofelia, in a later interview, called "legacy"; a space that offers the ambiguity necessary to make tribalism not seem like racism. Ofelia's aforementioned thoughts on her own Lamanite identity are illustrative of this ambiguity. She wonders to what extent one's propensity to be a faithful Mormon comes from one's covenant birth, one's Lamanite ancestry, or from one's own actions. Under these rarified valences of kin transmission and individual agency, being a *conversa* involves becoming heir to a new legacy that can be internalized or wasted. If internalized it becomes part of the blood, linking one to the promises to which that blood is bound through ancestral covenant. Heirs to this legacy become united, but the transmission of legacy through the mysterious idiom of blood risks profaning the Mormon project of universal tribalism—Zion. Impurities can travel through blood disguised as righteousness, and who will discern the difference? This risk parallels one that the Spanish brought to Peru: *limpieza de sangre* (blood purity). As historian Kathryn Burns (2011) noted,

> Spain's monarchs created the Spanish Inquisition in the late 1470s primarily to discipline ... people who were thought to practice Judaism clandestinely. And concerns began to fix on the supposed cleanliness of people's bloodlines ... the Castilian politics of race circa 1492 hinged on the purity of one's Christianity, increasingly defined as a matter not simply of belief and practice but of inheritance, or *limpieza de sangre*—something that could not be changed at the baptismal font.
>
> (p. 58)

For Mormonism's founder, Joseph Smith, on the other hand, the idea that "religion" is carried in the blood was precisely the point of the baptismal font. Baptism and Holy Ghost conferral literally changed blood if change was necessary. Blood change was not necessary for those who literally descended from Abraham, such as Amerindians, who would instead experience a skin color change. Those who were not Israelites, however, must have a violent "new creation by the Holy Ghost ... to purge out the old blood and make him actually the seed of Abraham" (Smith, 2016, p. 380). This caused physical convulsing in white Gentiles, whereas when the "Holy Ghost falls upon one of the literal seed of Abraham, it is calm and serene" (p. 380). Such a literal rewiring of past genealogies by Holy Ghost-induced blood transfusion seems to have the potential to change all tribes into one universally inclusive Zion citizenry.

Conversos in Saints' clothing

However, as Ofelia makes clear, universal inclusion is not happening in Periféricos Ward. On the surface level, this lack of inclusion seems to have very little to do with blood or lineage. The vast majority of members either sees blood purity as a relic of a racist past or does not know about it at all. Nevertheless, the correlate of blood purity and "lineage thinking," namely the notion that birth circumstances relate to worthiness, becomes a significant feature of Periféricos

Ward discourse when a future grandchild's Zion citizenship status is at stake. Ofelia alludes to this when she complains about the questioning of her daughter's covenant status. The only reason ward members would care to ask is to assess Shannon's worthiness as a potential daughter-in-law. They wondered if Shannon's outward appearance of righteousness matched the preexistent valor that is supposed to result in covenant birth. When they found she was not born in the covenant, they wondered if merging lineages with her family line might risk a future break in the great chain of sealings that tie all humanity together. In a religious tradition shot through with such ambiguities, navigating the riddle of "what the link might be between tribal identity and family history" (Cannell, 2013, p. 88) not only affects how Mormons imagine the ideal Zion citizen, it also affects how they rework Zion's boundaries to screen for that ideal.

Along Zion's boundaries where "tribe" can transmute from race to siblingship and back, there are many instances when geopolitical and historical borders unfortunately align. Since there are more generational Mormons in Utah and more *conversos* in Peru, the born-in-the-covenant versus *converso* divide maps closely onto the racial Ephraim (Euro-American) versus Manasseh (Amerindian) divide. This further maps onto the aforementioned ancestral divide regarding Peru's first *conversos*: the Spanish Crypto-Jews. What the Spanish Jewish *conversos* share with the Peruvian Mormon ones

> is a discursive process by which the excess or slippage produced by the *ambivalence* of mimicry (almost the same, *but not quite*) does not merely "rupture" the discourse, but becomes transformed into an uncertainty which fixes the colonial subject as a "partial" presence ... a proliferation of inappropriate objects that ensure its strategic failure, so that mimicry is at once resemblance and menace.
>
> (Bhabha, 1984, p. 127)

Assessing the authenticity of a *converso*'s conversion is ambiguous enough in a U.S. context where "seeing is believing." In an Andean context, however, mimicry, resemblance, and menace are a tripartite roulette behind the most mundane interactions. In Andean mythology, appearances are by definition deceiving and the gaze is a conduit for as much antireality as reality. Powerful, benevolent gods dress as poor people and provoke disgust among all but those who can intuit beyond the mimicry (Arguedas, 1975). Ontological ambiguity is, therefore a fundamental part of Andean place-making, and it exposes the authentic Zion citizenship of the growing number of Mormon *conversos* in Arequipa to significant scrutiny.

Ambivalence surrounding *conversos* finds expression in a phenomenon I witnessed in Periféricos Ward whereby even those who were proud of being *conversos* themselves drew the line at allowing their loved ones to marry *conversos*. On a pragmatic level, Mormons in Peru have sacrificed a lot for a Zion they believe that only their grandkids will live to fully experience. It is as if Arequipa itself is a *conversa* that will only "blossom as the rose" after a few more generations. If *conversos* cannot get their kids to marry someone born in the covenant then their grandkids will, in essence, be starting at the same level their kids were, propelling a second generation of Mormonism into perpetuity and never fully arriving at a third. On a structural level, if someone is a *converso* they are, as if filtered through Andean mythology, always suspect of being almost, *but not quite* Mormon.

Shannon and Ofelia embody the heart of this ambivalence. Ofelia represents the ambivalence of "blood" because, despite her descent from autochthonous Andeans with little-to-no European ancestry, she was ascribed the tribe of Ephraim in her patriarchal blessing. Shannon represents the ambivalence of *converso* status and its tension between destiny and agency because, despite her non-covenant birth status, she was set up to marry covenant-born Marco. Marco's parents do not subscribe to the importance of covenant birth, but other Periféricos Ward members who do subscribe very deeply, such as the bishop, still consider Shannon as complete a Mormon as it is possible to be. In their eyes, Shannon's saintliness outweighs her birth and whatever pre-birth cowardice this birth might represent. During Shannon's formative years in Periféricos Ward, everyone came to consider her as someone who was "the best of us." Yet, her triumph over birth status paradoxically perpetuated the tightening of Zion's borders because, as the best in the ward, she deserved nothing less than to marry the fullest Mormon imaginable. Shannon and her future husband were destined to produce children who would be the first full citizens of a local Arequipeño Zion. When "Plan A, Marco" backfired and "Plan B, Flavio: The Younger Brother" did not pan out, the bishopric decided to take matters into their own hands to design a Plan C. But what young man could possibly be "Mormon" enough for Shannon?

Zion's border police

There was one young man, but he was not a worthy Plan C, and may have even threatened Plan B. His name is Ayzo and he moved into the ward while Shannon was on her mission to Paraguay. He had only joined the church three years earlier and had just come back from his mission. He grew up in Lima, but moved on his own to Arequipa and into the boundaries of Periféricos Ward. Ofelia, old enough to be his mother, felt an immediate maternal connection to him. Over a year into their mother–son relationship, the substance of their cosmic intersubjectivity was revealed. Having never talked before about their tribes of Israel with each other, one day Ayzo mentioned that his patriarchal blessing ascribed him the tribe of Judá through biological descent but that, because his tribe was dispersed, he would be adopted by a woman from the tribe of Ephraim. To Ofelia, this could only mean one thing:

> "Look, you say that I am your *mamá*, am I right?" I ask him. "Yes, because you are my *mamá*, because you take care of me." "Ah, exactly. And have you ever asked yourself what tribe I'm from?" "Oh, that's true, I've never asked. So what tribe are you?" And I make him guess. He goes through all the tribes, but he doesn't get it. So I tell him, "I am from the tribe of Ephraim!" And we both sat there, stunned.

Ayzo had never met a Lamanite of the tribe of Ephraim before, so he never guessed that Ofelia would be his prophesied adoptive mother. Not that he needed any more solidification of their kinship. This had been constructed the way it often is in the Andes, through food.

> "You have to come eat lunch." "But, but–" "Don't give me any of your lip, Mister!" I tell him, "your lunch is all ready, you have to come and eat it." "But the doctor said, my diet–" "No excuses! I'm the one who will worry about your diet." And on Sundays he didn't want to come, he didn't want to impose, so I said, "hey, you come on Sunday, but I'm tired of cooking Monday through Friday, so you cook Sundays." So that was my way of getting him to come and eat, because otherwise he just doesn't eat. But the bishop didn't like that one bit.

Not everyone was excited by this new kinship formation. Bishop Paucar, one of the few ward members who lives in a "sealed" nuclear family, did not want Ayzo hanging around Ofelia's house because he feared what would happen when Shannon came back from her mission. Ayzo, already like a son-in-law to Ofelia, would surely fall for Shannon and endanger Plan B. The bishop's first line of defense would be to marry Ayzo off with someone else before Shannon even got back. He was "Mormon" enough for other young women in the ward, but not "Mormon" enough for Shannon:

> *Hermano* [Brother Jason], they premeditatively judge him in the sense that he is a recent *converso*. Unfortunately, that's the way it is. The bishop interviewed him and splayed the young women out in front of Ayzo on a tray as it were, "look, for example, we have Lizbeth Abedul, this is a young woman who was born in the covenant," and he actually told him that, Ayzo told me the story. The bishop said, "and her parents are sealed in the temple, her uncle has been a stake president and her other uncles are Fulano, Zutano, and Mengano, and her other uncle works in the temple, and she is from a stellar family and so this young woman suits you." All he said was, "thanks, Bishop for your recommendation." "But you have to get yourself a fiancé soon!" And Ayzo asked me, "but, why do they insist so much on me getting married? I mean, I don't even like that young woman and the bishop is the one who keeps insisting." "Just don't do it," I tell him. "I'm not going to." And during that time Shannon comes back and he says, "I want to go out with her," because he is very formal, I mean, he didn't say, "hey, want to go out with me?" No. I mean, he came, he sat down, he asked my permission to get to know her, to go out, and so he did things the way they should be done. And now the bishop is saying, "no, no, no, we will not permit you two to go out." And, I don't know in the end what it is the bishopric wants. I don't understand it. But sometimes they grab onto that idea, right? They say, "we don't know anything about his parents, he is a new *converso*, he was only a member for a year before his mission, he lives alone, we don't know what he does."

Thwarting this union was going to be more difficult than the bishop had expected.

Thinking Ayzo to be unworthy of Shannon because he lacked covenant birth, the bishop hoped Ayzo would feel that lack within himself and be tempted to heal it by marrying someone who was born in the covenant. Instead, Ayzo confirmed the bishop's worst fears and went immediately after Shannon. The bishop could not let this happen. It was time for phase two.

OFELIA: They called Shannon in to an interview. The bishop was bothered because she is going out with Ayzo. Not just the bishop either, his councilors, everyone is against her going out with him, and so she came back from her interview badly affected. And she expressed to me her sadness and said, "*Mamá*, I don't understand why so much resentment against Ayzo on the part of my leaders. They told me roundly, 'we want you to stop seeing him completely.' But what I feel— *Mamá*, I have prayed and I feel like he is a good young man and I want to go out with him." And I took this opportunity and said, "what do you think now after hearing from the bishop and listening to his councilors?" And she is a little close-minded at times, "no, if my leader tells me something, it is for a reason, *Mamá*, so I am going to pay heed." "Oh, really? Okay, so you are going to tell him that you aren't going to go out with him anymore?" "Yes, *Mamá*, I have to because my leader told me so." "Oh, really? And how do you feel about that, I mean, what do you feel inside yourself?" "But it's that, Mami, I really like him, I feel something very special." "Okay then, even though you feel something very special for him, you are going to throw that all away just because your bishop and his councilors told you to? You are going to stop going out with him?" "Yes, I know it is for the best because they are my leaders and they are counseling me for my benefit." "Alright, sounds perfect then," I told her, "but, you know what? The leaders are human beings, and they make mistakes and sometimes we as humans judge based on certain things, and we judge people as well. And do you know that they don't know Ayzo perfectly? Do you think for one second that if I knew that he was a disobedient young man and that he was really bad for you, that I would permit you to go out with him? I am your mother," I told her. "I know that young man, and you know it." "But my bishop said!" And she started to cry. I told her, "look. Pray. The bishop can tell you many things, but tell the Lord. What will the Lord tell you? You are forgetting that you are a missionary, that you have been a missionary, so make your decision, pray to the Lord. The leaders make mistakes, *Hijita*." And so she started to study, and she prayed and the next day when she woke up I asked her, "And? What did you think?" She said, "Mami. I am going to keep going out with him." "Alright, are you sure?" "Yes, *Mamá*." And so she told Ayzo, and it was very sad, *Hermano*. She told Ayzo.

JASON: So Ayzo knows that the bishop is against him?

OFELIA: "And you know what?" she told him, "it's not only the bishop, it is the councilors, the stake presidency."

Believing they had Shannon's best interests at heart in steering her away from someone who was almost, *but not quite* Mormon, the bishopric did not give up. Employing the rumor mill to turn the other "single young adults" against Ayzo, calling him in constantly for intimidating interviews, accusing him of being inactive and of not attending LDS institute classes, and even threatening to cut him off from the church's Perpetual Education Fund which paid for his mining engineering degree, the bishopric eventually succeeded in driving a wedge between Ayzo and Shannon. The couple resolved that it would be best for the social harmony of the ward if they began to see other people. Nevertheless, Ayzo remained a part of Ofelia's family. This confused the ward. Why would he still hang around Shannon so much if they had broken up? Was she available for a Plan C or not?

Shannon's love life is a microcosm of the greater Zion-building project and the productive and destructive tension that Zion's paradoxically exclusive inclusivity generates. Mormons are taught that their bodies are temples, and that the temple is the symbol for Zion. It is the place where God is able to seal humanity together under one united, coresident siblingship. It is universal *Pacha*. Yet, it is also extremely exclusive, complete with textual stipulations on who may and may not enter. In order to achieve the "temple recommend" card, required for temple entry, one must be baptized a Mormon, pay a full 10 percent of one's monthly income to the church corporation, and the list goes on. The last requirement on the list is that one must believe oneself to be worthy to enter. In Periféricos Ward, this would involve managing to not internalize the barrage of insinuations from global and local pulpits that true Mormon worthiness demands living in a U.S.-defined nuclear family, being born in the covenant, and most of all, being married—or striving to be married—to someone who also fulfills those requirements. In Periféricos Ward, if everyone's body is a temple, Shannon's is the Salt Lake City temple; the ultimate, central symbol of Zion in the ward. When they sing the hymns of Zion, they are singing to her: "youth of the promise, hope of Zion, listen to Jesus Christ and follow him in unity, youth of Israel" (Townsend, 1992, p. 168; translation mine). Shannon's body securely reserved as sacrosanct, the types of people the ward actively excludes from access to it reveal the unwritten rules that make up the true boundaries of their Zion—a city that, despite everything, still claims to be open to all.

Youth of Zion rise

The saga of Shannon and Ayzo is not over. After I left Arequipa in August 2018, I kept recording Skype conversations with Ofelia who had recently taken the 18-hour bus ride to the Lima temple with Shannon to help Ayzo do proxy baptismal rites on behalf of his sister who died while he was on his mission. Once inside the temple, Ofelia and Shannon emerged from the changing room dressed in white long before Ayzo, so they sat in the lobby. As they waited, the recommend card-checker's wife, an old Peruvian woman, came up to them and asked Shannon a question.

> "That little young man who you came in with, is that your brother?" "No, no. That's not my brother, he's only a friend," she tells him. And the sister gave her a long look and said, "ah, your friend, you don't say. You mean your boyfriend?" And Shannon told her, "he's just a friend, nothing more. He's a friend who asked that I be baptized on behalf of his sister." "Oh, but you are going to marry him." "No," Shannon tells her, "I am not going to marry him. There's nothing between us." "Yes, but you are going to marry him." And she looks at Shannon and laughs, and I also look at Shannon and smile. "You will go back to wherever you are from and you will marry him."

The elderly temple diviner did not err. About six months later, Ayzo and Shannon scheduled their temple marriage for December 19, 2019, four days after the Arequipa temple was to be dedicated. Against the directives of their "Judge In Israel"—an alternate title for bishop—they would be among the first couples sealed in that temple, the center of their own appropriately paradoxical piece of Peruvian Zion.

Periféricos Ward tensions between exclusive quasi-biological lineages and inclusive familial love scale broader than local matchmaking. These tensions link to the greater problem of family-making in today's world especially as they connect to race. As I conclude with a personal instantiation of Zion's multivalent endogamy, I ask a question that opens a larger realm of inquiry within tribalism's symbiosis with siblingship.

I received my patriarchal blessing at age 15 from an elderly, white, generational-Mormon in Utah. In it, I was ascribed to the tribe of Ephraim and promised that I would find a "mate of my own lineage." In the context of the blessing, I assumed this meant someone who was also ascribed to the tribe of Ephraim. I had no idea at the time that patriarchs tended to assign Ephraim to light-skinned people and other tribes to dark-skinned people, much less that I would one day want to marry a dark-skinned person. The type-written blessing also told me that if I did not follow the Lord's council, I would not receive my promised blessings. I never questioned His council until I became romantically involved with a Peruvian Mormon woman. Concerned by the "own lineage" statement for the first time, I asked her: "what's your tribe?" Unfortunately, she was from Manasseh, not Ephraim. Our future now depended upon deciphering what God could have meant by the term "lineage." Surely, we convinced ourselves, he could not be talking about tribe of Israel ascription. What sort of endogamy was he talking about? Was it not enough that I was marrying a Mormon? Did not that give us a common "lineage" according to spiritual transcendentalism? By this time, I knew full well what Ephraim symbolized for the patriarch who came of age during the height of apostolic rhetoric such as this:

> The Lord segregated the people both as to blood and place of residence. At least in the bases of the Lamanites and the Negroes, we have the definite word of the Lord himself that He placed a dark skin upon them: as a curse—as a sign to all others. He forbade inter-marriage with them under threat of extension of the curse.
>
> *(Peterson, 1954, p. 14)*

The question regarding the ambivalent nature of kin-making at the heart of Zion-building is this: was our eventual temple marriage in 2001 endogamous or exogamous? What kind of people embody Mormon worthiness to such an extent that they qualify unambiguously for Mormon endogamy? This lies at the root of the globally applicable question that Periféricos Ward matchmaking and match thwarting so contradictorily exemplify: Who gets to be one of "us?"

References

Arguedas, J.M., 1975. *Dioses y hombres de Huarochiri*. Mexico, D.F.: Siglo Veintiuno.
Bhabha, H.K., 1984. Of Mimicry and Man: The Ambivalence of Colonial Discourse. *October* 28: 125–33.
Burns, K., 2011. Unfixing Race. In L. Gotkowitz, ed. *Histories of Race and Racism: The Andes and Mesoamerica from Colonial Times to the Present*. Durham. NC: Duke University Press, pp. 58–70.
Canessa, A., 2012. *Intimate Indigeneities: Race, Sex, and History in the Small Spaces of Andean Life*. Durham, NC: Duke University Press.
Cannell, F., 2013. The Blood of Abraham: Mormon Redemptive Physicality and American Idioms of Kinship. *Journal of the Royal Anthropological Institute* 19(May): 77–94.
Lorde, A., 1984. *Sister Outsider: Essays and Speeches by Audre Lorde*. Berkeley, CA: Crossing Press.
Marin Benitez, C., 2015. *Filosofía Tawantinsuyana: Una Perspectiva Epistemica*. Lima, Peru: Juan Gutemberg.
Mauss, A.L., 2003. *All Abraham's Children: Changing Mormon Conceptions of Race and Lineage*. Urbana, IL: University of Illinois Press.
McKay-Lamb, T., and Jensen, E.W., 2015. Afterword. In T. McKay-Lamb and E.W. Jensen, eds. *A Book of Mormons: Latter-Day Saints on a Modern-Day Zion*. Ashland, OR: White Cloud Press, pp. 191–92.
Peterson, M.E., 1954. Race Problems as They Affect the Church. In *Brigham Young University Convention of Teachers of Religion on the College Level*. Provo, Utah. August 27.
Sarkisian, N., and Gerstel N., 2012. *Nuclear Family Values, Extended Family Lives: The Power of Race, Class, and Gender*. New York: Routledge.
Smith, J., 2016. *History of the Church of Jesus Christ of Latter-Day Saints*, vol. 3, ed. B.H. Roberts. CreateSpace.
Townsend, J.L., 1992. Juventud de Israel. In *Himnos de La Iglesia de Jesucristo de Los Santos de los Ultimos Dias*. Salt Lake City, Utah: La Iglesia de Jesucristo de los Santos de los Ultimos Dias, p. 168.
Weismantel, M., 1995. Making Kin: Kinship Theory and Zumbagua Adoptions. *American ethnologist* 22(4): 685–704.

Further reading

Bamford, S., 2007. *Biology Unmoored: Melanesian Reflections on Life and Biotechnology*. Berkeley, CA: University of California Press.
Bamford breaks down Euro-American "biogenetic" kinship into its component parts through comparison to a specific Melanesian kin system. Since Mormonism was incubated under the same Euro-American kin system that is hegemonic in much of the world, this text helps denaturalize kinship in ways that open new views into what a Peruvian Mormon kinship might mean.
Kim, E.J., 2010. *Adopted Territory: Transnational Korean Adoptees and the Politics of Belonging*. Durham, NC: Duke University Press.
Though in a very different context, this book continues the conversation on kin-making, community boundary policing, and counterintuitive inclusiveness that resonates with global Mormonism and its attempts to "adopt" the world into a universal lineage.

30
MORMON WOMEN AT WORK IN NICARAGUA

Amanda Talbot Tew

Working toward both spiritual and temporal self-reliance has long been an integral part of the tenets of Mormonism. Over 100 years ago church leader Joseph F. Smith taught that "Latter-day Saints believe not only in the gospel of spiritual salvation but also in the gospel of temporal salvation" (Smith, 1904, p. 74). Present-day church leaders have said church members have "a promise from the Lord that He will provide temporal blessings and open the door of self-reliance, which is the ability for us to provide the necessities of life for ourselves and our family members" (Message from the First Presidency, 2017). But is financial stability and progress possible for members who live in politically tumultuous or economically disadvantaged countries such as Nicaragua? Scholars examining Mormons in other Latin American countries have noted that members of the church face economic difficulties, which the gospel can somewhat temper, but the immense economic and political power of the wealthy elite keep poverty stable (Tullis, 2006; 1981). While LDS church leadership has implemented training and relief programs to address these disadvantages, members still must labor within the confines of the economic environment in which they live.

There is extensive research on the history and people of the LDS Church in Mexico as well as many South American countries, but research in Central America has focused mainly on Guatemala. Comparatively little work has been completed on the church in Nicaragua. As political tensions mount and the church prepares to build an LDS temple in the final Latin American country lacking one, it seems an appropriate time to expand our knowledge on the lives of Mormon women in Nicaragua. These women are at the center of economic progress in the family and view paid labor outside of the home as part of their standard duties of motherhood. For them, family finances and child rearing practices are shaped by the overarching need to reach temporal salvation in an environment where their male partners are often negligent or even absent. Even when their partners are present and providing financially, women still work to try to lift their families above the extremely depressed economy. Despite the challenges, these women gain a deep sense of purpose from their employment and sacrifice. They have come to view both paid labor and family nurturing as critical components for attaining temporal and spiritual salvation for their families.

During 2019, I conducted oral interviews of LDS women living in the southern Nicaraguan cities of Diriamba and Granada.[1] Of the eighteen women I interviewed, sixteen participate in the labor force, either running their own businesses or in other employment outside the home.

Of these, six have spent a significant portion of their adult lives being the sole providers for their children, either because there was no husband, the husband lost work, or the husband chose not to provide for the family. This high level of economic participation by these LDS women is not unusual for Nicaraguan women as a whole. The World Economic Forum's 2018 Global Gender Gap Report ranks Nicaragua 5th in the world for gender parity, based on four metrics (Zahidi, Geiger, and Crotti, 2018, pp. 10–11). Out of 149 countries, Nicaragua ranked 69th for gender parity in economic participation and opportunity, and 36th in educational attainment. Nicaragua's gender parity also ranks 1st in health/survival and 2nd in political empowerment (there are more women in Nicaraguan parliament, proportionally, than any other country measured). Women in Nicaragua seem to be doing well, particularly when compared to neighboring countries.[2]

While these statistics portray gender equality in Nicaragua in a positive light, some question the validity of Nicaragua's fifth place ranking in gender parity (Álvarez, 2016; Piper, 2018). After all, Nicaragua is a country that reports high rates of marital violence, infidelity, abdication of responsibility and abandonment by husbands and fathers, and a *machismo* culture that affects both the choices women can make about work and the control they have over the economic resources they earn. Nearly all of the women I interviewed indicated that violence against women was a major problem in Nicaragua, and many of them were abuse victims themselves. And though Nicaragua has enacted laws intended to protect women and their rights, this does not always translate into a better life. In their article on women at work in Latin America, Novta and Wong warn that "the mere existence of laws does not ensure de facto gender equality due to weak enforcement." They add that many women do not know the law well enough to realize their rights within it, or are unable to access justice when they do understand (2017, p. 14). If we are to accept Nicaragua's gender parity status, we must understand that it is a complex combination of both freedom and subjugation, where women's opportunities are often born out of an unequal burden of responsibility rather than respect for their gender.

Economy and employment in Nicaragua

My interest in the lives of Nicaraguan women developed out of my experience living in the country for a year with my husband and our four young children during 2017 and 2018. We lived in both Diriamba and Granada, and we participated in the local LDS congregations in those cities. I became part of the local LDS women's group, known as the Relief Society, and through worship participation, social activities, and joining in their humanitarian efforts, I developed close relationships with many of the women.[3] While living in Granada, I was asked to take a turn leading the group's efforts, including assisting with the economic and health issues of the women in that congregation. Through my experiences, I witnessed their lives firsthand and became acquainted with their struggles, ambitions, and resilience.

Moving to Nicaragua as a mother with dependent children opened my eyes to the challenge to provide in a country with a depressed economy and almost no social safety nets. Even then, as someone who had always lived a middle-class life in a First World economy—and took all of those benefits with me to Nicaragua—it took months of living in Nicaragua, and dealing intimately with families through the LDS Church's welfare program, to even begin to form a true picture of the local women's daily fight for the basics of life.[4]

With a GDP per capita of less than $2,000 per year, Nicaragua is the second poorest country in the western hemisphere, after Haiti (International Monetary Fund, 2019a). The country faces high unemployment, low wages, and widespread poverty. Only an estimated 25 percent of Nicaraguans are formally employed, while the other 75 percent survive through informal employment, such as selling wares on the streets and domestic work (COSEP/ILO, 2015; see also Freije, 2001, p. 56). Roughly half of all Nicaraguans live in poverty. And yet, Nicaragua is an enigma in that it has avoided the drug violence of its northern triangle neighbors (Honduras, Guatemala, and El Salvador), claiming the unusual combination of being both one of the poorest and one of the safest countries in Latin America (Schrader, 2017).

To more fully understand the temporal situation of families in Nicaragua, one must consider the reality of the country's cost of living. Basic life necessities in Nicaragua cost *nearly the same* as they do in the United States, and access to First World amenities is often even more expensive in comparison (Tullis, 1963, p. 12). Our family lived less comfortably in Nicaragua than we were accustomed to living in the United States, and yet our monthly expenditures in Nicaragua were not drastically less than our expenditures in the States had been. In comparison, the average wage for the Nicaraguan families we knew was about $250 per month, and for those without consistent work it was much less. The average Nicaraguan family is earning just enough for the most basic food and necessities, while luxuries such as meat and poultry, diverse fresh fruits and vegetables, electricity, plumbing, money for education, and public transportation are only infrequently accessible. While statistically many of the people are living in poverty, it's important to state that the majority of Nicaraguans we knew were optimistic and intelligent people with plans, schedules, and families. They are fully functioning individuals who have little choice but to live in an economic and political environment that has stagnated and stifled opportunity to the point that, though they have skills and personal ambitions, it is extremely difficult to progress.

We had lived in Nicaragua for nearly a year when anti-government protests erupted in the capital city of Managua on April 18, 2018. Many young student protesters were killed by government police, and over the following weeks violent political protests, rioting, and looting started spreading throughout all the major cities. We watched with amazement as the country that had been politically stable for thirty years quickly deteriorated. Commerce nationwide began to shut down and food and clean water became scarce. Eventually one night riots erupted within feet of the front door of our house. Imelda, a good friend who helped me lead the Relief Society in Granada, said *"hermana, hay que ir"* (sister, you need to leave), and we agreed. We left quickly and with mixed emotions: gratitude that we were able to escape the escalating danger and uncertainty, and sorrow for the families we knew who had no such option. During the months of violent unrest that followed, Nicaragua's already-struggling economy plummeted, leaving hundreds of thousands of Nicaraguans without work (Feinberg, 2018; International Monetary Fund, 2019b).[5]

As we flew away I regretted that I had not taken the opportunity to document the lives and stories of the women I had come to know. Returning to Nicaragua eight months later to conduct formal research felt like a chance to complete unfinished business, an important opportunity to chronicle at least a portion of what these women had experienced. I approached the trip with caution, knowing that the stability that had returned to the country was tenuous. Upon arrival, I immediately noticed that life had taken on a more normal appearance. The burning tires, brick barricades, and police in riot gear were all gone. The corner stores were again stocked with food and the evening streets were no longer chaotic. But the people would tell me it was all just a semblance of the freedom they once had. Many who spoke out against the government were being kidnapped, jailed, and some reportedly tortured. In reality, I returned to a Nicaragua with much less liberty and to a people in much worse economic conditions.

Nicaraguan motherhood and LDS women

One of my primary concerns during the oral interviews was how these women and families were surviving economically, day to day. From my own experience, I saw that the women shouldered much of this responsibility. When I interviewed Juana Lellany, a Cuban woman who moved to Nicaragua fifteen years ago, she explained, "I deeply admire Nicaraguan women, because they are women who fight, women who work hard" (Figueredo Garcés, 2019). The idea of the fighting Nicaraguan mother may stem from the era of the Sandinista Revolution. Karen Kampwirth notes that it was during the revolution that feminist thought flourished, aided by the strong egalitarian views of the revolutionaries and the women's own experiences as they organized into new networks of strength (Kampwirth, 2004). Kampwirth further explains that "empowered maternity" figured strongly in Nicaragua's revolutionary feminist ideal, pointing to the iconic photograph that emerged from this time period, one of a powerful and armed nursing mother (Kampwirth, 2004, pp. 5–9). Another woman I interviewed (Anonymous #21, 2019), who has spent most of her life raising her three sons on her own, spoke of this powerful, maternal Nicaraguan woman.

> In our country, Nicaragua ... sometimes women work so hard, they take the place of men. [But] women here are not sufficiently valued as those who are forging a society, who are working for the home, so that the home and family lack nothing ... The women of Nicaragua are hard workers, fighters. We are not perfect, but we work hard so that in my sixty decades of life in this country, I have seen how women successfully provide a better life for their families, and I think, wow ... they didn't have a father, they didn't have a husband to help them. I tell people, "Sometimes it's not necessary to have a husband ... You've experienced that, with effort, the Lord has made you more powerful than even a man."

While in Nicaragua, I observed that working for survival is inherently mothers' work.[6] As I came to know these women, I saw a divergence between the North American view of "ideal Mormon motherhood," and the "empowered maternity" of the working Mormon mother in Nicaragua. Leaders of the LDS Church have historically encouraged women to avoid paid labor outside of the home, and for a while many LDS women in the United States purposefully eschewed outside employment in favor of the religious ideal of stay-at-home motherhood.[7] The rhetoric targeting the idea of LDS women working has softened in recent years, and a greater number of LDS women in the States work, but strong cultural biases against women's paid employment remain. The LDS Church's official statement, "The Family: A Proclamation to the World," states that fathers are to "preside over their families in love and righteousness and are responsible to provide the necessities of life and protection for their families" and "mothers are primarily responsible for the nurture of their children." This landmark document is often interpreted in the United States as specifically mandating that women should not provide, but rather stay at home with children. However, after living in Nicaragua I began to wonder if this idea was a North American interpretation, born out of U.S. cultural experiences as well as exposure to more explicit rhetoric from past church leaders, rather than what the document actually states.[8] In the LDS Church in the United States, where generations of men have been providing in a stable, ample economy that allows for one-income households, there is a propensity to focus on what the document means for women's roles and decisions. But in a country where men often do not protect or provide, and women have always nurtured their children while concurrently working, I began to see that the interpretation of the Proclamation document for church members in this country might be more fully focused on what it mandates for men. While one of my interviewees (Leysan González, 2019) reported being taught by the LDS Church in Guatemala that it is best for women not to work, the Nicaraguan LDS women I interviewed did not seem aware of the church's past rhetoric against women working outside the home, nor did they speak of any doctrinal tension between paid employment and motherhood. For these women, employment is a fundamental part of life, and they believe that by bearing the weight of both spiritual and temporal salvation they are helping their families achieve both as well.[9]

"We share the responsibilities": dual earning and co-parenting in Nicaragua

Sinia (Hernández Mendieta, 2019) is an example of a woman who views employment as an important part of her life even though her husband is also present and providing for the family. Currently 37 years old, she has worked as a nurse for the past seventeen years. She is an active member of the church, and she serves as president of the children's group, known as the "Primary," in the Diriamba church congregation. While I lived in Diriamba, Sinia and I worked together leading the Primary, and I came to appreciate her steadiness and kindness. Some aspects of Sinia's life are atypical compared to other church members in the area. Her family is one of two in the church congregation that own a car. Her kitchen, where we sit for her interview, more closely resembles a U.S. kitchen than do those of most of the other members, including running water to the sink, a full-sized refrigerator, an oven, and tiles covering the floor instead of dirt or bare cement. Sinia's husband works full-time, is an ecclesiastical leader in the LDS Church for the larger Jinotepe area, and he is a very present husband and father for their two children.

Similar to many Nicaraguan women, Sinia's experience with women and employment began early. Her father died in the Sandinista wars when she was still young and, as she was the oldest of five children, she spent much of her youth taking care of her siblings while her mother worked.

> My mom was a secretary at an institute, and she worked Monday through Friday from 7:00 a.m. until 6:00 p.m. She had found someone to take care of us but had to let her go because she didn't have enough to pay her. So we took care of ourselves and attended school. My mom always left us food, and we learned to cook and prepare our meals when we were young.

Sinia decided from an early age to finish college and prepare for a career.

> We always had goals because my mom was on her own. We didn't have much. After my mother worked Monday through Friday, she worked an additional job [on the weekends] from 6:00 a.m. to 9:00 p.m. … She had to provide for the five of us children … So I already knew I must prepare myself to be able to help her … That's how we were raised.

She was 16 years old when her family was introduced to and baptized into the Mormon Church. As a young woman in the church, she received a church assignment to visit with and invite church members who were not actively attending to return to church. One of the people she visited was her future husband. Through her encouragement he returned to church and later became a missionary. A number of years after completing his mission, he and Sinia began dating and eventually married at the uncommonly older ages of 26 and 27, respectively.

During her young single adult years Sinia completed nursing school and began working at the main hospital in Granada, where she still works a twenty-four-hour shift every four days. I asked Sinia if she had been the one to support her husband once they married, since she had stable employment coming into the marriage. She said no, "we both work equally, and manage financially between the two of us; we work together." I knew Sinia and her husband were both very busy with careers, family, and church responsibilities. I wanted to know how they were able to balance everything together.

> We each help each other ... We schedule out our time. For example, in the morning when [the children] are going to school, if it's my turn to work he takes care of the children, making them breakfast, getting them ready, taking them to school ... Later he goes to work. If there is a church meeting ... we prepare to go together. And if we need to visit a brother or sister, or there is a church activity, we go. And I give thanks to God that I have his help, he is such a help as a husband, we share the responsibilities.

I felt like the gratitude Sinia expressed for her husband highlighted her understanding that their relationship is not the norm in Nicaragua. I asked Sinia if it has always been this way, or if it was a difficult process to arrive at this arrangement.

> No, it's been easy because we already know that we have to divide the responsibilities of the home. When we hold Family Home Evening we discuss the subject of housework. We always talk about that the work is not mine alone, I know I am the woman of the house, but the work is everyone's. Because we all live here and we all need to work so that one does not have to carry more weight than the other. We do our work quickly, we don't argue, there is peace in our home. We talk about things that aren't working well and how they should be, we converse, but we don't fight ... We always talk [as a family] about ... the food budget, everything.

And yet, despite her supportive partner and comparative financial stability, Sinia has ambitions that she cannot fully realize because of economic circumstances. Although she finished her nursing degree in 2004, she would like to get her license for promotion opportunities. However, she would have to pay 10,000 cordobas (about US$300) for the licensing program. Saving that amount of money seems far out of reach, especially now with the deteriorating political and economic situation. It used to be possible to get a loan from the Perpetual Education Fund, one of the LDS Church's small loans programs for developing countries, but sadly she said,

> Last year I talked to a leader in charge of the Perpetual Education Fund, and he told me that things are managed differently now, that they sent out a notice saying that if you are older than 30 you can no longer seek funds from the Perpetual Education Fund.

She acknowledges that there are other requirements at the university that she also does not meet, which complicates the goal of realizing her ambitions. Getting her license, she says, would allow for a higher salary or enable her to pursue a master's degree in nursing. But for now, she must wait and work.

Though she has been a member of the LDS Church since her youth, Sinia did not express any rhetoric that one's husband should be the main provider or that she should leave her employment to raise her children. For her, the balance she has with her husband results in an optimal situation in which they can both nurture their children, while also both working toward temporal security for their family.

Women supporting families

Sinia's view that her employment is an expected extension of her role as a mother is typical of the women I interviewed. Less typical in Sinia's experience is the equity and mutual financial provision in her marriage. I remember attending a small church meeting in one city where we discussed the topic of jobs and self-reliance. I knew that, for several families in that church unit, it was the women who worked to provide for their families, and childcare was often left to other female family members (mothers, sisters, etc.) rather than to the non-working husband. I also knew from talking to some of the women that, at times, their husbands turned down scarce job offers because of low pay. In this context I was chagrined when one leader stated that self-reliance was mainly the responsibility of the Relief Society. "Maybe we could teach the men how to find jobs, and make money?" I ventured. "It seems like none of the men work around here." This brought laughter from everyone, both men and women, but not much discussion.

Another day I went to visit a large family who were seeking church assistance for food. One of the men in the household answered the door and invited me into their house, which was one large room built of cement blocks, divided with tarps. When I asked for the main woman of the house, he said, "She's not here, she's out selling because there is no food for the children." He again emphasized, "We have no food," and then sat down next to another middle-aged man in the family and continued watching the tiny television in the front room. I could hear a baby and toddler fussing behind the tarp, being soothed by a young mom. Experiences like these were baffling to me. There were, of course, examples of men who did work as much or more than their wives, but an unspoken cultural rule in many families seemed to dictate that survival was the woman's responsibility. *If* the man found a job and he *liked* the job prospect and pay, he would work. But in the meantime, the woman needed to work doing whatever she could to provide the daily food.

Perhaps my pessimistic view is distorted by my own cultural expectations. Evelyn Stevens warned that "as culture-bound foreigners, we are not qualified to define the interests of Latin American women," nor can we say what would be best for them or their families (1973, p. 98). In reality, the number of women working in Nicaragua's depressed economy is consistent across all poor economies. Novta and Wong point out that there is a "well documented U-shaped relationship between female LFP [labor force participation] and log GDP per capita" (Novta and Wong, 2017, p. 8; see also Goldin, 1994).[10] In the most economically disadvantaged countries, women work in the labor force at high rates, and their income is a crucial part of meeting basic household needs. However, as a country's GDP per capita rises, more women stay home. Finally, as income levels rise even higher, the number of women participating in the labor force again rises (Novta and Wong, 2017, p. 8).

I noticed that upon my return to the country, even more women were saying that they needed to find employment because their husbands could not. Is it easier for women to find work during economic crises, I wondered? I spoke with Juana Lellany (Figueredo Garcés, 2019) about this during her interview. Though she grew up in Cuba, she married a Nicaraguan man whom she met while studying biochemistry in college in Havana. Due to political and economic problems in Cuba, they immigrated to Nicaragua. Juana, who has since divorced and remarried, is a natural leader who speaks with speed, confidence, and insight. She has been a member of the Mormon Church for only four years, but she has been given many assignments.

She currently leads the church's Self-Reliance Initiative for all the church units in Granada. When I pointed out that it seemed like the women were taking on even more responsibility for providing during this economic downturn, she agreed.

> We were analyzing this the other day. The principal sectors that have been affected by unemployment have been construction, transportation, and tourism. These sectors mainly employ men, and the majority have lost their jobs … But as women, we have the benefit that God has given us many talents. We work as housekeepers, nannies, teaching classes … as shopkeepers. Many women are good at selling. I, myself, survive right now by selling products. There are many women I have talked to who are supporting their spouses right now.

Research confirms what I casually observed and what Juana was saying. Sabarwal, Sinha, and Buvinic (2010, p. 3) report that during economic shocks "women have typically entered the labor force in response to declining household income. This effect seems to be particularly strong in lower income households, and in lower income economies where there is an informal labor market … to absorb additional workers."[11]

The degree to which women support families in Nicaragua is an inherent part of their economic status, and may be an important reason for more latitude in the church's rhetoric toward working women in this country. As Nicaragua continues to deal with political and economic upheaval, women's participation in the labor force may continue to increase, even as the church becomes more established.

Women's work as empowerment

I find Juana Lellany's perspective—as an educated outsider who is Latin American, and has lived in the country for many years—an important counterbalance to my own. While I often viewed the situation of women carrying the burden of work with frustration, Juana took a more positive view of the current situation, noting that "it's nice because we are seeing that women play an essential role in the family, in society … It's nice to see women contributing to the household and starting their own businesses."

> It's not because I am a feminist, but just that I enjoy being able to earn money for my household. I feel fulfilled, and I truly enjoy it. This is essential in society. It's important that each woman tries to become educated and improve. It's for the best. There is less conflict in marriage. It's nicer when both spouses contribute … At present, I feel satisfied and fulfilled, and I give thanks to God because I feel my capacity to serve has increased [through education and working]. I am not yet self-sufficient, but I am on the road to full self-sufficiency. And I would like all Nicaraguan women to be able to feel this way.

Juana's perspective that work can be part of a woman's identity and purpose-filled life is interesting. This rings true in the Global North, where work is seen as a privilege and an opportunity to progress. But does this hold true in economically disadvantaged countries? Nikki Craske has observed that while North American women seem to receive a sense of purpose or "efficacy" from employment, in an economically disadvantaged country the nature of work for many women is often oppressive and rarely viewed as uplifting (1999, p. 89). And yet, as I interviewed these women, they did seem to derive personal empowerment through employment, regardless of the type of work.

One woman I interviewed, Roxana (Quiroz Ortiz, 2019), has spent her adult life working in unskilled labor jobs to provide for her family. Yet she has found great satisfaction in providing for her children, and currently has ambitions of returning to school to study nursing. Now 37 years old, she is the president of the women's Relief Society in Diriamba. She is forthright, friendly, and confident, and yet she broke into tears several times throughout our interview as she quietly recounted the story of her life.

Growing up, Roxana and her two siblings were raised by her grandmother, as her mother always worked. Roxana married her first husband when she was only 15, and she had her first child one year later. She immediately started working, recalling, "I had to work; their father was not very responsible so I had to provide for my children." When I asked if he helped her, she said no, because "he had vices, such as alcohol, women, friends who were vagrants … I felt that if he were going to act like that, I could not act like that. I had to take care of my children." Her husband did not want to help care for children, so she moved back in with her mother when she became pregnant. She then started the life-long process of making money to feed her family.

> I started working very hard with my mother. I woke up when it was still dark, and we made enchiladas to fry and sell in a school. I left my studying. Afterwards I started working in a factory … cleaning the hallways and bathrooms.

Her second child was born only thirteen months after her first. She comments, "the load was very heavy for a young 17-year-old girl. But I had to work because I had to work. I felt that I could not leave my children to die." Roxana eventually moved in with her husband again, but over the years it was her younger sister who cared for her children while she worked in various jobs, which included selling, teaching, and working in another factory. She says she actually enjoyed the work, but at the same time "it was exhausting and I did not have time to see my children, but their father didn't care whether he worked or did not work."

Other women I interviewed shared similar experiences of having to take over all provider and childcare responsibilities, while still living with their husband and father of their children. Claudia (Elvir Baltodano, 2019), a young mother also in Diriamba, shared that at one point her taxi-driver husband began acting less reliably, drinking more, not coming home.

> Once he disappeared for about eight days, and I knew nothing of him, and I decided to act. I thought, it can't be like this, I need to work, I need to help my children progress. And thanks be to God for giving me this job [in a gas station], because truthfully in these times it's very difficult.

While her husband still lives with them and occasionally works, it is Claudia who essentially maintains the household, which includes her two young children as well as her parents.

While both Claudia and Roxana express some level of frustration with their husbands' irresponsibility, they also display a matter-of-fact acceptance of their behavior. Some of their attitudes may reflect Latin American *marianismo*, the "almost saint-like and superior-to-men" attitude contrasted with the husband's *machismo* abdication of responsibility (De Vos, 1995, p. 7). Evelyn Stevens says Latin American women identify strongly with this "moral superiority and spiritual strength," and adds that "no self-denial is too great … no limit can be divine to her vast store of patience with the men of her world" (Stevens, 1973, pp. 94–95). Unfortunately, sometimes a *marianismo* disposition is not enough to keep a husband's *machismo* from eventually fracturing the family.

Eventually, after losing a third child due to eclampsia, Roxana was hired to work at an orphanage for abandoned children with disabilities, a position she discovered she loved. While she worked with the children, her family was introduced to the LDS Church. She and her husband were baptized along with their two children. But despite Roxana's hopes, her husband's baptism into the church did not change his behavior. Eventually he stopped attending, and later Roxana and her children stopped attending as well. Finally one day, her husband told her he was leaving.

> He told me to go live my life, to keep working hard, that he no longer wanted to be with me. I fell into a deep depression, and asked him to return, but really he did not care about me.

I asked her why it was so hard, even though he had never been supportive of her. She talked about both her despair and how work helped her recover.

> I felt like I loved him, I don't know if I was obsessed, or infatuated, or simply accustomed. Maybe for these reasons, even though he treated me poorly and only I worked … I always wanted the father of my children to be my spouse forever. Working in the [orphanage] helped me overcome all of that.

One day two women from the Relief Society visited Roxana and encouraged her family to return to church. Roxana says they helped her realize she needed to seek help from God for her family, and she and her children started attending church again. In time, Roxana met and married another LDS man in the Diriamba ward. Both she and her new husband currently work, although some of his wages go to support his previous spouse and children.

Much of Roxana's life has centered on manual labor due to extreme necessity, and yet she talked during her interview about work and employment with purpose and ambition. In recent years, Roxana has been hired to care for the sick and elderly in their homes, and she feels she has found her true calling in this work.

> I would like to study rehabilitation to be able to help other people. Maybe I will decide to study nursing. Sometimes I think my age is a limiting factor, but I like to help other people, so I'm striving to complete my studies.

While Roxana's experience with her first husband was fraught, and she often was the only one contributing financially in that first marriage, she still derived great purpose from providing for her children and discovered her own talents and ambitions through her employment.

Work, poverty, and church support

In some situations, women deal with such poverty and lack of opportunity that they cannot provide even the basics of life during personal crises. During such times, the church's welfare program offers relief in the form of food and necessary medicine. Marta (Duarte Selva, 2019) became a mother at a young age almost four decades ago. Through the years, she and her husband worked together, side by side, as they tried to raise their eight children in the midst of substantial poverty. I interviewed Marta, now 57 years old, in the front room of her mud-brick house, where she told me she was preparing to undergo twenty-five rounds of radiation. When we lived in Granada she had gone through chemotherapy and a mastectomy, and I was disheartened that it was not over. A widow of two years, Marta still has young children and an aged mother at home who depend on her for support. Despite all her challenges, as she spoke with me she retained the same quiet optimism and faith that I had always observed in her.

Marta was introduced to the church in 1995 when her parents were invited to a church meeting by the missionaries. She says, "They took me [to the meeting] and it was beautiful ... From that time, we have been Mormons." She was baptized along with her father, mother, and many of her children. In spite of her hopes, her husband never joined the church. Yet he was a kind and present husband who always worked hard to provide, and wanted Marta to feel like she had equal access to the money that he earned. Despite the comparative economic equity in their marriage, Marta's family was quite impoverished and her life as a young mother was difficult. Through the 1990s Nicaragua's economy fell rapidly, and work was scarce. Her husband would often cross illegally into Costa Rica to find work and send money home to the family. Marta supplemented her husband's income by washing and ironing clothes, and cleaning houses, earning less than $1.00 for a full day's labor. She said one of the main challenges for Nicaraguan women is how hard they must work.

> In this society [the women] work. When they work, they are able to achieve and progress in society ... The women here are hard workers, we like to work. I still would like to work, but right now in my situation I can no longer work, I can't wash clothes anymore.[12] But I would like to, I have the desire to ... If women did not exist, men would not exist. We help them in their professional pursuits, to help them finish their studies, to have opportunities.

As she continued, Marta talked about the things she wishes she could do, and for a moment there was a hint of the ambitions that many women have, but that are so hard to fulfill in a Third World country.

> Due to our poverty, we can't achieve what we want to. Our dreams become stagnant and we can't progress. Because of the current situation in this country we can't get ahead because we, the women, are fighting only to survive.

One year Marta's husband had a construction accident in Costa Rica, and he could not work or send money. Marta struggled to find enough work to provide the daily food for her nine children and her aging parents. She had not been regularly attending the LDS church for quite a while, but a few weeks after her husband's accident, some leaders from the Granada church congregation arrived at their house, with two sacks and a box.

> They stopped and said, "Hello, is this the Selvas?" "Who are you looking for?" my mother asked. "We brought you a blessing, we want you to accept it." ... The brother tried to give us the food, but my children Rene and Juana took me inside and said, "Mom, don't take that, that's not ours, we don't want them to come back and take it away from us later." They were worried ... we had never seen so much food. Brother Gregorio said, "It's yours *hermana*, it says here 'Familia Duarte Selva.' Let me see your identification." Then they started to bring in the food. I was taken aback with joy, and my children began to cry because we had never seen so much food.

Marta's experience demonstrates how the church partners with its members to help them temporally when they cannot provide for themselves. In this way, the Mormon women in

Nicaragua are primarily responsible for the temporal salvation of their families but, as with spiritual salvation, the church strives to step in to help when one is desperate.

But as with all economic aid programs, there are instances of abuse in the church's welfare system in Nicaragua. In the weaker church units, I felt that money was often misappropriated and men in leadership often had more access to aid money than families where only women were members of the church. The church works to put restraints and controls to avoid such abuses, but in a deeply depressed economy it can be hard for those with access to the money to turn away from opportunities to get ahead. Despite these issues, I still saw the church welfare program provide much needed food and medicine to women and families in crisis.

Work and alternate constructs of motherhood

Motherhood is directly tied to providing both emotional and financial support in Nicaragua. However, not all of the women I interviewed constructed motherhood as being the *primary* nurturer for their children. Often women in Nicaragua must rely on relatives to help raise their children so that they can work to financially support their families. Marbelly (Cruz Glorío, 2019) has had steady employment as a grocery store brand stocker in local stores for Scott, Kotex, and Kimberly-Clark for most of her adult life. We met at the church for her interview, following a day-long children's program that she organized for all the Primary children in the church units in Granada. She is quiet, but speaks articulately and smiles easily. She was baptized as a child and participated in both the Primary and Young Women program and later married her husband when she was 20. As an adult she has been given many leadership assignments in the church because she is particularly reliable and diligent. Her husband is not a member of the church, and Marbelly's decision to attend church and accept time-consuming church assignments, in addition to her full-time work schedule, has been a point of deep tension in their marriage.

Marbelly's full-time work has affected other aspects of her family life, particularly her childcare decisions. When she and her husband finally had enough money to move out of her in-law's home, Marbelly's 8-year-old son stayed behind and lived with his grandmother until he was old enough to go to college. This situation is somewhat different from the other Nicaraguan women I interviewed. Marbelly was not a teen mother, nor was her husband a step-father, which would typically be situations in which the grandmother might take full-custody of the child. I asked Marbelly if it was difficult that her son did not live with them.

> Honestly, the truth is, since I was always working, it wasn't that hard. But yes, I did want him to have the same beliefs as me and the same customs that I was taught. And [the situation] made it difficult for me to teach him. But thankfully, he now knows the gospel, he has a testimony of the church, and he helps me press forward.

Marbelly places spiritual motherhood as paramount, a desire that her son learn her faith and customs, rather than him being raised in her home.

Work and unequal marital power dynamics

While Marbelly derives empowerment from her job, she still deals with a lack of equality in her marriage in regard to the economic resources she provides. At first, when I ask her who had provided the family's primary support, she explained that "we have both come to an agreement with our expenses … He pays a part of the expenses, and I pay the other." But this arrangement has not been easy to uphold. She told me that she had to save all the money to pay for her son to start attending college. When her husband did not want to help, she said

> I think it was because he didn't have any [money] to do it. We've had economic problems because he has had debts, and I never have any … I cover the majority of the expenses because he never has any [money]. I don't know what he does with his money.

Then she said, "I don't know how much he earns, but he does know how much I earn."

> *You don't know how much he earns?*
> Twenty-one years of marriage and I don't know how much he earns.
> *Why? Have you asked him?*
> He is *machista*. The thing is, here in Nicaragua, most of the men are *machista*.
> *He says he won't tell you?*
> Yes, and if I say, "Take my bank card, go take money out of my account," he does it. But he has never allowed me to use his bank card.

While both Sinia and Marta had relatively equitable money relationships with their husbands, the majority of the women I interviewed alluded to a lack of equal financial partnership similar to what Marbelly experienced. Even if both spouses were working, the wife was often expected to use *all* her wages to meet the household bills and expenses, while the husband would contribute a small allowance to his wife and keep the rest of his money for discretionary use. Couples not only kept their money separate, they also often did not share financial information with their spouses. And while Marbelly's husband would not tell her how much he earned, I also talked to wives who were secretive about extra jobs and the additional money they earned. The women feared that if their husbands knew about the money that they would spend it carelessly. In many (but not all) of the relationships I observed, money was considered a valuable asset that one must protect even from one's spouse.

Imelda (González Madrigal, 2019), my assistant in the Relief Society leadership in Granada, was a woman who sadly saw a portion of her wages spent on her husband's drinking. Pragmatic, yet prone to laughter, she has worked for years as a caretaker for her elderly neighbors, working seven days a week from early in the morning until late in the evening and making less than $150 a month. She was born to a very poor family in Granada's *Isletas*, the small volcanic islands that lie just offshore in Lake Cocibolca. Her parents were illiterate but worked hard to help her and her older sister move to the mainland and attend an excellent school. She later attended a private college where she received a title as a business executive secretary, and worked professionally for two years. Her husband asked her to stop working to birth and care for their children. When I asked her why he didn't want her to work, she said

> He was always that way. From the time we were young, he told me that he didn't want me to work. It's because of how we live in this country, the men are *machista*. He was too jealous and said he didn't like women to be around other people, especially men. So he wanted me at home.
> *And you liked working?*
> Of course!

And though she stayed home for many years, she eventually started working again as her husband lost employment due to alcoholism. After years of spending periods of weeks or months drinking daily, alcohol finally took his life. While there is some relief from the inequities and financial stress she experienced in her marriage, Imelda feels grief that their relationship did not improve, and that he is no longer there to see his children marry and have grandchildren. She says there was a time when he was younger and employed that he was very helpful, and assisted with their small children. But she recognizes that their marriage for many years was not a happy one.

> The biggest struggle of women in Nicaragua is to be happy in our marriages because the men are *machista* and this affects so much. Women suffer psychological abuse, verbal abuse. Very rarely can a woman say, "Yes, I'm in a happy marriage," because the husband always dominates, and is jealous, and this does not make a woman happy. Women suffer much here in Nicaragua.

"You are going to make your own decisions": work as autonomy and protection

For women who must deal with *machismo* in their marriages, paid employment and keeping money separate not only allows autonomy, but also protection from abuse. Juana del Socorro, whose family was one of the first families baptized into the LDS Church in Granada four decades ago, commented that violence against women often occurs when the women are economically reliant on their husbands.

> [The women] always have to do what the men say, even if they don't want to … they always must submit to them *because they are supported [economically] by the man in their home* … They are abused, violated, in their own home.

Elizabeth Brusco says that the role of *marianismo*, or the degree to which women accept *machismo* behavior in men, is "closely tied to the relative degree of female economic dependence" (Brusco, 1995). In a society where there are no economic or social safety nets, it can seem almost impossible to leave an abusive situation. In addition, if the husband is actually working and supporting the family, it seems that women will overlook abuse in order to maintain the economic stability. For this reason, Juana del Socorro (Martínez Baldelomar, 2019) says that her mother taught her to prepare for a career, and in this way protect herself against potential abuse from her future husband.

> My mom told me, "Daughter, first prepare for your career, get your certification, find work, *then* find a spouse … Because then you can say, 'I work, I can make decisions.' And no one is going to humiliate you because you have to say, 'Can I have money to buy salt? Can I have money to buy a dress? Can I have money for …?' No, you are going to make your own decisions … You have to study, you have to value yourself, and you have to be successful … you are not going to abase yourself to anyone." I kept her words with me. And so when I got married and had children, I worked.

Juana del Socorro's simple conclusion to her mother's advice—"when I got married and had children, *I worked*"—reflects the lives of so many LDS women in Nicaragua. These women are actively seeking temporal salvation. And while this seems to contradict the church's institutional narrative that spiritual salvation is based upon distinctly separate roles, including men as primary providers, these women are not questioning the institutional narrative or validity of the institutional authority or patriarchy. They work to take care of their families as a crucial part of their concept of maternity. Their employment, even when menial, often provides them fulfillment, autonomy, and protection.

The women I interviewed are committed members of the LDS Church. As the church becomes more established and more multigenerational in Nicaragua, will these women internalize church narrative regarding the importance of stay-at-home motherhood, and respond by working less? Will the tenets of the church in regard to men being the main providers ever alter Nicaraguan social constructs, prompting the majority of LDS Nicaraguan men to become the primary providers for their families? Further research into the issues facing LDS Nicaraguan women will help us develop a better understanding of the issues that LDS women face globally, and how the challenges of LDS women in Third World countries differ from those in more economically advantaged countries, including more stable and progressive Latin American nations.

Notes

1 I had received a grant from Claremont Graduate University to record oral interviews of LDS women in Nicaragua.
2 Gender parity for economic participation and opportunity in Honduras ranked 75th, Guatemala 100th, Costa Rica 105th. The large South American countries ranked even lower with Argentina 114th, and Chile 120th (World Economic Forum, Global Gender Gap Report, 2018, pp. 10–11).
3 Each geographical unit of the LDS Church has its own women's group, called a Relief Society. It is a spiritual, social, and humanitarian center for the women who all attend worship services in one particular congregation.
4 The LDS Church's welfare program provides resources for church members in economic distress. In Nicaragua it provides food and occasionally medicine. Recipients meet with an appointed ecclesiastical leader, often a Relief Society leader, who assesses needs and works with them to prepare a complete understanding of income and expenses as part of receiving temporary help.
5 Feinberg (2018, p. 12, fn 27):

> The IMF projected that the Nicaraguan real (inflation-adjusted) GDP would contract by 4 percent in 2018, an 8 percentage point reversal from an earlier, pre-crisis projection of a positive 4 percent expansion, and projected a further 1 percent decline in 2019. "World Economic Outlook," International Monetary Fund, October 2018, Table A4, 157, www.imf.org/en/Publications/WEO/Issues/2018/09/24/world-economic-outlook-october-2018.

In the World Economic Outlook (April 2019), the International Monetary Fund posted Nicaragua's unemployment rate at 23 percent, compared to rates in neighboring countries of the region, Costa Rica 9 percent, Panama 6 percent, El Salvador 6.7 percent, and Honduras 3.4 percent (IMF, 2019b).
6 This is similar to Caroline Kline's findings of women in Botswana and South Africa (Chapter 22, this volume).
7 This is beginning to change in the United States. Jana Riess (2019, p. 107) documents that 75 percent of LDS millennials report growing up with mothers who worked outside the home (with 54 percent of those working full-time), while only 57 percent of LDS baby boomers report that they grew up with mothers who worked outside the home (with 33 percent of those working full-time).
8 See Kline's chapter "Global Mormon Perspectives and Experiences of Familial Structures" (Chapter 22, this volume) for a more complete discussion of the shifting rhetoric within the LDS Church in regard to working women, as well as alternate interpretations of the Proclamation document and LDS women's roles in the international church.
9 See Kline's (Chapter 22, this volume) findings among mothers in Botswana, where working mothers are the norm. "Motherhood is a primary identity marker for Botswana women, but there is little sense in Botswana that motherhood should preclude paid labor. Women in Botswana associate motherhood not only with nurturing but also with production and provisioning of children."
10 This U-shaped phenomenon for women is not reflected in male labor force participation, where higher GDP per capita is "linearly associated with lower male LFP" (Novta and Wong, 2017, pp. 9–10). See also Goldin (1994).

11 Sabarwal, Sinha, and Buvinic (2010, pp. 8–9):

> Using household level data from Demographic Health Survey from sixty-six countries and across twenty-one years (1985–2006), Bhalotra and Umana (2009) show that globally, on average, a 10 percent drop in country GDP is associated with a 0.34 percentage point (69 percent) increase in women's work participation. Women's rising labor force participation during crisis emerges more reliably among low- and middle-income households than in upper-income ones (Cerutti 2000, Humphrey 1996, Judisman and Moreno 1990, Lee and Cho 2005). Women who exhibit the strongest increases in labor force participation are those with low education, who traditionally experience the lowest rates of economic participation in these low- and middle-income economies (Cerutti 2000).

12 Taking in clothes to wash is one of the most common jobs that women take, but she cannot use her dominant arm until she fully recovers from her mastectomy.

References

Álvarez, L., 2016. Mujeres en política: nada que celebrar. Laprensa.com. www.laprensa.com.ni/2016/03/08/politica/1998298-mujeres-politica-nada-celebrar (accessed June 24, 2019).

Anonymous, 2019. Oral History #21 (transcript). Interviewed by Amanda Tew, Nicaragua. Transcript forthcoming in the Claremont Mormon Women Oral History Collection, Special Collections, The Claremont Colleges Library, Claremont, California.

Brusco, E., 1995. *The Reformation of Machismo: Evangelical Conversion and Gender in Colombia.* Austin, TX: University of Texas Press.

Consejo Superior de la Empresa Privada (COSEP) and International Labor Organization (ILO), 2015. Encuesta de Empresas Sostenibles Nicaragua 2015: Identificación del obstaculos para el desarrollo empresarial. Geneva: OIT.

Craske, N., 1999. *Women and Politics in Latin America.* New Brunswick, NJ: Rutgers University Press.

Cruz Glorío, Marbelly del Carmen, 2019. Oral History #28 (transcript). Interviewed by Amanda Tew, Nicaragua. Transcript forthcoming in the Claremont Mormon Women Oral History Collection, Special Collections, The Claremont Colleges Library, Claremont, California.

De Vos, S., 1995. *Household Composition in Latin America.* New York: Plenum Press.

Duarte Selva, Marta Paula, 2019. Oral History #27 (transcript). Interviewed by Amanda Tew, Nicaragua. Transcript forthcoming in the Claremont Mormon Women Oral History Collection, Special Collections, The Claremont Colleges Library, Claremont, California.

Elvir Baltodano, Claudia Liseth, 2019. Oral History #26 (transcript). Interviewed by Amanda Tew, Nicaragua. Transcript forthcoming in the Claremont Mormon Women Oral History Collection, Special Collections, The Claremont Colleges Library, Claremont, California.

Feinberg, R.E., 2018, *Nicaragua: Revolution and Restoration.* Washington, D.C.: Brookings Institute. www.brookings.edu/wp-content/uploads/2018/11/FP_20181108_nicaragua.pdf.

Figueredo Garcés, Juana Lellany, 2019. Oral History #22 (transcript). Interviewed by Amanda Tew, Nicaragua. Transcript forthcoming in the Claremont Mormon Women Oral History Collection, Special Collections, The Claremont Colleges Library, Claremont, California.

Freije, S., 2001. Informal Employment in Latin America and the Caribbean: Causes, Consequences and Policy Recommendations. Instituto de Estudios Superiores de Administracion (ISEA), Venezuela.

Goldin, C., 1994. The U-Shaped Female Labor Force Function in Economic Development and Economic History. No. w4707. National Bureau of Economic Research.

González Madrigal, Imelda del Socorro, 2019. Oral History #29 (transcript). Interviewed by Amanda Tew, Nicaragua. Transcript forthcoming in the Claremont Mormon Women Oral History Collection, Special Collections, The Claremont Colleges Library, Claremont, California.

Hernández Mendieta, Sinia, 2019. Oral History #23 (transcript). Interviewed by Amanda Tew, Nicaragua. Transcript forthcoming in the Claremont Mormon Women Oral History Collection, Special Collections, The Claremont Colleges Library, Claremont, California.

International Monetary Fund, 2019a. GDP per capita, Current Prices. World Economic Outlook (April 2019). Washington, D.C. www.imf.org/external/datamapper/NGDPDPC@WEO/OEMDC/ADVEC/WEOWORLD/CMQ/WE?year=2019.

International Monetary Fund, 2019b. Unemployment Rate. World Economic Outlook (April 2019). Washington, D.C. www.imf.org/external/datamapper/LUR@WEO/OEMDC/ADVEC/WEOWORLD?year=2019.
Kampwirth, K., 2004. *Feminism and the Legacy of the Revolution: Nicaragua, El Salvador, Chiapas*. Ohio University Research in International Studies, Latin America Series No. 43. Ohio: Ohio University Press.
Leysan González, Chatai Qu, 2019. Oral History #24 (transcript). Interviewed by Amanda Tew, Nicaragua. Transcript forthcoming in the Claremont Mormon Women Oral History Collection, Special Collections, The Claremont Colleges Library, Claremont, California.
Martínez Baldelomar, Juana del Socorro, 2019. Oral History #30 (transcript). Interviewed by Amanda Tew, Nicaragua. Transcript forthcoming in the Claremont Mormon Women Oral History Collection, Special Collections, The Claremont Colleges Library, Claremont, California.
Message from the First Presidency, 2017. Personal Finances for Self-Reliance (2017), inside front cover. www.lds.org/manual/personal-finances-for-self-reliance/message-from-the-first-presidency?lang=eng.
Novta, N. and Wong, J.C., 2017. Women at Work in Latin America and the Caribbean. IMF Working Paper. International Monetary Fund.
Piper, A.T., 2018. An Investigation into the Reported Closing of the Nicaraguan Gender Gap. MPRA Paper 86769. University Library of Munich, Germany.
Quiroz Ortiz, Roxana, 2019. Oral History #25 (transcript). Interviewed by Amanda Tew, Nicaragua. Transcript forthcoming in the Claremont Mormon Women Oral History Collection, Special Collections, The Claremont Colleges Library, Claremont, California.
Riess, J., 2019. *The Next Mormons: How Millennials are Changing the LDS Church*. Oxford: Oxford University Press.
Sabarwal, S., Sinha, N., and Buvinic, M., 2010. How Do Women Weather Economic Shocks: A Review of the Evidence. Policy Research Working Paper, no. WPS 5496. World Bank. https://openknowledge.worldbank.org/handle/10986/3978 License: CC BY 3.0 IGO.
Schrader, S., 2017. Nicaragua: Central America's Security Exception. *NACLA Report on the Americas* 49(3): 360–65.
Smith, J.F., 1904. *President Joseph F. Smith*. Conference Report, April 1904. Salt Lake City, UT: Deseret Book.
Stevens, E.P., 1973. Marianismo: The Other Face of Machismo. In A. Pescatello, ed. *Female and Male in Latin America*. Pittsburgh, PA: University of Pittsburgh Press, pp. 89–101.
Tullis, F.L., 1963. *The Gospel in Central America: A Phenomenon of Response and Frustration*. L. Tom Perry Special Collections and Manuscripts, Harold B. Lee Library. Provo, UT: Brigham Young University.
Tullis, F.L., 1981. Three Myths about Mormons in Latin America. *Dialogue: A Journal of Mormon Thought* 7(1): 79–87.
Tullis, F.L., 2006. Writing about the International Church: A Personal Odyssey in Mexico. *Journal of Mormon History* 42(4): 1–30.
Zahidi, S., Geiger, T., and Crotti, R., 2018. Global Gender Gap Report. World Economic Forum. www3.weforum.org/docs/WEF_GGGR_2018.pdf.

Further reading

Altamirano Montoya, Á.J., and Teixeira, K.M.D., 2017. Multidimensional Poverty in Nicaragua: Are Female-Headed Households Better Off? *Social Indicators Research* 132: 1037–63. https://doi.org/10.1007/s11205-016-1345-y.
Francke, M., 1992. Women and the Labor Market in Lima, Peru: Weathering Economic Crisis. International Center for Research on Women Seminar on Weathering Economic Crises: Women's Responses to the Recession in Latin America, Washington, D.C.. August. Vol. 11.
Gibbons, J., and Luna, S., 2015. For Men Life Is Hard, for Women Life Is Harder: Gender Roles in Central America. In S. Safdar and N. Kosakowska-Berezecka, eds. *Psychology of Gender through the Lens of Culture*. Cham: Springer, pp. 307–26.
Gooren, H., 2007. Latter-day Saints under Siege: The Unique Experiences of Nicaraguan Mormons. *Dialogue: A Journal of Mormon Thought* 40(3): 134–55.
Kline, C., 2018. Navigating Mormonism's Gendered Theology and Practice: Mormon Women in a Global Context. Ph.D. Dissertation, Claremont Graduate University.

31
MORMON MASCULINITY, FAMILY, AND KAVA IN THE PACIFIC

Arcia Tecun and S. Ata Siuʻulua

"Isn't it about time?" is a phrase from a late twentieth-century campaign by the Church of Jesus Christ of Latter-day Saints (Mormon/LDS) that encouraged viewers to spend time with their families. The commercials created for this campaign displayed middle-class family activities such as a Western classical music recital or being in large U.S. suburban homes. The phrase "Family, isn't it about time?" is then heard at the end of these commercials. This assertion of spending time with family is based on the Victorian construct of family as primarily nuclear, rather than the complex communal extended family networks (e.g., village, clan) in Moana (Indigenous Pacific, Ocean/ic/ia) societies. By normalizing nuclear family constructs, criticisms emerge for activities that are viewed as obstacles to "family time." Moana men in Mormon communities are not collectively and intensely criticized for the amount of time they spend at their jobs, in church service, or even sport, but they are when they regularly attend kava drinking gatherings. Kava gatherings often include relatives, as well as kin-like relations between men through long-term meaningful communal relationships with non-biological kin. These kava gatherings also often include family members from outside one's own religious denomination, allowing for the *kāinga* (Tongan for *village family, clan, extended family group*) to be nurtured in these events, despite not all belonging to the same nuclear or congregational family. The Moana cultural values of nurturing socio-spatial relationships thus confront contested constructs of family and masculinity, which are negotiated in contemporary kava gatherings (Kaʻili, 2017; Tecun, 2017).

Kava is an ancestral elixir made from ground up *piper methysticum* plant roots, which is infused with water before imbibing. There are many kava traditions across the Moana that are diverse and unique (Lebot, Merlin, and Lindstrom, 1992). In this chapter we focus on the most common social gatherings that are increasingly pan-Moana and also found in large diaspora communities in the settler-colonial nation-states of the U.S., Australia, and New Zealand. Mormons are divided on the issue of kava and continue to negotiate what practices are constituted as acceptable within local and global communities. Kava is currently a predominantly cis-gendered heterosexual male space, although that is changing and dependent on different cultural traditions. The common kava settings we are focusing on for this chapter are rich sites of liminality where open conversations take place, which make them significant sites to explore constructs of masculinity and family among Moana peoples (Tecun, 2017). The data we are using for this chapter come from academic literature and personal lived experiences within diaspora communities of Moana Mormons. We were initially based in Utah and grew up there in Mormon communities, and we are now based in Aotearoa/New Zealand's north island (since 2015 and 2018). We also collectively draw from ethnographic research while living in Aotearoa and various trips to Utah and the Kingdom of Tonga between 2015 and 2019.

This chapter begins with a brief introduction to kava and the ambiguity of kava's place within Mormonism. We explore the negotiation between dominant constructs of masculinity with Moana Mormon nuances. We then offer a background of differing views of family between those introduced by "the West" and reinforced through Mormonism, alongside some of the Indigenous ideas of family across the Moana. We conclude with a discussion of how contested constructs of family and masculinity are negotiated within Mormon kava settings. We argue that although Mormon Moana kava events can reinforce hegemonic constructs of patriarchal social orders, they are also sites that subvert elements of masculinity and expand narrow definitions of family as exclusively nuclear or anthropocentric. Mormon men who participate in kava events engage in meaningful homosocial relationships and demonstrate evolving definitions of Indigenous kinship.

Kava background and Mormon contexts

Tomlinson (2004) explains that kava is a relaxer that leaves drinkers acutely mentally aware without emotional fluctuations, resulting in people discussing a variety of subjects that are important to them. He explains a Fijian kava setting that is also reflective of many of the Tongan and multi-ethnic pan-Moana contexts we have participated in:

> [As a] soporific, kava numbs its consumers and promotes feelings of relaxation and sociability. Unlike alcohol, it does not alter one's mood, and the mind of the drinker remains clear … However, those who have drunk a great deal grow tired, stare vacantly, and eventually get wobbly legs. Because one's mind remains sharp during kava-drinking, the fact of consumption remains accessible to contemplation. That is, in contrast to drinking alcohol, consuming a great deal of kava does not alter one's perceptions of the fact of consumption; even during the drinking, one is aware of the social milieu, the fact that one is drinking, and the conversation that takes place. In addition, kava is not addictive.
>
> (p. 657)

Tomlinson adds that meaningful discussions and kava are "intimately paired," citing that where kava stimulates conversation, good conversation demands more drinking of kava (2004, p. 659).

Kava is used for a variety of purposes and occasions across the Moana, known by many names such as 'ava, kava, sakau, yaqona, and more. Kava practices have a variety of levels of formality and protocols. Island nations like Tonga, Pohnpei, and Fiji maintain regular social gatherings in their spectrum of kava use (Lebot, Merlin, and Lindstrom, 1992; Aporosa, 2014). The strength and effects depend on the type and amount of kava that is infused with water (Lebot, Merlin, and Lindstrom, 1992; Aporosa, 2016). Kava gatherings are a space where constructions of marital, sibling, masculine, and homosocial relations are reinforced, negotiated, and transformed. Women have ancestrally participated in kava in many regions such as Fiji, Tonga, and Sāmoa, and in some cases still do or are revitalizing their place in kava circles (Lebot, Merlin, and Lindstrom, 1992). Although we are addressing more generally multi-ethnic Moana settings, we ground this chapter with our most common experiences within the global spectrum of Tongan perspectives. The social rituals and common gatherings we are focusing on take place most often and have the broadest range of participants in them, being more inclusive than elite ceremonies (e.g., ethnicity, age, religious affiliation, and social rank). We will refer to these more frequent kava gatherings for the remainder of this chapter as *faikava*, which is a term commonly known in Moana diaspora communities and what they are called in Tongan (Feldman, 1980; Helu, 1993).

Mormon stance on kava

Kava is absent in the Mormon canon or official global public policy. "A spokesman for the church's public affairs department, which fields all news-media inquiries, says there is no official policy on the drink" (Griffin, 2007, p. 3). The only available mention of kava found on the church's website is in the commentary for the "Mormon law of health" known as the Word of Wisdom, which prohibits and encourages the consumption of certain foods and substances (e.g., no alcohol, tobacco, coffee, black tea, etc. and yes to eating grains, fruits, and vegetables, etc.):

> D&C 89:9 Are Other Drinks Forbidden by the Word of Wisdom?
> What about cola drinks, kava, some health or sports drinks, or other drinks containing stimulants? An official statement by the Church's leaders reads: "With reference to cola drinks, the Church has never officially taken a position on this matter, but the leaders of the Church have advised, and we do now specifically advise against the use of any drink containing harmful habit-forming drugs under circumstances that would result in acquiring the habit. Any beverage that contains ingredients harmful to the body should be avoided."
>
> *(Doctrine and Covenants Student Manual, 2002)*

This association of kava is peculiar as it pairs a deeply significant cultural symbol and icon with commodities such as caffeinated drinks. Kava is not alcoholic, addictive, fermented, or caffeinated and does not fit in the context of this statement from both a chemical or cultural standpoint. Ultimately the official global church perspective leaves the choice to individuals to decide based on the principle of avoiding that which is harmful, which kava itself is not (Aporosa, 2016).

Regardless of what the official global stance of the church is or the lack of clarity or familiarity with it, kava is nonetheless controversial for Mormons, especially in Moana communities where kava gatherings are practiced. Kava controversy and stigma is derived mostly from polemic statements that are not binding and have no canonical authority. These statements are often made by prominent community leaders, local lay clergy, or other religious leaders with official titles in the church or by church-owned institutions themselves, such as Brigham Young University-Hawaii (BYU-H) (Griffin, 2007; Shumway, 2012; Sikahema, 2014). For example, Griffin (2007) mentions that the "Word in the Polynesian community is that ceremonial use is sometimes allowed but that drinking kava merely for recreation probably violates the church's Word of Wisdom" (p. 3). Further, the BYU-H Honor Code does not allow "kava clubbing or party drinking," but states

> This regulation should not be construed as anticulture, for kava has its vital place in the ceremonies and culture of Polynesia. But there is no doubt in our mind that there is a vast difference between ceremonial drinking of kava … and the party drinking of kava.
>
> *(Griffin, 2007, p. 3)*

This statement is colonizing in its assumption that Indigenous peoples are frozen, static, exotic, and incapable of adaptation, change, and transformation as contemporary subjects, which exacerbates kava stigmas in Moana communities. *Faikava* does not mean "kava party," and *kalapu* (*kava club*) does not mean "kava clubbing." A few possible interpretations that are more accurate to these oversimplified notions could include: kava session, kava gathering, to do kava, or to ingest the land, where kava is the metonym and metaphor of *fonua/vanua/honua* (Tongan, Fijian, Hawaiian words for land, heritage, and people). Even in the common social gatherings of *faikava*, these are significant sites of knowledge production and youth development (Fehoko, 2014). Additionally, Moana men are increasingly subject to mental health challenges, particularly in diaspora environments (Agee, McIntosh, and Culbertson, 2013; Marsters and Tiatia-Seath, 2019; Vaka et al., 2009). Vaka (2014) has demonstrated in his research how kava is a significant site for Tongan men to maintain positive mental health and well-being.

Kava controversies in Mormon communities are generally centered on social conflicts, such as men attending and leaving wives and children at home, rather than chemical effects. In some of the language-based Mormon congregations (e.g., Tongan speaking) there are often localized attempts to assert a ban on kava by lay clergy. These lay clergy will limit a church member's ability to obtain a "temple recommend," which grants access to the highest level of Mormon orthodox ceremonies within temples that are distinct from the church buildings of regular weekly worship. The controversy that continually arises is on whether Mormon kava participation in social kava rituals (vs. life event kava ceremonies or regal kava, etc.) gets in the way of time spent with families. The question of how masculinity is constructed and its relationship to however family is defined is thus vital to interrogate.

Intersecting masculinities

The hegemonic construct of masculinity that has penetrated the Moana is influenced by colonization, racism, sports, and the military, which has a history of static and essentialist notions of "different kinds of men," while privileging non-effeminate, stoic, heteronormative, homophobic, and transphobic masculinities standardized by white middle-class patriarchy (Besnier and Alexeyeff, 2014; James, 1994; Jolly, 2008; 2016; Presterudstuen and Schieder, 2016; Tengan, 2002; Tengan and Markham, 2009). Moana masculinities negotiate local agency with macro-historical forces such as "Christian conversion, market penetration and urbanization … which continue to contextualize the production of Pacific Island masculinities" (Biersack, 2016, p. 198). Tengan (2002) explains that dominant societal systems "legitimate patriarchal structures and subordinate feminities" (p. 241). Tengan also reminds that hegemonic and subaltern structures of masculinity are complex, not homogenous, and have no clear boundaries. Moana masculinities are thus multiple and plural, a mixture of hegemonic and subordinate elements. Biersack (2016) states that Moana societies today are "dynamic, filled with unprecedented potentialities and opportunities … more open to transnational influences, often nefarious, including the video stimulations of the male imagination" (p. 207). Hegemonies are incomplete and there is constant negotiation between structure and agency with gender and power. Tengan (2002) implores that we explore ways in which gender is "complexly situated in multiple contexts, [which] can draw upon dominant gender constructs for contradictory and even subversive purposes" (p. 239).

Historical Eurocentric portrayals of Moana men are based in being strong, active, and sexually dominant, while women were framed as weak and passive, being sexually restricted, yet also subject to sexual exoticism, and believed to cause "pollution" during menstruation (Suaalii, 1997; Tengan, 2002). Critics of these portrayals point to the role of high-ranking powerful and sacred women and the alternative explanation that rather than "polluting," women were highly potent during menstruation and attracted the Gods (Gunson, 1987; Tengan, 2002). Hokowhitu (2008) explains that in this gendered dichotomy between men and women, masculine Moana bodies have become socially normalized as "natural to sport." This construction of the Moana male body is derived from the same racist ideas of the African-American body. He adds that this idea has "unfortunately become part of a discourse that now informs [constructs of] the Pacific body, to the extent that Pacific peoples themselves are buying into such ... to explain the dominance of the Pacific *body* in sports" (p. 85). This allows for another stereotype associated with "natural physicality" to fester that assumes a normality of being physically violent, which overlooks socio-economic issues, historical trauma, and other factors in harmful displays of violence (Ahlburg, 2000; Hokowhitu, 2008; Kavapalu, 1991; Reyes, 2013). This has a tendency to excuse Moana masculine violence as an "evolutionary fact, as opposed to a symptom of social construction ... physical deviance, in a sense 'permits' ... male violence" (Hokowhitu, 2008, p. 90). This racist oversimplification of a "natural warrior-athlete" reinforces a normalization that tolerates child abuse as "discipline," and a culture of silence regarding physical and sexual violence against women and other men (Biersack, 2016; Hokowhitu, 2008; Tapu Podcast, n.d.). The documentary *Gangsters in Paradise: The Deportees of Tonga* (2019) includes a testimonial of the complex consequences of such constructs of masculinity. 'Ila Mo'unga, who is featured in this documentary, shares, "I get beaten by my dad I'm going to come and dish it out on somebody else. Because my dad was God, at least to me. He was God, and since I couldn't fight God I'd fight everybody else."

Dominant Mormon images of Moana men mirror global masculine hegemonies. Official and social representations of Mormon Moana men show idealized images of devout "simple and friendly" people on one hand, and as "violent, big brown bodies" on the other (*Father Lehi in Hawaii*, 2008; *From Heaven to Hell*, 2008; *In Football We Trust*, 2015; *The Other Side of Heaven*, 2001; *The R.M.*, 2003; *The Testaments of One Fold and One Shepherd*, 2000; Weaver, 2019). Additionally, dominant narratives of Moana men as either gangsters or athletes, such as in documentary films *From Heaven to Hell* (2008) and *In Football We Trust* (2015), continually re-center Moana identities on the male experience. *Faikava*, like church, also perpetuates this, as sites dominated by male conversations and perspectives. *Faikava* also has moments of subversion to hegemonic masculinities, however, which we will demonstrate later. If you do not fit the athlete/gangster discourse, the "exotic" alternative in stereotypical masculinities is to be a "ukulele playing happy go lucky native" (Aikau, 2012). During a *faikava* session a young Tongan Mormon man in his late twenties expressed that his survival strategy in "white Utah" was to be a "big funny teddy bear." As we discussed this further, he added that he felt that this made him appear less threatening as a large brown body. The dilemma is that subscribing to this masculinity also associated Moana men as being simple-minded and unintelligent, reduced to entertainers derived from "luau" culture, which is based on white gazes of exoticism and exploitation (*Father Lehi in Hawaii*, 2008; Trask, 1999).

Hoyt and Patterson (2011) argued that Mormon masculinity entered an identity crisis after the church abandoned polygynous practices, which were central to masculine identity (commonly referred to as "celestial," "plural marriage," "everlasting covenant," etc.). They explained that the new Mormon masculinity, which was catalyzed at the turn of the twentieth century, is based on four pillars: priesthood, Word of Wisdom adherence, going on missions as young adults, and monogamous heterosexuality. "The new ideal Mormon man was portrayed as an obedient follower who abstained from alcohol and tobacco, married one woman and entered into a career in which he would excel" (p. 73). While men began to transform into this new masculine construct, women were to assist and uphold this process. Additionally, Mormonism's historical experience of being outcast by the dominant protestant settler society would influence their efforts to become racially "white" to be accepted by the mainstream society (Reeve, 2015). Mormon masculinity desires acceptance and material success basing U.S. settler society as a universal model, along with its nationalist patriotism, while also remaining quietly uniquely set apart as chosen people who hold a divinely restored priesthood that is exclusive to Mormonism. In other words, to be a "good Mormon man" is to become a "white middle-class" consumer that is productive within neoliberal capitalism, and who simultaneously exercises exclusive religious priesthood to act and officiate on behalf of a presiding male deity. These white middle-class standards are transported and reinforced throughout the Moana as symbolic ideals to emulate. These symbols are visibly the material infrastructures of church buildings, schools, and church-owned properties that are leased to residents, often modeled after U.S. white suburbia. However, the project of Western modernity through colonial capitalism has not resulted in "success" for many Moana men who have become forcibly nomadic while looking for jobs in the metropoles, while women are often still barred to domestic life (Gailey, 1992; Young, 2000). Moana men's modern nomadism often means they have been severed from subsistence life skills. Men become physically visible in towns and urban centers because there is a lack of work or meaningful employment available. This often triggers a desire to flee overseas albeit to find demanding and stressful labor, yet where they at least have more work. In this context when men seek out the kava circle instead of loitering in town centers they are often accused of being "unproductive," thus distant from becoming a "white middle-class consumer" and worthy priesthood holder.

Kava controversies particularly but not exclusively for Mormons hinge on tensions caused in monogamous marriages and nuclear families, represented by men who frequent kava sessions and are often accused in Mormon communities of not spending enough time with their "family." When men are spending most of their time at work or church or even the gym they are not subject to such criticism as they are for going to *faikava*, in our observation. This is contradictorily reinforced by church and state systems that privilege men within hetero-reproductive partnerships and genealogies, in monogamous marriages, and exclusively nuclear families. When investigating further with men who were identified as problematic kava drinkers because of heavy daily participation, we found that they were carrying a heavy working-class burden. For example, these men expressed using kava as a remedy for their physical atrophy and emotional distress derived from their jobs. Several wives also expressed their stress from exclusively nuclear family structures that construct women as primarily responsible for child rearing, which is intensified when their husbands are away at *faikava* (Kalani, 2014). Women who had kāinga support nearby usually had less criticism of their husband's kava participation, however, with other women expressing that they had fewer issues with frequent kava attendance if it is brief (approximately two hours or less). There are some Mormon women who prefer their husbands abstain from *faikava* altogether. Victorian constructs of the nuclear family pressures partnerships and family relationships with the premise and notion that time is for making money rather than for nurturing complex kinship relationships (Kaʻili, 2017).

Another factor in kava controversies that should be mentioned is the assumption in Tongan *faikava* settings that there may be a *touʻa fefine (female kava server/preparer)*. Mormon commentators Shumway (2012) and Sikahema (2014) both point to marital discord when married men flirt with and infamously on rare occasions have extra-marital affairs with a *touʻa fefine*. When we have spoken with wives of kava participants they have often expressed that they do not want their husbands to be at a *faikava* where there is a *touʻa fefine* present. We do not focus more intently on the *touʻa fefine*, which is another complex element of contemporary kava culture, because we have not observed any to be present in the kava groups we have engaged with that are overtly Mormon (e.g., in values, identity, participants).

Homosociality

Kava settings often challenge hegemonic constructs of masculinity where rather than being stoic, men often speak openly and make themselves vulnerable. This act in turn strengthens bonds within the group, reinforcing comradery and a sense of brotherhood. Men often support each other materially and spiritually through difficult times, they mourn with each other, celebrate each other in good times, eat together, drink together, sing and pray together, openly debate one another, and collaborate and organize to help the collective in the kava group. These acts facilitate a strong homosociality, a collective social phenomenon similar to "religious communalism" (Gabriel, 2014, p. 54). Homosociality being "non-sexual positive social bonds" between men, expressing humanity towards same-sex/gender friends or mourning their loss(es) (Oware, 2011, p. 22). We once observed when a prominent member of a Mormon-based kava group entered into a rough set of events and difficulties in his life, and it was the members of his kava community that "rescued" him. They would call him or go physically look for him if he would not answer their calls. They would show up with kava or invite him back to talk and work through the struggle. This member after surviving his hardship shared that "kava [and this community] was healing to me." There is a deep sense of honest and authentic caring that is felt and expressed when someone shows up to one's house with a bag of kava during a hard time, to listen, share, and support you. There are countless stories, experiences, and observations we have made of such experiences that take place between men, including for their families and relations as well. Although there can be quite a bit of good humor and laughter in Mormon *faikava*, there are also solemn moments, crying, and open expressions of love where men are not strangers in saying *'ofa atu* to one another, which in Tongan means "I love you/ love to you."

Negotiating family constructs

Moana masculinities confront family constructs and the "Western" hegemonic standard of the "nuclear family" as "the family" within Mormonism. The globalizing cultural hegemony of gender and family is a homogenizing process in our contemporary global paradigms. Within it lies the legacy of the Victorian family, which has been challenged by those of and within the "West" as well as "others," yet it remains a powerful ideology that is accepted or contested as a universal norm. The Victorian family emerged from British imperialism where family became vital to the empire and an "economic strategy [for] capital accumulation … [and] the British empire became a 'family affair'" (Cleall, Ishiguro, and Manktelow, 2013, pp. 1–2). The nuclear construction of "the family" is a colonial construct upheld through religious projects that have arguably been the most influential in assimilating Indigenous peoples into the Victorian family to serve imperial goals (Jolly and Macintyre, 1989). Latai (2015) states:

> Missionaries imposed their own models of gender upon Samoan women based on Victorian ideals that promoted the roles of women as maternal and domestic … wives of missionaries who allegedly served as the perfect role models of the ideal woman [were] to be emulated by their local counterparts.
>
> *(p. 98)*

Jolly and Macintyre (1989) explain that different forms of Christianity also influenced a spectrum of family and gender constructs in the Moana. For example, Christian notions of female "pollution" ("impure polluting power of female sexuality") led to intensified gendered separation by Anglicans and Catholics, and a Protestant focus on unity within heteronormative monogamous marriage. For Moana cultures that had strict gendered sibling protocols, gendered separation intensified, while larger kinship networks were disrupted with the exclusive focus on fixed monogamous marriage that supported sedentary life. Jolly and Macintyre (1989) explain that domestic life has been largely overlooked as a site of colonialism, yet greatly informs the transmission of intergenerational knowledge and the possibilities of gender and family construct transformation. Although colonial experiences are complex and diverse, missionaries had an undeniable impact on domestic life. We only address some of the many issues in this realm of Moana life and their Mormon intersections.

Sister–brother

Sister–brother relationships are significant in several Moana cultures often informing an important element of rank within families (Kavapalu, 1991). Fijian, Tongan, and Sāmoan sister–brother relationships for example have a historical tension with the husband–wife focus in the Victorian family structure (Latai, 2015; Toren, 1994). Gifford (1929) explained that in Tonga "the sister is superior in rank to the brother, so also are her children ... The sister's children are fahu (Fijian vasu) to their mother's brother" (p. 22). The Tongan *fahu* was a welcomed introduction by Fijians and included the power that one's *fahu* had nearly unrestricted liberties to one's belongings, which included chiefly ranked individuals (Lātūkefu, 2014). This brother-sister relationship is a necessary principal in maintaining social balance, which includes having no indecent conversations, and an avoidance of everything sexual in each other's presence (Latai, 2015). Moana societies and cultures have complex social organizations where gender, age, and power are balanced through genealogical relationality and not as static top-down hierarchies of power. The brother-sister *tapu* (*sacred/set apart relationship*) is based in a sense of reverence for *mana fefine* (*transcendent power, authority, potency of women*). Marcus (1979) suggests:

> The brother's avoidance of his sisters has traditionally been associated with the broader cultural feature of combined avoidance of and respect for sacred or mystical power, embodied by persons of chiefly status. Brothers still refer to their sisters as 'eiki ("chiefly") in relation to themselves ... out of respect for the mystical or sacred qualities of the patriline, which females as sisters embody and pass to offspring.
>
> (p. 89)

The *mana* that sisters possess is derived from a divine spiritual order, where Tongan brothers are outranked as men, being linked to *ma'ama* (*earth*), while sisters and women are linked to *pulotu* (*spirit world, origin world, after world*) (Filihia, 2001; Herda, 1987). The ancient theology of sisters as vessels of divinity and with powers of attraction to the supernatural has shifted towards predominantly and in many cases exclusively male pastors and priests within Christianity (Latai, 2015). The male clergyman replaced or significantly subverted the centrality of the Indigenous "priestess/priest/spirit medium." A relational complimentary struggle for balance in gendered power transformed to an opposing competitive one; as women were not previously dependent on husbands for their material welfare, wives and sisters were pitted against each other (Gailey, 1980; 1987; 1992). The transformations of the sister–brother relationship thus brought a "decline in women's power as sisters," yet not a complete fall out of this Indigenous kinship structure that remains in some forms today (Kavapalu, 1991, p. 155). Marcus (1979) reminds us that a brother's *fatongia* (*sacred duty/responsibility/obligation*) to his sisters and their children still remains to some degree today, expressed as a cultural value and identifier of Tongan-ness. As Mormonism is increasingly popular in the Moana, the definition of family as primarily nuclear can create a dichotomy for people of the Moana, faced with the idea of having to choose between wife and nuclear family or brother–sister and *kāinga* (Kavapalu, 1991). This results in rifts and tensions as people negotiate these colliding gendered paradigms, while at the same time living a selective mix of them. Some Mormon Moana men have expressed that although there is an increased focus on nuclear families and spouses, when it comes to life events their sisters often reclaim their place within the *kāinga*. During these events (e.g., funerals), the highest-ranking *fahu* as determined by the *kāinga* performs her responsibilities and is sanctioned the privileges and respect due to her rank and title.

Mormon family

Mormons arrived in the eastern parts of the Moana in the seventeenth century, which was later then the first Christians in the region. Douglas (1974) explains that when Mormons finally arrived to the missionizing scene, many other Protestants had already had little success in attempting to eradicate "heathen" customs. These early Protestants had become more flexible and tolerant of Indigenous traditions and culture for these reasons. "The Mormons' overwhelming conviction of their own righteousness, however, did not permit them to learn from the experience or the mistakes of others" (p. 316). What became and arguably remains unique to Mormons is that they began with and maintained an attitude toward local customs that had long ceased with other missionaries. Douglas explains that, "there were few traditional practices that were not looked on with disfavour by L.D.S. missionaries. Kava drinking, the preparation of certain food and eating habits, tattooing, nudity, customary marriage, casual sexual relationships, and casual attitudes to property" (p. 317). Yet, out of all the traditions that concerned early Mormon missionaries, those which had to do with sexual relations are argued to have been the most disturbing to them, although they were also practicing a sexuality outside of dominant Western norms. For example, "the islanders" lack of inhibitions in sexual matters, and their seemingly nonchalant attitude to the obligations of marriage were shunned, while at the same time "Mormons had elevated polygamy to the status of spiritual law," teaching polygyny on one hand, while "nakedness and promiscuity" was interpreted to be inexcusable (Douglas, 1974, p. 318).

Today, the standard of the Mormon family is enforced through the global leaders of the church's official church declaration titled "The Family: A Proclamation to the World" in which they state:

> Gender is an essential characteristic of individual premortal, mortal, and eternal identity and purpose ... THE FAMILY is ordained of God ... Children are entitled to birth within the bonds of matrimony, and to be reared by a father and mother ... By divine design, fathers are to preside over their families ... [while] Mothers are primarily responsible for the nurture of their children ... Extended families should lend support when needed.
>
> *(The Church of Jesus Christ of Latter-day Saints, 1995)*

These vignettes of the Family Proclamation frame the Victorian ideology of gender and family as divine. The dominant gender constructs of cisgender heterosexual men and women are somehow imagined and relegated as "equal" within a family hierarchy of a presiding father and domestic mother. Kline (2016) explains that contemporary Mormonism is a discursive paradoxical space containing both the narratives of "presiding" men and "equal partnerships" between monogamous spouses. "The Family Proclamation" is thus "a simultaneous resistance and accommodation to egalitarian ideals" (Kline, 2016, p. 215). Additionally, the modern nuclear family structure is constructed as "THE" family structure, believed to be both divine and universal. Extended family is secondary to the nuclear base of a singular father and currently a singular mother. Gender is constructed as having been pre-determined prior to mortal existence/consciousness that will be ongoing postmortem, and marriage is ambiguously monogamous. Mormon canonical texts continue to include theology for polygynous marital unions although they are not currently practiced as living physical cohabitations and generally denounced publicly.

Discussion: Mormon kava adaptations of family and masculinity

Because of the controversies surrounding kava today, orthodox Mormons who participate in *faikava* often engage directly with church canon and official publications to interpret it for themselves or avoid the subject altogether covertly. In some cases, due to controversies and stigma, we have observed Mormon Moana men quit drinking kava altogether, quit drinking but still attend a kava gathering, or even take a kava fast and abstain for a time. There are a few yet growing number of groups, however, that have adapted kava to fit their Mormon responsibilities and likewise adapt their Mormonism to fit their Indigenous worldviews. For example, some groups have begun using kava as a medium for membership reactivation, retention, and ministering to those who are struggling or not regularly attending church. We have also met several men who have been baptized through Mormon kava circle networks and some who remain non-Mormons but have asked for and received Mormon priesthood blessings from kava community members. In one circumstance as well, a kava participant was referred to go to see a Tongan woman who was a known healer in their local community. After further discussion with other members of the kava group and broader Mormon Tongan community we discovered it was quite controversial, where some saw women healers as overstepping the bounds of male priesthood, yet others saw it as complementary and acceptable alongside Mormon priesthood healing rituals.

A friend of ours shared during a *faikava* how he remembers getting yelled at by some of his high school football ("American") coaches for playing love songs before a game. He recalls being instructed to listen to music that was "more fitting" (masculine) to pre-game preparation. He expressed his frustration with this experience, realizing how different views were colliding. His white football coaches who had made these types of comments were reinforcing the hegemonic masculinities for young brown men. He shared that he didn't need to get hyped up to play: "I was ready to go, my nerves were already fired up, so me and the other Poly [Moana] boys played love songs to calm us down" before the game. Similar to how Fijian, Sāmoan, and Tongan men's international rugby teams sing hymns together before or after their games, these young Moana football players drew from love songs that are often learned and sung in the common Tongan and Fijian kava gatherings (Iese, 2015; Mad Squirrels Rugby League, 2017; Pacific Warriors, 2015). Interestingly, in many kava settings where there is live music, the bands are composed primarily of men, which means all parts are sung or arranged to match the participants. Māhina (2017) explained that the falsetto part that men often sing in *faikava* string band groups is the women's part, the female role, but in the *faikava* men most often sing it because they are usually the only one's present. Tongan male falsetto and *hiva kakala* (*sweet fragrant singing/love songs*) is a distinguishing identifier of Tongan music, similar to the Hawaiian tradition of string bands and singing, which both subvert hegemonic notions of masculine musical performance (Low, 2016; Moyle, 1987). Additionally, in many kava circles complex comedy is performed by men, where the humor is often couched with political critique, historical nuance, and relational mindfulness (Hamilton, 2015; Māhina, 2008; Tecun, 2017). In some cases, men will comedically perform gender-bending identities, dance women's parts, cross-dress, or use homoerotic language that is softened and disguised with laughter, subverting momentarily hegemonic masculinities (Hereniko, 1994).

Although kava is still dominated by men's participation, some Mormons now drink together with wives because of the nuclear family emphasis. Some have expressed that this helps avoid potential stresses to their spouse or criticism from the community, while others have expressed their enjoyment to have their wives be part of the discussions and space. Another adaptation is kava taking place at someone's home where their spouses and children feel comfortable to come and go from the kava circle whether they drink it or not, which allows fathers to be available to attend to immediate family needs in their homes. There is also a midnight to midnight protocol that often exists during Sunday/Sabbath for Mormon kava drinkers. During this time discussions and songs often shift and include church issues, doctrine, and hymns. There are also common sayings among Mormon kava-drinking men to remind one another of their spousal responsibilities. This is often done through humor including, "did you get your passport stamped?" or "did your visa get approved?" or "are you in credit?" Each of these statements alludes to the status of your relationship with a partner or spouse when you arrive at a *faikava* and serve as reminders of both your nuclear family and *kāinga* responsibilities.

Despite the influences of church and state constructs of nuclear family and masculinity, complex communal extended family networks are covertly embedded within Moana cultures and communities. Among Tongans, for example, the *kāinga* holds on to some degree, beyond nuclear family constructs, often being deeply involved in broader kinship affairs (e.g., sharing of child rearing, shared economic support in life events, living in the same residence, etc.) (Korn, 1974; Gailey 1987). Throughout the Moana, this complex resistance to the quasi nuclear family is revealed in the use of the word "family" itself. In the Tongan language, the word *famili* is used as a transliteration of the English word family, which Helu (1995) explained was adopted because they did not have this concept, which differs from the kinship social structure of the *kāinga* in Tongan, *'aiga* in Sāmoan (Greenhill and Clark, 2011). The word *kāinga* is also used in the Māori language, meaning home, village, or dwelling. In exploring possibilities to remember and reimagine *kāinga/'aiga*, the Hawaiian equivalent of *'āina* helps us move beyond the hegemonic concepts that have confined even critical views of "family" within anthropocentrism. *'Āina* in Hawaiian is the word for land but they also have another word for land, *honua*, which is related to *fonua* (Tonga), *fanua* (Samoa), and *whenua* (Māori). Boggs (1977) explains that for Kanaka *'Ōiwi* (Native Hawaiians), "land was regarded as the center or basis of life" where the word broken down to its root *'ai* (to eat) is translated into that which nourishes (p. 22). Silva (2017) explains that the Hawaiian expression *aloha 'āina*, meaning the love of land and people, includes that land and people comprise a family and thus they are related. Tongan scholars also point to the deified ancestors of Tonga through living connections to land, sea, and people today (Ka'ili, 2017; Māhina, 1992). Additionally, this concept of land and people relationships includes spirits and deities that can manifest as animals, plants, or elements in natural phenomena. Ancestral bones and birth placentas that are commonly buried in many Moana traditions, intimately connect one to the ancestors that are in the land. The land or sea, particularly sacred sites and areas, may also be ancestors themselves or manifestations of ancestors and are thus included in Moana families. Masculinity, femininity, gender, and family take on different meanings and possibilities when they are detached from the hegemonic constructs we have discussed are negotiated in *faikava* events. Natural phenomena and environments thus can also be gendered as well as flora and fauna, broadening the concept of family and gender relations as relationships with both social and place-based kin. *Faikava* is potentially a powerful expression of intimacy with the *fonua* (*land, people, customs, placenta*), an act of nurturing not only social relationships but spatial/land/water/animal-based ones as well (Ka'ili, 2017; Tecun, 2017).

Conclusion

This chapter introduced kava and its ambiguous place within Mormonism that results in controversy and stigma for many Moana Mormons who participate. We explored the hegemonic constructs of masculinity and nuclear family structures, which stereotype Moana men as "naturally physical" and narrowly define family exclusively as nuclear. We also explored Moana concepts of masculinity and family that contest hegemonic ideas of masculinity and family through sister–brother relations, homosociality, and *kāinga*, *'aiga*, and *'āina*. Moana masculinities and family negotiate contested ideas that are often subverted within kava settings when men become vulnerable by opening up, expressing brotherly love, and broadening their gender constructs. By considering the Indigenous concepts and meanings of family, the possibilities for Mormon Moana masculinities expand to include natural environmental, social, and ancestral relationships. Indigenous kinship evolves in these intersections and tensions, as Mormons do not always adhere to Mormon constructs, as Moana people likewise do not always adhere to Moana constructs. Although Mormon kava events can reinforce hegemonic constructs of patriarchal and male-centered narratives, they are also sites that subvert elements of masculinity through alternative gender constructs and performances, meaningful homosocial relationships, spousal inclusion in kava, intimate relationships with ancestral land, and sibling respect.

Acknowledgments

Mālō 'Aupito 'Inoke Hafoka and Heather Louise Hernandez for your critical feedback on earlier drafts of this essay and to Amy Hoyt and Taylor Petrey for your guidance as editors.

References

Agee, M.N., McIntosh, T., and Culbertson, P., 2013. *Pacific Identities and Well-being: Cross-cultural Perspectives*. New York: Routledge.

Ahlburg, D., 2000. Poverty among Pacific Islanders in the United States: Incidence, Change, and Correlates. *Pacific Studies* 23(1): 51–74.

Aikau, H.K., 2012. *A Chosen People, a Promised Land: Mormonism and Race in Hawai'i*. Minneapolis, MN: University of Minnesota Press.

Aporosa, A., 2014. Yaqona (Kava) and Education in Fiji: Investigating "Cultural Complexities" from a Post-development Perspective. Ph.D. Dissertation, Massey University. https://mro.massey.ac.nz/handle/10179/4683.

Aporosa, A., 2016. Kava – Killer or Cure? In *Pasifika Medical Association 20th Anniversary Conference 2016 – The Pathway to Leadership is Service*. Auckland, New Zealand. August. http://pacifichealth.org.nz/wp-content/uploads/2016/04/Dr-Apo-Aporosa-Research-Fellow-Waikato-University.pdf.

Besnier, N., and Alexeyeff, K. eds., 2014. *Gender on the Edge: Transgender, Gay, and Other Pacific Islanders*. Hong Kong: Hong Kong University Press.

Biersack, A., 2016. Introduction: Emergent Masculinities in the Pacific. *The Asia Pacific Journal of Anthropology* 17(3–4): 197–212.

Boggs, S.T., 1977. The Meaning of 'Aina in Hawaiian Tradition. Scholar Space. http://hdl.handle.net/10125/34232 (accessed July 29, 2019).

The Church of Jesus Christ of Latter-day Saints, 1995. The Family: A Proclamation to the World. www.churchofjesuschrist.org/study/manual/the-family-a-proclamation-to-the-world/the-family-a-proclamation-to-the-world?lang=eng.

Cleall, E., Ishiguro, L., and Manktelow, E.J., 2013. Imperial Relations: Histories of Family in the British Empire. *Journal of Colonialism and Colonial History* 14(1): 1–16.

Doctrine and Covenants Student Manual, 2002. D&C 89:9: Are Other Drinks Forbidden by the Word of Wisdom? *The Word of Wisdom*. www.lds.org/manual/doctrine-and-covenants-student-manual/section-81-89/section-89-the-word-of-wisdom?lang=eng.

Douglas, N., 1974. Latter-Day Saints Missions and Missionaries in Polynesia, 1844–1960. Ph.D. Dissertation, Australian National University. https://trove.nla.gov.au/work/8277503.
Father Lehi in Hawaii (parts 1 and 2), 2008. YouTube. August 11. www.youtube.com/watch?v=JtrdmkXsY9g.
Fehoko, E., 2014. Pukepuke Fonua: An Exploratory Study on the Faikava as an Identity Marker for New Zealand-Born Tongan Males in Auckland, New Zealand. Master's Thesis, Auckland University of Technology. http://hdl.handle.net/10292/7723.
Feldman, H., 1980. Informal Kava Drinking in Tonga. *The Journal of the Polynesian Society* 89(1): 101–2.
Filihia, M., 2001. Men Are from Maama, Women Are from Pulotu: Female Status in Tongan Society. *The Journal of the Polynesian Society* 110(4): 377–90.
From Heaven to Hell, 2008. Directed by R Maguire. Ganglands Season 3, Episode 5. USA: History Channel.
Gabriel, K., 2014. Formulating Patriarchal Homosociality: Notes from India. *NORMA: International Journal for Masculinity Studies* 9(1): 45–59.
Gailey, C.W., 1980. Putting Down Sisters and Wives: Tongan Women and Colonization. In M. Etienne and E.B. Leacock, eds. *Women and Colonization: Anthropological Perspectives*. Santa Barbara, CA: Praeger, pp. 294–322.
Gailey, G.A., 1987. *Kinship to Kingship: Gender Hierarchy and State Formation in the Tongan Islands*. Austin, TX: University of Texas Press.
Gailey, G.W., 1992. A Good Man Is Hard to Find: Overseas Migration and the Decentered Family in the Tongan Islands. *Critique of Anthropology* 12(1): 47–74.
Gangsters in Paradise: The Deportees of Tonga, 2019. Directed by Vice, Zealandia, Series 1, Episode 4. February 6. www.youtube.com/watch?v=72u5q-0R48A.
Gifford, E.W., 1929. *Tongan Society*, vol. 16. Honolulu, HI: Bernice P. Bishop Museum.
Greenhill S.J., and Clark R., 2011. POLLEX-Online: The Polynesian Lexicon Project Online. *Oceanic Linguistics* 50(2): 551–59.
Griffin, G., 2007. Kava, Not Java: Will This Drink Cost You Your Temple Recommend? *Salt Lake City Weekly*. September 19. www.cityweekly.net/utah/kava-not-java/Content?oid=2131332.
Gunson, N., 1987. Sacred Women Chiefs and Female "Headmen" in Polynesian History. *The Journal of Pacific History* 22(3): 139–72.
Hamilton, S., 2015. "Pass the Ta'e Please." *Overland* 219 (Winter). https://overland.org.au/previous-issues/issue-219/feature-scott-hamilton/.
Helu, F., 1993. Identity and Change in Tongan Society since European Contact. *Journal de la Société des Océanistes* 97(2): 187–94.
Helu, F., 1995. Brother/Sister and Gender Relations in Ancient and Modern Tonga. *Journal de la Société des Océanistes* 100(1): 191–200.
Herda, P., 1987. Gender, Rank and Power in 18th Century Tonga: The Case of Tupoumoheofo. *The Journal of Pacific History* 22(4): 195–208.
Hereniko, V., 1994. Clowning as Political Commentary: Polynesia, Then and Now. *The Contemporary Pacific* 6(1): 1–28.
Hokowhitu, B., 2008. Understanding the Maori and Pacific Body: Towards a Critical Physical Education Pedagogy. *New Zealand Physical Educator* 41(3): 81–91.
Hoyt, A., and Patterson, S.M., 2011. Mormon Masculinity: Changing Gender Expectations in the Era of Transition from Polygamy to Monogamy, 1890–1920. *Gender and History* 23(1): 72–91.
Iese, J., 2015. *Manu Samoa Ua Faafetai*. YouTube. September 18. www.youtube.com/watch?v=8NrP1am9XQU.
In Football We Trust, 2015. Directed by Tony Vainuku and Erika Cohn.
James, K.E., 1994. Effeminate Males and Changes in the Construction of Gender in Tonga. *Pacific Studies* 17(2): 39–69.
Jolly, M., 2008. Moving Masculinities: Memories and Bodies across Oceania. *The Contemporary Pacific* 20(1): 1–24.
Jolly, M., 2016. Men of War, Men of Peace: Changing Masculinities in Vanuatu. *The Asia Pacific Journal of Anthropology* 17(3–4): 305–23.
Jolly, M., and Macintyre, M eds., 1989. *Family and Gender in the Pacific: Domestic Contradictions and the Colonial Impact*. Cambridge: Cambridge University Press.
Ka'ili, T.O., 2017. *Marking Indigeneity: The Tongan Art of Sociospatial Relations*. Tucson, AZ: University of Arizona Press.
Kalani, 2014. Faikava: One Woman's Thoughts. *Feminist Mormon Housewives: Angry Activists with Babies to Feed*. [blog] February 19. www.feministmormonhousewives.org/2014/02/faikava-one-womans-thoughts/.

Kavapalu, H., 1991. Becoming Tongan: An Ethnography of Childhood in the Kingdom of Tonga. Ph.D. Dissertation, Australia National University. https://trove.nla.gov.au/work/31745449.

Kline, C., 2016. Saying Goodbye to the Final Say: The Softening and Reimagining of Mormon Male Headship Ideologies. In P.Q. Mason and J.G. Turner, eds. *Out of Obscurity: Mormonism since 1945*. New York: Oxford University Press, pp. 214–33.

Korn, S.D., 1974. Tongan Kin Groups: The Noble and the Common View. *Journal of the Polynesian Society* 83: 5–13.

Latai, L., 2015. Changing Covenants in Samoa? From Brothers and Sisters to Husbands and Wives? *Oceania* 85(1): 92–104.

Lātūkefu, S., 2014. *Church and State in Tonga: The Wesleyan Methodist Missionaries and Political Development, 1822–1875*. St Lucia: University of Queensland Press.

Lebot, V., Merlin, M., and Lindstrom, L., 1992. *Kava, the Pacific Elixir: The Definitive Guide to Its Ethnobotany, History, and Chemistry*. New Haven, CT: Yale University Press.

Low, A.E., 2016. Sound Travels: Ernest Kaleihoku Kaai and the Transmission of Hawaiian Music in the Early Twentieth Century. Doctoral Thesis, University of Auckland. https://researchspace.auckland.ac.nz/handle/2292/31645.

Mad Squirrels Rugby League, 2017. Fiji vs Australia – Prematch Hymn NOQU MASU – RLWC 2017 Semi Final. YouTube. November 24. www.youtube.com/watch?v=BQtqLhxjqOg.

Māhina, H.'Ō., 2017. On the Matter of Kava: From the Past to the Present to the Future. In *KAVA: A Workshop for Kava Researchers and Enthusiasts: Anthropology and Pacific Studies Seminar Series*. The University of Waikato.

Māhina, 'Ō., 1992. The Tongan Traditional History Tala-Ē-Fonua: A Vernacular Ecology-Centred Historico-Cultural Concept. Ph.D. Dissertation, Australian National University. https://trove.nla.gov.au/version/245080238.

Māhina, 'Ō., 2008. Faiva Fakaoli: The Tongan Performance Art of Humour. *Pacific Studies* 31(1): 31–53.

Marcus, G., 1979. Elopement, Kinship, and Elite Marriage in the Contemporary Kingdom of Tonga. *Journal de la Société des Océanistes* 35(63): 83–96.

Marsters, C., and Tiatia-Seath, J., 2019. Young Pacific Male Rugby Players' Perceptions and Experiences of Mental Wellbeing. *Sports* 7(4): 1–19.

Moyle, R.M., 1987. *Tongan Music*. Oxford: Oxford University Press.

The Other Side of Heaven, 2001. Directed by Mitch Davis. USA: 3Mark Entertainment, Molen/Garbett Productions.

Oware, M., 2011. Brotherly Love: Homosociality and Black Masculinity in Gangsta Rap Music. *Journal of African American Studies* 15(1): 22–39.

Pacific Warriors, 2015. Pacific Warriors – Hymns. YouTube. September 21. www.youtube.com/watch?v=ubKG7oWy3DQ.

Presterudstuen, G.H., and Schieder, D., 2016. Bati as Bodily Labour: Rethinking Masculinity and Violence in Fiji. *The Asia Pacific Journal of Anthropology* 17(3–4): 213–30.

The R.M., 2003. Directed by Kurt Hale. USA: Produced by Dave Hunter.

Reeve, P., 2015. *Religion of a Different Color: Race, and the Mormon Struggle for Whiteness*. New York: Oxford University Press.

Reyes, E., 2013. L.A.'s Close-Knit Tongan Community Struggles with Poverty. *Los Angeles Times*. November 28. http://articles.latimes.com/2013/nov/28/local/la-me-tongan-community-20131129 (accessed September 2015).

Shumway, E., 2012. *Ki he kau Kava Tonga – Elder Shumway*. YouTube. May 25. www.youtube.com/watch?v=7XWS7_yK2F0.

Sikahema, V., 2014. Vai's View: Addressing Cultural Traditions That Oppose LDS Principles. *Deseret News*, Faith. September 5. www.deseretnews.com/article/865610309/Addressing-cultural-traditions-that-oppose-LDS-principles.html.

Silva, N.K., 2017. *The Power of the Steel-Tipped Pen: Reconstructing Native Hawaiian Intellectual History*. Durham, NC: Duke University Press.

Suaalii, T.M., 1997. Deconstructing the "Exotic" Female Beauty of the Pacific Islands and "White" Male Desire. *Women's Studies Journal* 13(2): 75–94.

Tapu Podcast, n.d. www.facebook.com/tapupodcast/.

Tecun, A., 2017. Tongan Kava: Performance, Adaptation, and Identity in Diaspora. *Performance of the Real E-journal* 1(1): 52–64. www.otago.ac.nz/performance-of-the-real/proceedings/index.html.

Tengan, T., 2002. (En)gendering Colonialism: Masculinities in Hawai'i and Aotearoa. *Cultural Values* 6(3): 239–56.

Tengan, T.P.K., and Markham, J.M., 2009. Performing Polynesian Masculinities in American Football: From "Rainbows to Warriors". *The International Journal of the History of Sport* 26(16): 2412–31.

The Testaments of One Fold and One Shepherd, 2000. Directed by Keith Merrill. USA: The Church of Jesus Christ of Latter-day Saints.

Tomlinson, M., 2004. Perpetual Lament: Kava—Drinking, Christianity and Sensations of Historical Decline in Fiji. *Journal of the Royal Anthropological Institute* 10(3): 653–73.

Toren, C., 1994. All Things Go in Pairs, or the Sharks Will Bite: The Antithetical Nature of Fijian Chiefship. *Oceania* 64(3): 197–216.

Trask, H.K., 1999. *From a Native Daughter: Colonialism and Sovereignty in Hawai'i*. Honolulu, HI: University of Hawai'i Press.

Vaka, S., 2014. A Tongan Talanoa about Conceptualisations, Constructions and Understandings of Mental Illness. Ph.D. Dissertation, Massey University. https://mro.massey.ac.nz/handle/10179/5777.

Vaka, S., Stewart, M.W., Foliaki, S., and Tu'itahi, M., 2009. Walking apart but towards the Same Goal? The View and Practices of Tongan Traditional Healers and Western-Trained Tongan Mental Health Staff. *Pacific Health Dialog* 15: 89–95.

Weaver, S.J., 2019. President Nelson Embarks on Pacific Ministry Tour. *Church News*. May 16. The Church of Jesus Christ of Latter-day Saints. www.churchofjesuschrist.org/church/news/president-nelson-embarks-on-pacific-ministry-tour?lang=eng.

Young, R., 2000. Gender, Mobility and Urban Place in Fiji: From Colonial to Post-colonial Wanderings. *Asia-Pacific Population Journal* 15(3): 57–71.

Further reading

Jolly, M., 2008. Moving Masculinities: Memories and Bodies across Oceania. *The Contemporary Pacific* 20(1): 1–24.

Jolly provides insights into Oceanic masculinities as plural and fluid rather than singular and unchanging. Oceanic masculinities are complex and are necessary to contextualize within "colonial histories, militarism, and globalization." Jolly provides opportunities to imagine masculinities in Oceania beyond singular masculinities subject to hegemonic Western influenced paradigms.

Ka'ili, T.O., 2017. *Marking Indigeneity: The Tongan Art of Sociospatial Relations*. Tucson, AZ: University of Arizona Press.

Ka'ili intimately explains one of Tonga's paramount cultural values, *tauhi vā*, which he defines as a "performance art of nurturing harmonious socio-spatial relationships." His research builds upon the *tā-vā* (time–space) Tongan theory of reality founded by 'Okusitino Māhina. He explains that tempo-spatial mediations are manifested socially through *tauhi vā*. Ka'ili also addresses masculinity, family, and Indigenous relationality.

Tecun, A., 2017. Tongan Kava: Performance, Adaptation, and Identity in Diaspora. *Performance of the Real E-journal* 1(1): 52–64. www.otago.ac.nz/performance-of-the-real/proceedings/index.html.

Tecun explores contemporary kava circles in diaspora. He analyzes how past common kava practices have consolidated to exist simultaneously in contemporary kava practices and events. He argues that kava is especially important to Moana peoples in diaspora as "transportable fonua (land)" allowing them to perform place-based identities.

Tengan, T., 2002. (En)gendering Colonialism: Masculinities in Hawai'i and Aotearoa. *Cultural Values* 6(3): 239–56.

This article analyzes the intersections of masculinity and colonialism within Hawai'i and Aotearoa. This work focuses on two of the most significant aspects of Indigenous masculinity production: military and sports. Tengan deconstructs hegemonic masculinities that privilege "patriarchal structures and subordinate femininities" towards decolonization and a revival of Indigenous constructs of gender in the Pacific.

Trask, H.K., 1999. *From a Native Daughter: Colonialism and Sovereignty in Hawai'i*. Honolulu, HI: University of Hawai'i Press.

This book is a powerful analysis and lyrical vendetta that critiques colonialism in Hawai'i. Trask organizes the book into five sections of essays that cover a broad range of topics including: the struggle for self-determination, the condemnation of neo-capitalism, and critiques of the exoticization of Indigenous Hawaiian's by "Western academia, paradise-seekers, and hula-lovers."

32
GENDERED DYNAMICS AND INSTITUTIONS WITHIN NIGERIAN MORMONISM

Russell W. Stevenson

Since 1978, the Church of Jesus Christ of Latter-day Saints in Nigeria has grown with surprising rapidity. In 2019, Nigeria continues to lead the globe in conversion rates, with nearly 180,000 members and fifty-four stakes—numbering in the hundreds of baptisms in the Enugu mission alone. As an increasing demographic presence, the experiences of African Latter-day Saints must be incorporated into any assessment of what defines the contemporary Church. Composed of less than 0.1 percent of Nigeria's population, the Church holds a visible presence through its temple in Aba and its myriad structures throughout the southern Nigerian landscape. Although the LDS Church in Africa mirrors its parental American ecclesiastical structures, the indigenous contexts render it a church distinct—and worthy of engagement on its own terms. Furthermore, although Latter-day Saint growth in sub-Saharan Africa has been exaggerated in devotional literature, even Church critic Phillip Jenkins has acknowledged that Nigerian Saints represent a notable case (Jenkins, 2009).

As a linguistically diverse country teeming with multiple ethnic communities, even most Nigerian scholars do not have the capacity to engage the full range of language sources. While this article will touch on four major ethno-linguistic groups (Yoruba, Hausa, Ibibio, and Igbo), it will primarily privilege the experiences of the Igbo, as Latter-day Saint theology found its earliest adherents among the Igbo populations. However, this privileging should *not* be taken to suppose Igbo ethnic supremacy.

This chapter seeks to highlight how the gender ideology of Nigerian Latter-day Saints has resonated against both indigenous worldviews as well as the post-independence present, producing an ambivalent system of gender construction that both builds upon and defies colonial gender scaffolding. Conceptualizing "gender" among Latter-day Saints in Nigeria faces a translation difficulty since the most contemporary teachings on gender, mainly General Conference addresses, have not been translated into Igbo, placing Igbo Latter-day Saints in the position of processing Latter-day Saint thought in Igbo and in English. Relatedly, the Igbo version of the Book of Mormon draws on multiple dialects rather than the commonly-accepted Igbo *izugbe* (central Igbo) devised for interchange between the Igbo villages. Because Igbo written language is generally not privileged in day-to-day commerce and discussion, analysis must be conducted from both English and Igbo texts as well as Igbo audio recordings of talks given by Latter-day Saint leaders.

Proper analysis of Latter-day Saint affiliation and gender identity in Nigeria requires that scholars complicate pristine notions of indigenous-ness, and, at the very least, reject that "indigenous" is a stable category, untouched by external forces. Scholars such as Chielezona Eze, Kwame Anthony Appiah, and Achille Mbembe have challenged scholars to reject "nativism" in favor of an Afro-centered identity capable of incorporating the full range of human experiences while retaining their African-ness. Derek Peterson has written of Christian conversions in East Africa that he seeks to engage the "technologies by which people are dislodged from their native provinces and propelled to live across linguistic and cultural frontiers"; in a similar vein, this chapter will demonstrate how mutually reinforcing gender norms have reinforced each other in the importation of Latter-day Saint theology into Nigerian lives through what Peterson has styled an "infrastructure of cosmopolitanism": in this instance, the process by which American gendered constructs mixed and mingled with indigenous Nigeria' milieus. In this regard, chroniclers must resist the temptation to dismiss Latter-day Saint identity as "un-African." By placing individual Africans at the center of their knowledge production, scholars acknowledge the individual full capacity to embrace layered identities not easily simplified—including the capacity to embrace an American-style religiosity and foreign gendered constructs (Eze, 2014; Appiah, 1992; Mbembe, 2002; Peterson, 2012).

Afro-politan Mormonism

For the past generation, scholarly discussion regarding African identity has relied on what Chielezona Eze has called the "relational model" of African identity, often defined through nationalist era literati: through construction of a narrative of pre-colonial order untouched by change, violence, or colonization as a mechanism for challenging Western hegemony. Charles Taylor, too, held that identity draws on an "inherent spatiality of the self"—an aspiration to connect to a particular kind of spatiality, be it abstract or literal. For the Afro-nationalist scholars, morality and wisdom could be tied to a particular stretch of land; indeed, the Igbo word for culture—*omenala* or *ọdịnanị*—may be translated as "that which the land does" or "that which is the land." *Ani*, the title for the land goddess, dictates all operations and mediates between mankind (*mmadu* lit. "good life") and *Chukwu* (lit. "the great God).

Homi Bhabha (1994) considers such narratives to be afflicted with "implacable oppositionality" and to be, ultimately, "an originary counter-myth" over and against Western erasure. By deploying this model, an importation of an externality must, of necessity, represent a mechanism of colonial oppression—and the arrival of American Latter-day Saint institutions to Igboland would certainly qualify. A body of scholars and commentators, ranging from Chielozona Eze to Taiye Selasi, has challenged this model, arguing that engagement with externalities—of a host of kinds—represents not colonial oppression but cultural richness. Simon Gikandi celebrates such "Afro-politanism" as a belief that African identities are "both rooted in specific local geographies" but "also transcendent of them"—to enjoy a "state of cultural hybridity—to be African and other worlds at the same time" (Gikandi, 2010). Kwame Anthony Appiah celebrates cultural "contamination" (Appiah, 1992). Eze writes: "The African is contaminated in the sense that she is not culturally or biologically pure. And this is good" (Eze, 2014).

Clearly, Nigerian Latter-day Saint thought alone does not represent "Afro-politanism" in a particularly robust form. Nigerian Latter-day Saints do not celebrate a poly-centric spiritual imaginary that draws on a host of linguistic traditions; indeed, English, rather than indigenous languages, serves as the common language of religious worship, with an acknowledged spiritual center in the American West, not in Nigeria. However, the acknowledgment of porous intellectual borders, of cultural hybridity, and a disavowal of ideology that insists on religiosity connected to one's immediate locale promote a discourse that allows Latter-day Saint thought to be one more manifestation of porous exchange in the contemporary world.

Gendered duality and indigenous religion in Nigeria

Understanding Latter-day Saint constructions of gender in Nigeria requires understanding the difference between Western and indigenous notions of gender identity and taking indigenous gender constructs seriously. While the Igbo proverb, *Ndị Igbo amaghị eze* (The Igbo know no king) speaks to the autonomous attributes of many small-hold farm lots, the sprawling kin network requires investment in family relationships. As Nigerian Latter-day Saint Christopher Chukwurah, observed: "We are our brother's keeper in Nigeria, and we don't let our relations suffer, if we can help. That is one thing I think is good about our culture, our society" (C. Chukwurah, 1988). Similarly, notions of male-ness and female-ness in Igbo society are construed through familial relationality.

Western notions of gender are largely based upon liberal ideals of autonomy and independence. Indigenous Igbo conceptualizations of the self do not allow for individuated sovereignty, be it gendered or otherwise. Chinua Achebe provides the most illuminating analysis on the Igbo theology of the self, arguing that the Igbo "postulate the concept of every man as both a unique creation and the work of a unique creator" (Achebe, 1975). However, the spiritual assumptions of the Igbo worldview do not allow for individuated *autonomy*. The Igbo proverb above concludes: *Ihe kwuru ihe akwudebe ya* (where one thing stands, another thing stands beside it). Notions of gender complementarity are rooted in Igbo indigenous fabric. Another widely used Igbo saying celebrates the two-ness of the universe: *ihe bụ abuo abuo: nwanyi na nwoke, mmuo na mmmadu, elu n'ala* (things exist in duality: women and man, spirit and humans, heaven and earth). No entity can be considered genuinely autonomous. All entities—even truth claims themselves—must be considered contingent upon other realities.

Traditional Igbo cosmos holds that each individual human enjoys a cosmic counterpart, called the *chi*: an individuated spiritual force that functions as an individualized spirit-god overseeing the individual affairs of individual destinies. The *chi* and the individual engage in a lifelong negotiation for his/her ultimate fate; as another Igbo proverb enjoins: *onye kwe, chi ya ga-ekwe* (if a person agrees, his/her *chi* will agree), thus bounding the absolute dominance of the *chi*. While traditional Igbo thought celebrated individual uniqueness, it did not allow for individual autonomy (Achebe, 2000). Achebe concludes: "Clearly, *chi* has unprecedented veto powers over man's destiny" (Achebe, 1975; Chukwukwere, 1983).

In pre-colonial (i.e., *tupu oge ndị ọcha bia* [before the white people came]) Igbo cosmology gendered interdependence played a substantial role in both social and cosmological formations. An adage holds: *ihe ụwa si n 'akala aka* (the things of the world emanate from an individual's hands) (Achebe, 2000). Nkiru Uwechia Nzegwu has argued that men and women enjoyed "separate political lines of governance," structured in order to render "men and women interdependent" (Nzegwu, 2006). Women and men wove gendered spirituality into the fabric of their daily lives. Masculinity and femininity were key attributes of deity. The supreme being, *Chukwu* (the great *Chi*) or, in some regions, *Ezechitoke* (the kingly spiritual creative force), derive their names from the notion of the *chi*, the individualized spirit-double accompanying each individual. Joseph Therese Agbasiere describes *ala* as a "complementary female vital force relating to earth divinity," and residing "at the apex of the pantheon of vital forces, particularly *chi* [personal spirit-deity], *ndichie* [the deified ancestors], and *umummuo* [minor divinities]." As Achebe concludes, female *mmuo* [spirits] "discerned the forces that abetted social disintegration (prevarication, thievery, infidelity, and violence) and worked toward societal cohesiveness."

While the *chi* was vague and gender-less, gender teemed throughout the natural landscape: entities in the sky (e.g., the sun, *anyanwụ* or lightning, *amadioha*) were male deities whereas the visible world teemed with feminine divine influence: *osmiri* (river), *ogba* (cave), and *agụ* (forested areas) (Agbasiere, 2000). The masculine felt distant, removed, and unreliable; the feminine seemed predictable, present, and enduring. To suppose that the "self" could be either "autonomous" or subservient undermines the fundamental existential claims of Igbo religion. As the Igbo expression goes, *igwe bụ ike*: in the community is strength.

However, Ifi Amadiume argues that in Nnobi, Igbo gender ideology is "flexible" and allows for men and women alike to fulfill similar responsibilities. Gender identities were fixed social relationships, not malleable constructs (Amadiume 1973); as Abosede George has noted, "women's lived experiences incorporated a relativity of status conditioned upon where women were and who else was present in that context" (George, 2019). As such, a woman could switch between functioning as a woman *as well as a father* depending upon the context. Thus, "to be a male" and "to be a female" (*ịbụ nwoke; ịbụ nwanyị*) or "to be a mother" or "to be a father" (*ịbụ nne; ịbụ nna*) does not pertain to biological sex but rather, to one's role in familial relationships.

Yoruba scholar Oyeronke Oyewumi has made the even more forceful argument: "the social categories 'men' and 'women' were nonexistent, and hence no gender system was in place" (Oyewumi, 1997). J. Lorand Matory has challenged Oyewumi, arguing that evidence of precolonial gender notions appear throughout the Yoruba diaspora in Brazil and Cuba. Matory considers sexuality to be evidence of what James Allen styles as a "hidden transcript": an unstated set of rules governing the lives—and suppressing the internal tensions—of communities. Similarly, as Steven Pierce (2007) observes, Nigerian Hausa gendered relationships should not be understood as "a taxonomy of different subcultural identities" but rather, that sexual relations are made up by a "set of polarities," such as male/female, masculine/feminine, older/younger, and rich/poor. "The avoidance of talk about sexuality," Matory observes, "is not an indication that gender hierarchy is unimportant. It's an indication of its deep importance" (Matory, 2017).

By contrast, in Western academe, notions of gendered autonomous selfhood have provided the intellectual grounds for the construction of "gender" as an independent context for analysis of behavior and identity. Situating the autonomous self at the center of identity construction re-frames discussion of the self in individual human beings, rather than in abstract iterations of femininity and masculinity. Embedded in Western gendered thought is the proposition that each individual is a sovereign entity equipped with constructing and negotiating their own identities on terms that they see fit; they are "autonomous selves." Joan Scott concludes: "there is no essence of womanhood (or of manhood) to provide a stable subject for our histories … only successive iterations of a word that doesn't have a fixed referent" (Scott, 2008). Alice Kessler-Harris observes: "The individual becomes the center, the tool that pries open an understanding of the tensions against which the historical process unfolds" (Kessler-Harris, 2012). Challenging the existence of universalizing narratives or theoretical lenses, and echoing Judith Butler's argument in *Gender Trouble*, Kessler-Harris considered notions of reified, static, and binary gendered identities to be unreliable, at best, and more often, harmful—gendered identity must be subsumed to individualized autonomy (Kessler-Harris, 2012). Thus, secular academic gender constructs do not allow for an externalized, mediating *chi* constraining an individual's impulses to transgress certain gender norms.

The idea of female spiritual leaders indigenous to Nigerian religiosity did not necessarily resonate with the contemporary Latter-day Saint missionaries. Latter-day Saint notions of gendered duality resonated well with indigenous Igbo gender cosmology. In Latter-day temple liturgy translated into Igbo, "opposite" has been rendered to be: *nwere ihe abuo* ("has duality").

Thus, while biological males and males may assume either male or female identities, duality and complementarity of gender identities enjoy a deep rootedness in Igbo language and cosmology.

The image of Latter-day Saint manhood in the colonial era

LDS Nigerian masculinity is both influenced by and presents a challenge to colonial masculinity. Ultimately, LDS masculinity is an agentive, hybrid masculinity. Both indigenous gendered constructs and the external gendered systems are the products of historical situations; neither should be viewed as inherently good or problematic. Chinua Achebe has illuminated the internal logics, laws, and identities bound up in indigenous Igbo identity of the *chi* and hints that not only did indigenous Igbo religion change over time but also had internalized mechanisms for incorporating change. Among Western Yoruba kingdoms such as the Oyo or Ife, the British delegated authority to the ruling *oba*. In the Hausa and Fulani North, emirs received British support. In the Igbo East, however, strict hierarchies did not govern village life; while titled men (*ndị isi*) enjoyed pre-eminence, the council of daughters (*otu umuada*) and *otu-ndiomu-ala* (council of wives) carried out key governmental responsibilities, ranging from functioning as courts of jurisdiction over disputes to serving as a credit union (*isusu*) for members.

As the British expanded their presence throughout the Niger Delta region, colonial officials such as Sir Frederick Lugard implemented a system of "indirect rule" in which they aspired to preserve "indigenous institutions." British colonial planners constructed male-driven polities, shifting the power from the relative equity between the *oha* and the *umuada* to male-driven "indigenous institutions." Although Lugard and others considered the "warrant chief" to be an "indigenous institution," most locals recognized it to be an externally imposed institution; in Mbaise, for instance, the warrant chief's nickname, "Waturuocha," meant "white sheep," illustrating his willingness to follow white officials at their beck and call. In 1914, Lugard contrived the amalgamation of the Southern and Northern Niger Delta regions, creating the modern construction known as "Nigeria," a name contrived by his wife, Flora Shaw from "Niger" and "area"; it has become cliché to echo Nigerian nationalist Obafemi Awolowo's observation that "Nigeria" is but a "mere geographical expression."

British and American educators and missionaries, such as Hope Waddell, Thomas Bowen, and Mary Slessor, too, cultivated a male-dominated ethos. In one instance, Mbaise Latter-day Saint proselyte Anthony Obinna recalled, with some embarrassment, that he grew up in a time when his community was "always afraid of white men and never wanted to appear before them or go near them." Obinna also enjoyed access to educational institutions as other young "Nigerian" men did. Anthony acknowledged the privileges his male-ness afforded. "It was very difficult to send girls to school," he later wrote, "for their work added to the income of the family" (A. Obinna, 1988). In 1937, an English traveler attempted to speak to his father, Obinna Ugochukwu. Recognizing that English was becoming a necessary skill in the colonial economy, Ugochukwu sent Anthony to school. He became a schoolteacher, educated through a correspondence course with Wolsey Hall at University of Oxford. Obinna reflected the gendered dynamics of the British regime. British officials promoted "progress," "civilization," and integration into the Anglophone imperial market. Although some masculinized institutions (e.g., secret societies) came under imperial critique, such critiques were less based on the fact that they were male-dominated but rather, the kind of masculine ethos they fostered.

Chinua Achebe's novels, *No Longer at Ease* and *A Man of the People*, highlight the transformation of Igbo men over the course of British colonization and into independence. Now locked into a new system of colonial patronage, Achebe's protagonist, Obi Okonkwo finds himself charged with bribery and fraud, a charge many Americans associate with contemporary Nigerian society. Once upwardly mobile with the colonial elite, Obi fell victim to the capriciousness of coloniality: the promise of "progress" through British institutions only proved his undoing. In *Man of the People*, Nigerian politicians manipulate democratic institutions through demagoguery and corruption, a remnant of British-constructed masculinity (Achebe, 1960; 1966). The collective voices of Nigerian Latter-day Saint men and women do not suggest that the Church of Jesus Christ of Latter-day Saints utilized colonial discourse or tools to impose gender norms. Instead, Nigerian men and women claim that they have actively cultivated Latter-day Saint identities and embraced their gendered implications.

For Nigeria's first president, Nnamdi "Benjamin" Azikiwe, American identity—whether religious or educational—represented an anti-colonial success story. Azikiwe modeled his University of Nigeria at Nsukka after Howard University to "restore the dignity of man"—to cultivate anew the masculinity that had been eroded by colonial rule. As a graduate of Storer College and Lincoln University Azikiwe considered historically Black Americana education to be a mechanism redefining British educational coloniality in Nigeria, such as the University of London and throughout the University College system—and heralded the contributions of American industrialists. Nigerian nationalist Mbonu Ojike urged Nigerian nationalists to "popularize our tongues like Patrick Henry of Virginia; our pens of national ideals like Thomas Jefferson; our swords of independence, like George Washington; [and] our fountains of economic stability like Henry Ford, John D. Rockefeller" (Ojiaku, 1972). In a similar fashion, some Nigerian elites saw Latter-day Saint men as masculine exemplars, the best that American anti-imperial manhood had to offer. As polygamist Christians who had shown their mettle in establishing railroads, banks, and immaculate temples independent of the federal regime, "Mormonism" conveyed a kind of anti-colonial flair. Their unwillingness to surrender their marital institutions inspired the *Lagos Weekly Record* (*LWR*, 1897) to opine: "If it is impossible to suppress that view of marriage among a highly cultivated people not born under the system," the British colonizers ought not "to suppress it among a people born to it and who for thousands of years have practiced it with wholesome results." Latter-day Saint men represented the idealized anti-colonial male: independent, sovereign, city-builders, and polygamists—all without the stigma of being "African." The *LWR* observed, wrongly but tellingly, that "to our knowledge there are no black Mormons." It celebrated Latter-day Saint men's industriousness, financial acumen, and commitment to institution.

In 1950, Reverend M.D. Opara, a vehement anti-colonial voice in the Eastern Region's parliament and head of the Zion Mission, looked to the LDS Church as an institution that valued self-sustenance from colonial authorities, ecclesiastical sovereignty, infrastructure-building, and dogged separatism; when he met Latter-day Saint missionaries while in New York, he highlighted that his Zion Mission "more or less kept themselves aloof" from the other faiths in Nigeria (Lund, 1950; Ekechi, 2010). In 1961, postal worker Charles Agu told a young Latter-day Saint missionary, Marvin Jones, that the Latter-day Saint faith was the next stage in Nigerians' plight of independence: "Now that they have independence, every one is growing financially, educationally," Jones recorded. "But they believe they should grow spiritually" (Jones, 1961; Stevenson, 2014). Christopher Chukwurah celebrated the association with the American faith:

> One thing about Americans is their spirit of hard work, and that's one concept that the Church of Jesus Christ of Latter-day Saints emphasizes—to teach them the principles and let them govern themselves. I think that's a beautiful aspect of American culture ... More so, the honesty that I find in American society, is what has made America great.

Obinna, too, celebrated that "religion, in the pure sense of it, is what makes America great" (C. Chukwurah, 1988).

Latter-day Saint lived masculinity connoted men-on-the-make, aspiring to economic independence and prosperity—capable of infrastructure-building, financial self-sustenance, and capitalist mobility, similar to their American masculine counterparts (Hoyt and Patterson, 2011). By affording priesthood ordination to all worthy males, Latter-day Saint theology emphasized individuated authority and access to titles typically reserved for local "big men": warrant chiefs, parish priests, or pastors. With loosened trade and immigration barriers, word of the Church of Jesus Christ of Latter-day Saints, considered a wealthy American sect—including the RLDS and Bickertonite versions—spread throughout southeastern Nigeria. A cohort of correspondents, mostly men, commenced a letter-writing campaign to solicit the establishment of the Church of Jesus Christ of Latter-day Saints in the country. Their narratives reflected the mythos promoted by Christian colonial educators: upwardly mobile men seeking stability on earth as well as in heaven by embracing Christianity and Christian educational institutions. While it is tempting to suppose that colonial Christianity established the framework against which Latter-day Saint congregations developed, national independence provides a more illuminating context. National sovereignty produced an environment in which Nigeria's national elite imagined the promotion of a masculinity informed to be suited to the needs of a global market. Despite similarities with their U.S. counterparts, Nigerian Latter-day Saint masculinity did not function as an *outpost* of an American faith but rather, its re-creation. The American dream was theirs, too. Anthony Obinna chided Church President Spencer W. Kimball: "The Spirit of God has called us to this church, and there is nothing that can keep us out" (Obinna, 1978; Stevenson, forthcoming).

Contemporary Latter-day Saint Nigerian men find themselves alienated from standard-fare Nigerian masculinity. Drinking *Schweppes*, water, or soda while other men imbibe strong alcohol, the same structure that celebrates heteronormativity at the highest levels in Latter-day Saint cosmology marginalizes Latter-day Saint men from man-making structures—and, to borrow from cultural anthropologist Rudolph Gaudio, citizen-making. District President Roger T. Curtis, a Scottish manager serving on the Lagos Sanitation Board, observed that if the LDS Church were "organize[d] properly" there, "it will be the saving of Nigeria." BYU Professor Spencer J. Palmer considered Nigeria to be the "next Mormon country."

LDS female authority in Nigeria

The arrival of Latter-day Saint missionaries marked no stark departure from historical precedent; Christian missionaries such as Hope Waddell and Mary Slessor had traversed Nigeria since the late nineteenth century. Composed of male and female missionaries—Rendell and Rachel Mabey as well as Edwin and Janath Cannon—Latter-day Saint missionaries heralded from Utah's blue-blood elite; Janath R. Cannon had served as a counselor in the auxiliary body for the Church's women's organization, the Relief Society General Board. At the height of their involvement in Nigeria, American missionaries constituted a tiny (albeit financially well-funded) minority; fifteen years earlier, American missionaries had been denied entrance visas out of hand based on the Church's reputation for racism. As a minority faith, with little to no political support from Western regimes, the Latter-day Saint church enjoyed no capacity to exert their will on Nigerian converts.

Women's institutions enjoyed a robust history in Igboland *tupu oge ndi ọcha biala* (pre-colonial times). Judith Van Allen has highlighted how the Igbo female institutions enjoyed indigenous autonomy, with exclusionary rights. Sprawling throughout semi-autonomous villages, Igbo residents formed local institutions of governance, eschewing the need for an overarching large-scale regime. Village councils (*oha*), women's councils (*umuada*), and age-groups (*ogbo*) held meetings to discuss the needs of the community; while the *oha* made final decisions regarding the governance of the village as a whole, other institutions decided particularized matters. In Onitsha, the women's society, *Otu Ogene* enjoyed power and status equivalent to the *Ndichie* (male elders serving in the *oha*). In Nnobi, the female *Ekwe* society, associated with Idemili, enjoyed *paramount* status among all political organizations in the area. As central players in the functioning of the market, women held *mikiri* meetings to discuss market rules. At times, Nigerian women had launched violent resistance to British colonial rule. When British colonial authorities attempted to carry out a tax census on women in Igbo communities in 1929, they launched a series of attacks throughout Igboland against the colonial authorities, burning the market and exposing themselves to police officers (an act so socially egregious that it prompted the male officers to flee). In Enyiogugu, Mbaise, Owerri District, women burned down the local courthouse. Frightened by the threat the Igbo women posed, the regime ended the system of warrant chieftaincy in eastern Nigeria. Called the *Ogu Umunwanyi* (Women's War), this episode reflected both the social acceptability of female violence as well as a weaponized use of female anatomy to achieve social ends. Similarly, in 1948–1949, Funmilayo Ransome-Kuti (mother of the famed Nigerian musician, Fela Kuti and aunt of famed author Wole Soyinka), orchestrated the Abeokuta women's market revolt against the ruling Alake male elite for excessive taxes; according to one political song, the women charged the Alake for "us[ing] your penis as a mark of authority that you are our husband ... O you men, vagina's head will seek vengeance" (Johnson-Odim and Mba, 1997) By 1977, the federal government had arrested the heads of the Nnobi Women's Council, as they had come to be seen as a subversive and excessively autonomous institution; Nnobi men had "discarded aspects of their traditional culture which guaranteed women full participation in the political structure" (Amadiume, 1973). Similar women's institutions experienced decline across the countryside.

Some Nigerian women embraced Latter-day gendered ideology because it placed bounds on their propensity to exhibit both masculine and feminine qualities. Independent churches had long produced environments for female spiritual leaders. Florence Chukwurah complained that the husbands in Aba "are difficult and don't want to join [their wives]" (F. Chukwurah, 1988). Susanna Ekpo in Akwa Ibom, a prayer house leader who later joined the Latter-day Saint faith, considered herself to be a visionary; she prophesied that "we would have missionaries come from overseas to Nigeria" and "got a voice in my heart that said 'there will be one day a stranger in the Church'" (Ekpo, 1988). When Nigeria's first Relief Society President, Fidelia Obinna met her husband, Anthony, "nobody showed him to me"; he "came to me in a dream ...When I saw him, I knew he was the man I saw in the dream" (F. Obinna, 1988). Rosemary Elendu, an Igbo proselyte from Nsirimo, was told that she "acted like a man in the other world" and that God "would also like me to continue that in this particular world." Her mother "always wanted me to be working ... because she said that I was the first daughter, and that if I was not brought up properly, that it would bring shame to the family." Elendu considered her masculine traits to be a positive feature: "There is no aspect of manual work that I cannot do." However, she believed the Latter-day Saint faith had disciplined her gendered impulses; she learned "how to compose [her]self" and disavowed alcohol: "I was trying to become masculine when I was doing these things." After adopting the Latter-day Saint health code prohibiting alcohol, she felt like "a mother and a wife, and [she] behaved like one" (Elendu, 1988). Caroline Ituma, a university-trained physician, also saw the benefits of the prescribed gender norms within the LDS faith and enjoyed activities for women that Latter-day Saint identity encouraged: "mak[ing] banana bread" and "learn[ing] how to knit . . we don't have that in any of the churches here" (Elendu, 1988).

The notion of female ritual authority troubled the American sister missionaries; while in Ghana, Janath R. Cannon blanched when one of the women cheerily told her that in the Ghanaian LDS Church, "we have prophetesses." In previous generations, the American Relief Society had enjoyed a similar relationship to the priesthood hierarchy as the *umuada* had enjoyed to the *oha*, including female ritual healings and sovereign governance over its own budget. The Relief Society's tradition reflected a tradition more congruent with the structures of indigenous Igboland than the missionaries supposed, even if the contemporary expressions of female spiritual leadership were lacking within the American headquarters.

Gender identities in Nigerian Latter-day Saint sacred texts

An analysis of gender in Latter-day Saint Igbo texts reveals these deeply-gendered implications of Latter-day Saint theology for Igbo-speakers. In translating gender pronouns, Latter-day Saint translations of the Book of Mormon, Doctrine and Covenants, and the Pearl of Great Price into Igbo and Yoruba have followed the conventions established by colonial-era translators such as Church Missionary Society missionaries, Thomas Dennis and Samuel Ajayi Crowther. This approach yields mixed results. In Igbo, *o kpere Chineke ekpe* could be translated, alternatively, as "she prayed to God" or "he prayed to God." Amadiume argues that the genderless-ness of the Igbo language has societal ramifications: a "system of few linguistic distinctions between male and female gender also makes it possible for men and women to play some social roles" which would "carry rigid sex and gender association" in other societies. Oyewumi echoes this argument. However, Matory rejects Oyewumi out of hand: "In English, as in Yoruba, one could recite an endless list of gender-free references to people without ever proving that the language or the culture is gender-free." Gender is manifested in language in a variety of ways; language invokes roles, values, and *en toto* imaginaries that invoke gendered identity. In other words, despite the lack of gendered linguistics, gendered norms and expectations shape the lives of Nigerians.

The Igbo translation of "The Family: A Proclamation to the World" highlights the Latter-day Saint deployment of gendered duality reflected in the indigenous Igbo sense of self. A statement articulating long-standing Latter-day Saint dogmas regarding gender identity and the pre-eminence of family bonds over all other social relationships, "The Family" was written, in part, to articulate existing Latter-day Saint theology in response to philosophical tectonic shifts (e.g., the post-structural turn, the rise of gender studies), and early legal initiatives to validate same-sex partnerships in the District of Columbia (1992), Hawaii (1997), and Vermont (1999). For most Nigerians, however, these legal initiatives and philosophical shifts are irrelevant, particularly in comparison to more pressing consideration of employment, infrastructure, and resource distribution.

"The Family" in Igbo highlights an entrenched heteronormativity that reveals the intent of Latter-day Saint terminology more starkly than the Proclamation's English counterpart. The Igbo translation of the sentence: "Each is a beloved spirit son or daughter of heavenly parents" expresses gender more explicitly than its English counterpart: *obula bu nwa nwoke* (Each is a male child) *ma-o bu nwa nwanyi muo* (or female child) *a hurun'anya* (that is beloved) *nke nne na nna nke eluigwe* (of a father and mother of Heaven). Thus, while the existence of Heavenly Mother is rarely discussed, Her existence is acknowledged more directly in the Igbo text of the Proclamation on the Family. Similarly, the sentence: "Gender is an essential characteristic of individual premortal, mortal, and eternal identity and purpose." Igbo gendered norms do not leave room for the same kind of gendered individualism; thus, *gender* is translated as: "*ibu nwoke ma-obu nwanyi*" ("to be a man or woman"). "Essential" is rendered as: "*ejirimara di mkpa*" ("an important feature" or "an important way of applying knowledge"). The Igbo rendering also articulates conventional notions of male rights to preside over the home: *site ncheptua dị nsọ* ("through holy design," or as *ncheputa* may also be translated, "concept"), *nne ga-achị isi* ("fathers will govern") *n'ezi-na-ụlọ ha nile n'ihu n'anya* ("in their homes in love").

Contemporary Latter-day Saint translation of Igbo language discourse illustrates the existence of Heavenly Mother more explicitly than the English language text does. In April 2019, President Russell M. Nelson's address, "Come, Follow Me" enjoined the congregants that Jesus Christ wanted them to "return to your Heavenly Parents." The Igbo interpretation renders the language: "*nna na nne gi n'eluigwe*" ("your father and mother in heaven"). Yet, it is ironic that when this author conducted interviews in summer 2016 with Igbo Latter-day Saints in Owerri and Aba, virtually no Latter-day Saints acknowledged—or claimed knowledge of—doctrines of Heavenly Mother.

Unlike in the United States, Latter-day Saint marital praxis celebrates heteronormative assumptions currently *en vogue* in Nigeria's legal structures. With an emphasis on procreation, ancestral connectivity, inter-generational binding, and heteronormativity, Latter-day Saint ritual worship resonates with prevailing Christian discourse regarding gender and sexuality, even as the temple itself is viewed with a mixture of opportunistic admiration (e.g., higher prices in the nearby market) alongside demonic foreboding. Understanding the significance of Latter-day Saint heteronormativity requires a discussion of the heated conversations on homosexuality over the past decade.

In 2014, Nigerian President Goodluck Jonathan signed the Same-Sex Marriage Prohibition Act (SSMPA) long-planned (since 2006), making same-sex unions punishable by up to fourteen years in prison and *advocacy* for same-sex unions punishable by up to seven years. Furthermore, it bans "public show of same sex amorous relationship" or same-sex cohabitation. Additionally, the SSMPA penalizes all who associate with, participate in, or support "gay clubs, societies, and organizations." A 2015 poll indicated that 87 percent of Nigerians support this law (BBC, 2015). Jonathan's successor in the 2015 election, Muhammad Buhari, the current president, continued the stridence,: homosexuality is "abhorrent to our culture," he told the press (Tshabalala, 2015). Nigerian columnist Bisi Olawumni situated LGBTQ-affirmative voices as cryptocolonialists: those who "come in the garb of human rights advocates" are "rationalizing and glamorizing sexual perversion … The urgent task now is to put up the barricades against this invading army of cultural and moral renegades before they overwhelm us" (Olawumni, 2004). Similar sentiments have been found elsewhere. In 1998, the Zambian government declared homosexuality to be a "Norwegian conspiracy," and the now-deposed Robert Mugabe spurned it as an "immoral import." During the colonial era, British officials attributed it to urbanization, the spread of the cash economy (allowing transactions between strangers), and the spread of prison and mining cultures. Whether perceived as a colonial import or the product of industrial urbanity, homosexuality is not socially acceptable within contemporary Nigeria.

A 2009 study by Marc Epprecht and Suye Egya reveals Nigerians' on-the-ground anxieties at a rural Nigerian university. Epprecht gave a thirty-minute presentation on the history of homosexuality in Africa and Epprecht and Egya reported that the students' first response was to "establish [his] anti-imperialist credentials." Only after Epprecht assured the students that he "empathize[d] with popular Nigerian critiques" did they begin to ask questions about the nature of homosexuality. The most frequent concern reflects a national dread: students feared that homosexuality would push Nigeria, "an already morally corrupt society," to "promote even more immorality." Moreover, homosexuality was "un-African," many assumed; when Epprecht assured them that homosexuality had, in fact, *originated* in Africa, a wave of laughter and scoffs filled the room. Same-sex sexuality, many supposed, was the stuff of the depraved underground. Many resisted Epprecht's lecture initially, considering it to be Western propaganda; however, by the conclusion, they accepted his presentation as sound research, even if they expressed a "significant amount of strongly hostile or overly homophobic sentiment," and, by a majority of three to one, rejected the notion that humans have a right to choose their sexual partners (Epprecht and Egya, 2009). No statistical data has been collected on Nigerian Latter-day Saint views on homosexuality; however, while American Latter-day Saints have shifted from firm opposition to LGBTQ unions, there is no documentable reason to believe that Nigerian Latter-day Saints differ from the Nigerian national trends. The fact that Latter-day Saint activism has never called for punitive action against those engaging in homosexual acts renders it as relatively moderate in comparison to many Nigerian churches.

Only recently has a current of LGBTQ-friendly literature published *in* Nigeria begun to challenge this trend (Dunton, 1989), and that only in the slowest of steps (Reuters, 2017). In Jude Dibia's ground-breaking 2005 novel, *Walking with Shadows*, Ebele Adrian Njoko, an Igbo businessman, is discovered to be gay. The book probes Adrian's haunted childhood, filled with abuse and neglect. When the protagonist's mother (Dibia, 2005), Ada (a name given to eldest daughters, related to *umuada* referenced above) learns of her son's orientation, she becomes flummoxed, dismissing homosexuality as "so foreign, so unnatural ... Being gay was certainly not in the African culture." Depicting a vexed childhood and abusive or neglectful parents—his father beats Adrian for having stolen some money—Dibia implies throughout that Adrian's gayness can be rooted in a dysfunctional family relationship. Religious authorities make matters worse; on Adrian's brothers pleading, a Pastor (likely based on Anglican minister, Peter Akintola) in Ikeja orders his guards to hold Adrian to the ground and rip his shirt off; the Pastor proceeds to whip Adrian while uttering a fervent—and eventually, fanatical—prayer. Sectional-religious divisions explain some of the hostility toward homosexuality. Southern Nigerians frequently attempt to trace homosexuality to Northern influence; in *The Interpreters*, when a Nigerian suggests to Golder that homosexuality is a Western imposition, Golder fires back: "Do you think I know nothing of your Emirs and their little boys?" (Soyinka, 1965). In a 2016 conversation with the author in Owerri, a Latter-day Saint male said curtly: "We don't want it here." Meanwhile, Northerners impugn Southern politicians as sexual libertines, opposed to a stable social order. Northern and Southern politicians, Gaudio explains, have thus engaged "in a competitive cycle of sexual innuendo, as each camp struggles to live down the other's implicit accusations of homosexuality by stepping up its own antigay rhetoric" (Gaudio, 2013).

Polygyny, which colonial-era Nigerian had seen as a bond between themselves and Latter-day Saints, shape Western perceptions of indigenous sexualities, of both hetero- and homo-variations. Some Western LGBTQ activists such as Audre Lorde have embraced indigenous Igbo woman–woman marriages and indigenous accommodations for homosexuality (Lorde, 1984). When this author discussed Western appropriation of Igbo female–female marriage with a female Igbo Latter-day Saint ecclesiastical figure in Enugu, same-sex sexuality-oriented interpretations were met with disdain. Similarly, Amadiume has rejected efforts to use indigenous women–women marriages as cause to justify homosexual relationships in Western countries; she maintains that male-ness and female-ness should be seen as social labels, rather than as biological constructs. Amadiume rejected such efforts as all too convenient:

> Black lesbians are using such prejudiced interpretations of African situations to justify their choices of sexual alternatives which have roots and meaning in the West ... How advantageous it is for lesbian women to interpret such practices as woman-to-woman marriages as lesbian.

Such readings, Amadiume observes, "would be totally inapplicable, shocking, and offensive" to women who engaged in such marriages. Nwando Achebe has similarly rejected the sexualization of these unions, highlighting that they relate to social standing and economic relationships rather than physical intimacy. The first and second wives of a polygynous husband are, thusly, considered to be married between each other (Achebe, 2011).

Work by scholars such as J. Lorand Matory and Rudolf Gaudio have highlighted that indigenous African societies *do*, in fact, have a history of same-sex relationships, even though the terms "gay" or "lesbian"—Western in origin—do not accord well with those on-the-ground experiences. Matory submits that indigenous Yoruba society accommodated same-sex relationships, maintaining that Afro-Brazilian Candomblé practitioners have "*reinterpreted* West African metaphors of spirit possession in light of Brazilian gender categories": deploying spiritual terms such as "mounting" and "possession" in sexualized contexts (Matory, 2005). Similarly, Gaudio observes of sexuality among the *yan daudu* of Kano (Hausa men who have sexual relationships with other men): "They marry, have children." An Ibadan gay rights organization even cites *yan daudu* as evidence of homosexuality that "has been existing before the advent of the Europeans." British officials had attributed *yan daudu* to the rise of urbanization, but their self-description is more simple: "Allah made us" (Gaudio, 2009).

Against Nigerian contexts, the notion of "same-sex attraction"—language familiar in American Latter-day Saint discourse—is not a slick way of dodging the label of "gay" but rather, a representation of a local, social reality that does not appropriate the "gayness" label. In this regard, Gaudio rejects the efforts of Western LGBTQ activists who project Western constructs onto local circumstances. When asked if the *yan daudu* are "gay," Gaudio offers no simple answers. As a gay man, he once had felt he could bond with *yan daudu* over shared sexual attractions, only to find their "social life differs in important ways from gay life in the West." Indeed, "gay" is a label used almost exclusively by urban-dwellers educated in Western theories. Many of these men identify as *masu harka*: "men who do the deed"—an umbrella term for both men who adorn themselves as women publicly, as well as "civilians," or men married to women who also seek the company of other men (*fararen-hula*). *Yan daudu*, while publicly acting as women, do seek to marry women and foster children. In Gaudio's 2009 study, before the passage of the SSMPA, he rejects the label "bisexual" or "transgender" in describing any of these groups, groups with which he had personal—and often, covert—contact; additionally, "gayness" holds cachet for primarily the globally minded elite but few others; after the Nigerian parliament had passed the SSMPA, Gaudio observed: "With very few exceptions, no one in Nigeria 'comes out' as gay … In a nation of over 160 million, Nigeria's gay-rights activists could fit in one room" (Gaudio, 2013).

Columbia Arabist Joseph Massad has warned international gay rights groups that projecting the label of "gay" onto men who have sex with men in Arab countries will lead to the persecution of "poor and nonurban men who practice same sex contact and who do not *necessarily* identify as homosexual or gay" (Massad, 2007). Neville Hoad labels the combined work of international/local gay rights activists and homophobic regimes to be an "unwitting conspiracy" that threatens to bound and suppress "the diversity of desires, practices, and possibly identities" (Hoad, 2007). Concerning West African sexuality, Nii Ajen observes: "Even the young men you may have done everything with sexually will say no if you ask him if he's gay" (Ajen, 2001).

The Nigerian government has exploited the lexical ambiguity undergirding the "who is gay?" question when responding to international human rights regimes on LGBTQ rights. When the Nigerian government reported the status of LGBTQ to the United Nations, the Minister of Foreign Affairs, Ojo Madueke, engaged in a bit of wordplay: "We went out of our way to look for gay, lesbian, and transgender groups but we could not come across Nigerians with such sexuality" (Green-Simms, 2016). Given the external origins of "gay" taxonomy, it is not surprising that Nigerian authorities would say that they could not find a label that most use.

While some voices in the Nigerian diaspora such as Bree and Chimamanda Adichie have presented more LGBTQ-affirming accounts, "gayness" remains the minority label rather than the rule. While the SSMPA almost certainly plays a role in discouraging the label, neither does it resonate well with local circumstances by engaging in same-sex sexual activity. Some observers may suppose that same-sex involved individuals *would* embrace "gay" if the law had not expressly criminalized the label; however, the term's stigmatization dates back well before the implementation of the law (Adichie, 2006; 2007). Situating the popularization of LGBTQ identity and the Proclamation against the post-structural critique and the gender turn holds merit; however, it must also deal with the experience of the local. While American Latter-day Saints are increasingly seen in the minority, retrograde in the United States, their gender theology enjoys the full backing of the Nigerian government—with no signs of change in the foreseeable future. Unlike their nineteenth-century American predecessors, Nigerian Latter-day Saints can rest at ease in their interpretation of gender theology, knowing that their ideas about gender enjoy political, legal, and ecclesiastical support in every sector of influence in Nigerian society. Court battles over same-sex marriage pose no legal or cultural threat to twenty-first-century Nigerian Latter-day Saint religious freedoms.

Yet, for all their rejection of LGBTQ expressions, Latter-day Saints have not benefited from the fruits of their theology—an irony embodied nowhere better than in the Aba Temple. As a structure funded with American resources (and thus, morally suspect—can Americans be trusted to understand African sexual morality?) dedicated to the celebration of a kind of cosmic heterosexuality, the rituals resonate with indigenous gender constructs while, simultaneously, conveying a message of American wealth and infrastructure. With a road built by church officials connecting the temple to the city, the temple produces a lived environment with increased commerce as well as ritualized heteronormativity. Neither at home in the American church nor well-suited to Nigerian religiosity, Nigerian Latter-day Saints gendered praxis reveals an embrace of a distant identity, an aspiration to externality rather than locality. Both in size and structure, the Aba Temple separates Latter-day Saints from the Nigerian public far more than its celebration of cosmic heteronormativity can offer.

Conclusion

If "global Mormonism" is to adhere to its vision, global stories must be incorporated into broader narratives and discourses, on their own terms; these stories may, at times, complicate efforts to leverage African identities in American Latter-day Saint cultural politics. Indeed, scholars who claim understanding of global Latter-day Saints must engage with the African challenge to Western Mormon discourse. Nigerian Latter-day Saint gender ideology offers a cross-pollination of indigenous gendered duality with American Latter-day cosmologies of family, marriage, and fixed gendered identity. Neither an extension of colonial religiosity *nor* a manifestation of indigenous Christianity, Latter-day Saint theology presents an identity that refuses to accord to strict geo-spatial boundaries. The body of "Afro-politan" literature offers a paradigm for understanding the complexities of Latter-day Saint identity: an ideology rooted in what Eze calls a "polychromatic, polymorphic, diverse, and open" sense of self.

Nigerian Latter-day Saint institutions and thought further offer a distinct case study: a society in which Latter-day Saint gender ideology *does not* stand at odds with the existing political structures and cultural discourse. With little allowance for or toleration of same-sex attraction, with rare invocations of Heavenly Mother, and with a discourse resonant with the national gendered dynamic, Latter-day Saint theology lacks the distinctiveness in Nigerian societies that many non-African Latter-day Saint positions offer.

Nigerian Mormon gender thought represents neither coloniality nor indigeneity but rather, a convergence—in the shaping of what Latter-day Saint gender ideology would be when backed by state ideology while, simultaneously, standing on the margins of Nigerian society. Such a combination of circumstances has been unknown throughout Mormon history: nineteenth-century Mormon polygamy challenged American monogamy, and twentieth-century Mormon monogamists identified largely with American nationalism. That Nigerian Latter-day Saints resonate with Nigerian sexual mores so thoroughly and stand apart from Nigerian society makes them a compelling case study in the history of the nexus between politics and religion in Mormon life.

References

Achebe, C., 1960. *No Longer at Ease*. Portsmouth, NH: Heinemann.
Achebe, C., 1966. *A Man of the People*. New York: John Day.
Achebe, C., 1975. Chi in Igbo Cosmology. In *Morning Yet on Creation Day*. Garden City, NY: Anchor Press.
Achebe, N., 2000. *Farmers, Traders, Warriors, and Kings: Female Power and Authority in Northern Igboland, 1900–1960*. Portsmouth, NH: Heinemann.
Achebe, N., 2011. *Female King of Colonial Nigeria*. Bloomington, IN: Indiana University Press.
Adichie, C., 2006. Jumping Monkey Hill. https://granta.com/jumping-monkey-hill/ (accessed July 13, 2019).
Adichie, C., 2007. On Monday Last Week. https://granta.com/on-monday-last-week/ (accessed July 13, 2019).
Agbasiere, J., 2000. *Women in Igbo Life and Thought*. New York: Routledge.
Ajen, N., 2001. West African Homoeroticism: West African Men Who Have Sex with Men. In S.O. Murray and W. Roscoe, eds. *Boy-Wives and Female-Husbands: Studies in African Homosexualities*. New York: Palgrave Macmillan, pp. 129–40.
Amadiume, I., 1973. *Male Daughters, Female Husbands*. New York: Zed Books.
Appiah, K.A., 1992. *In My Father's House: Africa in the Philosophy of Culture*. New York: Oxford University Press.
BBC, 2015. Nigeria Poll Suggests 87% Oppose Gay Rights. www.bbc.com/news/world-africa-33325899 (accessed June 19, 2019).
Bhabha, H., 1994. *The Location of Culture*. London: Routledge.
Chukwukwere, I., 1983. Chi in Igbo Religion and Thought: The God in Every Man. *Anthropos* 78: 519–34.
Dibia, J., 2005. *Walking with Shadows*. Lagos: Blacksands Books.
Dunton, C., 1989. "Wheyting be Dat?" The Treatment of Homosexuality in African Literature. *Research in African Literatures* 20: 422–48.
Ekechi, F.K., 2010. *Pioneer, Patriot, and Nigerian Nationalist: A Biography of the Reverend M.D. Opara, 1915–1965*. Durham, NC: Carolina Academic Press.
Epprecht, M., and Egya, S., 2009. Teaching about Homosexualities to Nigerian University Students: A Report from the Field. *Gender and Education* 23: 367–83.
Eze, C., 2014. Rethinking African Culture and Identity: The Afropolitan Model. *Journal of African Cultural Studies* 26: 234–47.
The Family: A Proclamation to the World. Igbo translation, 2008 [1995]. www.churchofjesuschrist.org/manual/the-family-a-proclamation-to-the-world/the-family-a-proclamation-to-the-world?lang=ibo (accessed June 20, 2019).
Gaudio, R., 2009. *Allah Made Us: Sexual Outlaws in an Islamic African City*. Malden, MA: Wiley-Blackwell.
Gaudio, R., 2013. Dire Straights in Nigeria. *Transition: An International Review* 114: 60–69.
George, A., 2019. A Philosopher with a Plan: Reflections on Ifi Amadiume's *Male Daughters, Female Husbands*. *Journal of West African History* 3: 124–30.

Gikandi, S., 2010. Foreword: On Afropolitanism. In J. Wawrzinek and J.K.S. Makokha, eds. *Negotiating Afropolitanism: Essays on Borders and Spaces in Contemporary African Literature and Folklore*. Amsterdam: Rodopi, pp. 9–11.

Green-Simms, L., 2016. The Emergent Queer: Homosexuality and Nigerian Fiction in the 21st-Century. *Research in African Literatures* 47: 139–61.

Hoad, N., 2007. *African Intimacies: Race, Homosexuality, and Globalization*. Minneapolis, MN: University of Minnesota Press.

Hoyt, A., and Patterson, S., 2011. Mormon Masculinity: Changing Expectations in the Era of Transition from Polygamy to Monogamy, 1890–1920. Gender and History 23(1): 72–91.

Jenkins, P., 2009. Letting Go: Understanding Mormon Growth in Africa. *Journal of Mormon History* 35: 1–26.

Johnson-Odim, C., and Mba, N.E., 1997. *For Women and the Nation: Funmilayo Ransome-Kuti of Nigeria*. Urbana, IL: University of Illinois Press.

Kessler-Harris, A., 2012. Gender Identity and the Gendered Process. *Journal of American History* 99: 827–29.

Lorde, A., 1984. *Sister Outsider: Essays and Speeches*. Trumansburg, NY: Crossing.

LWR, 1897. The Marriage Question in the State of Utah, United States of America, *Lagos Weekly Record*. December 18.

Massad, J., 2007. *Desiring Arabs*. Chicago, IL: University of Chicago Press.

Matory, J.L., 2005. *Black Atlantic Religion: Tradition, Transnationalism and Matriarchy in Afro-Brazilian Candomblé*. Princeton, NJ: Princeton University Press.

Matory, J.L., 2017. J. Lorand Matory at FIU on Gender in Yoruba Culture and Religion. www.youtube.com/watch?v=PPdD6PckRVE&t=942s (accessed June 19, 2019).

Mbembe, A., 2002. African Modes of Self-Writing. *Public Culture* 14: 239–73.

Nzegwu, N.U., 2006. *Family Matters: Feminist Concepts in African Philosophy of Culture*. Albany, NY: State University of New York Press.

Obinna, A., 1978. Letter to First Presidency. Edwin Cannon Correspondence, LDS Church History Library.

Ojiaku, M.O., 1972. Early Nigerian Response to American Education. *Phylon* 33: 380–88.

Olawumni, B., 2004. Homosexuality and Its Apostles. *Vanguard* (Lagos), March 10.

Oyewumi, O., 1997. *The Invention of Women: Making an African Sense of Western Gender Discourses*. Minneapolis, MN: University of Minnesota Press.

Peterson, D., 2012. *Ethnic Patriotism and the East African Revival*. Cambridge: Cambridge University Press.

Pierce, S., 2007. Identity, Performance, and Secrecy: Gendered Life and the "Modern" in Northern Nigeria. *Feminist Studies* 33: 539–65.

Reuters, 2017. LGBTQ Acceptance Slowly Grows in Nigeria, Despite Anti-Gay Laws, 2017. www.reuters.com/article/us-nigeria-lgbt-survey/lgbt-acceptance-slowly-grows-in-nigeria-despite-anti-gay-laws-idUSKCN18C2T8 (accessed June 19, 2019).

Scott, J., 2008. Unanswered Questions. *American Historical Review* 113: 1422–29.

Soyinka, W., 1965. *The Interpreters*. London: Collins, Fontana Books.

Stevenson, R., forthcoming. The Celestial City: "Mormonism" and American Identity in Post-Independence Nigeria. *African Studies Review*.

Stevenson, R., 2014. *For the Cause of Righteousness: A Global History of Blacks and Mormonism, 1830–2013*. Salt Lake City, UT: Greg Kofford.

Tshabalala, S., 2015. Nigeria's President Was Asked about Gay Marriage in the US. His Reply: "Sodomy" Is "Abhorrent." *Quartz*. July 22. https://qz.com/460923/nigerias-president-was-asked-about-gay-marriage-in-the-us-his-reply-sodomy-is-abhorrent/ (accessed July 12, 2019).

Manuscript Sources

Jones, M., 1961. Diary, Church History Library, Salt Lake City, UT.
Lund, G., 1950. Diary, Church History Library, Salt Lake City, UT.

LeBaron Oral Histories

Chukwurah, C. June 12, 1988, in Akwa Ibom State, Nigeria.
Chukwurah, F. June 2, 1988, in Ikot Ekpene, Akwa Ibom State, Nigeria.
Ekpo, S.C. June 2, 1988, in Okom, Eket Area, Nigeria.
Elendu, R. June 10, 1988, in Port Harcourt, Nigeria.
Obinna, A. June 4, 1988, in Aboh Mbaise, Imo State, Nigeria.
Obinna, F. June 4, 1988, in Aboh Mbaise, Imo State, Nigeria.

Further reading

Achebe, C., 2001. *Things Fall Apart*. New York: Penguin.
Afigbo, A.E., 1972. *The Warrant Chiefs*. London: Longman.
Ajayi, J., 1966. *Christian Missions in Nigeria 1841–1891: The Making of a New Elite*. London: Longman.
Ayendele, E., 1966. *The Missionary Impact on Modern Nigeria*. London: Longman.
Comaroff, J., 1985. *Body of Power, Spirit of Resistance: The Culture and History of a South African People*. Chicago, IL: University of Chicago Press.
Davis, K., Evans, M., and Lorber, J., 2006. *Handbook of Gender and Women's Studies*. New York: Sage.
Epprecht, M., 2008. *Heterosexual Africa? The History of an Idea from the Age of Exploration to the Age of AIDS*. Athens, OH: Ohio University Press.
Marshall, R., 2009. *Political Spiritualities: The Pentecostal Revolution in Nigeria*. Chicago, IL: University of Chicago Press.
Soyinka, W., 1986. Nobel Lecture. In H. Bloom, ed., 2010. *Chinua Achebe's Things Fall Apart*. New York: Bloom's Literary Criticism.
Sundkler, B., 1961. *Bantu Prophets in South Africa*. Cambridge: James Clarke and Co.
Sweet, J., 1996. Male Homosexuality and Spiritism in the African Diaspora. *Journal of the History of Sexuality* 7: 184–202.
Turner, H.W, 1967. *History of an African Independent Church: The Church of the Lord*, 2 vols. London: Oxford University Press.
Zabus, C., 2013. *Out in Africa: Same-Sex Desire in Sub-Saharan Literatures and Cultures*. London: James Currey.

PART IV

Theological approaches

33
SCRIPTURE AND GENDER

Joseph M. Spencer

Despite growing interest in gender in the Latter-day Saint context, Latter-day Saint scripture has received strikingly little gender-critical attention. A recent anthology of Latter-day Saint feminist writings, to illustrate, contains just three essays (out of sixty-two anthologized works) focused on scripture (see Brooks, Steenblik, and Wheelwright, 2016). The relative dearth of attention to scripture in this context has two facets. On the one hand, uniquely Latter-day Saint scripture—the Book of Mormon, the Doctrine and Covenants, and the Pearl of Great Price—has certainly received little gender-critical attention, whether from intellectually inclined believers or from academics more generally. On the other hand, scripture that Latter-day Saints share with the larger Christian world—the Christian Bible's two testaments—has received little gender-critical attention specifically from scholars and intellectuals working in and around the Latter-day Saint context (despite the existence of thriving relevant fields in biblical hermeneutics). Consequently, only the barest outlines of serious engagement with gender in Restoration scripture have so far been sketched. Yet, despite the underdeveloped state of the field, the scripture's textual resources are rich for productive study, as recent contributions attest, and foundational studies exist to orient future work.

In the following, I attempt to survey two things at once, before providing a theological assessment from my own perspective. I aim first to outline the presentation of gender in Latter-day Saint scripture, reviewing less flattering and less comfortable aspects of scripture along with aspects that lend themselves to a redemptive hermeneutic. Second, along the way, I mean to give a general impression of the current state of the field of gendered hermeneutics concerning Latter-day Saint scripture, focusing on work undertaken in the context of America's so-called second and third waves of feminism. Because the literature on gender in Latter-day Saint scripture—both conservative and liberal—focuses almost exclusively on women, I similarly narrow my focus here. In my concluding reflections, however, I not only sketch a theological proposal regarding scripture and gender, I gesture toward particularly underdeveloped models for gender-critical study in the context of Latter-day Saint scripture studies.

The Book of Mormon

Many have noted that the Book of Mormon, chief among uniquely Latter-day Saint volumes of scripture, is a book about men. In recounting the histories of two ancient New World civilizations, histories stretching over centuries, it seldom discusses women. Only three female characters unique to the volume receive names, and none of these three hails from among the book's protagonists, the Nephites. Certain female characters do receive more substantial roles, but as even believing defenders of the book admit, it contains "no stories told in as great detail as those of Ruth and Esther" in the Bible (Hurd, 1987, p. ix). In Book of Mormon narratives, women are "primarily accessories to men, dependent upon them not only for survival but also for identity, which is presented as a matter of relationship to a man, usefulness to a man, or use by men" (Bennion, 1990, p. 171). In fact, the "most frequently recorded actions" of women in the Book of Mormon are arguably "worrying for their families in peril or mourning for their families after disaster" (Charles, 1987, p. 50). With few exceptions, female characters hover in the story's background, mostly emerging only when the narrators report their abuse. As the text unfolds, women are mistreated by their sexually licentious husbands, kidnapped by power-hungry priests, reduced to prostitution, forced into oppressive marriages, placed in physical danger in defense of their oppressors, beaten by men of passion, made prisoners and put to death, burned alive for their faith, raped, tortured, and even cannibalized (see Pearson, 1996, p. 38).

One naturally sees how the textual data have spurred feminist critique, sometimes hoping to make devotional sense of this disturbing portrayal (see Bennion, 1990; Williams, 2002), and sometimes hoping to demonstrate that the book is misogynist or at least unwelcoming to female readers (see Anderson, 1994; Pearson, 1996). Yet, despite the obvious problem regarding women in the Book of Mormon, there are important countervailing tendencies in the volume as well. As one scholar notes, for instance, Book of Mormon texts are

> remarkable both for what they say and also for what they do not say. There is no suggestion that women are to be forever subservient to men because of Eve's choice in Eden … There is no statement that women are responsible for the sexual misconduct of men … There is no proclamation that gender determines communication from God, access to God, or inheritance in God's kingdom.
>
> *(Bennion, 1990, p. 172)*

In the context of Christian theological history, the absence in the Book of Mormon of such theologically misogynistic claims is noteworthy. Still more suggestively, however, another reader proposes that "the anti-female bias evident among the Nephites" may be less a simple feature of the storyline than something readers are meant to identify among "the numerous causes of [the Nephites'] downfall" (Pearson, 1996, p. 38). It may be that patterns of when and how women appear in the Book of Mormon support a more complex theology.

There is textual evidence for this last idea. Early in the volume, the prophet Jacob warns Nephites that they will be destroyed by their enemies, the Lamanites, if Nephite men do not repent of their sexual mistreatment of women: "Except ye shall repent, the land is cursed for your sakes; and the Lamanites, which are not filthy like unto you … shall scourge you even unto destruction" (Skousen, 2009, p. 161 [Jacob 3:3]). Further, Jacob predicts the survival of the Lamanites in the end, tying this promise to relative egalitarian gender relations among them: "Because of this observance in [rejecting sexual opportunism that victimizes women], the Lord God will not destroy them but will be merciful unto them, and one day they shall become a blessed people" (Skousen, 2009, p. 161 [Jacob 3:6]; see Hurd, 1987, p. 14). As if this provided a key to the subsequent history, women suffer throughout the Book of Mormon because of the actions of Nephite men, while the record's few glimpses of Lamanite society reveal relative gender equality and recount conspicuous stories of female agency. This leads some readers to claim that "as striking as the relatively infrequent mention of specific women in Mormon's accounts is the circumstance that many of the women he does mention are Lamanites." Further, readers may subtly be expected to suspect that Mormon, the volume's Nephite author-editor, was himself "impressed by the results of this contrast between his own culture and that of the Lamanites" (Christensen and Christensen, 1998, pp. 36–37). It is remarkable that the Book of Mormon's only speech from a Lamanite prophet pays particular attention to the suffering of Nephite women (see Berkey and Spencer, 2019). In the interstices of the narrative, it seems, are strategic resources for constructing an immanent critique of the volume's apparent androcentrism along lines sketched by the volume itself (see also Hardy, 2010, pp. 16–23). Further, such a critique, because it ties gender relations to political struggles between racially distinct peoples (the Nephites are portrayed as light-skinned, the Lamanites as dark-skinned), amounts to a redemptive hermeneutic that recognizes ways that race and gender intersect. Lamanite women may prove to be the Book of Mormon's subtly proffered heroes.

Can gender-driven interpretation of the Book of Mormon move beyond strictly feminist concerns? Certainly, it provides textual data for studies in masculinity. Yet only quite recently has anyone asked about how the volume understands or presents notions of masculinity (see Easton-Flake, 2019). The possibility of such work should have been obvious; the book first appeared in English during a major transformation of American understandings of masculinity, and early readers would likely have been attuned to gender dynamics in the volume (see Rotundo, 1993, pp. 10–30). It is to be hoped that more work on Book of Mormon masculinity is forthcoming. As for other approaches, moving beyond studies of women and men traditionally understood, little is likely to come from Book of Mormon studies, simply for lack of material. The Book of Mormon arguably assumes a gender binary. Further, the volume expresses strikingly little interest in sexuality, assuming but seldom thematizing traditional family structures. It is true that it occasionally mentions polygynous marital arrangements, as well as prostitution and rape, but these are all condemned as "grosser crimes" for which men are responsible (Skousen, 2009, p. 159 [Jacob 2:23]). Nonetheless, two passages regarding extramarital (or extra-monogamous) relations deserve at least brief notice. First, a particularly contentious passage appears to offer an exception clause for the practice of polygyny (see Jacob 2:30), although different Restoration traditions adhering to the Book of Mormon have interpreted the passage differently (see Ludlow, 1976, p. 159; and Hartshorn, 1964, p. 159). Second, the wording of a reference to rape late in the volume (see Moroni 9:9) lends itself to a problematic construal of chastity (see Kerr, 2017). On the whole, however, the Book of Mormon condemns what few non-traditional sexual relationships it mentions.

The Bible

Because the vast majority of believers date the Book of Mormon's origins to antiquity, when gender parity was largely unimaginable, interpreters occasionally argue that "the wonder is not that there is so little about women in the Book of Mormon but that there is so much, given the times and traditions" (Bennion, 1990, p. 177; see also Fronk, 2000, p. 6). But such arguments appear problematic in light of the fact that, "compared to the Bible, which mentions nearly 200 women by name, references to women in latter-day scripture are sparse" (Anderson, 1994, p. 186). As one interpreter points out, "in the Old Testament, 'he' and 'his' appear six-and-a-half times more often than do 'she' and 'her,'" while "in the Book of Mormon, the masculine pronouns appear, on average, thirty-five times more often than do the feminine ones" (Pearson, 1996, p. 35). In fact, the Hebrew Bible documents struggles by women against patriarchal structures and presuppositions (see LaCocque, 1990), and evidence suggests that women played a more central role in early Christianity than is often assumed (see Schüssler Fiorenza, 1983). In addition, as burgeoning biblical disciplines focused on non-binary conceptions of gender make clear (see Goss and West, 2000), the Bible is replete with narratives that are more obviously invested in the complexity of gender than those in uniquely Latter-day Saint scripture. Whatever this implies for the Book of Mormon, it suggests a ready source for reflection on gender in the Bible, which Latter-day Saints accept as canon. This is no place for a survey of gender criticism and the Bible, but places where Latter-day Saints might offer unique approaches to biblical texts deserve notice.

Biblical texts find their way into every volume of uniquely Latter-day Saint scripture through quotations and allusions, but they find their way most directly into the Pearl of Great Price. The latter is a late addition to the canon that contains, among other things, retellings of stories from Genesis. In the Book of Abraham, for instance, the fraught story of the biblical patriarch is recast in ways that emphasize gender. First, an account of Egyptian origins foreign to the Bible contrasts authorized and unauthorized priestly succession by distinguishing patrilineal priestly succession from usurped priestly succession tied to a woman whose name mysteriously "signifies, that which is forbidden" (Hauglid, 2010, p. 28 [Abraham 1:23]). Because these texts played a role in later justifications for withholding priesthood authority and temple blessings from believers of African descent (see throughout Harris and Bringhurst, 2015), here gender questions again intersect with racial concerns. Second, the Book of Abraham recasts the story of Abraham pleading with his wife to pose as his sister in Egypt. Because this portion of the book was reportedly dictated during 1842 while Joseph Smith wrestled with keeping his polygynous marriages secret (see Hauglid, 2020; cf., however, Muhlestein and Hansen, 2016), some critical interpreters find it significant that the story makes it God's idea (rather than Abraham's) to ask Sarah to dissimulate their marriage (see Staker, 1999). Finally, because, in explanations of vignettes from the papyri that spurred the Book of Abraham's production, Joseph Smith identified two Egyptian female figures as men, the book has raised interesting historical and theological questions about the stability of gender identities (see Nibley, 2000, pp. 425–42).

The Book of Abraham is especially complex, amplifying gendered concerns from within the biblical text and introducing new gendered (and intersectional) concerns in connection with biblical figures. Less fraught and more encouraging are alterations Smith made to the biblical text in what he called his "New Translation" of the Bible—small excerpts of which appear in the Pearl of Great Price. The New Translation is a large-scale revision of the English Bible, at least parts of which purport to restore lost texts (see Matthews, 1985, pp. 233–53). Generally, excerpts contained in the Pearl of Great Price do not significantly differ from their biblical counterparts on gender. In one noteworthy passage, however, Eve speaks about her role in Eden. "Were it not for our transgression," she tells Adam, "we should never had seed & should never had known good & evil & the joy of our redemption & the eternal life which God giveth unto all the obediant" (Faulring, Jackson, and Matthews, 2004, p. 93 [Moses 5:11]). This celebratory exclamation, combined with a Book of Mormon passage claiming that Adam and Eve "would have had no children" without their transgression (Skousen, 2009, p. 80 [2 Nephi 2:23]), grounds a strikingly positive assessment of Eve in the Latter-day Saint tradition (see Rockwood, 1987). These passages have also shaped a recent popular theology, conservatively feminist in orientation, making Eve's choice to eat Eden's forbidden fruit a knowing and brave decision in line with God's implicit but undisclosed intentions (see Campbell, 2010; and Cassler, 2016; for a literary-critical response, see Smith, 2017).

Much of Smith's New Translation, especially what lies outside the Pearl of Great Price, remains to be studied in depth. A recent study, however, shows that some of Smith's work on the Bible suggests interest in its portrayal of women. On ten occasions in just the revisions made to the Gospel of Mark, the New Translation "highlights the role of women or makes a passage gender neutral" in women's favor (Smith, 2015, p. 7). The most interesting of these is the replacement in Mark 15:21 of "Alexander," the child of Simon who carried Jesus' cross, with "Alexandria" (see Smith, 2015, p. 9; for the text, see Faulring, Jackson, and Matthews, 2004, p. 356). In a different vein, it has long been noted that Joseph Smith re-rendered 1 Corinthians 7, limiting the scope of Paul's recommendations regarding extreme chastity and affirming marital sexuality (see Sperry, 1955, pp. 130–32; for the full text, see Faulring, Jackson, and Matthews, 2004, pp. 500–505). Although the New Translation remains an understudied text, it lends itself to a specifically Latter-day Saint hermeneutic of the Bible. Given the volume of gender-critical studies on biblical texts, study of Smith's direct interactions with biblical texts about gender—in the uncanonized manuscripts of his New Translation or in canonized scripture that interacts with gender-rich biblical texts—promises to bear fruit. Present indications are that it promises to bear theologically satisfying fruit.

Beyond biblical interaction within uniquely Restoration scripture, there is important work undertaken by Latter-day Saint scholars on the biblical text itself in ways relevant to gender. Some such work addresses itself to the academy, expressing no obvious interest in Latter-day Saint concerns (although it draws attention from Latter-day Saints with intellectual leanings). Latter-day Saint biblical scholar David Bokovoy, for example, has published in the journal *Vetus Testamentum* an important essay analyzing the sexually complex story of the Garden of Eden (see Bokovoy, 2013). Similarly, Latter-day Saint scholar of early Christianity Taylor Petrey has published with Routledge his book *Resurrecting Parts*, a study of early Christian conceptions of sexuality and sexual difference (see Petrey, 2015). Less concerned with addressing the academy are other scholars working on the biblical text, attuned to questions of gender but writing for lay Latter-day Saints. Exemplary are two well-selling books on women in the Bible's two testaments by Camille Fronk Olsen (see Olsen, 2009; 2014). Further from the mainstream, yet still conservative in orientation, are occasional treatments of historical traces of female deity worship in the Hebrew Bible—often indebted to the marginal but inventive biblical scholar Margaret Barker (see, for example, Petersen, 2013). At the progressive pole are efforts like those of Cory Crawford to outline the Bible's gender-driven struggle for authority; Crawford explicitly argues that the Bible provides precedent for Latter-day Saint feminists seeking to change current institutional positions on women and authority (see Crawford, 2015; for an activist counterpoint, see Anderson, 1994). Positioned between the extremes are imaginative explorations of biblical women's voices gathered by Julie Smith, highlighting a range of hermeneutic possibilities (see Smith, 2016).

Given the literary richness of the Bible, as well as its wide readership and the many fields established for its critical study, it will remain—and likely become more central as—a site for gender-focused study in the Latter-day Saint scriptural context. Its complexity, providing readier grist for the interpretive mill, lends itself to a gendered hermeneutic.

The Doctrine and Covenants

Less germane to gender critique than either the Book of Mormon or the Bible is the collection of Joseph Smith's revelations known as the Doctrine and Covenants. Melodie Moench Charles explains the reason: "Because the Doctrine and Covenants had primarily one author (God mediated through the prophet, Joseph Smith), one genre (revelation), and for the most part a very limited span of time (about fifteen years), it has almost none of the diversity apparent" elsewhere in Restoration scripture (Charles, 1987, p. 45). Only one revelation is addressed to a woman—Section 25, to Emma Smith (Joseph Smith's wife)—and few others refer to women specifically or by name. Revelations addressed to men occasionally refer to their families, and commandments addressed to the whole Church sometimes include instruction for or regarding women (the care of widows, for example). In at least one case, specific application of a commandment to women seems to have been revealed only because Church members raised questions about the vagueness of an earlier commandment (see Charles, 1987, pp. 45–46; along with Underwood, 2008; the texts appear in MacKay et al., 2013, pp. 245–56, 264–67; and Jensen, Turley, and Lorimer, 2011, pp. 430–35). Nonetheless, "the Doctrine and Covenants contains no historical narratives showing women acting independently to balance against" standard or fluctuating nineteenth-century assumptions about gender roles (Charles, 1987, p. 45). Of course, much can be and has been read into the one revelation addressed to a woman—more moderately in recent decades than before (see Robinson and Garrett, 2000, pp. 168–73; and Newell and Avery, 1984, pp. 33–34). Further, there is potentially much to say about a revelation given partially in response to the Shaker idea that (as the text puts it) "the son of man cometh ... in the form of a woman" (MacKay et al., 2013, p. 302 [D&C 49:22]; for some orientation, see Foster, 1991). But there are relatively few places in the Doctrine and Covenants to which a feminist reading can turn. And serious work on how the Doctrine and Covenants conceives of masculinity has yet to begin, lacking even a preliminary study to orient further research.

Of course, one particularly potent text in the Doctrine and Covenants has often drawn the attention of gender critique: Joseph Smith's last-recorded revelation, concerning plural marriage (Section 132). This revelation was canonized only in 1876, more than three decades after the prophet's death and more than two decades after the practice of polygamy within the Church had become public knowledge. Although it has been controversial from the beginning, it has been controversial for different reasons at different times in the Church's history—at first simply because of the way it questioned establishment monogamy (see Foster, 1984), but more recently for overtly feminist reasons. Today it is contentious enough that one can find appeals for its removal from the canon (see Pearson, 2016, pp. 189–94) or, more moderately and in light of its being the source for quintessentially Latter-day Saint teachings about eternal marriage, appeals for a modern revision (see Smith, 2018, pp. 179–85). Such appeals are unlikely to gain favor with most Latter-day Saints, however. They appear alongside historical studies of polygamy that underscore the complexity of the abandoned institution and recommend resisting unilateral condemnations of the practice (see, for instance, Ulrich, 2017). And while more traditional treatments of the revelation concede that it is "potentially scandalous," these attempt to place it in historical context and salve the feelings of those offended by its "hard doctrine" by showing how it might be read as "the highest and deepest of Joseph's revelations" (Harper, 2008, pp. 480, 487, 489). Yet criticisms of the revelation express concern over more than its endorsement of polygyny, focusing also on its apparent elimination of female agency in plural marriage and the ostensibly harsh way the revelation speaks of Emma Smith (see Smith, 2018, pp. 141–51, 173–77). Those wishing to defend this particular revelation have much work to do.

Only recently has a serious textual study of Section 132 finally appeared in print (see Smith, 2018), and no detailed textual study of Section 25 has yet appeared. As with so much of the Doctrine and Covenants, historians who might provide close analysis of the canonical text have primarily focused on the history behind the scripture. Thus, although the study of Latter-day Saint women's history is a major focus in the field at present, it has contributed little to the study of gender-relevant texts in the Doctrine and Covenants. Given the paucity of references to women in the text and the abundance of documentary sources for extra-scriptural women's history, this situation is more than understandable. And anyway, scholarly work has yielded important reception-historical studies of the two revelations of most interest to feminists. Most work on the history of polygamy can be seen as contributing to the reception history of Joseph

Smith's revelation on plural marriage, and most histories of the subject give at least a few pages to analyzing key aspects of the text. As for the revelation to Emma Smith, probing and direct reception-historical work on it has already been undertaken. In the most remarkable analysis of the revelation to date, Carol Cornwall Madsen locates its significance in reconstructable historical events outside the text of the revelation. These include not only events and circumstances straightforwardly referred to in the text, but also events and circumstances occurring more than a decade after the original production of the text—like the original organization of the Church's women's association (the Relief Society). That event clearly changed and shaped the meaning and reception of the revelation in Latter-day Saint history (see Madsen, 2004). In at least this case, then, extra-scriptural interest in women's history has helped to clarify the scriptural text addressed to a woman in a forceful way. And the hermeneutic possibilities of the text of the revelation to Emma Smith seem real and redemptive, adaptable to changing circumstances for women.

In the end, however, the Doctrine and Covenants arguably has the least to offer a gender-critical reading of Restoration scripture. Not only does it have far less than the Bible and less even than the Book of Mormon to say about women, much of what it does have to say concerns one of the most controversial and uncomfortable topics in Latter-day Saint history (a topic, however, of obvious interest to sexuality studies). Even for a gendered hermeneutic interested in questions of masculinity, the Doctrine and Covenants arguably offers less than its companion volumes in the canon. Although much of it was originally addressed to men, the genre of revelation makes for less robust portrayals of the men involved and provides fewer resources for the interpreter.

Theological possibilities

The Latter-day Saint scriptural canon faces real challenges after political changes surrounding gender and sexuality during the twentieth century. Uniquely Latter-day Saint volumes of scripture straightforwardly assume a traditional gender binary, and they generally seem to endorse the normality—if not the normativity—of traditional patriarchy. This has led some to endorse a strong historicist program of interpretation, that is, a program of historical-critical interpretation that insists on the irrelevance of scripture to current institutional practice. As Lynn Matthews Anderson sums up this view,

> so long as Latter-day Saints continue to believe that women are included in our sacred stories when they are not … we perpetuate the larger myth that all the answers to contemporary questions pertaining to women can be found in our scriptures. This fundamental flaw in the basis for traditional and contemporary interpretation of LDS scripture prevents us from seeking new revelation and answers to old problems.
> (Anderson, 1994, p. 192; see also Petrey, 2020)

Such a view explicitly sets itself against any hermeneutic that would seek "to recover women's untold stories in sacred writ," preferring instead to criticize scriptural texts "that appear out of harmony with the life and mission of Jesus" (Anderson, 1994, pp. 194, 197). This viewpoint thus forecloses the alternative represented by Camille Fronk Olsen, also historicizing but in another fashion. Olsen insists that, "while cultural lenses may cloud the clarity and hide the deeper meaning of truth, to those willing to listen, God speaks through prophets" in the scriptures; this occurs when one uses historical sources to read scripture "through the eyes of the women" who largely go unmentioned in the text (Fronk, 2000, pp. 15, 5; see also Bennion,

1990). (It also arguably forecloses the program of a feminist midrash defended by Robert Rees, an inventive rewriting of scriptural stories that would recast the stories in line with twenty-first-century sensibilities; see Rees, 2011.)

These opposing interpretive programs both seem to me to overlook real textual possibilities. One might say, in fact, that they give up on the texts too quickly, or that they express too little confidence in the versatility of scripture. In essence, the two programs share a historical or historicist viewpoint that rapidly passes over what it means for scripture to be scripture. In the final few pages of this essay, therefore, I wish to sketch the possibility of a more strictly *scriptural* hermeneutic of gender, a gender-driven reading of Restoration scripture that focuses on what scripture, *as* scripture, might have to say about gender, and in a theologically productive way. The foregoing survey of the presentation of gender in the Latter-day Saint scriptural canon already provides, in faint outline, the basic lineaments of such a reading.

In his brilliant (but certainly still controversial) exposition of what it means to read scripture as scripture, Brevard Childs emphasizes the role that the notions of canon and especially of canonical shape must play. "The concern with canon," he explains, "resists the assumption that every biblical text has first to be filtered through a set historical critical mesh before one can even start the task of interpretation," but it also "seeks to challenge the interpreter to look closely at the biblical text in its received form and then critically to discern its function for a community of faith" (Childs, 1979, p. 83). The point here is to recognize the ways in which scripture's very shape—its large-scale structures, its volume-wide patterns, the tensions within it—help "to chart the boundaries within which the exegetical task is to be carried out" (Childs, 1979, p. 83). It is sadly true that the larger canonical shape of each volume of Restoration scripture has received strikingly little critical attention. Yet it is also true that even a preliminary investigation suggests the possibility of a gendered hermeneutic that points in promising directions.

The Book of Mormon provides a case in point. As already noted, prophetic voices within the book diagnose the volume's larger gender problem, identifying the Nephite men's tendency toward abuses of women and contrasting it with the relative gender parity that characterizes Lamanite society. The same prophetic voices further connect this contrast between gender relations in the Book of Mormon's racially distinguished peoples to the fact that the group who exhibits relative gender parity will survive to receive the full blessings of the gospel of Jesus Christ. If one takes these passages as providing a hermeneutic lens for the whole of the Book of Mormon, the troubling textual data read differently than they otherwise might. The appalling absence of female characters in the Nephite narrative can be read as part of the book's message, all the damning details adding up to a volume-level indictment of the book's supposed protagonists. Such a hermeneutic highlights the possibility that the Book of Mormon does not so much embody misogyny as portray it—and, however subtly, condemn it explicitly. In this way, as Jared Hickman has similarly argued with respect to race (rather than to gender), the Book of Mormon can be understood as outlining a metacritique of patriarchy, unraveling the orthodox patriarchal views of the Nephites that the book nonetheless *seems* to espouse (see Hickman, 2014). It is certainly significant that the Book of Mormon's eponymous author-editor himself gives the name of only one woman in the whole of the narrative he constructs: the Lamanite servant-woman Abish. This character might be read as the volume's real hero, triply other with respect to the volume's *apparent* heroes, the Nephites, because she is a woman, bears a "skin of blackness," and hails from the slave class (Skousen, 2009, p. 90 [2 Nephi 5:21]). Her actions—often recognized as constituting "the most powerful story involving a Book of Mormon woman" (Anderson, 1994, p. 187)—unmistakably mark the key turning point in the Book of Mormon's larger narrative. She is herself the first Lamanite convert to Christ, and she gathers a large multitude that becomes the first Lamanite people to convert to Christ. From there, the volume's promises to the Lamanite remnant of Israel begin to be fulfilled—promises that stretch beyond the story internal to the Book of Mormon, reaching into the modern context to which the volume is meant to speak (see Skousen, 2009, p. 3 [Book of Mormon title page]).

Similar hermeneutical programs might be spelled out for the other volumes of Latter-day Saint scripture, and for Joseph Smith's revision of the Bible in the New Translation. The revelation to Emma Smith in the Doctrine and Covenants speaks of God's historical dealings with women as wisely waiting for "a time to come" (MacKay et al., 2013, p. 162 [D&C 25:4]), and even the fraught texts of the Book of Abraham have given rise to a feminist hermeneutic that deserves more attention than it has yet received (see Nibley, 2000, pp. 343–81). Of course, it might be objected that all these scriptures—at the very least because they originated in pre-twentieth-century contexts—face "serious credibility issues by continuing to hold to precritical assumptions about sexual difference" (Petrey, 2011, p. 129). But the paths of theological inquiry cannot be decided in advance (especially without a metaethical defense). With an eye to gender concerns precisely, Adam Miller has proposed a helpful and illustrative thought experiment, a kind of hermeneutic with an eye to the future and textual possibility. In 1995, the Church issued "The Family: A Proclamation to the World," a document that insists on both irreducible sexual difference and irreducible gender equality. Miller imagines the situation in the year 2095, a hundred years after the Proclamation's first appearance. He imagines that the Proclamation has at that point "been officially canonized for more than sixty years" and so "has been enshrined as the cornerstone of a Mormon account of life in Christ." But, as many might predict, the same Proclamation at that point is "framed by a century of social and political upheaval" and "the document's original sense" is "increasingly obscure." And so Miller imagines a "generation of senior church leaders—all born decades after the proclamation's introduction and educated in a world where the predicted sea change in sexual mores and family structures was a fait accompli." He imagines them asking what would by then be old questions, but they ask them in a new way.

> What is gender? What does it mean to claim that sexual difference is eternal? How can men and women have gendered responsibilities and, yet, act as "equal partners"? In short, senior leaders are forced to ask, What is sexual difference, and what is sexual equality?

In my view, what is essential is Miller's insistence that any substantive answers to these questions would have to be "actively constructed rather than passively assumed"—that is, reading the Proclamation well requires as much rigor and imagination as reading scripture, and assumptions about what the Proclamation must mean are misplaced (Miller, 2017, p. 109). Theology inventively interacts with tradition and proposes possibilities framed by faith. Its future cannot be decided by worries about socially-determined credibility issues tied to a specific moment in history.

Largely, then, the theological possibilities regarding the Latter-day Saint scriptural presentation of gender remain to be explored in earnest. What emerges will depend on the care and fidelity with which scripture is read, as well as the honesty and imagination of the readers.

References

Anderson, L.M., 1994. Toward a Feminist Interpretation of Latter-day Scripture. *Dialogue: A Journal of Mormon Thought* 27(2): 185–203.

Bennion, F.R., 1990. Women and the Book of Mormon: Tradition and Revelation. In M. Cornwall and S. Howe, eds. *Women of Wisdom and Knowledge: Talks Selected from the BYU Women's Conferences*. Salt Lake City, UT: Deseret Book, pp. 169–78.

Berkey, K.M. and Spencer, J.M., 2019. "Great Cause to Mourn": The Complexity of *The Book of Mormon*'s Presentation of Gender and Race. In E. Fenton and J. Hickman, eds. *Americanist Approaches to the Book of Mormon*. New York: Oxford University Press, pp. 298–320.

Bokovoy, D.E., 2013. Did Eve Acquire, Create, or Procreate with Yahweh? A Grammatical and Contextual Reassessment of הנק in Genesis 4:1. *Vetus Testamentum* 63: 1–17.

Brooks, J., Steenblik, R.H., and Wheelwright, H. eds., 2016. *Mormon Feminism: Essential Writings*. New York: Oxford University Press.

Campbell, B., 2010. *Eve and the Choice Made in Eden*. Salt Lake City, UT: Deseret Book.

Cassler, V.H., 2016. The Two Trees. In J. Brooks, R.H. Steenblik, and H. Wheelwright, eds. *Mormon Feminism: Essential Writings*. New York: Oxford University Press, pp. 247–52.

Charles, M.M., 1987. Precedents for Mormon Women from Scriptures. In M.U. Beecher and L.F. Anderson, eds. *Sisters in Spirit: Mormon Women in Historical and Cultural Perspective*. Urbana and Chicago, IL: University of Illinois Press, pp. 37–63.

Childs, B.S., 1979. *Introduction to the Old Testament as Scripture*. Philadelphia, PA: Fortress Press.

Christensen, K., and Christensen, S., 1998. Nephite Feminism Revisited: Thoughts on Carol Lynn Pearson's View of Women in the Book of Mormon. *FARMS Review of Books* 10(2): 9–61.

Crawford, C., 2015. The Struggle for Female Authority in Biblical and Mormon Theology. *Dialogue: A Journal of Mormon Thought* 48(2): 1–66.

Easton-Flake, A., 2019. "Arise from the Dust, My Sons, and Be Men": Masculinity in the Book of Mormon. In E. Fenton and J. Hickman, eds. *Americanist Approaches to the Book of Mormon*. New York: Oxford University Press, pp. 362–90.

Faulring, S.H., Jackson, K.P., and Matthews, R.J. eds., 2004. *Joseph Smith's New Translation of the Bible: Original Manuscripts*. Provo, UT: BYU Religious Studies Center.

Foster, L., 1984. *Religion and Sexuality: The Shakers, the Mormons, and the Oneida Community*. Urbana and Chicago, IL: University of Illinois Press.

Foster, L., 1991. *Women, Family, and Utopia: Communal Experiments of the Shakers, the Oneida Community, and the Mormons*. Syracuse, NY: Syracuse University Press.

Fronk, C., 2000. Desert Epiphany: Sariah and the Women in 1 Nephi. *Journal of Book of Mormon Studies* 9(2): 4–15, 80.

Goss, R.E., and West, M. eds., 2000. *Take Back the Word: A Queer Reading of the Bible*. Cleveland, OH: Pilgrim Press.

Hardy, G., 2010. *Understanding the Book of Mormon: A Reader's Guide*. New York: Oxford University Press.

Harper, S.C., 2008. *Making Sense of the Doctrine and Covenants: A Guided Tour through Modern Revelations*. Salt Lake City, UT: Deseret Book.

Harris, M.L., and Bringhurst, N.G., 2015. *The Mormon Church and Blacks: A Documentary History*. Urbana, Chicago, and Springfield, IL: University of Illinois Press.

Hartshorn, C.B., 1964. *A Commentary on the Book of Mormon*. Independence, MO: Herald Publishing House.

Hauglid, B.M., 2010. *A Textual History of the Book of Abraham: Manuscripts and Editions*. Provo, UT: Neal A. Maxwell Institute.

Hauglid, B.M., 2020. "Translating an Alphabet to the Book of Abraham": Joseph Smith's Study of the Egyptian Language and His Translation of the Book of Abraham. In M. Ashurst-McGee, B.M. Hauglid, and H.H. MacKay, eds. *Producing Ancient Scripture: Joseph Smith's Translation Projects in the Development of Mormon Christianity*. Salt Lake City, UT: University of Utah Press, pp. 363–89.

Hickman, J., 2014. The Book of Mormon as Amerindian Apocalypse. *American Literature* 86(3): 429–61.

Hurd, J.W., 1987. *Our Sisters in the Latter-day Scriptures*. Salt Lake City, UT: Deseret Book.

Jensen, R.S., Turley, R.E., and Lorimer, R.M. eds., 2011. *The Joseph Smith Papers, Revelations and Translations*, vol. 2: *Published Revelations*. Salt Lake City, UT: Church Historian's Press.

Kerr, J.A., 2017. "Virtue" in Moroni 9:9. *Journal of Book of Mormon Studies* 26: 260–65.

LaCocque, A., 1990. *The Feminine Unconventional: Four Subversive Figures in Israel's Tradition*. Minneapolis, MN: Fortress Press.

Ludlow, D.H., 1976. *A Companion to Your Study of the Book of Mormon*. Salt Lake City, UT: Deseret Book.

MacKay, M.H. et al. eds., 2013. *The Joseph Smith Papers, Documents*, vol. 1: *July 1828–June 1831*. Salt Lake City, UT: Church Historian's Press.
Madsen, C.C., 2004. The "Elect Lady" Revelation (D&C 25): Its Historical and Doctrinal Context. In C.K. Manscill, ed. *Sperry Symposium Classics: The Doctrine and Covenants*. Provo, UT: BYU Religious Studies Center, pp. 117–32.
Matthews, R.J., 1985. *"A Plainer Translation": Joseph Smith's Translation of the Bible, A History and Commentary*. Provo, UT: Brigham Young University Press.
Miller, A.S., 2017. Christo-Fiction, Mormon Philosophy, and the Virtual Body of Christ. In S.J. Fluhman, K. Flake, and J. Woodworth, eds. *To Be Learned Is Good: Essays on Faith and Scholarship in Honor of Richard Lyman Bushman*. Provo, UT: Neal A. Maxwell Institute, pp. 101–10.
Muhlestein, K., and Hansen, M., 2016. "The Work of Translating": The Book of Abraham's Translation Chronology. In J.S. Fluhman and B.L. Top, eds. *Let Us Reason Together: Essays in Honor of the Life's Work of Robert L. Millet*. Salt Lake City and Provo, UT: Deseret Book, BYU Religious Studies Center, and Neal A. Maxwell Institute, pp. 139–62.
Newell, L.K., and Avery, V.T., 1984. *Mormon Enigma: Emma Hale Smith, Prophet's Wife, "Elect Lady," Polygamy's Foe, 1804–1879*. Garden City, NY: Doubleday.
Nibley, H., 2000. *Abraham in Egypt*. 2nd ed. Salt Lake City and Provo, UT: Deseret Book and FARMS.
Olsen, C.F., 2009. *Women of the Old Testament*. Salt Lake City, UT: Deseret Book.
Olsen, C.F., 2014. *Women of the New Testament*. Salt Lake City, UT: Deseret Book.
Pearson, C.L., 1996. Could Feminism Have Saved the Nephites? *Sunstone Magazine* 19(1): 32–40.
Pearson, C.L., 2016. *The Ghost of Eternal Polygamy: Haunting the Hearts and Heaven of Mormon Women and Men*. Walnut Creek, CA: Pivot Point Books.
Petersen, Z., 2013. Where Shall Wisdom Be Found? *Interpreter: A Journal of Mormon Scripture* 7: 97–112.
Petrey, T.G., 2011. Toward a Post-heterosexual Mormon Theology. *Dialogue: A Journal of Mormon Thought* 44(4): 106–41.
Petrey, T.G., 2015. *Resurrecting Parts: Early Christians on Desire, Reproduction, and Sexual Difference*. New York: Routledge.
Petrey, T.G., 2020. Theorizing Critical Mormon Biblical Studies: Romans 1:18–32. *Element: The Journal of the Society for Mormon Philosophy and Theology*, 8(1): 1–27.
Rees, R.A., 2011. The Midrashic Imagination and the Book of Mormon. *Dialogue: A Journal of Mormon Thought* 44(3): 44–66.
Robinson, S.E., and Garrett, H.D., 2000. *A Commentary on the Doctrine and Covenants*, vol. 1. Salt Lake City, UT: Deseret Book.
Rockwood, J.E., 1987. The Redemption of Eve. In M.U. Beecher and L.F. Anderson, eds. *Sisters in Spirit: Mormon Women in Historical and Cultural Perspective*. Urbana and Chicago, IL: University of Illinois Press, pp. 3–36.
Rotundo, E.A., 1993. *American Manhood: Transformations in Masculinity from the Revolution to the Modern Era*. New York: Basic Books.
Schüssler Fiorenza, E., 1983. *In Memory of Her: A Feminist Theological Reconstruction of Christian Origins*. New York: Crossroads.
Skousen, R. ed., 2009. *The Book of Mormon: The Earliest Text*. New Haven, CT: Yale University Press.
Smith, J.M., 2015. Five Impulses of the Joseph Smith Translation of Mark and Their Implications for LDS Hermeneutics. *Studies in the Bible and Antiquity* 7: 1–21.
Smith, J.M. ed., 2016. *As Iron Sharpens Iron: Listening to the Various Voices of Scripture*. Salt Lake City, UT: Greg Kofford Books.
Smith, J.M., 2017. Paradoxes in Paradise. In A.S. Miller, ed. *Fleeing the Garden: Reading Genesis 2–3*. Provo, UT: Neal A. Maxwell Institute, pp. 1–30.
Smith, W.V., 2018. *Textual Studies of the Doctrine and Covenants: The Plural Marriage Revelation*. Salt Lake City, UT: Greg Kofford Books.
Sperry, S.B., 1955. *Paul's Life and Letters*. Salt Lake City, UT: Bookcraft.
Staker, S., 1999. "The Lord Said, Thy Wife Is a Very Fair Woman to Look Upon": The Book of Abraham, Secrets, and Lying for the Lord. In B. Waterman, ed. *The Prophet Puzzle: Interpretive Essays on Joseph Smith*. Salt Lake City, UT: Signature Books, pp. 289–318.
Ulrich, L.T., 2017. *A House Full of Females: Plural Marriage and Women's Rights in Early Mormonism, 1835–1870*. New York: Alfred A. Knopf.
Underwood, G., 2008. "The Laws of the Church of Christ" (D&C 42): A Textual and Historical Analysis. In A.H. Hedges, J.S. Fluhman, and A.L. Gaskill, eds. *The Doctrine and Covenants: Revelations in Context,*

The 37th Annual Brigham Young University Sidney B. Sperry Symposium. Salt Lake City and Provo, UT: Deseret Book and BYU Religious Studies Center, pp. 108–41.

Williams, C.S., 2002. Women in the Book of Mormon: Inclusion, Exclusion, and Interpretation. *Journal of Book of Mormon Studies* 11: 66–79, 111–14.

Further reading

Anderson, L.M., 1994. Toward a Feminist Interpretation of Latter-day Scripture. *Dialogue: A Journal of Mormon Thought* 27(2): 185–203.

This pioneering essay provides an outline of a specifically Latter-day Saint feminist scriptural hermeneutic. It recommends a strong historicism with the aim of severing ties between scriptural authority and current institutional practice.

Charles, M.M., 1987. Precedents for Mormon Women from Scriptures. In M.U. Beecher and L.F. Anderson, eds. *Sisters in Spirit: Mormon Women in Historical and Cultural Perspective*. Urbana and Chicago, IL: University of Illinois Press, pp. 37–63.

This critical survey addresses all of Latter-day Saint scripture (including the Christian Bible) in terms of its presentation of women and of relationships between men and women. It concludes that Restoration scripture contains tensions between conservative and progressive tendencies and underscores the predilection among Latter-day Saints for texts that promote conservative viewpoints.

Fenton, E., and Hickman, J. eds., 2019. *The Book of Mormon: Americanist Approaches*. New York: Oxford University Press.

This collection of literary studies of the Book of Mormon features two important essays (A. Easton-Flake, K.M. Berkey and J.M. Spencer) outlining new hermeneutic approaches to gender and scripture. These focus on intersectionality and constructions of masculinity in uniquely Latter-day Saint scripture, pointing away from simpler hermeneutic investigations that mostly catalogue passages focused on women.

Hurd, J.W., 1987. *Our Sisters in the Latter-day Scriptures*. Salt Lake City, UT: Deseret Book.

This book is a traditional but responsibly imaginative encyclopedic treatment of uniquely Latter-day Saint scripture in terms of its presentation of gender. It was written for a lay believing audience and was published early in the development of gender-critical reflection on Restoration scripture, but it remains among the best repositories of many often-repeated textual insights regarding gender.

Williams, C.S., 2002. Women in the Book of Mormon: Inclusion, Exclusion, and Interpretation. *Journal of Book of Mormon Studies* 11: 66–79, 111–14.

This essay provides an excellent, balanced treatment of feminist hermeneutics and of its implications for uniquely Latter-day Saint scripture, in conversation with the best of contemporary feminist criticism at the beginning of the twenty-first century. It usefully combines feminist theory and hermeneutic practice responsibly while aiming at a readership with concrete concerns about reading scripture in a devotional context.

34
THEOLOGY OF THE FAMILY

Rosalynde Welch

Introduction

Perhaps no theme is as central to the self-understanding and public perception of the Church of Jesus Christ of Latter-day Saints as the family. Indelibly marked in the public eye by its early practice of polygamy, the church underwent in the twentieth century a remarkable turn in its relation to established North American family culture, welcoming its new image as an emblem of traditional "family values." In the twenty-first century, the church has again moved away from contemporary family culture in its resistance to the legal and cultural changes that have redefined the institution of marriage away from heterosexually gendered spousal roles. At every point, family models and domestic practices have marked the shifting distance between the church and its North American social context. The theology of family that informs Mormon family practices is no less contested a site. Mormon teachings on the family have been the arena in which dynamic tensions play out between different currents in Mormon thought. No single or systematic Mormon theology of family prevails. Rather, Mormon teachings on family might be better understood as a theological byproduct of the tradition's metaphysical propositions, and the staging ground for its competing soteriological visions. In particular, Mormonism's theological commitments to materialism, universalism, and sacramentalism radically transform its soteriology, and in the process the family becomes the very vehicle of Christian salvation.

Theology, history, and normativity

Any account of a Mormon theology of family must first contend with the difficulties of theology itself in a Mormon context. Mormonism's relative youth as a religious tradition, its belief in an ongoing stream of divine communication, and its open canon combine to make its official theology a (potentially) moving target. The Church of Jesus Christ of Latter-day Saints has no equivalent to the normative systematic theology of Catholicism, and this is likely to remain the case as the tradition matures for the epistemological reasons just suggested (Faulconer, 2010). Mormons are more likely to appeal to "doctrine" than to theology, and Mormon doctrine—normative interpretation of scripture and revelation—is established by the highest ecclesiastical councils of the church, through an implicit process of precedent, repetition, and official dissemination (Oman, 2006). Official discourse on family abounds in contemporary Mormonism, but most of it is informal or pastoral rather than theological in character. An important exception is the document "The Family: A Proclamation to the World" (1995), which currently occupies a quasi-canonical status as a venerated official interpretation of Mormon teachings on family.

Mormon doctrine draws in part, though not entirely, from its scriptural canon, composed of the Old and New Testaments, the Book of Mormon, the Doctrine and Covenants, and the Pearl of Great Price. The LDS canon, however, contains little material directly related to its unique theology of family. Several important scriptural texts, including Doctrine and Covenants 128, 131, 132, 137, and 138, gesture toward the centrality of marriage and family in Mormon theology of salvation, but these revelations—like most of Joseph Smith's revelatory corpus—are polysemous, allusive, occasional, and consequently open to widely differing interpretations. Further vexing a strictly scriptural approach, much of Smith's early revelation on family is bound up with the practice of polygamy or "celestial marriage," as it was known. Polygamy per se is not practiced in the contemporary Church of Jesus Christ of Latter-day Saints (though widowed men, but not women, who remarry may be sealed to their new spouse if she is unsealed, resulting in plural sealings in this circumstance). Because of this, the normative status of Smith's revelations on marriage remains undefined.

Furthermore, much of the significance of family in official Mormonism is not captured discursively in scriptural or official texts, but is enacted ritually in its temple rites. The church has not made these rites publicly available, and discussion of esoteric elements of temple practice is strictly curtailed in Mormon discourse in deference to the sacred significance it is believed to possess. With respect for the tradition, this article will observe those limits. In any case, analyses of textual reproductions of the rite generally fail to capture its ritual and sacramental meaning.

Given the epistemological and institutional impediments to producing a systematic theology of family, and the difficulties of a strictly scriptural method for this topic, most accounts of a Mormon theology of family take an historical approach. The last decade has seen important contributions to the intellectual, social, and ritual histories of Mormon theologies of the family. History has figured prominently in the young tradition's self-understanding and in its assessment by outsiders, due in part to the remarkable faith claims surrounding its modern origin and in part to the abundance and growing availability of primary source materials dealing with the early years of the church. From Joseph Smith's 1830 publication of the Book of Mormon onward, church leaders have prioritized record keeping, transmission, and publication, producing a rich trove of materials for historical analysis. Furthermore, the revelations and translations produced by Joseph Smith between 1829 and 1844 account for the vast majority of Mormonism's modern canon, and some scholars see these texts, not unreasonably, as the "original deposit of faith" that forms the core of Mormon theology and from which all later developments derive or depart. Any account of a Mormon theology of family must necessarily draw deeply from history, and this article will do so. But theology itself, particularly the elusive and ever-evolving theology of Mormonism, is not defined by its historical development, and it will not be the primary aim of this article to summarize such a history.

The ecclesiastical prerogative to define official Mormon doctrine *ex officio*, and the necessary-but-not-sufficient function of history vis-à-vis theology, create space for a creative or speculative approach to Mormon theology. Such an approach draws from official and historical discourses, and attempts in all cases to deploy them rigorously and in good faith, but does not aim to benchmark either orthodoxy or historical consensus, which lie outside the theologian's purview. Instead, a speculative theology makes wagers on key claims of the Mormon religious project, in this case, materialism, universalism, and sacramentalism. Speculative theology reasons conjecturally from those key claims, drawing on scripture, history, and tradition when germane, but ultimately making itself evaluable by different criteria. A speculative theology is successful to the extent that it exercises a persuasive and potent agency of its own, an agency that does not compete with official accounts for normativity or historical accounts for determinacy. The reader should be aware that what follows represents a particular interpretive rendering of Mormon theology, and while I attempt in good faith to represent normative LDS teachings where they are relevant, I make no authoritative claims. This disclaimer should not be read as merely defensive cover when treating a topic as sensitive and central to the CJCLDS as the theology of family. It should also be understood fundamentally as the methodological and disciplinary warrant that renders the field of speculative theology available to inquiry.

Parameters: materialism, universalism, sacramentalism

Of the several philosophical propositions of Mormonism, three in particular condition its characteristic theology of family: materialism, universalism, and sacramentalism. The salience and interpretation of these themes in Mormon teaching vary by context, and thus they function less as static determinants than as dynamic parameters inflecting the shape of LDS family theology in intersection. Mormon materialism, the assertion that "all spirit is matter, but it is more fine or pure," radically disrupts traditional neo-platonic Christian theism, which posits a strict ontological divide between God's eternal perfection of the spirit and the fallen realm of matter (D&C 131:7). Materialism entails several theological consequences, including the corporeality of God, the moral status of embodiment, and the metaphysics of being (Webb, 2013). Its metaphysical implications are especially relevant for theologies of the family. If a thoroughgoing religious materialism is to be wagered within Mormonism, it must deny the deeply ingrained Christian Platonism that bases ethics and ontology on an immaterial, eternal, and unitary Ideal, of which all material objects are merely derivative. That is, metaphysical materialism rules out essentialist theories that define objects by their self-coincidence with ideal forms or essences, which are necessarily immaterial and unrealized. Instead, a thoroughgoing materialism implies that ultimate reality is ontologically plural and particular, not unitary and general, and that any ethics (including an ethics of family) must be based on that plurality rather than on a Platonic notion of a general Good (say, an ideal family form). Thus, in a materialist framework, entities (including selves and families) are constituted from the outside by their relations to other entities and agencies, not from the inside by their essential coincidence with the Ideal. Mormon teaching readily embraces material social and sacred ontologies. Influential interpretations of Mormon theology posit the uncreated co-eternity of human substance with God, the dynamic plurality of the divine, and the fundamental relationality of human and divine subjectivity and being, as God organizes creation from co-eternal matter and invites the human soul into a familial relationship of growing parity (Givens, 2015, pp. 256–315). But LDS teaching has hesitated to countenance a material ethics. Most LDS accounts of righteousness and salvation draw on traditional Christian Platonist notions of eternal divine Law and Goodness, from which humanity falls short and toward which it must strive to comply, ultimately requiring divine mercy to be restored to full harmony with the Ideal. As a theological parameter, Mormon materialism currently informs several *ontological* claims about family—including the familial social structure of the cosmos, human identity founded on a filial relationship with God, and kinship as a vehicle of salvation—while it is largely absent from normative *ethical* discourse on the family, which tends to invoke the ideal form of the heterosexual, monogamous nuclear family.

Theological universalism, the claim that God will work a universal reconciliation of all creation through his divine love and mercy, has strongly marked Mormon teaching. The in- or exclusiveness of God's Christian covenant of salvation roiled the religious milieu of Mormonism's origin, in which universalist theologies claiming the eventual salvation of all human souls called into question traditional Calvinist doctrines of election. Mormon teaching came to embrace a form of universalism, based on Smith's visions of a capacious heaven encompassing multiple "degrees of glory" for virtually all people, including non-Christians and the unsanctified, as well as post-mortal opportunities for salvation (D&C 76, 137, and 128).[1] Smith's understanding of the salvation of the dead was occasioned by an 1836 vision of his cherished brother Alvin, who died in 1823 without baptism for the remission of sin, yet was revealed to Joseph Smith in post-mortal celestial splendor. Christian universalisms have struggled to reconcile the hope in universal salvation with scriptural accounts of the inevitability of sin and the necessity of baptism, and Smith's revelations suggested two possible resolutions: a graded heaven, wherein the righteous followers of Christ receive the greatest ("celestial") glory, which accommodates near-universal salvation while maintaining the soul's final accountability for sin; and proxy baptisms on behalf of departed kin which satisfy the exclusivist biblical demand for Christian baptism. Thus Mormon commitment to universalism invests kinship ties with great soteriological significance, as both the *raison d'être* of theological universalism and the logistical means by which near-universal salvation can be accomplished (Brown, 2012, pp. 203–47). Yet Mormonism, too, with its strong emphasis on personal moral choice and accountability, must reconcile the near-universalism of these revelations with other scriptural teachings on divine justice, retribution, and damnation. A latent anxiety around universalism and its threat to human agency is dramatized in an 1830 text produced by Smith, canonized as the Book of Moses, in which Satan advocates a strong form of universal salvation in a pre-mortal heavenly forum and is consequently expelled for "destroy[ing] the agency of man" (Moses 4:3). The import of the universalist theme in Mormon discourse varies by contexts both rhetorical and historical, at times approaching something like a traditional Christian heaven and hell, with the highest degree of glory highly sought as the reward of the righteous and lower degrees dreaded as the realm of sinners. Responsive to this variation, the soteriological function of family shifts contextually: where near-universalism is prominent in Mormon teaching, sacralized kinship ties become in themselves the motive and means of universal salvation; where it is not, family ties are valued no less but become an aspirational reward for righteousness contingent upon salvation in the celestial kingdom. Two familiar LDS hymns illustrate the modulation: in the former case, kinship bonds are the means by which, the Saints sing, "we'll … save ourselves with all our dead"; in the latter, "families can [might] be together forever" in a future heaven for the most righteous (*Hymns of the Church of Jesus Christ of Latter-day Saints*, 1985, pp. 5, 300).

Sacramentalism is the view that sacred rites such as baptism, Eucharist, and marriage are conduits of divine grace and necessary for salvation. Strong sacramental theologies, including Catholic and Latter-day Saint varieties, understand the rite not merely as a visible symbol or reminder of a more essential interior experience of grace or covenant, but as an "efficacious sign," the very means by which divine grace acts in the world. Perhaps the best known Christian instance of such sacramentalism is the Roman Catholic practice of eucharistic transubstantiation, by which the priest's performative ceremonial speech acts directly on the elemental substances of wafer and wine to transform them into the body and blood of Christ. Sacramental religious practices call forth the performative capacity of speech and ritual to act ontologically rather than representatively—that is, to bring realities into being directly rather than merely to represent a prior or underlying reality. Ironically, the Latter-day Saint eucharistic ritual, known simply as "the sacrament," is itself not highly sacramental: the doctrine of transubstantiation is not affirmed, and the faithful are enjoined to "partake of bread and wine in the remembrance of the Lord Jesus" and as a symbolic renewal of the personal baptismal covenant (D&C 20:75). Even baptism itself, though always necessary for salvation, often serves in LDS contexts as a symbolic commemoration of the personal covenant of faithfulness between the believer and God—the covenant being the morally efficacious element—rather than as a performative death and rebirth in itself.

Mormon sacramentalism shows itself most fully in the temple rites of family "sealing," a set of related rituals establishing matrimonial, generational, and adoptive bonds. Theologies of sealing metamorphosed continuously through the church's early years, assuming different forms and uniting different social and family configurations—plural marriage being the most notorious but not the only instance of retired LDS family configurations (Brown, 2012, p. 205). At every point, Latter-day Saint sealings evolved in tandem with models of heaven and were understood as necessary for salvation—eventually, indeed, as the condition of salvation itself. LDS sacraments are often conceived as a graded series, beginning in infancy with a christening-like ordinance and culminating in the temple rites, sealing being among the highest. Acting directly on the fabric of sacred space and time, the sealing sacrament marshals the performative power of ritual to create death-enduring bonds between individuals, including spouses, parents and children, siblings, and, historically, non-biological sacred kin. These bonds radiate outward from each sealed node to link kinship groups across time and space, promising eventually to unite the entire human family. The logics of Mormon universalism and sacramentalism thus closely inform one another, though they act independently in Mormon teaching. The resulting network is not only a cosmic familial structure but a salvific medium: the sealing bonds are sacramental conduits through which divine grace flows. As dramatized in the endowment rite, each individual's access to God routes through the social ties performed by the sealing. Heaven itself is structured—indeed, is brought into being—by sealed familial relationships. In this strand of theology, heaven is not the post-mortal, extra-terrestrial destination of the sealed and saved, but a condition generated immanently and sustained performatively by the sacrament of sealing itself. One theologian calls this the "materialization" of heaven (Stapley, 2018, p. 17). Mormonism might be understood to transfer a theology of transubstantiation from the sacrament of the Eucharist to the sacrament of matrimony (in its expanded Mormon form, encompassing various forms of kinship): by means of the transubstantive power of sealing, ordinary human biological, civil, or social ties become the Kingdom of Heaven.

Because sacramentalism is more prominent in temple rites than in other forms of LDS religious practice, discussion and development of sacramental theology is curtailed by the discursive limits the institution maintains around the temple. Comparative or historical contexts for sealing theology are generally absent from official discourse, and performative models of heaven are rarely integrated with scriptural teachings on obedience, judgment, and post-mortal reward that typically prevail in LDS chapels. As a result, the sacramental or performative dimension of Mormonism unevenly informs its theology of family. Where sacramentalism recedes, discussions of family tend to adopt a semi-Platonic framework in which a perfect, eternal family form governs all human family formation, with emphasis on affective ties of love and future heavenly reunion rather than ongoing cosmic construction. Heaven becomes the primordial origin of the divine family pattern and the site of eventual restitution and eternal reunion of particular human families within that cosmic-domestic model.

It is not my aim to imply a developmental arrow in these observations on materialism, universalism, and sacramentalism in LDS teaching. I suggest neither a declension nor an advancement of Mormon theology over time. While crucial historical factors have influenced the development of a Mormon theology of family, the trajectory is knotty and disjointed. In any case, those claims belong properly to history, not theology. By framing the theological parameters as something like a set of sliding switches that may be adjusted to varying intensities, I hope to suggest both the complexity and the dynamism of Mormon teachings on the family. My synchronic method, I hope, allows for generous critical description of all positions along the sliding parameter, but also for a meta-exploration of the generative capacity of religion itself, here instantiated in the fecund figure of the family. Theological sliders, conceptually related but independently variable, respond to the structural and cultural forces of history, but also to the nudges of rhetorical context, the pressure of personal religious practice, and the emergence of new energies and entities irreducible to strict causal reckoning. For the faithful, the breathings of divine inspiration may be at work in all.

Family and salvation

The Mormon theology of family is, in brief, a theology of salvation: to be sealed within a family is to be sealed up for salvation. The double function of the seal is the key to its theology. A dense cloud of meaning surrounds biblical images of seals, from the sealed book of Isaiah's prophecy to the Pauline seal of the Holy Spirit upon the righteous "unto the day of redemption" (Isaiah 29:11; Ephesians 4:30). Promising protection and belonging within the fold of the righteous at the last day, the seal of the Spirit marks the Christian as one named by God for redemption and eternal life. The seal of God wrinkles time, accomplishing the believer's post-mortal salvation before her death. Reformed theologies explored the biblical limits of God's assurance of salvation, debating the doctrines of election, the perseverance of conversion, and the surety with which the believer may rely on the election of grace: does the saving seal of the Spirit certify salvation? Once saved, can the converted be lost to God? Can the elect lose their sealed status through backsliding sin? The believer's anxious desire for certainty of salvation shows itself early in Latter-day Saint revelation. The question of the perseverance of salvation, or "retaining a remission of one's sins," figures prominently in an important passage of the Book of Mormon, which tacitly reflects both Methodist anxiety that the assurance of salvation may be lost and Calvinist conviction that salvation of the elect abides in the face of human unworthiness and nothingness (Mosiah 4:11–12).

Over the course of Joseph Smith's revelatory corpus, use of the term "seal," initially akin to the conventional Protestant assurance of salvation, grew to encompass new meanings centered on the salvific bonds uniting the Lord's people. These bonds initially took fraternal and civic forms developed in the early 1830s in several revelations on the priesthood (with an associated sacred fraternal order, the School of the Prophets) and the City of Zion (D&C 77:11; D&C 104:66–67). Shortly after, charismatic and ritual experiences kindled in the Kirtland temple introduced two crucial elements to the Latter-day Saints' concept of sealing: the sacramental power of ritual, and the priestly character of lineal family bonds. Within the Kirtland temple, Joseph Smith instituted, for members of the male missionary priesthood, sacramental ordinances of washing and anointing the body with oil, by virtue of which the priesthood was corporately sanctified for salvation (Brown, 2012, pp. 145–69). At the 1836 dedication of the temple, the Saints reported a series of charismatic manifestations that they associated with the New Testament Day of Pentecost. They discovered in these experiences the persevering seal of their salvation, imploring God to "forgive the transgressions of thy people, and let them be blotted out forever. Let the anointing of thy ministers be sealed upon them with power from on high … Let these thine anointed ones be clothed with salvation" (D&C 109:34–35; see also Malachi 4:5–6). During this fervent period, Smith recorded angelic visitations from several Old Testament figures including Elijah, who announced that he was come to fulfill the prophecy of Malachi to "turn the hearts of the fathers to the children, and the children to the fathers" and committing "the keys of this dispensation" to the latter-day prophet (D&C 110:15–16). The figure of Elijah thus became associated over time with a particular intergenerational form of patriarchy, directing the Saints' yearning for assured salvation toward a mode of universalism focused on a durable, lineal kinship bond, a "welding link," that would, like Elijah himself, evade death's reach (D&C 128:18).

Sacramental, universal, and familial themes were present in Mormon revelation from the beginning, but the Kirtland rites catalyzed further revelatory development that eventually took ritual and theological form in the Nauvoo temple rites (Stapley, 2018, pp. 17–23). The Nauvoo rites of the 1840s, which built upon and expanded Kirtland-era washings and anointings, introduced the sacrament of marriage, known as a "sealing," into an expanded liturgy that culminated, both ritually and theologically, in the sealing itself. The sealing rite, as the centerpiece of the Nauvoo endowment, required the inclusion of women within the priesthood order of the temple and integrated the genders in the faith's holiest religious practices and headiest theological explorations. Repurposing elements of the Freemason rite, Smith revealed a new liturgical complex that purified, ordained, and ritually inducted participants as priests, male and female, into the presence of God, instructing the company in the esoteric knowledge that assures their salvation through certain access to heaven. Once ushered into the presence of God, couples receive the sacrament of marriage, a final seal that securely links them within the highest realm of Mormonism's ample heaven.

Under the expansive logic of universalism, and given the crucial function of kinship connection in the Saints' networked heaven, Latter-day Saints set about in the decades after the introduction of the Nauvoo rite to maximize the density of sealed pairings within the community of the faithful. American norms of biological lineage and Victorian sexuality were set aside in the project of universal salvation. For several decades in the nineteenth century, adult males might secure their connection to heaven through a homosocial ritual adoption to a biologically unrelated church leader, aiming to tap into an unbroken line of priestly fatherhood extending through Adam to God himself.[2] More notorious was the Latter-day Saint practice of plural marriage, by which a man might be sealed polygynously to a succession of wives. Latter-day Saints explained the theology of plural marriage in several—occasionally conflicting—ways that varied by setting, but in sacramental contexts polygamy's *per capita* multiplication of sealed nodes (among the male religious elite) and kinship bonds (among wives and clans) amplified the expansive universalism of the sealing theology.[3] After the cessation of the social practice of polygamy in the early twentieth century, the Saints' theology of marriage shifted its emphasis from ontological performance to temporal duration: "celestial marriage"—that is, the instantiation of heaven in (polygamous) sealings—was reinterpreted as "eternal marriage," or monogamous sealings that, for the faithful, will survive death and remain in force forever (Hales, 2016). While the status of polygamous sealings in the afterlife remains an open question for Latter-day Saints, the church in 2013 revised the explanatory heading to Official Declaration 1, Wilford Woodruff's canonized 1890 announcement of the official end of polygamy, to read that "monogamy is God's standard for marriage unless He declares otherwise" (D&C Official Declaration 1). The social ontology of LDS sealing continues to extend its saving network in the present, but does so only by means of monogamous, heterosexual pairings.

Temple sealing, like other seals, assures salvation. Sealed couples are secured within a framework of sealed kinship connections that are linked intergenerationally and extended universally to encompass God the Father himself, whose saving grace flows, like electrons across a power grid, through adjacent nodes of the sacramental structure. The faithful gain certain access to God, but the divine presence is mediated by one's position within the priestly kinship network, a theme dramatized in the ritual performance of the endowment rites. Distinct from both Protestant notions of universal priesthood and the Catholic separation of ministerial priesthood from laity, the Latter-day Saint order of temple priesthood consists of all temple-sealed believers. By means of the sealing ordinance and the networked structure it produces, all supplicants are integrated into the priestly body. Now hardwired into the presence of God, the company of sealed Saints *becomes heaven* through the performative operation of the seal (Stapley, 2018, pp. 37–42). In this theological context, where universal and sacramental influences prevail, the mainspring of salvation is the "whole and complete and perfect union, and welding together of dispensations" performed by the sealing ordinance; individual piety, while enjoined in temple teaching, is not the means of salvation (D&C 128:18). Salvation is deliverance from separateness, not from sin per se. To be saved is to be sealed as a link in the networked cosmos; outside the sacramental net there is no salvation, because sealed relationships provide the only medium through which saving grace may travel. When one is sealed to one's kin, "their salvation is necessary and essential to our salvation" in order to preserve and extend the integrity of the sealed network in its approach to God (D&C 128:15).

The iterative, reticulate social structure produced by the seal—described variously by historians as the "sacerdotal heaven family," "the cosmological priesthood," the "divine order … of extended filiation," and similar—is, like a fractal figure, legible at spatio-temporal scales both cosmic and intimate (Brown, 2012, p. 146; Stapley, 2018, p. 17; Givens, 2015, p. 26). The grid is theologically universal in its limitless expansion, but it is ontologically local, performed by (and thus originating, temporarily, from) each and every sealed node. It is durable, expanding threefold on the traditional doctrine of perseverance. First, the sacramental seal ensures the perseverance of salvation with no possibility of loss by performing and re-performing that salvation perpetually, materializing heaven *in situ* and *in saecula*. Second, the seal promises the perseverance of family relationships by welding them directly into the always-materializing fabric of the cosmos. Third, the seal ensures the perseverance of the soul beyond death by decentering its locus from the finite boundaries of individual and distributing its value across the sealed network, beginning with the marital sealing and radiating through kinship bonds. For Mormon contexts in which a materialist metaphysics actively conditions its social ontology, the sealed network serves as a distributed, plural, and limitlessly local ground of being, the ontological substrate that makes relation itself possible, a function filled in creedal Christianity by the immaterial God of classical theism.

If Mormon theology of the family is a theology of salvation, what is its soteriology? Traditional substitution models of atonement regard the suffering and dying Christ as a substitute for the individual sinner, a surrogate who accepts the punishment consequent to a sin in the sinner's place and thus redeems her from hell. Mormon sacramental theology develops a related mechanism of proxy or agent surrogacy, but it transforms classical substitution theory in two decisive ways. First, Mormon soteriology divides the saving agency of Christ and distributes it, like the eucharistic host, among all the faithful. A Latter-day Saint may perform essential ordinances, including baptism, endowment and sealing, on behalf of another individual, because sacramental grace flows through sealed material channels "whether [the individuals] themselves have attended to the ordinances in their own *propria persona*, or by the means of their own agents" (D&C 128:8). The proxy actors become, in the Saints' gloss of Obadiah 1:21, "saviours on Mount Zion" to their deceased kin by opening the sacramental conduit of salvation. In effect, one person may bear the seal of salvation for a person to whom he is sealed, both by performing the sacramental ordinance on another's behalf and, more radically, by securing another's salvation, irrespective of sin, through the efficacy of his own position within the sealed network. Early Latter-day Saints treasured assurances that their wayward children would be saved at the last day by virtue of the temple sealing (Stapley, 2018, p. 37). That teaching has receded in official discourse, but the perseverance of the saving seal remains apparent in church leaders' reluctance to dissolve temple sealings: to dissolve a sealing is not simply to sever a personal relationship, but to revoke precisely what is understood to be irrevocable, God's promise of assured salvation.

The figure of the proxy savior who draws another into the immanent presence of God by the power of the seal, and the distribution of Christ's agency into chains and networks of such proxy saviors, remains central to the sacramental soteriology of Mormonism. Second, the Mormon soteriology of sealing transforms classical substitution theory by shifting the work of Christ's redemption from expiating sin (here, disobedience to divine law) to redeeming separation. While obedience to the law of the gospel is enjoined by covenant in the temple rite, its performance of salvation includes no scene of divine judgment. Instead, the faithful enter the divine presence by means of the esoteric knowledge conveyed by a proxy savior. The seal of salvation, in temple contexts, acts to rescue the faithful not from a retributive suffering consequent to their disobedience, but from an atomized isolation that would consign the unsealed to an eternity passed "separately and singly" (D&C 132:17). In sacramental contexts, it is Christ's redemption of the separation and finitude of death—a victory achieved by opening heaven in the present rather than delaying its opening as a final reward for the obedient—that kindles the familial soteriology of Mormonism. The saved rejoice "because they continue" (D&C 132:20). The condition of salvation is temporal, social, and developmental continuity.

This view of familial salvation has exposed LDS teaching to charges of heretical antinomianism, Pelagianism, and idolatry. Equipped with power over their own election and the salvation of their fellows, are the sealed not placed beyond strictures of law? Is the singularity of Jesus as the way, the truth, and the life of salvation not diminished by the partition and distribution of his agency? Is the performative sovereignty of God not usurped in the presumption that humans can sacramentally summon an immanent heaven into being and people it with their loved ones? These questions are not groundless. The near-universalism of Mormon sacramentalism is matched by a near-antinomianism: after receiving the seal of Christ, the believer's salvation will persevere despite "any sin or transgression ... whatever" except for the shedding of innocent blood, although he or she may suffer in the interim until the redemption of the seal (D&C 132:26). Western Christians are scandalized by the teaching that the company of the sealed will "pass by the angels, and the gods ... to their exaltation and glory in all things, as hath been sealed upon their heads ... Then shall they be gods" (D&C 132:19–20). The biblical God of Genesis summons the cosmos into being with the performative word of creation, and it is precisely this performative power that the Saints claim in their sacraments: what is bound by seal on earth—husband to wife, parent to child, kinsman to kinsman—must be bound irrevocably in heaven, ratified by God, never to be annulled. The Saints' ontological reading of Matthew 16:19 amounts to a radical rebuttal of the impassible, immutable, and sovereign God of Christian Platonism, who governs absolutely a heaven that is the origin and blueprint of all earthly things. With the saving power of the seal inherent in the sacramental kinship of the Saints, it is the earthly present that binds and conditions the heavenly future. Smith himself recognized the audacity of this "very bold doctrine that we talk of—a power which records or binds on earth and binds in heaven" (D&C 128:9). He pushed the logic of sacramental performance to its limits, perhaps with an air of jest, in an 1844 sermon:

> If you have power to seal on earth & in heaven then we should be crafty ... go & seal on earth your sons & daughters unto yourself & yourself unto your fathers in eternal glory ... use a little Craftiness & seal all you can & when you get to heaven tell your father that what you seal on earth should be sealed in heaven.
> (Woodruff, 1833–1898, p. 364)

Seal whom and how you can: the binding will hold here and hereafter. Whatever the scandal to traditional Christianity, however close Mormon sacramentalism skates to antinomianism or

Pelagianism, its excursion is propelled by the fusion of materialism, sacramentalism, and universalism that stands behind its theology of family.

To be sure, the boldness of Mormon sacramentalism scandalizes not only traditional Christianity but other currents within Mormonism itself. Where its performative parameter ebbs, Mormon teaching typically operates in what we might call its semantic or statement-oriented mode, concerned with stating what is or is not the case and evaluable on the accuracy of the statement. The semantic mode is often—but not always—salient in pedagogical contexts and official discourse; temple ritual, for instance, has important pedagogical and authoritative features, yet remains strongly performance-oriented. Statement-oriented and performance-oriented modes may alternate within the same scriptural texts and passages. Doctrine and Covenants 132, for instance, opens with a semantic reading of biblical polygamy, framed as the answer to a question of meaning: "Behold, and lo, I am the Lord thy God, and will answer thee as touching this matter" (D&C 132:2). Throughout the text, performance-oriented language arises intermittently, and where it recedes the statement-oriented mode prevails. Within LDS social contexts, the performative sacramentalism of temple practice remains highly insulated from other settings, and consequently meetinghouse Mormonism and ordinary LDS discourse tends to adopt the statement form. And where statement-orientation prevails, Mormon teachings on the family assume a normative character. Earthly human families are understood to possess a sacred nature and saving effect to the extent that they correspond with the divine template authorized and enacted by God. In the semantic mode, "that which is earthly conform[s] to that which is heavenly," whereas in the performative mode, that which is realized sacerdotally on earth *is* heaven (Givens, 2015, p. 269).[4] Semantic discourse on the family is rhetorically authorized by appeals to eternal laws and warnings about the consequences of infraction. The significance of the sealing sacrament is largely focused on the perpetuation of emotional ties between couples and among multi-generational family groups in the afterlife, and on the future theotic return and progression of the human personality within ongoing family relationships. In modern Mormon teaching, the heterosexual monogamous marriage form is prioritized over other kinship bonds, and the marriage relationship is structured according to normed gender roles. Salvation is understood as a process of obedience and purification, aided by Christ, that enables the individual soul's return to the presence of God in heaven. The theological parameters that shape LDS teachings on family remain present but muted. Universalism persists in the affirmation of Heavenly Parents as the universal creators and forebears of the human family; materialism persists in the valorization of divine embodiment and the perfection of the human soul's embodied state in the eternities; sacramentalism persists in the necessity of ritual ordinances and covenants for salvation, and of sealing for the highest degree of exaltation. Statement-oriented Mormon teachings on the family have proved coherent and motivational in fostering strong family formation and cohesion among North American Latter-day Saints over the course of significant demographic and cultural shifts in the twentieth and twenty-first centuries (Pew Research Center, 2012).

In both performative and semantic modes, Mormon teachings on family display a marked asymmetry with respect to gender. In particular, male and female agencies are constructed and engaged differently within the marital bond, though the nature of that difference varies by context. Textually, LDS scripture on family and sealing tends to take male agency for granted while it effaces female agency, yielding androcentric linguistic and narrative effects resembling those critiqued by feminist biblical scholars (Reuther, 1993). The discussion of plural marriage canonized as Doctrine and Covenants 132 takes the male subject as the default figure of human theotic exaltation conferred by the marital seal, with the female figure appearing primarily as a passive spouse (D&C 132:19).[5] In biblical language evoking the transfer of women between men as possessions or property, the text speaks of "virgins" "given" and "belong[ing]" to men as plural wives when authorized and sealed by God, though it should be noted that first wife's consent is explicitly required (D&C 132:61). Gender asymmetry pervades LDS ritual as well as scripture, but differently: the performative character of LDS temple rites produces a distinctive model of gendered agency unique to its sacramental spaces. In LDS sacred space, gender difference is produced and performed by the ways in which male and female persons are differently constituted, marked, and positioned by sacramental ordinances. Likewise, agency is not taken for granted as a feature of individual personality, but is constructed and performed within the soteriological dynamic of the seal itself, in particular through Mormonism's unique theology of salvation-by-agent or surrogate. Where temple rites invoke the figure of a proxy savior, it is typically the husband who acts in the role of surrogate Christ to draw his wife into the sealed network of heaven, and the sacramental power of that saving action redounds to the husband's exaltation (D&C 132:37, 55). Women may act in proxy ordinances on behalf of deceased women and thus fill the role of proxy savior in that capacity, but they do not act ritually as proxy savior to or for men. Although women are sealed together with men in the sacramental structure of heaven, a woman's priestly access to the sacramental conduit is always routed through her husband or father; her husband's priesthood, however, is routed through a patriarchal lineage (biological or adoptive), not through her. Thus the exaltation of men, dependent on the heterosexual marital seal, requires women's *spousal presence*, but within the current logic of the temple endowment a woman's *priestly agency* is not exercised mutually or symmetrically on behalf of her husband within the marriage seal.[6] These sacramental asymmetries exist in a complex relationship to present-day statement-oriented LDS discourse on family, which displays a differently inflected androcentrism. The discursive insulation of temple practices from ordinary religious practice means that pedagogical discourse on family outside the temple often relies on the model of the administrative ecclesiastical priesthood to organize its model of gender, rather than on the sacramental theology to which it is more closely (but covertly) related. Men are said to "preside" in the home, the word "preside" and "presidency" being central to the Melchizedek and Aaronic ecclesiastical orders (The Family: A Proclamation to the World, 1995).[7] The assumption often follows that men possess a spiritual authority in the family by virtue of their participation in the ecclesiastical priesthoods, but this logic is alien to the *sacramental* theology of family which relies on a performative, not an authoritative, notion of priesthood. In recent years, statement-oriented discourse on family, responding to pressure from Mormon feminists and broader changes in North American family and gender cultures, has emphasized the spiritual equality of men and women before God and the parity of husband and wife as equal partners within the marriage relationship, while maintaining distinct and hierarchical roles for each spouse. The performative roots of LDS theology have mostly remained submerged during this semantic evolution, though they have begun to emerge in recent discussions of the ecclesiastical authority exercised by women in and out of the temple (Oaks, 2014).

The gender difference produced and maintained by the structure of the sacramental seal also underlies its markedly heteronormative character. The Nauvoo temple rite integrated women into the previously fraternal company of the sealed and installed the marriage sacrament at the apex of the ritual series, and these key innovations inform the continued significance of heterosexual difference and union in Mormonism. The source of Mormonism's heteronormative commitment is available to various interpretations. Under a statement-oriented framework based on eternal law and heavenly ideals, heterosexual marriage reflects the ideal family order of heaven. Early Latter-day Saints inferred the existence of a Heavenly Mother, consort to Heavenly Father, from Joseph Smith's teachings on divine anthropology, theosis, and the marital seal. Under this inference, the irrevocably heterosexual nature of marriage derives from the divine union of Heavenly Father and Mother, itself governed by eternal law (Givens, 2015, p. 110). Though the existence of Heavenly Mother has never been explicitly revealed or canonized, Mormon teachings on the Heavenly Parents have become increasingly salient in response to both Mormon feminism and U.S. legal battles over the sexual character of marriage. Under a performative materialist framework, on the other hand, the heteronormative character of marriage responds to the inherent plurality of being itself, which is marked at every level by ontological difference and incommensurability. Heterosexual marriage thus produces and showcases sexual difference as a performance of the irreducible otherness, or plurality, of the world. It is precisely through the heterosexual couple's sealed adjacency to the irreducibly other—a gradient only possible under conditions of radical plurality—that sacramental grace flows (Miller, 2012, pp. 89–97). The *implications* of LDS heteronormativity are likewise available to differing interpretations. For some feminist theologians, heteronormativity guarantees the necessity of female bodies and female agency side by side with men in ecclesiastical, kinship, and cosmic structures. Without the indispensable functions for women guaranteed by the heteronormative structures of LDS soteriology and sacraments, it is believed, women would be relegated to the inferior status they occupied in much of historic Christianity (Cassler, 2010).[8] For other observers, the heteronormativity implied by a Heavenly Father and Mother and encoded in heterosexual sealing theology represents a needless and harmful marginalization of LGBTQ Saints, and a diminishment of the possibilities of Mormon sacramentalism (Petrey, 2011; 2016). The robust performative agency that powers Mormon sacramentalism, promising the faithful that "whatsoever you seal on earth shall be sealed in heaven," would seem to offer a justified theological warrant for re-opening the sealing ordinance to non-heterosexual forms, perhaps including same-sex marriages or ritual kinship adoptions between male and female couples who do not maintain a civil or sexual marriage relationship outside of the sealing. Such an innovation would allow LGBTQ Saints access to the sacramental network of grace and a recognized place within the ecclesiastical body. But Mormon sacramentalism as a theological parameter exists in dynamic tension with other soteriological models available in Mormon teaching and attested in Mormon scripture, which act in some cases to constrain the sacramental view. To this point, Mormon teaching has not re-explored its strong sacramental currents in light of current sexual and gender cultures.

Conclusion

The 1995 official document titled "The Family: A Proclamation to the World" stages the complex theological negotiation that shapes LDS discourse on the family. The LDS canon's teachings on family are diffuse, elliptical, and often textually entangled with other issues, so the Family Proclamation, as it is colloquially known, has assumed a quasi-canonical status as something like a systematic statement of belief. The 600-word document aims to synthesize Mormon teachings about family, bringing doctrines of the pre-mortal existence of the soul together with teachings on gendered responsibilities, family structure, and domestic life. The document is often read as a rehearsal of socially conservative political positions, including teachings on heterosexual marriage, gender essentialism, traditional gender roles, prohibition of sex outside of marriage, and discouragement of divorce. While these positions no doubt reflect the tone of much informal LDS discourse, the document lends itself poorly to a political reading. Gay marriage and divorce are never mentioned, much less denounced; gender is labeled as an "essential characteristic," but no particular male or female essence is specified; gender roles are laid out, but the differences in parental responsibilities are slight, and a prominent caveat allows for individual adaptation. Rather than a sacralization of social conservatism, the Proclamation is better understood as an enactment of the tensions between the semantic and performative modes of Mormon theology. Semantically, the document contains a strong strain of metaphysical idealism, inflected with Mormonism's characteristic vision of human theosis. The Proclamation appeals to a divine plan, an eternal blueprint of gender and family, which individual families are urged to emulate. Strong emphasis is placed on the perfection of the divine realm that bookends mortal experience: the human personality originates in the context of this divine perfection and will return to that realm if it succeeds in approximating the divine model. At the same time, the document assumes a strikingly performative linguistic mode. While explicit discussion of Mormon sacraments is limited to a single sentence and the word "seal" is conspicuously absent, the entire text is a *linguistic* performance, structured around serial performative formulas, including "we proclaim," "we declare," "we warn," and "we call." In effect, the semantic content of the document is formally subordinate to the performative dimension of the text, which exercises a direct and immanent agency upon the reader that is materialized at every occasion of its reading. Notwithstanding the document's statements on ideal family form, the performative character of family is unmistakable in the fundamental premise of the text: that a family is the kind of thing that must be proclaimed—that is, performed, re-made, materialized, brought to pass, sealed—rather than the kind of ideal form that abides, self-existent and eternal. The future of Mormon theology on the family will depend in large part on how this document is interpreted in future years. It contains and performs theological resources from divergent strains of Mormon thought, making it a pluripotent textual object that has the potential to shape (and in turn to be shaped by) a wide range of future courses for the Church of Jesus Christ of Latter-day Saints. The way forward will be determined by the ways in which the performative power of the seal makes itself known in the collective life of the Latter-day Saints.

Notes

1 See D&C 76, Smith's 1832 visionary experience known as "The Vision," for Mormonism's manifold heaven, from which only a small cohort of "sons of perdition" will be excluded. On the salvation of the dead, see D&C 137, Smith's 1836 vision of his unbaptized brother Alvin enjoying celestial glory. On proxy baptism for the salvation of the dead, see Smith's 1842 letter canonized as D&C 128.
2 For several recent discussions of LDS ritual adoption, see *Journal of Mormon History* 37(3) (Summer 2011).
3 Latter-day Saints have deployed a variety of sociological explanations for plural marriage as well as a number of theological justifications, including the opposing notions that polygamy represents a divine and eternal form of marriage and that the Saints' practice of polygamy constituted a temporary Abrahamic test of obedience. Both suggestions can find support in Latter-day Saint scripture. For an overview, see Givens (2015, pp. 279–90). Historical understanding of Joseph Smith's early practice of polygamy is still unfolding, but is probably best understood as a precursor to, not an instantiation of, the sacramental sealing theology of the Nauvoo rites.
4 Terryl Givens is the most influential contemporary theological proponent of the semantic model of family, in which earthly family forms are governed by pre-existent and eternal heavenly forms of social organization. Jonathan Stapley's performative model of sacerdotal "materialization" in his *The Power of Godliness* (2018) represents an important alternate theological interpretation.
5 D&C 132:19. Or see D&C 76:50–70, where the scriptural pronouns in the description of exaltation appear to be advisedly gendered.
6 For an important exception to this generalization, see Margaret Toscano's 1985 analysis of an esoteric Mormon rite, in which she argues, the wife's priestly authority and ceremonial agency achieve the husband's complete seal of salvation.
7 For scriptural uses of "preside," see the 1835 revelation on priesthood quorum organization canonized in D&C 107. The word "preside" does not occur in a familial context in the Doctrine and Covenants.
8 For a different approach to theorizing women's indispensability through heteronormative structures, see Toscano (1992).

References

Brown, S., 2012. *In Heaven as It Is on Earth: Joseph Smith and the Early Mormon Conquest of Death.* New York: Oxford University Press.

Cassler, V., 2010. The Two Trees. In J. Brooks, R. Steenblik, and H. Wheelwright, eds. 2016. *Mormon Feminism: Essential Writings.* New York: Oxford University Press, pp. 247–51.

The Family: A Proclamation to the World, 1995. The Church of Jesus Christ of Latter-day Saints. www.lds.org/topics/family-proclamation?lang=eng&old=true (accessed November 11, 2018).

Faulconer, J., 2010. Why a Mormon Won't Drink Coffee but Might Have a Coke: The Atheological Character of the Church of Jesus Christ of Latter-day Saints. In *Faith, Philosophy, Scripture.* Provo, UT: Neal A. Maxwell Institute for Religious Scholarship, Brigham Young University, pp. 87–107.

Givens, T., 2015. *Wrestling the Angel: The Foundations of Mormon Thought: Cosmos, God, Humanity.* New York: Oxford University Press.

Hales, L., 2016. Legal Briefs or Pastorals? The LDS Church's Three Official Statements on Marriage and Family. Paper presented to the Mormon History Association. Snowbird, Utah. June 9–12.

Hymns of the Church of Jesus Christ of Latter-day Saints, 1985. The Church of Jesus Christ of Latter-day Saints.

Miller, A., 2012. Love, Truth, and the Meaning of Marriage. In *Rube Goldberg Machines: Essays in Mormon Theology.* Draper, UT: Greg Kofford Books, pp. 89–97.

Oaks, D., 2014. The Keys and Authority of the Priesthood. *The Ensign.* May. www.lds.org/ensign/2014/05/priesthood-session/the-keys-and-authority-of-the-priesthood?lang=eng (accessed November 11, 2018).

Oman, N., 2006. Jurisprudence and the Problem of Church Doctrine. *Element* 2(2): 1–19.

Petrey, T., 2011. Toward a Post-Heterosexual Mormon Theology. *Dialogue: A Journal of Mormon Thought* 44(4): 106–41.

Petrey, T., 2016. Rethinking Mormonism's Heavenly Mother. *Harvard Theological Review* 109(3): 315–34.

Pew Research Center, 2012. Mormons in America: Certain in Their Beliefs, Uncertain of Their Place in Society. www.pewforum.org/2012/01/12/mormons-in-america-executive-summary/#family (accessed November 11, 2018).

Reuther, R., 1993. *Sexism and God-talk: Toward a Feminist Theology.* Boston, MA: Beacon Press.

Stapley, J., 2018. *The Power of Godliness: Mormon Liturgy and Cosmology.* New York: Oxford University Press.

Toscano, M., 1985. The Missing Rib: The Forgotten Place of Queens and Priestesses in the Establishment of Zion. In J. Brooks, R. Steenblik, and H. Wheelwright, eds. 2016. *Mormon Feminism: Essential Writings.* New York: Oxford University Press, pp. 133–43.

Toscano, M., 1992. Put on Your Strength, O Daughters of Zion: Claiming Priesthood and Knowing the Mother. In J. Brooks, R. Steenblik, and H. Wheelwright, eds. 2016. *Mormon Feminism: Essential Writings.* New York: Oxford University Press, pp. 181–88.

Webb, S., 2013. *Mormon Christianity: What Other Christians Can Learn from the Latter-day Saints.* New York: Oxford University Press.

Woodruff, W., 1833–1898. *Journals*, vol. 2. Wilford Woodruff journals and papers, Church History Library, The Church of Jesus Christ of Latter-day Saints, Salt Lake City, Utah.

Further reading

Brown, S., 2012. *In Heaven As It Is on Earth: Joseph Smith and the Early Mormon Conquest of Death.* New York: Oxford University Press.

This study of early Latter-day Saint death culture sheds light on the Saints' intertwined theologies of salvation and kinship, crystallized in what the author calls the "great chain of belonging."

Givens, T., 2015. *Wrestling the Angel: The Foundations of Mormon Thought: Cosmos, God, Humanity.* New York: Oxford University Press.

This study of Latter-day Saint theology interprets LDS teachings on family in light of its related theological claims about human theosis and the relational character of God as Heavenly Father.

Stapley, J., 2018. *The Power of Godliness: Mormon Liturgy and Cosmology.* New York: Oxford University Press.

This historical study of Latter-day Saint priesthood explores the sacramental and ontological dimensions of early LDS liturgical practices, which the author terms "the materialization of heaven."

35
THEOLOGY OF SEXUALITY

Taylor G. Petrey

In a special issue dedicated to sexuality and Mormonism in *Dialogue: A Journal of Mormon Thought* in 1976, Kenneth L. Cannon, a professor of Family Relations at Brigham Young University (BYU), wrote an article titled: "Needed: An LDS Philosophy of Sex." Worried about what he observed among many Latter-day Saints, the author called for a philosophy, "to develop healthy attitudes toward sex" (Cannon, 1976, p. 58). By that time, Latter-day Saints had spoken quite a bit on sexual morality. Indeed, the church president at the time, Spencer W. Kimball, was well-known for this. Cannon himself had been teaching at BYU for two decades and was the author of the textbook for BYU marriage classes, *Developing a Marriage Relationship* (1973). What could Cannon possibly mean that the previous 150 years of the LDS Church had not yet produced a philosophy of sex and why did he consider what had been said up to that point to be unhealthy?

Cannon's concern about "healthy attitudes" reflected a therapeutic approach to sex. He was asking that an LDS philosophy of sex discuss not simply pre-marital sexual prohibitions, but also the positive virtues of sexual love within marriage. Making the case for improved sex education for children and adults, a relaxation of taboos for using birth control, and encouragement of sexual exchange between spouses for the purpose of marital bonding, Cannon gave voice to a broader shift in attitudes about sexuality that had been happening in Latter-day Saint culture over the previous few decades. The new LDS theology that Cannon was both calling for and creating fractured a previously dominant theory of sexuality—that sex was essentially reproductive—into three separable purposes: pleasure, partner bonding, and procreation. The degree of separability and the interrelationship between these three purposes defines how Mormonism has accounted for sexuality as a theological topic.

An attempt to articulate an LDS theology of sexuality must examine both the normative sexual practices that Latter-day Saints enforce as well as the theological explanations that they have offered to describe sex. Both the practices and the theology have changed over time, sometimes quite dramatically, and should be historically situated. LDS theology of sex is not impermeable from its cultural context but is in dialogue with larger historical forces that give it meaning. This chapter then briefly discusses three historical periods where Latter-day Saints have defined new (to them) teachings about sexuality: the era of polygamy in the nineteenth century, the strict sexual morality that developed in the 1950s–1970s, and Mormonism's sexual revolution that has slowly taken place since the 1970s. Finally, this chapter reviews some of the contemporary issues in Mormon theologies of sex.

The era of plural marriage

The Church of Jesus Christ of Latter-day Saints arose at a time of both religious and sexual upheaval in America. There were numerous experimental movements seeking to found new societies that rejected the sexual order of the time. The Shakers and the Oneida community, along with Mormons, stand as the primary examples (Kern, 1981; Foster, 1981; 1991). The Shakers rejected sex altogether, practicing complete celibacy. The Oneida community, in contrast, rejected marriage and embraced communalism—of both property and sexual partners. Mormons joined these contemporaneous movements in sexual experimentation by reviving biblical polygamy. These groups all offered radically competing visions of a proper Christian sexuality, but they were all united in their search for a utopian alternative to the sexual status quo. Sex was not simply a private event, but defined the parameters of a whole social order around property, kinship, hierarchy, and gender.

The origins of LDS plural marriage and spiritual wifery can be traced to Joseph Smith, Jr., though initially these practices were confined to a small inner circle and not publicly taught. Smith had been thinking about plural marriage as early as 1831 and may have experimented with such a relationship in 1836 (Park, Chapter 6, this volume). The practice lay dormant for a while in Smith's life, but emerged again more fully articulated when he dictated a revelation to a close set of followers in 1843 (later canonized as Doctrine and Covenants 132). The revelation responded to Smith's inquiry to the Lord about the biblical practice of Abraham, Isaac, Jacob, Moses, David, and Solomon "having many wives and concubines." The Lord then answered in the form of a "new and everlasting covenant"—a new divine law. The document laid out a view that there are two kinds of marriage covenants: one lasts only in this world and the other remains in force in the afterlife. Those who do not enter into the eternal marriage covenant are "appointed angels in heaven" who will minister to those who are more worthy (D&C 132:16–17; cf. Mark 12:25; Luke 20:34–36; Matt 22:30). The primary feature of these plural spousal relationships was rooted in the promise to Abraham, a continuation of seed, "both in the world and out of the world should they continue as innumerable as the stars" (D&C 132:30; Hales, 2012).

In the liminal period of so-called "proto-polygamy," Smith was experimenting with new kinship formations that had many forms. In several well-known examples, he and his close associates were not only taking single women as "spiritual wives," but also women who were already married. Rather than the patriarchal, domestic household model of marriage, this kinship system was open to a variety of ways of making connections between couples and their extended kin. Rumors of the scandalous practices, however, spread not only among the Mormons, but among the surrounding communities. Smith sought to quell the controversy about the new teachings by smashing the press, the *Nauvoo Expositor*, that was publishing these stories.

The suppression of the *Nauvoo Expositor* was a last straw for the Mormons' neighbors—culminating in the arrest and mob-killing of Joseph Smith and his brother Hyrum. After the Smiths' death, the church Joseph had founded fractured in part over the question of plural marriage. The faction following Brigham Young out to the Utah Territory accepted a version of the practice, and announced it publicly to the world in 1852, nearly a decade after Joseph Smith first dictated the revelation on the subject (Whittaker, 1987).

By the time the teachings on plural marriage became public, the theology was even more explicit—plural marriage was a practice that mirrored biblical teachings. But biblical precedent was not enough to explain and defend the practice. Orson Pratt, who announced the doctrine publicly for the first time, claimed that there were other social benefits as well. Plural marriage would bring the end of whoredoms, adultery, fornication, and prostitution. Because of the "fallen nature" of men, sexual sin "is to be prevented in the way the Lord devised in ancient times; that is, by giving to His faithful servants a plurality of wives" (Pratt, 1852). In contrast, he warned, the practice of these sexual sins among other communities would ensure their eventual destruction. Sex was a social concern, and the controlled practices of Mormon polygamy were presented as an alternative to the social problems caused by monogamy (Stevenson, 2014). Specifically, an overabundance of male sexual desire was best cured by authorizing multiple sexual relationships for those who could provide for and support plural wives.

While the mores for marriage and sexuality represented an adaptation of conventional Christian assumptions about the limitations of acceptable sexual exchange, early Latter-day Saints actually developed a theology of sex that also built on beliefs in a domestic and material heaven. When Orson Pratt revealed publicly that Mormons practiced plural marriage, he indicated that it wasn't just the biblical patriarchs who were the models for such a practice, but even God himself was a polygamist. This materialist literalism about the true origin of human souls put reproduction at the center of a justification for plural marriage. Pratt grounded the teaching on polygamy in the pre-existence, describing how, through divine reproduction, human spirits were formed "by generation, the same as the body or tabernacle of flesh and bones." This view saw God as the "Father of our spirits" (Heb 12:9) in a biological sense, connecting marriage and sexual reproduction to a divine archetype. Pratt established Mormon polygamy in the order of the heavens themselves, alleging that God is married to multiple divine women and by this process the spirits of human beings are generated through sexual intercourse between a divine Father and his consorts.

Despite the apparent challenge to the Victorian sexual morality that plural marriage offered, nineteenth-century Mormons put forward a theology of sex that was defined by moral discourse. For instance, reproduction was a central theological justification for plural marriage. Early Mormons accepted the divine goodness of sexuality, but saw its purpose primarily as a means to fulfill the "commandment" to "multiply and replenish the earth" (cf. Gen 1:28; Whittaker, 1984). The idea that the phrase "multiply and replenish" is a "commandment" is introduced into Mormon texts through the revelation on polygamy. In this text the Lord explains to the righteous male that virgins, "are given unto him to multiply and replenish the earth, according to my commandment" (D&C 132:63). The "commandment"—a term used only in this text—to multiply and replenish was interpreted to mean that polygamy itself was commanded. Pratt's 1852 speech on plural marriage built on this explanation: "What is the object of this union? ... We are told the object of it; it is clearly expressed; for, says the Lord unto the male and female, *I command you to multiply and replenish the earth*" (Pratt, 1852).

At the same time, Mormon beliefs in a greater cosmological schema for sex and kinship animated their concerns to fulfill this imperative to procreate. They contended that human spirits pre-existed this mortal realm, awaiting embodiment here on earth. Brigham Young taught,

> There are multitudes of pure and holy spirits waiting to take tabernacles, now what is our duty?—to prepare tabernacles for them: to take a course that will not tend to drive those spirits into the families of the wicked ... It is the duty of every righteous man and woman to prepare tabernacles for all the spirits they can.
>
> *(Young, 1856, p. 8)*

The pronatalist duty not only encouraged large families, but then discouraged technologies that would curtail reproduction (Proctor, 2003).

The acceptance of a pronatalist theology of sexuality then started from a position that sex itself was not sinful, but was good and necessary to fulfill divine imperatives. However, this did not translate into a libertine view, but sought a balance. Mormon preaching in this context was wary of the "lusts of the flesh," but did not condemn them. In a sermon in 1885, apostle Erastus Snow taught:

> The lusts and desires of the flesh are not of themselves unmitigated evils. On the contrary they are implanted in us as a stimulus to noble deeds, rather than low and beastly deeds. These affections and loves that are planted in us are the nobler qualities that emanate from God. They stimulate us to the performance of our duties; to multiplying and replenishing the earth to assume the responsibilities of families, and rear them up for God … But all these instincts and desires of the flesh are susceptible of perversion, and when perverted result in sin.
>
> *(Snow, 1885)*

Snow took an approach to sex that it was not in itself evil, but could be perverted through excess. At the same time, he seemed more concerned that non-Mormons were not having enough sex—condemning both the Shakers for forbidding marriage and reproduction as well as "New England families" who have too few children, suspiciously disconnecting sex from reproduction.

Mormons believed that plural marriage was not just about maximizing reproductive output or providing an outlet for male sexual desires but was also a solution to women's urges as well. Mormons considered female sexual desire to be especially potent. Interpreting Genesis 3:16 which cursed Eve with sexual desire for Adam, George Q. Cannon noted,

> women, in their yearning after the other sex and in their desire for maternity, will do anything to gratify that instinct of their nature and yield to anything and be dishonored even rather than not gratify it; and in consequence of that which has been pronounced upon them they are not held accountable to the same extent as men are.
>
> *(Cannon, 1869)*

Because it was a man's responsibility to be the "head" of woman, he bore greater rationality and duty to set the boundaries of sexual desires outside of marriage. Fortunately, plural marriage made it easy for these lusty women to satisfy their desires with the men of their choice by marrying them.

The focus on reproductive sexuality, along with other kinds of temperate restraints from alcohol, coffee, tea, and tobacco, were hallmarks of a morally conservative American culture. In practice, nineteenth-century Mormon polygamy was often quite puritanical (Foster, 1981). At the same time, the innovative nature of plural marriage among white Americans and European immigrants lent itself to sexual experimentation. Marriage in this system proliferated into a number of new forms, with different sexual arrangements that were not necessarily tied to the traditional relationship between sex and marriage. Historian Kathryn M. Daynes notes seven varieties in the era of polygamy: civil marriage for time only, marriage for eternity only, marriage for time and eternity, sealing with postponed marriage, nominal marriage, proxy marriage, and convenience marriage (Daynes, 2001). Sex may have played a different role in each of these. The different forms of marriage, not including same-sex adoption and other ritualized bond-making, provided ways of thinking about kinship in much more broad terms than dyadic couples and nuclear families and disconnected sex from marriage in many cases. For instance, there would have been no sex between married partners in marriage for eternity only and proxy marriage.

Other forms of plural marriage expanded opportunity for sexual exchange. In one example of a convenience marriage, Mary Ann Darrow Richardson wrote to Brigham Young asking for advice about what to do when her husband, Edmund Richardson, had become a "eunuch." He could not produce children, and possibly could not engage in sexual intercourse at all. Rather than divorce, Young proposed a novel solution. He offered the names of three polygamous men, who would "marry" Mary Ann for the purpose of fathering children on behalf of her husband Edmund. The proxy father was not responsible for any marital duties, except sexual intercourse. Mary Ann selected one, Frederick Cox, who provided her with two children. Both offspring were considered to be the children of Edmund, the first husband (Daynes, 2001, pp. 80–82). This form of marriage seems to have been a uniquely Mormon innovation, not only for the practice itself but also the ritualization and formalization of it. Convenience marriages were like a kind of early reproductive technology for those in non-reproductive relationships, one that subordinates or even erases biological kinship when ritual kinship exists.

Besides some women having multiple male sexual partners and spouses, the kind of intense female bonding that occurred under polygamy may have also been occasion for romantic and sexual love between women, especially since these episodes may have taken place before the panic over same-sex relationships in the twentieth century. In one case, two prominent women May Anderson and Louie B. Felt were profiled in the *Children's Friend*, which was edited by Anderson, because of their close bond. In the profile, they expressed an admiration for each other's beauty, and even discussed that they were so close they shared the same bed (Quinn, 1994, pp. 242–44).

Strict sexual morality

In the era of monogamy at the dawn of the twentieth century, Mormons not only came to accept the monogamous sexual values of their new American compatriots, but more strictly enforced them (Hoyt and Patterson, 2011). After World War II, these efforts increased as LDS leaders developed new interrogation techniques and standards, and more forcefully condemned the sexual revolution of the postwar period. As a prominent example of this trend, LDS apostle and later Church President Spencer W. Kimball (d. 1985) made sexual morality one of the central messages of his ministry. He forbade masturbation; homosexuality; and pre-marital sex, petting, and passionate kissing. His magnum opus, *The Miracle of Forgiveness* (1969) lays out a harsh view of sexual transgression, and promises great spiritual, psychological, and societal blessings from a strict sexual morality. Sexual prohibitions were often couched in terms of danger and risk. Kimball warned of disease, shame, loss of virtue and purity, and divine punishment. His book remained immensely popular after fifty years and was often used in LDS leaders' counseling sessions.

One of Kimball's innovations was to establish greater ecclesiastical oversight of sexuality. Church structure places various male authorities in the position of monitoring and enforcing sexual standards, especially in teenage and young adult years. Such supervision takes the form of regular interviews for teenagers and the creation of specific church units for young single adults with their own dedicated ecclesiastical leaders. This monitoring is especially intense as young people prepare for missionary work. During this era, the church issued a new pamphlet, *For the Strength of Youth* (1965) that became a crucial tool in establishing uniform sexual standards before marriage (Fillmore, 2007).

For married Mormons, LDS leaders continued to interpret the phrase "multiply and replenish" as an injunction to have large families. Once monogamy became the only outlet for creating progeny, male Mormon leaders taught that their wives should not limit their output. There were various statements in the early twentieth century by church leaders objecting to birth control, artificial or natural. As birth control gained greater acceptance by the middle of the twentieth century, church leaders began to be more explicit in their denunciations (Proctor, 2003). In 1965, President Joseph Fielding Smith warned that those who use birth control "may be denied the glorious celestial kingdom" (Fielding Smith, 1965, p. 29). In 1969, the First Presidency sent a letter to church leaders explaining the official position. With the exception of risks to health of the mother or the possibility of genetic problems for children, they explained, "it is contrary to the teachings of the Church artificially to curtail or prevent the birth of children. We believe that those who practice birth control will reap disappointment by and by" (First Presidency, 1969).

Mormon experts outside of the official hierarchy echoed these teachings against birth control. BYU Religious Education professor Rodney Turner lamented that many Mormons were using birth control, and compared it to the adoption of Canaanite customs by the Israelites. He saw the use of birth control as a foreign influence upon the church and suggested that the LDS adoption of birth control would be an unholy mixture. He equated the use of birth control in marriage with pre-marital sex in terms of the gravity of the sin (Turner, 1972, p. 226). Turner taught that "the normal woman is theoretically capable of producing thirty or more children during her childbearing years," and suggested only that nature and custom dramatically reduced this number (Turner, 1972, p. 221). He quoted various church leaders who suggested the ideal number was eight to fifteen children. Turner captured a prominent message from many church leaders when he quoted apostle J. Reuben Clark: "As to sex in marriage, the necessary treatise on that for Latter-day Saints can be written in two sentences: Remember the prime purpose of sex desire is to beget children. Sex gratification must be had at that hazard" (Clark, 1949; quoted in Turner, 1972, p. 227).

The prohibition of birth control in this period was connected to the idea that the primary purpose of sex was for reproduction, an extension of the nineteenth-century pronatalist theology. The belief that non-reproductive sex was a moral evil then informed other restrictions on sexuality. Masturbation took on special significance, as Victorian-era theories that the practice caused mental insanity were repurposed in the era (Malan and Bullough, 2005). LDS Social Services frequently distributed suggestions for how to stop masturbation in these years, repeating many of the instructions from the masturbation panic of the Victorian period. These included practical suggestions such as avoiding privacy and "take cool brief showers," "keep your bladder empty," "reduce the amount of spices and condiments in your food," "wear pajamas that are difficult to open," and "in very severe cases it may be necessary to tie a hand to the bed frame with a tie in order that the habit of masturbating in a semi-sleep condition may be broken" (Albrecht, 1979). In the male-only session of General Conference on October 2, 1976, apostle Boyd K. Packer delivered a talk "To Young Men Only" against masturbation (Packer, 1976). The speech was widely distributed for decades afterward in ecclesiastical counseling sessions (Stack, 2016).

The most serious type of non-reproductive sex was same-sex relations. These were often connected to concerns about masturbation. Kimball developed his theories about the causes of homosexual activity based on his numerous interviews and counseling sessions, as well as his citation of popular media reports in his sermons and speeches (Petrey, 2020). He warned BYU students, "sometimes masturbation is the introduction to the more serious sins of exhibitionism and the gross sin of homosexuality" (Kimball, 1965; 1969). In this view, homosexuality had a clear cause, and could happen to anyone who was not exercising self-mastery over masturbation impulses.

The cultural panic about "homosexuality" (and the related panic over masturbation) that took hold in the United States after World War II has its roots in a medico-psychological theory of what is "normal." While this theory originally came from secular science and liberal Protestants who adopted therapeutic approaches to their faith, these groups slowly abandoned these beliefs while conservatives adopted them wholesale (White, 2015). In Latter-day Saint contexts, church leaders in the post-war period began a more severe opposition to same-sex sexual activity than they had done previously (Quinn, 1994; Prince, 2019; Petrey, 2020).

LDS opposition to birth control, masturbation, and same-sex relations pointed not only to a restriction of sexuality, but also that these restrictions rested on a presumption that sex was for the purpose of procreation alone. Such a theory of sexuality provided an ethical lens for authorizing certain kinds of sexual exchange and strictly forbidding others. Such a framework saw sexuality as both a divine commandment and a great source of danger and impurity.

The Mormon sexual revolution

In response to an exclusively reproductive ethic, many Latter-day Saints sought to articulate a theology that both confirmed LDS standards restricting sex to marriage but also expanding the types of sex married individuals might perform. There was a growing feeling that at least some of these restrictions were problematic and that a different theory of sex was needed. While Latter-day Saints did not accept the postwar sexual revolution in full, neither did they reject it. They merged their own traditional views with the values of the sexual revolution and critiqued it when they thought the sexual revolution went too far. As Klaus Hansen explains, there is a tension between the positive views of sex found in church teachings about the eternal possibility of sexual intercourse and the negative teachings that urge great control of sex both before and after marriage (Hansen, 2005).

LDS thinkers first responded to the sexual revolution in the 1960s. This moment provides some insights into how Latter-day Saints drew on their unique teachings to rearticulate a theology of sexuality. In an early example in the second issue of *Dialogue: A Journal of Mormon Thought* in 1967, Carlfred Broderick tried his hand at a "Gospel philosophy of sex." This approach set Mormon views of sexuality as the happy medium between an Augustinian/Catholic view of sex as sinful and a secular sexuality as recreation. But, Broderick also challenged the situational ethics of theologian Joseph Fletcher and others that was winning adherents in liberal Protestantism. The "new morality," so termed by Fletcher, attempted to offer a grounding for sexual ethics besides marriage (Fletcher, 1966). Broderick's interpretation of an LDS view started from the idea that humans and God would have sex in the eternities, proving that it was inherently good. At the same time, sex should also be governed by "self control." Thus, the continuation of sexuality was a contingent promise, based on the proper management of sexuality here on earth. In this way, Broderick sought to explain the tension between restriction and celebration as a productive one: "it is precisely because sex is seen as *good* rather than bad, as *divine* rather than devilish, that such importance is placed upon the restrictions surrounding its use" (Broderick, 1967, p. 101).

Resolving the tension between the positive view of sex and the restrictions placed on it has been the defining issue of a modern Mormon theology of sex. This tension has been manifest in a number of areas. In the 1960s and 1970s, LDS authors began to broach the American cultural discussions of "sex education," aimed first at children (e.g., Eberhard, 1967; Paxman, 1976). This was in part a response to the broader social efforts to establish reliable sex education in public schools, which church leaders opposed (*Priesthood Bulletin*, June 1971). LDS leaders taught that parents had the primary responsibility to provide sex education, but they often meant something quite different by that term. Along with other Christian opponents of sex education, LDS leaders expected parents to teach sexual morality, not necessarily the details of anatomy, forms of birth control, or reproductive health (Irvine, 2002). BYU Religious Education professor Rodney Turner expressed one extreme form of this concern: "It was the father of lies that introduced sex education into the world" (Turner, 1972, p. 55).

Despite initial LDS opposition to sex education, members of the church sought out new sources of information. The appetite for greater information on sexuality among Latter-day Saints in this period was certainly not restricted to children—it was also the parents who wanted a more complete sex education for themselves. The postwar cultural shift toward frank discussion about sexuality corresponded with the beginning of "intimacy guides" for LDS married couples. Like their evangelical counterparts, these sex manuals were not a rejection of the sexual revolution, but a repackaging of it in terms that made it compatible with traditional religious sensibility (DeRogatis, 2015). Glen C. Griffin and W. Dean Belnap's book, *About Marriage ... and More* (1968) was among the first in this new genre. Rather than focusing on prohibition or reproduction, this book laid out a positive view of sexuality based on emotional and relational goods. Sex is "the pinnacle of emotional experience and attainment that can possibly be reached" (Griffin and Belnap, 1968, p. 56). In terms of sex education, it included some anatomical drawings, and described the basics of intercourse and reproduction:

> When the penis is erect it can be admitted into the vagina of the female. This act of mating is called sexual intercourse or coitus. The husband and wife lie together, facing each other, during this process of the ultimate of married sexuality.

At the same time, reproduction remained central to the normative view of sexuality, especially female sexuality:

> The sexual relationship in marriage is a means to an end and not merely an end purpose in itself. It must also be remembered that the primary feeling and sexual motivations of the female are to have children. Much of the happiness and pleasure associated with this sacred relationship involves the anticipation of the creative role of the wife.
> *(Griffin and Belnap, 1968, p. 85)*

The interest in articulating a new LDS position on sex peaked in the 1970s and 1980s, helped along by psychological theories that gave subtle changes to LDS practices and teachings (Swedin, 1998). Since Freud and the popularization of psychology as a discipline after World War II, Americans were not only interested in sex, but were interested in the reasons they were interested in sex. These ideas took hold in LDS communities, especially in the newly redesigned LDS Social Services agency, which offered professional counseling services to assist ecclesiastical leaders in cases of sexual abuse and trauma, as well as homosexuality. The early head of this organization, Victor L. Brown, Jr., was a practitioner of "depth psychology," believing that sexual deviance was a manifestation of deeper emotional needs. Wanting to provide greater proof for his theories, Brown established a research arm at BYU in 1976. The Institute for Studies in Values and Human Behavior, also called the Values Institute, operated with its mission to produce empirical scholarship to validate LDS leaders' teachings on sexual morality and emotional health.

Brown did publish his research in 1981, *Human Intimacy: Illusion and Reality*. Brown's polemical book really tried to lay out a secular justification for LDS teachings on sexuality, with the hope that it could be adopted by non-LDS therapists. But the book was really embraced by LDS church leaders. LDS headquarters distributed a copy of the book to every bishop and stake president, granting it official sanction (Swedin, 1998, pp. 6–7). The book was widely used in pastoral and professional LDS counseling sessions. In opposition to the new LDS sex manuals, Brown cautioned against seeking pleasure in sexuality. He argued against masturbation, criticized American sexual values as selfish, and advocated for a view of human relationships that was less focused on sexuality and more on "intimacy." When sexual incompatibility was present in a relationship, he suggested working on relationship skills rather than sexual technique. By privileging emotional needs over what he saw as physical ones, he articulated an LDS view of sexuality as a distraction and even a hindrance to a true relationship bond (Brown, 1981).

Such advice was not enough to solve what was increasingly seen as a problem in modern LDS marriages: incompatible sexual expectations. One LDS sexual counselor noted, "however unintentional, Church membership can contribute to sexual problems for some members." It offered "conflicting messages" that saw some kinds of sexual activity as deeply sinful while accepting others as legitimate (Mackelprang, 1992). This conflict was compounded with relatively few tools or places to go for advice. LDS members increasingly turned to literature to address their sexual problems in marriage. For instance, Broderick found that his secular book on marital intimacy became a bestseller in LDS markets. In 1986, he wrote a book targeted toward an LDS audience, *One Flesh, One Heart: Putting Celestial Love into Your Temple Marriage*. The book was written to address what he saw as widespread unhappiness among LDS couples in their sex lives. Quoting Romans 12:1–2 ("present your bodies as a living sacrifice"), Broderick wrote,

> If a couple will take that the scripture for their guide, I testify that they will find the unity, grace, and joy in their intimate relationship that can occur only when their union is blessed by God and attended by the Spirit.
>
> *(Broderick, 1986, p. 7)*

Such sexual pleasure would also ensure that partners would not seek out alternative sources of emotional and sexual fulfillment in pornography, adultery, and homosexuality. In contrast to the earlier intimacy guides like Griffin and Belnap or Brown, Broderick's book did not suggest that the ultimate purpose of sex was reproduction, but spent much more time on the psychological benefits of a happy sex life. This turn inaugurated something else—sexual fulfillment as not only possible but also the result of living LDS standards. In this view, the sexual revolution in LDS culture promised that sex between a couple married in the temple and devoted to one another was actually more pleasurable and fulfilling than other kinds of sex. Rather than simply replacing sexual intimacy with emotional intimacy, as Brown taught, Broderick represented an ascendant view—celestial marriage was the key to the best sex.

These new sex-positive theologies among LDS psychologists and lay members occasionally came into conflict with restrictive pronatalism. On January 5, 1982, President Spencer W. Kimball sent a letter to local leaders explaining that, "the First Presidency has interpreted oral sex as constituting an unnatural, impure, or unholy practice" (First Presidency, 1982a). The letter sparked widespread controversy. Local church leaders began to ask married couples about their sexual practices, specifically whether they practiced oral sex, in their annual "worthiness" interviews. It was invasive and embarrassing for all involved. By October 15, 1982, the First Presidency issued a follow up letter and reversed course. Since January, they explained, "we have received a number of letters from members of the Church which indicate clearly that some local leaders have been delving into private, sensitive matters beyond the scope of what is appropriate." The clarification did not change the status of oral sex, but advised further discretion in the interview process. It explained to local leaders,

> you should never inquire into personal, intimate matters involving marital relations ... If in the course of such interviews a member asks questions about the propriety of specific conduct, you should not pursue the matter but should merely suggest that if the member has enough anxiety about the propriety of the conduct to ask about it, the best course would be to discontinue it.
>
> *(First Presidency, 1982b)*

The clarification traded on an impossible ambiguity. On one hand, oral sex was deemed to be forbidden and disqualifying for entering the temple. On the other hand, church leaders were forbidden from asking about it explicitly, and also prevented from explicitly forbidding it.

The controversy over oral sex between married people was a harbinger of the shift in sexual morality that was underway. LDS leaders and teachers increasingly moved away from reproduction as the sole purpose of sexual expression, and began to emphasize pleasure and spousal bonding as important in their own right. Birth control was another issue that changed as a part of this shift. From this period on, church leaders muted their condemnation of birth control, and began to teach that its use was a decision best left to the couple. Gordon B. Hinckley explained the change in 1984:

> The Lord has told us to multiply and replenish the earth that we might have joy in our posterity, and there is no greater joy than the joy that comes of happy children in good families. But he did not designate the number, nor has the Church. That is a sacred matter left to the couple and the Lord. The official statement of the Church includes this language: "Husbands must be considerate of their wives, who have the greater responsibility not only of bearing children but of caring for them through childhood, and should help them conserve their health and strength."
>
> *(Hinckley, 1984)*

This new teaching abandoned the threats to personal salvation for those who used birth control. At the same time, church leaders expanded the purpose of a sexual encounter between husband and wife to include partner bonding as a main objective. They now taught that sexual encounters need not all be procreative, "but also a means of expressing love and strengthening emotional and spiritual ties between husband and wife." The addition of "emotion" as a category for thinking about sexuality represented a new theological counterweight to the previously unconditional requirement of procreation.

The relaxation of earlier prohibitions on birth control or oral sex, as well as the new literature on marital intimacy, provided an alternative theory of sexuality to a supposedly secular one—commitment, not merely consent, was the key to sexual fulfillment. While they remained cautious in permitting any form of sexual practice between couples that were not mutually agreeable, Latter-day Saints were increasingly explicit not just in outlining principles of positive sexuality, but in providing greater detail on companionate sexual pleasure, including achieving orgasm, with special attention on women's preparation and pleasure. The new goal was not merely successful reproduction, but "strengthening marriage through sexual fulfillment" (e.g., Brotherson, 2004).

At the same time, the promise of "sexual fulfillment" was distinguished from a supposedly secular sex. LDS family therapist Wendy Nelson contrasts "worldly sex" with "marital intimacy," comparing the first to a "toot on the flute" and the second to the "grandeur of an orchestra" (Nelson, 2017). This dichotomy between two kinds of sex became a way of critiquing a secular sexual revolution, but also defining LDS sexual morality not in terms of prohibition but in terms of heightened pleasure. In its promise of better sex, Mormonism had come both to embrace the sexual revolution and also redefine its terms. Other LDS women have challenged these sexual scripts, critiquing the kind of sexuality provided by Mormon culture as unsatisfying (Peterfeso, 2011; Finlayson-Fife, 2002). Whether supporters of Mormonism's sexual norms or its critics, they both share the utopian values of better sex as the ultimate goal for a Mormon sexuality.

While reproductive sex faded from importance in the new LDS discourse on sexuality that emphasized sexual fulfillment and spousal bonding, these values did not extend to other kinds of sexual relationships. Instead, reproduction retained a central symbolic purpose for sex, even if in practice sex was not limited to reproduction for married partners. The symbolic place that reproductive sex held granted some continuity with past teachings that had been grounded in reproduction, but also functioned to fend off other forms of sexual exchange that might draw on spousal bonding as a stated value.

Though reproduction was declining in importance as the purpose of human sexual exchange, reproduction remained central to LDS theology of divine sexuality. God still lived by the older pronatalist concepts. In one classic example, Jeffrey R. Holland gave a speech in 1988 at BYU titled "Souls, Symbols, and Sacraments." Drawing on the LDS tradition that sexual intercourse is an eternal possibility for divine beings, Holland grounded earthly sexuality as a symbolic participation in a sacred act of creation. The symbol of sexual congress was of "total union" that pointed to all of the shared aspects of life together, joys and pains. But Holland went further by calling sex a "sacrament" and "ordinance," ritual terms in Latter-day Saint parlance. Sex was not only about creating intimacy with one's partner, but also with God: "sexual union is also, in its own profound way, a very real sacrament of the highest order, a union not only of a man and a woman but very much the union of that man and woman with God." What established sexuality in this realm was its reproductive dimension, not spousal bonding. This notion was distinctive in LDS teaching not just because God is a creator and procreation is connected to that, but specifically because God is a procreator: "*you will never be more like God at any other time in this life than when you are expressing that particular power*" (Holland, 1988; italics in original).

The most important document expressing an LDS theology of sexuality was produced in 1995, "The Family: A Proclamation to the World." It also showed the ways that the ideology of procreation continued to define legitimate sexual exchange. It declares,

> God's commandment for His children to multiply and replenish the earth remains in force. We further declare that God has commanded that the sacred powers of procreation are to be employed only between man and woman, lawfully wedded as husband and wife.

The emphasis on sex as essentially about procreation defined sexuality only in its procreative dimension, legitimating heterosexuality because of its reproductive potential, both in the mortal and divine realms. Human spirits are also described as a "beloved son or daughter of Heavenly Parents." The Proclamation did little to make permissible non-reproductive sexual exchange, whether through birth control, disability, age, or other forms of intercourse between married partners.

Theological issues

What kind of theologies of sexuality can both explain and even celebrate the reproductive, pleasurable, and relational aspects of sex? What theologies of sexuality can also make room for those who lead lives of celibacy, for whatever reason? What kinds of ethical considerations should influence sexual exchange with others or sexual practices with oneself? What resources does the tradition have for further adaptations to contemporary sexual norms, just as the tradition has adapted in the past? What, if any, limits on sexuality are appropriate and on what basis might those limits be justified?

The modern theology of sexuality in other Christian traditions generally embraces a positive evaluation of human sexuality, affirming its goodness and holiness in both Catholic and Protestant traditions (Thatcher, 2015). Rather than denominational labels being the most salient predictor of one's theology of sexuality, the debates between conservative and liberal theologians across denomination have defined the contemporary issues (Stuart, 2015). Today's sexual virtue ethics tend to value honesty and mutuality, and non-hierarchical, safe, and consensual sex as the basis for what should be socially (and legally) acceptable. Far from "anything goes," Christian debates about sexual ethics, especially in the last few decades, have increasingly emphasized verbal consent, respect, and equality, as essential features. Above all, ethical sex should be "loving." What that means is the key question. For many, long-term commitment and procreative intent may or may not be present in a "loving" sexual exchange, so long as all parties share the same perspective about the encounter. This approaches any sexual exchange as good or bad depending on the ethical conditions met—the normative questions may be answered in terms of whether they cause harm to oneself, one's partner, or society (Farley, 2008).

While some Protestant and Catholic theologies have developed along these lines, there is no existing example in contemporary Mormon theology that has seriously entertained a theology of sexual ethics that could legitimate sexual exchange between unmarried partners. Marital commitment still trumps consent as the basis of LDS sexuality. Instead, the theological issues for Latter-day Saints today tend to focus on four problems that have distinctive LDS considerations: celestial polygamy; celibacy; same-sex marriage; and materialism/biological literalism.

First, the notion of the eternal endurance of human marriages raises the possibility of polygamy in the next life, even if polygamy is not practiced (directly) in this life. Indeed, while the Church of Jesus Christ of Latter-day Saints abandoned polygamy at the turn of the twentieth century, in practice LDS men may still be sealed (ritually married in an LDS temple) to more than one woman in succession, either after civil divorce or death of a previous spouse. The same option of successive sealing is not available to women, who must be sealed to only one man at a time. It is possible to obtain a cancellation of a previous sealing for both women and men, but the process is lengthy and complicated. The result of this policy is that many LDS men are ritually connected to their successive wives (after divorce or death of a previous spouse) in eternal relationships—raising the issue that they are now polygamously married in the afterlife. The continuation of polygamy in this form is a great source of anxiety and controversy for many in the church (Pearson, 2016). Others, however, have sought to rehabilitate LDS polygamy in the context of contemporary queer polyamory movements that are critical of monogamy's failures, as nineteenth-century Mormons did as well (e.g., Ostler, 2019).

A second theological problem in Latter-day Saint approaches to sexuality is the place of celibacy. There is little room for a theologically valued celibacy—sexuality defines a crucial aspect of LDS theological anthropology. Foucault's classic *History of Sexuality: Volume 1* argues that the notion of modern sexuality helped define the idea that the self is a sexual being (Foucault, 1990). Mormonism certainly draws on these modernist notions of an essential sexual self, extending the sexual self to the afterlife. Yet, celibacy plays an increasingly important role in Mormonism. Changing geographic and economic pressures mean that North American Latter-day Saints are delaying marriage for longer. Divorce is increasingly common, meaning that extended periods of adult life are without any legitimate sexual access. Further, most gay, lesbian, queer, and trans Latter-day Saints are asked to forgo intimate relationships in order to practice celibacy. These situations all push against the grain of Mormonism's embrace of a positive sexuality. Even among the young and unmarried, people are having less sex than ever (Julian, 2018). Some Christians are suggesting, "theologians now need to focus more than they previously have on the dissatisfaction that sex inevitably induces because it is perhaps here in the very limits of sexual satisfaction that God is found" (Stuart, 2015, p. 30). Rather than the modernist, utopian search for "better sex," it may be the frustrations of this promise that create new theological space for divine encounter. Mormonism may come to embrace celibacy as a virtue in this new environment.

Third, modern Mormonism sees same-sex activities as especially problematic (Petrey, 2020; Prince, 2019). However, since the 1970s, many gay and lesbian Latter-day Saints have argued that the church should condone same-sex relationships (e.g., Jenkins, 1977). Contemporary LDS leaders, however, see Mormonism as inseparable from heterosexuality and that same-sex relationships are not theologically viable (Oaks, 2017). However, the argument that these relationships are not reproductive, and therefore illegitimate, is weak. Not only does the church condone non-reproductive sexual exchanges between married mixed-sex couples—whether due to disability, age, or choice—but same-sex couples raise children from previous relationships, and have access to reproductive technology and adoption just as many mixed-sex couples do. Further, the theological grounding for exclusively eternal heterosexual relationships is undercut by the same-sex relationship of the male Godhead, as well as the complications that trans identity raises for thinking of sexual difference as binary (Petrey, 2016).

Fourth, the question of reproduction and same-sex relationships also reveals another problem that LDS theologies must confront. Some have questioned the biological literalism of divine reproduction as a necessary aspect of Mormon theology (Bennion, 1967). Church leaders have long known about the problems of a materialist metaphysics and the doctrine of spirit birth. In 1966, apostle Joseph Fielding Smith responded to this very question, "If God has a body of flesh and bone, plus spirit, how is it that his children were spirits, in the pre-existence?" (Fielding Smith, 1979, vol. 5, pp. 186–87). In other words, how can a being of one substance be the parent to other beings of another substance? Fielding Smith focused on the conditional part of the statement, insisting that God does have a body of flesh and bone. He reversed the question: if God is only spirit, how can he create bodies of flesh and bone? But the reversal does not resolve the problem at all. Instead, it actually supports the premise that there is an irreconcilable gap between spiritual and material creation, namely, that beings who belong to one stage of materiality do not create beings who belong to another stage of materiality through reproductive means. If the materialist interpretation of Mormon thought does not hold that divine beings reproduce in the same ways that limited mortal bodies do so, as many scriptural examples suggest, the theological proposition for an exclusive heterosexual heaven is weakened (Petrey, 2011). Others, however, find value and meaning in notions of literal birth as a validation of women's birth experiences in this life as participating in a divine act (Cassler, 2016).

Conclusion

There is no single LDS theology of sexuality. The typical historical arc for developments and shifts is as follows: in the era of polygamy, Mormons challenged sexual norms in radical ways, even as they articulated such norms in the terms of a conservative American sexual morality. That is, polygamy promised to fulfill the goal for sexual morality in society where monogamy had failed. In the early twentieth century, Mormons converged with the broader society in their views of both sexuality and monogamy. Abandoning polygamy, Mormons attempted to assimilate to broader American culture by embracing the social ideals for a proper sexual morality. However, in the second half of the twentieth century, Mormons once again broke away from the dominant historical trajectory by rejecting the sexual revolution (Swedin, 1998, p. 5). The overview provided in this chapter suggests another aspect of the modern Mormon theology of sexuality—convergence with the values of the sexual revolution.

This adaptation of the sexual revolution calls into question the very premises of Cannon's plea that opened this chapter: can there be such a thing as an LDS philosophy of sex that is distinctive from the culture in which it is found? Not only have the dominant positions changed over time, but there are always multiple, coexistent positions—those that are vestiges of the past and those that are shaping a new future. Still, Mormons have often placed themselves in opposition to the sexual values of their host society as a part of the construction and shaping of their identity and distinctiveness. Yet, in historical and social analysis Mormon beliefs and practices of sexuality have both followed and rebelled against broader trends. Whatever the ultimate answer to that question may be, the attempt at distinctiveness in sexuality has been a recurrent feature of Latter-day Saint identity.

References

Albrecht, D.A., 1979. Seminar on Homosexuality. Washington D.C. Stake, December 1. Marriott Library Special Collections, Lester E. Bush Papers, Box 12, Folder 1.
Bennion, L.L., 1967. This-Worldly and Other-Worldly Sex: A Response. *Dialogue: A Journal of Mormon Thought* 2: 106–8.
Broderick, C., 1967. Three Philosophies of Sex, Plus One. *Dialogue: A Journal of Mormon Thought* 2: 97–106.
Broderick, C., 1986. *One Flesh, One Heart: Putting Celestial Love into Your Temple Marriage*. Salt Lake City, UT: Deseret Book.
Brotherson, L.M., 2004. *And They Were Not Ashamed: Strengthening Marriage Through Sexual Fulfillment*. N.p.: Inspire Book.
Brown, Jr., V.L., 1981. *Human Intimacy: Illusion and Reality*. Salt Lake City, UT: Parliament Publishers.
Cannon, G.Q., 1869. Celestial Marriage (October 9). *Journal of Discourses* 13: 197–209.
Cannon, K.L., 1973. *Developing a Marriage Relationship*. Provo, UT: Brigham Young University.
Cannon, K.L., 1976. Needed: An LDS Philosophy of Sex. *Dialogue: A Journal of Mormon Thought* 10(2): 57–61.
Cassler, V.H., 2016. The Two Trees: An LDS Revisiting of the Garden of Eden. *SquareTwo* 9(1). http://squaretwo.org/Sq2ArticleCasslerTwoTrees.html.
Daynes, K.M., 2001. *More Wives Than One: Transformation of the Mormon Marriage System, 1840–1910*. Urbana, IL: University of Illinois Press.
DeRogatis, A., 2015. *Saving Sex: Sexuality and Salvation in American Evangelicalism*. New York: Oxford University Press.
Eberhard, Jr., A.E., 1967. *Sacred or Secret? A Parents' Handbook for Sexuality Guidance of Their Children*. Salt Lake City, UT: Bookcraft.
Farley, M., 2008. *Just Love: A Framework for Christian Sexual Ethics*. New York: Bloomsbury.
Fielding Smith, J., 1965. *Conference Report*, p. 29.
Fielding Smith, J., 1979 [1966]. *Answers to Gospel Questions*, vol. 5. Salt Lake City, UT: Deseret Book.
Fillmore, B.D., 2007. Promoting Peculiarity: Different Editions of *For the Strength of Youth*. *Religious Educator* 8(3): 75–88.
Finlayson-Fife, J., 2002. Female Sexual Agency in Patriarchal Culture: The Case of Mormon Women. Ph.D. Dissertation, Boston College.
First Presidency of the Church of Jesus Christ of Latter-day Saints, 1969. (David O. McKay, Hugh B. Brown, N. Eldon Tanner) to Mission, Stake, and Ward Leaders. April 14.
First Presidency of the Church of Jesus Christ of Latter-day Saints, 1982a. Letter to All Stake, Mission, and District Presidents; Bishops; and Branch Presidents. January 5.
First Presidency of the Church of Jesus Christ of Latter-day Saints, 1982b. Letter to All Stake, Mission, and District Presidents; Bishops; and Branch Presidents. October 15.
Fletcher, J., 1966. *Situation Ethics: The New Morality*. Philadelphia, PA: Westminster Press.
Foster, L., 1981. *Religion and Sexuality: The Shakers, the Mormons, and the Oneida Community*. Urbana, IL: University of Illinois Press.
Foster, L., 1991. *Women, Family, and Utopia: Communal Experiments of the Shakers, the Oneida Community, and the Mormons*. Syracuse, NY: Syracuse University Press.
Foucault, M., 1990. *History of Sexuality*: vol. 1: *An Introduction*. New York: Vintage.
Griffin, G.C., and Belnap, W.D., 1968. *About Marriage ... and More*. Salt Lake City, UT: Deseret Book.
Hales, B.C., 2012. "A Continuation of the Seeds": Joseph Smith and Spirit Birth. *Journal of Mormon History* 38(4): 105–30.
Hansen, K., 2005. Mormonism. In C. Manning and P. Zuckerman, eds. *Sex and Religion*. Belmont, CA: Thomson Wadsworth, pp. 142–59.

Hinckley, G.B., 1984. *Cornerstones of a Happy Home*. Salt Lake City, UT: The Church of Jesus Christ of Latter-day Saints.

Holland, J.R., 1988. Souls, Symbols, and Sacraments. President of Brigham Young University. Devotional delivered January 12.

Hoyt, A. and Patterson, S.M., 2011. Mormon Masculinity: Changing Gender Expectations in the Era of Transition from Polygamy to Monogamy, 1890–1920. *Gender & History* 23(1): 72–91.

Irvine, J.M., 2002. *Talk about Sex: The Battles over Sex Education in the United States*. Berkeley, CA: University of California Press.

Jenkins, C., 1977. *Prologue: An Examination about the Mormon Attitude towards Homosexuality*. Pamphlet. Provo, Utah.

Julian, K., 2018. Why Are Young People Having So Little Sex? *The Atlantic*. December. www.theatlantic.com/magazine/archive/2018/12/the-sex-recession/573949/.

Kern, L.J., 1981. *An Ordered Love: Sex Roles and Sexuality in Victorian Utopias. The Shakers, the Mormons, and the Oneida Community*. Chapel Hill, NC: University of North Carolina Press.

Kimball, S.W., 1965. *Love vs. Lust*. Pamphlet. January 5.

Kimball, S.W., 1969. *The Miracle of Forgiveness*. Salt Lake City, UT: Bookcraft.

Mackelprang, R.W., 1992. "And They Shall Be One Flesh": Sexuality and Contemporary Mormonism. *Dialogue: A Journal of Mormon Thought* 25(1): 49–67.

Malan, M.K., and Bullough, V., 2005. Historical Development of New Masturbation Attitudes in Mormon Culture: Silence, Secular Conformity, Counterrevolution, and Emerging Reform. *Sexuality & Culture* 9(4): 80–127.

Nelson, W.W., 2017. January 2017 Worldwide Devotional for Young Adults. www.youtube.com/watch?v=uvou8o4DuEg.

Oaks, D.H., 2017. The Plan and the Proclamation. General Conference address. October. www.lds.org/general-conference/2017/10/the-plan-and-the-proclamation?lang=eng.

Ostler, B., 2019. Queer Polygamy. *Dialogue: A Journal of Mormon Thought* 52(1): 33–44.

Packer, B.K., 1976. *To Young Men Only*. Salt Lake City, UT: Church of Jesus Christ of Latter-day Saints.

Paxman, S.B., 1976. Sex Education Materials for Latter-day Saints. *Dialogue: A Journal of Mormon Thought* 10: 113–16.

Pearson, C.L., 2016. *The Ghost of Eternal Polygamy: Haunting the Hearts and Heaven of Mormon Women and Men*. Walnut Creek, CA: Pivot Point Books.

Peterfeso, J., 2011. From Testimony to Seximony, from Script to Scripture: Revealing Mormon Women's Sexuality through the Mormon Vagina Monologues. *Journal of Feminist Studies in Religion* 27(2): 31–49.

Petrey, T.G., 2011. Toward a Post-Heterosexual Mormon Theology. *Dialogue: A Journal of Mormon Thought* 44(4): 106–41.

Petrey, T.G., 2016. Rethinking Mormonism's Heavenly Mother. *Harvard Theological Review* 109(3): 315–41.

Petrey, T.G., 2020. *Tabernacles of Clay: Gender and Sexuality in Modern Mormonism*. Chapel Hill, NC: University of North Carolina Press.

Pratt, O., 1852. Celestial Marriage (August 29). *Journal of Discourses* 1: 53–66.

Prince, G., 2019. *Gay Rights and the Mormon Church*. Salt Lake City, UT: University of Utah Press.

Proctor, M., 2003. Bodies, Babies, Birth Control. *Dialogue: A Journal of Mormon Thought* 36(3): 171–87.

Quinn, D.M., 1994. *Same-Sex Dynamics among Nineteenth Century Americans: A Mormon Example*. Urbana, IL: University of Illinois Press.

Snow, E., 1885. Discourse delivered in the Tabernacle, Provo, Utah. Sunday Morning, May 31. Reported by John Irvine. *Journal of Discourses* 26: 213–17.

Stack, P.F., 2016. LDS Church "Retires" Mormon Apostle's "Little Factory" Pamphlet. *Salt Lake Tribune*. November 21.

Stevenson, R., 2014. Manly Virtue: Defining Male Sexuality in Nineteenth-Century Mormonism. *Dialogue: A Journal of Mormon Thought* 47(1): 48–82.

Stuart, E., 2015. The Theological Study of Sexuality. In A. Thatcher, ed. *The Oxford Handbook of Theology, Sexuality, and Gender*. Oxford: Oxford University Press, pp. 18–31.

Swedin, E., 1998. "One Flesh": A Historical Overview of Latter-day Saint Sexuality and Psychology. *Dialogue: A Journal of Mormon Thought* 31(4): 1–29.

Thatcher, A. ed., 2015. *The Oxford Handbook of Theology, Sexuality, and Gender*. Oxford: Oxford University Press.

Turner, R., 1972. *Woman and the Priesthood*. Salt Lake City, UT: Bookcraft.
White, H.R., 2015. *Reforming Sodom: Protestants and the Rise of Gay Rights*. Chapel Hill, NC: University of North Carolina Press.
Whittaker, D.J., 1984. Early Mormon Polygamy Defenses. *Journal of Mormon History* 11: 43–63.
Whittaker, D.J., 1987. The Bone in the Throat: Orson Pratt and the Public Announcement of Plural Marriage. *Western Historical Quarterly* 18(3): 293–314.
Young, B., 1856. The People of God Disciplined by Trials (September 21). *Journal of Discourses* 4: 51–57.

Further reading

Corcoran, B. ed., 1994. *Multiply and Replenish: Mormon Essays on Sex and Family*. Salt Lake City, UT: Signature Books.
Foster, L., 1991. *Women, Family, and Utopia: Communal Experiments of the Shakers, the Oneida Community, and the Mormons*. Syracuse, NY: Syracuse University Press.
Petrey, T.G., 2020. *Tabernacles of Clay: Gender and Sexuality in Modern Mormonism*. Chapel Hill, NC: University of North Carolina Press.
Swedin, E., 1998. "One Flesh": A Historical Overview of Latter-day Saint Sexuality and Psychology. *Dialogue: A Journal of Mormon Thought* 31(4): 1–29.
Swedin, E., 2003. *Healing Souls: Psychotherapy in the Latter-day Saint Community*. Urbana, IL: University of Illinois Press.

36
QUEER MORMONS

K. Mohrman

Why queer Mormons? Why not Mormons who are queer or queers who are also Mormon? Setting aside the obvious syntactical decision to title this chapter "Queer Mormons," the question remains. Why not gay and lesbian Mormons or LGBTQ+ Mormons? Or even LGBTQIA Mormons? And why write about this subject in a book about Mormonism and gender? One obvious answer to this last question is that very little academic writing has addressed queer Mormons, especially by those who would willingly accept or actively embrace such a label to describe themselves. Another is that even a cursory examination of the official views of the Church of Jesus Christ of Latter-day Saints on gender, sexuality, family, and exaltation betray an underlying anxiety about the naturalness of, and relationship between, gender and sexuality. But, while both the issue of self-description and the Church's official stance on gender and sexuality will be addressed in this chapter, there is another, perhaps less obvious—especially in view of the thinking, research, and writing that has been done in gender and sexuality studies and other interrelated fields over the last thirty years—but nonetheless more significant answer to the question, why queer Mormons?

That significance derives from the fundamental contributions queer theory has made in that thirty-year period. Queer theory's emergence between the late 1980s and early 1990s was the product of intersecting theoretical, disciplinary, and political developments in French philosophy; feminist theory and women's studies, including the often overlooked influence of women of color feminism; lesbian and gay studies; and activist responses to the HIV/AIDS epidemic in the U.S., among others. During this period questions about the stability of "women" as a conceptual category and therefore its legitimacy as the subject of feminism, and by extension the stability of and relationship between gender, sex, and sexuality, paralleled debates over lesbian and gay identity and history in the academy. These debates also coincided with the nominal and practical divisions emerging between "gay" versus "queer" activist groups responding to the crises of HIV/AIDS and severe attacks on and cuts to social welfare programming during the Reagan, Bush, and Clinton administrations.

Characterized by post-structuralist critiques of identity, knowledge, and power, queer theory emerged unevenly, but strongly critical of the assumed naturalness of heterosexual culture and its equation with society itself. As Michael Warner explained in his introduction to the seminal collection *Fear of a Queer Planet: Queer Politics and Social Theory*, het culture thinks of itself as the elemental form of human association ... as the indivisible basis of all community, and as the means of reproduction without which society wouldn't exist. Materialist thinking about society has in many cases reinforced these tendencies, inherent in heterosexual ideology, toward a totalized view of the social.

(1993, p. xxi)

Challenging this totalizing and normalizing view of heterosexual culture *as* society, queer theory has sought not to include LGBTQ+ people in social theory as it was already formulated, but rather to contest the heteronormative assumptions upon which such theory lies. In their essay "Sex in Public," Lauren Berlant and Michael Warner define heteronormativity as

the institutions, structures of understanding, and practical orientations that make heterosexuality seem not only coherent—that is, organized as a sexuality—but also privileged ... It consists less of norms that could be summarized as a body of doctrine than of a sense of rightness produced in contradictory manifestations—often unconscious, immanent to practice or to institutions.

(1998, p. 548)

In other words, in exposing and critiquing heteronormativity, among other kinds of normativity, queer theorists strive "to make theory queer, not just to have a theory about queers" (Warner, 1993, p. xxvi).

Understood in the context of queer theory's driving provocation to disrupt and upend assumptions about the naturalness, inevitability, and desirability of heterosexual culture, the phrase "queer Mormons" goes beyond queer's current colloquial meaning as an umbrella-like identificatory descriptor for non-normative sexual and gender identities to suggest that it is both desirable and necessary to challenge the assumptions, knowledges, practices, and institutions of heterosexual culture that dominate Mormonism; or to use "queer" as queer theorists do—as a verb rather than a noun—the phrase suggests that it is both desirable and necessary *to queer* Mormonism. This chapter then, while not denying the more common or less critical ways in which the term queer is used, explicitly employs it as a simultaneously theoretical and practical term that calls "into question conventional understandings of sexual identity by deconstructing the categories, the oppositions and equations that sustain them," primarily the two-sex system, the gender binary, and a fixed notion of sexual identity, as well as the apparently clear and stable relationship between all three (Jagose, 1997, p. 97). Thus, queering Mormonism is a task that challenges many of the fundamental ideas at the foundation of modern Mormon life, but it is also one that proposes alternative ways for historicizing, thinking, and living Mormonism. This is an especially important task given that the religious institution that often comes to stand in for the entirety of the Mormon faith tradition, the Church of Jesus Christ of Latter-day Saints, currently promotes heterosexuality as *the* organizing feature of all life, whether it be social, cultural, political, or spiritual life, not only in this world, but as the condition that made this world possible and that will characterize the next.

Queer(ing) Mormon history

The Church's contemporary stance on sex assignment, gender identity and roles, the gendered nature of the priesthood, sexuality, family organization, and the relationship between these things and exaltation and Godhood are often assumed by both Mormons and non-Mormons alike to be historically consistent, unchanged since the time of Joseph Smith; positions that if they have changed, have only shifted in minor and inconsequential ways. Predictably, the Church itself has promoted such a view of its own history: today it interprets this relationship as one characterized by explicitly (hetero)sexual reproductive practice, even to the point of institutionalizing heteronormativity as a fundamental condition of the preexistent, earthly, and eternal realms. For example, Taylor Petrey explains that the Church's definition of gender, which "suggests that men's role is being a 'breadwinner' and women's role is caring for children, cooking, cleaning, and other hallmarks of the twentieth-century American family division of labor … is meaningless in an eternal realm" since "dehistoricizing modern American divisions of labor" fails to account for the vast differences in how gender is understood and experienced "historically and cross-culturally." "The main problem" he argues, "for any theology that begins with a fixed notion of roles, gender binarism, or innate characteristics is that it [is] rooted in a fantasmatic [sic] idealization of such differences rather than any universal instantiation" (2011, p. 127). In a similar vein, Seth Payne points out that it is beyond question "that Joseph Smith taught that God is an exalted human being … as is the fact that Smith taught that some sort of relationship between the sexes—as it relates to creating familial ties—is essential to Godhood," but whether that relationship was meant to refer to reproductive sex, sexual orientation, and/or proscribed gender identity and roles is very much open for debate (2017, p. 50). It would be a mistake, Payne explains, to assume that there was a direct, or even inevitable, path between Smith's teachings in the early 1840s and the Church's current theological positions. In fact, significant and important transformations in its official teachings on and approaches to these issues, whether it be theologically, administratively, and/or practically, have been documented by numerous scholars (Cragun, Sumerau, and Williams, 2015; Payne, 2017; and Quinn, 1996).

Queer theory has helped to explain how many of the historical "facts" that are accepted about gender and sexuality are actually carefully crafted narratives that anachronistically apply contemporary ideas to explain or interpret past concepts, knowledges, practices, and events, thereby reinforcing the sense that modern paradigms of social organization are natural, inevitable, or even scientifically accurate. In the case of sexuality, in particular, queer theorists argue that "'queer' is not simply the latest example in a series of words,"—such as pederast, invert, homosexual, gay—"that describe and constitute same-sex desire transhistorically[,]" but rather that it is "a term that indexes precisely [sic] and specifically cultural formations" since the 1980s (Jagose, 1997, pp. 74–75). This view of queer reflects a now common and widely held scholarly opinion that both homosexuality and heterosexuality are not natural or ahistorical realities of human existence, but modern social concepts, with homosexuality predating the emergence of heterosexuality in both scientific discourse and urban subcultures in Europe and the U.S.

Separating notions of identity from practice, these scholars have demonstrated that something called "homosexuality"—or a notion of identity based on one's sexual desires or preferences for one's own sex—only appeared as a coherent, distinct concept in the late nineteenth century among sexologists and did not become a diffuse, commonly known, or accepted concept until the period between the turn of the century and the 1920s. This periodization is especially significant for thinking through gender and sexuality in Mormonism since Joseph Smith's church, founded in April 1830, had, by the 1920s, experienced substantial changes to the understanding, theologizing, administration, and practice of sexual activity, and did not yet recognize the concept of sexual identity. Smith's teachings, especially as encapsulated in the King Follett discourse and Sermon at the Grove on the nature of God, human potential for Godhood, and exaltation are now considered foundational doctrine in the Church of Jesus Christ of Latter-day Saints, despite the sermons' omission from official, canonized scripture. On the other hand, Smith's teachings on, and adoption of, the practice of plural marriage while officially recorded in Doctrine and Covenants has now been excised from the Church's public-facing theology concerning expected and acceptable earthly practice. During the Nauvoo period, when Smith gave both the Follett and Grove sermons and when polygamy began to be more widely shared and practiced among the upper echelons of Church leadership, he "taught that the practice of what he termed celestial marriage was essential in order for men and women to become exalted and become Gods," but he never linked *sexual* procreation, nor any notion of (hetero)sexuality to the possibility of Godhood (Payne, 2017, p. 48). Smith's failure to explicitly link sexual procreation to Godhood is critical for thinking through theological possibilities for, what Petrey (2011; also see Petrey, "Theology of Sexuality," Chapter 35, this volume) has termed, "post-heterosexual" theology in Mormonism—a theology that could recognize, accept, and even promote the instability of sex, gender, and sexuality. In a more historical and less theological vein, Smith's silence on the relationship between (hetero)sexuality and Godhood serves to queer Mormon history by highlighting the reality that Smith could not have explicitly connected sexuality to marriage, procreation, or exaltation because the concepts of homo- and heterosexuality did not even enter U.S. culture until the 1890s, almost fifty years after his death, and even then only in specialized medical journals.

Historian D. Michael Quinn has painstakingly documented the major difference between the Church's nineteenth- and twentieth-century views and approaches to same-sex activity concluding that between 1830 and the early twentieth century, "Mormon leaders ... were more tolerant of homoerotic behaviors than they were of every other nonmarital sexual activity" (1996, p. 265). Of course, the Church's relative tolerance of homoerotic behavior must be understood in the context of institutional expectations to only engage in sexual activity within marriage as well as the contradictory reality that the majority of nineteenth-century Latter-day Saints engaged in premarital sexual activity (1996, p. 199). Over the course of the nineteenth century leaders were much more concerned with preventing and punishing opposite-sex sexual activity, especially fornication and adultery, than they were with homoerotic behavior. Proposed or sanctioned punishment for activities like fornication and adultery were often quite violent, ranging from castration to decapitation, while such extreme responses were absent in cases of same-sex sex. In fact, authorities' responses to such activity were significantly milder (Quinn, 1996). Additionally, the Latter-day Saints did not pass an anti-sodomy law in Utah while they held control of the state's legal system. It was not until 1876, when federally selected anti-Mormon representatives controlled Utah's legislature and judiciary, that such a law was passed. While the Church by no means sanctioned or openly accepted same-sex sexual behavior, its "lighter" response to this activity must be contrasted with its openly homophobic, and often inhumane, responses to same-sex sexual behavior and gay identity beginning in the mid-twentieth century.

It is critical to scrutinize the Church's nineteenth-century attention to homoerotic behavior in the broader context of its promotion and practice of plural marriage, anti-Mormon sentiment, and the rapid development of sexual sciences during the last quarter of that century. Not only did the evolution of the Church's theology during this period mirror the increasing sex-consciousness of U.S. society, during which, as Payne (2017, pp. 48) explains, "Brigham Young and Mormon Apostle Orson Pratt, began to explicitly link 'eternal increase' and exaltation with sexual procreation ... in the process ... describ[ing] God in explicit[ly] sexual terms," but its leaders also explicitly drew on the latest scientific writings on sex to defend their sexual practices against an onslaught of public and federal pressure against their church and its practices (Hardy and Erickson, 2001). The driving forces that eventually culminated in the modern Church's views on the eternal nature of sex and gender and the role of sexual procreation in creating (eternal) life find their origin in its nineteenth-century response to national efforts to define citizenship (and not, coincidentally whiteness) in relationship to the gendered and sexualized dynamics of a private sphere that was characterized by a woman's consent to her husband's patriarchal authority in matters sexual, economic, and political (Bentley, 2002; Mohrman, 2017; Talbot, 2013). In other words, not only did the Church's views on sex, gender, and sexuality change significantly over time, but those changes, as well as the accompanying methods for defining and dealing with gender and sexual transgressions, were a product of earthly, modern historical developments in the U.S. more generally.

The Church's twentieth-century campaign for assimilation into and acceptance by U.S. society took the form not only of giving up polygamy, but of closely promoting and adhering to national norms around marriage, patriarchal gender relations, and reproductive sexuality using the language and logic of sexology which took popular hold during the twenty years before and after the fin de siècle (Mohrman, 2017). The early twentieth century was characterized by an increasing interest in defining, explaining, and regulating sexuality nationwide and the Church was no exception to this trend. In particular, the Church began to articulate "distinctly modern commitments" to heterosexuality and heteronormativity, "characterized by a divinely pre-ordained system of sexed difference, naturalized [patriarchal] gender roles, and opposite-sex desire that could only appropriately be expressed within marriage" (Mohrman, 2017, p. 181). While the Church had previously promoted marriage and sexual expression solely within its bonds, it had never before articulated views about innate sexual desire or identity, nor had it attempted to stringently and emphatically police gender roles. In fact, there is evidence the Church had actually held and promoted more liberal views of gender roles during the nineteenth century than it did in the twentieth (Mohrman, 2017). Relatedly, over the first half of the twentieth century, the Church developed, in tandem with a slow but steady process of bureaucratization that streamlined the administration, instruction, and experience of Mormonism for its members, a growing interest in homoerotic behavior, an interest that was critical in solidifying "certain behaviors, gender traits, and emotional ties as grounds for" reprimand, disfellowship, or excommunication and therefore served as "a catalyst in the formation of homosexual identity" itself, not just in the identification or regulation of homoerotic behavior (Canaday, 2009, p. 4). Thus, the Church's bureaucratic energies during the period between the turn of the twentieth century and World War II (much like the nation-state itself), focused as it was on identifying, counseling, and changing sexual behaviors considered sinful, were critical for incubating newly coalescing notions of homosexual and heterosexual identity as well as the leadership's strategies for moralizing, theologizing, and managing those identities (Mohrman, 2015).

Even as the Church was strengthening "heteronormative conventions of intimacy [to] block the building of nonnormative or explicit public sexual cultures," by ramping up its campaigns to reinforce distinct and complementary gender roles for men and women and the "naturalness" of opposite-sex attraction as the basis for marriage and procreation, both Mormon and non-Mormon queers resisted such attempted obstruction (Berlant and Warner, 1998, p. 553). Evidence of the creation of contingent, counterpublic spaces for queer life is present as early as the 1880s in Mormon Utah, although evidence of same-sex romantic and sexual activity dates back to the beginning of Mormonism (Quinn, 1996; O'Donovan, 1994). In 1882, when Oscar Wilde came to lecture at the Salt Lake Theater as part of his U.S. aesthetics tour, he was greeted by a fan club of "young men [i]n the front row, each adorned with an enormous sunflower" similar to those in other locations who the *Washington Post* reported had "'unmistakable rouge upon their cheeks.'" (Warner, 1987, p. 331; Quinn, 1996, pp. 314). Perhaps some of Wilde's young fanboys became members of the male-only Salt Lake Bohemian Club founded in 1886. Legally incorporated as a social club for both men and women in 1891 it became a "social haven for those who" defined themselves according to same-sex sexual identity by the 1920s. By the first decade of the twentieth century the club's membership included several prominent Latter-day Saint members (Quinn, 1996, p. 69). The club, at least through the 1920s if not beyond, served as a space for its middle- and upper-class members to openly socialize based on their non-normative sexual and gender identities. Other spaces associated with and run by the Church served as cruising sites for gay men in the first half of the nineteenth century such as the Deseret Gymnasium, now replaced by the Church Office Building in downtown Salt Lake City (O'Donovan, 1994; Winkler, 2008, p. 164).

As Quinn recounts, it was possible for some Latter-day Saints to engage in semi-public, if not explicitly acknowledged, homoerotic relationships during the early twentieth century (Mohrman, 2017). For example, well-loved director of the Mormon Tabernacle Choir between 1890 and 1916, Evan Stephens never married, engaged in several affairs with men, and openly used the then common language of "manliness" as code to describe his attraction to and love for men (Quinn, 1996). Similarly, Louie B. Felt and May Anderson's relationship was openly described in intimate, physical terms in biographical articles written about them for the Church publication *The Children's Friend*. They were widely known as "The Primary David and Jonathan" referencing their roles in the Church's Primary Association and intimating with the biblical reference, at least to those in the know, that they were more than friends and housemates (Quinn, 1996). Stephens, Felt, and Anderson were all in their sixties when Mormon publications featured their stories, tacitly referencing their same-sex desires and activities in 1919. Both their age and the still nascent public understanding of personal sexual identity gave them enough protection from being exposed as possibly engaging in homoerotic behavior, especially since they had grown up in a century when strong homosocial, even homoromantic, relationships were promoted and often venerated. But it is also clear that a younger generation in Utah, many of them Mormon, were developing a robust queer counterpublic as evidenced by a study conducted by Mildred Berryman in Salt Lake City between 1918 and 1939. A student first at Westminster College in Salt Lake City and then at Temple Bar College in Seattle, Berryman identified as homosexual and claimed to know at least 100 other self-identified homosexual women and men in the city, thirty-three of whom she anonymously interviewed for her unfinished thesis, "The Psychological Phenomena of the Homosexual" (Bullough and Bullough, 1977; Quinn, 1996). Other sites for cruising, socialization, and employment helped foment the formation of queer counterpublics in Mormon country. Comfort stations, or underground restrooms, were constructed downtown beginning in 1914 and, like Salt Lake City's Liberty Park, Wasatch Springs Plunge, a local bath and hot springs facility privately and publicly owned at various points between the 1850s and 1970s, and "Bare-Ass Beach," a stretch of shoreline on the Great Salt Lake, served as sites for cruising (Anderson, 2017). Later Auerbach's department store provided employment for openly gay men and gender non-conforming people, during the 1940s and 1950s, while several bars either catered to or tolerated queer clientele starting in the late 1940s, such as the Radio City Lounge, the Crystal Lounge, the Broadway Lounge, and the Tin Angel, among others (Anderson, 2017).

Following a successful period of rapid assimilation into U.S. society during the first half of the twentieth century, the evolution of the Church's understanding and approach to issues of same-sex sexuality progressed from relative tolerance of same-sex sexual activity in the nineteenth and early twentieth centuries (as late as 1948 Church President George Albert Smith advised "two young men to 'live their lives as decently as they could' within their homosexual companionship") to gradual and then severe condemnation of such activity and relationships between the 1950s and 1970s (Quinn, 1996, p. 372). Specifically, after World War II the Church began to overtly target homosexuality as both a sin in and of itself, and, as did the federal government, as a threat. Ryan Cragun, J.E. Sumerau, and Emily Williams have documented the Church leadership's changing discursive constructions of homosexuality between the 1950s and the 1990s noting that by the 1970s "LDS elites singled out homosexuality while listing social vices that were leading to the corruption of America," starkly contrasting with its relatively minor concern with same-sex sexual activity during the nineteenth century (Cragun, Sumerau, and Williams, 2015, p. 297). The late 1950s were the major turning point in the Church's treatment of same-sex sexual activity and the emergence of official, institutionalized homophobia on its part (Quinn, 1996). The Church's strong condemnation of same-sex sexuality and its identification with threats to (if not the outright destruction of) the family, society, the nation, and by the 1980s "divinely sanctioned" gender roles, eerily mirrored nineteenth-century anti-Mormon condemnation of polygamy as a familial, social, and national threat. Church leaders' increasingly vehement condemnation of same-sex sexuality in the 1960s and 1970s was paralleled by equally fervent, and at times violent, efforts to deny, reverse, or stymie individuals' homoerotic desires, including such tactics as aversion therapy and the promotion of opposite sex-marriage as a "cure" for homosexuality (Quinn, 1996). In 1976, one apostle, Boyd K. Packer, even advocated physical violence against gay men who attempted to "entice young men to join them in … immoral acts," leaving the interpretation of "entice" open for broad interpretation in a rampantly homophobic society. Packer's talk was widely published as a pamphlet until 2016 at which time it was discontinued. However, it was still available online at lds.org (Packer, 2012) at the time of writing.

The Church's transition from a focus on quiet reprimand, reassignment, and/or removal of those who were found to be engaging in same-sex sex to a response characterized by overt identification of gay individuals and condemnation of same-sex sex as more sinful than other kinds of sex outside marriage meant that the period between the late 1940s and the mid-1960s was characterized by several same-sex sex scandals. As in other cities, bars in Salt Lake City catering to a queer clientele were subject to frequent raids and their patrons to police harassment. Reporting on these raids during the late 1940s and 1950s, which were directly linked to anti-communist anxiety characteristic of the era, was supplemented by press coverage of several homophobic scandals that rocked the Mormon Corridor. Church-owned Ricks College, located in Rexburg, Idaho, fired the chairman of its music department in 1950 for engaging in sexual relations with male students, while in 1955 Boise, Idaho made national headlines for what became known as the Boys of Boise scandal in which city leaders, many of whom were Latter-day Saints, engaged in what has been described as a witch hunt against gay men in the city. In 1958 Salt Lake City's chief of police, the ultra-conservative, anti-communist, and John Birch Society supporter W. Cleon Skousen, instigated a concerted campaign against "moral perverts" that utilized bar raids and sting operations to expose queer people in the city (Anderson, 2017, p. 18; Quinn, 1996, p. 437). By the 1920s many Mormons had begun to identify according to their same-sex sexual desires, but it was not until the late 1960s—largely as a result of the extreme anti-communism embraced by the Church—that queer Mormons began to actively and publicly resist their treatment by both the Church and the state.

In 1966, David-Edward Desmond founded the United Order Family of Christ in Denver, a schismatic Mormon group for young gay men which operated on a platform of economic communalism. Desmond's group was only the second gay Christian church founded in the U.S. and was to be relatively short-lived, disbanding in the early 1970s, but its founding, paired with the coinciding rise in resistance to social and governmental homo- and transphobia nationwide, profoundly concerned Church leaders and marked a sharp increase in their public acknowledgment of and concern with same-sex sexuality (Quinn, 1996, p. 380; and Cragun, Sumerau, and Williams, 2015, pp. 296–97). Between the late 1960s and mid-1970s it is clear that queer activism burgeoning across the nation was beginning to take hold in Mormon-dominated Utah. Queer publications, organizations, and businesses sprung up at the University of Utah and in downtown Salt Lake City and an influential lesbian and gay Mormon presence even permeated the nationally recognized gay newspaper, *The Advocate*. Yet it is clear that by the time Leonard Matlovich, a Mormon, appeared on the cover of *Time* declaring "I Am a Homosexual" in 1975 protesting his discharge from the U.S. Airforce, queer activism in Salt Lake City was still nascent, highly circumscribed by the immense power of the Church to dictate social dialogue on the subject of sexuality.

As Douglas Winkler has demonstrated in his dissertation on the lives of gay men in Salt Lake City between the 1940s and 1970s, the conditions that helped foment vibrant community and viable organizing in other parts of the U.S. were either not present or were stifled by the conditions of a religiously dominated society and government. For example, bars did not have the same kind of community-building utility nor were they able to function as springboards for political organizing because of the Church's proscription against alcohol. Not only were queer Mormons less likely to frequent bars as a result of that proscription, but the Church actively worked to suppress the number of bars in the city, quelled the ability of those that did exist to serve alcohol, and shamed the public—both Mormon and non-Mormon—from patronizing them (Winkler, 2008, p. 150). This was but one of the many ways that the Church influenced the development of queer community formation and political organizing, the result being that queer Mormons were both reluctant and slow to develop any critique of the Church itself (Winkler, 2008, pp. 192–94).

Despite almost two decades of severe homo- and transphobic attacks (both in public discourse and in private experience), it was not until 1977 that queer Mormons began to openly challenge the Church policies and tactics. That year Cloy Jenkins, a student at BYU anonymously published *Prologue*, a lengthy response to Dr. I. Reed Payne's classroom contentions that homosexuality was chosen and therefore changeable. It was later that year that the first organization for queer Mormons was founded. Established during the inaugural Salt Lake Coalition for Human Rights convention in June that addressed gay rights specifically, Affirmation has become the largest and most visible organization for LGBTQ Mormons worldwide (see Gustav-Wrathall's "Mormon LGBTQ Organizing and Organizations," Chapter 16, this volume). It was also in 1977 that the Utah legislature passed its first bill banning same-sex marriage in Utah, reflecting the extent to which Latter-day Saint leaders had become concerned about and were actively working to minimize same-sex sexuality as a threat to the family, society, and the nation. This also helped to inspire the religious right's campaigns against gay rights in the 1970s.

Since the 1970s the Church has wavered back and forth on its view of even the possibility of homosexuality as a(n) (biological) identity. As late as 1976 Apostle Packer declared that it "is a falsehood that some are born with an attraction to their own kind, with nothing they can do about it" and even today the Church's official website addressing same-sex sexuality, Mormonandgay.churchofjesuschrist.org, favors and promotes the notion of same-sex attraction (SSA) over and above gay identity (Packer, 2012). Simultaneously, since the 1970s, the Church has exponentially strengthened adherence to the views of gender and sexuality that were introduced by leaders in the early twentieth century. In the Church's now (in)famous 1995 declaration, "The Family: A Proclamation to the World," to cite the most prominent example, gender (encompassing sex, gender identity, and patriarchal gender roles) has been declared to be a static characteristic of the premortal, mortal, and eternal realms, while a heteronormative vision of family, marriage, and procreation are all posited as essentially linked, "ordained of God," and required for exaltation (The Church of Jesus Christ of Latter-day Saints, The First Presidency and Council of the Twelve Apostles, 2019). While the Church's opposition to the Equal Rights

Amendment during the late 1970s and early 1980s was the first instance in which the Church articulated its understanding of sexuality to be causally related to gender roles, it was only in the battles over gay marriage during the early 1990s that it cemented its view of same-sex sexuality as fundamentally opposed to "proper" gender roles and expression, marriage, and procreation (Quinn, 1996, p. 382).

In response to the legalization of gay marriage in the U.S. in June 2015, the Church further fortified its position against same-sex sexuality and marriage, four months later introducing a new policy that qualified entering into a same-sex marriage as apostasy and, additionally, banning children "whose primary residence is with a couple living in a same-gender marriage or similar relationship" from being baptized, or receiving and participating in other rites and privileges of membership in the Church (The Church of Jesus Christ of Latter-day Saints, 2015). In an about-face, just three and a half years later, the Church reversed these policies (The Church of Jesus Christ of Latter-day Saints, 2019). Thus far, the Church's official position on transgender people and issues has remained substantially less explicit and specific compared to those it has on same-sex sexuality, but it does council the excommunication of those individuals that undergo sex-reassignment surgeries (see Potter's "Trans and Mutable Bodies," Chapter 37, this volume).

Mormon *and* queer?

Since the late 1970s, there has been a visible and growing population of queer Mormons. How these Mormons have been able to articulate their sexual and religious identities, form or participate in communities, and engage in social and political activism has largely been circumscribed by the power and influence of the Church. Sociologist Tina Fetner (2008) has described the formative impact the religious right has had on the agenda and success of gay and lesbian activism nationally, especially through the religious right's ability to sway the gay and lesbian movement's focus on, rhetoric about, and framing of particular issues. For example, Fetner demonstrates that gay marriage, far from being an original and central focus of gay and lesbian activism, was an issue thrust upon it by the religious right. "It is much more historically accurate," she explains, to say "that the lesbian and gay movement was pulled into the same-sex marriage battle by the religious right's massive campaign to reinforce the legal exclusion of same-sex couples from marriage" (Fetner, 2008, pp. 113–14). However, it was not until the 1990s that the religious right turned its attention toward marriage. As described above, it was more than a decade earlier that the Church of Jesus of Christ of Latter-day Saints had already initiated a campaign against gay marriage in Utah. In fact, in one of the earliest battles over marriage rights in the 1990s, the Church played a significant role, perhaps more significant than the religious right, in getting Hawai'i's legislature to pass a bill limiting marriage to heterosexual couples. Considering that the Church "actually raised concerns about 'homosexuality' prior to other Christian traditions (i.e., well before the rise of the religious right or the ex-gay movement), and [that it] may have influenced the discursive work of other Christian elites throughout the last 50 years," it becomes apparent that not only has the Church wielded a tremendous influence over the agenda and rhetoric of the lesbian and gay movement nationally, but that it has had an especially profound and limiting effect on queer Mormons' social and political activism (Cragun, Sumerau, and Williams, 2015, p. 296). Thus, by the time HIV/AIDS emerged in the early 1980s, the Church's power had already vastly delineated the terms and focus of debate over gender and sexuality in contemporary U.S. society, and in Utah particularly.

It is critical to acknowledge this history, not just for posterity or accuracy's sake, but for understanding the conditions that make it possible for both conceptualizing what it means to be, and for living as, a queer Mormon. In what remains one of the only scholarly challenges to the logic of "love the sinner, hate the sin" and the hegemonic influence of Christian morality that that phrase represents in U.S. society and law, Janet Jakobsen and Ann Pellegrini (2003) argue that accepting the terms of debate over same-sex sexuality and identity presented by conservative Christianity has problematic consequences with decidedly (hetero)normative results, and not just in terms of prioritizing queer inclusion in dominant institutions such as marriage rather than critically reassessing those institutions. In perhaps the most high-stakes example, Jakobsen and Pellegrini argue that responding to religious "opponents of lesbian and gay rights [who] overwhelmingly depict ... homosexuality as a behavior-based identity, as a lifestyle choice only, and a bad choice at that" with what they call the "born that way" argument, or the argument that "homosexual identity is innate, in some way rooted in an individual's essential nature," is a sometimes expedient, but ultimately dangerous argument with troubling implications, not least of which is that if one *could* change their identity or attractions they *should* (Jakobsen and Pellegrini, 2003, p. 76). This is not to deny that, as Jakobsen and Pellegrini point out, many queer (and I would add trans) people "describe their identities as inborn, something they were aware of from a very young age" and that they could not change even if they wanted to, but it is rather to highlight the deeply embedded social advantaging of heterosexuality and cisgender identity (2003, p. 77). The fact that many queer people try desperately to change their sexuality and/or their gender identity through prayer or other religiously driven means, highlights the continued and deeply embedded *social* privileging of heterosexuality and cisgender identity as preferable.

On Mormonandgay.churchofjesuschrist.org, several interconnected themes, including the "born this way" argument, are used to (re)emphasize non-heterosexuality as inferior and undesirable. In the website's section devoted to stories of individual Mormons who identify as gay, lesbian, or SSA and how they and their families handle their situations, "born this way" reasoning is reiterated repeatedly by gay and SSA individuals to demonstrate both their sincerity and worthiness for compassion. Just to give one example, in a story that features the Mackintosh family, Xian and his father Scott describe a conversation they had about Xian's sexuality several months after he originally came out. Scott recalled that before their conversation he thought gays and lesbians "had chosen this. And if they chose this, they deserved every bit of negativity I can give them." When confronted by Xian to discuss his son's sexuality Scott remembered that he "started letting him have all of the ammunition I had saved up," and "just blurted out ... 'Xian why would you chose this? *Why*?'" to which Xian replied, "'Dad I didn't choose this ... Why would anyone choose this?'" Xian reiterates what many queer Mormons express—whether or not they choose to remain active members of the Church—the sense that being queer is so difficult, apart from the specific religious challenges it poses, that it is a natural, but ultimately unfavorable and inferior identity to have. Emphasizing this idea, Xian further explains that "despite years and years of trying, [asking God,] 'show me a girl that I can be interested in,' I just knew eventually that that wasn't something that was going to happen for me" (The Church of Jesus Christ of Latter-day Saints, 2018b). At no time does Xian or any other individual who identifies as LGB or SSA featured on the Church's site question or challenge the notion that a non-heterosexual person would "deserve negativity," to use Scott Mackintosh's words, if they had chosen their sexuality.

Several other interrelated themes build on the "born this way" argument to reinforce the underlying assumption that non-heterosexual identity or sex is inferior and undesirable, including the Church's emphasis on love versus approval, chastity versus same-sex sexual activity, and salvation versus exaltation. Both the stories and official guidance provided on the website underscore that those people who identify as LGB or SSA should be loved and tolerated, but that any choices they make which conflict with the Church's official teachings should not be "condoned."

In other words, LGB or SSA individuals must either choose celibacy or marry someone of the opposite sex to remain in alignment with Church teachings, connecting to the explicit statement on the site that heterosexual marriage might not be necessary for salvation, but that it is necessary for exaltation—a more advantaged state of post-mortal existence in Mormon cosmology—not subtly communicating that heterosexuality is a privileged status over and above all other sexual identities. Although the Church has increasingly moved away from a view of SSA as unnatural and lesbian and gay identity as chosen (it is unclear what the view of bisexuality is), it has consequently and paradoxically embraced a more constructivist view that explains sexual activity and sexuality in terms of choice, variability, and nuance. Using phrases like "attraction is not identity. People can make their own choices about how to identify" and "sexual desire can be fluid and changeable" the Church's site sounds at times more like a post-structuralist, queer theoretical accounting of sexuality and identity than it does a conservative religious institution, illustrating both the appeal and danger of the "born this way" argument, especially for those queer people who identify with conservative Christian traditions (The Church of Jesus Christ of Latter-day Saints, 2018a; 2018c).

Although the realities of the Church's social and political power have circumscribed, and continue to circumscribe, the lived experience of queer Mormons, they and their allies have begun to exert significant influence culturally, religiously, socially, and politically, influence which has indeed drastically altered the experience for those who identify as both queer and Mormon. Numerous spaces have developed—both physical and digital—to help negotiate the complexities of what it means to live as a queer Mormon, whether it be a student group like Understanding Sexuality, Gender, and Allyship (USGA) at Brigham Young University, the globally active organization Affirmation, which serves "LGBTQ+ Mormons" and their "families and friends," or any number of queer Mormon Facebook groups. In these types of spaces, like other religious queers, queer Mormons take varying approaches to balancing their multiple identities. Many choose to accept and follow, or alternately disagree with, but still follow, Church teachings on sexuality, marriage, and family. Others do not follow, but do not officially break with the Church while continuing to attend their local ward. Still others choose to break completely with the Church, some maintaining their religious beliefs, while others completely reject the faith tradition altogether. However, a theme emerges when examining activism around queer issues within the Church and in Mormon culture more generally. The Church continues to exert a weighty influence on both social mores and political debates, but perhaps in more subtle and insidious ways than is typically accounted for. This is especially apparent in the reasoning contemporary Mormons deploy to challenge the erasure, ignorance, homophobia, and violence that have typically characterized Mormon responses to and treatment of queer people into the twenty-first century. For instance, efforts such as the "I'll Walk With You" video project (2019), which features filmed testimonials from Latter-day Saint families about how they came to prize the values of love and toleration for their "LGBT brothers and sisters," organizations like Mormons Building Bridges (2019), which focuses on "conveying love and acceptance to all those who identify as" LGBTI or SSA, or institutions like Encircle (2018), a community resource center located in Provo, Utah which works to "embrace and sustain every LGBTQ+ youth, every family and every community," reflect, albeit to varying degrees, the normalizing assumptions of heteronormativity that the Church has institutionalized as essential to its theology only in the twentieth century.

For example, emphases on love and tolerance, building lines of mutually respectful communication and understanding between straight, active Mormons and queer Mormons, as well as fighting for inclusion in the dominant institutions and practices of the Church and society all depend on essentialist logic ("born this way" or biological arguments) that often leaves intact hetero- and cissexist assumptions as valid and reasonable points of view and always leaves unquestioned and even reinforces heteronormativity as the commonsense way of interpreting and organizing society. In a typical video from the "I'll Walk with You" website Wesley Stephens, father to Tyler Stephens, describes his reaction to his son coming out, explaining that "it took some soul-searching for me to realize ... *I don't know if he's broken or if he needs to be fixed or what* [emphasis added], but I do know that I still love him. I mean that's my son." Throughout the testimonial Wesley Stephens reiterates his disapproval of and lack of understanding of same-sex sexuality, even admitting at the beginning of the video that he grew up "with a group of people, that we really didn't care for gays, at all ... I kinda hated 'em. I kinda just had this total disgust, I mean literal ... I couldn't stand 'em ... the thought of it just really made me sick" (I'll Walk With You, 2019). Yet, throughout the video he and his wife, Anita, continually reiterate that they love their son *despite* his sexuality. In other words, their emphasis on loving their son as more important than his sexuality—something they clearly disapprove of—does not require them to rethink their homophobic or heterosexist opinions, but simply requires them to prioritize communicating their love and not their disapproval to their son. Many other examples illustrate similar, although not always such stark, contradictions in the logic and assumptions that underlie Mormon approaches to negotiating, representing, and advocating for queer identities and rights whether it be pushing the Church to recognize marriage for couples of the same-sex or another Mormon father's statement in the popular documentary *Transmormon* (OHO Media, 2014) that because his trans daughter Eri *is* a woman she can conform to the heterosexual requirements of the Church's 1995 Proclamation which dictates only a woman and man can get married.

A queer Mormon future?

The effect, either knowingly or not, of repeating or relying on these assumptions and forms of reasoning is a reaffirmation of heteronormativity, the as yet still unchallenged commonsense framework for interpreting and organizing society which queer theory has sought to expose and contest. Berlant and Warner's descriptive definition of heteronormativity is especially helpful here: heteronormativity refers to the way "community is imagined through scenes of intimacy, coupling, and kinship" in which "a historical relation to futurity is restricted to generational narrative and reproduction," and "a whole field of social relations becomes intelligible as heterosexuality ... bestow[ed with] ... a tacit sense of rightness and normalcy," and that it is "produced in almost every aspect of the forms and arrangements of social life [including] nationality, the state, and the law; commerce; medicine; and education, as well as in the conventions and affects of narrativity, romance, and other protected spaces of culture" (1998, pp. 554–55). What would it mean then, indeed is it even possible, to queer the "commonsenseness" of heteronormativity, which has come to so profoundly structure mainstream Mormonism in the twenty-first century? While the consequences and possibilities for such a queer Mormon future are open for debate, and are best addressed by queer Mormons themselves, one potential point of departure is a consideration of the documented changes the Church has undergone in its attitude and approach to questions of gender and sexuality over its history—specifically, how those changes reflect broader political, social, and cultural patterns, and therefore potentially open up possibilities for historicizing, theologizing, and living Mormonism in significantly different ways. Indeed, the potential of queer, as Warner reminds us, is that the insistence on "a term initially generated in the context of terror—has the effect of pointing out a wide field of normalization, rather than simple intolerance, as the site of violence" (1993, p. xxvi). In the context of Mormonism then, queer's exposure of (hetero)normativity as a site of violence also invites a (re)consideration of its relationship to salvation and exaltation.

References

Anderson, J.S., 2017. *LGBT Salt Lake*. Charleston, SC: Arcadia Publishing.
Bentley, N., 2002. Marriage as Treason. In R. Weigman and D.E. Pease, eds. *The Futures of American Studies*. Durham, NC: Duke University Press, pp. 341–70.
Berlant, L., and Warner, M., 1998. Sex in Public. *Critical Inquiry* 24(2). Available through Auraria Library website https://library.auraria.edu/ (accessed March 13, 2019).
Bullough, V., and Bullough, B., 1977. Lesbianism in the 1920s and 1930s. *Signs* 2(4). Available through Auraria Library website https://library.auraria.edu/ (accessed March 13, 2019).
Canaday, M., 2009. *The Straight State*. Princeton, NJ: Princeton University Press.
The Church of Jesus Christ of Latter-day Saints, 2018a. About Sexual Orientation. https://mormonandgay.lds.org/articles/about-sexual-orientation?lang=eng (accessed March 13, 2019).
The Church of Jesus Christ of Latter-day Saints, 2018b. Becky's Story. https://mormonandgay.lds.org/articles/beckys-story?lang=eng (accessed March 13, 2019).
The Church of Jesus Christ of Latter-day Saints, 2018c. Frequently Asked Questions. https://mormonandgay.lds.org/articles/frequently-asked-questions?lang=eng (accessed March 13, 2019).
The Church of Jesus Christ of Latter-day Saints, 2019. First Presidency Shares Messages from General Conference Leadership Session. April 4. www.mormonnewsroom.org/article/first-presidency-messages-general-conference-leadership-session-april-2019 (accessed April 18, 2019).
The Church of Jesus Christ of Latter-day Saints, Office of the First Presidency, 2015. First Presidency Clarifies Church Handbook Changes. November 13. www.lds.org/pages/church-handbook-changes?lang=eng (accessed March 13, 2019).
The Church of Jesus Christ of Latter-day Saints, The First Presidency and Council of the Twelve Apostles, 2019. The Family. www.lds.org/topics/family-proclamation?lang=eng&old=true (accessed March 13, 2019).
Cragun, R.T., Sumerau, J.E. and Williams, E., 2015. From Sodomy to Sympathy. *Journal for the Scientific Study of Religion* 54(2). Available through Auraria Library website https://library.auraria.edu/ (accessed March 13, 2019).
Encircle, 2018. *Mission*. https //encircletogether.org/mission (accessed March 13, 2019).
Fetner, T., 2008. *How the Religious Right Shaped Lesbian and Gay Activism*. Minneapolis, MN: University of Minnesota Press.
Hardy, B.C., and Erickson, D., 2001. Regeneration—Now and Evermore! *Journal of the History of Sexuality* 10(1). Available through Auraria Library website https://library.auraria.edu/ (accessed March 13, 2019).
I'll Walk With You, 2019. *The Stephens*. http://ldswalkwithyou.org/the-stephens/ (accessed March 13, 2019).
Jagose, A., 1997. *Queer Theory*. New York: New York University Press.
Jakobsen, J., and Pellegrini, A., 2003. *Love the Sin*. New York: New York University Press.
Mohrman, K., 2015. Queering the LDS Archive. *Radical History Review* 122. Available through Auraria Library website https://library.auraria.edu/ (accessed March 13, 2019).
Mohrman, K., 2017. *Exceptionally Queer*. Ph.D. Dissertation, University of Minnesota.
Mormons Building Bridges, 2019. *Home*. http://mormonsbuildingbridges.org/ (accessed March 13, 2019).
O'Donovan, C., 1994. The Abominable and Detestable Crime against Nature. In B. Corcoran, ed. *Multiply and Replenish*. Salt Lake City, UT: Signature Books, pp. 123–70.
OHO Media, 2014. *Transmormon*. www.youtube.com/watch?v=iLjDgnGDV3g (accessed March 13, 2019).
Packer, B.K., 2012. *To Young Men Only*. Salt Lake City, UT: The Church of Jesus Christ of Latter-day Saints. https://web.archive.org/web/20151021234056/www.lds.org/manual/to-young-men-only/to-young-men-only (accessed March 13, 2019).
Payne, S., 2017. Mormonism and Same-Sex Marriage: Theological Underpinnings and New Perspectives. *Journal of Catholic Legal Studies* 51(1). Available through Auraria Library website https://library.auraria.edu/ (accessed March 13, 2019).
Petrey, T., 2011. Toward a Post-Heterosexual Mormon Theology. *Dialogue* 44(4). Available through Auraria Library website https://library.auraria.edu/ (accessed March 13, 2019).
Quinn, D.M., 1996. *Same-Sex Dynamics among Nineteenth-Century Americans*. Urbana, IL: University of Illinois Press.

Talbot, C., 2013. *A Foreign Kingdom*. Urbana, IL: University of Illinois Press.
Warner, H.L., 1987. Oscar Wilde's Visit to Salt Lake City. *Utah Historical Quarterly* 55(4). Available through Auraria Library website https://library.auraria.edu/ (accessed March 13, 2019).
Warner, M., 1993. *Fear of a Queer Planet*. Minneapolis, MN: University of Minnesota Press.
Winkler, D.A., 2008. Lavender Sons of Zion. Ph.D. Dissertation, University of Utah.

Further reading

Jagose, A., 1997. *Queer Theory*. New York: New York University Press.
Jakobsen, J., and Pellegrini, A., 2003. *Love the Sin*. New York: New York University Press.
Petrey, T., 2011. Toward a Post-Heterosexual Mormon Theology. *Dialogue* 44(4). Available through Auraria Library website https://library.auraria.edu/ (accessed March 13, 2019).
Quinn, D.M., 1996. *Same-Sex Dynamics among Nineteenth-Century Americans*. Urbana, IL: University of Illinois Press.
Warner, M., 1993. *Fear of a Queer Planet*. Minneapolis, MN: University of Minnesota Press.

37
TRANS AND MUTABLE BODIES

Kelli D. Potter

In contrast to the rest of the Christian tradition, Mormonism's theology is materialist (Webb, 2013, pp. 41ff). This materialism not only involves the claim that everything that exists is made of matter but also the claim that the human body has a positive valence in the moral order of the cosmos. For Latter-day Saints, bodies are one part of the soul, with the *material* spirit being the other part. Gaining a body in this mortal life is necessary in order to become as God is. Indeed, according to Mormon theology, even our Heavenly Parents have bodies. With this emphasis on embodiment and commitment to a kind of materialism, one might expect Mormonism to be quite progressive in its practices with respect to the body. A well-known feminist critique of traditional Christian theism is based on the fact that the latter pits embodied passion and desire against disembodied and dispassionate rationality, and then equates femininity with embodiment and masculinity with disembodiment. By contrast, feminist philosophers of religion such as Pamela Sue Anderson argue for an approach to understanding divinity that embraces embodiment and desire (1998, pp. 98ff). For Anderson, this would have implications for religious practice that would be more inclusive of women in the institutions of religious power. Her work makes clear that the connection between embodiment and gender issues is quite undeniable. However, far from drawing similarly radical conclusions, LDS orthodoxy has taken a rather conservative stance on practices relating to the body and body modification, especially regarding sex and gender.[1]

This chapter will explore Mormon theologies of embodiment with an eye to understanding how Mormon practice handles body modification, focusing primarily on those body modifications involved in medical procedures undergone and medications taken by transgender individuals. That is, this chapter will explore a particularly important intersection between Mormonism's theology of embodiment and its theology of gender. This exploration will reveal that the existence of transgender folk poses a problem for orthodox LDS theology. In the first section, I will give a brief overview of the transgender phenomenon and the nature of medical transitioning, including the role played by gender confirmation surgery (GCS). In the second section, I will identify some of the theological foundations of Mormonism's materialism and its connection to the theology of sex and gender, showing where lacunae and tensions exist in the orthodoxy as it stands. In the final section, I will explore several of the heterodox theologies of gender from within the LDS fold and identify an alternative Mormon theology of embodiment that would suggest a trans-friendly approach to the body and gender.

Mutable bodies

Humans modify their bodies in a myriad of ways: tattoos, piercings, surgical alterations (including altering sex organs), and psychotropic drugs (e.g., SSRIs, psilocybin). And these are just a few of the ways of modifying the body. Humans have a variety of reasons for body modification including, but not limited to, religious/spiritual, medical/therapeutic, and cosmetic. The LDS Church has taken positions on some types of body modifications. For example, the church has discouraged tattoos, cosmetic surgeries, and body piercings (Packer, 2000). But the most significant prohibition on body modification has been the aforementioned policy sanctioning those that have GCS. The 2010 edition of the *Church Handbook of Instructions: Book 1, Stake Presidencies and Bishoprics* states:

> Persons who are considering an elective transsexual operation should not be baptized. Baptism of a person who has already undergone an elective transsexual operation requires the approval of the First Presidency ... However, such persons may not receive the priesthood or a temple recommend.
> *(The Church of Jesus Christ of Latter-day Saints, 2010, p. 146)*

The word "elective" might seem to refer to the fact that these are surgeries that are sought out by transgender individuals rather than intersex newborns that undergo surgery due to having ambiguous genitalia. However, such surgeries on intersex babies *do* count as elective since they are not necessary for survival or good health. And, by contrast, GCS is often necessary in order to alleviate the gender dysphoria that often leads to suicide (Bockting and Goldberg, 2006). In this way, GCS is more medically necessary than surgery on an intersex baby's genitals, given that ambiguous genitalia are often perfectly functional and not an obstacle to good health. Perhaps the intent of the handbook is to emphasize the elective nature of the surgery because LDS doctrine emphasizes agency and the authors take undergoing GCS to be a matter of choice. However, a transgender individual might object that hormone replacement therapy (hereafter HRT), GCS, as well as other surgical procedures are not a matter of choice, but a matter of life or death. That is, HRT and GCS are no less necessary than antidepressants are for those living with depression. By referring to GCS as "elective," it seems clear that the church is categorizing GCS with cosmetic surgeries such as breast implants or liposuction. That is certainly misleading and it is inconsistent with the asymmetry in how they treat individuals who have undergone GCS and individuals that have had cosmetic surgery.

Given the seriousness of these sanctions against transgender individuals, it makes sense to take a look at possible theological justifications for such sanctions. But first let's review the facts and terminology related to transgender folk. "Transgender" applies to anyone that does not identify with their assigned gender and/or physical sex characteristics. This might include people that identify as the "opposite" gender and people that don't identify exclusively as a man or a woman. The umbrella term for transgender individuals of the latter sort is "nonbinary" and includes (but is not limited to) "genderqueer," "agender," "bigender," "genderfluid," and "androgyne." The word "transgender" is an adjective and is used to modify a noun, as in: "transgender woman" or "transgender man." It is not a verb nor is it a noun. Often "trans" is used as an abbreviated version of "transgender" (e.g., "trans man" or "trans woman"). The opposite of "trans" is "cis," where a cis person identifies with the gender assigned to them at birth.

Many, but not all, transgender folk experience what is commonly called "gender dysphoria" (or sometimes, "gender incongruence"). This is a state of mental dissonance in which one feels discomfort associated with one's assigned gender and/or one's primary and secondary sex characteristics. It usually arises in childhood or early puberty. In the DSM-V, gender dysphoria (previously called "gender identity disorder") is currently classified as a mental health condition in its own category. And it is worthy to note that gender dysphoria is not in the category of sexual disorders, although gender identity disorder *was* included in the DSM-IV (Parry, 2013).

Although this was not always the case, the currently accepted treatment affirms transgender identities. It includes psychological counseling which affirms one's inner sense of one's gender and access to various forms of medical transition, which include—but are not limited to—hormone replacement therapy, mastectomy, breast enhancement surgery, vaginoplasty, phalloplasty, facial feminization surgery, and vocal feminization surgery (WPATH, 2011). Those transgender individuals that engage in some form of medical transition are sometimes called "transsexuals," although that term is considered outdated by some. It is important to note that not all transgender individuals medically transition and not all of those that do medically transition choose to have GCS. This affirmative approach to the treatment of individuals with gender dysphoria has been shown to increase the well-being of the patient and to reduce the likelihood of suicide, which is extremely high in those that experience gender dysphoria (Haas, Rodgers, and Herman, 2014).

Given this background information, one might wonder what the handbook policy means by "transsexual operation." Indeed, there are several different operations that transsexuals might opt to undergo, including facial feminization surgery and breast implants for trans women and "top surgery" (i.e., mastectomy with breast reconstruction) for trans men. But since the cisgender world often assumes that the only relevant surgery is GCS, we can assume that this is the surgery to which the LDS handbook refers. It seems arbitrary that the handbook focuses only on surgeries related to genitalia unless we consider how this is related to their theological stance on gender and sexual relations. Many trans individuals medically transition without any surgeries and choose only the less risky HRT (Serano, 2016, pp. 31–32). What is the church's reason for singling out those that choose to have GCS, while ignoring those that don't?

There is a difference between medically transitioning and socially transitioning. A trans person socially transitions when they begin to live openly as the gender with which they identify. It is common for trans folk to change their names when they transition. And many seek to change their names and gender marker on their state ID, passport, birth certificate, and other legal documents. Not all transgender persons who socially transition undergo medical transition. So, it seems that the LDS Church's current policy doesn't include those that merely socially transition nor does it include those that medically transition but decide not to have GCS.

Mormonism, embodiment, and gender

In this section, I will give an overview of LDS orthodoxy on the subjects of embodiment and gender. As mentioned above, abstractly speaking, Mormon theology takes a quite heterodox approach to the body, at least when compared to traditional Christianity. It is clear that traditional Christianity has, for the most part, accepted a fundamental ontological dichotomy between body and spirit (soul) and that this dichotomy is a hierarchy with the body having a lesser valence than the spirit. Of course, God is immaterial on the traditional view. And rationality is associated with the spiritual while passion is associated with embodiment. On the traditional Christian view, God does not have body parts or passions. By contrast, according to LDS Mormonism, there is no fundamental ontological distinction between body and spirit. Joseph Smith taught that "all spirit is matter" but it is "more fine or pure" (D&C 131:7). Moreover, God the Father (i.e., "Heavenly Father") is embodied and was once a human like us. In the famous King Follet Discourse, Joseph Smith writes,

> God Himself who sits enthroned in yonder heavens is a Man like unto one of yourselves—that is the great secret! If the veil were rent today and the great God that holds this world in its sphere and the planets in their orbit and who upholds all things by His power—if you were to see Him today, you would see Him in all the person, image, fashion, and very form of a man, like yourselves. For Adam was a man formed in His likeness and created in the very fashion and image of God. Adam received instruction, walked, talked, and conversed with Him as one man talks and communicates with another man.
>
> ...
>
> He once was *a man* like one of us and that God Himself, the Father of us all, *once* dwelled on an earth the same as Jesus Christ himself did in the flesh *and like us*.
>
> *(Larsen, 1978, p. 7)*

If God is embodied, then there isn't a fundamental ontological dichotomy between the human and the divine. Moreover, it would seem that divinity is not incompatible with passion since, as Smith says, "That which is without body, parts, and passions is nothing. There is no other God in heaven but that God who has flesh and bones" (Smith, 1968, p. 181). Given that the Father has a body and we are to become like Him, Smith taught that the body was an essential element in our eternal progression. He says,

> We came to this earth that we might have a body and present it pure before God in the celestial kingdom. The great principle of happiness consists in having a body. The devil has no body, and herein is his punishment. He is pleased when he can obtain the tabernacle of man. ... All beings who have bodies have power over those who have not.
>
> *(1968, p. 181)*

Clearly, the body plays a positive role in Smith's theology. This means that there is no fundamental divide between the spirit world and the world of ordinary physical bodies.

It is important to note also that Mormonism's materialism differs from the materialism that was common in the philosophical world in the nineteenth century. The latter was deterministic (McMurrin, 1965, p. 44), where matter is understood to be unthinking and moved only by the laws of mechanics. By contrast, Mormonism's commitment to free will and an open future is incompatible with determinism and mechanism. And at least one Mormon theologian argues for a panpsychist view of the nature of matter (Pratt, 2014). So, instead of embracing a substance metaphysics in which *being* is the most fundamental ontological category, one could argue that Mormonism fits better with a metaphysics of *becoming* (McMurrin, 1959, pp. 20ff). In many ways, Mormonism's materialism is not unlike that of the so-called New Materialism (Coole and Frost, 2010, pp. 1ff).

Despite the fact that the materialist direction of Mormon theology seems like it could be the basis for a radical approach, LDS orthodoxy advocates a rather conservative practice regarding the body. Nowhere is this more obvious than in the late Apostle Elder Boyd K. Packer's General Conference talk entitled, "Ye Are the Temple of God." In this talk, Elder Packer takes a cue from Paul's 1 Corinthians and claims that our bodies are like the temple of God and should not be defiled in any way (Packer, 2000). In the LDS Church the temple is a sacred space and must be kept clean, both physically and spiritually. Non-members and unworthy members are not allowed to enter the temple since their presence would defile the building. So, if the body is like a temple of the Lord, then it should be kept clean as well, both literally and morally.

Some of the things that are prohibited in LDS practice are drugs, alcohol, coffee, tea, heterosexual sex outside of marriage, homosexual sex, masturbation, pornography, immodest dress, and (of course) "elective transsexual operations." Other things are sometimes discouraged, such as tattoos, multiple piercings (one piercing in each ear for women is deemed permissible), facial or long hair on men, and sodas with caffeine. Packer discusses most of these in his talk, saying about tattoos, for example, that "[y]ou would not paint a temple with dark pictures or symbols or graffiti or even initials" (2000). However, the most important part of his talk deals with sexual immorality. He gives a fairly typical set of instructions to the youth to avoid sex before marriage, and then he turns to discuss homosexuality. He says,

> With some few, there is the temptation which seems nearly overpowering for man to be attracted to man or woman to woman. The scriptures plainly condemn those who "dishonour their own bodies between themselves ... men with men working that which is unseemly" (Rom. 1:24, 27) or "women [who] change the natural use into that which is against nature" (Rom. 1:26).
>
> *(2000)*

So, on Packer's view, homosexual desire is unnatural and unseemly; it defiles the temple of the body. Packer goes on to admonish the youth:

> Do not experiment; do not let anyone of either gender touch your body to awaken passions that can flame beyond control. It begins as an innocent curiosity, Satan influences your thoughts, and it becomes a pattern, a habit, which may imprison you in an addiction, to the sorrow and disappointment of those who love you.
>
> *(2000)*

Elder Packer's approach to understanding sexual immorality is similar to what is sometimes called "purity culture" in the evangelical Christian world (Collins, 2014). This pattern of connecting sexual activity outside heterosexual marriage to a defilement of the body continues to play a significant role in other official LDS texts and practices. Purity culture has been criticized by feminists (Valenti, 2009) as well as by the well-known Mormon kidnap victim Elizabeth Smart.

The idea that the one can defile the body by engaging in unwed sexual activity implies that the body is morally mutable and that using the body for "unnatural and unseemly" purposes will reduce its moral goodness. And it is easy to see how one might use this "purity theology" to argue against allowing transsexuals into full fellowship. As with homosexuality, transsexuality could be seen as unnatural and unseemly since it involves a modification of the body's sexual characteristics motivated by the desire to "change sex." This desire is seen, according to this view, as being aroused by inappropriate touching or pornography. Of course, anyone acquainted with very many transgender individuals would know that sexual activity has very little to do with why trans folk transition (Serano, 2010).

There is, of course, an apparent incompatibility between the claim that temptations can be awoken by mere touch and the claim that the natural body has a positive valence. Where are these temptations coming from if not the body? Packer acknowledges as much when he describes these passions as being "awakened" in the body. We're back to thinking of the passions and the body as having a negative valence. But the body is also a temple of God, according to Packer. Purity culture emphasizes what one must *not* do with or to the body. Seeing the body as a temple seems to imply that it is, by nature, something separate from the world and something that must be kept clean of worldly influences. This approach to what one may do with or to one's body, then, is quite negative.

Packer connects the issue of the nature and purpose of the body to sexual morality. This connection is reinforced by the LDS church's official proclamation in 1995, the aforementioned "The Family: A Proclamation to the World" which states:

> All human beings—male and female—are created in the image of God. Each is a beloved spirit son or daughter of heavenly parents, and, as such, each has a divine nature and destiny. Gender is an essential characteristic of individual premortal, mortal, and eternal identity and purpose.
>
> In the premortal realm, spirit sons and daughters knew and worshipped God as their Eternal Father and accepted His plan by which His children could obtain a physical body and gain earthly experience to progress toward perfection and ultimately realize their divine destiny as heirs of eternal life. The divine plan of happiness enables family relationships to be perpetuated beyond the grave.
>
> *(The Church of Jesus Christ of Latter-day Saints, 1995)*

This text starts with the idea that humans, being male and female, are made in the image of God in a rather literal sense. Our bodies look like God's body—or better, the Gods' bodies; and these include male *and* female bodies. Moreover, if we assume that the reason for sexual differentiation is to allow for procreation, then it makes sense that we would literally have "Heavenly Parents." The Proclamation further states that "God has commanded that the sacred powers of procreation are to be employed only between man and woman, lawfully wedded as husband and wife." It is clear that the LDS view is that sex is for procreation. Of course, one might make the familiar Thomistic argument, on this basis, that homosexuality is immoral because it involves sex without the possibility of procreation (Pickett, 2015). Families are not limited to this life and if one lives righteously, one will live eternally with one's family. These families, of course, are understood to be heterosexual families and gender is taken to be an essential characteristic of our identities in premortal, mortal, and postmortal lives.

It is fairly clear that this theology excludes homosexuality and it *might seem* fairly clear that it excludes transgender individuals as well. Discussing bodily modification in the context of Mormon transhumanism, Adam S. Miller writes that "because it is seen as an essential characteristic of premortal, mortal, and postmortal identity, enhancements that rendered gender excessively plastic or inconsequential would be especially suspect" (2014, p. 132). However, this connection is not as tight as Miller seems to presuppose. The problem is that as soon as we say that the spirit has a gender, the theological possibility of a mismatch with the gender of the body arises. Moreover, this idea of a mismatch coheres with the well-known narrative in which a trans person feels like they were born in the wrong body (Prosser, 1998, p. 69). Finally, in the case of intersex folk, there *must* be a mismatch since their bodies are not unambiguously male or female.

To explore this idea of a mismatch, let's turn to Torben Bernhard's documentary film *Transmormon* which tells the coming out story of Eri Hayward, a trans woman raised by Mormon parents. Unlike many religious parents who reject their LGBTQ children, Eri's father, Edward Hayward, accepts her and even speculates that her spirit is actually female. He says,

> We believe that the Church leaders are receiving revelation that helps them to be able to better serve in the callings that we're given in the priesthood. We have the Proclamation to the World on the family which states very clearly that a marriage is between

a man and a woman. In my opinion, Eri's a woman and so, I don't see a problem with that. And, I'm hoping that the leaders of the Church are going to see it that way and that she'll be able to get married. And, she won't be able to have children but she can hopefully adopt children.

(Transmormon)

Hayward's interpretation of the Proclamation is quite reasonable theologically: gender can be essential to your spiritual nature and, yet, for whatever reason your body's sexual characteristics don't match your gender. Nothing in the Proclamation rules this out. And yet, the church doesn't allow transsexuals to be in full membership and, at least sometimes, excommunicates church members that have undergone GCS (Stack, 2017).

Heterodox possibilities

Of course, Hayward's interpretation of Mormon theology wouldn't allow for nonbinary and genderfluid folk. His approach to gender remains essentialist and binary: everyone is man or woman, not both and not neither. In the 1990s, Mormon feminists usually took a binary approach to gender as well. For example, in their groundbreaking book *Strangers in Paradox: Explorations in Mormon Theology*, Margaret Toscano and Paul Toscano write,

> A theology of a God of flesh and glory provides a model preserving binary opposites but refusing to favor one component over the other or to link the so-called less favorable component with the female. If God is both body and spirit, then we may believe that both are equally necessary and valuable.
>
> For us God is not only flesh and glory but also male and female. We disagree with those who assert that avoiding sexism means picturing God as being beyond gender and sexuality. A picture of God beyond all categories and relations encourages the very spirit/matter dichotomy which has denigrated women and sex. In our view the more salutary doctrine is one that sees God as spirit and body, male and female. For this reason, we have come to accept both a male God and a female God each of whom is simultaneously transcendent and immanent.
>
> *(1990, pp. 47–48)*

It's not clear whether this rules out the possibility of binary trans folk; but it certainly rules out the possibility of nonbinary and genderfluid individuals. However, Margaret Toscano has modified her view in more recent writings. In a Sunstone Symposium presentation from 2014, she begins,

> In this paper I will argue for the importance of diversity and valuing the wide variety of gender and sexual identities and expressions that are evident in the history of human cultures. I will also argue for the importance of male and female as biological, theological, social, and linguistic categories. I do not believe that divine perfection lies either in moving beyond the male female binary, or in moving beyond bodies that are sexed and gendered. But I also believe that we need to see all categories as fluid and that we need to increase our categories.
>
> *(Toscano, 2014, p. 1)*

Instead of acquiescing in the gender binary as she did before, Toscano takes the position that gender is still an essential part of our identities as humans and Gods-in-embryo, but that the genders need not be seen as exclusive opposites, nor do they need to be seen as fixed. We will return below to the idea that gender could be an essential part of our nature without a commitment to the gender binary.

Mormonism's extreme anthropomorphism raises interesting questions about the nature of the divine body and how it relates to human bodies. In addition to worries about God's skin color for example, Mormonism raises questions about whether God's body is sexed. Does God the Father have a penis and God the Mother a vagina? Of course, if procreation is indeed the manner in which deities produce spiritual children, then perhaps the Gods *do* have genitalia. At this point, Mormon theology starts to sound more like Greek or Norse religion than it does like Christianity. And we can push this sexiness even further, for our premortal spirits are supposed to have gender as well. Would this then imply that they have sex organs? Do we have spiritual penises and vaginas? And if we can become Gods, then do Gods have penises and vaginas?

Perhaps due to the strangeness of taking anthropomorphism this far, Mormon scholars have sometimes qualified their position on the similarity of divine and human bodies. For example, Taylor Petrey emphasizes some differences between human and divine bodies,

> [A] divine body is not constrained by space and time in the ways that mortal bodies are. From scriptural accounts, divine bodies can appear, disappear, pass through walls, and resist entropy. While these scriptural accounts affirm that it is possible for divine bodies to perform functions such as eating and drinking, they also suggest that there is no necessary requirement that they do so in order to sustain life.
>
> *(2011, p. 111)*

In a second example of such qualification, James Faulconer states:

> The bodies of flesh and bone with which I am familiar do not shine, have blood, cannot hover, can be wounded and die, must move through contiguous points of time-space—in short, they are not at all like the bodies of the Father and the Son. So what does it mean to say that the Father and the Son have bodies? In fact, does it mean anything at all? When I use the word *body* in any other context, I never refer to something that shines, can hover, is immortal, and moves through space seemingly without being troubled by walls and doors. Given the vast difference between what we mean by the word *body* in every other case and that to which the word refers in this case, one can legitimately ask whether the word *body* has the same meaning in this case that it has in the others.
>
> *(Faulconer, 2005, p. 1)*

It seems clear that the tendency to want to qualify the nature of God's embodiment is present in Mormon thought; and it is an understandable tendency. However, once this qualification begins then it is not clear that sexual differentiation is still part of the picture. And without sex being a part of the picture, it is not clear what justifies the heteronormative bias or the claim that gender is an essential and eternal part of one's identity.

In the article cited above, Petrey explores the possibility of a "post-heterosexual" approach to Mormon theology of sex and gender. He identifies the ambivalence concerning the role that sex plays in the divine life. He writes,

> The ambivalence on this point is a persistent tension in Mormon thought. That is, the doctrine of spiritual birth stands at odds with the doctrine of eternal intelligences, and

to this day Mormonism has not resolved this tension. On the one hand, "spirit birth" is a divine reproduction that mirrors human reproduction, requiring a male and female partner; and on the other hand, "spirit birth" is a more metaphorical "organization" that bears little resemblance to reproduction as a result of sexual intercourse.

(Petrey, 2011, p. 109)

Petrey goes on to argue against this view by pushing it to its logical extreme again. Petrey writes,

[If spirit birth is divine reproduction] then must we imagine that male gods deposit sperm in the bodies of female gods (who menstruate monthly when they are not pregnant), that the pregnant female god gestates spirit embryos for nine months and then gives birth to spirit bodies? While some LDS thinkers imagine an eternally pregnant Heavenly Mother, I see no reason why we must commit to this kind of literal pregnancy as the reason for divine female figures.

(Petrey, 2011, p. 110)

In addition to pointing to the ambivalence of Mormonism on divine sex, Petrey urges that there are many resources in the tradition that suggest that the spirit birth in the premortal life is not a literal birth, but rather another kind of production altogether (Petrey, 2011, p. 113). Without the need for divine sex for the reproduction of spirit children, then the central justification for Mormon heteronormativity fails. And this is how Petrey opens up the possibility for a post-heterosexual Mormon theology.

In addition to dealing with the divine reproduction model as a basis for heteronormativity, Petrey looks at the claim that gender is an essential and eternal characteristic of human identity. After pointing out that the meaning of the term "gender" in Mormon theology is quite unclear, Petrey argues that the claim that gender is essential and eternal is inconsistent with the church's emphasis on the necessity of teaching proper gender roles (Petrey, 2011, p. 124). If it is essential, then it doesn't need to be taught. However, since gender does need to be taught, Petrey takes this to be a reason to reject the Proclamation's gender essentialism in favor of Judith Butler's variety of social constructivism (Petrey, 2011, p. 124).

Petrey further develops his post-heterosexual approach in "Rethinking Mormonism's Heavenly Mother" (2016). After pointing to the heteronormativity and gender essentialism presupposed by the Mormon feminist theologies of Margaret Toscano and Janice Allred, among others, Petrey explores the possibility for a more fluid and pluralistic understanding of gender in the Mormon context. Interestingly for our purposes, he points to Mormon feminist discussions of the ways that Jesus transcends gender boundaries. He says,

Within the framework of sexual difference, many Mormon thinkers, in fact, point to Christ as transgressive with respect to his gender in order to enable female salvation. Such approaches undo the edifice of the gender binary that many of these same thinkers advance. I want to point out that it is not just fluidity as such that grounds this Mormon view of Jesus. Specifically, it is fluidity with respect to his maleness—"the most female of men." Mormon feminism has sought to retain such a female Christ as a point of identification for women. Surprisingly, then, notions of Christ's transgression of his maleness are ubiquitous in Mormon feminism, which deconstructs the rigidity of gender upon which these theologies have relied.

(2016, p. 23)

This emphasis on the fluid and plural nature of gender is certainly trans friendly since it is committed to the idea of transcending the boundaries that gender impose.

Petrey's approach is articulated with a Butlerian understanding of the nature of gender of which trans scholars and activists have sometimes been critical. According to Butler, gender is performative, where this means that the construction of gender depends on the repetition of actions such as certain bodily movements, ways of speaking, manners of dress, etc. (1990, pp. 174–81). Even our understanding of physical sex is mediated through the gender norms whose purpose it is to uphold heteronormativity (1993, pp. 9–10). Butler discusses transgender individuals often in her writings, using them as a way to show the conventionality and performativity of gender (2004). Nevertheless, there are problems with Butler's view from a trans perspective as well as from a Mormon perspective.

The main problem here is the fact that Butler's performative model of the nature of gender ignores the importance of the body for the transgender narrative (Prosser, 1998, pp. 21ff). In her book *Whipping Girl*, Julia Serano argues that both gender essentialism and social constructivism fail to adequately explain the existence of trans individuals. She says,

> Many girls who are masculine and boys who are feminine show signs of such behavior at a very early age (often before such children have been fully socialized with regard to gender norms), and generally continue to express such a behavior into adulthood despite the extreme amount of societal pressure that we place on individuals to reproduce gender expression appropriate for their assigned sex.
>
> *(2016, p. 98)*

Serano goes on to argue for a "bio-experiential" model of gender in which gender is rooted in inclinations that are "hard-wired" into our bodies and brains. However, these inclinations, in various dimensions and to varying degrees allow for the possibility of constructing gender in a plurality of ways. For Serano, gender is socially constructed but in a way that is grounded in our bodies and our experiences (2016, p. 100). Gender is not *merely* performative as Butler's view might seem to suggest.

Now one might suggest that something like Serano's model is not only better at explaining the existence of trans folk, it is also more in line with how Mormonism sees gender (i.e., as essential to who we are) than the view advocated by Petrey. Given what she says in her 2014 paper, Toscano would agree that gender is essential to identity even if it is not binary and not static. As with Toscano's later work, Serano's model sees gender as not being exclusively binary, since our gender is based on our psychological and biological inclinations which can themselves be a matter of degree (2016, p. 100).

Although we saw that the LDS Church has taken a rather negative approach to the praxis of the body, Mormonism has resources for emphasizing the positive potential in bodies. There are hints concerning how LDS theology could have taken a different direction in James Faulconer's essay "Divine Embodiment and Transcendence: Propaedeutic Thoughts and Questions" (2005). In this article, Faulconer argues that Mormonism's materialist theology requires a rejection of both substance dualism and reductive materialism. The problem is that reductive materialism misses something essential to the nature of the embodied experience. He states,

> We can speak of a body, animate or inanimate, in terms of its characteristics, in other words, scientifically, or we can speak of it in terms of its situatedness/interactions/activities/relations (what I will call shortly, openness). However, to see the body in terms only of characteristics is tantamount to seeing it as a corpse, even if the

characteristics discussed are the characteristics peculiar to a living being. To see the body only in terms of physical characteristics is to see it only in terms of the effects it produces as a material entity; its uses, its goals. It is not to see it in terms of its life and, so, it is to miss crucial aspects of what it means to be embodied.

(2005, p. 7)

Faulconer further argues that this openness of the body is what accounts for human and divine transcendence. He states,

As I see it, there are several things we can say about human transcendence, all of them implicitly matters of embodiment and, so, all of them candidates for helping us think about what divine embodiment means. A first is that humans are, qua humans, transcendent. A second is that for human beings transcendence means openness and exposure. It means the possibility of suffering.

(2005, p. 8)

This concept of openness is crucial for understanding divine and human embodiment. So, let's explore it a bit further. Openness is a characteristic of bodies that involves situatedness, activity, and relationships. *Situatedness* involves the fact that bodies are always already in the world, i.e., in an environment. Given that the human is essentially embodied, the human is not separate from the world, even in principle. Being in the world is part of what makes us what we are and so we are essentially relational. *Activity* implies dynamism, and the body is not a static entity with a timeless essence. Seeing bodies as active, relational, and situated seems to imply a rejection of substance metaphysics (i.e., "ontotheology"); our being is tied up with the being of others. Faulconer importantly notes that this openness that he ascribes to the lived body raises the possibility of suffering (2005, pp. 9–10).

Although Faulconer doesn't say anything about how his approach to Mormonism's theology of embodiment relates to issues of taking care of the body—including issues about bodily modification, I want to suggest that it could be the basis of a quite positive approach to the praxis of the body. The idea that the body is fundamentally dynamic is friendly to the idea that sexual features could themselves change. In fact, our bodily sexual features do change throughout our lives due to the influence of hormones and our environment (Roughgarden, 2004).

Moreover, the idea that the body *always* involves the possibility of suffering coheres with the view that the suffering involved in gender dysphoria is natural rather than a result of caving in to sinful temptation. Moreover, it is important to emphasize just how profound the suffering associated with gender dysphoria is. As an example, in *Transmormon*, we hear Eri Hayward recount her fantasy that she would one day cut off her penis and her parents would get her to the hospital in time to save her life. This is a story of deep suffering: her dysphoria was so intense that it might have led her to mutilate her own body. As many as 40 percent of trans individuals have attempted (successfully or unsuccessfully) to take their own lives (Haas, Rodgers, and Herman, 2014). Gender dysphoria is not an insignificant mental health issue.

Finally, Faulconer's idea that the body must be considered as something with a life, that includes irreducible subjective states, seems to indicate that we cannot understand trans bodies unless we understand the lived trans experience. Dovetailing with the LDS idea that each member of the church can receive revelation from God for personal issues (Hales, 2007), it would seem that we must trust trans folk when they testify about their own experience of their gender and their dysphoria. This is the only approach that respects trans folk as bodies with lives rather than bodies that are treated as mere objects, i.e., as if they are corpses.

Given the openness of human bodies, it seems natural to apply this openness to the nature of the sexed body and gender. The sexed body as we encounter it in scientific discourse is not what we think it is in everyday discourse (Roughgarden, 2004). In the latter, sex is male and female, exhaustively and exclusively. But biologically, the body itself defies this classical binary as is obvious with the case of intersex individuals. As mentioned above, the LDS Church has no official position on intersexuality; but their existence does seem to raise a significant problem for its binary approach to gender. Furthermore, they are often the victims of non-consensual but elective genital surgery, which sometimes doesn't conform to their subjective sense of their gender (Butler, 2004, pp. 59ff). These cases disrupt our everyday gender framework: material reality exceeds or transcends our conceptualization of it. Our conceptualization of sex and gender must allow for this disruption and, hence, must remain open ended. And it is hard to see how an approach that accounts for intersex individuals assigned to the wrong gender by ignorant doctors wouldn't also allow for the possibility of trans individuals. The fates of transgender and intersex members are tied together in their resistance to the gender binary in Mormonism.

At this point, we can see a coherent and trans-friendly interpretation of Mormon theology begin to emerge. An open approach to the body allows for sexual features to change over time and furthermore allows for the importance of suffering to the nature of the body. On the emerging view, gender is dynamic even if it remains an essential part of who we are, as Toscano argues. Of course, one might think that this approach doesn't allow for gender to be eternal, since it changes. On the contrary, gender can still be understood as eternal for in Mormon theology, "eternal" doesn't imply timelessness or a lack of change. Instead, "eternal" means "everlasting" and what is everlasting might nevertheless change (McMurrin, 1965, p. 36). To put it another way, Mormonism's doctrine of eternal progression is compatible with the idea that part of how we progress in the afterlife is in terms of how we manifest gender (see also Ostler, 2016).

Although the LDS Church has taken a rather negative stance toward the praxis of the body and—in particular—to transgender individuals that "elect" to undergo gender confirmation surgery, there are clearly resources within the tradition of Mormon theology that open up more progressive possibilities. Instead of seeing the body and bodily desire as a source of temptation or as a pure "temple" that must be kept clean of all worldly influences, Mormonism could opt for an approach that embraces the body as open, dynamic, and potentially divine in all of its complexities, including sexual ones.

Note

1 This chapter will follow the common practice in gender studies to distinguish between sex and gender, where the former refers to biological characteristics and the later to social role. However, it is important to note that this distinction between sex and gender can be problematized. For example, see Butler (1993).

References

Anderson, P.S., 1998. *A Feminist Philosophy of Religion*. Oxford: Blackwell.
Bockting, W.O., and Goldberg, J.M., 2006. Guidelines for Transgender Care (Special Issue). *International Journal of Transgenderism* 9(3/4).
Butler, J., 1990., *Gender Trouble: Feminism and the Subversion of Identity*. New York: Routledge.
Butler, J., 1993. *Bodies That Matter: On the Discursive Limits of Sex*. New York: Routledge.
Butler, J., 2004. *Undoing Gender*. New York: Routledge.
The Church of Jesus Christ of Latter-day Saints, 1995. The Family: A Proclamation to the World. www.lds.org/topics/family-proclamation (accessed August 30, 2018).

The Church of Jesus Christ of Latter-day Saints, 2010. *Church Handbook of Instructions: Book 1, Stake Presidencies and Bishoprics*. Salt Lake City, UT: The Church of Jesus Christ of Latter-day Saints.

The Church of Jesus Christ of Latter-day Saints, 2018. The Doctrine and Covenants of the Church of Jesus Christ of Latter-day Saints. www.lds.org/scriptures/dc-testament/dc/131?lang=eng (accessed August 31, 2018).

Collins, N., 2014. 7 Lies That Purity Culture Teaches Women. www.cbeinternational.org/blogs/7-lies-purity-culture-teaches-women (accessed August 30, 2018).

Coole, D., and Frost, S., 2010. Introduction to New Materialism. In D. Coole and S. Frost, eds. *New Materialisms Ontology, Agency, and Politics*. Durham, NC and London: Duke University Press, pp. 1–43.

Faulconer, J., 2005. Divine Embodiment and Transcendence: Propaedeutic Thoughts and Questions. *Element: The Journal for the Society for Mormon Philosophy and Theology* 1(1): 1–14.

Haas, A.P., Rodgers, P.L., and Herman, J.L., 2014. Suicide Attempts among Transgender and Gender Nonconforming Adults: Findings of the National Transgender Discrimination Survey. https://williamsinstitute.law.ucla.edu/wp-content/uploads/AFSP-Williams-Suicide-Report-Final.pdf (accessed August 31, 2018).

Hales, R.D., 2007. Personal Revelation: The Teachings and Examples of the Prophets. General Conference of The Church of Jesus Christ of Latter-day Saints. www.lds.org/general-conference/2007/10/personal-revelation-the-teachings-and-examples-of-the-prophets?lang=eng (accessed August 30, 2018).

Larsen, S., 1978. The King Follett Discourse: A Newly Amalgamated Text. *BYU Studies* 18(2): 1–18.

McMurrin, S.M., 1959. *The Philosophical Foundations of Mormon Theology*. Salt Lake City, Utah: University of Utah Press.

McMurrin, S.M., 1965. *The Theological Foundations of the Mormon Religion*. Salt Lake City, Utah: University of Utah Press.

Miller, A.S., 2014. Mormonism—Suffering, Agency, and Redemption: Mormonism and Transhumanism. In S. Fuller and C. Mercer, eds. *Transhumanism and the Body: The World Religions Speak*. New York: Palgrave MacMillan, pp. 121–36.

Ostler, B., 2016. Sexuality and Procreation. www.blaireostler.com/journal/2016/3/22/broadening-our-understanding-of-sexuality-and-procreation (accessed August 30, 2018).

Packer, B.K., 2000. Ye Are the Temple of God. www.churchofjesuschrist.org/study/general-conference/2000/10/ye-are-the-temple-of-god?lang=eng (accessed January 30, 2020).

Parry, W., 2013. Gender Dysphoria: DSM-5 Reflects Shift in Perspective on Gender Identity. *Huffington Post*. April 6. www.huffingtonpost.com/2013/06/04/gender-dysphoria-dsm-5_n_3385287.html (accessed August 31, 2018).

Petrey, T., 2011. Toward a Post-Heterosexual Mormon Theology. *Dialogue: A Journal of Mormon Thought* 44(4): 106–41.

Petry, T.G., 2016. Rethinking Mormonism's Heavenly Mother. *Harvard Theological Review* 109(3): 315–41.

Pickett, B., 2015. Homosexuality. *The Stanford Encyclopedia of Philosophy*. https://plato.stanford.edu/entries/homosexuality/ (accessed August 30, 2018).

Pratt, O., 2014. Absurdities of Immaterialism: Or, A Reply to T.W.P. Taylder's Pamphlet, Entitled, "The Materialism of the Mormons or Latter-Day Saints, Examined and Exposed." www.gutenberg.org/files/45005/45005-h/45005-h.htm (accessed August 31, 2018).

Prosser, J., 1998. *Second Skins: The Body Narratives of Transsexuality*. New York: Columbia University Press.

Roughgarden, J., 2004. *Evolution's Rainbow: Diversity, Gender, and Sexuality in Nature and People*. Berkeley, CA: University of California Press.

Serano, J.M., 2010. The Case against Autogynephilia. *International Journal of Transgenderism* 12(3): 176–87.

Serano, J., 2016. *Whipping Girl: A Transsexual Woman on Sexism and the Scapegoating of Femininity*. 2nd ed. Berkeley, CA: Seal Press.

Smith, J., 1968. *Teachings of the Prophet Joseph Smith*. Compiled by Joseph Fielding Smith. Salt Lake City, UT: Deseret Book.

Stack, P.F., 2017. After Leading LDS Congregations and Designing Mormon Temples, This Utah Dad Is Building a New Life—as a Woman. http://archive.sltrib.com/article.php?id=5522210&itype=CMSID (accessed August 30, 2018).

Toscano, M., 2014. The Gender of God and the Diversity of Human Sexuality. Paper presented at the 2014 Salt Lake Sunstone Symposium. Unpublished.

Toscano, M., and Toscano, P., 1990. *Strangers in Paradox: Explorations in Mormon Theology*. Salt Lake City, UT: Signature Books.

Transmormon, 2014. Directed by Torben Bernhard. OHO Media.

Valenti, J., 2009. *The Purity Myth: How America's Obsession with Virginity Is Hurting Young Women*. Berkeley, CA: Seal Press.

Webb, S.H., 2013. *Mormon Christianity: What Other Christians Can Learn from Latter-day Saints*. New York: Oxford University Press.

WPATH, 2011. *World Professional Association for Transgender Health, Standards of Care*. 7th ed.

Further reading

Butler, J., 2004. *Undoing Gender*. New York: Routledge.

In this collection of essays, Butler explores various topics relevant to transgender experience, including the role that the body plays with respect to gender.

Faulconer, J., 2005. Divine Embodiment and Transcendence: Propaedeutic Thoughts and Questions. *Element: The Journal for The Society for Mormon Philosophy and Theology* 1(1): 1–14.

This article explores some of the implications and possibilities for a Mormon understanding of the nature of the divine body.

Petrey, T., 2011. Toward a Post-Heterosexual Mormon Theology. *Dialogue: A Journal of Mormon Thought* 44(4): 106–41.

This article includes a comprehensive review of Mormonism's theology of sex and includes an exploration of the possibility of a queer-friendly interpretation.

Serano, J., 2016. *Whipping Girl: A Transsexual Woman on Sexism and the Scapegoating of Femininity*. 2nd ed. Berkeley, CA: Seal Press.

In this collection of essays, Serano explores theories of gender, the science and medicine of sex and gender, images of trans folk in the media, and the role that cissexism plays in everyday life. Serano also tackles the important issue of how trans activism and feminism relate.

Toscano, M., and Toscano, P., 1990. *Strangers in Paradox: Explorations in Mormon Theology*. Salt Lake City, UT: Signature Books.

This monograph explores Mormon theology on topics such as the nature of divinity, the roles of Heavenly Father and Heavenly Mother, Mormonism's theology of embodiment, and, of course, gender and its role in human and divine life.

38
FEMINISM AND HEAVENLY MOTHER

Fiona Givens

As a complete treatment of both subjects—Heavenly Mother and feminism—is beyond the scope of this chapter, I shall focus primarily on the initial flourishing of Mormon feminism against two contexts: the political context of the national feminist movement in America of the nineteenth century; and the 1840s theological context of Mormonism's unique doctrines of both Mother in Heaven and Mother Eve, as they are integrally related reconstructions. In the second half of the chapter I shall trace the various iterations of Heavenly Mother in Mormon thought, before concluding with a brief overview of ancient antecedents to a Heavenly Mother or divine feminine currently being excavated in early Christian and Jewish Studies.

While patriarchy may be as old as recorded history, with the production of the Christian canon male religious authority made the paradigm virtually impregnable. Appropriation of the Jewish creation narrative especially added a divine decree to social fact: "thy desire shall be to thy husband, and he shall rule over thee," the male deity informs the first woman (Gen 3:16 KJV). Pauline tradition reaffirmed that the original sin was female in origin: "Adam was not deceived, but the woman being deceived was in the transgression" (1 Tim 2:14 KJV). In addition to women's perceived innate susceptibility to deception and transgression, Saint Augustine of Hippo aggravated the negligible position of women by asserting that any and all sexual sin was likewise instigated by Eve. In his *Letter to Laetus*, he argued: "What difference does it make whether it is a wife or a mother, when a man has to guard against Eve in every woman?" (1956, p. 225).

Before Augustine's gospel, however, there was another, one which taught that humankind was inherently good and inherently divine and that mortality, rather than being a blameworthy Fall into depravity, was an ascent into the necessary educational experience that would empower humankind to become like God. Although not an admirer of Eve, the Greek Father, Irenaeus, found virtue in the Fall itself. In *Against Heresies*, he asks

> How then will any be a god, if he has not first been made a man? ... How immortal if he has not in his mortal nature obeyed his Maker? For one's duty is first to observe the discipline [teaching] of man and thereafter to share the glory of God.

Mortality, he opines, is the garden in which "man may at length reach maturity, becoming ripe, through these experiences" (Irenaeus, 2004, ch. 27, para. 7). Following Irenaeus, Origen also suggested that the Fall was necessary and educative, not tragic and misguided:

You (the soul) could not have reached the palm-groves unless you had experienced the harsh trials; you could not have reached the gentle springs without first having to overcome sadness and difficulties ... The education of the soul is an age-long spiritual adventure, beginning in this life and continuing after death.

(2009, 27.11).

Early Christian quasi-approbation of the Fall notwithstanding, from Augustine onward Philo of Alexandria's theology became the basis of traditional Christian theology and Western culture generally. Eve's "conduct [led] to all kind of wickedness; at which the Father of all was indignant. For their actions deserved his anger ... and accordingly he appointed them such a punishment as was befitting" (Philo, 2017, p. 27). The Fall was thereafter universally interpreted as the "wickedness" that followed Eve's reprehensible action.

The feminist response

In the Christian West, any challenge to patriarchal supremacy, any movement in the direction of equality between the sexes, could only emerge in defiance of, or in blatant disregard for, Christian dogma. In her vigorous push for female emancipation, Elizabeth Cady Stanton attempted to wrest the scriptural text from its patriarchal grip and re-frame it along feminist lines. Her weapon of choice was, naturally enough, a deeply revisionist, feminist reading of the Bible—one in which woman would be raised from her ignominy in the male-centric text. In her introduction to *The Woman's Bible*, Stanton writes:

From the inauguration of the movement for woman's emancipation the Bible has been used to hold her in the "divinely ordained sphere," prescribed by the Old and New Testaments ... Canon and civil law; church and state; priests and legislators; all political parties and religious denominations have alike taught that woman was made after man, of man, and for man, an inferior being, subject to man ... The fashions, forms, ceremonies and customs of society, church ordinances and discipline all grow out of this idea.

(1999, p. 7).

Stanton's truly brilliant insight, however—too radical even for many of her co-suffragettes who distanced themselves from the work—was in her recognition that the subservience attached to Eve and her descendants was inseparable from an absolute patriarchy in the heavens. The two were indissolubly connected. As she states without apology:

The first step in the elevation of woman to her true position, as an equal factor in human progress, is the cultivation of the religious sentiment in regard to her dignity and equality, the recognition by the rising generation of an ideal Heavenly Mother.

(1999, p. 14)

Stanton finds textual support for such a move in the plurality of gods indicated by the "let us" behind creation. "A Heavenly Father, Mother, and Son would seem more rational" than three male personages, as generally represented" (1999, p. 14). Her collaborator Lillie Devereux Blake also challenges the reading of "Elohim" as singular and inserts the plural form. She "attributes creation to a council of gods, acting in concert" (1999, p. 16) proving to her satisfaction that "Hebrews were in early days polytheists" (1999, p. 10).

If the Godhead consists of Father and Mother in holy equality, then from the creation, Adam and Eve made in their image would be fully equal in dignity and authority, she reasons. Consistent with Genesis 5:2 (God "called their name Adam"), she observers, "equal dominion is given to woman over every living thing, but not one word is said giving man dominion over woman" (1999, p. 15). Stanton and her collaborators, hostile reception notwithstanding, had correctly assessed the problem; female subordination and patriarchy *alike* rested on twin pillars: a male-gendered Trinity, and a human creation narrative that imputed a divine model behind only one half of the race, relegating Eve and her female progeny to secondary status.

A century later Virginia Ramey Mollenkott wrote that whereas women had made significant strides in the "secular" domain, "the language of Christian preaching, prayer, and hymnody is still laden with exclusive-sounding references, to men, man, brothers, sons, and the God of Abraham, Isaac and Jacob" (1983, p. 2). Second and then third generation feminist scholars continue to aver that while "a theme of male–female equality and mutuality informs the [biblical text] from beginning to end," it does not seem to have registered with a dominantly male religious leadership (1983, p. 7).

History, however, records some significant exceptions to this neglect. The feminine aspect of divinity had been championed by the earliest Christian writers, including Clement of Alexandria and John Chrysostom through the medieval writers Thomas Aquinas and Gregory Palamas, as well as by mystics such as the anchoress Julian of Norwich. It is Julian whom Mollenkott claims to have developed the image of a "Christian feminine divinity more fully [and] more centrally ... than any other medieval author" (1983, pp. 9–10). Aaron S. Fogleman writes that for the twelfth-century Cistercian monks the image of Christ "was that of a compassionate, loving, nurturing mother who creates and sacrifices" (2007, p. 84). Caroline Walker Bynum suggests that "a God who is mother and womb as well as father and animator could be a more sweeping and convincing image of creation than a father God alone." This image of Christ as the nurturing mother as well as the creator God also "became part of numerous radical pietist groups in the early modern period as well, including prophetesses and visionaries in England and mystics in Germany and some Puritan theologians in New England" (1982, p. 134). Shakers also posed an unusual challenge to divine patriarchy, positing a female incarnation of Jesus in Ann Lee. Shaker medium Paulina Bates took the next step: "The Deity consists of *two*," she wrote, "male and female ... the Eternal Father and [His] co-worker, Holy and Eternal Mother Wisdom" (Kvam, Schearing, and Ziegler, 1999, p. 361).

In all these cases, of course (with the possible exception of the Shakers), the constraints of a Trinitarian model allow, at most, for the addition of feminine dimensions to a unitary God. Extending Stanton's decisive break with an androgynous deity, Elizabeth A. Johnson proposes a feminist ethics that allows for the divine collaboration of differentiated selves.

> The self is rightly structured *not* in dualistic opposition to the other but in intrinsic relationship with the other. Rather than "we" meaning "not they," we and they are intertwined. Neither heteronomy (exclusive other directedness) nor autonomy in a closed egocentric sense but a model of relational independence, freedom in relation, full related selfhood becomes the ideal.
>
> *(1996, p. 68)*

In fact, a number of contemporary feminists suggest a reading of Genesis 1 that allows for the complete equality in the relationship of two distinct individuals.

> When the priestly author of Genesis 1 depicts God creating the human race in the divine image and likeness on the sixth day, the text makes clear that the compliment

is intended for male and female ... All members of the [human] species are equally favored with the theological identity of *imago dei*.

(Johnson, 1996, p. 70)

Duality, not androgyny, is implied.

Stanton, Mollenkott, and Johnson are arguing from embattled positions. It is a slow and arduous mode of engagement. Taking on the canon by storm as did Stanton and other first-wave feminists resulted in little, if any, movement for women on the ecclesiastical field of the nineteenth century, fortified as it was by resistant ranks of male clergy. Only rare exceptions advocated the feminization of deity. These include the influential Unitarian Theodore Parker, whose views of a gendered Trinity, Kathi Kern suggests, influenced Cady Stanton's own conception of a Mother in Heaven equal in power and glory to the Father (2001, p. 165). The courageous Quaker, Isaac Penington, propounded a similar view, echoing Philo of Alexandria, who wrote that Wisdom was the consort of God: "Moses, the friend of God ... uttered an oracle in the character of God ... showing most manifestly that God is ... the husband of wisdom" (Yonge, 1993, p. 85). The Moravians, radical pietists of the eighteenth century, also advocated a mixed-gendered Trinity, claiming the Holy Spirit to be the Mother. Her feast day, *Mutterfest*, was celebrated until 1774 (Fogleman, 2007, p. 84). The Puritan minister, Cotton Mather (1663–1728) also paused to consider that the Holy Spirit might be feminine. Laurel Thatcher Ulrich quotes sections of the sermon Mather gave at his mother's funeral. He employs the noun, "comforter" and the verb "comfort" so frequently that he pauses to make the following aside:

> It has been a little Surprising unto me to find that in some of the Primitive Writers, the Holy Spirit is called, The Mother. Tertullian uses this Denomination for the Holy Spirit; the Mother, who is Invoked with the Father and the Son.
>
> (Mather, 1714, p. 25)

Mather continues to explain the reasonableness of the metaphor. "It is through the Holy Ghost that we are born again. The Holy Ghost is spoken of in the scriptures as a comforter. Surely nothing is of greater comfort than a good mother" (Ulrich, 1976, p. 35).

Challenging *sola scriptura*

Without an authoritative text emerging to challenge more explicitly the doctrine of the Bible's sufficiency (*sola scriptura*), little space could be found to navigate a fully successful challenge to a male-centric deity, or the inferior position of womanhood's prototype, Eve. In 1830 just such a paradigm-shattering text emerged from Joseph Smith's mind, followed almost immediately thereafter by a second. Both emphatically resituate the Mother of all Living as the instigator of a human ascent rather than the precipitator of humanity's fall. The Book of Mormon and then the Book of Moses record an approbation of Eve's decision that turned Adamic catastrophe into divinely ordained progress. It would be hard to imagine a more potent basis for a religiously sanctioned feminism, than a reconstruction of Eve as valiant, courageous, and man's equal at the very least. The rehabilitation of Eve, occurs—indirectly—first in 2 Nephi, when the patriarch Lehi assesses the significance of the choice made to eat the fruit of the tree, which Eve recognized as "a tree to be desired to make one wise" (Gen 3:6 KJV)

> And now, behold, if Adam had not transgressed [they] would not have fallen, but [they] would have remained in the garden of Eden ... And they would have had no

children; wherefore they would have remained in a state of innocence, having no joy, for they knew no misery; doing no good, for they knew no sin. But behold, all things have been done in the wisdom of him who knoweth all things. Adam fell that men might be; and men are, that they might have joy.

(2 Nephi 2:22–25)

Eve's own voice on the matter is heard in the Book of Moses, which Smith produced mere months after publishing the Book of Mormon. Eve exclaims following the couple's transition into mortality: "Were it not for our transgression we never should have had seed, and never should have known good and evil, and the joy of our redemption, and the eternal life which God giveth unto all the obedient" (Moses 5:11). This move from Fall to Ascent represented a decisive break with Christian orthodoxy. Original sin may be, in the words of one contemporary theologian, "a cultural embarrassment" (Daly, 1972, p. 121). but it is nonetheless the mainstay of the Christian theology of human nature and the human condition alike, "a part of the faith of the whole Christian world," in the words of Charles Hodge (1970, p. 19).

By the late nineteenth century, female intellectuals of the LDS faith were trumpeting the significance of these paradigm shifts. As an example, Boyd Petersen notes that S.M.K. (presumably Sarah M. Kimball) exhibited a keen understanding of Mormonism's revolutionary theology in regard to Eve's role.

> Our great maternal progenitor is entitled to reverent honor for braving the peril that brought earth's children from the dark valley of ignorance and stagnation, and placed them on the broad, progressive plain, where they, knowing good and evil, joy and sorrow, may become Gods. Mother Eve, for taking initiative in this advance movement, should receive encomiums of praise ... shared by our great paternal who, though reluctantly, followed and aided in her heaven ordained enterprise.
>
> *(2014, pp. 155–56)*

However, as Stanton and her collaborators correctly deduced, this re-conceptualizing of Eve's (and woman's) status cannot be separated from the theology of divine gender implicit in any conception of the godhead. Any movement that went further than merely pasting onto a male deity trappings of the feminine would require a wholesale reconstruction of that Trinity. "Of the innumerable tenets over which Christians may disagree," argues Terryl Givens "none has been so central to the question of orthodoxy as the doctrine of the Trinity" (2014, p. 69). Smith rejected Trinitarianism outright when he stated:

> I have always declared God to be a distinct personage, Jesus Christ a separate and distinct personage from God the Father, and that the Holy Ghost was a distinct personage and a Spirit: and these three constitute three distinct personages and three Gods.
>
> *(Ehat and Cook, 1991, p. 378)*

While the 1830 texts described above challenge the bases of religiously founded earthly patriarchy, Smith's subsequent innovation of a Heavenly Mother threatened the patriarchal monopoly of heaven, assigning the feminine divine a status of potential equality with the male divine. The Book of Abraham, which was added to the LDS canon in 1880, moves beyond an explicit tritheism to a counsel of gods, among whom, it may be assumed, female deities are present. Erastus Snow succinctly argues the logic behind the LDS teaching: "There never was a god, and there never will be in all eternity, except they are made of these two component parts; a man and a woman; the male and the female" (1878, pp. 269–70). Smith's own recognition and elaboration of this explosive idea is impossible to trace precisely. This would suggest why, as Linda P. Wilcox notes, the "idea of a mother in heaven is shadowy and elusive, floating around the edge of Mormon consciousness" (1992, p. 3).

Smith's incorporation of a Heavenly Mother into his restoration theology first appeared in print through the intermediary of his close associate W.W. Phelps. In a letter published in the church newspaper, Phelps declared simply, "Thy father is God, thy mother is the Queen of Heaven," and imagined a scene where Christ "was anointed with holy oil in heaven, and crowned in the midst of brothers and sisters, while his mother stood with approving virtue" (1844, p. 758). It is unlikely that Joseph considered Christ's Mother, the "Queen of Heaven" to be Mary, for a few months later, Phelps elaborated the new doctrine in a hymn which proclaimed, through the persona of Joseph Smith, "the myst'ry that man hath not seen; Here's our Father in heaven, and Mother, the Queen" (1845, p. 794). Here the association is as divine consort rather than as Mother of the Lord.

While Phelps' hymn faded into oblivion, another hymn gave effective canonical status to the teaching of a Heavenly Mother as companion to Heavenly Father. Smith's plural wife Eliza R. Snow first propounded publicly a Heavenly Mother as God the Father's consort in a poem she wrote. It appeared first in the church's magazine in November 1845, and was then integrated into Mormon hymnody and is now known as "O My Father." Also titled "Invocation, or the Eternal Father and Mother," the pertinent lines are

> in the heavens are parents single? No the thought makes reason stare! Truth is reason; truth eternal tells me I've a mother there. When I lay this mortal by, Father, Mother, may I meet you in your royal courts on high? ... With your mutual approbation Let me come and dwell with you.
>
> *(Hymns, 1985, no. 292)*

Snow stated that the teaching of Heavenly Mother came from her first husband—Joseph Smith. Susa Young Gates added that Zina D.H. Young and Snow both learned the doctrine of a Heavenly Mother from Joseph Smith (Wilcox, 1992, pp. 65–66). President Wilford Woodruff, however, attributed the revelation directly to Snow, stating "that hymn is a revelation, though it was given unto us by a woman" (Hanks, 1992, p. 5).

The LDS doctrine of a Heavenly Mother, it must be emphasized, was—and remains, to a great extent—inchoate and inconsistent. The shadowy outlines of a divine feminine have been more fully, if tentatively, limned in several ways, in accordance with various and often competing agendas. For instance, Wilcox notes that Orson Pratt propounded a polygamous reading of the Heavenly Family—one in which God the Father's numerous wives and the children of those unions "were required to yield the upmost obedience to their great Head" (1992, p. 16). Gates, on the other hand, celebrated the singular "divine Mother" for her "equal sharing of equal rights, privileges and responsibilities" with the Father (Paulsen and Pulido, 2011, p. 78) and Snow suggested the efficacy of prayers offered "before the throne of the great eternal mother" (Paulsen and Pulido, 2011, p. 82). In response to the objections expressed by the Protestant community in regard to the Mormon inclusion of Heavenly Mother within their theological paradigm the *Latter-Day Saints' Millennial Star* quotes the following verse from Ann Taylor's poem, "My Mother" (erroneously attributed in the *Millennial Star* to William Wordsworth): "'Who taught my infant lips to pray,/ To love God's word and holy day,/ And walk in wisdom's pleasant way?/ My Mother.'" The writer then quotes the following by an "unknown author": "'Not only from the mouths of babes and sucklings has the cry gone forth for a Mother in Heaven. Men ... have yearned to adore her. The heart of man craves this faith and from time immemorial demanded the deification of woman.'" The writer, presumably Rudger Clawson, concludes "It doesn't take from our worship of the Eternal Father, to adore our Eternal Mother ... In fact, the love of one is a complement of our love for the other" (*Latter-Day Saints' Millennial Star*, 1910, pp. 619–20). Pushing this logic even further a *Deseret News* article opined that a general acceptance of Heavenly Mother would eventually result in the global emancipation of women (Hanks, 1992, p. 8).

The decade of the 1890s marked dramatic upheavals in Mormondom. Polygamy was formally abandoned in 1890, but would continue to be practiced surreptitiously until the early twentieth century. In 1894, the church relinquished its conception of a dynastic heaven, in which persons were sealed to prophets only; henceforth parents would be sealed to children and children to parents, in a manner consistent with the words of Malachi that had launched the entire theology of eternal sealing (Malachi 4:1–2). Also in this period, leading LDS female intellectuals were writing and publishing their views, and collaborating with national figures in the women's suffrage movement. In 1895, these women, most of whom were leaders in the Women's Relief Society, including the leading Mormon suffragette, Emmeline B. Wells, employed their own press to publish the opening chapter of Stanton's *Woman's Bible*, in which Stanton states categorically, "It is evident from the language that there was consultation in the Godhead, and that the masculine and feminine elements were equally represented ... Instead of three male personages, as generally represented, a Heavenly Father, Mother, and Son would seem more rational" (1999, p. 14). Likewise, the Book of Abraham challenges not only the male Trinitarian Godhead but also the traditional Genesis account of a single creator deity. A plurality of "gods went down [and] organized and formed the heavens and the earth" (Abraham 4:1). In addition, after taking "counsel among themselves" they form man in their image and likeness, "male and female ... form they them [and they] will cause them to be fruitful and multiply, and replenish the earth" (Abraham 4:26–28). Implicit in these verses is that the feminine divine is included in both the counsel and the formation of mankind. As Stanton remarks "The masculine and feminine elements, exactly equal and balancing each other are as essential to the maintenance of the equilibrium of the universe as positive and negative electricity" (1999, p. 15).

Lacking religious authority, however, Stanton and her colleagues invoked a scholarly community to make their case. Included among the pages of *The Woman's Bible* are references to biblical scholarship, experts in antiquity, language authorities, and commentators, all employed to buttress their vision of a Heavenly Mother and other feminist theological revisions. Cited sources range from Adam Clarke (frequently) and Bishop Colenso to Knorr von Rosenroth's translation of the Kabbalah Denudata and MacGregor Matthew's *Kabbalah Unveiled*. In a similar way, Joseph Smith had readily appropriated pertinent voices in support of his heterodox teachings, adding scholarly support to prophetic vision: Thomas Dick on eternal progression; Charles Buck on baptism for the dead; Adam Clarke on numerous topics; Hebrew lexicons for revisioning creation, and so forth (Givens, 2014, pp. 38–41). However, Smith's conception of an Adamic dispensation, in which the fullness of the gospel was taught to the couple, Eve and Adam, made ancient studies in particular an especially compelling resource for his claim that Mormonism was a Restoration, not an invention (Moses 5). Smith had clearly set the pattern, both with his production of ancient texts and his insistence that a wealth of lost truth was yet to be discovered. Intense interest in recovered ancient writings swept the church (*Times and Seasons*, 1843, p. 336).

Consonant with Smith's views and practice alike, church president Joseph F. Smith (1901–1918) could be seen as implicitly endorsing the search for antecedents to LDS doctrines now lost to the world, when he said, "If we find truth in broken fragments ... it may be set down as an incontrovertible fact that it originated at the fountain, and was given to philosophers, inventors ... reformers, and prophets by the inspiration of God" (1919, p. 38).

A number of LDS scholars have accepted the implicit challenge. David Paulsen has found early Christian antecedents for Mormonism's social trinity composed of distinct persons (1990, pp. 105–16); and Givens has traced dozens of Jewish, early Christian, and medieval varieties of human pre-existence (2010). Several LDS scholars have appropriated the work of Margaret Barker on temple theology to emphasize Joseph's appropriate re-situating of the Temple at the center of Mormon thought and praxis (Christensen, 2001). Hugh Nibley wrote thousands of pages on the subject of Egyptian studies to place Smith's Book of Abraham in a tradition of Abrahamic narratives (2005; 2009; 2010).

In light of such a ubiquitous pattern, one would expect Latter-day Saint scholars to be at the forefront in excavating the historical record, textual traditions, and archaeological discoveries for footprints of the divine feminine, as they have for a whole gamut of their other distinctive and unconventional doctrines. A possible explanation resides in events surrounding the resurgence of interest in both feminism and Heavenly Mother in the closing decades of the twentieth century. A number of prominent LDS women not only vocalized strong support for the Equal Rights Amendment, a bill which was strongly opposed by the leadership of the Church of Jesus Christ but they also advocated the public offering of prayer to Heavenly Mother (Stack, 2013). In addition, General Conference addresses were disrupted by women's vocal protests which served to embarrass publicly the male church leadership (Morril et al., n.d.). Wilcox points to an address in 1991, in which Gordon B. Hinckley, counselor in the First Presidency, warned against the invocation of Heavenly Mother by members of the Church of Jesus Christ and informed the gathered priesthood leadership to counsel their subordinates "to be on the alert ... and to make correction where necessary. Such correction ... should be firm and without equivocation" (1992, p. 16). A series of excommunications followed (Johnson, 1993). An official church website now states succinctly: "Latter-day Saints ... do not pray to Heavenly Mother" (Church of Jesus Christ, 2015). While there is growing textual and archaeological material to encourage Mormon engagement in the pursuit of a feminine divinity, the field continues to be a contested one. Margaret Barker (herself a lightning rod for controversy among non-LDS and LDS scholars alike), gives fair warning to those who would venture into the sphere of scholarship engaged in the theological excavation of Heavenly Mother. "The most cursory reading in the field reveals it to be a minefield of prejudices and assumptions which take precedence even over the archaeological evidence" (1992, p. 48).

With that admonition in mind, the rationale for and purpose of the following sections needs to be made clear. A survey of recent scholarship on the feminine divine, and her various manifestations in biblical and other ancient textual and archaeological records, may situate the LDS theology of Heavenly Mother within a longer historical narrative. At a minimum, such antecedents attest to the persistent longing by multitudes, across time and culture, to find "a Mother there." Against such a background, LDS doctrine of a Heavenly Mother emerges as a paradigm distinctive in contemporary Christianity but not in Judeo-Christian history. In what follows, the scholarship depicted does not represent uniform consensus. It does, however, typify a pattern of prominent voices who associate a feminine identity with one or more of the following divine epithets.

El Shaddai

Some of the earliest scholarly treatments of the Book of Genesis suggest that the deity known to the Patriarchs was not Yahweh. A nineteenth-century exegesis in German states succinctly that the only god known to and worshipped by Abraham, Isaac, and Jacob was El Shaddai or God Almighty (Shuckford, 1731, p. 275). The epithet "El Shadday," or "El Shaddai" occurs forty-eight times in the Hebrew Bible and is "third in frequency among the divine names (after Yahweh and Elohim)" (Lutzky, 1998, p. 15). David Biale notes "with the exception of the tetragrammaton YHWH, no divine name has generated [as] much controversy as El Shaddai or Shaddai" (Biale, 1982, pp. 240–41). Biale is also the "first in the contemporary literature to see the etymology 'breast' as key to understanding the name El Shadday," suggesting that the original form, the Hebrew compound *shad*, be read as "the God with breasts," or the God of the Breast (Lutzky, 1998, p. 18). Further, Frank Moore Cross states "the formation of the name ... plus the adjectival suffix—*ay* cannot be separated from the series of divine names known from Ugaritic sources," such as *Pidray*, *Tallay*, and *Arsay*, all of whom are feminine deities (1973, p. 56). Thus, the epithet "the One of [the breast] is wholly suitable" (1973, p. 56). Lutzky argues that when breast is privileged rather than mountain "the hypothesis that Shadday was originally the name or epithet of a goddess ... virtually imposes itself" (1998, p. 16). She argues further that this hypothesis is reinforced by the fact that "in the ancient Near East, breastfeeding was a divine act, imparting divinity, divine authority, and divine protection" suggesting that Shadday's divine powers extended far beyond nurturing only (1998, pp. 16, 18).

According to Biale, all the current biblical passages relating to El Shaddai in Genesis, with one exception, are covenantal promises of everlasting life. Lutzky prefers the term "imparting divinity," which in LDS thought, relates to the bestowal of "immortality and eternal life" (Moses 1:37). Of all the passages that mention El Shaddai in terms of the covenantal blessings of increase Biale considers Genesis 49:25 to be the most significant in establishing the feminine gender of Shaddai. As she is invoked together with the Father God, El, the implication that she is God, the Mother, is strongly implied. Mark S. Smith finds the following translation of Genesis 49:25–26 by Bruce Vawter compelling. Joseph is blessed "By El, your Father who helps you, / By Shadday who blesses you/With the blessings of Heavens, from above,/The blessings of the Deep, crouching below,/ The blessings of Breasts-and-Womb" (1990, p. 49). Biale concludes that the literary and archaeological evidence for the Genesis deity, Shaddai, acting both independently of and in concert with the Father, El, is "contextually and phonetically reasonable, if not scientifically persuasive" (1982, p. 248).

Shekhina

Another name for the female divine is "Shekhina." Originally, she "denoted the visible and audible manifestation of God's presence on earth. Ultimately she "stood for an independent, feminine divine entity" (Patai, 1990, p. 96). One of the names of the wilderness tabernacle was *mishkan*, meaning "dwelling" or "abode" (Patai, 1990, p. 97). According to Rabbi Yehoshua "as soon as the tabernacle was erected, the Shekhina descended and dwelt among" the people (Patai, 1990, p. 100). Therefore, any desecration of either the wilderness tabernacle or Temple was the height of disrespect to her personally (Patai, 1990, p. 101). As verbs in Semitic languages are also gendered together with adjectives and pronouns, Shekhina as the female entity was "kept in the forefront of consciousness by every statement made about her" (Patai, 1990, p. 107). So pervasive was her presence in the wilderness sojourn of the Israelites, that it was she who was seen to have taken up her abode in the "tent shrine" (Cross, 1973, p. 56). By contrast, Yahweh was the "visiting deity" (Patai, 1990, p. 97). According to Patai "it was an accepted article of faith that wherever their exile took the people of Israel ... the Shekhina went along with them and that she would remain with them until the time of redemption" (Patai, 1990, p. 103). According to Rabbi Aha when Shekhina left the wilderness sanctuary, she would return "to kiss its walls and columns, [and cried] Be in peace, O my Sanctuary ... O my royal palace ... O my precious house" (Patai, 1990, p. 108).

Additional possible epithets for Shekhina suggested by Margaret Barker include "shining" face and "Presence of the Lord" (Psalm 31:16; 67:1; 80:3; Barker, 2011, pp. 56–57). To support her claim Barker cites Psalm 67:1 "[May] God be merciful unto us, and bless us; and cause his face to shine upon us; Selah" (2011, p. 56).

The role of the Shekhina as divine feminine was dramatically celebrated by some Jews into the early modern period. In seventeenth-century Jerusalem, notes Simon Montefiore, every Friday "the Kabbalists, wearing white robes, would greet the 'bride of God,' the Shekhina, outside the city and then escort the divine presence back to their homes" (2011, pp. 311–12).

Asherah

Asherah as a name for the female deity has received considerable attention from scholars of the Hebrew Bible, bolstered by important discoveries at a number of archaeological sites, including a cult stand at Ta'nach, in which the first and third registers comprise Asherah imagery. The third and fourth registers contain images consistent with the God, Yahweh, suggesting to some scholars that Asherah and Yahweh were worshipped in the same locus (Ackerman, 2008, pp. 21–22). One of the strongest literary evidences for the legitimacy of Asherah's worship is to be found in 1 Kings 18:19. The prophet, Elijah, invites the priests of both Baal and Asherah to the contest of the gods, following which Elijah orders the execution of all the prophets of Baal but not those of Asherah (1 Kings 18:40). The text suggests that while Elijah found the worship of Baal offensive, the worship of the goddess was acceptable. Saul M. Olyan argues that anti-Asherah polemic is "restricted to the Deuteronomistic History or to materials which betray the influence of deuteronomistic language and theology" (1988, p. 3). Additionally, in countering the argument that Asherah was an imported deity, Olyan asks, "Why in the patriarchal narratives is it permissible for trees to be planted in Yahwistic cult places?" (1988, p. 5). Olyan argues further that the

> patriarchal narratives of cult founding at Bethel, Hebron and Beersheba indicate that the sacred tree and the pillar [associated with Asherah worship] ... were legitimate in the Yahwistic cult early on, and were not considered illegitimate in the time of the Yahwist or the Elohist.
>
> *(1988, p. 5)*

As with Shaddai, the worship of Asherah included the building of altars on which to burn incense, the setting up of pillars on which to pour libations and the making of bread or "cakes" (Jeremiah 7:17–21, 44:17–19). Trees in "high places," particularly, signified Asherah's presence. Mark S. Smith states that

> legal prohibitions and prophetic critiques indicate that the devotion of [Asherah] was observed as early as the period of the judges and as late as a few decades before the fall of the southern kingdom ... and her symbol (tree/pole/image) was a general feature of Israelite religion.
>
> *(1990, p. 108)*

During the Bicentennial Conference at the Library of Congress in 2005, Margaret Barker gave an address entitled "Joseph Smith and Pre-exilic Israelite Religion" in which she suggested that

Latter-day Saint texts, particularly the Book of Mormon, are more resonant with the texts pertaining to the pre-exilic tradition than those redacted by the Deuteronomists.

> If some of the wickedness in Jerusalem mentioned in the First Book of Nephi (1 Nephi 1:13) included parts of Josiah's temple purges we should expect to find information relevant to the Mormon tradition in texts outside the Bible. And we do.
>
> *(2005, p. 70)*

Barker theorizes that in light of Deuteronomic influence in the biblical text, "the Mother and her tree have almost been forgotten—but not in the Book of Mormon" (2005, p. 76).

Daniel Peterson also suggests that the textual references to Asherah and El as husband and wife were deliberately corrupted by the reforming Deuteronomists who were motivated to "oppose and suppress the veneration of Asherah, just as they opposed the veneration of the Nehushtan of Moses" (2000, p. 15). In his article, "Nephi and His Asherah: A Note on 1 Nephi 11:8–23," Peterson finds echoes of Asherah, symbolized by the Tree of Life in both Lehi's and Nephi's visions in which the Tree represents the "divine consort" and the fruit her "divine child" (2000, p. 15). While the Tree of Life (Asherah) figures in his father, Lehi's vision, the focus of his attention is the fruit, representing the divine child—the font of "exceedingly great joy" (1 Nephi 8:12). Nephi, on the other hand, is riveted to "the tree which is precious above all" (1 Nephi 10:9). Peterson notes that the Asherah vision is repeated by the prophet, Alma, who similarly writes of "the tree springing up unto everlasting life" whose fruit "is most precious ... sweet above all that is sweet ... and pure above all that is pure" (2000, p. 16). What is remarkable about these visions is that they appear to ground the Book of Mormon in the feminine divine tradition frequently represented by the Tree of Life, which may be a representation of Heavenly Mother. The apostle, John, records that in the vicinity of the throne of the Lamb, stands the Tree of Life, the leaves of which are for "the healing of the nations" (Rev. 22:1–2)

Wisdom

Another name for the female deity Asherah is Wisdom. Ackerman writes "although many goddesses have been nominated as Wisdom's primary antecedent, the most compelling arguments ... view Woman Wisdom as a reflex of ... Asherah" (2008, p. 10). The Wisdom tradition is voluminous. The entire book of Proverbs is a tribute to her gifts and attributes with myriad allusions to her divinity. Ackerman continues,

> Especially notable in this regard is the Proverbs 8 description of Woman Wisdom as present with, and the partner of, the Israelite God, Yahweh in the creation, a tradition that parallels closely Ugaritic materials that describe Asherah as "creatress" (*qnyt*), the consort of the creator God (*qny*) El.
>
> *(Ackerman, 2008, pp. 10–11)*

> That "happiness" accrues to those who hold fast to Woman Wisdom in [Proverbs] 3:18 further alludes to her identity as Asherah, as the Hebrew word for "happy" is a pun on the goddess's name.
>
> *(2008, p. 12)*

William G. Dever concurs. Citing Job 28:12–28; Proverbs 1:20–33; 3:7–19; 8:1–36; and 9:1–8, he states that "it is significant that Lady Wisdom is portrayed in these texts as a partner with

Yahweh in creation; that she goes about on her own speaking for Yahweh; that she brings specific blessings and long life" (2005, p. 301). "Length of days is in her right hand; and in her left hand riches and honour" (Proverbs 3:16–17) and those who find her are the recipients of life eternal (Proverbs 8:35). Seeking and living by her instruction is a form of worship (Wisdom of Solomon 6:17). By thus honouring Wisdom her children will reign forever (Wisdom of Solomon, 6:22).

The injunction to treasure up Wisdom appears in two of the introductory passages in the Doctrine and Covenants. Members of the Church of Jesus Christ are encouraged to seek wisdom, that "they might be instructed" (D&C 1:26). Echoing Proverbs 8:35, parishioners are again enjoined to seek for wisdom "[for] behold, the mysteries of God shall be unfolded to you, and then shall you be made rich. Behold, he that hath eternal life is rich" (D&C 6:7). This admonition is repeated verbatim in D&C 11:7. The Book of Mormon also strongly suggests that Wisdom is a sovereign deity. King Limhi attributes the lamentable condition of his people to their refusal "to walk in wisdom's paths" (Helaman 12:5). Elsewhere, the text explains, "They will not seek wisdom, neither do they desire that she should rule over them!" (Mosiah 8:20).

The Holy Spirit

The final name to be discussed is the Holy Spirit, whose position as a member of the Holy Trinity is universally accepted in the Christian tradition. With the exception of a few scholars, it is assumed that the Holy Spirit is the third male member of the Godhead. However, Johannes van Oort propounds: "The earliest Christians—most of whom were Jews spoke of the Holy Spirit as a feminine figure" (2016, p. 1). Robert Payne writes "the primitive semitic-Christian doctrine of the Holy Spirit as Mother" was propounded not only by early Syriac writers but by Aphrahat explicitly (Payne, 1966, p. 312). Origen's *Commentary on the Gospel of John*, in which he invokes the following passage from the *Gospel according to the Hebrews*, also suggests that the Holy Spirit is the Mother of the Lord, for "the Saviour Himself says, 'My Mother, the Holy Spirit, took me just now … and carried me off to the great Mount Tabor'" (Origen and Heine, 1989, p. 116). In his commentary on Isaiah (IV, on Is. 11:2) Jerome observes

> When the Lord came out of the water, the whole fount of the Holy Spirit descended up on him and rested upon him and said to him "My Son, in all the prophets I was waiting for thee that thou shouldst come … For thou art my rest; thou art my only begotten Son that reignest for ever."
>
> *(Scheck, 2015, p. 1)*

The Odes of Solomon, possibly of Jewish-Christian provenance, also suggest that "Spirit" may be read as "Mother" in addition to creatrix: "I rested on the Spirit of the Lord/and she raised me up to heaven (The Spirit) brought me forth before the … Lord's face/For according to the greatness of the Most High, so She made me" (Charlesworth, 1985, p. 765). Sebastian Brock notes that among the early Christian writers, one can find evidence "that there was once a fairly widespread tradition which associated the Holy Spirit with the image of mother" (1990, p. 81). Brock, as does Payne (1966, p. 314), finds the roots of this tradition to be in "the personalized figure of Wisdom" which we have seen above, as well as in "the Jewish concept of the Divine Presence or Shekinah" (1990, p. 81).

According to Susan Ashbrook Harvey, "it has become commonplace for church historians to point out that … prior to the year 400, the Holy Spirit was most often understood to be feminine" (1993, p. 111). The Syriac Christian tradition is based on Semitic sources in which the word for Spirit, *ruach*, is gendered feminine with accompanying feminine pronoun, adjective, and verb forms. Brock notes that the feminization of Spirit is the "norm in the three main monuments of early Syriac literature, the *Acts of Thomas*, and the writings of Aphrahat and Ephrem" (Brock, 1990, p. 74). Importantly, however, Brock stipulates that the feminization of the Spirit goes beyond mere grammatical form, citing the *Gospel According to Philip*, where the author "clearly sees the Spirit as female" as well as the *Gospel of Thomas*, in which "in the course of several prayers uttered by Judas Thomas, the ... text includes several invocations to the Holy Spirit as 'Mother'" (1990, p. 78). Brock concludes that the Syriac texts, in particular, show "clear evidence of a Trinity envisaged as consisting of Father, Mother, and Son" (1990, p. 79). Additionally, the church father, Epiphanius (c. 315–430) suggests a strong visible resemblance between the Mother and the Son. He transmits a revelation given to the Jewish Christian prophet Elxai in which "the Holy Spirit is ... like Christ ... but she is a female being" (Epiphanius and Williams, 2009, p. 50).

While the Church of Jesus Christ of Latter-day Saints currently tracks traditional Christian churches in gendering the Holy Spirit as masculine, room has already been made for a reading of the Holy Spirit as feminine. Early in the twentieth century church apostle, Charles Penrose, stated

> if the divine image, to be complete, had to reflect a female as well as a male element, it is self-evident that both must be contained in the Deity. And they are. For the divine Spirit that in the morning of creation "moved upon the face of the waters," bringing forth life and order, is ... the feminine gender, whatever modern theology may think of it.
>
> *(Millennial Star, 1902)*

In the Book of Abraham 4:2, the Holy Spirit is described as "brooding upon the waters." "Brooding" is generally acknowledged to be a feminine activity. In the Syriac tradition, Brock notes that the Hebrew verb *rahhef* (to hover), derived from Genesis 1:2 and Deuteronomy 32:1, "is frequently used to describe the action of the Holy Spirit," which, for Syriac writers is, like the verb "brooding," an essentially feminine action (Brock, 2008, p. 10).

Conclusion

Mormon feminism has seemed to many an oxymoron. The combined legacy of plural marriage (still officially a heavenly prospect) and an exclusively male priesthood seem to some observers irredeemably hostile to any possibility of a place for women that is fully equal to and commensurate with the status and dignity of men. At the same time, in two crucial regards, Mormonism has already achieved two feminist landmarks toward which Stanton could only wistfully aspire, and which no other Christian tradition has yet to accomplish: a scripturally warranted dogma that places Eve at humankind's forefront, as the initiator and bold champion of the entire human family's sojourn on earth; and a theological affirmation of a feminine counterpart to God the Father, suggesting a heaven where male and female share in glory and divinity. What remains at this point is for scholars belonging to the Church of Jesus Christ of Latter-Day Saints, who are invested in these and associated themes, to continue to collaborate with other scholars in excavating and expanding a theological framework that continues to challenge the model of unequivocal patriarchy, both on earth and in heaven above.

References

Ackerman, S., 2008. The West Semitic Godess of Spinning and Weaving. *Journal of Near Eastern Studies* 67(1): 1–29.
Augustine, and Parsons, Sister W., 1956. Letters, vol. 5, pp. 204–70. *The Fathers of the Church*, vol. 32. Washington, D.C.: The Catholic University of America Press. https://muse.jhu.edu/chapter/737770 (accessed July 30, 2019).
Barker, M., 1992. *The Great Angel: A Study of Israel's Second God*. Louisville, KY: Westminster John Knox Press.
Barker, M., 2005. Joseph Smith and Preexilic Israelite Religion. *BYU Studies Quarterly* 44(1): 69–82.
Barker, M., 2011. *Temple Mysticism: An Introduction*. London: Society for Promoting Christian Knowledge.
Biale, D., 1982. The God with Breasts: El Shaddai in the Bible. *History of Religions* 21(3): 240–56.
The Bible: King James Version, 2013. Salt Lake City, UT: The Church of Jesus Christ of Latter-day Saints.
Brock, S.P., 1990. The Holy Spirit as Feminine in Early Syriac Literature. In J.M. Soskice, ed. *After Eve*. London: Collins/Marshall Pickering, pp. 72–88.
Brock, S.P., 2008. *The Holy Spirit in the Traditional Syrian Baptismal Tradition*. Piscataway, NJ: Georgia's Press.
Bynum, C., 1982. *Jesus as Mother: Studies in the Spirituality of the High Middle Ages*. Berkeley, CA: University of California Press.
Charlesworth, J., 1985. *The Old Testament Pseudepigrapha*. Garden City, NY: Doubleday.
Christensen, K., 2001. *Paradigms Regained: A Survey of Margaret Barker's Scholarship and Its Significance for Mormon Studies*. Provo, UT: Foundation for Ancient Research and Mormon Studies.
Church of Jesus Christ of Latter-day Saints, 2013. *The Book of Mormon*. Salt Lake City, UT: Church of Jesus Christ of Latter-day Saints.
Church of Jesus Christ of Latter-day Saints, 2013. *The Doctrine and Covenants of the Church of Jesus Christ of Latter-Day Saints. The Pearl of Great Price*. Salt Lake City, UT: Church of Jesus Christ of Latter-Day Saints.
Church of Jesus Christ of Latter-day Saints, 2015. Mother in Heaven. October. www.lds.org/topics/mother-in-heaven?lang=eng.
Cross, F.M., 1973. *Canaanite Myth and Hebrew Ethic*. Cambridge, MA: Harvard University Press.
Daly, G., 1972. Theological Models in the Doctrine of Original Sin. *Heythrop Journal* 13(2): 121–42.
Dever, W., 2005. *Did God Have a Wife?* Grand Rapids, MI: Eerdmans.
Ehat, A., and Cook, L. eds., 1991. *The Words of Joseph Smith*. Orem, UT: Grandin Book Company.
Epiphanius, and Williams, F., 2009. *The Panarion of Epiphanius of Salamis*. Leiden: Brill. http://search.ebscohost.com/login.aspx?direct=true&db=nlebk&AN=312551&site=ehost-live&scope=site (accessed July 30, 2019).
Fogleman, A., 2007. *Jesus Is Female: Moravians and the Challenge of Radical Religion in Early America*. Philadelphia, PA: University of Pennsylvania Press.
Givens, T., 2010. *When Souls Had Wings: Premortal Existence in Western Thought*. New York: Oxford University Press.
Givens, T., 2014. *Wrestling the Angel: The Foundations of Mormon Thought*. New York: Oxford University Press.
Hanks, M. ed., 1992. *Women and Authority: Re-Emerging Mormon Feminism*. Salt Lake City, UT: Signature Books.
Harvey, S., 1993. Feminine Imagery for the Divine: The Holy Spirit. *St. Vladimir's Theological Quarterly* 37(2–3): 111–39.
Hodge, C., 1970. *Systematic Theology*, vol. 2. Grand Rapids, MI: Eerdmans.
Hymns of the Church of Jesus Christ of Latter-day Saints, 1985. Salt Lake City, UT: The Church of Jesus Christ of Latter-day Saints.
Irenaeus, 2004. *Adversus Haereses IV*. www.earlychristianwritings.com/text/irenaeus-book4.html (accessed August 8, 2019).
Johnson, D., 1993. As Mormon Church Grows, So Does Dissent from Feminists and Scholars. *The New York Times*. October 2. www.nytimes.com/1993/10/02/us/as-mormon-church-grows-so-does-dissent-from-feminists-and-scholars.html (accessed August 1, 2019).
Johnson, E., 1996. *She Who Is: The Mystery of God in Feminist Theological Discourse*. New York: Crossroad Publishing.

Kern, K., 2001. *Mrs. Stanton's Bible*. Ithaca, NY: Cornell University Press.
Kvam, K., Schearing, L., and Ziegler, V., 1999. *Eve and Adam: Jewish, Christian, and Muslim Readings on Genesis and Gender*. Bloomington, IN: Indiana University Press.
Latter-Day Saints' Millennial Star, 1910. vol. 72.
Lutzky, H., 1998. Shadday as a Goddess Epithet. *Vetus Testamentum* 48(1): 15–36.
Mather, C., 1714. *Maternal Consultations*. https://quod.lib.umich.edu/cgi/t/text/text-idx?c=evans;idno=N01426.0001.001;rgn=div1;view=text;cc=evans;node=N01426.0001.001:3 (accessed August 8, 2019).
Millennial Star, 1902. Women in Heaven. June 26. https://archive.org/stream/millennialstar6426eng#page/408/mode/2up (accessed August 8, 2019).
Mollenkott, V., 1983. *The Feminine Divine: The Biblical Imagery of God as Female*. New York: Crossroad Publishing.
Montefiore, S., 2011. *Jerusalem: The Biography*. New York: Knopf.
Morrill, K., Davis, D., Grieve, V., Andersen, R., Larsen, S., Gardner, A., … Miller, A., n.d. EXHIBITS. http://exhibits.usu.edu/exhibits/show/mormons-for-era (accessed August 1, 2019).
Nibley, H., 2005. *The Message of the Joseph Smith Papyri: An Egyptian Endowment*. Salt Lake City, UT: Deseret Books.
Nibley, H., 2009. *An Approach to the Book of Abraham*. Provo, UT: The Neal A. Maxwell Institute for Religious Scholarship.
Nibley, H., 2010. *One Eternal Round*. Provo, UT: The Neal A. Maxwell Institute for Religious Scholarship.
Olyan, S.M., 1988. *Asherah and the Cult of Yahweh in Israel*. Atlanta, GA: The Society of Biblical Literature.
Origen, 2009. *Origen Homilies on Numbers*, trans. T. Scheck. Madison, WI: InterVarsity Press.
Origen, and Heine, R.E., 1989. *Commentary on the Gospel of John, Books 1–10*. Washington, D.C.: Catholic University of America Press (The Fathers of the Church). http://search.ebscohost.com/login.aspx?direct=true&db=nlebk&AN=498822&site=ehost-live&scope=site (accessed July 30, 2019).
Patai, R., 1990. *The Hebrew Goddess*. 3rd ed. Detroit, MI: Wayne State University Press.
Paulsen, D.L., 1990. Early Christian Belief in a Corporeal Deity: Origen and Augustine as Reluctant Witnesses. *The Harvard Theological Review* 83(2): 105–16. www.jstor.org/stable/1509938.
Paulsen, D., and Pulido, M., 2011. A Mother There: A Survey of the Historical Teachings about Mother in Heaven. *BYU Studies* 50(1): 71–97.
Payne, R., 1966. *The Christian Centuries from Christ to Dante*. New York: Norton.
Petersen, B., 2014. Redeemed from the Curse Placed upon Her: Dialogic Discourse on Eve in the Woman's Exponent. *Journal of Mormon History* 40(1): 135–74.
Peterson, D., 2000. Nephi and His Asherah: A Note on 1 Nephi 11:8–23. *Journal of Book of Mormon Studies* 9(2): 80–81.
Phelps, W., 1844. The Answer. *Time and Seasons*. January 1, p. 758.
Phelps, W., 1845. A Voice from the Prophet, Come to Me. *Times and Seasons*, January 15.
Philo, 2017. *The Works of Philo Judaeus*, vol. 1, trans C. Yonge. Woodstock, NY: Devoted Publishing.
Scheck, T., 2015. *St. Jerome: Commentary on Isaiah*. New York: The Newman Press.
Shuckford, S., 1731. *Harmonie der Heiligen und Profanscribenten in den Geschichten der Welt*. Leipzig: Rüdiger.
Smith, J., 1919. *Gospel Doctrine*. Salt Lake City, UT: Deseret News.
Smith, M., 1990. *The Early History of God*. 2nd ed. Dearborn, MI: Wm. B. Eerdmans.
Snow, E., 1878. *Journal of Discourses*, vol. 19.
Stack, P.F., 2013. A Mormon Mystery Returns: Who Is Heavenly Mother? *The Salt Lake Tribune*. May 16. https://archive.sltrib.com/article.php?id=56282764&itype=CMSID (accessed August 1, 2019).
Stanton, E.C., 1999. *The Women's Bible*. New York: Prometheus Books.
Times and Seasons, 1843. History of Joseph Smith. October 1.
Ulrich, L., 1976. Vertuous Women Found: New England Ministerial Literature 1668–1735. *American Quarterly* 28(1): 20–40.
Van Oort, J., 2016. The Holy Spirit as Feminine: Early Christian Testimonies and Their Interpretation. *HTS Teologiese Studies/Theological Studies* 72(1): A3225. http://dx.doi.org/10.4102/hts.v72i1.3225.
Wilcox, L., 1992. *The Mormon Concept of a Mother in Heaven*. Salt Lake City, UT: Sunstone Education Foundation.
Yonge, C.D., 1993. *The Works of Philo: Complete and Unabridged*. Peabody, MA: Hendrickson Publishers.

Further reading

Barker, M., 2012. *Mother of the Lord*. London: T&T Clark.
In this volume Barker further buttresses her argument for the consistent presence of the divine female deity who resided in the Hebrew Temple until the reforms of King Josiah in the seventh century B.C.E.

Derr, J., Madsen C., Holbrook, K., and Grow, M., 2016. *The First Fifty Years of Relief Society: Key Documents in Latter-day Saint Women's History*. Salt Lake City, UT: Church Historian's Press.
This comprehensive volume includes not only the original version of the meeting minutes of the Female Relief Society of Nauvoo, it highlights the ecclesiastical, social, and political interests of Mormon women of the nineteenth century.

Irigaray, L., 2012. *In the Beginning, She Was*. London: Bloomsbury Academic.
In this book Irigaray argues for a conception of humanity as two halves in lieu of one whole, which is essentially masculine and promotes the recognition for "the between-us as an aspect that belongs to the core of our humanity" (p. 22).

McBaine, N., 2014. *Women at Church: Magnifying LDS Women's Local Impact*. Draper, UT: Greg Kofford Books.
This work examines the ecclesiastical position of women in the Mormon male gendered hierarchy and provides practical solutions for men and women to collaborate within the current ecclesiastical framework.

Schüssler Fiorenza, E., 1994. *In Memory of Her: A Feminist Theological Reconstruction of Christian Origins*. New York: Crossroad Publishing.
In this volume Schüssler Fiorenza explores the role of women in the early church, highlighting their various roles, including those of ecclesiastical leadership and ministry.

39
WOMEN AND PRIESTHOOD

Jonathan A. Stapley

[T]he priesthood in fullness is & shall be conferred upon you[.] you shalt Increase in wisdom & Knowledge & Intelligence be able to do miracles in the name of Jesus to heal the sick to drive the destroyer from thy habitations & shall be blest with Every comfort which you Desire to make you happy in Time & in Eternity.
  (John Smith, Patriarchal Blessing on Zina D.H. Young, 1850)

Any analysis of priesthood within the Church of Jesus Christ of Latter-day Saints must first acknowledge that church members and leaders have assigned meanings to "priesthood" that diverge dramatically from standard definitions. These meanings have also shifted over time, rendering various historical and contemporary usages incompatible. Studies, histories, and discussions that lack such an acknowledgment have often either projected presentist assumptions upon the past, or contained key categorical errors. In this chapter I review several analytical and definitional frameworks that address this problem when focused on the study of women and the Latter-day Saint priesthood. I then review the most significant historical and religious trends relating to Mormon women and priesthood for the nineteenth, twentieth, and twenty-first centuries.

Defining priesthood

Outside of the Church of Jesus Christ of Latter-day Saints, the word priesthood is similar to other words that terminate with -hood. This English suffix denotes either a state of being (childhood and knighthood), or a group with a shared state (neighborhood and brotherhood). This is similar to the suffix -dom (kingdom, freedom), the equivalent of which is incorporated into the German word for priesthood, "priestertum." Thus the Greek New Testament words translated as priesthood in English and the subsequent Christian usages of the term generally refer to priestdom—either the specific capacity of a priest, or to a group or body of priests. One becomes part of the neighborhood by buying a home and becoming a neighbor. One experiences motherhood by giving birth or adopting a child. And one experiences the community and state of priesthood by being ordained or consecrated a priest.

By contrast, current Latter-day Saint catechismal texts declare: "The priesthood is the power and authority of God. It has always existed and will continue to exist without end. Through the priesthood, God created and governs the heavens and the earth" (The Church of Jesus Christ of Latter-day Saints, 2010, p.8). This expansive power and authority is localized entirely within the church, as the church projects itself onto the cosmos. It is a mistake to assume that Latter-day Saint priesthood refers simply to a clerical station or government. And while members do sometimes employ standard non-Mormon usages to refer to a group of ordained priests or elders as "the priesthood," church leaders such as First Presidency member Dallin Oaks have stated that such usage is unequivocally outside of church order: "We should always remember that men who hold the priesthood are not 'the priesthood.' It is not appropriate to refer to 'the priesthood and the women.' We should refer to 'the holders of the priesthood and the women'" (Oaks, 2018, p. 69). As we will see, even these distinctions have become more complicated as aspects of priesthood ecclesiology have been extended to women in the last decade.

Ecclesiastical priesthood and cosmological priesthood

As described in my recently published work, priesthood in the Latter-day Saint tradition has had ecclesiastical and cosmological valences (Stapley, 2018). The earliest Mormon documentation of priesthood—primarily Joseph Smith's revelation texts—conform to the standard usages. For example when Joseph Smith revealed the office of church president, the revelation text describes it as the "President of the high Priest hood of the Church or in other words the Presiding high Priest over the high Priesthood of the Church."[1] Five years after organizing the church, however, Smith revealed a new taxonomy of priesthood within the church, namely the two organizational structures called the Aaronic Priesthood and the Melchizedek Priesthood. All existing ecclesiastical offices in the church were then organized within one of these priesthood hierarchies, essentially rendering these church offices to be different types of priests. This new framework was codified in the 1835 Doctrine and Covenants—a compilation of revelations that has served as a textual anchor since its publication. Throughout the first decades of the church the method of ordaining men to priesthood offices remained the same, and I refer to this conception of priesthood as the "ecclesiastical priesthood" of the church—priesthood associated with church office.

Smith had begun to reveal aspects of priesthood in the 1830s that expanded outside of ecclesiology, but in Nauvoo (1839–1844) Joseph Smith revealed a radical and expansive cosmology in association with a new temple liturgy, comprising washings and anointings, a dramatic presentation, and relational sealings. Here salvation, kinship, and government swirled together into a new conception of priesthood. Smith's temple liturgy included the "sealing" together of men and women, a ritual that after his death expanded to the joining of parents and children. This sealing was an eternal bond that materialized heaven. Heaven was not a destination or gift. It was created on earth by believers who entered into a network of relationality through sealing. Those believers were to ultimately be kings and queens, priests and priestesses.

As part of the temple liturgy, all initiates—male and female—dressed in priesthood robes and exchanged priesthood symbols. Contemporaneous documents indicate that these participants referred to themselves and to the heavenly network they created as "the priesthood." This priesthood was not, however, ecclesiastical in nature. Participating in the temple liturgy did not confer church office, but it did confer the ability to extend the heavenly chains of relation to one's family by birth, or by ritual. I refer to this conception of priesthood as the "cosmological priesthood." It is this cosmological priesthood that accounts for the patriarchal blessing of Zina Young which opened this chapter. "The priesthood in fullness is & shall be conferred upon you," the church patriarch declared to her. He was not declaring that Young was to have an ecclesiastical position. She was a priestess in heaven on earth and in the eternities, where ecclesiology passed away.

These categories are necessarily artificial—Joseph Smith did not use "ecclesiastical priesthood" and "cosmological priesthood." However these frameworks are useful to understand Latter-day Saint lived religion and historical theology. Ideas and terminology associated with the cosmological priesthood saturated discourse and thought for the years immediately after the Nauvoo era. It was integral to the trek West and the settlement of the Great Basin. Church leader sermons, baby blessings, patriarchal blessings, and diaries are filled with references to women being promised, receiving, or participating in this priesthood.

Women and priesthood authority

In a previously published study (Stapley, 2016), I employed a taxonomy to divide Mormon authority into three areas: (1) ecclesiastical authority, derived from church office; (2) liturgical authority, derived from membership in the church to participate in certain rituals of worship; and (3) priestly authority, derived from participation in the Nauvoo Temple liturgy or cosmological priesthood. I argued that over time church leaders and members have used the term "priesthood" in reference to shifting aspects of these authorities.

With the organization of the Relief Society in 1842, women were brought into the ecclesiastical structure of the church. Joseph Smith worked with prominent Nauvoo women to establish the Female Relief Society of Nauvoo. This organization was ecclesiastical in nature—it was part of the church—but Smith did not detail the relationship between this Relief Society and the church's established priesthood organizations, nor did he revise his ecclesiastical texts in the Doctrine and Covenants to accommodate (or include or encompass) it. Neither Smith nor any other female or male church leaders claimed that membership in the Relief Society conveyed a priesthood office in the church. However, they did repeatedly teach that the Relief Society was patterned after the priesthood and the presidency of the Relief Society was created through an ordination ritual nearly identical to those that created priesthood officers. Ordination was the means of creating an ecclesiastical office, and was not reserved to priesthood office until the twentieth century. Thus women in the Relief Society (and other church offices as they were created in the subsequent decades) held ecclesiastical positions in the church and wielded ecclesiastical authority.

Women have participated in various aspects of church liturgy since the creation of the church. In the early church women testified, exhorted, spoke in tongues, translated, and administered in the healing liturgy. In the late mid-twentieth century Melchizedek Priesthood officers became the only authorized administrators of the healing liturgy. Healings became a "priesthood ordinance"—a term within contemporary Mormonism that denotes a ritual necessarily performed by a priesthood officer. Women no longer had the liturgical authority to heal or bless. Church leaders have variously bestowed liturgical authority upon and removed it from women in the church (Stapley, 2018).

Since 1843 women in the church have participated in the temple liturgy as initiates, and have also performed select temple rituals as administrators. The temple liturgy is salvific and the authority to perform the liturgy in the temples and to extend temple relationships in one's body in the case of bearing children after being sealed, I argue, constitutes a particular type of authority that is distinct from the ecclesiastical and liturgical authorities of the church. As discussed, for the first several decades after the revelation of the Nauvoo temple liturgy, the temple and associated cosmology were understood in terms of priesthood—the cosmological priesthood. In order to distinguish the authority of temple participants, I have termed it a priestly authority.

Details of the shifting borders of priesthood over the ecclesiastical, liturgical, and temple/priestly terrains are complicated and do not follow simple narratives. Aspects of these developmental paths will be reviewed in the next sections of this chapter, one for each century in which the church has existed.

Jonathan A. Stapley

Women and priesthood in the nineteenth century

Ecclesiology

The history of a female ecclesiology in the Church of Jesus Christ of Latter-day Saints begins with a revelation that Joseph Smith dictated for his wife Emma three months after the church was organized, and which was canonized in the 1835 Doctrine and Covenants. This revelation included directions for Emma Smith to create a hymnal for church use, to comfort her husband, and to act as his scribe. The voice of the Lord also stated that she was to be "ordained under his hand to expound scriptures, and to exhort the church, according as it shall be given thee by my Spirit" (D&C 25). This language parallels the duties of deacons and teachers in the Articles and Covenants, the early ruling document of the church. The offices of deacons and teachers later became associated with the Aaronic Priesthood, and were "to warn, expound, exhort, and teach, and invite all to come unto Christ" (D&C 20). While Emma Smith was evidently ordained at this period, there is no documentation of an ecclesiastical office held by women until the organization of the Female Relief Society of Nauvoo over a decade later.

The foundational documents of the Nauvoo Relief Society and representative documents from the next fifty years of the Relief Society have been published by Derr et al. (2016) and Ulrich (2017) has narrated the lived experience of Mormon women during this time using contemporaneous documents. Through these minutes, sermons, letters, and journals we see how the Relief Society shifted within the ecclesiology of the church. When Joseph Smith first organized the society he said that "he would ordain" women "to preside over the Society—and let them preside just as the Presidency, preside over the church." He later told the Society that it "should move according to the ancient Priesthood." During his life the Relief Society exercised a significant amount of institutional autonomy and even played a role in the anti-polygamy agitation near the end of Joseph Smith's life.

Brigham Young, the president of the Quorum of Twelve Apostles, led the majority of the church after Smith's death. Young viewed the Relief Society's anti-polygamy efforts as being partly to blame for Smith's death. He shut down all semblances of a female ecclesiology in the church while expanding polygamy and the accessibility of the temple liturgy. Just as he shrewdly ordained all practicing adult men in Nauvoo to be Seventies, an office clearly subject to Apostolic priesthood authority within the ecclesiology of the period, Young reorganized church ecclesiology to be clearly and canonically under his direction. Even if church leaders had previously claimed that the church was not fully organized without the ecclesiastical structure of the Relief Society, Young was unequivocal that a female ecclesiastical structure was not only unnecessary, but also undesirable. He exercised his ecclesiastical priesthood authority to close it down.

Later in Utah Brigham Young grew to see the value of women organizing within the church and directed the re-establishment of local Relief Societies under the authority of ward bishops. Groups of wards were governed by priesthood officers known as stake presidencies, and Young later created stake Relief Society presidencies which had authority over the ward Societies within their respective stakes. After Young's death, his successor John Taylor established the general Relief Society presidency with Eliza R. Snow as the first general president in 1880. All of these Relief Society officers were ordained and set apart by their respective presiding priesthood officers—bishops, stake presidents, and church presidents.

In the later nineteenth century women also led the organization of the Primary Association, which was a children's ministry, and of the Ladies' Mutual Improvement Association, which was a youth ministry that also focused on cultural and social activities. These organizations became "auxiliaries" of the church over time and were ultimately integrated as ecclesiastical organizations under the authority of priesthood officers.

Cosmology

Within a few years of arriving in the Great Basin, the number of emigrants from Britain and Europe outnumbered the church members who had lived in Nauvoo. Within a few decades, settlers from Nauvoo were a small fraction of the population. Church leaders continued to make statements that referred to the cosmological priesthood, while maintaining clear ecclesiastical demarcations between men and women. In particular, church leaders frequently taught that temple marriage was an order of priesthood and that men and women shared priesthood through the temple. Patriarchs also commonly gave women blessings similar to the one given to Zina Young mentioned above, which made declarations of priesthood inheritance and conferral. Some church members began to interpret these statements to mean that women could in some measure, wield the ecclesiastical priesthood authority of their husbands to whom they had been sealed. Church leaders deprecated these beliefs but variations of them have persisted as Latter-day Saint folk beliefs and fundamentalist traditions (Stapley, 2018).

Women and priesthood in the twentieth century

Cosmology

As Brigham Young and other Nauvoo-era Saints passed away, the cosmological priesthood declined as an interpretive framework. Church leaders became less and less likely to refer to the temple in priesthood terms. By the turn of the twentieth century the cosmological priesthood was no longer a dominant lens for interpreting the temple. In its place a new priesthood cosmology arose through the championing of leaders like Church President Joseph F. Smith. Smith and others had begun to read the canonical 1835 revelation texts in new ways. They interpreted the concepts of the Aaronic and Melchizedek priesthood organizational structures as representing priesthood that exists outside of the particular offices of the church. This was coincidental with the rise of new priesthood definitions that equated priesthood with all the power and authority of God. Thus Smith changed the pattern of ordination in church to require, for example, the Melchizedek Priesthood to be conferred on an individual, and then in a separate linguistic act the person to be ordained to a particular office. Whereas the cosmological priesthood required the incorporation of women to be coherent, this new priesthood cosmology, which was based on the entirely male ecclesiastical priesthood, excluded women to maintain coherence (Stapley, 2018).

This new exclusively male priesthood cosmology resulted in many questions about the status of women in the church and in the cosmos. One prominent interpretive framework was incorporated into church lessons and teachings, being championed by several prominent women and men in the church beginning in the 1930s: the priesthood–motherhood dyad. Susa Young Gates[2] and Leah Widtsoe were foundational thinkers and proponents of this model. Widtsoe described pre-existent gendered spirits that receive corresponding gendered bodies that are complimentary and that both have a work to do that is not a mere biological accident. To wit, men were to receive the priesthood and women were to receive motherhood, and this reception was decided for each individual before the world existed. This was in some ways a sacralization of Victorian norms and despite being complementary, maintained a clear female deference to male priesthood partners who presided in the home (Shirts, 2018).

Whereas polygamy (a reification of the cosmological priesthood) had ordered the lives of church members in the nineteenth century, priesthood ecclesiology became the prime ordering principle for the twentieth century. In the nineteenth century "the patriarchal order" of the church was a euphemism for plural marriage. Church leaders repurposed the term to mean the priesthood system where a father was also an ecclesiastical officer, who baptized and blessed his own children (jobs generally performed by other priesthood officers in the past), and was the righteous head of the household. The male priesthood was to organize home and church. With regard to the temple, church leaders recognized that women could have authority to perform rituals in the temple, but they were clear to distinguish this authority from priesthood (Stapley, 2018). In 1965 Elder William Critchlow declared in a General Conference: "Priesthood is the power of God, presently and purposely denied to women for reasons which he has not revealed." Moreover he exhorted: "don't ever, Sister, make a pretense to priesthood power" (Critchlow, 1965, p. 38). Women did not hold priesthood in any sense.

Near the end of the century, when some conservative Protestant denominations were leaning into headship theologies drawn from the New Testament, church leaders released "The Family: A Proclamation to the World," a document designed to demarcate a formal and prophetic stance in the politics of same-sex marriage. The document did not include language about male headship, but did include language about husbands "presiding" in their homes alongside an exhortation that fathers and mothers were to be equal partners in all of their familial responsibilities. "Presiding" and "equal partnership" are not obviously compatible, but members around the world have found important liberating elements in the principles. This is particularly the case in areas where male family members have not always been traditionally active participants in childcare and family economy (Kline, 2016; McDannell, 2018).

Ecclesiology

Missionaries

Perhaps the single largest shift in the female ecclesiology of the church after the creation of the Relief Society was the calling of women to serve as missionaries beginning in 1898 (McBride, 2018). While women had testified and exhorted at church and in public on an informal basis since the organization of the church, evangelizing had always been the prerogative of priesthood officers. Joseph Smith's Articles of Faith, which he wrote to explain Latter-day Saint beliefs to a journalist, declared "we believe that a man must be called of God by 'prophesy, and by laying on of hands' by those who are in authority to preach the gospel and administer in the ordinances thereof" (Davidson et al., 2012, p. 500). For all but the last two years of the nineteenth century this belief was reified in the ordination of men to the priesthood office of seventy and their missionary labors throughout the world. Many believed that because women lacked priesthood office they could not preach the Restored gospel outside of the church.

Initially called to prove that Mormon women were not oppressed victims in the face of polygamy-focused anti-Mormon media, female missionaries were wildly successful evangelists and mission bureaucracies grew to clamor for more women to be called. While some questioned the possibility of women preaching the gospel on doctrinal grounds, and some resisted the expansion of female roles in the mission bureaucracies, pragmatic momentum obviated conservative discomfort. Female missionaries did still require a measure of authority and power that distinguished them from regular members to accomplish this work. When men who had already been ordained to the office of seventy before they were selected for missionary service, church leaders laid their hands on them to bless and "set them apart" for the work. Setting apart rituals began in the church in conjunction with ordination rituals and by the twentieth century became the standard method to create non-priesthood ecclesiastical offices. Thus women in the twentieth century were set apart and preached the gospel with authority, albeit an authority that was discrete from priesthood.

Correlation

Joseph F. Smith initiated the Priesthood Reform Movement at the beginning of the twentieth century, which comprised a set of progressive reforms designed to increase and improve the religious participation of men and boys in the church. These reforms included liturgical, ecclesiastical, and cosmological shifts, and continued for decades. These shifts were amplified and expanded in the Priesthood Correlation reforms of the 1960s and early 1970s. Church leaders realigned the church entirely based upon priesthood organization, from the priesthood-holding father, through priesthood home teachers, and through the various priesthood bureaucracies of the church to the church president at the apex. Church leaders focused on this "patriarchal order" as means to establish Zion—the temporal and spiritual salvation of the Saints (Bowman, 2016). Organizationally, these reforms transferred women's organizations and activities to be under the direction and approval of priesthood officers. All Relief Society magazines, lessons, projects, and finances, for example, were shifted outside of the Society's autonomy (McDannell, 2018).

"Keys" is another term that underwent significant shifts in the twentieth century. Its complicated lexical function in Latter-day Saint history can be traced to Joseph Smith, who used the term in different ways. One prominent usage was the idea that keys bestowed authority or power to do something—to open a metaphorical lock. Smith declared to the Female Relief Society in Nauvoo that he had "turned the key" to them in the name of God. By the mid-twentieth century church leaders used "keys" exclusively to denote a governing authority within the church and cosmos. As church leaders began to rationalize church ecclesiology they asserted how organizational presidents—church presidents, quorum presidents, Sunday school presidents, and Relief Society presidents—all held the keys of presidency (McConkie, 1950, p. 151; Yarn, 1964, p. 30). These keys were conferred upon them when they were set apart for their offices. Ultimately the church president held all the keys of the gospel kingdom on earth.

As part of the Correlation reforms church leaders maintained that "keys" were fundamental nodes for directing church authority, but asserted that only priesthood presidents held keys. This change was not only a theological assertion; in order for this reform to be coherent, high priest quorum presidencies were eliminated and stake presidents became the president of the high priest quorum. Another consequence of this reform was that women no longer held keys in the church. Whereas women had presided in Relief Society meetings up to this point, under Correlation, stake and ward priesthood officers presided at Society meetings, where they regularly attended. This realigned organizational paths of authority such that ward Relief Society presidencies became subject entirely to the ward priesthood ecclesiology. Stake and general Relief Society presidencies no longer communicated directly to local Societies but channeled communication through the priesthood bureaucracies of the church. Women did still operate Relief Societies throughout the world, and the centralized financing and bureaucracies of the church did enable and expand opportunities for the women's auxiliaries in many ways. Still ultimate decision making, from staffing to mission statements were required to be approved by all-male ecclesiastical leaders.

Liturgy

At the beginning of the twentieth century, women were prominent administrators in the healing liturgy of the church and by the end of the century they were barred from performing healing and blessing rituals, which became the explicit domain of Melchizedek priesthood officers. Current church members are largely unaware of female ritual healing in the church and the idea that women regularly performed what are now considered "ordinances" of the church has become nearly transgressive. This shift, however, is only part of a larger trend in the twentieth century to concentrate liturgical authority within the priesthood offices of the church. Other rituals, such as grave dedication and preparation of the Lord's Supper, which had historically been open to women, became priesthood ordinances during this time.

The Priesthood Reform Movement created a progressive structure to priesthood office; boys were to be ordained deacons, teachers, and then priests and elders at regular ages as they grew older. Church leaders also created jobs for these boys by assigning the preparing and passing of the Sacrament of the Lord's Supper to deacons and teachers respectively. There was no similar progressive ecclesiastical or liturgical structure for girls and women. The systematization of priesthood curricula and the training of younger and younger missionaries became an increased priority in church, and all literature produced was priesthood focused. Heber J. Grant began a liturgical formalization that resulted in significant changes to church ritual. As part of these changes, male and female healers were removed from the temples. And while Grant consistently allowed for female participation in the healing liturgy, he also emphasized the preference for the elders of the church to be called to administer. These and similar emphases were amplified under the Correlation movement, where all healing and blessing was considered a priesthood duty.

Most of the changes in female liturgical authority over the twentieth century were transfers of that authority to priesthood officers. In some cases, however, there have been some expansions as well. For example, while women preached and prayed in Relief Society meetings, ward Sacrament Meetings and General Conferences were the province of male ecclesiastical leaders. In some cases, women were explicitly barred from praying in public meetings. However, in the last quarter of the century, church leaders decided that women should pray at all meetings, which also regularly feature sermons by women (Stapley, 2018).

Mormon feminism

With Correlation, church leaders expanded priesthood bureaucracies and standardized simplified historical narratives and theology. In the 1970s many church members who were raised and educated in the correlated church began to discover the documents and stories of the early church that evinced a complexity not addressed in church literature. Professionalization in the church historical department resulted in new historical studies and increased archival accessibility. In particular a group of women in Boston including Laurel Thatcher Ulrich began to produce important scholarship on Mormon women and explore the relationships between feminism and the church. Complicating institutional narratives and exploring views outside of institutional mandates necessarily caused friction between scholars and church leaders. At the same time, church leaders began a campaign against the Equal Rights Amendment in the United States, which included mobilizing Relief Society members. Some members who supported the amendment protested against this activity. Sonia Johnson was a prominent church member activist who critiqued the church's politics, and leveled feminist critiques against its patriarchal structure. Johnson was excommunicated for her efforts, but continued to demonstrate against the church.

Throughout the 1980s and 1990s feminist scholars continued to produce a significant body of literature: historical studies, new theology, devotional literature, and literary criticism. These studies were the first to analyze women's historical roles in the church liturgy and ecclesiology. Two key works of this period are *Sisters in Spirit*, published by University of Illinois Press and *Women and Authority*, published by Signature Books—both edited volumes. Several of the chapter authors in the latter volume were excommunicated by church leaders for their work in this and other venues which critiqued the status quo within the church or proposed theology that discomfited church leaders (McDannell, 2018). Some of this scholarship employed historiography that in retrospect is problematic, and upon which some ongoing feminist critiques continue to rely. However, both women and men during this period produced scholarship that became the foundation for not only the disciplines of Mormon History and Mormon Studies today, but also for the historiography of the institutional church in subsequent decades.

Women and priesthood in the twenty-first century

The conflicts between feminist activism and the church continued after the 1990s and informed movements that have redefined the twenty-first-century church's relationship between women and the priesthood. The 2000s brought the rise of a new generation of feminist voices whose discourse was largely mediated online. As church members participated on the new social media—first blogs and then platforms such as Facebook—many feminists found access to likeminded peers and scholarship from previous decades, newly accessible and often digitized. Some of these women and men became activists, actively lobbying for change in the church. Some feminists lobbied for incremental change within the existing structure of the church, while others argued for an overhaul of every aspect of the church. The Ordain Women movement was one of these latter groups, harnessing social media to organize protests on Temple Square and advocate for female ordination to priesthood office. This conflict resulted in several organizers either resigning their church membership or being excommunicated (McDannell, 2018). At the same time many members, including church leaders, struggled to understand and articulate a constructive relationship between women and priesthood in the church. Church members largely did not have the tools to understand the history of women in the church, and some were not satisfied with seemingly stale "traditional" gender roles.

In 2013 male and female church leaders began speaking out on women and priesthood in expansive ways, actively engaging issues of gender, authority and power. This discourse culminated in then-apostle Dallin Oaks' April 2014 General Conference sermon entitled "The Keys and Authority of the Priesthood." Oaks redefined priesthood as any power or authority in the church: "We are not accustomed to speaking of women having the authority of the priesthood in their Church callings, but what other authority can it be?" (Oaks, 2014, p. 51). Thus women who receive authority and power to act in their callings wield both priesthood authority and priesthood power. While he did not explain how priesthood authority exists distinct from priesthood office, he clearly emphasized that the distribution of that authority was facilitated by those with keys—that is, presiding priesthood officers.

Oaks' priesthood paradigm immediately transformed the church lessons and discourse. For example, church leaders revised the instructional manual for missionary life in 2018 making explicit the idea that female missionaries preach the gospel with priesthood authority: "As a missionary, you have authority to preach the gospel. President Dallin H. Oaks has taught: 'Whoever functions in an office or calling received from one who holds priesthood keys exercises priesthood authority in performing her or his assigned duties'" (The Church of Jesus Christ of Latter-day Saints, 2018, p. 4). Leaders made practical changes in response as well—women's leadership roles have expanded in mission organizations over the same period.

This new priesthood framework has expanded into most aspects of church teaching. For example, the church-produced Gospel Topics Essay describing Joseph Smith's teachings on women and the temple adopted Oaks' framework. Moreover, the authority of women who administer the temple liturgy has become priesthood authority, returning priesthood language to the temple after more than a century. To revisit the taxonomy of authority introduced early in the chapter, Oaks redefined all ecclesiastical, liturgical, and priestly authority as priesthood authority (Stapley, 2018).

Conclusion

Priesthood has both ordered the worlds of the Saints and created them. Priesthood in the Church of Jesus Christ of Latter-day Saints is a capacious term with shifting and sometimes contradictory meanings. Perhaps no other relationship to this priesthood serves to better probe and illuminate this complexity and power than that of gender, particularly women's relationship to priesthood. When Joseph Smith first organized the church there were only four ecclesiastical offices, a simple liturgy with mostly written prayers, and no real conception of priesthood beyond those of contemporary churches. Smith was never static and he was quick to complicate every aspect of his new religion. Priesthood was, however, a subject of revelation upon revelation—a perennial focus—and was the center of his cosmos. At that center were women as well as men. Understanding these priesthoods, in their inceptions and in their various subsequent permutations, requires a vigilant anti-presentism and a careful contextualization to ensure that terms and concepts are not being ported between periods uncritically. It also requires skepticism of simplified narratives, both those arising from the institution and from those arising outside of it.

Notes

1 Revelation, November 11, 1831-B, in Godfrey et al. (2013, p. 134).
2 Lisa Olsen Tait has documented Susa Young Gates contribution to this framework in a forthcoming study.

References

Bowman, M., 2016. Zion: The Progressive Roots of Mormon Correlation. In P.Q. Mason, ed. *Directions for Mormon Studies in the Twenty-First Century*. Salt Lake City, UT: University of Utah Press, pp. 101–2.

The Church of Jesus Christ of Latter-day Saints, 2010. *Handbook 2: Administering the Church*. Salt Lake City, UT: The Church of Jesus Christ of Latter-day Saints.

The Church of Jesus Christ of Latter-day Saints, 2018. *Preach My Gospel: A Guide to Missionary Service*. 2nd ed. Salt Lake City, UT: The Church of Jesus Christ of Latter-day Saints.

Critchlow, W., 1965. The Priesthood and Women. *Conference Reports*. October.

Davidson, K., Whittaker, D., Ashurst-McGee, M., and Jensen, R., 2012. *Histories*, vol. 1: *Joseph Smith Histories, 1832–1844*. Salt Lake City, UT: Church Historian's Press.

Derr, J., Madsen, C., Holbrook, K., and Grow, M. eds., 2016. *The First Fifty Years of Relief Society: Key Documents in Latter-day Saint Women's History*. Salt Lake City, UT: Church Historian's Press.

Godfrey, M., Ashurst-McGee, M., Underwood, G., Woodford, R., and Hartley, W., 2013. *Documents*, vol. 2: *July 1831–January 1833*. Salt Lake City, UT: Church Historian's Press.

Kline, C., 2016. Saying Goodbye to the Final Say: The Softening and Reimagining of Mormon Male Headship Ideologies. In P.Q. Mason and J.G. Turner, eds. *Out of Obscurity: Mormonism since 1945*. New York: Oxford University Press, pp. 214–33.

McBride, M., 2018. Female Brethren: Gender Dynamics in a Newly Integrated Missionary Force 1898–1915. *Journal of Mormon History* 44(4): 40–67.

McConkie, B., 1950. The Relief Society and the Keys of the Kingdom. *Relief Society Magazine* 37(March): 151.

McDannell, C., 2018. *Sister Saints: Mormon Women since the End of Polygamy*. New York: Oxford University Press.

Oaks, D., 2014. The Keys and Authority of the Priesthood. *Ensign*. May, pp. 49–52.

Oaks, D., 2018. The Powers of the Priesthood. *Ensign*. May, p. 69.

Shirts, K., 2018. The Role of Susa Young Gates and Leah Dunford Widtsoe in the Historical Development of the Priesthood/Motherhood Model. *Journal of Mormon History* 44(2): 104–39.

Stapley, J., 2016. Women and Mormon Authority. In K. Holbrook and M. Bowman, eds. *Women and Mormonism: Historical and Contemporary Perspectives*. Salt Lake City, UT: University of Utah Press, pp. 101–20.

Stapley, J., 2018. *The Power of Godliness: Mormon Liturgy and Cosmology*. New York: Oxford University Press.

Ulrich, L., 2017. *House Full of Females: Plural Marriage and Women's Rights in Early Mormonism, 1835–1870*. New York: Knopf.

Yarn, D., 1964. The Function of Counselors. *Improvement Era* 67(1): 30.

40
MEN AND THE PRIESTHOOD

Margaret Toscano

The identity, subjectivity, and masculinity of male members of the Church of Jesus Christ of Latter-day Saints is defined, shaped, supported, but also problematized, by the powers, practices, beliefs, and discourse surrounding priesthood. But how? What issues and expectations, conformities, and resistances about maleness are evoked for church members—male and female—by LDS ecclesiastical and priesthood structures and by its historical narratives and theological paradigms?

The LDS Church trains its male members from their early youth to accept the doctrines and rituals of priesthood as part of their maturation. Mormon priesthood is a lay priesthood. Almost every boy is ordained by age 12, or now younger. Priesthood ordination serves as a male rite of passage that confers status in the church community, defines personal identity, and facilitates spirituality and worthiness that reinforce male bonding and organizational loyalty on a foundational level. Being a priesthood bearer is a normal and essential part of being a male member of the LDS Church. It is not something to question; it just is. The connection between priesthood and maleness is so deeply entrenched in Latter-day Saints that, in the past, LDS men as a group were often referred to as "The Priesthood"—though recently church leaders have rejected this equation and usage (Nelson, 2018). Whether Mormon men are called "The Priesthood" or more accurately "Priesthood holders," the two terms are interchangeable because only males—not females—can be ordained. Thus, priesthood defines those ordained against those unordained such that Mormon priesthood pits maleness against femaleness. Over time the rights, powers, privileges, and practices of the priesthood have become inextricably intertwined with Mormon male subjectivity and with how the Mormon male self is constructed. To be a Mormon priesthood bearer is to embody the divine. The ordained LDS male is the incarnation of godly power and, thus, enacts the authority of God even in his everyday actions. Both the doctrines and the practices surrounding priesthood provide the underlying framework that gives ordained Mormon men identity, purpose, and meaning, as well as setting patterns for how they should act within the LDS Church and community.

Mormon masculinity

Not only is LDS priesthood a lay priesthood, but it is multi-layered and hierarchical, with top leaders serving in priesthood offices into old age, supported by the centralized Church in Salt

Lake City, Utah. Mormon priesthood is divided into two general categories: the Aaronic Priesthood (typically for boys ages 11–18) and the Melchizedek Priesthood (for adult men). Ordination to the Aaronic offices of deacon, teacher, and priest and to the Melchizedek offices of elder and high priest, or more rarely of patriarch or apostle (the latter of which number fifteen in the entire Church), is presented and accepted in the LDS community as emblematic of male worthiness in the eyes of the Lord and of his "true and living" church (D&C 1:30).[1] Participating in the activities and rituals of the lesser Aaronic Priesthood, then receiving the greater Melchizedek Priesthood and serving a mission, marrying in the temple, exercising priesthood in the home, rearing faithful children, and serving in church callings constitute the expected path for every ordained LDS male. To deviate from this path is to wander beyond the acceptable margins of both LDS family and community life. The expectations of conformity to priesthood praxis and doxy can place on Mormon male priesthood bearers a heavy—and for some an overwhelming—burden made heavier by the contradictions that pepper the messages of LDS church leaders. Consequently, priesthood is a blessing and a burden. It assures and puzzles. It comforts and troubles. It can engender confidence and harmony as well as self-doubt and dissonance.

From an early age Mormon males are subjected to official church publications and pronouncements that often present images of the youthful and manly Joseph Smith or of physically robust and muscular Book of Mormon prophets as ideal priesthood men, along with photographs of LDS general authorities—old, mild-mannered, conservative, silver-haired, white, and presented in order of seniority. To these images must be added the official depictions of Jesus, Lord and Savior and head of the all-male priesthood order of the LDS Church (D&C 107). Mormon men and boys are told "the ideal example of manhood is Jesus Christ," whom they should follow by serving others "through love, work, priesthood callings, instruction, and example" (Ludlow, 1992, p. 888). In church art Jesus is depicted as a man of peace—blessing children, ordaining apostles, praying in Gethsemane, cradling lambs in his arms. He is presented as a male, but without sexuality, ambition, or material aspiration. He is neither lover nor husband nor father. His subservience to the Heavenly Father exemplifies how Mormon males should willingly subordinate their judgment to that of their priesthood superiors. Notwithstanding, Mormon men are also urged to date, court, marry, reproduce, be exemplary patriarchs, acquire worldly education and skills, be successful breadwinners for their immediate and even extended families. But they are not to aspire to church office, even though the Church's apostles and other top leaders are held up to them as models to emulate. Ordained Mormon men are to be obedient and humble, yet simultaneously assertive and valiant. The 1992 *Encyclopedia of Mormonism*'s entry entitled "Men's Roles" illustrates these contraries:

> LDS men are exhorted by their leaders to become strong yet mild, to be ambitious to serve yet selfless in order to add to another's eternal growth, and to measure their success by how they nurture others and how they teach and make possible the progress and growth of others rather than use others to feed their own needs.
> *(Ludlow, 1992, pp. 888–90)*

"Strong yet mild," "ambitious ... yet selfless"—these admonitions sum up the tensions in the notion of "true masculinity" that Mormon men are urged to achieve; and upon these notions arise the conflicting images of the ideal priesthood holder that Mormon males must somehow resolve.

The tensions surrounding religious masculinity are by no means unique to the LDS Church. In his 2008 article, "Muscular Mormonism," Richard Kimball describes how Mormon culture followed the movement of "Muscular Christianity" from the 1880s to the 1920s and beyond.

Building on the work of Clifford Putney, Kimball argues that Protestant Christianity, in response to the feminization of religion in the nineteenth century, attempted to rekindle men's interest in Christianity through manly sports, health, and recreation. A similar movement in the LDS Church took place in response to the emasculation caused both by the renunciation of polygamy and the desire to conform to mainstream American norms. Kimball explains that "Muscular Mormons … projected a manly image as the church moved from a maligned minority on the margins of American society to the respectability of the conservative middle class" (2008, p. 550). He further argues that stories of "athletic accomplishments by church members likewise provided a proof text for the LDS health code known as the Word of Wisdom." Thus the Mormon way of life promoted a version of American manliness that was athletic, vigorous, and competent. Kimball traces how Mormon priesthood leaders continue to idealize athletes (such as NFL star, Steve Young) as emblems of manliness—both spiritually and physically—that serve "a key role in the socialization of young men" in contemporary Mormonism (2008, p. 573).

With this historical background in mind, it is no surprise that Kristine Haglund, in a 2012 blogpost on the non-LDS "Religion and Politics" website, uses two Mormon male ritual acts to represent the contemplative and active as rival elements of Mormon masculinity: first, Mormon men's aggressive playing of basketball at the local church meetinghouses and, second, Mormon men sensitively weeping when speaking in public meetings. While she acknowledges that neither of these activities "is unique to Mormon culture," Haglund asserts that one element that "characterizes Mormon masculinity is a highly sentimentalized involvement with family, an often weepy public piety, and a soft-spoken homosociality in groups of Mormon men working together to administer the functions of the church." The contrasting elements represented by church basketball and weepy church talks occur in connected spaces in LDS buildings. Recreation halls adjoin the chapels in most LDS meeting houses, whose architecture symbolizes the competitive, powerful, athletic, and ambitious ideal of Mormon manhood on one hand, and the cooperative, subdued, non-contentious, and domesticated ideal on the other. Understanding this tension requires an understanding of LDS priesthood ordination, offices, and activities set within the context of Mormon history and beliefs about priesthood.

In their 2011 article "Mormon Masculinity," Amy Hoyt and Sarah M. Patterson argue that, in the nineteenth century, Mormon maleness was defined not only by polygamy but by the concepts and practices of the LDS lay priesthood that engaged all ordained LDS males and that were "central to the construction of Mormon masculinity" (2011, p. 74). The abandonment of polygamy dealt a serious blow to Mormon male identity, they argue. Priesthood had to be redefined for the LDS Church to move beyond plural marriage and frontier isolation in order to advance toward urbanization and accommodation with mainstream American culture and its ideals of masculinity. Hoyt and Patterson note how Mormon leaders remodeled priesthood by ordaining younger and younger men, who were then instructed "that the priesthood endowed them with the authority to perform sacred duties and that those duties were the purview of men in their faith" (2011, p. 81). Leaders also connected men's "worthiness" to hold priesthood with certain behaviors and activities, such as monogamous heterosexual fidelity, missionary service, and compliance with the Word of Wisdom (abstention from liquor, tobacco, coffee, and tea). Leaders began to stress individual social and business success, but not at the expense of commitment to the LDS religious community and church organization.

In his 2013 M.A. thesis, "'It'll Be Zion to Me': Ideal Mormon Masculinity in *Legacy*," David Newman defines contemporary Mormon masculinity "as the habitual enactment of faithfulness, tenderness, and competence primarily focused around the nuclear family and the local church community" (2013, p. 59). Newman, like others, sees Mormon men constructing their male identities both with and against American male patterns through the performance of actions and behaviors typically expected of men in LDS communities. Newman argues that Mormon masculinity is "complicit" with the dominant American position because it benefits from patriarchy and follows middle-class patterns of male success; however, it is a "subordinate" masculinity when it emphasizes sexual abstention, sentiment, strong attachment to parents, and subordination to other priesthood men (2013, pp. 48–63).

Mormon masculinity and the history of priesthood restoration

In his book, *Masculinities in Theory*, Todd W. Reeser argues that ideas and practices of masculinity are always in dialogue with a "series of others," that is, with other people, other ideas, and otherness itself (2010, p. 41). This means that masculinity cannot be static; nor is it monolithic, even when hegemonic. Mormon masculinity has changed and will continue to change, just as ideas about what priesthood is and how it should be used have changed and will continue to change. Though the scholars quoted above argue that the developments, expressions, and reformulations of ideal Mormon masculinity are highly performative (influenced, no doubt by current gender theorists, such as Judith Butler), it would be a mistake to reduce this to a set of ritualized actions and behaviors. Such a view ignores Mormonism's insistence on the reality of God and the spiritual realm, of the eternal destiny of humans as God's children, and of priesthood restoration as central to the mission of the LDS Church. These beliefs, deeply held by many Mormon men, are what cause them to remain active priesthood holders despite their personal struggles with conflicting images of their masculinity. The importance of belief and spirituality for the Mormon ideal of manhood can be appreciated only within the context of the complex and contested history and doctrines of priesthood restoration, which are primary sources of a priesthood holder's sense of purpose and meaning. This is fortified by priesthood structures and practices that create relationships crucial to Mormon men's self-concept, their connection to their religious paradigms, and their functions in the LDS community.

The authority of the LDS Church is predicated on its teaching that God dispensed to Joseph Smith and his successors the holy priesthood—the divine commission to speak and act in God's name. Over the years LDS church leaders have emphasized the ways male priesthood holders bear the burden of carrying out God's divine work on this earth. This was made explicit by apostle Rudger Clawson in the 1939 church manual *Priesthood and Church Government*, where he asserts that the

> spiritual condition of a man is determined by the degree to which he honors in his life the priesthood which has been conferred upon him. It follows that the prosperity of the Church itself may be measured by the activity of the priesthood bearers.
> *(Widtsoe, 1939, pp. v–vi)*

Clawson taught that when men live up "to the ideals of the priesthood, the Church advances rapidly: when they falter in their duties, the progress of the Church lags." This authoritative statement puts a "heavy responsibility" on holders of the Mormon lay priesthood because the way in which each man fulfills his duties affects the spirituality and success of the Church (Widtsoe, 1939, p. v). This connection also exalts ordained men to the center and apex of the divine work at the heart of the LDS restoration of God's true Church in the latter days. Mormon males become essential to God through their priestly callings that inform their sense of divine mission and purpose so crucial to their self-concept as males.

The Church's traditional and official narrative of God's dispensation of priesthood in the nineteenth century is straightforward. On May 15, 1829, while praying in the woods in upstate

New York, Joseph Smith and Oliver Cowdery were visited by the resurrected John the Baptist, who conferred upon them the lesser or Aaronic Priesthood with authority to preach the gospel and to baptize. Sometime during the first two weeks of June 1829 (the day has never been firmly fixed), Joseph and Oliver were visited by the resurrected apostles, Peter, James, and John, who ordained them to the greater or Melchizedek Priesthood with authority to confirm baptized members, to bless them with the gift of the Holy Ghost, and to organize and administer the Church.[2] It should be noted that scholars have disrupted this narrative by pointing out the absence of documentary evidence between 1829 and 1834 regarding these angelic visitations. In the earliest days of the Mormon movement, it was not the visitation of angels but the Book of Mormon that served as the offered proof of Joseph Smith's priesthood authority and prophetic calling. Most scholars see LDS priesthood concepts and practices developing and changing from 1830 to 1844 and beyond (Prince, 1995, pp. 3–21; Quinn, 2016; Bushman, 2005, pp. 57–143).

Three different but interrelated concepts of priesthood conferral emerge from the historical narratives. First is the notion of unmediated transmission of priesthood by the spirit or voice of God or by the visitation of angels—a mechanism usually reserved either to initiate a new dispensation of priesthood or to restore priesthood that has been lost. This may have been the actual method of priesthood transmittal during Mormonism's pre-ecclesiastical period of 1828 to 1830. Second is the concept of ordination by the laying on of hands by an individual accepted as holding priesthood authority. This has been the received and only accepted method of priesthood transmittal from at least 1832 to the present. Third, and perhaps least understood, is the doctrine of priesthood transmittal by ritual investiture, which has occurred by means of the Mormon temple endowment since May 1842. This last concept involves priesthood transmittal by a ritual rather than by an individual. It also involves the restoration of a more encompassing priesthood—the fullness of the priesthood—of which both the Aaronic and Melchizedek priesthoods are deemed parts of a greater whole. Joseph Smith also called the fullness of the priesthood the "Messianic" priesthood and associated it with the return of the prophet Elijah, prophesied in Malachi 4:5. Its purpose was to prepare its recipients to meet the Lord at the veil, to receive the promise of charismatic power, the power over nature, and to be sealed personally to God (Toscano and Toscano, 1990, pp. 143–208). While scholars debate the nature and purpose of temple priesthood, the LDS Church assures members that it connects only with family sealings and does not confer authority to act within the Church (Church Essay, n.d.).

The nuanced complexity of this history of priesthood restoration and the mixed-messages about the relationship of the various Mormon priesthood orders are a further source of tension in the ideal of Mormon masculinity because they set forth conflicts between private and public aspects of priestly power and identity. The early charismatic view of priesthood restoration emphasizes its spiritual, individualistic, and egalitarian nature. The conferral of priesthood by the laying on of hands of a superior priesthood holder emphasizes how priestly status and hierarchy are entwined with priesthood and with the contemporary corporate structure of the LDS Church. Joseph Smith's final revelation of the fullness of the Melchizedek Priesthood through temple rituals recaptures a more egalitarian spiritual model that includes women and focuses on divine mysteries, supernatural power, and extra-ecclesiastical authority that offer personal empowerment.

Paul Toscano and I developed this multi-leveled view of Mormon priesthood from Joseph Smith's many sermons and scriptural texts in our 1990 book, *Strangers in Paradox*. Not only did Smith see priesthood as charismatic, ecclesiastical, and messianic, but he discussed other levels and orders of priesthood connected with the various biblical figures and dispensation heads: Adam, Abraham, Moses, Elias, and Elijah (D&C 110)—each possessing certain priesthood keys and functions that relate to the salvation and exaltation of the human race and human history. Nevertheless, according to Smith, all of these priesthood orders and their functions are connected, centering on the messianic mission of Jesus Christ to transform the earth into the kingdom of God—to bring Zion above down to meet Zion below (Toscano and Toscano, 1990, pp. 143–53). The fullness of the priesthood as bestowed by the temple rituals was meant to bring together all the aspects of priesthood into one: the prophet/prophetess, priest/priestess, king/queen offices bestowed by the second anointing hold the keys to perform rituals in many contexts, govern righteously in the Church and kingdom of God, and exercise spiritual gifts, such as prophesy and revelation in the service of and for the benefit of all. The high priesthood of the temple, in this view, was more encompassing than the ecclesiastical high priesthood (Toscano, 2015, pp. 52–58). Nevertheless, the President of the Church is the head of the ecclesiastical priesthood, and therefore he determines how priesthood is used and who gets to use it in all church contexts.

In *The Power of Godliness: Mormon Liturgy and Cosmology*, Jonathan A. Stapley (2018) also describes three aspects of Mormon priesthood: ecclesiastical, liturgical, and cosmological. Though I agree that these three areas of priesthood are crucial for understanding early Mormon views about the nature of priesthood restoration, my own schema attempts to capture Joseph Smith's views through his language. Smith's texts demonstrate his concerns that priesthood should unite the spiritual and physical realms as equally valuable. Smith adamantly asserted the need for ordinances/liturgy as essential to redemption and sanctification. These rituals not only restored biblical patterns but memorialized inner transformative states and acted as conduits for God's spirit to connect heaven and earth. This view promotes a complex cosmology where gods, angels, and spirits of the unborn and the dead, and even devils interact with humans. The ecclesiastical priesthood was a central locus for liturgical acts, in Joseph Smith's view, but not the only one.

It is important to review this complicated history and theology to understand fully how and why priesthood is so engrained at every level of Mormon practice and in every level of theology and belief. Though orthodox LDS people most likely will not accept my understanding of priesthood, aspects of it still infiltrate current belief and practice because they are grounded in Mormon sacred texts, rituals, and history, whose multiple layers create confusion about how the ecclesiastical priesthood and the temple priesthood relate, and how personal priesthood relates to church priesthood. Importantly, power, privilege, and priesthood are interrelated in all the narratives of the restoration of the priesthood, as well as in all the orders and functions of the priesthood. Power is a particularly crucial noun that conjures spiritual, personal, and institutional power. Because priesthood is seen as divinely commissioned "power from on high," it serves as the basis for personal male empowerment and identity; its history and doctrines make it vital and compelling for men serving as God's priesthood holders in Mormonism.

D&C 121: the rights and power of the priesthood

The phrase "power from on high" denotes both institutional and personal authority. It not only creates a relationship between an individual priesthood bearer and God, but also relationships between that individual and his local religious community, as well relationships with the LDS Church, the greater Christian community, and the world at large. The Gospel of Luke presents the apparition of the glorified Jesus to his disciples after his resurrection to commission them to preach his gospel. But first he admonishes them to tarry in Jerusalem until they are endowed "with power from on high" (Luke 24:49), a phrase repeated several times in Joseph Smith's revelations. Each repetition signifies the transmission of divine authority and power from God to male priesthood holders commissioned to preach the Lord's gospel, establish his Church, expand the priesthood structure, and carry out the work of the Church (D&C 20, 38, 43, 95, 105, 107, 109, 135). Priesthood power, given from on high, is the "power of godliness" that spiritually transforms individuals (D&C 84:20–21). This holy power also can be subverted to unholy purposes by unholy means. D&C 121 contains a warning and admonition that certainly affects the ways priesthood shapes men's self-concepts in the LDS Church:

> 36. That the rights of the priesthood are inseparably connected with the powers of heaven, and that the powers of heaven cannot be controlled nor handled only upon the principles of righteousness.
> 37. That they may be conferred upon us, it is true; but when we undertake to cover our sins, or to gratify our pride, our vain ambition, or to exercise control or dominion or compulsion upon the souls of the children of men, in any degree of unrighteousness, behold, the heavens withdraw themselves, the Spirit of the Lord is grieved; and when it is withdrawn, Amen to the priesthood or the authority of that man.

Importantly, this revelation connects the spiritual with the physical. The two cannot be separated in Mormon theology, which argues for the positive nature of embodiment and refuses to see the bodily realm as inferior to the spiritual (D&C 88, 93). In Mormon thought, the supernatural element of priesthood power is as real as the corporate, political, or economic power of the Church and its ecclesiastical offices. Unrighteous dominion is not simply coercive action; it involves ungodly motives: pride, ambition, hypocrisy, and deception. Since real priesthood power depends on a man being a worthy vessel of the spirit of the Lord, priesthood holders must aspire to and attain godly attributes in themselves. This concept, while conveying power to males, also conveys daunting responsibilities and tasks that shape how priesthood holders see and define themselves.

In these verses, both the inner and outer aspects of priesthood are juxtaposed. The inner consists of "the powers of heaven," the "Spirit of the Lord." The outer consists of "the rights of the priesthood," the "authority of that man." A Mormon priesthood holder can have either or both. A man can hold a priesthood office but have no spiritual power, which means he can be administratively effective but without charismatic gifts. Or he can possess such gifts, but hold no ecclesiastical office or authority, which means he may be spiritually effective, but without official standing, and therefore may be perceived as a threat to the acknowledged leadership. Or a man may have both charisma and office, which is the ideal. It is understandable why the outer priesthood with its acknowledged ecclesiastical offices and callings is emphasized in the LDS Church since it is both managerial and manageable. Charisma is not; it is, therefore, downplayed.

Implied in these verses of D&C 121 are a series of connections established by the reception of the priesthood that include the fluid relationships between (1) the priest, God, and the supernatural world; (2) the priest, the communities he serves, and the world; and (3) the priesthood holder's inner and outer self as he matures and develops toward individuation. These verses warn that these relationships may be ruptured or destroyed by the abuse of priesthood "to gratify our pride, our vain ambition, or to exercise control or dominion or compulsion upon the souls of the children of men" (D&C 121:37). Priesthood concepts, rituals, and structures create mechanisms for interactions among the priesthood bearer, his God, his family, and his communities that define beneficially his identity and worth as a male. But these interactions can have the negative effect of making him feel inadequate or alienated. In either case, Mormon masculinity is constructed through these relationships. Throughout the following sections, I will emphasize both the positive and negative aspects of these relationships as seen by both supporters and critics.³

Priest and God

The priest-God relationship is central to the priesthood holder both as a person and as God's agent because his relationship with the divine lies at the heart of both his personal and institutional experience. His ecclesiastical office (i.e., his outer priesthood) confers upon him exceptional status, especially when it is perceived as a conduit through which God's spirit flows to members of his family and community. This status can inspire confidence in himself as well as his community's confidence in him; and it can provide him with opportunities to accomplish ends that might otherwise be out of reach. Of course, this status can easily be abused to gratify pride or to exercise dominion, or compulsion over others. The priesthood bearer's charisma or link with the divine (i.e., his inner priesthood) imbues even his most mundane duties with the sacred, thus encouraging others to yield to him allegiance they might withhold from a secular authority. The priest's belief in the spiritual dimension of priesthood encourages him to seek and do the will of God and inspires congregants to accomplish good through the priest's leadership. Even without belief in the inner dimensions of priesthood, its offices and callings confer respect and obedience. Of course, a corrupt or non-believing ambitious priest can play upon others' trust to achieve personal aggrandizement and elite status to the detriment of his congregation and even of the larger church community.

The link to the spiritual realm ascribed to priests, mystics, and magi is an old and widely accepted notion. In the Mormon sacred text entitled The Pearl of Great Price, the prophet Enoch is depicted as possessing the rare power over nature. He is able to command mountains to move, waters to part, and the earth to tremble in order to further God's work and even put at defiance God's enemies (Moses 7:13). Latter-day Saints in Joseph Smith's day not only believed such miraculous biblical stories, they claimed that such spiritual manifestations were happening to them, as in the appearance of God and angels during the Pentecostal dedication of the Kirtland temple in 1836 (Bushman, 2005, pp. 315–19). The connection of the priest to the spiritual world, however, is much more subtle and problematic in the contemporary world. Whether a faithful priesthood holder should be able to work miracles and manifest spiritual gifts is an oft-debated question both in contemporary Mormonism and in other Christian denominations. It is, of course, a notion rejected out of hand by the secular world. Most LDS accept the claim that top church leaders have divine manifestations in our contemporary age. But the lack of specific details and, some would say, of demonstrations of spiritual power, gives rise to two minority responses: some leave the Church to join groups that claim to have demonstrable spiritual gifts (Snuffer, 2015); while others leave the Church and become atheists, rejecting spiritual claims altogether (Schulson, 2014; Mormon Stories, n.d.). In both cases, the claim of inner or charismatic priesthood leads to criticism of those who claim to possess God's true priesthood but who fall short in some way.

Priest and community

The relationship between priest and community can be subdivided into four areas: family, community, corporation, and brotherhood. The LDS Church has encouraged men to be good husbands and fathers for generations, highlighting the benefits of the male priesthood structure for developing strong family groups (Kline, 2016, p. 217). While such emphasis on the family fortifies patriarchy and male domination, it has nevertheless encouraged Mormon men to be faithful husbands and responsible fathers with clear duties toward their wives and children. These teachings are especially beneficial in those cultures where these values tend to ameliorate and even neutralize machismo attitudes and abuses (Kline, 2018). The Church has recently softened slightly its patriarchal rhetoric by emphasizing the priesthood partnership of a husband and wife in their family—although feminist critics feel that LDS church leaders' continued denial of male and female priesthood equality subverts this notion of equality in the home.[4] However, Mormon couples—especially younger ones—work toward the goal of a true equal priesthood partnership in the family setting. In her 2016 essay, "Saying Goodbye to the Final Say: The Softening and Reimagining of Mormon Male Headship Ideologies," Caroline Kline argues that the tension between and emphasis on "both male/female equality and male headship within marriage is a recent development," perhaps first evident in the 1995 "The Family: A Proclamation to the World" (2016, p. 214). While leaders have softened the language of male headship and the link between priesthood and presiding in the home, the priesthood status of men still remains dominant in both ecclesiastical and family settings because it is crucial to encourage male commitment to the family and male participation in the Church (Kline, 2016, p. 222).

The priesthood holder's service to the community presents the most obvious benefits of priesthood to believers and non-believers alike. Sacerdotal structures create expectations for both individual and community service and facilitate charitable acts that can meet real needs and demonstrate true compassion toward others. Priesthood can create systemic good that spreads beyond personal service because it facilitates the rallying of group effort to address problems that surpass the ability or competence of any one individual: helping a neighbor move, providing food and services to a grieving family, lining up sand bags to diminish potential flood damage. The list goes on to include soup kitchens, raising funds for medical treatment, establishing endowments and scholarships, storing food and other necessaries to assist the poor, the disabled, or the victims of natural disaster. Even those who have lost faith often stay active in the Church so they can continue to participate in family and community social gatherings and service events. Of course, such participation can and does occur in the absence of priesthood in secular organizations. But the presence of priesthood insinuates into acts of charity a sense of a divine mandate to help each other in times of need and to establish a community based not on individual aggrandizement but on cooperation, mutual concern, and compassion. This sense of the spiritual in acts of service not only encourages men to offer physical assistance, but it also promotes the giving of spiritual and emotional support and comfort in the form of blessings, forgiveness and repentance, faith and hope, and other intangibles.

The rich, corporate LDS Church is both an object of praise and of criticism (Quinn, 2017). As is evident on lds.org, the Church is praised for its relief efforts during national and international disasters and for its welfare program. At the same time it is criticized for possessing so much real estate and managing so many large corporations. Critics ask whether a church should build shopping malls and accumulate large tracts of land when so much more could be done to relieve suffering among its own adherents and throughout the world. Some ask whether top church leaders have morphed from spiritual guides into corporate managers. Still others criticize the Church for covering over sexual abuses that have been perpetuated by some priesthood holders and even leaders (MormonLeaks documents both corporate abuse and sex-abuse cover-up). On the other hand, priesthood men in branches, wards, stakes, and missions throughout the Church have on many occasions demonstrated selfless willingness to set aside personal interests to aid the poor and destitute, especially in their local communities. Most priesthood leaders do not receive salaries for the countless hours they devote for the welfare of their congregations, but they do receive a sense of accomplishment and the respect of church members.[5]

The priesthood structure can also facilitate brotherhood: social contact and positive relationships among men who may tend not to gravitate to other same-sex social groups. Sports, guns, gambling, computer games, and the outdoors can bring about male bonding, it is true. But a priesthood structure can facilitate brotherhood not based on common interests alone, but upon commitment to higher purposes that engage men who might not otherwise have much in common. Such a brotherhood could include hunters and hymn writers, soccer enthusiasts and statisticians, filmmakers and fisherman and, thus, call upon talents and interests that not only promote personal growth but benefit others.

In his seminal 1992 essay, "On Mormon Masculinity," David Knowlton explores the ways priesthood structures create male bonding through church activities as well as through male priesthood rites of passage, such as missions (1992, pp. 23–24). Haglund and Newman also note the strong homosociality of Mormon priesthood structures manifest in many local and church-wide contexts: playing church ball, interacting with missionary companions, serving in quorums, in councils, in presidencies together, and in church welfare projects. Not surprisingly, these scholars describe the fear of homosexuality that is prevalent among homosocial LDS men and leaders, a phobic reaction that mainstream members and leaders do not characterize as fear but as the promotion of divinely ordained sex roles.

It is well-known that the Mormon priesthood is denied to females, to sexually active gay men, and to transgender folk. Apostle Dallin H. Oaks' 2018 conference talk, "Truth and Plan," reinforced traditional sex and gender identities, condemned same-sex unions, and denounced the altering of gender. Same-sex relationships, when framed as sins, precipitate not only individual crises for gay boys and men, but instigate such institutional campaigns as the 2008 Prop 8 movement in California against same-sex marriage and the November 2015 church policy that excluded the children of same-sex couples from church ordinances and activities. Though the LDS Church does not admit that the high-profile protests on Mormon blog sites influenced their 2019 rescinding of this policy, its LGBTQ negative campaigns and policies have led to various activist movements among church members, such as the Mama Dragons group (mamadragons.org), organized in 2014 out of concern for the well-being of their LGBTQ family members due to the high suicide rate among gay and lesbian LDS members. Taylor Petrey in his "Toward a Post-Heterosexual Mormon Theology" argues that theologically Mormon doctrine and ritual could incorporate same-sex relationships and sealings without damaging central tenets of the faith (2011). These activist movements and voices demonstrate how the church congregations, including their priesthood holders, can become not just sites of compliance but venues of resistance, where the muscular elements of priesthood are manifest in defiance of unpopular, or at least debated, edicts of church leaders.

Priest and self: development, maturation, status, and transformation

Whether in compliance with or in resistance to authority, faithful Mormon priesthood holders make strenuous efforts to live up to the ideals and expectations the Church sets for them. A significant impediment to men's efforts can be found in the arena of sexuality, where priesthood identity impinges upon competing notions of American masculine identity. Mormon doctrine is highly positive about sexuality and the body since it claims that both are eternal principles. But in practice these values get complicated. Church leaders feel obligated to send negative messages to males, especially to adolescent boys, about their sexuality, in order to encourage them to live the Church's morality code, known as the "law of chastity."[6] Knowlton argues that, despite the Mormon teaching that individuals will be resurrected as sexual beings, the LDS Church persists in organizing "anxiety, fear, faith, and hope around our penises, our libidos, and our sense of ourselves as gendered and religious beings" (1992, p. 26). Knowlton explains how this conflict begins early for Mormon boys because "sexual performance becomes one of the central competitive tests by which American men learn and prove their masculinity" (1992, p. 26). Young Mormon males learn that they have a choice: go along with the norms of American society and "suffer shame within the Church" or go along with church standards and "risk intense shaming and severe accusations of sissyness or worse from their peers" (1992, p. 26). While the Church promotes positive views about heterosexual marriage, it condemns all other sexual acts: masturbation, petting, pre-marital sex, pornography, promiscuity, homoerotic encounters, sex with prostitutes, etc. Even within marriage, unspoken taboos exist (Callister, 2014). Though church leaders emphasize negative messages in church discourse to prevent such behaviors, many LDS claim that their own positive attitudes about sex are an important part of their own Mormon faith and experience (Finlayson-Fife, 2002).[7]

Notwithstanding the cognitive dissonance sexuality creates for Mormon males, there are many positives for male maturation in priesthood structures and discourses. Mormon boys, who typically receive priesthood at age 12, begin at this early age to view themselves as playing important roles in their community and in God's kingdom. Newman emphasizes that "lay priesthood gives Mormon men authoritative status from a young age" (2013, p. 52). This is illustrated in a 2018 priesthood conference talk given by a top church leader, Douglas D. Holmes. He praises a young Aaronic Priesthood holder from New Guinea whose testimony inspired Holmes and other older men. Such a talk not only connects older and younger males with a sense of common purpose, but it also creates a context for male initiation into a priesthood brotherhood. Even for those LDS boys with good fathers, other male role-models, such as priesthood quorum and mission leaders, help adolescents explore their talents while learning valuable lessons. The power of multiple adult male role models for boys' positive development has been documented in other American groups (Gale, 2007).

Priesthood structures facilitate personal growth by presenting young men with opportunities to use their talents and to engage in rituals that demark their passage into young adulthood. The mission experience is a central rite of passage that cannot be underrated for its effectiveness over many generations in the construction of Mormon male identity.[8] In spite of some negative experiences, proselyting missions continue to serve as a potent program for helping young men (and more and more for young women) to accept responsibility for others, not just in a physical sense, but in a broader empathic and spiritual sense. The heavy burden that the expectations of mission service places upon young Mormon men often stimulates in them a personal sense of confidence and worth. Mission, church, and community service, when seen as coupled with God's power, can inspire Mormon males to feel that they have embarked upon a quest that promises to deepen personal spirituality, faith, hope, and purpose. The power of the quest archetype is well-attested through mythic narratives. Think of Luke Skywalker instructed by Obi Wan Kenobi to use the Force and become a Jedi Knight. If the essence of priesthood is the spirit of God, then a priesthood structure harnesses God's power systemically to achieve spiritual and righteous ends that involve the priesthood holder in a process of personal transformation, which though occasionally dramatic, usually manifests itself as the subtle development of patience, love, acceptance, forgiveness, gratitude, and desire to assist the poor and oppressed. At the same time, this system also provides opportunities for boys and men to develop self-confidence, leadership and public speaking skills, as well as a sense of belonging and purpose. All of this evidences the effect of both the inner and outer dimensions of priesthood on the Mormon male's inner and outer self.

Church discourse on the connection between male identity and priesthood

The structure of the Church emphasizes the centrality of maleness for reflecting God's image and for furthering God's work in bringing to pass the immortality and eternal life of humankind through the actions of priesthood holders. Thus, LDS church structure, rhetoric, and activities repeatedly connect priesthood, maleness, and divinity on a fundamental level in many contexts (Toscano, 2007). These connections have been talking points in the sermons of church leaders presented in priesthood meetings to male-only audiences for decades.[9] In 1974, Marion D. Hanks, a prominent general church leader, commented that the priesthood session filled with men and boys was "exciting and encouraging in its evidence of the tremendous priesthood potential in the Kingdom of God." He noted that the LDS Church can supply one of the most urgent needs of the time: "models of true manhood for boys who are on their way to becoming men" through "priesthood leadership." He asserted, "it takes men to make men" (Hanks, 1974). The theme of priesthood activity as a place of male initiation and masculine development is a constant one over the decades. In speeches, church leaders often repeat the phrase "Be Men!"—an exhortation taken from the Book of Mormon prophet Lehi, who admonishes his two wayward sons to forsake sin in order to be men of God (2 Nephi 1:21). These talks urging men to be men seem to reveal an underlying fear that manhood is fragile and must be fortified through sermons and actions.

In modern priesthood discourse, leaders also express the fear that the world will interpret the "righteousness" of priesthood holders as womanly or sissy, thus reflecting the concern of the earlier "Muscular Christianity" movement. In a 1992 discourse, LDS general authority Carlos Asay challenged this secular perception by giving scriptural and historical stories of godly men who are courageous. He concluded that address with the command, "Be men! Be men of Christ! Be men of God!" In his 2006 talk "Let Us Be Men," apostle D. Todd Christofferson also used this Book of Mormon scripture to characterize selfless service, accepting responsibility, and honoring commitments as examples of "true manhood."

Sometimes talks by church leaders to priesthood holders center on the theme of heroes, equating heroic qualities with the characteristics of good priesthood men. Church presiding bishop, H. David Burton, explained in a 1993 address that "carefully selected heroes can give us a pattern for our lives and serve as our role models. They can give us courage to walk the road of life righteously." Burton then listed his heroes: the Book of Mormon prophet Nephi, a contemporary sports star Nolan Ryan, then Church President Spencer W. Kimball, and each of his bishops over the years. Sometimes, the hero worship goes a bit awry, as in a 2014 talk entitled "The Priesthood Man," given by apostle and first presidency counselor Henry B. Eyring, in which he listed his boyhood heroes: his own father, Joe DiMaggio, and an ex-marine football player. Eyring then listed the qualities that make priesthood holders masculine: praying often, forgiving, being generous and kind, doing missionary and temple work, being honest and humble—qualities that many would not normally associate with sports stars and marines. Other male conference speakers express masculinity in royal or military language to emphasize the manliness of priesthood. A favorite hymn often sung in priesthood meetings is "Behold the Royal Army," which characterizes priesthood bearers as warriors and the entire priesthood assembly of the Church as God's host. The juxtaposition between the strong qualities of warriors and athletes with the soft qualities of priesthood service again highlights the tensions inherent in the competing models of Mormon masculinity.

Male priesthood and the exclusion of women

The relentless maleness of priesthood in the Church has raised concerns for decades by and about women and their roles in the LDS community. Ordain Women is the most recent group seeking the inclusion of women in the LDS priesthood structure (Shepherd et al., 2015). While this movement has opened up discussions about priesthood and gender even among mainstream, active Mormons, still the majority of active LDS people oppose women's ordination. In her 2014 book, *Women at Church: Magnifying LDS Women's Impact*, Neylan McBaine highlights the power of female agency within the already existing women's organizations that could be diluted if women were ordained. Others argue that men might lose interest in church activity without the sense of their special priesthood callings. In their 2010 study of the power of American religions to both divide and unite people, Putman and Campbell note the high rate of activity among LDS men (2010, pp. 24–25). The ongoing debates within Mormon culture about gender, sexuality, and priesthood reveal the strength of the idea of gendered identity within the Church and how disruptive it is to question accepted gender identities and roles, especially in regard to priesthood, which is seen as divinely organized around male ordination and leadership. The exclusion of women from priesthood continues to connect maleness with priesthood and to pit maleness against femaleness.

Recently church leaders have attempted to display sensitivity to the concerns of women and those who argue that priesthood keeps women in subordinate roles and that the spiritual power represented by priesthood should be available to all. For example, in a 2014 conference talk, apostle Dallin H. Oaks conceded that women have the power and authority of the priesthood, but not its keys or offices. This constitutes a more nuanced statement than past constructions that delineated women as mere recipients of the blessings of the priesthood. In April 2018, Church President Russell M. Nelson asked members not to refer to men as "The Priesthood" but only as holders of priesthood since the priesthood is the power of God, which is available to all worthy members, male and female. In this all-male meeting, Nelson declared that faithful women "know how to call upon the powers of heaven to protect and strengthen their husbands, their children, and others they love." He praised such "spiritually strong women who lead, teach, and minister fearlessly in their callings with the power and authority of God!" Then he thanked "faithful men who live up to their privileges as bearers of the priesthood ... They bless, guide, protect, and strengthen others by the power of the priesthood they hold."

Though President Nelson thanked and praised men and women equally, he undercut this manifestation of egalitarianism at the end of his talk by asking all the men in the priesthood session to stand up by rank from deacons to apostles. "I invite you literally to rise up with me in our great eternal brotherhood. When I name your priesthood office, please stand and remain standing." While they stood, he asked them to sing "Rise Up, O Men of God" and to "think of your duty as God's mighty army to help prepare the world for the Second Coming of the Lord. This is our charge. This is our privilege."

This powerful priesthood ritual devised by Nelson defines priesthood as a sign of masculine achievement while linking a man's rank in the church hierarchy with his standing in the community. Nelson also clearly delineates and separates male priesthood offices and duties from female authority and spirituality, thus reinforcing gendered roles in the Church. No matter how often church leaders praise women's worth and service, the sacred texts, the history, the doctrine, the leadership structure, and the control of resources all reinforce the centrality of men and maleness as God's priests. As Nelson's actions and words show, priesthood office and male privilege are still thoroughly entwined in church discourse, structure, and organizational purpose today. Scholars have argued that Mormon history and culture have produced a strong substrata of women's organizations, publications, and activities—a presence that cannot be ignored (McDannell, 2019; Holbrook and Bowman, 2016). Nevertheless, this chapter illustrates both the negatives and positives of the overwhelming connection between maleness and priesthood in the LDS tradition that is embedded at every level of Mormon practice and discourse.

Mormon men rejecting priesthood

Most LDS men continue to prize priesthood and express positive experiences in the Church that lead them to believe that whatever problems priesthood may pose are outweighed by the good done by male priesthood holders who are doing the best they can. Yet, in the last decade increasing numbers of priesthood holders have come to reject it, often for some of the same reasons stated by concerned Mormon women: lack of any rational justification for the connection between maleness and priesthood, aversion to hierarchical power structures, rejection of the responsibility to lead or judge others, fear of abusive power, and objection to the Church's maleness model as too narrow and exclusive.

Increasingly, rejection of priesthood accompanies or follows a faith crisis. If the sense of the supernatural and divine is lost, how then can a man of good conscience continue to function in the priesthood? If he no longer believes, should he persist in his priesthood duties, in helping others, while hiding his disbelief? Can he do this without being false or hypocritical? Is it ethical even to try without compromising integrity? Because LDS priesthood is saturated with maleness, the disappointment and anger that often follows loss of faith can provoke derision of Mormon models of manliness. If men have repressed expressions and explorations of their masculinity and sexuality at the behest of leaders they now deem false, their feelings of betrayal can fester into hostility and rage, or despair. This has obviously occurred with some gay men, but it can also be demonstrated by straight men.

In the online discussion group "Recovery from Mormonism," one of the participants explained that he was preparing an academic essay titled "Mormon Masculinity—Were You Man Enough?" His intent was to provide examples from the late apostle Boyd Packer, whose (in)famous "Little Factory" decried the evils of masturbation, from the late church president Spencer W. Kimball, whose book *The Miracle of Forgiveness* has induced sex guilt in generations of Mormons, and from the personal horror stories of gay Mormons. This participant claimed that his research would include responses to these questions: "What did you think the Church was telling you about what men are supposed to be? In what ways did you feel you didn't meet their ideal? How did it affect your sense of being a man?" Some respondents claimed that Mormon men are weak, subservient beta men too "quickly driven to tears." One respondent claimed that "there are two types of Mormon Masculinity, the users and the used, the Alpha males and the Beta males they exploit. They're Alphas by being more delusional and/or less principled than the rest of the Betas." Another respondent ridiculed Mormon men, stating that "masculinity isn't the first word that comes to mind when you see Mormon guys walking around." Yet another stated that Mormon men are "about as 'masculine' as David 'weenie ass' Bednar," who is a member of the Quorum of Twelve Apostles. One rare positive respondent stated: "I can honestly say that, truth claims aside, some of the members who taught me growing up were fantastic individuals who taught me … about self-reliance and responsibility" ("Mormon Masculinity—Were You Man Enough?" 2013).

Importantly, when Mormon men like these reject the truth claims of the Church, they sometimes reject Mormon definitions of masculinity that are expressed as faithfulness, service, obedience, humility, and gentleness; and they revert to mainstream American notions of hegemonic masculinity expressed as assertiveness, competitiveness, strength, sexual potency, and promiscuity (Messerschmidt, 2018). They rarely express awareness of the values that Mormon masculinity and American masculinity share: male privilege, power, independence, hard work, self-confidence, and athleticism. Many do not see that both the Mormon and American hegemonic definitions reinforce traditional gender roles.

A personal response

In conclusion, I want to contrast these responses of men who have left the LDS Church with the experience of my husband Paul. The comparison is relevant because he is no longer a member of the LDS Church, or any church for that matter. In 1993, he was excommunicated as one of the "September Six" for his acerbic criticism of top church leaders. Like the men in "Recovery from Mormonism," he too feels betrayed. But unlike them, he still sees value in the underlying belief claims of Mormonism and in the spiritual realm, though I have seen his life-long struggle with faith and doubt. Paul and I met in 1971 through my first husband, Guy. We were all students at BYU and were all zealous students of Mormon history and theology. It was then that I met Mike Quinn, now a well-known Mormon historian. We were the products of the idealistic 1960s; we wanted to build Zion, a classless society of equality and spirituality.

In 1972 I moved into Paul's BYU ward. He was the best example I had ever seen of a faithful priesthood holder. He exhibited both charisma and the dutiful execution of his priesthood responsibilities. He perfectly balanced the rights and powers of the priesthood. When Paul taught Sunday school lessons or gave speeches in our ward and stake, the spirit was palpable in the room, not just to me—who was falling in love with him—but to men in our ward and stake, too. Paul's favorite church job then was helping freshman Aaronic Priesthood holders prepare for their missions by teaching them the gospel. Decades later, some of these same men told me that it was because of Paul that they were converted to Christ and wanted to serve missions. While some of Paul's priesthood leaders appreciated his dedication and spirituality, others saw him as an upstart who did not know his proper place. Paul got in trouble at BYU at this time for preaching grace and criticizing the works-centered, judgmental, and perfection-obsessed policies of the Church. As a result, Paul began publicly criticizing church leaders for their materialism and hierarchal interpretation of priesthood authority. He experienced a slow but steady process of disillusionment.

Paul was not always the "angry apostate" some see him as today. Like others, he initially believed that, if he patiently worked in the Church, changes for the better would take place. He hoped he would be given a high church office that would allow him to facilitate such change. Paul always felt guilty about this desire, which he condemned in himself as ambition; and for years he avoided public expressions of his concerns. I remember how in the mid-1980s he came to the conclusion that he could remain silent no longer. So he joined me at the Sunstone Symposium in Salt Lake City. It is ironic that when Paul and I got married in 1978, I was expecting him to be a faithful, priesthood-holding husband who would make sure we held family home evenings and daily prayer. But even then he was too disillusioned for that; eventually I was too. I don't regret our journey out of the LDS Church. I'm just glad we made it together and that we have stuck together. It has been a transforming experience.

In preparing this chapter, I asked Paul to think back on what the priesthood meant to him in 1972 when I was in his BYU ward. I said,

> I know you will start with denial and say that you never did anything good and don't believe anymore. But you can't fool me. I've known you too long. I was there! Why was the priesthood so palpably powerful for you? How did it define the way you thought of yourself as a man in the Church?

I finally got him talking. He said it started with his spiritual allegiance to Jesus Christ. The message of Christ's gospel was visceral for him: "Christ comes down to us to raise us up to him. His love wipes away our sins and burdens like blowing dust off a table. Christ's grace is sufficient to help us endure our sufferings." Paul admitted,

I felt like I was on the Lord's errand. I was called by him to mediate the gospel to my generation. I didn't think that everything I said and did was right, but I had a sense of confidence that I would be guided to do and say what was needed in the very moment. His grace would be upon me. My priesthood was meaningful to me because I wanted to be an instrument for Christ. And I thought I felt his power was with me.

Paul was actually more eloquent than this, as usual. But these were the notes I jotted down. Paul's priesthood gave him a sense of purpose and identity as a Mormon male, even when he felt he was not successful as a man in mainstream American terms—athletic or rich.

On one level, thinking back on this period makes me sad. Since then, there has been a real loss for Paul and for the Church. This made me see some of the positive benefits of the Church's institutional priesthood. Without its structure, there is no venue or context for Paul's service—at least not to the extent he once had. On the other hand, Paul could never have become a prophet in exile, calling church leaders to repentance if he were still a church member. Grumpy old prophets sit alone in caves or, in Paul's case, in front of the TV in our bedroom watching the news, which these days could inspire anyone to make prophetic declarations. Paul always demurs regarding his belief in Christ and the supernatural. But I know he cannot help himself. The calling is in the blood and bones once it falls upon a person. Being Christ's priest is to swear personal allegiance to him, to further his work of redemption, whenever and however possible, no matter how small or invisible the task. Even after all the time that has passed since his excommunication and even in his old age, priesthood still undergirds Paul's identity and masculinity because it still subtly defines the ways he thinks, speaks, and acts as a soulful spirit in a failing male body.

Notes

1 Several headings under "Priesthood" in the *Encyclopedia of Mormonism* (Ludlow, 1992) give clear and orthodox explanations of the organizational structure of the Aaronic and Melchizedek priesthood orders and how they function in the Church.
2 The *Encyclopedia of Mormonism* (Ludlow, 1992) explains the LDS Church understanding of the restoration of the Aaronic and Melchizedek priesthood orders.
3 The LDS official website (lds.org) and publications give abundant evidence of the positive, while "Mormon Stories" (mormonstories.org) and "Mormon Leaks" (mormonleaks.io) are strong and popular critics. The "FairMormon" website (fairmormon.org) and conference give answers to the Church's critics. And the blog "By Common Consent" (bycommonconsent.org) gives a faithful yet thoughtful position.
4 Blog sites such as Exponent II (www.the-exponent.com), Feminist Mormon Housewives (fMh.org), and OrdainWomen (ordainwomen.org) keep the discussions around gender alive.
5 The status, honor, and respect given to LDS church leaders is evident in the conference talks I analyze below, as well as on the church website and in publications from Deseret Book.
6 Though church leaders frequently give such talks, a recent example is Tad R. Callister's "The Lord's Standard of Morality" (2014) that lists all the ways a person can commit sexual sins.
7 Though Finlayson-Fife focuses on women's sexuality, her dissertation also describes the Mormon men in their lives, illustrating the LDS tensions in beliefs and practices about sexuality.
8 As with the issues above, church publications highlight positive mission experiences, while blog sites like Mormon Stories give voice to the negative. The fact that more young women are serving missions today highlights the differences in the types of service that can be performed by women versus men with priesthood.
9 While I only examined priesthood conference talks from the 1970s to the present day, John A. Widtsoe's *Priesthood and Church Government in the Church of Jesus Christ of Latter-day Saints* traces the connection between priesthood and maleness back to 1939; and John Taylor's *The Government of God* traces it to 1852.

References

Asay, C.E., 1992. Be Men! General Conference. April. lds.org/general-conference/1992/04.
Burton, H.D., 1993. Heroes. General Conference. April. lds.org/general-conference/1993/04.
Bushman, R.L., 2005. *Joseph Smith: Rough Stone Rolling.* New York: Knopf.
Callister, T.R., 2014. The Lord's Standard of Morality. *Ensign.* March. lds.org/study/ensign/2014/03.
Christofferson, D.T., 2006. Let Us Be Men. General Conference. October. lds.org/general-conference/2006/10.
Church Essay, n.d. Joseph Smith's Teachings about Priesthood, Temple and Women. Church Essays. lds.org.
The Church of Jesus Christ of Latter-day Saints. Official website. lds.org.
Eyring, H.B., 2014. The Priesthood Man. General Conference. April. lds.org/general-conference/2014/04.
Finlayson-Fife, J., 2002. Female Sexual Agency in Patriarchal Culture: The Case of Mormon Women. Dissertation, Boston College.
Gale, C.E., 2007. Role Model Development in Young African American Males: Toward a Conceptual Model. Smith College, Theses, Dissertations, and Projects, 1274.
Haglund, K., 2012. Why Mormon Men Love "Church Ball" and Are Scared of Homosexuality. John C. Danforth Center on Religion and Politics. religionandpolitics.org/2012/09/10.
Hanks, M.D., 1974. Boys Need Men. General Conference. April. lds.org/general-conference/1974/04.
Holbrook, K., and Bowman, M. eds., 2016. *Women and Mormonism: Historical and Contemporary Perspectives.* Salt Lake City, UT: University of Utah Press.
Holmes, D.D., 2018. What Every Aaronic Priesthood Holder Needs to Understand. General Conference. April. lds.org/general-conference/2018/04.
Hoyt, A., and Patterson, S.M., 2011. Mormon Masculinity: Changing Gender Expectations in the Era of Transition from Polygamy to Monogamy, 1890–1920. *Gender & History* 23(1): 72–91.
Kimball, R., 2008. Muscular Mormonism. *The International Journal of the History of Sport* 25(5): 549–78.
Kline, C., 2016. Saying Goodbye to the Final Say: The Softening and Reimagining of Mormon Male Headship Ideologies. In P.Q. Mason and J.G. Turner, eds. *Out of Obscurity: Mormonism since 1945.* Oxford: Oxford University Press, pp. 214–33.
Kline, C., 2018. Navigating Mormonism's Gendered Theology and Practice: Mormon Women in a Global Context. Dissertation, Claremont Graduate University.
Knowlton, D., 1992. On Mormon Masculinity. *Sunstone Magazine.* August, pp. 19–31.
Ludlow, D.H., 1992. *Encyclopedia of Mormonism,* 5 vols. New Yok: Macmillan.
McBaine, N., 2014. *Women at Church: Magnifying LDS Women's Impact.* Salt Lake City, UT: Greg Kofford Books.
McDannell, C., 2019. *Sister Saints: Mormon Women since the End of Polygamy.* Oxford: Oxford University Press.
Messerschmidt, J.W., 2018. *Hegemonic Masculinity: Formulation, Reformulation, and Amplification.* Lanham, MD: Rowman & Littlefield.
Mormon Masculinity—Were You Man Enough? 2013. Recovery from Mormonism (RfM). exmormon.org.
Mormon Stories, n.d. www.mormonstories.org/podcast/tag-atheism.
Nelson, R.M., 2018. Ministering with the Power and Authority of God. General Conference. April. lds.org/general-conference/2018/04.
Newman, D.H., 2013. "It'll be Zion to Me": Ideal Mormon Masculinity in *Legacy.* Syracuse University Religion-Theses, Paper 3.
Oaks, D.H., 2014. The Keys and Authority of the Priesthood. *Ensign.* May, pp. 49–52.
Oaks, D.H., 2018. Truth and the Plan. General Conference. October. lds.org/general-conference/2018/10.
Petrey, T.G., 2011. Toward a Post-Heterosexual Mormon Theology. *Dialogue: A Journal of Mormon Thought* 44(4): 106–41.
Prince, G.A., 1995. *Power from On High: The Development of Mormon Priesthood.* Salt Lake City, UT: Signature Books.
Putnam, R.D., and Campbell, D.E., 2010. *American Grace: How Religion Unites and Divides Us.* New York: Simon & Schuster.
Quinn, D.M., 2016. *The Mormon Hierarchy: Origins of Power.* Salt Lake City, UT: Signature Books.

Quinn, D.M., 2017. *The Mormon Hierarchy: Wealth and Corporate Power*. Salt Lake City, UT: Signature Books.

Reeser, T.W., 2010. *Masculinities in Theory: An Introduction*. Oxford and Malden, MA: Wiley-Blackwell.

Schulson, M., 2014. Are Atheists the New Mormons? www.thedailybeast.com/are-atheists-the-new-mormons.

Shepherd, G., Anderson, L.F., and Shepherd, G., 2015. *Voices for Equality: Ordain Women and Resurgent Mormon Feminism*. Salt Lake City, UT: Greg Kofford Books.

Snuffer, D., 2015. *Passing the Heavenly Gift*. Salt Lake City, UT: Mill Creek Press.

Stapley, J.A., 2018. *The Power of Godliness: Mormon Liturgy and Cosmology*. Oxford: Oxford University Press.

Taylor, J., 2016 [1852]. *The Government of God*. London: Liverpool.

Toscano, M.M., 2007. Is There a Place for Heavenly Mother in Mormon Theology? An Investigation into Discourses of Power. In J.M. McLachlan and L. Ericson, eds. *Discourses in Mormon Theology: Philosophical and Theological Possibilities*. Salt Lake City, UT: Greg Kofford Books, pp. 193–223.

Toscano, M., and Toscano, P., 1990. *Strangers in Paradox: Explorations in Mormon Theology*. Salt Lake City, UT: Signature Books.

Toscano, P.J., 2015. *The Serpent and the Dove: Messianic Mysteries of the Mormon Temple*. 2nd ed. Amazon createspace.

Widtsoe, J.A., 1939. *Priesthood and Church Government in the Church of Jesus Christ of Latter-day Saints*. Salt Lake City, UT: Deseret Book.

Further reading

Messerschmidt, J.W., 2018. *Hegemonic Masculinity: Formulation, Reformulation, and Amplification*. Lanham, MD: Roman & Littlefield.

Messerschmidt's book shows how the concept of hegemonic masculinity, first formulated by Raewyn Connell, has developed over the past three decades in masculinity studies. His thorough analysis gives a theoretical basis for understanding how masculinity is constructed and performed in mainstream American culture.

Newman, D.H., 2013. "It'll be Zion to Me": Ideal Mormon Masculinity in *Legacy*. Syracuse University Religion-Theses, Paper 3.

Newman's thesis is a thoughtful study of how contemporary Mormons view ideal masculinity through pioneer narratives in an attempt to bridge the past with the present. Newman's definition of Mormon masculinity combines faithfulness, tenderness, and competency. While he focuses on the ways masculinity is performed in family and community settings, he also states that belief is crucial for LDS identity.

Ruchti, E., 2007. The Performance of Normativity: Mormons and the Construction of an American Masculinity. *Journal of Men, Masculinities and Spirituality* 1(2): 137–54.

Written for a non-LDS audience, Ruchti's article is one of the earlier scholarly attempts to place Mormon masculinity within the framework of American masculinity as it relates to religious belief and practice. Like Newman, she sees Mormons as constructing identity from the framework of a minority identity.

Toscano, M.M., 2015. Retrieving the Keys: Historical Milestones in LDS Women's Quest for Priesthood Ordination. In G. Shepherd, L.F. Anderson, and G. Shepherd, eds. *Voices for Equality: Ordain Women and Resurgent Mormon Feminism*. Salt Lake City, UT: Kofford Books, pp. 137–66.

My chapter in this book gives a chronology of the relationship between women and priesthood from Joseph Smith's sermons to the Relief Society to present-day debates. I also document my own involvement in Mormon feminism over the past thirty-five years. My chapter and this book in general are a counterpoint to male priesthood development, concepts, and identities.

41
MUJERISTA THEOLOGY

Sujey Vega

LDS Latinas through a *mujerista* theological lens

Had to settle a difficulty and iron it out between Elder Fred T. Ash and Sister Garcia, which was settled and hoped it would last.

H.W. Pratt (1936)

"Settle a difficulty," those words echoed in my mind as I sifted through microfilm at the Church History Library. In spite of the dim lighting and sleep-inducing glow from the microfilm readers, I carried on writing notes on annual reports, ward membership, home visits, and hymns sung at the Spanish branch in Mesa, Arizona. It was this line, "had to settle a difficulty and iron it out between Elder Fred T. Ash and Sister Garcia" that pushed the search for more. What was the difficulty? Who was Sister Garcia? How was it ironed out? The notes from the branch's annual reports hardly revealed anything beyond the quantity of members and recruitment efforts. The Mission Quarterly explained that soon after this journal entry, President Pratt reorganized the branch. Pratt was noted as saying this reorganization was "a real sign of growth of the Mesa Branch and the ability of the members to govern the branch, or better said to direct it." But what caused this re-organization and did the difficulty between Sister Garcia and Elder Ash have anything to do with it? Did she disagree with him, did she voice an unpopular opinion, or did she merely stop attending? Whatever it was, it was enough for President Pratt to visit with Sister Garcia on multiple occasions. The specifics of the "difficulty" are not clear, but what was evident was Sister Garcia's willingness to speak and have her voice heard.

I begin with Sister Garcia as a way to ground *mujerista* theology and *mujerista* approaches in quotidian lived experience. Far from some academic scholarly theological philosophy, *mujerista* theology was developed as a means to recognize the everyday lived reality of religious women. Sister Garcia's reality may be partial and filtered through the narrative written down by Pratt; however, unearthing her experience reveals the kind of *mujerista* theology that is possible in Mormon communities. *Mujerista* theology centers Latina voices and experiences to better understand how faith is lived and matters to the lives of *mujeres* who receive God's message in daily quotidian encounters.

Latinas in the Church of Jesus Christ of Latter-day Saints (LDS) are resourceful, are bound to help each other, and are tremendously conscious of the role of faith in their daily struggles, triumphs, and blessings. They inhabit their faith fully and enact what *mujerista* theologian Ada María Isasi-Díaz described as, "organic theologians, admirably capable of reflecting on and explaining their beliefs" (1996, p. x). LDS Latinas live out their doctrine every day. They see their faith enacted in daily blessings and turn to their scriptures when they confront challenges. Indeed, it is this experiential approach toward faith that grounds *mujerista* theology away from the metaphysical and toward a tangible divine enacted in material realities.

Like a quilting bee gathered around to socialize and suture their faith with their lived reality, approaching LDS Latinas through *mujerista* theology and Latina feminist theology provides an opportunity to explore the complex intersectional experiences of gender, ethnicity, immigration, class, and religion in this community. What began as an oral history project, a way to gather the voices of LDS Church members and document the century-long history of a Spanish-speaking congregation in Arizona, has evolved into a recognition of *mujerista* and Latina feminist theology to understand LDS Latinas. As I met LDS Latinas, I came to realize how migration, ethnicity, class, gender, and faith intersect for these women. LDS Latinas active in Spanish-speaking wards (congregations) discuss their hardships and good fortune through the lens of their faith. They utilize their doctrine along with their gendered ethnic social network to face multiple life stages and bolster one another during times of need. Far more than some rote memorization or trite recitation of their testimony, LDS Latinas speak from a place where faith is embodied and enacted to prevail.

My work looks to LDS Latinas/os, their agency, and their sense of spiritual and personal autonomy. I make use of intersectional theory to understand how the Latina/o community is raced, gendered, and classed simultaneously in their experiences with religion. I also interview the next generation of LDS Latino/a millennials and how they carry their faith forward or grow frustrated by the lack of adequate response to larger social justice issues like immigration, gender, and race politics. The following centers *mujerista* theology and Latina feminist theology as a means for understanding the complexity in all these narratives. First, a lesson in *mujerista* theology to ground how one can apply this concept to LDS Latinas. A *mujerista* lens will be applied to two LDS Latinas: Sister Garcia (from the archives) and Sister Veronica. Veronica is a pseudonym for one of the first LDS Latinas I met. During her interview she spoke of her testimony through the trauma of a dangerous border crossing. Finally, a critique of *mujerista* theology will introduce the distinct aspects of Latina feminist theology to provide a context for exploring LDS Latina/o millennials beyond *mujerista* framings.

Quotidian tenents of *mujerista* theology

To appreciate Ada María Isasi-Díaz' explanation of *mujerista* theology one must begin with an understanding of liberation theology, especially as it manifested in Latin America. Liberation theology is grounded on the direct relationship of faith with social justice. It problematized ecclesiastical authority and hierarchical deference to clergy. Instead, Latin American liberation theology acknowledged the poor, the dispossessed, the marginal as generators of faith. Religious leaders stepped down from places of authority and used their social position to work with the oppressed to advocate against violent dictatorships and economic exploitation.

Liberation theologians denoted how the teachings of Christ were grounded in salvific lessons against injustice. The Gospel and Christian doctrine were not secluded to the pulpit but were enacted in daily battles to end suffering. As such, the people were aligned with clergy in as much as they lived out Christ's teachings of peace, compassion, and equity. This democratized approach to faith informed how clerics worked with the laity to fight oppressive regimes and, in the case of Archbishop Óscar Romero in El Salvador, sacrificed their lives in the name of Christ's message to end suffering. This religious milieu inspired Isasi-Díaz to recognize the role of Latina American women in the struggle for justice. Isasi-Díaz explained *mujerista* theology as a means to:

> provide a platform for the voices of Latina grassroots women; to develop a theological method that takes seriously the religious understandings and practices of Latinas as a source for theology; to challenge theological understandings, church teachings, and religious practices that oppress Latina women, that are not life-giving, and, therefore, cannot be theologically correct.
>
> *(1996, p. 1)*

Prioritizing "life-giving" scriptures and highlighting Latina voices borrows from a liberation theology that placed Christ's blessings in the hands of those fighting oppression. Still, liberation theology was male centered in its approach and did not adequately engage in difficult conversations on gender and sexism. For Isasi-Díaz, a fight against oppression had to reconcile gender bias and provide a space to recognize the participation of women. Rather than perpetuate male-centered and male-controlled religious spaces, *mujerista* theology "is also about creating a voice for Latinas, not the only one but a valid one; and mujerista theology is also about capturing public spaces for the voices of Latinas" (Isasi-Díaz, 1996, p. 2). *Mujerista* theology shifted the focus to women, their perspectives, and their contributions for understanding scripture. *Mujerista* theologians noted how Latinas made up a majority of their church membership; yet, women were still excluded in leadership and major decision making of their congregations.

This Latina hermeneutical approach further prioritized how daily lived confrontations with multiplied oppressions, including sexism, informed the way they interpreted their faith. Thus, biblical verses were meaningful through their translation to lived reality. Latina lives were drastically different from the experiences of Latino men. As Isasi-Díaz explained, "For them la palabra de Dios [the word of God] referred not to what is written in the Bible, but to their understanding that their religious beliefs and practices could help them in their struggle for survival" (1996, p. 158). Importantly, the struggle for survival was not some abstract battle against sin. The struggle was in the everyday negotiations against injustices. *Lo cotidiano*, or quotidian confrontations left women especially equipped to speak on behalf of how they dealt with poverty, sexism, feeding their children, and overcoming constant tests of faith.

Both *mujerista* theology and Latina feminist theology agreed on the need to explore the quotidian or everyday lived realities of approaching faith, gender, feminism, and social justice. Theologian Jeanette Rodriguez explained how, "Latinas living in the United States face a daily struggle to maintain their identity as Latinas and as women in a society that explicitly discriminates against both" (2002, p. 116). Still, Rodriguez continues, there are Latinas who "credit their churches, primarily Roman Catholic, as being instrumental in identifying them as leaders, calling them to work in their communities, and offering them an opportunity to step into leadership roles" (2002, p. 116). These Latina feminist theologians or *mujerista* approaches, advocated for a deeper understanding of the way Latina struggles, survival, and lived experience informed their faith and how their very active presence in "comunidades de fe" shifted the paradigm of who could be credited as the heart, labor, and backbone of the Church.

Traditionally overlooked or devalued because of their attributed roles in domestic spaces, *mujerista* theology acknowledged that Latina women provided a rich viewpoint and quotidian examples of embodied faith. Isasi-Díaz expressed, "Instead of devaluing and rejecting our traditional roles in our families, what Latinas want is the opposite: we want the value of those roles to be recognized and their status to be enhanced" (1996, p. 139). God was not housed in rituals or repetitive prayer; instead, Latinas provided incredible opportunities to see faith enacted through mothering and domesticity. As Rodriguez emphasized, Latina women are "ordinary prophets and saints ... who live in the community, who act in the community for the same purpose: to give life. To give life abundantly. They do this against the discrimination and marginality of their social situation" (2002, p. 124). Reframing Latinas as prophets and saints whose daily activities manifest the divine, both Isasi-Díaz and Rodriguez turn theology toward a deeper appreciation for Latina contributions. The renowned theologian and scholar of womanism, Katie Cannon, similarly championed the inclusion of Black womanist voices. For Cannon, the experiences of women of color in the Church should no longer be "anecdotal evidence," instead they should be recognized "beyond serving as superfluous appendages, add-ons to ... the bottom of core course syllabi, as endnotes in church publications, or as impotent members" (2006, p. 20). Womanist, *mujerista*, and Latina feminist theological approaches validated the women's active participation in their church and highlighted how their experience in faith could contribute to ministerial lessons for all believers.

Applying a *mujerista* lens to LDS Latinas

The existing literature on LDS Latina/o experiences is limited, yet some authors do give credit to the work Latinas do in sustaining their wards. As Jared Tamez writes in "Our Faithful Sisters": Latina *hermanas* [sisters] "reveal a much more complicated landscape of agency and power" (2015, p. 84). Despite the structural limitations that these *hermanas* faced, Tamez recognized that they "were instrumental in weaving a cultural fabric that bound together the branches of the Mexican mission" (2015, p. 84). Importantly, Tamez wrote on the role of Mexican LDS women at the turn of the twentieth century and just after the LDS Church reopened its mission in Mexico. The Church withdrew its initial mission a decade earlier, but by 1901 Mormon missionaries returned to try once again to establish their gospel among Mexicans. It is in this moment of expansion that Mexican LDS women coordinated and united toward a faith journey that required much of their dedication to grow the faith. Though much of the history of the LDS Church in Mexico is known through the journals and notes of men, Tamez does a wonderful job detailing the labor of women who sutured together a community despite having to abdicate authority to men and leadership in Utah.

In the United States LDS Latinas faced their own set of struggles related to their raced, gendered, and classed position in society. Recalling the influence of his own mother, historian Ignacio García (2015) wrote in his memoir about the tenacity of Spanish-speaking Mormons whose wards were not as well funded as other Anglo members of the Church but whose faith and activities helped them persevere. In a later piece, García (2018) recognized the role of women, *las hermanas*, who led by example in his Mormon ward and taught him much about his own faith.

In my own research, I observed women organize and plan events that artfully wove faith and community. In Salt Lake City, women volunteered countless hours to place the finishing touches for Latino cultural events at the world-famous Mormon Tabernacle. In Phoenix, they planned folklorico dances, coordinated potluck Latin American meals, and taught their children that their faith and their culture were not oppositional. Critically, the act of maintaining positive ties to Latino identity for children raised in Arizona constitutes an important political act. Just in the last few years, the state of Arizona has enforced immigration laws targeting and discriminating Latina/o residents. Additionally, the state barred any discussion of Hispanic ethnic history or ethnic identity in its schools. These punitive laws result from a general culture of intolerance against Latina/o identified culture and identity. Interviews conducted in Arizona revealed parents and grandparents concerns with Latina/o youth who preferred English-dominant wards, refused to speak Spanish, and attempted to "pass" or blend to an Anglo/White Mormon identity. Adults felt this shaming of culture had a negative impact on their children, but felt they had to acquiesce in order to maintain teens active in the Church. Alternatively, there were Spanish-speaking LDS Latinas who worked tirelessly to create fun activities and culturally based events that celebrated Latin American heritage for their children. They knew their children would be exposed to an Anglo American church and an American identity, but they fought to maintain a rich positive sense of pride for their countries of origin, their culinary traditions, and their language while in the United States. These activities and conscious critique for the discrimination they faced in the United States resulted in a *mujerista* hermeneutic with their scriptures. Beyond event planning and coordinating a sense of community in their wards, their particular experience of being a Latina filtered into their faith explorations and testimony.

A *mujerista* hermeneutic was present in Veronica's memories of her border crossing. I met Veronica in 2006 when doing ethnographic fieldwork in Indiana. Her husband, Raul, was the president to a storefront *rama* (branch) where a dozen families gathered as Latter-day Saints. After attending several sacrament meetings and social events, Veronica invited me to dinner with the missionaries. I arrived on a cold Indiana evening and met the young missionary men in her living room. Shortly after I arrived we entered the dining room to share some delicious homemade pozole (hominy soup). The missionaries ate quietly and hardly spoke. Though their name badges identified them as elders, it was clearly Veronica and Raul who guided these young men into the meaning of enacted faith. Their spiritual commitment served as guiding post for these missionaries. Veronica and Raul were relatively new to the faith, yet they were already called to lead and grow their *rama* (branch). Their dedication to faith and community resulted in an expanding group of Spanish-speaking members.

The missionaries left directly after dinner and we transitioned to talking in the living room. We began discussing their conversion story and their journey into Mormonism. Veronica joined the Church while she was still in Mexico and used the transnational missionary network to keep tabs on her husband in the United States. It took some time for Raul to come around, but he eventually let the missionaries in and began learning more about the Book of Mormon. While he was meeting with missionaries in Indiana, Veronica was preparing to make the move with her children to join him. Lacking the financial resources and time to wait for a decades-long application process, they had to cross *sin papeles* (without documents). This was a difficult experience for the entire family. The crossing took weeks for Veronica and her children. Recalling the despair he felt while waiting for word of their arrival, Raul's voice began to crack. To fill the silence, Veronica described crossing the border with her children,

> fue una aventura terrible pero para ellos yo se les hice ver divertido—como que todo estaba bien ... Gracias a Dios estamos aqui, que si pasamos por todo fue porque El lo quiso asi que valoremos mas las cosas, lo que tenemos, nuestro hogar, la familia.
>
> [It was a terrible adventure, but for them [her children] I made it seem entertaining, like everything would be ok. Thank God we are here, what we went through was all because He wanted us to value things, value what we have, our home, and our family.]

Veronica courageously faced crossing into the country on foot with her children. Terrified herself, she referenced the crossing as "una Aventura," an adventure to compartmentalize the fear and transform it into excitement for her children. At this moment in the interview we paused to get tissues. As we dabbed our tears, Veronica repeated how her faith gave her strength to keep going. In the crossing she met another mother and her infant child. The mother had a fever and wanted to just rest or simply give up. Veronica would have none of that. Treacherous treks, near drownings, and jagged fences were dangerous, but they did not deter Veronica from reuniting with Raul.

A *mujerista* approach recognizes how faith was part and parcel to Veronica's tenacity. God was not simply present during Sacrament meetings but materialized in those frightening moments when Veronica was scared, when her children were bleeding, and when she woke up the next morning to try it again. Veronica felt the family learned to appreciate what they had because of this harrowing journey and perhaps that justified the trauma they went through. More importantly, Veronica asserted that this crossing was heavenly blessed, "El quiso" [He wished it]. Her faith, her God, was on her side. For Veronica, Raul, and many of the members in their *rama* (branch), God loved them and blessed them with or without visas.

This *mujerista* understanding recognizes how faith is embodied and religious beliefs evoked through daily blessings by God. This merger of religion with border crossings rings parallel with a Nepantla approach that acknowledges the importance of liminality. Latina feminist theologian Maria Pilar Aquino suggested that "entering Nepantla means for theologians that we are willing to engage in new explorations about God and ourselves from the creative 'border' locations" (2002, p. 149). The physicality of a geopolitical border crossing is important, but Nepantla speaks beyond the actual border crossing and accounts for navigating faith and feminism or the spiritual with the lived. Aquino further explained that Latina feminist thought "evolves everywhere, in rural and urban areas, in the kitchen and the streets, in our minds and our communities, in schools, hospitals, and churches, entre sábanas y libros" (2002, p. 134). Thus, for Aquino the intimacy of her feminist faith practices were both between the sheets and between the pages of a book, even if that book just so happens to be the Book of Mormon. I suggest that this Nepantla approach can equally be applied to the way LDS Latinas navigated their lives with their LDS scriptures. For Veronica, her Padre Celestial (Heavenly Father) was present and guided her and her children through hazardous landscapes. Reuniting the family was important to her, both in the secular present and in the spiritual beyond. She had been taught that a family could be eternally sealed in a Temple ceremony, but family unity also translated to earthly experiences. The journey or adventure for her and her children to reunite with Raul was blessed by her Creator and no unjust immigration laws would halt that union. Given the present reality that "Mormon women are not necessarily white, do not always speak English and span the economic as well as ethnic continuum," it is time that explorations of Mormon women account for women like Veronica who demonstrated a unique embodied experience with Mormonism (Hoyt, 2007, p. 94). Moreover, the framing of a Heavenly Father as advocate for family reunification is a tenet of the faith that LDS Latinas have long championed. *Mujeres* read their sacred texts and interpret the divine through their daily experiences and for too many of them the impact of unjust secular immigration laws creates obstacles that sever ties with relatives across national boundaries. In many ways, the notion that families are forever provides hope in an eternal reunification that man-made policies have barred.

Complicating *mujerista* approaches

An important distinction between *mujerista* theology and Latina feminist theology is precisely how to incorporate women and gender into theological inquiry. In Latin America, *mujeristas* focused on internal essentialized conceptualizations of female experiences. Isasi-Díaz echoes this exalting of femininity and domesticity by suggesting: "we want the value of those roles to be recognized and their status to be enhanced" (1996, p. 139). Here, the domestic, the familial, the strictly female experience is venerated rather than minimized. A Latina feminist theology includes Latina religious perspectives and champions emancipatory approaches to faith, but rejects romanticized feminine attributes. As the introduction to the *Reader in Latina Feminist Theology* explained,

> the term mujerista was coined in Peru as the name for a sectarian gynocentric group that, inspired by an essentialist ideology about women, turned away from the powerful Peruvian feminist movement in the late 1970s and gradually disappeared in the late 1980s.
>
> *(Aquino, Machado, and Rodríguez, 2002, p. xx)*

Furthermore, María Pilar Aquino notes that leading Mexican feminist Marta Lamas suggested that *mujerismo* "idealizes the 'natural' conditions of women and exalts the relationship among them" (2002, p. 139). Isasi-Díaz was well intentioned in demanding that Latin American *mujeres* must be included in theology, but her use of *mujerista* echoed essentialist arguments that marked women as inherently different in mind, body, and spirit from men. A similar reasoning is evident in religious conversations on complementarity, or the notion that there are only two genders (male and female) and that each fulfills a particular function for each other. Seeing someone as serving a function in your life does not automatically result in respect and certainly separate is not necessarily equal. The distinction between *mujerista* and Latina feminist theology prompts a unique comparison with LDS Latina experiences. The LDS Church promotes complementarity and the celebration of feminine, not feminist, gender identities. Thus, a *mujerista* approach lends itself to LDS Latina experiences perhaps more so than the Latina feminist critique. For instance, Sister Garcia and the "difficulties" she found herself in during the 1930s illustrated a particular *mujerista* feminine logic.

The peculiar reference to Sister Garcia in Harold W. Pratt's 1936 journal led to further searches for details on this woman's role in her ward. Combing through the pages of Relief Society minutes and Mesa Branch historical reports I finally came across a Sister Francesca de Garcia who was possibly married to an Elder Tomas Garcia.[1] The couple first appeared in the branch reports in October 1928 wherein Elder Garcia called the Sacrament meeting to order and Sister Garcia provided the closing prayer. Sister Garcia played a prominent role in the Mesa Branch between the years 1928–1935: leading prayer, giving lessons, and actively participating in both general branch meeting notes and Relief Society minutes. Importantly, the last moment Sister Garcia appeared in the records of the branch happened just a few months shy of Pratt's visit to "iron out" the difficulties. On September 8, 1935, Sister Garcia gave a lesson: "la hermana Francisca Garcia nos hablo tocante a 'La abnegación de la primera mujer – madre y hogar'" [Sister Garcia spoke to us on the topic of "The virtuous sacrifice of the first woman – motherhood and domesticity"]. A *mujerista* theology could be used to explore how this talk enhanced and celebrated the domestic role of women in the Church. Though emphasizing traditional gender roles and firmly identifying women as mothers and keepers of the home, Sister Garcia gave this talk to the entire ward and thus chose to highlight the virtues of Eve and the importance of her sacrifice for mankind. This rebranding of Eve as necessary figure rather than a fallen female was a century ahead of its time. For instance, Bruce C. Hafen (2004) of the First Quorum of the Seventy stated, "The Fall was not a disaster. It wasn't a mistake or an accident. It was a deliberate part of the plan of salvation ... Without tasting the bitter, we actually *cannot* understand the sweet." More recently, in 2019, Temple endowment ceremonies were changed to promote "more inclusive language, more gender equity, more lines for Mother Eve" (Stack and Noyce, 2019). In this sense, Sister Garcia's *mujerista* hermeneutic played out in her public talk to restore Eve and proclaim the abnegation, or giving up of priestly rights, to take an honorary role as mother and domestic. Though the archives only list the title of her talk, one could imagine a discussion surrounding elevating domesticity to a pillar of virtue.

Garcia's talk happened in September and by the following March Mission President Pratt took a special trip to Mesa to "settle a difficulty" between the branch president and Sister Garcia. At the time, Pratt was embroiled in succession politics and the splintering of the Church in Mexico (Gomez, 2004). Sister Garcia's presence in the archives demonstrated a self-assured Latina. Her message of complementarity and glorifying of female abnegation may not fall fully within a feminist ideal; still, Sister Garcia had some encounter with Elder Ash (male) that required the intervention by another male, President Pratt. I return to my previous driving questions about Sister Garcia and wonder how could a woman in 1936, and a Latina Spanish-speaking woman, command such attention? More to the point, what goes missing when we do not know the experiences of sisters like her and what is muted in her absences from those branch reports?

As stated earlier, President Pratt reorganized the branch shortly after this encounter. After this reorganization, the minutes and notes from the branch show a preponderance of European surname individuals leading prayer and Relief Society meetings. Though it was hoped at the time that the Mesa Mexican branch would be self-governing and able to direct themselves, what was present in the archives were several months where Latino surname members were not as active as they once were. It is possible that these growing pains were due to Sister Garcia's conflict and perhaps her sisters and other Latinos/as felt they needed some distance from the branch politics. Perhaps word of the conflicts with Mexican Saints spread to Mesa and frustration grew at appointing only English-surname individuals into leadership. Though we may never know the reason behind the reorganization or the lack of Latino participation in the weeks to follow; the fact that it was Sister Garcia, a female, who proved difficult for Elder Ash is, is still significant. Regretfully, Sister Garcia and so many other Latinas in the Church of Jesus Christ of Latter-day Saints demonstrate the complexity of their experience as gendered ethnic females whose faithful daily lives go often ignored. A *mujerista* theology enforces the need to look upon Latina experiences for religious lessons, spiritual knowledge, and advice on how to settle difficulties.

Conclusion

As a non-member, I constantly face moments of explaining my approach with the research, my interests, and most importantly my willingness to hear their voices. My work is all about listening and understanding without judgment. That means being attentive and empathizing with DACA students when they shed tears out of anger and frustration with right-leaning Mormon leadership. But this also means sitting across from a Spanish-speaking Relief Society president who speaks of Heavenly Father and the blessings of a restored gospel. The story, or rather stories, of LDS Latinas are complicated. There are tales of dissatisfaction, resiliency, and inspiration. *Mujerista* LDS Latina members need to be listened to and accounted for more fully for what they bring to the wider spectrum of LDS experiences.

Present-day LDS Latinas have a complex relationship with gender identity and are not a monolith. Some come to Mormonism as adults, others are born into it. In the U.S., there are international students, refugees, undocumented immigrants, permanent residents, citizens, and mixed-status families all in one Spanish-speaking ward. There are Republicans and Democrats, and even some progressive socialists. I have met LDS LGBT Latinas/os and those who echo the homophobia supported by the Church. There are also ex-LDS who have left the Church because they were critical of what they felt was a white supremacist undertone. For some Latinas, this emphasis with the feminine divine is a point of pride and community. For others, it is a reminder of being set apart, or rather set aside, as not fully worthy of leadership. Like Sister Garcia and Sister Veronica, these women all have a story to tell and strength waiting to be recognized. Their fortitude in faith gives us a glimpse at what Latina *hermanas* [sisters] might be encountering today as they intersect with gender, ethnicity, class, family, identity, sexuality, religion, and immigration. A *mujerista* and Latina feminist theology requires that their complicated gendered experience be centered in the conversation of scriptural interpretations and LDS ideology.

Note

1 Early membership rosters for the branch were not secured by the time this piece went into publication; however, considering Sister Garcia's participation in Relief Society there is a strong possibility that she was married to Elder Garcia, as opposed to their being father/daughter.

References

Aquino, M.P., 2002. Latina Feminist Theology: Central Features. In M. Pilar Aquino, D. Machado, and J. Rodríguez, eds. *A Reader in Latina Feminist Theology: Religion and Justice*. Austin, TX: University of Texas Press, pp. 133–60.

Aquino, M.P., Machado D., and Rodríguez J., 2002. *A Reader in Latina Feminist Theology: Religion and Justice*. Austin, TX: University of Texas Press.

Cannon, K., 2006. Structured Academic Amnesia: As If This True Womanist Story Never Happened. In S.M. Floyd-Thomas, ed. *Deeper Shades of Purple: Womanism in Religion and Society*. New York: New York University Press, pp. 19–28.

García, I.M., 2015. *Chicano While Mormon: Activism, War, and Keeping the Faith*. Madison, WI: Fairleigh Dickinson University Press.

García, I.M., 2018. Empowering Latino Saints to Transcend Historical Racialism: A Bishop's Tale. In G. Colvin and J. Brooks, eds. *Decolonizing Mormonism: Approaching a Postcolonial Zion*. Salt Lake City, UT: University of Utah Press, pp. 139–59.

Gomez, F., 2004. *The Church of Jesus Christ of Latter-day Saints and the Lamanite Conventions: From Darkness to Light*. Mexico City: El Museo de Historia del Mormonismo en México A.C.

Hafen, B.C., 2004. The Atonement: All for All. www.lds.org/general-conference/2004/04/the-atonement-all-for-all?lang=eng (accessed January 2, 2019).

Hoyt, A., 2007. Beyond the Victim/Empowerment Paradigm: The Gendered Cosmology of Mormon Women. *Feminist Theology* 16(1): 89–100.

Isasi-Díaz, A.M., 1996. *Mujerista Theology: A Theology for the Twenty-first Century*. Maryknoll, NY: Orbis Books.

Pratt, H.W., 1936. Journal. March 23. Manuscript Mexican Mission Manuscript History and Historical Reports, 1874–1977, Volume 5, Part 1. LR 5506 2. Salt Lake City, UT: Church History Library.

Rodríguez, J., 2002. Latina Activists: Toward an Inclusive Spirituality of Being in the World. In M. Pilar Aquino, D. Machado, and J. Rodríguez, eds. *A Reader in Latina Feminist Theology: Religion and Justice*. Austin, TX: University of Texas Press, pp. 114–30.

Stack, P.F., and Noyce D., 2019. LDS Church Changes Temple Ceremony: Faithful Feminists Will See Revisions and Additions as a "Leap Forward." *The Salt Lake Tribune*. January 2. www.sltrib.com/religion/2019/01/02/lds-church-releases/ (accessed January 4, 2019).

Tamez, J., 2015. "Our Faithful Sisters": Mormon Worship and the Establishment of the Relief Society in the Mexican Mission, 1901–1903. In J. Dormady and J.M. Tamez, eds. *Just South of Zion: The Mormons in Mexico and Its Borderlands*. Albuquerque, NM: University of New Mexico Press, pp. 73–88.

Further reading

Iber, J., 2000. *Hispanics in the Mormon Zion 1912–1999*. College Station, TX: Texas A&M University Press.

Pulido, E., 2015. Solving Schism in Nepantla: The Third Convention Returns to the LDS Fold. In J. Dormady and J.M. Tamez, eds. *Just South of Zion: The Mormons in Mexico and Its Borderlands*. Albuquerque, NM: University of New Mexico Press, pp. 89–110.

Smith, R.A., and Mannon, S.E., 2010. "Nibbling on the Margins of Patriarchy": Latina Immigrants in Northern Utah. *Ethnic and Racial Studies* 33(6): 986–1005.

Vega, S., 2015. *Latino Heartland: Of Borders and Belonging in the Midwest*. New York: NYU Press.

Vega, S., 2019. Intersectional Hermanas: LDS Latinas Navigate Faith, Leadership and Sisterhood. *Latino Studies* 17(1): 27–47.

Williams, P.J., and Fortuny-Loret de Mola, P., 2007. Religion and Social Capital among Mexican Immigrants in Southwest Florida. *Latino Studies* 5(2): 233–53.

INDEX

Aaronic priesthood 61, 63, 166, 505, 570, 572–3, 581, 584
Abildgaard, Nicolai 115
abortion 13, 23, 144, 205, 408
About Marriage ... and More (Griffin & Belnap) 516
abstinence-only education 291
Achebe, Chinua 466, 468
Achebe, Nwando 475
Ackerman, S. 563
activism: excommunication as response to 8; feminist 1, 43, 53, 408, 577; necessity of for institutional change 7; by the Relief Society 137; *see also* gay activism
Adichie, Chimamanda 476
adultery 62, 93–4, 189, 206, 510, 528
Affirmation: LGBTQ Mormons, Families, and Friends 43–4, 47, 70, 190–1, 223–5, 227–33, 532, 535
African Americans: impact of racism on 144–5; prohibition from the priesthood and temple blessing 63; treatment of families under slavery 26; *see also under* black
Against Heresies (Irenaeus) 553
Aha, Rabbi 561
AIDS 191–2, 234, 525
alcohol 62, 66–7, 115, 134, 372, 444–5, 453, 512, 532, 543
Alcott, William 91
Alger, Fanny 76
ALL Arizona 232
Allen, James 467
Allen, Judith Van 470
All Enlisted 164
Alliance for Therapeutic Choice and Scientific Integrity 199
Allred, Janice 163, 547
Amadiume, Ifi 467, 472, 474–5

American Baptists Concerned 223
American Community Survey (ACS) 350–1, 353, 355–6
American cultural practices, Mormon wariness of 133, 135
American Indian Movement 31
American Mormon customs, European criticisms 13
American Psychological Association 200
American Revolution 79, 88, 92
American values, complementary gender roles as distillation of 13–14
Andelin, Helen 148–9, 340
Andersen, Hans Christian 121
Anderson, Benedict 398
Anderson, George Edward 245
Anderson, Harry 252
Anderson, Lavina Fielding 2, 163, 341
Anderson, Lynn Matthews 489
Anderson, May 513, 530
Anderson, Pamela Sue 539
Anthony, Susan B. 86, 96
"Anti-Discrimination and Religious Freedom Amendments" 217
anti-polygamy agitation, by the Relief Society 572
anti-polygamy legislation 96, 105, 172, 243, 288, 336, 344–5
anti-sodomy legislation 208, 528
Aotearoa 17, 450; *see also* New Zealand
apostasy, entry into same-sex marriage as 198–9, 232, 342, 533
Appiah, Kwame Anthony 465
Aquinas, Thomas 555
Aquino, María Pilar 603–4
Arrington, Leonard 158, 162, 262, 393
art: Busath family portraits 239, 241; Captain Moroni 251; companion portraits of the first LDS

prophet and his wife 241–3; Elfie Huntington's life and work 245; Family Proclamation as part of Mormon visual culture 239, 343; Harriet Richards Harwood's life and work 246–7; the LDS family brand 241–4; Minerva Teichert's life and work 249–51; Mormon preferences 239–41; Mormon women artists 244–9; portrayal of Mormon masculinity 251–2; Trevor Southey's life and work 252–5; *see also* Scandinavian art
Art and Belief Movement 253
The Art of Homemaking (Hocle) 148, 340
Asad, Talal 314
Asay, Carlos 591
Asherah, as name for female deity 562–3
Asia, LDS gender ratios 20
Association of Mormon Counselors and Psychotherapists (AMCAP) 187–8
Augustine of Hippo, Saint 553
Australia 13
autonomy, women's work and 445–6
aversion therapy 190–1, 206, 225–6, 531
Avery, Valeen Tippetts 162
Awolowo, Obafemi 468
Azikiwe, Nnamdi "Benjamin" 469

Baden-Powell, Robert 132
Baehr v. *Lewin* 212
Bagley, Joseph 245
Ballard, Melvin J. 175
Banks, Dennis 31
Barber, Ian 18
Barker, Margaret 487, 560, 562–3
Barlow, B.A. 409
Barlow, Philip 109
Barney, Madi 293
Bartkowski, John 374–5
Bates, Paulina 555
Bathsheba Smith 89, 96
Bautista, Margarito 31
Beaman, Lori 396
beard restrictions 67
Bear River Massacre 287
Bednar, David 593
Beecher, Catharine 95
Beecher, Maureen Ursenbach 2
Beek, Walter Van 14
A Beginner's Boston (Relief Society) 158
"Behold the Royal Army" (hymn) 591
Belgium 13
Bell, Elouise 160
Bellecourt, Clyde & Vernon 31
Belnap, W. Dean 516
Bemon, Louisa 76
Bengtson, V.L. 406
Bennett, John C. 77
Benson, Ezra Taft 147, 162, 340–1
Bergin, Allen E. 188, 196

Berlant, Lauren 526, 536
Bernhard, Torben 544
Berryman, Mildred 222, 530
bestiality 206
Bhabha, Homi 465
Biale, David 561
the Bible: blending of passages into Mormon writings 102; changes in American understanding of 101; feminist reading of 554 (*see also The Woman's Bible*); gender critique 485–7, 491; "literal" readings 101, 110; and Mormon aversion to interracial marriage 35; in nineteenth-century America 100–1; plural marriage in 105–6; presentation of women in 108–9, 484; as primary religious text for LDS members 102; significance in American consciousness 100, 102; status in nineteenth-century Mormon thinking 102
Biersack, A. 452
biological sex, LDS conflation with heteronormative gendered behavior 52
birth control 6, 147, 163, 316, 509, 513–15, 518–19
bisexuality 196, 366, 475, 535
Bishop, Joseph 294
bishop's handbook 198
Bjørnson, Bjørnstjerne 124
Black, Kristeen 338, 343
black feminism, and intersectionality 38–9, 46
Blackhawk, Ned 29
black Mormons: eligibility for priesthood 16, 27, 32, 63, 178, 486; on the impact of racial restrictions 35; in Ireland 409; Spencer W. Kimball's revelation 161
blackness: explanations for 26, 32; "one drop" policy 33; *see also* race
Blake, Lillie Devereux 554
Bloch, Carl Heinrich 116–19
The Bloggernacle 164
blogs/blogging/bloggers 2, 22, 164, 200, 271, 278, 294, 342, 346
bodies, and worthiness 66–7
body modification: LDS Church positions 540; types of 540; *see also* transgender people
Boggs, S.T. 459
The Bohemian Club 222
Bokovoy, David 487
Book of Abraham 77, 79, 486, 491, 557, 559–60, 565
Book of Mormon: explanations for differences in skin color 26; failure to account for complexity of families within American history 26; first appearance in English 485; gender critique 483–5; as proof of Joseph Smith's priesthood authority 584; publication of 496; race and gender 485, 490–1; racialized vision of the family 26; theological importance 392; view of Native peoples 28

Book of Moses 498, 556–7
Borden, Bennett 233
Botswana 55–7; male behavior and family dynamics 330; non-nuclear family structures 327–8; working motherhood in 324
boundary maintenance: the home as marker of 346; and the Molly Mormon model 397
Bowen, Thomas 468
Boxer, Elise 28, 45, 337
Boy Scouts of America (BSA) 69–70, 132
Boys of Boise scandal 531
Brandes, Georg 124
Brasher, Brenda 397
Brassard, Brooke 338
Braude, Ann 365
bread baking 147, 395
Brekus, Catherine 339
bridewealth traditions 327–8
Brigham Young University (BYU): aversion therapy practised on gay students at 190–1, 206, 225; ban of homosexual students from 206; beard restriction 67; behavioral studies 188; LGBT Mormons group 223; response to sexual assault cases 293–4, 296; revised honor code 207
Britain 12, 94, 259, 393, 401, 573
Brock, Sebastian 564–5
Broderick, Carlfred 187, 515, 517
Brooks, Joanna 281, 406
Brotherton, Martha 82
Brown, Samuel 27
Brown, Victor L. 516
Brown v. Board of Education 34
Brusco, Elizabeth 311, 445
Bryant, Anita 209–10
Buck, Charles 559
Buddhism 306
Buehner, Alice 179
Buhari, Muhammad 473
Burns, Kathryn 425
Burton, H. David 591
Bush, Lester, Jr. 35
Bushman, Claudia L. 312, 316
Bushman, Richard 27
Butler, Judith 467, 547–8
Butterworth, Lisa 281
Buvinic, M. 439
Bynum, Caroline Walker 555
Byrd, A. Dean 195

caffeinated drinks 372; *see also* Word of Wisdom
California Marriage Protection Act 214
Campbell, David 166
Canada: cultural and racial assimilation in 345; establishment of LDS settlements 337; family practices of Saints in 337; William Shunn's experiences 65–6
Cannell, Fenella 309, 424

canning 147, 338, 343
Cannon, Edwin 470
Cannon, George Q. 245
Cannon, Janath 470, 472
Cannon, Katie 601
Cannon, Kenneth L. 509, 521
Cannon, Martha Hughes 244
Carter, Sarah 338
celestial marriage: primary purpose 273; sexual purity and the concept of 272–5
celibacy 80, 207, 226, 519–20, 535
Celtic Tiger 407–8
Central America 178; male behavior and family dynamics 329
Chambers, Alan 226
Chapman, Ruth 152
Charles, Melodie Moench 487
chastity: and the Book of Mormon 485; effects of loss 289, 292; guidelines 273–4; and its discontents 279–81; Kimball on 152, 189; as preparation for institutional investment 274–5; as primary LDS value 188–9, 272; problematic construal of 485; as religious imperative 68, 152; same-sex attraction and 196, 201, 226, 534; as women's responsibility 136, 152–3, 157, 278; *see also* Law of Chastity
Chen, C.H. 406
childbearing: Benson's instruction to prioritize 340–1; confinement rituals 264; delaying of 360; as LDS imperative 352; and salvation 272
children, couples without 354
children of same-sex couples: church restrictions on 198–9, 232–3, 342, 533, 589; reversal of 2015 policy 218
The Children's Friend 513, 530
child sexual abuse, LDS Church's response to 289–90
Chile, number of Latter-day Saints in 178
China 19
Chinese Exclusion Act (1882) 288
Cho, Sumi 39
Chou, Hui-Tzu Grace 181
Christensen, C.C.A. 118–21
Christensen, Danille Elise 346
Christianity 7, 20, 23, 132, 277, 306, 311, 425, 455–6, 546, 582
Christofferson, D. Todd 198, 235, 591
Christofferson, Tom 198
Christus (Thorvaldsen) 115–16
Christ with the Children (Anderson) 252
Chrysostom, John 555
Chukwurah, Christopher 466, 469
Chukwurah, Florence 471
The Church and the Proposed Equal Rights Amendment 208
Church History Department, prioritization of women's history 2

Church of Jesus Christ of Latter-day Saints: "Americanization" 337; change, speed of 6; close coupling with the U.S. 392; disincorporation 105; founding 1; gendered perspective of church attendance 372–3; gender roles 11; global membership 150; human fallibility of church leaders 63; meticulous record-keeping 4; as object of praise and of criticism 588; organizational and religious realities 307–8; standardization and correlation of church practice 16; women's influence 305 (*see also* women's influence in church)
Church Welfare Plan 138–9
Circling the Wagons (CTW) 227–8, 230
citizenship: flexible 19; training for 69–70
civil rights movement: Mormon concerns about 35; rise of 31
Claremont Women's Oral History Project 342, 346
Clark, J. Reuben 138–9, 157, 514
Clark, Spencer 229
Clark, Virginia 146
Clarke, Adam 559
Clawson, Rudger 559, 583
Clayton, William 82
Clement of Alexandria 555
clothing: instructions for women 278; Mormon concerns about 135–6, 152; wearing pants to church movement 164
Clyde, Aileen 21
Coalition for the Protection of Marriage 213
Coalition for Traditional Marriage 213
Cobb, Augusta 82, 94
coercion 52–3, 86, 127, 284
coffee, tea and 66, 134, 512, 543, 582
cohabitation 23, 131, 345, 352–3, 355, 359; statistical analysis 352–4
Cohen, Charles L. 308
Cold War 153, 206
Colenso, Bishop 559
Colombia 231, 311
colonialism: domestic life as a site of 456; impact on masculinity 332; and LDS masculinity in Nigeria 468–70
Colvin, Gina 45
Comfort Waiting (Southey) 254
Commentary on the Gospel of John (Origen) 564
Community of Christ 84
complementary gender roles: adoption by LDS families 340; Church promotion 340–1; as distillation of American values 13–14; liberating path argument 22; model of 60–1; reinforcement campaign 529; Saints' adherence to in the U.S. 337; view of as U.S. imposition 13
confession, mental health and gendered access to 387–8

Consenting Adult Sex Bill (California 1975) 209
conservatism 14, 205, 408
consumer culture, anxieties over 146
contraception *see* birth control
conversion therapy 195, 200, 225–6, 233–4; *see also* aversion therapy; reparative therapy
conversion to Mormonism 13, 15, 28, 30, 33, 114, 150, 179, 181, 259, 409, 420, 425–6, 500, 602
Cooper, B. 40
Corporation of the President of the Church of Jesus Christ of Latter-day Saints 175
correlation policy and reforms 16, 140, 150–1, 154, 306, 309, 407, 575–6
Costa Rica, male behavior and family dynamics 329
Cott, Nancy 86, 93
Council of Fifty 29
couples without children, statistical analysis 354
courtship, revitalization of Mormon courtship 134–6
covenant birth 420, 424–8
Cowdery, Oliver 76, 584
Cox, Frederick 513
Cragun, Ryan 531
Crapo, Mike 297
Craske, Nikki 439
Crawford, Cory 487
Crawford, Vesta 146
Crenshaw, Kimberlé Williams 39
Critchlow, William 574
Cropper-Rampton, Rebecca 181
Cross, Frank Moore 561
Crowther, Samuel Ajayi 472
cultural distinctiveness, of the LDS Church 18–20

Dalsgaard, Christen 117–18, 121, 123
Darwin, Charles 101
Das Mormonenmädchen (Möllhausen) 124
dating, instructions for 277–8
Davies, D.J. 407, 413
Davis, Kathy 39
Daynes, Kathryn M. 512
Decolonizing Mormonism (Colvin & Brooks) 45
Decoo, Wilfried 13
Decoo-Vanwelkenhuysen, Carine 13, 395–6
A Defence of Polygamy (Pratt) 91–2
Defense of Marriage Act (1996) 197, 212–14
Dehlin, John 229
De Hoyos, Arturo 188
De Hoyos, Genevieve 188
deity, feminization of 554–6 (*see also* Heavenly Mother)
DeLong, Lillian 14
de-marginalization, requirements for 47
DeMille, Cecil B. 251
Democratic Republic of Congo 309–10

Denmark 114
Dennis, Thomas 472
Dennison, McKenna 294
deprogramming 14
Derr, Jill & Brooklyn 309, 311, 572
Desmond, David-Edward 531
Developing a Marriage Relationship (Cannon) 509
Dever, William G. 563
Diagnostic and Statistical Manual of Psychiatric Disorder (DSM) 191, 541
Dialogue: A Journal of Mormon Thought 35, 159, 224, 509, 515
Dibia, Jude 474
Dick, Thomas 559
dietary code: women's adherence to 372; *see also* Word of Wisdom
Dignity USA 223
disaffiliation 181, 317
disclosure rules: mental health and 385–7, 389; potential for re-negotiation 389
"Divine Embodiment and Transcendence" (Faulconer) 548–9
division of labor: Irish Mormonism and 410; in non-traditional families 356–7; polygamy and 87–90
divorce: acceptance of 87; discouragement 506; legalization 124, 408; and legitimate sexual access 520; loosening of regulations 205; and non-traditional families 354–6; a novel solution 513; polygamy and 92–4; and sealing 83; and single-parent families 352; woman's right to 80; women's participation in the workforce and 340, 357, 359–60
Doctrine and Covenants: acceptance as Scripture 101; on biblical polygamy 504, 510, 528; contents 123; gender critique 487–9; rights and powers of the priesthood 585–7; on Wisdom 564
A Doll's House (Ibsen) 124
DOMA *see* Defense of Marriage Act (1996)
domesticity, postwar Mormon culture and women's attitudes to 147–8
domestic labor, importance of 147
domestic religious practice 342–4
domestic space, cultural meaning of 344–6
domestic violence 295, 329, 332, 338, 383, 386
domestic workers, church membership in migrant communities 19
Doss, Erika 247
Douglas, N. 457
Dow, Emily 78
Dragon Dads 229
drugs 543
Duke, James T. 374

ecclesiology 570, 572
Echo Hawk, Larry 32
Eden Farm (Southey) 255

Edmunds Act (1882) 105, 287, 344–5
Edmunds-Tucker Act (1887) 96, 105, 287
Egya, Suye 473
Ekpo, Susanna 471
Elendu, Rosemary 471
Elizabeth Smart Foundation 284
El Salvador 600
El Shaddai, as name for female deity 560–1
Embry, Jessie L. 181
Embryo (Southey) 254
employment, rates for Mormon women in Europe 13
employment and socioeconomic status, of U.S. Mormons 367
Employment Non-Discrimination Act (ENDA) 216
empowerment, women's work as 439–41
Encircle 232, 535
Encyclopedia of Mormonism 581
endowment 32, 77, 158, 502
England, teaching of Mormonism in 393
England, Eugene 159, 258
English Mormon women: comparisons with North American Mormon women 392; and depictions of Mormon women in England 393–5; and the navigation of secularized civic society 400–1; pragmatic egalitarianism 399–400; "third space" concept of home 399–400; and Utah's cultural significance 395–9
Epprecht, Marc 473–4
equality, generational differences in women's hopes for 22
Equality Utah 217
equal marriage: LDS Church's opposition to 342; *see also* gay marriage; Proposition 8; same-sex marriage
Equal Rights Amendment (ERA) 21, 160–2, 206, 208–13, 253, 289, 532–3, 576
eternal kinship, polygamy and 81–2
eternal kinship networks 27, 32–3
Eternal Marriage Student Manual 322
eternal relationships, reliance on heterosexuality 28
eternal significance of gender, universality of church teachings 15
Eubank, Sharon 14–16, 22–3
European progressivism, and American norms 13–14
evangelicalism 277
Eve, rehabilitation of 556–8, 605
Evergreen International, Inc. 194–5, 199, 225–7, 229–31, 233–4
evolution, Darwin's theory 101
excommunication: announcement of as penalty for polygamy 129; a personal experience 594–5; removal of as punishment for homosexual behavior 207; utilization for censorship of dissent 53

excommunications: church members that have undergone GCS 545; contributors to *Women and Authority* 577; of gay and lesbian Mormons 206; George P. Lee 31–2; John W. Taylor 131; Kate Kelly 8, 53, 165; of LDS scholars 2; of Maori LDS members 21; Mormon Alliance members 291; Ordain Women organizers 577; Paul Toscano 594; Philander Smartt 295; Sam Young 8, 296; the September Six 162–3; Sonia Johnson 161, 253; Trevor Southey 240, 254
ex-Mormon gays 230
ex-Mormons 231, 317
Exodus International 226
Exponent II 1, 159–60
Eyring, Henry B. 368, 591
Eze, Chielezona 465, 476

faikava 451–4, 458–9
FairMormon 23
the Fall 107, 553–4, 562, 604
family: and domesticity in postwar Mormon culture 144–5; gender and family structure 60–1; importance in LDS femininities 57; involvement with as characteristic of Mormon masculinity 582; Joseph Smith's revelations 61; LDS promotion of North American model 332; non-nuclear family structures 325–8 (*see also* non-traditional families); the nuclear model 350; patriarchal vs. egalitarian structures 328–32; racialized vision of in the Book of Mormon 26; transformations of family arrangements in the U.S. 350; women supporting families in Nicaragua 438–9; working mothers 322–5; *see also* Family Proclamation; home and family; non-traditional families; theology of family
"The Family: A Proclamation to the World" *see* Family Proclamation
family life, as basis of Mormonism 18
family planning 316
Family Proclamation: cultural interpretations 435–6; on family structure 61, 457–8; function 472, 574; on gender roles 11, 311, 341, 435, 457, 505, 519, 532–3, 588; and the Heavenly Mother 472; on homosexuality 211–12; introduction 21; on masculinity 64; Mormon feminism and 163; on the nature and purpose of the body 544; as part of Mormon visual culture 239, 321, 343; publication 21, 60, 163, 195, 212, 227, 321, 491; quasi-canonical status 496; and same-sex marriage 574; on sexual morality 544
family size, of U.S. Mormons 367
Farmer, Jared 29
Fascinating Womanhood (Andelin) 148–9, 340
fashion industry, George Richards' rebuke 135
Fatherhood (Southey) 254

fatherhood, sexuality and 68–9
Father Lehi in Hawaii (2008) 453
Faulconer, James 546, 548–9
Faust, James 368
Fear of a Queer Planet (Warner) 525
Featherstone, Vaughn 187
Felt, Louie B. 513, 530
female bonding, polygamy and 513
female deity *see* Heavenly Mother
female ecclesiology: in the nineteenth century 572–5; in the twentieth century 574–5
female emancipation movement, Mormon feminism and 554–6
female embodiment, the Mormon ideal 395
"Female Relief Society of Nauvoo" 95; *see also* Relief Society
femininities: challenges and limitations of the term 50; and hegemonic masculinity 52, 52–4; Helen Andelin's ideas on Mormon womanhood 148–9; importance of family in LDS femininities 57; lived experiences in the LDS 54–6; and the pervasive nature of patriarchy 51; and post-colonial feminist theory 51; and queer theory 51; theoretical framework 50–2; transformation of Mormon femininity 136–7; unifying themes 56–7
feminism: compatibility of Mormon principles with 406; Islamic 40; rebirth of Mormon feminism 159–60; *see also* Mormon feminism
feminist activism 1, 43, 53, 408, 577
Feminist Mormon Housewives (FMH) 280–1
feminization of deity: literature review 554–6; *see also* Heavenly Mother
Ferguson, Michael 226
Fetner, Tina 533
fiction, arrival in Utah 267
Fiji 450
Finland, working motherhood in 322–3
Flake, Jeff 297
Flanders, working motherhood in 322
Fletcher, Joseph 515
flexible citizenship 19
Florence, Nathan 239
Fogleman, Aaron S. 555
Ford, Stacilee 19, 46, 325–6
fornication 152, 189, 206, 510, 528
For the Strength of Youth 274–5, 277–8, 513
Foucault, M. 520
Frank, Robert 245
Frazer, Mabel Pearl 255n6
Frazier, Shirley 35
free agency 189, 196
Freece, Hans P. 125
French Polynesia 30
Freud, Sigmund 193
Friberg, Arnold 114–15, 251–2
Friedman, Susan Stanford 258

From Heaven to Hell (2008) 453
From Housewife to Heretic (Johnson) 2
Fundamentalist Church of Jesus Christ of Latter-Day Saints 84
fundraising, as women's responsibility 151

Gangsters in Paradise: The Deportees of Tonga (2019) 453
García, Ignacio 31, 45, 47, 601
Gardner, Marian 174
Garrett, Matthew 345–6
Gates, Susa Young 106, 132, 135–7, 139, 558, 573
gathering, North American settlements and the doctrine of 337–8
Gaudio, Rudolf 474–5
A Gauntlet (Bjørnson) 124
gay activism 191, 210, 533; *see also* Affirmation: LGBTQ Mormons, Families, and Friends
gay and lesbian civil rights movement 222
gay conversion therapy *see* aversion therapy; conversion therapy; reparative therapy
gay marriage: fight against the legalization of 205; LDS views on 222, 342; legalization 214, 216, 234, 342, 356, 533; legislation against 533; and therapeutic culture 197–9; *see also* equal marriage; Proposition 8; same-sex marriage
gay men, and the priesthood 589
gay Mormons, support websites 199, 207–8, 532, 534
Gay Pride 191, 223, 228–9, 233
gay rights 11, 190–1, 195–7, 199–201, 205–6, 209–11, 214, 532, 534
gender: Church's definition of 527; decoupling of from biological sex 51; flexibility of teachings on 20; historical approaches to 4–5; and mobility in a transnational religious community 18–20; reframing of Mormon gender in the progressive era *see* reframing of gender; social scientific approaches 5–6, 364–5; theological approaches to 6–7
gender comportment, imposition of international standards 21 (*see also* Family Proclamation)
gender confirmation surgery (GCS) 539–41, 545, 550
gender dysphoria 201, 224, 540–1, 549
gender equality: celestial marriage as pathway to 279; European perspective 13
gender inequality 278, 394, 396, 400–1
gender roles: in American culture's teaching 144; Brigham Young on 88–9; comparison of European and American LDS norms 13–14; comparison of values in the Global South 14–18; complementary *see* complementary gender roles; cultural context 79–81; the divine design 61; and family structure 60–1; gendered expectations of Mormon and American identities 11–12; Helen Andelin's perspectives on 148–9; the ideal unified LDS feminine subject 54; importance of balance for congregational life 19; official LDS teaching 11; as preoccupation of the post-war LDS church 146; separate spheres conception 136, 138, 239, 259, 263, 344; solidification of gendered spheres 138–9; U.S. responses and domestic divides 20–3; women 11
gender studies 1–4, 50–1, 58, 181, 472
Gender Trouble (Butler) 467
General Social Survey (GSS) 350–2, 354–7
George, Abosede 467
Getting Married (Strindberg) 124
Ghana 14–17, 20, 22, 46, 472
G.I. Bill 144, 145
Gifford, E.W. 101, 456
gifts of the spirit 16, 140, 171, 260
Gikandi, Simon 465
Givens, Terryl 557, 560
Glenn, Tyler 41
global perspectives, importance in the study of the LDS story 4
Global South: congruence with American Mormon values 14–18; culturally specific form of women's religious authority 17; definition 23n1; homosexuality's status 14
God Loveth His Children (Church) 196
Goodbye, I Love You (Pearson) 192
Goodman, K.L. 406
Gooren, Henri 329
gospel culture 18, 20
Gospel of Thomas 565
Gospel Topics essays 163
Gove, Mary 94
Graham, Sylvester 91
Graham-Russell, Janan 36
Gramsci, Antonio 51–2
Grant, Heber J. 34, 134, 137, 140, 175, 576
Great Basin Kingdom 29
Great Basin region, of North America 27, 29–30, 287, 337–8, 340, 345, 347, 571, 573
Great Depression 138
Green, Doyle L. 116
Griffin, Glen C. 516
Griffith, R.M. 189
Grimke, Angelina 94–5
Grimke, Sarah 94–5
Grundtvig, Elisabeth 124
Grundtvig, N.F.S. 121
Guatemala, male behavior and family dynamics 329

Hadlock, Neil 253
Haglund, Kristine 310, 582, 589
Hall, David 102, 336
Halrynjo, S. 40
Hana Pono Political Action Caucus 209, 212

Handbook 1: Stake Presidents and Bishops 198
Handbook of Instructions 207
Hangen, Tona 309
Hanks, Marion D. 591
Hanks, Maxine 2, 163
Hanks, Sara Katherine Staheli 281
Hansen, James V. 342
Hansen, Klaus 515
Harboe, Eleanore Christine 119
Hardy, Chad 255n4
Harris, S. 406
Hartmann, Debi 213
Hartwell, Rose 247
Harvey, Susan Ashbrook 564
Harwood, Harriet Richards 246–7
Hatch, Orrin 297
Hawaii 30, 116, 145, 161, 209, 212–13, 216, 227, 337, 342
Hawaii's Future Today (HFT) 213
Hayward, Eri 544–5, 549
The Hearth 228, 232
Heaton, T.B. 406
Heavenly Father, literal gender 64
Heavenly Mother: Asherah 562–3; divinity 64; El Shaddai 560–1; as feminine counterpart to God the Father 565; the Holy Spirit 564–5; Hoyt's argument 406; LDS doctrine 557–60; literature review 554–6; Shekhina 561–2; Stanton's insight 554–5; Wisdom 563–4
Hefner, Hugh 153
hegemonic masculinity: the concept 52, 52–3; femininities and 52, 52–4; priesthood as mechanism of 52–3, 55
hegemony, Gramsci's concept 51–2
Henri, Robert 249
heroes, talks by church leaders on the theme of 591
heteronormativity: definition 526, 536; divine reproduction model as basis for 547
heterosexuality, privileged status 535
heterosexual marriage: as cure for homosexuality 192, 206; federal legislation in the US 197
Hickman, Jared 28, 490
Hinckley, Gordon B. 11, 21, 60–1, 163, 176–7, 179, 192, 213–14, 226, 239, 289–91, 341–2, 518, 560
historical approaches to gender 4–5
historical transparency, the church's move towards 162–3
The History of Lucy Smith, Mother of the Prophet (Smith) 261
History of Sexuality: Volume 1 (Foucault) 520
HIV/AIDS 525
Hoad, Neville 475
Hoffmann, John 374–5
Hokowhitu, B. 453
Holland, LDS views of homosexuality in 14

Holland, Jeffrey R. 199, 519
Holman, T.B. 406
Holmes, Douglas D. 590
home: the concept 336; as site of significant cultural power 346; *see also* home and family
home and family: cultural meaning of domestic space 344–6; domestic religious practice 342–4; family structure and roles 338–42; housing arrangements and adaptations 339; LDS views on equal marriage 342; North American settlements and the doctrine of gathering 337–8; place in LDS religious practices 336–7; polygamous households 339, 344; publicization of LDS homes 344–6; and racial assimilation 345–6; and women's documentary practices 346; women's responsibilities 339 (*see also* gender roles)
Home Nights 135–6
homosexuality: born this way argument 195, 201, 534–5; the Church's distinction between behavior and orientation 207; church's first public pronouncement on 206; comparison of European and American views 14; comparison with fornication and adultery 189–90; early Mormon thinking on 222; eternal consequences 206; historical perspective 527; Irish attitudes and policies 408; LDS views on 14, 189–90, 222, 342; marriage as cure for 192, 206; Nigerian legislation and attitudes 473–6; and politics *see* homosexuality and politics; removal from list of psychiatric disorders 191, 225; roots of the post-war cultural panic 514–15; silence of Mormon scripture on 206; status in the Global South 14; and therapeutic culture *see* homosexuality and therapeutic culture; view of LDS church members in Holland 14; *see also under* gay; LGBTQ+; queer; same-sex
homosexuality and politics: anti-gay political strategy development 210–11; conservative view of homosexuality 205; Defense of Marriage Act 212–14; development of LDS policy 208–10; the Family Proclamation 211–12; and Mormon beliefs about homosexuality 206–8; Proposition 8 (California) 14, 197, 208, 214–16, 227, 229, 231, 234, 342, 589; the "Utah compromise" 216–17
homosexuality and therapeutic culture: AMCAP 187–8; attitudes towards homosexuality in the LDS community 189–90; aversion therapy 190–1, 206, 225–6, 531; BYU initiatives 188, 190–1, 206; ethical guidelines for therapists 228; and marriage equality 197–9; professionalization of therapy approaches 191–3; reparative therapy 192–3, 193–6, 199–200; and the resolution against SOCE therapy 199–200; sexuality and Mormonism 188–9; sympathetic approach 196–7

homosociality, in Pacific island kava settings 455
Hong Kong 18–20, 46, 325
Hoole, Daryl V. 148–9, 340
Hope for Transgressors 190
hormone replacement therapy (HRT) 540–1
Horne, Alice Merrill 248–9
Howells, Adele Cannon 115, 312
Hoyt, Amy 279, 339–40, 453, 582
Hudson, V.M. 243, 406
Human Intimacy: Illusion and Reality (Brown) 516
Human Rights Campaign 217
Huntington, Dimick B. 120
Huntington, Elfie 245
Huntington, Zina & Presendia 76

Ibsen, Henrik 124
identity, relationship between power and 39–40 (*see also* intersectionality)
identity politics 43
illegal drugs 372
Illinois Citizens for Family Life 209
"I'll Walk With You—LDS Parents of LGBT" 229, 535–6
imagined community 398
"I'm a Mormon" campaign 41, 180, 406
The Improvement Era 147
India: male behavior and family dynamics 329–30; non-nuclear family structures 328
Indian Farms 29
Indian Placement Program 27, 31
Indian Removal Act (1830) 29
Indian Student Placement Program 345–6
industrial revolution 27
In Football We Trust (2015) 453
Inouye, Melissa 19–20
institutional authority, male access to 52
Intercession at Gethsemane (Southey) 254
intermarriage, as root of civil rights struggles 34
international standards of gender comportment, imposition of 21 (*see also* Family Proclamation)
International Woman's Year (IWY) 160
internet: and church handling of same-sex marriage 198; and disaffiliation 317; Mormon feminism and 2, 164–5; Mormon women's mastery 310; support websites for gay Mormons 199, 207–8, 532, 534; and women's influence in the church 310
The Interpreters (Soyinka) 474
interracial marriage, Mormon rejection of legitimacy 35
interracial relationships, Mormon fears about 35
intersectional approach to gender studies 3
intersectionality: appearances of Mormonism in discussions of 38; between gender and religion 40; the concept 38–40; criticisms 39; de-marginalization, requirements for 47; of identity in a social system 42–3; of Mormon identity 40–2; Mormonism as a social system 42–6; movements opposing Mormonism's marginalizations 43–4; role of within Mormon Studies 44–6; social category/identity approach 40–2; of structural oppression 41–2
intersexuality, LDS Church's position 540, 550
interviews, policy change 8
Into Mortality (Southey) 254
Ireland: arrival of first missionaries 409; number of Mormons in 409; simultaneous liberalization and continued conservatism 408
Irenaeus 553
Irish Mormonism: contested understandings of female leadership in Church 410–14; in the context of Ireland's economic transformation 407–8; and division of labor 410; ethnic diversity 409; evaluating the place of gender in 416; and feminist practice 405–6; gender breakdown 409; gendered expectations 409–10; speaking of truth to power 414–16
Isasi-Díaz, Ada María 599–600, 603–4
Islam 306
Islamic feminism 40
Issues in Religion and Psychology (AMCAP journal) 188
"'It'll Be Zion to Me': Ideal Mormon Masculinity in *Legacy*" (Newman) 582
Ituma, Caroline 471

Jack, Elaine L. 21
Jackson, Andrew 27
Jacobs, Udney Hay 80
Jakobsen, Janet 534
James, Jane Manning 32–3, 36, 43, 265
Jefferson, Thomas 28, 469
Jeffs, Warren 84
Jenkins, Cloy 223, 532
Jenkins, Phillip 464
Jensen, Johannes V. 118, 123
Jenson, Andrew 125
Johnson, Barry L. 374
Johnson, Elizabeth A. 555–6
Johnson, Marinda Nancy 77
Johnson, Sonia 2, 161, 576
Jolly, M. 455–6
Jonathan, Goodluck 473
Jonker, M. 40
"Joseph Smith and Pre-exilic Israelite Religion" (Barker) 562–3
Journal of Mormon History 44
Julian of Norwich 555

Kabbalah Denudata 559
Kabbalah Unveiled (Matthew) 559
Kampwirth, Karen 435
Kane, Thomas 91
Kapp, Ardeth G. 290

kava: background and Mormon context 450–1; controversies for Mormons 454; cultural importance 451–2; definition 449; effects on the body 450; and homosociality 455; kava gatherings 449–52, 458; Mormon cultural adaptations 458–60; Mormon negotiation of kava culture 449; Mormon stance on 451–2; *see also* Pacific islands
Kavanaugh, Brett 296–7, 314
Kelly, Kate 8, 53, 165
Keohane, K. 408
Kern, Kathi 556
Kessler-Harris, Alice 467
keys, priesthood keys granted to women 262–4, 575
"The Keys and Authority of the Priesthood" (Oaks) 577
Kierkegaard, Peter Christian 121
Kierkegaard, Søren Aabye 121
Kimball, Heber C. 79, 81, 92, 161
Kimball, Helen Mar 81
Kimball, Richard 581–2
Kimball, Sarah 87, 95
Kimball, Spencer W. 16, 35, 65, 116, 152, 161, 188, 206–7, 210, 253, 274, 288–9, 322, 513, 593
Kimball, Vilate 92
King, Hannah Tapfield 100, 102–3, 110
King Follett Discourse 527–8, 541
kinship, tribal communities' definitions 26
kinship networks, ethnographic analysis 338, 343
Kirtland, Ohio 12, 29, 76, 171, 230, 261
Kitchen, Nathan R. 233
Kline, Caroline 36, 338, 340–1, 457, 588
Knight, Pete 214
Knowlton, David 11, 589–90
Kuhling, C. 408
Kunz, Calvin S. 181
Kuti, Fela 471

Ladies' Mutual Improvement Association 572
"A Lady to Her Husband" (Kimball) 92
Laman's curse 424
Lamas, Marta 604
Lamont, Ruby 107
Latin America 12, 30–1, 178, 433, 599, 603; dramatic growth of the LDS church 31; potential impact of conversion to Mormonism 15
Latina women: complex relationship with gender identity 605; enacting of faith through mothering and domesticity 601; experience of life in the US 600–1; *see also mujerista* theology
Latter-day Saint Women Stand 23
"Lavender Scare" 206, 222
Law of Adoption 32–3, 81–2
Law of Chastity 152, 196, 201, 226, 272–5, 277–8, 280–2, 589
LDS Family Fellowship 224, 229

LDS Handbook of Instructions 232
LDS practice, prohibitions 543
LDS Social Services 190–2, 201, 225, 514
Lee, Ann 555
Lee, George P. 31–2, 345
Lee, John D. 288
Lee, Mike 297
legalization of gay and same-sex marriage 210, 214, 216, 227, 234, 342, 356, 533
Lellany, Juana 438–9
Letter to Laetus (Augustine of Hippo) 553
"Let Us Be Men" (Christofferson) 591
LGBTQ+ community: acceptance into the LDS 189; anti-discrimination ordinances, LDS backing 227; and LDS views on equal marriage 342; oppression within Mormonism 43
LGBTQ organizing and organizations: evolution of 221–33; internationally 231; local groups 228; and the November 2015 Handbook policy change 232–3; parents' groups 229; past, present, and future 234–5
liberation theology 599–600
life choices, comparison of European and American Mormon women 13
Lighthouse International, Ghana 15
Liljefalk, Axel 125
literature: confinement rituals 264–5; Eliza Snow's writing 263–5; and female Mormon identity 268–9; Foundational Period 259–64; Home Literature 264–8; Josephine Spencer's writing 267–8; Lucy Mack Smith's writing 260–2; periodicals for Mormon adolescents 267; periods of Mormon literature 258–9; Susan Stanford Friedman on women's autobiography 258; *The Woman's Exponent* 265–6
liturgy, women's role 576
lived religion 2, 5, 61, 70, 260, 263, 308–9, 336, 339, 571
Lorde, Audre 420, 474
The Lord Jesus Christ (Parson) 252
The Lost Lamb (Parson) 252
Love, Mia 41
Loving v. *Virginia* 35
Lugard, Frederick 468
Luhrmann, Tanya 315–16
Lutherans Concerned 223
Lutzky, H. 561
Lyman, Amy Brown 137–8
Lyon, Sylvia Sessions 77, 81

Mabey, Rendell & Rachel 470
Macintyre, M. 455–6
Madueke, Ojo 475
Mahmood, Saba 40, 306–7
Majesty in Chains speech 286
male chastity, as women's responsibility 136, 153, 278

Mama Dragons 43–4, 47, 229, 589
A Man of the People (Achebe) 468–9
Mansfield, Ty 199, 226
Maori 17–18, 20–1, 30, 45
marital status, of U.S. Mormons 366
Marker, Mary 148
Marlboro Man 153
marriage: as cure for homosexuality 192, 206; emphasis on in the LDS Church 352; federal legislation in the U.S. 197; James Talmage on 135; missionary work as preparation for 275; seven varieties of 512
marriage equality 191, 197–9, 215, 229, 234; *see also* equal marriage; gay marriage; Proposition 8; same-sex marriage
masculinities: bodies and worthiness 66–7; chastity and self-control requirements 153–4; citizenship and success, training for 69–70; colonial era LDS masculinity in Nigeria 468–70; evolution in the early church 61–2; gender and family structure 60–1; gendered transformation of Mormon priesthood 139–40; homosociality in Pacific island kava settings 455; intersecting 452–4; male access to institutional authority 52; male identity in church discourse 591; missionary work 64–6; Mormon adaptations to kava culture 458–60; negotiating family constructs in the Pacific islands 455–8; post-polygamy emphasis on the Word of Wisdom 134; priesthood 62, 63–4, 453; sexuality and fatherhood 68–9; white hegemonic masculinity 54; *see also* Mormon masculinity; Myers, Wain; priesthood; Shunn, William
Masculinities in Theory (Reeser) 583
masculinity studies 3
massacre at Mountain Meadows 288
Massad, Joseph 475
masturbation 91, 190, 192, 206, 513–16, 543, 590, 593
matchmaking in Peru: *conversos* in Saint's clothing 425–7; covenant boundaries 422–5; and endogamy's threshold 420–2; youth of Zion rise 429–31; Zion's border police 427–9
materialism 158, 495, 497, 504, 539, 542, 594
Mather, Cotton 556
Matlovich, Leonard 532
Matory, J. Lorand 467, 472, 475
Matsuda, M.J. 47
Matthew, MacGregor 559
Matthias (Robert Mathews) 80
Mbembe, Achille 465
Mbiti, John 327
McBaine, Neylan 592
McBride, Matthew S. 181
McCall, Leslie 39
McDannell, Colleen 310, 312, 343, 367

McKay, David O. 146, 149, 153–4, 175–6, 289, 340
McLaughlin, Nancy C. 181
McLellin, William E. 170
meaningful labor, importance of in Mormon thought 147
media, commentary on Mormon culture and practices 284
media and entertainment, the Church's teachings 371–2
"Meet the Mormons" campaign 180
megachurches 15
Melchizedek priesthood 19, 61, 63, 505, 570–1, 573, 576, 581, 584
men and the priesthood: exclusion of women 591–2; facilitation of personal growth 590; gendered transformation of priesthood 139–40; history of priesthood restoration 583–5; male identity in church discourse 591; Mormon masculinity 580–3; overview of Mormon priesthood 580; a personal experience 594–5; priest-community relationship 587–9; priest-God relationship 587; priesthood as mechanism of masculine hegemony 52–3, 55; rejection of priesthood 593; rights and powers of the priesthood 585–7; sexuality and 589–90
mental health: and disclosure rules 385–7; experience of female members of religious organizations 378–9; and gendered access to confession 387–8; gendered access to resources in Mormon communities 379–81; gendered barriers to women's care-seeking in ecclesiastical settings 381–3; potential for improvement women's access to healthcare resources 388–90; and the potential re-negotiation of disclosure boundaries 389; Relief Society provision of healthcare for women 380–1, 383–5; religion and 378–9; religious organizations' care provisions 388
Merrick, Eliza Jane 259–60
Methodists 80
#MeToo movement 294–5
Metropolitan Community Churches 222
Mexico: attitudes and experiences of women of color 338, 340, 601; development of indigenous Mormonism 30–1; establishment of LDS settlements 337; expulsion of foreign missionaries from 31; male behavior and family dynamics 329; role of Mexican LDS women 601; Third Convention 337–8; working motherhood in 323–4
Miles, Carrie 322
Mill, John Stuart 124
Millennial Star 29, 259, 262
Miller, Adam S. 491, 544
The Miracle of Forgiveness (Kimball) 206, 224, 288–9, 513, 593

Missionary's Hand Book 176
missionary work: age of eligibility change 164, 177, 179; appearance and conduct standards 178–9; the British mission 172, 176; calculus of proselytizing effectiveness 169; and the concept of the priesthood 170–1, 569–71; contrasting experiences of male and female returned missionaries 180–1; early departure, consequences of 65–6; emigration era 171–3; the European mission 172; evolution of 169–70; freelance 170–1; goals and expectations 65; as grooming for callings and assignments 180; the Hawaiian mission 172; LDS female authority in Nigeria 470–2; length of service changes 179; literature review 170, 181–2; as masculine activity 149–50; Mormon feminism and women's eligibility for 164–5; multifaceted era 179–81; as preparation for marriage 275; program era 176–9; "reverse missions" phenomenon 178; as rite of passage 169; role of in Mormon masculinity 62, 64–6, 453; social media campaigns 180; success, measurement of 178; system era 173–6; theological prerequisite 171; women and 150, 169–70, 173–4, 177–80, 574–5; *see also* Shunn, William
Mitchell, Brian David 284–5
mixed orientation marriages 227, 230
Moana 450; *see also* Pacific islands
Moberly, Elizabeth R. 192–3
Model, Lisette 245
Moderate Mormon women 396
modest dress, George Richards on 135–6
modesty: in art 117; the concept of 278; criticisms of Mormon emphasis on 13, 32; indigenous peoples and 32; men's responsibilities 278; and the #MeToo movement 294; place of in postwar Mormon culture 152–4; women's responsibilities 157
Mollenkott, Virginia Ramey 555–6
Möllhausen, Balduin 124
"Molly Mormon" 393, 395–9, 401
monogamous heterosexuality, as pillar of Mormon masculinity 62, 453
Monson, Thomas S. 158
Montefiore, Simon 562
"Monument to Women" (Dennis Smith) 253
Moore, Russell 217
moral agency 189, 194
Moravians 80–1, 556
mormonandgay.churchofjesuschrist.org 208, 532, 534
mormonandgay.lds.org 199, 207 [TGP: These are the same site, just a different url. Combine entry with a /]
Mormon courtship, revitalization of 134–6
Mormon faith, key principles 406
Mormon femininity, transformation of 136–7

Mormon feminism: acceptance, growth of 166; alternative voices 162–3; background and context 157–9; and challenges to *sola scriptura* 556–60 (*see also* Heavenly Mother); and the Christian creation narrative 553–4; the Church's suspicion of 406; comparison with Christian feminism 7; contemporary Mormon women 165–7; critiques on the church 576–7; and dissent on purity teaching 279–81; and the Equal Rights Amendment 160–2; and the Family Proclamation 163; female behavior, broadening of the acceptable model for 165; and the female emancipation movement 554–6; and the internet 2, 164–5; and missionary work eligibility 164–5; Mormon feminist theologies 547; as oxymoron 565; rebirth 159–60; view of Christ's maleness 547
Mormon Feminism: Essential Writings (Brooks, Wheelwright, Steenblik) 281
Mormon Feminist Housewives 279
Mormon history, re-examination 162–3
Mormon identity: connotations of white American culture 42, 44; intersectionality of 40–2
Mormonism, populist roots 6
MormonLeaks 588
"Mormon Literature: Progress and Prospects" (England) 258
"Mormon Masculinity" (Hoyt & Patterson) 582
Mormon masculinity: family involvement as characteristic of 582; and the history of priesthood restoration 583–5; impact of abandonment of polygamy 453, 582; pillars of 62, 453; portrayal of 251–2; and postwar Mormon culture 149–50; priesthood as pillar of 62, 63–4, 453, 580–3; reconstruction of 132–4; role of missionary work 62, 64–6, 453; two types of 593; Word of Wisdom and 62, 66–7, 134, 453, 582
"Mormon Masculinity—Were You Man Enough?" 593
Mormon priesthood: overview 580; *see also* men and the priesthood; priesthood; women and the priesthood
Mormon Reformation 94
The Mormons (O'Dea) 364
Mormons Building Bridges (MBB) 228–9, 231–2, 535
Mormon settlements, ecological impact 29
Mormon sexual revolution 515–19
Mormons for Equality 229, 234
Mormons for Marriage Equality (M4ME) 228–9
Mormon Sisters, Women in Early Utah (Boston women's group) 159
Mormon Stories 227, 229
Mormon Studies: bias towards white American representations 44–6; female representation 364–5

Mormon theology, feminist credentials 406
Mormon womanhood, Helen Andelin's ideas on 148–9
Mormon Women for Ethical Government (MWEG) 297, 313–14
mortality 21, 27, 90, 553, 557
Mortensen, Paul 223
Mother and Child (Teasdel) 247
motherhood: as divine and sacred role 52, 139, 374; idealization of stay-at-home motherhood 322; LDS women's attitudes to 57, 435–6; presentation of the LDS ideal 146; women's reactions to Benson's 1987 discussion of 341; work and alternate constructs of 443
Mott, Elizabeth J. 343
Mould, Comfort 17
Mould, Rebecca (Prophetess Rebecca) 16–17, 46
Mountain Meadows Massacre 288
Moyle, Henry D. 149–50
Mugabe, Robert 473
mujerista theology: the concept 604; distinction from Latina feminist theology 603–5; Latina women's relationship with the Church 605–6; personal experiences of LDS Latinas 601–3; restoration of Eve 605; tenets 599–601; Veronica & Raul's story 602–3
multiply and replenish, the commandment to 147, 511, 513, 518–19
mundane tasks, religious value 147, 338
Murdock, Maxine 290
Murphy, Thomas 308
Muscular Christianity 115, 133, 153, 581, 591
Muscular Mormonism 581–2
Muslim women: British media attitudes to 393; understanding Western society's discrimination against 40
Mutterfest 556
Myers, Wain 60–1, 63–4

Nash, J.C. 40
National Association for Research and Therapy of Homosexuality (NARTH) 195, 199, 226
National Association for the Advancement of Colored People (NAACP), LDS Church's agreement on anti-poverty initiatives 47
National Organization for Marriage (NOM) 215
national unrest, and postwar Mormon culture 143–4
Native American cultures, kinship definitions 26
Native American Mormons, activism 31–2
Native Americans: acceptance of Mormon baptism 30; alignment of Mormon and American ideas about 28; assimilation into white families 345–6; Book of Mormon's view of 28; displacement by Mormon settlements 29; Eliza Snow's writing on 263–5; Mormon beliefs about 370; Mormon "civilizing" attempts 30; Mormon designation 170

Nauvoo, Illinois, exodus from 29
Nauvoo Expositor 510
"Needed: An LDS Philosophy of Sex" (Cannon) 509
Neilson, Reid L. 34, 181
Nelson, Merrill 217
Nelson, Russell M. 83–4, 200, 473, 592
Nelson, Wendy 518
Neon Trees 41
Newell, Linda King 162
Newell, Quincy 33, 36
New Era magazine 273, 275, 277
New Horizons for Homosexuals (Kimball) 206
Newman, David 582–3, 589–90
New York World's Fair 116, 252
New Zealand 5, 13, 17, 20, 30, 42, 310, 315, 449–50; *see also* Maori
Next Mormons Survey (NMS) 365–8, 373, 375
Nibley, Hugh 560
Nicaragua: abuse in the church's welfare system 443; anti-government protests 434; dual earning and co-parenting 436–41, 446; economy and employment in 433–4; employment opportunities for women 439; motherhood and LDS women 435–6; research on working Mormon women 432–3; safety record 434; Sandinista Revolution 435–6; women supporting families 438–9; women's work as empowerment 439–41; work, poverty, and church support 441–3; work and alternate constructs of motherhood 443; work and unequal marital power dynamics 443–5; work as autonomy and protection 445–6
Nichols, Thomas 94
Nicolosi, Joseph 226
Nigeria: Afro-politan Mormonism 465–6; colonial era LDS masculinity 468–70; denial of entrance visas to American missionaries on grounds of racism 470; ethno-linguistic groups 464; etymology 468; first president 469; gendered duality and indigenous religion in 466–8; growth of the LDS church 464; LDS female authority in 470–2; and LDS gender ideology 472–6, 477; LGBT-friendly literature published in 474; *Ogu Umunwanyi* (Women's War) 471; Same-Sex Marriage Prohibition Act (SSMPA) 473, 475–6
Noble, Joseph 76
NoH8 Campaign 215–16
Noll, M.A. 100–2
No Longer at Ease (Achebe) 468
non-nuclear family structures 325–8; *see also* non-traditional families
non-traditional families: the concept 350; couples without children 354; division of labor 356–7; divorce and 354–6; ethnographic study 5; and Mormon family values 352; same-sex couple households 356; single-parent families and

cohabitation 352–4; statistical overview 357–60; stepfamilies 355–6; study data sources 350–2
North American settlements, and the doctrine of gathering 337–8
North Star 199, 226–7, 230, 232–3
Notes on Virginia (Jefferson) 28
"November Policy" 198–9, 232, 342, 533, 589
Novta, N. 433, 438
Noyes, John Humphrey 80

Oaks, Dallin H. 162, 198, 210–11, 226, 410, 570, 577–8, 589, 592
Obergefell v. Hodges 229, 231, 342
Obinna, Anthony 468, 470–1
Obinna, Fidelia 471
O'Dea, Thomas 364–5
The Odes of Solomon 564
Oehlenschläger, Adam 121
Official Declaration 2; gendered road to 34–5
Ogles, Benjamin M. 295
Ojike, Mbonu 469
Okazaki, Chieko 21–2, 42, 291, 312
Olawumni, Bisi 473
Olsen, Camille Fronk 487, 489
Olsen, Merlin 69
Olsen, Ole 288
Olyan, Saul M. 562
Omith, George A. 262
"one drop" policy, of black African ancestry 33
One Flesh, One Heart: Putting Celestial Love into Your Temple Marriage (Broderick) 517
Oneida Community 75, 80, 510
"On Mormon Masculinity" (Knowlton) 589
Open Stories Foundation 227
oppression, intersectionality of structural oppression 41–2
oral history, Claremont Women's Oral History Project 342, 346
oral sex 517–18
Ordain Women movement 8, 70, 164, 577, 591–2
ordination, as male rite of passage 580
ordination of women: Emma Smith 572; questions about 53, 163; Relief Society officers 572; as source of tension 7
orgasm 518
Origen 553, 564
original sin 553; as "cultural embarrassment" 557; female origin 553
Orsi, Robert 336
orthodoxy and gender: demographic perspective 365–7; female representation in studies of Mormonism 364–5; gender as a factor in belief and behavior 373–6; gender differences in Mormons' religious practice 370–3; heterodox approach to embodiment 541–5; Mormon women as paragons of orthodoxy 368–70; social scientific approaches 364–5

The Other Side of Heaven (2001) 453
Otterson, Michael 216
"Our Faithful Sisters" (Tamez) 601
The Oxford Handbook of Mormonism 45, 241
Oyewumi, Oyeronke 467
Ozorak, Elizabeth Weiss 375

Pacific islands: family constructs 455–8; homosociality 455; intersecting masculinities 452–4; kava culture 449–52; Mormon family constructs 457–8; Mormon kava adaptations of family and masculinity 458–60; sister–brother relationships 456–7; *see also* kava
Packer, Boyd K. 116, 120, 160, 162, 225, 273, 514, 531, 542, 544, 593
Palamas, Gregory 555
pants, wearing pants to church movement 164
parental status, of U.S. Mormons 366
Parents and Friends of Lesbians and Gays (PFLAG) 224
Parker, Clyde A. 191
Parker, Jabari 41
Parker, Theodore 556
Parmley, LaVern 312
Parson, Del 252
Partridge, Eliza Maria 78
Pascal, Blaise 375
Patai, R. 561
patriarchy, the pervasive nature of 51
Patterson, Kelly 67
Patterson, S.M. 453, 582
Paul, Alice 160
Paulsen, David 560
Payne, Robert 564
Payne, Seth 527
Payne, Tally S. 181
Pearl of Great Price 472, 486, 587
Pearson, Carol Lynn 192
Pellegrini, Ann 534
Penington, Isaac 556
Pentecostal World Fellowship 15
Perpetual Emigrating Fund 173
Perry, Troy 223
persecution 103, 105, 285–7, 393–4, 475
Peru, matchmaking in *see* matchmaking in Peru
Petersen, Boyd 557
Petersen, Mark 210
Peterson, Daniel 563
Peterson, Dawn 30
Peterson, Derek 465
Peterson, John 29
Peterson, Mark E. 34, 190
Petrey, Taylor 487, 527–8, 546–8, 589
Phelps, W.W. 558
Philippines 42
Philo of Alexandria 554, 556
Pierce, Steven 467

Pieta (Southey) 254
pink-collar work 144, 151
Pioneer Day parade 88–9
Playboy 153
plural marriage *see* polygamy/plural marriage
Pohnpei 450
polyandry, definition 297n1
polygamy/plural marriage: announcement as official church practice 243; biblical precedent 105–6; and British attitudes to Mormonism 393–4; church's denouncement 83; conflict with U.S. government over 86; continuing practice 197; cultural context 79–81; definition 297n1; and division of labor in the household 87–90; divorce 92–4; ending of the practice 129–32; ending of the practice 62, 105, 340, 501 (*see also* reframing of gender); and eternal kinship 81–2; and female bonding 513; and the feminist argument for expanded gender roles 43; function of in Mormon culture 129–30; historical overview 76–9; housing arrangements and adaptations 339; impact of abandonment on Mormon male identity 453, 582; intersectional perspective 41; Joseph Smith's revelations 61–2, 76, 78–9, 83, 242, 488–9, 510; legislation against 96, 105, 172, 243, 288, 336, 344–5; literature review 75; Mary Lois Walker Morris's description 106; Mormon elevation to the status of spiritual law 457; Mormon women's attitudes 86–7, 106, 130, 131, 132, 370; and Mormon women's use of scripture 105–6; Native American practices vs Mormon 29; northern European commentary 124–7; origins 510; "patriarchal order" of the church as euphemism for 574; practice of in Canada and Mexico 337; and privacy 344–5; and proxy fatherhood 512–13; and relationships between husbands, wives, and household servants 90; relationship to the afterlife 83–4; relationship with women's rights 87; and the religion's public image 288; secrecy around 76; sexuality and reproduction 90–2; sexual violence and the doctrine of 284–5, 287; social benefits claimed for 510–11; theological legacy of Joseph Smith's teachings 83–4; theological perspective 501; theology of sexuality in the era of 510–13; and women's agency 339–40; women's suffrage and 94–7; women's support for as expression of agency 339; Woodruff's promise to end the public practice 33
polygyny: in the Book of Mormon 485; definition 297n1; Nigerian perspective 474–5
Polynesian Cultural Center 32
popular culture, the Church's teachings 371–2
pornography 543
postmodern theory 4
post-traumatic stress disorder (PTSD), experienced by LGBTQ Mormons 232

postwar Mormon culture: appropriate gender roles 146; babies and birth control 147; commodification of womanhood 148–9; domesticity/family life 144–5; and the economy in the American West 145–6; masculine roles 149–50; and mid-century national unrest 143–4; modesty and purity 152–4; volunteerism 154; ward culture 150–2; women's attitudes to domesticity 147–8
poverty: and church support for women 441–3; impact on expectations of working-class families 26; impact on family life 325–6, 332; LDS Church/NAACP agreement on 47; Nicaraguan experience 432–4
power, relationship between identity and 39–40 (*see also* intersectionality)
The Power of Godliness: Mormon Liturgy and Cosmology (Stapley) 585
Pratt, Harold W. 598, 604
Pratt, Addison 30
Pratt, Belinda Marden 91–3
Pratt, Mary Ann M. 107
Pratt, Orson 510–11, 558
Pratt, Parley 81
Price, Matt 223
priesthood: categories of 581; Celestial Marriage and 273; the concept 170–1, 569–71; democratic nature 63; ecclesiastical vs cosmological 570–1; eligibility of Africans and African-Americans 63; gendered transformation 139–40; imagery 581; introduction of youth ordination 133; Joseph Smith's revelations 61; male bonding activities 589; overview 580; as pillar of Mormon masculinity 62, 63–4, 453, 580–3; rejection of 593; rights and powers 585–7; two forms 61; women's feelings about Mormon doctrine 410, 412; *see also* Aaronic priesthood; Melchizedek priesthood; men and the priesthood; women and the priesthood
Priesthood and Church Government (Widtsoe) 140, 583
"The Priesthood Man" (Eyring) 591
Priesthood Reform Movement 575–6
Primary Association 19, 131, 309–10, 316, 398, 436, 572
Primary Children's Hospital 312
Primary Singing Time 316
Prince, Gregory 230, 313
Principles to Govern Possible Public Statement on Legislation Affecting Rights of Homosexuals 210
Pritt, Thomas & Ann 192–3
Proclamation on the Family *see* Family Proclamation
procreation, as primary LDS value 188
Prohibition movement 134
Prologue: An Examination of the Mormon Attitude Towards Homosexuality (Jenkins et al) 191, 223, 532

Prophetess Rebecca Mould 16–17, 46
Proposition 8, 14, 197, 208, 214–16, 227, 229, 231, 234, 342, 589
Proposition 22, 214
Psilander, Valdemar 126
"The Psychological Phenomena of the Homosexual" (Berryman) 530
psychology, critiques of secular ideas by LDS therapists 188
psychotherapists, relationship between the priesthood and 188
psychotherapy 187, 201; *see also* homosexuality and therapeutic culture
Public Vows: A History of Marriage and the Nation (Cott) 86
purity: as requirement for both women and men 153; *see also* sexual purity
"purity culture" 543
Putney, Clifford 582
Putney, N.M. 406

Q-Saints 233
queer Mormons: articulation of sexual and religious identity 533–6; the emergence of queer theory 525–6; possibilities for the future 536; queer (ing) Mormon history 526–33; social and cultural influence 535; terminology 525
queer theory, femininities and 51
quilting 147, 253
Quinn, D. Michael 206, 221–2, 528, 530, 594
Quorum of the Twelve Apostles 171–2

race: and attitudes towards Moana men 453; Book of Mormon's view of Native peoples 28; eligibility of Africans and African-Americans for the priesthood 16, 27, 32, 53, 178, 486; and racial assimilation into white families 345–6; racialized vision of the family in the Book of Mormon 26; of U.S. Mormons 366
race and gender: in the Book of Mormon 485, 490–1; and endowment and sealing ordinances 27–8; indigenous peoples in nineteenth-century Mormon thought 28–30; Japan, LDS Church's first years in 34; and the Mormon response to sexual violence 287; native Mormonisms in Oceania and Mexico 30–2; Official Declaration 2; gendered road to 34–5; "one drop" policy 33; popular resistance to racial restrictions 35; role of intersectionality within Mormon Studies 44–6; temple liturgy and racial restriction 32–3; theories about the origin of black skin 26, 32; white American women's experiences used as universal representation 44; *see also* Myers, Wain
racial categories, scriptural explanations 26
racism: impact on African-American family life 144; Nigeria's denial of entrance visas to American missionaries on grounds of 470

Radke, Andrea G. 181
Ransome-Kuti, Funmilayo 471
rape: common early legal standards for 289; culture of shame surrounding 286; Kimball's statement on victims' culpability 289; reference to in the Book of Mormon 485
Rebechi, Aldo 116
Reconciliation and Growth Project 227–8
"Recovery from Mormonism" 593–4
Reed Smoot hearings 288
Rees, Robert 224, 490
Reeser, Todd W. 583
Reeve, Paul 33
reframing of gender: the church welfare plan and the solidification of gendered spheres 138–9; the end of plural marriage 129–32; priesthood, gendered transformation 139–40; reconstruction of Mormon masculinity 132–4; revitalization of Mormon courtship 134–6; transformation of Mormon femininity 136–7
reframing of Mormon gender in the progressive era *see* reframing of gender
Reiss, Jana 279–80
Relief Society: activism 137; anti-polygamy agitation 572; "correlation" of 158; defense of Joseph Smith 95; demographic perspective 398; disclosure rules 385–7, 389; gendered access to confession 387–8; institutional autonomy 572; international survey 21; mental health care provision 380–1, 383–5; ordination of officers 572; reconstitution of 95; revision of minutes 262, 264
Relief Society Building 312
religious piety, as platform for empowerment 399
Religious Right, rise of 205
religious studies, contemporary historical conversations 4
religious transmission, in Mormon families 406
religious worship, in the home 342–4
Reorganized Church of Jesus Christ of Latter Day Saints 84
reparative therapy 192–6, 199–200
Republican Party, rise of the Religious Right 205
"Rethinking Mormonism's Heavenly Mother" (Petrey) 547
"reverse missions" phenomenon 178
Reynolds, George 115
Rich, Sarah DeArmon Pea 106
Richards, George 135–6
Richardson, Edmund 513
Richardson, Mary Ann Darrow 512–13
Richmond Jail incident 286
Riess, Jana 181, 311 [TGP: Duplicate- fix spelling above and in the manuscript]
Rigdon, Sidney 286
risk tolerance, as factor in gender gap in American religiosity 375

ritual adoption, of adults 28
The R.M. (2003) 453
Roberts, Brigham Henry 131–2
Rodriguez, Jeanette 600–1
Rogers, David W. 241
Rollins, Mary Elizabeth 77
Romero, Óscar 600
Rørbye, Martinus 117
Rosenroth, Knorr von 559
Roskelley, Samuel 287
Rutherford, Taunalyn 328–9, 407, 413
Rwanda 57

Sabarwal, S. 439
Salem, S. 40
same-gender attraction, comparison of European and American views 14
same-sex activity: historical perspective of the Church's views and approaches 222, 528; Kimball's theories 514; LDS opposition to 515
Same-Sex Dynamics among Nineteenth-Century Americans: A Mormon Example (Quinn) 221
same-sex households, statistical analysis 356, 359
same-sex marriage: as apostasy 198–9, 232, 342, 533; Californian campaign against 14 (*see also* Proposition 8); church restrictions on children of 198–9, 232–3, 342, 533, 589; Family Proclamation and 574; legislation for and against 208, 210–11, 213–14, 227, 234, 356, 473, 475–6; *see also* Proposition 8
Same-Sex Marriage Prohibition Act (SSMPA), Nigeria 473, 475–6
same-sex relationships: activism on 589; bonding between plural wives and 513; indigenous African societies' history of 475; Nigerian attitudes and legislation 473–6; theological issues 521
Same-sex Sex Dynamics among Nineteenth Century Americans (Quinn) 2 [TGP: Duplicate entry-standardize in the manuscript too]
Sāmoa 41, 450, 459
Sandinista Revolution, Nicaragua 435–6
Save our Children campaign 209
"Saying Goodbye to the Final Say" (Kline) 588
Scandinavian art: complicating the Mormon narrative 120–3; depiction of Mormon theology and gender ideals through 114–17; as visual historical record 117–20; *see also* art; Christensen, C.C.A.; Friberg, Arnold
Schroeder, Joy A. 108
Scott, Joan 467
Scott, Madelene 147
Scott, Richard G. 291
scrapbooking 346
scripture: as aid to women 106–9; the Bible in nineteenth-century America 100–1; biblical usage in the mainstream 103–5; comparison of Mormon and Protestant use of 105–6; levels of gender-critical attention 483; nineteenth-century Mormons and 101–3; nineteenth-century Mormon women's use of 102–3; "patchwork quoting" 102; silence of Mormon scripture on homosexuality 206
scripture and gender: the Bible 485–7; the Book of Mormon 483–5; the Doctrine and Covenants 487–9; theological possibilities 489–91
sealing: the concept of 273, 499, 500; relationship with salvation 501–2; the rite 501
"Seeking Sisterhood among Different Perspectives on Mormon Feminism" 23
self-discipline 67, 132, 134–5, 154
self-restraint 90, 135, 189
self-sufficiency 132, 145, 324, 439
Seneca Falls convention 1
separate-spheres conception of gender 136, 138, 239, 259, 263, 344
September Six 162–3, 594
Serano, Julia 548
sex education 13, 509, 515–16
"Sex in Public" (Berlant & Warner) 526
sexual abuse, church cover-ups 588
sexual immorality, as threat to the Mormon theological paradigm 275
sexuality: attitudes in the Global South 14–18; and fatherhood 68–9; and Mormonism 188–9; and the priesthood 589–90; and reproduction 90–2; *see also* theology of sexuality
sexual minorities 43, 196, 198, 200–1, 222
sexual orientation, of U.S. Mormons 366
sexual orientation change efforts (SOCE) 194–5, 199–200; *see also* aversion therapy; conversion therapy; reparative therapy
sexual pleasure, theology of sexuality and 517–18
sexual purity: alternative models 279–81; and the concept of celestial marriage 272–5; concerns about teachings 278–9; institutional expectations and teaching 271–2; instructions for dating 277–8; maintenance of as women's responsibility 136, 152–3, 157, 278; metaphors used in purity teaching 276; object lessons 276–9; Silver Ring Thing (SRT) 276–7
sexual revolution, Mormon 515–19
sexual violence: against children 289; Bishop and Smartt cases 294–5; Brett Kavanaugh investigation 296–7; common early legal standards for rape 289; complications of race 287; counselling and treatment guide for church leaders 291; culture of shame surrounding rape 286; and the doctrine of plural marriage 284–5, 287; Elizabeth Smart's experience 284–5; historical perspective 285–7; Joseph Bishop case 294; LDS Church's response to child sexual abuse 289–90; and media commentary on

Mormon culture and practices 284; and mental health support from religious leaders 379; Mormon responses to 287–97; secondary trauma related to gendered support provision 388; victim responsibility in LDS teachings 291
Shakers 75, 80, 90, 488, 510, 512, 555
Shea, Lolly 200
Shekhina, as name for female deity 561–2
Sheppard-Towner Act (1921) 137
Sherlock, Ingrid 322
Shumway, E. 454
Shunn, William 61, 63–8
Sidwell, Adelia B. Cox 108
Sikahema, V. 454
Silva, N.K. 459
Silver Ring Thing (SRT) 276–7
Singapore 19
Singh, Jakeet 40
single mothers 324, 326–7, 353, 419, 422
single-parent families, statistical analysis 352–4
single parenthood 325–7, 352–3; divorce and 354–6
single women 80, 90, 165, 169, 173, 177, 327, 343, 510
Sinha, N. 439
Sistas in Zion 43–4, 47
Sister Saints (McDannell) 310
Sisters in Spirit (Beecher & Anderson) 2, 577
Skinner, B.F. 193
Skousen, W. Cleon 531
slavery: adoption of Indian children and 29; Brigham Young's justification for the existence of 32; fragility of African American families under 26; polygamy as form of 288; women's activism against 94–5
Slessor, Mary 468, 470
Smart, Elizabeth Ann 278–9, 281–2, 284–5, 291, 297, 543
Smartt, Philander 294–5
Smith, Alvin 498
Smith, Barbara B. 160, 210
Smith, Dennis 253
Smith, Don Carlos 12
Smith, Emma: conflict with Brigham Young 95; empowered by the prophet 263; eviction of Joseph's first plural union 76; ignorance of Joseph's polygamous activities 78; Joseph's revelation to 242, 487–9, 491, 572; ordained 572; portrait 241; repatriation into the church story 163; sealing invitation to a person of African descent 32–3
Smith, Gary Ernest 253
Smith, George Albert 89, 530
Smith, Hyrum 78, 242, 286, 510
Smith, John 243
Smith, Joseph: Articles of Faith 574; and the close coupling of the Church with the U.S. 392; death 29, 95, 241–2, 510; early preaching methods 169; early revelations 171; founds Council of Fifty 29; function of religious innovations 27–8; introduction of eternal family doctrine 352; jail cell endurance of boastings about rape 286–7; King Follett Discourse 541; marriages 75–7, 130, 242; media commentary on marriages of 284–5; portrait of 241; publication of papers relating to 163; publication of the Book of Mormon 496; rehabilitation of Eve 556–8; revelation on Word of Wisdom 66–7; revelations on family 61; revelations on masculinity 61–2; revelations on plural marriage 61–2, 76, 78–9, 83, 242, 488–9, 510; revelations on priesthood 570–1; revelation to Emma 242, 487–9, 491, 572; silence on homosexuality 206; theological legacy of teachings on polygamy 83–4; turning key rhetoric 262–4, 575; validation role of women 315; visitation by resurrected apostles 584; wedding ring 255n1; white universalism 32; works regarded as scripture 101–2
Smith, Joseph, Sr. 12
Smith, Joseph F. 33, 133–5, 140; on birth control 514; initiates Priesthood Reform Movement 575; interpretation of the concepts of priesthood structures 573; speech on women's suffrage 96–7; on temporal salvation 432 [TGP: Joseph F. Smith and Joseph Fielding Smith are two different people and need to be distinguished with separate entries and these need to be pulled apart.]
Smith, Julie 487
Smith, Lucy Mack 102, 260–2, 264
Smith, Marilyn Y. 35
Smith, Tamu 43
Smith, Valerie 39
Snow, Eliza R. 77–8, 95–6, 102, 140, 170, 262–3, 265, 312, 558, 572
Snow, Erastus 116, 512, 557
social justice, relationship of faith with 599
social media: missionary work campaigns 180; participation of church members in 577
social problems, potential effects of church teachings on 15
social science perspectives: demographics of Mormon women and men in the U.S. 365–7; female representation in studies of Mormonism 364–5; gender as a factor in belief and behavior 373–6; gender differences in Mormons' religious practice 370–3; Mormon women as paragons of orthodoxy 368–70; social scientific approaches to gender 5–6, 364–5
sociological research, the concept 5
sociological surveys 5
Socorro, Juana del 445
soda, caffeinated 372

sodomy laws, and the constitutional right to privacy 210
"Souls, Symbols, and Sacraments" (Holland) 519
South Africa 13, 56–7; male behavior and family dynamics 330–2; non-nuclear family structures 326; working motherhood in 324–5
South America 178
Southern Poverty Law Center 199
Southey, Trevor 252–5
Spafford, Belle S. 145, 312
Spanish Inquisition 425
Spencer, Josephine 267–8
sport, as missionary tool 150
Stampe, Kirstine Marie Elisabeth 121–3
Stanton, Elizabeth Cady 86, 96, 554, 556–7, 559
Stapley, Jonathan A. 585
Steenblik, Rachel Hunt 281, 406
stepfamilies 355–6
Stephens, Evan 530
Stephens, Tyler 536
Stephens, Wesley 536
Stevens, Evelyn 438
Stevenson, Robert 35
Stevenson, Russell 46
Stonewall Riots 191, 222–3, 234
Strandberg, Julius 124
Strangers in Paradox (Toscano & Toscano) 2, 545, 584
Strindberg, August 124
structural oppression, intersectionality of 41–2
Sturdy Patriarchs 251
"The Subjection of Women" (Mill) 124
suicide 195, 232, 386, 540–1, 589
Sumerau, J.E. 531
Sunstone magazine 224

Taber, Susan 309
Taiwan 316–17
Talbot, Christine 344
Talmage, James 135
Tamez, Jared M. 338, 601
Tanner, Mary Jane Mount 103, 106
Taves, Ann 314
Taylor, Charles 465
Taylor, John 130–2, 243, 572
Taylor, John W. 131
tea and coffee 66, 134, 512, 543, 582
Teasdel, Mary 247
teen pregnancy 13
Teichert, Herman Adolph 249
Teichert, Minerva 115, 249, 249–51
temple clothing, function of uniformity 27
temple liturgy 26–7, 32–3, 35, 310, 570–2, 578
temple worthiness, requirements for 20
The Ten Commandments (1956) 251
Tengan, T.P.K. 452
Tertullian 556

The Testaments of One Fold and One Shepherd (2000) 453
Thacker, Randall 230
That We May Be One: A Gay Mormon's Perspective on Faith and Family (Christofferson) 198
theological approaches to gender 6–7
theology, Mormonism's lack of engagement with 6
theology of embodiment: body modification 540–1; heterodox possibilities 545–50; LDS orthodoxy on embodiment and gender 541–5; trans-friendly interpretation 550; *see also* transgender people
theology of family: and the Family Proclamation 496, 506–7; and the Heavenly Mother 505–6; implications for LGBTQ Saints 506; and Joseph Smith's early revelation on family 496; materialism 497; Mormon context of theology 495–7; parameters 497–500; and plural marriage 501; sacramentalism and 498–9; salvation 500–6; sealing and 499, 500, 501–3; universalism and 497–8, 501
theology of sexuality: celibacy 520; Family Proclamation 519; Kenneth Cannon's work 509; and LDS identity 521–2; the Mormon sexual revolution 515–19; in other Christian traditions 519–20; in the plural marriage era 510–13; in the post-war era of strict sexual morality 513–15; and sexual pleasure 517–18; theological issues 519–21; and the use of birth control 513–14
therapy, homosexuality and *see* homosexuality and therapeutic culture
Third Convention, Mexico 337–8
"Thirteen Articles of Healthy Chastity" (Butterworth) 281
Thorvaldsen, Bertel 115–16, 121
Tingey, Earl C. 68
tobacco 62, 66–7, 134, 372, 453, 512, 582
tobacco use 62
Tomlinson, M. 450
Tonga 41, 450, 453, 456, 459
Toscano, Margaret 2, 163, 545, 547–8, 584
Toscano, Paul 2, 545, 584, 594–5
"Toward a Post-Heterosexual Mormon Theology" (Petrey) 589
transgender people: the Church's position 533; denial of Mormon priesthood to 589; and the emergence of a trans-friendly interpretation Mormon theology 550; facts and terminology 540–1; Judith Butler's performative model 548; LDS orthodoxy on embodiment and gender 541–5; and marriage 536; medical transitioning vs social 541; and Mormon thinking on body modification 540–1
Transmormon (documentary) 536, 544–5
transnational religious community, mobility, gender, and 18–20
transparency, the church's move towards in its history 163

Index

Trump, Donald 298n3
"Truth and Plan" (Oaks) 589
Turner, Rodney 514–15
Turning Freud Upside Down (Jackson, Fischer, Dant) 188
Two Mormons (Dalsgaard) 117–18

Ugochukwu, Obinna 468
Ulrich, Laurel Thatcher 310, 339, 556, 572, 576
Understanding and Changing Homosexual Orientation Problems (LDS Social Services) 191
Understanding Sexuality, Gender, and Allyship (USGA) 535
United Families International (UFI) 23
United States (U.S.): chastity rhetoric 153; close coupling of the Church with 392; comparison of women's experiences with those in the Global South 22; and the concept of Zion 392; demographics of Mormon women and men 365–7; demographic transition 90; desegregation of Armed Forces 34; empire-building project 34; expansion of divorce in 94; Jefferson's vision 28; religious leaders as source of help for psychological distress 378; stay-at-home ideal of motherhood 322
Uruguay 42
Utah: cultural significance 395–9; enfranchisement of women 86; rise of a centralized bureaucratic structure in 16; understanding of women's roles in 13
"Utah compromise" 216–17

Van Beek, W. 328
Vanderpoel, John 249
van Oort, Johannes 564
Van Wagenen, Sterling 296
vegetarianism 115
A Victim of the Mormons 288
Victorian ideals of gender and family 259, 449, 454–7, 501, 573
Virginia Citizens Council 209
virginity 68, 289, 292
volunteerism, in postwar Mormon culture 154
Vranes, Zandra 43

Waddell, Hope 468, 470
Walking with Shadows (Dibia) 474
ward culture, in postwar Mormon culture 150–2
Warner, Michael 525–6, 536
Watson, Wendy 83
Watts, Gary & Millie 224
Weber, B.M. 40
Weber, Max 311, 316
Weed, Josh & Lolly 200
Wells, Emmeline B. 87, 266, 559
West Africa, LDS gender ratios 20
Wheelwright, Hannah 281, 406

When God Talks Back (Luhrmann) 315
Whipping Girl (Serano) 548
White, Dantzel 83
white hegemonic masculinity, femininities and 54
whiteness: as determinant of potential for godliness 33; privileging of 4; scriptural explanations 26
white slave trade, Mormon emigration and 124–7
Whitney, Helen Mar Kimball 109, 130
Whitney, Sarah Ann 77–8, 81
Why We Practice Plural Marriage (Whitney) 130
Wickman, Lance 226
Widtsoe, John A. 139–40
Widtsoe, Leah 139, 573
Wiedewelt, Johannes 115
Wieth, Clara 126
Wilcox, Linda P. 558, 560
Wilde, Oscar 529
Williams, Emily 531
Williams, Lee 223
Winkler, Douglas 532
Wirthlin, Joseph L. 153
Wisdom, as name for female deity 563–4
Wise, Jeff & Katherine 228
womanhood, commodification of in postwar Mormon culture 148–9
The Woman's Bible (Stanton) 554, 559
The Woman's Exponent 87, 96, 107, 159, 265–6
women: attitudes to domesticity in postwar Mormon culture 147–8; authority granted to and rescinded from 262–4; challenges of American society for LDS women 145–6; covenants with God 27; curbing of prophetic opportunities 16; disclosure rules and mental wellbeing of 385; disenfranchisement in Utah 96, 105; documentary practices 346; duty and calling 11; employment in post-war America 144, 145, 158; empowerment view of Mormonism 136; enfranchisement in Utah 86; exclusion from the priesthood 591–2; family responsibilities 339 (*see also* gender roles); feelings about exclusion from key leadership roles 410–11; fundraising role 151; influence in the church *see* women's influence in the church; mental health experience of female members of religious organizations 378–9; and missionary work 150, 169–70, 173–4, 177–80, 574–5; ordination *see* ordination of women; and the priesthood *see* women and the priesthood; religious authority in the Global South 17; representation in studies of Mormonism 364–5; responsibility for chastity and sexual purity 136, 152–3, 157, 278; spiritual leadership and participation in Ghanaian churches 15–16; supporting families in Nicaragua 438–9; view of Mormonism 166; and ward culture 151; women's work as empowerment 439–41; work as autonomy and protection for 445–6

Women and Authority (Hanks) 2, 577
women and the priesthood: and correlation reforms 575; defining priesthood 569–71; exclusion 591–2; female ecclesiology 572–3, 574–5; gendered transformation of priesthood 139–40; inclusion movements 591–2; liturgy 576; and male priesthood cosmology in the twentieth century 573–4; missionary work 574–5; Mormon feminist critiques 576–7; in the nineteenth century 572–3; priesthood keys granted to women 262–4, 575; in the twentieth century 573–7; in the twenty-first century 577–8; women and priesthood authority 571
Women at Church (McBaine) 592
women of color, attitudes and experiences 338, 340, 601
women preachers, in mainstream evangelical denominations 80
The Women's Exponent 1 [TGP: Should be "Woman's" as above. Fix in manuscript]
women's influence in the church: cultural context 308–11; and the internet 310; microbiological approach to the study of 305–8; ontological perspective 314–17; relational perspective 311–14; spheres of 317
"The Women's Movement: Liberation or Deception?" (Monson) 158
women's studies: emergence on college campuses 1; impact and influence on Mormon studies 2; influence of queer theory 525; intersectionality in 39; as response to androcentrism 3
women's suffrage 87, 127, 130–1, 197, 559; and polygamy 94–7
women's work, comparisons of LDS women with other American women 341
Wong, J.C. 433, 438
Woodhead, L. 365
Woodruff, Phoebe W. Carter 106
Woodruff, Wilford 33–4, 62, 96, 105, 129, 172–3, 181, 501, 558
Woodruff's Manifesto 131, 172
Woods, Fred E. 181
Word of Wisdom: acceleration of emphasis on 134; and the consumption of food in the home 343; gendered perspective of adherence 372–3; institutionalization as non-negotiable facet of Mormon identity 115; Joseph Smith's revelation 66–7; and kava 451; and Mormon masculinity 62, 66–7, 134, 453, 582; overlap with Guatemalan Mormons' cultural understandings of "hot" and "cold" in medicine 308
working motherhood: as alternate construct 443; Benson's discussion of 340–1; and cultural interpretations of the Family Proclamation 435–6; and family structure 322–5; Mormon attitudes towards 367; Nicaraguan experience 432–46; statistical analysis 357; and unequal marital power dynamics 443–5
working women, statistical analysis 357, 359
World Health Organization 388
World's Fair, New York 116, 252
worthiness, bodies and 66–7

Yehoshua, Rabbi 561
#YesAllWomen 294
Yoruba 308, 464, 472
Young, Brigham 32, 62, 77; announcement of polygamy as official church practice 243; conflict between Emma Smith and 95; demands destruction of Lucy Mack Smith's book 262; family arrangements 89; on gender roles 88–9; polygamous marriages 79, 82, 94, 338–9; reorganization of church ecclesiology 572; revision of Relief Society minutes 262–3; on women's role 157
Young, Gordon C. 20–1
Young, Sam 8, 296
Young, Steve 69, 582
Young, Zina D.H. 558
Young Woman's Manual 280
Young Women program 19, 309, 398
Young Women's Mutual Improvement Association 309
youth interviews, campaign to end 296
Yuval-Davis, N. 41

Zion: as global religious project 12; positioning the United States of America as 392; role of the "patriarchal order" 575; stakes outside of Utah 175
Ziser, Richard 213